Directory of U.S. Military Bases Worldwide

Third Edition

Directory of U.S. Military Bases Worldwide
Third Edition

Edited by William R. Evinger

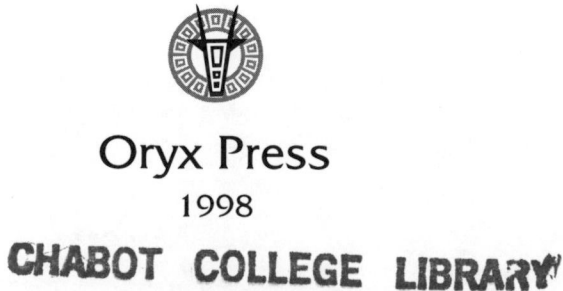

Oryx Press
1998

The rare Arabian Oryx is believed to have inspired the myth of the unicorn. This desert antelope became virtually extinct in the early 1960s. At that time several groups of international conservationists arranged to have 9 animals sent to the Phoenix Zoo to be the nucleus of a captive breeding herd. Today the Oryx population is over 800, and nearly 400 have been returned to reserves in the Middle East.

© 1998 by the Oryx Press
4041 North Central at Indian School Road
Phoenix, Arizona 85012-3397

The paper used in this publication meets the minimum requirements of American National Standard for Information Science—Permanence of Paper for Printed Library Materials, ANSI Z39.48, 1984.

Library of Congress Cataloging-in-Publication Data
Directory of U.S. Military bases worldwide / edited by William R.
Evinger. —[3rd ed.]
  Includes index.
  ISBN 1-57356-049-9 (alk. paper)
  1. Military bases, American—Directories. 2. United States—Armed
Forces—Facilities—Directories. I. Evinger, William R., 1943– .
  UA26.A2D57 1998
    355.7'0973—dc21   98-4143
                                                                   CIP

Contents

Appendixes   295

Indexes   307

Preface

This third edition of the *Directory of U.S. Military Bases Worldwide* lists nearly 1,200 active military bases and installations in the continental United States and overseas. It is the only single source providing a comprehensive, in-depth guide to U.S. military bases/installations. The contents reflect recent base closings and provide information on forthcoming scheduled base closures and realignments. All of the entries for the bases contained in the second edition have been updated, as of February 1998, and additional Coast Guard, National Guard, and Reserve bases have been identified and included.

The *Department of Defense Dictionary of Military and Associated Terms* defines military bases as "areas or localities containing installations that provide logistics or other support." It defines installations as "groupings of facilities located in the same vicinity, which support particular functions."

This general reference book provides information about base/installations of the Army, Navy, Air Force, Marine Corps, Coast Guard, National Guard, Reserve Forces, and Joint Service Installations, as well as Department of Defense agencies, military camps and stations, and command headquarters offices.

The research for this volume began in mid-1997 when requests were sent to the public affairs offices of the bases/installations listed in the second edition, as well as to additional bases that were identified through the Internet and other sources. Follow-up mailings were done, and many telephone calls were made to ensure the most complete coverage and response possible. All entries in this *Directory* were compiled from information obtained from completed surveys, pamphlets or publications supplied by the bases/installations, official Internet sites, and/or telephone responses.

The main section of this *Directory* lists the domestic bases/installations alphabetically, first by state, then by city, then by name. The entries for overseas bases/installations, including Puerto Rico and overseas possessions, follow the domestic bases and are listed alphabetically by country, then by city, then by name. Information in each entry profiles the official and popular names of the installation; address; main telephone and facsimile numbers; base e-mail address(es) and Internet Web site address(es); branch(es) of service; base location and size; major units; brief history; visitors' attractions; key contact persons with telephone numbers and e-mail addresses; number of personnel and estimates of payroll and contract expenditures; and services, including temporary housing, temporary housing, commissary and exchange, child care facilities, schools, libraries, medical facilities, and recreational opportunities on base or nearby. The entries in this edition also contain some information on changes to be expected resulting from future base closures and realignments. Some bases such as Cameron Station, Virginia; Philadelphia Naval Base and Shipyard, Pennsylvania; and Lowry Air Force Base, Colorado have been closed and are no longer included in the listings. Other bases may be gaining or losing major units due to a realignment of activities.

Two appendixes follow the main text. The first summarizes the major closures and realignments announced during the Defense Base Closure and Realignment Commission (BRAC) 1995 round. The second appendix provides information on the schedule as of September 30, 1997, for completing the recommendations of the 1988, 1991, 1993, and 1995 Defense Base Closure and Realignment Commissions.

There are four indexes in this *Directory*: (1) an alphabetical listing of all bases by official and popular base name; (2) a branch of service index, listing the bases by state (overseas by country); (3) an alphabetical index by state (overseas by country) of bases by branch of service; and (4) a numerical and alphabetical index by unit, listing major units and their home bases.

Within the time constraints for this project, the editor of this *Directory* has made every effort to identify and list as many bases/installations as possible. With scheduled closures and realignments, the updating of the database is a continuous process. Users of this *Directory* are urged to notify the editor of additional information for this inventory of bases.

While every effort has been made to ensure that all information is both accurate and current within the confines of format and scope, the publisher does not assume and hereby disclaims any liability to any party for loss or damage caused by errors or omissions in the *Directory of U.S. Military Bases Worldwide* whether such errors or omissions resulted from negligence, accident, or any other cause. In the event of a publication error, the sole responsibility of the publisher will be the entry of corrected information in succeeding editions. Please direct such information to: Editor, *Directory of U.S. Military Bases Worldwide,* The Oryx Press, 4041 North Central at Indian School Road, Phoenix, Arizona 85012.

Acknowledgements

This *Directory* would not have been possible without the help of the many Public Affairs Officers throughout the world who took the time to fill out my survey, provide me with brochures about their bases/installations, and/or answer my telephone inquiries. The author is also grateful for the support for this project provided by Jennifer Ashley and Magon Kinzie and the other members of The Oryx Press staff.

How to Use This Directory

The main section of this *Directory* is organized alphabetically by state for the domestic bases and alphabetically by country for overseas bases. Within each state's or country's section, the information is listed alphabetically first by city and then by the official name of the base or installation, regardless of branch of service. Each entry contains the following descriptive information:

BASE INFORMATION

Official name of the base/installation: Entries are organized within state and city by the official name of the base/installation. This name follows the entry number.

Abbreviated Name: Where available, the abbreviated names of installations are included.

Popular Name: Some bases/installations are not always known by their official names in ordinary usage. For example, the Marine Corps Combat Development Command is commonly known as Quantico, or Quantico Marine Base. To accommodate this, if the installation is also known by a "popular" name, that name is included in the entry (as provided by the installation). It is also indexed with the official names in the base name index.

Address and telephone number: This is the address of the base/installation, mailing address if applicable, and the commercial and DSN (Defense Switching Network, the military telephone network) telephone numbers.

E-mail and Internet: This field lists the e-mail address(s) of the base and the Internet World Wide Web address(s), if any.

Officer-of-the-day: The telephone number listed for officer-of-the-day is often usable 24 hours a day. Sometimes the officer-of-the-day is referred to by other titles: (Navy) Duty Officer, Command Duty Officer, Officer of the Deck, Quarterdeck; (Coast Guard) Group Duty Officer, Operations Center; (Air National Guard) Command Post; and (Army) Staff Duty Officer.

BASE PROFILE

Branch (of service): The *Directory* covers the Army, Navy, Air Force, Marine Corps, Army National Guard, Army Reserve, Naval Reserve, Air National Guard, Air Force Reserve, Air Force Civil Air Patrol, Marine Corps Reserve, Joint Service Installations, Department of Defense agencies such as the Defense Logistics Agency, and the U.S. Coast Guard.

Size and location: The approximate land area of the base/installation is given in acres. Some facilities are located in buildings and are listed as "Offices only." Directions to the base are included, giving main highways and/or distances from airports or nearby cities and towns.

Major units (located on the base/installation): Major commands, host commands, and tenant activities are listed. Some of these units may also have separate entries in the *Directory*, particularly if they have a separate geographic location, even though they may be technically part of a particular base. Conversely, users trying to locate a particular unit may find that it is included in the list of major units of the base to which it is assigned, but not as a separate entry.

Base history: A brief history of the base/installation is given, which was compiled from information provided by the base/installation.

Future closure/realignment: Future changes to major units and base activities resulting from the base closure and realignment process are identified.

Visitor attractions: Points of interests and museums, on base or off base but on land owned/leased by the base, are identified.

KEY CONTACTS

This section lists key personnel, their addresses and telephone numbers if different from that of the the main base, and e-mail addresses, if available. Included are Base Commander, Public Affairs Officer, Procurement Officer, Transportation Officer, and Director of Personnel and Community Activities.

PERSONNEL AND EXPENDITURES

This section lists the numbers of **Active Duty Personnel, Dependents living on the base/installation,** and **Civilian Personnel**. Total **Military Payroll Expenditures** and total **Contract Expenditures** for fiscal year 1997 in estimated and rounded dollar amounts are provided where available. When bases supplied this information for other fiscal years, that is indicated.

SERVICES

This part of the entry contains information on the services available on the base/installation including **Housing and Temporary Housing** for officers, enlisted personnel, families, and visitors; base **Commissary**, equivalent to a supermarket, with sizes varying depending on the base; and base **Exchange**, equivalent to a shopping center offering a variety of products and services, which is generally run on nonappropriated funds. **Child care facilities** and **capacities**, **Schools**, **Libraries**, and **Recreational facilities** are all listed when known.

SAMPLE ENTRY

OFFICIAL BASE NAME
ABBREVIATED NAME
POPULAR NAME

ADDRESS AND
TELEPHONE NUMBER

E-MAIL AND/OR
INTERNET

BRANCH(ES) OF SERVICE
FOUND ON THE BASE

MAJOR COMMANDS, HOST
COMMANDS, AND TENANT
ACTIVITIES

VISITOR ATTRACTIONS ON
OR NEAR THE BASE

NAMES AND TELEPHONE NUM-
BERS OF KEY CONTACTS OF
THE BASE

SUMMARY OF TYPES AND NUM-
BER OF HOUSING UNITS, SHOP-
PING SERVICES, CHILDCARE AND
EDUCATIONAL FACILITIES,
LIBRARIES, SCHOOLS, MEDICAL
AND RECREATIONAL FACILITIES

112. ABC Training Center, Pacific
ABCTCPAC

9999 N 9th St
San Diego, CA 92147-5080
619-555-5550; FAX 619-555-5551
Internet: http://www.fctcpac.navy.mil/
OFFICER-OF-THE-DAY: 619-553-8330,
   DSN 553-8330

Profile

BRANCH: Navy.
SIZE AND LOCATION: 95 acres. Ocean-front
   property on Point Loma, San Diego approx
   4 mi from intersection of I-5 & I-8; approx
   6 mi from downtown San Diego. *County:*
   San Diego.
MAJOR UNITS: Fleet Combat Training Center; Tactical Training Group, Pacific
   (TTGP); Naval Research and Development
   (NRAD); Naval Command, Control and
   Ocean Surveillance Center, Headquarters;
   Maritime Defense Zone Sector Southern
   California Operations Center.
BASE HISTORY: Origin of FCTC dates back
   to 1943 with a series of informal lectures on
   radar & Combat Information Center (CIC)
   concept. 1943-45, CIC instruction expanded
   to meet fleet's need to understand capabilities & tactical use of radar. 1945, CIC section established as separate command; designated CIC Indoctrination School. 1946,
   School moved to present location; designated CIC Group Training Center (later redesignated Fleet Air Defense Training Center in 1954, Fleet Anti-Air Warfare Training Center in 1960, & FCTC in 1976). Newest developments include integration of electronic warfare & long-range over-the-horizon weapons applications to counter changing threats, & Battlex, a multi-warfare area
   scenario simulation exercising battle group
   command & control.
VISITOR ATTRACTIONS: Beautiful view
   overlooking Pacific.

Key Contacts

COMMANDER: 619-553-8324, DSN 553-
   8324.
PUBLIC AFFAIRS: 619-553-0547, DSN 553-
   0547.
PROCUREMENT: 619-553-8202, DSN 553-
   8202.

Personnel and Expenditures

ACTIVE DUTY PERSONNEL: 510
CIVILIAN PERSONNEL: 70
MILITARY PAYROLL EXPENDITURE:
   $12.75 mil
CONTRACT EXPENDITURE: $2.8 mil

Services

 Housing: Family units 797; Unaccompanied officer
quarters 1; Unaccompanied enlisted quarters 10;
Barracks spaces. *Temporary Housing:* VIP units 3;
Unaccompanied officer/Enlisted quarters 74;
Transient quarters 62. *Commissary:* Yes; *Exchange:*
Retail store; Barber shop; Dry cleaners; Food shop;
Florist; Bank; Service station; Military clothing store;
Convenience store; Beauty shop; Credit union; ATM;
Post office; Fast food; Video rentals; Four seasons;
Class VI; Garden center; Tailor/Alterations; Cafeteria.
Child Care/Capacities: Day care center capacity 156,
6wks-6yrs; Summer day camp; Mattapany Day Camp.
Schools: College courses. *Base Library:* Yes. *Medical
Facilities:* Hospital; Medical clinic; Dental clinic;
Pharmacy; Veterinary services. *Recreational
Facilities:* Bowling center; Movie theater; Pool; Gym;
Recreation center; Golf course; Stables; Tennis courts;
Racquetball court; Fitness center/Weight room;
Softball field; Football field; Craft shop; Officers club;
Camping; Fishing/Hunting; Enlisted club; Picnic area;
Skeet range; Water sports; Playground.

OFFICER OF THE DAY

LAND AREA AND
GROUND TRANSPOR-
TATION DIRECTIONS
TO THE BASE

BRIEF HISTORY OF BASE

NUMBERS OF PERSONNEL
INCLUDING ACTIVE DUTY,
DEPENDENT, AND
CIVILIANS; AND PAYROLL AND
CONTRACT EXPENDITURES

Abbreviations Used in This Directory

A1c	Airman First Class		BMW	Bombardment Wing
AAFES	Army/Air Force Exchange Service		Bn	Battalion
ABFC	Advanced Base Functional Component		BOQ	Bachelor Officers Quarters
ABG	Air Base Group		BRAC	Defense Base Closure and Realignment Commission
ABW	Air Base Wing			
ACALA	Armament and Chemical Acquisition and Logistics Activity		Brig Gen	Brigadier General
			BUC	Chief Builder
ACC	Air Combat Command		BX	Base Exchange
adj	adjacent		Capt	Captain
Adj	Adjutant		CBT	Cadet Basic Training
Adj Gen	Adjutant General		CDR	Commander
Adm	Admiral		CEVG	Combat Evaluation Group
AEGIS	AEGIS Weapons System		CHPPM	Center for Health Promotion and Preventive Medicine (USA)
AF	Air Force			
AFB	Air Force Base		CID	Criminal Investigation Department
AFCENT	Allied Forces, Central Europe		CIDC	Criminal Investigation Command
AFRC	Armed Forces Reserve Center		CLANTFLT	Commander Atlantic Fleet
AFRES	Air Force Reserve		CMS	Central Materiel Service Team
AFS	Air Force Station		CMSgt	Chief Master Sergeant
AFSC	Air Force Systems Command		CNAVEUR	Commander US Naval Forces Europe
AHB	Attack Helicopter Battalion		CNCWU	Composite Naval Coastal Warfare Unit
AHC	Assault Helicopter Co		Co	Company
AKC	Aviation Storekeeper		Col	Colonel
AMC	Air Materiel Command		COM	Consolidate Open Mess
AMCCOM	Army Armament, Munitions, and Chemical Command		CONUS	Continental United States
			Cpl	Corporal
ANG	Air National Guard		CSM	Command Sergeant Major
APG	Army Planning Group		Ctr	Center
approx	approximately		CWO	Chief Warrant Officer
ARG	Air Reserve Guard		CW#	Chief Warrant Officer, # Class
ARNG	Air Reserve National Guard		DARCOM	Army Materiel Development and Readiness Command
ASOS	Automated Surface Observing System			
AT	Annual Training		DCAA	Defense Contract Audit Agency
ATM	Automatic Teller Machine		Dept	Department
Ave	Avenue		DESCOM	Army Depot System Command
BAQ	Basic Allowance for Quarters		Det	Detachment
Bde	Brigade		Div	Division
BEQ	Bachelor Enlisted Quarters		DLA	Defense Logistics Agency
bil	billion		DMZ	Demilitarized Zone
Blvd	Boulevard		DOD	Department of Defense

DODDS	Department of Defense Dependent Schools	MAW	Military Airlift Wing
DOE	Department of Energy	MCAS	Marine Corps Air Station
DPCA	Director of Personnel, Community Activities	METOC	Meteorology and Oceanography Command (USN)
DRMO	Defense Reutilization and Marketing Office		
DSN	Defense Switching Network (replaces AUTOVON)	MEWS	Early Warning Station Missile
		mi	mile(s)
DVQ	Distinguished Visitors Quarters	mil	million
E	East	MIUW	Mobile Inshore Underseas Warfare Craft
EMC	Electrician's Mate, Chief	MMCM	Machinist's Mate, Master Chief
Ens	Ensign	MP	Military Police
EOT	Emergency Operations Team	MSgt	Master Sergeant
Expy	Expressway	N	North
ext	extension	NAS	Naval Air Station
FIG	Fighter Interceptor Group	NATO	North Atlantic Treaty Organization
FIS	Fighter Interceptor Squadron	NAVSEA	Naval Sea System Command
FIW	Fighter Interceptor Wing	NAVSTA	Naval Station
FORSCOM	U.S. Army Forces Command	NCO	Noncommissioned Officer
FSSG	Force Service Support Group	NG	National Guard
ft	feet	NMCB	Naval Mobile Construction Battalion
Ft	Fort	NOAA	National Oceanic and Atmopsheric Administration
FY	Fiscal year		
Gen	General	NORAD	North American Air Defense Command
GOCO	Government Owned, Contractor Operated	NR	Naval Reserve
GOGO	Government Owned, Government Operated	NWS	Naval Weapons Station
HMC	Hospital Corpsman, Chief	OCONUS	Outside Continental United States
HS	Helicopter Antisubmarine Squadron	PACAF	Pacific Air Force
HSL	Helicopter Antisubmarine Squadron Light	PAO	Public Affairs Officer
HQ	Headquarters	PCS	Permanent Change of Station
hr(s)	hour(s)	Pfc	Private First Class
Hwy	Highway	PHCS	Senior Chief Photographer's Mate
IAP	International Airport	Pkwy	Parkway
IDT	Inactive Duty Training	Plt	Platoon
IEA	International Energy Agency	PO	Petty Officer
INSCOM	Intelligence and Security Command	PSB	Personnel Service Battalion
Intl	International	PSL	Physical Sciences Laboratory
ITT	Information, Tickets, Tours (Service)	Pvt	Private
JO#	Journalist, # Class	PX	Post Exchange
JO2	Petty Officer, 2nd Class	RADM	Rear Admiral
L	Light	Rear Adm	Rear Admiral
LCDR	Lieutenant Commander	REDCOM	Readiness Command
Lt	Lieutenant	ROTC	Reserve Officer Training Corps
LTC	Lieutenant Colonel	Rte	Route
Lt Gen	Lieutenant General	RV	Recreational vehicle
LTjg	Lieutenant Junior Grade	S	South
MAC	Military Airlift Command	SAC	Strategic Air Command
MACM	Master Chief Machine Accountant	SAR	Search and Rescue
MACS	Marine Air Control Squadron	SATAF	Site Activities Task Force
Maj	Major	SATO	Scheduled Airline Ticket Office
Maj Gen	Major General	SFC	Specialist First Class
MAP	Municipal Airport	Sgt	Sergeant
MARS	Military Affiliate Radio System	SK#	Storekeeper, # class
MASC	Marine Air-Ground Task Force Automated Services Center	SKCM	Master Chief Storekeeper
		SMSgt	Senior Master Sergeant
MASH	Mobile Army Surgical Hospital	SPT	Support
MATES	Mobilization and Training Equipment Site	sq	square
MATS	Military Air Transport Service	Sq	Squadron

SRW	Strategic Reconnaissance Wing	USCG	United States Coast Guard
SSgt	Staff Sergeant	USCGC	United States Coast Guard Cutter
St	Street	USCGR	United States Coast Guard Reserve
SUBASE	Submarine Base	USMC	United States Marine Corps
SUPRTCEN	Support Center	USN	United States Navy
TAACOM	Theater Army Area Command	USNR	United States Navy Reserve
TAC	Tactical Air Command	USPFO	United States Property and Fiscal Office
TACOM	Tank Automotive Command	VA	Attack Squadron
TAD	Tactical Air Direction	VAdm	Vice Admiral
TAD	Temporary Active Duty	VAQ	Tactical Early Warning Squadron
TAG	Tactical Airlift Group	VAQ	Visiting Airmen's Quarters
TAS	Tactical Airlift Squadron	VAW	Carrier Airborne Early Warning Squadron
TAW	Tactical Airlift Wing	VEQ	Visiting Enlisted Quarters
TECOM	U.S. Army Test and Evaluation Command	VF	Fighter Squadron
TFG	Tactical Fighter Group	VFA	Strike Fighter Squadron
TFW	Tactical Fighter Wing	VIP	Very Important Person
TMDE	test, measurement, and diagnostic equipment	VMA	Marine All Weather Attack Squadron
Tpke	Turnpike	VMFA	Marine Fighter Attack Squadron
TRACEN	Training Center	VOQ	Visiting Officers Quarters
TRADOC	Training and Doctrine Command	VP	Patrol Squadron
TRG	Tactical Reconnaissance Group	VQ	Fleet Air Reconnaissance Squadron
TSgt	Technical Sergeant	VRC	Fleet Logistics Support Squadron
Twp	Township	VS	Air Antisubmarine Squadron
Univ	University	VTU	Volunteer Training Unit
USA	United States Army	W	West
USAF	United States Air Force	WO	Warrant Officer
USAFE	United States Air Force Europe	WWI	World War I
USAFLO	United States Air Force Liaison Officer	WWII	World War II
USAR	United States Army Reserve	YN	Yeoman
USAREUR	United States Army, Europe	YNC	Yeoman, Chief
USARSO	US Army Forces Southern Command		

Profiles of Military Bases in the U.S.

Alabama

Anniston

1. Anniston Army Depot
ANAD
7 Frankford Ave
Anniston, AL 36201-4199
205-235-7501; FAX 205-235-4695; DSN
571-7501; DSN FAX 571-4695
Internet: http://www-anad.army.mil
Profile
BRANCH: Army.
SIZE AND LOCATION: 15,000 acres. Approx 50 mi E of Birmingham, AL; 90 mi W of Atlanta just off I-20. *County:* Calhoun.
MAJOR UNITS: Defense Distribution Depot, Anniston; Anniston Chemical Activity; Army Center of Military History; Defense Reutilization & Marketing Office; Defense Printing Service; Army TMDE Support Center.
BASE HISTORY: 1941, construction began. 1952, depot assigned maintenance mission, overhaul & repair combat vehicles. 1960, reconditioned tanks. 1963, maintenance & storage of chemical munitions (currently in process of disposal in accord with Chemical Weapons Convention). 1976, became part of Army Depot System Command (DESCOM). 1980s, missile maintenance included. 1992, general supply mission assumed by Defense Distribution Depot, Anniston (DDAA). 1995, DESCOM abolished & replaced by Industrial Operation Command (IOC) & chemical mission put under Anniston Chemical Activity. Current inventory of Depot is over $7.6 billion, ships/receives supplies, and produces over 600 combat vehicles annually.
Key Contacts
COMMANDER: Col Gregory F Potts, ATTN: SIOAN-CO, 205-235-7511, DSN 571-7511.
PUBLIC AFFAIRS: Joan C Gustafson, ATTN: SIOAN-PA, 205-235-6281, FAX 205-235-4735; DSN 571-6281, DSN FAX 571-4695, PAO@anniston-emh1.army.mil.
PROCUREMENT: Robert S Corrigan, 205-235-6532, DSN 571-6532.
TRANSPORTATION: Charles Reeves II, 205-235-6837, DSN 571-6837.
PERSONNEL/COMMUNITY ACTIVITIES: Billy Bickerstaff, Director of Resources, 205-235-6159, DSN 571-6159.
Personnel and Expenditures
ACTIVE DUTY PERSONNEL: 7
DEPENDENTS: 0
CIVILIAN PERSONNEL: 2,565

MILITARY PAYROLL EXPENDITURE: $130 mil (military/civilian)
CONTRACT EXPENDITURE: $76 mil
Services *Exchange:* Credit union; Class VI; Cafeteria. *Child Care/Capacities:* No day care facilities. *Schools:* No on-base schools. *Medical Facilities:* Medical clinic. *Recreational Facilities:* Gym; Racquetball court; Fitness center/ Weight room; Softball field; Auto shop; Craft shop; Fishing/Hunting; Picnic area; Community club.

2. Fort McClellan
Fort McClellan
Anniston, AL 36205-5000
205-848-4611; DSN 865-4611
OFFICER-OF-THE-DAY: 205-848-3821, DSN 865-3821
Profile
BRANCH: Army.
SIZE AND LOCATION: 46,000 acres. On Hwy 21, at N edge of Anniston, AL; 7 mi N of US-20, use Anniston-Oxford-Ft McClellan Exit, I-85. *County:* Calhoun.
MAJOR UNITS: Army Chemical School; Army Military Police School; 11th Chemical Bn; 787th Military Police Bn; DOD Polygraph Institute; Army Training Brigade; Army Reception Station; 701st Military Police Bn; Fort McClellan Military Police Co; Headquarters Bn; 14th Army Band; 46th Engineer (Combat) (Heavy), Co D; 365th Transportation Co (Light Truck); 702nd Ordnance Det; Army Medical Department Activity; Noble Army Health Clinic.
BASE HISTORY: 1912, National Guardsmen trained in area. 1917, federal government purchased land; began construction and mobilization. 1929, Camp McClellan became Fort. WWII, trained soldiers; served as POW camp for Germans & Italians. Following WWII, base inactivated; facilities deteriorated. 1951, reactivated as Chemical Corps School & Women's Army Corps Center and School; Military Police Corps added later.
FUTURE CLOSURE/REALIGNMENT: Scheduled for closure Sep 1999.
VISITOR ATTRACTIONS: Women's Army Corps Museum; Military Police Corps Regimental Museum; Chemical Corps Museum.
Key Contacts
COMMANDER: Commander, USACML&MPCEN&FM.
PUBLIC AFFAIRS: 205-848-5377, DSN 865-5377, Attn: ATZN-PAO, Bldg 51, Buckner Circle.

PROCUREMENT: 205-848-3622, DSN 865-3622.
TRANSPORTATION: 205-848-3020, DSN 865-3020.
PERSONNEL/COMMUNITY ACTIVITIES: 205-848-3827, DSN 865-3827.
Personnel and Expenditures
ACTIVE DUTY PERSONNEL: 1319; 1144 Guard & Reserve
DEPENDENTS: 3382
CIVILIAN PERSONNEL: 2301
Services
Housing: Family units 570; Unaccompanied enlisted quarters (double occupancy) 6; BAQ units 80; Duplex units 1. *Temporary Housing:* VIP units 4; VOQ units 342; VEQ units 80; Guesthouse units 138; Guest cottages 4; Apartment units 50; Lodge units 1. *Commissary:* Yes; *Exchange:* Retail store; Barber shop; Dry cleaners; Food shop; Florist; Bank; Service station. *Child Care/Capacities:* Day care center capacity 265. *Schools:* Elementary. *Base Library:* Yes. *Medical Facilities:* Medical clinic 60; Dental clinic. *Recreational Facilities:* Bowling center; Movie theater; Pool; Gym; Recreation center; Golf course; Tennis courts; Racquetball court; Fitness center/Weight room; Softball field; Football field; Auto shop; Craft shop; Officers club; NCO club; Camping; Fishing/Hunting.

Bessemer

3. Bessemer Naval & Marine Corps Reserve Readiness Center
NAVMARCORESCEN Bessemer
1001 4th Ave, SW
Bessemer, AL 35023-4731
205-424-4210; FAX 205-425-6517
Profile
BRANCH: Naval Reserve; Marine Corps Reserve.
SIZE AND LOCATION: 8 acres. 2 mi off I-20 at Academy Dr. Exit I-20/59 at Academy Dr, left, 1 mi to end, left, 1 mi to center; across street from Jess Lanier High School. *County:* Jefferson.
MAJOR UNITS: REDCOM NINE Activity; HQ Battery, 4th Bn, 14th Marine Regiment; L Battery, 4th Bn, 14th Marine Regiment; plus 20 other reserve units.
Key Contacts
COMMANDER: CDR Will M Christy, 205-424-4210, FAX 205-425-6517.

PUBLIC AFFAIRS: LCDR R J D Stevens, 205-424-4210, FAX 425-6517.

Personnel and Expenditures

ACTIVE DUTY PERSONNEL: 2 officers; 23 enlisted; 699 reservists

Services *Recreational Facilities:* Fitness center/ Weight room; Picnic area.

Birmingham

4. Birmingham Airport, Air National Guard Base

Sumpter Smith ANG Base

5401 E Lake Blvd

Birmingham, AL 35217-3595

205-841-9200; DSN 778-2210

Profile

BRANCH: Air National Guard.

SIZE AND LOCATION: 118 acres. Co-located with Birmingham Airport; within corporate limits of Birmingham off I-59; use Airport Hwy, Exit 129. *County:* Jefferson.

MAJOR UNITS: 117 Air Refueling Wing (ANG); 117th TAC RECON Wing (ANG); 252nd Transportation Unit; 307th Transportation Unit; Aviation Support Facility.

BASE HISTORY: Named for Col Sumpter Smith, who played an important part in promoting development of Birmingham's airport. 1994, converting to KC-135R.

Personnel and Expenditures

ACTIVE DUTY PERSONNEL: 964 Guard

CIVILIAN PERSONNEL: 323

MILITARY PAYROLL EXPENDITURE: $21.9 mil

Fort Rucker

5. Fort Rucker

US Army Aviation Center

Fort Rucker, AL 36362-5000

334-255-1110; DSN 558-1110

Internet: http://www-rucker.army.mil/

OFFICER-OF-THE-DAY: 334-255-3100, DSN 588-3100

Profile

BRANCH: Army.

SIZE AND LOCATION: 64,349 acres. In SE AL, approx 90 mi S of Montgomery and 30 mi NW of Dothan, AL; between US-231 and US-84. *County:* Dale; Coffee; Geneva; Houston.

MAJOR UNITS: Army Aviation Center; 1st Aviation Brigade; Army Aviation Logistics School; Aviation Training Brigade; Army Corps of Engineers, Ft Rucker; Defense Investigative Service, Ft Rucker; Army Dental Command, Ft Rucker; Army Aviation Center Noncommissioned Officer Academy; Operational Test and Evaluation Command; Army Reserve Center, Ft Rucker Regional Flight Center; Test, Measurement, Diagnostics, and Evaluation Center; Army Aeromedical Center; Army Aeromedical Research Laboratory; Army Traffic Control Activity; Army Aviation Technical Test Center; Air Force 23rd Flying Training Flight; Air Force Air Ground Operations School; Army School of Aviation Medicine; Army Safety School; Total Army Warrant Officer Career Center; Air Maneuver Battle Lab.

BASE HISTORY: 1935, land bought by federal government as Pea River Cooperative Land Use Area. 1942, opened as Ozark Triangular Division Camp, infantry training site. 1943, renamed Camp Rucker, to honor Gen Edmund Winchester Rucker, Confederate Army officer from TN & businessman, Montgomery, AL. 1946-50, Camp Rucker on inactive status until reactivated for Korean War. 1954, closed May-July, until Army Aviation School moved from Ft Sill, OK. 1955, designated Fort. During Vietnam War, provided primary training for Army Aviation. 1973, all Army aviation training consolidated here.

VISITOR ATTRACTIONS: Army Aviation Museum.

Key Contacts

COMMANDER: Maj Gen Daniel J Petrosky, 334-255-2600, DSN 588-2600; Col Laughlin, Garrison Commander, 334-255-2095.

PUBLIC AFFAIRS: Maj Yonts, ATZQ-PAO, Bldg 121/122, 334-255-2474, 334-255-2252, FAX 334-255-1004, ATZQPAO@ rucker-emh4.army.mil.

Personnel and Expenditures

ACTIVE DUTY PERSONNEL: 8000

DEPENDENTS: 3800

CIVILIAN PERSONNEL: 7000

Services

Housing: Family units 1515; Trailer spaces 43. *Temporary Housing:* VIP units 8; VOQ units 256. *Commissary:* Yes; *Exchange:* Retail store; Barber shop; Dry cleaners; Food shop; Florist; Bank; Service station; Furniture store; Bakery; Military clothing store; Convenience store; Beauty shop; Laundromat; Credit union; Video rental; Photo finishing; Jewelry/watch sales/repair; Optical shop; Car rental; Shoe repair; Tailor; Class VI; Rent all; Toys; Garden center; Ice cream; Snacks. *Child Care/Capacities:* Day care center; Home day care program; Latch key program. *Schools:* Preschool/Kindergarten; Elementary; College courses. *Base Library:* Yes. *Medical Facilities:* Hospital 72 beds; Medical clinic; Dental clinic; Pharmacy; Veterinary services; Lyster Army Community Hospital; Air Ambulance Division. *Recreational Facilities:* Bowling center; Movie theater; Pool; Gym; Recreation center; Golf course; Stables; Tennis courts; Racquetball court; Fitness center/Weight room; Softball field; Auto shop; Craft shop; Officers club; NCO club; Camping; Fishing/Hunting; Enlisted club; Youth center; Picnic area; Skeet range; Water sports; Playground; Post Wildlife Association; Lake Tholocco on post; Beach; Squash; Equestrian center; Basketball; Florida Recreation Area; ITT.

Gunter

6. Gunter Annex

Gunter, AL 36114

334-416-1110; DSN 596-1110

Internet: http://www.ssg.gunter.af.mil

Profile

BRANCH: Air Force.

SIZE AND LOCATION: 348 acres. Central AL, approx 5 mi NE of downtown Montgomery; between US-80 and US-231, off Dalraide. *County:* Montgomery.

MAJOR UNITS: Air Force Senior Noncommissioned Officer Academy; College for Enlisted Professional Military Education; Standard Systems Group, Headquarters; Air Force Reuse Center; Contracting Directorate; Electronic Software Distribution Center; Financial Management and Comptroller Systems; Flight Services Division; Global Combat Support System; Logistics Transportation; Sabre Drill Team; Small Computer Division.

BASE HISTORY: 1940, Army Air Corps Basic Flying Training School activated at Montgomery Municipal Airport. 1941, named Gunter Field for a mayor of Montgomery, William A Gunter. Flyer training began with American, British, Canadian, French, & Chinese pilots. Following WWII, training program transferred to Army Air Force's School, later training program Air University; used originally to house Maxwell AFB's personnel & tenant organizations. 1950, Medical Service School & Extension Course Institute established. 1957, Montgomery Air Defense Sector activated. 1960s, HQ, 14th Air Force & 32nd Air Division located here. 1971, Data Systems Design Center moved from Washington, DC, now subordinate unit of Materiel Command's Electronic Systems Center, Hanscom AFB, MA. 1972, Senior Noncommissioned Officer Academy established. Gunter's runways no longer active.

Key Contacts

COMMANDER: See Maxwell AFB.

PUBLIC AFFAIRS: Lt Kristi Beckman, 334-416-4323, DSN 596-4323, beckmank@ ssg.gunter.af.mil.

Services

Housing: See Maxwell AFB. *Exchange:* See Maxwell AFB.

Huntsville

7. Army Engineering & Support Center

Huntsville Center; CEHNC

Corps of Engineers/Huntsville

4820 University Square

Huntsville, AL 35816-1822

Mailing Address

PO Box 1600

Huntsville, AL 35807-4301

205-895-1200; FAX 205-895-1877; DSN 760-1300; DSN FAX 760-1877

E-mail: cehnd.usace.army.mil Internet:http:// www.cehnd.usace.army.mil

Profile

BRANCH: Army.

SIZE AND LOCATION: Offices only. At Research Park within city limits; 10 mi from Huntsville/Decatur IAP; 2 mi from Redstone Arsenal. *County:* Madison.

MAJOR UNITS: Army Engineering & Support Center.

BASE HISTORY: 1967, established to handle the SAFEGUARD ballistic missile defense system. Unlike other Corps Divisions/Districts, has no geographical/water basin boundaries. Current missions: chemical demilitarization; ordnance & explosive removal; energy contracts; medical equipment; Russian Chemical Demilitarization. Performs military & civil works construction.

Key Contacts
COMMANDER: Col Walter J Cunningham, 205-895-1300, FAX 205-895-1910, DSN 760-1300, CunninghamW_COL@smtp.hnd. usace.army.mil.
PUBLIC AFFAIRS: Robert DiMichele, 205-895-1691, FAX 205-895-1689, DSN 760-1691, dimicheler@hnc.usace.army.mil.
PROCUREMENT: Jim Reynolds, 205-895-1100.
TRANSPORTATION: Leonard Bynum, 205-895-1680.
PERSONNEL/COMMUNITY ACTIVITIES: Carol Dennis, Human Resources Officer, Redstone Arsenal, 205-876-7401; Judy Wilson, Community Relations Officer, 205-895-1693.

Personnel and Expenditures
ACTIVE DUTY PERSONNEL: 6
CIVILIAN PERSONNEL: 600
CONTRACT EXPENDITURE: $700 mil
Services *Base Library:* Yes. *Recreational Facilities:* Fitness center/Weight room.

Maxwell AFB

8. Maxwell Air Force Base
50 LeMay Plaza S
Maxwell AFB, AL 36112-6334
334-953-1110; DSN 493-1110
Internet: http://www.au.af.mil
Profile
BRANCH: Air Force.
SIZE AND LOCATION: 2487 acres. In central AL, between I-65, US-82 and Alabama River, approx 3 mi N-NW of downtown Montgomery; exits from I-65 & I-85 marked. *County:* Montgomery.
MAJOR UNITS: Air University; 42nd Air Base Wing; Air War College; Air Command and Staff College; College of Aerospace Doctrine, Research and Education; Ira C Eaker College for Professional Development; Air Force Quality Institute; 42nd Communications Squadron; Community College of the Air Force; Air University Library; Civil Air Patrol, HQ; Air Force Historical Research Agency; Academic Instructor School; Air Force Judge Advocate Generals School; Enlisted Heritage Research Institute; Human Resource Management School.
BASE HISTORY: 1910, Orville Wright started first school for instruction in aviation; Army purchased Wright Field. 1918, aircraft engine & repair depot established. 1922, named Maxwell Field for 2nd Lt William C Maxwell, Atmore, AL, native & aircraft accident victim. 1928, first permanent buildings completed. 1931-40, Air Corps Tactical School moved in from Langley Field, VA; Gunter Field airport acquired from city. 1946, Air University established. 1978-83 subordinate unit of Air Training Command established.
VISITOR ATTRACTIONS: Site of Indian Village of Towassa visited by DeSoto; Site of hanger used by Wright Brothers first flying school; Air Park; Heritage Hall.
Key Contacts
COMMANDER: Lt Gen Joseph J Redden, Air Univ; Col William S Cole Jr, 42 ABW.
PROCUREMENT: LTC Virgil L DeArmond, Contracting Officer, 42nd Contracting Squadron, 205-953-5319, DSN 493-5319.

Personnel and Expenditures
ACTIVE DUTY PERSONNEL: 4450; Reserve 1300
DEPENDENTS: 1530
CIVILIAN PERSONNEL: 4000
Services
Housing: Family units 957; Dormitory spaces 321; Senior NCO units 153; Junior NCO units 435; RV/Camper sites 30. *Temporary Housing:* VOQ units 1255; VAQ units 562; Transient quarters 41. *Commissary:* Yes; *Exchange:* Retail store; Barber shop; Dry cleaners; Food shop; Florist; Bank; Service station; Bookstore; Military clothing store; Convenience store; Beauty shop; Credit union. *Child Care/Capacities:* Day care center capacity 230, 6wks-5yrs; Before & after school youth activities. *Schools:* Preschool/Kindergarten; Elementary; College/University; College courses. *Medical Facilities:* Hospital 40 beds; Medical clinic; Dental clinic; Pharmacy; Veterinary services. *Recreational Facilities:* Bowling center; Movie theater; Pool; Gym; Recreation center; Golf course; Stables; Tennis courts; Racquetball court; Skating rink; Fitness center/Weight room; Softball field; Football field; Auto shop; Craft shop; Officers club; Camping; Enlisted club; Youth center; Picnic area; Skeet range; Water sports; Playground; Aero club; Fishing; Lake Pippin, 165 mi away.

Mobile

9. Mobile Coast Guard Aviation Training Center
USCG-ATC Mobile
8501 Tanner Williams Rd
Mobile, AL 36608-9682
334-639-6117; FAX 334-639-6435; DSN 649-3635
E-mail: ATCMOBILE@mailgatehq.comdt.uscg.mil
OFFICER-OF-THE-DAY: 334-639-6110
Profile
BRANCH: Coast Guard.
SIZE AND LOCATION: 231 acres. In city of Mobile on NW side of Mobile Regional Airport; entrance on Tanner Williams Rd; approx 6 mi from I-65 Airport Blvd Exit, follow signs. *County:* Mobile.
MAJOR UNITS: Coast Guard Aviation Training Center, Mobile; Coast Guard Gulf Strike Team.
BASE HISTORY: 1966, site commissioned as Air Station at former Bates Field Air Force Reserve facility as fixed-wing and rotary-wing pilot training unit. 1969, Helicopter Icebreaker Support Unit (IBSU) created; Aviation Training Center assumed current name, came under direct control of Coast Guard HQ. Operational divisions: Search & Rescue (supporting Eighth District), Training (providing training to all Coast Guard pilots), and Polar Operations (deployed on Icebreakers in AK, Arctic, and Antarctic). Largest air unit in Coast Guard.
VISITOR ATTRACTIONS: Coast Guard Aviation Hall of Fame (Memorial to Coast Guard aviators).
Key Contacts
COMMANDER: Capt Kurt A Carlson, 334-639-6101, FAX 334-639-6115.
PUBLIC AFFAIRS: Lt Carmen Bazzano, 334-639-6428, FAX 334-639-6435.

PROCUREMENT: LCDR Dave Walton, 334-639-6312, FAX 334-639-6315.
PERSONNEL/COMMUNITY ACTIVITIES: See Public Affairs Officer.
Personnel and Expenditures
ACTIVE DUTY PERSONNEL: 440
DEPENDENTS: 0
CIVILIAN PERSONNEL: 40
MILITARY PAYROLL EXPENDITURE: $17.9 mil
CONTRACT EXPENDITURE: $9.5 mil
Services
Housing: Unaccompanied enlisted quarters 15. *Temporary Housing:* VIP units (rooms) 2; Unaccompanied officer/Enlisted quarters 27; BAQ units 5. *Commissary:* Yes; *Exchange:* Retail store; Barber shop; Food shop; Bank; Service station; Convenience store; Beauty shop; Credit union; ATM; Class VI; Cafeteria. *Child Care/Capacities:* No day care facilities. *Schools:* No on-base schools. *Medical Facilities:* Medical clinic; Dental clinic; Pharmacy. *Recreational Facilities:* Pool; Tennis courts; Racquetball court; Fitness center/Weight room; Softball field; Football field; Auto shop; NCO club; Enlisted club; Picnic area; Consolidated club; Rental cottages and RV sites at Dauphin Island recreation area 25 mi S on Gulf of Mexico.

10. Mobile Coast Guard Group/ Station
Group Mobile
S Broad St
Mobile, AL 36615-1390
334-441-6217, 441-5051
Profile
BRANCH: Coast Guard.
SIZE AND LOCATION: 10 acres. S of I-10 in Mobile in Brookley Industrial Complex on Mobile Bay. *County:* Mobile.
MAJOR UNITS: Coast Guard Group, Mobile; Coast Guard Station, Mobile; Aids to Navigation (ANT) Team, Mobile; Fire & Safety Test Det, Mobile; USCGC *Chincoteague*; USCGC *Point Ledge*; USCGC *Sweetgum*; USCGC *Saginaw*; USCGC *Axe*; USCGC *White Pine*; Marine Safety Office, Mobile; Gulf Strike Team, Mobile; Electronic Support Det, Mobile.
BASE HISTORY: USCG Base established at Port City after Civil War, located at Choctaw Point approx 5 mi N of present location. 1966, present location, former Overseas Terminal of Brookley AFB, acquired. Group responsible for coastline from Biloxi, MS, to St Marks, FL, & Tennessee-Tombigbee Waterway & Chattahoochee, Flint, Mobile & other navigable rivers.
VISITOR ATTRACTIONS: Cutters located at base.

Personnel and Expenditures
ACTIVE DUTY PERSONNEL: 100
CIVILIAN PERSONNEL: 15
Services *Temporary Housing:* None. *Exchange:* Retail store; Barber shop; Bank; Service station; Military clothing store; Convenience store; *Child Care/Capacities:* No day care facilities. *Schools:* No on-base schools. *Medical Facilities:* Medical clinic. *Recreational Facilities:* Fitness center/Weight room; Softball field; NCO club.

11. Mobile Naval & Marine Corps Reserve Center
NMCRC Mobile
4851 Museum Dr
Mobile, AL 36608-2510
334-344-5341, 344-5395; FAX 334-341-0349
Profile
BRANCH: Naval Reserve; Marine Corps Reserve.
LOCATION: *County:* Mobile.
MAJOR UNITS: REDCOM NINE Activity; 4th SCAMP Platoon (MARFORRES); 3rd Force Reconnaissance Co (MARFORRES).
Key Contacts
COMMANDER: CDR R S Hixson.

12. US Army Corps of Engineers, Mobile District
CESAM
109 St Joseph St
Mobile, AL 36602-3630
Mailing Address
PO Box 2288
Mobile, AL 36628-0001
334-690-2505; FAX 334-690-2516; DSN 457-2511
E-mail: cesam-pa@sam.usace.army.mil Internet:http://www.sam.usace.army.mil/
Profile
BRANCH: Army.
SIZE AND LOCATION: Offices only. In city of Mobile. *County:* Mobile.
MAJOR UNITS: Corps of Engineers, Mobile District.
BASE HISTORY: 1815, Corps of Engineers officers reported to Mobile Gulf coastal area. 1888, present structure established. Mobile District is 1 of 6 district-level areas of South Atlantic Division, Atlanta. District includes parts of AL, MS, TN, FL, GA, & Latin America. Performs both civil works (water resources), military, & NASA construction/installation support.
Key Contacts
COMMANDER: Col William S Vogel, District Commander, 334-690-2511.
PUBLIC AFFAIRS: E Patrick Robbins, 334-690-2505.
PROCUREMENT: Edward M Slana, 334-441-6501.
TRANSPORTATION: Gloria Liggett, 334-690-2405.
PERSONNEL/COMMUNITY ACTIVITIES: Evelyn I Cave, Director of Personnel, 334-690-2521, evelyn.i.cave@sam.usace.army.mil.
Personnel and Expenditures
ACTIVE DUTY PERSONNEL: 9
CIVILIAN PERSONNEL: 1440
MILITARY PAYROLL EXPENDITURE: $82 mil
CONTRACT EXPENDITURE: $479 mil
Services *Base Library:* Yes.

Montgomery

13. Adjutant General of Alabama
PO Box 3711
Montgomery, AL 36109-0711
334-271-7200; FAX 334-271-7366
Profile
BRANCH: Army National Guard.
MAJOR UNITS: Alabama National Guard.
Key Contacts
COMMANDER: Maj Gen Clyde A Hennies.

14. Dannelly Field Air National Guard Base
PO Box 250284
Montgomery, AL 36125-0284
334-284-7100; DSN 742-9000
Profile
BRANCH: Air National Guard.
SIZE AND LOCATION: 42 acres. 7 mi SW of Montgomery, off US-80. *County:* Montgomery.
MAJOR UNITS: 187th Fighter Group (ANG).
BASE HISTORY: Named for Ens Clarence Dannelly, Navy pilot killed at Pensacola NAS during WWII.
Personnel and Expenditures
ACTIVE DUTY PERSONNEL: 1129
CIVILIAN PERSONNEL: 271
MILITARY PAYROLL EXPENDITURE: $12.9 mil
Services *Medical Facilities:* Dispensary.

15. Montgomery Marine Corps Reserve Center
1650 Federal Dr
Montgomery, AL 36107-1128
334-272-8843, 272-8152, 272-8228; FAX 334-272-7119; DSN 493-7798
Profile
BRANCH: Marine Corps Reserve.
LOCATION: SE Central AL. *County:* Montgomery.
MAJOR UNITS: L Co, 3rd Bn, 23rd Marine Regiment.

Redstone Arsenal

16. Redstone Arsenal
ATTN: AMSAM-RA-CF-FS-AC, Bldg 3491, Honest John
Redstone Arsenal, AL 35898
205-876-2151; DSN 746-0011
Internet: http://www.redstone.army.mil
Profile
BRANCH: Army.
SIZE AND LOCATION: 38,248 acres. In NW Alabama, adj to Huntsville, off Rte 231 on AL-20. *County:* Madison.
MAJOR UNITS: Army Aviation and Missile Command; Distributed Interactive Simulation Center (AMCOM); Corps of Engineers, Redstone Arsenal; Regional Civilian Personnel Center (CPOC), Redstone Arsenal; Defense Finance and Accounting Service, Redstone Arsenal; Defense Megacenter, Huntsville; Engineering Data Management Office, Army JEDMICS Component Office; Enhanced Fiber Optic Guided Missile; George C Marshall Space Flight Center; JTUAV Protect Office; Logistics Support Activity (LOGSA); Multi-User Engineering Change Proposal Automated Review System; Redstone Scientific Information Center (RSIC); Redstone Technical Test Center (RTTC); Regional Civilian Personnel Center, Redstone Arsenal; Army Space and Strategic Defense Command; Huntsville Virtual Reality Alabama; Missile and Munitions Center and School.

BASE HISTORY: 1941, established to make conventional ammunition & toxic chemicals. 1949-50, began work on missiles, with arrival of missile experts from Ft Bliss. 1958, Army Ordnance Missile Command established; supported by Redstone Arsenal. 1961, Army Ordnance Missile Support Agency established (replacing Redstone Arsenal). 1962, Army Missile Command activated. 1967, redesignated Army Missile Support Command. 1971, Arsenal Support Operations Directorate redesignated as Redstone Arsenal Support Activity. 1985, converted to contract mode of operations.
Key Contacts
COMMANDER: Col Duane F Brandt.
PROCUREMENT: Darrell Brewer, Logistics.
TRANSPORTATION: Margie S Wallace, 205-876-5161.
Personnel and Expenditures
ACTIVE DUTY PERSONNEL: 2025
CIVILIAN PERSONNEL: 16,750
Services
Housing: Family units 1120; Unaccompanied officer quarters 20; Senior NCO units 46. *Temporary Housing:* VIP units 6; VOQ units 76; VEQ units 16; Guesthouse units 21; No pets. *Commissary:* Yes; *Exchange:* Retail store; Service station; Convenience store; Credit union; Class VI. *Child Care/Capacities:* Day care center capacity 175; Home day care program. *Schools:* No on-base schools. *Medical Facilities:* Hospital 28 beds; Medical clinic; Dental clinic; Veterinary services. *Recreational Facilities:* Bowling center; Movie theater; Pool; Gym; Golf course; Tennis courts; Racquetball court; Fitness center/Weight room; Auto shop; Craft shop; Camping; Fishing/Hunting; Youth center; Boating; Aero Club.

Tuscaloosa

17. Tuscaloosa Armed Forces Reserve Center
2627 10th Ave
Tuscaloosa, AL 35401-6699
205-345-6910; FAX 205-759-5788
E-mail: tuscaloo@cnsrf.navy.mil
Profile
BRANCH: Army.
SIZE AND LOCATION: 4.3 acres. Approx 58 mi SW of Birmingham; approx 7 mi E of Tuscaloosa Municipal Airport. *County:* Tuscaloosa.
MAJOR UNITS: REDCOM NINE Activity; Naval Hospital Pensacola 2110 (NR); USS *Hayler* (DD-997)(9709NR); Volunteer Training Unit 0916 (NR); NCR-20th Naval Construction Regiment, Det E; 4th Force Service Support Group (USMC) (4FSSG); Armament Munitions and Chemical Command 10 ROTA 1009 (NR); Destroyer Tender (AD-41) Det 8 (NR); 75th Combat Support Hospital (US Army); Area Maintenance Support Activity 154G (US Army).
Key Contacts
COMMANDER: LCDR Alfred E Page, pagel@cnrf.nola.navy.mil; Capt Don S Colt (US Army) 205-750-2565, FAX 205-391-9220.
PUBLIC AFFAIRS: BMC(SW) Dennis G Tompkins, tompkins@cnrf.nola.navy.mil.

Personnel and Expenditures
ACTIVE DUTY PERSONNEL: 7; 200 guardsmen

Alaska

Anchorage

18. Anchorage Naval Reserve Center
2735 E Tudor Rd
Anchorage, AK 99507-1135
907-561-3003; FAX 907-561-0654; DSN
317-552-2486
Profile
BRANCH: Naval Reserve.
LOCATION: *County:* Anchorage.
MAJOR UNITS: REDCOM TWENTY-TWO
Activity.
Key Contacts
COMMANDER: Lt N H White.

19. Elmendorf Air Force Base
EAFB
6920 12th St
Anchorage, AK 99506-2530
907-552-1110; FAX 907-552-5111; DSN
317-552-1110
Internet: http://www.topcover.af.mil/
OFFICER-OF-THE-DAY: 907-552-5748, DSN
317-552-5748
Profile
BRANCH: Air Force.
SIZE AND LOCATION: 13,130 acres. N side
of Anchorage city limits; N off Glenn Hwy
on to Boniface Pkwy. *County:* Anchorage.
MAJOR UNITS: Alaskan Command, HQ; 11th
Air Force; 3rd Logistics Group; 3rd Logistics
Support Squadron; 3rd Equipment Mainte-
nance Squadron; 3rd Component Repair
Squadron; 3rd Supply Squadron; 3rd Trans-
portation Squadron; 3rd Contracting Squad-
ron; Air Force Engineering and Technical
Services; 3rd Security Forces Squadron; 19th
Fighter Squadron; 381st Intelligence Squad-
ron; 3rd Operations Squadron; 3rd Services
Squadron; 54th Fighter Squadron; 632nd Air
Mobility Support Squadron; 90th Fighter
Squadron; Air Force Band of the Pacific;
Alaska Weather Operations Center; 3rd Medi-
cal Group; E Co, 4th Reconnaissance Bn
(USMC Reserve).
BASE HISTORY: 1940, activated as Ft Richard-
son with Elmendorf Airfield, named for Capt
Hugh M Elmendorf, test pilot killed flying
new pursuit plane at Wright Field, OH, 1933.
Post WWII, 11th Air Force redesignated Alaskan Air Command. 1951, Ft Richardson
moved to present location & base redesig-
nated Elmendorf AFB; site of Alaska NO-
RAD Control Center. 1966, activation of 21st
Composite Wing (later 21st Wing). 1990, re-
designation of Alaskan Air Command as 11th
Air Force & Pacific Air Forces base. 1991, arrival of 90th Tactical Fighter & F-15Es; 3rd
Wing host unit. 1993, construction of new
hospital. 1993, Cope Thunder exercises
moved to ranges near Eielson. Currently, largest military installation in Alaska.
VISITOR ATTRACTIONS: Elmendorf Natural
Wildlife Museum.
Key Contacts
COMMANDER: Lt Gen Patrick K Gamble,
Alaska Command, 907-552-2100; Maj
Joseph E Mecadon, 11530 Q St, Suite 100,
99506-2830, 907-552-2341, DSN
317-552-2341; Capt Harris, 3rd Wing,
907-552-8151.
PUBLIC AFFAIRS: 6920 12th St, 99506-2530,
907-552-8151, DSN 317-552-8151.
PROCUREMENT: 6920 12th St, Suite 230,
99506-2570, 907-552-2810, DSN
317-552-2810.
TRANSPORTATION: 21900 2nd St, Suite 200,
99506-3385, 907-552-2312, DSN
317-552-2312.
PERSONNEL/COMMUNITY ACTIVITIES:
LTC Roger A Behringer, USA, 6920 12th St,
Suite 200, 99506-2550, 907-552-2820.
Personnel and Expenditures
ACTIVE DUTY PERSONNEL: 6900
DEPENDENTS: 10,370
CIVILIAN PERSONNEL: 2500
Services
Housing: Family units 1532; Barracks spaces;
Dormitory spaces 2608; Senior NCO units 230;
Junior NCO units 1070; RV/Camper sites 200;
total number of houses include duplexes, 4-
plexes, townhouses, and other units. *Temporary
Housing:* VIP units 5; VOQ units 80; VEQ units
300; VAQ units; Unaccompanied officer/En-
listed quarters; BAQ units; Transient quarters
48. *Commissary:* Yes; *Exchange:* Retail store;
Barber shop; Dry cleaners; Food shop; Florist;
Bank; Service station; Furniture store; Bakery;
Military clothing store; Convenience store;
Beauty shop; Laundromat; Credit union; Car
wash; Fast food; Class VI; Auto body/glass;
Fishing/Camping store; Arts/Crafts center. *Child
Care/Capacities:* Day care center capacity 250,
6wks-5yrs; Home day care program; Summer
day camp. *Schools:* Preschool/Kindergarten; Elementary; College courses; Special education.
Base Library: Yes. *Medical Facilities:* Hospital
75 beds; Dental clinic; Pharmacy; Refill pharmacy.

Recreational Facilities: Bowling center; Movie
theater; Pool; Gym; Recreation center; Golf
course; Stables; Tennis courts; Racquetball
court; Skating rink; Fitness center/Weight room;
Softball field; Football field; Auto shop; Craft
shop; Officers club; NCO club; Camping; Fish-
ing/Hunting; Enlisted club; Youth center; Picnic
area; Playground; Downhill/X-country skiing;
Teen center; Aero club; Recreation camp in Seward (130 mi S, open mid-May to mid-Sep, features cabins, trailers, motels, dining facilities,
campgrounds, scenic views, and fishing charters,
for info call 907-552-4015, reservations 552-
5526, space limited on weekends).

20. Kulis Air National Guard Base
5005 Raspberry Rd
Anchorage, AK 99502-1998
907-249-1176; DSN 317-626-1176
Profile
BRANCH: Air National Guard.
SIZE AND LOCATION: 129 acres. At Anchorage IAP off Raspberry Rd, approx 5 mi from
downtown. *County:* Borough of Anchorage.
MAJOR UNITS: 176th Composite Group; 210st
Air Rescue Squadron; 176th Medical Squadron; 144th Tactical Airlift Squadron.
BASE HISTORY: 1952, organized as 8144th
Air Base Squadron, Elmendorf AFB. 1953, redesignated 144th Fighter-Bomber Squadron.
1955, ANG moved to Kulis ANGB, named after 1st Lt Albert Kulis, ANG pilot killed during training mission. 1957, mission changed
to airlift. 1969, Squadron raised to group
level; renamed 176th TAG with 144th TAS
as mission unit. 1986, new flying squadron established and redesignated 176th Composite
Group; missions of refueling and airlift under
one group commander. 1990, 210th Air Rescue Squadron activated.
VISITOR ATTRACTIONS: Static aircraft display.
Key Contacts
COMMANDER: Col Van Williams.
PUBLIC AFFAIRS: Maj Sue A Stice,
907-249-1342, DSN 317-626-1342.
PROCUREMENT: MSG Karen Weidenbaugh,
907-249-1711, DSN 317-626-1711.
TRANSPORTATION: Capt Bonnie Carroll,
907-249-1406, DSN 317-626-1406.
PERSONNEL/COMMUNITY ACTIVITIES:
Maj James Campbell, 907-249-1403, DSN
317-626-1403.

Personnel and Expenditures
ACTIVE DUTY PERSONNEL: 1200 Guardsmen
CIVILIAN PERSONNEL: 245
MILITARY PAYROLL EXPENDITURE: $12 mil
CONTRACT EXPENDITURE: $45 mil
Services
Housing: None. *Medical Facilities:* Medical clinic. *Recreational Facilities:* None.

21. US Army Corps of Engineers, Alaska District
PO Box 898
Anchorage, AK 99506-0898
907-753-5700
Internet: http://www.usace.army.mil/alaska/
Profile
BRANCH: Army.
LOCATION: HQ on Elmendorf AFB, near Anchorage. *County:* Anchorage.
MAJOR UNITS: Corps of Engineers, Alaska District; Cold Regions Center of Expertise (CRCX).
BASE HISTORY: 1869, Corps surveyed territory. 1946, District created; covers entire state of Alaska, 586,000 sq mi; 3 field offices. Recently designed & constructed largest National Guard facility at Fort Richardson. 1996, CRCX established.
Key Contacts
COMMANDER: Col Sheldon L Jahn, Commander; Col Peter A Topp, District Engineer.
PUBLIC AFFAIRS: Salvatore Vitale, PAO; Dennis Hardy, POC, Alaska District, 907-753-5730, dennis.l.hardy@npa01.usace.army.mil; Pete Smallidge, CREEL POC, 603-646-4445, psmall@crrel.usace.army.mil.
Personnel and Expenditures
ACTIVE DUTY PERSONNEL: 10
CIVILIAN PERSONNEL: 500
CONTRACT EXPENDITURE: $250 mil

Clear Air Force Station

22. Clear Air Force Station
13th SWS
APO, AP AK 99704-5000
DSN 585-6416
Internet: http://www.spacecom.af.mil/21sw/13sws.htm
Profile
BRANCH: Air Force.
LOCATION: 40 mi N of Mount McKinley; 80 mi S of Fairbanks.
MAJOR UNITS: 13th Space Warning Squadron; Ballistic Missile Early Warning System (BMEWS Site II).
BASE HISTORY: Manages & operates three AN/FPS-50 detection radars & one AN/FPS-92 tracking radar. Continually watches fixed area of space for missile launches & orbiting satellites. Also responsible for portion of AF Space Command Space Surveillance Program; tracks 7,000+ space objects. Other stations at Thule AB, Greenland and RAF Fylingdales-Moor, UK.
Key Contacts
COMMANDER: LTC Jay G Santee.
PUBLIC AFFAIRS: 21st Space Wing, 775 Loring Ave, Ste 241, Peterson AFB, CO 80914-1294, 719-556-4696.

Eareckson Air Force Station

23. Eareckson Air Force Station
EAFS
673 ABG, Unit 12513
APO, AP AK 96512-2513
907-392-3000; DSN 317-392-3000
Profile
BRANCH: Air Force.
SIZE AND LOCATION: 7040 acres. Remote AFB, 1500 mi SW of Anchorage, AK, at westernmost tip of Aleutian Islands. *County:* Shemya Island.
MAJOR UNITS: 673rd Air Base Squadron (PACAF); 16th Space Surveillance Squadron (SPACECOM); 55th Operation Group, Det 1 (ACC).
BASE HISTORY: 1993, renamed after Col William O Eareckson; formerly Shemya AFB.
VISITOR ATTRACTIONS: WWII bunkers; Sea otters, sea lions, seals.
Key Contacts
COMMANDER: Personnel rotate every 12 months.
Personnel and Expenditures
ACTIVE DUTY PERSONNEL: 550
CIVILIAN PERSONNEL: 25
Services
Housing: Dormitory spaces 610. *Temporary Housing:* VIP units 4 units; VOQ units 10; VEQ units 35; Unaccompanied officer/Enlisted quarters 50. *Exchange:* Barber shop; Convenience store. *Child Care/Capacities:* No day care facilities. *Schools:* No on-base schools. *Base Library:* Yes. *Medical Facilities:* Medical clinic. *Recreational Facilities:* Bowling center; Movie theater; Gym; Recreation center; Racquetball court; Fitness center/Weight room; Softball field; Football field; Craft shop; Fishing/Hunting; Consolidated club.

Eielson AFB

24. Eielson Air Force Base
EAFB
3112 Broadway Ave, Ste 8
Eielson AFB, AK 99702-1830
907-377-1110; FAX 907-377-1412; DSN 317-377-1110
Internet: http://www.eielson.af.mil/
OFFICER-OF-THE-DAY: Wing Operations Center, 907-377-1500, DSN 317-377-1500
Profile
BRANCH: Air Force.
SIZE AND LOCATION: 63,110 acres. 26 mi SE of Fairbanks on Richardson Hwy. *County:* Fairbanks North Star Borough.
MAJOR UNITS: 354th Fighter Wing; 354th Operations Group; 354th Logistics Group; 354th Medical Group; 354th Support Group; 353rd Combat Training Squadron (Cope Thunder); 168th Air Refueling Wing (ANG); 354th Fighter Wing Publications Library; 355th Fighter Squadron; 18th Fighter Squadron; Air Force Technical Applications Center, Det 460; 354th Contracting Squadron; 66th Training Squadron; Arctic Survival School; 210th Rescue Squadron, Det 1 (ANG).
BASE HISTORY: 1943, opened as Mile 26 (from location of Signal Corps-operated telegraph station). WWII, operational facilities little used. 1948, named after Carl Ben Eielson, famed arctic pioneer & aviator. Until 1961, satellite of Ladd Field (Ft Wainwright); Strategic Air Command supported by 5010th Air Base Wing & Alaskan Air Command. 1981, 343rd Composite Wing activated as host. 1984, redesignated 343rd Tactical Fighter Wing. 1991, reorganized as 343rd Wing. 1993, 354th Fighter Wing from Myrtle Beach AFB became host. Mission: training & equipping tactical air support & close air support for Army forces in AK.
VISITOR ATTRACTIONS: Tours available upon request to public affairs office.
Key Contacts
COMMANDER: 907-377-1500, DSN 317-377-3259.
PUBLIC AFFAIRS: MSgt Christopher Shock, 907-377-1410, DSN 377-1410, shockc_at_354fw-cc@ccgate.eielson.af.mil.
PROCUREMENT: 354th Contracting Squadron, Suite 3, 907-377-2441, DSN 317-377-2441.
TRANSPORTATION: 354th Transportation Squadron, 3213 Division Ave, Suite 1, 99702-1560, 907-377-3376, DSN 317-377-3376.
PERSONNEL/COMMUNITY ACTIVITIES: 354th Services Squadron, Suite 4, 99702-1870, 907-377-1190, DSN 317-377-1190.
Personnel and Expenditures
ACTIVE DUTY PERSONNEL: 2740; Guard 400
DEPENDENTS: 4500
CIVILIAN PERSONNEL: 630
Services
Housing: Family units 1300; Unaccompanied officer quarters units, 8; BAQ units 7; Duplex units 43; Dormitory spaces 738; Senior NCO units 133; Junior NCO units 1065; Officer Units, 102. *Temporary Housing:* DVQ units 12; VOQ units 207; VAQ units 386; Guesthouse units 40; Cabins, 22. *Commissary:* Yes; *Exchange:* Barber shop; Dry cleaners; Food shop; Florist; Bank; Service station; Military clothing store; Convenience store; Beauty shop; Laundromat. *Child Care/Capacities:* Day care center capacity 150, infant-6yrs; Home day care program. *Schools:* Preschool/Kindergarten; Elementary; Intermediate/Junior high; High school. *Base Library:* Yes. *Medical Facilities:* Medical clinic; Dental clinic; Pharmacy; Veterinary services. *Recreational Facilities:* Bowling center; Movie theater; Pool; Gym; Recreation center; Tennis courts; Racquetball court; Skating rink; Fitness center/Weight room; Softball field; Football field; Auto shop; Craft shop; Officers club; Camping; Fishing/Hunting; Enlisted club; Youth center; Skeet range; Water sports; Playground; Hunting on federal lands away from base proper.

Fort Greely

25. Fort Greely
Fort Greely, AK 96508
Mailing Address
HQ US Army Alaska, APVP-GPC
APO AP, 96508-5811
907-873-1121; DSN 317-873-1121
OFFICER-OF-THE-DAY: 907-873-4720, FAX 907-873-2112, DSN 317-873-4720

Profile
BRANCH: Army.
SIZE AND LOCATION: 629,000 acres. 100 mi SE of Fairbanks at the junction of Alaska & Richardson Hwys; near end of ALCAN (Alaska/Canadian Hwy) at Delta Junction. *County:* Fairbanks.
MAJOR UNITS: Army Garrison, HQ Co; Northern Warfare Training Center; 526th Military Police Det; Cold Regions Test Center; 507th Signal Co.
BASE HISTORY: 1942, Army AFB established here at Station 17, Alaskan Wing, Air Transport Command. WWII, transfer point for American & Russian pilots under Lend-Lease. 1945, inactive status. 1947, designated site for 1st post-war cold weather maneuver, Exercise Yukon. 1948, transferred to Army; redesignated Army post, named US Troops, Big Delta, AK. 1948, named site for Arctic Training Center. Originally, Center consisted of Army Arctic Indoctrination School, Army Training Company & Test & Development Section. 1952, renamed Army Arctic Center; Army Chemical Corps-Arctic Test Team established. 1955, designated Ft Greely for Maj Gen Adolphus Washington Greely, arctic explorer & founder of AK Communications System. 1956, Chemical Corps-Arctic Test Team redesignated Class II activity; renamed Army Chemical Corps-Arctic Test Activity; Arctic Test Group renamed Arctic Test Board; Arctic Indoctrination School became Army Cold Weather & Mountain School, which became Northern Warfare Training Center in 1963. 1964, Arctic Test Board renamed Arctic Test Center. 1974, Ft Greely became part of 172nd Infantry Brigade. 1986, with activation of 6th Infantry Division (Light) and Army Garrison, AK, Ft Greely became one of three posts in single installation concept.
FUTURE CLOSURE/REALIGNMENT: Ft Greely to be realigned by relocating Cold Regions Test Activity (CRTA) & Northern Warfare Training Center (NWTC) to Ft Wainwright, AK, by July 2001.
Key Contacts
COMMANDER: LTC David L Anderson, APVR-GPC, APO AP 96568-6000, 907-873-4206, FAX 907-873-4631, DSN 317-873-4206.
PUBLIC AFFAIRS: Unit 45811, APO AP 96508, 907-873-4661, FAX 907-873-4638, DSN 317-873-4661.
TRANSPORTATION: Robert L Burns, 907-873-4453, FAX 907-873-4285, DSN 317-873-4453.
PERSONNEL/COMMUNITY ACTIVITIES: Director of Community Affairs, 907-873-4648, FAX 907-873-2112, DSN 317-873-4648.
Personnel and Expenditures
ACTIVE DUTY PERSONNEL: 311
DEPENDENTS: 456
CIVILIAN PERSONNEL: 291
Services
Housing: Family units 321; Unaccompanied officer quarters units 16; Unaccompanied enlisted quarters 16; Barracks spaces 572. *Temporary Housing:* Transient quarters 39. *Commissary:* Yes; *Exchange:* Retail store; Barber shop; Dry cleaners; Service station; Military clothing store; Credit union; Post office; Class VI; Tailor/Alterations.

Child Care/Capacities: Day care center capacity 58, 6wks-school age; Home day care program. *Schools:* Elementary. *Base Library:* Yes. *Medical Facilities:* Medical clinic; Pharmacy. *Recreational Facilities:* Bowling center; Movie theater; Pool; Gym; Recreation center; Tennis courts; Racquetball court; Skating rink; Fitness center/Weight room; Softball field; Auto shop; Craft shop; Youth center; Skeet range; Playground; Community club.

Fort Richardson

26. Adjutant General of Alaska
Camp Carroll
PO Box 5800
Fort Richardson, AK 99505-5800
907-428-6003; FAX 907-428-6019
Profile
BRANCH: Army National Guard.
MAJOR UNITS: Alaska National Guard; Camp Carroll (ARNG).
Key Contacts
COMMANDER: Maj Gen Jacob Lestenkof.

27. Fort Richardson
HQ, US Army Alaska, 600 Richardson Dr
Fort Richardson, AK 99505
907-384-1110; DSN 317-384-1110
Internet: http://143.213.12.254/home/htm
Profile
BRANCH: Army.
SIZE AND LOCATION: 62,000 acres. Approx 8 mi N of Anchorage on Glenn Hwy. *County:* Municipality of Anchorage.
MAJOR UNITS: HQ, US Army Alaska; Arctic Support Brigade; Army Garrison, Ft Richardson; 501st Infantry, 1st Bn (Airborne); 1st Brigade, 6th Infantry Division (L); 59th Signal Bn; 813th Engineer Bn (Reserve); Alaska National Guard.
BASE HISTORY: 1940-41, built on site of what is now post's sister installation, Elmendorf AFB; named for military pioneer explorer, Brig Gen Wilds P Richardson, served 3 tours of duty in AK Territory, 1897-1917. 1947, established as HQ of US Army AK (USARAL). 1950, moved to present location. 1959, 3 off-post Nike Hercules missiles built. 1961-73, home to US Modern Biathlon Training Center. 1974, HQ for 172nd Infantry Brigade (AK). 1986, established as HQ 6th Infantry Division (Light) & US Army Garrison, Alaska. 1990, HQ moved to Ft Wainwright. 1994, 6th Infantry Division (Light) inactivated; HQ US Army Alaska forces at Ft Richardson.
VISITOR ATTRACTIONS: Fish and Wildlife Center (museum); Ft Richardson National Cemetery; Ft Richardson Fish Hatchery (state run).
Key Contacts
COMMANDER: LTC Sammy G Wiglesworth; Post Commander, 600 Richardson Dr #6000, 99505-6000, 907-384-2280, DSN 317-384-2280; Col George Vakalis, Garrison Commander; Maj Gen David A Bramlett, Division Commander.
PUBLIC AFFAIRS: ATTN: APVR-RPO, 600 Richardson Dr, #5900, Ft Richardson, AK 99505-5900, 907-384-2072, DSN 317-384-2072.

PROCUREMENT: 600 Richardson Dr, #6400, 907-384-7087, DSN 317-384-7087.
TRANSPORTATION: 600 Richardson Dr, #7000, 907-384-1805, DSN 317-384-1805.
PERSONNEL/COMMUNITY ACTIVITIES: 600 Richardson Dr, #6600, 907-384-2017, DSN 317-384-2017.
Personnel and Expenditures
ACTIVE DUTY PERSONNEL: 2100; Guard 770; Reserve 190
DEPENDENTS: 3000
CIVILIAN PERSONNEL: 1400
Services
Housing: Family units 1757; Unaccompanied officer quarters 32; Unaccompanied enlisted quarters 19; Barracks spaces 2463. *Temporary Housing:* VOQ units 16; Transient quarters 130; 23 RV/camp spaces. *Commissary:* Yes; *Exchange:* Retail store; Barber shop; Dry cleaners; Food shop; Florist; Service station; Furniture store; Military clothing store; Convenience store; Beauty shop; Credit union; Fast food. *Child Care/Capacities:* Day care center capacity 120, 6wks-5yrs; Home day care program; Latch key program; Summer day camp; Preschool hourly care. *Schools:* Preschool/Kindergarten; Elementary; College courses; Noncommissioned Officer Academy. *Base Library:* Yes. *Medical Facilities:* Medical clinic; Dental clinic; Veterinary services. *Recreational Facilities:* Bowling center; Movie theater; Pool; Gym; Golf course; Tennis courts; Racquetball court; Skating rink; Fitness center/Weight room; Softball field; Football field; Auto shop; Craft shop; Officers club; NCO club & EM Club; Camping; Fishing/Hunting; Youth center; Picnic area; Skeet range; Playground.

Fort Wainwright

28. Fort Wainwright
Bldg 1555, Gaffney Rd
Fort Wainwright, AK 99703-5900
Mailing Address
1060 Gaffney Rd #5900
Fort Wainwright, AK 99703-5900
907-353-1100; DSN 317-353-1110
Internet: http://143.213.12.254/home.htm
OFFICER-OF-THE-DAY: 907-353-6701, FAX 907-353-6711, DSN 317-353-6701, DSN FAX 317-353-6711
Profile
BRANCH: Army.
SIZE AND LOCATION: 656,250 acres. Approx 0.25 mi from downtown Fairbanks off Rte 2 (Steese Hwy); approx 5 mi from Fairbanks IAP. *County:* North Star Borough.
MAJOR UNITS: Army Garrison, Ft Wainwright; 1st Brigade, 6th Infantry Division (Light); 1st Bn, 17th Infantry; 2nd Bn, 1st Infantry; Army Cold Regions Research & Engineering Laboratory; 3rd Squadron, 17th Cavalry; 46th Support Bn; 4th Bn, 11th Field Artillery; 41st Engineer Bn; 110th Military Intelligence F Co; 4th Bn, 123rd Theater Aviation; 203rd Personnel Service Bn; 198th Army Reserve Hospital; 813th Engineer Combat Bn.
BASE HISTORY: 1939, Congress appropriated funds for base near Fairbanks as a cold weather test site. Late 1941, begun as Ladd Army Airfield, link in AK Siberia Lend-Lease route. 1947, became part of Eielson AFB; used as resupply base for Distant Early

Warning radar sites and experimental ice stations in Arctic Ocean. 1961, Army reassumed command of Ladd Field; renamed Fort Wainwright for Gen Jonathan M Wainwright, defender of Bataan Peninsula in WWII. Today, home of 1st Brigade, 6th Infantry Division (Light) & the Arctic Support Brigade.

Key Contacts
COMMANDER: LTC Emmet E Holley, Post Commander, 1060 Gaffney Rd, 907-353-7660, DSN 317-353-7660.
PUBLIC AFFAIRS: Linda L Douglass.

Personnel and Expenditures
ACTIVE DUTY PERSONNEL: 4600
DEPENDENTS: 5600
CIVILIAN PERSONNEL: 1500
MILITARY PAYROLL EXPENDITURE: $185.2 mil

Services
Housing: Family units 1725; Unaccompanied officer quarters 40; Unaccompanied enlisted quarters 32. *Temporary Housing:* VIP units 4; VOQ units 43; VEQ units 27; Campground spaces 75. *Commissary:* Yes; *Exchange:* Retail store; Barber shop; Dry cleaners; Food shop; Florist; Service station; Furniture store; Bakery; Military clothing store; Convenience store; Beauty shop; Credit union; ATM; Optical store; Post office; Fast food; Video rentals; Thrift shop; Travel agency; Class VI; Computer store; Garden center; Tailor/Alterations; Laundry; Cafeteria; Photo store; Sports store. *Child Care/Capacities:* Day care center capacity 160, 6wks-12yrs; Home day care program; Summer day camp; Before & after school programs. *Schools:* Elementary; Intermediate/Junior high; College courses. *Base Library:* Yes. *Medical Facilities:* Bassett Army Community Hospital, 39 beds; Medical clinic; Dental clinic; Pharmacy; Veterinary services. *Recreational Facilities:* Bowling center; Pool; Gym; Golf course; Tennis courts; Racquetball court; Skating rink; Fitness center/Weight room; Softball field; Football field; Auto shop; Craft shop; Camping; Fishing/Hunting; Youth center; Picnic area; Skeet range; Playground; All ranks club; Consolidated club; Last Frontier Club; Arctic Oasis (club); Track; Snow sports; SATO; Information, tour, and registration office; Outdoor adventure center; Harding Lake, 40 mi SE.

Juneau

29. 17th Coast Guard District
709 W 9th St
Juneau, AK 99802
Mailing Address
PO Box 25517
Juneau, AK 99802-5517
907-463-2066; FAX 907-463-2072
Profile
BRANCH: Coast Guard.
SIZE AND LOCATION: Offices only. In Federal Bldg downtown Juneau. *County:* Juneau Borough.
MAJOR UNITS: 17th Coast Guard District; Civil Engineering Unit, Juneau; Director of Auxiliary, Juneau; Support Det, Juneau.
Key Contacts
COMMANDER: RADM Terry M Cross, 907-463-2025.
PUBLIC AFFAIRS: Lt Ray F Massey, 907-463-2071.

Personnel and Expenditures
ACTIVE DUTY PERSONNEL: 233
DEPENDENTS: 0
CIVILIAN PERSONNEL: 36
MILITARY PAYROLL EXPENDITURE: $4 mil
CONTRACT EXPENDITURE: $8 mil
Services *Child Care/Capacities:* No day care facilities. *Medical Facilities:* Medical clinic; Dental clinic; Pharmacy.

Ketchikan

30. Ketchikan Coast Guard Station
1300 Stedman St
Ketchikan, AK 99901-6698
907-228-0340; FAX 907-228-0347
OFFICER-OF-THE-DAY: 907-228-0375
Profile
BRANCH: Coast Guard.
LOCATION: In SE Alaska, 1 mi S of Ketchikan on Revillagigedo Island; not accessible by road. *County:* Borough of Ketchikan Gateway.
MAJOR UNITS: Coast Guard Station, Ketchikan; Integrated Support Command, Ketchikan; Coast Guard Forces, Ketchikan; Armory Det, Ketchikan; Electronic Shop, Ketchikan; Electronic Support Det, Ketchikan; USCGC *Planetree*; USCGC *Naushon*.
BASE HISTORY: 1911, base established as Lighthouse Service Depot. 1940, officially became part of Coast Guard. Today, an industrial base responsible for rehabilitation of navigation buoys & depot level support. Responsible for search & rescue from Canadian border to Cape Yagataga. Additional units on Sea Level Drive in Ketchikan & on Long Range Aids to Navigation Team at Shoal Cove, approx 20 mi SE of Ketchikan.
Key Contacts
PUBLIC AFFAIRS: 907-228-0298.
PROCUREMENT: 907-228-0240.
TRANSPORTATION: 907-228-0213.
PERSONNEL/COMMUNITY ACTIVITIES: 907-228-0227.
Personnel and Expenditures
ACTIVE DUTY PERSONNEL: 250
CIVILIAN PERSONNEL: 25
Services
Housing: Unaccompanied enlisted quarters; Barracks spaces. *Exchange:* Retail store. *Child Care/Capacities:* No day care facilities. *Schools:* No on-base schools. *Medical Facilities:* Medical clinic; Dental clinic; Pharmacy. *Recreational Facilities:* Gym; Fitness center/Weight room; Consolidated club.

King Salmon Airport

31. King Salmon Airport
643 SPTS, Unit 12526
APO, AP AK 96513-5000
907-721-3310; FAX 907-721-3474; DSN 721-3310
OFFICER-OF-THE-DAY: Capt Robert A Rennicker; 907-721-3301, DSN 721-3301
Profile
BRANCH: Air Force.
SIZE AND LOCATION: 727 acres. Just W of Aleutian Range approx 280 mi SW of Anchorage; 0.5 mi from town of King Salmon; 13 mi

from Naknek; not accessible by ground transportation. *County:* Bristol Bay Borough.
MAJOR UNITS: 643rd Support Squadron.
BASE HISTORY: 1941, constructed by Civil Aeronautics Authority (CAA) and turned over to Army for advanced staging base and refueling stop. Post WWII, returned to CAA, then State of Alaska in 1959. State continues to operate airport. 643rd Support Squadron under 11th AF Air Combat Wing, Elmendorf AFB. Tours for one year, unaccompanied (no dependents).
VISITOR ATTRACTIONS: Gateway to Katmai National Monument; Red Salmon capital of the world.
Key Contacts
COMMANDER: LTC William J Heinen; 907-721-3301, DSN 721-3301.
PUBLIC AFFAIRS: Maj Tom Burriss; 907-721-3302, DSN 721-3302.
PROCUREMENT: Capt Larry A Gunter; 907-721-3514, DSN 721-3514.
TRANSPORTATION: MSgt Mark A Kearney; 907-721-3509, DSN 721-3509.
Personnel and Expenditures
ACTIVE DUTY PERSONNEL: 290
CIVILIAN PERSONNEL: 17
Services
Housing: Dormitory spaces 291. *Temporary Housing:* VIP units 7; VOQ units 3; VEQ units 33. *Exchange:* Barber shop; Convenience store. *Child Care/Capacities:* No day care facilities. *Schools:* No on-base schools. *Base Library:* Yes. *Medical Facilities:* Medical clinic. *Recreational Facilities:* Bowling center; Movie theater; Gym; Racquetball court; Fitness center/Weight room; Softball field; Craft shop; Fishing/Hunting; Enlisted club.

Kodiak

32. Kodiak Coast Guard Integrated Support Command
Kodiak
Box 22
Kodiak, AK 99619-5020
907-487-5108; FAX 907-487-5275
OFFICER-OF-THE-DAY: 907-487-5267, DSN 487-5267
Profile
BRANCH: Coast Guard.
SIZE AND LOCATION: 23,000 acres. NE corner of Kodiak Island, 7 mi S of Kodiak, 1 mi S of Airport; 250 mi S of Anchorage. At beginning of Aluetian Island Chain; accessible by air from Anchorage, ferry boat from Homer or Seward. *County:* Kodiak Borough.
MAJOR UNITS: Coast Guard Support Center, Kodiak; Coast Guard Air Station, Kodiak; Coast Guard Communication Station, Kodiak; Marine Safety Det, Kodiak; Loran Station Narrow Cape; Loran Monitor Station, Kodiak; Electronic Support Unit, Kodiak; USCGC *Yocona* (WMEC-168); USCGC *Ironwood* (WLB-297); USCGC *Storis* (WMEC-38); USCGC *Firebush* (WLB-393); Coast Guard Public Affairs Det, Western Alaska.
BASE HISTORY: 1939, built by Navy as part of Aleutian campaign with small Coast Guard detachment assigned as tenant command. 1972, Coast Guard acquired base from Navy; changed to Support Center Kodiak. 1990s, re-

named Integrated Support Command, largest air station in Coast Guard.

VISITOR ATTRACTIONS: Historic site; strategic Navy base during WWII, bunkers & artillery sites still on base. Excellent hunting, fishing, crabbing, hiking & photographic opportunities nearby.

Key Contacts

COMMANDER: Box 14.

PUBLIC AFFAIRS: Box 22, 907-487-5542, DSN 487-5542.

Personnel and Expenditures

ACTIVE DUTY PERSONNEL: 1100

DEPENDENTS: 1500

CIVILIAN PERSONNEL: 62

Services

Housing: Family units 413; Unaccompanied officer quarters 8; Unaccompanied enlisted quarters 213. *Temporary Housing:* Unaccompanied officer/Enlisted quarters 8; Guesthouse units 44; Apartment units 27. *Commissary:* Yes; *Exchange:* Retail store; Barber shop; Dry cleaners; Food shop; Bank; Service station; Furniture store; Military clothing store; Convenience store; Beauty shop; Credit union; ATM; Post office; Video rentals; Travel agency; Tailor/Alterations; Cafeteria; Specialty crafts store; Pizza parlor. *Child Care/Capacities:* Day care center capacity 100; Home day care program. *Schools:* Preschool/Kindergarten; Elementary. *Base Library:* Yes. *Medical Facilities:* Medical clinic; Dental clinic. *Recreational Facilities:* Bowling center; Movie theater; Gym; Recreation center; Golf course; Tennis courts; Racquetball court; Fitness center/Weight room; Softball field; Football field; Auto shop; Craft shop; Officers club; NCO club; Fishing/Hunting; Skeet range; Sporting equipment & boats; Indoor pool; Indoor gazebo; Buskin River beach house for rent; Outdoor gazebo.

McGrath

33. Tatalina Air Force Station

General Delivery

McGrath, AK 99627

907-728-9001

Profile

BRANCH: Air Force.

SIZE AND LOCATION: 4970 acres. Approx 230 air mi NW of Anchorage; 150 mi W of Mt McKinley. *County:* Yukon-Koyukuk Borough.

MAJOR UNITS: Tatalina Long Range Radar Site (LRRS).

BASE HISTORY: Contract facility.

Key Contacts

COMMANDER: Site Supervisor, 907-728-9001, ext 1, FAX 907-728-9001, ext 5.

Personnel and Expenditures

CIVILIAN PERSONNEL: 4

Services *Recreational Facilities:* Softball field.

Arizona

Bellemont

34. Camp Navajo
1 Hughes Ave
Bellemont, AZ 86015-5000
Mailing Address
PO Box 16123
Bellemont, AZ 86015-6123
520-773-3205; FAX 520-773-3262; DSN
853-3205; DSN FAX 853-3262
OFFICER-OF-THE-DAY: 520-773-3202, DSN
853-3202
Profile
BRANCH: Army National Guard.
SIZE AND LOCATION: 28,600 acres (44 sq
mi). 12 mi W of Flagstaff Exit 185 on I-40;
20 mi E of Williams, AZ; 150 mi N of Phoenix. *County:* Coconino.
MAJOR UNITS: National Weather Service; Forest Service.
BASE HISTORY: 1942, construction of Navajo
Ordnance Depot began; Navajo Indian Reservation furnished much of unskilled labor; first
Navajo town on record built to house workers, later replaced by Indian Village, including trading post, sheep, weaving looms, and
Navajo interpreters. 1942, first ammunition received. 1953, strategic and critical materiels
mission assigned. 1955, general supply mission became back-up to Erie Ordnance Depot
and then to Benicia Arsenal. 1961, general
supplies mission phased out. 1967, assigned
physical distribution mission of Defense Logistics Administration. 1971, reserve status assigned and placed under Pueblo Army Depot.
1975, reassigned to Tooele Army Depot Complex. 1982, AZ Army NG took over direct
command of depot for training guard units in
ammunition operations. 1993, depot selected
as site for storage of Minuteman II/II rocket
motors. 1997, construction to modify storage
igloos for storage of Trident C4 motors for
Navy. BRAC 88 removed all federal ammunition stocks. 1992, installation turned over to
AZ NG.
VISITOR ATTRACTIONS: None on post;
within 160 mi radius of 52 National Parks &
Monuments.
Key Contacts
COMMANDER: Col Larry W Triphahn.
PUBLIC AFFAIRS: LTC Timothy J Cowan,
ATTN: AZXA-AS, 520-773-3300, FAX
520-773-3262, DSN 853-3300.
PROCUREMENT: Jack Darum, 520-773-3252,
FAX 520-773-3308.

TRANSPORTATION: CW3 Elizabeth West,
520-773-3223, FAX 520-773-3216.
PERSONNEL/COMMUNITY ACTIVITIES:
Maj Bruce Farley, 520-773-3229, FAX
520-773-3262, DSN 853-3229.
Personnel and Expenditures
ACTIVE DUTY PERSONNEL: 10
DEPENDENTS: 0
CIVILIAN PERSONNEL: 110
MILITARY PAYROLL EXPENDITURE: $3.5 mil
CONTRACT EXPENDITURE: $4 mil
Services
Housing: Family units 5; Barracks spaces 600;
Senior NCO units 52. *Temporary Housing:* Un-
accompanied officer/Enlisted quarters 20. *Ex-
change:* Seasonal exchange; Post office. *Medi-
cal Facilities:* Medical clinic. *Recreational Fa-
cilities:* Tennis courts; Fitness center/Weight
room; Softball field; Camping; Fishing/Hunting;
Picnic area; All ranks club.

Fort Huachuca

35. Fort Huachuca
USAIC & Fort Huachuca, ATTN: ATZS-CDR
Fort Huachuca, AZ 85613-6000
520-538-8604; DSN 879-8604
Internet: http://www.huachuca-usaic.army.mil/
Profile
BRANCH: Army.
SIZE AND LOCATION: 73,315 acres. 70 mi
SE of Tucson. I-10, Exit 302 (Hwy 90), ap-
prox 30 mi to Sierra Vista/Fort Huachuca af-
ter Huachuca City. *County:* Cochise.
MAJOR UNITS: Army Intelligence Center;
Army Intelligence School; 111th Military In-
telligence Brigade; Noncommissioned Officer
Academy; INSCOM Training and Doctrine
Support Det; 306th Military Intelligence Bn;
Battle Command Battle Lab, Huachuca;
Army Garrison, Ft Huachuca.
BASE HISTORY: Arizona's only active Army
post, established 1877, when Capt Samuel
Marmaduke Whitside, Sixth Cavalry, built
post in foothills of Huachuca Mountains.
1886, post was Gen Nelson A Miles' HQ &
forward supply base for campaign against
Geronimo and Apaches. 1913, 10th Cavalry's
Buffalo Soldiers arrived. 1916, joined Gen
Pershing's expedition into Mexico; assigned
mission of guarding border. 1933, 25th Infantry Regiment replace 10th Cavalry. WWII,
93rd Infantry Division then 92nd Infantry Division arrived for training. After WWII, de-

clared surplus transferred to State. Korean
War, activated by Army Engineers. 1954, con-
trol passed to Chief Signal Officer. 1967, be-
came HQ, Army Strategic Communications
Command. 1971, home of Army Intelligence
Center & School. 1973, Strategic Communica-
tion Command became Army Communica-
tions Command. 1984, renamed Army Infor-
mation Systems Command. 1990, Army
Training & Doctrine Command host; later,
Army Intelligence Center.
VISITOR ATTRACTIONS: Museum; WWII
buildings; Military cemetery dating to 1877;
Old post area designated National Historical
Landmark.
Key Contacts
COMMANDER: Col Theodore G Chopin,
Garrison Commander, 520-538-1562, FAX
520-533-5008, DSN 821-1562,
chopint%hua1@huachuca-emh11.army.mil.
PUBLIC AFFAIRS: ATZS-PA, 520-533-2752,
FAX 520-533-1280, DSN 821-2752; B Napp,
Media Relations, 520-533-1287.
Personnel and Expenditures
ACTIVE DUTY PERSONNEL: 7000
DEPENDENTS: 36,000 (dependents & retirees)
CIVILIAN PERSONNEL: 2900
Services
Housing: Family units 3524; Duplex units;
Townhouse units; Barracks spaces; Senior NCO
units 265; Junior NCO units 1304. *Temporary
Housing:* VOQ units 111; VEQ units 58; Unac-
companied officer/Enlisted quarters 147; Gues-
thouse units 33. *Commissary:* Yes; *Exchange:*
Retail store; Barber shop; Dry cleaners; Food
shop; Florist; Bank; Service station; Furniture
store. *Child Care/Capacities:* Day care center capacity 500; Home day care program; Latch key
program. *Schools:* Elementary; Intermediate/Jun-
ior high. *Base Library:* Yes. *Medical Facilities:*
Hospital 104 beds; Medical clinic; Dental clinic.
Recreational Facilities: Bowling center; Movie
theater; Pool; Gym; Recreation center; Golf
course; Stables; Tennis courts; Racquetball
court; Skating rink; Fitness center/Weight room;
Softball field; Football field; Auto shop; Craft
shop; Officers club; NCO club; Camping; Fish-
ing/Hunting; Hiking.

Gila Bend

36. Gila Bend Auxiliary Air Field
Gila Bend, AZ 85337-5000
DSN 853-5220

Profile
BRANCH: Air Force.
SIZE AND LOCATION: 2.7 mil acres. In Sonoran Desert of AZ; 65 mi SW of Phoenix on Hwy 85; 124 mi E of Yuma, AZ; 80 mi N of Lukeville, Mexico; small airport 4.5 mi from Gila Bend. *County:* Maricopa; Yuma.
MAJOR UNITS: 58th Support Squadron.
BASE HISTORY: 1941, site selected for gunnery range to serve advanced flying training for Luke Field & Williams Field. 1940s, control & use of range varied as requirements changed. 1942, small support base established S of Gila Bend. 1946-51, military site deactivated; later reactivated, range remained Williams Bombing & Gunnery Range. 1963, redesignated Luke Air Force Range. 1986, redesignated Barry M Goldwater Air Force Range (2.7 million acres). Gila Bend Auxiliary Field supports world's largest gunnery range. Run by civilian contractors; squadron oversees operation of facility for Air Combat Command.
VISITOR ATTRACTIONS: Aircraft static displays; Gillespie Dam; Painted Rocks; Butterfield stage route; Sonoran Desert; Oatman graves.

Key Contacts
PUBLIC AFFAIRS: See Luke AFB.

Personnel and Expenditures
CIVILIAN PERSONNEL: 93

Services
Housing: Family units 1; Duplex units 10; Dormitory spaces; Trailer spaces 20; 2/3 bedroom units 65. *Temporary Housing:* Guesthouse units 3; Transient quarters. *Commissary:* Yes; *Exchange:* Convenience store; Credit union. *Child Care/Capacities:* Day care center. *Schools:* No on-base schools. *Base Library:* Yes. *Medical Facilities:* Clinic w/technician. *Recreational Facilities:* Bowling center; Pool; Gym; Tennis courts; Racquetball court; Fitness center/Weight room; Softball field; Youth center; Picnic area; All ranks club.

Luke AFB

37. Luke Air Force Base
7383 N Litchfield Rd
Luke AFB, AZ 85309-1534
602-856-7411; DSN 896-1110
Internet: http://www.luk.aetc.af.mil
OFFICER-OF-THE-DAY: Luke AFB Command Post, 602-856-5800

Profile
BRANCH: Air Force.
SIZE AND LOCATION: 4198 acres. 20 mi W of Phoenix in Glendale; off I-10 on Litchfield Rd, Exit 128, then N 5 mi to intersection with Litchfield Rd. *County:* Maricopa.
MAJOR UNITS: 56th Fighter Wing; 944th Fighter Wing (AFRC); 56th Operations Group; 56th Logistics Group; 56th Support Group; 56th Medical Group; Training Support Squadron, Det 1 (ACC); Aircrew Training Research Division.
BASE HISTORY: 1941, Army Air Corps advanced training facility for pilots of fighter aircraft; called Luke Field, named for Lt Frank Luke Jr, Phoenix native & WWI pilot, first aviator to receive Medal of Honor. During WWII, nicknamed "Home of the Fighter Pilot." Luke personnel practiced aerial combat around Ajo Auxiliary Airfield (later Gila Bend Gunnery Range; today, Barry M Goldwater Air Force Range). 1946, closed. 1951, reactivated as Luke AFB under Air Training Command, home to 127th Pilot Training Wing. 1957, trained squadrons of German pilots until 1983. 1958, transferred to TAC, parent unit 4510th Combat Crew Training Wing. 1969, 58th Tactical Fighter Training Wing. 1977, HQ Tactical Training Luke (TTL) activated. 1980, HQ TTL became 832nd Air Division. 1991, 58th Fighter Wing became host; ended air-to-air Eagle training mission.
VISITOR ATTRACTIONS: Park with static display of aircraft.

Key Contacts
COMMANDER: Brig Gen Carrol H Chandler, 7224 N 139 Dr, 85309-1420.
PUBLIC AFFAIRS: 602-856-5853, FAX 602-856-6013, DSN 896-5853.

Personnel and Expenditures
ACTIVE DUTY PERSONNEL: 5250; Reserve 1000
DEPENDENTS: 12,300
CIVILIAN PERSONNEL: 1400

Services
Housing: Duplex units 874 (for Senior & Junior NCOs); Dormitory spaces 977. *Temporary Housing:* VIP units 16; VOQ units 136; VAQ units 122; Transient quarters 40. *Commissary:* Yes; *Exchange:* Retail store; Barber shop; Dry cleaners; Florist; Service station; Furniture store; Military clothing store; Convenience store; Beauty shop. *Child Care/Capacities:* Day care center capacity 120, 6wks-10yrs; Home day care program. *Schools:* No on-base schools. *Base Library:* Yes. *Medical Facilities:* Hospital 20 beds; Dental clinic; Pharmacy; Veterinary services. *Recreational Facilities:* Bowling center; Movie theater; Pool; Gym; Recreation center; Tennis courts; Fitness center/Weight room; Softball field; Auto shop; Craft shop; Officers club; NCO club; Youth center; Playground.

Mesa

38. Aircrew Training Research Division, Armstrong Laboratory
AL/HRA
6001 S Power Rd, Bldg 558
Mesa, AZ 85206-0904
602-988-6561
Internet: http://www.alhra.af.mil/

Profile
BRANCH: Air Force.
LOCATION: At Williams Gateway Airport (formerly Williams AFB); From Phoenix take I-10 S to US-60 E, S on Power Rd to Williams Field Rd Main Gate. *County:* Maricopa.
MAJOR UNITS: Aircrew Training Research Division.
BASE HISTORY: Part of Human Systems Center, AF Materiel Command. Premier organization for research & development in aircrew training techniques & technologies.

Key Contacts
COMMANDER: Col Lynn A Carroll, Division Chief, 602-988-6561, DSN 474-6109, carroll@alhra.af.mil.
PUBLIC AFFAIRS: Elizabeth Casey, casey@alhra.af.mil.

Personnel and Expenditures
CIVILIAN PERSONNEL: 150 (government & contractors)
Services *Recreational Facilities:* Running track.

Phoenix

39. Adjutant General of Arizona
Papago Military Reservation
5636 E McDowell Rd
Phoenix, AZ 85008-3495
602-267-2710; FAX 602-267-2715

Profile
BRANCH: Army National Guard.
MAJOR UNITS: Arizona National Guard; Papago Military Reservation; 385th Aviation Group, HQ (ANG); 98th Support Brigade Troop Command (ANG); 153rd Field Artillery Brigade (ANG); 923rd Medical Det; 108th Aviation.

Key Contacts
COMMANDER: Maj Gen Bill Van Dyke, 602-267-2710.
PUBLIC AFFAIRS: Capt Eileen Bienz, 602-267-2669.

40. Phoenix Naval & Marine Corps Reserve Readiness Center
NAVMARCORESCEN Phoenix; NMCRC Phoenix
Reserve Center
1201 N 35th Ave
Phoenix, AZ 85009-3398
602-484-7292; FAX 602-278-4993; DSN 602-896-1110 (ask for commercial number)

Profile
BRANCH: Naval Reserve; Marine Corps Reserve.
SIZE AND LOCATION: 8.1 acres. 7 mi from Phoenix Sky Harbor Airport; 15 mi from Tempe; 20 mi from Mesa. *County:* Maricopa.
MAJOR UNITS: REDCOM NINETEEN Activity; US Naval Reserve Recruiting; Prior Service Recruiting (USMC); Inspector-Instructor (USMC); Bulk Fuel Co D, 6th Engineer Support Bn.

Key Contacts
COMMANDER: Capt R J Canzonieri.
PUBLIC AFFAIRS: ENS Brook Dewalt, 602-484-7292, DSN 278-4993, DSN FAX 278-4993.

Personnel and Expenditures
ACTIVE DUTY PERSONNEL: 18; 700 Navy reservists

Services *Base Library:* Yes. *Recreational Facilities:* Facilities available at Luke AFB, 20 mi away.

41. Sky Harbor IAP, Air National Guard Base
3200 E Old Tower Rd
Phoenix, AZ 85034-6098
602-302-9000; DSN 853-9000
OFFICER-OF-THE-DAY: Command Post, DSN 853-9071

Profile
BRANCH: Air National Guard.
SIZE AND LOCATION: 58 acres. S side of Phoenix at Sky Harbor IAP, off Maricopa Fwy, I-17. *County:* Maricopa.

MAJOR UNITS: 161st Air Refueling Wing (ANG).

BASE HISTORY: 1946, 412th Fighter Squadron, redesignated 197th Fighter Squadron (Copperheads), first unit of AZ ANG. 1951, recalled to active duty for Korean War. 1950, base constructed at Sky Harbor. 1960, unit redesignated 161st Fighter Group. 1961-62, activated for Berlin Crisis; returned & redesignated 161st Air Transport Group (MATS). 1968, redesignated 161st Aeromedical Airlift Group. 1972, assumed present name & mission under Tactical Air Command. 1976, placed under Strategic Air Command. 1990-91, supported Operations Desert Shield/Storm.

Key Contacts
COMMANDER: Col William R Sherer, 602-302-9200, DSN 853-9200.
PROCUREMENT: Col George M Kelly, Logistics Group, 602-302-9280, DSN 853-9280.
PERSONNEL/COMMUNITY ACTIVITIES: DSN 853-9250.

Personnel and Expenditures
ACTIVE DUTY PERSONNEL: Guard 917
CIVILIAN PERSONNEL: 358
MILITARY PAYROLL EXPENDITURE: $24.2 mil

Tucson

42. Davis-Monthan Air Force Base
5275 E Granite St
Tucson, AZ 85707-3010
520-228-3900; DSN 228-1110
Internet: http://www.dm.af.mil/
Profile
BRANCH: Air Force.
SIZE AND LOCATION: 10,614 acres. In SE Tucson, approx 20 min from Tucson IAP; 3 mi off I-10, exit 268. *County:* Pima.
MAJOR UNITS: 355th Wing; 12th Air Force, HQ; 355th Operations Group; 355th Logistics Group; 355th Support Group; 355th Medical Group; 355th Wing Staff; 305th Rescue Squadron (AFRES); Aerospace Maintenance and Regeneration Center (AMARC).
BASE HISTORY: 1927, Charles Lindbergh flew *Spirit of St Louis* to dedicate present site; then, largest municipal airport in US. Army Air Corps established airfield, named for Tucson Air Corps officers, Lt Samuel H Davis (died in air crash at Carlstrom Field, FL, 1921) & Lt Oscar Monthan (died in crash near Honolulu, 1924). 1940, site selected for new Army base, Tucson Air Base; 1941, returned to original name. WWII, operational training base for B-17, B-24, & B-29 bomber aircrews. Post WWII, storage site for decommissioned aircraft. 1946, Strategic Air Command bombardment group established. 1960s, 390th Strategic Missile Wing & 18 Titan II sites activated (deactivated 1984). 1963-76, U-2 reconnaissance aircraft assigned. 1976, transferred to Tactical Air Command. 1992, 836th Air Division & 355th Fighter Wing deactivated; 355th Wing activated. More than 5000 aircraft in storage at AMARC.
VISITOR ATTRACTIONS: Tours of Aerospace Maintenance & Regeneration Center (storage yard for US military aircraft); most M-W-F at 9 & 10:30am reservations required

(reservations: 520-228-4570 between 2 & 4pm MST or in writing to PAO; Recorded information 520-228-3358).
Key Contacts
COMMANDER: Col John D W Corley, Commander, 355th Wing.
PUBLIC AFFAIRS: 1st Lt Keith Shepherd, Deputy Chief, 520-228-3204.
Personnel and Expenditures
ACTIVE DUTY PERSONNEL: 6200; Guard 162; Reserve 200
DEPENDENTS: 7000
CIVILIAN PERSONNEL: 600
Services
Housing: Family units Officer 133; Enlisted 1106; Unaccompanied officer quarters 168; Unaccompanied enlisted quarters 1426; RV/Camper sites Trailer spaces 100. *Temporary Housing:* VIP units 8; VOQ units 2; VEQ units 3; Transient quarters 12; RV spaces 72. *Commissary:* Yes; *Exchange:* Retail store; Barber shop; Dry cleaners; Food shop; Florist; Bank; Service station; Furniture store; Military clothing store; Convenience store; Beauty shop; Laundromat; Credit union; Optical shop. *Child Care/Capacities:* Day care center capacity 160; Home day care program; Latch key program; Summer day camp. *Schools:* Elementary; College courses. *Base Library:* Yes. *Medical Facilities:* Hospital 20 beds; Medical clinic; Dental clinic; Pharmacy; Veterinary services. *Recreational Facilities:* Bowling center; Movie theater; Pool; Gym; Recreation center; Golf course; Stables; Tennis courts; Racquetball court; Fitness center/Weight room; Softball field; Football field; Auto shop; Craft shop; Officers club; NCO club; Youth center; Picnic area; Skeet range; Playground.

43. Tucson IAP, Air National Guard Base
Tucson IAP
Tucson, AZ 85734
520-295-6210; DSN 924-6210
Profile
BRANCH: Air National Guard.
SIZE AND LOCATION: 84 acres. NW section of Tucson IAP. *County:* Pima.
MAJOR UNITS: 162nd Fighter Wing (ANG).
BASE HISTORY: 1939, 152nd Observation Squadron, predecessor to 162nd, originated with RI ANG. 1956, 152nd Fighter Interceptor Squadron of AZ ANG organized in Tucson. Began with old farmhouse & hangar for one airplane. End of 1950s, grew to Group status, first ANG unit designated Tactical Fighter Training Group; ANG Fighter Weapons School formed for advanced tactics & weapons employed for systems used by reserve air forces. Currently only A-7 & F-16 Combat Air-Crew Training Base in US.
Personnel and Expenditures
ACTIVE DUTY PERSONNEL: 1542 Guard
CIVILIAN PERSONNEL: 916
MILITARY PAYROLL EXPENDITURE: $67.7 mil
Services *Medical Facilities:* Medical clinic. *Recreational Facilities:* Officers club; NCO club.

44. Tucson Naval & Marine Corps Reserve Center
NMCRC Tucson
3655 S Wilmot Rd
Tucson, AZ 85730-3259

520-228-6289; FAX 520-228-6275; DSN 228-6289
Profile
BRANCH: Naval Reserve; Marine Corps Reserve.
LOCATION: *County:* Pima.
MAJOR UNITS: REDCOM NINETEEN Activity; Bulk Fuel Co A, 6th Engineer Support Bn.
Key Contacts
COMMANDER: LCDR P A Sloop.

Yuma

45. Yuma Marine Corps Air Station
MCAS Yuma
Box 99113
Yuma, AZ 85369-9113
520-341-2011; DSN 951-2011
OFFICER-OF-THE-DAY: 520-341-2252, DSN 951-2252
Profile
BRANCH: Marine Corps.
SIZE AND LOCATION: 3150 acres. In SW corner of AZ, 20 mi N of Mexican border, within Yuma city limits; 2 mi E of Yuma IAP. *County:* Yuma.
MAJOR UNITS: Marine Aircraft Group 13 (MAG-13); HQ & Maintenance Squadron 13; Marine Attack Squadron 211; Marine Attack Squadron 214; Marine Attack Squadron 311; Marine Attack Squadron 513; Marine Wing Support Squadron 371; Marine Fighter Training Squadron 401; 1st Light Antiaircraft Missile Bn; Marine Air Control Squadron 7.
BASE HISTORY: 1928, federal government leased 640 acres of desert land for flying field, Fly Field. WWII, taken over by Army Air Corps, renamed Yuma Army Airfield and designated site of flying school. Following WWII, all flight activities ceased. 1951, site reactivated as weapons proficiency center for fighter-interceptor units; named Yuma Air Base. 1956, renamed Vincent Air Force Base for Brig Gen Clinton D Vincent. 1959, facility signed over to Navy, and designated Marine Corps Auxiliary Air Station. 1962, designation changed to current Marine Corps Air Station.
Key Contacts
COMMANDER: Col C J Turner.
PUBLIC AFFAIRS: 1Lt W G Jimenez, 520-341-2275, DSN 951-2275.
PROCUREMENT: LCDR F M Deal, Supply Officer, Supply Dept, 520-341-2722, DSN 951-2722.
TRANSPORTATION: CWO3 J R Knipple, Traffic Management Officer, Traffic Management Office, 520-341-2019, DSN 951-2019.
PERSONNEL/COMMUNITY ACTIVITIES: D M Mitchell, MWR Director, 520-341-2422, DSN 951-2422.
Personnel and Expenditures
ACTIVE DUTY PERSONNEL: 5134
DEPENDENTS: 6281
CIVILIAN PERSONNEL: 1126
MILITARY PAYROLL EXPENDITURE: $103 mil
CONTRACT EXPENDITURE: $14.5 mil
Services
Housing: Family units 821; Unaccompanied officer quarters barracks rms 34; Unaccompanied en-

listed quarters barracks rms 887; BAQ units; Senior NCO units barracks rms 90. *Temporary Housing:* VIP units 3; VOQ units 282; VEQ units 594; VAQ units; Unaccompanied officer/ Enlisted quarters; BAQ units; Guesthouse units 13. *Commissary:* Yes; *Exchange:* Retail store; Barber shop; Dry cleaners; Bank; Service station. *Child Care/Capacities:* Day care center capacity 306; Home day care program. *Base Library:* Yes. *Medical Facilities:* Medical clinic; Dental clinic. *Recreational Facilities:* Bowling center; Movie theater; Pool; Gym; Stables; Tennis courts; Racquetball court; Fitness center/ Weight room; Softball field; Football field; Auto shop; Officers club; NCO club; Camping; Fishing/Hunting.

46. Yuma Proving Ground
USAYPG
Yuma, AZ 85365
520-328-1110
Internet: http://www.yuma.army.mil/
Profile
BRANCH: Army.
SIZE AND LOCATION: 850,000 acres. Approx 26 mi NE of Yuma; accessible from US-95, clearly marked. *County:* Yuma; LaPaz.

MAJOR UNITS: HQ, Support Troop, Military Freefall School; Yuma Proving Ground; Light Armored Vehicle Test Directorate.
BASE HISTORY: 1943, Yuma Test Branch activated under Corps of Engineers to test bridges, boats, vehicles, & well drilling equipment. 1944, Imperial Dam Engineer Station established. 1945, Engineer Station abolished; continued as Engineer Board, Engineer Research & Development Laboratories, Yuma Test Branch, until deactivation, 1950. 1951, reactivated as Yuma Test Station, Class I installation, Sixth Army. 1956, designated permanent Class I installation. 1962, redesignated & reassigned Yuma Test Station as Class II installation, AMC & TECOM. 1963, redesignated Yuma Proving Ground.
VISITOR ATTRACTIONS: Army Parachute Team, Golden Knights (winter training Jan-Feb); Asian-Pacific Islander Week (May); Hispanic Week (Sep); American Indian Pow-Wow; Black History Week (Jan); Military Appreciation Days (MADays).
Key Contacts
COMMANDER: Col Robert C Filbey, Garrison Commander, 520-328-2163, FAX 520-328-6249, DSN 899-2163, steypco@ yuma-emh1.army.mil.

PUBLIC AFFAIRS: Chuck Wullenjohn, 520-328-6189, DSN 899-6189, cwullenj@ yuma-emh1.army.mil.
PERSONNEL/COMMUNITY ACTIVITIES: Military Personnel, 520-328-3250, FAX 520-328-2089, DSN 899-3250, DSN FAX 899-2089; Civilian Personnel, 520-328-2611, FAX 520-328-3520, DSN 899-2611, DSN FAX 899-3520, civper@yuma-emh1.army. mil.

Personnel and Expenditures
ACTIVE DUTY PERSONNEL: 380
DEPENDENTS: 550
CIVILIAN PERSONNEL: 1400
Services
Housing: Family units 290; Barracks spaces 435; Mobile home units 8. *Temporary Housing:* Unaccompanied officer/Enlisted quarters 9; BAQ units 8; Guesthouse units 10. *Commissary:* Yes; *Exchange:* Retail store; Barber shop; Dry cleaners; Food shop; Bank; Service station; Bakery. *Child Care/Capacities:* Day care center capacity 100. *Schools:* Preschool/Kindergarten; Elementary, grades 1-5. *Base Library:* Yes. *Medical Facilities:* Medical clinic; Dental clinic. *Recreational Facilities:* Bowling center; Movie theater; Pool; Gym; Recreation center; Tennis courts; Racquetball court; Fitness center/Weight room; Softball field; Auto shop; Craft shop; Fishing/Hunting; Combined community club.

Arkansas

Fort Smith

47. Fort Smith Municipal Airport, Air National Guard Base
Fort Smith, AR 72906
501-648-5210; DSN 962-8210

Profile
BRANCH: Air National Guard.
SIZE AND LOCATION: 113 acres. In S Fort Smith, AR, off I-540. *County:* Sebastian.
MAJOR UNITS: 184th Fighter Wing (ANG).
BASE HISTORY: 1953, 184th Tactical Reconnaissance Squadron federally recognized at Fort Smith, AR. 188th Fighter Group activated during Berlin Crisis, 1961, supported Vietnamese airlift, 1975; Cuban boatlift, 1980.

Personnel and Expenditures
ACTIVE DUTY PERSONNEL: 991 Guard
CIVILIAN PERSONNEL: 298
MILITARY PAYROLL EXPENDITURE: $25.9 mil

Services *Medical Facilities:* Medical clinic; Dental clinic.

48. Reserve Base, Fort Chaffee
US Army Garrison
Fort Smith, AR 72905-0001
501-484-2141; DSN 962-2141

Profile
BRANCH: Army Reserve.
SIZE AND LOCATION: 72,000 acres. 5 mi SE of Ft Smith, AR, on AR State Hwy-22. From I-40, I-540W Exit, then Exit No 8 for AR State Hwy 22E. *County:* Sebastian; Franklin.
MAJOR UNITS: Reserve Training Site, Medical; Army Reserve NCO Academy.
BASE HISTORY: Most of present buildings date from 1941; named for Maj Gen Adna R Chaffee, first Chief of Armored Forces; first mission to train armored divisions. 1942-1945, German POWs imprisoned here. 1946-48, placed on inactive status until designated home of 5th Armored Division. Deactivated 1950, resumed operations with Korean War. 1956, redesignated as Fort Chaffee. 1957, 5th Armored Division again deactivated; became Army Training Center, Field Artillery; additional mission of training Reserve forces. 1959, placed in caretaker status with HQ XIX US Army Corps remaining. 1961, reopened as training center. 1965, inactivated; used for NG & Reserve summer training. 1975, Refugee Processing Center for Vietnamese refugees established. 1980-82, Resettlement Center for Cuban refugees established. 1986, Joint Readiness Training Center established. 1993, JRTC relocated to Ft Polk, LA; Reserve Training Site-Medical began operations training medical units on use of Deployable Medical System. 1997, deactivated; transferred to Reserve Component.

Key Contacts
COMMANDER: 501-484-2282, DSN 962-2282.

Services
Housing: Barracks spaces 359; RV/Camper sites 39. *Temporary Housing:* VIP units 9; VOQ units 141; VEQ units 208.

Little Rock

49. US Army Corps of Engineers, Little Rock District
CESWL
700 W Capitol St, Rm 7530
Little Rock, AR 72201
Mailing Address
PO Box 867
Little Rock, AR 72203-0867
501-324-5531; FAX 501-324-6968
Internet: http://www.usace.army.mil/swl/

Profile
BRANCH: Army.
SIZE AND LOCATION: Offices only. Near center of Little Rock. *County:* Pulaski.
MAJOR UNITS: Corps of Engineers, Little Rock District.
BASE HISTORY: 1881, established for work on limited navigation projects; investigations on Arkansas, St Francis, L'Anguille, Saline, White, Black, Current, & Fourche LaFave Rivers; dredging & channeling main projects. 1923, combined with Memphis District. 1937, reorganized as Little Rock District. 1939, Denison District formed; Tulsa District activated from Little Rock territory. 1980, territory added to District. Today, Corps manages Arkansas River watershed between Fort Smith & Pine Bluff, White River watershed above Peach Orchard Bluff, near Georgetown, AR, & Little River Basin in SW AR; responsible for developing & operating water resource projects in most of AR & southern MO, for flood control, recreation, hydroelectric power generation, and improvement of fish & wildlife. Performs military & civil works construction.

Key Contacts
COMMANDER: Col Philip S Morris.
PUBLIC AFFAIRS: ATTN: CESWL-PA, cesw1-pa@swl01.usace.army.mil.
PROCUREMENT: Annie McClintock, 501-324-5720.
TRANSPORTATION: 501-324-5651.
PERSONNEL/COMMUNITY ACTIVITIES: Human Resources, 501-324-5350.

Personnel and Expenditures
ACTIVE DUTY PERSONNEL: 6
CIVILIAN PERSONNEL: 875

Services *Base Library:* Yes.

Little Rock AFB

50. Little Rock Air Force Base
LRAFB
The Rock
1250 Thomas Ave
Little Rock AFB, AR 72099-5000
501-988-3131; DSN 731-3131
Internet: http://www.LittleRock.af.mil
OFFICER-OF-THE-DAY: 501-988-3200, DSN 731-3200

Profile
BRANCH: Air Force.
SIZE AND LOCATION: 6898 acres. 17 mi NE of Little Rock, adj to Jacksonville, AR. *County:* Pulaski.
MAJOR UNITS: 314th Airlift Wing; 314th Support Group; 314th Logistics Group; 314th Operations Group; 314th Medical Group; 463rd Airlift Group (AMC); 189th Airlift Group (ANG); Air Force Office of Special Investigations, Det 427; Air Force Combat Aerial Delivery School; 348th Recruiting Squadron.
BASE HISTORY: 1953, construction began, part of SAC. 1960s, served as support base for Titan II, ICBMs positioned around N central AR, as 308th Strategic Missile Wing. 1970, came under TAC, 64th TAW host until replaced by 314th TAW, 1971. 1970, returned to TAC; 64th TAW from Stewart AFB, TN, became host. 1971, unit redesignated 314th TAW, MAC. 1974, MAC assumed control. 1986, Army's Joint Readiness Training Center (JRTC) established here; trains non-mechanized infantry battalion task forces. 1986, AR ANG became 189th TAG. 1990s, 314th Airlift Wing becomes host.

Key Contacts

COMMANDER: Brig Gen Jack R Holbein, 1250 Thomas Ave, Ste 106, LRAFB, AR 72099, 501-988-6401, DSN 731-6401.

PUBLIC AFFAIRS: Maj Lisa Caldwell, 1250 Thomas Ave, Ste 151, LRAFB, AR 72099, 501-988-3601, DSN 731-3601, DSN FAX 731-6978, 314AW/PA@AW314-1. LITTLEROCK.AF.MIL.

PROCUREMENT: 501-988-3834, DSN 731-3834.

TRANSPORTATION: 501-988-6755, DSN 731-6755.

PERSONNEL/COMMUNITY ACTIVITIES: 501-988-6349, DSN 731-6349.

Personnel and Expenditures

ACTIVE DUTY PERSONNEL: 5108
DEPENDENTS: 5472
CIVILIAN PERSONNEL: 1455
MILITARY PAYROLL EXPENDITURE: $143 mil
CONTRACT EXPENDITURE: $71.8 mil

Services

Housing: Family units 1535; RV/Camper sites 24. *Temporary Housing:* VOQ units 201; VAQ units 149. *Commissary:* Yes; *Exchange:* Retail store; Barber shop; Dry cleaners; Food shop; Florist; Bank; Service station; Furniture store; Bakery; Military clothing store; Convenience store; Beauty shop; Credit union; ATM; Optical store; Post office; Fast food; Video rentals; Four seasons; Thrift shop; Travel agency; Class VI; Garden center; Tailor/Alterations; Cafeteria. *Child Care/Capacities:* Day care center capacity 185; Home day care program; Summer day camp; Before & after school programs. *Schools:* Preschool/Kindergarten; Elementary. *Base Library:* Yes. *Medical Facilities:* Hospital 10; Medical clinic; Dental clinic; Pharmacy; Veterinary services. *Recreational Facilities:* Bowling center; Movie theater; Pool; Gym; Recreation center; Golf course; Stables; Tennis courts; Racquetball court; Fitness center/Weight room; Softball field; Football field; Auto shop; Craft shop; Officers club; Camping; Fishing/Hunting; Enlisted club; Youth center; Picnic area; Playground.

North Little Rock

51. Adjutant General of Arkansas
Camp J T Robinson
North Little Rock, AR 72199-9600
501-212-5001; FAX 501-212-5009

Profile

BRANCH: Army National Guard.
MAJOR UNITS: Arkansas National Guard.

Key Contacts

COMMANDER: Maj Gen Don C Morrow.

52. Camp Joseph T Robinson
CJTR
Camp Robinson
North Little Rock, AR 72199-9600
501-212-5100; FAX 501-212-5909; DSN 962-5100; DSN FAX 962-5100

Internet: http://arkansas-guard/
OFFICER-OF-THE-DAY: Fire & Security Office, 501-212-5282, FAX 501-212-5281, DSN 962-5282

Profile

BRANCH: Army National Guard.
SIZE AND LOCATION: 48,188 acres. In N Little Rock, connecting roads from I-40, from Hwy 176 follow signs; 12 mi to Little Rock Regional Airport; 12 mi to Little Rock AFB. *County:* Pulaski.
MAJOR UNITS: Arkansas National Guard, HQ; 39th Infantry Brigade; State Area Command, AR ARNG; 87th Troop Command; Professional Education Center; National Guard Marksmanship Training Unit; Camp Pike, USAR 90th RSC; Army Reserve Center; Naval Reserve Center; Marine Corps Reserve Center.
BASE HISTORY: 1917, War Department constructed huge post named Camp Pike in honor of explorer Zebulon Pike. After WWI, closed. 1922, used as NG training area. 1937, renamed Camp Joseph T Robinson for US Senator Robinson of AR; basic training base & POW camp. In past decade, many of prewar structures replaced; open for year round training. All branches train here; brigade-sized infantry, artillery, engineer, or combat service support units in non-live fire exercises can be accommodated one at a time.
VISITOR ATTRACTIONS: Aircraft, flag, artillery, & equipment display; Museum; Annual Open House (fall).

Key Contacts

COMMANDER: Maj Gen Don C Morrow, Adjutant General, 501-212-5000, FAX 501-212-5009, DSN 962-5000.
PUBLIC AFFAIRS: LTC Cissy Lashbrook, State Public Affairs Officer, TAG-DZ-PA, 501-212-5020, FAX 501-212-5019, DSN 962-5020, lashbrookc@ar-arng.ngb.army. mil.
PROCUREMENT: Linda Barron, State Purchasing Agent, State Personnel/Purchasing, 501-212-5111, FAX 501-212-5119, DSN 962-5111.
TRANSPORTATION: Col Tom Thomas, State Maintenance Office, 501-212-5753, DSN 962-5753.
PERSONNEL/COMMUNITY ACTIVITIES: Col Philip Morriss, Director of Personnel, DPA, 501-212-4002, FAX 501-212-4009, DSN 962-4002; Community Activities see Public Affairs Officer.

Personnel and Expenditures

ACTIVE DUTY PERSONNEL: 523
CIVILIAN PERSONNEL: 148
MILITARY PAYROLL EXPENDITURE: $98 mil

Services

Housing: Family units 1136; Unaccompanied officer quarters; Mobile home units. *Temporary Housing:* VIP units 2; VOQ units 26; VEQ units 100; Dormitory units 360; Mobile home units 7. *Exchange:* Barber shop; Dry cleaners; Credit union; ATM; Post office; Travel agency; Canteen; Restaurant. *Schools:* Youth Challenge Program. *Base Library:* Yes.

Medical Facilities: Medical clinic. *Recreational Facilities:* Pool; Gym; Recreation center; Golf course; Tennis courts; Fitness center/Weight room; Softball field; Fishing/Hunting; All ranks club; Fitness trail.

Pine Bluff

53. Pine Bluff Arsenal
PBA
Pine Bluff, AR 71602
501-540-3000; FAX 501-540-3013; DSN 966-3000
Internet: http://www-ioc.army.mil/eq/maps/ sites/pbaa.htm

Profile

BRANCH: Army.
SIZE AND LOCATION: 14,454 acres. Bordered on W by Missouri Pacific RR and E by Arkansas River. Approx 8 mi NW of Pine Bluff; 35 mi SE of Little Rock. Main entrance (Plainview Gate) at terminal point of AR State Hwy 256, just N of White Hall, approx 1 mi off AR Hwy 365. *County:* Jefferson.
MAJOR UNITS: Pine Bluff Arsenal; GETN Training Site; TMDE Support Center; Ammunition Demilitarization Support Facility.
BASE HISTORY: 1941, established by War Department Chemical Warfare Service to manufacture and assemble incendiary munitions. Current missions: manufacture various types of conventional smoke, riot control, incapacitating agents, incendiary & pyrotechnic mixes; produce & test chemical defense equipment, such as masks, filters, & protective clothing; provide engineering & technology for design of facilities & equipment used in production of munitions & provide technical & engineering expertise for pollution abatement programs & demilitarization; operate a depot for receipt, storage, surveillance, renovation, & demilitarization of munitions & other government controlled materiel; keep in state of readiness to meet mobilization requirements & support Reserve Training Program. Plans call for $500 mil chemical weapons incinerator.

Key Contacts

COMMANDER: 501-540-3003, DSN 966-3461.
PUBLIC AFFAIRS: Peggy Rainwater, 10020 Kabrich Circle, 501-540-3016, DSN 966-3016.

Personnel and Expenditures

ACTIVE DUTY PERSONNEL: 8
CIVILIAN PERSONNEL: 875
CONTRACT EXPENDITURE: $44 mil

Services

Housing: Family units 26. *Exchange:* Credit union. *Child Care/Capacities:* Day care center; Summer day camp. *Schools:* No on-base schools. *Medical Facilities:* Medical clinic; Pharmacy. *Recreational Facilities:* Bowling center; Pool; Gym; Recreation center; Golf course; Stables; Racquetball court; Fitness center/Weight room; Softball field; NCO club; Fishing/Hunting; Youth center; Picnic area.

California

Alameda

54. Alameda Coast Guard Integrated Support Command
USCG ISC Alameda
Coast Guard Island
Commander, Coast Guard Island, Bldg 21
Alameda, CA 94501-5100
510-437-3156; FAX 510-437-2915
Internet: http://www.wenet.net/~uscg/; http://www.dot.gov/dotinfo/uscg/
OFFICER-OF-THE-DAY: 510-437-3151
Profile
BRANCH: Coast Guard.
SIZE AND LOCATION: 43 acres. In middle of Oakland Estuary between cities of Alameda & Oakland, CA. I-880 runs N-S only 2 blocks E of Island. Oakland IAP approx 5 mi S of Island. *County:* Alameda.
MAJOR UNITS: Coast Guard Pacific Area HQ; Joint Interagency Task Force West; Maintenance & Logistics Command, Pacific; Integrated Support Command, Alameda; Marine Safety Office, San Francisco Bay; USCGC *Munro*; USCGC *Sherman*; USCGC *Boutwell*; USCGC *Morgenthau*; 11th Coast Guard District; Coast Guard Forces; Coast Guard Administrative Law Judge; Electronic Support Det, Alameda; Investigative Services, Pacific Region; Coast Guard Reserve Group; Coast Guard Pacific Area Training Team; Coast Guard Armory Det, Alameda; Director of Auxiliary, Alameda; Maritime Defense Command 11, Coast Guard Pacific Region; Composite Naval Coastal Warfare Unit 111.
BASE HISTORY: 1913, former Government Island, artificial island, formed. 1926, Coast Guard Base 11 established. 1931, Executive Order gave title to 15 acre tract for permanent base. 1939, 35 added acres acquired from city of Alameda. 1942, additional 17 acres purchased. 1982, changed from Coast Guard Training Center to Support Center Alameda; renamed Coast Guard Island. 1996, realignment increased staff from San Pedro, former District Office.
VISITOR ATTRACTIONS: WWII Coast Guard Patrol Frigate Memorial Monument; 378-ft, high-endurance cutters open for tours when in port; Whale-boat races.
Key Contacts
COMMANDER: Capt Dick Clark, 510-437-3172.

PUBLIC AFFAIRS: CDR Jeff Robertson, Coast Guard Island, Bldg 42, Alameda, CA 94501, 510-437-3319, 437-5918, JROBERTSON@d11.uscg.mil.procurement; 510-437-3391, FAX 510-437-3392.
PROCUREMENT: 510-437-3391, FAX 510-437-3392.
TRANSPORTATION: 510-437-3050.
PERSONNEL/COMMUNITY ACTIVITIES: 510-437-3579.
Personnel and Expenditures
ACTIVE DUTY PERSONNEL: 700
DEPENDENTS: 0
CIVILIAN PERSONNEL: 350
Services
Housing: Permanent party barracks rooms 60 (E-6 & below). *Temporary Housing:* TAD barracks rooms 12 (E-6 & below). *Exchange:* Barber shop; Florist; Service station; Credit union; ATM; Post office; Travel agency; Tailor/Alterations. *Child Care/Capacities:* Day care center capacity 187, 6wks-12yrs; After-school programs. *Schools:* No on-base schools. *Medical Facilities:* Medical clinic; Dental clinic; Pharmacy. *Recreational Facilities:* Pool; Gym; Recreation center; Tennis courts; Racquetball court; Fitness center/Weight room; Softball field; Football field; Auto shop; Picnic area; Playground.

55. Alameda Naval & Marine Corps Reserve Readiness Center
2144 Clement Ave
Alameda, CA 94501-1486
510-814-2605; FAX 510-522-5645; DSN 993-9107
Profile
BRANCH: Naval Reserve; Marine Corps Reserve.
LOCATION: *County:* Alameda.
MAJOR UNITS: Naval Reserve Readiness Center, Alameda; Marine Corps Reserve Readiness Center, Alameda.
Key Contacts
COMMANDER: CDR N A Vaniman.

Bakersfield

56. Bakersfield Naval & Marine Corps Reserve Center
4201 Chester Ave
Bakersfield, CA 93301-1198
805-327-7194, 327-7195; FAX 805-327-2839

Profile
BRANCH: Naval Reserve; Marine Corps Reserve.
LOCATION: *County:* Kern.
MAJOR UNITS: REDCOM NINETEEN Activity; 3rd & 4th Bulk Fuel Platoons, B Co, 6th Engineer Support Bn.
Key Contacts
COMMANDER: Lt T E Simpson.

Barstow

57. Barstow, Marine Corps Logistics Base
MCLB Barstow
Barstow, CA 92311-5011
619-577-6430; FAX 619-577-6530; DSN 282-6430
Profile
BRANCH: Marine Corps.
SIZE AND LOCATION: 5687 acres. Off I-40 & I-15 near Barstow, CA, served by State Hwys 58 and 247; nearest commercial airport Ontario IAP, 90 mi SW; 120 mi from Los Angeles. *County:* San Bernardino.
MAJOR UNITS: Headquarters Bn; Base Support Division; Facilities and Services Division; Fleet Support Division; Maintenance Center; Repair Division; Resource Management Division; Human Resources Office; Morale, Welfare, and Recreation Division; Defense Distribution Depot, Barstow.
BASE HISTORY: 1942, established as naval supply depot; transferred to Marine Corps as storage site for supplies & equipment for Fleet Marine Forces in Pacific; known as Marine Corps Depot of Supplies under Commanding General, Marine Corps Depot of Supplies, San Francisco. 1946, outgrew original facilities; annexed Army holding & reconsignment point, Yermo Annex. 1954, Commanding General, San Francisco moved to Barstow. 1978, redesignated present title. 1992, distribution mission of base transferred to DDRW (Defense Distribution Region West). Site divided into Nebo (Little Shepherd) & Yermo (Desert Flower) Annex. HQ, administrative, storage, shopping, recreational & housing facilities at Nebo. Maintenance Center, stables, Obregon Park, & bulk of Fleet Support Division's outdoor storage at Yermo Annex. Current mission: to procure, maintain, repair, rebuild, store, & distribute

supplies & equipment as assigned; and to conduct such schools & training as directed. Defense Distribution Depot operates two facilities: Nebo (administration HQ) & Yermo Annex.

VISITOR ATTRACTIONS: Historic Route 66 runs through MCLB.

Key Contacts

COMMANDER: Col Dennis C McBride, 619-577-6555, DSN 282-6555.

PUBLIC AFFAIRS: Capt Eric R Carlson, 619-577-6426, DSN 282-6426.

PERSONNEL/COMMUNITY ACTIVITIES: James Dingeldein, 619-577-6886, DSN 282-6886.

Personnel and Expenditures

ACTIVE DUTY PERSONNEL: 350

DEPENDENTS: 337

CIVILIAN PERSONNEL: 2076

MILITARY PAYROLL EXPENDITURE: $105.1 mil

CONTRACT EXPENDITURE: $37.6 mil

Services

Housing: Family units 363; Unaccompanied officer quarters 15; Barracks spaces 179; Senior NCO units 23. *Temporary Housing:* VIP units 1; VOQ units 4; VEQ units 4. *Commissary:* Yes; *Exchange:* Retail store; Barber shop; Dry cleaners; Food shop; Bank; Service station; Convenience store; Credit union. *Child Care/Capacities:* Day care center capacity 115, 6mo-12yrs; Home day care program. *Schools:* No on-base schools. *Base Library:* Yes. *Medical Facilities:* Medical clinic; Dental clinic; Pharmacy. *Recreational Facilities:* Bowling center; Pool; Gym; Golf course; Tennis courts; Racquetball court; Fitness center/Weight room; Softball field; Auto shop; Craft shop; Youth center; Playground; Oasis Club (E-7 & up); NCO/E club (E6 & below).

Beale AFB

58. Beale Air Force Base

Beale AFB

Beale AFB, CA 95903-5000

916-634-3000; DSN 368-1110

Internet: http://www.beale.af.mil/welcome/arrival.htm

OFFICER-OF-THE-DAY: Command Post, 916-634-5700

Profile

BRANCH: Air Force.

SIZE AND LOCATION: 23,000 acres. Approx 40 mi N of Sacramento; 10 mi E of Marysville, CA. Hwy 65 runs S of Beale; Hwy 20 runs N (E-W); Hwy 70 runs W of Beale (N-S); Hwy 99 runs W of Beale (N-S). *County:* Yuba.

MAJOR UNITS: 9th Reconnaissance Wing; 9th Comptroller Squadron; 9th Operations Group; 9th Logistics Group; 9th Support Group; 9th Medical Group; 940th Air Refueling Wing (AFRES); 612th Air Operations Group; 7th Space Warning Squadron; Global Operations Center; 48th Intelligence Squadron; 13th Intelligence Squadron; Air Force Office of Special Investigations, Det 218.

BASE HISTORY: 1942, construction of Camp Beale; named for founder of US Camel Corps, Edward Fitzgerald Beale, Naval Academy graduate, Commissioner of Indian Affairs, Army Brig Gen, Surveyor Gen of CA & NV, & Minister to Austria (One of few USAF

bases not named for aviator). WWII, 13th Armored, 81st & 96th Infantry Divisions trained. Also served as personnel replacement depot, German POW camp, & West Coast separation center. Post WWII, declared surplus. 1948, Air Force used base for bombardier-navigator training. 1951, designated AFB; underwent several jurisdictional changes before becoming part of SAC. 1957, construction of first runway. 1958, 14th Air Division transferred in; support base for 851st Strategic Missile Squadron & Titan I missile sites (3) (discontinued, 1965). 1965, 4200th SRW (later 9th SRW) activated, flying SR-71. 1975, 17th BMW host unit. 1976, 100th SRW reassigned as 100th Air Refueling Wing & 99th Strategic Reconnaissance Squadron brought U-2s & later TR-1 aircraft. 1979, became SAC unit. 1980, site for PAVE PAWS (Phased Array Radar) with 7th Missile Warning Squadron (later 7th Space Warning Sq). 1983, 100th ARW inactivated, all personnel consolidated with 9th SRW; transferred to newly-formed Space Command. 1992, Air Combat Command base; responsible for U-2 flight line. 1994, added responsibility for SR-71s.

VISITOR ATTRACTIONS: Edward F Beale Museum; WWII POW Cell Block (Historic Monument); Aircraft exhibits.

Key Contacts

COMMANDER: Brig Gen Simpson, 9th RW/CC, 916-634-2311, DSN 368-2311.

Personnel and Expenditures

ACTIVE DUTY PERSONNEL: 4000

DEPENDENTS: 3400

CIVILIAN PERSONNEL: 800

Services

Housing: Family units 1708; Unaccompanied officer quarters 53; Unaccompanied enlisted quarters 743; Duplex units; Dormitory spaces; Senior NCO units; Junior NCO units; Trailer spaces 140; RV/Camper sites; Multiplex units 306. *Temporary Housing:* VIP units 6; VOQ units 53; VEQ units 48; Lodge units 17; RV Spaces 44. *Commissary:* Yes; *Exchange:* Retail store; Barber shop; Dry cleaners; Food shop; Florist; Bank; Beauty shop; Credit union; Fast food; Video rentals; Jewelry/watch sales/repair. *Child Care/Capacities:* Day care center capacity 180; Home day care program. *Schools:* Preschool/Kindergarten; Elementary; College courses. *Base Library:* Yes. *Medical Facilities:* Hospital 6 beds; Dental clinic. *Recreational Facilities:* Bowling center; Movie theater; Pool; Gym; Recreation center; Golf course; Stables; Tennis courts; Racquetball court; Fitness center/Weight room; Softball field; Auto shop; Craft shop; Officers club; NCO club; Fishing/Hunting; Rod & Gun club; Dry Creek Saddle Club.

Bridgeport

59. Marine Corps Mountain Warfare Training Center

MCMWTC

Pickel Meadows

Box 5003

Bridgeport, CA 93517-5003

760-932-7761; FAX 760-932-7706; DSN 985-7231; DSN FAX 985-7208

Internet: http://138.156.4.23./mwtc

OFFICER-OF-THE-DAY: 760-932-7761, DSN 985-7231

Profile

BRANCH: Marine Corps.

SIZE AND LOCATION: 46,000 acres (Toiyabe National Forest). In Sweetwater Mts of E central CA, 30 mi N of Bridgeport, CA; 4 mi W of intersection of Hwy 395 & Sonora Junction on Hwy 108 at Pickel Meadows in the Toiyabe National Forest; 110 mi S of Reno, NV. *County:* Mono.

MAJOR UNITS: Mountain Warfare Training Center (USMC).

BASE HISTORY: 1951, established as Cold Weather Bn to provide training for personnel bound for Korea. Post Korean War, renamed Marine Corps Cold Weather Training Center. 1963, renamed Marine Corps Mountain Warfare Training Center. 1967, placed in caretaker status. 1976, reactivated.

Key Contacts

COMMANDER: Col P W O'Toole, 760-932-7761, DSN 985-7231, DSN FAX 985-7208, O'TOOLE@pendleton.usmc.mil.

PUBLIC AFFAIRS: Capt E W Dunnick, 760-932-7761, ext 296, DSN 985-7296, DSN FAX 985-7208, CAPTE.W.DUNNICK@pendleton.usmc.mil.

Personnel and Expenditures

ACTIVE DUTY PERSONNEL: 241

DEPENDENTS: 325

CIVILIAN PERSONNEL: 46

MILITARY PAYROLL EXPENDITURE: $6.2 mil

CONTRACT EXPENDITURE: $2 mil

Services

Housing: Family units 111; Unaccompanied enlisted quarters 98; Barracks spaces 6; Senior NCO units 9. *Temporary Housing:* VIP units 1; Unaccompanied officer/Enlisted quarters 22; *Exchange:* Barber shop; Food shop; Convenience store; Post office; Video rentals; Travel agency. *Child Care/Capacities:* Day care center. *Schools:* No on-base schools. *Base Library:* Yes. *Medical Facilities:* Medical clinic. *Recreational Facilities:* Movie theater; Gym; Stables; Racquetball court; Fitness center/Weight room; Softball field; Camping; Fishing/Hunting; Playground; All ranks club.

China Lake

60. China Lake Naval Air Weapons Station

NAWS, China Lake; NAVAIRWPNSTA

One Administration Circle

China Lake, CA 93555-6001

760-939-9011; FAX 760-939-2056; DSN 437-9011

OFFICER-OF-THE-DAY: Quarterdeck LCPO, Code C8103, 760-939-2303, DSN 437-2303

Profile

BRANCH: Navy.

SIZE AND LOCATION: 1.126 mil acres (17,000 sq mi). In Mojave Desert, S-central CA, next to Ridgecrest, CA; 8 mi from US-395; 11 mi from Hwy 14; 150 mi NE of Los Angeles. *County:* Kern; Inyo; San Bernardino.

MAJOR UNITS: Naval Air Warfare Center Weapons Division, China Lake; Naval Air Weapons Test Squadron; Naval Air Weapons Station, China Lake.

BASE HISTORY: 1943, established as Naval Ordnance Test Station, Inyokern, with airstrip, Harvey Field. WWII, developed non-nuclear explosive components in support of Manhattan Project. 1950s, developed Sidewinder heat-seeking air-to-air missile. 1967, NOTS China Lake & Naval Ordnance Lab, Corona joined to form Naval Weapons Center here. 1979, acquired National Parachute Test Range. Site includes vast complex of laboratories & test-range facilities. Center situated under restricted military airspace of nearly 17,000 sq mi, making NAWS Navy's largest research development, test, & evaluation (RDT&E) activity. Complex covers 2 areas: China Lake Complex, in north; Randsburg Wash/Mojave "B" Complex, in south. Principal Navy RDT&E center for air warfare systems (except anti-submarine warfare systems), missile weapon systems, & national range/facility for parachute test & evaluation; permanent activity of Naval Air Systems Command.

VISITOR ATTRACTIONS: Weapons exhibit center (Open to public M-F 7:30-4:30, Sat 10-2).

Key Contacts
COMMANDER: Code CO8, 760-939-2211, DSN 437-2211.
PUBLIC AFFAIRS: Code CO803, 760-939-3511, DSN 437-3511.
PROCUREMENT: Code C65, 760-939-3801, DSN 437-3801.
TRANSPORTATION: Public Works Dept, Code C83, 760-939-2382, DSN 437-2382.
PERSONNEL/COMMUNITY ACTIVITIES: Human Resources Dept, Code C62, 760-939-8123, DSN 437-8123.

Personnel and Expenditures
ACTIVE DUTY PERSONNEL: 1000
DEPENDENTS: 2500
CIVILIAN PERSONNEL: 4000

Services
Housing: Family units 500; Unaccompanied officer quarters; Unaccompanied enlisted quarters; BAQ units; Duplex units; Barracks spaces. *Temporary Housing:* VIP units 4; VOQ units 7; VEQ units; Unaccompanied officer/Enlisted quarters 24. *Commissary:* Yes; *Exchange:* Retail store; Barber shop; Service station; Military clothing store; Military clothing store; Convenience store; Credit union. *Child Care/Capacities:* Day care center. *Schools:* Preschool/Kindergarten; Elementary; Intermediate/Junior high. *Base Library:* Yes. *Medical Facilities:* Medical clinic; Dental clinic. *Recreational Facilities:* Bowling center; Pool; Gym; Golf course; Tennis courts; Fitness center/Weight room; Softball field; Auto shop; Craft shop; Enlisted club; Youth center; Picnic area.

Concord

61. Concord Naval Weapons Station
WPNSTAC
10 Delta St
Concord, CA 94520-5100
510-246-5591; FAX 510-246-5454; DSN 350-5591; DSN FAX 350-5454
OFFICER-OF-THE-DAY: 510-246-2075 (pager 246-0756), DSN 350-2075

Profile
BRANCH: Navy.
SIZE AND LOCATION: 13,000 acres. Main gate on Port Chicago Hwy; 45 mi NE of San Francisco; 60 mi NE of San Francisco IAP. *County:* Contra Costa.
MAJOR UNITS: Naval Weapons Station, Concord; Naval Branch Medical Clinic; Naval Criminal Investigative Service; Naval Dental Clinic; Naval Ordnance Center, Pacific Division; Naval Sea Logistics Center, Det Pacific; Naval Undersea Warfare Center; Public Works Center, San Diego; US Coast Guard Marine Safety Det; Resident Officer-in-Charge of Construction; 1st United Services Credit Union.
BASE HISTORY: 1942, established as annex to Naval Ammunition Depot, Mare Island, later renamed Naval Ammunition Depot, Port Chicago, site of largest state-side disaster of WWII. Expanded to DOD West Coast Ammunition Ocean Terminal. Principal port for transshipment of ammunition during Korean & Vietnam Wars. Supported Operations JUST CAUSE & Desert Storm. Today, largest military facility on West Coast for transshipment of ammunition & other hazardous cargo; also provides materiel & technical support for ammunition, weapons & weapons systems; and, homeport & logistics support agency for Pacific Fleet auxiliary ammunition ships used for replenishment of Navy ships at sea. Divided into Tidal Area & Inland Area. Tidal Area has facility for sorting returned ordnance, railroad & truck classification yards, and 3 ocean terminal piers capable of berthing 6 large cargo ships simultaneously. Inland Area consists of administration buildings, military barracks, storage magazines.
VISITOR ATTRACTIONS: Port Chicago Memorial Site; Tule Elk & other wildlife conservation area.

Key Contacts
COMMANDER: Capt Paul N Bruno, 510-246-5575, FAX 510-246-2011, DSN 350-5575, DSN FAX 350-2011.
PUBLIC AFFAIRS: Linda Zukeran, 510-246-5591, DSN 350-5591, DSN FAX 350-5454.
PERSONNEL/COMMUNITY ACTIVITIES: See Public Affairs Officer.

Personnel and Expenditures
ACTIVE DUTY PERSONNEL: 400
CIVILIAN PERSONNEL: 1200

Services
Housing: Family units 297; Unaccompanied enlisted quarters 48. *Temporary Housing:* None. *Exchange:* Barber shop; Bank; Credit union; ATM; Thrift shop. *Child Care/Capacities:* Summer day camp; Child care providers available for all children. *Schools:* Preschool/Kindergarten; *Base Library:* Yes. *Medical Facilities:* Medical clinic; Dental clinic; Pharmacy. *Recreational Facilities:* Gym; Recreation center; Fitness center/Weight room; Softball field; Football field; Auto shop; Youth center; Picnic area; Playground; All ranks club; Morale, Welfare, & Recreation Dept; Recreation gear issue; Golf course nearby.

Dublin

62. Parks Reserve Forces Training Area
Camp Parks
Camp Parks, Bldg 790
Dublin, CA 94568-5201
510-803-5650; FAX 510-803-5637

Profile
BRANCH: Army Reserve.
SIZE AND LOCATION: 2900 acres. In Livermore Valley, central to greater San Francisco Bay Area; 18 mi E of Oakland; 44 mi E of San Francisco. Nearest major population centers Dublin, Pleasanton, San Ramon and Livermore. Served by I-580 and I-680. Nearest airports Livermore and Oakland. *County:* Alameda.
MAJOR UNITS: Regional Training Site, Medical (RTS-Med); 91st Division (Ex) 1st Brigade; 91st Division (Ex) Battle Projection Center; 319th Signal Bn, B Co; 159th Infantry (ARNG); AMSA/ECS 30; 6237th Army Reserve Forces School; 6th Area NCO Academy.
BASE HISTORY: 1942, comprised of two major areas, Camp Parks and Camp Shoemaker; served as Navy basic training center through WWII when deactivated and leased to Alameda County. Korean War, became known as Parks AFB, until 1958, when declared excess to Air Force requirements, then passed to Army control and became Camp Parks. 1975, redesignated sub-installation of Presidio of San Francisco and assigned mission of supporting Reserve Components training and readiness. 1983, status changed from inactive to semi-active for reserve forces local training area. 1992, made sub-installation of Ft Lewis, WA. 1993, made sub-installation of US Army Reserve Command (USARC).
VISITOR ATTRACTIONS: Small museum; Monument site/plaque honoring RADM Parks.

Key Contacts
COMMANDER: LTC Tom Brown.
PUBLIC AFFAIRS: Lynne Schaack, Public Affairs Specialist.

Personnel and Expenditures
ACTIVE DUTY PERSONNEL: 67
DEPENDENTS: 25
CIVILIAN PERSONNEL: 685
CONTRACT EXPENDITURE: Combined with Ft Lewis, WA

Services
Housing: Family units 14; Senior NCO units; Junior NCO units. *Exchange:* Retail store. *Child Care/Capacities:* No day care facilities. *Schools:* No on-base schools. *Medical Facilities:* Dispensary. *Recreational Facilities:* Tennis courts; Fitness center/Weight room; Softball field; Community club.

Edwards AFB

63. Edwards Air Force Base
Edwards AFB, CA 93523
805-277-1110; FAX 805-277-4392; DSN 527-4392
Internet: http://www.edwards.af.mil

Profile
BRANCH: Air Force.

SIZE AND LOCATION: 301,000 acres. In SW CA on western edge of Mojave Desert approx 100 mi NE of Los Angeles, 90 mi NW of San Bernardino, 80 mi SE of Bakersfield. *County:* Kern; Los Angeles.

MAJOR UNITS: Air Force Flight Test Center; 412th Test Wing; Air Force Test Pilot School; 412th Test Group; 420th Test Group; 716th Logistics Test Squadron; 545th Test Group; 501st Range Squadron; 514th Test Squadron; 412th Operations Support; 411th Test Squadron; 413rd Test Squadron; 415th Test Squadron; 416th Test Squadron; 417th Test Squadron; 418th Test Squadron; 419th Test Squadron; 445th Test Squadron; 412th Logistics Group; 412th Aircraft Generation Squadron; 412th Component Repair Squadron; 412th Equipment Maintenance Squadron; 412th Logistics Test Squadron; 95th Air Base Wing; 95th Civil Engineering Squadron; 95th Communications-Computer Systems Squadron; 95th Medical Group; 95th Mission Support Squadron; 95th Security Police; 95th Supply Squadron; 95th Transportation Squadron; Air Force Operational Test and Evaluation Center, Det 5; Area Defense Counsel; Civil Air Patrol; Federal Aviation Administration; NASA Ames Research Center/Dryden Flight Research Facility; Phillips Laboratory; Army Airworthiness Qualification Test Directorate; Corps of Engineers; 18th Test Squadron; 31st Test & Evaluation Squadron; 1275th Test & Evaluation Squadron; 374th Training Development Squadron; Utah Test and Training Range.

BASE HISTORY: 1933, bombing & gunnery training began at Muroc, CA, with detachment, March Field, CA. WWII, S end of dry lake used to train fighter pilots & bomber crews. 1942, portion of Muroc Dry Lake assigned to Materiel Command Flight Test Base; America's 1st jet tested. 1944, redesignated Muroc Flight Test Base. 1946, facilities merged into single flight test activity at Muroc Army Air Field under AMC. 1948, redesignated Muroc AFB. 1949, redesignated Edwards AFB for Capt Glen W Edwards, resident of Lincoln, CA, killed during performance test of YB-49, Flying Wing. 1950, Air Research & Development Command (ARDC) replaced AMC. 1951, AF Flight Test Center activated here. 1961, ARDC became AF Systems Command, responsible for research & development of aerospace weapons systems, from drawing board to operational readiness. Flight Test Center here also provides support functions to NASA space shuttle program, including secondary landing site for all space shuttle flights. 1992, AF Systems Command merged with AF Logistics Command into AF Materiel Command.

VISITOR ATTRACTIONS: NASA Tours (805-258-3449); NASA gift shop (805-258-3449); Edwards Tours (805-277-3517).

Key Contacts
COMMANDER: Maj Gen Richard Engel, 1 S Rosmand Blvd.
PUBLIC AFFAIRS: LTC Robert C Williams, 15 E Mojave, 805-277-3510, DSN 527-3510.

Personnel and Expenditures
ACTIVE DUTY PERSONNEL: 4741
DEPENDENTS: 6100
CIVILIAN PERSONNEL: 9655
MILITARY PAYROLL EXPENDITURE: $266 mil
CONTRACT EXPENDITURE: $279 mil

Services
Housing: Family units 1989; Dormitory spaces 208; Senior NCO units; Trailer spaces 164; Apartments 50. *Temporary Housing:* VOQ units 85; VAQ units 82; Transient quarters. *Commissary:* Yes; *Exchange:* Retail store; Barber shop; Dry cleaners; Florist; Bank; Service station; Military clothing store; Convenience store; Beauty shop; Laundromat; Credit union. *Child Care/Capacities:* Child development center. *Schools:* Preschool/Kindergarten; Elementary; Intermediate/Junior high; High school. *Base Library:* Yes. *Medical Facilities:* Hospital; Medical clinic; Dental clinic; Veterinary services. *Recreational Facilities:* Bowling center; Movie theater; Pool; Gym; Recreation center; Golf course; Stables; Tennis courts; Racquetball court; Fitness center/Weight room; Softball field; Football field; Auto shop; Craft shop; Camping; Youth center; Skeet range; Consolidated club; Rod & Gun club; Aero club; Tours & Tickets; Recreation equipment rental; Lake Isabella, 2 hr drive N; SATO.

El Centro

64. El Centro Naval Air Facility
NAF El Centro
1605 3rd St
El Centro, CA 92243-5001
619-339-2699; DSN 958-8699
OFFICER-OF-THE-DAY: 619-339-2524, DSN 958-8524

Profile
BRANCH: Navy.
SIZE AND LOCATION: 2289 acres (plus control of additional 54,000 acres). 120 mi E of San Diego off I-8, Drew Rd Exit at Seeley, CA; 62 mi W of Yuma, AZ off I-8. *County:* Imperial.
MAJOR UNITS: Strike Fighter Maintenance Unit.
BASE HISTORY: Since 1942, NAF El Centro has had several names: Marine Corps Air Station, Naval Air Facility, Naval Auxiliary Landing Field, Naval Air Station, & National Parachute Test Range. Facility involved in aeronautical escape system testing, evaluation, & design. 1947, Parachute Experimental Division moved here from Lakehurst, NJ. 1949, Fleet Gunnery Unit assigned. 1951, Joint Parachute Facility established. 1959, ejection seat from high-speed jet at altitudes under 1000 ft successfully tested; parachute system for Mercury Space Program tested. 1964, Naval Aerospace Recovery Facility designated (later combined with Naval Air Facility to form National Parachute Test Range). 1979, parachute test function transferred to Naval Weapons Center, China Lake; El Centro again NAF. 1986, much of film "Top Gun" shot here.
VISITOR ATTRACTIONS: Winter Home of Blue Angels Air Demonstration Team.

Key Contacts
COMMANDER: Capt Carlos S Badger, 619-339-2401, DSN 958-8401.
PUBLIC AFFAIRS: 619-339-2519, DSN 958-2519.
PROCUREMENT: 619-339-2219.
TRANSPORTATION: 619-339-2218, DSN 958-8218.

PERSONNEL/COMMUNITY ACTIVITIES: 619-339-2618, DSN 958-8618.
Personnel and Expenditures
ACTIVE DUTY PERSONNEL: 350
DEPENDENTS: 200
CIVILIAN PERSONNEL: 400
Services
Housing: Family units 172; Unaccompanied officer quarters 95 rooms; Unaccompanied enlisted quarters 452 rooms; Mobile home units 5; RV/Camper sites 40. *Temporary Housing:* Lodge units 400 rooms; Mobile home units 5. *Commissary:* Yes; *Exchange:* Retail store; Barber shop; Dry cleaners; Service station; Furniture store. *Child Care/Capacities:* Day care center capacity 80. *Schools:* No on-base schools. *Base Library:* Yes. *Medical Facilities:* Medical clinic; Dental clinic. *Recreational Facilities:* Bowling center; Movie theater; Pool; Recreation center; Tennis courts; Racquetball court; Fitness center/Weight room; Softball field; Football field; Auto shop; Craft shop; All hands club; Go-cart track; Golf driving range.

El Granada

65. Pillar Point Air Force Station
PO Box 609
El Granada, CA 94018-0609
415-728-3508
Profile
BRANCH: Air Force.
SIZE AND LOCATION: 50 acres. On Pillar Point near Half Moon Bay, 21 mi S of San Francisco. *County:* San Mateo.
MAJOR UNITS: Pillar Point Air Force Station.
BASE HISTORY: WWII, established coastal artillery installation. 1959, acquired by Navy for planned missile guidance station; site deactivated. 1962, reactivated for support of missile launches from Vandenberg AFB. 1965, transferred to Air Force. Currently, northernmost instrumentation facility of 30th Space Wing, Vandenberg AFB. Equipped to support ballistic, orbital, & aeronautical programs with radar tracking, telemetry reception & processing, command control, & communications services. Maintained and operated solely by contractor employees of ITT Federal Services Corp. Under caretaker status.
Key Contacts
COMMANDER: Dennis B Inch, Station Manager.

El Segundo

66. Defense Contract Management District West
DCMC West
222 N Sepulveda Blvd
El Segundo, CA 90245-4320
310-335-3001; FAX 310-335-4409; DSN 972-3001
E-mail: zd00000@dcmdw.dsl.mil
Profile
BRANCH: Defense Logistics Agency.
LOCATION: *County:* Los Angeles.
MAJOR UNITS: Defense Contract Management District West.

Encino

67. Encino Naval & Marine Corps Reserve Center
6337 Balboa Blvd
Encino, CA 91316-1584
818-344-5101; FAX 818-334-7329; DSN 833-1110

Profile
BRANCH: Naval Reserve; Marine Corps Reserve.
MAJOR UNITS: REDCOM NINETEEN Activity; HQ, 2nd Bn, 23rd Marine Regiment; HQ & Service Co, 2nd Bn, 23rd Marine Regiment.

Key Contacts
COMMANDER: LCDR J B Walsh.

Fallbrook

68. Fallbrook Naval Ordnance Center, Pacific Division
700 Ammunition Rd
Fallbrook, CA 92028-3187
619-731-3609

Profile
BRANCH: Navy.
LOCATION: 80 mi S of Seal Beach; adj to Camp Pendleton Marine Corps Base; along DeLuz River. *County:* San Diego.
MAJOR UNITS: Naval Ordnance Center, Pacific Division.
BASE HISTORY: Part of Naval Weapons Center Seal Beach. Stores, issues, & performs intermediate repair of air-launched weapons, including Phoenix, Sidewinder, Walleye, HARM, Hellfire, Maverick, Skipper, & Shrikes missiles. Statistical performance analysis of various air, surface, & sub-surface launched weapons conducted. Primary provisioner of conventional ordnance to Marine Corps.

Key Contacts
COMMANDER: CDR Richard Kelly Eley, 619-731-3609.
PUBLIC AFFAIRS: Capt Andrew Hammond, 909-273-4521.

Fort Hunter Liggett

69. Fort Hunter Liggett
Fort Hunter Liggett, CA 93928
408-386-3000; FAX 408-386-2011

Profile
BRANCH: Army.
SIZE AND LOCATION: 164,637 acres. In Santa Lucia Mountains; 23 mi SW of King City at intersection of Hwy G14 and G18 near Jolon, CA. *County:* Monterey.
MAJOR UNITS: Army Garrison, Ft Hunter Liggett; Test and Experimentation Command Experimentation Center.
BASE HISTORY: 1957, activated as sub-installation of Ft Ord military complex; named for Lt Gen Hunter Liggett, commander of 31st Army Division, AEF, in WWI; purchased from William Randolph Hearst & others. WWII, maneuver area & artillery range. Post

WWII, intermittent use for field training. 1969, construction of permanent facilities.
FUTURE CLOSURE/REALIGNMENT: Scheduled for major realignment by Sep 1999.
VISITOR ATTRACTIONS: Ranch house of William Randolph Hearst (used as guesthouse); Mission San Antonio.

Key Contacts
COMMANDER: LTC David V Hines, ATTN: AFRC-FMH-CDR, 408-386-2506, DSN 686-2506.
PUBLIC AFFAIRS: See Base Commander.

Personnel and Expenditures
ACTIVE DUTY PERSONNEL: 500
DEPENDENTS: 100
CIVILIAN PERSONNEL: 400

Services
Housing: Family units 32; Unaccompanied enlisted quarters; Barracks spaces 1044; Unaccompanied officer quarters units 60. *Temporary Housing:* VIP units 1; Guesthouse units 11. *Commissary:* Yes; *Exchange:* Retail store; Barber shop; Dry cleaners; Food shop; Service station. *Child Care/Capacities:* Day care center capacity 37, 6wks-5yrs; Summer day camp. *Schools:* College courses. *Base Library:* Yes. *Medical Facilities:* Medical clinic; Pharmacy; *Recreational Facilities:* Bowling center; Movie theater; Pool; Gym; Recreation center; Tennis courts; Racquetball court; Fitness center/Weight room; Softball field; Auto shop; Craft shop; Camping; Fishing/Hunting; Youth center; Picnic area; Skeet range; Playground; All ranks club.

Fort Irwin

70. Fort Irwin, National Training Center
NTC and Ft Irwin
PAO, Box 105067
Fort Irwin, CA 92310-5067
760-256-1071; DSN 470-1110, 470-1111

Profile
BRANCH: Army.
SIZE AND LOCATION: 636,182 acres (Ft Irwin 1000 acres). In Mojave Desert along I-15, halfway between Los Angeles & Las Vegas, 37 mi NE of Barstow, CA; only access via Ft Irwin Rd which joins I-15 just N of Barstow. *County:* San Bernardino.
MAJOR UNITS: National Training Center; Operations Group, Ft Irwin; 11th Armored Cavalry Regiment.
BASE HISTORY: 1860, small stone fort built. 1930s, Gen George Patton used area for maneuvers. 1940, reservation named Mojave Anti-Aircraft Range, subpost of Camp Haan, adjacent to later March AFB. 1942, renamed for Maj Gen Leroy Irwin, battle commander of 57th Field Artillery Brigade, WWI. 1944, deactivated. 1951, reactivated. 1961, designated permanent Class I installation; renamed Fort Irwin. 1971, deactivated; maintenance status. 1972, post assumed by CA ANG. 1980, NTC activated. 1981, Fort reactivated. Twelve scheduled rotations per year; infantry, armor, artillery, & support units train for 2 weeks.

Key Contacts
COMMANDER: LTC David A Ahrens, Garrison Commander, 760-380-6267, FAX 760-380-6269, DSN 470-6267, ahrensd@irwin.army.mil.

Personnel and Expenditures
ACTIVE DUTY PERSONNEL: 4700; Guard & Reserve 80
DEPENDENTS: 7800
CIVILIAN PERSONNEL: 3400

Services
Housing: Family units 306; Unaccompanied officer quarters 1157; Barracks spaces 1838; Senior NCO units 201; Trailer spaces 74; Officer 306. *Temporary Housing:* VIP units 9; Guesthouse units 21; Guest cottages 14; Mobile home units 14; Official mission TDY mobile home 1. *Commissary:* Yes; *Exchange:* Retail store; Barber shop; Dry cleaners; Food shop; Florist; Service station; Furniture store; Military clothing store; Convenience store; Beauty shop; Laundromat; Credit union; Fast food; Mini-mall; Delicatessen. *Child Care/Capacities:* Day care center capacity 150, 0-5yrs; Home day care program; Latch key program; Hourly care, capacity 27. *Schools:* Preschool/Kindergarten; Elementary; Intermediate/Junior high; College courses. *Base Library:* Yes. *Medical Facilities:* Hospital Weed Army Hospital, 27 beds; Dental clinic; Pharmacy; Veterinary services. *Recreational Facilities:* Bowling center; Movie theater; Pool; Gym; Recreation center; Skating rink; Fitness center/Weight room; Softball field; Football field; Auto shop; Craft shop; Officers club; NCO club; Enlisted club; Youth center; Playground.

Fresno

71. Fresno Naval Reserve Center
NRC Fresno
Armed Forces Reserve Center
5565 E Shields Ave
Fresno, CA 93727-7790
209-291-0204, 291-0205; FAX 209-291-0206

Profile
BRANCH: Naval Reserve; Army Reserve.
SIZE AND LOCATION: 3 acres. In downtown Fresno, approx 4 mi from Fresno Airport. *County:* Fresno.
MAJOR UNITS: REDCOM NINETEEN Activity.
BASE HISTORY: 1946, established. 1977, present center established.
VISITOR ATTRACTIONS: Quarter Deck.

Key Contacts
COMMANDER: LCDR George A Bowles, BOWLES@cnrf.nola.navy.mil.

Personnel and Expenditures
ACTIVE DUTY PERSONNEL: 230 reservists (8 reserve units)

Services *Base Library:* Yes. *Medical Facilities:* Medical clinic. *Recreational Facilities:* Gym; Fitness center/Weight room; Craft shop.

Fresno Air Terminal

72. Fresno Air National Guard Base
Fresno ANGB
5323 E McKinley Ave
Fresno Air Terminal, CA 93727-2199
209-454-5144; FAX 209-454-5385; DSN 949-9144
OFFICER-OF-THE-DAY: 209-454-5155, DSN 949-9155

Profile
BRANCH: Air National Guard.
SIZE AND LOCATION: 85 acres. Within city limits of Fresno, bounded by city on three sides and just S of Clovis, CA; main portion of base lies in E-W orientation adj to McKinley Ave and runway shared with Fresno Air Terminal on N. *County:* Fresno.
MAJOR UNITS: 144th Fighter Wing, Headquarters; 144th Operations Group; 144th Logistics Group; 144th Support Group; 144th Medical Squadron.
BASE HISTORY: 1955, three buildings built on site. 1975, current facility development program started when refueling function unified into single facility. Weapons storage area inherited from Marines; lies across runway on N portion of base.
VISITOR ATTRACTIONS: Static display of aircraft.
Key Contacts
COMMANDER: Col Douglas R Moore, 209-454-5144, DSN 949-9144.
PUBLIC AFFAIRS: MSgt Debbie Ayres, 209-454-5145, 454-5262, DSN 949-9154, 949-9262.
PROCUREMENT: SMS Win Downing, 209-454-5128, DSN 949-9128.
TRANSPORTATION: LTC Mike Pogey, 209-454-5109, DSN 949-9109.
PERSONNEL/COMMUNITY ACTIVITIES: LTC Dan Fernandez, Personnel, 209-454-5279, DSN 949-9279, Capt Dan Nation, Community Activities.
Personnel and Expenditures
ACTIVE DUTY PERSONNEL: 972
CIVILIAN PERSONNEL: 290
MILITARY PAYROLL EXPENDITURE: $3.6 mil
CONTRACT EXPENDITURE: $206,000
Services
Housing: None. *Temporary Housing:* None. *Exchange:* None. *Medical Facilities:* Emergency clinic. *Recreational Facilities:* Fitness center/Weight room; NCO club.

Herlong

73. Sierra Army Depot
SIAD
Herlong, CA 96113
916-827-4345; DSN 855-4345
Profile
BRANCH: Army.
SIZE AND LOCATION: 36,000 acres. In Honey Lake Valley among foothills of Sierra Nevadas; approx 55 mi NW of Reno, NV; 40 mi SE of Susanville, CA, off Hwy 395. *County:* Lassen.
MAJOR UNITS: Sierra Army Depot.
BASE HISTORY: 1942, designated Sierra Reserve Arsenal; primary mission: receipt, storage and issue of ammunition; also general supplies. 1947-1951, mission expanded to include renovation and demilitarization of ammunition and demolition of outdated and dangerous ammunition. 1962, renamed Sierra Army Depot; supply mission: ammunition; strategic and critical elements such as chromium, manganese, and tungsten; and, packed and crated household goods stored for military service personnel (only Army installation storing household goods for DOD personnel on nontemporary basis). Currently, depot under Industrial Operations Command (IOC); also provides training & facilities for Army Reserve & ANG units; Amadee Army Airfield in northern part of depot. Mission: provide cost effective operations in receipt, storage, issue & maintenance of equipment & components for operational project stocks; and receipt, storage, issue, maintenance & demilitarization of conventional ammunition.
FUTURE CLOSURE/REALIGNMENT: Major realignment to be completed by Sep 2001.
Key Contacts
PUBLIC AFFAIRS: Larry Rogers, 916-827-4343, DSN 855-4343.
Personnel and Expenditures
ACTIVE DUTY PERSONNEL: 30
CIVILIAN PERSONNEL: 668
Services
Housing: Unaccompanied officer quarters; Barracks spaces; Senior NCO units; Junior NCO units. *Temporary Housing:* Guesthouse units. *Commissary:* Yes; *Exchange:* Retail store; Barber shop; Dry cleaners; Food shop; Florist; Service station; Convenience store; Beauty shop; Laundromat; Credit union. *Child Care/Capacities:* Day care center; Home day care program; Latch key program; *Schools:* Preschool/Kindergarten; Elementary; Intermediate/Junior high; High school. *Base Library:* Yes. *Medical Facilities:* Medical clinic; Dental clinic; Pharmacy. *Recreational Facilities:* Bowling center; Pool; Gym; Recreation center; Tennis courts; Racquetball court; Fitness center/Weight room; Softball field; Football field; Youth center; Picnic area; Playground; Community club.

Lemoore

74. Lemoore Naval Air Station
NAS Lemoore
116 Catalina Ave
Lemoore, CA 93245-3000
209-998-0100; DSN 949-1110
Internet: http://www.lemoore.navy.mil/welcome.html
Profile
BRANCH: Navy.
SIZE AND LOCATION: 18,000 acres; 12,000 leased back to farmers. 40 mi S of Fresno at Lemoore off Hwy 198, 19 mi E of I-5; 30 mi W of Hwy 99 in San Joaquin Valley in central CA. *County:* Kings; Fresno.
MAJOR UNITS: Naval Air Station, Lemoore; Strike Fighter Wing, Pacific; Strike Fighter Squadron 22; Strike Fighter Squadron 25; Strike Fighter Squadron 27; Strike Fighter Squadron 94; Strike Fighter Squadron 97; Strike Fighter Squadron 113; Strike Fighter Squadron 115; Strike Fighter Squadron 125; Strike Fighter Squadron 137; Strike Fighter Squadron 146; Strike Fighter Squadron 147; Strike Fighter Squadron 151; Strike Fighter Squadron 192; Strike Fighter Squadron 195; Strike Fighter Weapons School; Strike Fighter Super Hornet Team; Carrier Air Wing 2; Carrier Air Wing 9; Carrier Air Wing 11; Carrier Air Wing 14; Construction Bn Unit 406; Fleet Imaging Facility, Pacific; Mobile Construction Bn 133; Naval Air Reserve Center, Lemoore; Naval Hospital Lemoore; Naval Pacific Meteorology and Oceanography Det, Lemoore; Aviation Survival Training Center; Fleet Aviation Specialized Operational Training Group, Pacific; Marine Aviation Training Support Group; Naval Air Maintenance Training Group, Det, Lemoore; Naval Aviation Engineering Service Unit; Naval Criminal Investigative Service, Lemoore; Personnel Support Activity Det, Lemoore.
BASE HISTORY: 1958, construction began about 1 mi W of Lemoore Army Air Field (LAAF), active during WWII. 1961, site commissioned; officially named Reeves Field for RADM Joseph M Reeves, who laid groundwork for modern aircraft carrier strike force. Navy's newest & largest master jet air station.
Key Contacts
COMMANDER: Capt Louis D Childress.
PUBLIC AFFAIRS: Dennis McGrath, 209-998-3393, DSN 949-3393.
Personnel and Expenditures
ACTIVE DUTY PERSONNEL: 5300
DEPENDENTS: 10,000
CIVILIAN PERSONNEL: 1900
Services
Housing: Family units 1250; Unaccompanied officer quarters 166; Unaccompanied enlisted quarters 1400; Barracks spaces 2688. *Temporary Housing:* VIP units 8; Lodge units 46. *Commissary:* Yes; *Exchange:* Retail store; Barber shop; Dry cleaners; Service station; Furniture store; Military clothing store; Convenience store; Beauty shop; Laundromat; Credit union; Optical store; Fast food; Class VI; Hobby store; Ice cream. *Child Care/Capacities:* Day care center capacity 120; Home day care program. *Schools:* Elementary. *Base Library:* Yes. *Medical Facilities:* Hospital 20 beds; Dental clinic; Veterinary services. *Recreational Facilities:* Bowling center; Movie theater; Pool; Gym; Recreation center; Tennis courts; Racquetball court; Fitness center/Weight room; Softball field; Football field; Auto shop; Craft shop; Officers club; Enlisted club; Youth center; Skeet range; Driving range; Stables for boarding; CPO club; Archery; Pistol range; Gear locker rental equipment; Cross country track; Flying club; Tours and Travel.

Los Angeles

75. Defense Contract Management Command, Hughes Los Angeles
DCMC Hughes LA
P.O. Box 92463
Los Angeles, CA 90009-2463
310-364-6404
Internet: http://www.dcmdw.dla.mil; http://rz.dcmdw.dla.mil
Profile
BRANCH: Defense Logistics Agency.
LOCATION: *County:* Los Angeles.
MAJOR UNITS: Defense Contract Management Command, Hughes Los Angeles.
Key Contacts
COMMANDER: Col Larry Rensing; Darryl J Jackson, Deputy, 310-416-5497.

76. Los Angeles Air Force Base
2430 E El Segundo Blvd, Ste 4049
Los Angeles, CA 90245-4687
Mailing Address
325 Challenger Way, Ste 1990
El Segundo, CA 90245-4659
310-363-1000; DSN 833-1000

Internet: http://www.laafb.af.mil/
OFFICER-OF-THE-DAY: SMC Command Post, 310-363-2353, DSN 833-2353; Base Locator 310-363-1876, DSN 833-1876; Staff Duty Officer, 310-363-0486, DSN 833-0486

Profile
BRANCH: Air Force.
SIZE AND LOCATION: 275 acres. 2 mi S of Los Angeles IAP in El Segundo; 1 mi W of I-405, on El Segundo Blvd, right on Douglas St, entrance on right. *County:* Los Angeles.
MAJOR UNITS: Space and Missile Systems Center; 61st Air Base Group; Air Force Audit Agency, Los Angeles; Air Force Office of Special Investigations, Det 110; Air Mobility Command Space-A Flight Information; Defense Contract Audit Agency; Defense Systems Management College, Western Regional Center; Defense Dissemination Program.
BASE HISTORY: 1954, Space & Missile Systems Center began as Western Development Division developing ICBMs. Mission: buys all Air Force & most DOD satellites & rocket boosters to launch them; focal point for development & acquisition of space-based support; and, designs & acquires space systems & completes on-orbit checkouts. Base has no flightline. Base divided into Area A (major units) & Area B (61st Air Base Group, clinic, BX, & commissary).

Key Contacts
COMMANDER: Lt Gen Roger G DeKok, 310-363-0667, DSN 833-0667; Col Dieter Barnes, 61st ABG, 310-363-5066, FAX 310-363-5069, DSN 833-5066.
PUBLIC AFFAIRS: SMC/PA, 310-363-0030, FAX 310-363-2549, DSN 833-0030; Chet R DelSinore, 310-363-6428, DSN 833-6428.
PROCUREMENT: Director of Contracting 310-363-0886, FAX 310-363-5507, DSN 833-0886.
TRANSPORTATION: Transportation Management Office, 310-363-3673, DSN 833-3673.
PERSONNEL/COMMUNITY ACTIVITIES: Military Personnel, 310-363-2314, DSN 833-2314; Civilian Personnel, 310-363-2321, DSN 833-2321.

Personnel and Expenditures
ACTIVE DUTY PERSONNEL: 1630
DEPENDENTS: 1987
CIVILIAN PERSONNEL: 1107

Services
Housing: Family units 348; Unaccompanied officer quarters None on base; Unaccompanied enlisted quarters 169; Townhouse units 370; Dormitory spaces required for E-4 & below; Senior NCO units 56; All housing at Ft MacArthur Annex, Pacific Heights & Pacific Crest located 20 mi S of base. *Temporary Housing:* VIP units Suites 4; Transient quarters 22; VOQ/VEQ units 29; Ft MacArthur Inn, TLF 22, VOQ 27. *Commissary:* Yes; *Exchange:* Retail store; Barber shop; Dry cleaners; Food shop; Florist; Bank; Service station; Military clothing store; Convenience store; Credit union; Optical store; Flower shop; Shoppette at Fort MacArthur housing. *Child Care/Capacities:* Day care center 2 centers, capacity 180, 6wks-6yrs, fully accredited; Home day care program; Summer day camp; Before & after school programs. *Schools:* No on-base schools. *Base Library:* Yes. *Medical Facilities:* Medical clinic; Dental clinic; Pharmacy. *Recreational Facilities:* Pool; Gym; Recreation center; Tennis courts; Racquetball court; Fitness center/Weight room 2 regular, 1 mini, 1 multipurpose; Softball field; Auto shop; Craft shop; Officers club; NCO club; Youth center; Picnic area 3 pavilions; Water sports; Playground; Equipment checkout; Tickets & Tours; Community center; Jogging path.

77. Los Angeles Naval & Marine Corps Reserve Center
USNMCRC Los Angeles
Los Angeles Fire Dept Training Ctr
1700 Stadium Way
Los Angeles, CA 90012-1498
213-485-6939; FAX 213-847-3440

Profile
BRANCH: Naval Reserve; Marine Corps Reserve.
SIZE: 10.75 acres. *County:* Los Angeles.
VISITOR ATTRACTIONS: California State historic site.

Key Contacts
PUBLIC AFFAIRS: Fire Captain Louis Roupoli.
Services *Recreational Facilities:* Pool; Gym; Softball field.

78. Navy Office of Information, West
11000 Wilshire Blvd, Ste 11100
Los Angeles, CA 90024
310-235-7481; FAX 310-235-7856

Profile
BRANCH: Navy.
MAJOR UNITS: Navy Office of Information, West.
BASE HISTORY: Serves AK, AZ, CA, HI, ID, MT, NV, OR, UT, & WA. Also liaison with film & television industry in Los Angeles area.

79. US Army Corps of Engineers, Los Angeles District
911 Wilshire Blvd
Los Angeles, CA 90017
Mailing Address
PO Box 532711
Los Angeles, CA 90053
213-452-3908

Profile
BRANCH: Army.
LOCATION: *County:* Los Angeles.
MAJOR UNITS: Corps of Engineers, Los Angeles District.
BASE HISTORY: 1898, began construction of breakwater in San Pedro Bay, now superport complex of Los Angeles-Long Beach. Today, covers 226,000 sq mi, southern CA & NV, & all of AZ; part of South Pacific Division.

Key Contacts
COMMANDER: 213-452-3967.
PUBLIC AFFAIRS: 213-452-3333.
Personnel and Expenditures
CIVILIAN PERSONNEL: 942

March ARB

80. March Air Reserve Base
MARB
March Field
March ARB, CA 92518-9000
909-655-1110; DSN 947-1110

E-mail: pa452@tecnet2.jcte.jcs.mil Internet: http://www.afres.com/march.field
OFFICER-OF-THE-DAY: 909-655-4137, DSN 947-4137, DSN FAX 947-4113

Profile
BRANCH: Air Force Reserve.
SIZE AND LOCATION: 2300 acres. In cities of Riverside & Moreno Valley off I-215; approx 8 mi from downtown Riverside; 22 mi from Ontario IAP; 2 mi S of intersection of CA Hwy 60 and I-215. *County:* Riverside.
MAJOR UNITS: 452nd Air Mobility Wing; 303rd Air Refueling Squadron; 729th Airlift Squadron; 730th Airlift Squadron; 163rd Air Refueling Wing; 119th Fighter Wing; 452nd Medical Squadron; 452nd Aeromedical Patient Staging Squadron; 4th Combat Camera; US Customs.
BASE HISTORY: 1917, Alessandro Field established near Riverside; part of national build-up of aviation training facilities. 1918, March Field established & renamed for Lt Peyton C March, killed in 1918 aircraft accident. 1st base established in West. 1923-26, inactive. 1927, Army flying school established. 1931, became operational base. WWII, trained bombardment units for Pacific duty; added Camp Hahn as anti-aircraft artillery training facility with both facilities supporting as many as 160,000 troops. 1946, reverts to Tactical Air Command base. 1949-53, became part of Strategic Air Command with B-29s. 1957, nonstop around the world "Power Flight" ends at March. 1960, 1st reserve unit assigned & conversion to B-52B bombers & KC-135 Stratotankers. Vietnam War, March served as logistical springboard for supplies to the Pacific & a reception center for returning prisoners of war & return to SAC duties. 1982, last B-52 wing replaced by KC-10 tankers. 1993, March begins realignment. 1996, becomes March Air Reserve Base.
VISITOR ATTRACTIONS: March Field Museum, displays of military aircraft (outside of base, free admission) for info call 909-655-3725.

Key Contacts
COMMANDER: Brig Gen Clayton T Gadd, 452 AMW/CC, 2145 Graeber St, Ste 117, March ARB CA 92518-1667, 909-655-4520, DSN 947-4520, DSN FAX 947-2875.
PUBLIC AFFAIRS: Capt Stephen M Razo, 452 AMW/PA, 2145 Graeber ST, Ste 211, March ARB CA 92518-1671, 909-655-4137, DSN 947-4137, DSN FAX 947-4113, srazo@riv.afres.af.mil.
PROCUREMENT: R Chapman, 909-655-2046, DSN 947-2046, DSN FAX 947-3772.
TRANSPORTATION: Maj Williams Woody, 909-655-7466, DSN 947-7466, DSN FAX 947-3182.
PERSONNEL/COMMUNITY ACTIVITIES: Maj Nancy Robinson, 909-655-3023, DSN 947-3023,.

Personnel and Expenditures
ACTIVE DUTY PERSONNEL: 3727 guard & reservists
CIVILIAN PERSONNEL: 1335
MILITARY PAYROLL EXPENDITURE: $23 mil
CONTRACT EXPENDITURE: $16.5 mil

Services
Housing: None. *Temporary Housing:* VOQ units 85; VEQ units 194; Lodge units 24.

Commissary: Yes; *Exchange:* Barber shop; Dry cleaners; Florist; Military clothing store; Credit union; ATM; Travel agency. *Child Care/Capacities:* No day care facilities; *Schools:* No on-base schools. *Medical Facilities:* Medical clinic; *Recreational Facilities:* Pool; Gym; Recreation center; Fitness center/Weight room; Craft shop; Officers club.

McClellan AFB

81. McClellan Air Force Base
McClellan AFB, CA 95652-1089
916-643-1110; DSN 633-1110
Internet: http://www.mcclellan.af.mil/homex. html
Profile
BRANCH: Air Force.
SIZE AND LOCATION: 3755 acres. 9 mi NE of Sacramento; main gate on Watt Ave, just N of I-80. *County:* Sacramento.
MAJOR UNITS: Sacramento Air Logistics Center; 940th Air Refueling Wing; 4th Air Force, HQ; 77th Communications Squadron; Coast Guard Air Station, Sacramento.
BASE HISTORY: 1937, Sacramento Air Depot commissioned. 1939, renamed McClellan Field for Maj Hezekiah McClellan, pioneer in charting Alaskan air routes; depot kept name and became primary unit at McClellan. During WWII, site bore brunt of air logistics to Pacific. Following WWII, stored surplus aircraft and supplies. 1947, renamed McClellan AFB. One of five centers of Air Force Materiel Command; assumed world-wide responsibility for management of Air Force electrical components, communications-electronics systems, flight control instruments, fluid drive accessories, and tactical shelters. 1985, completed land exchange; selling Splinter City, S of base and across railroad and Roseville Rd, in exchange for land W of base. Growth of space logistics continued; supports Space Shuttle. 1988, base assigned F-15 Eagle workload. 1992, alternate support for KC-135; full responsibility for A-10, F-111, F-117 Stealth, and F-22.
FUTURE CLOSURE/REALIGNMENT: Scheduled for closure by Jul 2001 by BRAC 95. 940th Air Refueling Wing & HQ 4th Air Force to transfer to Beale AFB.
VISITOR ATTRACTIONS: McClellan Aviation Museum (open Mon-Sat 9-3).
Key Contacts
COMMANDER: Maj Gen Eugene L Tattini, SLAC.
PUBLIC AFFAIRS: SM-ALC/PA, 5241 Arnold Way, Suite 3, 95652-1089, 916-643-6127, DSN 633-6127.
Personnel and Expenditures
ACTIVE DUTY PERSONNEL: 2792; Guard 200; Reserve 1159
CIVILIAN PERSONNEL: 10,227
MILITARY PAYROLL EXPENDITURE: $450 mil
Services
Housing: Family units 645; BAQ units 14; Senior NCO units 24. *Temporary Housing:* VIP units 8; VOQ units 63; VAQ units 8; Transient quarters 21. *Commissary:* Yes; *Exchange:* Retail store; Barber shop; Dry cleaners; Food shop; Florist; Bank; Service station; Bakery; Framing; One-hour photo; Fast food; Video rental. *Child Care/Capacities:* Day care center capacity 99.

Base Library: Yes. *Medical Facilities:* Medical clinic; Dental clinic; Hospital at Mather AFB location. *Recreational Facilities:* Bowling center; Movie theater; Pool; Gym; Recreation center; Golf course; Tennis courts; Racquetball court; Auto shop; Craft shop; Officers club; NCO club; Youth center; Health club; Aero club; Hobby shop; Archery; Outdoor recreation; Equipment rental; Sports fields.

Moffett Federal Airfield

82. Santa Clara, Naval Air Reserve
NAR Santa Clara
500 Shenandoah Plaza
Moffett Federal Airfield, CA 94035
Mailing Address
PO Box 128
Moffett Federal Airfield, CA 94035
415-603-9540; FAX 415-603-9546; DSN 359-9540
OFFICER-OF-THE-DAY: 415-603-9527, DSN 359-9527
Profile
BRANCH: Naval Reserve.
LOCATION: 35 mi S of San Francisco; 7 mi N of San Jose; at intersection of Hwy 101 & 237. *County:* Santa Clara.
MAJOR UNITS: Naval Air Reserve, Santa Clara.
BASE HISTORY: 1933, commissioned as Sunnyvale NAS. 1942, renamed for Rear Adm William A Moffett, killed in crash of dirigible USS *Akron*. Visitors from airship era would still recognize many buildings; Hangar One, built to hold dirigible USS *Macon*, and Hangars Two & Three, built in WWII era for blimps.
Key Contacts
COMMANDER: 415-603-9525, DSN 359-9525.

Monterey

83. Naval Postgraduate School
NPS
1 University Circle
Monterey, CA 93943-5001
408-656-2023; FAX 408-656-3238; DSN 878-2023
Internet: http://www.nps.navy.mil/
OFFICER-OF-THE-DAY: 408-656-2441, DSN 878-2441
Profile
BRANCH: Navy.
SIZE AND LOCATION: 615 acres. In Monterey, CA, on Hwy 1; 60 mi S of San Jose; 120 mi S of San Francisco; 5 mi N of Carmel; 300 mi N of Los Angeles; small commercial airport at Monterey. *County:* Monterey.
MAJOR UNITS: Naval Postgraduate School; Defense Manpower Data Center; Defense Resources Management Institute; Fleet Numerical Oceanography Center; Naval Research Laboratory; Naval Telecommunications Center; Naval Support Activity Monterey Bay.
BASE HISTORY: 1909, started as School of Marine Engineering at Naval Academy, Annapolis, MD. 1912, renamed Postgraduate Department. 1919, renamed US Naval Postgradu-

ate School. 1951, NPS officially moved to Monterey into the former luxury Hotel Del Monte, renamed Herrmann Hall, used for administrative offices, bachelor officer's quarters, Officers' & Faculty Club, & classrooms. Presently, more than 1800 students enrolled in over 30 academic programs, representing all services, NOAA, DOD civilians, & 20 allied countries with four graduations per year.
VISITOR ATTRACTIONS: Part of school in old Del Monte Hotel, historic site; small museum in old hotel.
Key Contacts
COMMANDER: RADM Marsha Johnson Evans, 408-656-2511, DSN 878-2511.
PUBLIC AFFAIRS: CDR Drew Malcomb, Code 004, 408-656-2023, DSN 878-2023, DMalcomb@nps.navy.mil.
Personnel and Expenditures
ACTIVE DUTY PERSONNEL: 2000
DEPENDENTS: 2141
CIVILIAN PERSONNEL: 602
MILITARY PAYROLL EXPENDITURE: $121.2 mil
CONTRACT EXPENDITURE: $15.2 mil
Services
Housing: Family units 877; Unaccompanied officer quarters 181; Unaccompanied enlisted quarters 42; Family units at Ft Ord reserved for NPS enlisted members. *Temporary Housing:* Rooms for transit personnel available in Herrmann Hall. *Exchange:* Retail store; Barber shop; Dry cleaners; Florist; Bank; Service station; Bookstore; Military clothing store; Convenience store; Beauty shop; Credit union. *Child Care/Capacities:* Day care center. *Base Library:* Yes. *Medical Facilities:* Dental clinic. *Recreational Facilities:* Pool; Gym; Golf course; Tennis courts; Racquetball court; Fitness center/Weight room; Softball field; Officers club; NCO club; Enlisted club.

84. Naval Research Laboratory, Marine Meteorology Division
7 Grace Hopper Ave, Stop 2
Monterey, CA 93943-5502
Internet: http://www.nrlmry.navy.mil/
Profile
BRANCH: Navy.
LOCATION: From Hwy 1 take N Fremont east, right onto Airport Rd, right on to Grace Hopper Ave to Bldg 702 on left. *County:* Monterey.
MAJOR UNITS: Marine Meteorology Division, Monterey.
BASE HISTORY: 1971, established as Naval Environmental Prediction Research Facility (NEPRF). 1989, changed status & designation as combined Naval Oceanographic Research & Development Activity, Stennis Space Center, MS. 1992, consolidated into NRL. Today, NRL Monterey, only scientific center in Navy dedicated to atmospheric research.
Key Contacts
COMMANDER: Capt Bruce Buckley.
Personnel and Expenditures
ACTIVE DUTY PERSONNEL: 5
CIVILIAN PERSONNEL: 100 contractors & research personnel

85. Presidio of Monterey
POM
Monterey, CA 93944-5006

408-242-5119, 5000; DSN 878-5119, 5000
OFFICER-OF-THE-DAY: 242-647-5119, DSN
878-5119
Profile
BRANCH: Army.
SIZE AND LOCATION: 128 acres. On Light-
house Ave, in city limits of Monterey.
County: Monterey.
MAJOR UNITS: Defense Language Institute;
Foreign Language Center; 229th Military In-
telligence Bn; Association of the US Army
#6102.
BASE HISTORY: 1941, Army instituted formal
Japanese language instruction for Japanese-
American recruits in abandoned airplane han-
gar at San Francisco's Crissy Field; school
named 4th Army Intelligence School; Navy
began teaching Japanese to officers at
Berkeley. 1942, Navy school moved to Univ
of Colorado, Boulder; Army school moved to
Camp Savage, MN, and later to Ft Snelling,
MN; Army school renamed Military Intelligence Service Language School. After WWII,
Navy school combined with Naval Intelligence School, Anacostia, Washington, DC.
1947, Army school moved to Presidio of Monterey; renamed Army Language School.
1963, consolidation of all service language
programs resulted in establishment of Defense Language Institute; East Coast Branch
established in Washington, DC; Army Language School in Monterey became West
Coast Branch. 1974, branches merged into Defense Language Institute Foreign Language
Center, Presidio of Monterey. DLI now offers
41 foreign languages and dialects and enrolls
approximately 5000 students annually.
VISITOR ATTRACTIONS: Museum.
Key Contacts
COMMANDER: Col Daniel D Devlin,
Installation commander; Col David F Gross,
Garrison Commander.
PUBLIC AFFAIRS: Michael Murphy, murphy@
pom\emh1.army.mil; Robert
Britton,Command Information Officer; Kay
Rodrigues, Media Relations Officer; Bldg
614, Rm 142; 408-242-4104.
Personnel and Expenditures
ACTIVE DUTY PERSONNEL: 3000
DEPENDENTS: 2800
CIVILIAN PERSONNEL: 1400
Services
Housing: Family units 1681; Unaccompanied of-
ficer quarters 93; Unaccompanied enlisted quar-
ters 2500. *Temporary Housing:* VIP units 2;
VOQ units 51; VEQ units 34; Guesthouse units
8. *Exchange:* Barber shop; Dry cleaners; Service
station; Commisary and Exchange at Annex; Exchange on Post. *Child Care/Capacities:* Day
care center capacity 200. *Schools:* Elementary;
Intermediate/Junior high; High school. *Base Library:* Yes. *Recreational Facilities:* Movie theater; Gym; Recreation center; Fitness center/
Weight room; Softball field; Football field; Officers club; NCO club.

Norco

86. Naval Warfare Assessment Division
NWAD
2300 5th St
Norco, CA 91760-1950

909-273-5000
Internet: http://www.corona.navy.mil
Profile
BRANCH: Navy.
LOCATION: 40 mi E of Seal Beach; off I-15,
exit at 6th St, W on 6th to Hamner Ave, S on
Hamner to 5th St, W on 5th St to main gate
on left. *County:* Riverside.
MAJOR UNITS: Naval Warfare Assessment Di-
vision; Warfare Assessment Laboratory; Fleet
Analysis Center.
BASE HISTORY: Navy's only independent
analysis & assessment center. On site of 700-
acre luxury resort of Lex Clark (1928-41).
1941, bought by Navy; converted to hospital.
WWII, hospital & missile development, NBS
Corona Laboratories. 1953, designated Naval
Ordnance Laboratory. 1960s, Fleet Missile
System Analysis & Evaluation Group
(FMSAEG) established. 1971, became Annex
of NWS, Seal Beach. 1976, renamed Fleet
Analysis Center; later Naval Warfare Assess-
ment Center, Corona. 1994, Warfare Assess-
ment Laboratory dedicated.
Key Contacts
COMMANDER: Capt Michael G Mathis; Dr
Wayne Meeks, Director.
PUBLIC AFFAIRS: Curt Sandberg,
909-273-4326, DSN 933-4326, sandberg.
curt@corona.navy.mil.
Personnel and Expenditures
ACTIVE DUTY PERSONNEL: 950 (military &
civilians)
CIVILIAN PERSONNEL: 700 (contractors)
CONTRACT EXPENDITURE: $180 mil

Novato

87. Coast Guard Pacific Strike Team
CGPST
Hangar 2, Hamilton Rd
Novato, CA 94949-5082
415-883-3311; FAX 415-883-7814
Profile
BRANCH: Coast Guard.
SIZE AND LOCATION: 5.6 acres. Off US-101
at Hamilton Field Exit. *County:* Marin.
MAJOR UNITS: Coast Guard Pacific Strike
Team.
BASE HISTORY: Small facility.
Personnel and Expenditures
ACTIVE DUTY PERSONNEL: 35
Services
Housing: None.

88. Department of Defense Housing Facility
Novato, CA 94949
415-382-4110
Profile
BRANCH: DOD; Coast Guard; Navy.
SIZE AND LOCATION: 1600 acres. Just N of
San Francisco. *County:* Marin.
MAJOR UNITS: Coast Guard Pacific Strike
Team; Navy Public Works Center, Oakland
Det.
BASE HISTORY: Originally Hamilton AFB.
1984, name changed; Navy Public Works
Center, Oakland took charge of housing;
Coast Guard established Strike Team, Bldg
390. Remainder acquired by Army; sub-instal-

lation of Presidio Garrison San Francisco.
Current facility established when Hamilton
Army Airfield closed; sub-unit of Navy Pub-
lic Works in Oakland.
Key Contacts
COMMANDER: John Scales, Installation
Coordinator, 415-382-4112; Tom Flugg,
Housing Manager, 415-382-4123.
Services
Housing: Housing units 1500.

Oakland

89. Military Traffic Management Command, Western Area
MTMC-WA
100 Alaska St
Oakland, CA 94626-1000
510-466-3021; DSN 859-3021
Internet: http://www.mtmc.army.mil
OFFICER-OF-THE-DAY: Staff Duty Officer:
510-466-3421, DSN 859-3421
Profile
BRANCH: Army.
MAJOR UNITS: Military Traffic Management
Command, Western Area; Army-Air Force
Exchange Service, Western Region Distribu-
tion Center; Training Support Brigade-Travis.
BASE HISTORY: 1965, MTMC established to
serve as DOD Single Manager Operating
Agency under Secretary of Army for Military
Traffic Management, Land Transportation, &
Common User Ocean Terminals. MTMC-
WA headquartered at Oakland Army Base,
CA. One of four area commands of Military
Traffic Management Command HQ, Falls
Church, VA. 1987, MTMC became compo-
nent of US Transportation Command (US-
TRANSCOM) along with Military Sealift
Command (MSC) and Military Airlift Com-
mand (MAC). See Oakland Army Base for
more information.
Key Contacts
PUBLIC AFFAIRS: 510-466-3021, FAX
510-466-3023, DSN 859-3021, DSN FAX
859-3023.

90. Oakland Army Base
OARB
100 Alaska St, Ste 2001
Oakland, CA 94626-5000
510-466-9111; DSN 859-9111
Internet: http://mtmc.army.mil/wa.htm
OFFICER-OF-THE-DAY: 510-466-3131, DSN
859-3131
Profile
BRANCH: Army.
SIZE AND LOCATION: 422 acres. On E shore
of San Francisco Bay, within city limits of
Oakland. Immediately S of toll gates of San
Francisco-Oakland Bay Bridge where I-80
(Eastshore Fwy), I-580 (MacArthur Fwy),
and State Hwy 880 (Nimitz Fwy) converge;
OARB/Navy Supply Center off ramp from I-
80. *County:* Alameda.
MAJOR UNITS: Military Traffic Management
Command, Western Area, HQ; Army Garri-
son, Oakland Army Base; 1302nd Major Port
Command (Army); Army Reserve Center,
Oakland Army Base.
BASE HISTORY: 1941, site commissioned;
1943, base completed. Korean & Vietnam

Wars, busiest port on Pacific Coast. Today, more than 75 percent of DOD cargo moving through Bay Area managed by Military Traffic Management Command, Western Area. FUTURE CLOSURE/REALIGNMENT: Scheduled for closure, Jul 2001.

Key Contacts
COMMANDER: Capt D Scott Ensminger, 510-466-2282.
PUBLIC AFFAIRS: Donna Shepard, 510-466-3053, DSN 859-3053.
PROCUREMENT: Joyce Cavaler, 510-466-2703.

Personnel and Expenditures
ACTIVE DUTY PERSONNEL: 53
DEPENDENTS: 65
CIVILIAN PERSONNEL: 503

Services
Housing: Family units 112; Junior NCO units 25; RV storage. *Temporary Housing:* Guesthouse units 52. *Commissary:* Yes; *Exchange:* Retail store; Barber shop; Dry cleaners; Service station. *Child Care/Capacities:* Day care center capacity 84, 6wks-12yrs; Home day care program; Latch key program; Summer day camp. *Base Library:* Yes. *Medical Facilities:* Medical clinic; No services for retirees. *Recreational Facilities:* Bowling center; Movie theater; Gym; Tennis courts; Fitness center/Weight room; Craft shop; Officers club; Youth center; Community club; Officers' club at Ft Mason, San Francisco.

Oceanside

91. Camp Pendleton Marine Corps Base
Camp Pendleton
Camp Pendleton
Oceanside, CA 92055-5001
760-725-4111; DSN 365-4111
Profile
BRANCH: Marine Corps.
SIZE AND LOCATION: 125,000 acres. 35 mi N of San Diego; just E of I-5 N of Oceanside. *County:* San Diego.
MAJOR UNITS: Marine Corps Base, Camp Pendleton; 1st Marine Expeditionary Force (I MEF); 1st Marine Division; 1st Force Service Support Group (1st FSSG); Marine Aircraft Group 39 (MAG-39); Assault Craft Unit 5 (Navy); Army Reserve Center, Camp Pendleton; Marine Corps Mountain Warfare Training Center; 1394th Deployment Support Brigade.
BASE HISTORY: 1941, Navy bought SE corner of Rancho Santa Margarita to establish Naval Ammunition Depot. Mid-1942, government purchased remainder of Rancho; 9th Marines & 1st Battalion, 12th Marines. Named after Gen Joseph H Pendleton, Corps veteran; General's full name with initial to distinguish between Army facility, Camp Pendleton, VA; for years, correspondence from Base maintained Santa Margarita Rancho designation part of address. WWII, training site for elements of 3rd Marine Division, entire 4th, 5th Marine Divisions, & replacements for all divisions. Korean War, 1st Provisional Brigade replaced by reservists. Mid-1950s to mid-1960s, site of variety of training exercises. 1965, 1st Marine Division departed for Vietnam. 1969, 4th Marine Division moved to

New Orleans; 5th Marine Division deactivated.
VISITOR ATTRACTIONS: Rancho Santa Margarita y Las Flores (built circa 1830); El Camino Real ruins; Amphibian Vehicle Museum; Las Flores Adobe; Las Flores Asistencia (auxiliary mission).
Key Contacts
PUBLIC AFFAIRS: Joint Public Affairs Office, Bldg #1160, 760-725-5566, DSN 365-5566.
Personnel and Expenditures
ACTIVE DUTY PERSONNEL: 37,500
DEPENDENTS: 51,600
CIVILIAN PERSONNEL: 3600
Services
Housing: Family units 5920; Unaccompanied officer quarters 117; Unaccompanied enlisted quarters 27,500; Mobile home units 250; Trailer spaces 149; RV/Camper sites 237. *Temporary Housing:* VIP units 5; VOQ units 89; VEQ units 42; Unaccompanied officer/Enlisted quarters 117; Lodge units 64; Cabins 100. *Commissary:* Yes; *Exchange:* Retail store; Barber shop; Dry cleaners; Florist; Bank; Service station; Furniture store; Military clothing store; Convenience store; Beauty shop; Credit union. *Child Care/Capacities:* Day care center capacity 900; Home day care program; *Schools:* Elementary; College/University. *Base Library:* Yes. *Medical Facilities:* Hospital 156 beds; Medical clinic; Dental clinic; Dispensary; Veterinary services. *Recreational Facilities:* Bowling center; Movie theater; Pool; Gym; Recreation center; Golf course; Stables; Tennis courts; Racquetball court; Fitness center/Weight room; Softball field; Football field; Auto shop; Craft shop; Officers club; NCO club; Camping; Fishing/Hunting; Enlisted club; Youth center; Picnic area; Skeet range; Water sports.

Ontario

92. 18th Cavalry, 1st Squadron, HQ
HQ/18 CAV
ANG Armory
950 N Cucamonga Ave
Ontario, CA 91764-2999
909-983-3699; FAX 909-983-1174
Profile
BRANCH: Army National Guard.
LOCATION: 2 mi W of Ontario Airport; 5 mi W from I-10 & I-15 freeway intersection. *County:* San Bernardino.
MAJOR UNITS: 1st Squadron, 18th Cavalry, HQ; HHT, 1st Squadron, 18th Cavalry; Troop C, 1st Squadron, 18th Cavalry.
Key Contacts
COMMANDER: LTC Jacob A Van Goor, 909-984-5560.
PUBLIC AFFAIRS: Cpt William Hanley, 909-983-9880.
Personnel and Expenditures
ACTIVE DUTY PERSONNEL: 8; Reserve 290
DEPENDENTS: 0
CIVILIAN PERSONNEL: 0

93. Ontario Air National Guard Station
Ontario ANGS
1280 Tower Rd
Ontario, CA 91761-7627

909-390-7400; FAX 909-390-7490; DSN 947-3559; DSN FAX 947-3559, ext 7490
Profile
BRANCH: Air National Guard.
SIZE AND LOCATION: 11 acres. Between I-10 & Ontario Blvd at Archibald Ave, adj to Ontario Airport. *County:* San Bernardino.
MAJOR UNITS: 148th Combat Communications Squadron (ANG); 210th Weather Flight.
FUTURE CLOSURE/REALIGNMENT: Scheduled for closure Sep 1998.
Key Contacts
COMMANDER: LTC Dean A Cunningham, 909-390-7411, FAX 909-390-7490, DSN 947-3559, dcunningham@cariv.ang.af.mil.
PUBLIC AFFAIRS: Cpt Joe Wilburn, 909-390-7415, FAX 909-390-7490, DSN 947-3559, jwilburn@cariv.ang.af.mil.
Personnel and Expenditures
ACTIVE DUTY PERSONNEL: 3; Guard 140
CIVILIAN PERSONNEL: 27

Palmdale

94. Production Flight Test Installation, Air Force Plant 42
PFTI AF Plant 42
2503 E Ave P
Palmdale, CA 93550-2196
805-272-6700; FAX 805-273-7558
OFFICER-OF-THE-DAY: Kathleen Cook
Profile
BRANCH: Air Force.
SIZE AND LOCATION: 5800 acres. At 25th St E & Ave P; 5 mi from Palmdale; approx 60 mi N of Los Angeles; in Mojave Desert 40 mi SW of Edwards AFB. *County:* Los Angeles.
MAJOR UNITS: Aeronautical Systems Division (AFSC) Det 1; Lockheed Martin Skunk Works; Northrop Grumman; Boeing North American.
BASE HISTORY: A government owned, contractor-operated facility with 10 different production sites sharing a common runway complex; 2 runways 12,000 ft; Runway 25 strongest in world. Each site responsible for their assigned facility (aerospace company who occupies site). 1989, Air Force entered into joint-use agreement with Los Angeles Dept of Airports; operate Palmdale Regional Airport on 54 acres leased to them by AF.
VISITOR ATTRACTIONS: Blackbird Airpark (SR-71 & YF12 displays); Facility not open to public.
Key Contacts
COMMANDER: LTC Peter L Drinkwater.
PUBLIC AFFAIRS: Lorraine H Sadler, sadler1%p42-ascdet1@mhs.elan.af.mil.
Personnel and Expenditures
ACTIVE DUTY PERSONNEL: 60
DEPENDENTS: 0
CIVILIAN PERSONNEL: 8500
MILITARY PAYROLL EXPENDITURE: $434 mil
CONTRACT EXPENDITURE: $17 mil
Services
Housing: None. *Exchange:* None. *Child Care/Capacities:* No day care facilities.

Paso Robles

95. Western Mobilization & Training Complex
Camp Roberts
7700 Hwy 101,Bldg 109
Paso Robles, CA 93446-7393
805-238-3100; FAX 805-238-8116; DSN
949-8210; DSN FAX 949-8116
E-mail: cprbtsim@calguard.ca.gov Internet:
http://www.concentric.net/~Armor149/
bcom.htm

Profile
BRANCH: Army National Guard.
SIZE AND LOCATION: 54,000 acres. In central CA, directly off Hwy 101; 7 mi N of San Miguel; 14 mi N of Paso Robles. *County:* San Luis Obispo; Monterey.
MAJOR UNITS: Western Mobilization & Training Complex; United Defense; Mobilization and Training Equipment Site (MATES); Satellite Communication Station (SATCOM); 1st Bn, 149th Armor Division, Co B.
BASE HISTORY: 1902, area studied for possible location of military post. 1940, land purchased, including Rancho Nacimiento, part of historic Mission San Miguel; construction of Main (west) Garrison cantonment area as Camp Nacimiento Replacement Training Center; renamed Camp Roberts for Corporal Harold W Roberts, WWI tank driver; one of few posts named for enlisted man & only active one. 1941, began operations as one of world's largest military training facilities; parade ground possibly largest (14 football fields long). 1943, final land purchased. WWII, 436,000 infantry & field artillery troops trained; 45,000 at one time; housed Italian & German POWs. 1946, outprocessing center; reverted to caretaker status; summer drills only. 1950, activated for troop & armor training; 300,000 trained. 1954, reverted to caretaker status. Vietnam era, "most active, inactive Post in US." 1970, officially closed by Army. 1971, California ANG received control.
VISITOR ATTRACTIONS: Museum; Old Mission Trail, El Camino Real, historic area.

Key Contacts
COMMANDER: LTC Lawrence Kimmel, 805-238-8202, DSN 949-8202.
PUBLIC AFFAIRS: 1Lt Nicole M Balliet, 805-238-8203, DSN 949-8203.
TRANSPORTATION: SSgt Scott Witt, 805-238-8280, FAX 805-238-8022, DSN 949-8280.
PERSONNEL/COMMUNITY ACTIVITIES: See Public Affairs Officer.

Personnel and Expenditures
ACTIVE DUTY PERSONNEL: 125
DEPENDENTS: 20
CIVILIAN PERSONNEL: 100

Services
Housing: None. *Temporary Housing:* VIP units 5; VOQ units 3; VEQ units 12; Guest cottages 9. *Exchange:* Barber shop; Dry cleaners; Military clothing store; Convenience store; Laundromat; Video rentals; PX. *Child Care/Capacities:* No day care facilities. *Schools:* No on-base schools. *Medical Facilities:* Troop medical clinic during training. *Recreational Facilities:* Gym; Recreation center; Fitness center/Weight room; Softball field; Camping; Fishing/Hunting; Picnic area; Consolidated club.

Petaluma

96. Petaluma Coast Guard Training Center
USCG TRACEN Petaluma
599 Tomales Rd
Petaluma, CA 94952-5000
707-765-7211; FAX 707-765-7329
OFFICER-OF-THE-DAY: 707-765-7215

Profile
BRANCH: Coast Guard.
SIZE AND LOCATION: 800 acres. 58 mi N of San Francisco; area known as Two Rock. *County:* Sonoma; Marin.
MAJOR UNITS: Coast Guard Training Center, Petaluma.
BASE HISTORY: 1971, Coast Guard acquired site from Army; training command established; West Coast's resident training facility. Mission to provide training for Coast Guard personnel including entry level petty officer technical skills, advance petty officer technical & leadership skills, & program support training. Facilities available for conferences & workshops. 1989, addition of Electronics Technician & Telephone Technician schools. Center now operates 10 schools offering 50 courses for 6000 students a year. Basic & specialized training for Coast Guard Reserve personnel also conducted.

Key Contacts
COMMANDER: 707-765-7320.
PUBLIC AFFAIRS: 707-765-7379.
PROCUREMENT: 707-765-7283.
TRANSPORTATION: 707-765-7368.
PERSONNEL/COMMUNITY ACTIVITIES: 707-765-7340.

Personnel and Expenditures
ACTIVE DUTY PERSONNEL: 420
DEPENDENTS: 400
CIVILIAN PERSONNEL: 50

Services
Housing: Family units 140; RV/Camper sites 9. *Temporary Housing:* Guesthouse units 6. *Exchange:* Retail store; Barber shop; Dry cleaners; Bank; Service station. *Child Care/Capacities:* Day care center capacity 75. *Base Library:* Yes. *Medical Facilities:* Medical clinic; Dental clinic. *Recreational Facilities:* Bowling center; Movie theater; Pool; Gym; Tennis courts; Racquetball court; Softball field; Auto shop; NCO club; Camping.

Point Arena AFS

97. Point Arena Air Force Station
32750 Eureka Hill Rd
Point Arena AFS, CA 95468-5000

Profile
BRANCH: Air Force.
LOCATION: 12 mi from Point Arena, CA, 160 mi N of San Francisco. *County:* Mendocino.
BASE HISTORY: 1997, disestablished & put in caretaker status.

Key Contacts
COMMANDER: Contact: LTC Martin Lewis, Commander, 9th Civil Engineer Sq, 6451 B St, Beale AFB, CA 95903, 916-634-2943, DSN 368-2943, DSN FAX 368-3298.

Point Mugu

98. Point Mugu, Naval Air Weapons Station
NAWS
521 9th St
Point Mugu, CA 93042-5001
805-989-1110; DSN 351-1110
Internet: http://iwd.mugu.navy.mil/97html/
About_NAWC_Mugu.html; www.
nawcwpns.com/overview.html
OFFICER-OF-THE-DAY: 805-989-7209

Profile
BRANCH: Navy.
SIZE AND LOCATION: 4500 acres. Approx 60 mi NW of Los Angeles; near cities of Oxnard & Camarillo; on Pacific Coast Hwy; from Ventura Fwy to Las Posas Exit in Camarillo, Las Posas to Point Mugu. *County:* Ventura.
MAJOR UNITS: Naval Air Weapons Station; Naval Air Warfare Center, Weapons Division (NAWCWPNS); Naval Air Reserve, Point Mugu; Antarctic Development Squadron 6; Weapons Test Squadron; Air Test and Evaluation Squadron, 9th Det; Information Warfare Division; Visioneering Laboratory; Tactical Automated Mission Planning System; Tactical Electronic Reconnaissance Processing and Evaluation System; Advanced Tactical Information Management System; Intelligence Analysis System; Tactical Exploitation Group; Laser and Surveillance Systems Group; San Nicholas Island, Outlying Landing Field.
BASE HISTORY: 1946, founded as Naval Air Missile Test Center; site of early post-war missile & drone efforts. 1949, NAS Point Mugu established. 1958, Pacific Missile Range established. 1975, Pacific Missile Test Center established. 1991, Naval Air Weapons Station, Point Mugu, established with Weapons Division major tenant. Many Air Force, Army, Marine Corps & NASA programs use facilities. Fleet elements supported during training exercises on range.
VISITOR ATTRACTIONS: Missile Park (Wood Rd Exit, Hwy 1).

Key Contacts
PUBLIC AFFAIRS: 805-989-8094, DSN 351-8094.

Personnel and Expenditures
ACTIVE DUTY PERSONNEL: 1450; Reserve 340
DEPENDENTS: 2600
CIVILIAN PERSONNEL: 3200
MILITARY PAYROLL EXPENDITURE: $30.2 mil

Services
Housing: Family units 1451; Unaccompanied officer quarters 32; Unaccompanied enlisted quarters 766; BAQ units; Barracks spaces; RV/Camper sites. *Temporary Housing:* VOQ units 6 (cabins, max stay 5 nights); VEQ units 12; Unaccompanied officer/Enlisted quarters 87; Transient quarters 183; Beach cottages, Beach motel rooms/suites (including handicap access suite). *Commissary:* Yes; *Exchange:* Retail store; Barber shop; Dry cleaners; Food shop; Bank; Service station; Convenience store; Beauty shop; Credit union; Laundry; Personal services. *Child Care/Capacities:* Day care center capacity 50; Child development center. *Base Library:* Yes. *Medical Facilities:* No medical facilities. *Recreational Facilities:* Bowling center; Movie thea-

ter; Pool; Gym; Recreation center; Golf course (driving range); Tennis courts; Racquetball court; Fitness center/Weight room; Softball field; Auto shop; Craft shop; Camping; Fishing/Hunting; Youth center; Picnic area; Skeet range; Playground; Rod & Gun club; Jogging; Beach; RV park; Beach motel.

Point Reyes Station

99. Coast Guard Communication Station Pacific, San Francisco
CAMSPAC San Francisco
17000 Sir Francis Drake Blvd
Point Reyes Station, CA 94956
Mailing Address
PO Box 560
Point Reyes Station, CA 94956-0560
415-669-2047; FAX 415-669-2096
Profile
BRANCH: Coast Guard.
SIZE AND LOCATION: 266 acres. From Hwy 37 or Hwy 1010, S Novato Blvd Exit, follow S Novato Blvd to Point Reyes-Petaluma Rd, left, follow signs to Point Reyes Station, entering Point Reyes Station, left on Mesa to Coast Guard sign, turn left. *County:* Marin.
MAJOR UNITS: Coast Guard Communication Station Pacific San Francisco.
BASE HISTORY: 1943, original Radio Station San Francisco located in San Bruno, CA. 1973, present station site at Point Reyes National Seashore activated. 1978, name changed to present CAMSPAC. Consists of 3 separate sites: Receiver Site (RX) approx 5 mi W of small town of Inverness; housing complex in town of Point Reyes; & Transmitter Site (TX) near town of Bolinas.
Personnel and Expenditures
ACTIVE DUTY PERSONNEL: 90
Services
Housing: Unaccompanied enlisted quarters; Townhouse units 36. *Temporary Housing:* Guest house at TRACEN, Petaluma 8. *Exchange:* This is a satellite exchange of TRACEN, Petaluma. *Medical Facilities:* Dispensary at Petaluma; Letterman Hospital is 1 hr away. *Recreational Facilities:* Recreation center (pool table); Fitness center/Weight room (& hot tub); Tennis courts; Auto shop; Morale locker equipment checkout; Participates with TRACEN, Petaluma; Bear Valley Visitor Center, 5 mi away.

100. Coast Guard Communication Station Pacific, Transmitter Site
CAMSPAC TX
PO Box 560
Point Reyes Station, CA 94956-0560
415-868-2514; FAX 415-868-2514
Profile
BRANCH: Coast Guard.
SIZE AND LOCATION: 75 acres. 25 mi SE of Point Reyes housing site near town of Bolinas. *County:* Marin.
MAJOR UNITS: Coast Guard Communication Station Transmitter Site.
BASE HISTORY: See Coast Guard Communication Area Station Pacific, San Francisco
Services
Housing: See USCG CAMSPAC, San Francisco.

Pomona

101. Pomona Naval Industrial Reserve Ordnance Plant
PO Box 2507
Pomona, CA 91769-2507
909-623-0725
Profile
BRANCH: Navy.
LOCATION: 40 mi NE of Seal Beach. *County:* Los Angeles.
BASE HISTORY: Division of Naval Weapons Center Seal Beach. Site is Navy's Gage and Standards Center for developing and maintaining more than 18,000 unique ordnance gages that ensure weapons can be assembled into ready-to-fire rounds. Facility is quality assurance agent for Navy's metrology and calibration program, and designs and applies measurement science disciplines to national standards.
Key Contacts
COMMANDER: See Naval Weapons Center Seal Beach.
PUBLIC AFFAIRS: ATTN: Code 01P, Naval Weapons Center Seal Beach, Seal Beach, CA 90740-5000, 213-594-7215, DSN 873-7215.

Port Hueneme

102. Naval Facilities Engineering Service Center
NFESC
1100 23rd Ave
Port Hueneme, CA 93043-4370
805-982-1393; FAX 805-982-4429; DSN 551-1393; DSN FAX 551-4429
E-mail: help@nfesc.navy.mil Internet:http://www.nfesc.navy.mil
Profile
BRANCH: Navy.
LOCATION: Approx 65 mi NW of Los Angeles; tenant of Naval Construction Battalion Center, Port Hueneme. *County:* Ventura.
MAJOR UNITS: Naval Facilities Engineering Service Center.
BASE HISTORY: 1948, Naval Civil Engineering Laboratory established at Solomons, MD, to test commercial equipment for Naval Mobile Construction Battalions. 1950, moved to Port Hueneme; known as Naval Civil Engineering Research & Evaluation Laboratory. 1993, Naval Facilities Engineering Service Center established to consolidate missions of 6 former Naval Facilities Engineering Command (NAVFAC) organizations. Navy's center for specialized engineering & technology.
VISITOR ATTRACTIONS: Point Hueneme historical lighthouse.
Key Contacts
COMMANDER: Capt Donald G Morris.
PUBLIC AFFAIRS: Lori Lee, 805-982-1271, FAX 805-982-1594, DSN 551-1271, DSN FAX 551-1594, llee@nfesc.navy.mil.
PROCUREMENT: 805-982-1114, DSN 551-1114.
PERSONNEL/COMMUNITY ACTIVITIES: 805-982-1134, DSN 551-1134.
Personnel and Expenditures
ACTIVE DUTY PERSONNEL: 12
CIVILIAN PERSONNEL: 520

CONTRACT EXPENDITURE: $140 mil
Services *Base Library:* Yes.

103. Port Hueneme Division, Naval Surface Warfare Center
NSWC-PHD
4363 Missile Way
Port Hueneme, CA 93043-4307
805-982-7202; FAX 805-382-1459; DSN 551-7977
Internet: http://www.nswses.navy.mil/
Profile
BRANCH: Navy.
LOCATION: 60 mi N of Los Angeles, 45 mi S of Santa Barbara; on Port Hueneme, Naval Construction Battalion Center (NCBC). *County:* Ventura.
MAJOR UNITS: Naval Surface Warfare Center; AEGIS Combat Systems Det; Underway Replenishment Test Site; Surface Warfare Engineering Facility; Self Defense Test Ship; Integrated Combat System Test Facility, San Diego; Technical Information Innovation Center for JCALS/JEDMICS.
BASE HISTORY: 1963, established as Naval Ship Missile Systems Engineering Station for in-service engineering & logistics support of Terrier, Tartar, & Talos missile systems. 1972, renamed Naval Ship Weapon Systems Engineering Station. 1992, current name; consolidated with former Integrated Combat Systems Test Facility, San Diego, Fleet Combat Direction System Support Activity, Dam Neck, & Naval Mine Warfare Engineering Activity, Yorktown, VA. Today, supports Naval Sea Systems Command (Washington, DC) to provide test, evaluation, in-service engineering, & integrated logistics support for surface & mine warfare combat systems.
Key Contacts
COMMANDER: Capt Nicholas L Richards, 805-982-8238, DSN 551-8238.
PUBLIC AFFAIRS: Shirley Bradley, Code 0003, 805-982-7976, DSN 551-7976.
PROCUREMENT: Code 5F00, 805-982-0646, DSN 551-0646.
TRANSPORTATION: Code 0140, 805-982-8362, DSN 551-8362.
PERSONNEL/COMMUNITY ACTIVITIES: Peggy Murillo, Director of Personnel, Code 0600, 805-982-7202.
Personnel and Expenditures
ACTIVE DUTY PERSONNEL: 107
CIVILIAN PERSONNEL: 2400
Services
Housing: See Port Hueneme, Naval Construction Bn Center (NCBC). *Temporary Housing:* See NCBC. *Commissary:* Yes; *Exchange:* See NCBC. *Base Library:* Yes. *Medical Facilities:* See NCBC. *Recreational Facilities:* See NCBC.

104. Port Hueneme, Naval Construction Battalion Center
NCBC Port Hueneme
1000 23rd Ave
Port Hueneme, CA 93043-4301
805-982-4711; DSN 551-4001
Internet: http://www.cbcph.navy.mil/cbcframe.html
OFFICER-OF-THE-DAY: Duty Officer, 805-982-2007, 982-4576; Quarterdeck, 805-982-4571
Profile
BRANCH: Navy.

SIZE AND LOCATION: 1615 acres. In Oxnard & Port Hueneme; 60 mi NW of Los Angeles; on Pacific Coast Hwy & 101 Fwy. *County:* Ventura.

MAJOR UNITS: Naval Construction Bn Center; Naval Mobile Construction Bn 3; Naval Mobile Construction Bn 4; Naval Mobile Construction Bn 5; Naval Mobile Construction Bn 40; Underwater Construction Team Two; 31st Naval Construction Regiment HQ; 1st Naval Construction Regiment; Naval Support Force Antarctica; Naval Construction Training Center; Naval Civil Engineer Corps Officers School; Naval Facilities Engineering Service Center; Naval Surface Warfare Center, Port Hueneme Division; Naval Construction Force Support Unit TWO; Engineering Duty Officers School; Naval Reserve Center, Port Hueneme; Weapons Co, 2nd Bn, 23rd Marine Regiment.

BASE HISTORY: 1942, began operations to train, stage, & supply newly created Seabees. WWII, shipped more construction supplies than any other port in US. Active in Korean & Vietnam War. Mission remains same today, support for Seabees. Only deep-water port between Los Angeles & San Francisco.

VISITOR ATTRACTIONS: CEC/Seabee Museum.

Key Contacts
COMMANDER: Capt Daniel L Hambrock, 805-982-4741.
PUBLIC AFFAIRS: 805-982-4493, pao@cbcph.navy.mil.
PROCUREMENT: Supply Dept, 805-982-2183.
PERSONNEL/COMMUNITY ACTIVITIES: Human Resources Office, 805-982-2416.

Personnel and Expenditures
ACTIVE DUTY PERSONNEL: 3800
DEPENDENTS: 1500
CIVILIAN PERSONNEL: 4500

Services
Housing: Family units 800; Unaccompanied officer quarters 97; Unaccompanied enlisted quarters 1050; Trailer spaces 20. *Temporary Housing:* VIP units 1; Lodge units 47. *Commissary:* Yes; *Exchange:* Retail store; Barber shop; Dry cleaners; Florist; Service station; Furniture store; Military clothing store; Convenience store; Beauty shop; Optical store; Shoe repair; Personalized services; Hardware/Garden shop. *Child Care/Capacities:* Day care center capacity 153, 3mo-6yrs; Home day care program. *Schools:* Preschool/Kindergarten. *Base Library:* Yes. *Medical Facilities:* Medical clinic; Dental clinic. *Recreational Facilities:* Bowling center; Movie theater; Pool; Gym; Golf course; Tennis courts; Skating rink; Fitness center/Weight room; Softball field; Auto shop; Craft shop; Officers club; Enlisted club; Youth center; Picnic area; Community center; ITT office; Gear issue rental.

Sacramento

105. Adjutant General of California
9800 S Goethe Rd
Sacramento, CA 95826-9101
916-854-3500; FAX 916-854-3671
Profile
BRANCH: Army National Guard.
MAJOR UNITS: California National Guard.
Key Contacts
COMMANDER: Maj Gen Tandy K Bozeman.

106. Sacramento Naval & Marine Corps Reserve Readiness Center
8277 Elder Creek Rd
Sacramento, CA 95828-1799
916-387-7100, 387-7124; FAX 916-387-7101
Profile
BRANCH: Naval Reserve; Marine Corps Reserve.
LOCATION: *County:* Sacramento.
MAJOR UNITS: REDCOM TWENTY-TWO Activity; Motor Transport Maintenance Co (-), 4th Maintenance Bn.
Key Contacts
COMMANDER: Capt J R Kirwan.

107. US Army Corps of Engineers, Sacramento District
CESPK
1325 J St
Sacramento, CA 95814-2922
916-557-5100, 557-7490; FAX 916-557-7853
Internet: http://www.usace.army.mil/cespk.html
Profile
BRANCH: Army.
SIZE AND LOCATION: Offices only. In city of Sacramento. *County:* Sacramento.
MAJOR UNITS: Corps of Engineers, Sacramento District.
BASE HISTORY: 1929, became a separate district of Corps of Engineers. Before 1929, known as Sacramento Sub-office of San Francisco District. 1929-41, performed civil works projects only. 1968, became second largest district in contiguous US when territory transferred from Los Angeles District. Covers all or part of 8 western states, CA, NV, UT, OR, ID, WY, CO, and AZ; also operates 13 recreation areas in CA. Currently, military works call for design and construction of projects at 34 military installations. Performs military & civil works construction & real estate.
Key Contacts
COMMANDER: Col Dorothy F Klasse.
Personnel and Expenditures
ACTIVE DUTY PERSONNEL: 1100
CONTRACT EXPENDITURE: $200 mil

San Bruno

108. San Bruno Naval & Marine Corps Reserve Center
NMCRC San Bruno
900 Commodore Dr, Bldg 1
San Bruno, CA 94066-0727
415-244-1701, 244-1740; FAX 415-244-1725;
DSN 494-1701
Profile
BRANCH: Naval Reserve; Marine Corps Reserve.
LOCATION: *County:* San Mateo.
MAJOR UNITS: REDCOM TWENTY-TWO Activity; HQ, 23rd Marine Regiment; HQ Co, 23rd Marine Regiment; E Co, 2nd Bn, 23rd Marine Regiment.
Key Contacts
COMMANDER: Lt M R Hunt.

San Diego

109. Coronado Naval Amphibious Base
NAVPHIBASE Coronado
3420 Guadalcanal Rd
San Diego, CA 92155-5000
619-437-2011; DSN 577-2011
OFFICER-OF-THE-DAY: 619-437-3432, DSN 577-3432
Profile
BRANCH: Navy.
SIZE AND LOCATION: 1006 acres. On Silver Strand between San Diego Bay and Pacific Ocean; Hwy 5 S over Coronado-San Diego Bay Bridge, left on Orange (becomes Hwy 75), left at sign to front gate. Approx 7 mi from downtown San Diego; 10 mi from San Diego Airport; 1 mi from Coronado. *County:* San Diego.
MAJOR UNITS: Naval Amphibious Base, Coronado; Commander, Naval Air Force Pacific Fleet, HQ; Commander, 3rd Fleet; Naval Special Warfare Command (SEALs); Naval Aviation Depot; USS *Kitty Hawk*; USS *Constellation*; Naval Surface Force; Expeditionary Warfare Training Group, Pacific; Tactical Air Control Group.
BASE HISTORY: 1943, establishment of Amphibious Training Base to train landing craft crews. 1946, renamed Naval Amphibious Base (NAB), Coronado; mission changed to providing administrative & logistical support to amphibious units on base, conduct research & test amphibious equipment. Property formed by land fill, dredged from San Diego Bay. Remained in active operational status since initial establishment. 1994, Naval Amphibious School, Coronado & Landing Force Training Command, Pacific, consolidated as Expeditionary Warfare Training Group, Pacific. Today, major shore command supporting some 30 tenant commands.
Key Contacts
COMMANDER: Capt Donald Stuer, Commanding Officer, Bldg 16, 619-437-2078, DSN 577-2078.
PUBLIC AFFAIRS: Ken Mitchell, Bldg 16, 619-437-3024, DSN 577-3024.
PROCUREMENT: Bldg 16, 619-437-2094, DSN 577-2094.
TRANSPORTATION: Bldg 16, 619-437-3036, DSN 577-3036.
PERSONNEL/COMMUNITY ACTIVITIES: Director of Personnel, Bldg 16, 619-437-3230, DSN 577-3230.
Personnel and Expenditures
ACTIVE DUTY PERSONNEL: 16,000
CIVILIAN PERSONNEL: 8800
Services
Housing: Family units 54; Unaccompanied officer quarters 280; Unaccompanied enlisted quarters 3200; Barracks spaces; Senior NCO units 62. *Temporary Housing:* VIP units 3; VOQ units 10; BAQ units 5; Guesthouse units; Transient quarters 90. *Commissary:* Yes; *Exchange:* Retail store; Barber shop; Dry cleaners; Food shop; Florist; Service station; Beauty shop; Credit union. *Child Care/Capacities:* Day care center capacity 90. *Base Library:* Yes. *Medical Facilities:* Medical clinic; Dental clinic. *Recreational Facilities:* Bowling center; Movie theater; Pool; Gym; Golf course; Tennis courts; Racquetball court; Fitness center/Weight room; Softball field; Football

field; Auto shop; Officers club; NCO club; Marina; Beach; Recreation gear locker, rentals; RV Park; Flying club.

110. Defense Contract Management Command, San Diego
DCMC San Diego
7675 Dagget St, Ste 200
San Diego, CA 92111-2241
619-495-7651
Internet: http://www.dcmdw/dla.mil/sndao/sndao.htm
Profile
BRANCH: Defense Logistics Agency.
LOCATION: *County:* San Diego.
MAJOR UNITS: Defense Contract Management Command, San Diego.
Key Contacts
COMMANDER: Cmd Rob Robbins, USN, 619-495-7411, DSN 972-7411.

111. Fleet Antisubmarine Warfare Training Center, Pacific
FLEASWTRACENPAC
32444 Echo Lane, Ste 100
San Diego, CA 92147-5199
619-524-1011; FAX 619-524-1674; DSN 524-1011
E-mail: fasw.00@netpsa.cnet.navy.mil Internet: http://192.101.121.120/ndcsd/asw.htm
OFFICER-OF-THE-DAY: 619-524-1689, DSN 524-1689
Profile
BRANCH: Navy.
SIZE AND LOCATION: 37.5 acres. Approx 3 mi W of downtown San Diego, adj to San Diego Bay; approx 1.5 mi W of San Diego IAP. *County:* San Diego.
MAJOR UNITS: Fleet Antisubmarine Warfare Training Center; Afloat Training Group; Fleet Intelligence Training Center; Naval Education Support Center; Total Quality Leadership Team, Pacific; Navy Campus; Mess Specialist School.
BASE HISTORY: 1939, Fleet Sound School established at Destroyer Base (now Naval Station) San Diego. 1942, Fleet Sound School, San Diego constructed/occupied. 1960, renamed Fleet Antisubmarine Warfare School. 1973, changed to Fleet Antisubmarine Warfare School Pacific. 1994, renamed current name. Currently, primary center for training sonar technicians.
Key Contacts
COMMANDER: Capt James S Snyder, 619-524-1665; DSN 524-1665.
PUBLIC AFFAIRS: STGC Philip Robert, 619-524-1696, DSN 524-1696.
PROCUREMENT: Jim Conrad, 619-532-3439.
TRANSPORTATION: 619-524-1579, DSN 524-1579.
Personnel and Expenditures
ACTIVE DUTY PERSONNEL: 1300
CIVILIAN PERSONNEL: 100
Services
Housing: Unaccompanied enlisted quarters 8; Barracks spaces 1047. *Temporary Housing:* Transient quarters 139. *Exchange:* Barber shop; Dry cleaners; Food shop; Military clothing store; Convenience store; ATM; Post office. *Child Care/Capacities:* No day care facilities. *Schools:* No on-base schools. *Base Library:* Yes. *Medical Facilities:* Dental clinic. *Recreational Facilities:* Pool; Tennis courts; Racquetball

court; Fitness center/Weight room; Softball field; Picnic area; Weight room; Sand volleyball courts; Martial arts; Sailing center.

112. Fleet Combat Training Center, Pacific
FCTCPAC
53690 Tomahawk Dr, Ste 144
San Diego, CA 92147-5080
619-553-8330; FAX 619-553-0063
Internet: http://www.fctcpac.navy.mil/
OFFICER-OF-THE-DAY: 619-553-8330, DSN 553-8330
Profile
BRANCH: Navy.
SIZE AND LOCATION: 95 acres. Ocean-front property on Point Loma, San Diego approx 4 mi from intersection of I-5 & I-8; approx 6 mi from downtown San Diego. *County:* San Diego.
MAJOR UNITS: Fleet Combat Training Center; Tactical Training Group, Pacific (TTGP); Naval Research and Development (NRAD); Naval Command, Control and Ocean Surveillance Center, Headquarters; Maritime Defense Zone Sector Southern California Operations Center.
BASE HISTORY: Origin of FCTC dates back to 1943 with a series of informal lectures on radar & Combat Information Center (CIC) concept. 1943-45, CIC instruction expanded to meet fleet's need to understand capabilities & tactical use of radar. 1945, CIC section established as separate command; designated CIC Indoctrination School. 1946, School moved to present location; designated CIC Group Training Center (later redesignated Fleet Air Defense Training Center in 1954, Fleet Anti-Air Warfare Training Center in 1960, & FCTC in 1976). Newest developments include integration of electronic warfare & long-range over-the-horizon weapons applications to counter changing threats, & Battlex, a multi-warfare area scenario simulation exercising battle group command & control.
VISITOR ATTRACTIONS: Beautiful view overlooking Pacific.
Key Contacts
COMMANDER: 619-553-8324, DSN 553-8324.
PUBLIC AFFAIRS: 619-553-0547, DSN 553-0547.
PROCUREMENT: 619-553-8202, DSN 553-8202.
Personnel and Expenditures
ACTIVE DUTY PERSONNEL: 510
CIVILIAN PERSONNEL: 70
MILITARY PAYROLL EXPENDITURE: $12.75 mil
CONTRACT EXPENDITURE: $2.8 mil
Services *Exchange:* Retail store; Barber shop; Dry cleaners; Food shop; Bank; Cafeteria. *Recreational Facilities:* Tennis courts; Fitness center/Weight room; Softball field; PAR course; Basketball/Volleyball facilities.

113. Miramar Marine Corps Air Station
MCAS Miramar
PO Box 402013
San Diego, CA 92145-5000
619-537-1011; DSN 577-1011
Internet: http://www.usmc.mil/
Profile
BRANCH: Marine Corps.

SIZE AND LOCATION: 25,000 acres. 10 mi N of San Diego near I-15 & I-805. *County:* San Diego.
MAJOR UNITS: 3rd Marine Aircraft Wing; Marine Aircraft Group 11; Marine Aircraft Group 46; 4th Tank Bn; Marine Aviation Logistics Squadron 11; VMFA (AW)-225; VMFA(AW)-242; Marine Fighter Attack Squadron 232; VMFA-314; VMFA-323; VMFA-134; Commander, Marine Corps Bases Western Area.
BASE HISTORY: Present site owned by Federal government since WWI; purchased for Camp Kearny, Army Infantry Training Center. Used for variety of military functions, including lighter-than-air aircraft base and target bombing range. WWII, southern half of station commissioned Auxiliary Air Station; North Island and northern half designated Marine Corps Air Depot Miramar. 1946, activities combined; designated Marine Corps Air Station Miramar. 1947, Marine air units moved to MCAS El Toro. 1952, designated NAS Miramar. 1961, support base for fighter squadrons only. Home base for all Pacific Fleet fighter and airborne early warning squadrons. 1997, NAS replaced by MCAS.
Key Contacts
COMMANDER: Col Tom Caughlan.
PUBLIC AFFAIRS: Cpl Jason W Dequenne, PAO, Bldg M-250, MCAS Miramar, San Diego, CA 92145-5005, 619-537-6021, DSN 577-6021, DSN FAX 537-6001.
Personnel and Expenditures
ACTIVE DUTY PERSONNEL: 12,000
DEPENDENTS: 5000
CIVILIAN PERSONNEL: 1500
Services
Housing: Family units 88; Unaccompanied officer quarters 200; Unaccompanied enlisted quarters 26; Trailer spaces 108. *Temporary Housing:* VIP units 4 units; Unaccompanied officer/Enlisted quarters 1; Lodge units 90. *Commissary:* Yes; *Exchange:* Barber shop; Dry cleaners; Food shop; Florist; Bank; Service station; Furniture store; Military clothing store; Convenience store; Laundromat; Credit union; ATM; Optical store; Post office; Fast food; Video rentals; Travel agency; Garden center; Tailor/Alterations; Photo store. *Child Care/Capacities:* Day care center capacity 200; Home day care program; Before & after school programs. *Schools:* No on-base schools. *Base Library:* Yes. *Medical Facilities:* Medical clinic; Dental clinic; San Diego Naval Hospital, 15 mi away. *Recreational Facilities:* Bowling center; Movie theater; Pool; Gym; Recreation center; Golf course; Stables; Tennis courts; Racquetball court; Fitness center/Weight room; Softball field; Auto shop; Craft shop; Officers club; NCO club; Camping; Fishing/Hunting; Youth center; Picnic area; Jogging course; Camp gear; RV storage lot; RV park spaces, 24.

114. Naval Health Research Center
NHRC
271 Catalina Blvd, Bldg 306
San Diego, CA 92152
Mailing Address
PO Box 85122
San Diego, CA 92186-5122
DSN 553-8429, DSN FAX 553-9389

Internet: http://mac088.nhrc.navy.mil/Headline/Welcome/Overview.html

Profile

BRANCH: Navy.

LOCATION: *County:* San Diego.

MAJOR UNITS: Naval Health Research Center.

BASE HISTORY: Bureau of Medicine & Surgery laboratory supporting fleet operational readiness through research, development, test, & evaluation on biomedical & psychological aspects of Navy & Marine Corps.

Key Contacts

COMMANDER: Capt Larry M Dean, MSC, USN, co@nhrc.navy.mil.

PUBLIC AFFAIRS: CDR T Luz, 619-553-8480, Luz@vax309.nhrc.navy.mil.

115. North Island Naval Air Station

NASNI

San Diego, CA 92135-5000

619-545-2672; FAX 619-545-2162; DSN 735-2672

OFFICER-OF-THE-DAY: 619-545-2673, DSN 735-2673

Profile

BRANCH: Navy.

SIZE AND LOCATION: 2802 acres. Off Hwy I-5; Coronado Bay Bridge Exit, through toll booths, down Third St to main gate. Coronado approx 5 min from base; San Diego Airport approx 15 min N. *County:* San Diego.

MAJOR UNITS: Commander, Naval Air Force, US Pacific Fleet; Commander, Carrier Group 1; Commander, Carrier Group 7; Commander, Sea Control Wing Pacific; Commander, Helicopter Antisubmarine Light Wing Pacific; Commander, Helicopter Antisubmarine Wing Pacific; Commander, Helicopter Tactical Wing Pacific; USS *Constellation* (CV-64); Naval Air Station, North Island; Naval Auxiliary Landing Field, San Clemente Island; Antisubmarine Warfare Operations Center (ASWOC); Commander, Helicopter Wing Reserve; Fleet Area Control and Surveillance Facility (FACSFAC); Fleet Aviation Specialized Operational Training Group, Pacific; Fleet Electronic Warfare Support Group; Marine Corps Security Force Co; Naval Air Maintenance Training Group Dets, North Island; Naval Aviation Depot; Naval Aviation Engineering Service Unit; Naval Oceanography Command Facility; Navy Regional Data Automation Center, San Diego; Naval Telecommunications Center; Nuclear Weapons Training Group, Pacific (NUWPNTRAGRUPAC); Operational Test and Evaluation Force, Pacific (OPTEVFOR); Pacific Fleet Imaging Command (FLTIMAGCOMPAC); Personnel Support Activity Det; Submarine Rescue Unit; US Customs Service.

BASE HISTORY: 1917, North Island commissioned; until 1937, shared facilities with Army Signal Corps. 1927, Charles Lindbergh took off from North Island for St Louis on way to Paris. Before WWII, area called Spanish Bight separated base from city of Coronado; area filled in with sand from San Diego harbor, 1940s. Site important training, staging, & deployment center, especially during WWII, and Korean War.

Key Contacts

COMMANDER: 619-545-2667, DSN 735-2667.

Personnel and Expenditures

ACTIVE DUTY PERSONNEL: 16,200

DEPENDENTS: 7044

CIVILIAN PERSONNEL: 7300

Services

Housing: Unaccompanied officer quarters; Unaccompanied enlisted quarters; No base housing at NAS North Island. *Temporary Housing:* VIP units; Unaccompanied officer/Enlisted quarters; Lodge units. *Commissary:* Yes; *Exchange:* Retail store; Barber shop; Dry cleaners; Food shop; Florist; Bank; Service station. *Child Care/Capacities:* Day care center capacity 90. *Base Library:* Yes. *Medical Facilities:* Medical clinic; Dental clinic. *Recreational Facilities:* Bowling center; Movie theater; Pool; Gym; Recreation center; Golf course; Tennis courts; Racquetball court; Fitness center/Weight room; Softball field; Football field; Auto shop; Craft shop; Officers club.

116. Region Nineteen, Naval Reserve Readiness Command

REDCOM 19

960 N Harbor Dr

San Diego, CA 92132-5108

619-532-1837; FAX 619-532-3031; DSN 522-1837

Internet: http://mork.nosc.mil/~redcom19/

Profile

BRANCH: Naval Reserve.

LOCATION: *County:* San Diego.

MAJOR UNITS: Naval Reserve Readiness Command, Region 19.

Key Contacts

COMMANDER: RADM J E Kerr, 619-532-1842, DSN 522-1842.

117. San Diego Coast Guard Activities

Air Station San Diego

2710 N Harbor Dr

San Diego, CA 92101-1079

619-683-6300; FAX 619-683-6324

OFFICER-OF-THE-DAY: 619-683-6470, FAX 619-683-6474

Profile

BRANCH: Coast Guard.

SIZE AND LOCATION: 22.5 acres. Directly across N Harbor Dr from San Diego Lindbergh Field; near corner of Laurel St & Harbor Dr off I-5. *County:* San Diego.

MAJOR UNITS: Coast Guard Group, San Diego; Coast Guard Air Station, San Diego; Marine Safety Office, San Diego; Aids to Navigation (ANT) Team, San Diego; Coast Guard Station, San Diego; USCGC *Tybee*; USCGC *Point Hobart*; Colorado River Patrol.

BASE HISTORY: 1934, Coast Guard Air Patrol Detachment supported anti-smuggling operations. 1937, Air Station established on tideland adjacent to Lindbergh Field. 1948, cutters & boats added creating Coast Guard Group. Currently, Air Station maintains 4 Dolphin helicopters & 3 Falcon jets. Today, operating as "One Coast Guard Team" with men/women working as one integrated chain of command in all areas. Responsible for 60 mi of coastline from Mexican border to San Mateo, CA, and 200 mi out to sea.

Key Contacts

COMMANDER: Capt William M Hayes, 619-683-6301, FAX 619-683-6324.

PUBLIC AFFAIRS: Lt Elizabeth D Blow, 619-683-6322, FAX 619-683-6324, PAO@interest.uscg.mil.

PROCUREMENT: CWO David Lewis, 619-683-6401, FAX 619-683-6407, S.LEWIS@internet.uscg.mil.

PERSONNEL/COMMUNITY ACTIVITIES: LCDR Scott Pollock, 619-683-6331, FAX 619-683-6338, S.POLLOCK@internet.uscg.mil.

Personnel and Expenditures

ACTIVE DUTY PERSONNEL: 300

DEPENDENTS: 0

CIVILIAN PERSONNEL: 2

Services

Housing: Unaccompanied enlisted quarters. *Temporary Housing:* None. *Exchange:* Retail store; Military clothing store; Convenience store. *Child Care/Capacities:* No day care facilities. *Schools:* No on-base schools. *Medical Facilities:* Small medical clinic with corpsman. *Recreational Facilities:* Gym; Recreation center; Tennis courts; Racquetball court; Fitness center/Weight room; Picnic area.

118. San Diego Fleet and Industrial Supply Center

FISC San Diego

937 N Harbor Dr

San Diego, CA 92132-5044

619-532-2203; FAX 619-532-2828; DSN 522-2203

E-mail: fiscsdcic@fmso.navy.mil Internet:http://www.sd.fisc.navy.mil

Profile

BRANCH: Navy.

SIZE AND LOCATION: 16 acres. HQ at Broadway Complex, downtown San Diego; along the bay a few miles from Lindbergh Field (Airport); N of Seaport Village. *County:* San Diego.

MAJOR UNITS: Fleet & Industrial Supply Center, San Diego; Commander, Naval Base San Diego, Personnel Support Activity San Diego; Reserve Readiness Command Region 19; Naval Computer & Telecommunications Center; MARS.

BASE HISTORY: 1904, coaling station at Point Loma, first permanent Navy logistics shore establishment in San Diego; today, site occupied by NSC Fuel Department. 1922, Naval Supply Depot opened here; Supply Depot building also HQ, Commander, Naval Base, San Diego. 1952, redesignated Naval Supply Center. 1973, sister Supply Center in Long Beach closed. 1980, consolidation gave NSC responsibility for functions previously accomplished by supply department, NAS North Island. 1992, redesignated FISC. Currently, provides wide variety of supplies & services to naval activities throughout the SW with 20 regional offices throughout southern CA (San Diego, Seal Beach, Corona, Fallbrook, & El Toro), Yuma, AZ, and Ingleside, TX.

Key Contacts

COMMANDER: Capt Bill Bickert, CO FISC San Diego, 937 N Harbor Dr, Ste 01, San Diego, CA 92132-0001, 619-532-2203, DSN 522-2203.

PUBLIC AFFAIRS: Mary Markovinovic, FISC San Diego, Public Affairs, Code 05, Ste 14, San Diego, CA 92132-0014, 619-532-1931, DSN 522-1931.

PROCUREMENT: CDR John Qua, FISC San Diego, Regional Contracts, Code 200, Ste 60, San Diego, CA 92132-0060, 619-532-3435, DSN 522-3435.

PERSONNEL/COMMUNITY ACTIVITIES: Lynne Lester, FISC San Diego, Human Resources, Code 020, San Diego, CA 92132-0026, 619-532-2730, DSN 522-2730.

Personnel and Expenditures
ACTIVE DUTY PERSONNEL: 24 officers, 77 enlisted
CIVILIAN PERSONNEL: 960
CONTRACT EXPENDITURE: $500 mil

Services
Housing: None on base, available through housing office. *Exchange:* Barber shop; Convenience store; ATM. *Child Care/Capacities:* No day care facilities. *Schools:* No on-base schools. *Medical Facilities:* Dental clinic. *Recreational Facilities:* Gym.

119. San Diego Marine Corps Recruit Depot
MCRD San Diego
1600 Henderson Ave, #120
San Diego, CA 92140-5001
619-524-8762; DSN 524-8762

Profile
BRANCH: Marine Corps.
SIZE AND LOCATION: 433 acres. Off I-5 just S of I-8; joined by Washington St, Pacific Hwy, Witherby St (also joined by Old Town Ave), & Barnett St; 2 mi from downtown San Diego, between I-5 & Lindbergh Field Airport. *County:* San Diego.
MAJOR UNITS: Western Recruiting Region; Recruit Training Regiment; HQ & Service Bn; HQ, 12th Marine Corps District; Coast Guard Pacific Area Tactical Law Enforcement Team; Recruiters School; Drill Instructor School.
BASE HISTORY: 1919, ground-breaking at "Dutch Flats" marshlands; Marine Corps' oldest operating installation on West Coast. 1921, designated Advanced Marine Corps Expeditionary Base. 1923, Recruit Depot for western half of US moved to San Diego. Served as home for Marine Expeditionary Forces in China & Fleet Marine Forces between two world wars. WWII, trained about 223,000 recruits. 1948, designated MCRD. Graduates 19,000 Marines each year.
VISITOR ATTRACTIONS: Command Museum; Graduation ceremonies.

Key Contacts
COMMANDER: Brig Gen Henry Osmond, 619-524-8727.
PUBLIC AFFAIRS: Maj Benjamin Owens, 619-524-8762.

Personnel and Expenditures
ACTIVE DUTY PERSONNEL: 2100
DEPENDENTS: 2300
CIVILIAN PERSONNEL: 850

Services
Housing: Family units Officer 5; Unaccompanied enlisted quarters 300; Navy housing available off base. *Temporary Housing:* VIP units; VOQ units 10; VEQ units 32. *Exchange:* Retail store; Barber shop; Dry cleaners; Service station; Military clothing store; Convenience store; Beauty shop; Credit union; Class VI; Garden center; Household store; Commissaries nearby. *Child Care/Capacities:* Day care center capacity 80. *Schools:* No on-base schools. *Base Library:* Yes. *Medical Facilities:* Medical clinic; Naval Medical Center, 8 mi. *Recreational Facilities:* Bowling center; Movie theater; Gym; Fitness center/Weight room; Softball field; Football

field; Officers club; NCO club; Enlisted club; Boat house.

120. San Diego Naval & Marine Corps Reserve Center
NAVMARCORESCEN San Diego; NMCRC SD
9955 Pomerado Rd
San Diego, CA 92131-5293
619-537-8040; FAX 619-537-8042; DSN 577-8040; DSN FAX 577-8042
Internet: http://www.cts.com/browse/nrcstaff

Profile
BRANCH: Naval Reserve; Marine Corps Reserve.
SIZE AND LOCATION: 21 acres. Approx 3 mi E of MCAS Miramar. *County:* San Diego.
MAJOR UNITS: REDCOM NINETEEN Activity; I & I Staff (USMC); MIUW 106; MIUW 107; PSD Miramar Reserve Dept; CNRRC Det 1, Zone 9, Station 1.

Key Contacts
COMMANDER: Capt G M Erickson, 619-537-8022, DSN 577-8022, DSN FAX 577-8042.
PUBLIC AFFAIRS: PN2 A L Thuys, 619-537-8040, DSN 577-8040, DSN FAX 577-8042.

Personnel and Expenditures
ACTIVE DUTY PERSONNEL: 2900 Navy reservists; 418 USMC reservists

Services *Recreational Facilities:* Gym; Fitness center/Weight room; Picnic area.

121. San Diego Naval Medical Center
NAVMEDCENSD
34800 Bob Wilson Dr
San Diego, CA 92134-5000
619-532-9380; FAX 619-532-9059
OFFICER-OF-THE-DAY: 619-532-6400, DSN 522-6400

Profile
BRANCH: Navy.
SIZE AND LOCATION: 70 acres. Off Florida Canyon Dr, adj to Balboa Park; 8 mi from San Diego IAP. *County:* San Diego.
MAJOR UNITS: Naval Medical Center, San Diego; Naval School of Health Sciences; Naval Drug Screening Laboratory.
BASE HISTORY: 1914, 4th Regiment, USMC, established field hospital in Balboa Park. 1917, medical facility officially established on Balboa Park Exposition Grounds. 1919, designated US Naval Hospital, San Diego. 1922, permanent facility commissioned on nearby Inspiration Point. During WWII, patient census reached as high as 12,000. 1988, new facility dedicated; world's largest & most technologically advanced military health care complex.

Key Contacts
COMMANDER: RADM R A Nelson, MC, USN; 619-532-6400, DSN 522-6400.
PUBLIC AFFAIRS: Doug Sayers.
PROCUREMENT: CDR V E Liebold, MSC, USN; 619-532-6625, DSN 522-6625.

Personnel and Expenditures
ACTIVE DUTY PERSONNEL: 3000
CIVILIAN PERSONNEL: 1200

Services
Housing: Family units 4; Unaccompanied enlisted quarters 1300.

Exchange: Retail store; Barber shop; Dry cleaners; Florist; Military clothing store; Convenience store; Beauty shop. *Child Care/Capacities:* Day care center for employees, 6wks-5yrs; Hourly drop off for children of outpatients. *Base Library:* Yes. *Medical Facilities:* Hospital 562 beds; Medical clinic; Dental clinic; Pharmacy. *Recreational Facilities:* Pool; Gym; Recreation center; Tennis courts; Racquetball court; Fitness center/Weight room; Softball field; All hands club.

122. San Diego Naval Station
NAVSTA San Diego
32nd St Naval Station
3455 Senn Rd
San Diego, CA 92136-5084
Mailing Address
NAVSTA SAN DIEGO
SAN DIEGO, CA 92136-5084
619-556-2400; FAX 619-556-2423; DSN 562-2400; DSN FAX 526-2423
OFFICER-OF-THE-DAY: 619-556-1246, DSN 562-1246

Profile
BRANCH: Navy.
SIZE AND LOCATION: 1029.45 acres. In city of San Diego at intersection of Harbor Dr & 32nd St, portions of southern end of base in National City; all major freeways within a few min drive. *County:* San Diego.
MAJOR UNITS: Naval Station, San Diego; Fleet Training Center; Navy Public Works Center; Shore Intermediate Maintenance Activity; Personnel Support Activity Det; Transient Personnel Unit.
BASE HISTORY: 1923, commissioned as destroyer base, then repair base. 1945, named Naval Station, San Diego. Currently homeport to 65 surface ships.
VISITOR ATTRACTIONS: Surface Navy Museum (in Public Affairs Office).

Key Contacts
COMMANDER: Capt Vison E Smith.
PUBLIC AFFAIRS: H Sam Samuelson, Public Affairs Office, Code OP, 3445 Surface Navy Blvd, San Diego, CA 92136-5059, 619-556-7356, FAX 619-556-7357, DSN 526-7356.

Personnel and Expenditures
ACTIVE DUTY PERSONNEL: 35,969
DEPENDENTS: 0
CIVILIAN PERSONNEL: 7088
MILITARY PAYROLL EXPENDITURE: $1.1 bil
CONTRACT EXPENDITURE: $140 mil

Services
Housing: Unaccompanied enlisted quarters 7; BAQ units 3; *Commissary:* Yes; *Exchange:* Retail store; Barber shop; Dry cleaners; Food shop; Florist; Bank; Service station; Furniture store; Bakery; Bookstore; Military clothing store; Convenience store; Beauty shop; Laundromat; Credit union; ATM; Optical store; Post office; Fast food; Video rentals; Thrift shop; Travel agency; Shoe repair; Computer store; Garden center; Tailor/Alterations; Laundry; Cafeteria; Photo store. *Child Care/Capacities:* Day care center capacity 440, 6wks-5yrs; Home day care program. *Schools:* College courses. *Medical Facilities:* Medical clinic; Dental clinic; Dispensary; Pharmacy. *Recreational Facilities:* Bowling center; Movie theater; Pool; Gym; Recreation center; Golf course; Tennis courts; Racquetball court; Fitness center/Weight room;

Softball field; Football field; Auto shop; Craft shop; Officers club; Enlisted club; Picnic area.

123. San Diego Naval Submarine Base
SUBASE San Diego
140 Sylvester Rd
San Diego, CA 92106-3521
Mailing Address
Submarine Pacific West Coast
San Diego, CA 92106-3521
619-553-1011; FAX 619-553-7400; DSN 553-1011
Profile
BRANCH: Navy.
SIZE AND LOCATION: 330 acres. At tip of Ballast Point (harbor entrance) on Point Loma peninsula; approx 8 mi from downtown San Diego, Lindbergh Field and I-5 & I-8. *County:* San Diego.
MAJOR UNITS: Submarine Squadron 11; Submarine Development Squadron 5; Submarine Training Facility; USS *McKee*; USNS *Mercy*.
BASE HISTORY: 1852, President Fillmore set aside southern portion of Point Loma for military use. Subsequently, land assigned to Army; named for Civil War Gen William Rosecrans, later known as Camp San Diego. 1959, Ft Rosecrans, designated historic landmark, turned over to Navy. 1963, Submarine Support Facility established. 1974, Submarine Support Facility became shore command. 1981, site redesignated Naval Submarine Base.
VISITOR ATTRACTIONS: Ft Rosecrans/ Cabrillo National Monument nearby; SUBASE Chapel; Fort Guijarros historic site.
Key Contacts
COMMANDER: Capt Jeffrey Cassias, 619-553-7400.
PUBLIC AFFAIRS: Lt Lydia Leporte, 619-553-8643.
PROCUREMENT: Shirley Mitchell, 619-553-7148.
TRANSPORTATION: 619-553-7370.
PERSONNEL/COMMUNITY ACTIVITIES: 619-553-7162.
Personnel and Expenditures
ACTIVE DUTY PERSONNEL: 3800
DEPENDENTS: 4000
CIVILIAN PERSONNEL: 200
Services
Housing: Family units 15; Unaccompanied enlisted quarters 576; Senior NCO units 6; Junior NCO units 129. *Temporary Housing:* VIP units 6; Unaccompanied officer/Enlisted quarters 135. *Exchange:* Barber shop; Dry cleaners; Florist; Bank; Service station; Military clothing store; Convenience store; Laundromat; Credit union. *Child Care/Capacities:* Day care center capacity 267. *Schools:* College courses. *Base Library:* Yes. *Medical Facilities:* Dental clinic. *Recreational Facilities:* Pool; Gym; Recreation center; Tennis courts; Racquetball court; Fitness center/ Weight room; Softball field; Auto shop; Picnic area; Playground.

124. Space & Naval Warfare Systems Command
COMSPAWARSYSCOM
SPAWAR
4301 Pacific Hwy
San Diego, CA 92110-3127
619-524-3470

Internet: http://www.nosc.mil/spawar/welcome.page
Profile
BRANCH: Navy.
LOCATION: In old Air Force Plant 19 Complex, Old Town, San Diego. *County:* San Diego.
MAJOR UNITS: Space & Naval Warfare Systems Center, San Diego.
BASE HISTORY: Relocated from Arlington, VA, to new HQ, Oct 1997.
Key Contacts
COMMANDER: RADM George F A Wagner, 619-524-7000, wagnerg@nosc.mil.
PUBLIC AFFAIRS: 619-524-3470.
Personnel and Expenditures
ACTIVE DUTY PERSONNEL: 291
CIVILIAN PERSONNEL: 721
Services
Housing: None. *Temporary Housing:* None. *Exchange:* Convenience store. *Child Care/Capacities:* No day care facilities. *Schools:* No on-base schools. *Medical Facilities:* No medical facilities.

San Francisco

125. San Francisco Coast Guard Air Station
CGAS-SFO; Air Stat San Fran
Bldg 1020, San Francisco IAP
San Francisco, CA 94128-3099
415-876-2911, 399-3455, 399-3415
OFFICER-OF-THE-DAY: 415-876-2929, DSN 859-6929
Profile
BRANCH: Coast Guard.
SIZE AND LOCATION: 24 acres. 1 mi N of San Francisco IAP Exit, off North Access Rd between United Airlines and Flying Tigers Airlines. *County:* San Francisco.
MAJOR UNITS: Coast Guard Air Station, San Francisco; USCGC *Point Brower*; USCGC *Buttonwood*.
BASE HISTORY: 1941, site established at Mills Field, CA. Through WWII, under operational command of Navy; conducted search & rescue missions & coastal patrols. Mission: maritime search & rescue along 300 miles of coastline, from Point Conception to Ft Bragg, CA; drug & fisheries law enforcement missions; aids to navigation, such as offshore lighthouses; & aerial surveillance for marine environmental protection.
Key Contacts
COMMANDER: 415-876-2910, DSN 859-6910.
PUBLIC AFFAIRS: 415-876-2925, DSN 859-6925.
Personnel and Expenditures
ACTIVE DUTY PERSONNEL: 99
CIVILIAN PERSONNEL: 2
Services
Services Medical Facilities: Clinic limited to assigned personnel. *Recreational Facilities:* Gym; Recreation center; Tennis courts; Racquetball court; Fitness center/Weight room; Auto shop.

126. San Francisco Coast Guard Group
Group San Francisco
YBI (Yerba Buena Island)
Yerba Buena Island
San Francisco, CA 94130-5103
415-399-3400
E-mail: ODO@dot.uscg.mil/internet
OFFICER-OF-THE-DAY: 415-399-3529
Profile
BRANCH: Coast Guard.
SIZE AND LOCATION: 9 acres. Yerba Buena Island in center of entrance to San Francisco Bay connected to Treasure Island and access to I-80 San Francisco Oakland Bay Bridge (mid-span), with San Francisco and Oakland 5 min away; bus service available. *County:* San Francisco.
MAJOR UNITS: Coast Guard Group, San Francisco; Coast Guard Station, San Francisco; Aids to Navigation (ANT) Team, San Francisco; USCGC *Point Brower*; USCGC *Buttonwood*; Vessel Traffic Service, San Francisco; Electric Shop, San Francisco; Coast Guard Reserve Center, San Francisco.
BASE HISTORY: Yerba Buena is a natural island. Treasure Island was built for 1939-40 Golden Gate International Exposition, to become San Francisco's airport after fair. Spaniards named island Yerba Buena for "good herb" growing there, mint used to flavor tea. Americans called it "Goat Island" for goat herds kept there by ship captains. Island's history includes tales of pirates, buried treasure, and ghosts. 1866, government set aside Yerba Buena Island for military; US Lighthouse Service established Pacific Coast depot on island. 1898, Yerba Buena Island site for first West Coast naval training school (transferred to San Diego, 1923), island became Navy receiving station. Today, part of Yerba Buena Island site of Navy family housing; remainder of island is Coast Guard's San Francisco base, Yerba Buena Island lighthouse, and Vessel Traffic Service, which monitors movement of all ships between Golden Gate and Sacramento.
Key Contacts
COMMANDER: Capt Hall.
PUBLIC AFFAIRS: Lt Cooley, 415-399-3504.
Personnel and Expenditures
ACTIVE DUTY PERSONNEL: 200
DEPENDENTS: 0
CIVILIAN PERSONNEL: 6
Services
Housing: Unaccompanied enlisted quarters 40; Senior NCO units 1. *Temporary Housing:* None. *Child Care/Capacities:* No day care facilities. *Schools:* No on-base schools. *Medical Facilities:* No medical facilities. *Recreational Facilities:* Gym; Recreation center; Tennis courts; Fitness center/Weight room; Picnic area.

127. US Army Corps of Engineers, San Francisco District
333 Market St
San Francisco, CA 94105
415-977-8659
Internet: http://www.spn.usace.army.mil/
Profile
BRANCH: Army.
LOCATION: *County:* San Francisco.
MAJOR UNITS: Corps of Engineers, San Francisco District.

BASE HISTORY: 1866, established with authority for river & harbor work on Pacific Coast W of Rocky Mts. Covers 600 mi of coastline from Oregon border to S of Monterey & Klamath River Basin in Oregon.

Key Contacts
COMMANDER: LTC Richard G Thompson, 415-977-8500, rthompson@smtp.spd.usace.army.mil.
PUBLIC AFFAIRS: Doug Makitten, 415-977-8659, dmakitten@smtp.spd.usace.army.mil.

128. US Army Corps of Engineers, South Pacific Division
CESPD
333 Market St, Rm 923
San Francisco, CA 94105-2195
415-977-8322; FAX 415-977-8315
Internet: http://www.spd.usace.army.mil/
Profile
BRANCH: Army.
SIZE: Offices only. *County:* San Francisco.
MAJOR UNITS: Corps of Engineers, South Pacific Division.
BASE HISTORY: Oversees 4 districts: Albuquerque; Sacramento; Los Angeles; & San Francisco. Performs military & civil works construction.
Key Contacts
COMMANDER: Brig Gen Joseph R Capka, Commander, 415-705-1414.
PUBLIC AFFAIRS: Frank Rezac, 415-705-2405.
PROCUREMENT: Ray Suderman, 415-705-2413.
TRANSPORTATION: Roy Hovey, 415-705-2419.
Personnel and Expenditures
ACTIVE DUTY PERSONNEL: 5
CIVILIAN PERSONNEL: 250
Services *Base Library:* Yes. *Medical Facilities:* Health unit in bldg. *Recreational Facilities:* Fitness center/Weight room.

San Jose

129. San Jose Naval & Marine Corps Reserve Center
NAVMARCORESCEN San Jose
N&MCRC San Jose
995 E Mission St
San Jose, CA 95112-1699
408-294-3070; FAX 408-294-7915; DSN 462-0111 (ask for commercial number)
Profile
BRANCH: Naval Reserve; Marine Corps Reserve.
SIZE AND LOCATION: 6.2 acres. Approx 3 mi from downtown San Jose; 5 mi from San Jose IAP; 4 blocks from 880/101 hwy interchange. *County:* Santa Clara.
MAJOR UNITS: REDCOM TWENTY-TWO Activity.
BASE HISTORY: 1948, main facility completed as San Jose Armory. Korean War, redesignated Naval Reserve Training Center. Vietnam War to present, survived several BRAC surveys.
Key Contacts
COMMANDER: LCDR C R Giudice, 408-294-3070, FAX 294-7915.

Personnel and Expenditures
ACTIVE DUTY PERSONNEL: 10 Navy, 15 Marine; 415 Navy Reservists, 200 Marine Reservists
Services *Recreational Facilities:* Fitness center/Weight room.

San Luis Obispo

130. Camp San Luis Obispo
CSLO
PO Box 4209
San Luis Obispo, CA 93403-4209
Profile
BRANCH: Army National Guard.
SIZE AND LOCATION: 4160 acres. 5 mi NE of San Luis Obispo on Hwy 1. *County:* San Luis Obispo.
MAJOR UNITS: US Property and Fiscal Office for California; 649th Military Police Co.
BASE HISTORY: 1928, established as Camp Merriam, named after Gov Frank F Merriam. 1940, renamed Camp San Luis Obispo by Army. 1940-41, most construction of cantonment area completed. 1946, site returned to state; provides logistical & fiscal support for CA National Guard; training site for 40th & 49th Infantry Divisions, ARNG. 1950, Army leased camp as Class I installation & Southwest Signal Corps Training Center as Class II activity. 1965, camp returned to state. Site of California Military Academy, Sixth Army sponsored unit training schools, & other state activities.
VISITOR ATTRACTIONS: Small aircraft museum.
Key Contacts
COMMANDER: Capt Steve Morgan, 805-782-7642, FAX 805-782-7645.
Personnel and Expenditures
CIVILIAN PERSONNEL: 47
Services
Housing: Unaccompanied officer quarters 5; Barracks spaces 12; Dormitory spaces 79; RV/Camper sites 12; 2-person huts 101. *Temporary Housing:* VIP units 4; VOQ units 5; Apartment units 8; *Exchange:* Retail store. *Recreational Facilities:* Fitness center/Weight room; Officers club; NCO club; Camping.

San Pedro

131. San Pedro Coast Guard Support Center
USCG SUPRTCEN San Pedro
RC PO Box 8
San Pedro, CA 90731-0811
310-732-7404
OFFICER-OF-THE-DAY: 310-514-6400
Profile
BRANCH: Coast Guard.
SIZE AND LOCATION: 27 acres. On W end of Reservation Point, southerly extension of Terminal Island in San Pedro; 30 min drive from Los Angeles IAP, Long Beach Municipal Airport, or Torrance Municipal Airport. *County:* Los Angeles.
MAJOR UNITS: Coast Guard Support Center, San Pedro; Coast Guard Station, San Pedro; Aids to Navigation (ANT) Team, San Pedro;

Integrated Support Command, San Pedro; Coast Guard Reserve Group, Terminal Island; Armory Det, San Pedro; Director of Auxiliary, San Pedro; Electronic Support Det, San Pedro.
BASE HISTORY: 1933, Lighthouse Service first tenant of Reservation Point with lighthouse & industrial depot. 1950s, boat basin & barracks/administration bldg constructed. Parts of the facility have been used for Public Health Service quarantine station, immigration center, Navy brig, & Army Quartermaster Corps facility.
Personnel and Expenditures
ACTIVE DUTY PERSONNEL: 480
CIVILIAN PERSONNEL: 25
Services
Housing: Barracks spaces 30. *Exchange:* Retail store; Barber shop; Credit union. *Child Care/Capacities:* No day care facilities. *Schools:* No on-base schools. *Medical Facilities:* Medical clinic; Dental clinic; Pharmacy. *Recreational Facilities:* Recreation center; Tennis courts; Softball field; Enlisted club; Picnic area; Basketball court; Horseshoe pit.

Santa Ana

132. El Toro Marine Corps Air Station
MCAS El Toro
PO Box 95002
Santa Ana, CA 92709-5002
714-726-2100; DSN 997-3011
Internet: http://www.ordnance.org/eltoro.htm; http://www.usmc.mil/baseguid/eltoro.htm
OFFICER-OF-THE-DAY: 714-726-3901, DSN 997-3901
Profile
BRANCH: Marine Corps.
SIZE AND LOCATION: 4738 acres. Between Irvine & El Toro; approx 1 mi from I-5, Sand Canyon Exit; S of I-5/H-55 intersection & N of I-5/H-133 intersection; John Wayne Airport approx 12 mi NW. *County:* Orange.
MAJOR UNITS: HQ, Marine Corps Air Bases, Western Area; 3rd Marine Aircraft Wing; Marine Aircraft Group 46, Det B; Marine Medium Helicopter Squadron 764; Marine Heavy Helicopter Squadron 769; Marine Wing Support Squadron 473.
BASE HISTORY: 1943, commissioned as temporary Marine Corps Air Station; built on former Irvine Ranch. 1945, made permanent West Coast Marine Corps Air Station. 1968-74, major support base for President Nixon's visits to Western White House at San Clemente. 1975, first point of arrival for 50,000 Vietnamese refugees. 1984, one of 15 DOD "Model Installations" test sites to reduce bureaucracy & inefficiency. Today, showcase for Marine Corps Aviation & reserve mobilization site. "Flying Bull" insignia designed by Disney Studios in 1944.
FUTURE CLOSURE/REALIGNMENT: To be closed, Jul 1999. Relocate: aircraft & dedicated personnel, equipment, & support to other naval air stations, primarily NAS Miramar, CA, & MCAS Camp Pendleton, CA; Marine Corps Reserve Center to relocate to NAS Miramar. Data Processing Center to be closed.

VISITOR ATTRACTIONS: Historical aircraft display throughout air station.

Key Contacts

COMMANDER: Brig Gen R Magnus, 714-726-3622, DSN 997-3622.

PUBLIC AFFAIRS: Maj Margaret Kuhn, 714-726-2937.

PROCUREMENT: LTC Steven Carlson, Supply Division, 714-726-3855, DSN 997-3855.

TRANSPORTATION: 714-726-2178, DSN 997-2178.

PERSONNEL/COMMUNITY ACTIVITIES: Community Plans and Liaison, 714-726-3702, DSN 997-3702.

Personnel and Expenditures

ACTIVE DUTY PERSONNEL: 5000; Reservists 300

DEPENDENTS: 2350

CIVILIAN PERSONNEL: 900

Services

Housing: Family units 1188; Unaccompanied officer quarters 110; Unaccompanied enlisted quarters 1274; RV/Camper sites 16. *Temporary Housing:* VIP units 4; VOQ units 100; VEQ units 400; Lodge units 24; Transient quarters 970. *Commissary:* Yes; *Exchange:* Retail store; Barber shop; Dry cleaners; Food shop; Florist; Bank; Service station; Thrift shop. *Child Care/Capacities:* Day care center capacity 100; Home day care program. *Schools:* Elementary. *Base Library:* Yes. *Medical Facilities:* Medical clinic; Dental clinic. *Recreational Facilities:* Bowling center; Movie theater; Pool; Gym; Recreation center; Golf course; Stables; Tennis courts; Racquetball court; Fitness center/Weight room; Softball field; Football field; Auto shop; Craft shop; Officers club; NCO club; Big Bear Lake facility, 100 mi NE in San Bernardino Mts.

Seal Beach

133. Seal Beach Naval Weapons Station

NWSSB

800 Seal Beach Blvd

Seal Beach, CA 90740-5000

562-594-7011; DSN 873-7011

Internet: http://www.sbeach.navy.mil/

OFFICER-OF-THE-DAY: 562-594-7101, DSN 873-7101

Profile

BRANCH: Navy.

SIZE AND LOCATION: 14,000 acres (all 4 sites). Los Angeles IAP to NWSSB: Hwy 405 S (Long Beach) to Seal Beach Blvd, left, head SE to NWSSB, main gate 3 blocks on left. *County:* Orange.

MAJOR UNITS: Naval Weapons Station, Seal Beach; EOT HQ Det 1; EOT Det 2; EOT Det 3; EOT Det 4; EOT Det 5; MASC MAG OPS Det 1; MASC PIER OPS Det 1; HQ Battery, 5th Bn, 14th Marine Regiment; O Battery, 5th Bn, 14th Marine Regiment.

BASE HISTORY: 1944, commissioned as Naval Ammunition and Net Depot, to receive, store and load ammunition for fleet. 1962, renamed Naval Weapons Station; readies approx 365 ships each year with missiles, torpedoes, and conventional ammunition for deployment. Organized into five centers: Seal Beach, Corona, Pomona, Fallbrook, and Detachment Port Hadlock, WA. Seal Beach is

Navy's major southern West Coast port facility for storing weapons and loading them onto ships. Overhaul depot for key combat systems; depot level repair of more than 500 vital weapon system components, surface missile and antisubmarine combat systems.

VISITOR ATTRACTIONS: Seal Beach National Wildlife Refuge (1000 acres).

Key Contacts

COMMANDER: CDR Mike Brolchino, Reserve Program Manager, 562-626-7872, DSN 837-7872.

PUBLIC AFFAIRS: Code 01P, 562-594-7215, DSN 873-7215.

PROCUREMENT: Supply Officer, Code 11, 562-594-7202, DSN 873-7202.

Personnel and Expenditures

ACTIVE DUTY PERSONNEL: 277

DEPENDENTS: 200

CIVILIAN PERSONNEL: 1507

Services

Housing: Handled by Long Beach Naval Station Housing Office, 213-547-7840. *Exchange:* Barber shop; Food shop; Bank; Service station. *Child Care/Capacities:* No day care facilities. *Schools:* No on-base schools. *Base Library:* Yes. *Medical Facilities:* Medical clinic. *Recreational Facilities:* Bowling center; Gym; Tennis courts; Fitness center/Weight room; Softball field; Fishing/Hunting; Golf driving range.

Stockton

134. Defense Distribution Region West

DDRW

PO Box 960001

Stockton, CA 95296-0002

209-982-2839; FAX 209-982-2827; DSN 462-2839

Profile

BRANCH: Joint Service Installation; Defense Logistics Agency; DOD.

SIZE AND LOCATION: 1172 acres. 75 mi E of San Francisco; 60 mi S of Sacramento; 7 mi S of Stockton, CA; 1 mi E off Hwy 5 and 2 mi W off Hwy 99; Stockton Airport 5 mi N; Modesto Airport 35 mi S from Depot. *County:* San Joaquin.

MAJOR UNITS: Defense Distribution Depot, San Joaquin; Medical Equipment Maintenance Division; Army Medical Material Agency; 6th Army Veterinary Food Inspection Det, Tracy Branch.

BASE HISTORY: 1942, Lathrop Holding & Reconsignment Point commissioned. 1943, site major wartime installation. 1948, renamed Sharpe General Depot for Maj Gen Henry Granville Sharpe, Commissioner & Army Quartermaster General, 1905-18. 1959, airstrip, hangar, & shop facilities built to support air maintenance support mission for Army aircraft. 1962, renamed Sharpe Army Depot; depot assigned to Army Supply & Maintenance Command; petroleum lab dedicated here. 1965, mission expanded to include maintenance of air delivery items & personnel parachutes for depot stocks. 1990, consolidation of distribution functions at Sharpe Army Depot, Naval Supply Center Oakland, & DLA's Defense Depot Tracy. 1991, distribution functions at Sacramento Army Depot & Sacramento Air Logistics Center at McClellan

AFB joined DDRW. 1992, Naval Supply Centers in Puget Sound, WA, San Diego, CA, & Marine Corps Logistics Base, Barstow, CA, added. 1993, Defense Depot Ogden, Hill AFB, Tooele Army Depot, Oklahoma City Air Logistics Center (Tinker AFB), San Antonio Air Logistics Center (Kelly AFB), Corpus Christi Army Depot, & Red River Army Depot, Texarkana, TX, added to DDRW. Sharpe & Tracy locations primary hub for receiving, issuing, & storage. Defense Distribution Depot San Joaquin consists of former Sharpe Army Depot, Defense Depot Tracy, & storage facilities on Rough & Ready Island, near Stockton.

VISITOR ATTRACTIONS: Display (clothing, food, night vision goggles, circuit boards) from each of consolidated family of DDRW (Lobby, Bldg 330).

Key Contacts

COMMANDER: Mike Casey, 209-982-2001, DSN 462-2001.

PUBLIC AFFAIRS: Douglas J Imberi, 209-982-2837, 982-2838.

PROCUREMENT: Kathie Weatherford, 209-982-2401, DSN 462-2401.

TRANSPORTATION: Capt Steigleman, 209-832-9001, DSN 462-9001.

PERSONNEL/COMMUNITY ACTIVITIES: Alan Brewer, Director of Personnel, 209-982-2215, DSN 462-2215.

Personnel and Expenditures

ACTIVE DUTY PERSONNEL: 20

DEPENDENTS: 66

CIVILIAN PERSONNEL: 1100

Services

Housing: Family units 30; Unaccompanied enlisted quarters 6; Barracks spaces 100; Trailer spaces; RV/Camper sites 12. *Temporary Housing:* Apartment units; Barracks spaces 100. *Exchange:* Retail store; Military clothing store; Convenience store; Credit union. *Child Care/Capacities:* Day care center. *Schools:* No on-base schools. *Base Library:* Yes. *Medical Facilities:* Industrial clinic. *Recreational Facilities:* Pool; Gym; Recreation center; Racquetball court; Fitness center/Weight room; Softball field; NCO club; Youth center; Playground.

135. Stockton Naval Communications Station

NAVCOMMSTA Stockton

305 W. Fyffe St.

Stockton, CA 95203-5000

209-944-0494, DSN 466-7494

OFFICER-OF-THE-DAY: 209-944-0494, DSN 466-7494

Profile

BRANCH: Navy.

SIZE AND LOCATION: 1433 acres. On Rough & Ready Island approx 10 mi from downtown Stockton; approx 3 mi from I-5; 2 mi from Hwy 4; 10 mi from Stockton Airport. *County:* San Joaquin.

MAJOR UNITS: Naval Communications Station; General Services Administration; Armed Forces Reserve Center.

BASE HISTORY: 1943, Navy acquired Rough & Ready Island; owns all except for two 13-acre parcels owned by Shell & Mobil. WWII, site developed into major supply annex. Currently, major communications station for eastern Pacific Fleet.

Key Contacts
COMMANDER: CDR M V Steadley, 209-944-0225, DSN 466-7225, DSN FAX 466-7301.
PUBLIC AFFAIRS: YNC I M Estevez, 209-944-0513, DSN 466-7513, DSN FAX 466-7512.
Personnel and Expenditures
ACTIVE DUTY PERSONNEL: 40
DEPENDENTS: 40
CIVILIAN PERSONNEL: 315
Services
Housing: Family units 43; Unaccompanied enlisted quarters 3. *Commissary:* Yes; *Exchange:* Retail store; Barber shop; Food shop; Service station; Convenience store; Credit union. *Child Care/Capacities:* No day care facilities. *Schools:* No on-base schools. *Medical Facilities:* No medical facilities. *Recreational Facilities:* Pool; Gym; Golf course; Tennis courts; Racquetball court; Fitness center/Weight room; Softball field; Camping; Picnic area; Fishing.

Sunnyvale

136. Onizuka Air Station
1080 Lockheed-Martin Way
Sunnyvale, CA 94089
Mailing Address
1080 Lockheed-Martin Way, Box 053
Sunnyvale, CA 94089-1236
408-752-4027; FAX 408-752-4024; DSN 561-4027; DSN FAX 561-4024
Internet: http://oafb.af.mil
OFFICER-OF-THE-DAY: 408-752-3840, DSN 561-3841
Profile
BRANCH: Air Force; Air Force Reserve; Naval Reserve.
SIZE AND LOCATION: 23 acres. Adj to intersection of CA 237 & US-101; 8 mi N of San Jose; 40 mi S of San Francisco; 0.5 mi from Moffett Federal Airfield. *County:* Santa Clara.
MAJOR UNITS: 750th Space Group; 750th Logistic Support Squadron; 750th Mission Support Squadron; 21st Space Operations Squadron; 5th Space Operations Squadron; 750th Medical Squadron; 750th Communications Squadron.
BASE HISTORY: 1960, established as Satellite Test Annex in SW corner of Lockheed complex. 1971, renamed Sunnyvale AFS. 1987, renamed Onizuka AFB for LTC Ellison S Onizuka who died aboard space shuttle *Challenger*. Today, one of the centers for US military satellite operations. Monitors & controls on-orbit military spacecraft. Operates & maintains worldwide network of 9 satellite tracking & command stations.
FUTURE CLOSURE/REALIGNMENT: Deactivation of 750th Space group scheduled for Sep 2000.
Key Contacts
COMMANDER: Col James E Dill, Box 041, 408-752-3234, DSN 561-3234, DSN FAX 561-6082.
PUBLIC AFFAIRS: Arthur C Haubold, 408-752-4026, DSN 561-4026, DSN FAX 561-4024, Haubolac@gemini.oafb.af.mil.
TRANSPORTATION: 408-752-4641, DSN 561-4641, DSN FAX 561-4679.

Personnel and Expenditures
ACTIVE DUTY PERSONNEL: 600
DEPENDENTS: 1400
CIVILIAN PERSONNEL: 2300
MILITARY PAYROLL EXPENDITURE: $41.2 mil
CONTRACT EXPENDITURE: $52.5 mil
Services
Housing: Unaccompanied enlisted quarters 96; Dormitory spaces 164; Senior NCO units 75; Junior NCO units 525. *Temporary Housing:* VIP units 5; VOQ units 44; VEQ units 28. *Commissary:* Yes; *Exchange:* Barber shop; Dry cleaners; Service station; Military clothing store; Credit union; ATM; Post office; Class VI; Garden center; Tailor/Alterations. *Child Care/Capacities:* Day care center capacity 170, 6wks-5yrs; Latch key program; Summer day camp; Before & after school programs; Family day care. *Schools:* No on-base schools. *Medical Facilities:* Medical clinic; Dental clinic. *Recreational Facilities:* Pool; Gym; Recreation center; Golf course; Tennis courts; Racquetball court; Fitness center/Weight room; Softball field; Youth center; Playground.

Travis AFB

137. Travis Air Force Base
TAFB
Travis
60 AMW
Travis AFB, CA 94535-2127
707-424-1110; FAX 707-424-5936; DSN 837-1110
Internet: http://www.travis.af.mil
Profile
BRANCH: Air Force; Air Force Reserve.
SIZE AND LOCATION: 6277 acres. 50 mi NE of San Francisco; within corporate limits of Fairfield; off I-80, Airbase Pky turnoff leading directly to main gate; served by San Francisco & Oakland IAPs. *County:* Solano.
MAJOR UNITS: 15th Air Force, HQ; 60th Air Mobility Wing; 349th Air Mobility Wing.
BASE HISTORY: 1943, established as Fairfield-Suisun Army Air Base assigned to Air Transport Command. 1949, Strategic Air Command host unit. 1950, renamed for Brig Gen Robert F Travis, killed in B-29 crash. 1950s reorganizations, SAC replaced by 150th Air Transport Wing (MATS, later MAC). 1966, 60th Military Airlift Wing activated here. Vietnam War, primary aerial port on west coast; also participated in return of POWs, war children (Operation Babylift), & SE Asian refugees (Operation New Life). Since 1960s, supported resupply of research teams in Antarctic (Operation Deep Freeze). 1980s, supported space program. 1990, major participation in Operations Desert Shield/Storm. 1992, MAC becomes Air Mobility Command (AMC) & 60th MAW redesignated 60th Airlift Wing.
VISITOR ATTRACTIONS: Air Force Museum; Parks.
Key Contacts
COMMANDER: Brig Gen George N Williams, 400 Brennon Circle, 707-424-2452, DSN 837-2452, DSN FAX 837-1078.
PUBLIC AFFAIRS: Lt Craig A Heighton, 60th AMW/PA, 540 Airlift Dr, Travis AFB, CA 94535-2127 St, 94535-2406, 707-424-2011,

DSN 837-2011, DSN FAX 837-5936, cheighton@bcmsc04.travis.af.mil.
Personnel and Expenditures
ACTIVE DUTY PERSONNEL: 8482, 4371 reservists
DEPENDENTS: 9040
CIVILIAN PERSONNEL: 2890
MILITARY PAYROLL EXPENDITURE: $545.5 mil
CONTRACT EXPENDITURE: $197.3 mil
Services
Housing: Family units 2467; Unaccompanied enlisted quarters; BAQ units; Duplex units; Townhouse units; Dormitory spaces; Senior NCO units; Junior NCO units; Trailer spaces; RV/Camper sites. *Temporary Housing:* BAQ units; Lodge units; Dormitory units; Mobile home units; Transient quarters. *Commissary:* Yes; *Exchange:* Retail store; Barber shop; Dry cleaners; Food shop; Florist; Bank; Service station; Furniture store; Bakery; Bookstore; Military clothing store; Convenience store; Beauty shop; Laundromat; Credit union; ATM; Optical store; Post office; Fast food; Video rentals; Travel agency; Class VI; Shoe repair; Computer store; Garden center; Tailor/Alterations; Laundry; Cafeteria; Photo store. *Child Care/Capacities:* Day care center; Home day care program; Summer day camp; Before & after school programs. *Schools:* Elementary; Intermediate/Junior high; High school; College/University; College courses. *Base Library:* Yes. *Medical Facilities:* Hospital 350; Medical clinic; Dental clinic; Dispensary; Pharmacy; Veterinary services. *Recreational Facilities:* Bowling center; Movie theater; Pool; Gym; Recreation center; Golf course; Stables; Tennis courts; Racquetball court; Fitness center/Weight room; Softball field; Football field; Auto shop; Craft shop; Officers club; NCO club; Camping; Fishing/Hunting; Enlisted club; Youth center; Picnic area; Skeet range; Water sports; Playground; All ranks club; Consolidated club; Rod & Gun club; Aero club; Equipment loan center.

Tustin

138. Tustin Marine Corps Air Station
MCAS Tustin
Tustin, CA 92710-5001
714-726-2100; DSN 997-3011
OFFICER-OF-THE-DAY: 714-726-7501, DSN 997-7501
Profile
BRANCH: Marine Corps.
SIZE AND LOCATION: 1558 acres. In coastal alluvial plain area, elevation 54 ft. Santa Ana Mts approx 17 mi N-NW; San Joaquin Hills 5 mi to SE; approx 7 mi NW of El Toro MCAS; 50 mi S of Los Angeles, off I-5 at Red Hill exit. *County:* Orange.
MAJOR UNITS: Marine Aircraft Group 16 (MAG-16).
BASE HISTORY: 1942, commissioned as Naval Lighter-than-Air-Base for helium-filled airships conducting anti-submarine patrols off CA coast. Two hangars still world's largest freestanding structures; served as blimp base until decommissioned, 1949. 1951, air station reactivated, as Marine Corps Air Facility Santa Ana, country's first activity devoted to helicopter operations. 1969, renamed Marine

Corps Air Station (Helicopter) Santa Ana. 1978, annexation by city of Tustin; redesigned MCAS(H) Tustin. 1985, renamed MCAS Tustin; under jurisdiction of Commander, Marine Corps Air Bases Western Area, MCAS El Toro. Station major training site for Marine transport helicopter aircrews destined for duty in Western Pacific. FUTURE CLOSURE/REALIGNMENT: To close by Jul 1999.

Key Contacts
PROCUREMENT: 714-726-3855, DSN 997-7501.
TRANSPORTATION: 714-726-3952, DSN 997-3952.
PERSONNEL/COMMUNITY ACTIVITIES: Community Plans and Liaison, 714-726-3703, DSN 997-3703.

Personnel and Expenditures
ACTIVE DUTY PERSONNEL: 2350; Reserve 20
DEPENDENTS: 3765
CIVILIAN PERSONNEL: 150

Services
Housing: Family units 1500; Unaccompanied officer quarters 15; Unaccompanied enlisted quarters 950; Senior NCO units 30. *Temporary Housing:* VIP units 1. *Exchange:* Retail store; Barber shop; Dry cleaners; Food shop; Florist; Bank; Service station; Bookstore. *Child Care/Capacities:* Day care center capacity 25. *Schools:* No on-base schools. *Base Library:* Yes. *Medical Facilities:* Medical clinic; Dental clinic. *Recreational Facilities:* Bowling center; Pool; Fitness center/Weight room; Softball field; Football field; Auto shop; Officers club; NCO club.

Twentynine Palms

139. Twentynine Palms Marine Corps Air Ground Combat Center
MCAGCC
Box 788100, Bldg 1551
Twentynine Palms, CA 92278-8100
760-830-6000; DSN 957-6000

Profile
BRANCH: Marine Corps.
SIZE AND LOCATION: 596,480 acres. Southern tip of Mojave Desert, 60 mi NE of Palm Springs; 150 mi E of Los Angeles. E on I-10, exit on State Hwy 62, continue for approx 50 mi; W on I-40, exit at Amboy Rd to Twentynine Palms (Note: no service stations between Amboy Rd & Twentynine Palms). Bus service available from San Diego & Palm Springs. *County:* San Bernardino.
MAJOR UNITS: Marine Corps Air Ground Combat Center; 7th Marine Regiment (Reinforced); Marine Corps Communication-Electronics School; Combat Service Support Group 1; Aviation Ground Support Element; Marine Unmanned Aerial Vehicle Squadron 1; HQ Bn, Twentynine Palms; 3rd Bn, 4th Marine Division.
BASE HISTORY: 1940, Army used area for training glider crews. 1943, training fighter pilots; Navy for bombing & gunnery ranges until end of WWII. 1945, inactive. 1952, designated HQ, Marine Corps Training Center, Twentynine Palms. 1957, commissioned Marine Corps Base. 1979, became Marine Corps Air Ground Combat Center. 1980, Combined Arms Command activated, command HQ for

Fleet Marine Force, Pacific units garrisoned here; home HQ Nucleus of 7th Marine Amphibious Brigade, Near Term Prepositioning Ships Program. 1981, 27th Marine Regiment HQ Nucleus reactivated as Ground Combat Element of 7th Marine Amphibious Brigade. Exercise Support Base, formerly Camp Wilson, added major improvements for units participating in combined arms training exercises.

Key Contacts
COMMANDER: Maj Gen R G Richard, 760-830-7070.
PUBLIC AFFAIRS: Capt Yates, 760-830-5471.

Personnel and Expenditures
ACTIVE DUTY PERSONNEL: 9895
DEPENDENTS: 6500
CIVILIAN PERSONNEL: 1500

Services
Housing: Family units 2300; Mobile home units 75; Highrise (hotel-style barracks) 12; Unaccompanied officer suites 31. *Temporary Housing:* VIP units 6; VOQ units 51; VEQ units 38; Guesthouse units; Temporary lodging facility 24 units. *Commissary:* Yes; *Exchange:* Retail store; Barber shop; Dry cleaners; Food shop; Florist; Bank; Service station; Furniture store; Bakery; Bookstore; Class VI. *Child Care/Capacities:* Day care center capacity 336; Home day care program. *Schools:* No on-base schools. *Base Library:* Yes. *Medical Facilities:* Hospital 40 beds; Dental clinic. *Recreational Facilities:* Bowling center; Movie theater; Pool; Gym; Recreation center; Golf course; Stables; Tennis courts; Racquetball court; Fitness center/Weight room; Softball field; Football field; Auto shop; Craft shop; Officers club; NCO club; Youth center; Skeet range; Basketball courts; Volleyball courts; Miniature golf; Motocross.

Van Nuys

140. Sepulveda Air National Guard Station
SANGS
261CBCS
15900 Victory Blvd
Van Nuys, CA 91406-6499
818-909-2300; FAX 818-909-2312; DSN 893-7300; FAX DSN 893-7300, ext 312
E-mail: 261CCS@cantd.af.mil

Profile
BRANCH: Air National Guard.
SIZE AND LOCATION: 62 acres. Off I-405, W of intersection with Roscoe Blvd; approx 25 mi N of Los Angeles IAP; take I-405 S, exit at Victory Blvd. *County:* Los Angeles.
MAJOR UNITS: 261st CBCS.

Key Contacts
COMMANDER: LTC L Denise Yogt, 818-909-2311, FAX 818-909-2312, DSN 893-7300, ext 311, dvogt@cantd.af.mil.
PUBLIC AFFAIRS: LTC Ritz, 805-986-7495, DSN 893-7495.

Personnel and Expenditures
ACTIVE DUTY PERSONNEL: 6, reserve/guard 120
CIVILIAN PERSONNEL: 20

Vandenberg AFB

141. Vandenberg Air Force Base
VAFB
747 Nebraska Ave
Vandenberg AFB, CA 93437-6228
805-734-8232 (extension last five digits of DSN number); DSN 276-3595
E-mail: vafb3.vafb.af.mil Internet:http://www.30.vafb.af.mil/index.htm

Profile
BRANCH: Air Force.
SIZE AND LOCATION: 98,500 acres. 55 mi N of Santa Barbara on central coast of CA. From N, Hwy 101 to Betteravia Exit in Santa Maria, left off Broadway (CA State Hwy in Orcutt), approx 6 mi to Lomoc/Vandenberg Exit, 12 mi to main gate. From S, Hwy 101 to Hwy 246 Exit in Buellton (Buellton Lompoc Rd), approx 20 mi, exit at State Rte 1, exit for Vandenberg AFB, main gate approx 10 mi. *County:* Santa Barbara.
MAJOR UNITS: 30th Space Wing; 381st Training Group; 14th Air Force.
BASE HISTORY: 1941, built as training center for rapid development of armored forces in Burton Mesa area; designated Camp Cooke for Maj Gen Phillip St George Cooke, pioneer cavalry officer. WWII, armored and infantry divisions trained here. 1944, POW camp established; German & Italian prisoners; 16 branch POW camps; maximum security Army Disciplinary Barracks (now US Penitentiary, Lompoc) constructed. 1946, camp deactivated. 1950, reactivated. 1953, inactivated again; disciplinary barracks transferred to US Bureau of Prisons for civilian use. 1955, reactivated. Mid-1957, Air Force took control of northern two-thirds of site for nation's first combat-ready missile base. 1958, Cooke AFB became Vandenberg AFB, for Gen Hoyt S Vandenberg, second Air Force Chief of Staff, early advocate of aerospace preparedness. 1958, first launch; southern portion of former camp transferred to Navy for Naval Missile Facility, Point Arguello. 1964, area transferred back to AF. 1966, acquisition of additional 15,000 acres (Sudden Ranch). Since then, more than 1700 launches of Atlas, Titan, Minuteman, and Peacekeeper missiles have been conducted. Only military installation in US from which unmanned government & commercial satellites launched.
VISITOR ATTRACTIONS: Space & Missile Museum (SLC-10) National Historic Landmark (1987); Areas of interest close-by: Hearst Castle; Little Denmark (Solvang); Los Padres National Forest; La Purisma Mission; Lake Cachuma; Mequelito Park; Jamala Beach; Ocean Beach; Najoqui Falls; Gaviota Beach.

Key Contacts
COMMANDER: Col C Robert Kehler, DSN 276-2000, DSN FAX 276-4979, Kehler@vafb3.vafb.af.mil.
PUBLIC AFFAIRS: Maj Brad Peck, 805-734-8232 ext 63595; DSN 276-3595, DSN FAX 276-8303, peck@vafb3.vafb.af.mil.
PERSONNEL/COMMUNITY ACTIVITIES: Laureen Freeman, DSN 276-3595, DSN FAX 276-8303, FreemanL@vafb3.vafb.af.mil.

Personnel and Expenditures
ACTIVE DUTY PERSONNEL: 3765

DEPENDENTS: 4783
CIVILIAN PERSONNEL: 4759
MILITARY PAYROLL EXPENDITURE: $66.8 mil
CONTRACT EXPENDITURE: $0.4 mil (excluding construction)

Services

Housing: Family units 1740; Dormitory spaces 1032; Senior NCO units 137; Junior NCO units 1118; Trailer spaces 172. *Temporary Housing:* VIP units 2. *Commissary:* Yes; *Exchange:* Retail store; Barber shop; Dry cleaners; Food shop; Florist; Bank; Service station; Furniture store; Military clothing store; Convenience store; Beauty shop; Laundromat; Credit union; ATM; Optical store; Post office; Fast food; Video rentals; Four seasons; Travel agency; Class VI; Shoe repair; Garden center; Tailor/Alterations; Laundry. *Child Care/Capacities:* Day care center all, 6 mo-up; Before & after school programs. *Schools:* Preschool/Kindergarten; Elementary; Intermediate/Junior high; High school; College courses. *Base Library:* Yes.

Medical Facilities: Hospital 20; Medical clinic; Dental clinic; Pharmacy; Veterinary services. *Recreational Facilities:* Bowling center; Movie theater; Pool; Gym; Recreation center; Golf course; Stables; Tennis courts; Racquetball court; Fitness center/Weight room; Softball field; Football field; Auto shop; Craft shop; Camping; Fishing/Hunting; Enlisted club; Youth center; Picnic area; Skeet range; Water sports; Playground; Community club; Consolidated club.

Colorado

Aurora

142. Buckley Air National Guard Base
18500 E Sixth Ave
Aurora, CO 80011-9599
303-340-9555; DSN 877-9011

Profile
BRANCH: Air National Guard; Joint Service Installation.
SIZE AND LOCATION: 3835 acres. 8 mi E of Denver on E-central edge of Aurora; 2.5 mi E of intersection of I-225 and Hwy 6 (Sixth Ave). *County:* Arapahoe.
MAJOR UNITS: 140th Wing (ANG); Colorado ANG, HQ; Army Aviation Support Facility (ARNG); Marine Reserve Units; Naval Reserve Readiness Center; 227th Air Traffic Control Flight (ANG); 240th Civil Engineering Flight (ANG).
BASE HISTORY: 1942, activated for Army Air Corps Technical School; named Buckley Field for 1st Lt John H Buckley, WWI pilot killed in Meuse-Argonne Offensive; former CO Guardsman. 1946, transferred from Army to CO ANG. 1947, transferred to Navy. 1959, decommissioned as NAS. 1960, CO ANG assumed command. 1968, 120th Tactical Fighter Squadron assigned; first ANG unit sent to combat since WWII. Provides combat readiness training of tactical units of CO ANG; area's only military flying base, charged with aircraft search & rescue activities. One of three ANG bases solely owned & operated by National Guard.

Personnel and Expenditures
ACTIVE DUTY PERSONNEL: 1165 Guard
CIVILIAN PERSONNEL: 485
MILITARY PAYROLL EXPENDITURE: $42.1 mil

Services *Exchange:* Barber shop; Credit union. *Medical Facilities:* Medical clinic. *Recreational Facilities:* Softball field; Skeet range; All ranks club; Flying club.

143. Denver Naval Reserve Readiness Center
PO Box 111802
Aurora, CO 80042-1802
303-340-6203; FAX 303-340-6215

Profile
BRANCH: Naval Reserve.
LOCATION: *County:* Adams; Arapahoe.
MAJOR UNITS: Naval Reserve Center, Denver.

Key Contacts
COMMANDER: Capt J Denardo.

144. Fitzsimons Army Medical Center
FAMC
Aurora, CO 80045-5001
303-361-8241; FAX 303-361-3333; DSN 943-8241

Profile
BRANCH: Army.
SIZE AND LOCATION: 577 acres. In city of Aurora off I-225; approx 7 mi E of downtown Denver. *County:* Arapahoe.
MAJOR UNITS: Fitzsimons Army Medical Center; Army Medical Equipment & Optical School; Civilian Health & Medical Program for Uniformed Services, HQ (CHAMPUS).
BASE HISTORY: 1918, ground broken. 1920, named after 1st Lt William Thomas Fitzsimons, doctor & first American officer killed in action in WWI.
FUTURE CLOSURE/REALIGNMENT: Scheduled to close, Sept 1999.

Key Contacts
COMMANDER: Col John M Bull, 303-361-8311.
PUBLIC AFFAIRS: Helen W Littlejohn, 303-361-3192, DSN 943-3192.

Personnel and Expenditures
ACTIVE DUTY PERSONNEL: 1723
DEPENDENTS: 2000
CIVILIAN PERSONNEL: 2019

Services
Housing: Family units 181; Unaccompanied officer quarters 35; Unaccompanied enlisted quarters 40. *Temporary Housing:* VIP units 10; Guesthouse units 35. *Commissary:* Yes; *Exchange:* Retail store; Barber shop; Dry cleaners; Food shop; Florist; Service station; Military clothing store; Convenience store; Beauty shop; Credit union. *Child Care/Capacities:* Day care center capacity 200; Home day care program. *Medical Facilities:* Hospital 504 beds; Medical clinic; Dental clinic; Dispensary; Pharmacy; Veterinary services. *Recreational Facilities:* Bowling center; Pool; Gym; Recreation center; Golf course; Tennis courts; Racquetball court; Fitness center/Weight room; Softball field; Auto shop; Craft shop; Officers club; NCO club; Youth center.

Colorado Springs

145. Cheyenne Mountain Air Force Station
1 NORAD Rd, Ste 5304
Colorado Springs, CO 80914-6064
719-474-4010

Profile
BRANCH: Air Force Reserve.
SIZE AND LOCATION: 4.5 acres (interior chambers). Approx 6 mi from city of Colorado Springs. From Denver, I-25S to Exit 148B (Colorado Springs), right on Nevada Ave, 5 mi to Hwy 115, CMAFB Exit (1,000 ft paved road climb leading to underground complex; 7,200 ft above sea level). *County:* El Paso.
MAJOR UNITS: US Space Command; 721st Support Group; Air Force Space Command; North American Aerospace Defense Command (NORAD); Air Weather Service, Military Airlift Command; Federal Emergency Management Agency; Missile Warning Center; Space Defense Operations Center; Space Surveillance Center; Air Defense Operations Center; Civil Defense National Warning Center.
BASE HISTORY: 1961, original construction of Cheyenne Mountain AFB. 1966, first opened. Cheyenne Mountain AFB & Cheyenne Mountain Complex tightly secured, special access only, military installations just outside & inside hollowed mountainside of CO Rocky Mountains. Inside 15 steel buildings which function 24 hours a day. Parking for 600 vehicles outside. Operational centers keep watch on aircraft, missiles, & space systems that might pose threat to US & Canada. Jointly operated with Canada. 1996, changed from AFB to Station.
VISITOR ATTRACTIONS: Tour Programs for public, classified & distinguished visitors.

Key Contacts
COMMANDER: Maj Gen Jeffrey Grime, 719-474-3429.
PUBLIC AFFAIRS: Maj Colleen Ryan, 719-474-2242; Peter Locke, 719-474-3592.
PROCUREMENT: Contracting through Peterson AFB.

Services *Temporary Housing:* All facilities at Peterson AFB. *Exchange:* Retail store; Barber shop. *Child Care/Capacities:* No day care facilities. *Schools:* No on-base schools.

Medical Facilities: Medical clinic; Dental clinic; Dispensary. *Recreational Facilities:* Gym; Racquetball court; Fitness center/Weight room; Softball field; Dining facility, Granite Inn.

146. US Air Force Academy
USAFA
Colorado Springs, CO 80840-5151
719-472-1818; DSN 259-3110
Internet: http://www.usafa.af.mil or http://mustang.usafa.af.mil/
OFFICER-OF-THE-DAY: 34th TRW Operations Center, 719-333-2910, DSN 333-2910
Profile
BRANCH: Air Force.
SIZE AND LOCATION: 18,500 acres. W of I-25, just N of Colorado Springs; two gates, about 5 mi apart, access from I-25, clearly marked. *County:* El Paso.
MAJOR UNITS: Air Force Academy, HQ; Dean of the Faculty; 34th Training Wing (Cadet Wing); 10th Air Base Wing; 557th Flying Training Squadron; DOD Medical Exam Review Board.
BASE HISTORY: 1948, board of civilian & military educators planned curriculum for USAF Academy. 1954, Congress authorized USAF Academy creation. 1955, first class entered, temporary facilities, Lowry AFB, Denver. 1958, cadet wing moved into permanent home. 1959, Commission of Colleges & Universities of North Central Association of Colleges and Secondary Schools accredited academy's degree program; first graduating class of 206. 1964, expanded from 2529 to 4417 cadets. 1976, women entered academy.
VISITOR ATTRACTIONS: Barry Goldwater USAF Academy Visitor Center (open every day, 9am-5pm in winter, 9am-6pm Memorial Day through Labor Day); self-guided tour available (recording 719-333-8723); nature trail; American Legion Memorial Tower; Cadet Chapel (open M-Sat 9am-5pm, Sun 1pm-5pm, closed occasionally for private services; service times 719-333-4515); Special events: Noon Formation, Cadet Parades, Graduation, Sporting events, & Center for Educational Multimedia (schedule 719-333-2778).
Key Contacts
COMMANDER: Lt Gen Tad J Oelstrom, Superintendent, 719-333-4140, DSN 333-4140; Brig Gen Stephen R. Lorenz, Commandant of Cadets.
PUBLIC AFFAIRS: LTC Douglas D McCoy Jr, Director of Public Affairs, HQ USAFA/PA, 2304 Cadet Dr, Ste 320, USAF Academy, CO 80840-5016, 719-333-2990, DSN 333-2990.
PROCUREMENT: HQ USAFA/LGC, 8110 Industrial Dr, Ste 200, USAFA, CO 80840-2315.
TRANSPORTATION: Col Frederick L Williams, Dir of Personnel, HQ USAFA/LGT, 719-333-3504, DSN 333-3504.
PERSONNEL/COMMUNITY ACTIVITIES: 10th Services Squadron, 719-333-4801, DSN 333-4801.
Personnel and Expenditures
ACTIVE DUTY PERSONNEL: 2560, plus 4043 cadets
DEPENDENTS: 4260
CIVILIAN PERSONNEL: 2045
Services
Housing: Family units 1229; Dormitory spaces 202. *Temporary Housing:* VIP units 10; VOQ units 78; Guesthouse units 26; Senior enlisted

suites 2; Rampart Lodge reservations 719-333-4910, DSN 333-4910. *Commissary:* Yes; *Exchange:* Retail store; Barber shop; Dry cleaners; Florist; Bank; Service station; Credit union. *Child Care/Capacities:* Day care center capacity 144; Home day care program. *Schools:* Pre-school/Kindergarten; Elementary; High school. *Base Library:* Yes. *Medical Facilities:* Hospital 55; Medical clinic; Dental clinic. *Recreational Facilities:* Bowling center; Pool; Gym; Recreation center; Golf course; Stables; Tennis courts; Racquetball court; Fitness center/Weight room; Softball field; Football field; Auto shop; Craft shop; Officers club; Camping FAMCAMP; Fishing/Hunting; Enlisted club; Youth center; Aero club; Farish Recreation Area; Outdoor recreation center; Outdoor adventure program; Ski shop; Sporting events 800-666-8723.

Commerce City

147. Rocky Mountain Arsenal
RMA
Arsenal
72nd Ave & Quebec St
Commerce City, CO 80022-1748
303-289-0136; FAX 303-289-0582; DSN 749-2136
Internet: http://www.pmrma_http://www.army.mil
Profile
BRANCH: Army.
SIZE AND LOCATION: 17,000 acres. In Commerce City; 2 mi W of Denver IAP; 10 mi NE of downtown Denver. *County:* Adams.
MAJOR UNITS: Rocky Mountain Arsenal; Fish & Wildlife Service.
BASE HISTORY: 1942, land purchased for production of chemical weapons and munitions during WWII. 1945-50, site used for reconditioning and demilitarization of mustard shells. Korean War, production of white phosphorous-filled munitions and incendiary cluster bombs. 1953-57, production of GB nerve gas here. Late 1950s-mid1960s, demilitarization programs. 1970, disposal of chemical warfare material here. Current mission, contamination cleanup.
FUTURE CLOSURE/REALIGNMENT: BRAC 92, RMA will become National Wildlife Refuge upon completion of remediation.
VISITOR ATTRACTIONS: Visitor's Center; Eagle Watch (winter months); Rattlesnake Hill
Key Contacts
COMMANDER: Col Eugene H Bishop, Program Manager.
PUBLIC AFFAIRS: Ruth Mecham, Relations Manager, rmecham@pmrma-emh1.army.mil.
Personnel and Expenditures
ACTIVE DUTY PERSONNEL: 3
DEPENDENTS: 0
CIVILIAN PERSONNEL: 140
MILITARY PAYROLL EXPENDITURE: $100,000
CONTRACT EXPENDITURE: $43 mil
Services
Housing: None. *Base Library:* Yes. *Medical Facilities:* Medical clinic.

Denver

148. Air Force Reserve Command Personnel Center
Denver, CO 80280-5000
303-370-4631
Profile
BRANCH: Air Force.
SIZE: Offices only. *County:* Denver.
MAJOR UNITS: Personnel Center (AFRES).
BASE HISTORY: 1953, established as Detachment 1, HQ Continental Air Command, to centralize custody & maintenance of master personnel records of AFRES members not on extended active duty. 1954, detachment began operations, responsible for wide variety of personnel actions, including administrative capability for mobilization of AFRES. 1957, became HQ Air Reserve Records Center, within Continental Air Command. 1965, renamed Air Reserve Personnel Center. 1968, ARPC designated separate operating agency. 1971, personnel records of ANG officers added. 1978, airmen records added. 1978, status changed to currently named unit & organizational element of AFRES. 1983, separate operating agency status reestablished. Remains in operation at current location after Lowry AFB closed Sep 1994.
Key Contacts
PUBLIC AFFAIRS: Capt Robin Grantham, Media Rep, 912-327-1761; Office of PA, 155 2nd St, Robins AFB, GA 31098-1635, 912-327-1750, DSN 497-1750.

149. Defense Finance and Accounting Service, Denver Center
DFAS-DE
6760 E Irvington Place
Denver, CO 80279
303-676-7741; FAX 303-676-6194; DSN 926-7741
Internet: http://www.dfas.mil
Profile
BRANCH: DOD.
SIZE AND LOCATION: Offices only. In Bldg 444, on SW corner of former Lowry AFB. *County:* Denver.
MAJOR UNITS: Defense Finance and Accounting Service, Denver Center.
BASE HISTORY: 1951, site of former Army Medical Depot; designated Air Force Finance Center. 1957, accounting & finance functions merged; name changed to Air Force Accounting and Finance Center (AFAFC). 1976, moved to Lowry AFB, into Gilchrist Building, named in honor of Center's first commander. 1991, consolidated into DFAS. Maintains pays systems for Air Force & Army active duty, Guard & Reserve, Navy Midshipmen & ROTC. Largest single pay system. Also responsible for pay of Army, Navy, Air Force, Marine Corps annuitants, & 295,000 DOD civilians.
Key Contacts
COMMANDER: John S Nabil, Director, 303-676-7461, DSN 926-7461.
PUBLIC AFFAIRS: Linda R Winkler, 303-676-7741.
PROCUREMENT: Thomas Carrol, Director of Support Services, 303-676-7545, DSN 926-7545.

PERSONNEL/COMMUNITY ACTIVITIES:
James B Hohman, Jr, Director of Human
Resources, 303-676-6472, DSN 926-6472.
Personnel and Expenditures
ACTIVE DUTY PERSONNEL: 137
CIVILIAN PERSONNEL: 1900
Services *Schools:* College courses. *Base Library:* Yes.

Englewood

150. Adjutant General of Colorado
6848 S Revere Pky
Englewood, CO 80112-6703
303-397-3023; FAX 303-397-3281
Profile
BRANCH: Army National Guard.
MAJOR UNITS: Colorado National Guard.
Key Contacts
COMMANDER: Brig Gen William A
Westerdahl.

Falcon AFB

151. Falcon Air Force Base
300 O'Malley Ave, Suite 24
Falcon AFB, CO 80912-3024
719-567-1110; DSN 560-1110
Internet: http://www.fafb.af.mil
Profile
BRANCH: Air Force.
SIZE AND LOCATION: 3840 acres. 15 mi E of
Colorado Springs off State Hwy 94. *County:*
El Paso.
MAJOR UNITS: 50th Space Wing; Joint National Test Facility; Space Warfare Center;
50th Operations Group; 50th Logistics
Group; 50th Support Group; 750th Space
Group; 7th Space Operations Squadron
(USAFR); Defense Support Program; Defense Satellite Communications System; Military Strategic and Tactical Relay (Milstar);
Fleet Satellite Communications System;
NATO III; Defense Meteorological Satellite
Program; NAVSTAR Global Positioning System.
BASE HISTORY: 1985, AFS (newest in Air
Force) activated as backup to Onizuka (CA)
AFB. 1987, 2nd Space Wing took operational
control of Air Force Satellite Control Network. 1988, redesignated Falcon AFB. 1992,
50th Space Wing activated here.
VISITOR ATTRACTIONS: Priority A, restricted facility. Visitors only by request for
specific reasons.
Key Contacts
COMMANDER: Col Elwood C Tircuit, Suite
20, 80912-3020, 719-550-5000, DSN
560-5000.
Personnel and Expenditures
ACTIVE DUTY PERSONNEL: 2340
DEPENDENTS: 3491
CIVILIAN PERSONNEL: 435; contractors 2000
Services
Housing: At Peterson AFB. *Temporary Housing:* None. *Exchange:* At Peterson AFB. *Child
Care/Capacities:* At Peterson AFB. *Base Library:* Yes. *Medical Facilities:* Dental clinic;
Medical Aid Station; other care at USAF Academy & Evans Army Community Hospital.

Recreational Facilities: Gym; Tennis courts;
Racquetball court; Fitness center/Weight room;
Softball field; Picnic area; Outdoor volleyball &
basketball courts; Par course.

Fort Carson

152. Fort Carson and 4th Infantry Division (Mechanized)
Ft Carson
ATTN: AFZC-GC
Fort Carson, CO 80913-5011
719-526-5811; DSN 691-5811
Internet: http://www.carson.army.mil; http://
www.hqda.army.mil/acsim/gcdirect/garrisns/
fortscars.htm
Profile
BRANCH: Army.
SIZE AND LOCATION: 137,391 acres. Bordering S side of Colorado Springs; approx 40 mi
from Pueblo; I-25, adj to Fort, runs N to Denver. *County:* El Paso.
MAJOR UNITS: 4th Infantry Division, 3rd Brigade (Mechanized); 43rd Area Support
Group; 3rd Armored Cavalry Regiment; 10th
Special Forces Group; Pinon Canyon Maneuver Site.
BASE HISTORY: 1942, Cheyenne Valley
Ranch purchased; donated to Federal government for camp named for Brig Gen Christopher "Kit" Carson, frontiersman; buildings
turned over to 89th Infantry Division; also
constructed Camp Hale, 20 mi W of Leadville, first US training post for mountain
troops. WWII, largest hospital center in US;
POW camp. 1954, made permanent Fort; air
operations based at Peterson Field until 1954,
when moved to Camp Hale. 1956, air operations relocated to Mesa Air Strip. 1957,
Mountain & Cold Weather Training Command transferred to Ft Greely, AK, & Camp
Hale training site for Carson ski teams. 1965,
Camp Hale declared surplus; traded for land
on Ft Carson's S border. 1966, present facility, Butts Field completed. 1970, initial test
site for modern Volunteer Army concept (VO-
LAR). 1983, Pinon Canyon Maneuver Site acquired (245,000 acres, about 100 air mi SE of
main Fort).
VISITOR ATTRACTIONS: Listed historic site.
Key Contacts
COMMANDER: Col Lawrence E Davis, Bldg
1430, 719-526-5600, FAX 719-526-5524,
DSN 691-5600, 4idgarrcdr@carson-emh1.
army.mil.
PERSONNEL/COMMUNITY ACTIVITIES:
Civilian Personnel Advisory Center, 6223
Prussman, 80913-5020, 719-526-4524, FAX
719-526-2962.
Personnel and Expenditures
ACTIVE DUTY PERSONNEL: 15,000
DEPENDENTS: 32,000
CIVILIAN PERSONNEL: 3300
Services
Housing: Family units 1828; Unaccompanied officer quarters 25; Unaccompanied enlisted quarters 6. *Temporary Housing:* VIP units 5; VOQ
units 155; VEQ units 105; Guesthouse units 1.
Commissary: Yes; *Exchange:* Retail store; Barber shop; Dry cleaners; Food shop; Florist;
Bank; Service station. *Child Care/Capacities:*
Day care center capacity 500; Home day care
program.

Schools: Elementary; Intermediate/Junior high.
Base Library: Yes. *Medical Facilities:* Hospital
195 beds; Medical clinic; Dental clinic. *Recreational Facilities:* Bowling center; Movie theater;
Pool; Gym; Recreation center; Golf course; Stables; Tennis courts; Racquetball court; Fitness
center/Weight room; Softball field; Football
field; Auto shop; Craft shop; Officers club; NCO
club; Fishing/Hunting.

153. Fort Carson Naval Reserve Center
Bldg 8932
Fort Carson, CO 80913-5040
719-526-2964; FAX 719-526-2965
Profile
BRANCH: Naval Reserve.
LOCATION: *County:* El Paso.
Key Contacts
COMMANDER: LCDR Greg A Smith (USNR).

Golden

154. Camp George West
15000 S Golden Rd
Golden, CO 80401-3953
303-273-1659
Profile
BRANCH: Army National Guard.
LOCATION: Near intersection of I-70 & Colfax
Ave. *County:* Jefferson.
MAJOR UNITS: Camp George West (ARNG);
1st Bn, 157th Field Artillery, B Battery;
193rd Military Police Bn; 220th Military Police Co.
BASE HISTORY: Also houses State Emergency
Operations Center & training facility Colorado State Patrol
Key Contacts
COMMANDER: Capt Richard Brence,
303-279-3529, FAX 303-273-9503.

La Junta

155. 99th Range Support Squadron, OL-B
99 RANSS OL-B
30800 1st Ave, Industrial Park
La Junta, CO 81050-9501
719-384-4419; FAX 719-556-7783; DSN
834-4123, 834-4126; DSN FAX 834-7783
Profile
BRANCH: Air Force.
SIZE AND LOCATION: 35 acres. Operations
facilities on E ramp of La Junta Municipal
Airport off Hwy 109, approx 9 mi N of La
Junta; 67 mi E of Pueblo. *County:* Otero.
MAJOR UNITS: 99th Range Support Squadron,
Operating Location-B (Nellis AFB, NV).
BASE HISTORY: Small SAC installation with
very limited facilities. 1960, moved from Denver. 1988-89, facilities upgraded. 1996, transferred to civilian contractor, Lockheed-Martin.
Key Contacts
COMMANDER: Mr. Roger Fate, Site Manager.
Personnel and Expenditures
CIVILIAN PERSONNEL: 3 civil service; 27
contractors

Peterson AFB

156. Peterson Air Force Base
775 Loring Ave, Ste 219
Peterson AFB, CO 80914-5000
719-556-7321; FAX 719-556-7848; DSN
834-7321; DSN FAX 834-7848
Internet: http://www.spacecom.af.mil
OFFICER-OF-THE-DAY: Command Post,
719-556-4555, FAX 719-556-8151, DSN
835-8555

Profile
BRANCH: Air Force.
SIZE AND LOCATION: 1278 acres. 5 mi E of
Colorado Springs and 60 mi S of Denver. Col-
located with Colorado Springs' Municipal
Airport. *County:* El Paso.
MAJOR UNITS: HQ Air Force Space Com-
mand; North American Aerospace Defense
Command; US Space Command; 21st Space
Wing; Army Space Command, HQ; 302nd
Airlift Wing (Reserve); Air Force Audit
Agency; Air Force Office of Special Investigations; 84th Airlift Flight (AMC).
BASE HISTORY: 1925, established as civil airport for Colorado Springs. 1941, large portion
of airport taken for Army air base. 1942,
named Peterson Field for 1st Lt Edward J Peterson, native of Englewood, CO, photo reconnaissance pilot killed in 1942. Post WWII,
city took control of site and dismantled barracks. 1948, flying facility for 15th Air Force
established at Ent AFB, Colorado Springs.
1949, Air Force portion of Peterson Field inactive status. 1951, Aerospace Defense Command reactivated Field. 1976, renamed Peterson AFB. 1979, transferred to SAC. 1983,
transferred to Air Force Space Command, 1st
Space Wing. 1986, 3rd Space Support Wing
host of Peterson Complex. 1992, 21st Space
Wing host. Peterson "Complex" includes military and civilian personnel at Peterson AFB,
Cheyenne Mountain AFB, and Falcon AFB.
VISITOR ATTRACTIONS: Peterson Air and
Space Museum (WWII & space exhibits)
open Tue-Fri, 8:30-4:30 and Sat 9:30-4:30.
Medal of Honor Grove.

Key Contacts
COMMANDER: Brig Gen Franklin Blaisdell,
775 Loring Ave, Ste 205, Peterson AFB, CO
80914, 719-556-2100, DSN 834-2100, DSN
FAX 834-2109.
PUBLIC AFFAIRS: Capt Robyn Chumley,
719-556-4696, FAX 719-556-7848, DSN
834-4696, 21swpa@spacecom.af.mil.
PROCUREMENT: 21st Logistics Group, 135 E
Ent Ave, Ste 103, 80914-1380,
719-556-7493, FAX 719-556-6242, DSN
834-7493.
TRANSPORTATION: Transportation Flight;
621 W Stewart Ave, 80914-2310,
719-556-4307, FAX 719-556-4717, DSN
834-4307.
PERSONNEL/COMMUNITY ACTIVITIES:
21st Services Squadron, 675 Suffolk St, Ste 6,
80914-1110, 719-556-4881, DSN 834-4881.

Personnel and Expenditures
ACTIVE DUTY PERSONNEL: 4295
DEPENDENTS: 6222
CIVILIAN PERSONNEL: 5478
MILITARY PAYROLL EXPENDITURE: $245 mil
CONTRACT EXPENDITURE: $189 mil

Services
Housing: Family units 491; Duplex units 12;
Townhouse units 362; Dormitory spaces 358;
Senior NCO units 70; Junior NCO units 314.
Temporary Housing: VIP units 4; VOQ units 66;
VEQ units 8; Unaccompanied officer/Enlisted
quarters 2; BAQ units 6; Dormitory units 40.
Commissary: Yes; *Exchange:* Retail store; Bar-
ber shop; Dry cleaners; Florist; Bank; Service
station; Furniture store; Bakery; Military cloth-
ing store; Convenience store; Beauty shop;
Credit union; ATM; Optical store; Post office;
Fast food; Video rentals; Thrift shop; Travel
agency; Class VI; Garden center; Photo store.
Child Care/Capacities: Day care center capacity
336, 6mo-5yrs; Before & after school programs.
Schools: College/University; College courses.
Base Library: Yes. *Medical Facilities:* Medical
clinic. *Recreational Facilities:* Bowling center;
Pool; Gym; Recreation center; Golf course; Tennis courts; Racquetball court; Fitness center/
Weight room; Softball field; Football field; Auto
shop; Craft shop; Officers club; NCO club; Fish-
ing/Hunting; Youth center; Skeet range; Playground; Rod & Gun club.

Pueblo

157. Pueblo Chemical Depot
Bldg 1, SCBPU-PA, 45825 Hwy 96 E
Pueblo, CO 81006-9330
719-549-4135; FAX 719-549-4866; DSN
749-4135

Profile
BRANCH: Army.
SIZE AND LOCATION: 23,121 acres. 14 mi E
of Pueblo, via US-50 near Pueblo Airport.
County: Pueblo.
BASE HISTORY: 1942, Pueblo Ordnance Depot began to receive, store and issue general
supplies to support WWII. 1946, mission of
maintaining and overhauling artillery, fire
control, and optical equipment. 1948, renovation and demilitarization of ammunition here.
1962, renamed Pueblo Army Depot. 1976,
given Depot Activity status and assigned to
Tooele Army Depot. 1988-91, responsible for
destroying Pershing missile rocket motors.
1996, renamed Pueblo Chemical Depot; no
longer under Tooele Army Depot. One of 8
CONUS sites storing chemical stockpile. Depot remains active as long as chemical stockpile is stored.
VISITOR ATTRACTIONS: "Hi-Pardner" Park
just outside main gate, antique munitions on
display.

Key Contacts
COMMANDER: LTC Patrick Fogleson,
SCBPU-CO, 719-549-4141, DSN 749-4141.
PUBLIC AFFAIRS: Marilyn M Thompson.

Personnel and Expenditures
ACTIVE DUTY PERSONNEL: 1
DEPENDENTS: 50
CIVILIAN PERSONNEL: 200

Services
Housing: Family units 15; Duplex units 2. *Tem-
porary Housing:* VIP units 1. *Medical Facilities:*
Medical clinic. *Recreational Facilities:* Pool;
Gym; Tennis courts; Racquetball court; Fitness
center/Weight room; Softball field.

Connecticut

Groton

158. New London Naval Submarine Base
SUBASE NLON
Box 00
Groton, CT 06349-5000
860-449-4636; DSN 241-4636
Internet: http://www.csg2.navy.mil
OFFICER-OF-THE-DAY: 860-449-3444, FAX 860-449-4489, DSN 241-3444

Profile
BRANCH: Navy.
SIZE AND LOCATION: 1325 acres. Situated on E bank of Thames River about 6 mi upstream from estuary and within townships of Ledyard and Groton. Main gate 0.5 mi off Rte 12, 3 mi from I-95, Exit 86, on Crystal Lake Rd. 60 mi SE of Hartford; nearest airports, Groton/New London (10 mi), Hartford/Bradley IAP (60 mi). *County:* New London.
MAJOR UNITS: Submarine Group 2; Naval Submarine School; Submarine Squadron 2; Submarine Development Squadron 12; Naval Submarine Support Facility, New London/Groton; Supervisor of Shipbuilding, Conversion and Repair; Naval Submarine Medical Research Laboratory; Naval Undersea Medical Institute; Personnel Support Activity Det; Naval Security Group Activity, Groton; Naval Underwater Systems Center, New London Laboratory; Naval Legal Service Office, Groton; Naval Investigative Service.
BASE HISTORY: Birthplace of submarine force. 1868, CT donated 112 acres. 1872, buildings and pier built as Navy Yard. 1881, downgraded to coaling station. 1915, monitor *Ozark*, brought 4 submarines to pier. 1916, converted to submarine base. Between WWI and WWII, schools and training facilities established.
VISITOR ATTRACTIONS: Nautilus Memorial; Submarine Force Library and Museum (located adjacent to Main Gate).

Key Contacts
COMMANDER: Capt Robert N Nestlerode, 860-449-3400, FAX 860-449-2653, DSN 241-3400, cosubase@mindport.net.
PUBLIC AFFAIRS: JOC(SW) William Polson, ATTN: PAO, Box 44, Groton, CT 06349-5044, 860-449-3889, FAX 860-449-5012, DSN 241-3889.

Personnel and Expenditures
ACTIVE DUTY PERSONNEL: 10,000
DEPENDENTS: 20,000
CIVILIAN PERSONNEL: 975
MILITARY PAYROLL EXPENDITURE: $330 mil (military & civilian)

Services
Housing: Family units 2627; Unaccompanied enlisted quarters 12 bldgs; Barracks spaces 3300. *Temporary Housing:* Unaccompanied officer/Enlisted quarters 1 bldg; Transient quarters 63 combined officer/enlisted at O'Kane Hall; Susse Chalet 150 units. *Commissary:* Yes; *Exchange:* Retail store; Barber shop; Dry cleaners; Food shop; Florist; Bank; Service station; Bakery; Military clothing store; Convenience store; Beauty shop; Credit union; ATM; Post office; Fast food; Video rentals; Thrift shop; Travel agency; Computer store; Garden center; Tailor/Alterations; Laundry; Cafeteria. *Child Care/Capacities:* Day care center capacity 25, 6wks-6yrs; Home day care program; Summer day camp; Before & after school programs; Day care off base: capacity 244, 2 full time, 1 part time; Child care not all on base but all affiliated.. *Schools:* No on-base schools. *Base Library:* Yes. *Medical Facilities:* Hospital; Medical clinic; Dental clinic. *Recreational Facilities:* Bowling center; Movie theater; Pool; Gym; Recreation center; Golf course; Tennis courts; Fitness center/Weight room; Softball field; Football field; Auto shop; Enlisted club; Picnic area; Lake for swimming/ice skating; Marina with boat slips.

Hartford

159. Adjutant General of Connecticut
National Guard Armory, 360 Broad St
Hartford, CT 06105-3795
860-524-4953; FAX 860-524-4898

Profile
BRANCH: Army National Guard.
MAJOR UNITS: Connecticut National Guard.

Key Contacts
COMMANDER: Maj Gen David W Gay.

New Haven

160. New Haven Naval & Marine Corps Reserve Center
NMCRC
30 Woodward Ave
New Haven, CT 06512-3658
203-467-1618; FAX 203-468-6739

Profile
BRANCH: Naval Reserve; Marine Corps Reserve.
LOCATION: S Connecticut. *County:* New Haven.
MAJOR UNITS: REDCOM ONE Activity; 1st Truck Plt, Direct Support Co A&B, 6th Motor Transport Bn.

Key Contacts
COMMANDER: CDR B P Morgan.

New London

161. Coast Guard Academy
CGA
15 Mohegan Dr
New London, CT 06320-4195
860-444-8500

Profile
BRANCH: Coast Guard.
SIZE AND LOCATION: 100 acres. 5 minutes N of downtown New London, across Thames River from Groton, located N of I-95 in SE CT. *County:* New London.
MAJOR UNITS: Research & Development Center, Avery Point; Central Oil Identification Laboratory, Groton; International Ice Patrol, Avery Point, Groton; USCGC *Eagle*; USCGC *Point Francis*.
BASE HISTORY: 1876, founded as Revenue Cutter School of Instruction. 1878, Barque *Chase* served as seagoing Academy until 1900. 1910, Arundel Cove, MD, became second land-based Academy site. Academy relocated to Ft Trumbull, former Army installation, New London, CT. 1915, Life Saving & Revenue Cutter Services merged as Coast Guard, providing Academy with current name. 1922, Academy moved to current location to accommodate increased corps size. 1932, construction of new facility completed.
VISITOR ATTRACTIONS: Coast Guard Museum located in Waesche Hall, open year round, 9-4 weekdays, 9-5 weekends & holidays (May-Oct); Visitors Pavilion open 9-5 (May-Oct); Barque *Eagle*, America's Tallship, Fri, Sat, Sun 12-5 when in port; Dress parades in Spring & Fall on Washington parade field.

Key Contacts
COMMANDER: Superintendent.

Personnel and Expenditures
ACTIVE DUTY PERSONNEL: 600/900 cadets
CIVILIAN PERSONNEL: 160
Services
Housing: Family units 5. *Exchange:* Retail store;
Barber shop; Dry cleaners; Food shop; Florist;
Bank; Service station. *Base Library:* Yes. *Medical Facilities:* Medical clinic; Dental clinic. *Recreational Facilities:* Bowling center; Pool; Gym;
Tennis courts; Racquetball court; Softball field;
Auto shop; Officers club; NCO club.

162. Naval Undersea Warfare Center
NUSC
New London Laboratory
New London, CT 06320
203-440-4000
Profile
BRANCH: Navy.
LOCATION: On Naval Submarine Base, New
London. *County:* New London.
BASE HISTORY: 1970, Center result of merger
between Naval Underwater Sound Laboratory, New London and Naval Underwater
Weapons Research and Engineering Station,
Newport (formerly NUOS). Also see Naval
Education and Training Center, Newport, RI.
Personnel and Expenditures
ACTIVE DUTY PERSONNEL: 19
CIVILIAN PERSONNEL: 1506
Services
Housing: See New London Naval Submarine
Base, Groton. *Temporary Housing:* See New
London Naval Submarine Base, Groton.

Niantic

163. Camp Rowland
Smith St
Niantic, CT 06357-2597
Internet: http://ct.ang.af.mil/CtANG/ngact.htm
Profile
BRANCH: Army National Guard.
SIZE AND LOCATION: 88 acres; Stone's
Ranch Training Area, 2200 acres.

In SE CT, near Niantic, SW of New London;
off I-95, exit 74, follow CT Rte 161; Stone's
Ranch Training Area, 3 mi. *County:* Hartford.
MAJOR UNITS: 169th Leadership Regiment;
Co C, 280th Signal Bn; 208th Personnel Det.
BASE HISTORY: 1881, CT Legislature authorized purchase of National Guard Training
Site; named Camp Niantic. Named after sitting governor since 1930s. First used as recruiting station, later hospitalization site during Spanish-American War & training site for
coastal artillery units. Today, 1000-person,
year-round cantonment facility used by reserve component units, state & federal government organizations. Also serves as main cantonment area for units conducting tactical
training at nearby Stone's Ranch Training
Area & East Haven Rifle Range.
Key Contacts
COMMANDER: Maj John Whitford, Facility
Manager, 860-691-6001, FAX
860-691-6065.
Personnel and Expenditures
ACTIVE DUTY PERSONNEL: 2; Guard/Reserve 8
CIVILIAN PERSONNEL: 7
Services
Housing: Unaccompanied officer quarters 40;
Barracks spaces 800; Senior NCO units 60. *Exchange:* PX. *Medical Facilities:* Dispensary.
Recreational Facilities: Fitness center/Weight
room; Football field; Softball field; Playground;
Picnic area.

Plainville

164. Plainville Naval & Marine Corps Reserve Center
1 Linsley Dr
Plainville, CT 06062-2918
203-747-4563, 747-4564; FAX 203-747-1176
Profile
BRANCH: Naval Reserve; Marine Corps Reserve.
LOCATION: N Connecticut. *County:* Hartford.
MAJOR UNITS: REDCOM ONE Activity; C
Co, 1st Bn, 25th Marine Regiment.

Key Contacts
COMMANDER: CDR M P Argo.

Stratford

165. Defense Contract Management Command, Stratford
DCMC Stratford
550 Main St
Stratford, CT 06497
203-385-4393; FAX 203-385-4355
E-mail: dlarocque@dcrb.dla.mil Internet:http://
33.1.105.80/DCMCSTRAT/home.htm
Profile
BRANCH: Defense Logistics Agency.
LOCATION: Off I-95 at exit 33; approx 4 mi N
of Bridgeport. *County:* Fairfield.
MAJOR UNITS: Defense Contract Management
Command, Stratford; Defense Contract Management Command, Sikorsky.
Key Contacts
COMMANDER: LTC Christopher R Mihok,
USAF; LCDR Michael J Cerneck, USN
(Sikorsky).

Windsor Locks

166. Bradley IAP Air National Guard Base
Bradley IAP
Windsor Locks, CT 06096
203-623-8291; DSN 636-8310
Profile
BRANCH: Air National Guard.
SIZE AND LOCATION: 158 acres. 15 mi N of
Hartford, exit 40 off I-91. *County:* Hartford.
MAJOR UNITS: 103rd Tactical Fighter Group
(ANG); Army National Guard Aviation Bn.
BASE HISTORY: Named for Lt Eugene M
Bradley, killed in aircraft crash in 1941.
Personnel and Expenditures
ACTIVE DUTY PERSONNEL: 878
CIVILIAN PERSONNEL: 197

Delaware

Dover AFB

167. Dover Air Force Base
DAFB
201 Eagle Way
Dover AFB, DE 19902-7219
302-677-3372; FAX 302-677-2901; DSN
445-3372, DSN FAX 445-2901
Internet: http://www.dover.af.mil
OFFICER-OF-THE-DAY: Command Post:
302-677-4201, DSN 445-4201, DSN FAX
445-4201
Profile
BRANCH: Air Force; Air Force Reserve.
SIZE AND LOCATION: 3900 acres. From
Dover, DE, follow US-113 S, a few miles
past Blue Hen Mall, Dover AFB on left.
County: Kent.
MAJOR UNITS: 436th Airlift Wing; 436th Aer-
ial Port Squadron; 436th Comptroller Squad-
ron; 436th Security Police Squadron; 436th
Supply Squadron; 436th Transportation
Squadron; 3rd Airlift Squadron; 9th Airlift
Squadron; Air Force Hospital; 512th Airlift
Wing (Reserve Associate); Air Force Office
of Special Investigations; Air Force Civil Air
Patrol Liaison; Army and Air Force Exchange
Service; Defense Reutilization & Marketing
Office; US Air Force Judiciary Area Defense
Counsel; 219th Field Training Det; 436th
Contracting Squadron; 436th Logistics Sup-
port Squadron; 436th Component Repair
Squadron; 436th Aircraft Generation Squad-
ron; 436th Services Squadron; 436th Commu-
nications Squadron; 436th Civil Engineer
Squadron; 436th Medical Operations Squadron; 436th Aerospace Medicine Squadron;
436th Medical Support Squadron; 436th Operations Support Squadron; 436th Dental
Squadron; AMC Museum; US Air Force Port
Mortuary.
BASE HISTORY: 1941, newly completed
Dover Municipal Airfield leased to Army Air
Corps; assigned to Eastern Defense Command as coastal patrol base. 1942, antisubmarine patrols conducted by base personnel. Feb
to Aug 1943, closed to complete construction
on main runway. Following reopening, along
with fighter pilot training, base became site
for development of air launched rockets. Following WWII, became a preseparation processing center; deactivated. Reactivated in
1951, and assigned to Air Defense Command.

1952, MATS (later MAC) assumed command; Dover strategic airlift base. 1971, 9th
Military Airlift Squadron reactivated. 1973,
exchanged with Charleston AFB brought 3rd
MAS & C-5s to Dover. 1989, 31st MAS reactivated; only all C-5 base in AMC. 1991,
436th MAW redesignated 436th Airlift Wing.
VISITOR ATTRACTIONS: AMC Museum.
Key Contacts
COMMANDER: Col Felix Grieder, 436 Airlift
Wing Commander, 302-677-4360, DSN
445-4360, DSN FAX 445-2948.
PUBLIC AFFAIRS: Capt Donna Nicholas,
302-677-3372, DSN 445-3372, DSN FAX
445-2901, Nicholas@aw436.dover.af.mil.
PROCUREMENT: LTC Darryl Middleton,
302-677-4447, DSN 445-4447, DSN FAX
445-4451.
TRANSPORTATION: Maj Victor Parker,
302-677-4906, DSN 445-4906, DSN FAX
445-2956.
PERSONNEL/COMMUNITY ACTIVITIES:
Maureen Sealund, 302-677-3355, DSN
445-3355, DSN FAX 445-2901, Sealund@
AW436.dover.af.mil.
Personnel and Expenditures
ACTIVE DUTY PERSONNEL: 4500; 2500 re-
servists
DEPENDENTS: 6500
CIVILIAN PERSONNEL: 1100
MILITARY PAYROLL EXPENDITURE: $470 mil
CONTRACT EXPENDITURE: $56.5 mil
Services
Housing: Family units 1549; Dormitory spaces
1860; Senior NCO units 211; Junior NCO units
1230; Officers 108. *Temporary Housing:* VOQ
units 14; VAQ units 164. *Commissary:* Yes; *Ex-
change:* Retail store; Barber shop; Dry cleaners;
Food shop; Florist; Bank; Service station; Bak-
ery; Military clothing store; Convenience store;
Beauty shop; Credit union; ATM; Optical store;
Post office; Fast food; Video rentals; Thrift
shop; Travel agency; Class VI; Tailor/Altera-
tions. *Child Care/Capacities:* Day care center
Capacity 119, 6mos-5yrs; Summer day camp;
Before & after school programs. *Schools:* Pre-
school/Kindergarten; Elementary; Intermediate/
Junior high; College/University; College
courses. *Base Library:* Yes. *Medical Facilities:*
Hospital; Medical clinic; Dental clinic; Phar-
macy; Veterinary services. *Recreational Facili-
ties:* Bowling center; Movie theater; Pool; Gym;
Recreation center; Golf course; Tennis courts;
Racquetball court; Fitness center/Weight room;
Softball field; Football field; Auto shop; Craft

shop; Youth center; Picnic area; Skeet range;
Water sports; Playground; Community club;
Consolidated club.

Wilmington

168. Adjutant General of Delaware
First Regiment Rd
Wilmington, DE 19808-2191
302-326-7001; FAX 302-326-7196, 326-7119
Profile
BRANCH: Army National Guard.
MAJOR UNITS: Delaware National Guard.
Key Contacts
COMMANDER: Maj Gen George K Hastings.

169. New Castle County Airport, Air National Guard Base
Wilmington, DE 19720
302-323-3500; DSN 445-7500
Profile
BRANCH: Air National Guard; Army National
Guard.
SIZE AND LOCATION: 57 acres. 5 mi S of
Wilmington, off I-95, exit 5 (Basin Rd).
County: New Castle.
MAJOR UNITS: 166th Airlift Wing (ANG);
Army National Guard Aviation Co.
Personnel and Expenditures
ACTIVE DUTY PERSONNEL: 991 Guard
CIVILIAN PERSONNEL: 240
MILITARY PAYROLL EXPENDITURE: $16.8
mil
Services *Medical Facilities:* Dispensary.

170. Wilmington (DE) Naval & Marine Corps Reserve Center
3920 Kirkwood Hwy
Wilmington, DE 19808-5194
302-998-3328, 998-3329, 999-1462; FAX
302-992-9347
Profile
BRANCH: Naval Reserve; Marine Corps Re-
serve.
LOCATION: N Delaware. *County:* New Castle.
MAJOR UNITS: REDCOM FOUR Activity;
3rd Beach & Terminal Operations Co, 2nd
Longshoreman Plt; 3rd & 4th Plt, Bulk Fuel
Co C, 6th Engineer Support Bn.
Key Contacts
COMMANDER: LCDR E S Howard.

District of Columbia

171. Anacostia Naval Station

NS Anacostia
NAVSTA Washington, 9th & M St SE
Washington, DC 20374
202-433-2219
Internet: http://www.ndw.navy.mil/navsta.html

Profile
BRANCH: Navy.
SIZE AND LOCATION: 78 acres. Adj to Bolling AFB; along Anacostia River; take Naval Station Exit off I-295, follow signs. *County:* City of Washington, DC.
MAJOR UNITS: Naval Military Personnel Command; Seabees; Naval Reserve Center, Washington; Marine Corps Reserve Center, Washington; Marine Helicopter Squadron 1 (HMX-1); Naval Imaging Command; Family Housing Welcome Center, Naval Station Washington.
BASE HISTORY: 1997, became part of NAVSTA Washington.

Key Contacts
COMMANDER: See Naval Station Washington.

Personnel and Expenditures
ACTIVE DUTY PERSONNEL: 250

Services *Exchange:* At Bolling AFB. *Recreational Facilities:* Gym; Racquetball court; Fitness center/Weight room (sauna); Softball field.

172. Armed Forces Institute of Pathology

AFIP
6925 16th St, NW (WRAMC, Bldg 54)
Washington, DC 20306-6000
202-782-2100; DSN 662-2100
Internet: http://www.afip.mil/

Profile
BRANCH: Joint Service Installation; DOD.
LOCATION: On grounds of Walter Reed Army Medical Center. *County:* City of Washington, DC.
MAJOR UNITS: Armed Forces Institute of Pathology.
BASE HISTORY: Evolved from Army Medical Museum founded in 1862 to undertake systematic collection & study of anatomical & disease related specimens produced as a result of Civil War. Also see Walter Reed Army Medical Center.
VISITOR ATTRACTIONS: National Museum of Health & Medicine, AFIP in S wing of Bldg 54, WRAMC, open daily, 10-5 every day, incl holidays; for tours, lectures, & seminars call 202-576-2348.

Key Contacts
COMMANDER: Col Michael J Dickerson.
PUBLIC AFFAIRS: Christopher C Kelly.
Services *Base Library:* Yes.

173. Bolling Air Force Base

11th Wing
Washington, DC 20332-5100
202-767-4600; 202-767-4522 (information); DSN 297-4600
Internet: http://www.bolling.af.mil/

Profile
BRANCH: Air Force.
SIZE AND LOCATION: 604 acres. SW portion of DC, on E side of Potomac River, off Rte I-295. *County:* City of Washington, DC.
MAJOR UNITS: 11th Wing; Air Force Band; Air Force Honor Guard; Defense Intelligence Agency; Air Force Office of Special Investigations; Office of Scientific Research; Air Force Chaplain, HQ; Air Force Surgeon General; Air Force Historian; 11th Civil Engineering Squadron; 11th Communications Squadron; 11th Mission Support Squadron; 11th Security Forces Squadron.
BASE HISTORY: 1918, field opened; named for first high-ranking Air Service officer killed in WWI, Col Raynal C Bolling. Flying field originally located where Anacostia NAS is today; moved S following severe floods in 1930s. 1927, Lindbergh's *Spirit of St Louis* returned to Bolling after transatlantic flight. 1933, Wiley Post completed round-the-world flight on Bolling's runway. 1946, became first HQ of SAC. 1948, redesignated HQ Command Air Force. 1962, to decrease air congestion around National Airport, fixed-wing & later, helicopter flying activities moved to Andrews AFB; Bolling changed to support base. 1976, assigned to MAC. 1985, became official HQ Air Force District of Washington. Now serves as administrative & technological center of Air Force in Washington, DC. 11th Wing responsible for base level & major command level manpower, personnel, financial management support and general courts-martial convening authority for 35,000 Air Force personnel; offices also in Pentagon.
VISITOR ATTRACTIONS: F-105 static display.

Key Contacts
COMMANDER: Col Peter Sutton, 202-767-4109.
PUBLIC AFFAIRS: Capt Thomas Wessel, 202-767-7561, twessels@mail.bolling.af.mil; Cali Coulthard, Chief of Media Relations, 202-404-7205, ccoulthar@mail.bolling.af.mil.
PROCUREMENT: 202-767-7986, 767-8086.

Personnel and Expenditures
ACTIVE DUTY PERSONNEL: 1470
DEPENDENTS: 3500
CIVILIAN PERSONNEL: 1040

Services
Housing: Family units Officer 240; Enlisted 947; Senior NCO units; General officers' quarters. *Temporary Housing:* VIP units 23; VOQ units 78; VEQ units 51; Transient quarters 50. *Commissary:* Yes; *Exchange:* Retail store; Barber shop; Dry cleaners; Food shop; Florist; Service station; Military clothing store; Convenience store; Beauty shop; Optical store; Video rentals; Tailor/Alterations. *Child Care/Capacities:* Day care center capacity 100; Home day care program. *Schools:* No on-base schools. *Base Library:* Yes. *Medical Facilities:* Medical clinic; Dental clinic. *Recreational Facilities:* Bowling center; Pool; Gym; Recreation center; Tennis courts; Racquetball court; Fitness center/Weight room; Softball field; Auto shop; Craft shop; Officers club; NCO club; Youth center; Picnic area; Marina; Driving range.

174. Coast Guard Headquarters

CG HQ
Transpoint
2100 Second St, SW
Washington, DC 20593-0001
202-267-2229, 267-1340 (Personnel Locator)
Internet: http://www.dot.gov/dotinfo/uscg/welcome.html
OFFICER-OF-THE-DAY: 202-267-2100

Profile
BRANCH: Coast Guard.
SIZE AND LOCATION: 1 city block. Six-story leased office building in SW Washington, DC; adj to Ft McNair; 5 mi from National Airport. *County:* City of Washington, DC.
MAJOR UNITS: Coast Guard Personnel Command; Coast Guard Support Command, HQ; Coast Guard Reserve Group.
BASE HISTORY: HQ moved here in 1982.

Key Contacts
COMMANDER: Capt Catherine Kelly, 202-267-2329, cKelly@comdt.uscg.mil.

PUBLIC AFFAIRS: Capt Bud Schneeweis, 202-267-1587, FAX 202-267-4307, wschneewies@comdt.uscg.mil.
PROCUREMENT: G-A, 202-267-2007.
TRANSPORTATION: G-CCS, 202-267-1642.
PERSONNEL/COMMUNITY ACTIVITIES: Community Activities, G-CP-3, 202-267-0936; Military Personnel, G-CAS-1, 202-267-2320; Civilian Personnel, 202-267-2059.

Personnel and Expenditures
ACTIVE DUTY PERSONNEL: 1200
CIVILIAN PERSONNEL: 1000
Services *Exchange:* Military clothing store; Snacks. *Medical Facilities:* Medical clinic. *Recreational Facilities:* Fitness center/Weight room; Facilities available at nearby Ft McNair.

175. Commanding General, DC National Guard
National Guard Armory, 2001 E Capitol St
Washington, DC 20003-1719
202-433-5220; FAX 202-433-5105
Profile
BRANCH: Army National Guard.
MAJOR UNITS: District of Columbia National Guard.
Key Contacts
COMMANDER: Maj Gen Warren L Freeman.

176. District of Columbia National Guard, HQ
DC Armory
2001 E Capitol St
Washington, DC 20003-1719
202-433-5100
Profile
BRANCH: Air National Guard; Army National Guard.
SIZE AND LOCATION: Offices only. At DC Armory adj to RFK Stadium.
MAJOR UNITS: HQ, District Area Command, DC Army National Guard; HQ, DC Air National Guard; 260th Military Police Command (DC ARNG); 74th Troop Command (DC ARNG); Health & Dental Clinic, Det 3 (DC ARNG); Recruiting (DC ARNG).
VISITOR ATTRACTIONS: DC Armory hosts several large public events each year, antique show, super sale, Ringling Bros Circus, Christmas show. Drill floor/arena available for public use; rates & schedule—DC Sports Commission, 202-547-9077.
Key Contacts
COMMANDER: Maj Gen Warren L Freeman.
PUBLIC AFFAIRS: LTC Mike Milord, 202-433-4304.
Services
Housing: None. *Recreational Facilities:* None.

177. Fort Lesley J McNair
Fort McNair
HQ, Army Military District of Washington 103 Third Ave Ft Lesley J McNair
Washington, DC 20319-5058
202-685-2886; FAX 202-685-1999; DSN 325-2886; DSN FAX 325-2886
E-mail: ANPA@mcnair-emh2.army.mil Internet:http://www.mdw.army.mil
Profile
BRANCH: Army.
SIZE AND LOCATION: 98 acres. In Washington, DC; where Anacostia River empties into Potomac River in SW portion of city; approx 6 mi from Washington National Airport.
MAJOR UNITS: Military District of Washington, HQ; Army Garrison, Fort McNair; 3rd Infantry, Co A, 1st Bn; National Defense University; Inter-American Defense College; 67th Ordnance Det.
BASE HISTORY: In continuous use as military reservation since 1794; known as Turkey Buzzard Point (later Greenleaf Point). During War of 1812, US Arsenal at Greenleaf's Point destroyed when stored powder ignited. 1826, land purchased N of Arsenal as site for first Federal penitentiary; conspirators in Lincoln assassination imprisoned and executed here. 1881, became Washington Barracks, transferred to Quartermaster Department. 1898-1909, general hospital, forerunner of Walter Reed Army Hospital, located here; Maj Walter Reed did research here. 1935, name changed to Ft Humphreys. 1939, changed back to Army War College (Post), and Army War College (School). 1942, home of Army Military District of Washington, HQ. 1943, joint Army-Navy Staff College established (forerunner of National War College). 1948, renamed for commander of Army Ground Forces during WWII, Lt Gen Lesley J McNair, killed at Normandy, 1944. 1954, Industrial College of Armed Forces founded to prepare officers for top level posts in future wartime supply organization and to study problems of industrial mobilization. 1962, Inter-American Defense College opened here; curriculum includes study of international situation and world blocs, and planning for hemispheric defense.
VISITOR ATTRACTIONS: National War College building a National Historic Landmark.
Key Contacts
COMMANDER: Carlton Freese, Post Coordinator, 202-685-3089, DSN 325-3089, freesec@mcnair-emh2.army.mil.
PUBLIC AFFAIRS: Ned Christensen, Ft Myer Military Community, ATTN: PAO, 204 Lee Ave, Ft Myer, VA 22211-1199, 703-696-3944, FAX 703-696-2678, DSN 226-3944, christenn@myer-emh2.army.mil.
PROCUREMENT: Tom Watchko, 703-696-7098, DSN 226-7098.
TRANSPORTATION: Ed Brown, 703-696-3102, DSN 656-3102, ebrown@belvoir.army.mil.
PERSONNEL/COMMUNITY ACTIVITIES: 703-696-3305, DSN 426-3305.
Personnel and Expenditures
ACTIVE DUTY PERSONNEL: 820
DEPENDENTS: 63
CIVILIAN PERSONNEL: 1300
Services
Housing: Family units 25; Duplex units 12. *Temporary Housing:* Transient quarters 20. *Commissary:* Yes; *Exchange:* Barber shop; Dry cleaners; Service station; Bookstore; Beauty shop; Credit union. *Medical Facilities:* Medical clinic; Dental clinic. *Recreational Facilities:* Bowling center; Pool; Gym; Golf course; Softball field; Craft shop; Officers club; NCO club.

178. Marine Barracks Washington DC
MarBks
8th & I Sts, SE
Washington, DC 20390-5000
202-433-4073; FAX 202-433-5269; DSN 288-4073
Internet: http://www.usmc.mil/opages/divpa.htm
Profile
BRANCH: Marine Corps.
SIZE AND LOCATION: 2 acres. SE Washington, DC, near Washington Navy Yard. *County:* City of Washington, DC.
MAJOR UNITS: Marine Band; Marine Drum and Bugle Corps; Marine Corps Silent Drill Platoon; Marine Corps Color Guard; Marine Corps Institute.
BASE HISTORY: 1801, site established; oldest post of Marine Corps; residence of Commandant of Marine Corps since 1805. Site chosen by President Jefferson. Arranged in quadrangle as today. Commandant's house only original building. 1900-71, most buildings rebuilt. Training of new officers & recruits continued throughout 19th century. Location of Marine Corps HQ until 1901. 1976, designated National Historic Landmark. Home of Marine Band, "The President's Own," since 1801. Duties: official ceremonies of State, Evening Parades, special security for President, & operate Marine Corps Institute (Corps' correspondence school founded 1920 by Maj Gen John A Lejeune). 1934, Marine Drum & Bugle Corps "Commandant's Own" formed.
VISITOR ATTRACTIONS: Evening Parade, every Fri, May through Aug, 8:45pm, call/write for reservations; Sunset Parade, every Tue, May through Aug at 7:00pm at Marine Corps Memorial (Iwo Jima Memorial), just N of Arlington National Cemetery; Summer Concert Series, Wed, Jun through Aug at 8:00pm on W steps of Capitol & Sun evenings, at Sylvan Theater, on Washington Monument grounds; Marine Corps Museum located in Bldg 58, Washington Navy Yard.
Key Contacts
COMMANDER: Col Dennis Hejlik, 202-433-4073, DSN 288-4073; Commandant Gen Charles C Krulak, HQ Marine Corps, 2 Navy Annex, Washington, DC 20380-1775.
PUBLIC AFFAIRS: Capt Richard Luehrs, 202-433-4173, DSN 288-4173; Commandant's PAO, Maj E A Arends, HQ, USMC, 2 Navy Annex, Washington, DC 20380-1775, 703-693-6199, FAX 703-614-2358, DSN 224-2358.
Personnel and Expenditures
ACTIVE DUTY PERSONNEL: 1168
DEPENDENTS: 40
CIVILIAN PERSONNEL: 20
Services
Housing: Family units 5; Unaccompanied officer quarters 4; Unaccompanied enlisted quarters 127. *Temporary Housing:* See Military District of Washington. *Exchange:* Convenience store. *Child Care/Capacities:* No day care facilities. *Schools:* No on-base schools. *Medical Facilities:* Clinic at Washington Naval Yard. *Recreational Facilities:* Gym.

179. Military District of Washington
MDW
Washington, DC 20319-5050
202-475-0855; DSN 335-0855

Internet: http://www.mdw.army.mil/cominfo.
htm

Profile
BRANCH: Army.
SIZE AND LOCATION: 91,889 acres. At Ft
McNair, SE Washington, DC. *County:* City
of Washington, DC.
MAJOR UNITS: Army Military District of
Washington; Fort Myer; Fort McNair; Ar-
lington National Cemetery; Fort Meade; Fort
Ritchie; Fort Belvoir; Fort AP Hill; Fort Ham-
ilton, NY; 3rd U.S. Infantry (The Old Guard);
Army Band (Pershing's Own); Operational
Support Airlift Command (OSAC); Joint Per-
sonal Property Shipping Office, Washington
Area (JPPSOWA); White House Transporta-
tion Agency; MDW Engineer Co.
BASE HISTORY: 1921, began as District of
WA; within Third Corps Area and included
DC, Ft Washington, MD, and Ft Hunt and Ft
Myer, VA. 1927, District of Washington dis-
solved; responsibility for military ceremonies
and troops in DC assigned to Commanding
General, 16th Infantry Brigade, Ft Hunt.
1939, new organization, Washington Provisional Brigade created. May 1942, brigade became MDW. 1966, HQ moved to Ft McNair.
1971, functions consolidated and performed
by MDW HQ. Command's missions: respond
to crisis, disaster, or security requirements of
National Capital Region (NCR); provide base
of operations to Army and DOD throughout
NCR, including personal property shipping,
nationwide airlift, and operation of Arlington
National Cemetery; and conduct official ceremonies. Although MDW's mission has remained the same, it has gained, lost, and regained various installations and support responsibilities over the years. Vint Hill Farms,
Arlington Hall Station, Walter Reed Army
Medical Center, Cameron Station, and The
Pentagon once were part of MDW. Currently
emcompasses Ft Myer Military Community
(Ft Myer & Ft McNair), Ft Belvoir (including
Ft AP Hill), Ft Meade, Ft Ritchie, 12th Aviation Battalion (Davison Army Airfield), & Arlington National Cemetery.
VISITOR ATTRACTIONS: See individual
bases.

Key Contacts
COMMANDER: Maj Gen Robert F Foley.
PUBLIC AFFAIRS: Col Douglas R Coffey, HQ
Military District of Washington, ATTN:
PAO, 103 Third Ave, Fort McNair, DC
20319-5058, 202-685-2886, FAX
202-685-1999, DSN 325-2886.

Personnel and Expenditures
ACTIVE DUTY PERSONNEL: 16,531
CIVILIAN PERSONNEL: Approx 5000

180. Naval District Washington, Washington Navy Yard
NDW
901 M St, SE
Washington, DC 20374
202-433-2218
Internet: http://www.ndw.navy.mil/ndwhome.
html

Profile
BRANCH: Navy.
SIZE AND LOCATION: 66.3 acres. In SE
Washington on the Anacostia River. *County:*
City of Washington, DC.

MAJOR UNITS: Naval District Washington;
Washington Naval Yard; Military Sealift
Command; Naval Criminal Investigative Service; Navy Band.
BASE HISTORY: 1799, Washington Navy
Yard opened; longest, continuously operated
federal facility in US; Navy's oldest shore station. 1803, homeport for entire fleet. Latrobe
Gate Marine Corps' oldest sentry post. 1860s,
mission shifted to ordnance production. 1886,
redesignated Naval Gun Factory Washington.
1961, industrial production ceased; became
supply & administrative center. 1964, renamed Washington Navy Yard. 1965, Naval
District Washington (NDW) established; Potomac River Naval Command & Severn River
Naval Command combined. Responsible for
15,000 military & 50,000 civilian employees.
VISITOR ATTRACTIONS: Navy Museum;
Marine Corps Museum; Serves as ceremonial
"quarterdeck" in Washington area.

Key Contacts
COMMANDER: RADM Robert L Ellis Jr.
PUBLIC AFFAIRS: Lt David Waterman,
202-433-2678, FAX 202-433-6278, david.
waterman@ndw.navy.mil.

181. Naval Medical Command, Bureau of Medicine & Surgery
BUMED
2300 E St, NW
Washington, DC 20372-5120
202-762-3211; DSN 762-3211
E-mail: nmc9jan@bms230.navy.mil Internet:
http://support1.med.navy.mil/bumed

Profile
BRANCH: Navy.
LOCATION: In NW Washington, just W of De-
partment of State at 23rd & E Sts. *County:*
City of Washington, DC.
MAJOR UNITS: Office of the Surgeon General,
USN.
BASE HISTORY: Directs provision of medical
& dental services for Navy & Marine Corps
personnel.
VISITOR ATTRACTIONS: Site of old Naval
Obseratory (not open to public).

Key Contacts
COMMANDER: VADM Harold M Koenig,
Chief of BUMED, Surgeon General of the
Navy.
PUBLIC AFFAIRS: Capt Sheila A Graham,
202-762-3218, FAX 202-762-3218, DSN
762-3224.

182. Naval Research Laboratory
NRL
4555 Overlook Ave, SW
Washington, DC 20375-5320
202-767-3200; FAX 202-404-7419, 767-2541;
DSN 297-3200
Internet: http://www.nrl.navy.mil
OFFICER-OF-THE-DAY: 202-767-2505, DSN
297-2505

Profile
BRANCH: Navy.
SIZE AND LOCATION: 130 acres. In Washing-
ton, DC; 9 mi to Washington National Air-
port; 38 mi to Dulles IAP; 38 mi to Baltimore-
Washington IAP; 5 mi to Union Station.
County: City of Washington, DC.
MAJOR UNITS: Executive Directorate; Busi-
ness Operations Directorate; General Science
and Technology Directorate; Warfare Sys-

tems and Sensors Research Directorate; Materials Science and Component Technology Directorate; Ocean and Atmospheric Science
and Technology Directorate; Naval Center for
Space Technology.
BASE HISTORY: 1923, established with two divisions: Radio & Sound. WWII, produced
practical equipment, sonar sets, direction-find-
ing devices, & first practical radar equipment
built in US. 1946, placed under Office of Naval Research, in-house research laboratory.
Accomplishments include: Deep Ocean
Search System; space investigations; 78 satellites, including Vanguard I; experiments
aboard Skylab; HEAO spacecraft; & several
space shuttle missions, TIMATION project,
NAVSTAR Global Positioning System program. Designated major shore command.
Navy's lead laboratory for space systems, fire
research, tactical electronic warfare, & artificial intelligence.
VISITOR ATTRACTIONS: Exhibit room on
site; Tours available of research facilities.

Key Contacts
COMMANDER: Capt Bruce W Buckley,
Commanding Officer; Timothy Coffey,
Director of Research.
PUBLIC AFFAIRS: Dick Thompson (acting),
Code 1230, 202-767-2542, FAX
202-767-6991, DSN 297-2542, nrl1230@ccf.
nrl.navy.mil.
PROCUREMENT: Cindy Hartman,
202-767-3446, DSN 297-3446.
TRANSPORTATION: Steve Harrison,
202-767-3371, DSN 297-3371.
PERSONNEL/COMMUNITY ACTIVITIES:
Betty A Duffield, 202-767-3421, DSN
297-3421.

Personnel and Expenditures
ACTIVE DUTY PERSONNEL: 116
DEPENDENTS: 0
CIVILIAN PERSONNEL: 3963

Services
Housing: None. *Exchange:* Credit union. *Child
Care/Capacities:* No day care facilities.
Schools: College courses. *Base Library:* Yes.
Medical Facilities: Medical clinic. *Recreational
Facilities:* Pool; Gym; Fitness center/Weight
room; Recreation club.

183. Naval Security Station
NAVSECSTA
NSS
3801 Nebraska Ave NW
Washington, DC 20393-5440
202-764-2296; FAX 202-764-2651; DSN
764-2296
OFFICER-OF-THE-DAY: 202-764-0211, DSN
764-0211

Profile
BRANCH: Navy.
SIZE AND LOCATION: 38 acres. At Nebraska
& Massachusetts Aves NW; off Ward Circle.
County: City of Washington, DC.
MAJOR UNITS: Naval Security Station; Naval
Computer and Telecommunications Com-
mand; Communications Security Material
System; Naval Surface Warfare Center Det,
Dahlgren Division.
VISITOR ATTRACTIONS: Navy Chapel.

Key Contacts
COMMANDER: CDR Lawrence L Lehman,
202-764-0522, FAX 202-764-2651, DSN
764-0522.

PUBLIC AFFAIRS: LCDR Christine E Buswell, 202-764-2296, FAX 202-764-2651, DSN 764-2296.

Personnel and Expenditures
ACTIVE DUTY PERSONNEL: 200
DEPENDENTS: 0
CIVILIAN PERSONNEL: 250

Services
Housing: Unaccompanied enlisted quarters 1. *Temporary Housing:* None. *Exchange:* Barber shop; Credit union. *Child Care/Capacities:* No day care facilities. *Schools:* No on-base schools. *Medical Facilities:* Medical clinic; Dental clinic. *Recreational Facilities:* Gym; Recreation center; Tennis courts; Racquetball court; Fitness center/ Weight room; Picnic area; All ranks club.

184. Region Six, Naval Reserve Readiness Command
REDCOM 6
901 M St SE, Washington Navy Yard, Bldg 200-3
Washington, DC 20374-5009
202-433-3822; FAX 202-433-5561
Internet: http://www.spawar.navy.mil/nr/cnsrf/rc06/

Profile
BRANCH: Naval Reserve.
MAJOR UNITS: Naval Reserve Readiness Command, Region 6.
BASE HISTORY: Responsible for 14 reserve centers with 9000 reservists.

Key Contacts
COMMANDER: RADM Pierce J Johnson, 202-433-6220.

185. US Army Corps of Engineers, Headquarters
CECG
20 Massachusetts Ave NW
Washington, DC 20314-1000
202-761-0010; FAX 202-761-4752; DSN 763-0001
Internet: http://www.hq.usace.army.mil/

Profile
BRANCH: Army.
SIZE AND LOCATION: Offices only. In downtown Washington, DC. *County:* City of Washington, DC.
MAJOR UNITS: HQ, Corps of Engineers.

Key Contacts
COMMANDER: Lt Gen Joe N Ballard, Chief of Engineers & Commander, CECG-ZA, 202-761-0660.
PUBLIC AFFAIRS: Col Wm L Mulvey, 202-761-0010.

186. US Naval Observatory
USNO
3450 Massachusetts Ave NW
Washington, DC 20392-5100
202-762-1467; FAX 202-653-1497
Internet: http://www.usno.navy.mil/

Profile
BRANCH: Navy.
SIZE AND LOCATION: 72 acres. In NW Washington, DC; 5 mi from National Airport. *County:* Washington, DC.
MAJOR UNITS: Residence of Vice President; Oceanographer of the Navy.
BASE HISTORY: 1830, founded as Depot of Charts & Instruments, one of oldest scientific agencies in US; original mission included caring for Navy's chronometers, charts, & other navigational equipment. 1844, Depot reestablished as US Naval Observatory; located on hill N of where Lincoln Memorial now stands. 1893, moved to present site. 1966, old Observatory in Foggy Bottom declared National Historic Landmark. 1977, Walter Mondale first vice-president to live at newly created official residence on grounds of Observatory. Today, in Astrometry, Observatory uses astro-graphic telescopes in Washington, DC, Flagstaff, AZ, and Black Birch, New Zealand. Few institutions make such fundamental observations regularly.
VISITOR ATTRACTIONS: Public tours of Observatory, Mon 8:30 pm except Federal holidays and overcast days; One of the leading astronomical libraries in the world; Master clock for US (Digital time for modems, 202-762-1594; Voice time, 202-762-1401)

Key Contacts
COMMANDER: Capt Kent W Foster, 202-762-1437; Dr Ken Johnston, Scientific Director, 202-762-1437.
PUBLIC AFFAIRS: 202-762-1438.

Personnel and Expenditures
ACTIVE DUTY PERSONNEL: 6
CIVILIAN PERSONNEL: 160

Services
Housing: None. *Temporary Housing:* Guest cottages 1. *Base Library:* Yes. *Recreational Facilities:* Tennis courts.

187. US Soldiers' and Airmen's Home
USSAH
Soldiers Home
3700 N Capitol St, NW
Washington, DC 20317
800-422-9988; FAX 202-722-9087
OFFICER-OF-THE-DAY: Security Office, 202-722-3111

Profile
BRANCH: Joint Service Installation.
SIZE AND LOCATION: 320 acres. 2.5 mi N of the Capitol. *County:* City of Washington, DC.
MAJOR UNITS: Soldier's & Airmen's Home.
BASE HISTORY: 1851, opened as asylum for old & disabled veterans. Founded by Gen Winfield Scott, who appropriated land with money from Mexican War. Today, funded by active-duty soldiers & airmen (not tax money). Modern retirement community housing nearly 1400 retirees & veterans. Eligibility: veterans with active-duty service at least 50% enlisted or warrant officer, and: 1) retirees with 20 or more years active service, & at least 60 yrs old; 2) veterans unable to earn livelihood due to service-connected disability; or 3) veterans who served in war theater or received hostile-fire pay, & unable to earn livelihood due to a non-service-connected disability.
VISITOR ATTRACTIONS: Four bldgs on National Historic Register, including Anderson Cottage, summer White House for presidents Hayes, Arthur, & Lincoln. Emancipation Proclamation final draft written here.

Key Contacts
COMMANDER: Maj Gen Donald C Hilbert, USA, Retired, 202-722-3226.
PUBLIC AFFAIRS: Kerri J Childress, 202-722-3556.
PROCUREMENT: 202-722-3393.

PERSONNEL/COMMUNITY ACTIVITIES: Joan R Esch, 202-722-3209.

Personnel and Expenditures
CIVILIAN PERSONNEL: 700

Services
Housing: Dormitory spaces 1400. *Temporary Housing:* Guesthouse units 32. *Exchange:* Retail store; Barber shop; Bank; Beauty shop; Laundromat; Credit union. *Base Library:* Yes. *Medical Facilities:* Medical clinic; Dental clinic; Dispensary; Pharmacy; Long-term health care, 220 beds. *Recreational Facilities:* Bowling center; Movie theater; Gym; Recreation center; Golf course; Tennis courts; Fitness center/Weight room; Softball field; Auto shop; Craft shop; Picnic area; Fishing.

188. Walter Reed Army Medical Center
WRAMC
7100 Georgia Ave NW
Washington, DC 20307-5001
202-782-3501; DSN 662-3501
Internet: http://www.wramc.amedd.army.mil/
OFFICER-OF-THE-DAY: 202-782-7309, DSN 662-7309

Profile
BRANCH: Army.
SIZE AND LOCATION: 113 acres; 164 acres (Forest Glen). Main section of WRAMC between Rock Creek Park and Georgia Ave near MD-DC boundary, approx 3 mi from I-495. Ground transportation available between WRAMC and Andrews AFB (for info contact Air Evacuation 782-6141). *County:* City of Washington DC; Montgomery, MD (Forest Glen).
MAJOR UNITS: Walter Reed Army Medical Center; Walter Reed Army Institute of Research; Armed Forces Institute of Pathology; North Atlantic Regional Medical Command; North Atlantic Regional Dental Command; North Atlantic Veterinary Command; Army Dental Activity; Armed Forces Pest Management Board; Army Information Systems Command; Army Office for Defense Medical Information Systems; Army Physical Disability Agency; Borden Institute; Tri-Care Northeast Region.
BASE HISTORY: May 1, 1909, first patients admitted. Medical center, named for Maj Walter Reed, established to integrate patient care, teaching, & research. WWI, capacity grew from 80 patient beds to 2500. 1977, new Walter Reed Army Medical Center dedicated; 5500 rooms, 28 acres of floor space, maximum capacity 1280 patients, admissions of 22,000 a year. Outlying clinics at Pentagon & Ft McNair. Forest Glen Annex 3 mi N of Main Section home to shopping complex with PX, commissary, clothing sales store, bowling center, craft shop, service station, restaurant, speciality shops, food inspection service, motor pool, engineer facilities, laundry, family housing, research, administration buildings, & large outdoor picnic area. Also see Armed Forces Institute of Pathology.
VISITOR ATTRACTIONS: National Museum of Health & Medicine.

Key Contacts
COMMANDER: Brig Gen Michael J Kussman, 202-782-6394, DSN 662-6394.
PUBLIC AFFAIRS: Ben M Smith, 202-782-7177, DSN 662-7177.

PROCUREMENT: Contracting, 202-782-1262, DSN 662-1262.

TRANSPORTATION: 202-782-3430, DSN 662-3430.

PERSONNEL/COMMUNITY ACTIVITIES: 202-782-4946, DSN 662-4946.

Personnel and Expenditures

ACTIVE DUTY PERSONNEL: 2100

CIVILIAN PERSONNEL: 2250

Services

Housing: Family units 211; Barracks spaces 321. *Temporary Housing:* VIP units suites; Guesthouse units; Hotel 200 rooms. *Commissary:* Yes; *Exchange:* Retail store; Barber shop; Dry cleaners; Food shop; Florist; Service station; Military clothing store; Convenience store; Beauty shop; Credit union; Optical store; Tailor/Alterations; Four Seasons store. *Child Care/Capacities:* Day care center capacity 11, Child Development Center. *Base Library:* Yes. *Medical Facilities:* Hospital 500 beds; Medical clinic; Dental clinic; Pharmacy; Veterinary services. *Recreational Facilities:* Bowling center; Recreation center; Tennis courts; Fitness center/Weight room; Softball field; Auto shop; Craft shop; Offi-cers club; NCO club; Community center; Patient recreation center; ITT services.

189. Washington, Naval Station

NAVSTA Washington

9th & M Sts, SE

Washington, DC 20374

202-545-6700; DSN 288-6700

Internet: http://www.ndw.navy.mil/nswhome.html

Profile

BRANCH: Navy.

SIZE AND LOCATION: 572 acres. In Washington Navy Yard. *County:* City of Washington, DC.

MAJOR UNITS: Naval Station, Washington; Washington Navy Yard; Public Works Center; Naval Reserve Readiness Command, Region 6; Naval Computer and Telecommunications Station, Washington, DC.

BASE HISTORY: 1917, land for Washington Navy Yard acquired. 1996, NAVSTA Washington created out of NAVSTA Anacostia & Washington Navy Yard. Previously part of Naval District of Washington (NDW).

VISITOR ATTRACTIONS: Navy Yard; Marine Corps Museum; Navy Memorial Museum; Combat Art Gallery; Willard Park Naval Weapons Collection; Display ship *Barry* (DD 933).

Key Contacts

COMMANDER: CDR Jackie M Y Arrowood, 202-433-3495; LCDR A E Whitaker, Executive Officer.

PUBLIC AFFAIRS: PAO, Washington Navy Yard, 202-433-2218.

Services *Temporary Housing:* Apartment units (at Bolling AFB) 50. *Exchange:* Barber shop; Dry cleaners; Bank; Service station; Convenience store; Beauty shop; Laundromat; Also use nearby Bolling AFB exchange. *Child Care/Capacities:* Day care center capacity 75; Home day care program. *Medical Facilities:* Dental clinic; Dispensary. *Recreational Facilities:* Pool; Tennis courts; Racquetball court; Fitness center/Weight room; Auto shop; Officers club; NCO club; Picnic area; Marina; Recreation center at Solomons.

Florida

Astor

190. Cecil Field Naval Air Station, Detachment Astor

PO Box 84
Astor, FL 32102-0084
904-759-2111; DSN 860-5456

Profile
BRANCH: Navy.
SIZE AND LOCATION: 124 acres. 1.5 mi S of
Hwys 19 & 40; 10 mi W of Astor, FL; approx
65 mi N of Orlando, FL. *County:* Marion;
Lake.
MAJOR UNITS: NAS Cecil Field.
BASE HISTORY: Opened about 1950, served
as Army, Air Force, and Naval installation.
Only Navy bombing range on east coast open
for live ordnance.

Key Contacts
COMMANDER: CDR G Blocker;
904-759-2902.

Personnel and Expenditures
ACTIVE DUTY PERSONNEL: 100
CIVILIAN PERSONNEL: 70

Services
Housing: Unaccompanied enlisted quarters 12.
Exchange: Retail store; Service station. *Recreational Facilities:* Pool; Tennis courts; Fitness
center/Weight room; Softball field.

Boca Chica Key

191. Key West Naval Air Facility

NAS Key West
Bldg A-418
Boca Chica Key, FL 33040-9001
Mailing Address
PO Box 9001
Key West, FL 33040-9001
305-293-2268; FAX 305-293-2230; DSN
483-2268; DSN FAX 483-2230
OFFICER-OF-THE-DAY: 305-293-2268, FAX
305-293-2230, DSN 483-2268, DSN FAX
483-2230

Profile
BRANCH: Navy.
SIZE AND LOCATION: 5215 acres. 6 separate
annexes on Key West & Boca Chica Key; approx 130 mi S of Miami. *County:* Monroe.
MAJOR UNITS: Joint Interagency Task Force
East (JIATF East); Caribbean Regional Operating Center (CARIBROC); US Coast Guard

Group, Key West; Army Special Forces Underwater Operations School; Naval Air Warfare Center Det; Naval Computer and Telecommunications Area Master Station, Atlantic Det; Naval Personnel Support Activity
Det; Fighter Squadron 101; Air Force Aerostat Site (Cudjoe Key); Naval Oceanography
Command Det.
BASE HISTORY: 1917, site began as coastal air
patrol station 1918, training base for seaplane
pilots and blimp facility established. WWI,
NAS Key West commissioned as HQ Seventh
Naval District. After WWI, caretaker status
until 1939. 1940, NAS reestablished with major additions: satellite Meacham Field (now
Key West IAP), for lighter-than-air, Boca
Chica Field for land planes, Seaplane Base,
and operating & training base for fleet aircraft
squadrons. 1945, satellite fields disestablished
and combined into one aviation activity under
current designation and maintained as training and experimental site. 1962, major player
in Cuban Missile Crisis with reconnaissance
& operational flights. Currently, serves as premier pilot training facility for transient tactical aviation squadrons, conducts Search &
Rescue duty. Country's southernmost naval
base.
VISITOR ATTRACTIONS: Super powerboat
offshore races (twice a year); Air Show/Open
House (Apr).

Key Contacts
COMMANDER: Capt Scott T Johnson,
305-293-2107, DSN 483-2107.
PUBLIC AFFAIRS: Lt Jonathan Hupp,
305-293-2425, FAX 305-293-2230, DSN
483-2425, naskwpao@norfolk.navy.mil.
PROCUREMENT: CMDR Jack E Cloud, Jr,
305-293-2189, FAX 305-293-2129, DSN
483-2189, dsn fax 483-2129.
TRANSPORTATION: CMDR James Cruz,
305-293-2304, FAX 305-293-2502, DSN
483-2304, DSN FAX 483-2502.
PERSONNEL/COMMUNITY ACTIVITIES:
Daryl K Dye, Director Welfare, Morale &
Recreation, 305-293-2112, FAX
305-293-2416, DSN 483-2112, DSN FAX
483-2416.

Personnel and Expenditures
ACTIVE DUTY PERSONNEL: 1293
DEPENDENTS: 942
CIVILIAN PERSONNEL: 1126

Services
Housing: Family units 1391; Unaccompanied officer quarters 40; Unaccompanied enlisted quarters 226.

Temporary Housing: VIP units 1; Unaccompanied officer/Enlisted quarters 257; Guesthouse
units 8; BEQ units 518. *Commissary:* Yes; *Exchange:* Main retail store (Sigsbee Park Annex)-
Barber/Beauty Shop, Snack Bar, Uniform Shop,
Personalized Services, Laundry/Dry Cleaning,
Furniture Store, ATM, Video Rentals, Class VI,
Garden Center, Tailor/Alterations, Photo Processing, Cellular Phone Center, Photocopying,
Gas Station, IT&T, Laundromat; Boca Chica Annex minimart. *Child Care/Capacities:* Day care
center; Home day care program; Summer day
camp. *Schools:* Elementary. *Medical Facilities:*
Medical clinic; Dental clinic; Pharmacy; Veterinary services. *Recreational Facilities:* Bowling
center; Pool; Gym; Recreation center; Tennis
courts; Racquetball court; Fitness center/Weight
room; Softball field; Football field; Auto shop;
Craft shop; Officers club; NCO club; Fishing/
Hunting; Youth center; In-line skating Rink
(Sigsbee Park); Sunset Lounge (Sigsbee Park);
Marinas (Boca Chica/Sigsbee Park).

Clearwater

192. Clearwater Coast Guard Air Station

15100 Rescue Way
Clearwater, FL 34622-2990
813-535-1437; FAX 813-535-1437
OFFICER-OF-THE-DAY: 813-535-1210

Profile
BRANCH: Coast Guard.
SIZE AND LOCATION: 40 acres. At St Petersburg/Clearwater IAP; from Tampa I-275 to
Exit 18 to Roosevelt Blvd; Air Station on
Fairchild Dr off Roosevelt Blvd. *County:*
Pinellas.
MAJOR UNITS: Coast Guard Air Station, Clearwater; Coast Guard Station, Clearwater.
BASE HISTORY: 1934, Albert Whitted Airport, downtown St Petersburg, became homebase for Coast Guard amphibious aircraft &
helicopters. 1976, moved to St Petersburg/
Clearwater Airport for longer runways; renamed Coast Guard Air Station, Clearwater.
1987, became Coast Guard's largest Air Station; motto, "Anytime, Anywhere," describes
current operation. Missions in support of
search & rescue, law enforcement, aids to
navigation, marine environmental protection,
& others flown on daily basis; involved in Cuban Boatlift, Grenada Rescue Mission, interagency & international narcotics interdiction

efforts, & response to Space Shuttle *Challenger* disaster.

Key Contacts
PUBLIC AFFAIRS: 813-535-1145.
PROCUREMENT: 813-535-1500.
TRANSPORTATION: 813-535-1570.
PERSONNEL/COMMUNITY ACTIVITIES: 813-535-1112.

Personnel and Expenditures
ACTIVE DUTY PERSONNEL: 580
CIVILIAN PERSONNEL: 50

Services
Housing: None. *Temporary Housing:* Duty crew berthing. *Exchange:* Retail store; Barber shop; Dry cleaners; Food shop; Military clothing store; Convenience store. *Child Care/Capacities:* No day care facilities. *Schools:* No on-base schools. *Medical Facilities:* Medical clinic; Dental clinic; Pharmacy. *Recreational Facilities:* Gym; Tennis courts; Fitness center/Weight room; Softball field.

193. St Petersburg Naval Reserve Center
15400 Fairchild
Clearwater, FL 34622-3532
813-531-7033; FAX 813-539-8050
Profile
BRANCH: Naval Reserve.
LOCATION: *County:* Pinellas.
MAJOR UNITS: REDCOM EIGHT Activity.
Key Contacts
COMMANDER: CDR A A Ramirez.

Cocoa Beach

194. Cape Canaveral Air Force Station
Cocoa Beach, FL 32925
407-853-1110; DSN 467-1110
Profile
BRANCH: Air Force.
MAJOR UNITS: Cape Canaveral AFS (AFSC).

Cortez

195. Cortez Coast Guard Station
4530 124th St Court West
Cortez, FL 34215-9999
941-794-1261
Profile
BRANCH: Coast Guard.
SIZE AND LOCATION: 1.5 acres. In Cortez, FL, on N side of Sarasota Bay. *County:* Charlotte.
MAJOR UNITS: Coast Guard Station, Cortez.
BASE HISTORY: 1976, commissioned; housed in building constructed 1890 as Albion Inn. 1992, new 2-story multistation dedicated. Area of responsibility from Skyway Bridge to southern tip of Gasparilla Island.
Personnel and Expenditures
ACTIVE DUTY PERSONNEL: 26
CIVILIAN PERSONNEL: 3
Services
Housing: 10, 2-person rooms for duty personnel. *Exchange:* Retail store; Military clothing store; Convenience store. *Recreational Facilities:* Fitness center/Weight room; Boating; Volleyball; Horseshoe pit.

Fort Myers Beach

196. Fort Myers Beach Coast Guard Station
719 San Carlos Dr
Fort Myers Beach, FL 33931-2221
941-463-5754; FAX 941-463-3535
Profile
BRANCH: Coast Guard.
SIZE AND LOCATION: 10 acres. In Ft Myers Beach off State Rte 865; 2 mi from beach. *County:* Lee.
MAJOR UNITS: US Coast Guard Station, Ft Myers Beach; USCGC *Point Steele.*
BASE HISTORY: 1979, remodeled & recommissioned. Southernmost station in Group St Petersburg; area of responsibility from S of Sarasota to Everglades City, FL.
Key Contacts
COMMANDER: CWO4 Red Henson.
PUBLIC AFFAIRS: See CG Group/Station, 600 8th Ave SE, St Petersburg, FL 33701.
Personnel and Expenditures
ACTIVE DUTY PERSONNEL: 40
DEPENDENTS: 0
Services
Housing: Family units 8; Government leased housing. *Exchange:* Convenience store. *Child Care/Capacities:* No day care facilities. *Schools:* No on-base schools. *Medical Facilities:* No medical facilities. *Recreational Facilities:* Recreation center; Fishing/Hunting; Basketball.

Fort Walton Beach

197. Eglin Air Force Base
Fort Walton Beach, FL 32542
904-882-3931; FAX 904-882-4894; DSN 872-3931
Internet: http://www.eglin.af.mil/pa
Profile
BRANCH: Air Force.
SIZE AND LOCATION: 463,704 acres. Eglin 26 mi S of I-10, Crestview, FL. Hwy 85 runs S from Crestview and junctions with Hwy 20 at Niceville, FL; right turn on Hwy 20 to E gate. *County:* Okaloosa, FL; Santa Rosa, FL; Walton, FL; Escambia, FL; Washington, FL; Escambia, AL; Covington, AL; Geneva, AL.
MAJOR UNITS: Air Force Development Test Center; 33rd Fighter Wing; Air Warfare Center; Wright Laboratory; 46th Test Wing; Army Ranger Training Bn; Naval EOC/DOD School.
BASE HISTORY: 1935, established as Valparaiso Bombing and Gunnery Base. 1937, redesignated Eglin Field for LTC Frederick I Eglin, Army Air Corps. 1940, Forestry Service ceded Choctawhatchee National Forest to Air Force. 1941, Air Corps Proving Ground activated; Eglin became site for gunnery training & major testing center for aircraft, equipment, & tactics; pioneer in missile development, First Experimental Guided Missiles Group. 1950, Air Research & Development Command established (now Air Force Systems Command). 1951, Air Force Armament Center brought development & testing together. 1957, Air Proving Ground Center formed & built Eglin Gulf Test Range. 1968, redesignated Armament Development & Test

Center. 1975, base one of 4 Vietnamese Refugee Processing Centers. 1979, Center renamed Armament Division. 1980, processing center for Cuban refugees. 1990, became Air Force Development Test Center.
VISITOR ATTRACTIONS: Air Force Armament Museum.
Key Contacts
COMMANDER: Col James F Shambo, 646 ASW/CC, 904-882-3333, DSN 872-3333.
PUBLIC AFFAIRS: Maj Matt Durham, AFDTC/PA, 904-882-3931, DSN 872-3931.
PROCUREMENT: Col William Borchardt, AFDTC/PK, 904-882-4398, DSN 872-4398.
TRANSPORTATION: Maj Jo A Alfaro, 646 TRANS/CC, 904-882-4581, DSN 872-4581.
PERSONNEL/COMMUNITY ACTIVITIES: Shirley Pigott, 646 MSSQ/CC, 904-882-3933, DSN 872-3933.
Personnel and Expenditures
ACTIVE DUTY PERSONNEL: 10,000
DEPENDENTS: 13,600
CIVILIAN PERSONNEL: 4850
MILITARY PAYROLL EXPENDITURE: $208.7 mil
Services
Housing: Family units 2359; Unaccompanied officer quarters 20; Dormitory spaces 4100; Senior NCO units 21; Mobile home units 225; RV/Camper sites 15. *Temporary Housing:* VIP units 3; VOQ units 147; VAQ units 188; Transient quarters 88. *Commissary:* Yes; *Exchange:* Retail store; Barber shop; Dry cleaners; Food shop; Florist; Bank; Service station; Furniture store; Bakery; Bookstore; Military clothing store; Convenience store; Beauty shop; Laundromat; Credit union; ATM; Optical store; Post office; Fast food; Video rentals; Thrift shop; Travel agency; Class VI; Computer store; Garden center; Tailor/Alterations; Laundry; Cafeteria; Photo store. *Child Care/Capacities:* Day care center; Home day care program; Latch key program; Summer day camp; Before & after school programs. *Schools:* Preschool/Kindergarten; Elementary; College/University; College courses. *Base Library:* Yes. *Medical Facilities:* Hospital; Medical clinic; Dental clinic; Dispensary; Pharmacy; Veterinary services. *Recreational Facilities:* Bowling center; Movie theater; Pool; Gym; Recreation center; Golf course; Stables; Tennis courts; Racquetball court; Fitness center/Weight room; Softball field; Football field; Auto shop; Craft shop; Officers club; NCO club; Camping; Fishing/Hunting; Enlisted club; Youth center; Picnic area; Skeet range; Water sports; Playground; Community club; All ranks club; Rod & Gun club; Health & wellness center.

Hialeah

198. Miami Naval & Marine Corps Reserve Readiness Center
NMCRTC
18650 NW 62nd Ave
Hialeah, FL 33015-6009
305-628-5150, 628-5151; FAX 305-628-5154
Profile
BRANCH: Naval Reserve; Marine Corps Reserve.
LOCATION: *County:* Dade.
MAJOR UNITS: REDCOM EIGHT Activity; TOW & Scout Platoons, 8th Tank Bn; 33rd

Interrogator Translator Team (MARFOR-RES).
Key Contacts
COMMANDER: CDR R J Swanson.

Homestead ARB

199. Homestead Air Reserve Base
Homestead ARB
482nd Fighter Wing/PA
Homestead ARB, FL 33039-1299
305-224-7000; DSN 791-7000
Internet: http://www.homestead.af.mil
Profile
BRANCH: Air Force Reserve.
SIZE AND LOCATION: 1000 acres. Approx 25 mi S of Miami, 2 mi E on Biscayne Dr from US-1; 5 mi NE of Homestead, FL. *County:* Dade.
MAJOR UNITS: 482nd Fighter Wing; 125th Fighter Wing, Det 1 (FL ANG); US Southern Command; US Customs Miami Air Branch.
BASE HISTORY: 1941, airstrip deeded to government by Pan American Airways; used as maintenance stopover point for aircraft ferried to Caribbean and North Africa; runway, Homestead Army Air Field, belonged to Caribbean Wing, Air Transport Command. 1943, home of 2nd Operational Training Unit, providing advanced training for air crews. 1945, base closed due to massive hurricane. 1955, reactivated as Homestead AFB with 823rd Air Division; growing threat from Cuba brought 31st TFW from George AFB, CA, and tent city of 10,000 Army troops. 1968, TAC took control. 1985, 31st TFW returns to host. Aug 24, 1992, base closed due to Hurricane Andrew. 1994, reopened as reserve base.
Key Contacts
COMMANDER: Col Richard J Eustace, 305-224-7442, DSN 791-7442.
PUBLIC AFFAIRS: Maj Bobby D'Angelo, 305-224-7303, DSN 791-7303, DSN FAX 791-7302, rdangelo@homestead.af.mil.
Personnel and Expenditures
ACTIVE DUTY PERSONNEL: 1500 reservists
Services *Recreational Facilities:* Gym; Tennis courts; Racquetball court; Fitness center/Weight room; Softball field; All ranks club.

Hurlburt Field

200. Hurlburt Field
131 Bartley St, Ste 315
Hurlburt Field, FL 32544-5269
850-884-1110; DSN 579-1110
Internet: http://www.hurlburt.af.mil/
OFFICER-OF-THE-DAY: Command Post, 850-884-7774, DSN 579-7774
Profile
BRANCH: Air Force.
SIZE AND LOCATION: 6634 acres. In panhandle of FL on US-98; 7 mi W of Ft Walton Beach on Santa Rosa Sound. *County:* Okaloosa.
MAJOR UNITS: Air Force Special Operations Command; 16th Special Operations Wing (SOW); Air Force Special Operations School; Special Missions Operations Test & Evaluation Center; Joint Warfare Center; 823rd Civil Engineering Squadron (Red Horse);

505th Command and Control Evaluation Group; 18th Test Flight Squadron; 720th Special Tactics Group; Combat Weather Facility; 335th Training Squadron, Det 1; Field Training Det 327; Air Force Office of Special Investigations.
BASE HISTORY: 1940s, originally designated Auxiliary Field No. 9, as small pilot & gunnery training field, part of Eglin AFB complex; named for 1st Lt Donald W Hurlburt, killed in aircraft crash at Eglin Army Airfield. 1955, 17th Light Bombardment Wing training. 1958, 4751st Missile Wing of Air Defense Command tested surface-to-air missiles. 1961, 4400th Combat Crew Training Squadron (later Group & 1st Air Commando Wing) trained as counterinsurgency force. 1968, became 1st Special Operations Wing. 1983, personnel led Operation Urgent Fury in Grenada. 1989, mobilized for Operation Just Cause in Panama. 1991, took active role in Operation Desert Shield/Storm, suffering largest single loss by any unit. 1990, 23rd Air Force redesignated as Air Force Special Operations Command.
VISITOR ATTRACTIONS: Hurlburt Field Air Park.
Key Contacts
COMMANDER: Gen Peter Schoomaker, AFSOC.
PUBLIC AFFAIRS: 16 SOW/PA, 131 Bartley St, Ste 326, 850-884-7464, DSN 579-7464.
Personnel and Expenditures
ACTIVE DUTY PERSONNEL: 7500
DEPENDENTS: 11,300
CIVILIAN PERSONNEL: 775
Services
Housing: Family units 366; Dormitory spaces 900 rooms; 300 leased housing units off base. *Temporary Housing:* VIP units 7; VOQ units 115; VAQ units 84; 0-6 Suites 16, Temp Living Facilities 24. *Commissary:* Yes; *Exchange:* Retail store; Barber shop; Dry cleaners; Food shop; Florist; Bank; Service station; Military clothing store; Convenience store; Beauty shop; Credit union; Travel agency. *Child Care/Capacities:* Day care center capacity 200, 6mo-5yrs; Home day care program; Summer day camp. *Schools:* College courses. *Base Library:* Yes. *Medical Facilities:* Medical clinic; Dental clinic; Pharmacy; Eglin Regional Hospital nearby. *Recreational Facilities:* Bowling center; Movie theater; Pool; Gym; Recreation center; Golf course; Tennis courts; Racquetball court; Fitness center/Weight room; Softball field; Auto shop; Craft shop; Officers club; NCO club; Camping; Fishing/Hunting; Enlisted club; Youth center; Picnic area; Skeet range; Water sports; Scuba diving club; Marina.

Jacksonville

201. Blount Island Command
5880 Channel View Blvd
Jacksonville, FL 32226
904-696-5100
Internet: http://192.156.21.137/bic.htm
Profile
BRANCH: Marine Corps.
SIZE AND LOCATION: 726 acres (262 acres exclusive use, 500 controlled use). On the St Johns River in Jacksonville, FL; 6 mi from Atlantic Ocean. *County:* Duval.

MAJOR UNITS: Blount Island Command.
BASE HISTORY: Plans, coordinates, & executes logistics efforts in support of Maritime Prepositioning Ships (MPS) & Norway Geo-Prepositioning Programs. Three Maritime Prepositioning Ship (MPS) squadrons with 13 ships strategically located to provide Marine Corps supplies in event of war or other contingency.
Key Contacts
COMMANDER: Col Dennis E Long, 904-696-5100.
PUBLIC AFFAIRS: SSgt Michael Giannetti, 904-696-5051.

202. Cecil Field Naval Air Station
NAS Cecil Field
Jacksonville, FL 32215-5000
904-778-5626; DSN 860-5626
Internet: http://www.cecilfield.com
OFFICER-OF-THE-DAY: 904-778-5626, DSN 860-5626
Profile
BRANCH: Navy.
SIZE AND LOCATION: 30,000 acres. SE of Jacksonville off State Rte 228. *County:* Duval.
MAJOR UNITS: Commander, Strike Fighter Wing, US Atlantic Fleet; Commander, Sea Control Wing, US Atlantic Fleet; Naval Atlantic Meteorology & Oceanography Det; Legal Service Office Det, Cecil Field (NLSO); Naval Air Maintenance Training Group Det; Naval Aviation Engineering Service Unit; Marine Aircraft Group 42, Det a; Marine Aviation Training Support Group; Strike Fighter Weapons School, Atlantic; VFA-15; VFA-34; VFA-37; VFA-81; VFA-82; VFA-83; VFA-86; VFA-87; VFA-105; VFA-106; VFA-131; VFA-136; VS-22; VS-24; VS-30; VS-31; VS-32; VQ-6.
BASE HISTORY: 1941, auxiliary training base for NAS Jacksonville. 1943, commissioned as Naval Auxiliary Air Station. Post WWII, decommissioned. 1950, returned to active status; designated south's only master jet base.
FUTURE CLOSURE/REALIGNMENT: Closure to be completed by Sep 1999.
Key Contacts
COMMANDER: Capt Frank T Bossio.
PUBLIC AFFAIRS: 904-778-6055, DSN 860-6055.
PROCUREMENT: Supply Officer, 904-778-5770, DSN 860-5770.
TRANSPORTATION: Transportation Officer, 904-778-5912, DSN 860-5912.
Personnel and Expenditures
ACTIVE DUTY PERSONNEL: 6,434
CIVILIAN PERSONNEL: 695
MILITARY PAYROLL EXPENDITURE: $250.4 mil
CONTRACT EXPENDITURE: $9 mil
Services
Housing: Family units 297; Unaccompanied officer quarters Temporary 81; Permanent 50; Unaccompanied enlisted quarters 3343; Duplex units 90; Townhouse units 200; Barracks spaces 3344; Trailer spaces 36; RV/Camper sites 4. *Temporary Housing:* Lodge units At NAS Jax. *Commissary:* Yes; *Exchange:* Retail store; Barber shop; Dry cleaners; Food shop; Florist; Service station; Military clothing store. *Child Care/Capacities:* Day care center capacity 104; Home day care program. *Schools:* No on-base schools. *Base Library:* Yes.

Medical Facilities: Medical clinic; Dental clinic.
Recreational Facilities: Bowling center; Pool;
Gym; Golf course; Tennis courts; Racquetball
court; Fitness center/Weight room; Softball
field; Football field; Auto shop; Officers club;
NCO club; Youth center; SATO; ITT.

203. Fleet and Industrial Supply Center
FISC
Box 97, NAS Jacksonville
Jacksonville, FL 32212-0097
904-542-1220; FAX 904-772-5166
OFFICER-OF-THE-DAY: 904-542-1001, DSN
942-1001

Profile
BRANCH: Navy.
SIZE AND LOCATION: 180 acres. On NAS
Jacksonville on west side of city. *County:* Du-
val.
BASE HISTORY: 1982, established by consoli-
dating supply departments of Naval Station
Mayport, NAS Jacksonville, and Jacksonville
Fuel Depot. One of eight major supply cen-
ters where supplies and repairs are purchased
and stored. Main site on St John's River at
NAS Jacksonville. 19 mi N of main site is
Fuel Directorate, and 40 mi NE of main site is
NSC Jacksonville Fleet Support Center, on
Mayport Naval Station, providing direct sup-
port to Fleet customers.

Key Contacts
COMMANDER: Capt E J Fishburne,
904-542-1263, DSN 942-1263.
PUBLIC AFFAIRS: Richard Crews, Code CA.
PROCUREMENT: LCDR D O'Rear,
904-542-1073, DSN 942-1073.

Personnel and Expenditures
ACTIVE DUTY PERSONNEL: 30
CIVILIAN PERSONNEL: 250
MILITARY PAYROLL EXPENDITURE: $10 mil
CONTRACT EXPENDITURE: $80 mil

Services
Housing: See Jacksonville NAS. *Exchange:* See
Jacksonville NAS. *Recreational Facilities:* See
Jacksonville NAS.

204. Jacksonville IAP, Air National Guard Base
Jacksonville, FL 32229
904-741-7100; DSN 460-7100

Profile
BRANCH: Air National Guard.
SIZE AND LOCATION: 332 acres. On W end
of Jacksonville IAP; 3 mi W of I-95, approx
10 mi N of Jacksonville. *County:* Duval.
MAJOR UNITS: 125th Fighter Wing (ANG).
BASE HISTORY: 1968, built to replace original
1947 facility.

Personnel and Expenditures
ACTIVE DUTY PERSONNEL: 1009 Guard
CIVILIAN PERSONNEL: 383
MILITARY PAYROLL EXPENDITURE: $27.1
mil

Services *Medical Facilities:* Medical clinic.
Recreational Facilities: Softball field; Officers
club; NCO club.

205. Jacksonville Naval Air Station
NAS Jax
Jacksonville, FL 32212-5000
Mailing Address
Box 102, Naval Air Station

Jacksonville, FL 32212-5000
904-542-2340; FAX 904-542-2413; DSN
942-4032; DSN FAX 942-2413
E-mail: NASJAX.ORG Internet:http://www.nas-
jax.org
OFFICER-OF-THE-DAY: 904-542-2338, DSN
942-2338

Profile
BRANCH: Navy.
SIZE AND LOCATION: 3896 acres. Approx 13
mi S of downtown Jacksonville. I-295 around
Jacksonville to intersection of I-295 and US-
17 (Roosevelt Blvd), US-17 N Exit (marked
NAS Jacksonville), main gate about 3 mi N
of intersection. Jacksonville IAP approx 35
mi. *County:* Duval.
MAJOR UNITS: Naval Air Station, Jackson-
ville; Patrol Wing 11, Commander; Naval
Base Jacksonville, Commander; Naval Hospi-
tal Jacksonville; Naval Supply Center; Naval
Aviation Depot; Naval Air Reserve Unit; Patrol Squadron 5 (VP-5); Patrol Squadron 16
(VP-16); Patrol Squadron 24 (VP-24); Patrol
Squadron 30 (VP-30); Patrol Squadron 45
(VP-45); Patrol Squadron 49 (VP-49); Patrol
Squadron 56 (VP-56); Helicopter Antisubma-
rine Wing, US Atlantic; Helicopter Antisub-
marine Squadron 3; Helicopter Antisubmarine Squadron 5; Helicopter Antisubmarine
Squadron 11; Helicopter Antisubmarine
Squadron 15; Naval Air Reserve, Jacksonville; Naval Oceanography Command Facility; Naval Reserve Readiness Command, Region 8; Fleet & Industrial Supply Center;
Navy Band, Jacksonville; Naval Oceanography Command Facility.
BASE HISTORY: During WWI, area named
Camp Joseph E Johnston (Army) and later
Camp Foster (National Guard). 1940, commissioned. WWII, base provided training for aviation cadets & served as POW camp for German soldiers. 1945, separation center & Naval Hospital. 1946, 1st home of Navy's Flight
Demonstration Team, Blue Angels. 1948, mission changed to fleet units support. 1950s, establishment of Patrol Squadrons with mission
of antisubmarine warfare. Today, air station
stands at forefront of antisubmarine warfare
readiness.
FUTURE CLOSURE/REALIGNMENT: To
gain aircraft & personnel (Sea Control Wing,
US Atlantic Fleet) from Cecil Field; lose HS-
1 to decommissioning by 1998.

Key Contacts
COMMANDER: Capt Robert D Whitmire, Box
102, 32212-0102, 904-542-2334, DSN
942-2334.
PUBLIC AFFAIRS: Charles P Dooling, Box 2,
904-542-4032, FAX 904-542-2413, DSN
942-4032.
PROCUREMENT: Supply Office,
904-542-5420, DSN 942-5420.
TRANSPORTATION: 904-542-2461, DSN
942-2461.
PERSONNEL/COMMUNITY ACTIVITIES:
Steven Scott, Director of Personnel,
904-542-3253, FAX 904-542-3091, DSN
942-3253.

Personnel and Expenditures
ACTIVE DUTY PERSONNEL: 8097
DEPENDENTS: 610
CIVILIAN PERSONNEL: 9532
MILITARY PAYROLL EXPENDITURE: $250 mil
CONTRACT EXPENDITURE: $549 mil

Services
Housing: Family units 407; Unaccompanied officer quarters 325; Unaccompanied enlisted quarters 2200; Duplex units; Barracks spaces; Senior
NCO units; Junior NCO units; Mobile home
units 50; Trailer spaces; RV/Camper sites full
service 8; partial service 5; primitive 13. *Temporary Housing:* VIP units; Unaccompanied offi-
cer/Enlisted quarters; Lodge units; Transient
quarters. *Commissary:* Yes; *Exchange:* Retail
store; Barber shop; Dry cleaners; Photo shop; Florist; Bank; Service station; Furniture store; Military clothing store; Convenience store; Beauty
shop; Laundromat; Credit union; ATM; Optical
store; Post office; Fast food; Video rentals;
Thrift shop; Travel agency; Class VI; Shoe repair; Computer store; Garden center; Tailor/Al-
terations; Laundry; Cafeteria; Photo store; Ice
cream; Exchange equipment rental. *Child Care/
Capacities:* Day care center preschool-kindergar-
ten; Home day care program; Before & after
school programs. *Schools:* College/University;
College courses. *Base Library:* Yes. *Medical Facilities:* Hospital 263; Medical clinic; Dental
clinic; Pharmacy; Veterinary services. *Recreational Facilities:* Bowling center; Movie theater;
Pool; Gym; Recreation center (game room);
Golf course; Tennis courts; Racquetball court;
Fitness center/Weight room; Softball field; Auto
shop; Craft shop; Officers club; NCO club;
Camping (summer day); Fishing/Hunting; Enlisted club; Youth center; Picnic area; Skeet
range; Water sports; Playground; Community
club; All ranks club; Consolidated club; Rod &
Gun club; ITT office; Youth and family program; Marina; Equipment rental.

206. Jacksonville Naval Hospital
NAVHOSPJAX
2080 Child St
Jacksonville, FL 32214-5000
904-777-7300 (Information Desk); FAX
904-777-7792; DSN 942-7300; DSN FAX
942-7300
Internet: http://199.208.118.32/
OFFICER-OF-THE-DAY: 904-777-7301, DSN
942-7301

Profile
BRANCH: Navy.
SIZE AND LOCATION: 25 acres. On Naval
Air Station, Jacksonville, FL, off US-17.
County: Duval.
BASE HISTORY: 1941, originally constructed
for in-patient care of military personnel,
gradually changed to provide care for dependents and retired personnel. 1967, present 8-
story facility constructed. 1972, Naval Regional Medical Center Command established
here. 1983, decommissioned & Naval Hospital commissioned; Naval Regional Medical
Clinic, Key West, FL, made separate entity.
Currently, general medical & surgical hospital with Navy's largest Family Practice Training Program; tenant of NAS Jacksonville.

Key Contacts
COMMANDER: Capt Milt Benson, Hospital
Commander.
PUBLIC AFFAIRS: Bob Hines.

Personnel and Expenditures
ACTIVE DUTY PERSONNEL: 1000
CIVILIAN PERSONNEL: 500

Services *Exchange:* See Jacksonville NAS.
Child Care/Capacities: Day care center capacity
40.

Medical Facilities: Hospital 176; Medical clinic; Dental clinic; Dispensary; Pharmacy; Veterinary services.

207. Region Eight, Naval Reserve Readiness Command
REDCOM 8
Box 90, Bldg 966 NAS
Jacksonville, FL 32212-0090
904-772-2486; 1-800-201-4199; FAX
904-772-4180; DSN 942-2486
Internet: http://www.navy.mil/homepages/
redcom8/

Profile
BRANCH: Naval Reserve.
MAJOR UNITS: Naval Reserve Readiness Command, Region 8.

Key Contacts
COMMANDER: Capt Stan Halter.

208. US Army Corps of Engineers, Jacksonville District
CESAJ
400 W Bay St
Jacksonville, FL 32202-4412
Mailing Address
PO Box 4970
Jacksonville, FL 32232-0019
904-232-2241; FAX 904-232-1213
Internet: http://www.saj.usace.army.mil/

Profile
BRANCH: Army.
SIZE AND LOCATION: Offices only. In downtown Jacksonville at intersection of Bay & Julia Sts, in Charles E Bennet Federal Bldg; approx 15 mi from Jacksonville IAP. *County:* Duval.
MAJOR UNITS: Corps of Engineers, Jacksonville District.
BASE HISTORY: Established 1947, Jacksonville District, one of six districts in South Atlantic Division, responsible for civil works mission in peninsular FL (entire state for regulatory functions) & Antilles (PR & US Virgin Islands). Current projects include navigation, flood control, beach erosion control, regulatory functions, recreation, hurricane protection, water supply, water pollution control, hydroelectric power, flood plain management services, urban studies program, environmental quality policy, & emergency operations. Part of South Atlantic Division, HQ in Atlanta. Performs civil works construction.

Key Contacts
COMMANDER: Col Joe R Miller, Commander & District Engineer, 904-232-2241, FAX 904-232-2237.
PUBLIC AFFAIRS: Jacquelyn Griffin, 904-232-2235, FAX 904-232-2237, jacquelyn.j.griffin@saj02.usace.army.mil.

Personnel and Expenditures
ACTIVE DUTY PERSONNEL: 4
CIVILIAN PERSONNEL: 750
Services *Base Library:* Yes. *Recreational Facilities:* Boating, camping, picnicking available at recreation sites.

MacDill AFB

209. MacDill Air Force Base
8208 Hanger Loop Dr, Ste 51
MacDill AFB, FL 33621-5502
813-280-1110; DSN 968-1110
E-mail: webmaster@macdill.af.mil Internet:
http://www.macdill.af.mil
OFFICER-OF-THE-DAY: Command Post, 813-828-4361, DSN 968-4361

Profile
BRANCH: Air Force.
SIZE AND LOCATION: 5700 acres. Approx 5 mi S of Tampa on tip of Interbay Peninsula; I-75 to I-275 S, exit at Dale Mabry Hwy (US-92S), 5 mi S to main gate. *County:* Hillsborough.
MAJOR UNITS: 6th Air Refueling Wing; US Central Command; US Special Operations Command; Joint Communications Support Element; NOAA Air Operations Center.
BASE HISTORY: 1939, construction began. 1941, activated as MacDill Army Air Base, named for Col Leslie MacDill, aviation pioneer. WWII, mission transitional training B-17s & B-26s. 1946, training in B-29s, SAC base, flew bombers. 1950-63, 306th Bombardment Group in command. Scheduled to close in 1962, renewed activity with Cuban Missile Crisis and activation of US Strike Command & transition from SAC to Tactical Air Command. 1963, 1st F-4C base. 1970, mission changed from replacement training to combat-ready operational. 1972, US Readiness Command activated. 1981, became 56th Tactical Training Wing and converted to F-16s. 1980, Rapid Deployment Task Force activated, until 1983, US Central Command replaced it. 1987, US Special Operations Command activated. 1994, major staging area for Operation Restore Democracy in Haiti. BRAC 95, recommended keeping base open and relocate active flying back. 1996, 6th Air Base Wing redesignated 6th Air Refueling Wing under 21st Air Force & Air Mobility Command.
FUTURE CLOSURE/REALIGNMENT: BRAC 95 returned control of air field to Air Force; called for 12 KC-135 Stratotankers from Malmstrom AFB, MT to relocate; 6th Air Base Wing designated 6th Air Refueling Wing; aligned under Air Mobility Command.

Key Contacts
COMMANDER: Brig Gen John D Becker, Wing Commander, 813-828-4444, 813-828-5407, DSN 968-4444.
PUBLIC AFFAIRS: Capt Edwina Walton, 813-828-2215, FAX 813-828-3653, DSN 968-2215.
PROCUREMENT: LTC Richard McHargue, Supply Officer, 813-828-3249, DSN 968-3249.
TRANSPORTATION: LTC Michael Kane, 813-828-2771, DSN 968-2771.
PERSONNEL/COMMUNITY ACTIVITIES: Capt Alan Gladfelter, Director of Personnel, 813-828-3311, FAX 813-828-3311, DSN 968-3311.

Personnel and Expenditures
ACTIVE DUTY PERSONNEL: 5170
DEPENDENTS: 12,279
CIVILIAN PERSONNEL: 1937
MILITARY PAYROLL EXPENDITURE: $190 mil
CONTRACT EXPENDITURE: $95 mil

Services
Housing: Family units 804; Barracks spaces / Dormitories 2076; Trailer spaces with hookups 191; RV/Camper sites without hookups 285; Tent sites 35; Housing renovations underway, 10 yr project, numbers will vary. *Temporary Housing:* VIP units suites 20; VOQ units 112; VAQ units 62; Transient quarters 25; Chief suites 3. *Commissary:* Yes; *Exchange:* Barber shop; Dry cleaners; Food shop; Florist; Bank; Service station; Furniture store; Bakery; Military clothing store; Convenience store; Beauty shop; Laundromat; Credit union; ATM; Optical store; Post office; Fast food; Video rentals; Thrift shop; Travel agency; Class VI; Tailor/Alterations; Laundry; Photo store. *Child Care/Capacities:* Day care center capacity 192, 6mos-5yrs; Home day care program; Summer day camp; Before & after school programs. *Schools:* Preschool/Kindergarten; Elementary; College/University; College courses. *Base Library:* Yes. *Medical Facilities:* Hospital 55; Dental clinic; Pharmacy; Veterinary services. *Recreational Facilities:* Bowling center; Movie theater; Pool; Gym; Golf course; Tennis courts; Racquetball court; Fitness center/Weight room; Softball field; Football field; Auto shop; Craft shop; Officers club; NCO club; Camping; Fishing/Hunting; Enlisted club; Youth center; Picnic area; Skeet range; Water sports; Playground; Marina; Miniature golf; Model airplanes.

Mayport

210. Mayport Naval Air Station
NAVSTA Mayport
Mayport, FL 32228-0112
904-270-5011; DSN 960-5011
Internet: http://www.navy.mil/pwcjax/myphis.htm

Profile
BRANCH: Navy.
SIZE AND LOCATION: 3409 acres. At mouth of St Johns River, 18 mi E of downtown Jacksonville; accessible from Rte A1A or Rte 10-W; Beaches Exit from I-95, Atlantic Blvd to Mayport Rd, left onto Mayport Rd dead ends at NS. *County:* Duval.
MAJOR UNITS: Cruiser-Destroyer Group 12; Carrier Group 6; Destroyer Squadron 12; Destroyer Squadron 14; Destroyer Squadron 24; Helicopter Antisubmarine Light Wing; Helicopter Antisubmarine Squadron Light 40; Helicopter Antisubmarine Squadron Light 42; Helicopter Antisubmarine Squadron Light 44; Helicopter Antisubmarine Squadron Light 46; Helicopter Antisubmarine Squadron Light 48; Western Hemisphere Group; Afloat Training Group, Mayport; Fleet Training Center; Shore Intermediate Maintenance Activity; Regional Support Group; USS *John F Kennedy*; NAMTRAGRUDET Mayport.
BASE HISTORY: 1942, commissioned as second SE naval installation. 1943, reclassified Naval Section Base; landing field added; fueling facility for submarines. 1944, Naval Auxiliary Air Station commissioned; encompassed entire site. 1945, decommissioned; placed in caretaker status. 1948, reactivated as Naval Outlying Landing Field. By 1951, more than doubled in size, serving first carrier. 1955, Auxiliary Air Station reactivated. 1959, designated Naval Station. 1962, ad-

vanced staging area, Cuban Missile Crisis. 1982-1984, ships homeported at Mayport involved in operations off coast of Beirut, Lebanon, & Operation Urgent Fury in Grenada; Naval Air Facility established. 1987, USS *Stark* (homeported at Mayport), struck by Iraqi missiles in Persian Gulf. 1988, redesignated Naval Air Station. 1990, homeported ships deployed in Middle East. 1992, Naval Air Station consolidated with Naval Station. Homeport to 20 ships.
VISITOR ATTRACTIONS: Weekend ship visit, 904-241-6289.

Key Contacts
COMMANDER: Capt Jan C Gaudio, 904-270-5201.
PUBLIC AFFAIRS: LCDR Conrad C Chun, PO Box 205, Mayport, FL 32228-0205, 904-270-5226, DSN 960-5226.
PROCUREMENT: Joanne Cruz, 904-772-5031.

Personnel and Expenditures
ACTIVE DUTY PERSONNEL: 11,000
DEPENDENTS: 45,000
CIVILIAN PERSONNEL: 1700

Services
Housing: Family units Officer 150; Enlisted 1130; Unaccompanied officer quarters 100; Unaccompanied enlisted quarters 1050; Townhouse units 628; RV/Camper sites 50. *Temporary Housing:* VIP units 10; VEQ units 250; Lodge units 19. *Commissary:* Yes; *Exchange:* Retail store; Barber shop; Dry cleaners; Food shop; Florist; Bank; Service station. *Child Care/Capacities:* Day care center capacity 375; Home day care program. *Schools:* No on-base schools. *Base Library:* Yes. *Medical Facilities:* Medical clinic; Dental clinic; NAVCARE, approx 5 mi at Naval Hospital, Jacksonville. *Recreational Facilities:* Bowling center; Pool; Gym; Recreation center; Golf course; Tennis courts; Racquetball court; Softball field; Auto shop; Craft shop; Officers club; Fishing/Hunting; Chief club; Track; EM club; Beach; Boat rentals; Car wash.

Miami

211. US Southern Command
SOUTHERN COMMAND
3511 NW 91st
Miami, FL 33172
Internet: http://www.ussouthcom.com/southern

Profile
BRANCH: Joint Service Installation.
LOCATION: 4 mi W of Miami IAP; off Florida Turnpike in Westpointe Business Park. *County:* Dade.
MAJOR UNITS: US Southern Command.
BASE HISTORY: Oct 1997, new HQ dedicated; relocated from Quarry Heights, Panama. Mission: oversees US military activity in South and Central America and Caribbean area.

Key Contacts
COMMANDER: Gen Charles E Wilhelm, USMC; RADM Walter F Doran, USN, Deputy Commander; Gen Weley K Clark, US Army.
PUBLIC AFFAIRS: Lt Jane Campbell, 305-437-1206, 437-1200; fax: 305-597-4744.

Personnel and Expenditures
ACTIVE DUTY PERSONNEL: 850
CIVILIAN PERSONNEL: 130
CONTRACT EXPENDITURE: $50 mil (local impact)

Services
Housing: None. *Schools:* No on-base schools.

Miami Beach

212. Miami Beach Coast Guard Group/Station
GRUMIA/BMB; BMB, GROUP Miami
100 MacArthur Causeway
Miami Beach, FL 33139-5101
305-535-4301; FAX 305-535-4493
OFFICER-OF-THE-DAY: 305-535-4315, 535-4316

Profile
BRANCH: Coast Guard.
SIZE AND LOCATION: 14 acres. On Mac Arthur Cswy (I-395) approx 1 mi W of Miami Beach; 4 mi E from Miami; 12 mi E from Miami IAP. *County:* Dade.
MAJOR UNITS: Coast Guard Group, Miami; Coast Guard Station, Miami Beach; Aids to Navigation (ANT) Team, Miami; USCGC *Valiant*; USCGC *Farallon*; USCGC *Manitou*; USCGC *Matagorda*; USCGC *Maui*; USCGC *Barnof*; USCGC *Chandeleur*; Coast Guard Reserve Center, Miami; Naval Engineering Support Unit, Miami; Electronic Support Det, Miami; Coast Guard Reserve Unit CNCWU 207; Integrated Support Command, Miami.
BASE HISTORY: 1941, Coast Guard acquired man-made island to replace beach facilities previously located at Ft Lauderdale & Miami Beach; named Coast Guard Depot, Causeway Island until 1946, when designated as Base Miami Beach. 1993, commissioned station. Current multimission responsibility: command & control center for Coast Guard Group Miami; serves Greater Miami area as world's busiest search & rescue & law enforcement unit; services Aids to Navigation; industrial plant (second largest in Coast Guard), services units throughout 7th Coast Guard District.
VISITOR ATTRACTIONS: Tours available upon request subject to operational commitments.

Key Contacts
COMMANDER: 305-535-4301.
PUBLIC AFFAIRS: 305-535-4312.
PROCUREMENT: 305-535-4322.
TRANSPORTATION: 305-535-4342.

Personnel and Expenditures
ACTIVE DUTY PERSONNEL: 400
CIVILIAN PERSONNEL: 75

Services
Housing: Barracks spaces 33. *Temporary Housing:* Transient quarters 1. *Exchange:* Retail store; Barber shop; Dry cleaners; Military clothing store; Military clothing store; Convenience store; ATM. *Child Care/Capacities:* No day care facilities. *Schools:* No on-base schools. *Medical Facilities:* Medical clinic; Dental clinic; Dispensary. *Recreational Facilities:* Pool; Gym; Recreation center; Racquetball court; Fitness center/Weight room (workout room); NCO club; Enlisted club; Basketball courts; Indoor firing range; Volleyball courts.

Milton

213. Whiting Field Naval Air Station
NAS Whiting Field; NASWF Whiting Field
7550 USS Essex St
Milton, FL 32570-6155
904-623-7201; FAX 904-623-7625; DSN 868-7201; DSN FAX 868-7625
E-mail: nday1@navtap.navy.mil Internet:http://www.ncts.navy.mil/naswf
OFFICER-OF-THE-DAY: 904-623-7331, DSN 868-7331

Profile
BRANCH: Navy.
SIZE AND LOCATION: 3973 acres. 8 mi NE of Milton, FL. *County:* Escambia, Santa Rosa, Fl; Conecuh, South Baldwin, AL.
MAJOR UNITS: Naval Training Air Wing 5; Naval Oceanographic Command; Training Squadron 2 (VT-2); Training Squadron 3 (VT-3); Training Squadron 6 (VT-6); Helicopter Training Squadron 8; Helicopter Training Squadron 18; Navy Resale; Branch Medical Clinic.
BASE HISTORY: 1943, commissioned; named for Naval hero Kenneth Whiting. 1945, POW camp established with Camp Rucker, AL. After WWII, reverted to NAS and became known as backbone of Navy's flight program. 1949-50, home of Blue Angels, precision flying team, and Navy's first jet training unit, JUT ONE, commissioned. 1972, home of Training Air Wing 5 and established helicopter training at South Field and North Field, home of three fixed-wing squadrons. Above includes all of NASWF's Outlying Landing Fields; Barin, Brewton, Choctow, Evergreen, Harold, Holley, Pace, Santa Rosa, Saufley, Site 6, Site 8, Silverhill, Spencer, Summerdale, and Wolf.
VISITOR ATTRACTIONS: Naval Aviation Atrium Museum.

Key Contacts
COMMANDER: Capt Richard L Dick, 7550 USS Essex St, Ste 100, 32570-6155, 904-623-7121, FAX 904-623-7757, DSN 868-7121.
PUBLIC AFFAIRS: JOCS(SW) Dave Youngquist, 7550 USS Essex St, Ste 201, 32570-6155, 904-623-7651, FAX 904-623-7601, DSN 868-7651.
PROCUREMENT: Lt George Degener, 904-623-7727, DSN 868-7727.
TRANSPORTATION: Marian Williams, Public Works, 7151 USS Wasp St, 32570-6159, 904-623-7268, DSN 868-7268.
PERSONNEL/COMMUNITY ACTIVITIES: Ed Dee, MWR, 7180 Langley St, 32570-6149, 904-623-7221, DSN 868-7221.

Personnel and Expenditures
ACTIVE DUTY PERSONNEL: 1708
DEPENDENTS: 4300
CIVILIAN PERSONNEL: 1164
MILITARY PAYROLL EXPENDITURE: $86 mil
CONTRACT EXPENDITURE: $60 mil

Services
Housing: Family units 412; Unaccompanied officer quarters 232; Unaccompanied enlisted quarters 305; Duplex units 100. *Temporary Housing:* VIP units 2; Unaccompanied officer/Enlisted quarters 62; BEQ 12.

Commissary: Yes; *Exchange:* Retail store; Barber shop; Dry cleaners; Food shop; Florist; Bank; Service station. *Child Care/Capacities:* Day care center capacity 32. *Schools:* College courses. *Base Library:* Yes. *Medical Facilities:* Medical clinic; Dental clinic. *Recreational Facilities:* Bowling center; Pool; Gym; Recreation center; Golf course; Tennis courts; Racquetball court; Fitness center/Weight room; Softball field; Auto shop; Craft shop; Officers club; Camping; Fishing/Hunting; Enlisted club; Water sports.

Old Town

214. Operating Location Alpha Bravo South East Air Defense Sector
OLAB SE AD SECTOR
Rte 2, Box 321
Old Town, FL 32680-9710
904-542-7457
Profile
BRANCH: Air Force.
SIZE AND LOCATION: 5 acres. From Cross City, FL, US-19 turn E on County Rd 351, approx 12 mi on N side of road. *County:* Dixie.
MAJOR UNITS: Southeast Air Defense Sector, OL-AB; Federal Aviation Administration.
BASE HISTORY: Joint FAA/USAF radar site.
Key Contacts
COMMANDER: Site Chief.
Personnel and Expenditures
CIVILIAN PERSONNEL: 7

Opa-Locka

215. Miami Coast Guard Air Station
CGAS Miami
15000 NW, 42nd Ave, Opa-Locka Airport
Opa-Locka, FL 33054-2397
305-953-2105
Profile
BRANCH: Coast Guard.
SIZE AND LOCATION: 20 acres. On Opa-Locka Airport. *County:* Dade.
MAJOR UNITS: Coast Guard Air Station, Miami; Coast Guard Tactical Law Enforcement Team.
BASE HISTORY: 1932, commissioned on Biscayne Bay, first aviation unit in Coast Guard. Today, world's busiest air/sea rescue unit. Now at Opa-Locka Airport, mission includes search & rescue, maritime law enforcement, & environmental protection.
VISITOR ATTRACTIONS: Air Station tours conducted by Public Affairs Office.
Key Contacts
COMMANDER: 305-953-2101.
PUBLIC AFFAIRS: 305-953-2151.
Personnel and Expenditures
ACTIVE DUTY PERSONNEL: 339
CIVILIAN PERSONNEL: 2
Services
Housing: BAQ units Two person rooms 26. *Commissary:* Yes; *Exchange:* Retail store; Barber shop. *Medical Facilities:* Medical clinic; Dental clinic. *Recreational Facilities:* Pool; Gym; Tennis courts; Auto shop; NCO club.

Orlando

216. Naval Air Warfare Center, Training Systems Division
NAWCTSD
12350 Research Pkwy
Orlando, FL 32826-3224
407-380-4000
Internet: http://www.ntsc.navy.mil/
Profile
BRANCH: Navy.
SIZE AND LOCATION: 40 acres. In Central FL Research Park, just off Alafaya Trail, approx 1.5 mi N of State Rd 50; approx 15 mi from downtown Orlando; approx 12 mi E of Naval Training Center, Orlando; about 17 mi NE of Orlando IAP; adj to Univ of Central FL; facility also known as de Florez Complex. *County:* Orange.
MAJOR UNITS: Naval Training Systems Division; Army Project Manager for Training Devices (PM TRADE).
BASE HISTORY: Early 1940s, began as three-man desk in Navy's Bureau of Aeronautics; evolved into complex, multidisciplinary organization that annually procures about a billion dollars in training systems. Pioneered development of simulation devices for military training. At de Florez Building since 1988.
Key Contacts
COMMANDER: Capt W Mark Yerkes.
PUBLIC AFFAIRS: Code 75, 407-380-8208, 380-8372, PAO@ntsc.navy.mil.
Personnel and Expenditures
ACTIVE DUTY PERSONNEL: 50
CIVILIAN PERSONNEL: 1200
Services *Base Library:* Yes. *Medical Facilities:* Naval Hospital, Orlando. *Recreational Facilities:* Bowling center; Movie theater; Golf course; Tennis courts; Softball field; Auto shop; Officers club; NCO club.

217. Orlando Naval & Marine Corps Reserve Readiness Center
NAVMARCORESCEN Orlando
595 N Primrose Dr, Ste 1
Orlando, FL 32803-5074
407-646-5991; FAX 407-898-7514; DSN 791-5991
Profile
BRANCH: Naval Reserve; Marine Corps Reserve.
SIZE AND LOCATION: 1 acre. By Executive Airport in Orlando. *County:* Orange.
MAJOR UNITS: REDCOM EIGHT Activity.
Key Contacts
COMMANDER: Capt Virginia D Joosten.
PUBLIC AFFAIRS: QM2 A Jenkins, 407-897-8161.
Personnel and Expenditures
ACTIVE DUTY PERSONNEL: 750 Reservists
Services *Recreational Facilities:* Gym; Fitness center/Weight room.

218. Orlando, Naval Training Center
NTC
4701 Holland St
Orlando, FL 32813
407-646-4501; DSN 791-4501
Profile
BRANCH: Navy.

LOCATION: NTC on N side of Orlando; Annex on S (formerly McCoy AFB). *County:* Orange.
MAJOR UNITS: Naval Training Center, Orlando; Naval Nuclear Power Training Command.
BASE HISTORY: 1940, commissioned as Army Air Corps base. 1968, recommissioned NTC.
Key Contacts
COMMANDER: Capt Southgate.
PUBLIC AFFAIRS: Ens Davis, 407-646-5053, DSN 791-5053.
Services
Housing: Family units; *Temporary Housing:* Lodge units. *Commissary:* Yes; *Exchange:* Retail store. *Child Care/Capacities:* Day care center capacity 150; *Schools:* No on-base schools. *Recreational Facilities:* Bowling center; Pool; Gym; Golf course; Auto shop; Craft shop; NCO club; Picnic area.

Panama City

219. Naval Coastal Systems Station
NCSC
6703 W Hwy 98
Panama City, FL 32407-7001
850-234-4011; DSN 436-4011
Internet: http://www.ncsc.navy.mil/
Profile
BRANCH: Navy.
SIZE AND LOCATION: 580 acres. 1 mi W of Panama City on US-98; 1 mi W of Gulf Coast Community College and Florida State Univ-Panama City Campus; on St Andrew Bay. *County:* Bay.
MAJOR UNITS: Navy Diving & Salvage Training Center (NDSTC); Navy Experimental Diving Unit (NEDU); US Coast Guard Station; Florida Marine Patrol.
BASE HISTORY: 1942, base established to provide safe harbor for WWII convoy ships. 1944, established training center for amphibious vessel crews, including crews in D-Day invasion. 1945, training center closed; forerunner of Naval Coastal Systems Center moved to site; equipment & personnel from deactivated Mine Warfare Test Station, Solomons Island, MD, nucleus of new facility; station redesignated Navy Mine Defense Laboratory. 1968, renamed Naval Ship Research & Development Laboratory, Panama City. 1972, renamed Naval Coastal Systems Laboratory. 1978, received present name.
Key Contacts
COMMANDER: Capt Richard J Parish, 850-234-4201, DSN 436-4201.
PUBLIC AFFAIRS: Steve Applegate, 850-234-4817, DSN 436-4817.
Personnel and Expenditures
ACTIVE DUTY PERSONNEL: 670
DEPENDENTS: 1200
CIVILIAN PERSONNEL: 1400
Services
Housing: Family units 65; Unaccompanied enlisted quarters rooms 6; BAQ units 13; Junior NCO units 15; Mobile home units 15. *Temporary Housing:* VIP units suites 5; VOQ units 36; VEQ units 184; RV Trailer rentals 11. *Exchange:* Retail store; Barber shop; Dry cleaners; Food shop; Florist. *Child Care/Capacities:* No day care facilities. *Schools:* No on-base schools. *Base Library:* Yes.

Medical Facilities: Medical clinic; Dental clinic. *Recreational Facilities:* Bowling center; Pool; Gym; Tennis courts; Racquetball court; Fitness center/Weight room; Softball field; Auto shop; Officers club; NCO club; Camping; Fishing/ Hunting.

220. Tyndall Air Force Base

500 Minnesota Ave
Panama City, FL 32403-5000
850-283-1110; DSN 523-1110
Internet: http://www.tyndall.af.mil/
OFFICER-OF-THE-DAY: 850-283-1110, DSN 523-1110

Profile
BRANCH: Air Force.
SIZE AND LOCATION: 29,000 acres. 12 mi E of Panama City, FL on US-98; Bay County/ Panama City Municipal Airport approx 15 mi. *County:* Bay.
MAJOR UNITS: 325th Fighter Wing; Air Education and Training Command; 1st Air Force; Air Force Civil Engineering Support Agency; Southeast Air Defense Sector; 475th Weapons Evaluation Group; Wright Laboratories; 148th Fighter Wing, Det 1 (MN ANG); Armstrong Laboratories; 1st Fighter Squadron; 2md Fighter Squadron; 325th Logistics Group; 325th Supply Squadron; 325th Medical Group; 84th Test Squadron; Environics Directorate; NORAD Systems Support Facility; Canadian Forces Det; Air Force Water Survival School.
BASE HISTORY: 1941, commissioned as Air Corps' first flexible gunnery school named for Lt Frank B Tyndall, native of FL & WWI flying ace. 1946, site of Air Training Command base, home of Air University's Air Tactical School. 1957, transferred to Air Defense Command shifting mission to weapons center. 1968, Air Defense Weapons Center activated here. 1979, transferred to TAC. 1981, 325th Fighter Weapons Wing (later renamed 325th Tactical Training Wing) activated. Home of Air Force Air-to-Air Weapons Meet, William Tell, since 1958. 1983, TAC's first Region Operations Control Center (ROCC) established. 1991, Weapons Center deactivated; 325th Tactical Fighter Wing (later 325th FW) host. 1992, part of Air Combat Command. 1993, part of Air Force Education & Training Command.
VISITOR ATTRACTIONS: Located in resort area with unlimited fresh & salt water activities available.

Key Contacts
COMMANDER: Brig Gen Gary M Rubus, 325th FW/CC, 500 Minnesota Ave, Suite 1, 32403-5426, 850-283-2668, DSN 523-2668.
PUBLIC AFFAIRS: Jim Weslowski, 325th FW/PA, 500 Minnesota Ave, Suite 3, 32403-5425, 850-283-2983, DSN 523-2983.
PROCUREMENT: Contracting Officer; 325th CONS/CC, 501 Illinois Ave, Suite 5, 32403-5526, 850-283-3266, DSN 523-3266.
TRANSPORTATION: 325th TRANS/CC, 244 Alabama Ave, 32403-5120, 850-283-2304, DSN 523-2304.
PERSONNEL/COMMUNITY ACTIVITIES: 325 MSSQ/CC, 445 Suwannee Rd, Suite 211, 32403-5536, 850-283-3241, DSN 523-3241.

Personnel and Expenditures
ACTIVE DUTY PERSONNEL: 4600; Guard 270; Reserve 140
DEPENDENTS: 5500

CIVILIAN PERSONNEL: 2500
Services
Housing: Family units 1069; RV/Camper sites 50. *Temporary Housing:* VOQ units 239; BAQ units 864; Guest cottages 3; Transient quarters 40. *Commissary:* Yes; *Exchange:* Retail store; Barber shop; Dry cleaners; Food shop; Florist; Service station; Military clothing store; Convenience store; Beauty shop; Credit union. *Child Care/Capacities:* Day care center capacity 300, 6wks-5yrs; Home day care program; Summer day camp; Before & after school program (K-3rd grade). *Schools:* Preschool/Kindergarten; Elementary; College courses. *Base Library:* Yes. *Medical Facilities:* Hospital 30 beds; Medical clinic; Dental clinic; Pharmacy; Veterinary services. *Recreational Facilities:* Bowling center; Movie theater; Pool; Gym; Recreation center; Golf course; Stables; Tennis courts; Racquetball court; Fitness center/Weight room; Softball field; Auto shop; Craft shop; Officers club; NCO club; Camping; Fishing/Hunting; Youth center; Picnic area; Skeet range; Water sports; Playground; Aero club.

Patrick AFB

221. Patrick Air Force Base

45th Space Wing
Patrick AFB, FL 32925-3237
407-494-1110; DSN 854-1110
Internet: http://www.pafb.af.mil

Profile
BRANCH: Air Force.
SIZE AND LOCATION: 2342 acres. 2 mi S of Cocoa Beach on Rte A1A. *County:* Brevard.
MAJOR UNITS: 45th Space Wing; 45th Operations Group; 45th Logistics Group; 45th Support Group; 45th Operations Support Group; 45th Range Squadron; 45th Weather Squadron; 45th Civil Engineer Squadron; 45th Communications Squadron; 45th Mission Support Squadron; 45th Security Forces Squadron; 45th Services Squadron; 1st Space Launch Squadron; 3rd Space Launch Squadron; 5th Space Launch Squadron; 23rd Intelligence Squadron; 114th Combat Communications Squadron; 333rd USAF Recruiting Squadron; Air Force Technical Applications Center; Defense Equal Opportunity Management Institute; 920th Rescue Group; DOD Manned Space Flight Support Office; Eastern Range.
BASE HISTORY: 1940, established as Banana River NAS. 1948, Air Force took over; renamed it for Maj Gen Mason M Patrick, Chief of Army Air Service, 1921-27.

Key Contacts
COMMANDER: Brig Gen F Randall Starbuck, 45th Space Wing, 407-494-6204, FAX 407-494-2516.
PUBLIC AFFAIRS: Lynda Yezzi, lynda-yezzi@ pafb.af.mil.

Personnel and Expenditures
ACTIVE DUTY PERSONNEL: 1400
DEPENDENTS: 4500
CIVILIAN PERSONNEL: 700
Services
Housing: Family units Officer 197; Enlisted 1352; Unaccompanied enlisted quarters 278. *Temporary Housing:* VIP units 8; VOQ units 100; VEQ units Senior NCO 26; Enlisted 74; Lodge units 51; Mobile home units 55; Tent spaces at campgrounds 5.

Commissary: Yes; *Exchange:* Retail store; Barber shop; Dry cleaners; Food shop; Florist; Service station; Military clothing store; Convenience store; Furniture store; Beauty shop; Optical store; Video rentals; Laundry; Mini-mall; Car rental; Toys. *Child Care/Capacities:* Day care center capacity 157; Home day care program. *Schools:* No on-base schools. *Base Library:* Yes. *Medical Facilities:* Hospital 25 beds; Veterinary services. *Recreational Facilities:* Bowling center; Movie theater; Pool; Gym; Golf course; Stables; Tennis courts; Racquetball court; Fitness center/Weight room; Auto shop; Craft shop; Officers club; NCO club; Camping; Fishing/Hunting; Youth center; Picnic area; Skeet range; Water sports; Aero club; Beach; Yacht club; Boat marina.

Pensacola

222. Corry Station Naval Technical Training Center

NAVTECHTRACEN Pensacola FL
640 Roberts Ave
Pensacola, FL 32511-5138
850-452-6516; FAX 850-452-6633; DSN 922-6516
OFFICER-OF-THE-DAY: 850-452-6512, DSN 922-6512

Profile
BRANCH: Navy.
SIZE AND LOCATION: 349.3 acres. On FL panhandle Gulf Coast, 3 mi from Pensacola, FL; access via New Warrington Rd (State Rd 295) and US-98. *County:* Escambia.
MAJOR UNITS: Naval Technical Training Center; Audio Visual/Photo Office; Defense Investigative Service; Naval Criminal Investigative Service; Naval Security Group Activity; 313th Training Squadron (USAF); Marine Support Bn, Co K.
BASE HISTORY: 1923, opened; originally Corry Field, named for LCDR William M Corry Jr, naval pioneer aviator. 1928, moved to present site, as aviation training command. After WWII, facility active as auxiliary air station. 1958, decommissioned. 1960, recommissioned Naval Communications Training Center. 1973, Navy electronic warfare training schools consolidated at Corry and Naval Schools of Photography detachment here; renamed Naval Technical Training Center. 1990, Opticalman and Instrumentman Applied Instruction transferred from Great Lakes, IL. 1995, Joint Aviation Electronic Warfare School added. Current mission entry- & advanced-level training of all services officer/enlisted personnel.

Key Contacts
COMMANDER: Capt Hugh Doherty, 850-452-6516, FAX 850-452-6633, DSN 922-6516.
PUBLIC AFFAIRS: Sandra E Bansemer, 850-452-6318, FAX 850-452-6053, DSN 452-6053.

Personnel and Expenditures
ACTIVE DUTY PERSONNEL: 1040
CIVILIAN PERSONNEL: 594
MILITARY PAYROLL EXPENDITURE: $76.2 mil
CONTRACT EXPENDITURE: $1.7 mil

Services

Housing: Unaccompanied enlisted quarters; Barracks spaces; Senior NCO units; Junior NCO units. *Commissary:* Yes; *Exchange:* Retail store; Barber shop; Dry cleaners; Food shop; Florist; Bank; Service station; Credit union; ATM; Post office; Fast food; Thrift shop; Travel agency. *Child Care/Capacities:* Day care center capacity 250, new born-8 yrs. *Schools:* No on-base schools. *Base Library:* Yes. *Medical Facilities:* Medical clinic; Dental clinic. *Recreational Facilities:* Bowling center; Pool; Gym; Recreation center; Tennis courts; Racquetball court; Fitness center/Weight room; Football field; Auto shop; Craft shop; CPO club; Camp site on Perdido Bay.

223. Naval Education and Training Professional Development and Technology Center
NETPDTC
Saufley Field
6490 Saufley Field Rd
Pensacola, FL 32509-5237
850-452-1313; DSN 922-1313
Internet: http://www.cnet.navy.mil/netpdtc/saufax.htm

Profile
BRANCH: Navy.
SIZE AND LOCATION: 866 acres. 7 mi NW of Pensacola, FL; Approx 2.5 mi W of junction of US-90 and Saufley Field Rd; approx 8 mi W of Pensacola Municipal Airport. *County:* Escambia.
MAJOR UNITS: Naval Education and Training Professional Development and Technology Center; Defense Activity for Non-traditional Education Support (DANTES); Defense Finance and Accounting Service Financial Systems Activity (DFAS-FFAPE); Naval Reserve Center, Saufley Field; Navy Advancement Center.
BASE HISTORY: 1940, Saufley Field opened. 1943, commissioned Naval Auxiliary Air Station. 1968, redesignated NAS. 1976, decommissioned; caretaker status; airfield designated Outlying Landing Field. 1979, reactivated for Naval Education and Training Program Development Center & Navy's first Federal Prison Camp, operated by Bureau of Prisons. 1986, NETPDTC host. Airfield currently used as outlying field with touch-and-go landings for pilot training by NAS Whiting Field.

Key Contacts
COMMANDER: Capt Barbara J Stankowski, 850-452-1310, FAX 850-452-1307, DSN 922-1310, DSN FAX 922-1307, netpdtc.00@smtp.cnet.navy.mil.
PUBLIC AFFAIRS: Media Resources Division, 850-452-1825, DSN 922-1825, netpdtc.n72@smtp.cnet.navy.mil; cnet.pao@smtp.cnet.navy.mil.

Personnel and Expenditures
ACTIVE DUTY PERSONNEL: 1000
CIVILIAN PERSONNEL: 530; Federal Prisoners 500

Services
Housing: None. *Temporary Housing:* None. *Exchange:* Retail store; Barber shop; Dry cleaners. *Child Care/Capacities:* No day care facilities. *Schools:* No on-base schools. *Medical Facilities:* No medical facilities. *Recreational Facilities:* Gym; Golf course (par three); Tennis courts; Racquetball court; Fitness center/Weight

room; Softball field; Consolidated dining facility (limited hours).

224. Pensacola Coast Guard Station
21 Slemmer Ave
Pensacola, FL 32508-5231
850-453-8282

Profile
BRANCH: Coast Guard.
LOCATION: On NAS Pensacola. *County:* Escambia.
MAJOR UNITS: Coast Guard Station, Pensacola; Aids to Navigation (ANT) Team, Pensacola; Coast Guard Liaison, Pensacola; USCGC *Point Lobos.*
BASE HISTORY: 1885, original US Life Saving Service located on Santa Rosa Island. 1979, following two hurricanes, Station relocated on Big Lagoon, W of Pensacola Pass. 1987, present site dedicated. Mission: search & rescue, law enforcement, aids to navigation, & safety & marine environment coverage extends along FL Panhandle.

Personnel and Expenditures
ACTIVE DUTY PERSONNEL: 45

Services
Housing: Crew's quarters only. *Exchange:* Also uses Pensacola NAS. *Recreational Facilities:* Shares facilities with Pensacola NAS.

225. Pensacola Naval Air Station
NASP; NAS Pensacola
190 Radford Blvd
Pensacola, FL 32508-5217
850-452-0111 (Operator); FAX 850-452-2760; DSN 922-0111
E-mail: naspoob12@netpmsa.cnet.navy.mil Internet:http://www.cnet.mil/NASPCOLA/NASPCOLA.HTM
OFFICER-OF-THE-DAY: Command Duty Office, 850-452-2353, DSN 922-2353

Profile
BRANCH: Navy.
SIZE AND LOCATION: 5800 acres. Approx 11 mi SW of Pensacola, FL, on Navy Blvd; approx 12 mi E of AL state line; from I-10, Exit 2 S on Hwy 297 (Pine Forest Rd) merges with Hwy 90 (Mobile Hwy), S on Hwy 90 to Hwy 295 (New Warrington Rd) becomes Navy Blvd to Main Gate. *County:* Escambia.
MAJOR UNITS: Naval Air Station; Chief of Naval Education & Training; Naval Air Technical Training Center; Naval Aviation Schools Command; Commander, Training Wing Six; Navy Recruiting Orientation Unit; Marine Aviation Training Support Group; Naval Air Maintenance Training Group; Naval Operational Medical Institute; Navy Flight Demonstration Squadron (Blue Angels).
BASE HISTORY: "Cradle of Naval Aviation," established 1914, oldest NAS. 1826, Pensacola Navy yard established on original site. 1861, some claim first shots of Civil War fired here. 1911, decommissioned. 1914, selected as first Aeronautic Center. WWI, nicknamed "Annapolis of the Air" and known for development of balloons, blimps, and dirigibles at Chevalier Field. 1928, auxiliary base, Corry Field, constructed 5 mi N of main station. WWII, auxiliary fields added: Bronson, Barin, and Whiting, FL. 1948, designated Naval Air Basic Training Command HQ. 1971,

Chief of Naval Education and Training here. Today, all naval aviators begin training here.
VISITOR ATTRACTIONS: Naval Aviation Museum; Fort Barrancas; Fort Redoubt; Barrancas National Cemetery; Lighthouse Tours.

Key Contacts
COMMANDER: Capt J Michael Denkler, 850-452-2713, DSN 922-2713.
PUBLIC AFFAIRS: GS-12 Harry C White, Code OOBOO, 850-452-2311, FAX 850-452-2760, DSN 922-2311, NASPOOBOO@Netpmsa.cent.navy.mil..

Personnel and Expenditures
ACTIVE DUTY PERSONNEL: 12,004
CIVILIAN PERSONNEL: 4502
MILITARY PAYROLL EXPENDITURE: $411 mil
CONTRACT EXPENDITURE: $160 mil

Services
Housing: Family units adequate 585, substandard 198; Unaccompanied officer quarters 220; Unaccompanied enlisted quarters 4908; Senior NCO units 22; Junior NCO units 365; RV/Camper sites 42; Tent sites 14. *Temporary Housing:* VIP units 38; VOQ units 485; VEQ units 725; Unaccompanied officer/Enlisted quarters 220; Lodge units 12; Mobile home units 12. *Commissary:* Yes; *Exchange:* Retail store; Barber shop; Dry cleaners; Food shop; Florist; Bank; Service station; Furniture store; Bakery; Military clothing store; Convenience store; Beauty shop; Laundromat; Credit union; ATM; Optical store; Post office; Fast food; Video rentals; Four seasons; Thrift shop; Class VI; Tailor/Alterations; Laundry; Cafeteria; Commissary located on Hwy 98 nearby; Florist at NEX Mall on Hwy 98. *Child Care/Capacities:* Day care center capacity 182, 6wks-6yrs; Summer day camp. *Schools:* College courses; No on-base schools. *Base Library:* Yes. *Medical Facilities:* Hospital 161 beds; Medical clinic; Dental clinic; Dispensary; Pharmacy; Veterinary services; Navy Hospital on Hwy 98 nearby. *Recreational Facilities:* Bowling center; Movie theater; Pool; Gym; Recreation center; Golf course; Stables; Tennis courts; Racquetball court; Fitness center/Weight room; Softball field; Football field; Auto shop; Craft shop; Officers club; Camping; Fishing/Hunting; Enlisted club; Youth center; Picnic area; Water sports; Playground; Community club; All ranks club; Consolidated club.

226. Pensacola Naval Hospital
6000 W Hwy 98
Pensacola, FL 32512-0003
850-452-6601

Profile
BRANCH: Navy.
SIZE AND LOCATION: 78 acres. On Hwy 98, between Navy Blvd and Fairfield Dr; 3 mi N of NAS Pensacola. *County:* Escambia.
MAJOR UNITS: Naval Hospital Pensacola.
BASE HISTORY: Since early 19th century, Navy medicine practiced in 6 different facilities in Pensacola area. 1976, newest, 8-story, structure dedicated. 1983, redesignated Naval Hospital Pensacola. Also, responsible for branch hospital & 8 branch medical clinics in MS & FL.

Key Contacts
COMMANDER: Capt Lockhart, Commander.
PUBLIC AFFAIRS: 850-452-6601, DSN 922-6601.

Services
Housing: See Pensacola NAS. *Temporary Housing:* See Pensacola NAS.

Exchange: Retail store; Barber shop; Food shop; Florist; Convenience store; Beauty shop; Laundry; Tailor; Optical shop; Video rental. *Child Care/Capacities:* No day care facilities. *Medical Facilities:* Hospital 342 beds; Medical clinic. *Recreational Facilities:* Tennis courts.

227. Pensacola Naval Reserve Center
550 Raby Ave
Pensacola, FL 32509-5246
850-452-1341, 452-1342; FAX 850-452-1405; DSN 922-1341
Profile
BRANCH: Naval Reserve.
LOCATION: *County:* Escambia.
MAJOR UNITS: Naval Reserve Center, Pensacola.
Key Contacts
COMMANDER: CDR G A Dacosta.

Saint Augustine

228. Adjutant General of Florida
St Francis Barracks
Dept of Military Affairs, PO Box 1008
Saint Augustine, FL 32085-1008
904-823-0100; FAX 904-823-0125
Profile
BRANCH: Army National Guard.
MAJOR UNITS: Florida National Guard.
Key Contacts
COMMANDER: Maj Gen Ronald O Harrison.
PUBLIC AFFAIRS: Crystal Sauls, 904-823-0166.

Saint Petersburg

229. Defense Contract Management Command, Clearwater
DCMC Clearwater
9549 Koger Blvd, Ste 200
Saint Petersburg, FL 33702-2455
Internet: http://33.33.100.174/
Profile
BRANCH: Defense Logistics Agency.
LOCATION: *County:* Pinellas.
MAJOR UNITS: Defense Contract Management Command, Clearwater.
Key Contacts
COMMANDER: LTC R Mark Brown.

230. Egmont Key Coast Guard Light Station
LTSTA Egmont Key
C/O USCG Station, Saint Petersburg
Saint Petersburg, FL 33701
813-823-5588
Profile
BRANCH: Coast Guard.
SIZE AND LOCATION: 1.5 acres. On island of Egmont Key, 1.5 mi W of entrance to Tampa Bay; only access by boat. *County:* Hillsborough.
MAJOR UNITS: Light Station, Egmont Key.
BASE HISTORY: 1940, land set aside for military use; established as Coast Guard Station.

Primary mission upkeep of light (6th brightest in FL), grounds, radiobeam, foghorn, and assisting in search & rescue around island.
VISITOR ATTRACTIONS: Remains of Spanish-American War fort; Lighthouse dating to 1858; 55 acre bird sanctuary.
Key Contacts
COMMANDER: Officer in Charge.
PUBLIC AFFAIRS: See CG Group/Station, St Petersburg, FL.
Personnel and Expenditures
ACTIVE DUTY PERSONNEL: 4
Services
Housing: Crew's quarters only.

231. St Petersburg Coast Guard Group/Station
Group St Petersburg
600 8th Ave, SE
Saint Petersburg, FL 33701-5099
813-824-7505
Profile
BRANCH: Coast Guard.
SIZE AND LOCATION: 10 acres. Approx 20 mi from Tampa Airport; bounded by Albert Whitted Airport to N, Univ of S FL, St Petersburg campus to W, Bayboro Harbor to S, separated from Tampa Bay to E by airport runway. *County:* Pinellas.
MAJOR UNITS: Coast Guard Group, St Petersburg; Coast Guard Station, St Petersburg; Aids to Navigation (ANT) Team, St Petersburg; Electronic Support Det, St Petersburg; USCGC *Durable;* USCGC *Resolute;* USCGC *White Sumac;* USCGC *Vise;* USCGC *Venturous.*
BASE HISTORY: 1928, originally commissioned on S side of Bayboro Harbor; relocated to Clearwater. 1976, moved to vacated Air Station facilities across harbor. Old site, still part of station, serves as South Moorings for ships. Old Station office building serves as Reserve training facility. Group Offices colocated at Station. Missions: search & rescue, law enforcement, & industrial support.
Personnel and Expenditures
ACTIVE DUTY PERSONNEL: 120
CIVILIAN PERSONNEL: 6
Services *Exchange:* Retail store; Barber shop; Food shop. *Medical Facilities:* Medical clinic; Dental clinic. *Recreational Facilities:* Pool; NCO club.

Starke

232. Camp Blanding Training Site
CBTS/ISU
Rt 1, Box 465
Starke, FL 32091-9703
904-533-2268; DSN 960-3100
OFFICER-OF-THE-DAY: 904-533-2268, DSN 960-3100
Profile
BRANCH: Army National Guard.
SIZE AND LOCATION: 76,000 acres. In N central FL, off State Rd 16, 5 mi E of Starke, on Kingsley Lake. *County:* Clay.
MAJOR UNITS: 653rd Engineer Det (Utilities); 221st Ordnance Det; Florida Regional Training Institute (OCS); 202nd Civil Engineering Squadron (CES), Florida Air National Guard; 3rd Bn, 20th Special Forces Group (Air-

borne), HQ & HQ Det; Support Co, 3rd Bn; 20th Special Forces Group (Airborne); 853rd Supply & Service Co; US Property and Fiscal Office; State Maintenance Office (SMO); Combined Support Maintenance Shop; Mobilization and Training Equipment Site (MATES); 159th Weather Flight (ANG); 631st Maintenance.
BASE HISTORY: Site was location of FL NG, Camp Foster. 1939, named for Lt Gen Albert H Blanding, distinguished FL soldier. 1940, leased to Army as active duty training center. During WWII, served as infantry replacement training center, induction center, POW compound, & separation center. Following WWII, 30,000 acres returned to armory board. 1950-70, limited use by military. 1970s, expansion began. 1981, redesignated as Class A military installation. Site includes parachute drop zone & airfield expanded training capacity; Navy uses bombing & strafing target in southern portion of post. E I DuPont de Nemours & Co mines restricted area on western edge of post (ilmenite & other heavy minerals).
VISITOR ATTRACTIONS: Camp Blanding Museum of World War II.
Key Contacts
COMMANDER: Col John F Holechek Jr.
PUBLIC AFFAIRS: Maj Gregory A Moore, 904-823-0168, DSN 860-7168.
PROCUREMENT: Maj Drexel Bullivant; 904-533-3507, DSN 960-3507.
PERSONNEL/COMMUNITY ACTIVITIES: Maj Bruce J Cornelison, 904-533-3457.
Personnel and Expenditures
ACTIVE DUTY PERSONNEL: 41
CIVILIAN PERSONNEL: 50
Services *Temporary Housing:* VIP units 3; Officer/enlisted quarters for temporary use during training 80. *Exchange:* Retail store; Barber shop; Tailor/Alterations. *Medical Facilities:* Medical clinic. *Recreational Facilities:* Tennis courts; Racquetball court; Softball field; Football field; NCO club; Camping; Fishing/Hunting; Picnic area; Water sports.

Summerland Key

233. Cudjoe Key Air Force Station
Cudjoe Key AFS
PO Box 420235
Summerland Key, FL 33042
305-745-3844
Profile
BRANCH: Air Force.
SIZE AND LOCATION: 65 acres. Off US-1 on FL Keys approx 30 mi N of Key West; 130 mi S of Homestead AFB; at end of State Rd 5 (unmarked) on N side of US-1 by mile marker 21.5. *County:* Monroe.
MAJOR UNITS: Southeast Air Defense Sector, Det 3.
BASE HISTORY: 1959, activated as missile tracking station for Eglin Test Range. 1960, designated Cudjoe Key AFS. 1967, transferred to Air Force Security Service. 1971, reassigned to Aerospace Defense Command for testing of medium range balloon-borne radar surveillance system, Seek Skyhook. 1980, home to fully operational continuous air defense radar surveillance. 1982, Project Seek Skyhook redesignated Tethered Aerostat Radar System (TARS). Detachment 3, Opera-

tion Location AM, 20th Air Defense Squadron went through several redesignations until receiving current designation, 1987.

Key Contacts
PUBLIC AFFAIRS: Information Specialist.

Personnel and Expenditures
CIVILIAN PERSONNEL: 42
CONTRACT EXPENDITURE: $3.7 mil

Tallahassee

234. Tallahassee Naval & Marine Corps Reserve Center
NAVMARCORESCEN Tallahassee;
  NCRTC Tallahassee
2910 Roberts Ave
Tallahassee, FL 32304-5098
904-576-6194, 576-6195, 574-3149; FAX
904-574-3615

Profile
BRANCH: Naval Reserve; Marine Corps Reserve.
SIZE AND LOCATION: 1 acre. Approx 5 mi from downtown Tallahassee. *County:* Leon.
MAJOR UNITS: REDCOM EIGHT Activity; Voluntary Training Unit; Naval Reserve FFG Support 208; Naval Hospital Jacksonville; Naval Reserve Shore Intermediate Maintenance Activity, Det 908; Naval Reserve CINCUSNVAEUR (Commander in Chief U.S. Naval Forces Europe) Det 108; NMCB 14, Det 1114; Explosive Ordnance Department Mobilization Unit; Tallahassee Training Unit; Naval Reserve NSC (Navy Supply Corps) Pensacola 108; Naval Reserve SCONTGRP 0814; 4th Air Naval Gunfire Liaison Co (MARFORRES).
BASE HISTORY: Post WWII, Marine Corps reserve center; Naval reserves added later. Small facility for classroom training & administrative support.

Key Contacts
COMMANDER: LCDR W T Carney.

Personnel and Expenditures
ACTIVE DUTY PERSONNEL: 27; 384 reservists

Services *Temporary Housing:* Lodging for reservists coordinated with local hotel. *Medical Facilities:* Corpsman.

Recreational Facilities: Gym; Fitness center/ Weight room.

Tampa

235. Tampa Coast Guard Marine Safety Office
MSO Tampa
155 Columbia Dr
Tampa, FL 33606-3598
813-228-2191; FAX 813-228-2399

Profile
BRANCH: Coast Guard.
SIZE AND LOCATION: 1.25 acres. In city of Tampa on Davis Island; approx 10 mi from Tampa IAP. *County:* Hillsborough.
MAJOR UNITS: Marine Safety Office, Tampa.
BASE HISTORY: Jurisdiction encompasses almost entire W coast of FL from Stake Point in N to Everglades City on S; extending inland generally to center of state.

Personnel and Expenditures
ACTIVE DUTY PERSONNEL: 42
CIVILIAN PERSONNEL: 3

236. Tampa Naval Reserve Center
1325 York St
Tampa, FL 33602-4298
813-209-4001, 209-4003; FAX 813-228-2557

Profile
BRANCH: Naval Reserve.
LOCATION: *County:* Hillsborough.
MAJOR UNITS: REDCOM EIGHT Activity.

Key Contacts
COMMANDER: CDR S Zivovic.

West Palm Beach

237. West Palm Beach Naval & Marine Corps Reserve Center
NAVMCRC West Palm Beach; MCRTC
1227 Marine Dr
West Palm Beach, FL 33409-6298
561-687-3954; FAX 561-687-3961

E-mail: ndas1@navtap.navy.mil

Profile
BRANCH: Naval Reserve; Marine Corps Reserve.
LOCATION: 4 mi from downtown West Palm Beach, directly across from Miami IAP. *County:* Palm Beach.
MAJOR UNITS: REDCOM EIGHT Activity; Navy Reserve Recruiters; 4th Air Naval Gunfire Liaison Co (MARFORRES).

Key Contacts
COMMANDER: LCDR Robert McKenna, 561-688-9194, FAX 561-687-3961, ndas1@ navtap.navy.mil.

Personnel and Expenditures
ACTIVE DUTY PERSONNEL: 11; 340 reservists

Services *Recreational Facilities:* Fitness center/ Weight room.

Yankeetown

238. Yankeetown Coast Guard Station
P.O. Box 360
Yankeetown, FL 34498-0360
352-447-6901

Profile
BRANCH: Coast Guard.
SIZE AND LOCATION: 3.4 acres. Approx 3.5 mi from Gulf of Mexico; approx 3 mi from US-19; 40 mi from I-75; 100 mi from Tampa IAP. *County:* Levy; Citrus.
MAJOR UNITS: Coast Guard Station, Yankeetown.
BASE HISTORY: 1963, houseboat commissioned CG Lifeboat Station Islamorada, FL. 1975, houseboat refurbished; recommissioned Station Yankeetown. 1990, permanent station commissioned (replaced houseboat); responsible for search & rescue, law enforcement, & aids to navigation from Bayport to Fenholloway River, FL.

Key Contacts
PUBLIC AFFAIRS: See CG Group/Station, St. Petersburg, FL.

Personnel and Expenditures
ACTIVE DUTY PERSONNEL: 21

Services
Housing: Barracks spaces 6.

Georgia

Albany

239. Albany Marine Corps Logistics Base

MCLB Albany
814 Radford Blvd
Albany, GA 31704-1128
912-439-5000; DSN 567-5000
Internet: http://www.hqmc.usmc.mil
OFFICER-OF-THE-DAY: 912-439-5206, DSN
567-5206

Profile
BRANCH: Marine Corps.
SIZE AND LOCATION: 3330 acres. In SE corner of Albany; accessible from US-19; road signs to base; Albany/Dougherty County Airport approx 12 mi SW of Albany. *County:* Dougherty.
MAJOR UNITS: Deputy Commander for Logistics Operations; Corporate Information Management Office; Integrated Logistics Support Directorate; Information Resources Management Directorate; Contracts Directorate; Storage and Distribution Directorate; Prepositioning Programs Support Directorate; Blount Island Command; Marine Corps Band, Marine Corps Logistics Base; Mobile Equipment Ordnance Center.
BASE HISTORY: 1952, commissioned as Marine Corps Depot of Supplies. 1954, large depot repair facility completed; renamed Marine Corps Supply Center. 1954-1967, controlled supplies at storage & issue locations in eastern half of US, Atlantic, Caribbean, & Mediterranean areas. 1976, renamed Marine Corps Logistics Support Base, Atlantic. 1978, present name. 1990, assumed command of Marine Corps Logistics Base, Barstow, CA, & Blount Island Command, Jacksonville, FL. 1990-91, major support of Operations Desert Shield/Storm. Today, inventory control point of Marine Corps.
VISITOR ATTRACTIONS: Indian Lake Wildlife Refuge dedicated to Native Americans (area hunting ground). Deer, bobcat, raccoon, opossum, & waterfowl protected inside refuge; fishing & boating permitted. Refuge open year-round to MCLB personnel & tour groups on request.

Key Contacts
COMMANDER: LTC Catkin Burton, Battalion Commander.
PUBLIC AFFAIRS: 912-439-5215, DSN 567-5215.

Personnel and Expenditures
ACTIVE DUTY PERSONNEL: 900
DEPENDENTS: 1700
CIVILIAN PERSONNEL: 3175

Services
Housing: Family units Officer 97; Enlisted 572; Unaccompanied officer quarters 12; Unaccompanied enlisted quarters 32; Trailer spaces 20. *Temporary Housing:* VIP units 3; VOQ units 10; VEQ units 4; Guesthouse units 6. *Commissary:* Yes; *Exchange:* Retail store; Barber shop; Dry cleaners; Food shop; Bank; Service station. *Child Care/Capacities:* Day care center 3 centers, capacity 244; Home day care program. *Schools:* No on-base schools. *Base Library:* Yes. *Medical Facilities:* Medical clinic; Dental clinic; Local civilian hospitals provide in-patient care. *Recreational Facilities:* Bowling center; Movie theater; Pool; Gym; Recreation center; Golf course; Tennis courts; Racquetball court; Fitness center/Weight room; Softball field; Football field; Auto shop; Officers club; NCO club; Fishing/Hunting; Youth center; Soccer field.

Athens

240. Navy Supply Corps School

NAVSCSCOL
1425 Prince Ave
Athens, GA 30613
706-354-4111; FAX 706-354-7239; DSN 588-4111

Profile
BRANCH: Navy.
SIZE AND LOCATION: 58.5 acres. Corner of Prince & Oglethorpe Aves, Athens, GA; accessible from Hwy 29, Athens Bypass or Hwys 78 & 316 from Atlanta; 60 mi NE of Atlanta; served by Ben Epps (Clarke Co) Airport 3.5 mi away. *County:* Clarke.
MAJOR UNITS: Navy Supply Corps School; Personnel Support Det.
BASE HISTORY: 1860s, first used as Univ of GA High School. Civil War, Confederate Training site, Federal Garrison, & hospital/school for disabled Civil War veterans. 1891, became State Normal School; 1932, Univ of GA, Dept of Ed. WWII, Army & Navy training site. 1954, commission as sole training location for Navy Supply Corps officers to receive basic supply corps qualifications training; 17 other courses offered, including Marine Corps Aviation Supply Officer Qualification Course. Only Navy training site with complete set of afloat automated systems.
VISITOR ATTRACTIONS: Navy Supply Corps Museum (in Carnegie Library on National Historic Register); entire base part of Oglethorpe Historic District on Georgia's Antebellum Trail.

Personnel and Expenditures
ACTIVE DUTY PERSONNEL: 356; plus 250 students
DEPENDENTS: 300
CIVILIAN PERSONNEL: 146
MILITARY PAYROLL EXPENDITURE: $6.3 mil
CONTRACT EXPENDITURE: $1.4 mil

Services
Housing: Family units 56; Townhouse units. *Temporary Housing:* VIP units 5; Unaccompanied officer/Enlisted quarters 169; Barracks. *Commissary:* Yes; *Exchange:* Retail store; Barber shop; Service station; Military clothing store; Convenience store; Credit union. *Child Care/Capacities:* Day care center capacity 22, 1-5yrs. *Schools:* Preschool/Kindergarten; College courses. *Base Library:* Yes. *Medical Facilities:* Medical clinic; Dental clinic; Dispensary. *Recreational Facilities:* Pool; Gym; Recreation center; Tennis courts; Racquetball court; Fitness center/Weight room; Softball field; Officers club; NCO club; Camping; Fishing/Hunting; Enlisted club; Youth center; Water sports; Playground.

Atlanta

241. Adjutant General of Georgia

935 E Confederate Ave, SE
Atlanta, GA 30316
Mailing Address
GA Dept of Defense, PO Box 17965
Atlanta, GA 30316-0965
404-624-6001; FAX 404-624-6005

Profile
BRANCH: Army National Guard.
MAJOR UNITS: Georgia National Guard.

Key Contacts
COMMANDER: Maj Gen William P Bland Jr, 404-624-6024.

242. Navy Office of Information, Southeast

100 Alabama St SW, Ste 4R10
Atlanta, GA 30303
404-562-1630; FAX 404-562-1635

Profile
BRANCH: Navy.
MAJOR UNITS: Navy Office of Information, Southeast.
BASE HISTORY: Serves AL, FL, GA, KY, MS, NC, SC, VA, WV, US Virgin Islands, & Puerto Rico.

243. US Army Corps of Engineers, South Atlantic Division
CESAD
77 Forsyth St, SW, Rm 322
Atlanta, GA 30303-3490
404-331-6711; FAX 404-331-1269
Internet: http://www.usace.army.mil/sad/
Profile
BRANCH: Army.
SIZE AND LOCATION: Offices only. In city of Atlanta; SAD Lab, 611 S Cobb Dr, Marietta, GA 30060-3112, 770-919-5296; FAX 770-919-4977. *County:* Fulton.
MAJOR UNITS: Corps of Engineers, South Atlantic Division.
BASE HISTORY: Responsible for execution of Corps missions in southeastern US, Caribbean, & Latin America; 260,000 sq mi; all or part of 8 states. Five district offices: Wilmington, NC; Charleston, SC; Savannah, GA; Jacksonville, FL; & Mobile, AL. Performs military & civil works construction and real estate.
Key Contacts
COMMANDER: Brig Gen Robert L VanAntwerp.
Personnel and Expenditures
ACTIVE DUTY PERSONNEL: 35 (division)
CIVILIAN PERSONNEL: 4400 (division)

Augusta

244. Augusta Naval & Marine Corps Reserve Center
NAVMARCORESCEN Augusta
2869 Central Ave
Augusta, GA 30909-3904
706-733-2249; FAX 706-733-2695
Profile
BRANCH: Naval Reserve; Marine Corps Reserve.
SIZE AND LOCATION: 2 acres. 1 block N of Wrightsboro Rd at Daniel Field. *County:* Richmond.
MAJOR UNITS: REDCOM EIGHT Activity; FFG22 2207 (NR); NCFSU 3 Det E; NH Jacksonville 1408 (NR); NWS CHAS EOT Det 5 (NR); 4FSSG 4th Maintenance Bn CCB MSE5 (NR); NH Jacksonville PO80 (NR); 2nd Direct Support Platoon, Motor Transport Maintenance Co, 4th Maintenance Bn.
Key Contacts
COMMANDER: LCDR J D Croce, USNR.
PUBLIC AFFAIRS: YN2 T L Burton.
Personnel and Expenditures
ACTIVE DUTY PERSONNEL: 8; 200+ reservists

Columbus

245. Columbus Naval Reserve Center
PO Box 1539
Columbus, GA 31902-1539
706-324-5298, 324-9185; FAX 706-327-7254
Profile
BRANCH: Naval Reserve.
LOCATION: *County:* Muscogee.
MAJOR UNITS: REDCOM EIGHT Activity.
Key Contacts
COMMANDER: LCDR B K Lowe.

Dobbins AFB

246. Atlanta Naval & Marine Corps Reserve Readiness Center
1210 Sea Services Rd
Dobbins AFB, GA 30069-5000
770-218-9939; FAX 770-218-0297; DSN 925-5816
Profile
BRANCH: Naval Reserve; Marine Corps Reserve.
LOCATION: *County:* De Kalb; Fulton.
MAJOR UNITS: REDCOM EIGHT Activity.
Key Contacts
COMMANDER: CDR D L Upton.

Forest Park

247. Fort Gillem
Fort McPherson/Gillem
4705 N Wheeler Dr
Forest Park, GA 30050-5000
404-363-7311; DSN 797-7311
Internet: http://www.mcphersn.army.mil/fortgill.htm
OFFICER-OF-THE-DAY: 404-464-3602, DSN 367-3602
Profile
BRANCH: Army.
SIZE AND LOCATION: 1500 acres; Lake Allatoona 85 acres. 15 min S of downtown Atlanta off I-75 and I-85; Hartsfield IAP 15 min W; installation just outside Exchange 285 which goes around Atlanta and just off Bypass 675 which connects I-75 to 285 and I-85. *County:* Clayton.
MAJOR UNITS: 1st US Army, HQ; Army Criminal Investigation Command, HQ, Third Region; Army Criminal Investigation Laboratory, HQ; Army Criminal Investigation Laboratory-CONUS (Continental US); 547th Ordnance Det (Explosive) Ordnance Disposal Control Center; 13th Ordnance Det; Army 2nd Recruiting Brigade; Readiness Group, Atlanta; Army & Air Force Exchange System Distribution Center; 52nd Ordnance Group; 81st Regional Support Command; Georgia National Guard Armory.
BASE HISTORY: 1941, site established when Atlanta General Army Depot moved Candler Warehouse to now Ft Gillem; many name changes serving as trainer & supplier. 1973, responsibility transferred from Army Materiel Command to Forces Command; renamed Ft Gillem (subpost of Ft McPherson), named for

Lt Gen Alvan C Gillem Jr, who began as private at Ft McPherson in 1910 & retired as commanding general 3rd Army. Fort serves as staging area for Red Cross Disaster Action Team & storage space for federally owned house trailers to be used as temporary homes in national emergency.
Key Contacts
COMMANDER: LTC Mike Butt, Ft McPherson, Garrison Commander, Bldg 65, Ft McPherson, GA 30330-5000, 404-464-2206, DSN 367-2206.
PUBLIC AFFAIRS: Barb Govert, 1386 Troop Row SW (PAO), Atlanta GA 30330-1069, 404-464-3392, DSN 367-3392, DSN FAX 367-3392, ext 3659, govert@ftmcphs-emh2.army.mil.
PROCUREMENT: Tom Rolka, 404-464-3258, DSN 367-3258.
TRANSPORTATION: W Looney, 404-363-5581, DSN 797-5581.
PERSONNEL/COMMUNITY ACTIVITIES: Pat Gould, Director of Community Activities, 404-646-2555, DSN 367-2555.
Personnel and Expenditures
ACTIVE DUTY PERSONNEL: 830
CIVILIAN PERSONNEL: 2000
Services
Housing: Family units (Officer and NCO sets) 10; Unaccompanied officer quarters 18; Barracks spaces 70; Senior NCO units 48. *Temporary Housing:* VIP units 1; Transient quarters Officer or enlisted 6. *Commissary:* Yes; *Exchange:* Retail store; Barber shop; Dry cleaners; Food shop; Florist; Bank; Service station; Furniture store; Beauty shop; Credit union; ATM; Optical store; Post office; Fast food; Video rentals; Four seasons; Thrift shop; Travel agency; Class VI; Computer store; Garden center; Laundry; Photo store. *Child Care/Capacities:* Latch key program; Summer camp and before- & after-school programs at Ft McPherson. *Schools:* College courses; No on-base schools. *Medical Facilities:* Medical clinic; Pharmacy. *Recreational Facilities:* Pool; Gym; Tennis courts; Racquetball court; Fitness center/Weight room; Softball field; Picnic area; Skeet range; Community club; Recreation area at Lake Allatoona (45 mi N); Marchman and Stevens recreational lakes with picnicking; Soccer field (formerly Morris Airfield).

Fort Benning

248. Fort Benning
USAIC
HQ, US Army Infantry Center
Fort Benning, GA 31905-5000
706-545-2011; DSN 835-2011
Internet: http://www-benning.army.mil/
Profile
BRANCH: Army.
SIZE AND LOCATION: 182,000 acres. I-185 runs into Ft Benning less than 1 mi S of Columbus, GA. *County:* Muscoger, GA; Chattahooche, GA; Russell, AL.
MAJOR UNITS: Army Infantry Center & School; 3rd Brigade, 3rd Infantry Division (Mechanized); 11th Infantry Regiment; 29th Infantry Regiment; 36th Engineer Group; 75th Ranger Regiment; 718th Engineer Det; 89th Explosive Ordnance Disposal Det; 2145th Garrison Support Unit, Det 11; 1207th

Army Hospital; Army Marksmanship Unit; Army Research Institute, Ft Benning; CIDC, Ft Benning Dist, 3rd MP Group; Combined Arms and Tactics Directorate; Corps of Engineers, Savannah District; Dismounted Battleship Battle Lab; 249th Engineer Bn, B Co, 3rd Plt; Ft Benning Field Office, Region II, US Army Trial Defense Service; Ft Benning Resident Office, 902nd Military Intelligence Group; Infantry Training Brigade; Noncommissioned Officer Academy, Ft Benning; Physical Fitness School; Medical Department Activity (MEDDAC); Ranger Training Brigade; School of the Americas; Special Forces Recruiting; Southeast Civilian Personnel Center (CPOC); TMDE Support Center; TRADOC System Manager, Antitank Missiles; TRADOC Systems Manager, Bradley Fighting Vehicle System; Canadian Infantry School; Soldier Systems Command; 17th Air Support Operations Squadron; Lawson Army Airfield; Drill Sergeant School.

BASE HISTORY: 1918, established with move of School of Musketry (later, Infantry School of Arms) from Ft Sill, OK, to Camp Benning; known as "Home of the Infantry," named for Confederate Maj Gen Henry Lewis Benning. Original site proved unsuitable; Bussey Plantation, S of Columbus, purchased. Following WWI, camp abandoned. 1922, camp renamed Ft Benning; permanent construction of Infantry School began. 1930s, Public Works Administration, Works Progress Administration, & Civilian Conservation Corps built new buildings; Tank School moved from Ft Meade; Officer Candidate Program, & Parachute School. 1950, Ranger Training Command organized. 1958, Martin Army Hospital opened. 1961, airborne training consolidated at Infantry School. 1970, Army Training Center closed; HQ, US Army Infantry Center, reorganized under CONUS Installation Management Study (CIMS). Following Vietnam War, activities phased down; emphasis shifted to more conventional warfare, especially VOLAR concept (Volunteer Army).

VISITOR ATTRACTIONS: National Infantry Museum (Free, M-F, 8-4:30, Sat-Sun & holidays, 12:30-4:30); Airborne and Ranger shows.

Key Contacts
COMMANDER: Maj Gen Carl F Ernst, Commanding General, 650-545-5111; Brig Gen Walter Wojdakowski, Assistant Commandant, Army Infantry School, 650-545-5296; Col John C Latimer, Chief of Staff, Army Infantry School, 650-545-5231; Col Byron D Greene III, Garrison Commander, 650-545-1500 835-5111.
PUBLIC AFFAIRS: Rich McDowell, ATZB-PAO, 31905-5065, 608-545-2211.

Personnel and Expenditures
ACTIVE DUTY PERSONNEL: 21,100; Reservists 12,400
DEPENDENTS: 20,800
CIVILIAN PERSONNEL: 6500

Services
Housing: Family units 4100; Unaccompanied officer quarters 108; Unaccompanied enlisted quarters 26; Barracks spaces 19,000; RV/Camper sites 65; Tent spaces 32. *Temporary Housing:* VIP units 30; VOQ units 1160; VEQ units; Unaccompanied officer/Enlisted quarters 48; Guesthouse units 114; Hotel 1144.

Commissary: Yes; *Exchange:* Retail store; Barber shop; Food shop; Bank; Service station; Bookstore. *Child Care/Capacities:* Day care center capacity 685; Home day care program; Latch key program; Summer day camp. *Schools:* Preschool/Kindergarten; Elementary; Intermediate/Junior high; College/University; College courses. *Base Library:* Yes. *Medical Facilities:* Hospital 167 beds; Medical clinic; Dental clinic; Dispensary; Pharmacy; Veterinary services. *Recreational Facilities:* Bowling center; Movie theater; Pool; Gym; Recreation center; Golf course; Stables; Tennis courts; Racquetball court; Fitness center/Weight room; Softball field; Football field; Auto shop; Craft shop; Officers club; NCO club; Camping; Fishing/Hunting; Enlisted club; Youth center; Picnic area; Skeet range; Water sports; Playground.

Fort Gordon

249. Army Signal Center & Fort Gordon
USASC&FG
Fort Gordon
Chamberlain Ave, Bldg 29808
Fort Gordon, GA 30905-5000
Mailing Address
HQ, US Army Signal Center & Ft Gordon
Fort Gordon, GA 30905-5000
706-791-0110; DSN 780-0110
Internet: http://www.gordon.army.mil
OFFICER-OF-THE-DAY: Duty Officer: 706-791-4517, DSN 780-4517
Profile
BRANCH: Army.
SIZE AND LOCATION: 55,588 acres. 8 mi SW of Augusta, GA; between US-78 & 278 & US-1; gates on both US-78 & US-1. *County:* Richmond; Columbia; McDuffie; Jefferson.
MAJOR UNITS: 15th Regimental Signal Brigade; Army Signal Center; Regimental Noncommissioned Officer Academy; Regimental Officer Academy; Dwight David Eisenhower Army Medical Center; Army Southeastern Regional Dental Command; Army Dental Activity; Army Dental Laboratory; Southeast Regional Veterinary Command; 73rd Ordnance Bn; 63rd Signal Bn; 67th Signal Bn; 93rd Signal Bn; 513th Military Intelligence Brigade; Regional Signal Intelligence Operations Center.
BASE HISTORY: 1941, Camp Gordon, named for Confederate Lt Gen John Brown Gordon, activated for infantry & armor training. WWII, used for divisional training base, 4th & 26th Infantry Divisions, 10th Armored Division, US Disciplinary Barracks, & POW camp for Germans & Italians. Post WWII, almost deserted. 1948, Signal Corps Training Center, Military Police School, & Engineer Aviation Unit Training Center established. 1950s, Military Government Training, Army Criminal Investigation Laboratory, Rehabilitation Training Center, & US Disciplinary Barracks added. 1953, Basic Replacement Training Center; Advanced Leader's School established. 1956, made permanent Army installation; designated Ft Gordon. 1957-58, Army Training Center (Basic) & Civil Affairs School activated. Vietnam War, infantry, military police & signal soldiers trained. 1962, Signal Corps Training Center reorganized under Army Southeastern Signal School. 1974, communications training consolidated at Ft Gordon with relocation of Signal School from Ft Monmouth, NJ; redesignated present name. 1988, Army Computer Science School relocated from Ft Benjamin Harrison, IN. Presently world's largest communications electronics facility & communications electronics training facility. Home of Army Signal Corps.
VISITOR ATTRACTIONS: Signal Corps Museum; Preview Discovery Center; Fort Discovery.

Key Contacts
COMMANDER: MG Michael W Ackerman, Army Signal Center, 706-791-4588, DSN 780-4588; Col Michael W Karpinsky, Brigade Commander, 706-791-7837, DSN 780-7837, Karpinsm@emh1.gordon.army.mil.
PUBLIC AFFAIRS: James L Hudgins, PAO, Bldg 29808, Rm 130, 30905-5283, 706-791-7003, FAX 706-791-2061, DSN 780-7003, hudginsj@emh.gordon.army.mil.
PROCUREMENT: Patsy Wallace, Directorate of Contracting, Bldg 2102, 30505-5110, 706-791-3896, wallacep@emh.gordon.army.mil.
TRANSPORTATION: Winnie Skelton, Directorate of Public Works, Bldg 33720, 30905-5040, 706-791-5144, DSN 780-5144.
PERSONNEL/COMMUNITY ACTIVITIES: Chuck Large, Dir of Community Activities, Bldg 29808, 30905-5020, 706-791-4140, FAX 706-791-2486, DSN 780-4140, largec@emh.gordon.army.mil.

Personnel and Expenditures
ACTIVE DUTY PERSONNEL: 11,228
DEPENDENTS: 2129
CIVILIAN PERSONNEL: 4840

Services
Housing: Family units Officer 153; Enlisted 723; Barracks spaces 10,746; *Temporary Housing:* VIP units 5; VOQ units 463; VEQ units 380; Guesthouse units 110 units; *Commissary:* Yes; *Exchange:* Retail store; Barber shop; Dry cleaners; Food shop; Florist; Bank; Service station; Bakery; Bookstore; Military clothing store; Convenience store; Beauty shop; Credit union; Optical store; Post office; Fast food; Four seasons; Thrift shop; Shoe repair; Class VI; Garden center; Tailor/Alterations; Laundry; Cafeteria; SATO; Car rental; Snack bar. *Child Care/Capacities:* Day care center Hourly care capacity 340; FAmily Child care capacity 250; Home day care program. *Schools:* College courses; No on-base schools. *Base Library:* Yes. *Medical Facilities:* Hospital 176; Medical clinic; Dental clinic; Veterinary services. *Recreational Facilities:* Bowling center; Movie theater; Pool 3; Gym 6; Recreation center; Golf course 9 & 18 Hole; Stables; Tennis courts; Racquetball court; Fitness center/Weight room; Softball field; Football field; Auto shop; Officers club; NCO club; Camping; Fishing/Hunting; Youth center; Recreation area at Thurmond Lake, Leitner Lake, & Mirror Lake; Dinner theater; Nature trail.

Fort McPherson

250. Fort McPherson
1386 Troop Row SW
Fort McPherson, GA 30330-1069

404-464-2206; FAX 404-464-3659; DSN
367-2206; DSN FAX 367-3659
Internet: http://www.mcphersn.army.mil/
OFFICER-OF-THE-DAY: 404-464-3602, DSN
367-3602

Profile
BRANCH: Army.
SIZE AND LOCATION: 487 acres. Borders
southern portion of Atlanta; about 10 min
from downtown and 10 min from airport.
County: Fulton.
MAJOR UNITS: Army Forces Command, HQ
(FORSCOM); Army Reserve Command, HQ;
3rd Army, HQ; Army Garrison, Ft McPherson; Army Medical Command.
BASE HISTORY: Named after Civil War Gen
James Birdseye McPherson, who died nearby.
1889, permanent Army station. Spanish-
American War, served as General Hospital,
jail for spies, Spanish POWs, & recruit training center. 1914, troop garrison ordered to
TX; post nearly abandoned. WWI, again
served as General Hospital & War Prison Barracks. 1920-1923 & 1927-1934, HQ for IV
Corps Area, 8th Infantry Brigade, & 22nd Infantry Regiment (last major troop regiment at
post). Camp Jessup, automobile depot, established along S border; 1927 incorporated into
Fort. 1930s, hospital expanded; post known
as rehabilitation center. WWII, served as hospital center, general supply depot & reception
center for processing recruits (later major
separation center). 1947, home of Third
Army. 1973, reorganization brought Army
Forces Command here (FORSCOM). 1974,
Ft Gillem, GA, designated sub-installation;
1977, Ft Buchanan, PR. 1982, Third Army reactivated Army component HQ, US Central
Command.
VISITOR ATTRACTIONS: Post historic district features 40 buildings on National Register of Historic Places, date from 1887-1910.

Key Contacts
COMMANDER: Col Steven R West,
404-464-2206, DSN 367-2206; Gen David A
Bramlett, Commanding Gen FORSCOM.
PUBLIC AFFAIRS: Barbara Govert, ATTN:
AFRD-PAO, HQ, USARCENT & 3rd Army,
1881 Hardee Ave, SW, 30330-1064,
404-464-3392, DSN 367-3392; Col Rausch,
PAO FORSCOM.
PERSONNEL/COMMUNITY ACTIVITIES:
Marcia T Lance, 404-464-2814, DSN
367-2814.

Personnel and Expenditures
ACTIVE DUTY PERSONNEL: 2500
DEPENDENTS: 6477
CIVILIAN PERSONNEL: 2850
MILITARY PAYROLL EXPENDITURE: $201
mil (includes Ft Gillem)

Services
Housing: Family units 110; Unaccompanied offi-
cer quarters 20; Unaccompanied enlisted quar-
ters 348; BAQ units 20; Barracks spaces 300.
Temporary Housing: VIP units (suites) 8; VOQ
units 49; VEQ units 8; *Commissary:* Yes; *Exchange:* Retail store; Barber shop; Dry cleaners;
Service station; Military clothing store; Convenience store; Beauty shop; Credit union. *Child
Care/Capacities:* Day care center capacity 110.
Schools: No on-base schools. *Base Library:* Yes.
Medical Facilities: Medical clinic; Dental clinic;
Pharmacy; Veterinary services. *Recreational Facilities:* Bowling center; Pool; Gym; Recreation
center; Golf course; Tennis courts; Racquetball

court; Fitness center/Weight room; Softball
field; Football field; Auto shop; Craft shop;
Youth center; Playground; Community club.

Garden City

251. Savannah IAP Air National Guard Base
Travis Field ANGB
1401 Robert B Miller Jr Dr
Garden City, GA 31402
912-966-8201; DSN 860-8210

Profile
BRANCH: Air National Guard.
SIZE AND LOCATION: 20 acres. Co-located
with Savannah IAP; approx 4 mi NW of Sa-
vannah off I-95. *County:* Chatham.
MAJOR UNITS: 165th Airlift Wing (ANG);
Field Training Site (GA ANG).
BASE HISTORY: 1946, site originally named
Chatham Field, home of 158th Fighter Squad-
ron. Early 1950s, named changed to Travis
Field. 1958, home of 165th Group. 1974, re-
designated 165th Tactical Airlift Group.

Personnel and Expenditures
ACTIVE DUTY PERSONNEL: 988 Guard
CIVILIAN PERSONNEL: 300
MILITARY PAYROLL EXPENDITURE: $22.3
mil

Services
Housing: Barracks spaces. *Temporary Housing:*
VOQ units 156; VEQ units 736. *Exchange:* Con-
venience store. *Child Care/Capacities:* No day
care facilities. *Schools:* No on-base schools.
Medical Facilities: Medical clinic. *Recreational
Facilities:* Fitness center/Weight room; Softball
field; Picnic area.

Hinesville

252. Fort Stewart
Hinesville, GA 31314-5000
912-767-1411; FAX 912-767-7939; DSN
870-1411; DSN FAX 870-7939
OFFICER-OF-THE-DAY: 912-767-8666, DSN
870-8666

Profile
BRANCH: Army.
SIZE AND LOCATION: 279,270 acres. In Hinesville, GA; take I-95 S from Savannah IAP;
41 mi SW of Savannah; near US-17, I-16, & I-
95; bisected by GA Hwy 144 & US-17; Savannah & Jessup served by Amtrak; Hinesville 1 mi from main gate; Claxton 37 mi
NW; Glenville 19 mi; Pembroke 18 mi N;
Richmond Hill midway between post & Savannah. *County:* Liberty; Long; Bryan;
Evans; Tattnall.
MAJOR UNITS: 3rd Infantry Division (Mechanized); 24th Corps Support Group; 1st Bn,
75th Ranger Division; 103rd Military Intelligence Bn; Division Support Command; Division Artillery; Aviation Brigade; Engineer
Brigade; 123rd Signal Bn.
BASE HISTORY: 1940, Camp Stewart activated as Anti-aircraft Artillery Center. After
WWII, separation center of redeployed
troops, then inactive. 1950, reopened as Third
Army Anti-aircraft Artillery Training Center.
1953, tank training added. 1956, became permanent military installation, Ft Stewart Anti-

aircraft Artillery & Tank Training Center.
1966, Army Aviation School relocated from
Ft Rucker, AL; new mission: helicopter gunnery courses & helicopter pilot. 1971, designation changed to US Army Garrison, Ft Stewart. 1974, home to infantry units. 1975, 24th
Infantry Division, the Victory Division, officially activated at Stewart's Donovan Field,
motto "First to Fight," heavy element of the
18th Airborne, Combined Contingency
Forces (CCF). Largest Army installation E of
Mississippi River. 1996, 3rd Infantry makes
Ft Stewart home.
VISITOR ATTRACTIONS: Ft Stewart Museum; tour of WWII building area.

Key Contacts
COMMANDER: Maj Gen James Riley,
Commander, 3rd ID(M) & Ft Stewart,
912-767-5606, FAX 912-767-7967, DSN
870-5606, Riley,MGJames@Stewart-emh5.
army.mil.
PUBLIC AFFAIRS: Maj William R Oaks, PAO,
Bldg 294, 912-767-5457, FAX 912-767-4951,
DSN 870-5457, Oaks,WilliamR@
Stewart-emh5.army.mil.
PROCUREMENT: Stephen Kandul, Director of
Contracting, 912-767-8420, FAX
912-767-2966, DSN 870-8420, AFZP-DC@
Stewart-emh5.army.mil.
TRANSPORTATION: Robert J Wagner, Chief
of Transportation Division, 912-767-3278,
FAX 912-767-7896, DSN 870-3275,
AFZP-DIT@Stewart-emh5.army.mil.
PERSONNEL/COMMUNITY ACTIVITIES:
Bo Boram, 912-767-8660, FAX
912-767-9015, DSN 870-8660, boramb@
Stewart-emh5.army.mil 870-2401.

Personnel and Expenditures
ACTIVE DUTY PERSONNEL: 15,917
DEPENDENTS: 5936
CIVILIAN PERSONNEL: 3381
MILITARY PAYROLL EXPENDITURE: $555 mil
CONTRACT EXPENDITURE: $85 mil

Services
Housing: Family units 227; Unaccompanied officer quarters 2700; Barracks spaces 9591; Trailer
spaces 109. *Temporary Housing:* VIP units 4;
Guesthouse units 70; Transient quarters 75; Temporary duty personnel without families at Hunter
AAF 13. *Commissary:* Yes; *Exchange:* Retail
store; Barber shop; Dry cleaners; Food shop; Florist; Bank; Service station; Bakery; Bookstore;
Convenience store; Credit union; ATM; Optical
store; Post office; Fast food; Video rentals;
Thrift shop; Travel agency; Class VI; Tailor/Al-
terations; Laundry; Cafeteria; Photo store; Car
rental; Ice cream parlor; Watch repair shop.
Child Care/Capacities: Day care center capacity
300; Home day care program. *Schools:* Pre-
school/Kindergarten; Elementary. *Base Library:*
Yes. *Medical Facilities:* Hospital 109; Medical
clinic; Dental clinic; Pharmacy; Veterinary services. *Recreational Facilities:* Bowling center;
Movie theater; Pool; Gym; Recreation center;
Golf course; Stables; Tennis courts; Racquetball
court; Fitness center/Weight room; Softball
field; Auto shop; Craft shop; Officers club; NCO
club; Camping; Fishing/Hunting; Enlisted club;
Youth center; Picnic area; Skeet range; Water
sports; Playground; Rod & Gun club; Performing arts center; Track; Garden plots.

Kings Bay

253. Kings Bay Naval Submarine Base

NAVSUBASE Kings Bay
1063 USS Tennessee Ave
Kings Bay, GA 31547-2606
912-673-2001; DSN 573-2001
Internet: http://www.kingsbay.org/kbayhist.htm
Profile
BRANCH: Navy.
SIZE AND LOCATION: 16,000 acres. On outskirts of St Marys, GA, about 5 mi E of I-95, Exits 1, 2, and 2A; nearby towns: Kingsland, about 8 mi W, Woodbine, 18 mi N, Brunswick, GA, about 35 mi N and Jacksonville, FL, about 35 mi S. *County:* Camden.
MAJOR UNITS: Naval Submarine Base, Kings Bay; Strategic Weapons Facility, Atlantic; Submarine Group 10; Submarine Squadron 16; Submarine Squadron 20; TRIDENT Training Facility; Marine Corps Security Force Co, Kings Bay; Construction Base Unit 412; USS *Tennessee* (SSBN 734); USS *Pennsylvania* (SSBN 735); USS *West Virginia* (SSBN 736); USS *Kentucky* (SSBN 737); USS *Maryland* (SSBN 738); USS *Nebraska* (SSBN 739); USS *Rhode Island* (SSBN 740); USS *Maine* (SSBN 741); USS *Wyoming* (SSBN 742); USS *Louisiana* (SSBN 743).
BASE HISTORY: 1954-58, acquired by Army for military ocean terminal. Following completion placed in inactive ready status; Army base never activated. Used twice: 1964, shelter from Hurricane Dora & Cuban Missile Crisis. Following withdrawal of Fleet Ballistic Missile Submarine Squadron from Rota, Spain, Kings Bay selected for relocation. 1978, base transferred from Army to Navy. 1980, named Atlantic Fleet homeport of ballistic submarines. 1982, name changed from Naval Submarine Support Base to Naval Submarine Base.
Key Contacts
COMMANDER: Capt Jim Alley, 912-673-4700.
PUBLIC AFFAIRS: LCDR Robert Raine, 912-673-4714.
PROCUREMENT: Sandra White, 912-673-4609.
Personnel and Expenditures
ACTIVE DUTY PERSONNEL: 4967
DEPENDENTS: 15,650
CIVILIAN PERSONNEL: 4035
MILITARY PAYROLL EXPENDITURE: $115.4 mil
CONTRACT EXPENDITURE: $52.6 mil
Services
Housing: Family units 660; Unaccompanied officer quarters 154; Unaccompanied enlisted quarters 1225; Barracks spaces 461. *Temporary Housing:* VIP units 12; VEQ units 435; Unaccompanied officer/Enlisted quarters 34; Lodge units 26. *Commissary:* Yes; *Exchange:* Retail store; Barber shop; Dry cleaners; Food shop; Florist; Bank; Service station; Beauty shop. *Child Care/Capacities:* Day care center capacity 178; Home day care program. *Schools:* No on-base schools. *Base Library:* Yes. *Medical Facilities:* Medical clinic; Dental clinic. *Recreational Facilities:* Bowling center; Movie theater; Pool; Gym; Tennis courts; Racquetball court; Fitness center/Weight room; Softball field; Football field; Auto shop; Craft shop; Officers club; NCO club.

Marietta

254. Atlanta Naval Air Station

NAS Atlanta
Marietta, GA 30060-5099
770-421-5392; FAX 770-421-5416; DSN 925-5392
Internet: http://www.mindspring.com/~nasatlis/
OFFICER-OF-THE-DAY: 770-421-5392, DSN 925-5392
Profile
BRANCH: Naval Reserve; Marine Corps Reserve.
SIZE AND LOCATION: 184 acres. In Marietta, GA, on Hwy 75, about 20 mi N of Atlanta between Marietta and Smyrna, adj to Dobbins AFB. *County:* Cobb.
MAJOR UNITS: Attack Squadron 205 (VA-205); Fleet Logistics Support Squadron 46 (VR-46); Marine Air Group 42 (MAG-42); Marine Observation Squadron VMO-4; Marine Attack Helicopter Squadron HMLA-773; CAG-20; VAW-77; VFA-203; VMFA-142; RIPO/RIAC-14; MACG-48; MWSS-472; 4th LAAD.
BASE HISTORY: 1941, commissioned as Naval Reserve Aviation Base on part of Fort Gordon. 1943, designated NAS. Post WWII, reverted to Naval Air Reserve Training Program; base area insufficient for safety. 1955-9, moved to present site adjoining Dobbins AFB. Currently, training center for Navy & Marine Corps Reservists; air station provides services, training & support for drilling reservists. NAS Atlanta adjacent to, but not part of, Dobbins AFB; shares runways with Dobbins AFB & Lockheed.
Key Contacts
COMMANDER: Capt Ike Puzon, 770-421-5413, DSN 925-5413.
PUBLIC AFFAIRS: 770-421-5406, DSN 925-5406.
PROCUREMENT: Supply Officer, 770-421-5533, DSN 925-5533.
TRANSPORTATION: Public Works, 770-421-5512, DSN 925-5512.
PERSONNEL/COMMUNITY ACTIVITIES: See Public Affairs Officer.
Personnel and Expenditures
ACTIVE DUTY PERSONNEL: 900; reservists 2300
DEPENDENTS: 20
CIVILIAN PERSONNEL: 190
MILITARY PAYROLL EXPENDITURE: $20 mil
CONTRACT EXPENDITURE: $10 mil
Services
Housing: Family units 10; Barracks spaces (bldgs) 2. *Temporary Housing:* VIP units 4; Unaccompanied officer/Enlisted quarters (bldg) 1. *Exchange:* Retail store; Barber shop; Food shop; Florist; Service station. *Child Care/Capacities:* Day care center capacity 20. *Medical Facilities:* Medical clinic; Dental clinic. *Recreational Facilities:* Bowling center; Pool; Recreation center; Tennis courts; Racquetball court; Fitness center/Weight room; Auto shop; Officers club; NCO club; Camping; Fishing/Hunting; Lakeside recreation site with cabins.

255. Defense Contract Management Command, Lockheed Martin, Marietta

DCMC Lockheed Martin, Marietta
86 S Cobb Dr
Marietta, GA 30063-0260
770-494-3271; FAX 770-494-5215
E-mail: arl8734@dcmds.dla.mil Internet:http://www.galinks.com/dcmclmm/
Profile
BRANCH: Defense Logistics Agency.
LOCATION: *County:* Cobb.
MAJOR UNITS: Defense Contract Management Command, Lockheed Martin, Marietta; Office of Special Investigations (USAF); Defense Contract Audit Agency.

256. Defense Contract Management District South

805 Walker St
Marietta, GA 30060-2789
770-590-6411; DSN 697-6411
E-mail: dsmds-d@dcmds.dls.mil Internet:http://www.dcmc.dcrb.dla.mil/Cassites/Atlanta/cmdr.htm
Profile
BRANCH: Defense Logistics Agency.
SIZE: Offices only. *County:* Cobb.
MAJOR UNITS: Defense Contract Management District South.
Key Contacts
COMMANDER: Col Charles J Guta.

257. Dobbins Air Reserve Base

Marietta, GA 30069-5010
770-919-5000; DSN 925-5000
Profile
BRANCH: Air Force Reserve; Air National Guard.
SIZE AND LOCATION: 1800 acres. In Marietta, GA, 16 mi NW of Atlanta. *County:* Cobb.
MAJOR UNITS: 94th Airlift Wing (AFRC); 22nd Air Force, HQ (AFRC); 151st Medical Bn (ARNG); Army Reserve Center.
BASE HISTORY: 1943, built as Rickenbacker Field. 1950, named for Capt Charles Dobbins, flyer from Marietta killed, 1943. Busiest Air Reserve training base; owned by Air Force Reserve. Lockheed Martin Aeronautical Systems Co, NAS Atlanta, & USAF Plant 6 share runways, control tower, & weather facilities.
Personnel and Expenditures
ACTIVE DUTY PERSONNEL: 25 USAF; 8 USA; AFRC 2011; Army Reserve 100
CIVILIAN PERSONNEL: 678
MILITARY PAYROLL EXPENDITURE: $52 mil
Services
Housing: Unaccompanied officer quarters; BAQ units; RV/Camper sites. *Temporary Housing:* VOQ units 1; VAQ units 1. *Exchange:* Retail store; Barber shop; Bank. *Medical Facilities:* Medical clinic; Dental clinic. *Recreational Facilities:* Gym; Recreation center; Tennis courts; Racquetball court; Softball field; Camping.

Moody AFB

258. Moody Air Force Base

Moody AFB, GA 31699-5000

912-257-4211; DSN 460-4211
Internet: http://www.moody.af.mil
OFFICER-OF-THE-DAY: Command Post
257-3501

Profile

BRANCH: Air Force.
SIZE AND LOCATION: 5039 acres. 10 mi NE
of Valdosta, GA, on GA-125. S on I-75, Exit
7 to GA-122, E through Hahira, GA toward
Lakeland, GA, right (S) onto GA-125, 4 mi to
base. N on I-75, Exit 4 to US-84, east on US-
84 (Hill Ave) to downtown Valdosta, left (N)
onto GA-7 (Ashley St), Ashley St N to GA-
125 (Bemiss Rd), 9 mi to base, extreme right-
hand lane. *County:* Lowndes.
MAJOR UNITS: 347th Fighter Wing; 347th
Medical Group; 347th Logistics Group; 347th
Support Group; 347th Operations Group;
347th Composite Wing; 343rd Supply Squadron; 69th Fighter Squadron; Grand Bay Weapons Range.
BASE HISTORY: 1942, established as Moody
Field Advanced Pilot Training School; named
for Maj George Putnam Moody, early Air
Force pioneer. 1946, placed on inactive
status. 1951, reactivated for Korean conflict;
Air Force Pilot Instrument School & Instrument Flying School. 1958, Air Training Command training all-weather interceptor pilots.
1960, pilot training combined into one element as 3550th Pilot Training Wing, later
38th Flying Training Wing. 1975, 347th Tactical Fighter Wing transferred from Thailand.
1992, part of Air Combat Command with 71st
Air Control Squadron. 1994, 347th redesignated 347th Wing. 1995, conversion to composite wing completed.

Key Contacts

COMMANDER: 347 FW/CC, 5113 Austin
Ellipse, Ste 1, 31699-1599; 912-257-3400,
460-3400.
PUBLIC AFFAIRS: 347 FW/PA, 5251 Berger
St, Ste 3, 31699-1795, 912-257-3395, DSN
460-3395.

Personnel and Expenditures

ACTIVE DUTY PERSONNEL: 4275
DEPENDENTS: 2300
CIVILIAN PERSONNEL: 370

Services

Housing: Family units 304; Mobile home units
39. *Temporary Housing:* VIP units 6 units; VOQ
units 28; VEQ units 16. *Commissary:* Yes; *Exchange:* Retail store; Barber shop; Dry cleaners;
Food shop; Florist; Service station; Military
clothing store; Convenience store; Beauty shop;
Laundromat; Credit union. *Child Care/Capaci-
ties:* Day care center capacity 105; Home day
care program. *Schools:* College courses. *Base Library:* Yes. *Medical Facilities:* Hospital 15
beds; Dental clinic; Pharmacy; Veterinary services. *Recreational Facilities:* Bowling center;
Movie theater; Pool; Gym; Golf course; Tennis
courts; Racquetball court; Fitness center/Weight
room; Softball field; Football field; Auto shop;
Craft shop; Officers club; Enlisted club; Youth
center; Picnic area.

Robins AFB

259. Robins Air Force Base
RAFB
78th Air Base Wing
Robins AFB, GA 31098-1662

912-926-1110; DSN 468-1110
Internet: http://www.robins.af.mil

Profile

BRANCH: Air Force.
SIZE AND LOCATION: 8722 acres. Adj to
Warner Robins, GA; 15 mi SE of Macon on
Hwy GA 247. *County:* Houston.
MAJOR UNITS: Warner Robins Air Logistics
Center; 78th Air Base Wing; 19th Air Refuel-
ing Group; Air Force Reserve Command,
HQ; 93rd Air Control Wing; 116th Bomb
Wing; 5th Combat Communications Group;
Defense Reutilization & Marketing Office.
BASE HISTORY: Early 1941, Army Air Corps
established maintenance and supply depot.
1942, original construction completed and air
depot named Wellston Air Depot. City of
Wellston changed name to Warner Robins for
Brig Gen Augustine Warner Robins, native of
VA and chief of Materiel Division of Army
Air Corps. 1942, depot redesignated Warner
Robins Army Air Depot. Depot underwent
other name changes: Warner Robins Air De-
pot Control Air Command; Warner Robins
Air Service; Warner Robins Air Technical
Service Command; and Warner Robins Air
Materiel Area; and current name, Warner
Robins Air Logistics Center, 1974. Installa-
tion remained Robins Field until 1978 when
renamed Robins AFB. Jan 1996, main US op-
erating base for E-8 Joint STARS aircraft.
Apr 1996, GA ANG 116th Fighter Wing relo-
cated to Robins as 116th Bomb Wing with
B1B bombers.
VISITOR ATTRACTIONS: Museum of Avia-
tion adjacent to base.

Key Contacts

COMMANDER: Col William "Jack" Evans,
912-926-2177, FAX 912-926-2170, DSN
468-2177, wjevans@sct.robins.af.mil.
PUBLIC AFFAIRS: Maj Harriet D Camejo,
WR-ALC/PA, 912-926-2137, DSN 468-2137,
DSN FAX 468-9597, dcamejo@cag.robins.
af.mil.
PROCUREMENT: David D Burton,
912-926-3916, FAX 912-926-9504, DSN
468-3916, dburton@pk.robins.af.mil.
TRANSPORTATION: Maj Phil Nardi,
912-926-6081, FAX 912-926-0128, DSN
468-6081.
PERSONNEL/COMMUNITY ACTIVITIES:
Col Ronald D Jones, 912-926-3441, FAX
926-6249, DSN 468-3441.

Personnel and Expenditures

ACTIVE DUTY PERSONNEL: 5000
DEPENDENTS: 7400
CIVILIAN PERSONNEL: 12,000
MILITARY PAYROLL EXPENDITURE: $218.6
mil
CONTRACT EXPENDITURE: $1.62 bil

Services

Housing: Family units 1396; Dormitory spaces
1169. *Temporary Housing:* VIP units 15; VOQ
units 134; VAQ units 111; *Commissary:* Yes;
Exchange: Retail store; Barber shop; Dry cleaners; Florist; Bank; Service station; Furniture
store; Military clothing store; Convenience
store; Beauty shop; Credit union; ATM; Post office; Fast food; Video rentals; Thrift shop;
Travel agency; Class VI; Computer store; Garden center; Tailor/Alterations; Cafeteria; *Child
Care/Capacities:* Day care center capacity 270,
6wks-5yrs; Home day care program; Summer
day camp. *Schools:* Preschool/Kindergarten; Elementary; College/University; College courses.

Base Library: Yes. *Medical Facilities:* Hospital
10; Dental clinic; Dispensary; Pharmacy. *Recreational Facilities:* Bowling center; Movie theater; Pool; Gym; Recreation center; Golf course;
Stables; Tennis courts; Racquetball court; Fitness center/Weight room; Softball field; Football field; Auto shop; Craft shop; Officers club;
Fishing/Hunting; Enlisted club; Youth center;
Picnic area; Skeet range; Playground.

Savannah

260. Hunter Army Air Field
HAAF
Hunter Army Air Field
Savannah, GA 31409-5000
912-352-6217, 352-5876; DSN 971-6217,
971-5876

Profile

BRANCH: Army.
SIZE AND LOCATION: 5400. In business/resi-
dential area of SW Savannah; Exit 16 off I-
95, to GA Hwy 204, Main Gate located off
White Bluff Rd; 40 mi NE of Fort Stewart.
County: Chatham.
MAJOR UNITS: 1st Bn, 75th Ranger Regiment;
260th Quartermaster Bn; 24th Aviation Bri-
gade; 3rd Bn, 160th Special Operations Avia-
tion Regiment (ABN); 224th Military Intelli-
gence Bn; 559th Quartermaster Bn; Coast
Guard Air Station; Defense Investigative
Service, Savannah Field Office; 5th Weather
Squadron, Det 21; 1160th Transportation Co
(Heavy Helicopter) GA ANG; 117th Tactical
Air Command Control Squadron; Army Na-
tional Guard; DARCOM Logistics Asst Of-
fice; Army Information Systems Command;
Army Criminal Investigation Command, 3rd
Region, Field Office; M1 Abrams Tank Mate-
riel Fielding Team; Navy Space Surveillance
Station; 507th Tactical Air Command Air
Control Wing, Det 2; District Corps of Engi-
neers, Resident Engineer Office, Savannah;
Georgia Army National Guard.
BASE HISTORY: In Apr 1967, Army took con-
trol of former Hunter Air Force Base; became
Army Flight Training Center. Jul 1967,
Hunter reopened with 145th Aviation Battal-
ion (Combat). 1973, due to reconsolidation at
Ft Rucker, AL, Hunter placed in caretaker
status. 1974, Hunter (along with Ft Stewart)
entered new era as home to infantry units;
used by transport aircraft for units of Ft Stewart.
VISITOR ATTRACTIONS: Small museum.

Key Contacts

COMMANDER: LTC William T Wolf,
912-352-5668, FAX 352-6000.

Personnel and Expenditures

ACTIVE DUTY PERSONNEL: 3900
DEPENDENTS: 6100
CIVILIAN PERSONNEL: 840

Services

Housing: Family units 488; Trailer spaces 20.
Temporary Housing: VOQ units 2; VEQ units
13; Guesthouse units 41. *Commissary:* Yes; *Exchange:* Retail store; Barber shop; Dry cleaners;
Florist; Bank; Furniture store; Military clothing
store; Convenience store; Beauty shop; Laundromat; Credit union; Video rentals; Class VI; Arcade; Watch repair. *Child Care/Capacities:* Day
care center capacity 198, 6wks-12yrs; Home day
care program. *Schools:* No on-base schools.

Medical Facilities: Medical clinic; Dental clinic; Pharmacy; Veterinary services. *Recreational Facilities:* Bowling center; Pool; Gym; Recreation center; Golf course; Tennis courts; Racquetball court; Fitness center/Weight room; Softball field; Auto shop; Craft shop; Officers club; NCO club; Camping; Fishing/Hunting; Youth center; Picnic area; Skeet range; Water sports; Playground; Marina.

261. Savannah Naval & Marine Corps Reserve Center

N&MCRC Savannah
1407 S Wheaton St
Savannah, GA 31404-1799
912-233-6127, 233-6131, 233-8010; FAX
912-234-5889; DSN 971-6094

Profile
BRANCH: Naval Reserve; Marine Corps Reserve.
LOCATION: In SE GA. *County:* Chatham.
MAJOR UNITS: 1st Longshoreman Plt, 2nd Beach & Terminal Operations Co, 4th Landing Support Bn.

262. US Army Corps of Engineers, Savannah District

PO Box 889
Savannah, GA 31402

Profile
BRANCH: Army.
MAJOR UNITS: Corps of Engineers, Savannah District.
BASE HISTORY: 1829, Robert E Lee, Corps Engineer, commanded Savannah Station to build Ft Pulaski. 1888, district formally established. Serves military bases in NC & SC; navigation in Savannah & Brunswick harbors, intracoastal waterway, GA coastline, & Savannah River.

Key Contacts
COMMANDER: Col Grant M Smith, District Engineer, CESAS-DX, 912-652-5270.
PUBLIC AFFAIRS: James N Parker, Jr, Chief, CESAS-PA, 912-652-5770; G Jeanne Hodge, Public Information Officer; Debra E Egan, 912-652-5756, Debra.H.Egan@SAS02.usace.army.mil.

Tunnel Hill

263. Catoosa Area Training Center

CATC
43 Pistol Range Rd
Tunnel Hill, GA 30755-9998
706-935-4897; FAX 706-965-3508
E-mail: Jerry@tn-ngnet.army.mil

Profile
BRANCH: Army National Guard.
SIZE AND LOCATION: 1630 acres. Approx 14 mi SE of Chattanooga, TN off of GA Hwy 2; exit 139 off I-75. *County:* Catoosa.
MAJOR UNITS: Tennessee Army National Guard.
BASE HISTORY: 1906-1907, original training reservation acquired, formerly Ft Oglethorpe Rifle Range & Training Site. 1919-41, used by "Fighting" 6th Calvary. WWII, used by Woman Army Corps (WAC) & German POWs. 1945, Georgia NG assumed operational control. 1960, Tennessee NG assumed operational control through license from Corps of Engineers. 1966, renamed NG Catoosa Rifle Range. 1976, assigned present name. Accommodations for up to one battalion of infantry, armor, artillery, engineers, or combat service support units available for non-live fire training. Terrain hilly to mountainous.

Key Contacts
COMMANDER: Facility Manager.
Personnel and Expenditures
ACTIVE DUTY PERSONNEL: 12 guard
CIVILIAN PERSONNEL: 9
Services
Housing: Family units 1; Dormitory spaces 240.
Temporary Housing: VOQ units 35; VEQ units 25. *Recreational Facilities:* Fitness center/Weight room; Softball field; Football field; Camping; Fishing/Hunting; Picnic area.

Winder

264. Army Aviation Support Facility

AASF
PO Box 545
Winder, GA 30680-0545
770-867-4400

Profile
BRANCH: Army National Guard.
SIZE AND LOCATION: 23 acres. On Winder-Barrow County Airport, 4 mi from Winder, GA; 18 mi W of Athens, GA; 50 mi E of Atlanta, GA. *County:* Barrow.
MAJOR UNITS: 244th Aviation Bn, Det 1, Co B; 148th Medical Co; 171st CSAB.

Key Contacts
COMMANDER: LTC Rex Spitler, 770-867-6214.
Services
Housing: None. *Recreational Facilities:* Fitness center/Weight room.

Hawaii

Barbers Point

265. Barbers Point Naval Air Station

Barbers Point, HI 96862-5050
808-684-6266; DSN 315-484-6266
Internet: http://www.bptnas.navy.mil/

Profile

BRANCH: Navy.

SIZE AND LOCATION: 3700 acres. On SW tip of island of Oahu; 25 mi SW of Honolulu, S of Hwy H-1. *County:* Ewa District.

MAJOR UNITS: Patrol Wings Pacific Fleet; Patrol Squadron 4 (VP-4); Patrol Squadron 9 (VP-9); Patrol Squadron 47 (VP-47); Patrol Squadron Special Projects Unit 2 (VPU-2); Helicopter Antisubmarine Squadron Light 37 (HSL-37); Coast Guard Air Station; Hawaii Air National Guard; 297th Air Traffic Control Flight (ATCF); Navy Reserve Naval Air Station, Barbers Point Det 187.

BASE HISTORY: 1942, hurriedly commissioned; used to train pilots & service planes from aircraft carriers in Pacific Theater, USS *Lexington*, USS *Yorktown*, & USS *Enterprise*. Following WWII, served as rapid demobilization center & support functions of all area aviation activities. 1949, adjacent Ewa MCAS incorporated into NAS boundary. 1950, Patrol Squadron Six arrived from NAS Whidbey Island, WA; others follow; establish Barbers Point as major antisubmarine warfare aviation center. Korean War, served as major cargo forwarding & personnel replacement center for UN forces. 1973, operational shore command of Commander, Patrol Wings, US Pacific Fleet. Today, primarily Patrol Squadron support; hosts transient aircraft; known as "Crossroads of Pacific" and "Home of Rainbow Fleet."

FUTURE CLOSURE/REALIGNMENT: Scheduled to close Jul 1999, with 1100 acres retained for family housing, commissary, exchange, & golf course.

Key Contacts

COMMANDER: Capt Robert F Kernan, 808-684-3176, FAX 808-684-7350.
PUBLIC AFFAIRS: Sandy Miller, 808-684-7101, FAX 808-684-2385, DSN 315-484-7101, pao@bptnas.navy.mil.

Personnel and Expenditures

ACTIVE DUTY PERSONNEL: 2700
DEPENDENTS: 2668
CIVILIAN PERSONNEL: 1124
MILITARY PAYROLL EXPENDITURE: $140 mil

Services

Housing: Family units 1067; Unaccompanied officer quarters 149; Unaccompanied enlisted quarters 1007; BAQ units; Townhouse units; Barracks spaces. *Temporary Housing:* VIP units 12; VOQ units 100; VEQ units 50; Unaccompanied officer/Enlisted quarters; BAQ units; Guesthouse units; Guest cottages; Transient quarters 113; Cabins 24; Tent spaces 15. *Commissary:* Yes; *Exchange:* Retail store; Barber shop; Dry cleaners; Food shop; Florist; Bank; Service station; Furniture store; Bakery; Convenience store; Beauty shop; Credit union; Fast food; Class VI. *Child Care/Capacities:* Day care center 120; Home day care program. *Schools:* Preschool/Kindergarten; Elementary; College courses. *Base Library:* Yes. *Medical Facilities:* Medical clinic; Dental clinic. *Recreational Facilities:* Bowling center; Movie theater; Pool; Gym; Recreation center; Golf course; Tennis courts; Racquetball court; Fitness center/Weight room; Softball field; Football field; Auto shop; Craft shop; Officers club; NCO club; Camping; Fishing/Hunting.

Camp Smith

266. Camp H M Smith

Camp Smith, MARFORPAC
MARFORPAC
Camp Smith, HI 96861-5001
808-477-0081; FAX 808-477-5053; DSN 477-5053
Internet: http://www.mcbh.usmc.mil/smith.html
OFFICER-OF-THE-DAY: 808-477-8363, DSN 477-8363

Profile

BRANCH: Marine Corps.

SIZE AND LOCATION: 220.5 acres; Puuloa Rifle Range, Ewa Beach 137 acres; Manana Housing 62 acres. On Halawa Heights Rd, off Rte H-1, NW of Honolulu; overlooking Pearl Harbor, near community of Aiea. *County:* Ewa District.

MAJOR UNITS: Marine Forces Pacific (MARFORPAC); Fleet Marine Force, Pacific; Commander-in-Chief, US Pacific Command; Camp H M Smith, HQ & Service Bn; Special Operations Command, Pacific; Joint Task Force, Full Accounting.

BASE HISTORY: 1942, originally Aiea Naval Hospital. 1949, hospital deactivated; medical facilities consolidated into Tripler AMC. 1955, acquired by Marine Corps for Fleet Marine Force Pacific. 1956, dedicated; named for Lt Gen Holland McIntyeire "Howlin' Mad" Smith, pioneer of amphibious warfare techniques & camp's first commander. 1957, became HQ, Commander-in-Chief US Pacific Command. 1994, Marine Corps Base HI assumed operational responsibility for Camp Smith. Serves as nerve center of all US military forces in region. Only Marine Corps installation supporting unified commander (CinCPac).

Key Contacts

COMMANDER: Col Sheryl Murray.
PUBLIC AFFAIRS: 808-477-8309, FAX 808-477-5053, DSN 477-8309.
PROCUREMENT: Lt Carnes, 808-477-0490, DSN 477-0490.
TRANSPORTATION: GYSgt Molina, 808-477-0155, DSN 477-0155.
PERSONNEL/COMMUNITY ACTIVITIES: CWO4 McPherson, 808-477-8383, DSN 477-8383.

Personnel and Expenditures

ACTIVE DUTY PERSONNEL: 10,302
DEPENDENTS: 4865
CIVILIAN PERSONNEL: 385

Services

Housing: Family units 4; Unaccompanied officer quarters 9; Barracks spaces 124. *Temporary Housing:* See Pearl Harbor Naval Complex & Hickam AFB. *Exchange:* Retail store; Barber shop; Dry cleaners; Bank; Service station. *Child Care/Capacities:* Provided by other services. *Schools:* Other services' schools and civilian. *Base Library:* Yes. *Medical Facilities:* Medical clinic; Dental clinic. *Recreational Facilities:* Bowling center; Pool; Gym; Stables; Tennis courts; Racquetball court; Fitness center/Weight room; Softball field; Officers club; NCO club; Camping; Enlisted club; SNCO club.

Fort Shafter

267. Fort Shafter

HQ US Army, Pacific, Bldg T-100
Fort Shafter, HI 96858-5100
808-471-7110; DSN 315-471-7110
Internet: http://www.usarpac.army.mil

Profile

BRANCH: Army.

SIZE AND LOCATION: 592 acres. Adj to junction of Moanalua Fwy & H-1 Fwy, Diamond Head bound; approx 7 mi from Honolulu

IAP; overlooks airport, Hickam AFB, and Pearl Harbor. *County:* Honolulu.

MAJOR UNITS: US Army, Pacific (USAR-PAC); Army Support Command, Hawaii (USASCH); Pacific Ocean Division, Army Corps of Engineers; 4th Special Operations Support Command (Prov); Army Readiness Group, Pacific.

BASE HISTORY: 1907, first permanent Army post in HI. 1909, companion installation, Schofield Barracks, built on Leilehua Plain in central region of Oahu.

VISITOR ATTRACTIONS: Palm Circle, WWII; Hawaii Monarchy Cannon; Decorative fountains (built by Italian POWs WWII); Home of Army Community Theater Group.

Key Contacts

COMMANDER: Lt Gen William M Steele, 808-438-2206, FAX 808-438-2469, DSN 438-2206, leew@shafter-emh3.army.mil.

PUBLIC AFFAIRS: Col John W Reitz, 808-438-9375.

PROCUREMENT: William Y Ikemoto, Contracting, 808-438-6535.

PERSONNEL/COMMUNITY ACTIVITIES: 808-438-2333, DSN 438-2333.

Personnel and Expenditures

ACTIVE DUTY PERSONNEL: 1270

DEPENDENTS: 1300

CIVILIAN PERSONNEL: 500

Services

Housing: Family units 669; Unaccompanied officer quarters 10; Unaccompanied enlisted quarters 400; BAQ units 70; Duplex units 50; Townhouse units 60; Barracks spaces 400; Dormitory spaces 40; Senior NCO units 20; Junior NCO units 15. *Temporary Housing:* VIP units 10; VOQ units 5; VEQ units 5; VAQ units 5; Unaccompanied officer/Enlisted quarters 12; BAQ units 11; Guesthouse units 12; Guest cottages 10. *Commissary:* Yes; *Exchange:* Retail store; Barber shop; Dry cleaners; Food shop; Florist; Bank; Service station; Bakery; Bookstore; Military clothing store; Beauty shop. *Child Care/Capacities:* Day care center capacity 75; Home day care program. *Schools:* Preschool/Kindergarten; Elementary. *Base Library:* Yes. *Medical Facilities:* Dental clinic; Tripler Army Medical Center, approx 10 min away. *Recreational Facilities:* Bowling center; Pool; Gym; Recreation center; Golf course; Tennis courts; Racquetball court; Fitness center/Weight room; Softball field; Football field; Auto shop; Craft shop; Fishing/Hunting; Community theater (stage productions); Community club.

268. US Army Corps of Engineers, Honolulu District

Fort Shafter, HI 96858

Internet: http://www.pod.usace.mil/hed/hedwelc.html

Profile

BRANCH: Army.

LOCATION: Co-located with Pacific Division. *County:* Honolulu.

MAJOR UNITS: Corps of Engineers, Honolulu District.

BASE HISTORY: 1905, founded; largest geographic responsibility of any district, across 5 time zones, from Polynesia through Micronesia.

Key Contacts

COMMANDER: LTC Ralph Graves, Commander.

Personnel and Expenditures

CIVILIAN PERSONNEL: 550 (District & Division)

269. US Army Corps of Engineers, Pacific Ocean Division

CEPOD

Bldg 230, Ft Shafter

Fort Shafter, HI 96858-5440

808-438-1500; FAX 808-438-8387; DSN 314-438-1500

Internet: http://www.pod.usace.army.mil/

Profile

BRANCH: Army.

SIZE AND LOCATION: Offices only. On Fort Shafter. *County:* Honolulu.

MAJOR UNITS: Corps of Engineers, Pacific Ocean Division.

BASE HISTORY: 1957, Division established; covers 9 mil sq mi; responsible for military construction programs from Hawaii to Korea, including Okinawa, Taiwan, & Pakistan. Performs military & civil works construction and military and civil works real estate.

Key Contacts

COMMANDER: Col Robin R Cababa (Acting), Division Engineer.

PUBLIC AFFAIRS: Larry Hawthorne, 808-438-8319.

Hawaii National Park

270. Kilauea Military Camp, Joint Services Recreation Center

KMC

Hawaii National Park, HI 96718-5000

808-967-8333

Profile

BRANCH: Joint Service Installation.

SIZE AND LOCATION: 52 acres. At 4000 ft atop Kilauea Summit; approx 30 mi from Hilo, HI, heading due S along Hwy 11. *County:* Hawaii.

MAJOR UNITS: Joint Services Recreation Center.

BASE HISTORY: Started out as business venture by group of Hilo businessmen, investing to create maneuvering ground for NG and vacation spot for HI's Army. 1916, opened and offered officer's building, eating and cooking facilities, latrines, and tents for sleeping; military members received special rates. KMC, however, was not profitable and Army took over management in 1921. 1936, received 20-year lease for major projects and expansion, and operated under special use permit from National Park Service. Also used as POW camp, facility for mentally depressed, and bombing site.

VISITOR ATTRACTIONS: Located on edge of Kilauea Caldera, home of Madame Pele, world's most active volcano; tours to all parts of island. For information/reservations 808-438-6707 (from Oahu) & 808-967-8334 (all other places) or write KMC Reservation Office, Hawaii Volcanoes National Park, HI 96718 (FAX 808-967-8343).

Key Contacts

COMMANDER: Randy A Hart, General Manager.

PUBLIC AFFAIRS: Marsha Lee.

PROCUREMENT: Sue Morita-Rodrigues.

Personnel and Expenditures

ACTIVE DUTY PERSONNEL: 14

DEPENDENTS: 7

CIVILIAN PERSONNEL: 120

Services *Temporary Housing:* Dormitory units 2 large; Cabin & apartment units 68. *Exchange:* Retail store; Service station; Laundry; Cafeteria; Gift shop. *Base Library:* Yes. *Medical Facilities:* Dispensary; Ambulance service. *Recreational Facilities:* Bowling center; Gym; Recreation center; Golf course; Tennis courts; Softball field; Lounge; Rental equipment; Nature walks; Hiking; Mini health center; Basketball/volleyball.

Hickam AFB

271. Hickam Air Force Base

HAFB

15th Air Base Wing

Hickam AFB, HI 96853-5000

808-471-7100; DSN 471-7100

Profile

BRANCH: Air Force.

SIZE AND LOCATION: 2700 acres. 9 mi from downtown Honolulu, between Pearl Harbor Naval Base and Honolulu IAP; 12 mi from Waikiki. *County:* Honolulu District; Ewa District.

MAJOR UNITS: 15th Air Base Wing; Pacific Air Forces, HQ.

BASE HISTORY: 1934, Quartermaster Corps hacked airfield from tangled brush and sugar cane fields, became Hickam Field named for LTC Horace Meek Hickam, killed in aircraft accident, 1934. Japanese attack, Dec 7, 1941, resulted in 124 killed, 37 missing, 274 wounded at Hickam. WWII, hub of Pacific aerial network. Hawaiian Air Depot supported transient aircraft ferrying troops and supplies to forward areas; also played major role in training and staging, and supply center for both air and ground troops. After WWII, represented almost exclusively by Air Transport Command and its successor, MATS (today's Air Mobility Command), until 1957, when HQ Far East Air Forces moved from Japan to Hawaii, redesignated Pacific Air Forces. 1985, Hickam designated National Historic Landmark.

Key Contacts

COMMANDER: 15 ABW/CC, 808-449-6341, DSN 449-6341.

PUBLIC AFFAIRS: 15 ABW/PA, 808-449-2490, DSN 449-2490; Pacific Air Forces, 25 E St, Ste I-106, Hickam AFB, HI 96853-5496, 808-449-2490, DSN 449-2490.

PROCUREMENT: 15 ABW/LGC, 808-449-6860, DSN 449-6860.

TRANSPORTATION: 15 ABW/LGT, 808-449-6570, DSN 449-6570.

PERSONNEL/COMMUNITY ACTIVITIES: Director of Personnel, 15 ABW/MS, 808-449-5696, DSN 449-5696.

Personnel and Expenditures

ACTIVE DUTY PERSONNEL: 4638

DEPENDENTS: 6605

CIVILIAN PERSONNEL: 1333

MILITARY PAYROLL EXPENDITURE: $212.3 mil

CONTRACT EXPENDITURE: $25.8 mil

Services

Housing: Family units 2946; Unaccompanied officer quarters 8; Unaccompanied enlisted quarters 546; Dormitory spaces 988; Senior NCO units 50. *Temporary Housing:* VIP units 12; VOQ units 156; VEQ units 172. *Commissary:* Yes; *Exchange:* Retail store; Barber shop; Dry cleaners; Food shop; Florist; Bank; Service station; Furniture store. *Child Care/Capacities:* Day care center; Home day care program. *Schools:* Preschool/Kindergarten; Elementary. *Base Library:* Yes. *Medical Facilities:* Medical clinic; Dental clinic. *Recreational Facilities:* Bowling center; Movie theater; Pool; Gym; Recreation center; Golf course; Tennis courts; Racquetball court; Skating rink; Fitness center/ Weight room; Softball field; Football field; Auto shop; Craft shop; Officers club; NCO club; Fishing/Hunting.

Hilo

272. Pohakuloa Training Area
PTA
36 Mile Marker Saddle Rd
Hilo, HI 96720
Mailing Address
Commander, USAG-HI-PTA
APO AP, 96556-5703
808-969-2400; FAX 808-538-3501
E-mail: apvggp@shafter-emh3.army.mil
Profile
BRANCH: Army.
SIZE AND LOCATION: 108,000 acres. Approx halfway between Hilo and Kona on Island of Hawaii; on Saddle Rd between Mauna Kea and Mauna Loa at 6400 ft level on S flank of Mauna Kea (13,976 ft); 36 mi E to Hilo airport; 25 mi W to Waimea small airport; 50 mi NW to Kailua-Kona (airport); bounded on E & W by Parker Ranch; 200 mi from Honolulu. *County:* Hawaii.
MAJOR UNITS: 25th Infantry Division (L); 3rd Marine Regiment; 29th Brigade (SEP).
BASE HISTORY: 1955, cantonment facilities constructed from WWII prefabricated quonset huts. PTA can accommodate all live fire of a light infantry division and can support a brigade task force. Currently training site in mountain area; approx 27,000 troops train here a year; principally 25th Infantry Div, 1st Marine Amphibious Brigade, 45th Support Group, IXth Corps (USAR), Hawaii National Guard, and USAF forces Pacific. Largest sub-installation of US Army Support Command, HI.
VISITOR ATTRACTIONS: Rare plants; archaeological sites; remote site.
Key Contacts
COMMANDER: LTC David Hergenroeder.
PUBLIC AFFAIRS: HQ 25th ID (L), ATTN: APVG-PAO, Schofield Barracks, HI 96857-6007.
Personnel and Expenditures
ACTIVE DUTY PERSONNEL: 25
DEPENDENTS: 0 (Unaccompanied tour)
CIVILIAN PERSONNEL: 119
MILITARY PAYROLL EXPENDITURE: $1 mil
CONTRACT EXPENDITURE: $20 mil
Services
Housing: Barracks spaces 1600; Senior NCO units 100. *Temporary Housing:* Unaccompanied officer/Enlisted quarters 4; Transient quarters 4.

Exchange: Service station; ATM; Fast food. *Child Care/Capacities:* No day care facilities. *Schools:* No on-base schools. *Medical Facilities:* Dispensary. *Recreational Facilities:* Tennis courts; Fitness center/Weight room; Community club.

Honolulu

273. Fort DeRussy
Honolulu, HI 96858
808-438-1824
Profile
BRANCH: Army; Army Reserve.
SIZE AND LOCATION: 72 acres. On beach at Waikiki, 10 mi from Honolulu Airport. *County:* Honolulu.
MAJOR UNITS: Armed Forces Recreation Center; 9th Army Reserve Command.
BASE HISTORY: Built on land once duck ponds for Hawaiian royalty. Fort an open post, park, & beach area enjoyed by Hawaiian residents, tourists, & all service personnel. About 2 million people visit each year. 1995, new hotel. Satellite installation of Fort Shafter.
VISITOR ATTRACTIONS: Army Museum of the Pacific; Hale Koa Hotel, first-class resort reserved for active duty, reserve component, & retired military personnel of all services. 420 rooms, restaurants, shows, & white sand beach on Waikiki. Room rates depend on pay grade, status, & room location. Reservations accepted up to year in advance (recommended); active duty personnel given priority.
Key Contacts
COMMANDER: LTC John V Sutter, 808-438-6996.
PUBLIC AFFAIRS: US Army Support Command, Hawaii (USASCH), Ft Shafter, HI 96858-5000, 808-471-7110, DSN 315-471-7110.
Personnel and Expenditures
ACTIVE DUTY PERSONNEL: 25 (including Military Police)
Services *Temporary Housing:* Hale Koa Hotel 420 rooms, 14-story hotel, reserve 6 months to 1 year in advance. *Exchange:* Retail store; Barber shop; Dry cleaners; Food shop; Florist; Bank; Bookstore; Convenience store; Beauty shop; Laundromat; Car rental. *Medical Facilities:* Tripler Medical Center nearby. *Recreational Facilities:* Pool; Tennis courts; Racquetball court; Picnic area; Skeet range; Recreation equipment storage.

274. Fort Kamehameha
Ft Kam
Honolulu, HI 96853
808-438-2227
Profile
BRANCH: Air Force; Air National Guard.
LOCATION: At Hickam Air Force Base next to Honolulu IAP. *County:* Ewa District.
MAJOR UNITS: Hawaii Air National Guard; Central Identification Laboratory, Hawaii.
BASE HISTORY: Primarily a housing area located within Hickam AFB. 1992, became part of Hickam AFB.
Key Contacts
PUBLIC AFFAIRS: See 15 ABW/PA, 800 Scott Circle, Hickam AFB, HI 96853-5321.

Personnel and Expenditures
ACTIVE DUTY PERSONNEL: See Hickam AFB
Services *Recreational Facilities:* Tennis courts.

275. Honolulu Coast Guard Base/ Station
Sand Island Access Rd
Honolulu, HI 96819-5000
808-541-2454, 541-2480; FAX 808-541-2452
Profile
BRANCH: Coast Guard.
SIZE AND LOCATION: 1 acre. On Honolulu Harbor across from Aloha Tower; 6 mi E of Pearl Harbor. *County:* Honolulu.
MAJOR UNITS: Coast Guard Group, Honolulu; Coast Guard Base, Honolulu; Coast Guard Station, Honolulu; Armory Det, Honolulu; Integrated Support Command, Honolulu; Electronic Support Unit, Honolulu; Naval Engineering Support Unit; Aids to Navigation (ANT) Team, Honolulu; USCGC *Washington*; USCGC *Assateague*; USCGC *Mallow*; USCGC *Sassafras*; USCGC *Rush*; USCGC *Jarvis*; Marine Safety Office, Honolulu.
BASE HISTORY: 1926, Sand Island's mud flats fortified with coral & mud dredged from harbor channel; first buildings medical treatment stations for victims of leprosy. Currently, station's helicopters operate out of Barbers Point NAS. Sand Island also called Anuenue (Rainbow) Island.
Personnel and Expenditures
ACTIVE DUTY PERSONNEL: 23
Services
Housing: Family units 200; Unaccompanied enlisted quarters 40. *Exchange:* Barber shop; Dry cleaners; Food shop; Service station; Military clothing store. *Medical Facilities:* Medical clinic. *Recreational Facilities:* Pool; Gym; Tennis courts; Racquetball court; Fitness center/ Weight room; Softball field; NCO club; Playground; Marina; Boating.

276. Honolulu Naval & Marine Corps Reserve Readiness Center
NAVMARCORESCEN Honolulu
Reserve Center
530 Peltier Ave
Honolulu, HI 96818-3753
808-471-0091; FAX 808-474-4816
E-mail: nrc@pearlharbor.navy.mil Internet:http://www.Pearlharbor.navy.mil/NRC
Profile
BRANCH: Naval Reserve; Marine Corps Reserve.
SIZE AND LOCATION: 7 acres. Approx 1.5 mi from Honolulu IAP on Peltier Ave. *County:* Honolulu.
MAJOR UNITS: REDCOM NINETEEN Activity; Military Affiliate Radio System (MARS); Naval Recruiting (Reserve); Intel Programs Office (NR).
Key Contacts
COMMANDER: CDR Anthony J Abbruzzi, 808-471-4558, FAX 808-474-4816, abbruzzi@cnrf.nola.navy.mil.
PUBLIC AFFAIRS: HM1(FMF) Randy E Burris, 808-474-4819, FAX 808-474-4816, burrisr@cnrf.nola.navy.mil.
Personnel and Expenditures
ACTIVE DUTY PERSONNEL: 525 reservists
Services *Base Library:* Yes.

Recreational Facilities: Fitness center/Weight room; Volleyball court.

277. State of Hawaii, Department of Defense HQ
Fort Ruger
3949 Diamond Head Rd
Honolulu, HI 96816-4495
808-733-4258; FAX 808-733-4238
Internet: http://www.dod.hawaii.gov
Profile
BRANCH: Air National Guard; Army National Guard.
LOCATION: On southern coast of Oahu off H-1, near Diamond Head. *County:* Honolulu.
MAJOR UNITS: Hawaii Army National Guard, HQ; Hawaii Air National Guard, HQ.
BASE HISTORY: Originally a coastal defense post built, 1908-1911. Currently office building.
VISITOR ATTRACTIONS: Officer's Club, Mon-Tue, Private Parties only; Wed-Sat, 6-9pm; Sun, Brunch 10am-1pm.
Key Contacts
COMMANDER: Maj Gen Edward V Richardson, State Adj Gen.
PUBLIC AFFAIRS: Capt Charles Anthony, 808-733-4258, pao@dod.hawaii.gov.
Personnel and Expenditures
ACTIVE DUTY PERSONNEL: 3126 Army Guard; 2391 Air Guard

Kaneohe Bay

278. Kaneohe Bay Marine Corps Base
MCBH Kaneohe Bay
Box 63002
Kaneohe Bay, HI 96863-3002
808-471-7110; DSN 471-7110
Internet: http://www.mcbh.usmc.mil/
Profile
BRANCH: Marine Corps.
SIZE AND LOCATION: 2951 acres. 11 mi from Honolulu on N shore of Oahu (windward side) on Mokapu Peninsula. *County:* Honolulu.
MAJOR UNITS: III Marine Expeditionary Force, HI; 3rd Marine Regiment; 1st Marine Aircraft Wing; HQ Bn, Marine Corps Base, HI; 1st Radio Bn; Combat Service Support Group 3; Marine Forces, Pacific Band; 1st Marine Aircraft Wing, Aviation Support Element; Marine Aviation Logistics Support Element, Kaneohe; Marine Helicopter Training Squadron 301; Marine Heavy Helicopter Squadron 362; Marine Heavy Helicopter Squadron 363; Marine Heavy Helicopter Squadron 366; Marine Heavy Helicopter Squadron 463.
BASE HISTORY: 1918, Ft Hase commissioned (known as Kuwaaohe Military Reservation). 1939, Navy constructed small seaplane base; NAS role expanded to administration of Kaneohe Bay Naval Defense Sea Area. 1941, Army artillery unit. Dec 7, 1941, NAS Kaneohe Bay attacked first. Post-WWII, NAS limited to small air operations, small security detachment, & federal communications center. 1951, Marines assumed control of NAS combined air-ground team; naval operations moved to Barbers Point NAS. Location ideal for deployment to Far East as well as intermediate refueling & maintenance stop for tactical & support aircraft during transpacific flights. 1994, MCAS Kaneohe Bay, Camp HM Smith, Molokai Training Support Facility, Manana Family Housing Area, Puuloa Range, & Pearl City Warehouse Annex consolidated to form this new command.
FUTURE CLOSURE/REALIGNMENT: To gain aircraft from NAS Barbers Point, HI, by Jul 1999.
VISITOR ATTRACTIONS: Hawaiian Burial Grounds; Site of first attack on Dec 7, 1941.
Key Contacts
COMMANDER: Brig Gen David F Bice, 808-257-2378.
PUBLIC AFFAIRS: Capt John Milliman, 808-257-2728.
Personnel and Expenditures
ACTIVE DUTY PERSONNEL: 7375
DEPENDENTS: 4300
CIVILIAN PERSONNEL: 1200
Services
Housing: Family units 1921; Unaccompanied officer quarters 48; Unaccompanied enlisted quarters 4400. *Temporary Housing:* VIP units 3; VOQ units 72; VEQ units 14; Guesthouse units 12; Lodge units 24. *Commissary:* Yes; *Exchange:* Retail store; Barber shop; Dry cleaners; Food shop; Florist; Bank; Service station; Furniture store. *Child Care/Capacities:* Day care center capacity 240; Home day care program. *Schools:* Elementary. *Base Library:* Yes. *Medical Facilities:* Medical clinic; Dental clinic. *Recreational Facilities:* Bowling center; Movie theater; Pool; Gym; Recreation center; Golf course; Tennis courts; Racquetball court; Fitness center/Weight room; Softball field; Football field; Auto shop; Craft shop; Officers club; NCO club; Fishing/Hunting; Surfing; Boating; Marina.

Kekaha

279. Pacific Missile Range Facility
PMRF; PMRF Barking Sands
PO Box 128
Kekaha, HI 96752-0128
808-335-4740; FAX 808-335-4660; DSN 471-6740
Internet: http://www.pmrf.navy.mil/greetings.html
OFFICER-OF-THE-DAY: Command Security, 808-335-4476, DSN 471-6476
Profile
BRANCH: Navy.
SIZE AND LOCATION: 1885 acres; 42,000 sq mi of sea & airspace. On W side of island of Kauai, off Hwy 50; approx 26 mi from nearest commercial airport; 6 mi W of Kekaha on Kaumualii Hwy; Kukui Grove Ctr primary mall area in Lihue approx 30 mi. *County:* Kauai.
MAJOR UNITS: 30th Range Squadron; Hawaii Air National Guard; National Bureau of Standards; Naval Undersea Warfare Center, Det; Sandia National Laboratories, Kauai Test Facility.
BASE HISTORY: 1940, acquired by Army; named Mana Airport. During WWII, heavily used by military. 1941-1948, used by Hawaiian Airlines & Pan American Clippers. 1954, established as Bonham Airfield under Air Force. 1958, transferred to Navy; first PMRF instrumentation vans positioned near airstrip. 1965, responsibility transferred NAS, Barbers Point to Pacific Missile Range; renamed PMRF, Barking Sands. Today, trains fleet under realistic open ocean war-at-sea scenarios; maintains facilities at Makaha Ridge, Port Allen, Mauna Kapu, & unmanned radar site on Niihan Island.
VISITOR ATTRACTIONS: Barking Sands sand dunes.
Key Contacts
COMMANDER: Capt James Bollin, 808-335-4251, DSN 471-6251.
PUBLIC AFFAIRS: Vida N Mossman, 808-335-4560, FAX 808-335-4484, DSN 471-6560.
Personnel and Expenditures
ACTIVE DUTY PERSONNEL: 122
DEPENDENTS: 120
CIVILIAN PERSONNEL: 550
Services
Housing: Family units 56; Unaccompanied officer quarters 1; Unaccompanied enlisted quarters 23. *Temporary Housing:* VIP units 1; Guest cottages 4; Transient quarters 15. *Exchange:* Retail store; Barber shop; Dry cleaners; Service station; Furniture store; Convenience store. *Child Care/Capacities:* Day care center capacity 25, 2yrs-5yrs. *Schools:* No on-base schools. *Medical Facilities:* Dispensary. *Recreational Facilities:* Bowling center; Movie theater; Pool; Recreation center; Tennis courts; Racquetball court; Fitness center/Weight room; Softball field; Auto shop; Craft shop; NCO club; Fishing/Hunting; Mini golf; All-hands club.

Kihei

280. Maui Space Surveillance Complex
535 E Lipoa Pkwy, Ste 200
Kihei, HI 96753
808-875-4500; FAX 808-874-1600
Internet: http://ulua.mhpcc.af.mil/~set3/
OFFICER-OF-THE-DAY: Security Manager, TSgt James Jezek, 808-874-1538
Profile
BRANCH: Air Force.
LOCATION: Site on the Island of Maui atop 10,023-ft summit of Mt Haleakala; approx 90 mi E of Hickam AFB; offices in Kihei; warehouse facility in Kahului. *County:* Maui.
MAJOR UNITS: 18th Space Surveillance Squadron, Det 3; Phillips Laboratory, Maui.
BASE HISTORY: 1979, Detachment activated as OL-AA, 46th Aerospace Defense Wing. 1981, renamed Det 3, 1st Strategic Aerospace Division, SAC. 1983, made part of 1st Space Wing, AFSC. 1990, assigned to 18th Space Surveillance Squadron, Peterson AFB. 1995, parent reassigned to Edwards AFB; assigned to 21st Space Wing. Operates, maintains, & supports the Maui Space Surveillance System (MSSS) & Ground-based Electro-Optical Deep Space Surveillance System (GEODSS). Both systems search, detect, track & identify manmade objects in space. Largest DOD telescope. Facility identified as military location requiring proper military uniform by visitors.
VISITOR ATTRACTIONS: Visitor's desk at RTS Kihei Facility (Premier Place); all visitors must be cleared in advance.

Key Contacts

COMMANDER: Maj David Simmons; MSgt Shawn Coughlar, Det Superintendent, 808-874-1548.

PUBLIC AFFAIRS: SSgt Steven Erwin, Information Management, 808-874-1537.

Personnel and Expenditures

ACTIVE DUTY PERSONNEL: 5

CIVILIAN PERSONNEL: 160

Services

Housing: None.

Pearl Harbor

281. Afloat Training Group, Western Pacific

ATG WESTPAC

Pearl Harbor, HI 96860-7600
808-472-8881; FAX 808-472-8666; DSN 430-0111, ask for 472-8881
Internet: http://www.atgwp.navy.mil/
OFFICER-OF-THE-DAY: 808-472-8881

Profile

BRANCH: Navy.

LOCATION: Fire-fighting unit on NAVBASE Pearl Harbor, remainder on Ford Island middle of Pearl Harbor; must take ferry/small boat. ATG WESTPAC tenant command on NAVSTA Pearl Harbor. *County:* Ewa District.

MAJOR UNITS: Afloat Training Group, Western Pacific.

BASE HISTORY: Mission to provide training ashore & afloat to Navy, Marine, & Coast Guard commands in HI, & Navy & Coast Guard ships homeported at Pearl Harbor, Guam, & AK. Average of 1500 students graduate monthly with studies ranging from Basic Damage Control to Advanced Transistor & Solid State Theory. Training facility available for students to operate antisubmarine warfare attack trainer, mobile multithreat environmental control trainer, & Battle Force Tactical Trainer, along with complete fire-fighting school complex near Dry Dock No 4.

Key Contacts

COMMANDER: Capt Michael A Calhoun, calhounm@yokipc-emh1.navy.mil.

PUBLIC AFFAIRS: R Wall, 808-472-8881, ext 317, wallr.atgwp@yokipc-emh1.navy.mil.

PROCUREMENT: R Martin, martinr.atgwp@yokipc-emh1.navy.mil.

Personnel and Expenditures

ACTIVE DUTY PERSONNEL: 200

CIVILIAN PERSONNEL: 7

Services

Housing: See Pearl Harbor Naval Complex. *Exchange:* See Pearl Harbor Naval Complex. *Child Care/Capacities:* Run by SUBASE Pearl Harbor. *Medical Facilities:* Maklapa Branch Medical Clinic, Pearl Harbor & Naval Shipyard Medical Clinic, Pearl Harbor. *Recreational Facilities:* Facilities located on NAVSTA & SUBASE Pearl Harbor.

282. Marine Barracks, Hawaii

MARBKS HI

Pearl Harbor, HI 96860-5440
808-471-0672; DSN 471-0672
OFFICER-OF-THE-DAY: DSN 471-3626

Profile

BRANCH: Marine Corps.

SIZE AND LOCATION: 49 acres. On Naval Base, Pearl Harbor. *County:* Ewa District.

MAJOR UNITS: Marine Barracks, HI; Headquarters and Service Co; Guard Co Pearl Harbor.

BASE HISTORY: 1904, detachment of Marines arrived in Honolulu for duty as guard force; for four years quartered in empty coal shed fitted for temporary use before moving into tents on site, in the area now known as Fort Armstrong. 1914, quarters moved from Honolulu to Pearl Harbor. Over the years, site improved to include over 50 buildings; one of largest in Marine Corps. 1976, three Marine barracks (Pearl Harbor, Barbers Point, and Lualualei) consolidated into one named Marine Barracks, Hawaii. 1976, reorganization to include deactivation of Guard Company Barbers Point, Guard Company Lualualei, and turning over security responsibilities for gates at Naval Station, Pearl Harbor. 1993, deactivated Guard Company, Westloch.

VISITOR ATTRACTIONS: See Naval Base, Pearl Harbor.

Key Contacts

COMMANDER: Col W W North, DSN 471-0672.

PUBLIC AFFAIRS: Capt J R Denney, DSN 474-6518.

PROCUREMENT: See Public Affairs Officer.

Personnel and Expenditures

ACTIVE DUTY PERSONNEL: 154

Services

Housing: See Pearl Harbor Naval Complex.

Temporary Housing: See Pearl Harbor Naval Complex.

283. Pearl Harbor Naval Complex

NAVSTA Pearl Harbor

Commander Naval Base, Box 110
Pearl Harbor, HI 96860-5020
808-474-7110; FAX 808-474-0771; DSN 315-471-7110
Internet: http://www.hawaii.navy.mil
OFFICER-OF-THE-DAY: 808-474-6249, DSN 471-6249

Profile

BRANCH: Navy.

SIZE AND LOCATION: 12,600 acres (land & water). 2 mi W of Honolulu IAP; 9 mi from downtown Honolulu; 12 mi from downtown Waikiki. From H-1 Fwy, follow segment passing next to Honolulu Airport, exit at 15B to Nimitz Gate. *County:* Honolulu District; Ewa District.

MAJOR UNITS: Commander in Chief, US Pacific Command; Commander in Chief, US Pacific Fleet; Commander, Naval Surface Group Middle Pacific; Naval Station, Pearl Harbor; Submarine Force, US Pacific Fleet; Submarine Base, Pearl Harbor; Navy Public Works Center, Pearl Harbor; Personnel Support Det, Pearl Harbor; Barbers Point Naval Air Station; Barbers Point Squadron Naval Sea Cadet Corps; Commander, Antisubmarine Warfare Force, Pacific Fleet; Commander, Task Force 12; Commander, Naval Facilities Engineering Command, Pacific Division; Commander, Third Naval Construction Brigade; Explosive Ordnance Disposal Mobile Unit 3.

BASE HISTORY: 1860s, coaling station established in Honolulu. 1887, treaty with King Kalakaua granted rights to Pearl Harbor. 1899, Naval Coal Depot built; channel

dredged. 1901, shore establishment created. 1908, Congress authorized establishment of naval station at Pearl Harbor, named for pearl oysters in its waters. 1912, began as Receiving Ship at Hospital Point. 1916, 14th Naval District established. 1937-40, NAVSTA Pearl transferred to small barge near Submarine Base. 1940, renamed Receiving Station; moved to present HQ, Bldg 150. Dec 7, 1941, Japanese attacked sinking four battleships, badly damaging four more, & other warships permanently or temporarily put out of commission; 2113 Navy & Marines died, 987 wounded. By 1954, nearly 90% of Navy's personnel en route to or from duty in Pacific processed through Receiving Station. 1955, Naval Station established; absorbed functions of Receiving Station; under Commander, Naval Logistics, Pacific Fleet. Today, facility is Navy's largest base in Pacific; 40 homeported fleet units & 70 shore commands (major commands listed separately).

VISITOR ATTRACTIONS: *Arizona* Memorial; USS *Bowfin Park*; Pacific Submarine Museum; Ship open-house.

Key Contacts

COMMANDER: RADM William G Sutton, Commander; Capt William Rigby, Chief of Staff.

PUBLIC AFFAIRS: Frank A DeSilva, Box 110, Pearl Harbor, HI 96860-5020, 808-471-0281, FAX 808-471-5400.

PROCUREMENT: Code 40, Supply Officer, Naval Station Box 23, Pearl Harbor, HI 96860, 808-471-1220, DSN 471-9187.

TRANSPORTATION: Code 22, Transportation Officer, Naval Station Box 21, Pearl Harbor, HI 96860, 808-474-4084.

PERSONNEL/COMMUNITY ACTIVITIES: MWR, Code 90, Naval Station Box 20, Pearl Harbor, HI 96860-6000, 808-474-0787.

Personnel and Expenditures

ACTIVE DUTY PERSONNEL: 27,500

DEPENDENTS: 40,000

CIVILIAN PERSONNEL: 13,800

Services

Housing: Family units Flag Officer 18; Officer 1105; Enlisted 6941; Unaccompanied officer quarters 3; Unaccompanied enlisted quarters 9; Barracks spaces 9 bldgs; Dormitory spaces 9 bldgs; Senior NCO units 62. *Temporary Housing:* Transient quarters 207. *Commissary:* Yes; *Exchange:* Retail store; Barber shop; Dry cleaners; Food shop; Florist; Bank; Service station; Furniture store; Bakery; Bookstore; Military clothing store; Convenience store; Beauty shop; Laundromat; Credit union; ATM; Optical store; Post office; Fast food; Video rentals; Four seasons; Thrift shop; Travel agency; Class VI; Shoe repair; Computer store; Garden center; Tailor/Alterations; Laundry; Cafeteria; Photo store; *Child Care/Capacities:* Day care center capacity 274. *Schools:* No on-base schools; *Base Library:* Yes. *Medical Facilities:* Medical clinic; Dental clinic. *Recreational Facilities:* Bowling center; Movie theater; Pool; Gym; Recreation center; Golf course; Tennis courts; Racquetball court; Fitness center/Weight room; Softball field; Football field; Auto shop; Officers club; Fishing/Hunting; Enlisted club; Youth center; Water sports.

284. Pearl Harbor Naval Submarine Base
SUBASE Pearl
Pearl Harbor, HI 96860-6500
808-471-2770; FAX 808-471-2752; DSN
471-2770; DSN FAX 471-2752
E-mail: @subase.hnl.mrms.navy.mil Internet:
http://www.pearlharbor.navy.
mil\subase\subase.html
OFFICER-OF-THE-DAY: 808-471-2770, FAX
808-471-2716, DSN 471-2770
Profile
BRANCH: Navy.
SIZE AND LOCATION: 125 acres. Off Kame-
hameha Hwy, approx 3 mi from Honolulu
IAP; approx 16 mi from downtown Waikiki.
County: Honolulu.
MAJOR UNITS: Commander, Submarine
Force, US Pacific Fleet (COMSUBPAC);
Commander Submarine Squadron 1 (CSS-1);
Commander Submarine Squadron 3 (CSS-3);
Commander Submarine Squadron 7 (CSS-7);
Naval Submarine Training Center, Pacific
(NSTC); Naval Intermediate Maintenance Fa-
cility (NAVIMFAC).
BASE HISTORY: 1914, submarines operated
from Pier 5 across from old Naval Station,
downtown Honolulu. 1915, submarines as-
signed to operate out of Pearl Harbor using
temporary submarine base on Kuahua Island,
site of today's Naval Supply Center. 1919,
Submarine Division Fourteen arrived and
moored at Quarry Point, site of present base.
1923, first permanent building constructed.
1932, Escape Training Tank completed here.
1985, last diesel submarine transferred out.
Subase Pearl Harbor will merge with Naval
Station Pearl Harbor FY-98.
VISITOR ATTRACTIONS: Submarine Memorial; Dive Tower; Historic trail.
Key Contacts
COMMANDER: Capt George B Covington,
808-471-9962, FAX 808-471-2752, COO@
subase.hnl.mrms.navy.mil.
PUBLIC AFFAIRS: Lt G Duncan,
808-471-2730, FAX 808-471-2752, C10@
subase.hnl.mrms.navy.mil.
PROCUREMENT: CDR C T Switzer,
808-471-8120, FAX 808-471-2752.
Personnel and Expenditures
ACTIVE DUTY PERSONNEL: 247
DEPENDENTS: 0
CIVILIAN PERSONNEL: 63
Services
Housing: Unaccompanied officer quarters units
112; Unaccompanied enlisted quarters 1100.
Temporary Housing: Unaccompanied officer/En-
listed quarters 43; BEQ units 46. *Exchange:* Barber shop; Dry cleaners; Food shop; Service station; Convenience store; Credit union; ATM;
Post office; Video rentals; Laundry; SATO;
Navy campus. *Child Care/Capacities:* Day care
center capacity 70, 6wks-6yrs. *Schools:* No on-
base schools. *Base Library:* Yes. *Medical Facilities:* Medical clinic; Dental clinic. *Recreational
Facilities:* Bowling center; Movie theater; Pool;
Gym; Recreation center; Tennis courts; Racquetball court; Softball field; Auto shop; All ranks
club.

285. Pearl Harbor Navy Public Works Center
PWC Pearl
Pearl Harbor, HI 96860-5470

808-471-3926; FAX 808-471-5024
Internet: http://www.pwcpearl.navy.mil
OFFICER-OF-THE-DAY: 808-471-8481
Profile
BRANCH: Navy.
SIZE AND LOCATION: 71 acres. Above Kame-
hameha Hwy & Makalapa Gate into Pearl
Harbor Naval Base, on Radford Dr; about 15
mi from downtown Honolulu. *County:* Hono-
lulu.
MAJOR UNITS: Public Works Center, Pearl
Harbor.
BASE HISTORY: 1933, general services shop
established for Submarine Base, Pearl Harbor. WWII, facility served Shipyard & other
Naval activities. 1946, moved to present site.
1954, officially established under control of
Commander, Naval Base, Pearl Harbor. 1967,
came under Commander, Pacific Division,
Naval Facilities Engineering Command. 1960-
83, underwent several consolidations, extended area of responsibility from Pearl Harbor to many other major Oahu-based Navy
commands; also provided public works support to other Pacific commands. 1987, control
returned to COMNAVBASE Pearl; became
Navy Industrial Fund/Defense Business Operating Fund activity. Center provided services
on basis of set rates & payment received for
services used to pay employees' salaries &
for materials used.
Key Contacts
COMMANDER: Capt James L Delker,
808-471-3926, FAX 471-5024, delker@
central.pwcpearl.navy.mil.
PUBLIC AFFAIRS: Denise M Emsley, Public
Affair Office (Code 09R), 808-471-7300,
FAX 474-5479, emsled@central.pwcpearl.
navy.mil.
PROCUREMENT: Ken Bucher, 808-474-2153,
FAX 808-474-6808, buchek@central.
pwcpearl.navy.mil.
TRANSPORTATION: Peter Ricci,
808-474-3134, FAX 808-474-0153, riccip@
central.pwcpearl.navy.mil.
Personnel and Expenditures
ACTIVE DUTY PERSONNEL: 15
DEPENDENTS: 0
CIVILIAN PERSONNEL: 1500
MILITARY PAYROLL EXPENDITURE: $1 mil
CONTRACT EXPENDITURE: $132 mil
Services
Housing: Available from Pearl Harbor Naval
Complex, Housing Office. *Medical Facilities:*
Naval Clinic, Makalapa on Pearl Harbor Naval
Base. *Recreational Facilities:* Tennis courts;
Softball field; Picnic area; Horseshoe pits; Vol-
leyball court.

Schofield Barracks

286. Schofield Barracks
SB
US Army Hawaii
Schofield Barracks, HI 96857-6000
808-471-7110; DSN 315-471-7110
Internet: http://www.usarpac.army.mil; http://
150.137.10.101/usarhawteam.htm
OFFICER-OF-THE-DAY: 808-655-0461, DSN
455-0461
Profile
BRANCH: Army.

SIZE AND LOCATION: 14,000 acres (includes
Wheeler Army Airfield & Helemano Military
Reservation). In center of Oahu off H-2 Fwy;
17 mi NW of Honolulu. *County:* Oahu.
MAJOR UNITS: 25th Infantry Division (L);
Army Garrison, Hawaii; 45th Corps Support
Group (Forward); 703rd Military Intelligence
Brigade; Hawaii National Guard; Army Law
Enforcement Command.
BASE HISTORY: Home of 25th Infantry Divi-
sion since establishment, Oct 1941.
VISITOR ATTRACTIONS: Tropic Lighting
Museum; site of film *From Here to Eternity.*
Key Contacts
COMMANDER: Maj Gen James Hill,
808-655-0025; Col James T Hirai, Garrison
Commander; LTC Donald K Birdseye,
Schofield Barracks Community Commander.
PUBLIC AFFAIRS: Maj Aileen Ahearan,
808-655-2918.
PROCUREMENT: William Y Ikemoto,
808-438-6535.
TRANSPORTATION: 808-655-0489, DSN
455-0489.
PERSONNEL/COMMUNITY ACTIVITIES:
808-438-2333, DSN 438-2333.
Personnel and Expenditures
ACTIVE DUTY PERSONNEL: 12,100; Re-
serve 1250; Guard 3000
DEPENDENTS: 11,225
CIVILIAN PERSONNEL: 2700
Services
Housing: Family units 5196; Unaccompanied of-
ficer quarters 36; Unaccompanied enlisted quar-
ters 26. *Temporary Housing:* Guesthouse units
190. *Commissary:* Yes; *Exchange:* Retail store;
Barber shop; Dry cleaners; Food shop; Florist;
Bank; Service station; Furniture store; Military
clothing store; Convenience store; Beauty shop;
Laundromat; Credit union; Toys; Car center;
Class VI; Car rental; Thrift shop; Shoe repair;
Optical shop. *Child Care/Capacities:* Day care
center capacity 310; Home day care program;
Latch key program; Summer day camp. *Schools:*
Preschool/Kindergarten; Elementary; High
school. *Base Library:* Yes. *Medical Facilities:*
Medical clinic; Dental clinic; Veterinary serv-
ices. *Recreational Facilities:* Bowling center;
Movie theater; Pool; Gym; Recreation center;
Golf course; Tennis courts; Racquetball court;
Fitness center/Weight room (spa); Softball field;
Football field; Auto shop; Craft shop; Officers
club; NCO club; Youth center (activities); Equip-
ment rentals.

Tripler AMC

287. Tripler Army Medical Center
Tripler AMC
Tripler AMC, HI 96859-5000
808-433-2778; DSN 315-433-6662
Internet: http://www.tamc.amedd.army.mil
Profile
BRANCH: Army.
LOCATION: On island of Oahu, top of
Moanalua Ridge overlooking S shore; approx
7 mi from Waikiki and 5 mi from downtown
Honolulu; approx 3 mi to Honolulu IAP and
Pearl Harbor. *County:* Honolulu.
MAJOR UNITS: Troop Command, Tripler
Army Medical Center; Military Personnel Di-
vision Tripler Army Medical Center; Health
Care Region 12.

BASE HISTORY: 1907, several wooden structures at Ft Shafter used as hospital. 1920, named for Brevet Brig Gen Charles Stuart Tripler, Civil War contributions to Army medicine. WWII, 450 bed capacity expanded to 1000. 1948, new Tripler construction completed. Architecturally distinctive coral pink structure atop Moanalua Ridge, a familiar landmark on S side of Oahu. Currently, largest military medical treatment facility in Pacific; only Army medical center not located on US mainland. Major teaching center for graduate training. Operates Army Health Clinic at Schofield Barracks, Troop Medical Clinic at Armed Forces Recreation Center, Kilauea Military Camp,.& Troop Medical Clinic, Pohakuloa Training Area. Administrative & logistical support to Army Dental Activity, HI, HQ on Moanalua Ridge near medical center. Veterinary support, & sanitary inspection program throughout Pacific Basin.

Key Contacts

COMMANDER: Col Ronald C Kershner, Commander, Troop Command, Bldg 215.
PUBLIC AFFAIRS: ATTN: MCHK-IO, 1 Jarrett-White Rd, Tripler AMC, HI 96859-5000, 808-433-5785, 808-433-6661 (24-hrs), web_tmac@smtplink.tamc.amedd. army.mil.

Personnel and Expenditures

ACTIVE DUTY PERSONNEL: 1700
CIVILIAN PERSONNEL: 1150

Services

Housing: Family units 216; Unaccompanied officer quarters 9; Unaccompanied enlisted quarters 10. *Temporary Housing:* Guesthouse units 97. *Exchange:* Small exchange/mall. *Child Care/Capacities:* Day care center capacity 21, employees children. *Schools:* No on-base schools. *Base Library:* Yes. *Medical Facilities:* Hospital 358 beds. *Recreational Facilities:* Bowling center; Pool; Gym; Tennis courts; Fitness center/ Weight room; Softball field; Football field; Officers club; NCO club; Under USASCH Ft Shafter.

Wahiawa

288. Naval Computer & Telecommunications Area Master Station, Eastern Pacific

NCTAMS EASTPAC

500 Center St
Wahiawa, HI 96786-3050
808-653-5345; FAX 808-653-0202; DSN 453-5345
Internet: http://nctamsep.navy.mil/
OFFICER-OF-THE-DAY: 808-653-5385, DSN 453-5385

Profile

BRANCH: Navy.
SIZE AND LOCATION: 2421 acres. 20 mi N of Pearl Harbor and Pearl City at Kamehameha Hwy and Whitmore Village. *County:* Honolulu.
MAJOR UNITS: Naval Computer and Telecommunications Area Master Station, Eastern Pacific; Naval Security Group Department; Naval Branch Medical Clinic, Wahiawa; Naval Branch Dental Clinic, Wahiawa; US Coast Guard Communication Station, Honolulu; USAF Satellite Management Center, Pacific; Personnel Support Activity Det, Wahiawa.

BASE HISTORY: 1906, Naval Radio Station, Pearl Harbor operational. 1916, new station operational at Hospital Point. Dec 7, 1941, Naval radio stations proved to be highly vulnerable to attack; all equipment was moved to Wahiawa; excellent, protected receiving site. Dec 17, 1941, relocation completed with Security Group Unit moved from Heeia. 1943, Communications Security Unit established at Wahiawa under Chief of Naval Operations, to assist in cryptographic security, traffic control, & analysis. Following WWII, central radio station returned to Pearl Harbor; Wahiawa relegated to receiver site. 1956, central station relocated to Wahiawa site. 1959, radio station at Heeia turned over to Marine Corps Air Station, Kaneohe; Haiku station was placed in nonoperational status. 1967, consolidation with message centers at Pearl Harbor (NAVSHIPYD), Makalapa (CINCPACFLT), Camp Smith (CINCPAC), Moanalua (FLEWEACEN), Secure Voice Pearl Harbor, & Consolidated Maintenance under NAVCOMMACTS Pearl Harbor, department of NAVCOMMSTA Honolulu. 1977, NAVCOMMACTS Pearl Harbor disestablished. 1974, Naval Communications Processing & Routing System (NAVCOMPARS) at Wahiawa activated with dual access to AUTODIN switches at Wahiawa & Norton AFB, CA. 1976, Common User Digital Information Exchange System (CUDIXS), automated communication system using satellites, became operational.

Key Contacts

COMMANDER: Capt Elaine Fishburne, 808-653-5345, DSN 453-5345.
PUBLIC AFFAIRS: Lt Absolon S Kent, 808-653-5569, DSN 453-5569.
PROCUREMENT: 808-653-5286, DSN 453-5286.
TRANSPORTATION: 808-653-5473, DSN 453-5473.

Personnel and Expenditures

ACTIVE DUTY PERSONNEL: 828
DEPENDENTS: 3500
CIVILIAN PERSONNEL: 217

Services

Housing: Family units Officer units 16; enlisted units 122; Unaccompanied enlisted quarters 85. *Exchange:* Barber shop; Dry cleaners; Food shop; Service station; Military clothing store; Convenience store. *Child Care/Capacities:* Day care center capacity 53, 6wks-5yrs. *Base Library:* Yes. *Medical Facilities:* Medical clinic; Dental clinic; Dispensary. *Recreational Facilities:* Bowling center; Movie theater; Pool; Gym; Tennis courts; Racquetball court; Fitness center/ Weight room; Softball field; Football field; Auto shop; Craft shop; Officers club; Enlisted club; Playground.

Waianae

289. Lualualei Naval Magazine

NAVMAG LLL

3 Constellation St
Waianae, HI 96792-4300
808-653-1200; 808-474-4340
OFFICER-OF-THE-DAY: Senior Watch Officer, 808-668-3185, DSN 315-668-3185

Profile

BRANCH: Navy.

SIZE AND LOCATION: 11,590 acres. In Lualualei Valley approx 38 mi from Honolulu; on H-1 approx 20 min from Honolulu Airport. *County:* Honolulu.
MAJOR UNITS: Lualualei Naval Magazine; Calibration Lab; Ordnance Det Mobile Unit One; Ordnance Det Training and Evaluation Office; MK 48/ADCAP Torpedo Division; MK 48 Shop Admin; Mobile Mine Assembly Group OIC (MOMAG); Naval Undersea Warfare Command (NUWC); Director of Logistics, Munitions Branch (US Army Support Command, Hawaii, DOL); Radio Transmitter Facility, Lualualei.
BASE HISTORY: 1929, property acquired from McCandles estates; land (now West Loch, Waipio Peninsula) set aside from Pearl Harbor Reservation. 1934, commissioned, Naval Ammunition Depot, Oahu. 1974, Naval Ammunition Depot disestablished; Naval Magazine Lualualei established, tri-service facility. Facility receives, renovates, maintains, stores, & issues ammunition, explosives, expendable ordnance items, weapons & technical ordnance materiels. Command composed of HQ at Lualualei, West Loch (shipping & receiving center) & Waikele (storage) branches.

Key Contacts

COMMANDER: Capt Rollin Lippert, 808-668-3211; DSN 315-668-3066.
PUBLIC AFFAIRS: Lt Jeneane Fiallo, 808-668-3185.
PROCUREMENT: 808-668-3348.
TRANSPORTATION: 808-668-3251, DSN 315-668-3251.

Personnel and Expenditures

ACTIVE DUTY PERSONNEL: 155
CIVILIAN PERSONNEL: 274

Services

Housing: Family units 29; Unaccompanied enlisted quarters 93; Duplex units 15. *Exchange:* Convenience store. *Child Care/Capacities:* No day care facilities. *Schools:* No on-base schools. *Medical Facilities:* Dental clinic. *Recreational Facilities:* Pool; Tennis courts; Fitness center/ Weight room; ; All hands club (off base).

290. Waianae Army Recreation Center

WARC

85-010 Army St
Waianae, HI 96792
808-696-6026; FAX 808-696-7841;
Reservations: 1-800-333-4158 (Mainland), 1-800-847-6771 (Outer Islands); 808-696-2811 (Emergencies)

Profile

BRANCH: Army.
SIZE AND LOCATION: 13.5 acres. W coast of Oahu, 35 mi from Waikiki. *County:* Oahu.
MAJOR UNITS: Army Recreation Center.
BASE HISTORY: A beach vacation camp constructed during WWII to provide soldiers R&R.
VISITOR ATTRACTIONS: Operated for enjoyment of Army members & families. Other service members, retired military personnel, & DOD civilians welcome on space available basis. Cabin charges modest, vary according to cabin type & individual's rank; 14-day stay limit per visit. Maid service not provided; no pets.

Personnel and Expenditures

CIVILIAN PERSONNEL: 50

Services *Temporary Housing:* Guest cottages 33. *Exchange:* Food shop; Class VI; Laundry. *Medical Facilities:* First aid station. *Recreational Facilities:* Recreation center; Tennis courts; Softball field; Football field; Fishing/ Hunting; Water sports; Community club; Recreation center; Scuba diving; Equipment rental; Beach; All ranks club; Special services (MWR).

Waimanalo

291. Bellows Air Force Station

Bellows
515 Tinker Rd
Waimanalo, HI 96795
808-259-8080
OFFICER-OF-THE-DAY: 808-259-4215, FAX 808-259-4227

Profile
BRANCH: Air Force.
SIZE AND LOCATION: 1500 acres. On NE coast of Oahu on windward side of island approx 16 mi from business district of Honolulu; 19 mi from downtown Waikiki with access from Kalanianaole Hwy; 25 mi from Hickam AFB. *County:* Honolulu.
MAJOR UNITS: 15th SPT6, Det 1; Bellows Recreation Center; Hawaii ANG Military Academy.
BASE HISTORY: 1917, established by presidential order as Waimanalo Military Reservation. Renamed Bellows Field after 2nd Lt F B Bellows, aviator killed in WWI. Station personnel credited for capturing first POW of WWII. 1958, flying activities terminated. Used as interference-free site for AF Communications Command Transmitter Complex. Presently, recreational facility for military; training area for Marine Corps; & site of HI ANG Military Academy.
VISITOR ATTRACTIONS: Cottage reservations: 808-259-8080; 1-800-437-2607 (US Mainland only). Camping reservations: 808-259-4121.

Key Contacts
COMMANDER: Capt Jara Allen, 808-259-4215, FAX 808-259-4227.
PUBLIC AFFAIRS: Kelly Bortles, 808-259-4210, 808-259-4227.
PERSONNEL/COMMUNITY ACTIVITIES: E Ann Rodrigue-Bailey, 808-259-4218, FAX 808-259-4227.

Personnel and Expenditures
ACTIVE DUTY PERSONNEL: 29
DEPENDENTS: 3
CIVILIAN PERSONNEL: 75
Services
Housing: Family units 4; Barracks spaces 14. *Temporary Housing:* VIP units 3; Guest cottages 100; Campsites 50. *Exchange:* Convenience store; Laundromat; ATM. *Child Care/Capacities:* No day care facilities. *Schools:* No on-base schools. *Medical Facilities:* No medical facilities. *Recreational Facilities:* Recreation center; Tennis courts; Camping; Picnic area; All ranks club; Beach cottages; Mini-golf; Golf driving range; Equipment checkout; Conference room; Paintball; Best beach on Oahu.

Waimea

292. Kokee Air Force Station

PO Box 909
Waimea, HI 96796-0909
808-335-6501

Profile
BRANCH: Air National Guard.
SIZE AND LOCATION: 10 acres. Approx 20 mi from Waimea Town; 50 mi W of Lihue airport. *County:* Kauai.
MAJOR UNITS: 150th Aircraft Control & Warning Flight.
BASE HISTORY: 1961, established as 109th ACWS, Detachment 1. 1960-1983, 24hr air defense surveillance conducted; part of NW Anchor/Flank & NW Approaches. 1984-present, 24hr air defense (back-up).

Key Contacts
COMMANDER: Maj Wayson Iwaski.
PUBLIC AFFAIRS: TSgt Leona T Chandler.
PROCUREMENT: 808-655-7727, DSN 315-455-7727.

Personnel and Expenditures
ACTIVE DUTY PERSONNEL: 0; Guard 30
CIVILIAN PERSONNEL: 0
Services
Housing: None. *Temporary Housing:* Lodge units 2. *Child Care/Capacities:* No day care facilities. *Schools:* No on-base schools. *Medical Facilities:* No medical facilities.

Wheeler Army Airfield

293. Wheeler Army Airfield

Wheeler Army Airfield, HI 96854-5155
808-656-1414; DSN 455-7411
OFFICER-OF-THE-DAY: MPs, 808-655-0022

Profile
BRANCH: Army.
SIZE AND LOCATION: 1389 acres. 22 mi from Honolulu, near Wahiawa; off Rte 99, next to Schofield Barracks. *County:* Honolulu.
MAJOR UNITS: 15th Air Base Squadron; 22nd Tactical Air Support Squadron; 326th Air Division; Military Traffic Management Command, Pacific; 25th Infantry Division (L) Aviation Brigade; 2/25 AVN, B Co; 3/4 CAV, B Troop; 193rd Aviation Bn, C Co (ANG); Defense Information Systems Agency; 6010th Aerospace Defense Group; Aviation Support Facility (ANG).
BASE HISTORY: 1922, established as part of Schofield Barracks; named after Maj Sheldon H Wheeler, killed in aircraft accident. 1935, first solo flight HI to CA by Amelia Earhart. 1941, sustained extensive damage during attack on Pearl Harbor. During WWII-1949, under command of 7th Air Force & successor commands. 1949-51, inactivated on minimum caretaker status. During Korean War reactivated. Army responsible for airfield operations; Navy for crash & rescue operations. 1987, designated National Historic Landmark. 1991, Army assumed operational control; renamed Wheeler Army Airfield.

Personnel and Expenditures
ACTIVE DUTY PERSONNEL: 970
DEPENDENTS: 1300
CIVILIAN PERSONNEL: 500
Services
Housing: Family units 491; Unaccompanied officer quarters; Barracks spaces. *Exchange:* Barber shop; Credit union. *Child Care/Capacities:* Day care center capacity 86. *Schools:* Preschool/Kindergarten; Elementary; Intermediate/Junior high. *Base Library:* Yes. *Medical Facilities:* Medical clinic; Dental clinic; Dispensary; Veterinary services. *Recreational Facilities:* Bowling center; Movie theater; Pool; Gym; Recreation center; Tennis courts; Racquetball court; Fitness center/Weight room; Softball field; Football field; Auto shop; Craft shop; Officers club; NCO club; Youth center; Skeet range; Aero Club; Game room; Horseback riding; Scuba classes; Volleyball.

Idaho

Boise

294. Adjutant Genral of Idaho
4040 W Guard St
Boise, ID 83705-5004
208-422-5225; FAX 208-422-6179
Profile
BRANCH: Army National Guard.
MAJOR UNITS: Idaho National Guard.
Key Contacts
COMMANDER: Maj Gen John F Kane.

295. Boise Air Terminal, Air National Guard Base
Gowen Field
PO Box 45
Boise, ID 83707-0045
208-422-5011; DSN 941-5011
Profile
BRANCH: Joint Service Installation.
SIZE AND LOCATION: 1994 acres; 138,000 acres (Orchard Training Area). On S side of Boise Municipal Airport; approx 6 mi S of downtown Boise. *County:* Ada; Elmore.
MAJOR UNITS: Idaho Army National Guard, HQ; State Area Command, HQ; 124th Wing (ANG); 4th Tank Bn, Co C (Marine Corps Reserve); Army Field Training Site.
BASE HISTORY: 1940, Army Air Corps selected site as operations & training center for medium bombardment wing, named Boise Air Field. 1941, name changed to Gowen Field, to honor Lt Paul Gowen, Army aviator killed in aircraft accident in Panama. 1946, ID ANG formed. 1953, ARNG 240 sq mi range used as armor training/maneuver area. 1990, Multi-Purpose Range Complex (MPRC) built; Gowen becomes major armor training site for total army. Home of National Guard Armor Training Center, accredited by Ft Knox Armor School; Combat Vehicle Transition Training Team for M1-M1A1 Abrams tanks; Region Training Site-Maintenance; F4G "Wild Weasel" training all Air Force & National Guard Reserve pilots in F4-G SEAD mission. MPRC most advanced & difficult armor training/certification range in world.
VISITOR ATTRACTIONS: Static displays of military vehicles & aircraft.
Personnel and Expenditures
ACTIVE DUTY PERSONNEL: 1123 Guard
CIVILIAN PERSONNEL: 423

MILITARY PAYROLL EXPENDITURE: $35.2 mil
Services
Housing: Unaccompanied officer quarters 17; Barracks spaces 2820. *Temporary Housing:* Limited transient facilities during ARNG camps. *Exchange:* Retail store; Barber shop; Dry cleaners; Military clothing store; Convenience store; Laundromat; Credit union. *Medical Facilities:* Medical clinic. *Recreational Facilities:* Movie theater; Pool; Tennis courts; Fitness center/ Weight room; Softball field; Officers club; NCO club.

296. Boise Naval & Marine Corps Reserve Center
4087 W Harvard Ave
Boise, ID 83705-6289
208-422-6289; DSN 422-6288
Profile
BRANCH: Naval Reserve; Marine Corps Reserve.
LOCATION: *County:* Ada.
MAJOR UNITS: REDCOM TWENTY-TWO Activity; C Co, 4th Tank Bn, 4th Marine Division.
Key Contacts
COMMANDER: LCDR M E Kidd.

Idaho Falls

297. Idaho Falls Naval Nuclear Power Training Unit
Idaho Falls, ID 83403-2751
208-533-5334
Profile
BRANCH: Navy.
LOCATION: 65 mi W of Idaho Falls off Rte 20 on Department of Energy Federal Reservation. *County:* Jefferson; Madison; Butte; Bingham.
MAJOR UNITS: Nuclear Power Training Unit; Naval Reactors Facility.
VISITOR ATTRACTIONS: Access restricted to staff and students.
Personnel and Expenditures
ACTIVE DUTY PERSONNEL: 1200
DEPENDENTS: 1000
Services *Medical Facilities:* Medical clinic.

Mountain Home AFB

298. Mountain Home Air Force Base
MHAFB
366th Wing
Mountain Home AFB, ID 83648-5000
208-828-2111; DSN 728-2111
OFFICER-OF-THE-DAY: Command Post, 208-828-5800, DSN 728-5800
Profile
BRANCH: Air Force.
SIZE AND LOCATION: 9106 acres. 10 mi SW of town of Mountain Home; 49 mi from Boise; 13 mi from I-84 access between Boise and Twin Falls. *County:* Elmore.
MAJOR UNITS: 366th Wing.
BASE HISTORY: 1943, opened with 396th Bombardment Group. 1944, designated Mountain Home Army Air Field, replacement training unit for B-24s (later B-29s). 1945, deactivated. 1948, SAC reactivated base with 311th Air Division, Reconnaissance. 1949, again deactivated. 1951, MATS assumed control. 1953, SAC returned. 1962, three Titan I ICBM launch complexes constructed. 1966, TAC assumed jurisdiction. 1972, 366th TFW replaced 347th, to train aircrews and maintain aircraft. Home to Air Force's only air intervention composite wing. Only Air Force unit equipped with F-16C, F-15C, F-15E, B-52, and KC-135R aircraft. Also responsible for Saylor Creek Air Force Training and Electronic Combat Range (110,000 acres), Owyhee County approx 20 mi SE of base.
VISITOR ATTRACTIONS: F-111 Monument near main gate; Heritage Park.
Key Contacts
COMMANDER: Brig Gen William A Peck Jr, Wing Commander, 366th WG/CC, 208-828-2366, DSN 728-2366.
PUBLIC AFFAIRS: Capt Melissa L Miller, 366th WG/PA, 366 Gunfighter Ave, 83648-5298, 208-828-6800, DSN 728-6800.
PROCUREMENT: Col William Clark, Logistics Group Commander, 366th LG/CC, 208-828-2093, DSN 728-2093.
TRANSPORTATION: Maj Darcy Lilley, 366th TRNS/CC, 208-828-2088, DSN 728-2088.
PERSONNEL/COMMUNITY ACTIVITIES: Col Paul Daigle, Support Group Commander, 366th SPTG/CC, 208-828-6366, DSN 728-6366.
Personnel and Expenditures
ACTIVE DUTY PERSONNEL: 3977

DEPENDENTS: 5568
CIVILIAN PERSONNEL: 847
MILITARY PAYROLL EXPENDITURE: $134.4 mil
CONTRACT EXPENDITURE: $33.5 mil

Services
Housing: Family units 1525; Dormitory spaces 908; Senior NCO units 134; Junior NCO units 1207; RV/Camper sites 12. *Commissary:* Yes; *Exchange:* Retail store; Barber shop; Dry cleaners; Florist; Bank; Service station; Furniture store; Military clothing store; Service station; Beauty shop; Laundromat; Credit union. *Child Care/Capacities:* Day care center capacity 148, 6wks-6yrs. *Schools:* Preschool/Kindergarten; Elementary; Intermediate/Junior high; College courses. *Base Library:* Yes. *Medical Facilities:* Hospital 20 bed; Medical clinic; Dental clinic; Pharmacy; Veterinary services.

Recreational Facilities: Bowling center; Movie theater; Pool; Gym; Recreation center; Golf course; Stables; Tennis courts; Racquetball court; Fitness center/Weight room; Softball field; Auto shop; Craft shop; Youth center; Skeet range; Playground; Consolidated club.

Pocatello

299. Pocatello Naval Reserve Facility
NAVRESFAC Pocatello
Armed Forces Reserve Center
611 W Quinn Rd
Pocatello, ID 83202-1954
208-238-0490; FAX 208-237-3007

Profile
BRANCH: Naval Reserve.
LOCATION: On I-15; 160 mi N of Salt Lake City. *County:* Bannock.
MAJOR UNITS: REDCOM TWENTY-TWO Activity; Fleet Hospital Det F; CD Det 0918; Volunteer Training Unit; SUPSHIP 1122; AS-40 *Cable* Det B; WEPSTA Concord.
BASE HISTORY: Tenant of Army.

Key Contacts
COMMANDER: LCDR Norman Finnel, 208-238-0490, FAX 208-237-3007.
PUBLIC AFFAIRS: LCDR Skinner, 208-238-0490, FAX 208-237-3007.

Personnel and Expenditures
ACTIVE DUTY PERSONNEL: 6; 87 reservists
Services *Recreational Facilities:* Fitness center/Weight room.

Illinois

Champaign

300. US Army Corps of Engineers, Construction Engineering Research Laboratories
USACERL
2902 Newmark Dr
Champaign, IL 61826
Mailing Address
PO Box 9005
Champaign, IL 61826-9005
217-373-7216; 1-800-USA-CERL
Internet: http://www.cecer.army.mil/
Profile
BRANCH: Army.
LOCATION: From I-57, exit 238 (Olympian Dr), turn left off ramp, left at stop sign (Mattis Ave), left at stoplight (Interstate Dr), right into visitor's parking. *County:* Champaign.
MAJOR UNITS: Corps of Engineers, Construction Engineering Research Laboratories; Planning & Management Laboratory; Utilities & Industrial Operations Laboratory; Land Management Laboratory; Facilities Technology Laboratory.
BASE HISTORY: 1969, Laboratory dedicated at Univ of Illinois at Urbana-Champaign. 1972, added environmental research mission. 1991, reorganized; renamed Laboratories (with two-lab structure).
Key Contacts
PUBLIC AFFAIRS: Dana Finney, ATTN: CECER-TR-PA, 217-373-6714, FAX 217-373-7222, d-finney@cecer.army.mil.
Personnel and Expenditures
CIVILIAN PERSONNEL: 350 government; 200 university

Chicago

301. Defense Contract Management Command, PLAS
DCMC PLAS
10601 W Higgins Rd, PO Box 66911
Chicago, IL 60666-0911
1-888-752-7463
Internet: http://www.plas.dcmdc.dla.mil/
Profile
BRANCH: Defense Logistics Agency.
LOCATION: *County:* Cook.
MAJOR UNITS: Defense Contract Management Command, PLAS (Performance Labor Accounting System).
Key Contacts
COMMANDER: Don Peterson, Program Manager, 773-825-6590, dpeterson@dcmdc.dla.mil.

302. Navy Office of Information, Midwest
55 E Monroe St, Ste 1402
Chicago, IL 60603-5705
312-606-0360; FAX 312-606-0653
Profile
BRANCH: Navy.
MAJOR UNITS: Navy Office of Information, Midwest.
BASE HISTORY: Serves IL, IN, IA, MI, MN, NE, ND, SD, OH, & WI.

303. US Army Corps of Engineers, Chicago District
CELRC
111 N Canal St, River Center Bldg, Ste 1200
Chicago, IL 60606-7206
312-353-6400; FAX 312-353-2525
Internet: http://www.usace.army.mil/ncc
Profile
BRANCH: Army.
SIZE AND LOCATION: Offices only. Corner of Washington & Canal Sts. *County:* Cook.
MAJOR UNITS: Corps of Engineers, Chicago District.
BASE HISTORY: Performs civil works construction & civil works real estate.
Key Contacts
COMMANDER: LTC Roger A Gerber, District Engineer.
PUBLIC AFFAIRS: 312-353-6400, ext 1302.
TRANSPORTATION: 312-353-6400, ext 1202.
Services *Base Library:* Yes.

304. US Army Corps of Engineers, Great Lakes Regional Office
CELRD
111 N Canal St, Ste 1200
Chicago, IL 60606-7205
312-353-6308; FAX 312-353-5233
Internet: http://www.usace.army.mil/ncd/
Profile
BRANCH: Army.
SIZE AND LOCATION: Offices only. In downtown Chicago. *County:* Cook.
MAJOR UNITS: Corps of Engineers, Great Lakes Regional Office.
BASE HISTORY: Performs civil works construction & real estate.
Key Contacts
COMMANDER: Brig Gen VanWinkle, Commander, Great Lakes and Ohio River Division, 513-684-3000.
PUBLIC AFFAIRS: Donna Strachn, 513-684-3010, FAX 513-684-6218.
Services *Base Library:* Yes. *Recreational Facilities:* Fitness center/Weight room.

Decatur

305. Decatur Naval Reserve Center
NRC Decatur
2595 Federal Dr
Decatur, IL 62526-2162
217-875-1733; FAX 217-875-6958
Profile
BRANCH: Naval Reserve.
SIZE AND LOCATION: 2.19 acres. On Hwy 72; 40 mi E of Springfield, IL; 200 mi S of Chicago; 120 mi NE of St Louis; 200 mi W of Indianapolis. *County:* Macon.
MAJOR UNITS: REDCOM THIRTEEN Activity; Volunteer Training Unit 1604G; USS *Frank Cable* (AS-40) Det E; NMCB 26 Det 1326; NAVHOSP GLAKES Det 113.
Key Contacts
COMMANDER: LCDR Michael T Simmons.
PUBLIC AFFAIRS: YN2 R L Oker.
Personnel and Expenditures
ACTIVE DUTY PERSONNEL: 10; 219 reservists
Services *Recreational Facilities:* Fitness center/Weight room.

Forest Park

306. Forest Park Naval Reserve Center
7410 W Roosevelt Rd
Forest Park, IL 60130-2592
708-771-7010, 771-7011; FAX 708-771-7046
Profile
BRANCH: Naval Reserve.
LOCATION: *County:* Cook.
MAJOR UNITS: REDCOM THIRTEEN Activity.

Key Contacts
COMMANDER: CDR D D Thetford.

Granite City

307. Charles Melvin Price Army Support Center
CMPSC
The Price Center; The Depot
Hwy 3 & Niedringhaus
Granite City, IL 62040-1801
Mailing Address
ATTN: PAO
Granite City, IL 62040-1801
618-452-4212; FAX 618-452-4283; DSN 892-4212; DSN FAX 892-4283
Profile
BRANCH: Army.
SIZE AND LOCATION: 686 acres. On IL Rte 3 at Niedringhaus in Granite City, IL; 10 mi NE of St Louis, MO; 5 mi S of I-270 on IL Rte 3; 15 mi E of St Louis Lambert IAP. *County:* Madison.
MAJOR UNITS: Army Reserve Personnel Command; Army Recruiting Command HQ Co; 84th Division (IT); 226th Transportation Co; 376th Engineer Plt (FF); 936th HOT Mission (Maint); 226th Transportation Co (RR Engr); Naval Air Warfare Center Det (DAMO); US Coast Guard Naval Engineering Support Unit.
BASE HISTORY: WWI, site selected. 1942, Granite City Engineer Depot opened. Except Korean War, sharp drop in activity during postwar decades. 1962, renamed Granite City Army Depot; control from Corps of Engineers to Army Materiel Command. Mission unchanged until 1966, assumed support missions for Greater St Louis area from deactivated Army Support Center. 1971, depot proper closed, merged with various Army Aviation Systems Command support services to become Headquarters and Installation Support Activity. 1975, Granite City element changed again, became St Louis Area Support Center (SLASC). Currently, supports approx 55 military and federal agencies in St Louis area. Named for late Congressman Charles M Price. Subordinate command of Aviation Missile Command, Redstone Arsenal, AL.
VISITOR ATTRACTIONS: St Louis Area Armed Forces Museum; St Louis Arch (10 mi).
Key Contacts
COMMANDER: Keith A Armstrong, armstrong-keith@cmpsc.stl.army.mil.
PUBLIC AFFAIRS: Jack E Joyner, joyner-jack@cmpscstl.army.mil.
PROCUREMENT: James McInroe, 618-452-4496, DSN 892-4496, mcinroe-james@cmpsc.stl.army.mil.
TRANSPORTATION: Vernon Shelby, 618-452-4404, DSN 892-4404, shelby-vernon@cmpsc.stl.army.mil.
PERSONNEL/COMMUNITY ACTIVITIES: Debra Grady, Community Activities, 618-452-4523, DSN 892-4523, grady-debra@cmpsc.stl.army.mil.
Personnel and Expenditures
ACTIVE DUTY PERSONNEL: 200
DEPENDENTS: 500
CIVILIAN PERSONNEL: 250
CONTRACT EXPENDITURE: $12 mil

Services
Housing: Family units 164; Unaccompanied officer quarters 7; Unaccompanied enlisted quarters 7; Barracks spaces 52. *Commissary:* Yes; *Exchange:* Retail store; Barber shop; Food shop; Bank; Military clothing store; Credit union; ATM; Thrift shop; Class VI. *Child Care/Capacities:* Day care center capacity 52, 6wks-5yrs; Home day care program; Before & after school programs; Computer/homework lab. *Schools:* No on-base schools. *Base Library:* Yes. *Medical Facilities:* No medical facilities. *Recreational Facilities:* Bowling center; Movie theater; Pool; Gym; Golf course; Tennis courts; Softball field; Auto shop; Craft shop; Youth center; Playground; Community club.

Great Lakes

308. Great Lakes Naval Training Center
NTC Great Lakes
2701 Sheridan Rd, Bldg 1
Great Lakes, IL 60088-5000
847-688-3500; DSN 792-3501
E-mail: ntc-grl.n1@smtp.cnet.navy.mil Internet:http://www.ntcpao.com
OFFICER-OF-THE-DAY: 847-688-3939, DSN 792-3939
Profile
BRANCH: Navy.
SIZE AND LOCATION: 1628 acres. On shore of Lake Michigan approx 35 mi N of Chicago on I-94, exit Rte 137; 40 mi S of Milwaukee; serviced by O'Hare IAP 25 mi SW. *County:* Lake.
MAJOR UNITS: Construction Bn Unit 401; Defense Accounting Office, Cleveland Center; Defense Printing Service; Defense Reutilization & Marketing Office; Naval Hospital Corps School; Marine Corps Absentee Collection Unit; Naval Criminal Investigative Service; Naval Dental Center; Naval Dental Research Institute; Naval Hospital NTC; Naval Legal Service Office Det; Naval Trial Service Office Det; Naval Office of Medical/Dental Affairs; Naval Reserve Readiness Command, Region 13; Naval Training Center; Navy Computer & Telecommunications Det; Navy Drug Screening Laboratory; Navy Recruiting Area 5; Personnel Support Activity; Personnel Support Det, Naval Training Center; Personnel Support Det, Recruit Training Command; Public Works Center/Engineering Field Activity; Recruit Training Command; Reserve Readiness Center; Selective Service System, Region III; Service School Command; Supply Department NTC; Transient Personnel Unit; HQUSMEPCOM.
BASE HISTORY: 1911, dedicated by President Taft; Navy's largest training facility. Site divided by 4 natural plateaus: main training camp; receiving camp; Naval hospital; & Marine barracks. WWI, Seabees originated with 12th Regiment, "Fighting Tradesmen." John Philip Sousa, age 62, commissioned Lt, USNR, commanding officer of band, formed 14 regimental bands. Following WWI, baseball team included major leaguers. 1918, football team undefeated against major college opponents; won 1919 Rose Bowl game. WWI, established aviation school, Great Lakes Aeronautical Society, nicknamed "The Millionaire

Squadron," with members from wealthy Chicago families who built their own hangar. 1918, made NAS; Commandant Moffett became known as "Father of Naval Aviation." 1923, Naval Reserve Air Base established. 1933-1935, reduced to maintenance status. 1937, operations transferred to NAS Glenview. 1942, first WAVE (Women Accepted for Volunteer Emergency Service) unit established. 1944, changed from Station to Center. 1948, 1st recruit school here for women "regulars." 1954, Gunnery School dedicated; largest all-glass bldg in world. 1960, hospital dedicated. 1982, 1st base with cable TV & military access TV channel for all residents. 1991, Naval Training Station decommissioned; consolidated with Naval Training Center. 1993, BRAC supports consolidation of naval recruit training at Great Lakes. 1997, Service School Consolidation complete. Currently, Service School Command largest single command in Navy.
VISITOR ATTRACTIONS: Recruit graduation review held every Friday afternoon; Command Exhibit (operated by Great Lakes Naval Museum Association).
Key Contacts
COMMANDER: RADM Kevin Green, Rm 209.
PUBLIC AFFAIRS: LCDR W Curry Graham, Bldg 1, Rm B25, 847-688-2201, FAX 847-688-4945, DSN 792-2201.
PROCUREMENT: NTC Comptroller, Bldg 3200, 847-688-3371, DSN 792-3371.
TRANSPORTATION: Public Works Center/Engineering Field Activity, Bldg 1H, 847-688-6895, DSN 792-6895.
PERSONNEL/COMMUNITY ACTIVITIES: Personnel Support Activity, Bldg 122, 847-688-3301, DSN 792-3301.
Personnel and Expenditures
ACTIVE DUTY PERSONNEL: 21,800
DEPENDENTS: 6300
CIVILIAN PERSONNEL: 4060
MILITARY PAYROLL EXPENDITURE: $191 mil
CONTRACT EXPENDITURE: $86 mil
Services
Housing: Family units 2707; Unaccompanied officer quarters 117; Unaccompanied enlisted quarters 1152; Mobile home units 150. *Temporary Housing:* Unaccompanied officer/Enlisted quarters 52; Recruits 15,000; Student enlisted 8634. *Commissary:* Yes; *Exchange:* Retail store; Barber shop; Dry cleaners; Food shop; Bank; Service station; Furniture store; Bakery; Military clothing store; Convenience store; Credit union; ATM; Post office; Fast food; Video rentals; Thrift shop; Travel agency; Garden center; Tailor/Alterations; Laundry; Cafeteria. *Child Care/Capacities:* Day care center capacity 390, 6wks-5yrs; Before & after school programs; *Schools:* Elementary. *Base Library:* Yes. *Medical Facilities:* Hospital 139; Medical clinic; Dental clinic; Veterinary services. *Recreational Facilities:* Bowling center; Movie theater; Pool; Gym; Recreation center; Golf course; Tennis courts; Racquetball court; Fitness center/Weight room; Softball field; Football field; Auto shop; Craft shop; NCO club; Fishing/Hunting; Enlisted club; Youth center; Picnic area; Water sports; Playground; All ranks club; All hands club; Marina; Cable TV; YMCA; Sailing.

309. Recruit Training Command Great Lakes

RTC Great Lakes
Great Lakes, IL 60088
847-688-2445
Internet: http://www.cnet.navy.mil/greatlks/rtc.htm

Profile

BRANCH: Navy.

SIZE AND LOCATION: 140 acres. I-94 N to Rte 137, E 3 mi RTC on right. From WI: exit I-94 at IL State Line, Rte 41 S to Rte 137, Buckley Rd, left 1.5 mi, RTC on right. *County:* Lake.

MAJOR UNITS: Recruit Training Command; Navy Recruiting Area Five; Combat Systems School; Naval Hospital Corps School; Engineering Field Activity, Midwest; Enlisted Sailor Program; Navy Band, Great Lakes; Naval Hospital Great Lakes; Public Works Center, Great Lakes; Service School Command.

BASE HISTORY: 1994, became Navy's only Recruit Training Command, "boot camp."

VISITOR ATTRACTIONS: RTC is a restricted base; general visitation not permitted. Recruit graduation review every Fri, open to the public, visitors welcome (100,000 annually); held on parade field, Camp Porter (weather permitting) or Gallery Hall, Drill Hall 1200 (winter & inclement weather).

Key Contacts

COMMANDER: RADM Kevin P Green, Commander NTC, Bldg 1127, RTC Great Lakes, IL 60088-5300.

PUBLIC AFFAIRS: JOC Paul Engstrom, Bldg 1313, 847-688-2430, rtc.public-affairs@smtp.cnet.navy.mil.

Personnel and Expenditures

ACTIVE DUTY PERSONNEL: 493
CIVILIAN PERSONNEL: 4

Services

Housing: Barracks spaces 1000 beds; Staff quarters 350. *Commissary:* Yes; *Exchange:* See Great Lakes Naval Training Center. *Base Library:* Yes. *Medical Facilities:* Hospital 136 beds. *Recreational Facilities:* Bowling center; Movie theater; Pool; Gym; Recreation center; Golf course; Tennis courts; Racquetball court; Fitness center/Weight room; Softball field; Auto shop; Craft shop; Officers club; NCO club; Enlisted club.

310. Region Thirteen, Naval Reserve Readiness Command

REDCOM 13
2701 Sheridan Rd
Great Lakes, IL 60088-5026
847-688-5313; DSN 792-5313
Internet: http://www.navy.mil/homepages/navresfor/navsurf/redcom13.html

Profile

BRANCH: Naval Reserve.

MAJOR UNITS: Naval Reserve Readiness Command, Region 13.

Key Contacts

COMMANDER: RADM J J Mumaw.

O'Hare IAP ARS

311. O'Hare International Airport Air Reserve Station

O'Hare IAP ARSK
928th Airlift Group
O'Hare IAP ARS, IL 60666-5010
312-825-5980; FAX 312-825-6229; DSN 930-5980

Profile

BRANCH: Air Force Reserve.

SIZE AND LOCATION: 346 acres. On N side of O'Hare IAP in suburbs of Des Plaines & Rosemont; Main gate on Higgins Rd off Mannheim Rd off Northwest Tollway; approx 15 mi from downtown Chicago. *County:* Cook.

MAJOR UNITS: 928th Airlift Group; 928th Operations Group; 64th Airlift Squadron; 63rd Aeromedical Evacuation Squadron; 28th Mobile Aerial Port Squadron; 928th Operations Support Flight; 928th Logistics Group; 928th Support Group; 928th Civil Engineering Squadron; 928th Communication Flight; 928th Morale Welfare & Recreation Squadron; 928th Security Police Squadron; 928th Medical Group; 928th Medical Squadron; 36th Aero Patient Staging Squadron; Illinois Air National Guard, Headquarters; Army Reserve Units; Civil Air Patrol; Defense Contract Management District North Central; Aeronautical Systems Division.

BASE HISTORY: This Air Force Reserve complex can be traced back to 141st AFBU(RT) at Douglas-Orchard Airport, Park Ridge, IL, former name for O'Hare IAP. 1963, 928th TAG (now 928th AG) activated, component of 64th TAS. Holds Air Force's top record, 45 years accident-free flying. Major activity hosting VIPs. Since Eisenhower, unit received every American president and vice-president, the Pope, royalty, and foreign presidents and government officials visiting Chicago area.

FUTURE CLOSURE/REALIGNMENT: O'Hare ARS to be closed as proposed by city of Chicago, and assigned Air Reserve Component units to be relocated to Greater Rockford Airport, or another location acceptable to Secretary of Air Force (in consultation and agreement with the receiving location); provided the City of Chicago can demonstrate that it has financing in place to cover the full cost of replacing facilities (except for FAA grants for airport planning and development that would otherwise be eligible for federal financial assistance to serve needs of civil aviation at receiving location), environmental impact analyses, moving, and any added costs of environmental cleanup resulting from higher standards or a faster schedule than DOD would be obliged to meet if base did not close, without any cost whatsoever to federal government, and further provided that the closure/realignment be completed by Jun 1999. Chicago would also have to fund the cost of relocating the Army Reserve activity, or leave it in place. If these conditions are not met, the units should remain at O'Hare IAP.

Key Contacts

COMMANDER: Col Peter K Sullivan; Group Commander, 928th AG/CC, 312-825-6050, DSN 930-6050.

PUBLIC AFFAIRS: Maj Gary T Strasburg; 928th AG/PA, 312-825-5980, DSN 930-5980; Defense Contract Management District, 312-825-6014.

Personnel and Expenditures

ACTIVE DUTY PERSONNEL: 1500 Reservists
CIVILIAN PERSONNEL: 1400
MILITARY PAYROLL EXPENDITURE: $48 mil

Services

Housing: Family units None. *Exchange:* Barber shop; Convenience store. *Medical Facilities:* Medical clinic. *Recreational Facilities:* Fitness center/Weight room; Softball field; NCO club.

Peoria

312. Greater Peoria Regional Airport Air National Guard Base

182 AW
2416 S Falcon Blvd
Peoria, IL 61607-5023
309-633-3000; FAX 309-633-3085; DSN 724-4000
E-mail: COMCENTER@ILPIA.ANG.AF.MIL
Internet:http://132.94.50.31/air/182/ang.html

Profile

BRANCH: Air National Guard.

SIZE AND LOCATION: 340 acres. Off IL Rte 474, take Airport Rd exit, left onto Airport Rd, right on Smithville Rd, 2 mi to main gate. *County:* Peoria.

MAJOR UNITS: 182nd Airlift Wing (ANG); 182nd Operations Group (ANG); 182nd Support Group (ANG); 182nd Logistics Group (ANG).

BASE HISTORY: 1946, 169th Fighter Squadron formed. 1958, redesignated 169th Fighter Interceptor Squadron. 1961-62, active duty during Berlin Crisis. 1962, reorganized as part of 182nd Tactical Fighter Group. 1990-91, 5 squadrons activated for Operation Desert Shield/Storm. 1992, present designation. 1993, 500 units members activated for Midwest Flood relief. 1994, move to new facility. 1997, celebrated 50 years of service.

VISITOR ATTRACTIONS: Memorial Park with static aircraft displays.

Key Contacts

COMMANDER: Col Alan L Paige, 309-633-3200, DSN 724-4200, DSN FAX 724-4085, APAIGE@ILPIA.ANG.AF.MIL.

PUBLIC AFFAIRS: 1Lt William D Soddy, 309-633-3253, DSN 724-4253, DSN FAX 724-4360, WSODDY@ILPIA.AF.MIL.

PROCUREMENT: 2Lt Edith J Obryan, 309-633-3017, DSN 724-4017, DSN FAX 724-4064, EOBRYAN@ILPIA.ANG.AF.MIL.

TRANSPORTATION: See Procurement Officer.

PERSONNEL/COMMUNITY ACTIVITIES: LTC Alan L Bowman, 309-633-3017, DSN 724-4017, DSN FAX 724-4107, ABOWMAN@ILPIA.ANG.AF.MIL.

Personnel and Expenditures

ACTIVE DUTY PERSONNEL: 945; Guard 63; Air Technician 202
DEPENDENTS: 0
CIVILIAN PERSONNEL: 1
MILITARY PAYROLL EXPENDITURE: $19.7 mil

Services
Housing: None. *Temporary Housing:* None.
Child Care/Capacities: No day care facilities.
Medical Facilities: Medical clinic.

313. Peoria Naval & Marine Corps Reserve Center
7117 W Plank Rd
Peoria, IL 61604-5297
309-697-8244, 697-8491; FAX 309-697-0339
Profile
BRANCH: Naval Reserve; Marine Corps Reserve.
LOCATION: *County:* Peoria.
MAJOR UNITS: REDCOM THIRTEEN Activity; A Co, 6th Engineer Support Bn.
Key Contacts
COMMANDER: LCDR M A Wenzel.

Rock Island

314. Rock Island Arsenal
Rock Island, IL 61299-5000
309-786-6001; FAX 309-782-6037; DSN
793-6001
E-mail: ria-emh2.army.mil Internet:http://www.
ria-emh2.army.mil
OFFICER-OF-THE-DAY: 309-782-5621, DSN
793-5621
Profile
BRANCH: Army.
SIZE AND LOCATION: 946 acres. Metropolitan area of Moline & Rock Island, IL, and Davenport & Bettendorf, IA; off I-74 & I-80; served by Quad City Airport, Moline. *County:* Rock Island.
MAJOR UNITS: Industrial Operations Command, HQ; Army War Reserves; Armament & Chemical Acquisition & Logistics Activity; Corps of Engineers, Rock Island; Defense Information Service Organization-Defense Megacenter; Army Industrial Engineering Activity; Rock Island National Cemetery.
BASE HISTORY: 1862, established. Civil War site for Confederate prison. Produced military equipment almost since inception; supplier of each national conflict. Currently, state-of-the-art manufacturing center of tool kits & shop sets. Island National Historic Landmark.
VISITOR ATTRACTIONS: Rock Island Arsenal Museum; Ft Armstrong; Bridge Monument; Clock Tower Building; Arsenal sun dial; Davenport House; National & Confederate cemeteries.
Key Contacts
COMMANDER: Col Steven L Roop,
309-782-6035, DSN 793-6035, DSN FAX
793-6037.
PUBLIC AFFAIRS: Vicki M Stapes, External Affairs Officer, 309-782-4786, DSN
793-4786, DSN FAX 793-6782, riapao@
ria-emh2.army.mil.
PROCUREMENT: Gary Wagler,
309-782-8509, DSN 793-8509.
TRANSPORTATION: Les Black,
309-782-1587, DSN 793-1587, DSN FAX
793-0892.
PERSONNEL/COMMUNITY ACTIVITIES:
Pat Broderick, 309-782-1221, DSN 793-1221,
DSN FAX 793-1292.
Personnel and Expenditures
ACTIVE DUTY PERSONNEL: 270

DEPENDENTS: 150
CIVILIAN PERSONNEL: 6700
Services
Housing: Family units 58; Unaccompanied enlisted quarters 20. *Temporary Housing:* Transient quarters 1. *Commissary:* Yes; *Exchange:* Retail store; Barber shop; Food shop; Credit union; Thrift shop; Travel agency; Cafeteria. *Child Care/Capacities:* Day care center capacity 120, new born-7yrs; Home day care program; Summer day camp. *Schools:* No on-base schools. *Medical Facilities:* Medical clinic. *Recreational Facilities:* Gym; Fitness center/Weight room; Softball field; Auto shop; Craft shop; Fishing/Hunting; Youth center; Picnic area; Skeet range; Playground.

315. Rock Island Naval & Marine Corps Reserve Center
Rock Island Arsenal
Rock Island, IL 61299-7620
309-782-6084; DSN 793-6084; DSN FAX
793-6166
Profile
BRANCH: Naval Reserve; Marine Corps Reserve.
LOCATION: *County:* Rock Island.
MAJOR UNITS: REDCOM THIRTEEN Activity.
Key Contacts
COMMANDER: CDR C L Wilson.

316. US Army Corps of Engineers, Rock Island District
CEMVR
PO Box 2004, Clock Tower Bldg
Rock Island, IL 61204-2004
309-794-5900; FAX 309-794-5793
Internet: http://www.ncr.usace.army.mil
Profile
BRANCH: Army.
SIZE AND LOCATION: Offices only. HQ building in Rock Island, IL, W end of Arsenal Island. *County:* Rock Island.
MAJOR UNITS: Corps of Engineers, Rock Island District; Industrial Operations Command; Army Armament and Chemical Acquisition and Logistics Activity (ACALA).
BASE HISTORY: 1866, established to improve shallow upper Mississippi River into major inland waterway capable of handling rapidly increasing river traffic following Civil War. 1930, District outgrew its location in federal building in Rock Island, above post office; one office moved to Liberty Building, another to Safety Building. 1931, HQ moved into Clock Tower Building. Operates and maintains 23 public recreation areas along 314 mi stretch of Mississippi River from Guttenberg, IA, to Saverton, MO, and at 3 reservoirs in IA. Covers 78,000 sq mi in portions of five states (IA, IL, MO, MN, and WI).
VISITOR ATTRACTIONS: Headquarters located in Clock Tower Building, completed in 1867 on National Register of Historic Places. Two visitors centers at Lock and Dam 15 in Quad Cities on Mississippi River and at Starved Rock Lock and Dam on Illinois River. Visitors centers at 3 reservoirs. Also, site of Fort Armstrong, Col Davenport House, Rock Island Arsenal Museum, Confederate prison, Bridge Monument, & National Cemetary with Gen Rodman's grave.

Key Contacts
COMMANDER: Col James V Mudd,
309-794-5224, FAX 309-794-5181.
PUBLIC AFFAIRS: Ron Fournier,
309-794-5274, FAX 309-794-5793, ronald.f.
fournier@mvr02.usace.army.mil.
TRANSPORTATION: Mary Strassburger.
PERSONNEL/COMMUNITY ACTIVITIES:
Virginia DeMarce.
Personnel and Expenditures
ACTIVE DUTY PERSONNEL: 4
DEPENDENTS: 14
CIVILIAN PERSONNEL: 700-800
Services *Commissary:* Yes; *Base Library:* Yes.
Recreational Facilities: Fitness center/Weight room; Rock Island Arsenal, nearby, has many recreational facilities.

Savanna

317. Savanna Army Depot Activity
SVDA
3700 Army Depot Rd
Savanna, IL 61074-9639
815-273-8700, 273-8901; FAX 815-273-6093;
DSN 585-8700, 585-8901; DSN FAX 585-6025
E-mail: savanna-ad@ri3903S1 Internet:http://
www.dac.army.mil/
OFFICER-OF-THE-DAY: 815-273-8000, DSN
585-8000, DSN FAX 585-6120
Profile
BRANCH: Army.
SIZE AND LOCATION: 13,172 acres. In NW IL on Mississippi R; 8 mi N of Savanna, IL; accessible off Rte 84 which connects 12 mi N to US-20; 30 mi S to US-30 & 55 mi S to I-80. *County:* Jo Daviess; Carroll.
MAJOR UNITS: Defense Ammunition Center, Savanna; Ammunition School, Savanna; Technical Center for Explosives Safety; Demil Technology Office; Army Management Career Program Office.
BASE HISTORY: 1918, opened. 1919-20, building expansion (18 warehouses still in use). 1920-WWII, 52nd Ordnance Ammunition Company assigned. 1921, Savanna Ordnance Depot became independent of Rock Island Arsenal. WWII, manufacturing & storage facilities greatly expanded; loaded special bombs for Gen Doolittle's Tokyo raid. 1941, designated to study & develop safe & adequate loading, bracing & staying of all types of ammunition, & explosives for shipment. Since then, associated functions added to require development of outloading & storage procedures for all ammunition within Army Ammunition Supply System.
FUTURE CLOSURE/REALIGNMENT: Major closure to be completed by Sep 2000. Defense Ammunition Center moves to McAlester Army Ammunition Plant.
Key Contacts
COMMANDER: Capt Thomas S Schorr Jr,
815-273-8700, DSN 585-8700, DSN FAX
585-6093, tschorr@ria-emh2.army.mil.
PUBLIC AFFAIRS: Jean R Kean,
815-273-8701, DSN 585-8701, DSN FAX
585-6025, jkean@ria-emh2.army.mil.
PROCUREMENT: Marcia J Hanson,
815-273-8341, DSN 585-8341, DSN FAX
585-6024, mhanson@letterkenn-emh1.army.
mil.

TRANSPORTATION: Kathleen A Sproule, 815-273-8722, DSN 585-8722, DSN FAX 585-6017, siosv-mt@letterkenn-emh1.army. mil.

PERSONNEL/COMMUNITY ACTIVITIES: Judith L Ide, 815-273-8856, DSN 585-8856, DSN FAX 585-8753, jide@ria-emh2.army. mil.

Personnel and Expenditures
ACTIVE DUTY PERSONNEL: 1
DEPENDENTS: 4
CIVILIAN PERSONNEL: 396
MILITARY PAYROLL EXPENDITURE: $13.2 mil
CONTRACT EXPENDITURE: $4 mil

Services
Housing: Family units 11; Unaccompanied enlisted quarters 4. *Temporary Housing:* None. *Child Care/Capacities:* No day care facilities. *Schools:* No on-base schools. *Medical Facilities:* Occupational Health Nursing Office. *Recreational Facilities:* Pool; Gym; Tennis courts; Fitness center/Weight room; Camping; Fishing/ Hunting; Picnic area; Playground.

Scott AFB

318. Scott Air Force Base
Scott AFB, IL 62225-5000
618-256-1110; DSN 576-1110
Internet: http://www.safb.af.mil

Profile
BRANCH: Air Force.
SIZE AND LOCATION: 3297 acres. Shiloh Gate 1.5 mi SE of I-64, exit 19A, at Rte 158, approx 25 mi E of St Louis, MO; commercial service through Lambert Airport, St Louis. *County:* St Clair.
MAJOR UNITS: 375th Airlift Wing; US Transportation Command, HQ; Air Mobility Command, HQ; Air Force Weather Service; Air Force Communications Agency; 375th Operations Group; 375th Support Group; 375th Medical Group; 375th Logistics Group; 375th Communications Group; 375th Public Affairs; Air Force Command, Control, Communications and Computer Agency; Defense Information Technology Contracting Office; 375th Supply Hazmat Pharmacy.
BASE HISTORY: Active installation since 1917, named after Army Cpl Frank S Scott, killed in Wright biplane crash, 1912. WWI & WWII training base; once housed dirigibles. Now, home to 5 major commands with worldwide commitment. Current missions are managing a domestic aeromedical evacuation system, commanding all operational support airlift in US, and providing initial qualification training for C-9 & C-21 pilots.
VISITOR ATTRACTIONS: Tours on request.

Key Contacts
COMMANDER: Col Thomas P Kane, Commander, 375 AW/CC, 618-256-5309.
PUBLIC AFFAIRS: 375 AW/PA, 618-256-5309; AFNCC help desk DSN 576-4395.

Personnel and Expenditures
ACTIVE DUTY PERSONNEL: 7100; Reserve 945
DEPENDENTS: 10,200 (25,000 incl retirees)
CIVILIAN PERSONNEL: 3000
MILITARY PAYROLL EXPENDITURE: $1.1 bil (incl contracts & civilian payroll)

Services
Housing: Family units 1778; Mobile home units 104; Dorms 6. *Temporary Housing:* VOQ units 6; VAQ units 2; Transient quarters bldgs 2. *Commissary:* Yes; *Exchange:* Retail store; Barber shop; Dry cleaners; Florist; Bank; Service station. *Child Care/Capacities:* Day care center capacity 100; Home day care program. *Base Library:* Yes. *Medical Facilities:* Regional AF Medical Ctr 115 beds. *Recreational Facilities:* Bowling center; Movie theater; Pool; Gym; Recreation center; Golf course; Tennis courts; Racquetball court; Fitness center/Weight room; Softball field; Auto shop; Craft shop; Officers club; NCO club; Camping; Fishing/Hunting.

Springfield

319. Adjutant General of Illinois
1301 N MacArthur Blvd
Springfield, IL 62702-2399
217-785-3500; FAX 217-785-3736

Profile
BRANCH: Army National Guard.
MAJOR UNITS: Illinois National Guard.

Key Contacts
COMMANDER: Maj Gen Richard G Austin.

320. Camp Lincoln
1301 N MacArthur Blvd
Springfield, IL 62702-2317
217-761-3569; FAX 217-761-3527; DSN 555-3569; DSN FAX 555-3527
OFFICER-OF-THE-DAY: 217-761-3502 (after hours IL State Police take calls)

Profile
BRANCH: Army National Guard; Air National Guard.
SIZE AND LOCATION: 640 acres. On N side of Springfield, bordering Rte 29, 0.5 mi from airport; near Lincoln's Tomb in Oak Ridge Cemetery. *County:* Sangamon.
MAJOR UNITS: State Area Readiness Command (STARC); 139th Public Affairs Det; State Area Readiness Command, Det 3; State Area Readiness Command, Det 4; 144th Army Band; 744th Engineer Det; 3637 Maintenance Bn; 232nd S & S Bn; 634th FSB, Co C; 1144th Transportation Bn.
BASE HISTORY: 1886, Camp Lincoln first used. Currently, used by Illinois Army & Air NG, law enforcement agencies, & community organizations.
VISITOR ATTRACTIONS: Military museum and static equipment display; Lincoln's tomb (nearby).

Key Contacts
COMMANDER: Maj Gen Richard G Austin, Adjutant General, 217-785-3500, DSN 555-3500, austinr@il-arng.ngb.army.mil.
PUBLIC AFFAIRS: Maj Mark Hurley, 217-761-3569, DSN 555-3569, DSN FAX 555-3527, hurleym@il-arng.ngb.army.mil.
PROCUREMENT: Capt Kurtis Dorethy, 217-761-3553, DSN 555-3553.
TRANSPORTATION: Col John Wyatt, 217-761-3597, DSN 555-3597.
PERSONNEL/COMMUNITY ACTIVITIES: LTC Terry Downen, Director of Personnel, 217-761-3558, DSN 555-3558.

Personnel and Expenditures
ACTIVE DUTY PERSONNEL: 3; Guard 347

CIVILIAN PERSONNEL: 85 State; 347 Federal
MILITARY PAYROLL EXPENDITURE: $9.6 mil
CONTRACT EXPENDITURE: $2.1 mil

Services
Housing: Barracks spaces 80; Mobile home units 6; for TDY soldiers only. *Temporary Housing:* None. *Exchange:* Retail store; Military clothing store. *Child Care/Capacities:* No day care facilities. *Medical Facilities:* No medical facilities. *Recreational Facilities:* Fitness center/ Weight room; NCO club; All ranks club; Running track; Small arms range.

321. Capital Municipal Airport, Air National Guard Base
Springfield, IL 63707-5000
217-753-8850; DSN 892-8210

Profile
BRANCH: Air National Guard.
SIZE AND LOCATION: 91 acres. In NW section of Springfield off State Rte 29. *County:* Sangamon.
MAJOR UNITS: 183rd Fighter Wing (ANG).

Personnel and Expenditures
ACTIVE DUTY PERSONNEL: 1033 Guard
CIVILIAN PERSONNEL: 306
MILITARY PAYROLL EXPENDITURE: $22.1 mil

Services *Medical Facilities:* Dispensary.

Wilmington

322. Joliet Army Ammunition Plant
JOAAP
29401 S State Rte 53
Wilmington, IL 60481-8879
815-423-2870; FAX 815-423-2871
E-mail: joliet-aap@ria-emh2.army.mil

Profile
BRANCH: Army.
SIZE AND LOCATION: 7482 acres. In Des Plaines River Valley, 12 mi S of Joliet, IL, on IL Rte 53. *County:* Will.
MAJOR UNITS: Joliet Army Ammunition Plant.
BASE HISTORY: 1940, constructed as Kankakee Ordnance Works & Elwood Ordnance Plant. Sanderson & Porter Co built & operated ammunition loading line at EOP until 1945. E I DuPont built & operated high explosive line at KOW until 1942; US Rubber Co retained as contractor. 1945, KOW & EOP consolidated; renamed facility Joliet Arsenal, one of nation's largest munitions producers. 1945-65, operated by federal government. 1965, Elwood unit put on standby status; US Rubber Co responsible for all Joliet AAP. 1966-76, reactivated. 1976, inactive status with Uniroyal, Inc (formerly US Rubber Co) as contractor. 1993, placed in excess status & in process of being disposed. 1997, 15,080 acres transferred to USDA, Forest Service, for Midwest National Tallgrass Prairie; 982 acres to VA for cemetery. Currently in modified caretaker status pending disposal. Pending, 2900 acres to State of IL, 455 acres to Will Co for landfill, & 4000 more acres to Forest Service.

Key Contacts
COMMANDER: Arthur M Holz, Commander's Rep, SIOJO-CR.

Indiana

Charlestown

323. Indiana Army Ammunition Plant
INAAP
Charlestown, IN 47111-9667
812-284-7707; FAX 812-284-7820; DSN
366-7707

Profile
BRANCH: Army.
SIZE AND LOCATION: 8600 acres. In southern IN, near Louisville, KY. Bounded on E by Ohio River and W by IN State Hwy 62. *County:* Clark.
BASE HISTORY: A military industrial installation; one of largest ammunition plants in Army Armament, Munitions & Chemical Command; a government owned, contractor operated (GOCO) facility. Operated by ICI Americas Inc. 1992, production ceased; currently inactive; in modified caretaker status.

Key Contacts
COMMANDER: Vernon H Huss Jr, Commander's Representative, 812-284-7707, DSN 366-7707.

Personnel and Expenditures
ACTIVE DUTY PERSONNEL: 0
DEPENDENTS: 0
CIVILIAN PERSONNEL: 5 government; 61 contractor

Services
Housing: Housing closed 1994. *Temporary Housing:* None.

Crane

324. Crane Division, Naval Surface Warfare Center
NSWC Crane
300 Hwy 361
Crane, IN 47522-5001
812-854-1640; FAX 812-854-4388
Internet: http://www.crane.navy.mil
OFFICER-OF-THE-DAY: 812-854-1225, DSN 482-1225

Profile
BRANCH: Navy.
SIZE AND LOCATION: 62,609 acres (97.8 sq mi). On Hwy 45 in S-central IN, 35 mi SW of Bloomington, 75 mi SW of Indianapolis, 71 mi NW of Louisville; direct access via Hwy 58 & Hwy 45. *County:* Martin.

MAJOR UNITS: Naval Surface Warfare Center; Crane Army Ammunition Activity; Coast Guard Small Arms Repair Facility; Naval Security Group Det; Explosive Ordnance Disposal Mobile Unit 2.
BASE HISTORY: 1941, commissioned as Naval Ammunition Depot, Burns City, to supply ammunition. 1943, renamed Crane for Commodore William Montgomery Crane, first Chief of Naval Ordnance; mission expanded to include applied sciences, weapons engineering, & quality evaluation. 1959, merger of Bureau of Ordnance & Bureau of Aeronautics into Bureau of Weapons gave Crane responsibility for providing scientific & engineering support. 1975, renamed Naval Weapons Support Center Crane; production & storage transferred to Crane Army Ammunition Activity. 1977, Crane Army Ammunition Activity established. 1992, Crane merged with Naval Ordnance Station at Louisville, KY to form present organization. Center comprises area larger than DC. 400 mi of roads & trails, 170 mi of railroad, 800 acre lake, & 3000 buildings.
VISITOR ATTRACTIONS: Small arms museum; Natural Resources Nature Center.

Key Contacts
COMMANDER: Capt Stephen Gootee, USN, Bldg 1, Code A; J M Carney, Exec Director.
PUBLIC AFFAIRS: Bldg 1, Code 052, 812-854-1511, FAX 812-854-4388.
PROCUREMENT: Bldg 64, Code 116, 812-854-1449, DSN 482-1449.
TRANSPORTATION: Bldg 2713, Code 096, 812-854-3136, DSN 482-3136.
PERSONNEL/COMMUNITY ACTIVITIES: Bldg 5, Code 064, 812-854-1602, DSN 482-1602.

Personnel and Expenditures
ACTIVE DUTY PERSONNEL: 1
CIVILIAN PERSONNEL: 610

Services
Housing: Family units 31; Unaccompanied enlisted quarters 24. *Temporary Housing:* VIP units 1; Unaccompanied officer/Enlisted quarters 19. *Commissary:* Yes; *Exchange:* Retail store; Barber shop; Service station; Military clothing store; Home appliances. *Child Care/Capacities:* Summer day camp. *Schools:* No on-base schools. *Base Library:* Yes. *Medical Facilities:* Dispensary; Pharmacy. *Recreational Facilities:* Bowling center; Pool; Gym; Recreation center; Golf course; Tennis courts; Racquetball court; Fitness center/Weight room; Softball field; Craft shop; Camping; Fishing/Hunting; Picnic area; Playground; Marina; Hiking trails.

Edinburgh

325. Camp Atterbury
National Guard Armory
Edinburgh, IN 46124-1096
812-526-1526; DSN 569-2526

Profile
BRANCH: Army National Guard.
SIZE AND LOCATION: 33,132 acres. In central IN, 45 mi S of Indianapolis; I-65, 5 mi from post. *County:* Bartholomew; Brown; Johnson.
MAJOR UNITS: 81st Troop Command, HQ; Atterbury Reserve Forces Training Area; 1015th Adjutant General Co; 149th Mobile Army Surgical Hospital; 38th Air Traffic Control Platoon; 120th Public Affairs Det; 838th Transportation Det; 1413th Engineer Det; 138th Finance Bn; 176th Finance Det; 177th Finance Det; 178th Finance Det; 1438th Transportation Co; 1313th Engineer Co.
BASE HISTORY: 1942, post constructed. 1946, post inactivated. 1950, reactivated for Korean War. 1954, inactivated again. 1969, licensed to Military Department of Indiana. 1980s, considerable construction; 26,364 acres of training area, 6113 acres of ranges, impact areas, & 655 acres of cantonment area. Terrain gently rolling with brigade size combat arms or combat service support area available for unlimited indirect fire or limited direct live fire exercises. Used 260 days a year by 40 different agencies, including federal, police, ROTC, active & reserve components of Air Force, Army, Marines, & Navy. 1987, Atterbury Armory built as 800 man, one-story facility.

Key Contacts
PUBLIC AFFAIRS: 812-526-1306.

Services
Housing: Barracks spaces. *Temporary Housing:* VOQ units; VEQ units; Unaccompanied officer/Enlisted quarters. *Exchange:* Retail store; Barber shop; Laundromat. *Child Care/Capacities:* No day care facilities. *Schools:* No on-base schools. *Medical Facilities:* Medical clinic; Dispensary. *Recreational Facilities:* Pool; Gym; Recreation center; Stables; Racquetball court; Fitness center/Weight room; Softball field; Officers club; NCO club; Camping; Fishing/Hunting.

Evansville

326. Evansville Naval & Marine Corps Reserve Center

NMCRC Evansville
2900 E Division St
Evansville, IN 47711-6897
812-479-6824; FAX 812-479-0258

Profile
BRANCH: Naval Reserve; Marine Corps Reserve.
SIZE AND LOCATION: 1 acre (administration & classroom spaces). Next to Roberts Stadium in Evansville. *County:* Vanderburg.
MAJOR UNITS: REDCOM THIRTEEN Activity; AD Det 2 (NR); NMCB 26 Det 1826; NAVHOSP GLAKES 513 (NR); PHIB CB 1 Det 313 (NR); Volunteer Training Unit 1307G (NR).

Key Contacts
COMMANDER: LCDR John M Randolph.
PUBLIC AFFAIRS: LCDR Beverly Lowery.

Personnel and Expenditures
ACTIVE DUTY PERSONNEL: 140 reservists

Fort Wayne

327. Defense Contract Management Command, Indianapolis, HDC

DCMC Indianapolis HDC
1010 Production Rd
Fort Wayne, IN 46808-4106
219-429-5596
Internet: http://209.22.54.3/hughes/hughes.htm

Profile
BRANCH: Defense Logistics Agency.
LOCATION: *County:* Allen.
MAJOR UNITS: Defense Contract Management Command, Indianapolis, Hughes Defense Communications.

Key Contacts
COMMANDER: Maj James E Guyll.
PUBLIC AFFAIRS: H K Friedrich, Single Process Initiative Point of Contact, 219-429-8269.

328. Fort Wayne IAP, Air National Guard Base

Fort Wayne, IN 46809-5000
219-478-3210; DSN 786-1210

Profile
BRANCH: Air National Guard.
SIZE AND LOCATION: 138 acres. 5 mi SSW of Fort Wayne. *County:* Allen.
MAJOR UNITS: 122nd Fighter Wing (ANG).

Personnel and Expenditures
ACTIVE DUTY PERSONNEL: 965 Guard
CIVILIAN PERSONNEL: 303
MILITARY PAYROLL EXPENDITURE: $22.5 mil

329. Fort Wayne Marine Corps Reserve Center

MCRC Fort Wayne
1903 St Mary's Ave
Fort Wayne, IN 46808-2331
219-426-5743; FAX 219-420-1004

Internet: http://www.marforres.usmc.mil (see unit pages)

Profile
BRANCH: Marine Corps Reserve.
SIZE AND LOCATION: 2 acres. In Fort Wayne, approx 1.5 mi NW of downtown; approx 4 mi from Exit 109A, Rt 69 via Goshen Rd & West State Blvd. *County:* Allen.
MAJOR UNITS: Inspector-Instructor Staff; Det 1, Communications Co, HQ and Service Bn; 4th Force Service Support Group; Peace-Time War-Time Support Team (PWST) Fort Wayne.
BASE HISTORY: Established following WWII. Located in former Franklin Middle School; hosted Navy & Marine Corps until 1994 when Navy unit disbanded. Facility transferred to city & colocated with city functions. Relocation likely in future.

Key Contacts
COMMANDER: Capt T E Arnold, Jr, arnold@marforres.usmc.mil.

Personnel and Expenditures
ACTIVE DUTY PERSONNEL: 10; 105 reservists

Services *Recreational Facilities:* Pool lounge; Gym; Fitness center/Weight room.

Gary

330. Gary Naval & Marine Corps Reserve Center

860 N Lake St
Gary, IN 46403-1098
219-938-2541, 938-2544; FAX 219-938-8116

Profile
BRANCH: Naval Reserve; Marine Corps Reserve.
LOCATION: *County:* Lake.
MAJOR UNITS: REDCOM THIRTEEN Activity.

Key Contacts
COMMANDER: LCDR Anthony S Bradley.

Grissom ARB

331. Grissom Air Reserve Base

Grissom ARB, IN 46971
317-688-2104; FAX 317-688-8222; DSN 928-2104
Internet: http://www.gus.afres.af.mil/Homepage/gusnet.htm

Profile
BRANCH: Air Force Reserve.
SIZE AND LOCATION: 3100 acres. On Hwy 31 approx 15 mi N of Kokomo, IN, 50 mi N of Indianapolis. *County:* Miami.
MAJOR UNITS: 434th Air Refueling Wing (AFRC); 434th Headquarters Squadron; 434th Operations Group; 434th Operations Support Squadron; 72nd Air Refueling Squadron; 74th Air Refueling Squadron; 434th Logistics Group; 434th Logistics Support Squadron; 434th Maintenance Squadron; 434th Aircraft Generation Squadron; 434th Support Group; 434th Mission Support Squadron; 434th Security Police Squadron; 434th Civil Engineering Squadron; 434th Communications Squadron; 434th Medical Squadron.

BASE HISTORY: 1942, began as Bunker Hill Naval Station, named after nearby hamlet of Bunker Hill; used to train carrier pilots, incl Ted Williams. Post WWII, closed. 1954, redesignated Bunker Hill AFB, Tactical Air Command (title to base held by Navy until 1982); later joined by Strategic Air Command. 1968, renamed for LTC Virgil I Grissom, Indiana native, one of three astronauts who died in *Apollo* spacecraft, Jan 1967. 1970, became home of largest aerial refueling wing in Air Force. 1994, deactivated; realigned as Reserve facility. One of 4 Reserve Bases; operates year around.
VISITOR ATTRACTIONS: Aircraft museum located just outside main gate.

Key Contacts
COMMANDER: Col Anthony Tassone Jr.
PUBLIC AFFAIRS: Gary Lockard, 434th ARW, PAO Office, Bldg 667, Rm 111, Grissom ARB, IN 46971, 765-688-3348, FAX 765-688-9033, DSN 928-3348, Leafs@netusa1.net.

Personnel and Expenditures
ACTIVE DUTY PERSONNEL: Reservists/civilians 700 full time
CIVILIAN PERSONNEL: 719
MILITARY PAYROLL EXPENDITURE: $44.6 mil
CONTRACT EXPENDITURE: $400,000

Services *Temporary Housing:* Base billeting, 765-688-2844. *Commissary:* Yes; *Exchange:* Retail store; Barber shop; Dry cleaners; Food shop; Florist; Service station; Military clothing store; Convenience store; Beauty shop; Credit union. *Child Care/Capacities:* Day care center capacity 94, 6mo-12yrs; Home day care program; Summer day camp. *Schools:* Preschool/Kindergarten; Elementary. *Base Library:* Yes. *Medical Facilities:* Medical clinic; Dental clinic; Pharmacy; Veterinary services. *Recreational Facilities:* Bowling center; Movie theater; Pool; Gym; Recreation center; Golf course; Stables; Tennis courts; Racquetball court; Fitness center/Weight room; Softball field; Football field; Auto shop; Craft shop; Youth center; Picnic area; Playground; Combined Officer/NCO club; one of world's largest swimming pools.

Indianapolis

332. Adjutant General of Indiana

ATTN: MDI-AG, 2002 S Holt Rd
Indianapolis, IN 46241-4839
317-247-3279; FAX 317-247-3540

Profile
BRANCH: Army National Guard.
MAJOR UNITS: Indiana National Guard.

Key Contacts
COMMANDER: Maj Gen Robert J Mitchell.

333. Defense Contract Management Command, Indianapolis

DCMC Indianapolis
8899 E 56th St
Indianapolis, IN 46249-5701
317-542-2044; DSN 699-2044
Internet: http://209.22.54.3/

Profile
BRANCH: Defense Logistics Agency.
LOCATION: *County:* Marion.

MAJOR UNITS: Defense Contract Management Command, Indianapolis.
Key Contacts
COMMANDER: LTC John A Merkwan.
PUBLIC AFFAIRS: R L Briggs, Single Process Initiative Point of Contact, 317-542-2044, DSN 699-2044.

334. Defense Finance and Accounting Service, Indianapolis Center
DFAS-IN
8899 E 56th St
Indianapolis, IN 46249-0001
317-510-2163; FAX 317-510-1134; DSN 699-2163; DSN FAX 699-1134
Internet: http://www.dfas.mil
Profile
BRANCH: DOD.
LOCATION: In Lawrence Township, NE of Indianapolis; on site of former Ft Benjamin Harrison. *County:* Marion.
MAJOR UNITS: Defense Finance and Accounting Service, Indianapolis.
BASE HISTORY: 1991, activated as US Army Finance & Accounting Center. 1996, renamed; bldg managed by GSA. Manages seven operating locations: Lawton, OK; Bluegrass, KY; Orlando, FL; Rock Island, IL; Rome, NY; Seaside, CA; St Louis, MO.
VISITOR ATTRACTIONS: Ft Harrison State Park.
Key Contacts
COMMANDER: Gregory P Bitz, Director, 317-510-2135.
PUBLIC AFFAIRS: Virginia Johnson, 317-510-2163.
Personnel and Expenditures
CIVILIAN PERSONNEL: 2888 (in house); 8100 (network/military & civilian)

335. Indianapolis Naval & Marine Corps Reserve Readiness Center
NAVMARCORE; NMCRRC Indianapolis
Heslar Naval Armory
3010 White River Pky E Dr
Indianapolis, IN 46208-4998
317-924-6389; FAX 317-924-1735
Profile
BRANCH: Naval Reserve; Marine Corps Reserve.
SIZE AND LOCATION: 5 acres. 3 mi SW of Indianapolis. *County:* Marion.
MAJOR UNITS: REDCOM THIRTEEN Activity; I & I Staff HQ Bn; Det, Communications Co; Det 2, Electronic Maintenance Co, 4th Maintenance Bn.
VISITOR ATTRACTIONS: Historic artifacts of *USS Indianapolis.*
Key Contacts
COMMANDER: CDR Mark D Savignac.
Personnel and Expenditures
ACTIVE DUTY PERSONNEL: 385 reservists

Services *Recreational Facilities:* Fitness center/ Weight room; Officers club; NCO club; Enlisted club; All ranks club.

336. Old Fort Benjamin Harrison
Indianapolis, IN 46216
Finance: 317-543-7061; DSN 699-4198. Band 317-542-2413
Internet: http://www.ai.org/ing/ranger/
Profile
BRANCH: Army.
SIZE AND LOCATION: 2501 acres. NE side of Indianapolis on 56th St 1 mi E of I-465; adj to town of Lawrence; 12 mi from Indianapolis IAP. HQ, 138th Finance Bn, IN ARNG, 8899 E 56th St, 46249-1179. 38th Band Div, IN ARNG, 8210 Otis Ave, 46216-1033. *County:* Marion.
MAJOR UNITS: 138th Finance Bn, HQ; 176th Finance Det; 177th Finance Det; 178th Finance Det; 38th Band Division; Reserve Forces Center, Old Fort Benjamin Harrison.
BASE HISTORY: 1903, established, remained nameless until 1906; President Theodore Roosevelt named it after predecessor & friend. Originally intended as station for one infantry regiment. WWI, officers' training camp. WWI-WWII, infantry post, housing at one time or another 10th, 11th, 20th, 23rd, 40th, 45th, & 46th Infantry Regiments. WWII, site used as reception center, Finance Replacement Training Center, part of Army Finance School, Army Chaplain's School, Cook & Baker's School, Military Police Disciplinary Barracks, & POW camp for German & Italian prisoners. 1947, placed on inactive list. 1948, Indiana Military District HQ; Army released control to Air Force, name changed to Benjamin Harrison AFB; 10th Air Force HQ. 1950, Army regained control. 1951, Army Finance Center here. 1957, location of Adjutant General & Finance Schools. 1965, Defense Information School. 1973, placed under Army Training & Doctrine Command (TRADOC), designed Army Administration Center; Adjutant General & Finance Schools merged as Army Institute of Administration. 1980, post reorganized; renamed Army Soldier Support Center; Institute of Administration became Institute of Personnel & Resource Management. 1984, Institute renamed Army Soldier Support Institute. 1995, Fort closed. 1996, Garrison deactivated; site Reserve Forces Center.
VISITOR ATTRACTIONS: Army Finance Corps Museum (317-542-2169).
Key Contacts
COMMANDER: LTC Patrick M Carney, 138th Finance Bn.
Services *Commissary:* Yes; *Exchange:* PX.

South Bend

337. Defense Contract Management Command, Indianapolis-South Bend
501 E Monroe St, Ste 100
South Bend, IN 46601-2341
219-236-8111
Internet: http://209.22.54.3/sb/contacts.htm
Profile
BRANCH: Defense Logistics Agency.
LOCATION: *County:* St Joseph.
MAJOR UNITS: Defense Contract Management Command, Indianapolis-South Bend.
Key Contacts
COMMANDER: Maj Jamie Harris.

338. South Bend Naval & Marine Corps Reserve Center
1901 S Kemble Ave
South Bend, IN 46613-1799
219-233-2375, 233-2434; FAX 219-289-8229
Profile
BRANCH: Naval Reserve; Marine Corps Reserve.
LOCATION: *County:* St Joseph.
MAJOR UNITS: REDCOM THIRTEEN Activity; B Co (REIN), 6th Engineer Support Bn.
Key Contacts
COMMANDER: LCDR G M Wirtz.

Terre Haute

339. Hulman Regional Airport, Air National Guard Base
Terre Haute, IN 47803-5000
812-877-5210; DSN 724-1210
Profile
BRANCH: Air National Guard.
SIZE AND LOCATION: 279 acres. 5 mi E of Terre Haute; S of US-40, off State Rte 42. *County:* Vigo.
MAJOR UNITS: 181st Fighter Wing (ANG).
Personnel and Expenditures
ACTIVE DUTY PERSONNEL: 1001 Guard
CIVILIAN PERSONNEL: 296
MILITARY PAYROLL EXPENDITURE: $21.4 mil
Services *Medical Facilities:* Dispensary.

340. Terre Haute Marine Corps Reserve Center
200 S Fruitridge Ave
Terre Haute, IN 47803-1695
812-235-8636, 235-8724; FAX 812-235-2912
Profile
BRANCH: Marine Corps Reserve.
LOCATION: *County:* Vigo.
MAJOR UNITS: K Co, 3rd Bn, 24th Marine Regiment.

Iowa

Cedar Rapids

341. Cedar Rapids Naval Reserve Center
Armed Forces Reserve Center
2525 Matterhorn Dr
Cedar Rapids, IA 52402-3798
319-363-1791, 363-5363; FAX 319-363-7216
Profile
BRANCH: Naval Reserve.
LOCATION: *County:* Linn.
MAJOR UNITS: REDCOM SIXTEEN Activity.
Key Contacts
COMMANDER: LTC W Caldbeck.

Des Moines

342. Des Moines IAP, Air National Guard Base
3100 McKinley Ave
Des Moines, IA 50321
515-287-9210; DSN 939-8210
Profile
BRANCH: Air National Guard.
SIZE AND LOCATION: 113 acres. In SW quadrant of Des Moines. Des Moines IAP adj to base. Army Post Rd (Hwy 5) intersects with Fleur Dr at SE corner of airport, approx 5 mi from downtown Des Moines. *County:* Polk.
MAJOR UNITS: 132nd Fighter Wing (ANG).
BASE HISTORY: 1941, IA ANG & 132nd TFW began with 124th Observation Squadron at Des Moines Municipal Airport. Korean War, called to active duty; served 21 months. 1988, 132nd TFW first ANG unit deployed to Far East for multi-national exercise.
Personnel and Expenditures
ACTIVE DUTY PERSONNEL: 958 Guard
CIVILIAN PERSONNEL: 296
MILITARY PAYROLL EXPENDITURE: $25.9 mil
Services *Exchange:* Retail store.

343. Des Moines Naval & Marine Corps Reserve Center
Fort Des Moines, Bldg 47, Hickman Rd
Des Moines, IA 50315-6213
515-253-4977 (Duty beeper); FAX
515-285-2401
Profile
BRANCH: Naval Reserve; Marine Corps Reserve.
LOCATION: *County:* Polk.
MAJOR UNITS: REDCOM SIXTEEN Activity; E Co (-), 2nd Bn, 24th Marine Regiment.
Key Contacts
COMMANDER: LCDR R B Monroe.

Dubuque

344. Dubuque Naval Reserve Center
NAVRESCEN Dubuque
10677 Airport Rd
Dubuque, IA 52003-9556
319-556-2144; FAX 319-556-3423
Profile
BRANCH: Naval Reserve.
SIZE AND LOCATION: 15 acres. 6 mi S of Dubuque on Hwy 61; .25 mi from Dubuque regional airport. *County:* Dubuque.
MAJOR UNITS: REDCOM SIXTEEN Activity; 389th Engineering Bn (Heavy)(Army); FISC Yokosuka, Det 313 (NR); FH 500 CBTZ23, Det F (NR) NMCB 25 Det 1425 (NR); VTU 1606G (NR).
Key Contacts
COMMANDER: LCDR Thomas C Rieckens, 319-556-7243, FAX 319-556-3423.
Services *Recreational Facilities:* Gym; Fitness center/Weight room.

Johnston

345. Adjutant General of Iowa
7700 NW Beaver Dr, Camp Dodge
Johnston, IA 50131-1902
515-252-4211; FAX 515-252-4656
Profile
BRANCH: Army National Guard.
MAJOR UNITS: Iowa National Guard.
Key Contacts
COMMANDER: Maj Gen Warren G Lawson.

346. Camp Dodge Iowa
Cp Dodge, IA
7700 NW Beaver Dr
Johnston, IA 50131-1902
515-252-4011; FAX 515-252-4656; DSN 946-2011; DSN FAX 946-2656
E-mail: kingr@ia-arng.ngb.army.mil Internet: http://www.guard.state.ia.us
Profile
BRANCH: Air National Guard; Army National Guard.
SIZE AND LOCATION: 4400 acres. 5 mi N of Des Moines; 2 mi N of Johnston, IA; Hwy 401, 4 mi N of I-80 exchange. *County:* Polk.
MAJOR UNITS: Iowa Army National Guard, Headquarters; Iowa Air National Guard; Headquarters, 67th Troop Command; 185th Supply & Service Bn; 113th Cavalry, Troops A & B, 1st Squadron; 1034th Quartermaster Supply Co; 3655th Maintenance Co, Det 1; 3654th Maintenance Co, Det 3; Equipment Maintenance Center—Continental US; Regional Training Site, Maintenance (Camp Dodge); 194th Infantry Det (ABN); 3657th Maintenance Co; 135th Public Affairs Det; 334th Forward Support Bn, Co C; 185th Regional Training Institute.
BASE HISTORY: 1907, site purchased for training of state militia; named Camp Dodge for Maj Gen Grenville M Dodge, from Council Bluffs, IA, active in organizing early IA militia. WWI-WWII, Federal use, during interim periods leased portions to state. 1955, title conveyed to IA State. Currently, Annual Training Site and weekend training of IA NG, and Logistical Support Center for IA. Terrain flat to rolling. One battalion-sized infantry, artillery, engineer or combat type service type unit conducting non-live fire exercises, can be accommodated at one time. Usually three to four large annual training periods. Used by Army and Navy Reserve, ANG, ROTC, and USMC Reserve.
VISITOR ATTRACTIONS: Iowa Gold Star Military Museum (open Tue-Fri, 1:30-4:30); Adjacent to Saylorville Recreation Area; 11th largest wildlife refuge in state, third largest outdoor filtered swimming pool in the world.
Key Contacts
COMMANDER: Maj Gen Warren G Lawson, The Adjutant General of the Iowa National Guard, 515-252-4211, DSN 946-2211.
PUBLIC AFFAIRS: LTC Robert C King, 515-252-4582, DSN 946-2582.
PROCUREMENT: Maj Susan L Ziegenfuss, 515-252-4248, DSN 946-2248.
TRANSPORTATION: Capt David R Verdi, 515-252-4355, DSN 946-2355.

PERSONNEL/COMMUNITY ACTIVITIES:
Col Mark E Zirkelbach, Director of
Personnel, 515-252-4360, DSN 946-2360.
Personnel and Expenditures
ACTIVE DUTY PERSONNEL: 140
DEPENDENTS: 35
CIVILIAN PERSONNEL: 330
Services *Temporary Housing:* VIP units 1;
VEQ units 28; VAQ units 46. *Exchange:* Retail
store; Credit union. *Base Library:* Yes. *Medical
Facilities:* Medical clinic during scheduled train-
ing weekends. *Recreational Facilities:* Pool; Fit-
ness center/Weight room.

Middletown

347. Iowa Army Ammunition Plant
Iowa AAP
ATTN: SMCIO-CO
Middletown, IA 52638-5000
Mailing Address
17571 State Hwy 79
Middletown, IA 52638-5000
319-753-7200; DSN 585-7200
Profile
BRANCH: Army.
SIZE AND LOCATION: 19,000 acres. 8 mi W
of Burlington, IA. *County:* Des Moines.
MAJOR UNITS: Iowa Army Ammunition Plant.
BASE HISTORY: A GOCO military industrial
installation under jurisdiction of Army Arma-
ment, Munitions, and Chemical Command.
Original plant constructed Feb 1942. Highest
employment 12,200 in 1941.
Key Contacts
COMMANDER: LTC John R Stefanovich.
PUBLIC AFFAIRS: Larry R Johnson.

TRANSPORTATION: Thomas Hauck.
Personnel and Expenditures
ACTIVE DUTY PERSONNEL: 2
DEPENDENTS: 5
CIVILIAN PERSONNEL: 24; 825 contractor
personnel
CONTRACT EXPENDITURE: $48.3 mil
Services
Housing: Family units 41. *Medical Facilities:*
Hospital 1; Numerous examining tables. *Recrea-
tional Facilities:* Tennis courts; Fitness center/
Weight room; Softball field; Fishing/Hunting.

Sergeant Bluff

348. Sioux Gateway Airport, Air National Guard Base
Sergeant Bluff, IA 51110
712-279-7500; DSN 939-6500
Profile
BRANCH: Air National Guard.
SIZE AND LOCATION: 118 acres. In W IA; 7
mi S of Sioux City, IA; off I-29 at Sioux Gateway Airport. *County:* Woodbury.
MAJOR UNITS: 185th Fighter Wing (ANG).
BASE HISTORY: Began as 174th Fighter
Squadron; federally recognized 1946, unit of
Iowa ANG. 1951, called to active duty;
moved to Dow AFB, Bangor, ME, reactivated
to that base. 1952, released from active duty;
returned to state control. 1968, after series of
reorganizations & redesignations, 185th recalled to active duty as result of Pueblo Crisis. 1969, returned to Sioux City; released
from active duty.
Personnel and Expenditures
ACTIVE DUTY PERSONNEL: 980 Guard

CIVILIAN PERSONNEL: 336
MILITARY PAYROLL EXPENDITURE: $25.4
mil
Services
Housing: Barracks spaces; Dormitory spaces.
Medical Facilities: Medical clinic.

Sioux City

349. Sioux City Naval Reserve Center
2501 S Lewis Blvd
Sioux City, IA 51106-5103
712-276-0130; FAX 712-276-4678; DSN
939-6210
Profile
BRANCH: Naval Reserve.
LOCATION: *County:* Woodbury.
MAJOR UNITS: REDCOM SIXTEEN Activity.
Key Contacts
COMMANDER: Lt C Gerkin.

Waterloo

350. Waterloo Marine Corps Reserve Center
MCRC
1689 Burton Ave
Waterloo, IA 50703-2181
319-233-8731, 233-5114; FAX 319-233-1417
Profile
BRANCH: Marine Corps Reserve.
LOCATION: *County:* Black Hawk.
MAJOR UNITS: D Battery, 2nd Bn, 14th Ma-
rine Regiment.

Kansas

Atchison

351. Defense Industrial Plant Equipment Facility
DIPEF
RR 1, PO Box
Atchison, KS 66002-9801
913-367-4300; DSN 886-1520

Profile
BRANCH: Army.
SIZE AND LOCATION: 125 acres. 1 mi S of Atchison, KS, on old Hwy 73. *County:* Atchison.
MAJOR UNITS: AMCCOM Vault 1; AMCCOM Vault 2; Industrial Plant Equipment Machines; Clothing & Medical Supplies.
BASE HISTORY: 1944, War Food Administration leased limestone mine for perishable foods. 1952-63, Army took over operation for storage of industrial plant equipment. Currently, GOCO industrial activity under Defense Industrial Plant Equipment Center, Memphis, TN; also off-site storage facility for Defense Reutilization and Marketing Offices (DRMOs) at Ft Leavenworth, and Ft Riley, KS.

Key Contacts
COMMANDER: Richard Everett.

Personnel and Expenditures
CIVILIAN PERSONNEL: 30

Services *Medical Facilities:* First Aid Room.

Fort Leavenworth

352. Fort Leavenworth
CAC & Ft Leavenworth
US Army Combined Arms Center & Fort Leavenworth
Fort Leavenworth, KS 66027
913-684-4021; DSN 552-4021
OFFICER-OF-THE-DAY: 913-684-4154, DSN 552-4154

Profile
BRANCH: Army.
SIZE AND LOCATION: 5600 acres. Adj to Leavenworth, KS, on US-73 and KS Rte 92, approx 30 mi NW of Kansas City, MO. *County:* Leavenworth.
MAJOR UNITS: Command and General Staff College; Combined Arms Command, US Disciplinary Barracks; TRADOC Analysis Command, Headquarters; 35th Infantry Division, Headquarters (Mobilized)(ANG).
BASE HISTORY: Established by Col Henry Leavenworth in 1827. In 1830s-1840s branches of Santa Fe and Oregon Trails traversed post, carrying settlers west. During Mexican War (1846-48), important Army HQ. Mid-1850s, saved from abandonment by US Secretary of War, Jefferson Davis. George A Custer and his brother Tom, who was first man to earn two Medals of Honor, served here. Tom Custer buried in National Cemetery here. In May 1881, what is today US Army Command and General Staff College was established.
VISITOR ATTRACTIONS: Ft Leavenworth is a National Historic Landmark; Frontier Army Museum (open 10-4, Mon-Sat, 12-4, Sun & Holidays, except New Year's, Christmas, Thanksgiving, and Easter); Buffalo Soldier Monument.

Key Contacts
COMMANDER: Lt Gen L D Holder.
PUBLIC AFFAIRS: LTC James W Gleisberg, Bldg 198, 600 Thomas Ave, Ft Leavenworth, KS 66027-1399, 913-684-5604, DSN 552-5604.
PROCUREMENT: Elizabeth Bornman, Bldg 198, 913-684-3383, DSN 552-3383.
TRANSPORTATION: John Self, Bldg 198, 913-684-5631, DSN 552-5631.
PERSONNEL/COMMUNITY ACTIVITIES: Timothy Laster, Bldg 198, 913-684-3719, DSN 552-3719.

Personnel and Expenditures
ACTIVE DUTY PERSONNEL: 3200
DEPENDENTS: 4600
CIVILIAN PERSONNEL: 2300
MILITARY PAYROLL EXPENDITURE: $124 mil
CONTRACT EXPENDITURE: $150 mil

Services
Housing: Family units 1586; Unaccompanied enlisted quarters 6; BOQ units 4; Unaccompanied officer quarters units 4. *Temporary Housing:* VIP units 31; VOQ units 701; Guesthouse units 12. *Commissary:* Yes; *Exchange:* Retail store; Barber shop; Dry cleaners; Food shop; Bank; Service station; Bookstore; Military clothing store; Beauty shop; Computer shop; Optical shop; Video rental. *Child Care/Capacities:* Day care center capacity 279; Home day care program. *Schools:* Elementary; Intermediate/Junior high. *Base Library:* Yes. *Medical Facilities:* Hospital 20; Dental clinic. *Recreational Facilities:* Bowling center; Movie theater; Pool; Gym; Recreation center; Golf course; Stables; Tennis courts; Racquetball court; Fitness center/Weight room; Softball field; Football field; Auto shop; Craft shop; Camping; Fishing/Hunting; Picnic area; Club.

Fort Riley

353. Fort Riley
Huebner Rd, Bldg 500
Fort Riley, KS 66442-5016
785-239-2672, 239-3911; DSN 856-1110
Internet: http://www.riley.army.mil; http://144.246.28.35/

Profile
BRANCH: Army.
SIZE AND LOCATION: 100,752 acres. Between Manhattan & Junction, KS; Manhattan 15 mi E; Junction City at W gate; Ogden at E gate. *County:* Geary; Riley.
MAJOR UNITS: 1st Brigade, 1st Infantry Division (MECH); 1st Armor Division, 3rd Brigade; 937th Engineer Group (Combat); 541st Maintenance Bn; Defense Military Pay Office and 1st Finance Bn; 1st Personnel Services Bn; Law Enforcement Command; 82nd Medical Co.
BASE HISTORY: 1852, temporary quarters named "Camp Center" set up. 1853, permanent post established, named Ft Riley in honor of Maj Gen Bennett Riley, Mexican War hero. 1855, construction of more permanent buildings. 1861, 4th Cavalry served tour. 1866, 7th Cavalry organized under Col Smith & LTC George A Custer. Since 1917, 1st Infantry Division, "No Mission Too Difficult, No Sacrifice Too Great, Duty First." 1955-65, "Big Red One" stationed; first division to go to Vietnam. 1970, 1st Infantry Division returned. 1990, fort personnel deployed to Operation Desert Shield/Storm.
VISITOR ATTRACTIONS: US Cavalry Museum; Custer House; Combat Air Museum; 1st Infantry Division Museum; 1st Territorial Capital of KS; Buffalo herd.

Key Contacts
COMMANDER: Maj Gen Michael L Dodson, 785-239-3516, DSN 856-3516.
PUBLIC AFFAIRS: Bldg 405, 785-239-2022, DSN 856-2022.

Personnel and Expenditures
ACTIVE DUTY PERSONNEL: 10,000; Guard 40; Reserves 20
DEPENDENTS: 9500
CIVILIAN PERSONNEL: 3400

Services

Housing: Family units 3180; Unaccompanied officer quarters 32; Unaccompanied enlisted quarters 16; BAQ units; Barracks spaces; Senior NCO units. *Temporary Housing:* VIP units 8; VOQ units 111; BAQ units; Guesthouse units 38; Transient quarters. *Commissary:* Yes; *Exchange:* Retail store; Barber shop; Dry cleaners; Food shop; Florist; Bank; Service station; Bakery; Military clothing store; Convenience store; Beauty shop; Laundromat; Credit union; Optical store; Fast food; Thrift shop; Class VI; Sports shop; 1 Hr Photo; Ice cream shop; Auto parts; Delicatessen. *Child Care/Capacities:* Day care center capacity 300, 4wks-12yrs; Home day care program; Latch key program; Summer day camp. *Schools:* Preschool/Kindergarten; Elementary; Intermediate/Junior high. *Base Library:* Yes. *Medical Facilities:* Hospital 106 beds; Medical clinic; Dental clinic; Veterinary services. *Recreational Facilities:* Bowling center; Movie theater; Pool; Gym; Recreation center; Golf course; Stables; Tennis courts; Racquetball court; Skating rink; Fitness center/Weight room; Softball field; Football field; Auto shop; Craft shop; Officers club; NCO club; Camping; Fishing/Hunting; Youth center; Picnic area; Playground; Ft Riley parks; Moon Lake; Community Center; Activities center; Outdoor recreation equipment checkout center; Camping at nearby State Lake.

McConnell AFB

354. McConnell Air Force Base
57837 Coffeyville St, Ste 240
McConnell AFB, KS 67221-3504
316-652-3141; FAX 316-652-3148; DSN
743-3141; DSN FAX 743-3148
Internet: http://www.mcconnell.af.mil
OFFICER-OF-THE-DAY: Command Post,
316-652-3251, DSN 743-3251

Profile
BRANCH: Air Force.
SIZE AND LOCATION: 3066 acres. In SE corner of Wichita. From N: on Kansas Tpke S, use E Wichita Exit, W 0.5 mi on US-54 (Kellogg Ave), left at Rock Rd. From S: on Kansas Tpke, K-15 Exit, right, gate approx 1 mi straight ahead. From I-35: Kellogg E to Rock Rd, S to E gate. *County:* Sedgwick.
MAJOR UNITS: 22nd Air Refueling Wing; 184th Bomb Wing (KS ANG); 931st Air Refueling Group (AFRES).
BASE HISTORY: 1929, ground broken for Wichita Municipal Airport, current site of base. 1941, KS ANG assigned to SE corner of airport. 1942-45, Army Air Force Materiel Center established at airport; replaced by 4156th AAF unit for short time. 1950, Air Force began federal court action to convert airport to military facility. 1952, city of Wichita builds new airport, now known as Mid-Continent Airport. 1953, became Wichita AFB. 1954, renamed in honor of Fred & Thomas McConnell of Wichita. 1951-58, hosted by Air Training Command. 1958-63, hosted by Strategic Air Command. 1963-72, Tactical Air Command host & 381st Strategic Missile Wing, SAC, major tenant. 1972, 384th Air Refueling Wing (Heavy) activated at McConnell assigned to 12th Strategic Missile Division and HQ 15th Air Force; 384th

aircraft have supported many TAC and ANG fighter deployments all over the world. 1987, 384th ARW redesignated 384th BMW (SAC), making McConnell fourth base to host B-1B bomber, reporting to HQ SAC, Offutt AFB, NE, through HQ 8th Air Force, Barksdale AFB, LA. 1992, McConnell began reporting to HQ ACC, Langley, VA; host unit renamed 384th Bomb Wing. 1994, redesignated 384th Bomb Group, tenant activity; 184th Fighter Group renamed 184th Bomb Group. 1995, 931st ARG activated; 184th Bomb Group redesignated 184th Bomb Wing (KS ANG).
VISITOR ATTRACTIONS: Several static displays of aircraft & memorabilia; displays of civil & military aviation; Kansas Aviation Museum (nonprofit, non-Air Force, outside west gate).

Key Contacts
COMMANDER: Col Larry Stevenson.
PUBLIC AFFAIRS: 1Lt Amber Young, younga@emh.mcconnell.af.mil.
PROCUREMENT: Capt Donna Toole, 316-652-3275, DSN 743-3275, Tooled@ emh.mcconnell.af.mil.
TRANSPORTATION: Maj Greg White, 316-652-5250, DSN 743-5250, Whitea@emh. mcconnell.af.mil.
PERSONNEL/COMMUNITY ACTIVITIES: Capt Daniel PonceDeLeon, 316-652-3761, DSN 743-3761, ponced@emh.mcconnell.af. mil.

Personnel and Expenditures
ACTIVE DUTY PERSONNEL: 2969
DEPENDENTS: 6481
CIVILIAN PERSONNEL: 463
MILITARY PAYROLL EXPENDITURE: $87 mil
CONTRACT EXPENDITURE: $60 mil

Services
Housing: Family units 486; Dormitory spaces 655. *Temporary Housing:* VIP units 9; VOQ units 34; VAQ units 30; Transient quarters 24. *Commissary:* Yes; *Exchange:* Retail store; Barber shop; Dry cleaners; Food shop; Florist; Bank; Service station; Military clothing store; Convenience store; Beauty shop; Credit union; ATM; Optical store; Post office; Fast food; Video rentals; Thrift shop; Travel agency; Class VI; Computer store; Garden center; Tailor/Alterations; Laundry. *Child Care/Capacities:* Day care center capacity 86, 6mo-10yrs; Home day care program; Summer day camp; Before & after school programs. *Schools:* Elementary; College courses. *Base Library:* Yes. *Medical Facilities:* Medical clinic; Dental clinic; Pharmacy; Veterinary services. *Recreational Facilities:* Bowling center; Movie theater; Pool; Gym; Golf course; Tennis courts; Racquetball court; Fitness center/Weight room; Softball field; Auto shop; Craft shop; Officers club; Fishing/Hunting; Enlisted club; Youth center; Picnic area; Playground; Combined club.

Overland Park

355. Marine Corps Reserve Support Center
MCRSC
10950 El Monte
Overland Park, KS 66211
913-481-7500; DSN 465-3101; 465-3102 plus ext

OFFICER-OF-THE-DAY: 913-491-7500, DSN 465-3101, ext 7500

Profile
BRANCH: Marine Corps.
SIZE AND LOCATION: Office bldg with annex. In SW section of Kansas City Metro area, off I-435, first exit W of State Line Rd (KS/MO border); Roe exit S to 109th (immediate left) in Fox Hill Office complex, follow into El Monte, sign on parking lot marks facility. *County:* Johnson.
BASE HISTORY: 1965, originally established as Reserve Records Branch (Class III), under USMC Reserve Data Services Center, administrative support center for Reserve of USMC. 1972, redesignated Marine Corps Reserve Forces Records Branch (Class III), subordinate branch of Division of Reserve under Reserve Automated Systems Manpower Branch for Systems Management. 1973, redesignated Marine Corps Reserve Forces Administrative Activity (MCRFAA). 1976, redesignated Marine Corps Reserve Forces Administrative Center (MCRFAC). Basic mission remained constant until 1981; Marine Corps Reserve Forces Administration Center amalgamated into administrative and management complex designated MCRSC. 1982, moved into current facility. Provides Marine Corps with pre-trained individual manpower, consisting of IRR, Standby Reserve, Fleet Marine Corps Reserve not on active duty, regular and retired Reservists, and Individual Mobilization Augmentees (IMAs); recruits prior service Marines for drilling SMCR units within 4th Marine Division/4th Marine Aircraft Wing team (4th DWT).

Key Contacts
COMMANDER: Director; 913-491-7502, DSN 465-3101, ext 7502.
PUBLIC AFFAIRS: 913-491-7905, DSN 465-3101, ext 7905.
PROCUREMENT: 913-491-7900, DSN 465-3101, ext 7900.
PERSONNEL/COMMUNITY ACTIVITIES: Personnel, Head, HQ Division, 913-491-7710, DSN 465-3101, ext 7710; Community Activities see Public Affairs Officer.

Personnel and Expenditures
ACTIVE DUTY PERSONNEL: 312
CIVILIAN PERSONNEL: 90

Services
Housing: Facilities located at Richards-Gebaur AFB. Housing maintained by Marine Corps Finance Ctr, Kansas City, MO.

Parsons

356. Kansas Army Ammunition Plant
KSAAP
23018 Rooks Rd, Ste AA
Parsons, KS 67357-8403
316-421-7447; FAX 316-421-7387; DSN 956-1447; DSN FAX 956-1387

Profile
BRANCH: DOD.
SIZE AND LOCATION: 13,727 acres. In SE KS, 3 mi E and 0.5 mi S of Parsons, KS, just off US-160; 60 mi NW of Joplin, MO municipal airport; Tulsa IAP approx 100 mi S. *County:* Labette.

BASE HISTORY: 1941-42, established as GOCO military industrial installation under AMCCOM. Operated by Day & Zimmermann on facilities contract. Current workload includes Load, Assemble & Pack (LAP) of Air Force Combined Effects Munition & other contracts.

FUTURE CLOSURE/REALIGNMENT: Although on the BRAC 91 list, KAAP remains active through a facility contract.

Key Contacts
COMMANDER: Don Dailey, Commander's Representative, 316-421-7449, DSN 956-1449, DSN FAX 956-1387, ddailey@dzikansas.com.
PUBLIC AFFAIRS: Jerry Fager, 316-421-7447, DSN 956-1447, DSN FAX 956-1387, jfager@dzikansas.com.
PROCUREMENT: Jerry G Riley, 316-421-7391, DSN 956-1391, jriley@dzikansas.com.
TRANSPORTATION: Patrick McCall, 316-421-7453, DSN 956-1453, pmccall@dzikansas.com.
PERSONNEL/COMMUNITY ACTIVITIES: See Public Affairs Officer.

Personnel and Expenditures
ACTIVE DUTY PERSONNEL: 0
DEPENDENTS: 0
CIVILIAN PERSONNEL: 9

Services
Housing: None. *Child Care/Capacities:* No day care facilities. *Medical Facilities:* No medical facilities.

Salina

357. Nickell Barracks Training Center
1844 Jumper Rd
Salina, KS 67401-8123
785-825-0203
Profile
BRANCH: Army National Guard.
LOCATION: On Smoky Hill River, 58 mi NNE of Hutchinson. *County:* Saline.
MAJOR UNITS: Nickell Barracks Training Center (ARNG).

Shawnee Mission

358. 9th Marine Corps District
9th MarCorDist
10000 W 75th St
Shawnee Mission, KS 66204-2219
913-236-3511; FAX 913-236-3501; DSN 465-3511
Profile
BRANCH: Marine Corps.
SIZE AND LOCATION: Offices only. Off I-35 and 75th St in city of Shawnee Mission; 20 mi S of Kansas City. *County:* Johnson.
MAJOR UNITS: 9th Marine Corps District, Headquarters Unit.
BASE HISTORY: Recruiting District Headquarters for 11 Midwestern states.
Key Contacts
COMMANDER: Col Robert S Robichaud.
PUBLIC AFFAIRS: CWO Douglas C Hauth; 913-236-3515, DSN 465-3515.

PROCUREMENT: Capt L D Singleton; 913-236-3520, DSN 465-3520.
TRANSPORTATION: GySgt R W Pierce; 913-236-3520, DSN 465-3520.
Personnel and Expenditures
ACTIVE DUTY PERSONNEL: 60
CIVILIAN PERSONNEL: 20

Topeka

359. Adjutant General of Kansas
2800 SW Topeka Blvd
Topeka, KS 66611-1287
913-274-1001; FAX 913-274-1682
Profile
BRANCH: Army National Guard.
MAJOR UNITS: Kansas National Guard.
Key Contacts
COMMANDER: Maj Gen James F Rueger.

360. Coast Guard Human Resources Service & Information Center
HRS&IC
444 SE Quincy St
Topeka, KS 66683-3591
913-357-3600; FAX 913-295-2721
E-mail: Admin/HRSIC@internet.uscg.mail
Profile
BRANCH: Coast Guard.
SIZE AND LOCATION: Offices only. In downtown Topeka in Carlson Federal Bldg; take 3rd St exit from I-70E or 5th St exit from I-70W. *County:* Shawnee.
MAJOR UNITS: Coast Guard Human Resources Service & Information Center.
BASE HISTORY: 1982, moved from Riverdale, MD; 1997 changed name from Pay & Personnel Center.
Key Contacts
COMMANDER: Capt Robert J Williamson, 913-357-3603, CO/HRSIC@internet.uscg.mail.
PUBLIC AFFAIRS: CDR J Dennis Williamson, 913-357-3603, FAX 913-295-2721, XO/HRSIC@internet.uscg.mail.
PROCUREMENT: CWO Wes Smyth, 913-357-3620, FAX 913-295-2721, R.Smyth/HRSIC@internet.uscg.mail.
Personnel and Expenditures
ACTIVE DUTY PERSONNEL: 175
DEPENDENTS: 0
CIVILIAN PERSONNEL: 95
CONTRACT EXPENDITURE: $4 mil
Services *Child Care/Capacities:* No day care facilities. *Schools:* No on-base schools. *Medical Facilities:* No medical facilities.

361. Forbes Field Air National Guard Base
Forbes Field 190 AREFW
190th Air Guard
5920 Coyote Dr
Topeka, KS 66619-5000
913-862-1234; DSN 720-4791
E-mail: hqaii@air@agks
Profile
BRANCH: Air National Guard.
SIZE AND LOCATION: 140 acres. Adj to US-75; adjoins Pauline, KS, to E; 3 mi S of

Topeka, KS; adjoins Topeka Airport (MTAA). *County:* Shawnee.
MAJOR UNITS: 190th Air Refueling Group; 117th Refueling Squadron; 127th Weather Flight; 190th Air Force Clinic.
BASE HISTORY: 1942, opened as Topeka Army Air Corps Base. Closed at end of WWII. 1948, reopened; renamed after Maj Daniel H Forbes, native Topekan killed 1948 test flying Northrup YB-49, "Flying Wing." 1949-51, facility closed. 1961, site location of Atlas E missiles; deactivated 4 years later. TAC base until deactivation. 1973, most of base turned over to city of Topeka for municipal airport. Forbes ANGB licensed to state of KS. 1942, 190th ARG began as 440th Bombardment Squadron, Light; deactivated following WWII; reorganized as 117th Bombardment Squadron, Light, PA NG; Korean War activated as training unit, Langley AFB, VA. Came to Hutchinson, KS 1957 as 117th FIS. 1967, 190th TRG transferred to Forbes as tactical bombardment unit.
VISITOR ATTRACTIONS: Restored EB-57 on display at new base gate.
Key Contacts
COMMANDER: Col Steve Thomas, 913-861-4791, DSN 720-4791, SThomas@cc@190ARG.
PUBLIC AFFAIRS: 1Lt Cindy Marcello, 913-861-4195, DSN 720-4195, CAntolik@CC@190ARG.
PROCUREMENT: 913-861-4490, DSN 720-4490.
TRANSPORTATION: 913-861-4618, DSN 720-4618.
PERSONNEL/COMMUNITY ACTIVITIES: 913-861-4134, DSN 720-4134.
Personnel and Expenditures
ACTIVE DUTY PERSONNEL: 1100
CIVILIAN PERSONNEL: 85
Services
Housing: Local motels for UTA drill. *Temporary Housing:* Local motels for weekend guests. *Exchange:* Retail store. *Child Care/Capacities:* No day care facilities. *Schools:* No on-base schools. *Medical Facilities:* Medical clinic. *Recreational Facilities:* Fitness center/Weight room; Softball field; Recreation Center for Alert Crews only.

362. Topeka Naval & Marine Corps Reserve Center
2014 SE Washington St, Ste 3
Topeka, KS 66607-1398
913-233-7434; FAX 913-233-7469
Profile
BRANCH: Naval Reserve; Marine Corps Reserve.
LOCATION: *County:* Shawnee.
MAJOR UNITS: REDCOM SIXTEEN Activity; Det 2, Supply Co, 4th Supply Bn.
Key Contacts
COMMANDER: LCDR Gopp.

Wichita

363. Defense Contract Management Command, Wichita
DCMC Wichita
271 W 3rd St N, Ste 6000
Wichita, KS 67202-1212

Internet: http://www.dcmdw.dla.mil/dcmcwch/
homepage.htm

Profile
BRANCH: Defense Logistics Agency.
LOCATION: *County:* Sedgwick.
MAJOR UNITS: Defense Contract Management
Command, Wichita.

Key Contacts
COMMANDER: LTC Charles E Snavely,
USAF; James Rose, Deputy.

364. Wichita Naval & Marine Corps Reserve Center
NAVMARCORESCEN Wichita
3026 George Washington Blvd
Wichita, KS 67210-1599
316-683-3481; FAX 316-683-5115

Profile
BRANCH: Naval Reserve; Marine Corps Reserve.
SIZE AND LOCATION: 7 acres. 0.5 mi from
back gate of McConnell AFB. *County:* Sedgwick.
MAJOR UNITS: REDCOM SIXTEEN Activity; NMCB 15 Det 1215; FH 500 CBTZ 23

Det K (NR); AD 42 Det 9 (NR); VTU (NR);
Electrical Maintenance Co, 4th Maintenance
Bn; Engineer Maintenance Co, Det 1, 4th
Maintenance Bn.
BASE HISTORY: Naval Reserve Ctr built 1972-
73; DC Trainer added 1989-90. Marine Corps
section added 1990.

Key Contacts
COMMANDER: LCDR D B Foster.
PUBLIC AFFAIRS: ENC T L Smith.

Personnel and Expenditures
ACTIVE DUTY PERSONNEL: 7; 175 reservists

Services *Base Library:* Yes. *Recreational Facilities:* Uses facilities on McConnell AFB.

Kentucky

Fort Campbell

365. Fort Campbell
ATTN: AFZB-PO
Fort Campbell, KY 42223-5000
502-798-3427; FAX 502-798-6247; DSN 635-3427
OFFICER-OF-THE-DAY: 502-798-9793, DSN 635-9793

Profile
BRANCH: Army.
SIZE AND LOCATION: 105,068 acres. On KY/TN border; adj to Clarksville, TN, and Oak Grove, KY; 9 mi S of Hopkinsville, KY; approx 60 mi NW of Nashville; US 41-A runs along post's E boundary; exits from I-24 lead to post. *County:* Christian, Trigg, KY; Montgomery, Stewart, TN.
MAJOR UNITS: 101st Airborne Division (Air Assault); 5th Special Forces Group (Airborne); 160th Special Operations Aviation Regiment (Airborne).
BASE HISTORY: 1942, Camp Campbell constructed, named for William Campbell, Army veteran of Seminole & Mexican Wars, TN congressman, & governor. Base two-thirds in TN, Post Office in KY; TN first designated as official address; 6 months later, without explanation, KY named permanent address. WWII, location of training ground for 12th, 14th & 20th Armored Divisions, HQ IV Armored Corps & 26th Infantry Division. 1949-56, 11th Airborne arrived; center for assembly & redeployment of troops. 1950, designated Fort Campbell, permanent status. 1951-1953, command under 2nd Army. 1953, transferred to Third Army. 1956, 101st Airborne Division moved in from Ft Jackson, SC. 1966-72, location of Basic Combat Training Center. 1969, Training Center & Ft Campbell combined. 1972, 101st Airborne Division *Screaming Eagles* returned.
VISITOR ATTRACTIONS: 101st Airborne Division Museum; Don F Pratt Museum.

Key Contacts
COMMANDER: Maj Gen William F Kernan, Commander, 101st Airborne Division, 502-798-9915, DSN 635-9915.
PUBLIC AFFAIRS: Maj Billy J Buckner, 502-798-3427, DSN 635-3427.
PROCUREMENT: Carl J Heckmann, Directorate of Contracting, 502-798-7126, DSN 635-7126.

TRANSPORTATION: Mike Bowers, Directorate of Logistics, 502-798-3424, DSN 635-3424.
PERSONNEL/COMMUNITY ACTIVITIES: LTC(P) Jeffrey Earley, Directorate of Personnel and Community Activities, 502-798-9953, DSN 635-9953.

Personnel and Expenditures
ACTIVE DUTY PERSONNEL: 23,299
DEPENDENTS: 39,114
CIVILIAN PERSONNEL: 4149
MILITARY PAYROLL EXPENDITURE: $613 mil
CONTRACT EXPENDITURE: $256 mil

Services
Housing: Family units 4153. *Temporary Housing:* VOQ units 78; Guesthouse units 142; DVQ suite 1. *Commissary:* Yes; *Exchange:* Retail store; Barber shop; Dry cleaners; Food shop; Florist; Bank; Service station; Furniture store; Bakery; Military clothing store; Convenience store; Beauty shop; Laundromat; Credit union; Fast food; Ice cream shop. *Child Care/Capacities:* Day care center capacity 606, 1mo-12yrs; Home day care program; Latch key program. *Schools:* Preschool/Kindergarten; Elementary; Intermediate/Junior high; High school; College/University; College courses. *Base Library:* Yes. *Medical Facilities:* Hospital 241 beds; Medical clinic; Dental clinic; Dispensary; Pharmacy; Veterinary services. *Recreational Facilities:* Bowling center; Movie theater; Pool; Gym; Recreation center; Golf course; Stables; Tennis courts; Racquetball court; Fitness center/Weight room; Softball field; Football field; Auto shop; Craft shop; Officers club; NCO club; Camping; Fishing/Hunting; Enlisted club; Youth center; Picnic area; Skeet range; Playground.

Fort Knox

366. Army Armor Center & Fort Knox
Ft Knox
Fort Knox, KY 40121-5000
Mailing Address
ATZK PAO 131, PO Box 995
Fort Knox, KY 40121-5000
502-624-1181, operator; FAX 502-624-6434;
DSN 464-1181, operator

E-mail: harrisr@knox-emh3.army.mil (webmaster) Internet:http://www.knox.army.mil or 147.238.100.101
OFFICER-OF-THE-DAY: HQ Staff Duty Office (night/weekend emergencies), 502-624-4421, DSN 464-4421, DSN FAX 464-6434

Profile
BRANCH: Army.
SIZE AND LOCATION: 109,054 acres. From N, I-65 to Gene Snyder Expy, S on 31W/US-60 to Ft Knox. From S, I-65 to Elizabethtown, N on 31W to Ft Knox. 45 min drive from Louisville; 40 min from Standiford Field, Louisville Airport. *County:* Hardin; Meade; Bullitt.
MAJOR UNITS: Army Armor Center & Fort Knox; Army Armor School, HQ; 16th Cavalry Regiment; 1st Armor Training Brigade; 43rd Ordnance Det (EOD); Army Dental Activity, Ft Knox; Defense Investigative Service, DOD Central Region, Midwest Sector; Mounted Maneuver Battlespace Lab; Ireland Army Community Hospital; NCO Academy; Office, Chief of Armor; Readiness Group, Knox; Armor Branch Safety Office; Staff Judge Advocate; Office of Total Army Quality; 100th Division (Training), 4th Brigade (Training Support); 1287th Logistical Support Bn; 244th Aviation Brigade, Aviation Support Facility Knox; 3rd Bn, 345th Regiment; 3rd Regional Training Brigade; G1/46th Adjutant General Bn (Reception); 81st Regional Support Command; 244th Aviation Brigade, 8th Bn/229th Aviation Regiment; Army Counterintelligence, Army INSCOM, Fort Knox Resident Office, 902nd Military Intelligence Group; Army & Air Force Exchange Service; Allied Liaison Office; AMC Logistics Assistance Office; 280th MP Det (CID), 3rd MP Group; Army Support Det, Columbus; DOD Commissary, Fort Knox; Corps of Engineers, Fort Knox Area Office; HQ First United States Army forward (West); Defense Accounting Office; Defense Printing Service Det Office, Knox; Defense Reutilization & Marketing Office; Federal Bureau of Investigation; US Bullion Depository; Kentucky Army National Guard, Military Academy; Navy Mobile Construction Bn 20; Operational Support Airlift Command (OSAC), Fort Knox Regional Flight Center; 2nd Region (ROTC) Army Cadet Command; Army Command Test & Evaluation Coordination; Army Test Measuring Diagnostic Equipment Support Activity CONUS, Region 2; TRADOC Regional Coordinating Element

(DELTA); TRADOC System Manager (TSM) for Abraams; Close Combat Tactical Trainer (CCTT) Project Office; TRADOC System Manager (TSM) for Force XXI; US Army Research Institute, Armored Forces Training Research Unit, Fort Knox; Army Recruiting Command; 3rd Recruiting Brigade; Army Research Lab, Fort Knox Field Element; A Co, 8th Tank Bn (USMC); Operating Location C, 18th Weather Squadron (USAF); 113th Army Band (Dragoons).

BASE HISTORY: 1918, established as Camp Henry Knox, field artillery training center, named for Maj Gen Henry Knox, Chief of Artillery Continental Army, American Revolution, and 1st Secretary of War. 1922, closed as permanent installation. 1922-32, served as training center for 5th Corps area, Citizens Military Training Camps, & National Guard. 1925-28, designated Camp Henry Knox National Forest. 1932, designated permanent garrison; name changed to Ft Knox. 1930s, center for cavalry mechanization. 1937, Gold Vault opened. 1940, Armored Force School & Armored Force Replacement Center established. Home of Armor & Cavalry to this day. Every soldier in Armored Force serves here at least once during term of service.

FUTURE CLOSURE/REALIGNMENT: 1997, 19th Combat Engineers inactivated.

VISITOR ATTRACTIONS: Patton Museum of Cavalry and Armor; No visitors are permitted at US Bullion Depository owned by Treasury Department.

Key Contacts
COMMANDER: Maj Gen George H Harmeyer, Bldg 1101, 502-624-2121, DSN 464-2121, DSN FAX 464-6434, harmeyer@ftknox-emh7.army.mil.
PUBLIC AFFAIRS: Maj Michael Pond, Bldg 474, 502-624-4788, DSN 464-4788, DSN FAX 464-6074, pondm@ftknox-emh3.army.mil.
PROCUREMENT: Reba Watson, Director of Contracting, 502-624-7152, DSN 464-7152, DSN FAX 464-7165, watsonr@ftknox-emh3.army.mil.
TRANSPORTATION: Terry Bird, 502-624-2506, DSN 464-2506, dsn fax 464-3315, birdt@ftknoxdol-emh10.army.mil.
PERSONNEL/COMMUNITY ACTIVITIES: Sam Jones, Director of Human Resources (Family Support) 502-624-2028, DSN 464-2028, DSN FAX 464-6223, joness@ftknox2-emh3.army.mil.

Personnel and Expenditures
ACTIVE DUTY PERSONNEL: 11,574 (including soldiers in training)
DEPENDENTS: 7833
CIVILIAN PERSONNEL: 6429
MILITARY PAYROLL EXPENDITURE: $287.2 mil (military & civilian)
CONTRACT EXPENDITURE: $107.3 mil

Services
Housing: Family units 4232; Unaccompanied officer quarters 54; Unaccompanied enlisted quarters 8662; Senior NCO units 38. *Temporary Housing:* VIP units 1; Guesthouse units 76; Transient quarters 614. *Commissary:* Yes; *Exchange:* Retail store; Barber shop; Dry cleaners; Food shop; Florist; Bank; Service station; Furniture store; Bakery; Bookstore; Military clothing store; Convenience store; Beauty shop; Laundromat; Credit union; ATM; Optical store; Post office; Fast food; Video rentals; Four seasons;

Thrift shop; Travel agency; Class VI; Computer store; Garden center; Tailor/Alterations; Laundry; Cafeteria; Photo store. *Child Care/Capacities:* Day care center capacity 650, 6wks-12yrs; Home day care program; Latch key program; Summer day camp; Before & after school programs; Hourly care, preschool special needs available. *Schools:* Preschool/Kindergarten; Elementary; Intermediate/Junior high; High school; College/University; College courses. *Base Library:* Yes. *Medical Facilities:* Hospital 100; Medical clinic; Dental clinic; Pharmacy; Veterinary services. *Recreational Facilities:* Bowling center; Movie theater; Pool; Gym; Golf course; Stables; Tennis courts; Racquetball court; Fitness center/Weight room; Softball field; Football field; Auto shop; Craft shop; Officers club; NCO club; Camping; Fishing/Hunting; Enlisted club; Youth center; Picnic area; Skeet range; Water sports; Playground; Community club; Camp Carlson outdoor recreation area; Equipment rental center; Tioga Falls National Recreational Trail.

Frankfort

367. Adjutant General of Kentucky
100 Minuteman Pky, Bldg 100
Frankfort, KY 40601-6168
502-564-8558; FAX 502-564-6271
Profile
BRANCH: Army National Guard.
MAJOR UNITS: Kentucky National Guard.
Key Contacts
COMMANDER: Brig Gen John R Groves Jr.

Lexington

368. Lexington Naval Reserve Center
NAVRESCEN Lexington
NRC Lexington
151 Vo Tech Rd
Lexington, KY 40510-1002
606-255-1041; 255-1042; FAX 606-253-9366
Profile
BRANCH: Naval Reserve.
LOCATION: In Lexington approx 15 min from Bluegrass Airport. *County:* Fayette.
MAJOR UNITS: REDCOM NINE Activity; NAVHOSP CLEJEUNE 0209 (NR); CG54 Antietam 5409 (NR); NAVSTA Panama Det 409 (NR); VOLTRAUNIT 0908 (NR); AS-33 Simon Lake 3309C (NR); AD-41 Yellowstone Det 16 (NR); NMCB 24 Det 0924.
Key Contacts
COMMANDER: LCDR R J Patterson, 606-255-8013.
PUBLIC AFFAIRS: PNC(AW) D A Perez.
Personnel and Expenditures
ACTIVE DUTY PERSONNEL: 10; 260 reservists
Services *Base Library:* Yes. *Recreational Facilities:* Gym; Fitness center/Weight room.

Louisville

369. Army Corps of Engineers, Louisville District
CELRL
PO Box 59
Louisville, KY 40201-0059
Internet: http://www.orl.usace.army.mil/ceorl1/
Profile
BRANCH: Army.
SIZE AND LOCATION: Offices only. In downtown Louisville. *County:* Jefferson.
MAJOR UNITS: Corps of Engineers, Louisville District.
BASE HISTORY: 1886, established. Covers states of IL, IN, KY, MI, & OH with civil works & military construction mission.
Key Contacts
COMMANDER: Col Harry Spear, District Engineer, 502-582-5601.
PUBLIC AFFAIRS: Ken Crawford, 502-582-5736, FAX 502-582-5270, kcrawford@smtp.orl.usace.army.mil.

370. Louisville Naval Ordnance Station
NAVSURFWARCEN ORDSTA
5403 Southside Dr
Louisville, KY 40214-5000
502-364-5456; FAX 502-364-6333; DSN 989-5456
OFFICER-OF-THE-DAY: 502-364-5203, DSN 989-5203
Profile
BRANCH: Navy.
SIZE AND LOCATION: 142 acres. 7 mi S of downtown Louisville and 1 mi W of Standiford Field Airport; 3 mi SW of intersection of I-65 & I-264. *County:* Jefferson.
MAJOR UNITS: Naval Ordnance Station, Crane Division, Naval Surface Warfare Center.
BASE HISTORY: 1941, commissioned as Naval Ordnance Plant Louisville, GOCO, operated by Westinghouse Electric Co until after WWII; produced gun systems and munitions. 1946, Station became Navy operated/owned. 1950, reactivation during Korean War. 1966, renamed Naval Ordnance Station Louisville. 1986, designated overhaul and repair facility for Phalanx Close-In Weapons System. 1992, merged with Naval Surface Weapons Center, Crane, IN. Today, only government-owned, government-operated facility working to overhaul and maintain naval gun systems, missile launchers, and gun control radars and computers; operates under Naval Sea Systems Command, Washington, DC.
Key Contacts
COMMANDER: Capt Richard Gilbert, 502-364-5211, DSN 989-5211.
PUBLIC AFFAIRS: William J Meers.
PROCUREMENT: Charles Buccola, 502-364-5828, DSN 989-5828.
TRANSPORTATION: Tom Mason, 502-364-5743, DSN 989-5743.
PERSONNEL/COMMUNITY ACTIVITIES: Ed Simmerman, Crane Division, NSWC, Crane, IN 47522.
Personnel and Expenditures
ACTIVE DUTY PERSONNEL: 15
DEPENDENTS: 8
CIVILIAN PERSONNEL: 2280
MILITARY PAYROLL EXPENDITURE: $1.2 mil

CONTRACT EXPENDITURE: $197.5 mil

Services

Housing: Family units 8. *Base Library:* Yes. *Medical Facilities:* Medical clinic. *Recreational Facilities:* Pool; Tennis courts; Softball field.

371. Louisville Naval Reserve Center

NAVRESCEN Lousiville; NRC Louisville
5401 Southside Dr
Louisville, KY 40214-2674
502-364-5074; 364-5075; 364-5076; FAX
502-361-5901; DSN 989-5074

Profile

BRANCH: Naval Reserve.

SIZE AND LOCATION: 4.098 acres. 3 mi SW of junction of I-264 & I-65; approx 5 mi SW of metro Louisville. *County:* Jefferson.

MAJOR UNITS: REDCOM NINE Activity; PHIB CB 1 Det 309 (NR); VOLTRAUNIT 0909 (NR); NAVHOSP CLEJEUNE P0921; NAVHOSP CLEJEUNE P0109 NR; AD-41 Yellowstone Det 1309 (NR); 4MD 8 Tank Bn A (NR); NAVAIRTERM NORVA Det 609 (NR); COMPHIBRON 8 Det 809 (NR); AS-39 Land Det 309 (NR); FLTSUPTRA Det 1409 (NR); NDCL NORFOLK Det 809 (NR); NWS York Det 709 (NR).

Key Contacts

COMMANDER: CDR Irvin F Norwood, 502-364-6370, FAX 502-361-5901, DSN 989-6370.

PUBLIC AFFAIRS: YN2 M L Slaughter.

Personnel and Expenditures

ACTIVE DUTY PERSONNEL: 15; 380 reservists

Services *Base Library:* Yes. *Recreational Facilities:* Fitness center/Weight room; Picnic area; Basketball court; Volleyball court.

372. Standiford Field Air National Guard Base

1019 Grade Lane
Louisville, KY 40213-2678
502-364-9400; DSN 989-9400
Internet: http://www.kyang.win.net

Profile

BRANCH: Air National Guard.

SIZE AND LOCATION: 36 acres. In heart of Louisville near I-65 and I-264. *County:* Jefferson.

MAJOR UNITS: 123rd Airlift Wing; 165th Airlift Squadron; 205th Combat Communication Squadron.

BASE HISTORY: 1946, 359th Fighter Group and 368th Fighter Squadron (Army Air Corps) designated 123rd Fighter Group and 165th Fighter Squadron respectively; allotted to KY. 1950, activated for Korean War; moved from Standiford Field to Godman Field, Ft Knox, KY. 1951, Wing assigned to Manston RAF Station, Margate, England. 1952, deactivated; returned to ANG status. 1968-69, Pueblo Crisis precipitated recall to federal service, Tactical Air Command. 123rd TAC Reconnaissance Wing, renamed 123rd Tactical Airlift Wing, 1989. Only Air Force installation in KY.

Key Contacts

COMMANDER: 502-364-9404, DSN 989-9404.

Personnel and Expenditures

ACTIVE DUTY PERSONNEL: 300
CIVILIAN PERSONNEL: 14

Services *Exchange:* Credit union.

Richmond

373. Blue Grass Army Depot

2091 Kingston Hwy
Richmond, KY 40475-5001
606-293-3011, 293-4211; FAX 606-293-3217
Internet: http://www-bgad.army.mil

Profile

BRANCH: Army.

SIZE AND LOCATION: 15,499 acres. Lexington facility 10 mi E of Lexington; I-64, 2 mi from main gate, access to I-75. Blue Grass facility 4 mi S of Richmond, KY, on US-421 off US-25; from I-75 Eastern KY Univ bypass. Located on portion of Richmond Civil War Battle Site. *County:* Fayette; Madison.

MAJOR UNITS: Materiel Readiness Support Activity (MRSA); Central Test, Measurement, & Diagnostic Equipment (TMDE) Activity; Army Depot System Command (DESCOM) Quality Systems and Engineering Center; Defense Reutilization and Marketing Office; Army Calibration Repair Center; Ionizing Radiation Dosimetry Center; 1st Combat Evaluation Group, Strategic Air Command, Det 8; Federal Emergency Management Agency.

BASE HISTORY: 1941-42, originally created as two separate installations, Lexington Signal Depot & Blue Grass Ordnance Depot. 1964, depots merged. 1966, facility under Army Materiel Command. 1977, change in mission & function; assigned as depot activity under Red River Army Depot, TX. 1980, depot responsibility transferred to Anniston Army Depot, AL. 1985, full depot status.

VISITOR ATTRACTIONS: Closed to public.

Key Contacts

COMMANDER: 606-293-3911, DSN 745-3911.

PUBLIC AFFAIRS: Clara Moraga, 606-625-6221, DSN 745-3039, siobgpao@bluegrass-emh1.army.mil.

Personnel and Expenditures

ACTIVE DUTY PERSONNEL: 4
DEPENDENTS: 20
CIVILIAN PERSONNEL: 428

Services

Housing: Family units 15; BAQ units 6. *Temporary Housing:* Guesthouse units 1. *Commissary:* Yes; *Exchange:* Retail store; Barber shop; Credit union. *Medical Facilities:* Medical clinic. *Recreational Facilities:* Recreation center; Golf course; Softball field; Officers club; Fishing/Hunting; Small game hunting at Blue Grass.

Louisiana

Barksdale AFB

374. Barksdale Air Force Base
BAFB
2d Bomb Wing/PA, 841 Fairchild Ave, Ste 103
Barksdale AFB, LA 71110-2270
318-456-3065; FAX 318-456-5986; DSN
781-3065; DSN FAX 781-5986
Internet: http://www.barksdale.af.mil
OFFICER-OF-THE-DAY: 318-456-2151, FAX
  318-456-5770, DSN 781-2151
Profile
BRANCH: Air Force.
SIZE AND LOCATION: 22,361 acres (including 18,000 acre recreation area & game preserve). 4 mi E of Shreveport, in corporate limits of Bossier City; 2 mi S of I-20 off Airline Dr, on Barksdale Blvd. *County:* Bossier Parish.
MAJOR UNITS: 8th Air Force, HQ; 2nd Bomb Wing; 917th Wing (AFRES); 49th Test Squadron; Det 5, 57th Wing; Air Force C4 Agency (OLB, AFC4A/MB); Det 1, 307th Red Horse Squadron (AFRES); Navy Mobile Construction Bn 28 SEABEES (NR); Air Force Office of Special Investigations, Det 219; Defense Commissary Agency (SO/BAR); Air Combat Command (ACC) Training Support Squadron, Det 13; Navy Resident Officer-in-Charge of Construction (ROICC); 29th Training Systems Squadron (OLAB); Det 2, 11th Contingency Hospital.
BASE HISTORY: 1931, construction began. 1932, 20th Pursuit Group arrived from Mather Field CA. 1933, field formally dedicated, named for Lt Eugene H Barksdale, killed in flight test, 1926. 1935, 3rd Attack Wing from Ft Crockett, TX, arrived. 1940, became Air Corps Flying School & later HQ Army AF Training Command. 1949, Strategic Air Command began operations. 1975, home of HQ, 8th Air Force. 1981, added 2nd Bombardment Wing. 1990-1, deployed in support of Desert Shield/Storm & redesignated 2nd Wing. 1992, 264 buildings placed on National Registry of Historic Places; 1st Russian bombers to land on American soil flew in; changed from SAC to Air Combat Command base. 1994, through realignment received aircrew training & retired remaining KC-135s.
VISITOR ATTRACTIONS: 8th Air Force Museum.
Key Contacts
COMMANDER: Col Andrew W Smoak, Ste
  100, 318-456-2170, DSN 781-2170, DSN

FAX 781-2439, smoaka@bw2.barksdale.af.
  mil.
PUBLIC AFFAIRS: LTC Temple H Blakc,
  318-456-3001, DSN 781-3001, DSN FAX
  781-5986, black@bw2.barksdale.af.mil.
PROCUREMENT: Maj Arnold Holcomb,
  318-456-8946, FAX 318-456-8945, DSN
  781-8946, holcomba@sups2.barksdale.af.
  mil.
TRANSPORTATION: Maj Steven Amato,
  318-456-5452, FAX 318-456-5494, DSN
  781-5452, amatos@trnss2.barksdale.af.mil.
PERSONNEL/COMMUNITY ACTIVITIES:
  LTC Daniel Yinger, 318-456-2635, DSN
  781-2635, DSN FAX 742-5236, yingerd@
  gendel.barksdale.af.mil.
Personnel and Expenditures
ACTIVE DUTY PERSONNEL: 6155
DEPENDENTS: 6300
CIVILIAN PERSONNEL: 1366
MILITARY PAYROLL EXPENDITURE: $267.6
  mil
CONTRACT EXPENDITURE: $65.3 mil
Services
Housing: Family units 429; Dormitory spaces 1650; RV/Camper sites 18; Primitive tent sites 20. *Temporary Housing:* VOQ units 139; VAQ units 102; Guesthouse units 24. *Commissary:* Yes; *Exchange:* Retail store; Barber shop; Dry cleaners; Food shop; Florist; Bank; Service station; Military clothing store; Convenience store; Beauty shop; Credit union; ATM; Optical store; Post office; Fast food; Video rentals; Four seasons; Thrift shop; Travel agency; Class VI; Garden center. *Child Care/Capacities:* Day care center capacity 156, 6 wks-5yrs; Home day care program; Summer day camp; Before & after school programs. *Schools:* Preschool/Kindergarten. *Base Library:* Yes. *Medical Facilities:* Hospital 45; Dental clinic; Pharmacy; Veterinary services. *Recreational Facilities:* Bowling center; Movie theater; Pool; Gym; Golf course; Stables; Tennis courts; Racquetball court; Fitness center/Weight room; Softball field; Football field; Auto shop; Craft shop; Officers club; NCO club; Camping; Fishing/Hunting; Enlisted club; Youth center; Picnic area; Skeet range; Playground; Aero club.

Baton Rouge

375. Baton Rouge Naval & Marine Corps Reserve Center
NMCRTC Baton Rouge
8410 Gen Chennault Dr
Baton Rouge, LA 70807-8000
504-356-1369, 356-4109; FAX 504-358-0699
Profile
BRANCH: Naval Reserve; Marine Corps Reserve.
LOCATION: *County:* East Baton Rouge Parish.
MAJOR UNITS: REDCOM NINE Activity; Weapons Co, 3rd Bn, 23rd Marine Regiment.
Key Contacts
COMMANDER: CDR D A Tezza.

Bossier City

376. Shreveport Naval & Marine Corps Reserve Center
1440 Swan Lake Rd
Bossier City, LA 71111-5334
318-746-9657, 746-9659; FAX 318-746-9580;
DSN 781-1142
Profile
BRANCH: Naval Reserve; Marine Corps Reserve.
LOCATION: E suburb of Shreveport. *County:* Bossier Parish.
MAJOR UNITS: REDCOM NINE Activity; B Co, 1st Bn, 23rd Marine Regiment.
Key Contacts
COMMANDER: LCDR D M Robertson.

Fort Polk

377. Fort Polk
JRTC & Ft Polk
Joint Readiness Training Center
Fort Polk, LA 71456-5000
318-531-2911; DSN 863-2911
Internet: http://146.53.33.3/
OFFICER-OF-THE-DAY: 318-531-1726, DSN
  863-1726
Profile
BRANCH: Army.
SIZE AND LOCATION: 198,000 acres.

In W-central LA, 8 mi S of Leesville, on Hwy 171; Alexandria, 50 mi, Lake Charles, 70 mi. *County:* Vernon Parish.

MAJOR UNITS: Joint Readiness Training Center; 2nd Armored Cavalry Regiment; Warrior Brigade; 519th Military Police Bn; Army Garrison, Ft Polk; 1st Bn, 509th Parachute Infantry Regiment (JRTC Opposing Force).

BASE HISTORY: 1941, camp built; named after Confederate General and Episcopal Bishop Leonidas Polk; established to support famous LA Maneuvers prior to WWII. Post-WWII until 1960s, series of closings and reopenings; opened only in summer for reserve training. Active Army units stationed on temporary basis during Korean War and Berlin Crisis. 1962-76, active as Infantry Training Center. Vietnam years, trained soldiers in basic and advanced infantry skills. Has varying terrain, from jungle-type vegetation to broad, rolling plains. 1974, home of 5th Infantry Division (Red Devils), and largest military construction expenditure ever for single installation. 1993, JRTC relocated from Little Rock AFB and Ft Chaffee, AK; 5th Armored Division relocated to Ft Hood, TX.

VISITOR ATTRACTIONS: 2nd Armored Cavalry Regiment Museum; Ft Polk Military Museum; 5th Infantry Division Memorial Park.

Key Contacts
COMMANDER: Brig Gen Samuel S Thompson III, 318-531-1706; 863-1706.
PUBLIC AFFAIRS: 318-531-2714, DSN 863-2714.
PROCUREMENT: 318-531-2684, DSN 863-2684.
TRANSPORTATION: 318-531-1415, DSN 863-1415.
PERSONNEL/COMMUNITY ACTIVITIES: Director of Community and Family Activities, 318-531-1272, DSN 863-1272.

Personnel and Expenditures
ACTIVE DUTY PERSONNEL: 8100; Guard, Reserve, ROTC 23,000
DEPENDENTS: 12,900
CIVILIAN PERSONNEL: 2250

Services
Housing: Family units 4604; Unaccompanied officer quarters 128; Unaccompanied enlisted quarters 5380; Senior NCO units 712; Junior NCO units 2486; Mobile home units 297; Trailer spaces 150. *Temporary Housing:* VIP units 9; VOQ units 80; Guesthouse units 70; Guest cottages 8; Transient quarters 180. *Commissary:* Yes; *Exchange:* Retail store; Barber shop; Dry cleaners; Food shop; Florist; Bank; Service station; Furniture store; Bakery; Military clothing store; Convenience store; Beauty shop; Laundromat; Credit union. *Child Care/Capacities:* Day care center capacity 350, 6wks-12yrs; Home day care program. *Schools:* Elementary. *Base Library:* Yes. *Medical Facilities:* Hospital 169; Dental clinic; Pharmacy; Veterinary services. *Recreational Facilities:* Bowling center; Movie theater; Pool; Gym; Recreation center; Golf course; Stables; Tennis courts; Racquetball court; Fitness center/Weight room; Softball field; Football field; Auto shop; Craft shop; Officers club; NCO club; Camping; Fishing/Hunting; Youth center; Picnic area; Skeet range; Water sports; Playground; Music & theater center; Dinner theater; Beach, boat rental & water skiing at Toledo Bend Lake Recreation Area.

Hammond

378. Hammond Air National Guard Station
236 CCS
901 N Airport Rd
Hammond, LA 70401
Mailing Address
PO Box 1438
Hammond, LA 70404-1438
504-429-3200; FAX 504-429-3299; DSN 457-8676, DSN FAX 457-8676, ext 3299
E-mail: Postmaster%cc%236ccs@lanbg.ang.af.mil

Profile
BRANCH: Air National Guard.
SIZE AND LOCATION: 30 acres. In SE LA, 1 mi E of Hammond, LA, on Hwy 190 at Hammond Municipal airport; 55 mi NE of New Orleans. *County:* Tangipahoa Parish.
MAJOR UNITS: 236th Combat Communications Squadron; 122nd Weather Flight; US Space Flight.
BASE HISTORY: A former WWII auxiliary field. 1953, 236th Combat Communications Squadron organized & received federal recognition as 236th Airways & Air Communications Flight Mobile. 1954, moved to present site.

Key Contacts
COMMANDER: Maj Charles M Munley Jr, M_Munley@lanbg.ang.af.mil.
PUBLIC AFFAIRS: Lt Paul Perron, P_Perron@lanbg.ang.af.mil.

Personnel and Expenditures
ACTIVE DUTY PERSONNEL: 7; 200 ANG
CIVILIAN PERSONNEL: 29
CONTRACT EXPENDITURE: $150,000

Services
Housing: None. *Temporary Housing:* None.

Minden

379. Longhorn/Louisiana Army Ammunition Plant
LHAAP/LAAP
Gate 4, Hwy 80 E
Minden, LA 71055
Mailing Address
PO Box 658
Doyline, LA 71023-0658
318-459-5100; FAX 318-459-5114; DSN 637-5100; DSN FAX 637-5114
E-mail: LOUISIANA-AAP@RIA-emh2.army.mil

Profile
BRANCH: Army.
SIZE AND LOCATION: 15,000 acres. On US-80 approx 25 mi E of Shreveport, LA. *County:* Webster Parish; Bossier Parish.
MAJOR UNITS: LA National Guard; Goex.
BASE HISTORY: 1941, site acquired by federal government; facility constructed and operated by Silas Mason Company. WWII, 65 different ammunition items produced. 1945, placed in standby status. 1951, Remington Rand assumed GOCO contract for reactivation in support of Korean War. 1958, production ceased with Sperry Rand Corporation preserving LAAP facilities. 1961, reactivated to support Vietnam War. 1975, Thiokol Corp assumed

operation. 1994, production ceased. Plant is currently inactive. 1998, Valentec awarded facility use contract.

Key Contacts
COMMANDER: James McPherson, Commander's Representative.

Personnel and Expenditures
ACTIVE DUTY PERSONNEL: 0
DEPENDENTS: 0
CIVILIAN PERSONNEL: 13 government; 21 contractor

Services
Housing: None. *Child Care/Capacities:* No day care facilities. *Schools:* No on-base schools. *Medical Facilities:* No medical facilities.

New Orleans

380. 8th Coast Guard District
CCGD8; USCG 8th District
501 Magazine St, Rm 1324
New Orleans, LA 70130-3396
504-589-6198; FAX 504-589-5142
OFFICER-OF-THE-DAY: 504-589-6225

Profile
BRANCH: Coast Guard.
SIZE AND LOCATION: Offices only. In New Orleans central business district; top 3 floors of Hale Boggs Federal Bldg. *County:* Orleans Parish.
MAJOR UNITS: 8th Coast Guard District; Coast Guard Reserve Unit CNCWU 208; Coast Guard Reserve Group; Investigative Services, Gulf Region; Director of Auxiliary, New Orleans; Coast Guard Administrative Law Judge.
BASE HISTORY: Administrative command for Coast Guard District 8.
VISITOR ATTRACTIONS: French Quarter nearby.

Key Contacts
COMMANDER: RADM Timothy W Josiah, 504-589-6198.
PUBLIC AFFAIRS: CWO Ron Mench, 504-589-6198, FAX 504-589-2142.
PROCUREMENT: Carmen Ziolkouski, 504-589-4941.
TRANSPORTATION: E T Crawford, 504-589-4926.
PERSONNEL/COMMUNITY ACTIVITIES: 504-589-6220.

Personnel and Expenditures
ACTIVE DUTY PERSONNEL: 250
CIVILIAN PERSONNEL: 50

Services *Recreational Facilities:* Contract gym with YMCA & Holiday Inn.

381. Adjutant General of Louisiana
Jackson Barracks, HQ Bldg
New Orleans, LA 70146-0330
504-278-8211; FAX 504-278-6554

Profile
BRANCH: Army National Guard.
MAJOR UNITS: Louisiana National Guard.

Key Contacts
COMMANDER: Maj Gen Ansel M Stroud Jr.

382. Jackson Barracks
Office of the AG, LA ARNG
New Orleans, LA 70146-0330
504-271-6262
OFFICER-OF-THE-DAY: 504-271-6262

Profile

BRANCH: Air National Guard; Army National Guard.

SIZE AND LOCATION: 200 acres. Divides St Bernard & Orleans Parish; sprawls across 3 city streets (Dauphine, St Claude, & Claiborne) & runs from Mississippi River to Florida Ave; bounded by Delery & Angela streets. Approx 15 min from downtown New Orleans; about 30 min from New Orleans IAP. *County:* Orleans Parish.

MAJOR UNITS: 141st Field Artillery, 1st Bn; 204th Area Support Group; State Area Command (STARC), HQ; 214th Engineering Installation Squadron; 159th MASH; 3673rd Maintenance Co; Louisiana Air National Guard, HQ; 39th Military Police Co.

BASE HISTORY: 1834-35, constructed as training post for troops of forts along Mississippi. Initially named New Orleans Barracks and referred to as "US Barracks." 1866, renamed Jackson Barracks for Andrew Jackson, hero of Battle of New Orleans and President. Mexican War, embarkation point for troops bound for Mexico. 1847, made general hospital for wounded returning from Mexico and forerunner to veterans hospitals. 1861-62, occupied by Confederate troops. 1866-81, infantry units occupy site. 1881-1914, location of Third Artillery. WWI, active processing and training center. 1922, turned over to LANG. 1930s, renovation by WPA. Shortly before WWII, federal government repossessed Jackson Barracks and operated as part of New Orleans Port of Embarkation. After WWII, returned to state control. 1955, full ownership vested in LA State.

VISITOR ATTRACTIONS: Entire facility historical site. Military museum with multi-media theater housed in old powder magazine, circa 1837; Residential plantation (antebellum) homes; HQ buildings date back to 1830s & 1940s.

Key Contacts

COMMANDER: Maj Gen Ansel M Stroud, Jr, Adj Gen, 504-278-8212, DSN 485-8212.

PUBLIC AFFAIRS: Maj Maria L LoVasco, ATTN: LANG-PAO, 504-278-8281, DSN 485-8281.

PROCUREMENT: LTC Willie Hymel, ATTN: LANG-DLS-P, 504-278-8412, DSN 485-8412.

TRANSPORTATION: Dan McDonnel, ATTN: LANG-DLS-T, 504-278-8442, DSN 485-8442.

PERSONNEL/COMMUNITY ACTIVITIES: Col Glenn Appe, ATTN: LANG-DPA, 504-278-8300, DSN 485-8300.

Personnel and Expenditures

ACTIVE DUTY PERSONNEL: 248
DEPENDENTS: 118
CIVILIAN PERSONNEL: 30
MILITARY PAYROLL EXPENDITURE: $16.2 mil
CONTRACT EXPENDITURE: $1.5 mil

Services

Housing: Family units 37; Unaccompanied officer quarters 2; Unaccompanied enlisted quarters 5; Townhouse units 7; Senior NCO units 3; Trailer spaces 28. *Temporary Housing:* VIP units 2; Unaccompanied officer/Enlisted quarters 30; BAQ units 25; Apartment units 5; Dormitory units 80. *Exchange:* Military clothing store; Convenience store; Credit union. *Base Library:* Yes.

Recreational Facilities: Recreation center; Tennis courts; Fitness center/Weight room; Softball field; Officers club; NCO club; Playground.

383. New Orleans Naval Air Station Joint Reserve Base, Air Force Reserve
NAS JRB NOLA
Callendar Field

HQ, 926th Fighter Wing
New Orleans, LA 70143-5400
Mailing Address
PO Box 50, Bldg 261
NAS JRB New Orleans, LA 70143-0050
504-678-3293; FAX 504-678-3247; DSN 678-3293; DSN FAX 678-3247

Profile

BRANCH: Air Force Reserve.

LOCATION: Tenant on New Orleans Naval Air Station Joint Reserve Base. *County:* Plaquemines Parish.

MAJOR UNITS: 926th Fighter Wing (AFRC); 159th Fighter Wing (LA ANG); Civil Air Patrol; [See New Orleans Naval Air Station Joint Reserve Base, Naval Air Station for other units.].

BASE HISTORY: Air Force History: 1958, 357th Troop Carrier Squadron first AFRES unit at NAS. 1961, 706th Troop Carrier Squadron moved here from Barksdale AFB, LA. 1963, assigned to 926th Troop Carrier Group, TAC. 1976, designation changed to 926th TAG. 1977, converted to combat mission and 926th TFG, parent wing, 917th TFW, Barksdale AFB. 1990, recalled to active duty (1st Air Force Reserve unit recalled) in support of Operations Desert Shield/Storm both in Middle East and to backfill stateside bases. 1992, redesignated 926th Fighter Group (Air Combat Command) with F-16s. 1994, redesignated 926th Fighter Wing. 1996, converted from F-16s to A-10 Thunderbolt II. Today, a completely self-supporting tenant unit of NAS New Orleans. Also see New Orleans Naval Air Station Joint Reserve Base, Naval Air Station, for history of Naval Station.

Key Contacts

COMMANDER: Col Robert Lytle, USAFRC, 926th FW/CC.

PUBLIC AFFAIRS: Capt Thomas Deall, USAFRC, 926th FW/PA, 504-678-3493, DSN 678-3493.

PROCUREMENT: Phil Lysiak, 926th LG/LGS, 504-678-3441, DSN 678-3441.

TRANSPORTATION: Greg Richards, 926th LG/LGT, 504-678-3831, DSN 678-3831.

PERSONNEL/COMMUNITY ACTIVITIES: Lovie Smith, 926th FW/DPC, 504-678-3482, DSN 678-3482.

Personnel and Expenditures

ACTIVE DUTY PERSONNEL: 3 AFRC recruiters; 225 Air Reserve Technicians; 700 reservists
CIVILIAN PERSONNEL: 150
MILITARY PAYROLL EXPENDITURE: $35 mil

384. New Orleans Naval Air Station Joint Reserve Base, Naval Air Station

400 Russell Ave
New Orleans, LA 70143-5012
504-678-3253; DSN 678-3253

Internet: http://www.164.105.130.21
OFFICER-OF-THE-DAY: 504-678-3253, DSN 678-3253

Profile

BRANCH: Navy; Joint Service Installation.

SIZE AND LOCATION: 4900 acres. In Belle Chase, LA on LA Hwy 23, approx 15 mi SW of New Orleans. From I-10, US-90 across Mississippi River Bridge (Crescent City connection) to LA Hwy 23, base approx 8 mi S. *County:* Plaquemines Parish.

MAJOR UNITS: Naval Air Station, New Orleans; Fleet Logistic Support Squadron 54 (VR-54); Patrol Squadron 94 (VP-94)(NR); Strike Fighter Squadron 204 (VFA-204)(NR); Marine Air Group 46 (Marine Reserve); 926th Tactical Fighter Group (AFRES); 159th Tactical Fighter Group (LA ANG); Coast Guard Air Station, New Orleans; Customs Service, Air Operations Branch, New Orleans; Civil Air Patrol.

BASE HISTORY: 1941, Naval Air Reserve Air Base, on shores of Lake Pontchartrain, commissioned. 1942, designated NAS, as primary training base for student aviators. 1946, facility mission of training Naval Air Reservists. 1957, first Naval contingent assigned to new field. 1958, installation dedicated to Alvin Andrew Callender, native of New Orleans, killed in WWI. Since then, known to public as Alvin Callender Field. Unique facility with each branch of military represented.

VISITOR ATTRACTIONS: Annual Air Show (late Oct).

Key Contacts

COMMANDER: 504-678-3201, DSN 678-3201.
PUBLIC AFFAIRS: 504-678-3260, DSN 678-3260.

Personnel and Expenditures

ACTIVE DUTY PERSONNEL: 1200; Guard/Reserve 3400
DEPENDENTS: 850
CIVILIAN PERSONNEL: 900

Services

Housing: Family units 215; Unaccompanied enlisted quarters 149; RV/Camper sites 17; Unaccompanied officer quarters suites 8. *Temporary Housing:* VOQ units 8; VEQ units 78; Unaccompanied officer/Enlisted quarters 62; RV 17. *Exchange:* Barber shop; Food shop; Service station; Convenience store; Credit union; ATM; Small exchange; Military clothing store, Navy only; Commissary at New Orleans Support Activity. *Child Care/Capacities:* Day care center capacity 65, 1yr-5yrs; Home day care program; Latch key program; Summer day camp. *Schools:* No on-base schools. *Medical Facilities:* Medical clinic; Dental clinic; Pharmacy. *Recreational Facilities:* Bowling center; Pool; Gym; Recreation center; Golf course; Tennis courts; Racquetball court; Fitness center/Weight room; Softball field; Football field; Auto shop; Camping; Youth center; Picnic area; Playground; All hands club/Restaurant.

385. New Orleans Naval & Marine Corps Reserve Readiness Center

5020 Lakeshore Dr
New Orleans, LA 70146-3310
504-678-1070, 288-2322; FAX 504-283-4441; DSN 678-1040

Profile

BRANCH: Naval Reserve; Marine Corps Reserve.

LOCATION: *County:* Orleans Parish.

MAJOR UNITS: REDCOM NINE Activity; HQ, 3rd Bn, 23rd Marine Regiment; HQ & Service Co, 3rd Bn, 23rd Marine Regiment.

Key Contacts
COMMANDER: CDR F K Amacker.

386. New Orleans Naval Support Activity

NAVSUPPACT New Orleans
4400 Dauphine St
New Orleans, LA 70146-5000
504-678-5011; FAX 504-678-2111; DSN 678-5011

Profile
BRANCH: Naval Reserve.
SIZE AND LOCATION: 228 acres. On W bank of Mississippi River approx 2 mi from downtown New Orleans; 13 mi from Moisant IAP. Main gate at intersection of Gen Meyer Ave and Shirley Dr in Algiers section of New Orleans. *County:* Orleans Parish.
MAJOR UNITS: Commander, Naval Reserve Force; Commander, Naval Air Reserve Force; Commander, Naval Surface Reserve Force; Commander, Marine Reserve Force; 4th Marine Aircraft Wing; 4th Marine Division; 8th Marine Corps District, Headquarters; Military Traffic Management Command, Gulf Outport; Naval Reserve Personnel Center; Naval Reserve Readiness Command, Region 10; Special Boat Unit 22; Supervisor of Shipbuilding, Conversion and Repair.
BASE HISTORY: 1849, Naval Support Activity on land purchased for intended Navy yard. 1901, Naval Dry Dock (YFD #2) arrived; Naval Station established. 1911-1915, closed. 1915, reopened as industrial Navy yard for repair of vessels. 1933, placed in maintenance status. 1939, reactivated to handle transient naval personnel. WWII, facility provided general naval indoctrination, fire fighting, antiaircraft gunnery, & other special courses. 1944, designated Naval Repair Base. 1947, redesignated Naval Station. 1962, location of HQ, Support Activity, New Orleans, Eighth Naval District. 1960s, HQ disestablished for Naval Support Activity. 1966, New Orleans Army Base (18.64 acres on E bank) transferred to Navy. Today, Naval Support Activity provides logistical support for activities & tenant commands on both sides of Mississippi.

Key Contacts
PUBLIC AFFAIRS: LCDR Dave Wells, 504-678-1240, wellsd@cnrf.nola.navy.mil.

Personnel and Expenditures
ACTIVE DUTY PERSONNEL: 3433
DEPENDENTS: 815
CIVILIAN PERSONNEL: 1993

Services
Housing: Family units 286; Unaccompanied officer quarters 73 units; Unaccompanied enlisted quarters 445; RV/Camper sites 16. *Temporary Housing:* Lodge units 22. *Commissary:* Yes; *Exchange:* Retail store; Barber shop; Dry cleaners; Food shop; Florist; Bank; Service station; Furniture store; Military clothing store; Convenience store; Beauty shop; Credit union; Optical shop; Fast food. *Child Care/Capacities:* Day care center capacity 62, 8wks-5yrs; Home day care program; Summer day camp. *Schools:* College courses. *Base Library:* Yes. *Medical Facilities:* Medical clinic; Dental clinic; Dispensary; Pharmacy; Veterinary services (routine shots only). *Recreational Facilities:* Bowling center; Pool; Gym; Tennis courts; Racquetball court; Fitness center/Weight room; Softball field; Football field; Auto shop; Craft shop; Officers club; NCO club; Camping (RV park); Enlisted club; Youth center; Picnic area; Playground; ITT.

387. US Army Corps of Engineers, New Orleans District

PO Box 60267
New Orleans, LA 70160-0267
Internet: http://www.lmn.usace.army.mil/

Profile
BRANCH: Army.
LOCATION: *County:* Orleans Parish.
MAJOR UNITS: Corps of Engineers, New Orleans District.
BASE HISTORY: Mission to plan, design, construct, operate & maintain federally sponsored navigation, flood control, hurricane protection, environmental enhancement & water resource development projects in 30,000 sq mi of southern LA. One of 4 districts in Lower Mississippi Valley Division.

Key Contacts
COMMANDER: Col William Conner.
PUBLIC AFFAIRS: Jim Addison, 504-862-2201, FAX 504-862-1724, addisonj@smtp.lmn01.usace.army.mil.

Pineville

388. Camp Beauregard

409 F St
Pineville, LA 71360-8726
318-641-8211; FAX 318-641-3341

Profile
BRANCH: Air National Guard; Army National Guard.
SIZE AND LOCATION: 700 acres. 6 mi N of Alexandria, LA, on Hwy 165N. *County:* Rapides.

MAJOR UNITS: Combined Support Maintenance Shop; US Property and Fiscal Office Warehouse Facility for LA; Louisiana Military Academy (NCOA & OCS); 225th Engineer Group, HQ and HQ Co; 527th Engineer Bn, Co A; 3671st Heavy Equipment Maintenance Co; 165th Transportation Bn, HQ and HQ Det; 399th Medical Det; 935th Engineer Det; 3673rd Maintenance Co, Det 1; 1086th Transportation Co, Det 1; 225th Engineer Group (Aviation), Det 1; 256th Infantry Brigade, Det (Aviation); Branch State Civil Defense, HQ.
BASE HISTORY: 1917, designated one of 16 original camp sites training troops in WWI; named for Pierre Gustav Toutant Beauregard, LA's "Napoleon in Gray," Confederate commander; Adj Gen of LA. 1919, deactivated. 1940, reactivated with formation of 3rd Armored Division; Camps Livingston, Clairborne, & Polk established; Esler Field, Alexandria Air Base, & Pollock Air Field constructed within 10 mile radius. Post WWII, Camp & satellite camps deactivated & allowed to deteriorate. 1948, Camp Beauregard became State Military Reservation. 1972, NG Bureau funded expansion of facilities. Maintained with inmate trainees from Work Training Facility-North, LA Department of Corrections. Camp is a major training center for Army NG.
VISITOR ATTRACTIONS: Stafford House.

Key Contacts
PUBLIC AFFAIRS: Lonna A Guillory.

Personnel and Expenditures
CIVILIAN PERSONNEL: 451

Services
Housing: Family units 79; Unaccompanied officer quarters; Unaccompanied enlisted quarters; Barracks spaces; Male soldiers 720; Female soldiers 40. *Exchange:* Small exchange. *Medical Facilities:* Dispensary. *Recreational Facilities:* Movie theater; Pool; Gym; Tennis courts; Softball field; Officers club; NCO club; Basketball; Volleyball.

Slidell

389. Camp Villere

60034 Camp Villere Rd
Slidell, LA 70460-4218
FAX 1-800-486-3375

Profile
BRANCH: Army National Guard.
LOCATION: SE Louisiana, 30 mi NE of New Orleans. *County:* Saint Tammany Parish.
MAJOR UNITS: Camp Villere (ARNG).

Maine

Auburn

390. Auburn Range
Auburn, ME 04210
Mailing Address
Maine Military Bureau, c/o Camp Keyes,
    ATTN: MSG NEWBEGINBldg 7
Augusta, ME 04330-0033
207-626-4330; 207-626-4309
Profile
BRANCH: Army National Guard.
LOCATION: SW Maine on Androscoggin
    River, near Lewiston; 30 mi N of Portland.
    County: Androscoggin.
MAJOR UNITS: Auburn Range (ARNG).

Augusta

391. Adjutant General of Maine
Military Bureau, Camp Keyes
Augusta, ME 04333-0033
207-626-4205; FAX 207-626-4509
Profile
BRANCH: Army National Guard.
MAJOR UNITS: Maine National Guard.
Key Contacts
COMMANDER: Maj Gen Earl L Adams.

392. Camp Keyes
Augusta, ME 04333-0033
207-626-4205; FAX 207-626-4509; DSN
476-4205
Profile
BRANCH: Air National Guard; Army National
    Guard.
LOCATION: Across street from Augusta Air-
    port; 0.5 mi from Augusta Armory. *County:*
    Kennebec.
MAJOR UNITS: State Area Command, HQ,
    ME ARNG; HHD Stare Area Readiness Com-
    mand; Maine Military Academy; HHC, 213
    Medical Bde, Health Service Liaison Det.
VISITOR ATTRACTIONS: Maine Military
    Museum.
Key Contacts
COMMANDER: Maj Gen Earl L Adams,
    Adjutant General MEANG.
PUBLIC AFFAIRS: Maj Dale Gilbert,
    207-626-4390, Gilbert@me-ngnet.army.mil.
PROCUREMENT: CW2 Frank Robinson,
    207-626-4267.

TRANSPORTATION: SSgt Steve Mullett,
    207-626-4365.
PERSONNEL/COMMUNITY ACTIVITIES:
    LTC Bond, 207-626-4221, FAX
    207-626-4246, DSN 476-4221, HROME@
    me-ngnet.army.mil.
Services
Housing: None. *Temporary Housing:* None. *Exchange:* Exchange. *Child Care/Capacities:* No
day care facilities. *Schools:* No on-base schools.
Medical Facilities: No medical facilities. *Recreational Facilities:* Fitness center/Weight
room.

Bangor

393. Bangor IAP Air National Guard Base
Bangor ANG Base
101st ARW/MEANG
103 Maineiac Ave, Ste 505
Bangor, ME 04401-3099
207-990-7700; FAX 207-990-7088; DSN
698-7224; DSN FAX 698-7088
OFFICER-OF-THE-DAY: Air Commander,
    207-990-7201, DSN 698-7201
Profile
BRANCH: Air National Guard.
SIZE AND LOCATION: 418 acres. City of Ban-
    gor at airport; 2 mi W on Rte 222 (Union St)
    from I-95. *County:* Penobscot.
MAJOR UNITS: 101st Air Refueling Wing,
    HQ; 101st Civil Engineering Squadron; 101st
    Consolidated Aircraft Maintenance Squadron;
    101st Mission Support Squadron; 101st Mis-
    sion Support Flight; 101st Resource Manage-
    ment Squadron; 101st Security Police Flight;
    132nd Air Refueling Squadron; OTH-B
    (Over-the-Horizon Backscatter) Program.
BASE HISTORY: Feb 1947, 101st Fighter
    Group & 132nd Fighter Squadron allotted to
    MEANG; received federal recognition at
    Camp Keyes, Augusta, & Dow AFB, Bangor,
    respectively. 1946, 101st Fighter Group acti-
    vated. 1951-2, active service & returned to
    MEANG. 1976, Group converted from
    fighter interceptor mission to air refueling.
    1994, Northeast Tanker Task Force formed.
VISITOR ATTRACTIONS: Wing HQ, histori-
    cal gallery.

Key Contacts
COMMANDER: Col John H Bubar, Wing
    Commander, 207-990-7224, DSN 698-7224,
    jbubar@mebgr.ang.af.mil.
PUBLIC AFFAIRS: Lt Mark Champagne,
    207-990-7225, DSN 698-7225.
PROCUREMENT: MSgt Robert Busch,
    207-990-7419, DSN 698-7419, rbusch@
    mebgr.ang.af.mil.
TRANSPORTATION: SMSgt Colby Gordon,
    207-990-7491, DSN 698-7491, cgordon@
    mebgr.ang.af.mil.
PERSONNEL/COMMUNITY ACTIVITIES:
    Maj Richard Gilman, 207-990-7128, DSN
    698-7128, rgilman@mebgr.ang.af.mil.
Personnel and Expenditures
ACTIVE DUTY PERSONNEL: 102
DEPENDENTS: 0
CIVILIAN PERSONNEL: 274
MILITARY PAYROLL EXPENDITURE: $23 mil
CONTRACT EXPENDITURE: $8.8 mil
Services
Housing: None. *Commissary:* Yes; *Exchange:*
Retail store; Food shop. *Child Care/Capacities:*
No day care facilities. *Schools:* No on-base
schools. *Medical Facilities:* Medical clinic. *Rec-
reational Facilities:* Gym; Racquetball court;
Softball field; All ranks club.

394. Bangor Naval Reserve Center
300 Hildreth St N, Ste 300
Bangor, ME 04401-5777
207-942-4388; FAX 207-942-6751
Profile
BRANCH: Naval Reserve.
LOCATION: *County:* Penobscot.
MAJOR UNITS: REDCOM ONE Activity.
Key Contacts
COMMANDER: LCDR C A Stowell.

Bath

395. Bath Supervisor of Shipbuilding, Conversion and Repair
SUPSHIP Bath
574 Washington St
Bath, ME 04530-1916
207-442-2253; FAX 207-442-3092
Profile
BRANCH: Navy.

LOCATION: Off US-1 near Bath Iron Works, within corporate limits of Bath, ME. *County:* Sagadahoc.

MAJOR UNITS: Naval Sea Systems Command, Field Office.

BASE HISTORY: Field office of Naval Sea Systems Command (NAVSEA), Washington, DC. Mission to ensure that Navy receives complete and fully operational ships on time and within cost and design constraints of contract.

Key Contacts
COMMANDER: Capt Ralph E Staples, Jr.
PUBLIC AFFAIRS: Patricia H Cavender, 207-442-2946, FAX 207-442-3092.
PERSONNEL/COMMUNITY ACTIVITIES: Cheryl Pooler, 207-442-3547, FAX 207-442-3119.

Personnel and Expenditures
ACTIVE DUTY PERSONNEL: 23
CIVILIAN PERSONNEL: 212

Services
Housing: None. *Temporary Housing:* None. *Child Care/Capacities:* No day care facilities. *Schools:* No on-base schools. *Medical Facilities:* No medical facilities.

Brunswick

396. Brunswick Naval Air Station
NASB
2 Alpha Ave
Brunswick, ME 04011-5000
207-921-1110; FAX 207-921-2256; DSN 476-1110; DSN FAX 476-2256
OFFICER-OF-THE-DAY: 207-921-2214, DSN 476-2214

Profile
BRANCH: Navy.
SIZE AND LOCATION: 3087 acres. I-95 Exit 9, follow 95 N Thru Traffic-Brunswick, continue on Rte 95 for approx 18 mi to Exit Coastal Rte 1, Brunswick, take exit "Cooks Corner-NAS" right at light, after 0.2 mi left into main gate. *County:* Cumberland.
MAJOR UNITS: Patrol Squadron 8 (VP-8); Patrol Squadron 10 (VP-10); Patrol Squadron 11 (VP-11); Patrol Squadron 23 (VP-23); Patrol Squadron 26 (VP-26); Patrol Squadron 44 (VP-44); Patrol Wings Atlantic (Topsham Annex); Naval Security Group Activity, Det Winter Harbor.
BASE HISTORY: 1943, commissioned; trained Royal Canadian Air Force Pilots in formal flying, gunnery procedures & carrier landings. Satellite landing fields at Sanford, Rockland, Portsmouth, Bar Harbor, & Augusta; sea plane ramp in Casco Bay. 1947, deactivated. 1951, reactivated antisubmarine warfare & Fleet Air Wing 3 (later Patrol Wing 5). 1971, Commander Patrol Wings, US Atlantic Fleet established HQ. 1970, acquisition of former Topsham AFB. Support to over 30 off-station & tenant activities including Naval Communications Unit Cutler, East Machias; Naval Survival School, Rangeley; and Department of Naval Sciences, Maine Maritime Academy, Castine. Under operational control of Commander Naval Air Force, US Atlantic Fleet, Norfolk, VA.

Key Contacts
COMMANDER: 207-921-2203, DSN 476-2203.

PUBLIC AFFAIRS: 207-921-2527, DSN 476-2527, 476-2327.

Personnel and Expenditures
ACTIVE DUTY PERSONNEL: 4800 (military & civilian)
DEPENDENTS: 3100

Services
Housing: Family units; BAQ units; Dormitory spaces; Trailer spaces. *Temporary Housing:* Unaccompanied officer/Enlisted quarters; Lodge units; Transient quarters. *Commissary:* Yes; *Exchange:* Retail store; Barber shop; Dry cleaners; Food shop; Florist; Bank; Service station; Beauty shop; Main cafeteria; Laundry; Optical shop. *Child Care/Capacities:* Day care center capacity 96; Home day care program. *Schools:* No on-base schools. *Base Library:* Yes. *Medical Facilities:* Medical clinic; Dental clinic. *Recreational Facilities:* Bowling center; Movie theater; Pool; Gym; Recreation center; Golf course; Tennis courts; Racquetball court; Skating rink; Fitness center/Weight room; Softball field; Football field; Auto shop; Craft shop; Officers club; NCO club; Picnic area; Hobby center; Woodworking shop; Metal shop; Ski shop.

Buxton

397. Hollis Plaines
Buxton, ME 64042
Mailing Address
Military Bureau, c/o Camp Keyes, Bldg 7, ATTN: MSG NEWBEGIN
Augusta, ME 04330-0033
207-626-4330; 626-4309

Profile
BRANCH: Army National Guard.
LOCATION: SW Maine, 15 mi W of Portland. *County:* York.
MAJOR UNITS: Hollis Plaines (ARNG).

Caribou

398. Caswell Range
Caribou, ME 04736
Mailing Address
Military Bureau, c/o Camp Keyes, Bldg 7, ATTN: MSG NEWBEGIN
Augusta, ME 04330-0033
207-626-4330; 207-626-4309

Profile
BRANCH: Army National Guard.
LOCATION: N Maine, along Aroostook River; 13 mi N of Presque Isle. *County:* Aroostook.
MAJOR UNITS: Caswell Range (ARNG).

Cutler

399. Cutler Naval Computer & Telecommunications Station
NCTS Cutler; NAVCOMTELSTA Cutler
Cutler, ME 04626-9603
207-259-8203; DSN 476-7203
OFFICER-OF-THE-DAY: 207-259-8229, DSN 476-7229

Profile
BRANCH: Navy.
SIZE AND LOCATION: 3000 acres.

Approx 90 mi E of Bangor, ME on Rte 191; within corporate limits of Cutler. *County:* Washington.
MAJOR UNITS: Naval Computer and Telecommunications Station, Cutler.
BASE HISTORY: Late 1940s, site chosen for very high-powered, low-frequency transmitter for broadcast to North Atlantic & Arctic Oceans. 1958-61, transmitter constructed. World's most powerful transmitter, over 2 million watts, provides link between high-level command authority ashore & ships, planes, & submarines operating in northern latitudes. Also operates primary High Frequency Transmitter site in NE.
VISITOR ATTRACTIONS: "Downeast" area of ME famous for beautiful scenery.

Key Contacts
COMMANDER: Commanding Officer, 207-259-8211, DSN 476-7211.
PUBLIC AFFAIRS: 207-259-8226, DSN 476-7226.
PROCUREMENT: Supply Officer, 207-259-8215, DSN 476-7215.
TRANSPORTATION: See Procurement.
PERSONNEL/COMMUNITY ACTIVITIES: See Public Affairs Officer.

Personnel and Expenditures
ACTIVE DUTY PERSONNEL: 110
DEPENDENTS: 90
CIVILIAN PERSONNEL: 90
MILITARY PAYROLL EXPENDITURE: $3.7 mil
CONTRACT EXPENDITURE: $871,000

Services
Housing: Family units 60; Unaccompanied enlisted quarters 19; RV/Camper sites 4. *Commissary:* Yes; *Exchange:* Retail store; Barber shop; Dry cleaners; Florist. *Child Care/Capacities:* Home day care program. *Base Library:* Yes. *Medical Facilities:* Medical clinic. *Recreational Facilities:* Bowling center; Gym; Tennis courts; Racquetball court; Skating rink; Softball field; Auto shop; NCO club; Camping; Fishing.

Portland

400. Portland Naval Reserve Readiness Center
NRC Portland
350 Commercial St
Portland, ME 04101-4665
207-775-6555, 775-6556; FAX 207-828-0734

Profile
BRANCH: Naval Reserve.
SIZE AND LOCATION: 8 acres. On waterfront in downtown Portland, approx 2 mi from US-295, approx 7 mi from Portland Airport. *County:* Cumberland.
MAJOR UNITS: REDCOM ONE Activity.
BASE HISTORY: Sept 1973, commissioned to train & administer naval units & coordinate naval surface reserves throughout northern New England; provide training hub for units assigned to reserve centers at Bangor & Augusta, ME, Manchester, NH, & Lawrence, MA, and act as Commander, Second Fleet's representative for naval vessels visiting port of Portland, ME.
VISITOR ATTRACTIONS: Old Port shopping; Children's museums; L L Bean.

Key Contacts
COMMANDER: LCDR Roger D Perkins.

Personnel and Expenditures
ACTIVE DUTY PERSONNEL: 9
CIVILIAN PERSONNEL: 1

South Portland

401. South Portland Air National Guard Station
SPANGS
50 Western Ave
South Portland, ME 04106-2499
207-756-7800; FAX 207-756-7890; DSN 698-7800; DSN FAX 698-7890
Internet: http://www.meang.ang.af.mil
(subpage off)
Profile
BRANCH: Air National Guard.
SIZE AND LOCATION: 12 acres. At intersection of Western Ave & I-295; 2 mi from South Portland; 3 mi from Portland. *County:* Cumberland.
MAJOR UNITS: 243rd Engineering Installations Squadron; 265th Combat Communications Squadron.
BASE HISTORY: 1964, Training Center dedicated.
Key Contacts
COMMANDER: Maj Don McCormack, 265 CBCS/CC.
Personnel and Expenditures
ACTIVE DUTY PERSONNEL: 11
DEPENDENTS: 0
CIVILIAN PERSONNEL: 25
MILITARY PAYROLL EXPENDITURE: $0.5 mil
CONTRACT EXPENDITURE: $1.2 mil
Services
Housing: None. *Temporary Housing:* None. *Child Care/Capacities:* No day care facilities. *Schools:* No on-base schools. *Medical Facilities:* No medical facilities.

Southwest Harbor

402. Southwest Harbor Coast Guard Group
Clark Paint Rd
Southwest Harbor, ME 04679
Mailing Address
PO Box 5000
Southwest Harbor, ME 04679-5000
207-244-4204; FAX 207-244-4256

E-mail: Kdenman/Gruswhbrn2@maillant.uscg.mil
Profile
BRANCH: Coast Guard.
SIZE AND LOCATION: 2 acres. In town of Southwest Harbor across Mt Desert Island from resort area of Bar Harbor; 20 mi from Ellsworth, ME; 50 mi from Bangor IAP; Bar Harbor Airport 12 mi. *County:* Hancock.
MAJOR UNITS: Coast Guard Group, SW Harbor; Coast Guard Station, SW Harbor; Coast Guard ESD SW Harbor; Aids to Navigation (ANT) Team, Southwest Harbor; USCGC *Bridle.*
BASE HISTORY: Complex established as lighthouse depot. 1945-66, mission expanded; group concept established. 1966, 1968, 1984, and 1994, new construction & renovations. Responsible for area from Port Cylde, ME, to Canadian border.
Key Contacts
COMMANDER: CDR James F Murray, 207-244-4201, JMurray/Gruswhbrn2@maillant.uscg.mil.
PUBLIC AFFAIRS: LTjg Ryan D Allain, 207-244-4297.
Personnel and Expenditures
ACTIVE DUTY PERSONNEL: 120
CIVILIAN PERSONNEL: 17
Services
Housing: Family units 7; Senior NCO units 1; Barracks spaces. *Temporary Housing:* None. *Exchange:* Retail store; Military clothing store. *Child Care/Capacities:* No day care facilities. *Schools:* No on-base schools. *Medical Facilities:* Contracted. *Recreational Facilities:* Gym; Fitness center/Weight room; Auto shop; Playground.

Winter Harbor

403. Winter Harbor Naval Security Group Activity
NSGA; NAVSECGRUACT Winter Harbor
Main St
Winter Harbor, ME 04693-0010
207-963-5534; FAX 207-963-2219; DSN 476-9202
OFFICER-OF-THE-DAY: 207-963-5534, DSN 476-9534
Profile
BRANCH: Navy.
SIZE AND LOCATION: 110 acres.

Main base at tip of Schoodic Peninsula, operations site near Corea, ME, 10 mi from main base, and 3 housing areas in town of Winter Harbor. In Acadia National Park, approx 280 mi NE of Boston and about 60 mi SE of Bangor, ME on Rte 1. *County:* Hancock.
MAJOR UNITS: Naval Security Group Activity.
BASE HISTORY: Aug 1917, began as Otter Cliffs Radio Station on Mt Desert Island, approx 5 mi from present site. 1933, station closed due to deterioration of buildings. 1935, moved to Winter Harbor as Navy Radio & Direction Finding Station; buildings donated by John D Rockefeller. Post WWII, expanded including land near Corea, ME; addition of cryptologic operations. Name changes: 1944, Supplementary Navy Radio Station; 1950, Naval Radio Station (R); & 1958, current name. Serves as a station in Navy's High Frequency Direction Finding Network, part of Classic Wizard Tactical Ocean Surveillance System; trains all personnel who maintain & operate the system.
VISITOR ATTRACTIONS: Schoodic Point Section of Acadia National Park; Fraser Point Picnic Area.
Key Contacts
PUBLIC AFFAIRS: 207-963-7502, ext 205.
PERSONNEL/COMMUNITY ACTIVITIES: 908-532-7810, DSN 992-7810.
Personnel and Expenditures
ACTIVE DUTY PERSONNEL: 16 officers; 365 enlisted & civilians
Services
Housing: Family units 123; Unaccompanied officer quarters 20; Unaccompanied enlisted quarters 32; Duplex units 30; RV/Camper sites 7; Apartment units 41. *Temporary Housing:* Unaccompanied officer/Enlisted quarters 4; Mobile home units 4; Cabins 3. *Commissary:* Yes; *Exchange:* Retail store; Barber shop; Dry cleaners; Florist; Service station; Military clothing store; Convenience store; Laundry. *Child Care/Capacities:* Day care center capacity 28, 6wks-6yrs; Home day care program; Summer day camp. *Schools:* College courses. *Medical Facilities:* Medical clinic; Dental clinic; Pharmacy. *Recreational Facilities:* Bowling center; Gym; Tennis courts; Racquetball court; Skating rink; Fitness center/Weight room; Softball field; Auto shop; Camping; Youth center; Picnic area; Playground; Consolidated club; Gear issue; Car wash; Horseshoe pits; Ski program; Camp grounds & trailer hook-ups; Recreational cabins.

Maryland

Aberdeen Proving Ground

404. Aberdeen Proving Ground
Aberdeen Proving Ground, MD 21005-5001
410-278-5201; FAX 410-278-2570; DSN
298-1110
Internet: http://www.apg.army.mil/
OFFICER-OF-THE-DAY: 410-278-4500, DSN
298-4500; Post Locator 410-306-1403
Profile
BRANCH: Army.
SIZE AND LOCATION: 72,518 acres. 25 mi
NE of Baltimore; 3 mi E from Aberdeen Exit
85 on I-95; 1 mi E from US-40 in Aberdeen,
MD. *County:* Harford.
MAJOR UNITS: Army Test and Evaluation
Command; Army Ordnance Center & School;
Army Aberdeen Test Center; Army Chemical
& Biological Defense Command; Army Envi-
ronmental Center; Army Center for Health
Promotion and Preventive Medicine; North-
east Region Civilian Personnel Operations
Center; Army Medical Research Institute for
the Chemical Defense; Program Manager
Chemical Demilitarization; 203rd Military In-
telligence Bn; Army Garrison, Aberdeen
Proving Ground; 520th Theater Army Medi-
cal Laboratory; 902nd Military Intelligence
Group, APG Military Intelligence Det; 3rd
Military Police Group, APG Resident
Agency; Army Aviation Support Activity
(ANG); 29th Infantry Division (Light) Avia-
tion Brigade (ANG); 29th Air Traffic Serv-
ices Group, HQ (ANG); Material Operations
Division, Army National Ground Intelligence
Center; National Guard Bureau, Installation
Restoration Program Branch; Project Man-
ager Abrams Tank Systems; School of Mili-
tary Packaging Technology; Corps of Engi-
neers, Aberdeen Field Office; Army Edge-
wood Chemical Activity; Army Materiel
Command Surety Field Activity, HQ; Army
Materiel Systems Analysis Activity; Army
Publications Center; Army Research Laboratory, Aberdeen Site; Army Special Security
Office, Aberdeen; Army Technical Escort
Unit; Army TMDE Support Center.
BASE HISTORY: 1917, established; home of
Army Ordnance. 1971, former Edgewood Arsenal (established 1917, chemical weapons research, development, & testing facility)
merged with Aberdeen Proving Ground; that
section of post referred to as Edgewood Area.

Remaining section referred to as Aberdeen
Area. Other areas include Churchville Test
Site, Harford County, Caroll Island & Grace's
Quarters, Baltimore County. Center for Army
materiel testing, laboratory research, and mili-
tary training. All tanks & wheeled vehicles
for Army tested for last 50 years. "Home of
Ordnance." Center for chemical warfare re-
search & development.
VISITOR ATTRACTIONS: Army Ordnance
Museum.
Key Contacts
COMMANDER: Col Roslyn M Glantz,
410-278-4006, DSN 298-4006.
PUBLIC AFFAIRS: Gary A Holloway, Chief,
Public Affairs Office, 1142 Ryan Bldg,
410-278-1142, DSN 298-1142, amstepa@
tec1.apg.army.mil Command, 410-278-1142,
DSN 298-1142; John Yaquint, Media
Queries, 410-278-1154.
PROCUREMENT: 410-278-3497, DSN
298-3497.
TRANSPORTATION: 410-278-3896, DSN
298-3896.
PERSONNEL/COMMUNITY ACTIVITIES:
410-298-2281, DSN 298-5793.
Personnel and Expenditures
ACTIVE DUTY PERSONNEL: 4500
DEPENDENTS: 2900
CIVILIAN PERSONNEL: 10,600
MILITARY PAYROLL EXPENDITURE: $529.6
mil (military & civilian)
CONTRACT EXPENDITURE: $342.7 mil
Services
Housing: Family units 1477; Unaccompanied of-
ficer quarters 374; Unaccompanied enlisted quar-
ters 100; Barracks spaces 4500; Trailer spaces
90; Contract rooms 35. *Temporary Housing:*
VIP units 10; Guesthouse units 35; Camp-
ground. *Commissary:* Yes; *Exchange:* Retail
store; Barber shop; Dry cleaners; Food shop; Flo-
rist; Service station; Convenience store. *Child
Care/Capacities:* Day care center capacity 280;
Home day care program. *Schools:* No on-base
schools. *Base Library:* Yes. *Medical Facilities:*
Medical clinic; Dental clinic. *Recreational Facilities:* Bowling center; Movie theater; Pool;
Gym; Recreation center; Golf course; Stables;
Tennis courts; Racquetball court; Softball field;
Football field; Auto shop; Craft shop; Officers
club; NCO club; Fishing/Hunting; Youth center;
Picnic area; Flying; Minature golf; Batting
cages; Go-carts.

Adelphi

405. Adelphi Laboratory Center, Army Research Laboratory
2800 Powder Mill Rd
Adelphi, MD 20783-1197
301-394-2515; DSN 290-2515
Internet: http://www.arl.mil/EA/alcvisitpg.html
OFFICER-OF-THE-DAY: 301-394-4476, DSN
290-4476
Profile
BRANCH: Army.
SIZE AND LOCATION: 137 acres. Off New
Hampshire Ave, just outside I-495 (Capital
Beltway) on Powder Mill Rd; accessible to I-
95, Baltimore/Washington Pkwy, Baltimore/
Washington IAP, Washington National Air-
port, Dulles Airport. *County:* Montgomery.
MAJOR UNITS: Ballistic Research Laboratory;
Harry Diamond Laboratory; Sensors and Elec-
tron Devices Directorate; Information Sci-
ences and Technology Directorate; Weapons
and Materials Research Directorate; Corpo-
rate Information and Computing Center.
BASE HISTORY: 1989, Adelphi Laboratory
Center officially established. Harry Diamond
Laboratories (HDL) occupied research facil-
ity since 1975. HDL shared site with HQ,
Electronics Research & Development Com-
mand (ERADCOM) from 1978 to 1985,
when ERADCOM disestablished & Army
Laboratory Command (LABCOM) activated.
1992, LABCOM disinstalled; Army Research
Laboratory (ARL) established. Adelphi Labo-
ratory Center provides identity for site of
ARL. Location for Aurora, world's largest
full-threat gamma radiation simulator, oper-
ated by ARL under Defense Nuclear Agency.
ARL controls test range in Blossom Point,
MD.
Key Contacts
COMMANDER: John W Lyons, 301-394-1600.
PUBLIC AFFAIRS: Judith Johnston, ARL,
301-394-4368, jjohnston@arl.mil.
PROCUREMENT: 301-394-3690, DSN
290-3690.
PERSONNEL/COMMUNITY ACTIVITIES:
Director of Personnel, 301-394-3310, DSN
290-3310.
Personnel and Expenditures
ACTIVE DUTY PERSONNEL: 30
CIVILIAN PERSONNEL: 1200
Services *Medical Facilities:* Nurse's clinic dur-
ing duty hrs.

406. Adelphi Naval Reserve Center
NAVRESCEN Adelphi
NRC Adelphi
2600 Powder Mill Rd
Adelphi, MD 20783-1198
301-394-3966, 394-3967; FAX 301-394-4847;
DSN 290-3966; DSN FAX 290-4847
Internet: http://www.mil.org/adelphi/a00.html

Profile
BRANCH: Naval Reserve.
SIZE AND LOCATION: 4.3 acres. Exit 28A on I-495 (Capital Beltway). Junction of New Hampshire Ave & Powder Mill Rd. 50 mi S of Baltimore; 20 mi N of Washington, DC. *County:* Prince George's.
MAJOR UNITS: REDCOM SIX Activity.

Key Contacts
COMMANDER: CDR Jack J McCarry, 301-394-3685, FAX 301-394-4847, DSN 290-3685, Mcgarry@erols.com.
PUBLIC AFFAIRS: Lt Beth M Kikla, 301-394-3424, FAX 301-384-4847, DSN 290-3424, Kikla@smtp.cnrf.nola.navy.mil.

Personnel and Expenditures
ACTIVE DUTY PERSONNEL: 20; 521 reservists

Services *Recreational Facilities:* Fitness center/Weight room.

Andrews AFB

407. Andrews Air Force Base
AAFB
Andrews AFB, MD 20331-5000
301-981-1110; DSN 858-1110
Internet: http://www.aon.af.mil
OFFICER-OF-THE-DAY: Command Post, 301-981-5058, DSN 858-5058

Profile
BRANCH: Air Force.
SIZE AND LOCATION: 4332 acres. Approx 11 mi SE of Washington, DC, Exit 9 (Allentown Rd, Andrews AFB) State Rte 337 off Rte I-95. Approx 50 mi S of Baltimore, MD. *County:* Prince George's.
MAJOR UNITS: 89th Airlift Wing; Malcolm Grow Medical Center; 10th Aeromedical Staging Flight; 459th Airlift Wing (AFRES); 113th Fighter Wing (DC ANG); Naval Air Facility; Marine Aircraft Group 49 (MAG-49); Air National Guard Readiness Center (ANGRC); Combat Camera, Det 9 (1st CTLS).
BASE HISTORY: Aug 25, 1942, established as Camp Springs Army Airfield. May 1943, became operational. Named for Lt Gen Frank M Andrews, European commander of operations for Army Air Forces. Post WWII, served largely as HQ base; home of Continental Air Command, SAC, and MATS and Air Forces Systems Command. Korean War, provided combat readiness training for B-25 medium bomber crews; served as main port of entry for foreign military and government officials. July 1961, established as home of official presidential aircraft, *Air Force One.* 1963, Naval Air Facility, Anacostia, moved headquarters to E side of base. 1992, became 89th Airlift Wing under Air Mobility Command (AMC). Historic visits: body of assassinated President Kennedy, 1963; US prisoners of war returning from Vietnam, 1973; Pope John Paul II, 1979; and US hostages returning from Iran, 1981. Arrival/departure site for troops in Operation Desert Shield/Storm and arrival site for most foreign dignitaries.
VISITOR ATTRACTIONS: Located near Washington, DC.

Key Contacts
COMMANDER: Brig Gen Arthur J Lichte, 1535 Command Dr, Andrews AFB, MD 20762, 301-981-5702, DSN 858-5702.
PUBLIC AFFAIRS: Maj James L Stratford, 1535 Command Dr, Andrews AFB, MD 20762, 301-981-4424, FAX 301-981-9039, DSN 858-4424, Stratfordj@emh.aon.af.mil.

Personnel and Expenditures
ACTIVE DUTY PERSONNEL: 10,009
CIVILIAN PERSONNEL: 3201
MILITARY PAYROLL EXPENDITURE: $402.8 mil

Services
Housing: Family units 2082; Unaccompanied officer quarters 21; Unaccompanied enlisted quarters 100; BAQ units 56; Dormitory spaces 974; Mobile home units 209; RV/Camper sites 10. *Temporary Housing:* VIP units 21; VOQ units 180; VAQ units 56; Transient quarters 69. *Commissary:* Yes; *Exchange:* Retail store; Barber shop; Dry cleaners; Food shop; Florist; Bank; Service station; Furniture store; Military clothing store; Convenience store; Beauty shop; Laundromat; Credit union; ATM; Optical store; Post office; Fast food; Video rentals; Four seasons; Thrift shop; Travel agency; Shoe repair; Garden center; Tailor/Alterations; Laundry; Cafeteria; Photo store. *Child Care/Capacities:* Day care center 6wks-5yrs; Home day care program; Before & after school programs. *Schools:* No on-base schools. *Base Library:* Yes. *Medical Facilities:* Hospital 235; Medical clinic; Dental clinic; Pharmacy; Veterinary services. *Recreational Facilities:* Bowling center; Movie theater; Pool; Gym; Recreation center; Golf course; Tennis courts; Racquetball court; Fitness center/Weight room; Softball field; Football field; Auto shop; Officers club; NCO club; Enlisted club; Youth center; Picnic area; Skeet range; Playground; Community club.

408. Washington, DC, Naval Air Facility
NAF Washington
1 San Diego Loop, Bldg 3198
Andrews AFB, MD 20762-5518
301-981-4880; FAX 301-981-3806; DSN 858-4880; DSN FAX 858-3806
OFFICER-OF-THE-DAY: 301-981-4880, FAX 301-981-3806, DSN 858-4880

Profile
BRANCH: Navy; Joint Service Installation; Naval Reserve.
SIZE AND LOCATION: 119 acres. Immediately off I-95 at Camp Springs, MD; tenant command on Andrews AFB, MD; approx 10 mi S/SE of Washington, DC. *County:* Prince Georges.
MAJOR UNITS: Fleet Logistics Squadron 48 (VR-48); Fleet Logistics Squadron 1 (VR-1); Marine Aircraft Group 41 (MAG-41); Tactical Electronic Warfare Squadron 209 (VAQ-209); Marine Aircraft Support Det HQ (MASD).
BASE HISTORY: 1958-61, functions of Anacostia NAS moved to Andrews AFB, concurrent with commissioning of new Naval Air Facility (NAF) at Andrews. 1972, Naval Air Reserve Training Unit, Washington (NARTU) became Naval Air Reserve Unit (NARU) Washington. Since 1976, support mission of NAF Washington included administrative & transport flight operations & transient service to fleet & logistics aircraft. 1978, NAF Washington transferred to Chief of Naval Reserve.
VISITOR ATTRACTIONS: See Andrews AFB.

Key Contacts
COMMANDER: Capt E A "Skip" Perry, 301-981-3783, FAX 301-981-3806, DSN 858-3783.
PUBLIC AFFAIRS: Lt Sean Carty, 301-981-3749, FAX 301-981-3806, DSN 858-3749.
PROCUREMENT: CDR Varner, 301-981-4470, FAX 301-981-2619, DSN 858-4470.
TRANSPORTATION: Mr. Tarpley, 301-981-4371, FAX 301-981-2878, DSN 858-4371.
PERSONNEL/COMMUNITY ACTIVITIES: Mrs. Hoffman, 301-981-5705, FAX 301-981-3806, DSN 858-5705.

Personnel and Expenditures
ACTIVE DUTY PERSONNEL: 700
DEPENDENTS: 0
CIVILIAN PERSONNEL: 140

Services
Housing: See Andrews AFB. *Exchange:* See Andrews AFB. *Child Care/Capacities:* Day care center capacity 202, 6wks-5yrs; Before & after school programs. *Medical Facilities:* Medical clinic; Dental clinic; Veterinary services; Access to Malcom Grow AF Hospital. *Recreational Facilities:* See Andrews AFB.

Annapolis

409. Annapolis Naval Station
NAVSTA Annapolis
58 Bennion Rd
Annapolis, MD 21402-5054
410-293-2385; DSN 281-2385

Profile
BRANCH: Navy.
SIZE AND LOCATION: 275.5 acres. On Severn River, adj to US Naval Academy; W border Rte 50/301; S border runs down Annapolis Neck Peninsula area just S of Forest Dr; 27 mi from Washington, DC & Baltimore, MD; from Rte 50 E, 450 S to NAVSTA. *County:* Anne Arundel.
MAJOR UNITS: Naval Station, Annapolis; Naval Construction Bn Unit 403; Defense Commissary Agency, Annapolis; Naval Surface Warfare Center, Carderock Division; US Marine Corps Naval Academy Co.
BASE HISTORY: 1851, 6 years after founding of US Naval Academy, 1st midshipmen training ship USS *Preble* arrived at what was then Ft Severn. 1911, completion of NAS, Greenbury Point, home of Naval Aviation, 1st NAS. 1939, 1st Yard Patrol Craft arrived. 1941, Severn River Naval Command established; Naval Air Facility reestablished. 1947, Severn River Command expanded to include Naval Small Craft Facility, Naval Air Facility, Naval Station, and Naval Barracks. 1962, Severn River Naval Command disestablished; all missions transferred to Naval Station. Mission: general support, including underway seamanship & sail training, small arms weapons familiarization, navigation & engineering de-

velopment for Midshipmen at Naval Academy.

VISITOR ATTRACTIONS: US Naval Academy; Chesapeake Bay; historic Annapolis, MD.

Key Contacts
COMMANDER: Capt Gerard M Farrell.
PUBLIC AFFAIRS: William Karditzas.

Personnel and Expenditures
ACTIVE DUTY PERSONNEL: 850; 300 Reservists
CIVILIAN PERSONNEL: 120

Services
Housing: Family units 413; Unaccompanied enlisted quarters 91; Mobile home units 16; RV/Camper sites 10. *Temporary Housing:* Unaccompanied officer/Enlisted quarters 16. *Commissary:* Yes; *Exchange:* Retail store; Barber shop; Dry cleaners; Food shop; Florist; Bank; Service station; Military clothing store; Convenience store; Beauty shop; Credit union; ATM; Optical store; Fast food; Video rentals; Thrift shop; Class VI; Garden center; Laundry; Photo store. *Child Care/Capacities:* Day care center capacity 80, new born–5yrs; Home day care program; Summer day camp; Before & after school programs. *Schools:* No on-base schools. *Base Library:* Yes. *Medical Facilities:* No medical facilities; *Recreational Facilities:* Movie theater; Pool; Gym; Recreation center; Golf course; Tennis courts; Racquetball court; Fitness center/Weight room; Softball field; Football field; Officers club; Camping; Fishing/Hunting (and crabbing); Youth center; Picnic area; Skeet range; Water sports; Playground.

410. Naval Surface Warfare Center, Carderock Division, Annapolis Detachment
NSWCCD, Annapolis Det
Annapolis, MD 21402-5067
410-267-2776
Internet: http://www.dt.navy.mil/sites/annap.html

Profile
BRANCH: Navy.
LOCATION: On Severn River directly opposite Naval Academy. *County:* Anne Arundel.
MAJOR UNITS: Machinery Research and Development Directorate; Survivability, Structures and Materials Directorate.
BASE HISTORY: 1908, former Naval Engineering Experiment Station (EES) established under guidance of Rear Adm George W Melville. Post WWII, testing evolved into research & development. 1963, renamed Marine Engineering Laboratory. 1967, merged with David Taylor Model Basin to form Naval Ship Research & Development Center. 1969-70, several functions of Brooklyn Naval Shipyard acquired. Active in machinery silencing, propulsion machinery, anti-fouling coatings, metallic & composite materials, piping systems, fuels & lubricants, & pollution abatement systems.
FUTURE CLOSURE/REALIGNMENT: Major closure/realignment to be completed by Dec 1999.

Personnel and Expenditures
ACTIVE DUTY PERSONNEL: 900 (military & civilians)

411. United States Naval Academy
Annapolis, MD 21402

410-293-1000; 410-293-3109 (recorded events); 410-263-6933 (Information & Guided Tours); DSN 281-1000
Internet: http://www.nada.navy.mil

Profile
BRANCH: Navy.
SIZE AND LOCATION: 1747 acres. Near downtown Annapolis on S bank of Severn River; 30 mi S of Baltimore; 40 mi E of Washington, DC; follow signs off US-50. *County:* Anne Arundel.
MAJOR UNITS: Brigade of Midshipmen.
BASE HISTORY: 1845, established as Naval School, undergraduate college of Navy at Fort Severn in Annapolis; instruction required 5 years, first & last at Annapolis, middle years at sea. 1850, Naval School became US Naval Academy. 1851, adopted current course of instruction; 4 consecutive years at Annapolis with at-sea training during summers. During Civil War, Academy moved to Newport, RI. 1865, reestablished at Annapolis. During WWI (until 1921) & WWII, courses shortened to 3 years; reserve officers also trained. 1976, first women midshipmen entered. Naval Academy & Naval Station (separate commands) share many personnel support & recreational facilities.
VISITOR ATTRACTIONS: National tourist attraction; many buildings, statues & monuments, represent highlights in Navy history. Several buildings & most of Academy grounds (the Yard) open to visitors from 9-sunset. Academic buildings & residences closed to general public except special occasions. Marine Barracks, quartered across Severn River, provide honor guard for superintendent, tomb of John Paul Jones & Naval Academy Museum, Preble Hall. Visitors center in Ricketts Hall.

Key Contacts
COMMANDER: Adm Charles R Larson, Superintendent.
PUBLIC AFFAIRS: 410-293-2291, pao@nada.navy.mil.

Personnel and Expenditures
ACTIVE DUTY PERSONNEL: 1134; 4000 Midshipmen
DEPENDENTS: 2700

Services
Housing: Family units 413; Unaccompanied enlisted quarters 247; Trailer spaces 16. *Temporary Housing:* VIP units 1; VOQ units 15. *Commissary:* Yes; *Exchange:* Retail store; Barber shop; Dry cleaners; Military clothing store; Beauty shop; Shoe repair; Computer store; Laundry; Midshipmen store; Tailor; Personal services shop; Travel agency; All other services at Annapolis Naval Station and Naval Hospital. *Child Care/Capacities:* Day care center. *Schools:* See Annapolis Naval Station. *Base Library:* Yes. *Medical Facilities:* Medical clinic; Dental clinic; See Annapolis Naval Station. *Recreational Facilities:* Bowling center; Movie theater; Pool; Gym; Recreation center; Golf course; Tennis courts; Racquetball court; Fitness center/Weight room; Softball field; Football field; Auto shop; Craft shop; Officers club; NCO club; Camping; Fishing/Hunting; Youth center; Picnic area; Sailing marina; Archery range; Equipment checkout; Soccer field.

Baltimore

412. Adjutant General of Maryland
5th Regiment Armory
Baltimore, MD 21201-2288
410-576-6097; FAX 410-576-6079

Profile
BRANCH: Army National Guard.
MAJOR UNITS: Maryland National Guard.

Key Contacts
COMMANDER: Maj Gen James F Fretterd.

413. Baltimore Naval Reserve Readiness Center
NAVRESCEN Baltimore; NRC Baltimore
1201 Halsey Pl
Baltimore, MD 21230-5392
410-752-4561; FAX 410-752-8352

Profile
BRANCH: Naval Reserve.
SIZE AND LOCATION: 0.875 acre. Next to Ft McHenry National Monument; 10 min from Inner Harbor/Camden Yards. *County:* Baltimore.
MAJOR UNITS: REDCOM SIX Activity; MIUWU 210; NRC Baltimore (17 units); Naval Reserve Recruiting Command, Det Five (NRC Baltimore).
BASE HISTORY: 1947, former immigrant detention center, becomes Naval Reserve Armory. 1962, largest reserve center in Fifth Naval District. 1972, Naval Reserve Training Center, Fort McHenry, Baltimore, redesignated Naval Reserve Center, Ft McHenry & center renovated.

Key Contacts
COMMANDER: CDR J J Turonis, turonis@cnrf.nda.navy.mil.

Personnel and Expenditures
ACTIVE DUTY PERSONNEL: 32; 650 reservists

Services *Recreational Facilities:* Fitness center/Weight room.

414. Martin State Airport, Air National Guard Base
Glenn L Martin State Airport
Baltimore, MD 21220-8270
410-780-8270; DSN 243-6210

Profile
BRANCH: Air National Guard.
SIZE AND LOCATION: 175 acres. 8 mi E of Baltimore; 1 mi NE of Middle River. *County:* Baltimore.
MAJOR UNITS: 175th Wing (ANG).

Personnel and Expenditures
ACTIVE DUTY PERSONNEL: 1757 Guard
CIVILIAN PERSONNEL: 476
MILITARY PAYROLL EXPENDITURE: $31.3 mil

415. US Army Corps of Engineers, Baltimore District
USCOE Baltimore; CENAB
10 S Howard St, Rm 11000
Baltimore, MD 21201
Mailing Address
PO Box 1715
Baltimore, MD 21203-1715
410-962-2089; FAX 410-962-3660

Internet: http://www.nab.usace.army.mil

Profile

BRANCH: Army.

SIZE AND LOCATION: Offices only. City Crescent Bldg, 4 blocks from Inner Harbor; approx 12 mi from Baltimore-Washington IAP. *County:* Baltimore.

MAJOR UNITS: Corps of Engineers, Baltimore District.

BASE HISTORY: Baltimore District largest of 5 districts in North Atlantic Division, HQ in NYC. Ft McHenry, National Historical Site, built by Baltimore District. Robert E Lee first Baltimore District Engineer. Today, supports military construction projects at over 30 installations in MD, PA, DE, WV, DC, and part of VA. Supports civil works projects over 49,000 sq mi including drainage basins of Susquehanna and Potomac Rivers and part of the Chesapeake Bay. Performs military & civil works construction and military & civil works real estate. Includes office of Supervisor of Baltimore Harbor.

VISITOR ATTRACTIONS: Near Ft McHenry, Inner Harbor, Aquarium & MD Science Center.

Key Contacts

COMMANDER: Col Bruce A Berwick, 410-962-4545, FAX 410-962-7516.

PUBLIC AFFAIRS: Lucy Lather, Chief, CENAB-PA, 410-962-2089, FAX 410-962-3660.

PROCUREMENT: Jerry Rifkin, Chief, CENAB-CT, 410-962-2196.

TRANSPORTATION: Pat Dockery, Chief, CENAB-LO, 410-962-4091.

PERSONNEL/COMMUNITY ACTIVITIES: Wayne Richardson, CENAB-HR, 410-962-2087.

Personnel and Expenditures

ACTIVE DUTY PERSONNEL: 15

CIVILIAN PERSONNEL: 750

Services *Exchange:* Cafeteria. *Base Library:* Yes. *Recreational Facilities:* Fitness center/Weight room.

Bethesda

416. National Imagery & Mapping Agency, Dissemination Division

4600 Sangamore Rd
Bethesda, MD 20816-5003
301-227-2495; 800-826-0342; FAX 301-227-2498
Internet: http://www.nima.mil

Profile

BRANCH: DOD.

SIZE AND LOCATION: 40 acres. Suburb of Washington, DC.. *County:* Montgomery.

MAJOR UNITS: NIMA, Dissemination Division.

BASE HISTORY: 1995, replaced Defense Mapping Agency, Hydrographic & Topographic Center.

Key Contacts

PUBLIC AFFAIRS: Michele Williams, Office of Congressional & Public Liaison, 8613 Lee Hwy, Fairfax, VA 22031-2137, 703-275-5864, FAX 703-275-8561.

Personnel and Expenditures

ACTIVE DUTY PERSONNEL: 161

CIVILIAN PERSONNEL: 3400

417. National Naval Medical Center

NNMC
8901 Wisconsin Ave
Bethesda, MD 20889-5600
301-295-4611; DSN 295-4611

Profile

BRANCH: Navy.

SIZE AND LOCATION: 250 acres. On Wisconsin Ave, just inside I-495; across from National Institutes of Health (NIH); at Medical Center Metrorail stop. *County:* Montgomery.

MAJOR UNITS: Naval Medical Research and Development Command; Naval Health Sciences Education and Training Command; National Naval Dental Center; Armed Forces Radiobiology Research Institute; Naval School of Health Sciences; Uniformed Services University of the Health Sciences.

BASE HISTORY: 1802, first naval medical facility in Washington area; established in rented building near Washington Navy Yard. 1935, established at 23rd & E Sts, NW, Washington, DC (present site of Naval Medical Command). 1938, present site chosen by President Franklin D Roosevelt; personally sketched elevation & ground plan which became architect's guide. 1942, dedicated by FDR as National Naval Medical Center. Capacity: WWII, 2464 beds; Korean War, 1167; Vietnam War, 1122. 1973, Naval Hospital & National Naval Medical Center consolidated into National Naval Medical Center. 1980, replacement hospital dedicated. 1982, Naval Medical Command National Capital Region established; Naval Hospital, Bethesda, reestablished as regional activity; Naval Dental Clinic reorganized, both under Naval Medical Command.

Key Contacts

COMMANDER: RADM Bonnie B Potter, 301-295-5800, DSN 295-5800.

PUBLIC AFFAIRS: Capt Ryland Dodge, 301-295-5727, DSN 295-5727.

Personnel and Expenditures

ACTIVE DUTY PERSONNEL: 4835

CIVILIAN PERSONNEL: 2150

Services

Housing: Family units 8; Unaccompanied officer quarters 107; Unaccompanied enlisted quarters 319. *Temporary Housing:* Lodge units 22. *Exchange:* Retail store; Barber shop; Dry cleaners; Food shop; Bank; Service station; Beauty shop; Optical store; Tailor/Alterations. *Child Care/Capacities:* Day care center capacity 80. *Schools:* No on-base schools. *Base Library:* Yes. *Medical Facilities:* Hospital 427 beds; Dental clinic. *Recreational Facilities:* Bowling center; Pool; Gym; Tennis courts; Officers club; NCO club.

Cheltenham

418. Cheltenham Naval Communication Detachment

NAVCOMM DET Cheltenham
9190 Commo Rd, Washington, DC 20397-5520
Cheltenham, MD 20397-5310
301-238-2335; FAX 301-238-2007; DSN 251-2335

Profile

BRANCH: Navy.

SIZE AND LOCATION: 559 acres. In Naval District of Washington; in suburban MD, adj to community of Cheltenham, 3 mi from Andrews AFB. Exit 7A from I-95, left onto MD 223 (Woodward Rd), abrupt right onto Dangerfield Rd; NCU approx 12 mi from Washington, DC. *County:* Prince George's.

MAJOR UNITS: Joint Interoperability Test Center (JITC); Naval Telecommunications Station, Washington; Navy—Marine Corps Military Affiliate Radio Station; Naval Telecommunications Center, Cheltenham; Naval Investigative Service Command.

BASE HISTORY: 1938, commissioned. Preceding WWII, steadily grew to handle mounting communications requirements in and out of Washington, DC, area. Following WWII, continued to grow, but encroaching population density reduced effectiveness as receiving site. 1975, designated as Naval Communication Unit. Of original land, 125 acres transferred to county and 17 acres leased to county for a firefighter training academy. Today, provides communications support to over 300 military, DOD, and federal government agencies throughout Washington, DC, area, as well as military installations in Newport, RI, and Great Lakes, IL. Under operational control of Commander, Naval Telecommunications Command.

Key Contacts

COMMANDER: LCDR Lilia L Ramirez; 301-238-2228, DSN 251-2228.

PROCUREMENT: Lt Jane F Mills; 301-238-2361, DSN 251-2361.

TRANSPORTATION: See Procurement Officer.

Personnel and Expenditures

ACTIVE DUTY PERSONNEL: 140

DEPENDENTS: 20

CIVILIAN PERSONNEL: 250

Services

Housing: Family units 39; Townhouse units 32. *Exchange:* Convenience store. *Child Care/Capacities:* No day care facilities. *Schools:* No on-base schools. *Medical Facilities:* No medical facilities. *Recreational Facilities:* Bowling center; Movie theater; Gym; Tennis courts; Fitness center/Weight room; Softball field; Football field; Enlisted club; Picnic area; Playground.

Cumberland

419. Cumberland Naval Reserve Center

NAVRESCEN, Cumberland
#1 Navy Way
Cumberland, MD 21502-2598
301-777-3141, 777-3142; FAX 301-777-1874

Profile

BRANCH: Naval Reserve.

SIZE AND LOCATION: 13 acres. In city limits of Cumberland, MD; Rte 40/48 use Willowbrook Rd Exit. *County:* Allegany.

MAJOR UNITS: REDCOM SIX Activity; RNMCB 23 Det 0623; AD-41 Yellowstone Det 0966 (NR); FF-1084 McCandless Det 8406 (NR); NH Bethesda Det 2606 (NR); CHB-10 Det D-106 (NR); Volunteer Training Unit Det 0623 (NR).

BASE HISTORY: 1946, Director of Naval Reserve for Fifth Naval District visited Cumberland to secure site for Naval Armory; arrangements made to use training facilities at Fort Hill High School until Armory completed. Nov 20, 1946, division activated.

Key Contacts
COMMANDER: LCDR D Meinheit.
Personnel and Expenditures
ACTIVE DUTY PERSONNEL: 11
Services *Recreational Facilities:* Softball field.

Curtis Bay

420. Curtis Bay Coast Guard Yard
SUPCEN Baltimore
2401 Hawkins Point Rd
Curtis Bay, MD 21226-1797
410-508-3913; FAX 410-508-3919
Profile
BRANCH: Coast Guard.
SIZE AND LOCATION: 112 acres. On Curtis Creek 2 mi E of Baltimore; 5 mi from Baltimore-Washington IAP. *County:* Anne Arundel.
MAJOR UNITS: Coast Guard Yard, Curtis Bay; Coast Guard Station, Curtis Bay; Aids to Navigation (ANT) Team, Curtis Bay; Support Det, Curtis Bay; Director of Auxiliary, Curtis Bay; Engineering Logistics Center, Curtis Bay; Coast Guard Reserve Group, Curtis Bay.
BASE HISTORY: 1899, founded; only shipbuilding & repair facility of Coast Guard. Until 1910, Yard permanent home of Coast Guard Academy (now New London, CT). Today, Coast Guard's largest, most modern industrial plant, responsible for construction, repairs & renovation of vessels, various aids to navigation, manufacturing of miscellaneous Coast Guard peculiar equipment, provide logistics support to Coast Guard Fleet as ships Inventory Control Point; also storage facility for decommissioned vessels.
Personnel and Expenditures
ACTIVE DUTY PERSONNEL: 250
CIVILIAN PERSONNEL: 830
Services
Housing: Unaccompanied officer quarters 7; Unaccompanied enlisted quarters 144; Trailer spaces 4. *Temporary Housing:* Transient quarters 5. *Exchange:* Retail store; Barber shop; Food shop. *Medical Facilities:* Medical clinic; Dental clinic. *Recreational Facilities:* Bowling center; Pool; Gym; Recreation center; Tennis courts; Racquetball court; Softball field; Auto shop; Officers club; NCO club.

Fort Detrick

421. Fort Detrick
810 Schreider St
Fort Detrick, MD 21702-5000
301-619-8000; DSN 343-8000
E-mail: ftdtrck-ccmail.army.mil Internet:http://www.medcom.amedd.army.mil/detrick/
Profile
BRANCH: Army.
SIZE AND LOCATION: 1200 acres. Off US-15 within city limits of Frederick, MD; 50 mi from Washington, DC and Baltimore, MD. *County:* Frederick.
MAJOR UNITS: Army Garrison; Army Medical Research & Materiel Command; Army Research Institute of Infectious Diseases; 1110th Army Signal Bn.
BASE HISTORY: Army Medical Command installation traces its roots to small municipal airport, Detrick Field, in 1930s; 104th Observation Squadron, MD NG, set up summer camp; Ft Detrick, named after Army medical officer, Maj Frederick L Detrick. 1969, biological warfare laboratories closed. Today, multi-mission installation providing space for offices, laboratories, and advanced communication facilities; Army Medical Department's leading microbiological containment research campus.
FUTURE CLOSURE/REALIGNMENT: BRAC 95: Military & civilian employees of 1108th Army Sig Bde, 1111th Army Signal Bn, ISEC CONUS will be relocating to Ft Detrick with closure of Ft Richie, MD, Sep 1998.
VISITOR ATTRACTIONS: Historical buildings.
Key Contacts
COMMANDER: Col Albert E Kinkead, Commander, 301-619-7314, DSN 343-7314, DSN FAX 343-2515.
PUBLIC AFFAIRS: Norman M Covert, 301-619-2018, DSN 343-2018, FAX 343-3320, COVERTN@ftdetrck-ccmail.army.mil.
PROCUREMENT: LTC John L Chafee, 301-619-2183.
TRANSPORTATION: Kaye L Murray, 301-619-2708.
PERSONNEL/COMMUNITY ACTIVITIES: Rafael Santaliz, Jr, 301-619-2711, DSN 343-2711, FAX 343-3227.
Personnel and Expenditures
ACTIVE DUTY PERSONNEL: 841
DEPENDENTS: 384
CIVILIAN PERSONNEL: 3646
MILITARY PAYROLL EXPENDITURE: $23.8 mil
CONTRACT EXPENDITURE: $10 mil
Services
Housing: Family units 155; Barracks spaces 300. *Temporary Housing:* VOQ units 1; Guesthouse units 16; Apartment units 4. *Commissary:* Yes; *Exchange:* Retail store; Barber shop; Dry cleaners; Food shop; Service station; Military clothing store; ATM; Video rentals; Thrift shop; Travel agency; Class VI; Garden center; Tailor/Alterations; Cafeteria. *Child Care/Capacities:* Day care center 6wks-5yrs; Home day care program; Summer day camp; Before & after school programs. *Schools:* No on-base schools. *Base Library:* Yes. *Medical Facilities:* Medical clinic; Dental clinic; Pharmacy; Veterinary services. *Recreational Facilities:* Pool; Gym; Tennis courts; Racquetball court; Fitness center/Weight room; Softball field; Football field; Auto shop; Youth center; Picnic area; Skeet range; Playground; Community club.

Fort Meade

422. Fort George G Meade
Ft Meade; FGGM
Fort Meade, MD 20755-5000
301-677-6261; DSN 923-1110
Internet: http://www.mdw.army.mil/meade.htm
Profile
BRANCH: Army.
SIZE AND LOCATION: 6000 acres.
Almost midway between Baltimore & Washington, DC; 7 mi from I-95; 2 mi from Baltimore-Washington Pkwy; just off MD State Rte 175 & 198. *County:* Anne Arundel.
MAJOR UNITS: Army Garrison, Ft Meade; National Security Agency; 694th Intelligence Group (USAF); 902nd Military Intelligence Group; 704th Military Intelligence Brigade; Naval Security Group Activity, Ft Meade; 1st Recruiting Brigade; Defense Information School; Defense Courier Service, HQ; Army Field Band; 1st Army-East, HQ; Army Claims Service; 55th Signal Co (Combat Camera); Army Central Personnel Security Clearance Facility; Army Intelligence & Security Command; Army Intelligence Materiel Activity; Army Environmental Hygiene Activity-North; Defense Commissary Agency, Northeast Region HQ; Readiness Group, Meade; Kimborough Ambulatory Care Center.
BASE HISTORY: 1917, built for troops drafted for WWI; originally named Camp Meade for Maj Gen George Gordon Meade, Civil War general. 1928, renamed Ft Leonard Wood, but Pennsylvanians protested resulting in change to Ft Meade. WWII, served as training center. 1947, Second Army HQ arrived. 1966, Second Army merged with First Army; HQs moved in from Ft Jay, NJ. 1973, Army reorganization provided for transition from Active Army organization to Reserve Components. 1990, began processing Reserve & ARNG units for Operation Desert Shield. Today, provides support for 114 tenant units; one of six Army installations under command of Military District of Washington.
VISITOR ATTRACTIONS: Ft Meade Army Museum (301-677-6966); National Cryptologic Museum (301-688-5849).
Key Contacts
COMMANDER: Brig Gen Charles R Viale, Installation Commanding General & Deputy Commanding Gen 1st Army-East; Col David H Troops, Garrison Commander.
PUBLIC AFFAIRS: Garrison Public Affairs, ATTN: ANME-PA, 2837 Ernie Pyle St, 20755-5025, 301-677-1433, FAX 301-677-1305, DSN 923-1433.
Personnel and Expenditures
ACTIVE DUTY PERSONNEL: 12,000
DEPENDENTS: 5700
CIVILIAN PERSONNEL: 25,000
Services
Housing: Family units Officer 619, Enlisted 1981; Unaccompanied officer quarters 62; Unaccompanied enlisted quarters 30. *Temporary Housing:* VIP units 7; VOQ units & Enlisted 162; Guesthouse units 54. *Commissary:* Yes; *Exchange:* Retail store; Barber shop; Dry cleaners; Food shop; Florist; Bank; Service station; Bakery. *Child Care/Capacities:* Day care center capacity 568; Home day care program; Child development centers 303. *Schools:* Preschool/Kindergarten; Elementary; Intermediate/Junior high; High school. *Base Library:* Yes. *Medical Facilities:* Medical clinic; Pharmacy; Veterinary services; Kimborough Ambulatory Care Center; Dental clinic. *Recreational Facilities:* Bowling center; Movie theater; Pool; Gym; Recreation center; Golf course; Stables; Tennis courts; Racquetball court; Fitness center/Weight room; Softball field; Football field; Auto shop; Craft shop; Officers club; NCO club.

Fort Ritchie

423. Alternate Joint Communications Center/Site R
AJCC
c/o Fort Ritchie
Fort Ritchie, MD 21719-5010
Profile
BRANCH: Joint Service Installation.
LOCATION: 6 mi NE of Ft Ritchie, MD. *County:* Franklin.
MAJOR UNITS: Alternate National Military Command Center (ANMCC); 1111th Signal Bn; 1108th Signal Brigade.
BASE HISTORY: 1950, construction of AJCC, also called Site R. 1954, became operational. Tenants represent each of military departments & Joint Chiefs of Staff. Housekeeping, logistical, & engineering support responsibility of HQ, Army Garrison, Ft Ritchie. Scheduled buses provide daily transportation from post to Site R. Most military personnel working at site live on Ft Ritchie.
Services
Housing: See Ft Ritchie, MD. *Exchange:* Barber shop; Food shop; Post office; Cafeteria; Snacks; Additional facilities at Ft Ritchie, MD. *Medical Facilities:* Medical clinic; Dental clinic. *Recreational Facilities:* See Ft Ritchie, MD.

424. Fort Ritchie
Fort Ritchie, MD 21719-5010
301-878-5874; FAX 301-878-5025; DSN 277-5874
Internet: http://www.mdw.army.mil/ritchie.htm
Profile
BRANCH: Army.
SIZE AND LOCATION: 638 acres. Near PA border approx 75 mi from Washington, DC; 65 mi from Baltimore, MD; and 80 mi from Harrisburg, PA. I-270 N from Washington, DC, to Frederick, MD, Rte 15 N to Thurmont, MD Rte 550 to Ft Ritchie's main gate. Washington County Regional Airport approx 12 mi. *County:* Washington.
MAJOR UNITS: Army Garrison, Ft Ritchie; Army Information Systems Engineering Command-CONUS; 1108th Signal Brigade; Defense Information Systems Agency, Western Hemisphere.
BASE HISTORY: 1926, area chosen as training site for MD NG; facilities built; HQ building built to resemble castle on Army Corps of Engineers insignia; named Camp Albert C Ritchie for governor of MD. WWII, Army leased Camp for centralized Military Intelligence Training Center; name shortened to Camp Ritchie; German & Japanese POWs housed; camp used for training purposes; soldiers trained as interrogators, military interpreters, translators, aerial photography interpreters & order of battle specialists. By 1944, all Counter Intelligence Corps personnel trained here. 1946, center moved to Ft Riley, KS; Camp Ritchie returned to state. 1946-50, used for state's Chronic Disease Hospital. 1948, Army needed post for support of Alternate Joint Communications Center (AJCC), known as Site R. 1964, redesignated Class II Installation under Army Strategic Communications Command. 1971, USASTRATCOM-CONUS HQ relocated from Alexandria, VA. 1973, name changed to Army Communica-

tions Command. 1975, renamed 7th Signal Command. 1993, transferred to Military District of Washington.
FUTURE CLOSURE/REALIGNMENT: Scheduled to close by Sep 1998.
VISITOR ATTRACTIONS: Post Historical Collection; Brig Gen Leonard J Riley Historical Holding; Ft Ritchie Museum.
Key Contacts
COMMANDER: LTC Francis Clepper Jr, ATTN: UAA, 301-878-5666, DSN 277-5666.
PUBLIC AFFAIRS: ATTN: ANRT-PA, 343 Banfill Ave, 301-878-5729, FAX 301-878-5025, DSN 277-5729.
PROCUREMENT: 301-878-4301, DSN 277-4301.
TRANSPORTATION: ATTN: ANRT-LG, 301-878-4434, DSN 277-4434.
PERSONNEL/COMMUNITY ACTIVITIES: ATTN: ANRT-CA, 301-878-5233, DSN 277-5233.
Personnel and Expenditures
ACTIVE DUTY PERSONNEL: 1020
DEPENDENTS: 780
CIVILIAN PERSONNEL: 1025
Services
Housing: Family units 341; Barracks spaces 454. *Temporary Housing:* VOQ units 10; Unaccompanied officer/Enlisted quarters 18; Guesthouse units 21. *Commissary:* Yes; *Exchange:* Retail store; Barber shop; Dry cleaners; Food shop; Bank; Service station; Military clothing store; Convenience store; Beauty shop; Credit union; Thrift shop; Class VI; *Child Care/Capacities:* Day care center capacity 120, 6wks-6yrs; Home day care program; Latch key program; Summer day camp. *Schools:* No on-base schools. *Base Library:* Yes. *Medical Facilities:* Medical clinic; Dental clinic; Pharmacy; Veterinary services. *Recreational Facilities:* Bowling center; Movie theater; Pool; Gym; Recreation center; Golf course; Tennis courts; Racquetball court; Skating rink; Fitness center/Weight room; Softball field; Football field; Auto shop; Craft shop; Fishing/Hunting; Youth center; Playground; Community club; Lake Royer, Upper and Lower.

Glen Arm

425. Gunpowder Military Reservation
GPMR
10901 Notchcliff Rd
Glen Arm, MD 21057
410-576-6065, 592-8633
Profile
BRANCH: Army National Guard.
LOCATION: 3 mi NE of Parkville, MD. *County:* Baltimore.
MAJOR UNITS: Gunpowder Target Range (ARNG).
BASE HISTORY: Supports year-round field training exercises for ARNG, Reserves, ROTC, and active duty Aberdeen Proving Ground soldiers.

Indian Head

426. Indian Head Division, Naval Surface Warfare Center
NSWC Indian Head; IHDIV
101 Strauss Ave
Indian Head, MD 20640-5000
301-743-4000
E-mail: webmaster@mail.ih.navy.mil Internet: http://www.ih.navy.mil
Profile
BRANCH: Navy.
SIZE AND LOCATION: 3401 acres. 25 mi S of Washington, DC, at end of Rte 210; On a peninsula with Potomac on W, Mattawoman Creek on E; from I-495 at Woodrow Wilson Bridge take exit to MD 210 S (Indian Head Hwy) 20 mi to Main Gate. *County:* Charles.
MAJOR UNITS: Naval Ordnance Center; Naval Explosive Ordnance Disposal Technology Division; Naval School, Explosive Ordnance Disposal; Ordnance Environmental Support Office; Technical Center for Explosive Safety; Energetic Manufacturing Technology Center.
BASE HISTORY: 1890, established by Bureau of Ordnance under supervision of Ensign Robert Dashiell; began testing guns & ammunition. 1900, powder factory added. WWI, expansion (Stump Neck). 1915, ammonium picrate plant added. 1919, railroad connection added. 1921, lost Naval Proving Ground designation; referred to as Naval Powder Factory. Depression years, 325th Co of Civilian Conservation Corps. WWII, facilities added; Explosives Investigation Lab examined captured ordnance; ballistite powder plant added. Post war, research labs opened; experimental propellants developed. 1954, nitroglycerin & cordite plants added. 1958, renamed Naval Propellant Plant. 1966, renamed Naval Ordnance Station; produced plastic explosives. 1980s, concentrated on products/processes too unprofitable, too dangerous, or too difficult for private sector. Today, principal Navy RDT&E facility for energetics & energetic materials.
Key Contacts
COMMANDER: Capt Wayne J Newton, Commander.
PUBLIC AFFAIRS: Christina Adams, 301-743-4627, FAX 301-743-6524, pao@mail.ih.navy.mil; Sandy Schroeder, PAO Assistant, pa1@mail.ih.navy.mil.
Personnel and Expenditures
ACTIVE DUTY PERSONNEL: 500
DEPENDENTS: 700
Services
Housing: Family units 20; Unaccompanied enlisted quarters 1; BAQ units 2; RV/Camper sites; Apartment units 206. *Exchange:* Small exchange. *Child Care/Capacities:* Day care center capacity 100. *Medical Facilities:* Medical clinic; Dental clinic. *Recreational Facilities:* Bowling center; Pool; Gym; Golf course; Tennis courts; Racquetball court; Fitness center/Weight room; Auto shop; Craft shop; Fishing/Hunting; Picnic area.

Patuxent River

427. Patuxent River, Naval Air Station
NAS Patuxent River
PAX River
22268 Cedar Point Rd, Unit NASAD
Patuxent River, MD 20670-1154
301-342-1018; FAX 301-342-3537; DSN
342-1018
Internet: http://www.nawcad.navy.mil/pax
OFFICER-OF-THE-DAY: Command Duty Office,
Bldg 409, 301-342-1097, FAX 301-342-6613,
DSN 342-1097

Profile
BRANCH: Navy; DOD.
SIZE AND LOCATION: 7000 acres. On
Chesapeake Bay, 60 mi SE of Washington,
DC; about 35 mi S of Waldorf, MD just off
Rte 235. *County:* St Mary's.
MAJOR UNITS: Naval Air Station; Naval Air
Warfare Center Aircraft Division (NAW-
CAD); Air Test and Evaluation Squadron 1
(VX-1); Naval Aviation Maintenance Office;
Aerospace Materials Division, NAWCAD;
Naval Research Laboratory Flight Support
Det; Naval Aviation Depot Operations Cen-
ter; Aviation Board of Inspection & Safety;
Naval Atlantic Meteorology & Oceanography
Det; Special Trials Unit; Marine Aviation
Det; VC-6 UAC Det; Naval Air Systems
Command (NAVAIR).
BASE HISTORY: 1942, established by Navy
Bureau of Aeronautics to consolidate 5 di-
verse Navy aircraft test facilities. 1943, test
operations begun. 1944, first US all jet-pow-
ered airplane, XP-59A, flight-tested. 1945,
Naval Air Test Center established. 1958, Naval Test Pilot School established. 1975, reorganized, NATC became Naval Air Systems
Command (NAVAIR) principal site for aircraft developmental testing; comprising
Strike Aircraft, Antisubmarine Aircraft, Rotary Wing Aircraft, & Systems Engineering
Test with Computer Services, Technical Support & Naval Test Pilot School. 1991, consolidated as Naval Air Warfare Center with two
divisions: Aircraft at Patuxent and Weapons
at Point Mugu, CA. 1992, NATC reorganized
as part of NAWCAD; established as Navy's
center for full spectrum RDT&E, engineering, & fleet support for air platforms.
FUTURE CLOSURE/REALIGNMENT: Under
BRAC 1991, NAWCAD Warminster, PA,
Lakehurst, NJ, Trenton, NJ, and Indianapolis,
IN have consolidated with NAWCAD
Patuxent River. Naval Air Systems Command, Arlington, VA, transfer finalized Sept
97. Lakehurst, NJ transfer scheduled for 1998.
VISITOR ATTRACTIONS: Naval Air Test &
Evaluation Museum, outside main gate; Pear-
son Pavillion; Mattapany.

Key Contacts
COMMANDER: Capt Paul Roberts, Bldg 304,
301-342-1020, FAX 301-342-3537, DSN
342-1020.
PUBLIC AFFAIRS: Cathy Partusch, 47122
Liljencrantz Rd, #440, Patuxent River, MD
20670, 301-342-7512, FAX 301-342-7509,
DSN 342-7512, PartuschCA%am5@mr.
nawcad.navy.mil.

PROCUREMENT: Deborah Raley, Bldg 588,
20620, 301-342-1824, FAX 301-342-1866,
DSN 342-1857, Raley_Debbie%am3@mr.
nawcad.navy.mil.
TRANSPORTATION: Donald Goddard,
301-342-3288, FAX 301-342-3833, DSN
342-3288, Goddard_Don%Pax9@mr.nawcad.
navy.mil.
PERSONNEL/COMMUNITY ACTIVITIES:
William Wagoner, 301-342-3330, FAX
301-342-1069, DSN 342-3330,
Wagoner_Bill%Paxcc@mr.nawcad.navy.mil.

Personnel and Expenditures
ACTIVE DUTY PERSONNEL: 2500
DEPENDENTS: 1500
CIVILIAN PERSONNEL: 17,000
MILITARY PAYROLL EXPENDITURE: $75.7
mil
CONTRACT EXPENDITURE: $188.5 mil

Services
Housing: Family units 797; Unaccompanied offi-
cer quarters 1; Unaccompanied enlisted quarters
10; Barracks spaces. *Temporary Housing:* VIP
units 3; Unaccompanied officer/Enlisted quar-
ters 74; Transient quarters 62. *Commissary:* Yes;
Exchange: Retail store; Barber shop; Dry cleaners; Food shop; Florist; Bank; Service station;
Military clothing store; Convenience store;
Beauty shop; Credit union; ATM; Post office;
Fast food; Video rentals; Four seasons; Class VI;
Garden center; Tailor/Alterations; Cafeteria.
Child Care/Capacities: Day care center capacity
156, 6wks-6yrs; Summer day camp; Mattapany
Day Camp. *Schools:* College courses. *Base Library:* Yes. *Medical Facilities:* Hospital; Medi-
cal clinic; Dental clinic; Pharmacy; Veterinary
services. *Recreational Facilities:* Bowling cen-
ter; Movie theater; Pool; Gym; Recreation center; Golf course; Stables; Tennis courts;
Racquetball court; Fitness center/Weight room;
Softball field; Football field; Craft shop; Officers club; Camping; Fishing/Hunting; Enlisted
club; Picnic area; Skeet range; Water sports;
Playground.

Solomons

428. Solomons, Navy Recreation Center
NRC Solomons
PO Box 147
Solomons, MD 20688
410-326-4217; 1-800-NAVY-230
Internet: http://www.ndw.navy.mil/dept/code91/
mwrsolomons.html

Profile
BRANCH: Navy.
SIZE AND LOCATION: 295 acres. Off MD Rte
2 and 4, 65 mi SE of Washington, DC.
County: Calvert.
MAJOR UNITS: Navy Recreation Center.
BASE HISTORY: Activity of Naval Station
Washington. Recreation area established to
provide affordable recreational programs &
facilities for Navy personnel (active duty, re-
tired, reserve, & DOD civilians) in National
Capital Region. Reservations required.

Key Contacts
COMMANDER: See Naval Station
Washington.

Personnel and Expenditures
ACTIVE DUTY PERSONNEL: 13
CIVILIAN PERSONNEL: 100

CONTRACT EXPENDITURE: Primarily funded
by nonappropriated funds
Services *Temporary Housing:* Guesthouse units
21; Guest cottages 7; Apartment units 15; Campsites 350; Log cabins (new 1996). *Recreational
Facilities:* Bowling center; Movie theater; Pool;
Recreation center; Golf course (driving range,
miniature); Tennis courts; Racquetball court;
Skating rink; Fitness center/Weight room; Softball field; Camping; Picnic area; Water sports;
Playground; Fishing; Crabbing; Marina; Boat
rentals; Beach; Outdoor picnic tables; Grills; No
telephones or television provided.

West Bethesda

429. Carderock Division, Naval Surface Warfare Center
NSWCCD
David Taylor Model Basin (DTMB)
9500 MacArthur Blvd
West Bethesda, MD 20817-5700
301-227-1142; FAX 301-227-3574; DSN
287-1142; DSN FAX 287-3574
E-mail: webmaster@www50.dt.navy.mil In-
ternet:http://www.dt.navy.mil

Profile
BRANCH: Navy.
SIZE AND LOCATION: 185 acres. Just outside
Capital Beltway, I-495, Exit 41, on to Clara
Barton Pky; 20 min from downtown Washington, DC. *County:* Montgomery.
MAJOR UNITS: Total Ship Systems Director-
ate; Materials, Structures & Survivability Di-
rectorate; Machinery Research and Development Directorate; Hydromechanics Director-
ate; Signatures Directorate; Machinery In-
Service Engineering Directorate; Business Di-
rectorate.
BASE HISTORY: 1898, original model basin
built at Washington Navy Yard; used for 40
years; named for RADM David W Taylor,
who urged Congress to establish towing tanks
to study scale models of ships before construction; Navy's first wind tunnels occupied same
site. 1940, operations at Carderock began
with complex of towing tanks still used today.
With 7 technical departments, laboratory remains largest facility of its kind in western
world. 1992, merger of David Taylor Research Center & Naval Ship Systems Engineering Station, Philadelphia. Detachments,
which provide environment for both model &
full-scale trials, include Acoustic Research
Detachment, Bayview, ID; Acoustic Trials
Detachment, Cape Canaveral, FL; Puget
Sound Detachment, Bremerton, WA; Underwater Explosions Research Division,
Portsmouth, VA.
FUTURE CLOSURE/REALIGNMENT: Transfer Machinery R&D capability from
CONSWC Annapolis to CDNSWC Philadelphia; close CDNSWC Annapolis in 2000.
VISITOR ATTRACTIONS: Tours available by
request.

Key Contacts
COMMANDER: Capt John Preisel Jr,
301-227-1515, DSN 287-1515, DSN FAX
287-3557, preisel@oasys.dt.navy.mil;
Richard Metrey, Director.
PUBLIC AFFAIRS: James M Scott,
301-227-1137, DSN 287-1137, DSN FAX
287-3574, scott@oasys.dt.navy.mil.

PROCUREMENT: CDR Kevin O'Connor, 301-227-2793.
PERSONNEL/COMMUNITY ACTIVITIES: Marsha Thurman, Human Resources Office, 301-227-2880.

Personnel and Expenditures
ACTIVE DUTY PERSONNEL: 9
CIVILIAN PERSONNEL: 1745

Services *Schools:* Satellite graduate engineering program. *Base Library:* Yes. *Recreational Facilities:* Tennis courts; Fitness center/Weight room; Softball field; Picnic area.

Massachusetts

Bedford

430. Hanscom Air Force Base

Hanscom AFB
Bedford, MA 01731
Mailing Address
9 Eglin St
Hanscom AFB, MA 01731-2118
617-377-4441; DSN 478-5980
Internet: http://www.hanscom.af.mil
OFFICER-OF-THE-DAY: 617-377-5144, DSN
478-5144

Profile
BRANCH: Air Force.
SIZE AND LOCATION: 850 acres. 20 mi NW
of Boston within boundaries of towns of Bedford, Concord, Lexington, and Lincoln. Take
I-95 to Rte 2A W Exit, 1 mi towards Concord
to Hanscom exit, turn right about .5 mi on
right. *County:* Middlesex.
MAJOR UNITS: Electronic Systems Center,
Headquarters; Geophysics Directorate; 360th
Air Force Recruiting Group; 2014th Information Systems Squadron; 85th Aerial Port
Squadron; Air Force Office of Special Investigations, Det 102; Civil Air Patrol.
BASE HISTORY: WWII, built and turned over
to Commonwealth of MA; named for
Laurence G Hanscom, civil aviation enthusiast and political editor of *Worcester Telegram*; Hanscom Field operated as Reserve
Training Center and Test Support Wing. After WWII, base became leader in electronics.
1951, Air Force Cambridge Research Center
(AFCRC) established MIT's Lincoln Laboratory. 1957, Air Defense Systems Management Office (ADSMO) established. All systems development/acquisition activities
merged into Air Force Systems Command,
Andrews AFB, MD. Electronic Systems Division formed at Hanscom. 1973, all active
squadrons left.

Personnel and Expenditures
ACTIVE DUTY PERSONNEL: 2537
DEPENDENTS: 1960
CIVILIAN PERSONNEL: 1715

Services
Housing: Family units 859; Unaccompanied enlisted quarters; BAQ units; Barracks spaces; Dormitory spaces; Senior NCO units; Junior NCO
units; Mobile home units; Trailer spaces; RV/
Camper sites; Family units; Unaccompanied officer quarters; Unaccompanied enlisted quarters;
BAQ units; Duplex units; Townhouse units; Barracks spaces; Dormitory spaces; Senior NCO
units; RV/Camper sites. *Commissary:* Yes; *Exchange:* Retail store; Barber shop; Dry cleaners;
Food shop; Florist; Bank; Service station; Bakery; Beauty shop; Optical shop; Garden center;
Lunch bar. *Child Care/Capacities:* Day care center capacity 390; Home day care program.
Schools: Preschool/Kindergarten; Elementary;
Intermediate/Junior high. *Base Library:* Yes.
Medical Facilities: Medical clinic; Dental clinic.
Recreational Facilities: Bowling center; Movie
theater; Pool; Gym; Recreation center; Golf
course; Tennis courts; Racquetball court; Fitness
center/Weight room; Softball field; Auto shop;
Craft shop; Officers club; NCO club; Camping.

Boston

431. 1st Coast Guard District

408 Atlantic Ave
Boston, MA 02110-3350
617-223-8480; FAX 617-223-8523

Profile
BRANCH: Coast Guard.
SIZE AND LOCATION: Offices only. In Federal Bldg, downtown Boston, near Financial
District & South Station. *County:* Suffolk.
MAJOR UNITS: First Coast Guard District; Investigative Services, Boston; Coast Guard Reserve Unit CNCWU 201.

Personnel and Expenditures
ACTIVE DUTY PERSONNEL: 233
CIVILIAN PERSONNEL: 100

Services *Recreational Facilities:* Fitness center/
Weight room.

432. Boston Coast Guard Reserve Center

427 Commercial St
Boston, MA 02109-1027
617-223-3190; FAX 617-223-3166; DSN
324-3190

Profile
BRANCH: Coast Guard.
SIZE AND LOCATION: 12.7 acres (plus 5.5
acres in South Weymouth). Inner Boston Harbor, on Commercial St, North End-Hanover
Exit; 5 mi from Boston Logan Airport; 6
blocks off Hwy 93. *County:* Suffix.
MAJOR UNITS: USCGC *Escanaba* (WMEC-907); USCGC *Seneca* (WMEC-906); USCGC
Spencer (WMEC-905); Coast Guard Group,
Boston; Marine Safety Office, Boston; Naval
Engineering Support Unit; Coast Guard Station, Boston; Aids to Navigation Training
Team; District Armory, Boston; Naval Reserve Unit; Immigration & Naturalization
Service; Navy COOPMINE Unit.
BASE HISTORY: 1944, original site acquired
by condemnation; expansion to N by purchase in 1972. 1976, Base Boston redesignated SUPRTCEN Boston.
VISITOR ATTRACTIONS: Major structures
1890s vintage.

Personnel and Expenditures
ACTIVE DUTY PERSONNEL: 70
CIVILIAN PERSONNEL: 100

Services
Housing: Barracks spaces 44. *Temporary Housing:* Transient quarters 5. *Exchange:* Retail
store; Barber shop; Dry cleaners; Food shop; Florist; Military clothing store; Convenience store;
Beauty shop. *Child Care/Capacities:* No day
care facilities. *Schools:* No on-base schools.
Base Library: Yes. *Medical Facilities:* Medical
clinic; Dental clinic; Dispensary; Pharmacy. *Recreational Facilities:* Gym; Fitness center/Weight
room; All hands club.

433. Defense Contract Management District Northeast

495 Summer St
Boston, MA 02210-2183
617-753-4093
Internet: http://www.dcmc.dcrb.dla.mil

Profile
BRANCH: Defense Logistics Agency.
SIZE AND LOCATION: Offices only. In downtown Boston. *County:* Suffolk.
MAJOR UNITS: Defense Contract Management
District Northeast.

Key Contacts
COMMANDER: Brig Gen Malishenko.

434. Navy Office of Information, New England

408 Atlantic Ave, Rm 222
Boston, MA 02110-3316
617-951-2690; FAX 617-951-2693

Profile
BRANCH: Navy.
MAJOR UNITS: Navy Office of Information,
New England.
BASE HISTORY: Serves CT, ME, MA, NH,
RI, & VT.

435. Navy Recruiting District New England
NRD New England
495 Summer St
Boston, MA 02210-2103
617-753-4683; FAX 617-542-2906; DSN
955-4683
E-mail: navyneof@tiac.net Internet:http://www.
tiac.net/users/navyne
Profile
BRANCH: Navy.
SIZE AND LOCATION: Offices only. Downtown Boston, in Barnes Bldg. *County:* Suffolk.
MAJOR UNITS: Navy Recruiting District, New
England.
BASE HISTORY: 1970, established as Navy Recruiting District Boston. 1993, renamed current name. HQs for all Navy Recruiting Stations in ME, NH, VT, RI, MA, northern CT,
and Europe. Currently, 50 recruiting stations
& 3 processing stations in Portland, Spring-
field & Boston.
Key Contacts
COMMANDER: Cmdr G E Argerake,
617-753-4791, FAX 617-542-2906, DSN
955-4791.
PUBLIC AFFAIRS: JOC(SW) Edward Buczek,
617-753-4793, FAX 617-753-4793, DSN
955-4793, navyneof@tiac.net.
PROCUREMENT: SKC Paul Rump,
617-753-4797, FAX 617-350-7629, DSN
955-4797.
TRANSPORTATION: See Procurement
Officer.
PERSONNEL/COMMUNITY ACTIVITIES:
PNC Bruce Johnson, 617-753-4319, FAX
617-542-2906, DSN 955-4319.
Personnel and Expenditures
ACTIVE DUTY PERSONNEL: 200
DEPENDENTS: 0
CIVILIAN PERSONNEL: 7
Services *Child Care/Capacities:* No day care
facilities. *Recreational Facilities:* Fitness center/
Weight room.

Cape Cod

436. Cape Cod Coast Guard Air Station
USCG Air Station Cape Cod
Cape Cod, MA 02542-5024
508-968-6300; FAX 508-968-6315; DSN
557-6300
OFFICER-OF-THE-DAY: 508-968-6330, DSN
557-6330
Profile
BRANCH: Coast Guard.
SIZE AND LOCATION: 1200 acres. On upper
cape; 15 mi from Hyannis; 65 mi from Bos-
ton; 60 mi from Providence, RI. *County:*
Barnstable.
MAJOR UNITS: Coast Guard Air Station, Cape
Cod; 102nd Fighter Wing; Camp Edwards Re-
serve Training Site (Army); Army Aviation
Brigade; 26th (Yankee) Infantry Division; NE
Regional Fisheries Training Center; Coast
Guard Ordnance Support Facility, Cape Cod;
Coast Guard Reserve Group, Cape Cod.
BASE HISTORY: 1970, established as tenant
under command of Otis AFB; consolidation
of Air Station, Salem, MA, and Air Detach-

ment, Quonset Point, RI. 1973, Air Force de-
parted leaving Air Station largest active-duty
military command on Massachusetts Military
Reservation/Otis ANGB. Primary mission is
search and rescue from Canadian border to
central NJ.
VISITOR ATTRACTIONS: Cape Cod National
Cemetery; Cape Cod National Seashore.
Key Contacts
COMMANDER: Capt R Willie Clark.
PUBLIC AFFAIRS: Lt B Washborn,
508-968-6317.
PROCUREMENT: CDR Sena, 508-968-6520,
DSN 557-6520.
PERSONNEL/COMMUNITY ACTIVITIES:
LCDR A Berehorn, 508-968-6447, DSN
557-6447.
Personnel and Expenditures
ACTIVE DUTY PERSONNEL: 300
DEPENDENTS: 1500
CIVILIAN PERSONNEL: 50
Services
Housing: Family units; Duplex units; Town-
house units; Barracks spaces; 635 units total.
Temporary Housing: Apartment units; Lodge
units. *Commissary:* Yes; *Exchange:* Retail store;
Barber shop; Dry cleaners; Food shop; Service
station; Bakery; Military clothing store; Conven-
ience store; Beauty shop. *Child Care/Capaci-
ties:* Day care center capacity 100. *Schools:* Pre-
school/Kindergarten; Elementary. *Base Library:*
Yes. *Medical Facilities:* Medical clinic; Dental
clinic; Dispensary; Pharmacy. *Recreational Facilities:* Movie theater; Gym; Golf course; Tennis courts; Racquetball court; Fitness center/
Weight room; Softball field; Auto shop; NCO
club; Youth center.

437. Massachusetts Military Reservation/Otis Air National Guard Base
MMR/OTIS ANGB
Otis ANGB
Cape Cod, MA 02542-5001
508-968-4667; DSN 557-4667
OFFICER-OF-THE-DAY: USCG AS Cape Cod:
508-968-5306 (Weekdays), 508-968-5330 (all
other)
Profile
BRANCH: Air Force; Coast Guard; Air Na-
tional Guard; Army National Guard; Marine
Corps Reserve.
SIZE AND LOCATION: 22,000 acres. On up-
per Cape Cod, 4 mi S of Bourne Bridge; Fal-
mouth 7 mi S, Sandwich 5 mi NE. Nearest air-
port Hyannis located 20 mi E of base, served
by commuter airlines only; major airports
Boston & Providence, RI about 1.5 hrs away.
I-495 connects Cape with western & central
MA & I-95 points S. Coastal Rte 3 connects
to Boston Expy & Beltways & I-95 to/from
points N. *County:* Barnstable.
MAJOR UNITS: Coast Guard Air Station Cape
Cod; 102nd Fighter Interceptor Wing (ANG);
26th Aviation Brigade; Army Aviation Sup-
port Group (ARNG); Camp Edwards Army
National Guard Training Site; 1st Bn, 25th
Marines (Reserves); Cape Cod Air Force Sta-
tion; 567th Air Force Band (ANG); 101st
Weather Flight (ANG); 202nd Weather Flight
(ANG); 6th Missile Warning Squadron;
2165th Communications Squadron; Aviation
Flight Facility (ARNG).

BASE HISTORY: 1940, established as state
Army NG training site; named Camp Ed-
wards for Maj Gen Clarence R. Edwards,
WWI 26th "Yankee" Infantry Division, MA.
WWII & Korean War convalescent facility
for troops. 1945, Otis Field completed; named
for Boston City Hospital surgeon Lt Frank
Jesse Otis Jr. 1953, Air Force took over most
of base; Camp Edwards reduced to small
area, northern corner Otis AFB. 1970, Coast
Guard consolidated Salem, MA, & Quonset
Point, RI, to USCG Air Station Cape Cod,
Otis. 1973, Otis AFB deactivated; control of
airfield to 102nd FIW. Later, Cape Cod AFS
(Flat Rock area of Camp Edwards) added.
1980, Otis AFB renamed Otis ANGB. Installation designated Massachusetts Military Reservation (MMR) with all commands operating independently (shared responsibilities &
maintenance); none designated as senior.
VISITOR ATTRACTIONS: Massachusetts National Cemetery.
Key Contacts
COMMANDER: LTC Sam Shiver,
508-968-4667; USCG AS Cape Cod:
508-968-5300, DSN 557-5300; 102nd FIW:
508-968-4667; Army Post Commander:
508-968-5885, DSN 557-5902.
PUBLIC AFFAIRS: Frank Adinolf,
508-968-4003, USCG AS Cape Cod PAO:
508-968-5316, DSN 557-5316; 102nd FIW,
PAO: 508-968-4003; Camp Edwards PAO:
508-968-5975.
Personnel and Expenditures
ACTIVE DUTY PERSONNEL: Coast Guard
313; Air National Guard 1252; Camp Edwards 167
DEPENDENTS: 1200
CIVILIAN PERSONNEL: Coast Guard 195;
Air National Guard 300; Camp Edwards 65
MILITARY PAYROLL EXPENDITURE: $54.3
mil (USAF)
Services
Housing: Family units 150; Townhouse units
74; Barracks spaces 408. *Temporary Housing:*
Guest cottages 4; Apartment units 4; Lodge units
14; Hotel-style rooms 7. *Commissary:* Yes; *Ex-
change:* Retail store; Barber shop; Dry cleaners;
Food shop; Florist; Bank; Service station; Bak-
ery. *Child Care/Capacities:* Day care center ca-
pacity 50. *Schools:* Elementary; Intermediate/
Junior high. *Base Library:* Yes. *Medical Facili-
ties:* Medical clinic; Dental clinic. *Recreational
Facilities:* Movie theater; Golf course; Stables;
Tennis courts; Racquetball court; Softball field;
Auto shop; Craft shop; Fishing/Hunting; All
services/rank activities center (limited hrs).

Chicopee

438. Westover Air Reserve Base
WARB
Westover ARB
Chicopee, MA 01022-1825
413-557-3588; FAX 413-557-2099; DSN
589-3588
Internet: http://www.afres.af.mil/~439aw/list.
htm
OFFICER-OF-THE-DAY: 413-557-3571, DSN
589-3571
Profile
BRANCH: Air Force Reserve.
SIZE AND LOCATION: 2456 acres.

Exit 5 off I-90 (Massachusetts Tpke) in Chicopee, to Rte 91 to Rte 291 Springfield to Fuller Rd exit, follow signs. 35 mi N of Bradley IAP, Windsor Locks, CT. *County:* Hampden.
MAJOR UNITS: 439th Airlift Wing; 439th Operations Group; 439th Medical Group; 439th Support Group; 439th Logistics Group; Naval Reserve Center, Westover ARB; Armed Forces Reserve Center, Westover ARB; 739th Security Police Flight.
BASE HISTORY: 1940, activated and served as bomber training site and transition station for overseas missions; named for Maj Gen Oscar Westover, then top-ranking US military pilot and first Chief of Air Corps. 1946-55, served as staging point for Berlin Airlift and as freight and passenger terminal for Military Transport Service. 1955-74, was a major Strategic Airlift Command base; HQ Eighth Air Force tenant until 1970. 1974, Air Force Reserve base established. From 1974-87, 439th Tactical Airlift Wing operated C-130 Hercules aircraft until converting to Galaxy at Westover, eventually becoming 439th Airlift Wing.

Key Contacts
COMMANDER: Col Elizabeth A Grote, Commander, 439th Logistics Group, 413-557-3816, DSN 589-3816.
PUBLIC AFFAIRS: Gordon A Newell, 439th Airlift Wing, PAO, 100 Lloyd St, 413-557-3500, DSN 589-3500.
PROCUREMENT: Michael LaFortune, 100 Logistics Dr, 2nd Fl, Ste 200, 01022-1531, 413-557-3508, DSN 589-3508.
TRANSPORTATION: Shari MacDonald, 439th LSSQ/LGT, 450 Hangar Ave, South Wing, 1st Fl, Ste 1, 01022-1772, 413-557-2121, DSN 589-2121.
PERSONNEL/COMMUNITY ACTIVITIES: 439th MSSQ/MSC, South Wing, Ste 106, 01022-1843, 413-557-2871, DSN 589-2871.

Personnel and Expenditures
ACTIVE DUTY PERSONNEL: 1
CIVILIAN PERSONNEL: 1200
MILITARY PAYROLL EXPENDITURE: $59.8 mil
CONTRACT EXPENDITURE: $17.2 mil

Services
Housing: None. *Temporary Housing:* VOQ units 80; BAQ units 356; All quarters transient. *Commissary:* Yes; *Exchange:* Food shop; Military clothing store; Convenience store; Credit union. *Child Care/Capacities:* No day care facilities. *Schools:* No on-base schools. *Medical Facilities:* Medical clinic. *Recreational Facilities:* Bowling center; Pool; Tennis courts; Racquetball court; Fitness center/Weight room; Softball field; Picnic area; Consolidated club.

Devens

439. Devens Reserve Forces Training Center
31 Quebec St, Box 1
Devens, MA 01433-4424
508-796-3307; FAX 796-3163; DSN 256-3307
OFFICER-OF-THE-DAY: 508-796-3711, DSN 256-3711

Profile
BRANCH: Army Reserve.
SIZE AND LOCATION: 11,602 acres.

Off Rte 2, 35 mi NW of Boston adj to four towns: Ayer, Lancaster, Shirley, Harvard; 25 mi from Worcester. *County:* Worcester; Middlesex.
MAJOR UNITS: 94th Regional Support Command.
BASE HISTORY: Sept 1917, Fort Devens established as infantry training center. Named for Brevet Maj Gen Charles Devens, Union Army general and attorney general during presidency of Rutherford B Hayes. 1990, NE step-off point for Operation Desert Storm. Mar 3, 1996, closed as active duty installation.
VISITOR ATTRACTIONS: Self-guided tour of historical sites; Museum.

Key Contacts
COMMANDER: H Carter Hunt Jr, 508-796-2126.
PUBLIC AFFAIRS: Linda Jeleniewiski, 508-796-3307.
PROCUREMENT: James Dijak, 508-796-2430.

Lawrence

440. Lawrence Marine Corps Reserve Center
67 N Parish Rd
Lawrence, MA 01843-2999
508-682-0049, 685-3828; FAX 508-683-2363; DSN 686-1043
Internet: http://www.marforres.usmc.mil/Webpa

Profile
BRANCH: Marine Corps Reserve.
LOCATION: In NE corner of MA. *County:* Essex.
MAJOR UNITS: Ordnance Contact Team 1, 4th Force Service Support Group (FSSG).

Key Contacts
COMMANDER: Capt Scott W Wassel.

Natick

441. Army Soldier Systems Command
SSCOM
Natick Labs
Kansas St
Natick, MA 01760-5000
508-223-4001; FAX 508-233-5390; DSN 256-4001; DSN FAX 256-5390
E-mail: amsscpa@natick-emh2.army.mil Internet:http://www-sscom.army.mil

Profile
BRANCH: Army.
SIZE AND LOCATION: 78 acres. 16 mi W of Boston; Exit 13 MA Turnpike at intersection of Rte 27 & Kansas St. *County:* Middlesex.
MAJOR UNITS: Army Natick Research, Development, and Engineering Center; Army Research Institute of Environmental Medicine; Navy Clothing and Textile Research Facility; US Coast Guard Health Services Command.
BASE HISTORY: WWI and WWII, mission scattered under Army Quartermaster Corps. 1952, operational combined at Natick. 1963, Quartermaster Research & Engineering Center at Natick changed to Army Natick Laboratories. 1983, renamed Army Natick Research & Development Center, subordinate command of Army Troop Support Command

(TROSCOM), St Louis, MO, & subsequently redesignated as USANRDEC. 1994, Soldier Systems Command (SSCOM) activated to develop, integrate, acquire, & sustain soldier & related support systems to modernize, balance, & improve soldier's warfighting capabilities. SSCOM subordinate activities: Army Natick Research, Development & Engineering Center (NRDEC) Natick, MA; Project Manager-Soldier (PM-Soldier) Ft Belvoir, VA; & Army Support Activity (ARSO) Philadelphia, PA.
VISITOR ATTRACTIONS: Located in Boston metro area.

Key Contacts
COMMANDER: Col Richard Ross, 508-233-5519, FAX 508-233-5384, DSN 256-5519.
PUBLIC AFFAIRS: Susan Aninger, 508-233-5340, FAX 508-233-5390, DSN 256-5340, saninger@natick-emh2.army.mil.
PROCUREMENT: Cheryl Deluca, 508-233-4514, FAX 508-233-5286, DSN 256-4514, cdeluca@natick-emh2.army.mil.
TRANSPORTATION: Sandra Fitch, 508-233-4236, FAX 508-233-4684, DSN 256-4236, sfitch@natick-emh2.army.mil.
PERSONNEL/COMMUNITY ACTIVITIES: Edward Falkowski, 508-233-5555, FAX 508-233-5105, DSN 256-5555, efalkowski@natick-emh2.army.mil.

Personnel and Expenditures
ACTIVE DUTY PERSONNEL: 104
DEPENDENTS: 0
CIVILIAN PERSONNEL: 850

Services *Temporary Housing:* Guesthouse units. *Exchange:* Barber shop; Credit union; Travel agency; Cafeteria. *Child Care/Capacities:* Day care center. *Base Library:* Yes. *Medical Facilities:* Medical clinic. *Recreational Facilities:* Pool; Softball field; Officers club; NCO club;

442. Navy Clothing and Textile Research Facility
NCTRF
P.O. Box 59
Natick, MA 01760-0001
508-233-4172; FAX 508-233-4783; DSN 256-4172

Profile
BRANCH: Navy.
SIZE AND LOCATION: 1 acre. 20 mi W of Boston in Natick, MA; just off Rte 9, less than 1 mi from Exit 13 of MA Tpke, off Rte 27; laboratory building located 3 mi E on grounds of Army Natick Research, Development and Engineering Center. *County:* Middlesex.
MAJOR UNITS: Materials Research Division; Clothing Development Division; Environmental Sciences Division; Quality Assurance Division; Technical Support Division.
BASE HISTORY: 1879, began as Clothing Manufacturing Department of Naval Clothing Depot, Brooklyn, NY. 1943, Textile and Clothing R&D Division formed. 1947, served as research arm of Clothing Supply Office (CSO). 1958, CSO reorganized; Clothing and Textile Research and Development Division remained in Brooklyn as division of Naval Supply Research and Development Facility, Bayonne, NJ. 1962, division moved to Bayonne. 1967, division closed; renamed

Navy Clothing and Textile Research Unit and relocated in Natick, MA. March 1976, unit received current title.

Key Contacts
PUBLIC AFFAIRS: Cleveland A Heath, 508-233-4189.

Personnel and Expenditures
ACTIVE DUTY PERSONNEL: 1
CIVILIAN PERSONNEL: 52

Services *Exchange:* Retail store. *Base Library:* Yes.

Reading

443. Adjutant General of Massachusetts
Camp Curtis Guild, 25 Haverhill St
Reading, MA 01867-1999
617-944-0500, ext 2201; FAX 617-727-5574

Profile
BRANCH: Army National Guard.
MAJOR UNITS: Massachusetts National Guard.

Key Contacts
COMMANDER: Maj Gen Raymond A Vezina.

444. Camp Curtis Guild
CCGD
25 Haverhill St
Reading, MA 01867-1999
617-944-0500

Profile
BRANCH: Army National Guard.
LOCATION: 2 mi NE of Reading; 20 mi N of Boston. *County:* Middlesex.
MAJOR UNITS: Camp Curtis Guild (ARNG).
BASE HISTORY: Primarily weapons training site.

Key Contacts
COMMANDER: Brig Gen Frank P Baran.

Waltham

445. US Army Corps of Engineers, New England District
CENAE
424 Trapelo Rd
Waltham, MA 02254-6300
617-647-8220; FAX 617-647-8821
Internet: http://www.ned.usace.army.mil

Profile
BRANCH: Army.
SIZE AND LOCATION: 12 acres. In Frederick C Murphy Federal Bldg, 12 mi W of Boston; 1.5 mi E of I-95/Rte 128 at Trapelo Rd exit. *County:* Middlesex.
MAJOR UNITS: Corps of Engineers, New England District; Federal Emergency Management Agency.
BASE HISTORY: Site originally constructed as WWII-era Murphy Army Hospital; used for

offices since late 1950s; water resource responsibilities in all 6 New England states (66,000 sq mi). Plans, designs, constructs, maintains, & operates water resource projects. Civilian workforce located at HQ & at 31 dams, 2 hurricane barriers, Cape Cod Canal, & field offices. Performs military & civil works construction.
VISITOR ATTRACTIONS: Corps visitor center.

Key Contacts
COMMANDER: Col Michael S Meuleners, Division Engineer.
PUBLIC AFFAIRS: Larry Rosenberg, Chief, 617-647-8238, FAX 617-647-8850, larry.b.rosenberg@ned01.usace.army.mil; Sue Douglas, Media Relations Specialist, 617-647-8264, susan.i.douglas@ned01.usace.army.mil.

Personnel and Expenditures
ACTIVE DUTY PERSONNEL: 7
CIVILIAN PERSONNEL: 600 (total district)

Services *Child Care/Capacities:* Day care center capacity 50, 6mo-6yrs. *Base Library:* Yes. *Medical Facilities:* Medical clinic. *Recreational Facilities:* Gym; Fitness center/Weight room; Softball field.

Westfield

446. Barnes Municipal Airport, Air National Guard Base
Westfield, MA 01085-1385
413-568-9151; DSN 636-9210

Profile
BRANCH: Air National Guard.
SIZE AND LOCATION: 186 acres. 3 mi N of Westfield; N of I-90, off exit 3, Southampton Rd. *County:* Hampden.
MAJOR UNITS: 104th Fighter Wing (ANG).
BASE HISTORY: 1952, base dedicated with 131st Tactical Fighter Squadron. 1956, 104th Fighter Group (Air Defense) activated. 1958, mission changed to Tactical Air Command. 1961, called to active duty for Berlin Crisis.

Personnel and Expenditures
ACTIVE DUTY PERSONNEL: 339 full-time; 986 Guard

Services *Medical Facilities:* Medical clinic; Dental clinic. *Recreational Facilities:* Fitness center/Weight room; Officers club; Enlisted club.

Woods Hole

447. Woods Hole Coast Guard Group
Group Woods Hole
Little Harbor Rd
Woods Hole, MA 02543-1099

508-457-3219, 457-3250

Profile
BRANCH: Coast Guard.
SIZE AND LOCATION: 2 acres. In Village of Woods Hole; town of Falmouth. From center of Falmouth, follow Woods Hole Rd approx 4 mi, enter facility on left. *County:* Barnstable.
MAJOR UNITS: Coast Guard Group, Woods Hole; Aids to Navigation (ANT) Team, Woods Hole; Coast Guard Station, Woods Hole; USCGC *Bittersweet*; USCGC *Sanibel*; USCGC *Monomoy*; Support Det, Woods Hole.
BASE HISTORY: 1966, established as "Supergroup." One of largest units in Coast Guard; covers over 600 mi of coastline from Plymouth, MA, to RI/CT border. Mission: Search & Rescue, Maritime Law Enforcement, Aids to Navigation, administrative & operational center.
VISITOR ATTRACTIONS: Strictly a working facility with no berthing or recreational facilities. Public tours after work day/weekends. Groups contact Public Affairs Officer for guided tours.

Personnel and Expenditures
ACTIVE DUTY PERSONNEL: 200
CIVILIAN PERSONNEL: 20

Services *Medical Facilities:* Corpsman assigned.

Worcester

448. Worcester Naval & Marine Corps Reserve Center
640 Plantation St
Worcester, MA 01605-2098
508-853-5522, 853-5523; FAX 508-852-6987
E-mail: worcest@cnsrf.navy.mil

Profile
BRANCH: Naval Reserve; Marine Corps Reserve.
SIZE AND LOCATION: 6.6 acres. At NE corner of intersection of Rt 290 & Plantation St. *County:* Worcester.
MAJOR UNITS: REDCOM ONE Activity; 25th Marine Regiment HQ; Naval Criminal Investigation Service Office; US Marine Corps Recruiting Office; US Navy Recruiting Office.

Key Contacts
COMMANDER: LCDR A T Obrien.

Personnel and Expenditures
ACTIVE DUTY PERSONNEL: Navy 250 Reservists; Marine Corps 350 Reservists

Services *Base Library:* Yes. *Recreational Facilities:* Gym; Fitness center/Weight room.

Michigan

Alpena

449. Alpena Combat Readiness Training Center
Alpena CRTC
Phelps Collins ANG
5884 A St
Alpena, MI 49707
517-354-6203; FAX 517-354-6333; DSN 741-3203; DSN FAX 741-3333
Profile
BRANCH: Air National Guard.
SIZE AND LOCATION: 2711 acres. 7 mi W of Alpena, MI, off State Rte 32. *County:* Alpena.
MAJOR UNITS: ANG Field Training Site, Headquarters.
BASE HISTORY: Named for Capt W H Phelps Collins, American Flying Corps, killed in France in 1918. Facilities used by ANG and AFRES units for annual field training and ARNG and Marine Reserve for special training.
Key Contacts
COMMANDER: COL Terry McKenna, 517-354-6291, DSN 741-3291, tmckenna@M1BTL.ANG.AF.MIL.
Personnel and Expenditures
ACTIVE DUTY PERSONNEL: 88; 22 reservists
Services *Medical Facilities:* Hospital 14 beds; Dispensary. *Recreational Facilities:* Tennis courts; Fitness center/Weight room; Softball field; Camping; Fishing/Hunting; Picnic area; Water sports; All ranks club.

Battle Creek

450. Battle Creek Naval & Marine Corps Reserve Center
NMCRC, Battle Creek
101 Base Ave
Battle Creek, MI 49105-1242
616-968-9216, 968-0415; FAX 616-968-9859
Profile
BRANCH: Naval Reserve; Marine Corps Reserve.
LOCATION: *County:* Calhoun.
MAJOR UNITS: REDCOM THIRTEEN Activity; Bridge Co A, 6th Engineer Support Bn; Engineer Support Co, 6th Engineer Support Bn.

Key Contacts
COMMANDER: LCDR W G Breznau.

451. Defense Logistics Services Center
DLSC
74 Washington Ave N
Battle Creek, MI 49017-3084
616-961-7014
Internet: http://www.dlsc.dla.mil/welcome.htm
Profile
BRANCH: Defense Logistics Agency.
SIZE: Offices only. *County:* Calhoun.
MAJOR UNITS: Defense Logistics Services Center.
Key Contacts
COMMANDER: Rick Maison, Program Manager, 616-961-4170, DSN 932-4170, rmaison@dlsc.dla.mil.

452. Defense Reutilization and Marketing Service
DRMS
74 N Washington St
Battle Creek, MI 49017-3092
616-961-7015; FAX 616-961-5907; DSN 932-7015; Information on sales: 800-468-8289; Customer Service: 888-352-9333
Internet: http://www.drms.dla.mil/; http://www.drms.com
Profile
BRANCH: Defense Logistics Agency.
SIZE AND LOCATION: Offices only. In Battle Creek. *County:* Calhoun.
MAJOR UNITS: Defense Reutilization and Marketing Service.
BASE HISTORY: DRMS, Defense Logistics Agency (DLA) supports US military logistics community by redistributing, selling & disposing of excess DOD personal property. Established 1972, worldwide organization with more than 200 field offices (Defense Reutilization and Marketing Offices) located on or near major military installations employs more than 3800 civilian & military personnel.
Key Contacts
PUBLIC AFFAIRS: Carol J Simpson, 616-961-7015, FAX 616-961-7410, DSN 932-7015, pubaff@drms.dla.mil.
Personnel and Expenditures
ACTIVE DUTY PERSONNEL: 20 (worldwide)
CIVILIAN PERSONNEL: 435
Services *Exchange:* Food shop; Bank; Credit union.

Child Care/Capacities: Day care center capacity 36, 6wks-6yrs. *Medical Facilities:* Medical clinic. *Recreational Facilities:* Fitness center/Weight room.

453. W K Kellogg Airport, Air National Guard Base
3367 W Dickman Rd
Battle Creek, MI 49015-1291
616-963-1596; DSN 580-3210
Profile
BRANCH: Air National Guard.
SIZE AND LOCATION: 315 acres. At W K Kellogg Regional Airport, near I-94, Helmer Rd Exit; 3 min W of downtown Battle Creek. *County:* Calhoun.
MAJOR UNITS: 110th Fighter Wing (ANG); 172nd Fighter Squadron; 110th Resource Management Squadron.
BASE HISTORY: 1928, Kellogg Regional Airport, largest municipally-owned airport in MI, built. 1946, Battle Creek NG Air Corps organized. 1947, Governor designated Kellogg Regional Airport as HQ, 172nd Fighter Squadron with federal recognition; first of its type. 1951, mobilized for Korean War. 1950s-70s, mission changed from fighter bomber, to fighter interceptor, to tactical reconnaissance, to fighter group. 1991, began transition to A-10 and OA-10 Thunderbolt II aircraft.
VISITOR ATTRACTIONS: Ft Custer Recreational Park (nearby); International Balloon Championship (4th of July week).
Personnel and Expenditures
ACTIVE DUTY PERSONNEL: 910 Guard
CIVILIAN PERSONNEL: 273
MILITARY PAYROLL EXPENDITURE: $24.1 mil
Services
Housing: None. *Exchange:* Retail store. *Medical Facilities:* Medical clinic. *Recreational Facilities:* All ranks club.

Calumet

454. Calumet Naval Reserve Facility
NAVRESFAC Calumet
2 Airport Rd
Calumet, MI 49913
Mailing Address
RR 1, Box 94F
Calumet, MI 49913-9717

906-482-4677; FAX 906-482-1880
E-mail: NRFCAL@up.net
Profile
BRANCH: Naval Reserve.
SIZE AND LOCATION: Leased portion of
bldg. 7 mi from Hancock & Calumet, on road
with Houghton County Airport. *County:*
Houghton.
MAJOR UNITS: REDCOM SIXTEEN Activity.
Key Contacts
COMMANDER: Lt Knuth.
PUBLIC AFFAIRS: MRC Parks.
Personnel and Expenditures
ACTIVE DUTY PERSONNEL: 6; 90 reservists

Detroit

455. Detroit Coast Guard Group/ Base
USCG Group Detroit
110 Mt Elliot Ave
Detroit, MI 48207-4380
313-568-9525; FAX 313-568-9469
Profile
BRANCH: Coast Guard.
SIZE AND LOCATION: 1 acre. Downtown De-
troit, on Detroit River, directly N of western
tip of Belle Isle and Windsor, Canada; approx
1 mi E of Renaissance Center. *County:*
Wayne.
MAJOR UNITS: Coast Guard Group, Detroit;
Coast Guard Base, Detroit; USCGC *Bristol
Bay* (WTGB-102); Aids to Navigation (ANT)
Team, Detroit; Marine Safety Office, Detroit
(Captain of the Port); Coast Guard Air Station, Detroit.
BASE HISTORY: 1859, obtained by Lighthouse
Service; passed to Coast Guard; most buildings replaced with single multipurpose building. Missions include supply & logistics sup-
port; maintenance/repair aids-to-navigation;
& communication with all vessels in Group's
area; parent command for 10 search & rescue
stations, support base, 2 aids-to navigation
teams, electronics support facility, & 2 ice-
breakers; responsible for all US waters in
lower two-thirds of Lake Huron, including
Saginaw Bay, St Clair River, Lake St Clair,
Detroit River, & approx western two-thirds of
Lake Erie; helicopters housed at Selfridge
ANG Base.
Key Contacts
COMMANDER: Capt James J Collin,
313-568-9500.
PUBLIC AFFAIRS: LCDR A J Keith,
313-568-9521.
PROCUREMENT: CWO3 Jay Hatcher,
313-568-9513.
TRANSPORTATION: CWO4 Guntenaar,
313-568-9523.
PERSONNEL/COMMUNITY ACTIVITIES:
CDR Joe Castillo.
Personnel and Expenditures
ACTIVE DUTY PERSONNEL: 80
DEPENDENTS: 0
CIVILIAN PERSONNEL: 11
Services
Housing: None. *Temporary Housing:* None. *Ex-
change:* Retail store. *Child Care/Capacities:* No
day care facilities. *Schools:* No on-base schools.
Medical Facilities: Dispensary. *Recreational Fa-
cilities:* Fitness center/Weight room.

456. US Army Corps of Engineers, Detroit District
CELRE
Engineer Corps, Detroit
497 Michigan Ave
Detroit, MI 48226-2575
Mailing Address
PO Box 1027
Detroit, MI 48231-1027
313-226-6413; FAX 313-226-5993; DSN
346-5763
Internet: http://www.sparky.nce.usace.army.mil
Profile
BRANCH: Army.
SIZE AND LOCATION: Offices only. HQs in
downtown Detroit. *County:* Wayne.
MAJOR UNITS: Corps of Engineers, Detroit
District.
BASE HISTORY: Detroit District conducts fed-
eral water resources activities throughout
Great Lakes Region. Performs civil works
construction.
VISITOR ATTRACTIONS: Soo Locks at Sault
Ste Marie, MI; Lake Superior Maritime Visi-
tor Center, Duluth, MN.
Key Contacts
COMMANDER: LTC Thomas C Haid,
313-226-6762.
PUBLIC AFFAIRS: Lynn Duerod,
313-226-4680.
PROCUREMENT: Wanda Carter Davis,
313-226-5148.
TRANSPORTATION: Jacqueline Berninger,
313-226-7236.
PERSONNEL/COMMUNITY ACTIVITIES:
Henry Garcia, 313-226-6423.
Personnel and Expenditures
ACTIVE DUTY PERSONNEL: 3
DEPENDENTS: 0
CIVILIAN PERSONNEL: 600

Grand Rapids

457. Grand Rapids Naval & Marine Corps Reserve Center
1863 Monroe Ave, NW
Grand Rapids, MI 49505-6294
616-363-6889, 363-5465, 363-1694; FAX
616-363-1488
Profile
BRANCH: Naval Reserve; Marine Corps Re-
serve.
LOCATION: *County:* Kent.
MAJOR UNITS: REDCOM THIRTEEN Activ-
ity; A Co, 1st Bn, 24th Marine Regiment.
Key Contacts
COMMANDER: CDR S R Wilson.

Grayling

458. Camp Grayling Maneuver Training Center
CGMTC
Camp Grayling
HQ Bldg #117
Grayling, MI 49739-0001
517-348-7621; FAX 517-348-3855; DSN
623-3200; DSN FAX 623-3855

Internet: http://www.voyager.net/goguard/
grayhom2.htm
OFFICER-OF-THE-DAY: 517-348-3601, DSN
623-3601, DSN FAX 623-3855
Profile
BRANCH: Air National Guard; Army National
Guard.
SIZE AND LOCATION: 147,000 acres. Along
I-75, 3 mi W of Grayling, MI, 200 mi NW of
Detroit; 250 mi NE of Chicago; 55 mi due E
of Traverse City, MI. *County:* Crawford; Kal-
kaska; Otsego.
MAJOR UNITS: Camp Grayling Manuever
Training Center; 1071st Maintenance Co;
1438th Engineering Det (Utilities); 1439th En-
gineering Det (Fire Fighting); 1440th Engineering Det (Fire Fighting); 745th Ordnance
Det (Explosive Ordnance Disposal); 1183rd
Ordnance TM (MLRS Maintenance); Mobilization and Training Equipment Site
(MATES); TMC Team, Det 6, HQ STARC
(AMMED); State Environmental Section.
BASE HISTORY: 1913, originated with 14,000-
acre grant of private land to state of MI from
lumber baron Rasmus Hanson for permanent
military encampment, forest preserve, &
game refuge. Continuously used as military
training site, now encompassing wooded &
rolling terrain; all conventional Army weapons can be fired on ranges, with maneuver
space for entire division, including infantry,
armor, artillery, & aerial gunnery; largest National Guard training center in US.
VISITOR ATTRACTIONS: Historic buildings,
including Officers Club in continuous operation since 1917; military cemetery (2 graves).
Hartwick Pines State Park, 93-acre stand of
virgin pines. Hanson Hills recreation Area
with downhill & cross country skiing. Heart
of Michigan's vacation land; trout fishing on
nearby rivers (headwaters of Manistee & Aus-
able rivers).
Key Contacts
COMMANDER: Col Gary J McConnell,
517-348-3611, DSN 623-3611, DSN FAX
623-3855, cgcdrmi@ng-net.army.mil.
PUBLIC AFFAIRS: Maj Thomas F Lamie,
517-348-3603, DSN 623-3603, DSN FAX
623-3855, isupaomi@ng-net.army.mil.
PROCUREMENT: LTC Timothy J Swope,
517-348-3662, DSN 623-3662, DSN FAX
623-3844, isudolmi@ng-net.army.mil.
PERSONNEL/COMMUNITY ACTIVITIES:
Maj James E Gardiner, 517-348-3650, DSN
623-3650, DSN FAX 623-3749, isudpcmi@
ng-net.army.mil.
Personnel and Expenditures
ACTIVE DUTY PERSONNEL: 22
DEPENDENTS: 0
CIVILIAN PERSONNEL: 193
MILITARY PAYROLL EXPENDITURE: $6.1 mil
CONTRACT EXPENDITURE: $18.3 mil
Services
Housing: Unaccompanied officer quarters 4;
Barracks spaces 6800; Mobile home units 4; RV/
Camper sites 90. *Temporary Housing:* VIP units
3; VOQ units 10; Unaccompanied officer/En-
listed quarters 50; Guest cottages 4. *Exchange:*
Retail store; Military clothing store; Laundro-
mat; ATM; Post office; Class VI; Barber shop
(summer only). *Child Care/Capacities:* No day
care facilities. *Schools:* No on-base schools.
Medical Facilities: Troop medical clinic; Dental clinic; Pharmacy available summer only. *Recreational Facilities:* Tennis courts; Fitness cen-

ter/Weight room; Softball field; Officers club; NCO club; Camping; Fishing/Hunting; Enlisted club; Picnic area; Water sports; Beach with water recreation equipment; Boat launch.

Lansing

459. Adjutant General of Michigan
2500 S Washington Ave
Lansing, MI 48913-5101
517-483-5507; FAX 517-482-0356
Profile
BRANCH: Army National Guard.
MAJOR UNITS: Michigan National Guard.
Key Contacts
COMMANDER: Maj Gen E Gordon Stump.

460. Lansing Naval & Marine Corps Reserve Center
1620 E Saginaw St
Lansing, MI 48912-2396
517-482-9150, 482-9688; FAX 517-482-7556
Profile
BRANCH: Naval Reserve; Marine Corps Reserve.
LOCATION: *County:* Clinton; Eaton; Ingham.
MAJOR UNITS: REDCOM THIRTEEN Activity; C Co, 1st Bn, 24th Marine Regiment.
Key Contacts
COMMANDER: LCDR Andrew P Dougherty.

Saginaw

461. Saginaw Naval & Marine Corps Reserve Center
Armed Forces Reserve Center
3500 Douglas St
Saginaw, MI 48601-4799
517-754-1375, 754-3091; FAX 517-754-7331
Profile
BRANCH: Naval Reserve; Marine Corps Reserve.
LOCATION: *County:* Saginaw.
MAJOR UNITS: REDCOM THIRTEEN Activity; B Co, 1st Bn, 24th Marine Regiment.
Key Contacts
COMMANDER: Lt J R Blaylock.

Sault Ste Marie

462. Sault Ste Marie Coast Guard Group
USCG Group Sault
337 Water St
Sault Ste Marie, MI 49783
906-635-3217; FAX 906-635-3219
OFFICER-OF-THE-DAY: 906-635-3228
Profile
BRANCH: Coast Guard.
SIZE AND LOCATION: 5 acres. Eastern Upper Peninsula of MI on St Mary's River, bordering Canada. I-75N exit just before Canadian border. *County:* Chippewa.
MAJOR UNITS: Coast Guard Group, Sault; Coast Guard Base, Sault; USCGC *Katmai Bay*; USCGC *Buckthorn*; Coast Guard Station, Sault; Aids to Navigation (ANT) Team,

Sault; Marine Safety Office, Sault; Vessel Traffic Service, Sault.
Key Contacts
COMMANDER: Capt Richard A Rooth.
PUBLIC AFFAIRS: Executive Officer, 906-635-3214.
PROCUREMENT: CWO Kevin Sandvig, 906-635-3240.
TRANSPORTATION: See Procurement Officer.
PERSONNEL/COMMUNITY ACTIVITIES: See Public Affairs Officer.
Personnel and Expenditures
ACTIVE DUTY PERSONNEL: 148
CIVILIAN PERSONNEL: 6
MILITARY PAYROLL EXPENDITURE: $2.8 mil
CONTRACT EXPENDITURE: $0.5 mil
Services *Exchange:* Retail store. *Medical Facilities:* Medical clinic.

Selfridge ANG Base

463. Detroit Naval Reserve Readiness Center
25154 Plattsburg St, Center Selfridge Bldg 1408
Selfridge ANG Base, MI 48045-4915
810-307-6148, 307-6174; FAX 810-307-5562
Profile
BRANCH: Naval Reserve.
MAJOR UNITS: REDCOM THIRTEEN Activity.
Key Contacts
COMMANDER: CDR V L Kainz.

464. Selfridge Air National Guard Base
SANGB
28947 Wilbur Wright Blvd
Selfridge ANG Base, MI 48045-5046
313-307-5553; DSN 273-5553
Profile
BRANCH: Joint Service Installation; Air National Guard; Coast Guard; Army Reserve; Naval Reserve.
SIZE AND LOCATION: 3700 acres. Main gate approx 1.5 mi E of junction I-94 and MI-59; 25 mi NE of Detroit; nearest city, Mount Clemens, 2.5 mi W. *County:* Macomb.
MAJOR UNITS: 127th Wing (ANG); 927th Air Refueling Wing (AFRC); Naval Air Facility, Detroit; Coast Guard Group/Base, Detroit; Marine Wing Support Group 47; Army Tank Automotive Command Support Activity Selfridge; Army Readiness Group Selfridge.
BASE HISTORY: Originally built as Joy Aviation Field; later used by Packard Motor Co as test field. 1917, leased by government; named Selfridge Field for 1st Lt Thomas E Selfridge, first person to die from engine-driven aircraft accident. 1922, named permanent installation. 1920s, first night landing. WWII, training of many units including 332nd Fighter Group, all-black unit commanded by Col Benjamin O Davis Jr. 1946, 56th Fighter Group reactivated. 1947, became Selfridge AFB. 1950s, HQ 10th Air Force, in charge of training, recall & records of all Air Reservists, 13-state area. 1960s, Coast Guard Station, Detroit & Marine Air Reserve Training Detachment added; 5th Air Force Reserve Region transferred; SAC refueling tankers & Nike missiles removed. Nicknamed "Home of the Gen-

erals." 1970, added Naval Air Facility, Detroit. 1970, MI ANG. 1971, became Selfridge ANG Base.
VISITOR ATTRACTIONS: Selfridge Military Air Museum (open every Sun except Easter, Apr-Oct, 1-5pm).
Personnel and Expenditures
ACTIVE DUTY PERSONNEL: 1686 Guard; 811 AFRC; 176 Air Reserve Technicians
CIVILIAN PERSONNEL: 449 ANG; 60 AFRC
MILITARY PAYROLL EXPENDITURE: $61.8 mil (ANG); $18.8 mil (AFRC)
Services
Housing: Family units 967; Unaccompanied officer quarters 17; Unaccompanied enlisted quarters 21; Townhouse units 40; Barracks spaces 54; Senior NCO units 218; Junior NCO units 407. *Temporary Housing:* Guesthouse units 15; VOQ/VEQ Lufberry Hall (Bldg 410) 27 rooms. *Commissary:* Yes; *Exchange:* Retail store; Barber shop; Dry cleaners; Food shop; Bank; Service station; Furniture store; Bakery; Military clothing store; Convenience store; Beauty shop; Credit union. *Child Care/Capacities:* Day care center capacity 123, 6wks-12yrs; Home day care program; Latch key program; Summer day camp. *Schools:* College courses. *Base Library:* Yes. *Medical Facilities:* Medical clinic; Dental clinic; Dispensary; Pharmacy; Veterinary services (limited). *Recreational Facilities:* Bowling center; Movie theater; Pool; Gym; Recreation center; Golf course.

Traverse City

465. Traverse City Coast Guard Air Station
AIRSTA Traverse City
Airport Access Rd
Traverse City, MI 49684-3586
616-922-8300; FAX 616-922-8213
E-mail: CGAIRSTA@GTII.COM Internet:http://www.dot.gov/dotinfo/uscg/d9/astc/astc.htm
OFFICER-OF-THE-DAY: 616-922-8217
Profile
BRANCH: Coast Guard.
SIZE AND LOCATION: 70 acres. Within city limits of Traverse City, 2 mi from downtown; adj to Cherry Capital Airport on Airport Access Rd (crosses Parsons Rd) meets Hwy 31 & 72. *County:* Grand Traverse.
MAJOR UNITS: Coast Guard Air Station, Traverse City.
BASE HISTORY: 1938, established as one plane detachment to provide search & rescue service for Great Lakes. WWII, Navy constructed airfield as secret drone site. 1946, commissioned permanent air station. 1991, operated 3 Sikorsky HH-60J "Jayhawk" helicopters & provided operational response from Duluth, MN, on Lake Superior to Lake Michigan, Lake Huron, Lake Erie, and, on occasion, Lake Ontario. Currently, operates 5 HH65A helicopters.
Key Contacts
COMMANDER: CDR Barry A Harner, 616-922-8222.
PUBLIC AFFAIRS: LT Thomas L Kaye, 616-922-8273.
PROCUREMENT: CWO2 Peter J Fleury, 616-922-8320.
PERSONNEL/COMMUNITY ACTIVITIES: 616-922-8224.

Personnel and Expenditures

ACTIVE DUTY PERSONNEL: 130
DEPENDENTS: 0
CIVILIAN PERSONNEL: 6
CONTRACT EXPENDITURE: $250,000

Services

Housing: None. *Temporary Housing:* Rooms for duty pilots, air crews & duty standers. *Exchange:* Retail store; Military clothing store. *Child Care/Capacities:* No day care facilities. *Schools:* No on-base schools. *Medical Facilities:* Medical clinic; Dental clinic; Pharmacy. *Recreational Facilities:* Tennis courts; Racquetball court; Fitness center/Weight room; Softball field; Auto shop; Craft shop; Picnic area; Playground; All hands club; Camping, fishing & hunting nearby; Volleyball courts.

Warren

466. Army Tank-Automotive & Armaments Command

TACOM
Detroit Arsenal
11 Mile Rd
Warren, MI 48397-5000

Mailing Address

ATTN: AMSTA-CS-CT
Warren, MI 48397-5000
810-574-5000; FAX 810-574-5097; DSN 786-5000; DSN FAX 786-5097
E-mail: amstact@cc.tacom.army.mil Internet: http://www.tacom.army.mil

Profile

BRANCH: Army.

SIZE AND LOCATION: 350 acres. At Detroit Arsenal in Warren, MI; E on I-696 to Van Dyke exit, take service drive, first left over freeway to Westbound service drive, 0.5 mi to first right after railroad tracks, 11 Mile Rd gate on right. *County:* Macomb.

MAJOR UNITS: Army Tank-Automotive & Armaments Command (TACOM); Ground Combat & Support Systems.

BASE HISTORY: 1967, TACOM established. 1975, TACOM responsible for Army Garrison, Selfridge Air National Guard Base. Currently responsible for all military wheeled & tracked vehicles & armaments. Mission involves research, development, procurement, distribution, repair parts supply, preparation of maintenance doctrine & operational training. Foreign military sales program lists more than 60 friendly nations as customers. National inventory control & maintenance point for 1.2 million vehicles. Most of TACOM's facilities housed at Detroit Arsenal, Warren, MI. Other sites include Armament Research Development & Engineering Center (ARDEC) Picatinny Arsenal, NJ, and Chemical Acquisition & Logistics Activity (ACALA) Rock Island, IL.

FUTURE CLOSURE/REALIGNMENT: Major realignment to be completed Sep 1999; Tank plant closed Dec 1996.

Key Contacts

COMMANDER: Maj Gen Roy E Beauchamp, 810-574-5133, FAX 810-574-5038, DSN 786-5133.
PUBLIC AFFAIRS: Eric P Emerton, 810-574-5663, FAX 810-574-5097, DSN 786-5663, emertone@cc.tacom.army.mil.

Personnel and Expenditures

ACTIVE DUTY PERSONNEL: 91
CIVILIAN PERSONNEL: 3580

Services *Medical Facilities:* Medical clinic.

Minnesota

Arden Hills

467. Twin Cities Army Ammunition Plant
TCAAP
4700 Hwy 10, Ste A
Arden Hills, MN 55112-3928
612-633-2301, ext 1661; FAX 612-633-2308;
DSN 798-1500, ext 1661
Internet: http://147.217.15.5/rm/iocfact/tcaap.htm

Profile
BRANCH: Army.
SIZE AND LOCATION: 2383 acres. Approx 10 mi from downtown Minneapolis-St Paul on I-35W. *County:* Ramsey.
MAJOR UNITS: Twin Cities Army Ammunition Plant.
BASE HISTORY: 1941-42, constructed as part of DOD military industrial complex to produce small caliber ammunition. Produced munitions during WWII, Korean War, and Vietnam War. 1976, production completed. No longer a producing facility; inactive, modified caretaker. Contractor: Alliant Techsystems.
FUTURE CLOSURE/REALIGNMENT: Internal Army (88th RSC & MN ARNG) land transfer of approx 1500 acres proceeding.
VISITOR ATTRACTIONS: Installation restoration program activities.

Key Contacts
COMMANDER: Michael R Fix, SIOTC_CR, Commander's Representative, 612-633-2301, ext 1661, FAX 612-633-2308, DSN 798-1500, Ext 1661, DSN FAX 798-2308, mfix@ria-emh2.army.mil; Ervin Barrett, 1607 Christie Place, St Paul, MN 55106, 612-774-8944; Robin Rockney, Plant Manager; Martin R McCleery, Installation Co-Chair, 612-633-2301, ext 1651, FAX 612-633-3129, DSN 798-1500, ext 1651, DSN FAX 798-3129, mmccleer@ria-emh2.army.mil.

Personnel and Expenditures
CIVILIAN PERSONNEL: 6
CONTRACT EXPENDITURE: $11.8 mil

Services
Housing: None.

Duluth

468. Duluth IAP Air National Guard Base
148th FW
4680 Viper St
Duluth, MN 55811-6031
218-727-6886; DSN 825-7210
E-mail: helpdesk@mndlh.ang.af.mil Internet: http://www.dlh.ang.af.mil

Profile
BRANCH: Air National Guard.
SIZE AND LOCATION: 152 acres. 5 mi NW of Duluth, off US-53. *County:* St Louis.
MAJOR UNITS: 148th Fighter Wing; 179th Fighter Squadron; Defense Reutilization Management Office.

Key Contacts
COMMANDER: Col Kenneth Stromquist, 218-723-7200, DSN 825-7200, kstromquist@mndlh.ang.af.mil.
PUBLIC AFFAIRS: Maj Suzan Lane, 218-723-7227, DSN 825-7227, slane@mndlh.ang.af.mil.
PROCUREMENT: SMSgt Mark Horngren, 218-723-7241, DSN 825-7241, DSN FAX 825-7403, mhorngren@mndlh.ang.af.mil.
TRANSPORTATION: MSgt Robyn Randall, 218-723-7240, DSN 825-7240, DSN FAX 825-7261, rrandall@mndlh.ang.af.mil.
PERSONNEL/COMMUNITY ACTIVITIES: Maj Penny Dieryck, 218-723-7205, DAN 825-7205, DSN FAX 825-7433, pdieryck@mndlh.ang.af.mil.

Personnel and Expenditures
ACTIVE DUTY PERSONNEL: 970
DEPENDENTS: 0
CIVILIAN PERSONNEL: 233

Services
Housing: None. *Exchange:* Convenience store. *Child Care/Capacities:* No day care facilities. *Schools:* No on-base schools. *Medical Facilities:* No medical facilities.

469. Duluth Naval Reserve Center
5019 Airport Rd
Duluth, MN 55811-1546
218-722-3454; FAX 218-722-2423

Profile
BRANCH: Naval Reserve.
LOCATION: *County:* St Louis.
MAJOR UNITS: REDCOM SIXTEEN Activity.

Key Contacts
COMMANDER: LCDR T H Hopkins.

Little Falls

470. Camp Ripley
PO Box 150
Little Falls, MN 56345-0150
320-632-7337

Profile
BRANCH: Army National Guard.
SIZE AND LOCATION: 53,000 acres. 100 mi NW of Minneapolis; 7 mi N of Little Falls, MN; bordering on Mississippi & Crow Wing rivers. *County:* Morrison.
MAJOR UNITS: Camp Ripley (ARNG).
BASE HISTORY: Year-round training post with capacity of 12,000.

Personnel and Expenditures
CIVILIAN PERSONNEL: 530

Minneapolis

471. Fridley Naval Industrial Reserve Ordnance Plant
5001 E River Rd
Minneapolis, MN 55421-1400
612-572-6360; FAX 612-572-3345

Profile
BRANCH: Navy.
SIZE AND LOCATION: 82.6 acres. On the Mississippi River just N of Minneapolis. *County:* Anoka.
MAJOR UNITS: Fridley Naval Industrial Reserve Ordnance Plant.

Key Contacts
COMMANDER: Patrick K Morrow, Co-Chair, 612-572-6360, FAX 612-572-3345, morrow_patrick_k@hq.navsea.navy.mil; John Flora, Co-Chair.

472. Minneapolis Naval Air Reserve Center
6201 32nd Ave S
Minneapolis, MN 55450-28982800
612-725-5055, 725-5058; FAX 612-725-5062;
DSN 825-5055, 825-5058
OFFICER-OF-THE-DAY: 612-725-5061, DSN 825-5061

Profile
BRANCH: Naval Reserve; Marine Corps Reserve.
LOCATION: *County:* Hennepin.
MAJOR UNITS: Naval Air Reserve Center, Minneapolis; Det A, Marine Wing Support

Squadron 471 (MWSS-471); Maintenance Det A, 4th Maintenance Bn.

Key Contacts
COMMANDER: 612-725-5061, ext 5.

473. Region Sixteen, Naval Reserve Readiness Command

REDCOM 16
715 Apollo Ave
Minneapolis, MN 55450-2018
612-713-1567; FAX 612-713-1558; DSN 783-1567
Internet: http://www.navy.mil/homepages/navresfor/navsurf/redcom16.html

Profile
BRANCH: Naval Reserve.
MAJOR UNITS: Naval Reserve Readiness Command, Region 16.

Key Contacts
COMMANDER: Capt R R Lustman.

Minneapolis-Saint Paul IAP

474. Minneapolis-Saint Paul IAP, Air National Guard Base/ARS

Minneapolis-Saint Paul IAP, MN 55450-2000
ANG: 612-725-5631, DSN 825-5631; AFRC: 612-725-5011, DSN 825-5110

Profile
BRANCH: Air National Guard; Air Force Reserve.
SIZE AND LOCATION: 130.5 acres (ANG); 300 acres (AFRC). Off I-494 in S Minneapolis on Minneapolis-St Paul IAP. *County:* Hennepin.

MAJOR UNITS: 133rd Airlift Wing (ANG); 210th Engineering Installation Squadron (ANG); 237th Air Traffic Control Flight (ANG); 934th Airlift Wing (AFRC); Naval Reserve Readiness Command, Region 16; US Air Force Civil Air Patrol.
BASE HISTORY: ANG considered nation's oldest federally recognized ANG unit. 1921, established by Brig Gen Ray S Miller, 109th Observation Squadron assigned to Army NG. First airfield at what is now Larpenteur and Snelling Avenues, St Paul. Later, state rented airfield near Fort Snelling called Speedway Field, current Minneapolis-St Paul IAP. 1930, moved to Holman Field, downtown St Paul. After WWII, unit returned to St Paul as 109th Fighter Squadron. 1957, ANG took over former Air Force site at IAP. 1960s, Wing carried cargo to Vietnam.

Personnel and Expenditures
ACTIVE DUTY PERSONNEL: 150; Guard 1250; Reserve 1150
CIVILIAN PERSONNEL: 274 ANG; 199 AFRC
MILITARY PAYROLL EXPENDITURE: $19.3 mil (ANG); $24 mil (AFRC)
Services *Temporary Housing:* Temporary quarters provided by 934th TAG, Air Force Reserve. *Exchange:* BX.

Saint Paul

475. Adjutant General of Minnesota

20 W 12th St, 4th Fl Veterans Services Bldg
Saint Paul, MN 55155
612-282-4666; FAX 612-282-4541

Profile
BRANCH: Army National Guard.

MAJOR UNITS: Minnesota National Guard.
Key Contacts
COMMANDER: Maj Gen Eugene R Andreotti.

476. St Paul Naval & Marine Corps Reserve Center

NMCRC
Twin Cities, Fort Snelling
Fort Snelling, 6400 Bloomington Rd
Saint Paul, MN 55111-4051
612-726-9391, 726-1707; FAX 612-726-9416

Profile
BRANCH: Naval Reserve; Marine Corps Reserve.
LOCATION: *County:* Ramsey.
MAJOR UNITS: REDCOM SIXTEEN Activity; Military Police Co, HQ Bn, 4th Marine Division.

Key Contacts
COMMANDER: CDR S Reynolds.

477. US Army Corps of Engineers, St Paul District

CEMVP
190 E 5th St
Saint Paul, MN 55101-1638
612-290-5200; FAX 612-290-5478
Internet: http://www.mvp.usace.army.mil

Profile
BRANCH: Army.
SIZE AND LOCATION: Offices only. In Army Corps of Engineers Centre. *County:* Ramsey.
MAJOR UNITS: Corps of Engineers, St Paul District.
BASE HISTORY: Performs civil works construction.

Key Contacts
COMMANDER: Col J M "Mike" Wosnik.

Mississippi

Camp Shelby

478. Camp Shelby Training Site
CSTS; Camp Shelby
Bldg 1001, CSTS-DPCA
Camp Shelby, MS 39407-5500
601-558-2000; FAX 601-558-2859; DSN
921-2100; DSN FAX 921-2859
Internet: http://ngms.state.ms.us/

Profile
BRANCH: Army National Guard.
SIZE AND LOCATION: 134,820 acres. 10 mi S
of Hattiesburg, MS, on Hwy 49, on N edge of
De Soto National Forest. *County:* Forrest.
MAJOR UNITS: Installation Support Unit,
Camp Shelby; Regional Training Institute;
Maintenance Readiness Branch; RETRO
FVR; Regional Training Brigade (AC); Director of Logistics, Camp Shelby; MATES; 3rd
Brigade, 87th Division; CSMS; 704th Ordnance (EOD).
BASE HISTORY: 1917, Camp Shelby established; named for Isaac Shelby, Indian
fighter, Revolutionary War hero, & first Governor of KY. Following WWI, demobilized &
deactivated. 1934, state acquired site for summer camp by National Guard. 1940, reopened
as federal installation. WWII, site of largest
tent city in world; trained Japanese-American
442nd Regimental Combat Team; convalescent hospital; & POW camp for German Africa Corps. After WWII, closed until Korean
War when developed as Emergency Railhead
Facility. 1956, Continental Army Command
designated it as Permanent Training Site, directed by 3rd Army HQ; site of Hagler Army
Air Field. State Operated Mobilization Site
(SOMS); approx 110,000 National Guard &
USAR troops train each year. Today, largest
state-owned & operated field training & mobilization site in US.
VISITOR ATTRACTIONS: Camp Shelby
Armed Forces Museum.

Key Contacts
COMMANDER: LTC James I Pylant,
601-558-2764, FAX 601-558-2859, pylanti@
ngms.state.ms.usDSN 921-2764.

Personnel and Expenditures
ACTIVE DUTY PERSONNEL: 100; guard 117
AGR
CIVILIAN PERSONNEL: 616
MILITARY PAYROLL EXPENDITURE: $4.4 mil
CONTRACT EXPENDITURE: $4 mil

Services
Housing: Unaccompanied officer quarters 9;
Barracks spaces 11,000; Senior NCO units 95;
RV/Camper sites 25. *Temporary Housing:* Unaccompanied officer/Enlisted quarters 140. *Exchange:* Retail store; Barber shop; Bank; Military clothing store; Laundromat; Credit union.
Medical Facilities: Hospital 20; Medical clinic;
Dental clinic; Dispensary; Pharmacy. *Recreational Facilities:* Movie theater; Pool; Gym; Tennis courts; Fitness center/Weight room; Softball
field; Officers club; NCO club; Camping; Fish-
ing/Hunting; Picnic area; All ranks club.

Columbus AFB

479. Columbus Air Force Base
CAFB
14 FTW/PA, 555 Seventh St, Ste 203
Columbus AFB, MS 39710-1009
601-434-7322; FAX 601-434-7009; DSN
742-7322; DSN FAX 742-7009
E-mail: 14ftwpa@colgate1.col.aetc.af.mil In-
ternet:http://www.col.aetc.af.mil
OFFICER-OF-THE-DAY: Command Post,
601-434-7020, FAX 601-434-7023, DSN
742-7020

Profile
BRANCH: Air Force.
SIZE AND LOCATION: 6027 acres. On US-45,
10 mi N of junction with US-82 at city of Columbus. *County:* Lowndes.
MAJOR UNITS: 14th Flying Training Wing
(AETC); 14th Support Group; 14th Operations Group; 37th Flying Training Squadron;
50th Flying Training Squadron; 48th Flying
Training Squadron; 49th Flying Training
Squadron; 14th Medical Group.
BASE HISTORY: Began as training facility for
fighter and bomber crews. 1942, pilot training
began; closed after WWII. 1951, reopened as
contract flying school providing flight training for pilots during Korean War. 1955-69,
Strategic Air Command Base. 1969, returned
to Air Training Command. Serves as reception base for NASA's Space Shuttle on return
journey from Edwards AFB to Kennedy
Space Center. Primary mission to provide undergraduate pilot training to qualified Air
Force officers, ANG, Air Force Reserve, &
foreign officers. 1993, introduction to fighter
fundamentals course taught.

Key Contacts
COMMANDER: Col Jack J Cotton Jr, Ste 201,
39710-1000, 601-434-7006, DSN 742-7006,
DSN FAX 742-2827.
PUBLIC AFFAIRS: Sherry Medders,
medderss@colgate1.aetc.af.mil.
PROCUREMENT: Maj Donna Heinz,
601-434-7802, DSN 742-7802, DSN FAX
742-7764, heinzd@colgate1.aetc.af.mil.
TRANSPORTATION: Jimmy Helton,
601-434-2684, DSN 742-2684, DSN FAX
742-2576, heltonje@col3B201.af.mil.
PERSONNEL/COMMUNITY ACTIVITIES:
LTC Richard J Gaydos Jr, 601-434-2615,
DSN 742-2615, DSN FAX 742-2610,
richardgaydos@mss.

Personnel and Expenditures
ACTIVE DUTY PERSONNEL: 1398
DEPENDENTS: 1097
CIVILIAN PERSONNEL: 1318
MILITARY PAYROLL EXPENDITURE: $63.8
mil
CONTRACT EXPENDITURE: $29.3 mil

Services
Housing: Family units 735; Unaccompanied officer quarters 136; Unaccompanied enlisted quarters 57; Dormitory spaces 224. *Temporary Housing:* VIP units 4; VOQ units 59; VEQ units 31;
Transient quarters 26. *Commissary:* Yes; *Exchange:* Retail store; Barber shop; Dry cleaners;
Florist; Bank; Service station; Military clothing
store; Convenience store; Beauty shop; Credit
union; ATM; Post office; Fast food; Video rentals; Four seasons; Thrift shop; Travel agency;
Class VI; Tailor/Alterations; Laundry. *Child
Care/Capacities:* Day care center capacity 64,
4mo-5yrs; Home day care program; Summer
day camp; Before & after school programs.
Schools: College courses. *Base Library:* Yes.
Medical Facilities: Medical clinic; Dental clinic;
Pharmacy; *Recreational Facilities:* Bowling center; Movie theater; Pool; Gym; Recreation center; Golf course; Stables; Tennis courts;
Racquetball court; Fitness center/Weight room;
Softball field; Football field; Auto shop; Craft
shop; Fishing/Hunting; Youth center; Picnic
area; Skeet range; Playground; Consolidated
club; Enlisted lounge.

Elliott

480. Camp McCain Training Site
3152 Camp McCain Rd
Elliott, MS 38926

601-227-3611; FAX 601-227-3616
Profile
BRANCH: Army National Guard.
LOCATION: N-central Mississippi; 105 mi N of
Jackson. *County:* Grenada; Montgomery.
MAJOR UNITS: Camp McCain (ARNG).
Key Contacts
COMMANDER: Maj Sam Massey.

Gulfport

481. Gulfport-Biloxi Regional Airport, Air National Guard Base
Gulfport, MS 39501
601-868-6200; DSN 363-8200
Profile
BRANCH: Air National Guard.
SIZE AND LOCATION: 269 acres. Within city
limits of Gulfport, off US-90 at Hewes Rd;
Air-to-ground gunnery range 70 mi N.
County: Harrison.
MAJOR UNITS: Mississippi Air National
Guard Field Training Site, HQ; 255th Tacti-
cal Control Squadron (ANG); 1108th Avia-
tion Repair Depot (ARNG); 173rd Civil Engi-
neering Flight.
Personnel and Expenditures
ACTIVE DUTY PERSONNEL: 406 Guard
CIVILIAN PERSONNEL: 118
MILITARY PAYROLL EXPENDITURE: $6.4 mil
Services *Medical Facilities:* Dispensary.

482. Gulfport Naval Construction Battalion Center
Seabee Center
Gulfport, MS 39501-5000
601-871-2555; DSN 868-2555
OFFICER-OF-THE-DAY: 601-871-2555, DSN
868-2555
Profile
BRANCH: Navy.
SIZE AND LOCATION: 1100 acres. Off I-10 in
Gulfport, MS, 70 mi E of New Orleans and
60 mi W of Mobile, AL. *County:* Harrison.
MAJOR UNITS: 1st Naval Mobile Construction
Bn; 7th Naval Mobile Construction Bn; 74th
Naval Mobile Construction Bn; 133rd Naval
Mobile Construction Bn; 20th Naval Con-
struction Regiment; Naval Construction Train-
ing Center; Naval Reserve Center.
BASE HISTORY: 1942, Advanced Base Depot
established: Armed Guard School, Cooks and
Bakers School, Advanced Base Receiving
Barracks added. 1944, Naval Training Center
established. 1945, depot became US Naval
Storehouse. 1946, training center decommis-
sioned. 1948, national stockpile: bauxite, tin,
copper, sisal, and abaca. 1952, Naval Storehouse disestablished; Naval Construction Battalion Center established. Since 1969, center
in constant state of construction.
VISITOR ATTRACTIONS: Seabee Museum.
Key Contacts
COMMANDER: Capt Louis Marchette,
601-871-3320, DSN 868-3320.
PUBLIC AFFAIRS: Nancy C Brooks, Code 15,
601-871-2699, FAX 601-871-2975, DSN
868-2699, ncbrooks@cbcgulf.navfac.navy.
mil.
Personnel and Expenditures
ACTIVE DUTY PERSONNEL: 3388
CIVILIAN PERSONNEL: 775

MILITARY PAYROLL EXPENDITURE: $91.3
mil (military and civilian)
CONTRACT EXPENDITURE: $215 mil (eco-
nomic impact)
Services
Housing: Family units 107; Unaccompanied officer quarters 56; Unaccompanied enlisted quarters 2112; Trailer spaces 25; Navy lodge. *Temporary Housing:* Lodge units 13. *Commissary:*
Yes; *Exchange:* Retail store; Barber shop; Dry
cleaners; Florist; Bank; Service station; Family
service center. *Child Care/Capacities:* Day care
center capacity 180. *Base Library:* Yes. *Medical
Facilities:* Medical clinic; Dental clinic. *Recreational Facilities:* Bowling center; Movie theater;
Pool; Gym; Recreation center; Golf course; Tennis courts; Racquetball court; Fitness center/
Weight room; Softball field; Auto shop; Craft
shop; NCO club; Fishing.

483. US Naval Home
USNH
1800 Beach Dr
Gulfport, MS 39507-1597
1-800-332-3527; FAX 601-896-8526; DSN
868-2727
Internet: http://www.afrh.com/navyhome.htm
Profile
BRANCH: Navy.
SIZE AND LOCATION: 38 acres. On the beach
(Frontage Rd) Hwy 90, Gulfport, MS; approx
6 mi from Naval Construction Battalion Cen-
ter, Gulfport, and Keesler AFB, Biloxi, MS.
County: Harrison.
MAJOR UNITS: US Naval Home; Armed
Forces Retirement Home (AFRH).
BASE HISTORY: 1834, original Naval Asylum
(renamed Naval Home in 1880) opened in
Philadelphia, PA, on land owned by William
Penn family. 1976, relocated to Gulfport facil-
ity, 11-story highrise on grounds of former
Gulf Coast Military Academy, military pre-
paratory school for boys & annex 3, Kessler
AFB. Armed Forces Retirement Home main-
tained in part by pay contribution of 50 cents
per month from all active duty enlisted per-
sonnel, warrant officers & limited duty offi-
cers.
Key Contacts
COMMANDER: Frederick M Fox, Jr, Director.
PUBLIC AFFAIRS: Jim Laudermilk.
PROCUREMENT: Resource Management
Officer, 601-896-1323.
Personnel and Expenditures
CIVILIAN PERSONNEL: 183
Services
Housing: Private resident rooms 550. *Exchange:* Retail store; Barber shop; Bank; Convenience store; Beauty shop; Post office. *Base
Library:* Yes. *Medical Facilities:* Medical &
dental care limited to resident care; 60 long-term
care beds. *Recreational Facilities:* Bowling center; Movie theater; Pool; Recreation center; Fitness center/Weight room; Auto shop; Craft
shop; Full range of activities; Transportation to
special events, shopping trips, recreational out-
ings; Bar & lounge; Beach access.

Jackson

484. Adjutant General of Mississippi
PO Box 5027
Jackson, MS 39296-5027
601-973-6232; FAX 601-973-6251
Profile
BRANCH: Army National Guard.
MAJOR UNITS: Mississippi National Guard.
Key Contacts
COMMANDER: Maj Gen James H Garner.

485. Jackson Naval Reserve Center
NAVRESCEN Jackson
181 S Jefferson St
Jackson, MS 39201-2806
601-352-3912; FAX 601-948-5623
Profile
BRANCH: Naval Reserve.
SIZE AND LOCATION: 1.7 acres. Off I-55, ap-
prox 10 mi from Jackson IAP; on edge of
State Fairgrounds. *County:* Hinds.
MAJOR UNITS: REDCOM NINE Activity.
BASE HISTORY: 1949, center activated as
joint Navy/Marine Corps facility. 1979, Ma-
rine Corps moved to Armed Forces Reserve
Center, Jackson.
Key Contacts
COMMANDER: Lt James C Heilman,
heilman@cnrf.nola.navy.mil.
PUBLIC AFFAIRS: LCDR William P Harris.
Personnel and Expenditures
ACTIVE DUTY PERSONNEL: 8; 200 reservists

486. Allen C Thompson Air National Guard Base
172nd AW
Thompson Field
141 Military Dr
Jackson, MS 39208-8881
601-939-3633; FAX 601-936-8634; DSN
731-9310; DSN FAX 731-9634
E-mail: MSJAN.ANG.AF.MIL Internet:http://
172aw.ang.af.mil
Profile
BRANCH: Air National Guard.
SIZE AND LOCATION: 84 acres. Adj to Jack-
son Municipal Airport, 7 mi E of Jackson, off
hwy 475; off I-20 to hwy 475. *County:*
Rankin; Hinds.
MAJOR UNITS: 172nd Tactical Airlift Group
(ANG); 172nd Operations Group (ANG);
172nd Logistics Group (ANG); 172nd Sup-
port Group (ANG).
Key Contacts
COMMANDER: Col William J Lutz,
601-936-8730, FAX 601-936-8634; DSN
731-8730, blutz@msjan.ang.af.mil.
PUBLIC AFFAIRS: Col James L Catt Jr,
601-936-8311, FAX 936-8634, DSN
731-9311, jcatt@msjan.ang.af.mil.
Personnel and Expenditures
ACTIVE DUTY PERSONNEL: 1097 guards-
men
CIVILIAN PERSONNEL: 183
Services *Base Library:* Yes. *Medical Facilities:*
Dispensary. *Recreational Facilities:* Softball
field; All ranks club.

Keesler AFB

487. Keesler Air Force Base

KAFB
720 Chappie James Ave, Rm 106
Keesler AFB, MS 39534-2603
601-377-1110; DSN 597-1110
E-mail: webmaster@www.kee.aetc.af.mil Internet:http://www.kee.aetc.af.mil
OFFICER-OF-THE-DAY: Base Command Post, 601-377-4330, DSN 597-4330

Profile

BRANCH: Air Force.
SIZE AND LOCATION: 3554 acres. Within city limits of Biloxi, between I-10 and US-90. Signs on I-10, US-90, and I-110. Transportation from New Orleans and Gulfport airports; approx 60 mi W of Mobile, AL and 90 mi E of New Orleans. *County:* Harrison.
MAJOR UNITS: 2nd Air Force, HQ; 403rd Air Force Reserve; 53rd Weather Reconnaissance Squadron (Hurricane Hunters); 738th Engineering Installation Squadron; 81st Training Wing; 81st Technical Training Group; 81st Support Group; 81st Logistics Group; 81st Medical Group; 7th Airborne Command & Control Squadron (ACC); 1839th Engineering Installation Group; 1872nd Training Development Squadron; Air Weather Squadron, Det 5; First Sergeant Academy; Navy Technical Training Unit; Air Force Office of Special Investigations, Det 407; Keesler Area Audit Office.
BASE HISTORY: 1941, founded; named for 2nd Lt Samuel Reeves Keesler, aerial observer from Greenwood, MS, killed in action in France, WWI. During WWII, site of Air-Sea Rescue School, Chemical Warfare School, first Rotary Wing School. 1943, women and foreign nationals began training. 1947, became "Electronics Center of the Air Force" with addition of radar school. 1967-73, provided flying training. 1968, personnel administration, astronautics, and space systems courses added. 1980s, added training in Airborne Warning and Control Systems (AWACS), Ground-Launched Cruise Missile & Air Traffic Control Training Program. 1990s, weather observation & forecasting training transferred here from Chanute AFB, IL, and Instrumentation, Calibration, and Space Maintenance Systems Management training from Lowry AFB, CO. 1993, inactivation of Training Center & replacement by 81st Training Wing from England. Currently has courses in avionics, computer systems, radio systems, and radar systems.
VISITOR ATTRACTIONS: Guided/self-guided tours, drive-through tours available by calling Community Relations Office 601-377-7329, 377-2254, DSN 597-7329, 597-2254. 24-hour arrival point is Muse Manor or Shaw House. Second largest Medical Center in Air Force.

Key Contacts

COMMANDER: Brig Gen Andrew J Pelak, Jr, Wing Commander, 81st TRW/CC, Rm 204, 601-377-2411, DSN 597-2411.
PUBLIC AFFAIRS: Anne B Gunter, 81st TRW/PA, 601-377-2783, FAX 601-377-3940, DSN 597-2783.
PROCUREMENT: Maj Lonnie Ford, 81st Contracting Squadron, 601-377-3131, DSN 597-3131.
TRANSPORTATION: LTC J H Rainey, 81st Transportation Squadron, 601-377-2525, DSN 597-2525.
PERSONNEL/COMMUNITY ACTIVITIES: LTC Nancy Weaver, 81st Mission Support Squadron, 601-377-3185, DSN 597-3185.

Personnel and Expenditures

ACTIVE DUTY PERSONNEL: 11,521
DEPENDENTS: 5078
CIVILIAN PERSONNEL: 4302
MILITARY PAYROLL EXPENDITURE: $212 mil
CONTRACT EXPENDITURE: $14 mil

Services

Housing: Family units 1951; Duplex units 1236; Townhouse units 400; Dormitory spaces 2786; Mobile home units 49. *Temporary Housing:* VIP units 8 enlisted, 6 officer units; VOQ units 342; VAQ units 958; Transient quarters 73. *Commissary:* Yes; *Exchange:* Retail store; Barber shop; Dry cleaners; Food shop; Florist; Bank; Service station; Furniture store; Bakery; Military clothing store; Convenience store; Credit union; ATM; Optical store; Post office; Fast food; Video rentals; Thrift shop; Travel agency; Class VI; Garden center; Tailor/Alterations; Laundry. *Child Care/Capacities:* Day care center capacity 1076, 12mos-5yrs; Home day care program; Before & after school programs. *Schools:* College courses; No on-base schools. *Base Library:* Yes. *Medical Facilities:* Hospital 135; Medical clinic; Dental clinic; Dispensary; Pharmacy; Veterinary services. *Recreational Facilities:* Bowling center; Movie theater; Pool; Gym; Recreation center; Golf course; Tennis courts; Racquetball court; Fitness center/Weight room; Softball field; Football field; Auto shop; Craft shop; Officers club; NCO club; Enlisted club; Youth center; Picnic area; Playground; Marina with boat rentals.

Meridian

488. Key Field, Air National Guard Base

6225 M St
Meridian, MS 39302-1825
601-484-9000; DSN 778-9210

Profile

BRANCH: Air National Guard.
SIZE AND LOCATION: 117 acres. Within city limits of Meridian, on Hwy 11 S between I-59 and US-11 near Municipal Airport. *County:* Lauderdale.
MAJOR UNITS: 186th Air Refueling Wing (ANG); 238th Combat Communications Squadron (ANG).
BASE HISTORY: 1939, activated as 153rd Observation Squadron at Key Field, named for Al & Fred Key, pioneers in air refueling techniques (their plane, the *Ole Miss*, permanently displayed in Air & Space Museum, Washington, DC). 1940, active duty as part of 67th Observation Group; redesignated 153rd Liaison Squadron. 1945, reorganized into MS ANG. 1946, federal recognition as 153rd Fighter Squadron. 1951-52, active duty as escort squadron, SAC. 1952, returned to state control as 153rd Tactical Reconnaissance Squadron. 1956-58, moved to Gulfport, MS. 1962, renamed 186th Tactical Reconnaissance Group. 1992, converted to 186th Air Refueling Group Air Mobility Command. Oldest ANG unit in MS.

Personnel and Expenditures

ACTIVE DUTY PERSONNEL: 1069 Guard
CIVILIAN PERSONNEL: 329
MILITARY PAYROLL EXPENDITURE: $21.1 mil

489. Meridian Naval Air Station

NASMER
1155 Rosenbaum Ave, Ste 13
Meridian, MS 39309-5003
601-679-2211; FAX 601-679-2160; DSN 637-2211

Profile

BRANCH: Navy.
SIZE AND LOCATION: 8064 acres; plus 5000 acres outlying fields. Approx 89 mi from Jackson, MS, 15 mi NE of Meridian, MS, on Hwy 39 N, clearly marked access road to main gate. *County:* Lauderdale; Kemper; Neshoba.
MAJOR UNITS: Naval Technical Training Center; Marine Aviation Training Support Group; Training Air Wing 1; Training Squadron 19 (VT-19); Training Squadron 23 (VT-23); Training Squadron 7 (VT-7); Regional Counterdrug Training Academy.
BASE HISTORY: 1961, commissioned Naval Auxiliary Air Station (NAAS), home to VT-7, & VT-9 to train fleet jet pilots (1 of 2 in US). 1968, full NAS. 1971, Training Air Wing 1 commissioned. 1982, upgraded to Major Shore Command. Additional mission to train all of Navy's enlisted supply & administrative personnel. Main base largely undeveloped forest land; improved area: administration area, family housing area, & air operations area (Centroid Area). Outlying sites: Outlying Landing Field (OLF) Bravo in NW Kemper County, 18 mi NW of station, and OLF Alpha, in S-central Noxubee County, 22 mi N of main base (currently leased to Air Force under host-tenant agreement, 1978). Multipurpose Target Range, in W-central Noxubee County, 33 mi NW of main base.
FUTURE CLOSURE/REALIGNMENT: Recommended to remain open by BRAC 95.

Key Contacts

COMMANDER: Capt Bernard M Satterwhite, Jr, 601-679-2111, DSN 637-2111.
PUBLIC AFFAIRS: Susan Junkins, 601-679-2602, DSN 637-2602.
PROCUREMENT: John Eldridge, 601-679-3169, DSN 637-3169.
TRANSPORTATION: Ed Dempsey, 601-679-2463.

Personnel and Expenditures

ACTIVE DUTY PERSONNEL: 2500
DEPENDENTS: 1170
CIVILIAN PERSONNEL: 1450

Services

Housing: Family units 518; Unaccompanied enlisted quarters 140; Duplex units 320; Townhouse units 18; Barracks spaces 92; Dormitory spaces 1354; Senior NCO units 32; Junior NCO units 277. *Temporary Housing:* VIP units 5; VOQ units 115; Unaccompanied officer/Enlisted quarters 120. *Commissary:* Yes; *Exchange:* Retail store; Barber shop; Dry cleaners; Food shop; Florist; Bank; Service station; Military clothing store; Convenience store; Beauty shop; Credit union. *Child Care/Capacities:* Day care center; Home day care program; Summer day camp. *Schools:* College courses. *Base Library:* Yes. *Medical Facilities:* Medical clinic; Dental clinic; Dispensary; Pharmacy; Veterinary services.

Recreational Facilities: Bowling center; Pool; Gym; Recreation center; Golf course; Stables; Tennis courts; Racquetball court; Fitness center/ Weight room; Softball field; Football field; Auto shop; Officers club; NCO club; Camping; Fishing/Hunting; Youth center; Picnic area; Skeet range; Water sports; Playground; Wood shop.

Pascagoula

490. Pascagoula Naval Station
NAVSTA PAS
Pascagoula, MS 39595
601-761-2140; FAX 601-761-2025; DSN 358-2140
Internet: http://www.datasync.com/navsta/
Profile
BRANCH: Navy.
SIZE AND LOCATION: 187 acres. On Singing River Island, on Gulf Coast, 10 mi S of I-10; 35 mi E of Gulfport, MS; 30 mi W of Mobile, AL. *County:* Jackson.
MAJOR UNITS: Naval Station, Pascagoula; Shore Intermediate Maintenance Activity; Naval Supply Center Det, Pensacola; USS *Ticonderoga*; USS *Yorktown*; USS *John L Hale*; USS *Stephen W Groves*; USS *Thomas S Gates*.
BASE HISTORY: 1987-88, causeway & station construction. 1992, dedicated; first ship arrived; Shore Intermediate Maintenance Activity opened. 1993, ammunition magazines opened.
VISITOR ATTRACTIONS: Mississippi Medal of Honor Park. Tours of NS scheduled through PAO.
Key Contacts
COMMANDER: CDR Christy J Wheeler.
PUBLIC AFFAIRS: 601-761-2019, DSN 358-2019.
PROCUREMENT: Supply Officer, 601-761-2006, DSN 358-2006.
Personnel and Expenditures
ACTIVE DUTY PERSONNEL: 1600
CIVILIAN PERSONNEL: 160
Services
Housing: Unaccompanied enlisted quarters 154. *Temporary Housing:* None. *Exchange:* Minimart; Class VI; Some uniform items. *Child Care/ Capacities:* No day care facilities. *Schools:* No on-base schools. *Medical Facilities:* Medical clinic; Dental clinic. *Recreational Facilities:* Gym; Tennis courts; Fitness center/Weight room; Softball field; Nature trail.

491. Pascagoula, Supervisor of Shipbuilding, Conversion and Repair
SUPSHIP PAS
PO Box 7003
Pascagoula, MS 39568-7003
601-769-6160; DSN 457-6160
Internet: http://www.datasync.com/~sospasc/
Profile
BRANCH: Navy.
SIZE AND LOCATION: 611 acres (shipyard). At Ingalls Shipyard, Pascagoula. *County:* Jackson.
MAJOR UNITS: Supervisor of Shipbuilding, Conversion, and Repair, Pascagoula.
BASE HISTORY: 1951, established. Navy activity housed in contractor facility with responsibility for administering Navy shipbuilding contracts of 11 private shipyards along Gulf Coast. Navy owns property at Lakeside Manor which supports ships' crews when in port for overhaul & repair of naval vessels at contractor's facilities.
Key Contacts
COMMANDER: Capt Harry J Rucker, Supervisor of Shipbuilding, 601-769-4242, DSN 457-4242.
PUBLIC AFFAIRS: 601-769-4375, DSN 457-4375.
PROCUREMENT: Contracts, 601-769-4250, DSN 457-4250.
TRANSPORTATION: 601-769-4809, DSN 457-4809.
PERSONNEL/COMMUNITY ACTIVITIES: 601-769-4186, DSN 457-4186; MWR, 601-769-4604.
Personnel and Expenditures
ACTIVE DUTY PERSONNEL: 59
CIVILIAN PERSONNEL: 354
Services
Housing: Unaccompanied enlisted quarters; BAQ units 84; *Exchange:* Retail store; Military clothing store. *Medical Facilities:* Medical clinic; Dental clinic. *Recreational Facilities:* Softball field.

Stennis Space Center

492. Mississippi Army Ammunition Plant
MSAAP
AH: SMCMS-CO
Stennis Space Center, MS 39529-7000
601-689-8902
Profile
BRANCH: Army.
SIZE AND LOCATION: 5000 acres. In Stennis Space Ctr, 15 mi from Picayune, MS; 40 mi from Gulfport, MS; 60 mi from New Orleans. *County:* Hancock.
BASE HISTORY: 1978, established as GOCO ammunition plant as part of NASA space complex, which includes other Navy, contractor, and NASA installations. 1990, an inactive plant with no military functions.
Personnel and Expenditures
ACTIVE DUTY PERSONNEL: 0
CIVILIAN PERSONNEL: 65

493. Naval Meteorology and Oceanography Command
COMNAVMETOCCOM
1020 Balch Blvd
Stennis Space Center, MS 39529-5005
601-688-2211
Internet: http://www.cnmoc.navy.mil/
Profile
BRANCH: Navy.
SIZE AND LOCATION: Offices only. At John C Stennis Space Center, near Bay St Louis, MS. *County:* Hancock.
MAJOR UNITS: Naval Meteorology and Oceanography Command.
BASE HISTORY: Command began as Depot of Charts & Instruments. 1970s, Navy's meteorology & oceanography programs merged.
Key Contacts
COMMANDER: RADM Paul G Gaffney II.

494. Naval Research Laboratory, Stennis Space Center
NRL-SSC
Director, Code 7030
Stennis Space Center, MS 39529-5004
601-688-5328; FAX 601-688-5552
Internet: http://www.nrlssc.navy.mil/
Profile
BRANCH: Navy.
SIZE AND LOCATION: 200,000 sq ft. At Stennis Space Center in SW corne of MS; 50 mi NE of New Orleans; 30 mi from Mississippi Gulf Coast. *County:* Hancock.
MAJOR UNITS: Naval Research Laboratory, Stennis Space Center; Naval Meteorology and Oceanography Command, Commander; Naval Oceanographic Office, Stennis Space Center.
Key Contacts
COMMANDER: Capt Buckley; Grant R Bower, Director.
PUBLIC AFFAIRS: Sherryl Carbonaro, Head, Public Affairs Office, Code 7030.3, SSC, MS 39529-5004; Becky Rotundo, 601-688-5328, FAX 601-688-5552, becky.rotundo@nrlssc. navy.mil.

Vicksburg

495. US Army Corps of Engineers, Mississippi Valley Division/ Mississippi River Commission
CEMVD
1400 Walnut St
Vicksburg, MS 39180
Mailing Address
PO Box 80
Vicksburg, MS 39181-0080
601-634-57580; FAX 601-634-7110
E-mail: webmaster@smtp.lmk.usace.army.mil
Internet:http://www.lmv.usace.army.mil/
Profile
BRANCH: Army.
SIZE AND LOCATION: Offices only. LMVD Laboratory at 3909 Halls Ferry Rd, Vicksburg, MS 39180 (601-634-2122). *County:* Warren.
MAJOR UNITS: Corps of Engineers, Mississippi Valley Division; Corps of Engineers, Mississippi River Commission.
BASE HISTORY: 1879, created by Act of Congress. Responsible for civil works in Mississippi Valley. Performs civil works construction & civil works real estate.
Key Contacts
COMMANDER: Brig Gen(P) Robert B Flowers, Commander.
PUBLIC AFFAIRS: Karen Buehler, 601-634-7729, CEMVD-PA@USACE. ARMY.MIL.

496. US Army Corp of Engineers, Vicksburg District
Vicksburg, MS 39180-5191
601-631-5042
E-mail: webmaster@smtp.lmk.usace.army.mil
Internet:http://www.lmk.usace.army.mil/
Profile
BRANCH: Army.
LOCATION: *County:* Warren.

MAJOR UNITS: Corps of Engineers, Vicksburg District.

Key Contacts

COMMANDER: Col Gary W Wright, Commander.

PUBLIC AFFAIRS: Michael Logue, 601-631-5052.

497. US Army Corps of Engineers, Waterways Experiment Station
CEWES
WES

3909 Halls Ferry Rd
Vicksburg, MS 39180-6199
601-636-3111; FAX 601-634-2388
Internet: http://www.wes.army.mil

Profile

BRANCH: Army.

SIZE AND LOCATION: 700 acres. Main entrance 2 mi S of I-20 on Halls Ferry Rd. *County:* Warren.

MAJOR UNITS: Corps of Engineers, Waterways Experiment Station.

BASE HISTORY: 1929, established as hydraulics laboratory to help control floods in lower MS Valley. Today, principal research and development facility of Corps of Engineers. 5-laboratory complex: Environmental, Coastal & Hydraulics, Geotechnical, Information Technology, and Structures laboratories. Solves engineering & scientific problems for federal, state & local government, industry, or individuals on a reimbursable basis. Performs military & civil works construction.

VISITOR ATTRACTIONS: Water resources demonstration model; Nature trail; Niagara River & Falls model; Landing mat & membrane display & experimental vehicles; Special services are provided for reception of official & casual visitors; Guided tours conducted twice daily on weekdays for general public, special tours conducted for professional & civic groups.

Key Contacts

COMMANDER: Robert W Whalin, Director, 601-634-2513; COL Bruce K Howard, Deputy Dir.

PUBLIC AFFAIRS: Billy C Bridges, Chief, Public Affairs Office, PO Box 631, Bldg 1000, 601-634-2504, FAX 634-2361, bridgesb@ex1.wes.army.mil.

PROCUREMENT: Chief, Contracting Office, PO Box 631, Bldg 3072, 601-634-2624.

TRANSPORTATION: Chief, Transportation and Travel Management Branch, PO Box 631, Bldg 2059, 601-634-2933.

PERSONNEL/COMMUNITY ACTIVITIES: Chief, Vicksburg Area Engineer Consolidated Civilian Personnel Office, PO Box 80, 601-634-5133.

Personnel and Expenditures

ACTIVE DUTY PERSONNEL: 10

CIVILIAN PERSONNEL: 1400

Services

Housing: Family units 12. *Exchange:* Retail store; Two concession areas. *Base Library:* Yes. *Medical Facilities:* Health and safety services, First aid center. *Recreational Facilities:* Tennis courts; Racquetball court; Softball field; Fishing/Hunting; Soccer field; Jogging track.

Missouri

Bridgeton

498. Lambert Field Air National Guard Base
10800 Lambert International Blvd
Bridgeton, MO 63044
314-263-6331; DSN 693-6331

Profile
BRANCH: Air National Guard.
SIZE AND LOCATION: 50 acres. In NW St
Louis, near intersection of I-70 & US-67 at St
Louis IAP. *County:* St Louis.
MAJOR UNITS: 131st Fighter Wing (ANG);
110th Weather Flight.

Key Contacts
COMMANDER: Col George D Graves,
314-263-6200, DSN 693-6200.

Personnel and Expenditures
ACTIVE DUTY PERSONNEL: 1235
CIVILIAN PERSONNEL: 306

499. Saint Louis Naval & Marine Corps Reserve Center
NMCRC St Louis
10810 Lambert International Blvd
Bridgeton, MO 63044-2314
314-263-6490; FAX 314-263-6419; DSN
693-6490

Profile
BRANCH: Naval Reserve; Marine Corps Re-
serve.
SIZE AND LOCATION: 9 acres. On MO ANG
base at Lambert Field. *County:* St Louis.
MAJOR UNITS: REDCOM NINE Activity;
HQ, 3rd Bn, 24th Marine Regiment; HQ &
Service Co, 3rd Bn, 24th Marine Regiment;
Det 5, MARFORPAC.
BASE HISTORY: Naval reserves in Saint Louis
date back to 1904. 1961, present building con-
structed on site of old naval air station. 1996,
22,000-ft addition added.

Key Contacts
COMMANDER: Capt Vernon Bothwell.

Personnel and Expenditures
ACTIVE DUTY PERSONNEL: 24
DEPENDENTS: 0
CIVILIAN PERSONNEL: 0

Services *Recreational Facilities:* Consolidated
club.

Cape Girardeau

500. Cape Girardeau Naval Reserve Center
2530 Maria Louise Lane
Cape Girardeau, MO 63701-4393
573-335-3051; FAX 573-335-4231

Profile
BRANCH: Naval Reserve.
SIZE AND LOCATION: 4.85 acres. Approx
120 mi S of St Louis, MO; just off I-55; ap-
prox 8 mi from Cape Girardeau Regional Air-
port. *County:* Cape Girardeau.
MAJOR UNITS: REDCOM NINE Activity;
NMCB 28 Det 0428; SIMA San Diego 2318
(NR); Food Service FUNC TM 2 (NR);
NAVHOSP CLEJEUNE 0309 (NR); Volun-
teer Training Unit 1801 (NR).
BASE HISTORY: 1965, moved to present loca-
tion.

Key Contacts
COMMANDER: CDR T J Gunnell.
PUBLIC AFFAIRS: LCDR M K Casetta.

Personnel and Expenditures
ACTIVE DUTY PERSONNEL: 171 reservists

Fort Leonard Wood

501. Fort Leonard Wood
US Army Engineer Center & Fort Leonard
Wood
Fort Leonard Wood, MO 65473-5000
573-596-0131; DSN 581-0131
Internet: http://www.wood.army.mil/

Profile
BRANCH: Army.
SIZE AND LOCATION: 62,910 acres. 125 mi
SW of St Louis, MO, off I-44 at Waynesville/
St Robert Exit. *County:* Pulaski; Laclede.
MAJOR UNITS: Army Engineer Center; Army
Engineer School; 1st Engineer Brigade; 3rd
Training Brigade; Army Garrison, Ft Leonard
Wood; Libby Noncommissioned Officer
Academy; 43rd Adjutant General Bn; 399th
Army Band; 463rd Military Police Co; 35th
Engineer Bn; 169th Engineer Bn; 554th Engi-
neer Bn; 58th Transportation Bn; 577th Engi-
neer Bn; 5th Engineer Bn (Combat)(Mecha-
nized); 10th Infantry Regiment.
BASE HISTORY: 1940, Seventh Corps Area
Training Center completed. 1941, renamed
for Maj Gen Leonard Wood, Army surgeon,

Rough Rider, Military Gov of Cuba & Philip-
pines & Medal of Honor recipient. 1941, HQ
designation changed to Engineer Replacement Training Center (ERTC). 1943, served
as POW camp. 1946, inactivated; used for
summer training of NG. 1950, reactivated under 6th Armored Division (Training). 1953,
Army Reception Station established. 1955,
5th Army training camp established. 1956, redesignated US Army Training Center, Engineer; only temporary post until then (original
orders designated it "Fort"), made permanent
military installation. 1965, Gen Leonard
Wood Army Hospital built. Mission of Engineer School to train Army Engineer Officers.
School began with US Military Academy,
West Point. 1866, Essayons Club founded at
Willets Point, NY, out of that Engineer
School of Application established (recognized
by War Dept, 1885). 1901, school moved to
Washington Barracks, DC. After WWII,
moved to Camp Humphreys (later Ft
Belvoir), VA. 1988, transferred to Ft Leonard
Wood.
VISITOR ATTRACTIONS: Army Engineer
Museum; WWII display barracks.

Key Contacts
COMMANDER: Maj Gen Robert Flowers; Brig
Gen Edwin J Arnold Jr, Deputy
Commanding General; Col M Stephen
Rhoades, Chief of Staff.
PUBLIC AFFAIRS: 573-563-4013.
PROCUREMENT: Directorate of Contracting,
573-596-0266.
TRANSPORTATION: Directorate of Logistics,
573-596-0614.
PERSONNEL/COMMUNITY ACTIVITIES:
Civilian Personnel Advisory Center,
573-596-0280.

Personnel and Expenditures
ACTIVE DUTY PERSONNEL: 10,900; Guard
100; Reserve 200
DEPENDENTS: 5100
CIVILIAN PERSONNEL: 4400

Services
Housing: Family units 2864; Barracks spaces;
Senior NCO units; Junior NCO units; Trailer
spaces 20; BOQ/BEQ 2680. *Temporary Housing:* VIP units 9; VOQ units 510; VEQ units 70;
Guesthouse units 70; *Commissary:* Yes; *Exchange:* Retail store; Barber shop; Dry cleaners;
Florist; Service station; Furniture store; Bookstore; Convenience store; Beauty shop; Optical
store. *Child Care/Capacities:* Day care center
284; Home day care program.

Schools: Preschool/Kindergarten; Elementary; Intermediate/Junior high. *Base Library:* Yes. *Medical Facilities:* Hospital 75 beds; Dental clinic; Dispensary; Pharmacy; Veterinary services. *Recreational Facilities:* Bowling center; Pool; Golf course; Fitness center/Weight room; Auto shop; Stables; Movie theater; Gym; Tennis courts; Racquetball court; Softball field; Craft shop; Camping; Fishing/Hunting; Officers club; NCO club; Consolidated club.

Independence

502. Lake City Army Ammunition Plant
LCAAP
ATTN: SIOLC-AO
Independence, MO 64051-0250
816-796-7156; FAX 816-796-7124; DSN
463-9156, DSN FAX 463-9124
E-mail: LAKE-CITY-AAP@ria-emh2.army.mil
OFFICER-OF-THE-DAY: 816-796-7114, DSN
   463-9114
Profile
BRANCH: Army.
SIZE AND LOCATION: 3935 acres. Approx 23
   E of Kansas City, MO; 7 mi E of Inde-
   pendence, MO, on Rte 7 off I-70; 30 mi from
   Richards-Gebaur AFB, MO; 45 mi from
   Whiteman AFB, MO; 5 mi N of Blue
   Springs, MO; 3 mi W of Buckner, MO.
   Served by Kansas City IAP & Kansas City
   Municipal Airport. *County:* Jackson.
MAJOR UNITS: Corps of Engineers; Defense
   Contract Audit Agency.
BASE HISTORY: 1941, plant opened as GOCO
   facility, owned by government, controlled by
   Army Industrial Operations Command (IOC);
   operated by Remington Arms Co, Inc. 1946-
   51, plant inactive. 1985, Olin Corp-Winches-
   ter Group took over operations. Plant is only
   active US manufacturer of military small cali-
   ber ammunition. Present production approx
   40 mil rounds/month.
Key Contacts
COMMANDER: LTC Richard R Thibodeau,
   816-796-7111, DSN 463-9111.
PUBLIC AFFAIRS: debbie m parks,
   816-796-7156, dsn 463-9156, dsn FAX
   463-9124, dparks@ria-emh2.army.mil.
PROCUREMENT: Paul D Anthamatten,
   816-796-7131, DSN 463-9131.
TRANSPORTATION: Paul E Hill,
   816-796-7151, DSN 463-9151.
PERSONNEL/COMMUNITY ACTIVITIES:
   See Public Affairs Officer.
Personnel and Expenditures
ACTIVE DUTY PERSONNEL: 2
DEPENDENTS: 30
CIVILIAN PERSONNEL: 1234
CONTRACT EXPENDITURE: $140 mil
Services
Housing: Family units 11. *Temporary Housing:*
None. *Child Care/Capacities:* No day care facili-
ties. *Schools:* No on-base schools. *Medical Fa-
cilities:* Dispensary.

Jefferson City

503. Adjutant General of Missouri
2302 Militia Dr
Jefferson City, MO 65101-1203
573-526-9710; FAX 573-526-9929
Profile
BRANCH: Army National Guard.
MAJOR UNITS: Missouri National Guard.
Key Contacts
COMMANDER: Brig Gen John D Havens.

Kansas City

504. Defense Finance and Accounting Service Center, Kansas City
1500 E 95th St
Kansas City, MO 64197-0001
1-800-449-DFAS; TDD 1-800-558-DFAS; DSN
465-3116
Internet: http://www.dfas.mil/
Profile
BRANCH: DOD.
SIZE: Offices only. *County:* Jackson.
MAJOR UNITS: Defense Finance and Account-
   ing Service Center, Kansas City.
BASE HISTORY: Former Marine Corps Fi-
   nance Center. 1991, consolidated into DFAS.
   Coordinates & supervises pay of all active
   duty, Reserve, retired & survivor annuitants.
   1997, consolidated to present location.
Key Contacts
COMMANDER: Steve E Turner, 816-926-7102.
PUBLIC AFFAIRS: 816-926-2793.
Personnel and Expenditures
CIVILIAN PERSONNEL: 1000 (Total Work-
   force)

505. Kansas City Naval Reserve Readiness Center
3100 E Brush Creek Blvd
Kansas City, MO 64130-2499
816-923-2341; FAX 816-924-4261
Profile
BRANCH: Naval Reserve.
LOCATION: *County:* Jackson.
MAJOR UNITS: REDCOM SIXTEEN Activity.
Key Contacts
COMMANDER: CDR J Lumetta.

506. US Army Corps of Engineers, Kansas City District
CENWK
601 E 12th St
Kansas City, MO 64106-2896
Mailing Address
700 Federal Bldg
Kansas City, MO 64106-2896
816-983-3201; FAX 816-983-5575
Internet: http://www.nwk.usace.army.mil/
Profile
BRANCH: Army.
SIZE AND LOCATION: Offices only. In down-
   town Kansas City. *County:* Jackson.
MAJOR UNITS: Corps of Engineers, Kansas
   City District.
BASE HISTORY: Performs military & civil
   works construction and real estate.

Key Contacts
COMMANDER: Col Robert E Morris, District
   Engineer, 816-983-3201.
PUBLIC AFFAIRS: George F Hanley, Chief,
   Rm 736, 816-983-3486.

Neosho

507. Fort Crowder
890 Carver Ave
Neosho, MO 64850-9169
417-451-5444
Profile
BRANCH: Army National Guard.
LOCATION: SW Missouri; 16 mi SSE of Jop-
   lin. *County:* Newton.
MAJOR UNITS: Fort Crowder.
Key Contacts
COMMANDER: Donald Snyder, Site Manager.

Nevada

508. Camp Clark
RR 3, Box 77
Nevada, MO 64772
417-667-2357
Profile
BRANCH: Army National Guard.
LOCATION: 50 mi N of Joplin. *County:* Ver-
   non.
MAJOR UNITS: Camp Clark (ARNG).

Saint Joseph

509. Rosecrans Memorial Airport, Air National Guard Base
Saint Joseph, MO 64503
816-236-3300; DSN 956-3300
Profile
BRANCH: Air National Guard.
SIZE AND LOCATION: 302 acres. 4 mi W of
   St Joseph. *County:* Buchanan.
MAJOR UNITS: 139th Airlift Wing (ANG).
Personnel and Expenditures
ACTIVE DUTY PERSONNEL: 905 Guard
CIVILIAN PERSONNEL: 291
MILITARY PAYROLL EXPENDITURE: $21.2
   mil

Saint Louis

510. Army Reserve Personnel Center
ARPERCEN
9700 Page Blvd
Saint Louis, MO 63132-5200
314-538-3828; DSN 698-3828
Profile
BRANCH: Army; Army Reserve.
SIZE AND LOCATION: 85 acres. From Hwy
   270 and Page Blvd, 2 mi E on Page; From
   Hwy I-270 and Page Blvd, 0.25 mi W on
   Page; served by St Louis IAP, 10 mi. *County:*
   St Louis.
MAJOR UNITS: Officer Personnel Manage-
   ment Directorate; Enlisted Personnel Manage-

ment Directorate; Mobilization, Operations and Training Directorate; Information Management Directorate; Resource Management Directorate; Personnel Actions & Services Directorate.

BASE HISTORY: 1919, Adjutant General established agency to maintain records of soldiers; demobilized after WWI. After WWII, moved to Saint Louis. 1956, moved to current building. 1971, named Reserve Components Personnel and Administration Center (RCPAC), including Army Reserve; first central nationwide administrative agency for Army Reserve soldiers, including Individual Ready Reserve (IRR). 1983, Army Reserve Personnel Center (ARPERCEN) established as field operating agency of Chief Army Reserve. 1985, RCPAC mission assumed by ARPERCEN: to provide life cycle personnel management services for Army Reserve soldiers to support defined readiness requirements, with focus on mobilization.

Key Contacts
COMMANDER: Col Donald G Condway.
PUBLIC AFFAIRS: LTC Jim Allen, 314-538-3828, DSN 698-3828.

Personnel and Expenditures
ACTIVE DUTY PERSONNEL: 400
CIVILIAN PERSONNEL: 816

Services *Exchange:* Barber shop. *Recreational Facilities:* Fitness center/Weight room; Softball field; Community club.

511. National Imagery and Mapping Agency, Saint Louis
NIMA, St Louis
3200 S 2nd St
Saint Louis, MO 63118-3399
800-455-0899 (24 hours); 314-260-1236; FAX 314-260-1128; DSN 490-1236; DSN FAX 490-1128
E-mail: chdesk@nima.mil Internet:http://www.nima.mil

Profile
BRANCH: DOD.
SIZE: Offices only. *County:* St Louis.
MAJOR UNITS: National Imagery and Mapping Agency, St Louis.
BASE HISTORY: 1995, established replacing Defense Mapping Agency, Aerospace Center.

Key Contacts
PUBLIC AFFAIRS: Michele Williams, NIMA, Office of Congressional & Public Liaison, 8613 Lee Hwy, Fairfax, VA 22031-2137, 703-275-5864, FAX 703-275-8561.

512. Saint Louis Army Publications Distribution Center
USAPDC St Louis
1655 Woodson Rd
Saint Louis, MO 63114-6181
314-263-7305; FAX 314-263-7395; DSN 693-7305
OFFICER-OF-THE-DAY: 314-263-7301, DSN 693-7301

Profile
BRANCH: Army.
SIZE AND LOCATION: 35 acres. 15 mi W of downtown St Louis; 4 mi S of St Louis IAP. *County:* St Louis.
MAJOR UNITS: Army Publications Distribution Center, St Louis.
BASE HISTORY: Serves as primary storage & distribution point for Army technical & sup-

ply publications, recruiting publicity items, classified publications, accountable forms & Army personnel testing materials.
VISITOR ATTRACTIONS: Tour of facilities.

Key Contacts
COMMANDER: 314-263-7300, DSN 693-7300.
PUBLIC AFFAIRS: 314-263-7305, ext 220, DSN 693-7305, ext 220.
PROCUREMENT: 314-263-7305, ext 230, DSN 693-7305, ext 230.
TRANSPORTATION: 314-263-7305, ext 275, DSN 693-7305, ext 275.

Personnel and Expenditures
ACTIVE DUTY PERSONNEL: 2
CIVILIAN PERSONNEL: 120

Services *Recreational Facilities:* Fitness center/Weight room.

513. Saint Louis Coast Guard Base
USCG Base St Louis
Foot of Iron St
Saint Louis, MO 63111
314-832-5941; FAX 314-832-5910

Profile
BRANCH: Coast Guard.
SIZE AND LOCATION: 4.5 acres. On Mississippi Riverfront in S St Louis; 1 mi S of 4200 S Broadway Exit of Hwy 55 S. *County:* St Louis.
MAJOR UNITS: Coast Guard Base, Saint Louis; USCGC *Sumac*; USCGC *Cheyenne*; USCGC *Obion*; 2nd Coast Guard District Armory; Coast Guard Reserve Unit A; Coast Guard Reserve Unit B; Coast Guard Director of Auxiliary.
BASE HISTORY: 1942-44, small buildings constructed to support naval vessels. Since WWII, primarily involved in search and rescue, aids to navigation, logistics, and industrial support.
VISITOR ATTRACTIONS: Weekend tours of base and moored Coast Guard river tenders (Cutters).

Key Contacts
COMMANDER: LCDR R A Rendon; 314-832-5941.
PUBLIC AFFAIRS: Lt R F Olson, Jr.

Personnel and Expenditures
ACTIVE DUTY PERSONNEL: 51
DEPENDENTS: 0
CIVILIAN PERSONNEL: 7

Services
Housing: Barracks spaces 24. *Temporary Housing:* Transient quarters 1. *Exchange:* Florist; Military clothing store; Convenience store; Class VI. *Recreational Facilities:* Pool; Fitness center/Weight room.

514. US Army Corps of Engineers, St Louis District
CEMVS
1222 Spruce St
Saint Louis, MO 63103-2833
314-331-8010; FAX 314-331-8770
Internet: http://www.mvs.usace.army.mil/

Profile
BRANCH: Army.
SIZE: Offices only. *County:* St Louis.
MAJOR UNITS: Corps of Engineers, St Louis District.
BASE HISTORY: 1872, officially established. Comprises about 28,000 sq mi in eastern MO & southwestern IL. Major missions: flood damage reduction, navigation, recreation, en-

vironmental engineering, water supply, hydropower, & others. Performs civil works construction.

Key Contacts
COMMANDER: Col Thomas J Hodgini.
PUBLIC AFFAIRS: Sandra Clawson, 314-331-8002, clawson@smtp.mvs.usace.army.mil.

Personnel and Expenditures
CIVILIAN PERSONNEL: 850

Springfield

515. Springfield Naval & Marine Corps Reserve Center
1110 N Fremont Ave
Springfield, MO 65802-3591
417-869-5721, 869-2858; FAX 417-862-5604

Profile
BRANCH: Naval Reserve; Marine Corps Reserve.
LOCATION: *County:* Greene.
MAJOR UNITS: REDCOM NINE Activity; Weapons Co, 3rd Bn, 24th Marine Regiment.

Key Contacts
COMMANDER: LCDR L D Grippin.

Whiteman AFB

516. Whiteman Air Force Base
WAFB
509 Sprit Blvd, Ste 111
Whiteman AFB, MO 65305-5097
816-687-6123; FAX 816-687-7948; DSN 975-6123; DSN FAX 975-7948
E-mail: bw509pa@hqbw509.whiteman.af.mil
  Internet:http://www.whiteman.af.mil
OFFICER-OF-THE-DAY: Command Post, 816-687-3778, DSN 975-3778

Profile
BRANCH: Air Force.
SIZE AND LOCATION: 5300 acres. 65 mi SE of Kansas City, MO. From E: I-70 to Sedalia Exit onto US-65 S, right on US-50 W in Sedalia, approx 20 mi to Knob Noster Exit, Rte J, left on Rte J (State St) approx 2 mi S to main gate. From W: I-70 to Warrensburg Exit onto State Hwy 13 S, approaching Warrensburg, left onto US-50 E (at end of Hwy 13 overpass), approx 10 mi to State Hwy 132 Exit, right onto State Hwy 132 S for approx 2 mi to Warrensburg entrance. *County:* Johnson.
MAJOR UNITS: 509th Bomb Wing (AFRES); 442nd Fighter Wing (MO NG); Army Aviation Support Facility.
BASE HISTORY: 1942, site selected for Sedalia Army Air Field, a training base for WACO glider pilots. 1947, inactivated. 1951, SAC reactivated base to support B-47 bomber & KC-47 aerial refueling tanker. 1952, 340th BMW activated at redesignated Sedalia AFB. 1955, renamed Whiteman AFB for 2nd Lt George A Whiteman, Sedalia native who died in attack on Pearl Harbor. 1962, 351st Strategic Missile Wing activated. 1980s, 1st female Minuteman missile crew; 1st male/female crew; 1st female squadron commander. 1993, 509th Bomb Wing host with B-2 bombers & active flight operations. 1994, 442nd Fighter Wing comes from Richards-Gebaur AFRB,

Kansas City. 1995, 351st Missile Wing inactivated; Whiteman responsible for network of unused Minuteman II missiles in central MO.

VISITOR ATTRACTIONS: Heritage Center, exhibits of base's history; Peace Park, B-47 Stratojet & Minuteman I missile on display; Only on-base launch control facility (Oscar-1) for MMII missile; B-2 facility.

Key Contacts

COMMANDER: Brig Gen Thomas B Goslin Jr, Ste 509, 816-687-5090, DSN 975-5090.

PUBLIC AFFAIRS: Capt Bruce J Sprecher, 816-687-6124, DSN 975-6124.

PROCUREMENT: Doris Cavanuss, 816-687-5402, DSN 975-5402.

TRANSPORTATION: LTC Sorenson, 816-687-4186, DSN 975-4186.

PERSONNEL/COMMUNITY ACTIVITIES: SSgt Dee Ann Poole, 816-687-6128, DSN 975-6128.

Personnel and Expenditures

ACTIVE DUTY PERSONNEL: 2979
CIVILIAN PERSONNEL: 778
MILITARY PAYROLL EXPENDITURE: $98 mil

Services

Housing: Family units 991; Unaccompanied enlisted quarters 50; Dormitory spaces 674; Senior NCO units 38; Junior NCO units 811. *Temporary Housing:* VIP units; VOQ units; VEQ units; VAQ units; BAQ units; Dormitory units. *Commissary:* Yes; *Exchange:* Retail store; Barber shop; Dry cleaners; Food shop; Florist; Bank; Service station; Military clothing store; Convenience store; Beauty shop;

Child Care/Capacities: Day care center capacity 90, 6mos-5yrs; Home day care program; Latch key program; Summer day camp. *Schools:* Preschool/Kindergarten; Elementary; College courses. *Base Library:* Yes. *Medical Facilities:* Hospital 30; Medical clinic; Dental clinic; Pharmacy; Veterinary services. *Recreational Facilities:* Bowling center; Movie theater; Pool; Gym; Recreation center; Golf course; Tennis courts; Racquetball court; Fitness center/Weight room; Softball field; Football field; Auto shop; Officers club; NCO club; Enlisted club; Youth center; Picnic area; Playground; Fishing; Knob Noster State Park just outside gate.

Montana

Billings

517. Billings Naval & Marine Corps Reserve Center
NAVMARCORESCEN Billings
NMCRC Billings
717 N 22nd St
Billings, MT 59101-6507
406-248-2090; FAX 406-248-2042
E-mail: bil@salts.icpphil.navy.mil Internet:http:/
/www.billings@cnsrf.navy.mil
Profile
BRANCH: Naval Reserve; Marine Corps Reserve.
SIZE AND LOCATION: 1 acre. Marine Reserve 2 mi from Billings (at 2120 8th Ave N, Billings, MT 59101-0398, 406-248-1100, FAX 406-248-9316); Army Reserve 4 mi from Billings; Malstrom AFB 250 mi NW on Hwy 87. *County:* Yellowstone.
MAJOR UNITS: REDCOM TWENTY-TWO Activity; 4th Reconnaissance Bn, Co B (Marine Corps Reserve).
Key Contacts
COMMANDER: CDR Richard Z Ladao.
Personnel and Expenditures
ACTIVE DUTY PERSONNEL: 6; 101 reservists
Services *Base Library:* Yes. *Recreational Facilities:* YMCA.

Forsyth

518. 99th Electronic Combat Range Group
DET 18, RANSS
PO Box 5026
Forsyth, MT 59327-5026
406-356-7935; FAX 406-356-297; DSN 675-5216
E-mail: Flo@MCW.NET
Profile
BRANCH: Air Force.
SIZE AND LOCATION: Housing area, 53 acres; Operational area, 25 acres. Operations area: 22 mi NW of Forsyth MT on US-12, near ghost town of Vananda; 281 mi from support base, Ellsworth AFB, SD. Housing area: E side of Forsyth Mt. *County:* Rosebud.
MAJOR UNITS: 99th Electronic Combat Range Group, Det 18.
BASE HISTORY: Mar 15, 1986, Detachment 18 activated. Jun 4, 1986, began full scoring

operations. 1986-1992, SAC facility established. 1992-present Air Control Center facility.
Personnel and Expenditures
ACTIVE DUTY PERSONNEL: 75
DEPENDENTS: 95
CIVILIAN PERSONNEL: 2
Services
Housing: Family units 50; Dormitory spaces 12. *Temporary Housing:* None. *Commissary:* Yes; *Exchange:* Military clothing store. *Child Care/Capacities:* No day care facilities. *Schools:* No on-base schools. *Medical Facilities:* No medical facilities. *Recreational Facilities:* Recreation center; Tennis courts; Racquetball court; Fitness center/Weight room; Softball field; Football field; Auto shop; Craft shop; Playground.

Great Falls

519. Great Falls Naval Reserve Center
NAVRESCEN Great Falls
2825 Airport Ave B
Great Falls, MT 59404-5571
406-452-3936; FAX 406-452-9765
Profile
BRANCH: Naval Reserve.
LOCATION: *County:* Cascade.
MAJOR UNITS: REDCOM TWENTY-TWO Activity.
FUTURE CLOSURE/REALIGNMENT: Minor closure/realignment to be completed by Sep 1998.
Key Contacts
COMMANDER: CDR T L Schmidt.

520. Malmstrom Air Force Base
Great Falls, MT 59402-5000
406-731-1110; DSN 632-1110
Internet: http://www.malmstrom.af.mil
Profile
BRANCH: Air Force.
SIZE AND LOCATION: 29,067 acres. E of Great Falls, MT, off Hwy 89 Bypass; Great Falls in N-central MT about 75 mi E of Rocky Mts. *County:* Cascade.
MAJOR UNITS: 341st Missile Wing; 819th Red Horse Squadron.
BASE HISTORY: May 1942, construction began on East Base, assigned to training 2nd Air Force bombardment groups. 1943, Station 5, Alaskan Wing, Air Transport Command

(ATC) organized, transferred to Air Service Command, then moved from Gore Field (Great Falls Municipal Airport) to base. 1944, reassigned to Air Transport Command, ferried lend-lease aircraft to USSR; Station 5 deactivated to 1455th Army Air Force Base Unit. Following WWII, supported personnel assigned to Alaskan airbases. 1948, served as training site for Operation Vittles, Berlin Air-Lift. 1954, SAC replaced MATS. 1956, dedicated for Col Einar Axel Malmstrom, Vice Wing Commander, died in air crash; 341st Strategic Missile Wing, dubbed America's "Ace in the Hole" by Pres Kennedy during Cuban Missile Crisis, activated (341st SMW has 200 Minuteman missiles across MT). 1988, first flying wing since 1961, 301st Air Refueling Wing, responsible for KC-135 stratotankers. 1996, KC-135s reassigned to MacDill AFB, FL. 1997, 819th RHS activated.
VISITOR ATTRACTIONS: Malmstrom Heritage Center & Air Park, just inside main gate; sponsored by Malmstrom Historical Foundation (open noon to 3, Mon-Sat, summer, get pass at gate); display of aircraft & missiles previously deployed.
Key Contacts
COMMANDER: Col Glenn C Waltman, 21 77th St N, Rm 144, 59402-7538, 406-731-3411, DSN 632-3411.
PUBLIC AFFAIRS: Capt David W Honchul, 7015 Goddard Dr, Rm 159, 406-731-4044, DSN 632-4044, DSN FAX 632-4048, 34pa@malmstrom.af.mil.
PROCUREMENT: Maj David Schiller, 406-731-3744, DSN 632-3744, DSN FAX 632-4005.
TRANSPORTATION: Maj Kevin Gamaehe, 406-731-6324, DSN 632-6324, DSN FAX 632-6331.
Personnel and Expenditures
ACTIVE DUTY PERSONNEL: 3473
DEPENDENTS: 4727
CIVILIAN PERSONNEL: 407
MILITARY PAYROLL EXPENDITURE: $129 mil
CONTRACT EXPENDITURE: $8 mil
Services
Housing: Family units 1406; Dormitory spaces 1036; Trailer spaces 93. *Temporary Housing:* VOQ units 34; VAQ units 36; Transient quarters 195. *Commissary:* Yes; *Exchange:* Retail store; Barber shop; Dry cleaners; Florist; Bank; Service station; Military clothing store; Convenience store; Beauty shop; Laundromat; ATM; Optical store; Post office; Fast food; Video rentals;

Thrift shop; Travel agency; Class VI; Tailor/Alterations; Laundry; Cafeteria. *Child Care/Capacities:* Day care center capacity 90, 6mos-6yrs; Home day care program; Before & after school programs. *Schools:* College courses. *Base Library:* Yes. *Medical Facilities:* Medical clinic; Dental clinic; Pharmacy; Veterinary services. *Recreational Facilities:* Bowling center; Movie theater; Pool; Gym; Stables; Tennis courts; Racquetball court; Fitness center/Weight room; Softball field; Football field; Auto shop; Craft shop; Camping; Fishing/Hunting; Youth center; Picnic area; Playground; Consolidated club.

521. Montana Air National Guard
MANG
120th Fighter Wing
2800 Airport Ave B
Great Falls, MT 59404-5570
406-791-6202; FAX 406-791-6488; DSN
279-2202; DSN FAX 279-2488
OFFICER-OF-THE-DAY: 406-791-6202, DSN
279-2202
Profile
BRANCH: Air National Guard.
SIZE AND LOCATION: 139 acres. Co-located with Great Falls IAP, W of Great Falls, MT. *County:* Cascade.
MAJOR UNITS: 120th Fighter Wing (ANG); 186th Fighter Squadron (ANG).
BASE HISTORY: 1947, 186th Fighter Squadron formed; equipped with P-51 Mustang aircraft. When unit returned from Korean War, reformed at Great Falls IAP. 1953, 1st Air Guard unit assigned F-86 Sabrejet; unit entered Air Defense role it still performs today. 1956, 120th Fighter Group established. 1984, mission expanded; assigned operation of alert detachment permanently stationed at Davis-Monthan AFB, Tucson, AZ.
Key Contacts
COMMANDER: Col James W Higgins, 406-791-6282, DSN 279-2282, DSN FAX 279-2488, JHIGGINS@MTGTF.ANG.AF. MIL.
PUBLIC AFFAIRS: Maj Iver Johnson, 406-791-6330, DSN 279-2330, DSN FAX 279-2488, IJOHNSON@MTGTF.ANG.AF. MIL.
PROCUREMENT: MSG Patti Seibel, 406-791-6246, DSN 279-2246, PSEIBEL@ MTGTF.ANG.AF.MIL.
TRANSPORTATION: CMS Larry McEwen, 406-791-6315, DSN 279-2315, DSN FAX 279-2488, LMCEWEN@MTGTF.ANG.AF. MIL.

PERSONNEL/COMMUNITY ACTIVITIES: Capt Bryan P Fox, 406-791-6281, DSN 279-2281, DSN FAX 279-2488, BFOX@ MTGTF.ANG.AF.MIL.
Personnel and Expenditures
ACTIVE DUTY PERSONNEL: 75 reservists; 286 technicians
DEPENDENTS: 0
CIVILIAN PERSONNEL: 10
MILITARY PAYROLL EXPENDITURE: $13.3 mil
CONTRACT EXPENDITURE: $6.3 mil
Services
Housing: None. *Exchange:* Convenience store; Credit union; ATM; Cafeteria. *Child Care/Capacities:* No day care facilities. *Schools:* College/University. *Medical Facilities:* Medical clinic. *Recreational Facilities:* Fitness center/Weight room; All ranks club.

Helena

522. Adjutant General of Montana
1100 N Main St
Helena, MT 59604
Mailing Address
PO Box 4789
Helena, MT 59604-4789
406-444-6910; FAX 406-444-6973
Profile
BRANCH: Army National Guard.
MAJOR UNITS: Montana National Guard.
FUTURE CLOSURE/REALIGNMENT: Minor closure/realignment to be completed by Sep 1998.
Key Contacts
COMMANDER: Maj Gen John E Prendergast.

523. Fort William Henry Harrison
Ft Harrison
PO Box 4789
Helena, MT 59604-4789
406-444-6910; FAX 406-444-6973; DSN 747-3010; DSN FAX 747-3073
Profile
BRANCH: Army National Guard.
SIZE AND LOCATION: 2912 acres. 11 mi W of Helena city limits, adj to Veterans Administration Hospital; US-12 W, exit at sign marked VA Hospital & National Guard. *County:* Lewis; Clark.
MAJOR UNITS: State Area Readiness Command, HQ; 1049th Engineer Plt (FFTG);

103rd Public Affairs Det; 208th Regional Training Institute; AHC 1-189th Aviation Co A; AHC 1-189th Aviation Co B; AHC 1-189th Aviation Co C; 163rd Armored Bn; 3669th Maintenance Co.
BASE HISTORY: Late 1800s, established for MT volunteers. 1942, Special Forces (Devil's) Brigade training. 1980s, began to modernize, replacing many pre-WWII structures; added many small arms ranges. Ideal post for winter & mountain terrain training.
Key Contacts
COMMANDER: Maj Gen John E Prendergast, Adjutant General, 406-444-6910, DSN 747-3010.
PUBLIC AFFAIRS: Col Ray Reed, Dept of Military Affairs, State of Montana, PO Box 4789, Helena, MT 59604-4789, 406-444-6995, DSN 747-3095.
PROCUREMENT: Maj Warden, USPFO, PO Box 1157, 59624-1157, 406-444-7920, DSN 747-3120.
TRANSPORTATION: Lt Strom, USPFO, PO Box 1157, 59624-1157, 406-444-7927, DSN 747-3127.
PERSONNEL/COMMUNITY ACTIVITIES: LTC Dwyer, 406-444-6925, DSN 747-3025.
Personnel and Expenditures
ACTIVE DUTY PERSONNEL: 1; Guard 3600 (State)
Services
Housing: BAQ units 12; Dormitory spaces 8. *Temporary Housing:* Dormitory units 4. *Exchange:* Convenience store; Credit union. *Medical Facilities:* Dispensary. *Recreational Facilities:* Officers club; Enlisted club; Picnic area.

Missoula

524. Missoula Naval Reserve Center
Fort Missoula, Bldg 26A
Missoula, MT 59801-7299
406-329-3802; FAX 406-329-3905
Profile
BRANCH: Naval Reserve.
LOCATION: *County:* Missoula.
MAJOR UNITS: REDCOM TWENTY-TWO Activity.
FUTURE CLOSURE/REALIGNMENT: Minor closure/realignment to be completed by Sep 1998.
Key Contacts
COMMANDER: CDR T L Schmidt.

Nebraska

Ashland

525. Camp Ashland
Ashland, NE 68003
402-944-2479
Profile
BRANCH: Army National Guard.
LOCATION: E Nebraska. *County:* Saunders.
MAJOR UNITS: Camp Ashland (ARNG).
Key Contacts
COMMANDER: Maj Schrook.

Grand Island

526. Cornhusker Army Ammunition Plant
102 N 60th Rd
Grand Island, NE 68803
308-381-0313; DSN 939-3690
Profile
BRANCH: Army.
SIZE AND LOCATION: 12,000 acres. Grand Island, NE, near I-80 and NE-281. *County:* Hall.
BASE HISTORY: 1942, WWII ammunition plant built. Base in active production, 1942-1945; during Korean War, 1950-1957; and during Vietnam War, 1965-1973. Current status: excess.
Key Contacts
COMMANDER: Thomas L Jamieson, Commander's Representative.
Personnel and Expenditures
ACTIVE DUTY PERSONNEL: 0
CIVILIAN PERSONNEL: 3
CONTRACT EXPENDITURE: $100,000
Services
Housing: Family units 10 (excess).

Lincoln

527. Adjutant General of Nebraska
1300 Military Rd
Lincoln, NE 68508-1090
402-471-7114; FAX 402-471-7171
Profile
BRANCH: Army National Guard.
MAJOR UNITS: Nebraska National Guard.
Key Contacts
COMMANDER: Maj Gen Stanley M Heng.

528. Lincoln Air National Guard Base
155th ARG
2420 W Butler Ave
Lincoln, NE 68524-1897
402-471-3241; DSN 946-1210
OFFICER-OF-THE-DAY: 402-471-1266, DSN 946-1266
Profile
BRANCH: Air National Guard.
SIZE AND LOCATION: 163 acres. NW corner of city of Lincoln, approx 3 mi from downtown; adj to city airport and parallels I-80. *County:* Lancaster.
MAJOR UNITS: 155th Air Refueling Group (ANG).
BASE HISTORY: Second oldest ANG unit in nation. 1943, began as 401st Fighter Squadron at Westover Field, MA. 1948, NE ANG held first summer field training in Lincoln. Korean War, active service at Dow AFB, Bangor, ME; completed service at Alexandria AFB, LA. 1954, squadron redesignated 173rd FIS, Air Defense Command. 1956, moved to present facilities as SAC base. 1964, mission changed from air defense to tactical photo-reconnaissance. 1994, redesignated 155th Air Refueling Group flying KC-135Rs.
VISITOR ATTRACTIONS: T-33, F-86, and RF-84 static aircraft display.
Key Contacts
COMMANDER: Col Mark R Musick, 402-458-1111, DSN 946-1111, mmusick@ nelink.ang.af.mil.
PUBLIC AFFAIRS: Maj Drew Miller, 402-458-1120, DSN 946-1120, UTA weekends only.
PROCUREMENT: 402-471-1214, DSN 946-1214.
TRANSPORTATION: 402-471-1280, DSN 946-1280.
PERSONNEL/COMMUNITY ACTIVITIES: Capt Dennis Gries, 402-471-1324, DSN 946-1324.
Personnel and Expenditures
ACTIVE DUTY PERSONNEL: 1100 guardsmen
CIVILIAN PERSONNEL: 225
CONTRACT EXPENDITURE: $0.9 mil
Services *Exchange:* Retail store; Food shop. *Recreational Facilities:* Softball field; Officers club; NCO club; Running track.

529. Lincoln Naval Reserve Center
NAVRESCEN Lincoln
4511 NW 42nd St
Lincoln, NE 68524-2241
402-470-2142, 470-2136; FAX 402-0480, 470-2564
E-mail: us82456@navix.net
Profile
BRANCH: Naval Reserve.
LOCATION: Approx 5 mi from downtown Lincoln; follow I-80 to Exit 395, N on NW 48th to Airpark Rd, turn right to NW 42nd, turn left. 3 mi from airport. *County:* Lancaster.
MAJOR UNITS: REDCOM SIXTEEN Activity; VTU 1809G (NR); LST-1184 Support Unit Det B (NR); FH 500 CBTZ 23 Det C (NR); ABFC NOACT D29A (NR); RNMCB 15 Det 0415 (NR); Readiness Unit (NR).
Key Contacts
COMMANDER: CDR Jeffrey K Olson.

Offutt AFB

530. Offutt Air Force Base
OAFB
55 WG
Offutt AFB, NE 68113-5000
402-294-1110; DSN 271-1110
Profile
BRANCH: Air Force.
SIZE AND LOCATION: 4040 acres. 10 mi S of Omaha off I-75; 1 mi S of Fort Crook; 3 mi N of La Platte on US-75. *County:* Sarpy.
MAJOR UNITS: 55th Wing; US Strategic Command; Air Force Global Weather Center; 6949th Electronic Security Squadron; 6th Space Operations Squadron; National Airborne Operations Center; Air Combat Command Band; Ehrling Bergquist Hospital; 343rd Recruiting Squadron; Defense Finance & Accounting Service, Omaha.
BASE HISTORY: 1896, originally intended to replace Ft Omaha, base began as Ft Crook, named for Gen George Crook; many original buildings still in use. WWI, first air unit, 61st Balloon Company, assigned to post. 1920, first flying field established. 1924, field dedicated for Omaha's first air casualty during WWI, Lt Jarvis J Offutt. Following WWI, used mostly for training air reservists. 1930s, aircraft manufacturing plant, Glenn L Martin Nebraska Bomber Assembly Plant, constructed at Offutt Field. WWII, Italian POW

camp established. After WWII, reverted to training facility for Army Reservists. 1948, Offutt Field and Ft Crook designated Offutt AFB, host base for HQ, Strategic Air Command (from Andrews AFB, MD). 1959-65, 566th Strategic Missile Squadron, later 549 SMS, responsible for operations of 3 Atlas D missile launcher sites. 1992, SAC disestablished; US Strategic Command activated.

VISITOR ATTRACTIONS: Fort Crook Historic Distirct.

Key Contacts

COMMANDER: Brig Gen (Sel) Gary A Ambrose, 205 Looking Glass Ave, Ste 121, 402-294-5533, FAX 402-294-7706, DSN 271-5533.

PUBLIC AFFAIRS: Maj Cynthia B Colin, 55 WG/PA, 906 SAC Blvd, Ste 1, 68113-3206, 402-294-3663, FAX 402-294-7172, DSN 271-3663.

PROCUREMENT: 55 CONS/CC, 402-294-2455, DSN 271-2455.

TRANSPORTATION: 55 TRNS/CC, 402-294-4659, DSN 271-4659.

PERSONNEL/COMMUNITY ACTIVITIES: 55 Services Squadron, 402-294-4719, DSN 271-4719.

Personnel and Expenditures

ACTIVE DUTY PERSONNEL: 7415
DEPENDENTS: 15,131
CIVILIAN PERSONNEL: 1621
MILITARY PAYROLL EXPENDITURE: $294.8 mil
CONTRACT EXPENDITURE: $13.1 mil

Services

Housing: Family units 2612. *Temporary Housing:* VOQ units 171; VAQ units 60. *Commissary:* Yes; *Exchange:* Retail store; Barber shop; Dry cleaners; Food shop; Florist; Bank; Service station; Bakery; Military clothing store; Convenience store; Beauty shop; Laundromat; Credit union; ATM; Optical store; Post office; Fast food; Video rentals; Four seasons; Thrift shop; Travel agency; Class VI; Tailor/Alterations; Laundry; Cafeteria. *Child Care/Capacities:* Day care center; Home day care program; Latch key program. *Schools:* No on-base schools. *Base Library:* Yes. *Medical Facilities:* Hospital 60; Medical clinic; Dental clinic; Pharmacy; Veterinary services. *Recreational Facilities:* Bowling center; Movie theater; Pool; Gym; Recreation center; Golf course 2; Stables; Tennis courts; Racquetball court; Fitness center/Weight room;

Softball field; Auto shop; Craft shop; Officers club; Camping; Fishing/Hunting; Enlisted club; Youth center; Picnic area; Skeet range; Water sports; Playground; Community club; Rod & Gun club.

Omaha

531. Omaha Naval & Marine Corps Reserve Center
NNAVMARCORESCEN Omaha; MCRC Omaha
5808 N 30th St
Omaha, NE 68111-1299
402-451-2098; FAX 402-451-6681
E-mail: OMAHA@cnsrf.navy.mil

Profile

BRANCH: Naval Reserve; Marine Corps Reserve.

SIZE AND LOCATION: 10 acres. In N Omaha, 5 mi W of Epply Air Field, 15 mi N of Offutt AFB. *County:* Douglas.

MAJOR UNITS: REDCOM SIXTEEN Activity; NOACT (NR); USSTRATCOM (NR); NEAT (NR); NMCB 15; FLT HOSPITAL 23 Det N (NR); CNAVEUR (NR); Engineer Maintenance Co, 4th Maintenance Bn.

Key Contacts

COMMANDER: CDR John F Kadlec.
PUBLIC AFFAIRS: YN1 Brian K Morse.

Personnel and Expenditures

ACTIVE DUTY PERSONNEL: 10; 300 reservists

Services *Recreational Facilities:* Fitness center/Weight room.

532. US Army Corps of Engineers, Missouri River Regional Office
12565 West Center Rd
Omaha, NE 68144-3869
402-697-2400; FAX 402-697-2720
Internet: http://www.mrd.usace.army.mil/

Profile

BRANCH: Army.

SIZE AND LOCATION: 0.5 acre. In western portion of city of Omaha. *County:* Douglas.

MAJOR UNITS: Corps of Engineers, Missouri River Regional Office.

BASE HISTORY: 1833, Corps began work on Missouri River, pulling snags. 1933, estab-

lished; division office, Kansas City, MO, responsible for improvement of Missouri River & tributaries from Hermann, MO, to headwaters in MT. 1942, moved to Omaha. Today, maintains & operates 45 dams, 600 mi of levees & other flood control structures. Design & construction agent for Army & Air Force in 11 Midwestern states. Home of Centers of Expertise for Transportation systems & Protective Design. 1997, renamed from Missouri River Division to Northwestern Division, Missouri River Regional Office. Performs military & civil works construction and real estate.

Key Contacts

COMMANDER: Col Richard W Craig.

Personnel and Expenditures

ACTIVE DUTY PERSONNEL: 25
CIVILIAN PERSONNEL: 3000

533. US Army Corps of Engineers, Omaha District
CENWO
215 N 17th St
Omaha, NE 68102-4978
402-221-3900; FAX 402-221-3128
Internet: http://wwwcemro.mro.usace.army.mil/

Profile

BRANCH: Army.

SIZE AND LOCATION: Offices only. In downtown Omaha. *County:* Douglas.

MAJOR UNITS: Corps of Engineers, Omaha District.

BASE HISTORY: Military & civil works boundaries encompass more than 700,000 sq mi of northern plains states & upper midwest; part of Missouri River Region of Northwestern Division. Responsible for engineering service for civil works, military design & construction, & hazardous, toxic & radioactive waste.

Key Contacts

COMMANDER: Col Robert D Volz.
PUBLIC AFFAIRS: Betty M White, 402-221-3916.
PROCUREMENT: Donald Robinson, 402-221-4100.
TRANSPORTATION: Norma I Kolbe, 402-221-3241.
PERSONNEL/COMMUNITY ACTIVITIES: Larry Boehm, Human Resources, 402-221-4071.

Services *Base Library:* Yes.

Nevada

Carson City

534. Nevada National Guard Headquarters
2525 S Carson St
Carson City, NV 89701-5502
702-887-7331; FAX 702-887-7333; DSN
830-5331

Profile
BRANCH: Air National Guard; Army National Guard.
SIZE AND LOCATION: 13 acres. In center of Carson City, NV; 3 mi S of junction Hwy 50 & 395. *County:* Carson.
MAJOR UNITS: State Area Readiness Command, HQ; Nevada Army National Guard, HQ; Nevada Air National Guard, HQ; US Property and Fiscal Office; 150th Maintenance Co.
BASE HISTORY: 1883, state militia designated National Guard of Nevada.

Key Contacts
COMMANDER: Maj Gen Drennan A Clark, The Adjutant General, 702-887-7302, DSN 830-5302.
PUBLIC AFFAIRS: Maj Cindy Kirkland.
PROCUREMENT: Col Robert J Hayes, 702-887-7201, DSN 830-5201.
TRANSPORTATION: MSG Larry W Miller, 702-887-7220, DSN 830-5220.
PERSONNEL/COMMUNITY ACTIVITIES: Col Joseph R Rooney, 702-887-7258, DSN 830-5258.

Personnel and Expenditures
ACTIVE DUTY PERSONNEL: 365 guardsmen
CIVILIAN PERSONNEL: 50
MILITARY PAYROLL EXPENDITURE: $800,000

Services *Recreational Facilities:* Gym; Fitness center/Weight room.

Fallon

535. Fallon Naval Air Station
NAS Fallon
4755 Pasture Rd
Fallon, NV 89406-5000
702-426-5161; DSN 890-5161
OFFICER-OF-THE-DAY: 702-426-2715, 890-2715

Profile
BRANCH: Navy.
SIZE AND LOCATION: 57,584 acres; 118,000 acres including ranges.

65 mi E of Reno, NV; 8 mi S of Fallon, NV. *County:* Churchill.
MAJOR UNITS: Naval Air Station, Fallon; Explosive Ordnance Disposal, Group 3, Det Fallon; Naval Pacific Meteorology Oceanography Command Det; Naval Strike & Air Warfare Center; Strike Fighter Wing, Det Fallon; Fighter Squadron Composite 13 (VFC-13); NPMOD (Weather Det).
BASE HISTORY: 1942, Army Air Corps built 4 air bases on eastern side of Sierras for defensive facilities. When threat of Japanese invasion ended, facility at Fallon offered to Navy for training torpedo, attack, and fighter pilots. Designated as Naval Auxiliary Air Station for aircraft operating out of Naval Air Center Alameda. WWII, placed in caretaker status until Korean War; redesignated Auxiliary Landing Field for NAS Alameda. 1953, reestablished as Naval Auxiliary Air Station under Fleet Air Alameda. 1958, landing field named for LCDR Bruce Van Voorhis, Fallon native killed in Battle of Solomon Islands. 1960s, expanded and associated Bombing and Electronic Warfare Ranges (Ranges B-16, B-17, B-19, and B-20) added to prepare air crews for Vietnam. 1972, designated major NAS. 1984, Naval Strike Warfare Center established and expansion of Carrier Battle Groups.
VISITOR ATTRACTIONS: Churchill County Museum in Fallon.

Key Contacts
COMMANDER: Capt S C Ronnie, 702-426-2700, DSN 890-2700, DSN FAX 890-2930.
PUBLIC AFFAIRS: Amme McMillin, APR, 702-426-2880, DSN 890-2880, DSN FAX 890-2930, amcmilli@fallon.navy.mil.
PROCUREMENT: CDR Chet Burton, 702-426-2812, DSN 890-2812, DSN FAX 890-2993, burtone@fallon.navy.mil.
TRANSPORTATION: LCDR Jim Souba, Public Works, 702-426-2712, DSN 890-2712, DSN FAX 890-2680.

Personnel and Expenditures
ACTIVE DUTY PERSONNEL: 1200
DEPENDENTS: 1800
CIVILIAN PERSONNEL: 1300
CONTRACT EXPENDITURE: $42 mil

Services
Housing: Family units mix of townhomes/Duplexes 360; Unaccompanied enlisted quarters bldgs 9; RV/Camper sites; BOQ/BEQ permanent party 350. *Temporary Housing:* Lodge units 6; Transient quarters officer/Enlisted 2000.

Commissary: Yes; *Exchange:* Retail store; Barber shop; Dry cleaners; Food shop; Service station; Furniture store; Military clothing store; Convenience store; Beauty shop; Laundromat; Credit union; ATM; Post office; Four seasons; Thrift shop; Travel agency; Tailor/Alterations; Car rental; Snacks. *Child Care/Capacities:* Day care center capacity 130, 6mos-5yrs; Home day care program; After-school programs. *Schools:* No on-base schools. *Base Library:* Yes. *Medical Facilities:* Medical clinic; Dental clinic; Pharmacy. *Recreational Facilities:* Bowling center; Movie theater; Pool; Gym; Stables; Tennis courts; Racquetball court; Fitness center/Weight room; Softball field; Football field; Auto shop; Craft shop; Officers club; NCO club; Camping Rentals; Enlisted club; Youth center; Picnic area; Playground; All ranks club; Go-cart track; Ski equipment rental.

536. Nevada Army National Guard, Fallon
NVANG
895 E Richards
Fallon, NV 89406
702-423-2452
Internet: http://members.aol.com/ar1221/index.html

Profile
BRANCH: Army National Guard.
SIZE AND LOCATION: 2.0 acres. In W Nevada; at junction of SR-50 & US-95; 53 mi E of Reno. *County:* Churchill.
MAJOR UNITS: 221st Armor, 1st Bn, Det 1, HQ and HQ Co.
BASE HISTORY: Command & train units in Nevada ANG.

Key Contacts
COMMANDER: LTC Arron R Kenneston, 702-887-7243.
PUBLIC AFFAIRS: SSgt Paul J Pishnak, 702-423-2452.

Personnel and Expenditures
ACTIVE DUTY PERSONNEL: 2; Guard 80
CIVILIAN PERSONNEL: 0

Services *Recreational Facilities:* Gym; Fitness center/Weight room.

Hawthorne

537. Hawthorne Army Depot
HWAD
PO Box 5000
Hawthorne, NV 89415-5000
702-945-7001; FAX 702-945-7948; DSN
830-7001; DSN FAX 830-7948
E-mail: hawthorne-ad@ria-emh2.army.mil
Profile
BRANCH: Army.
SIZE AND LOCATION: 147,000 acres. 135 mi
SE of Reno, NV, on Hwy 95, 1 mi from Haw-
thorne; US-95 and State Hwy 359 divide
plant into three separate ammunition storage
and production areas, plus industrial area.
County: Mineral.
MAJOR UNITS: Naval Undersea Warfare Cen-
ter; Marine Corps Program Office.
BASE HISTORY: 1926, following fire at Navy
Ammunition Depot, Lake Denmark, NJ, Hawthorne selected as ammunition storage site;
arid climate & close proximity to West Coast.
1930, Naval Ammunition Depot (NAD) Hawthorne commissioned. 1977, Army designated
as Single Manager for Conventional Ammunition & NAD Hawthorne transferred to Army
Armament, Munitions & Chemical Command
(AMCCOM); renamed Hawthorne Army Am-
munition Plant (HWAAP). 1980, converted to
GOCO installation. Claims to be "World's
Largest Ammunition Depot." Current contrac-
tor, Day & Zimmerman/Hawthorne Corp.
Key Contacts
COMMANDER: LTC James E Ewing, ATTN:
SIOHW-XO, jewing@hawthorne-dz.com.
PUBLIC AFFAIRS: Cpt Gerald M Muhl,
702-945-7018, DSN 830-7018, DSN FAX
830-7948, muhlg@hawthrone-dz.com.
Personnel and Expenditures
ACTIVE DUTY PERSONNEL: 5
CIVILIAN PERSONNEL: 635
Services
Housing: Family units 30; Unaccompanied en-
listed quarters 16; BAQ units; Duplex units 50.
Recreational Facilities: Golf course; Fishing/
Hunting.

Henderson

538. Nevada National Guard
Henderson
PO Box 90759, Pacific & Black Mountain Ave
Henderson, NV 89009-0759
Profile
BRANCH: Army National Guard.
SIZE AND LOCATION: 8.3 acres. In SE corner
of Nevada; 13 mi SE of Las Vegas on US-93/
95. *County:* Clark.
MAJOR UNITS: 221st Armor, 1st Bn, Compa-
nies B, C, and D.
BASE HISTORY: Train armor crew.
Key Contacts
COMMANDER: Maj Gen Drennan A Clark;
The Adjutant General, 702-887-7302, DSN
830-5302.
PUBLIC AFFAIRS: LTC Chris A Anastassatos;
2525 S Carson St, Carson City, NV,
89701-5502.

Personnel and Expenditures
ACTIVE DUTY PERSONNEL: 176 (Guards-
men)
CIVILIAN PERSONNEL: 20
CONTRACT EXPENDITURE: $2.8 mil

Las Vegas

539. Las Vegas Naval & Marine Corps Reserve Center
NMCRC Las Vegas
2801 E Sahara Ave
Las Vegas, NV 89104-4119
702-457-6528; FAX 702-457-4507; DSN
682-4312
Profile
BRANCH: Naval Reserve; Marine Corps Re-
serve.
SIZE AND LOCATION: 1 acre. In city limits of
Las Vegas. *County:* Clark.
MAJOR UNITS: REDCOM NINETEEN Activ-
ity; Camp Pendleton (NR); CB 17 Det 0817
(NR); AD-42 (NR); China Lake (NR).
Key Contacts
COMMANDER: LCDR Resnicke.
Personnel and Expenditures
ACTIVE DUTY PERSONNEL: 8; 216 reservists

540. Nevada National Guard Las Vegas
5150 Boulder Hwy
Las Vegas, NV 89122
Profile
BRANCH: Army National Guard.
SIZE AND LOCATION: 20.9 acres. In SE cor-
ner of Nevada on US-93/95. *County:* Clark.
MAJOR UNITS: Battle Born Brigade; 122nd
Smoke Co; 137th Decontamination Co; 72nd
Military Police Co; 1st FWD, Co B, Det 1;
150th Maintenance Co, Det 1; 221st Armor,
1st Bn, Headquarters and Headquarters Co;
144th Field Artillery, Headquarters and Head-
quarters Bn 2nd Bn, Det 1.
BASE HISTORY: Command and train soldiers
of Nevada ANG.
Key Contacts
COMMANDER: Maj Gen Drennan A Clark;
The Adjutant General, 702-887-7302, DSN
830-5302.
PUBLIC AFFAIRS: LTC Chris A Anastassatos;
2525 S Carson St, Carson City, NV,
89701-5502.
Personnel and Expenditures
ACTIVE DUTY PERSONNEL: 593 (Guardsmen)
CIVILIAN PERSONNEL: 40
CONTRACT EXPENDITURE: $6.9 mil

Nellis AFB

541. Nellis Air Force Base
HQ AWFC/CC, 4370 N Washington Blvd, Ste
117
Nellis AFB, NV 89191-7076
702-652-1110; DSN 682-1110
Internet: http://www.nellis.af.mil
Profile
BRANCH: Air Force.
SIZE AND LOCATION: 11,000 acres; ranges
3.0 mil acres.

Take Craig Rd Exit off I-15, follow signs ap-
prox 8 mi NE of Las Vegas. *County:* Clark.
MAJOR UNITS: Air Warfare Center, HQ; 57th
Wing; 53rd Wing; Air Force Air Demonstra-
tion Squadron (Thunderbirds); Air Force
Weapons School; 57th Logistics Group; 57th
Operations Group; 57th Component Repair
Squadron; 57th Equipment Maintenance
Squadron; 57th Logistics Support Squadron;
57th Operations Support Squadron; 414th
Training Squadron; 422nd Test and Evalu-
ation Squadron; 549th Combat Training
Squadron; 99th Air Base Wing; 99th Logistics Group; 99th Medical Group; 99th Range
Group; 99th Support Group; 11th Reconnaissance Squadron; 39th Intelligence Squadron;
57th Aircraft Generation Squadron; 66th Rescue Squadron; 99th Civil Engineering Squadron; 99th Communications Squadron; 99th
Comptroller Squadron; 99th Contracting
Squadron; 99th Mission Support Squadron;
99th Range Squadron; 99th Range Support
Squadron; 99th Security Forces Squadron;
99th Services Squadron; 99th Supply Squadron; 99th Transportation Squadron; 547th Intelligence Squadron; 820th Red Horse Squadron; 896th Munitions Squadron; Directorate
of Tactics.
BASE HISTORY: 1941, Army Air Corps Flexible Gunnery School training B-17 gunners.
1945, crew training for B-29. Following
WWII, changed to temporary standby status.
1947, closed. 1949, reopened. 1950, renamed
for Lt William Harrell Nellis, NV resident
killed in action over Luxembourg. Korean
War, virtually every fighter pilot trained here.
1958, assigned to TAC. 1966, Tactical
Fighter Weapons Center established. 1990s,
several name changes. 1995, AWC established; manages advanced pilot training & in-
tegrates test & evaluation requirements; pro-
vides realistic training in combined air,
ground, and electronic threats.
VISITOR ATTRACTIONS: Air Force Demonstration Squadron (Thunderbirds) Hangar &
Museum.
Key Contacts
COMMANDER: Maj Gen Marvin R Esmond.
PUBLIC AFFAIRS: AWC 702-652-6448,
652-2750, DSN 682-6448, 682-2750.
PERSONNEL/COMMUNITY ACTIVITIES:
4420 Grissom Ave, Ste 216, 702-652-8184.
Personnel and Expenditures
ACTIVE DUTY PERSONNEL: 6400
CIVILIAN PERSONNEL: 2600
Services
Housing: Duplex units 1467; Dormitory spaces
2000; Mobile home units 100. *Temporary Hous-
ing:* VOQ units; VEQ units; Trailer park. *Com-
missary:* Yes; *Exchange:* Retail store; Barber
shop; Dry cleaners; Food shop; Florist; Bank;
Service station; Furniture store; Bakery; Military
clothing store; Convenience store; Beauty shop;
Laundromat; Credit union. *Child Care/Capaci-
ties:* Day care center capacity 200, 6-10yrs;
Home day care program. *Schools:* Elementary.
Base Library: Yes. *Medical Facilities:* Hospital
35 beds; Dental clinic; Pharmacy; Veterinary
services. *Recreational Facilities:* Bowling center; Movie theater; Pool; Gym; Recreation center; Golf course; Stables; Tennis courts;
Racquetball court; Fitness center/Weight room;
Softball field; Football field; Auto shop; Craft
shop; Officers club; NCO club; Enlisted club;
Youth center; Skeet range; Playground.

Reno

542. Reno Naval & Marine Corps Reserve Center
4601 Cocoa Ave
Reno, NV 89506-1298
702-972-5600; FAX 702-972-5568
Profile
BRANCH: Naval Reserve; Marine Corps Reserve.
LOCATION: *County:* Washoe.
MAJOR UNITS: REDCOM TWENTY-TWO Activity; Det, 4th Force Reconnaissance Co (MARFORRES).
Key Contacts
COMMANDER: LCDR D E Sloat.

543. Reno Nevada Army National Guard Armory
Reno Armory
1000 N Wells Ave
Reno, NV 89512
702-329-0283; FAX 702-329-0584; DSN 830-5412
OFFICER-OF-THE-DAY: 702-329-0283
Profile
BRANCH: Army National Guard.
SIZE AND LOCATION: 2.9 acres. 1 block from I-80 on Wells Ave. *County:* Washoe.
MAJOR UNITS: 422nd Signal Bn, HQ; 321st Signal Co.
BASE HISTORY: Command and control of units in Nevada ARNG.
FUTURE CLOSURE/REALIGNMENT: Armory closed Nov 1997, moved to new armory in Stead, NV. Contact Maj Sullivan 702-887-7353.

Key Contacts
COMMANDER: LTC Felix Castagnola, 702-329-0573.
PUBLIC AFFAIRS: 2Lt Wilson Dasilva, 702-329-0284.

544. Reno/Tahoe IAP, Air National Guard Base
May Field
1776 ANG Way
Reno, NV 89502
702-788-4500; DSN 830-4500
Profile
BRANCH: Air National Guard.
SIZE AND LOCATION: 123 acres. On SW side of Reno-Cannon IAP; 5 mi SE of Reno, off of I-80. *County:* Washoe.
MAJOR UNITS: 152nd Airlift Wing (ANG).
BASE HISTORY: 1948, ANG unit established at Reno Army Air Base (later Stead AFB). 1953-54, Guard moved to Hubbard Field (later Reno-Cannon IAP); named for Maj Gen James A May, state Adjutant General. Activated for Korean War, Pueblo Crisis, and Operation Desert Shield/Storm. Nickname "High Rollers."
Personnel and Expenditures
ACTIVE DUTY PERSONNEL: 1009 Guard
CIVILIAN PERSONNEL: 322
MILITARY PAYROLL EXPENDITURE: $22.6 mil
Services *Medical Facilities:* Dispensary.

545. Stead Training Center
STC
4600 Alpha Ave
Reno, NV 89506-1287

702-677-5228, 677-5213; FAX 702-677-5203; DSN 830-5413
Profile
BRANCH: Army National Guard.
SIZE AND LOCATION: 360 acres. In NW Nevada; take Hwy 395 N from airport to Stead Blvd Exit (approx 10 mi), right on Stead Blvd (3.5 mi) to Alpha Ave, right to main bldg 8205 (0.25 mi). *County:* Washoe.
MAJOR UNITS: Regional Training Institute; Drug Demand Reduction; 113th Aviation Bn, Det 1, HQ & HQ Co; 1255th Medical Co, Det 1; 113th Aviation Det 1, Co D.
BASE HISTORY: National Guard Training Facility oriented to training soldiers during weekend training periods. Personnel usually accommodated for short periods (30 days). Not hotel or active duty installation. Not all amenities available.
Key Contacts
COMMANDER: SFC John L Mahfredi, Base Manager.
PROCUREMENT: Sgt Carl Adams.
Personnel and Expenditures
ACTIVE DUTY PERSONNEL: 12
DEPENDENTS: 0
CIVILIAN PERSONNEL: 3
Services
Housing: None. *Temporary Housing:* VOQ units 23; VEQ units 14; Troop barracks 145 each. *Exchange:* Convenience store; Laundromat; Video rentals. *Child Care/Capacities:* No day care facilities. *Schools:* No on-base schools. *Medical Facilities:* No medical facilities. *Recreational Facilities:* Fitness center/Weight room; Volleyball court; Horseshoe pit.

New Hampshire

Bedford

546. Manchester Naval & Marine Corps Reserve Center
25 Constitution Dr
Bedford, NH 03110-6000
603-471-0085, 471-0579; FAX 603-471-0183
Profile
BRANCH: Naval Reserve; Marine Corps Reserve.
LOCATION: In Bedford, 3 mi SW of Manchester. *County:* Hillsborough.
MAJOR UNITS: REDCOM ONE Activity; B Co, 1st Bn, 25th Marine Regiment.
Key Contacts
COMMANDER: LCDR D J Hurley.

Concord

547. Adjutant General of New Hampshire
State Military Reservation, 4 Pembroke Rd
Concord, NH 03301-5652
603-225-1200; FAX 603-225-1257
Profile
BRANCH: Army National Guard.
MAJOR UNITS: New Hampshire National Guard; Camp La Bonte State Military Reservation.
Key Contacts
COMMANDER: Brig Gen John E Blair.

Hanover

548. Army Cold Regions Research & Engineering Laboratory
CRREL; CECRL
CRREL
72 Lyme Rd
Hanover, NH 03755-1290
603-646-4100; FAX 603-646-4448; DSN 220-4100
E-mail: mdarling@crrel.usace.army.mil Internet:http://www.usace.army.mil/crrel
Profile
BRANCH: Army.
SIZE AND LOCATION: 31 acres. 2 mi N of Hanover, NH. *County:* Grafton.

MAJOR UNITS: Army Cold Regions Research & Engineering Laboratory.
BASE HISTORY: Feb 1961, established by Corps of Engineers, combining Snow, Ice, and Permafrost Research Establishment (SIPRE) with Arctic Construction and Frost Effects Laboratory (ACFEL). 1962, transferred from Corps of Engineers to Army Materiel Command. 1963, laboratory fully operational. 1969, reassigned to Corps of Engineers. 1970-85, Ice Engineering Facility and Frost Effects Research Facility added. 1992-94, Remote Sensing/Geographical Information Systems Center and Technical Information Analysis Center added.
Key Contacts
COMMANDER: LTC Mark C Nelson, Commander & Deputy Director.
PUBLIC AFFAIRS: Marie Darling.
PROCUREMENT: Charles Zdynczyk.
TRANSPORTATION: Thomas B Ladd.
PERSONNEL/COMMUNITY ACTIVITIES: Beryl Dixon.
Personnel and Expenditures
ACTIVE DUTY PERSONNEL: 4
CIVILIAN PERSONNEL: 319
MILITARY PAYROLL EXPENDITURE: $13.9 mil
CONTRACT EXPENDITURE: $5.2 mil
Services *Child Care/Capacities:* Day care center capacity 55; 6wks-6 yrs. *Schools:* Preschool/Kindergarten. *Base Library:* Yes. *Recreational Facilities:* Fitness center/Weight room.

New Boston AS

549. New Boston Air Station
317 Chestnut Hill Rd
New Boston AS, NH 03070-5125
603-471-2000; FAX 603-471-2213; DSN 881-1550
Profile
BRANCH: Air Force.
SIZE AND LOCATION: 2826 acres. In SW NH, approx 7 mi W of Manchester, NH, off Rte 114; 50 mi from Hanscom AFB. *County:* Hillsborough.
MAJOR UNITS: 23rd Space Operations Squadron.
BASE HISTORY: 1960, satellite support operations began at New Boston Satellite Tracking Station using van-mounted equipment. 1991, 23rd Space Operations Squadron activated; assigned to 750th Space Group; one of nine

worldwide satellite tracking stations of USAF Satellite Control Network; AFSPC facility. Located on former military bombing range (Grenier Field, deactivated 1956); live munitions still found.
Key Contacts
COMMANDER: LTC Cavalli, 603-471-2201.
Personnel and Expenditures
ACTIVE DUTY PERSONNEL: 22
CIVILIAN PERSONNEL: 150
Services
Housing: Dormitory spaces 2 units. *Temporary Housing:* Mobile home units 4. *Recreational Facilities:* Bowling center; Fitness center/Weight room; Softball field; Auto shop; Camping; Fishing/Hunting; Picnic area; All ranks club; Sport court; Executive health club; Outdoor recreation.

Pease ANGB

550. Pease Air National Guard Base
302 Newmarket St
Pease ANGB, NH 03803-6505
603-430-2453; DSN 852-2453
Profile
BRANCH: Air National Guard.
SIZE AND LOCATION: 229 acres. Located 3 mi NW of downtown Portsmouth, NH, and 50 mi NE of Boston. Take I-95 to Spaulding Tpke to maingate. *County:* Rockingham.
MAJOR UNITS: 157th Air Refueling Wing (ANG).
BASE HISTORY: June 1956, opened. 1957, renamed Pease for Capt Harl Pease Jr, NH native & graduate of Univ of NH. 1991, closed; New Hampshire Air National Guard retained cantonment area for operation of KC-135E tankers; base remained under control of Pease Development Authority (PDA). July 1991, airfield opened to civilian aviation. Plans for aviation center for worldwide trade, high technology business center & Great Bay National Wildlife Refuge.
Personnel and Expenditures
ACTIVE DUTY PERSONNEL: 320 full time; 922 Guard
MILITARY PAYROLL EXPENDITURE: $24.1 mil
Services *Exchange:* Retail store.

Portsmouth

551. Portsmouth Naval Shipyard
PNS
Portsmouth, NH 03804-5000
207-438-1000; FAX 207-438-1266; DSN
684-1000

Profile
BRANCH: Navy.
SIZE AND LOCATION: 298 acres (including
30 acre family housing site). On Seavey's Is-
land at mouth of Piscataqua River on border
of ME (telephone exchange) and NH (ZIP
Code); 1 mi off I-95; 50 mi N of Boston; ac-
cess by two federally-owned bridges; 8 mi
from Pease International Tradeport (airport).
County: York.
MAJOR UNITS: Portsmouth Naval Shipyard;
Submarine Maintenance Engineering Planning & Procurement (SUBMEEP); NSLC
Det, Portsmouth, NH.
BASE HISTORY: 1690s, on shore of Piscataqua
River, first warship, HMS *Falkland*, built in
North America. American Revolution, several
ships constructed for Continental Navy. 1799,
shipyard authorized by Federal government;
established in 1800. USS *Washington* first
vessel built in shipyard. 1917, first submarine
constructed at government-owned facility.
1969, last submarine built at Portsmouth. Mission today, overhaul, conversion & repair of
nuclear-powered submarines. Base has 3 dry
docks; river deep enough to allow large vessels to enter; current prevents freezing.
FUTURE CLOSURE/REALIGNMENT: Submarine Maintenance, Engineering Planning
and Procurement to close/realign by Jun 1998.
VISITOR ATTRACTIONS: Open to public by
appointment only; active duty/retired personnel, dependents, or civilian workers authorized use of all facilities on base.

Key Contacts
COMMANDER: Capt Vernon Williams,
207-438-2700.
PUBLIC AFFAIRS: Deborah Holton,
207-438-1525.
PROCUREMENT: CDR Stephen Ober,
207-438-2500.

Personnel and Expenditures
ACTIVE DUTY PERSONNEL: 400 permanent;
approx 1000 active duty sailors in port
DEPENDENTS: 950
CIVILIAN PERSONNEL: 3575

Services
Housing: Family units 234; Unaccompanied en-
listed quarters 34; BAQ units 211. *Temporary
Housing:* VIP units 3; VOQ units 23; VEQ units
165; Guesthouse units 3. *Commissary:* Yes; *Ex-
change:* Retail store; Barber shop; Florist; Bank;
Military clothing store; Credit union. *Child Care/
Capacities:* Day care center capacity 80; Home
day care program; Summer day camp. *Schools:*
No on-base schools. *Base Library:* Yes. *Medical
Facilities:* Medical clinic. *Recreational Facilities:* Bowling center; Gym; Recreation center;
Tennis courts; Racquetball court; Fitness center/
Weight room; Softball field; Auto shop; Officers
club; Picnic area; Playground; Billiards; Ice skating; Marina; Swimming & picnicking on Ja-
maica Island on base.

New Jersey

Bayonne

552. Bayonne Military Ocean Terminal
MOTBY
Foot of 32nd St
Bayonne, NJ 07002-5302
201-823-5111, 800-526-1465; FAX
201-823-6715; DSN 247-5111
OFFICER-OF-THE-DAY: Staff Duty Officer,
201-823-7207, DSN 247-7207

Profile
BRANCH: Army.
SIZE AND LOCATION: 432 acres. City of
Bayonne lies right outside terminal's main
gate. Bayonne has 9 mi of waterfront; New-
ark Bay lies W of city and Upper New York
Bay lies to E, Staten Island lies to S. 1.5 mi to
Statue of Liberty; approx 8 mi to Newark IAP
via NJ Tpke. *County:* Hudson.
MAJOR UNITS: Military Traffic Management
Command, Eastern Area; Military Sealift
Command, Atlantic; Army Garrison,
Bayonne; 1301st Major Port Command.
BASE HISTORY: 1942, commissioned US Na-
val Supply Depot, Bayonne. WWII, served as
principal transshipment point, including Pacific Theater. 1959, designated as Naval Supply Center. 1965, Military Ocean Terminal
Bayonne (MOTBY) established under Military Traffic Management and Terminal Service (MTMTS); became operational as tenant
of Naval Supply Center, Bayonne; assumed
operations from MOT Brooklyn. 1967, Naval
Supply Center disestablished, title transferred
to Army, and officially designated MOTBY.
MOTBY became world's largest military
water terminal in physical area/facilities.
1974-75, HQ, MTMTS, Eastern Area moved
from Brooklyn Army Terminal to MOTBY.
FUTURE CLOSURE/REALIGNMENT: BRAC
95: MOTBY to close by Jul 2001. Military
Traffic Management Command, Eastern Area
scheduled to merge with western area at
MTMC CONUS Command, Ft Eustis, VA.
VISITOR ATTRACTIONS: Ready access to a
rich diversity of activities, cultural events,
sports, and attractions in NYC/NJ area.

Key Contacts
COMMANDER: Brig Gen Gilbert S Harper,
201-823-6341, DSN 247-6341.
PUBLIC AFFAIRS: June M Pagan,
201-823-6351, DSN 247-6351.

PERSONNEL/COMMUNITY ACTIVITIES:
Mike Lupacchino, Chief, Family &
Community Division, 201-823-5566,
823-5650, DSN 247-5566, 247-5650; Craig
Hawley, Personnel Officer, 201-823-7958,
DSN 247-7958.

Personnel and Expenditures
ACTIVE DUTY PERSONNEL: 94
DEPENDENTS: 220
CIVILIAN PERSONNEL: 1700

Services
Housing: Family units 124; Unaccompanied enlisted quarters 3; Dormitory spaces 66. *Temporary Housing:* VIP units 1; VOQ units 1; Guesthouse units 40, Liberty Lodge 201-823-8700.
Exchange: Retail store; Barber shop; Dry cleaners; Food shop; Service station. *Child Care/Ca-
pacities:* Day care center capacity 46; Home day
care program; School-age latchkey program
available through youth activities center. *Base
Library:* Yes. *Medical Facilities:* Medical clinic.
Recreational Facilities: Bowling center; Movie
theater; Pool; Gym; Tennis courts; Racquetball
court; Fitness center/Weight room; Softball
field; Auto shop; Craft shop; Youth center; Community club; Woodworking shop; Bocce courts;
Miniature golf.

Cape May

553. Cape May Coast Guard Training Center
USCG TRACEN Cape May
1 Munro Ave
Cape May, NJ 08204-5082
609-898-6900
OFFICER-OF-THE-DAY: 609-898-6915

Profile
BRANCH: Coast Guard.
SIZE AND LOCATION: 500 acres. At Cape
May on NJ's southernmost point. At end of
Garden State Pkwy over bridge on Rte 109,
follow signs. From Lewes, DE, ferry take a
right on Rte 109 for approx 5 mi. *County:*
Cape May.
MAJOR UNITS: Coast Guard Training Center,
Cape May; Coast Guard Group, Cape May;
Coast Guard Air Station, Cape May; Small
Boat Station, Cape May; USCGC *Matinicus*;
USCGC *Hornbeam*; USCGC *Point Batan*;
USCGC *Point Franklin*; USCGC *Vigorous*;
Uniform Distribution Center, Cape May; Aids
to Navigation (ANT) Team, Cape May; Sup-

port Det, Cape May; Electronic Shop, Cape
May.
BASE HISTORY: Area used by Navy as harbor
in Revolutionary era. 1917, Navy training
base established at Sewell's Point. 1924,
Coast Guard used for patrols. 1941, served as
training site for aircraft carrier pilots. 1948,
commissioned. Current mission is to provide
recruits with basic skills; eight-week curriculum embraces military customs & courtesies,
Coast Guard organization & history, training
in small-arms marksmanship, seamanship,
physical conditioning, fire fighting & lifesaving techniques. Only basic training center in
Coast Guard.
VISITOR ATTRACTIONS: Recruit graduation
each Fri at 11am; Sunset parades (5) during
summer.

Key Contacts
COMMANDER: 609-898-6901.
PUBLIC AFFAIRS: 609-898-6914.
PROCUREMENT: 609-898-6930, 898-6306.
TRANSPORTATION: 609-898-6931.

Personnel and Expenditures
ACTIVE DUTY PERSONNEL: 800
DEPENDENTS: 500
CIVILIAN PERSONNEL: 50
MILITARY PAYROLL EXPENDITURE: $25 mil
CONTRACT EXPENDITURE: $6.8 mil

Services
Housing: Family units 173; Duplex units 5;
Townhouse units; Barracks spaces 12; Senior
NCO units; Junior NCO units. *Temporary Housing:* VOQ units; VEQ units 6; Apartment units
173; Transient quarters 6; VOQ/VEQ combined.
Commissary: Yes; *Exchange:* Retail store; Barber shop; Dry cleaners; Food shop; Tailor/Altera-
tions. *Child Care/Capacities:* Day care center capacity 30. *Medical Facilities:* Hospital 46 beds;
Medical clinic; Dental clinic. *Recreational Facilities:* Movie theater; Pool; Gym; Recreation
center; Racquetball court; Fitness center/Weight
room; Softball field; Football field; Auto shop;
Officers club; NCO club; Fishing; No hunting
on USCG property.

Colts Neck

554. Earle Naval Weapons Station
NWS Earle
201 Hwy 34 S
Colts Neck, NJ 07722-5005
908-866-2000; DSN 449-2000

OFFICER-OF-THE-DAY: 908-866-2500, DSN 449-2500

Profile
BRANCH: Navy.
SIZE AND LOCATION: 11,000 acres. On Hwy 34 S in Colts Neck. From N take NJ Tpk S to exit 11, follow Garden State Parkway S to exit 123, S on Rte 9 to Rte 18S, S on Rte 18 to Hwy 34 S to main entrance; from S or W take NJ Tpke to exit 8, follow Hwy 33 to Freehold & take Monmouth County Rte 537 to Rte 34, S on Rte 34 to main gate. 54 mi S of NYC, 79 mi N of Philadelphia, Newark airport approx 45 min away. *County:* Monmouth.
MAJOR UNITS: USS *Seattle* (AOE-3); USS *Detroit* (AOE-4); USS *Supply* (AOE-6); Shore Intermediate Maintenance Activity, NY Det; Mobile Mine Unit; Combat Logistics Squadron 2; Explosive Ordnance Disposal (EOD).
BASE HISTORY: 1943, commissioned as Naval Ammunition Depot, named after RADM Ralph Earle, Chief of Bureau of Ordnance during WWI. 1974, mission expanded to homeport for USS *Nitro* and redesignated NWS (Naval Weapons Station) Earle. 1980s, more ships added and housing areas added. 1990s, new facilities added.

Key Contacts
COMMANDER: Capt John C Shick.
PUBLIC AFFAIRS: Michael K Brady, 908-866-2171, DSN 449-2171.
PROCUREMENT: Noel Zimms, 908-866-2238, DSN 449-2238.
TRANSPORTATION: CDR Ginger Rice, 908-866-2317, DSN 449-2317.
PERSONNEL/COMMUNITY ACTIVITIES: Mrs Wendy Bovja, 908-866-2350, DSN 449-2350.

Personnel and Expenditures
ACTIVE DUTY PERSONNEL: 2800
DEPENDENTS: 1300
CIVILIAN PERSONNEL: 450
MILITARY PAYROLL EXPENDITURE: $5.5 mil
CONTRACT EXPENDITURE: $25.5 mil

Services
Housing: Family units 565; Trailer spaces 20. *Temporary Housing:* Mobile home units 8. *Exchange:* Retail store; Barber shop; Military clothing store; Convenience store; Credit union. *Child Care/Capacities:* Day care center capacity 104, 6wks-5yrs; Home day care program; Latch key program; Summer day camp. *Schools:* No on-base schools. *Base Library:* Yes. *Medical Facilities:* Medical clinic; Dental clinic; Dispensary; Pharmacy. *Recreational Facilities:* Bowling center; Movie theater; Pool; Gym; Recreation center; Tennis courts; Racquetball court; Fitness center/Weight room; Softball field; Auto shop; Craft shop; Officers club; Fishing/Hunting; Enlisted club; Youth center; Picnic area; Water sports; Playground.

Fort Dix

555. Fort Dix
ATTN: AFTZ-CO
Fort Dix, NJ 08640-5001
609-562-1011; DSN 944-1011
Internet: http://www.dix-emh5.army.mil
OFFICER-OF-THE-DAY: Staff Duty Officer, 609-562-2643, DSN 944-2643

Profile
BRANCH: Army.
SIZE AND LOCATION: 30,997 acres (14,000 acres for maneuvers & training; 13,765 acres of ranges & impact area). 15 mi E of NJ Tpke Exit 7; 25 mi SE of Trenton; 50 mi E of Philadelphia; on NJ-68, 1 mi SE of intersection of NJ-68 & Burlington Co-528 spur or 1 mi SW of intersection of NJ-68 & Burlington Co-545; near Wrightstown off Rte 528 spur. *County:* Burlington; Ocean.
MAJOR UNITS: Military Personnel & Adjutant General Services; Combat Readiness Division (FPD); Directorate of Information Management; Joint Interservice Regional Support Group (North 14); 1079th Garrison Support Unit; Defense Fuel Office; 2nd Brigade, ROTC; Training & Training Technology Battle Lab (T3BL); Federal Bureau of Prisons; Walson Air Force Medical Facility; 3rd Regional Military Police Group (CID); Ft Dix Resident Engineer Office; 542nd Explosive Ordnance Disposal; 60th Explosive Ordnance Disposal; Army Reserve Center, Ft Dix; TMDE Support Group; Readiness Group, Dix; Equipment Concentration Site (AMSA 27); Northeast Army Regional Intelligence Support Center (NEARISC); Mills Dental Clinic; Unit Training Equipment Site (UTES); Army Reserve NCO Academy; Battle Projection Center; Air Mobility Warfare Center; Naval Readiness Command Region Four; Mobile Undersea Warfare Unit; Coast Guard Atlantic Strike Team; NOAA Weather Station.
BASE HISTORY: 1917, Camp Dix established; named after Maj Gen John Adams Dix, 19th-century soldier-statesman; built as training & staging camp; later demobilization center for WWI troops. 1939, designated permanent installation, Fort Dix. 1947, designated basic training center; home of 9th Infantry Division. 1954, renamed US Army Training Center, Infantry. 1973, Overseas Replacement Station closed; Reception Station opened under Training & Doctrine Command. 1975, NY Area Command/Fort Hamilton became sub-installations of Ft Dix. 1988, Army/Air Force training course for Air Force Security Police opened. 1990, deployed troops (mostly reserve component units) for Desert Shield/Storm. 1991, trained Kuwaiti civilians basic military skills. 1992, Air Force assumed control of hospital; base realigned. Ft Dix largest military installation in NE; shares common boundaries with McGuire AFB & Lakehurst NAS. Remains stand-alone installation with New York Area Command as sub-installation. Mission: regional center of training; provide regional area support; provide base operations support for tenants; & maintain 1,197 units of Army family housing.
VISITOR ATTRACTIONS: Infantry Park Museum.

Key Contacts
COMMANDER: Col Timothy A Peterson, Post Commander, 609-562-2458, DSN 944-2458.
PUBLIC AFFAIRS: Robert Warner, ATTN: AFZT-PAZ, 5407 Pennsylvania Ave, 08640-5075, 609-562-4034, DSN 944-4034.
PROCUREMENT: 609-562-4252, DSN 944-4252.
TRANSPORTATION: ATZD-GDT, 609-562-3574, DSN 944-3574.

PERSONNEL/COMMUNITY ACTIVITIES: DCFA, 609-562-3353, DSN 944-3353.

Personnel and Expenditures
ACTIVE DUTY PERSONNEL: 1300
DEPENDENTS: 2304
CIVILIAN PERSONNEL: 2000; inmates 4296 (NJ Dept of Corrections)

Services
Housing: Family units 1197; Unaccompanied officer quarters 72; Unaccompanied enlisted quarters 212. *Temporary Housing:* VIP units 10; VOQ units 16; VEQ units 90; Guesthouse units 2; Guest cottages 169. *Commissary:* Yes; *Exchange:* Retail store; Barber shop; Dry cleaners; Food shop; Florist; Bank; Service station; Bakery; Bookstore; Military clothing store; Convenience store; Beauty shop; Credit union. *Child Care/Capacities:* Day care center; Home day care program; Latch key program; Summer day camp. *Schools:* Preschool/Kindergarten; Elementary; College courses. *Base Library:* Yes. *Medical Facilities:* Hospital 464 beds; Pharmacy; Veterinary services. *Recreational Facilities:* Bowling center; Movie theater; Pool; Gym; Golf course; Tennis courts; Fitness center/Weight room; Softball field; Football field; Craft shop; Officers club; NCO club; Fishing/Hunting; Youth center; Picnic area; Skeet range; Playground.

556. Region Four, Naval Reserve Readiness Command
REDCOM 4
5957 New Jersey Ave
Fort Dix, NJ 08640-8000
609-724-7698; FAX 609-724-7652; DSN 944-7698
Internet: http://www.navy.mil.homepages/navresfor/navsurf/redcom04.html

Profile
BRANCH: Naval Reserve.
MAJOR UNITS: Naval Reserve Readiness Command, Region 4.

Key Contacts
COMMANDER: RADM J W Eastwood, 609-724-7700, DSN 944-6107.

Fort Monmouth

557. Fort Monmouth
Fort Monmouth, NJ 07703-5000
732-532-9000; DSN 992-9000
Internet: http://www.monmouth.army.mil/c4iews.htm
OFFICER-OF-THE-DAY: 732-532-2110, DSN 992-2110

Profile
BRANCH: Army.
SIZE AND LOCATION: 1560 acres. NJ Tpke to I-95; E to Garden State Pkwy; S to Exit 105 for Eatontown & Fort Monmouth; New Brunswick, 23 mi NW; 10 min from Atlantic Ocean beaches; nearby Monmouth Park Race Track; 1.5 hrs S of New York City. *County:* Monmouth.
MAJOR UNITS: Team C4IEWS; Army Communications-Electronics Command (CECOM); Program Executive Office for Command, Control & Communications Systems (PEO C3S); Program Executive Office for Intelligence & Electronic Warfare (PEO IEW); Joint Interoperability & Engineering Organi-

zation (JIEO); Joint Computer-aided Acquisition & Logistics Systems (JCALS); Army Research Laboratory, Human Research & Engineering Directorate (ARL, HRED); Patterson Army Health Clinic.

BASE HISTORY: July 20, 1917, Army established reserve officers training battalion at Signal Corps Camp, Little Silver. Sept 1917, renamed Camp Alfred Vail. Aug 1925, made permanent military post, Fort Monmouth, in honor of soldiers of American Revolution who fought in nearby fields. Ft Monmouth is leading military technological & logistics center.

VISITOR ATTRACTIONS: Army Communications-Electronics Museum, equipment & documents, trace developments of Army communications, 1860 to present; Army Chaplains Museum; Post Chapel.

Key Contacts
COMMANDER: Commander Communications-Electronics Command & Fort Monmouth, AMSEL-CG, 732-532-1515, FAX 732-532-8685, DSN 992-1515, Amsel-Cg@Cecom3.Monmouth. Army.Mil.
PUBLIC AFFAIRS: AMSEL-IO, 732-532-1258, FAX 732-532-6262, DSN 992-1258, Amsel-Io@Cecom3.Monmouth. Army.Mil.

Personnel and Expenditures
ACTIVE DUTY PERSONNEL: 2000
DEPENDENTS: 3516
CIVILIAN PERSONNEL: 7646
MILITARY PAYROLL EXPENDITURE: $445 mil
CONTRACT EXPENDITURE: $556 mil

Services
Housing: Family units 881; Duplex units 186; Senior NCO units 100; Trailer spaces 24. *Temporary Housing:* VIP units 6; VOQ units 60; Guesthouse units 70; Off-base hotel/motel rooms w/ year-round rates 135. *Commissary:* Yes; *Exchange:* Retail store; Barber shop; Dry cleaners; Food shop; Bank; Service station; Furniture store; Military clothing store; Laundromat; Credit union; Optical store; Tailor/Alterations; Cafeteria; Jewelry/Watch sales/Repair. *Child Care/Capacities:* Day care center 250; Home day care program; Certified child care homes 57. *Base Library:* Yes. *Medical Facilities:* Hospital 35 beds; Medical clinic; Dental clinic. *Recreational Facilities:* Bowling center; Movie theater; Pool; Gym; Recreation center; Golf course; Tennis courts; Racquetball court; Fitness center/ Weight room; Softball field; Football field; Auto shop; Craft shop; Officers club; NCO club; Fishing/Hunting; Marina.

Gibbsboro

558. Gibbsboro Air Force Station
Gibbsboro, NJ 08026-1299
609-783-1449
Profile
BRANCH: Air Force.
SIZE AND LOCATION: 21.8 acres. On Rte 561 approx 14 mi E of Camden, NJ; 2 mi W of Berlin, NJ; 50 mi W of Atlantic City, NJ; 33 mi S of McGurie AFB, NJ. *County:* Camden.
BASE HISTORY: In caretaker status.
Key Contacts
COMMANDER: Bruno Kneucker, Site Chief.

Kearny

559. Kearny Naval Reserve Readiness Center
NRC Kearny
53 Hackensack Ave
Kearny, NJ 07032-4619
973-690-5906; FAX 973-690-5527
Profile
BRANCH: Naval Reserve.
LOCATION: 5 min from NJ Turnpike, Exit 15E; 10 min from Newark Airport. *County:* Hudson.
MAJOR UNITS: REDCOM FOUR Activity.
Key Contacts
COMMANDER: CDR Richard Delaquis, 973-690-5906, FAX 973-690-5527.
PUBLIC AFFAIRS: LCDR Boylan, 609-724-7718, CBOYLAN@mtahqexec.mta. ny.us.
Personnel and Expenditures
ACTIVE DUTY PERSONNEL: 17; 650 reservists

Lakehurst

560. Lakehurst Naval Air Engineering Station
NAES Lakehurst
Lakehurst, NJ 08733-5000
732-323-2011; FAX 732-323-7676; DSN 624-2011
Internet: http://www.lakehurst.navy.mil
OFFICER-OF-THE-DAY: 732-323-2308, DSN 624-2308
Profile
BRANCH: Navy.
SIZE AND LOCATION: 7420 acres. 54 mi E of Philadelphia; 60 mi N of Atlantic City; 68 mi S of NYC; 14 mi from Atlantic Ocean. From NJ Tpke take either Rte 70 E or Rte 524 E to Rte 539 E to base. From Garden State Pky take Exit 11 (Shore Areas) W to base. *County:* Ocean.
MAJOR UNITS: Lakehurst Naval Air Engineering Station; Naval Air Technical Training Center, Det; Army Communications-Electronics Command, Electronics Integration Directorate/Airborne Engineering Evaluation Support Activity; Naval Mobile Construction Bn 21; Naval Air Warfare Center Aircraft Division, Trenton; Defense Printing Service Branch Office; Naval Investigative Service; Personnel Support Det; Defense Reutilization & Marketing Office; Naval Facilities Command Northern Division Philadelphia; Naval Dental Clinic; Naval Medical Clinic; Ocean County Vocational Technical School.
BASE HISTORY: 1915-17, ammunition proving ground for Russian Imperial government. 1917, acquired by Army as ammunition proving ground; named Camp Kendric. 1921, commissioned Naval Air Station. 1921-61, Lighter Than Air (LTA) center. 1937, Hindenburg crashes. 1958, Naval Air Test Facility (NATF) created. 1967, NAEC reorganized; transferred to Naval Air Station, Lakehurst; made host command. 1973, NAEC relocated from Philadelphia. 1977, NAS & NATF disestablished & merged into NAEC. 1992, Naval Air Warfare Center (NAWC) established;

NAEC becomes Naval Air Warfare Center Aircraft Division Lakehurst (NAWCADLKE). 1994, NAWCADLKE becomes Naval Air Engineering Station (NAES); remainder reorganized. 1997, Aircraft & Weapons divisions integrated into Naval Aviation Systems Team's Competency Aligned Organization. Mission to ensure effectiveness of Navy's air arm by researching, developing & testing innovative technologies & equipment needed to support sophisticated aircraft. One of Navy's largest research, engineering, development, test & evaluation complexes; includes world's only in-ground low pressure catapult.
VISITOR ATTRACTIONS: Hindenburg Memorial; Hangar 1, Registered National Historic Landmark.
Key Contacts
COMMANDER: Capt Dougherty, 732-323-2380, DSN 624-2380.
PUBLIC AFFAIRS: 732-323-2620, DSN 624-2620.
PROCUREMENT: Business Development Office, 732-323-7684, FAX 732-323-1364.
TRANSPORTATION: 732-323-7540, DSN 624-7540.
PERSONNEL/COMMUNITY ACTIVITIES: 732-323-2587, DSN 624-2587.
Personnel and Expenditures
ACTIVE DUTY PERSONNEL: 429; reservists 103
CIVILIAN PERSONNEL: 2356
MILITARY PAYROLL EXPENDITURE: $110 mil (military & civilian)
CONTRACT EXPENDITURE: $205 mil
Services
Housing: Family units 219; Unaccompanied officer quarters; Unaccompanied enlisted quarters; Barracks spaces; Mobile home units 40. *Temporary Housing:* VIP units 1; Unaccompanied officer/Enlisted quarters; BAQ units; Dormitory units; Navy Lodge. *Commissary:* Yes; *Exchange:* Retail store; Barber shop; Food shop; Bank; Convenience store; Credit union. *Child Care/Capacities:* Day care center; Home day care program; Latch key program; Summer day camp. *Schools:* Preschool/Kindergarten; Graduate courses. *Base Library:* Yes. *Medical Facilities:* Medical clinic; Dental clinic. *Recreational Facilities:* Bowling center; Movie theater; Pool; Gym; Recreation center; Golf course; Tennis courts; Racquetball court; Fitness center/Weight room; Softball field; Auto shop; Fishing/Hunting.

McGuire AFB

561. McGuire Air Force Base
305th Air Mobility Wing
McGuire AFB, NJ 08641-5002
609-724-1110; DSN 440-1110
Profile
BRANCH: Air Force.
SIZE AND LOCATION: 3598 acres. 45 mi NE of Philadelphia; 20 mi SE of Trenton, NJ; Exit 7 NJ Tpke. *County:* Burlington.
MAJOR UNITS: 305th Air Mobility Wing; 21st Air Force; 514th Air Mobility Wing (AS-SOC); 108th Air Refueling Wing (ANG); Air Mobility Warfare Center; 621st Air Mobility Operations Group; Non-commission Officer Academy.

BASE HISTORY: Largest Military Airlift Command port of embarkation/debarkation on East Coast. Named for Maj Thomas B McGuire, native of Ridgewood, NJ, second leading WWII flying ace. 1937, began as Rudd Field, under control of Ft Dix. WWII, antisubmarine patrols flown and aircraft shuttled to Europe. 1945, served as reception center for returning forces. 1949, became McGuire AFB. 1966, MATS redesignated Military Airlift Command, and 438th Military Airlift Wing activated and host. Until 1973 cease-fire, McGuire aircrews moved men and supplies to and from Vietnam. 1973, brought out American POWs from N Vietnam. 1980s, participated in airlift operations in Beirut, Grenada, and Panama. 1990-91, Wing deployed to Persian Gulf for Desert Shield/Storm. 1991, 438th aircrews airlifted Terry Anderson, longest-held Western hostage in Iran, and remains of hostages Col William R Higgins and CIA agent William R Buckley back to US. 1992, 438th aircrews airlifted supplies and equipment to Commonwealth of Independent States under Operation Provide Hope; assigned to newly activated Air Mobility Command. 1993, made East Coast Mobility Center. 1994, site for new Air Mobility Warfare Center; 305th Air Mobility Wing formed.

Key Contacts
COMMANDER: Gen Craig R Rasmussen, 2901 Falcon Lane, 609-724-3051, FAX 609-724-6999, DSN 440-3051, rasmussc. 305hqamw@smpt-gwl.mcguire.af.mil.
PUBLIC AFFAIRS: Capt Kris Frazier, 2901 Falcon Lane, 609-724-2104, FAX 609-724-6999, DSN 440-2104, frazierk. 305hqamw@smpt-gwl.mcguire.af.mil.
PERSONNEL/COMMUNITY ACTIVITIES: 305th Support Group Commander, 609-724-3455, DSN 440-3455, DSN FAX 440-2441, reverk.305hqamw@smpt-gwl. mcguire.af.mil.

Personnel and Expenditures
ACTIVE DUTY PERSONNEL: 5500
DEPENDENTS: 8400
CIVILIAN PERSONNEL: 1400
MILITARY PAYROLL EXPENDITURE: $170 mil
Services
Housing: Family units 1754; Dormitory spaces 2000; Mobile home units 20; Trailer spaces 20. *Temporary Housing:* VOQ units 128; VAQ units 922; Lodge units 30; Transient quarters 30. *Commissary:* Yes; *Exchange:* Barber shop; Dry cleaners; Florist; Bank; Service station; Furniture store; Bakery; Military clothing store; Convenience store; Beauty shop; Credit union; ATM; Optical store; Post office; Fast food; Video rentals; Thrift shop; Class VI; Garden center; Tailor/Alterations; Cafeteria; Photo store. *Child Care/Capacities:* Day care center capacity 300, 6wks-5yrs; Home day care program; Summer day camp; Before & after school programs. *Schools:* Preschool/Kindergarten; Elementary. *Base Library:* Yes. *Medical Facilities:* Medical clinic; Pharmacy; Veterinary services; Uses Walson AF Hospital on neighboring Ft Dix. *Recreational Facilities:* Bowling center; Movie theater; Gym; Recreation center; Golf course; Tennis courts; Racquetball court; Fitness center/Weight room; Softball field; Auto shop; Officers club; NCO club; Enlisted club; Youth center; Playground; Aero club.

Picatinny Arsenal

562. Armament Research, Development, and Engineering Center, US Army TACOM
Picatinny Arsenal
AMSTA-AR-CG
Picatinny Arsenal, NJ 07806-5000
Internet: http://www.pica.army.mil
Profile
BRANCH: Army.
SIZE AND LOCATION: 6500 acres. 28 mi NW of New York City at intersection of I-80 and NJ Hwy 15; take I-80 west, exit 34B, follow signs to Arsenal. *County:* Morris.
MAJOR UNITS: Armament Research, Development, and Engineering Center (TACOM-ARDEC); Army Garrison, Picatinny Arsenal; Army Fuze Management Office (AFMO); Close Combat Armaments Center (CCAC); Defense Ammunition Logistics Activity (DALA); Fire Support Armaments Center (FSAC); Program Executive Officer, Ground Combat and Support Systems (PEOGCSS); 902nd Military Intelligence Group; Program Executive Officer, Field Artillery Systems (PEOFAS); Program Executive Officer, Armored Systems Modernization (PEOASM); Battle Labs.
BASE HISTORY: 1880, Dover Powder Depot established; renamed Picatinny Powder Depot. 1891, portion of depot transferred to Navy. 1907, renamed Picatinny Arsenal; moved into research and development. 1911, weaponry sciences school started. 1926, lightning strike on Navy Hill set off major explosion. WWII, arsenal produced munitions. 1948, Navy Air Rocket Test Station established. 1960, Navy portion returned to Army. 1977, HQ, Armament Research and Development Command established. 1983, changed to Armament Research and Development Center. 1986, renamed Armament Research, Development, and Engineering Center.
Key Contacts
COMMANDER: Brig Gen Joseph W Arbuckle, AMSTA-AR-CG, 973-724-6000, DSN 880-6000; Col Daniel M Prescott, Deputy Commander, AMSTA-AR-DC, 973-724-7000, DSN 880-7000; Carmine J Spinelli, Technical Director, AMSTA-AR-TD, 973-724-7012, DSN 880-7012.
PUBLIC AFFAIRS: AMSTA-AR-INP.
Personnel and Expenditures
ACTIVE DUTY PERSONNEL: 4000 (military and civilian)
Services
Housing: Family units. *Commissary:* Yes; *Exchange:* Retail store. *Child Care/Capacities:* Day care center; Home day care program. *Base Library:* Yes. *Recreational Facilities:* Pool; Golf course; Softball field; Officers club; Picnic area; Skeet range; Soccer field; Camping area; Archery range.

Pleasantville

563. Atlantic City Airport, Air National Guard Base
400 Langley Rd
Pleasantville, NJ 08232-9500
609-645-6000; DSN 445-6000
Profile
BRANCH: Air National Guard.
SIZE AND LOCATION: 286 acres. 10 mi NW of Atlantic City, NJ on Tilton Rd; Exit 9 off Atlantic Expy; Exit 36 N off Garden State Pkwy, Exit 37 S. *County:* Atlantic.
MAJOR UNITS: 177th Fighter Wing (ANG).
BASE HISTORY: 1917, 119th Aero Squadron established at Langley Field, VA. Inactivated until 1928, when reorganized as 119th Observation Squadron, NJ ANG, at Metropolitan Airport, Newark, NJ, part of 44th Division Aviation. 1930, squadron received federal recognition. 1940, active service as 490th Fighter Squadron. 1945, redesignated 119th Fighter Squadron (SE). 1946, redesignated ANG Newark. 1958, moved to former Atlantic City Naval Air Station, now Federal Aviation Administration Technical Center. Berlin Crisis 1961, rotated to Chaumont AB, France. Pueblo Crisis, assigned to 113th TFW, Myrtle Beach AFB, SC. 1969, returned to Atlantic City. 1972, reorganized as 177th FIG and 119th FIS.
VISITOR ATTRACTIONS: Base tour available for groups with advanced reservations.
Personnel and Expenditures
ACTIVE DUTY PERSONNEL: 910 Guard
CIVILIAN PERSONNEL: 305
MILITARY PAYROLL EXPENDITURE: $23.8 mil
Services *Exchange:* Retail store.

Sea Girt

564. Sea Girt National Guard Training Center
Sea Girt
PO Box 251
Sea Girt, NJ 08750-0251
732-974-5950
Profile
BRANCH: Army National Guard.
SIZE AND LOCATION: 1500 acres. 20 mi E of Fort Monmouth; along Atlantic Coast. *County:* Monmouth.
MAJOR UNITS: Sea Girt National Guard Training Center.
BASE HISTORY: Administrative & tactical training installation; also used by NJ State Police.
Key Contacts
COMMANDER: Mr Beck, Superintendent.

Trenton

565. Adjutant General of New Jersey
Eggert Crossing Rd, CN 340
Trenton, NJ 08625-0340
609-530-6957; FAX 609-530-7097

Profile
BRANCH: Army National Guard.
MAJOR UNITS: New Jersey National Guard.
Key Contacts
COMMANDER: Maj Gen Paul J Glazar.

566. Naval Air Warfare Center, Aircraft Division
NAWCAD TRN
PO Box 7176
Trenton, NJ 08628-0176
609-538-6633; FAX 609-538-6604; DSN 442-7633
Profile
BRANCH: Navy.
SIZE AND LOCATION: 67 acres. I-95 exit 2 at Bear Tavern Rd, off of Upper Ferry Rd; NW of Trenton, NJ; Within corporate limits of Ewing Township; adj to Mercer County Airport. *County:* Mercer.
BASE HISTORY: Begun in 1917. One of world's premier facilities for research, development, testing, and evaluation of air breathing propulsion systems. Test facilities can simulate any atmospheric condition an aircraft may encounter in flight. Off-site facility for power plant testing maintained at Naval Air Engineering Center, Lakehurst, NJ. NAEC houses fully instrumented chemistry lab for analysis of aviation fuels and lubricants.
FUTURE CLOSURE/REALIGNMENT: Minor closure/realignment to be completed by Dec 1998.
Key Contacts
COMMANDER: Capt David C Offerdahl; 609-538-6602, DSN 442-7602.
PUBLIC AFFAIRS: David B Polish; 609-538-6633, DSN 442-7633.
PROCUREMENT: LCDR James Hurley; 609-538-6640, DSN 442-7640.
PERSONNEL/COMMUNITY ACTIVITIES: Fred Olsen; 609-538-6613, DSN 442-7613.
Personnel and Expenditures
ACTIVE DUTY PERSONNEL: 7
CIVILIAN PERSONNEL: 610
Services
Housing: None. *Base Library:* Yes. *Medical Facilities:* Dispensary. *Recreational Facilities:* Tennis courts; Softball field.

West Trenton

567. West Trenton Marine Corps Reserve Center
Marine Scotch Rd
West Trenton, NJ 08628-1395
609-882-5133; FAX 609-882-7921
Profile
BRANCH: Marine Corps Reserve.
LOCATION: W-central NJ at Mercer County Airport. *County:* Mercer.
MAJOR UNITS: G Battery, 3rd Bn, 14th Marine Regiment.

New Mexico

Albuquerque

568. Albuquerque Naval & Marine Corps Reserve Center
NAVMARCORESCEN ABQ
400 K Wyoming Ave, NE
Albuquerque, NM 87123-1099
505-292-4141; FAX 505-275-9504; DSN
246-8348
Profile
BRANCH: Naval Reserve; Marine Corps Reserve.
LOCATION: *County:* Bernalillo.
MAJOR UNITS: REDCOM ELEVEN Activity; D Co, 4th Reconnaissance Bn.
Key Contacts
COMMANDER: CDR J M Daniels.

569. US Army Corps of Engineers, Albuquerque District
4101 Jefferson Plaza NE
Albuquerque, NM 87109-3435
505-342-3432
Internet: http://www.swa-wc.usace.army.mil/
Profile
BRANCH: Army.
LOCATION: *County:* Bernalillo.
MAJOR UNITS: Corps of Engineers, Albuquerque District.
Key Contacts
COMMANDER: LTC Lloyd S Wagner, Commander, 505-342-3432.
PUBLIC AFFAIRS: J H Bryant, 505-342-3171.

Cannon AFB

570. Cannon Air Force Base
CAFB
100 SDL Ingram Blvd, Ste 102
Cannon AFB, NM 88103-5216
505-784-3311; DSN 681-3311
Internet: http://www.cannon.af.mil/
Profile
BRANCH: Air Force.
SIZE AND LOCATION: 77,689 acres. In High Plains of eastern NM near TX Panhandle; 7 mi W of Clovis, NM, on US-60/84; 17 mi SW of Clovis Airport; altitude 4,295 ft. *County:* Curry.
MAJOR UNITS: 27th Fighter Wing; 27th Operations Group; 27th Support Group; 27th Logis-

tics Group; 27th Security Forces Squadron; 522nd Fighter Squadron; 27th Medical Group; 27th Civil Engineering Squadron; 27th Equipment Maintenance Squadron; 27th Communications Squadron.
BASE HISTORY: Late 1920s, civilian passenger facility for commercial transcontinental flights, Portair Field, established. 1930s, Portair renamed Clovis Municipal Airport. WWII, Clovis Army Air Base; glider detachment took over. 1943, 16th Bombardment Operational Wing arrived; trained B-24, B-17, and B-29 heavy bombers; renamed Clovis Army Air Field. 1947, inactivated. 1951, reassigned to TAC, with 140th Fighter-Bomber Wing; airfield renamed Clovis AFB. 1957, renamed Cannon AFB for Gen John K Cannon, former commander of TAC. 1959, 312th Fighter-Bomber Group deactivated; replaced by 27th TFW. 1965, mission changed to replacement training unit. 1968-73, trained forward air controllers & air liaison officers in AT-33s. 1988, base given expanding mission under Air Combat Command. 1995, home for F-16 Fighting Falcon aircraft.
VISITOR ATTRACTIONS: Memorial Park with vintage planes flown at Cannon.
Key Contacts
COMMANDER: Col David E Clary, 27 FW/CC, 505-784-2727, DSN 681-2727.
PUBLIC AFFAIRS: 27 FW/PA, 505-784-4131, FAX 505-784-2338, DSN 681-4131.
PROCUREMENT: 27 CONS/CC, N 100 Torch Blvd, 88103-5131, 505-784-2321, DSN 681-2321.
TRANSPORTATION: 27 TRANS/CC, 114 E Argentia Ave, 88103-5132, 505-784-2683, DSN 681-2683.
PERSONNEL/COMMUNITY ACTIVITIES: 27 FW/MWRSS, 101 W Eureka Ave, 88103-5013, 505-784-2381, DSN 681-2381.
Personnel and Expenditures
ACTIVE DUTY PERSONNEL: 4050
DEPENDENTS: 10,000
CIVILIAN PERSONNEL: 700
Services
Housing: Family units 1211; Dormitory spaces 1137; Trailer spaces 56. *Temporary Housing:* VOQ units 16; VAQ units 16; VIP units 14; TLF 45. *Commissary:* Yes; *Exchange:* Retail store; Barber shop; Dry cleaners; Food shop; Florist; Bank; Service station; Furniture store; Military clothing store; Convenience store; Beauty shop; Credit union. *Child Care/Capacities:* Day care center capacity 102, 6mo-12yrs; Home day

care program; Summer day camp; Enrichment program. *Schools:* Preschool/Kindergarten; College courses. *Base Library:* Yes. *Medical Facilities:* Hospital 20 beds; Medical clinic; Dental clinic; Pharmacy; Veterinary services. *Recreational Facilities:* Bowling center; Movie theater; Pool; Gym; Recreation center; Golf course; Tennis courts; Racquetball court; Fitness center/ Weight room; Softball field; Football field; Auto shop; Officers club; NCO club; Youth center; Picnic area; Skeet range; Playground.

Holloman AFB

571. Holloman Air Force Base
HAFB
49 FW/PA, 490 First St, Ste 2800
Holloman AFB, NM 88330-8287
505-475-5406; FAX 505-475-5908; DSN
867-5406
Internet: http://www.holloman.af.mil
OFFICER-OF-THE-DAY: Command Post, 505-475-7575, DSN 867-7575
Profile
BRANCH: Air Force.
SIZE AND LOCATION: 46,449 acres. Approx 10 mi from Alamogordo Municipal Airport; El Paso approx 85 mi S on Hwy 54; Las Cruces approx 60 mi SW on Hwy 70; Junction of Hwys 70 and 54 approx 5 mi from base gate. Shuttle service from El Paso airport; no public transportation with Alamorgordo. *County:* Otero.
MAJOR UNITS: 49th Fighter Wing; 49th Operations Group; 49th Logistics Group; 49th Support Group; 49th Medical Group; 49th Bare Base Systems Group; 7th Fighter Squadron; 8th Fighter Squadron; 9th Fighter Squadron; 49th Training Squadron; 1st German Air Force.
BASE HISTORY: 1942, Alamogordo Army Airfield began to train heavy bombardment groups. 1944, became Combat Crew Training Center, training replacement crews for bombardment groups. 1945, first atomic bomb detonated in NW corner of airfield's bombing range, known as Trinity Site. Following WWII, inactivated until 1946, when base was reactivated by AMC. 1948, renamed Holloman AFB for Col George V Holloman, pioneer in guided missile research. 1952, became Holloman Air Development Center and designated a permanent Air Force installation; Holloman test range integrated with White Sands

Proving Grounds, under Army. 1968, 49th TFW assigned to base. 1970, Missile Development Center deactivated and 49th TFW assumed host responsibilities. 1971, TAC assumed command. 1977, Tactical Training Center established. 1980, renamed 833rd Air Division. Since 1981, has provided contingency support for Space Shuttle at White Sands Space Harbor. 1991, 49th Fighter Wing became host after 833rd Air Division deactivated; base became home of F-117 Stealth Fighter. 1992, Air Combat Command activated, replacing Tactical Air Command.
VISITOR ATTRACTIONS: Heritage Park, static display of F-84F, F-86E, F-104C, F-100D, and F-105D.

Key Contacts
COMMANDER: Brig Gen Dennis R Larsen, 49 FW/CC, 505-475-5571, DSN 867-5571.
PUBLIC AFFAIRS: Capt Lawrence J Cox.
PROCUREMENT: LTC Jack Grubb, 49th Contracting Squadron, 505-475-3040, DSN 867-3040.
TRANSPORTATION: Maj Steven Gregorcyk, 49th Transportation Squadron, 505-475-5529, DSN 867-5529.
PERSONNEL/COMMUNITY ACTIVITIES: LTC Janet R Middleton, 49th Mission Support Squadron; 505-475-5855, DSN 867-5855.

Personnel and Expenditures
ACTIVE DUTY PERSONNEL: 4500
DEPENDENTS: 2450
CIVILIAN PERSONNEL: 2700
MILITARY PAYROLL EXPENDITURE: $144 mil
CONTRACT EXPENDITURE: $50.7 mil

Services
Housing: Family units 1551; Unaccompanied officer quarters 5; Unaccompanied enlisted quarters 3; Dormitory spaces 14. *Temporary Housing:* Lodge units 50. *Commissary:* Yes; *Exchange:* Retail store; Barber shop; Dry cleaners; Food shop; Florist; Bank; Service station; Bakery; Military clothing store; Convenience store; Beauty shop; Laundromat; Credit union; Video rental; Optical shop. *Child Care/Capacities:* Day care center; Home day care program. *Schools:* Preschool/Kindergarten; Elementary; Intermediate/Junior high. *Base Library:* Yes. *Medical Facilities:* Hospital 8; Medical clinic; Dental clinic; Dispensary; Pharmacy; Veterinary services. *Recreational Facilities:* Bowling center; Movie theater; Pool; Gym; Recreation center; Golf course; Stables; Tennis courts; Racquetball court; Fitness center/Weight room; Softball field; Football field; Auto shop; Craft shop; Officers club; Enlisted club; Youth center; Picnic area; Skeet range; Playground.

Kirtland AFB

572. Kirtland Air Force Base
KAFB
2000 Wyoming Blvd SE
Kirtland AFB, NM 87117-5606
505-846-0011; DSN 246-0011
Internet: http://www.kirtland.af.mil/
OFFICER-OF-THE-DAY: 505-846-4676, DSN 246-4676
Profile
BRANCH: Air Force.
SIZE AND LOCATION: 52,000 acres. 8 mi from Albuquerque on SE side of US-66.

From I-40/US-66, S on Wyoming Blvd. From I-25, E on Gibson Blvd to main gate. *County:* Bernalillo.
MAJOR UNITS: 377th Air Base Wing; Sandia National Laboratories; Air Force Operational Test and Evaluation Center; Phillips Laboratory; Department of Energy Det; Air Force Safety Center; Air Force Inspection Agency; Defense Special Weapons Agency's Field Command; Air Force Research Laboratory; 58th Special Operations Wing; NM Air National Guard; Defense Nuclear Agency's Field Command; Air Force Security Forces Center.
BASE HISTORY: 1939, began servicing transient military aircraft; large bomber crew training base; named for Col Roy C Kirtland, military aviation pioneer; established training depot for aircraft mechanics E of Kirtland Field, near original private airport, Oxnard Field, Sandia Base (later used as convalescent center for wounded air crewmen & storage & dismantling facility for surplus aircraft); Armed Forces Special Weapons Project (later Defense Atomic Support Agency, then Defense Nuclear Agency) operated Sandia Base. 1949, Air Force Special Weapons Command established at Kirtland; Navy established weapons test detachments that evolved into Naval Weapons Evaluation Facility. 1952, Air Force Special Weapons Command redesignated Air Force Special Weapons Center. 1960s, Air Force Weapons Laboratory created. Late 1970s, the Trestle, largest simulation facility ever built, completed. 1971, Kirtland & Sandia merged, under control of Air Force; replaced Field Command, Defense Nuclear Agency, as host unit. 1976, Special Weapons Center disestablished; Contract Management Division & 4900th ABW, became host. 1977, 1606th ABW created; MAC took over operation. 1982, Air Force Space Technology Center activated, under Air Force Systems Command's Space Division, HQ, Los Angeles. 1991, 1606th & 1550th combined into "super wing," 542nd Crew Training Wing (CTW). 1993, Air Force Materiel Command became major command; 377th Air Base Wing(ABW) became host wing and 542nd CTW, a tenant wing; Air Force Inspection Agency moved in from Norton AFB. 1994, 542nd Crew Training Wing redesignated 58th Special Operations Wing under Air Education & Training Command.
VISITOR ATTRACTIONS: National Atomic Museum.
Key Contacts
COMMANDER: Col Gary Dills, 377 ABW/CC, 505-846-7377, DSN 246-7377.
PUBLIC AFFAIRS: 505-846-5991, FAX 505-846-4897, DSN 246-5991.
Personnel and Expenditures
ACTIVE DUTY PERSONNEL: 4500; Guard 1060
DEPENDENTS: 10,700
CIVILIAN PERSONNEL: 15,040
MILITARY PAYROLL EXPENDITURE: $785.9 mil
CONTRACT EXPENDITURE: $53.9 mil
Services
Housing: Family units 1599; RV/Camper sites 40; General's quarters 4. *Temporary Housing:* VOQ units 238; VAQ units 249; Dormitory units 16; Transient quarters 40.

Commissary: Yes; *Exchange:* Retail store; Barber shop; Dry cleaners; Food shop; Florist; Bank; Service station. *Child Care/Capacities:* Day care center; Home day care program. *Schools:* Preschool/Kindergarten; Elementary. *Base Library:* Yes. *Medical Facilities:* Hospital; Medical clinic; Dental clinic. *Recreational Facilities:* Bowling center; Movie theater; Pool; Gym; Recreation center; Golf course; Stables; Tennis courts; Racquetball court; Skating rink; Fitness center/Weight room; Softball field; Football field; Auto shop; Craft shop; Officers club; NCO club.

Santa Fe

573. New Mexico National Guard State Headquarters
NMARNG
47 Bataan Blvd
Santa Fe, NM 87505-3258
505-474-1200; FAX 505-474-1674; DSN 867-1200; DSN FAX 867-8674
Profile
BRANCH: Army National Guard; Air National Guard.
SIZE AND LOCATION: 313.27 acres. I-25 N from Albuquerque, approx 51 mi, take exit 271; 5 mi from Santa Fe airport. *County:* Santa Fe.
MAJOR UNITS: HQ State Area Readiness Command (STARC), NM ARNG; HQ State Area Readiness Command, Det 1; Regional Training Institute; Operational Support Airlift Command, Det 44; HQ State Area Readiness Command, Det 4 (Medical); 93rd Troop Command; 123rd Public Affairs Det 1; 717th Medical Co; 3631st Maintenance Co; HHB, 6th Bn (MUA) 200th ADA; 6th Bn MESS Augmentation; HQ, 515th Regiment; 1st Bn (AD) 515th Regiment; 2nd Bn, 515th Regiment; 44th Army Band.
BASE HISTORY: Origin of New Mexico Army NG can be traced back to 1606, local militia, the "Neighbors," took over home defense. 1851, Territorial Legislature created Office of Adjutant General for central control of local militia units during peacetime. Served in every war since Civil War with commanders such as Kit Carson & Teddy Roosevelt. 111th Air Defense Brigade located in Albuquerque & five Chaparral air defense battalions headquartered in Belen, Las Cruces, Roswell, Clovis, and Springer. Other units in Santa Fe, Las Cruces, and Las Vegas, NM, have maintenance, aviation & transportation missions.
VISITOR ATTRACTIONS: Bataan Memorial Museum (off base).
Key Contacts
COMMANDER: Maj Gen Melvyn S Montano, Adjutant General of New Mexico, 505-474-1202, FAX 505-474-1289, DSN 867-8202.
PUBLIC AFFAIRS: Thomas O Koch, paonm@nm-ngnet.army.mil, 505-474-2785, FAX 505-474-1674, DSN 867-8785.
TRANSPORTATION: Frank Cordova (for Col John Alvarado) 505-474-1665, FAX 505-474-1664, DSN 846-8665.
PERSONNEL/COMMUNITY ACTIVITIES: CWO Juan Espinoza, Dir of Personnel, 505-474-1573, DSN 867-8573.

Personnel and Expenditures
ACTIVE DUTY PERSONNEL: 385; Guardsmen 3800
DEPENDENTS: 0
CIVILIAN PERSONNEL: 365
MILITARY PAYROLL EXPENDITURE: $19 mil
CONTRACT EXPENDITURE: $ 0.2 mil
Services *Temporary Housing:* BAQ units 1.
Child Care/Capacities: No day care facilities.
Schools: College courses. *Medical Facilities:*
No medical facilities. *Recreational Facilities:*
Gym; Fitness center/Weight room.

White Sands Missile Range

574. White Sands Missile Range
WSMR
White Sands
US Army White Sands Missile Range
White Sands Missile Range, NM 88002-5047
505-678-2121; DSN 258-2121
Internet: http://www.wsmr.army.mil
OFFICER-OF-THE-DAY: 505-678-2031, DSN
258-2031

Profile
BRANCH: Army.
SIZE AND LOCATION: 2.0 mil acres. In Tularosa Basin between Sacramento Mountains on E and San Andres on W. Main post at base of Organ Mountain Range. From El Paso: Alamogordo/Hwy 54 Exit off I-10, off-ramp Gateway N, continue NE until Gateway N becomes War Hwy, WSMR straight ahead approx 40 mi. From Las Cruces: Hwy 70/82 E Exit from I-10 or I-25, about 25 mi to missile range exit. From Alamogordo: Hwy 70/82 W, approx 47 mi to missile range exit. *County:* Dona Ana; Otero; Sierra; Socorro; Lincoln; Torrance.
MAJOR UNITS: Test & Evaluation Command; National Range Operations Directorate; Materiel Test Directorate; Instrumentation Development Directorate; Nuclear Effects Directorate; Support Troops Bn; Air Operations Directorate; Naval Air Warfare Center, Weapons Division, White Sands; Army Research Laboratory Battlefield Environments Division & Electronic Warfare Branch; Army Training & Doctrine Command Analysis Center; NASA White Sands Test Facility.
BASE HISTORY: Much of WSMR was once part of San Augustin Ranch, owned by Cox family since late 1800s, who still live a few miles W of main post. 1945, opened as White Sands Proving Ground to test feasibility of using missiles in warfare; world's first atomic bomb detonated in area known as Trinity Site; missile testing with Tiny Tim firings. Army airfield is Condron Field, SE of main post in dry lake bed. Today, designated as national test range, largest over land test facility in US. Supports missile development & test programs for DOD, other government agencies, some foreign governments, and private companies. White Sands Space Harbor alternate landing site for space shuttle & training site for NASA shuttle pilots. Mar 30, 1982, Space Shuttle *Columbia* ended third mission at range's Northrup Strip.
VISITOR ATTRACTIONS: Visitors center; Museum gift shop; Outdoor missile display; Trinity Site (open 1st Sat in Apr and Oct); Launch Site 33, National Historic Landmark (visits on special occasions).

Key Contacts
COMMANDER: Commanding General, 505-678-1101, DSN 258-1101.
PUBLIC AFFAIRS: Public Affairs Office, 88002-5047, 505-678-1134, DSN 258-1134.
PROCUREMENT: Contracting Directorate, 505-678-1215, DSN 258-1215.
TRANSPORTATION: 505-678-5924, DSN 258-5924.
PERSONNEL/COMMUNITY ACTIVITIES: Directorate of Personnel and Community Activities, 505-678-6103, DSN 258-6103.
Personnel and Expenditures
ACTIVE DUTY PERSONNEL: 707
DEPENDENTS: 1593
CIVILIAN PERSONNEL: 3579 government civilians; 2695 contractors
MILITARY PAYROLL EXPENDITURE: $17.5 mil
CONTRACT EXPENDITURE: $347.4 mil
Services
Housing: Family units 848; Unaccompanied officer quarters 16; Duplex units SEQ 10; Barracks spaces 492; SEQ apartments 20; OQ apartments 16. *Temporary Housing:* VIP units 3; VOQ units 32; VEQ units 16; Guesthouse units 15; DVQ 3. *Commissary:* Yes; *Exchange:* Retail store; Barber shop; Dry cleaners; Florist; Bank; Service station; Convenience store; Optical store; Gift shop. *Child Care/Capacities:* Day care center capacity 125. *Schools:* Preschool/Kindergarten; Elementary; Intermediate/Junior high; Army education center. *Base Library:* Yes. *Medical Facilities:* Medical clinic; Dental clinic. *Recreational Facilities:* Bowling center; Movie theater; Pool; Gym; Golf course; Stables; Tennis courts; Racquetball court; Skating rink; Softball field; Football field; Auto shop; Craft shop; Youth center; Community club; Community center.

New York

Albany

575. Albany Naval & Marine Corps Reserve Readiness Center
780 Washington Ave
Albany, NY 12203-1492
518-482-1133, 489-5441; FAX 518-489-0841
Profile
BRANCH: Naval Reserve; Marine Corps Reserve.
LOCATION: Approx 145 mi N of NYC. *County:* Albany.
MAJOR UNITS: REDCOM ONE Activity; F Co, 2nd Bn, 25th Marine Regiment.
Key Contacts
COMMANDER: CDR T G Smith.

Amityville

576. Amityville Naval & Marine Corps Reserve Center
Armed Forces Reserve Center
600 Albany Ave
Amityville, NY 11701-1124
516-842-4850, 842-3209, 842-1994; FAX 516-842-3083
Profile
BRANCH: Naval Reserve; Marine Corps Reserve.
LOCATION: SE New York. *County:* Suffolk.
MAJOR UNITS: REDCOM FOUR Activity; A Co, 6th Communications Bn; Communications Co, 6th Communications Bn.
Key Contacts
COMMANDER: LCDR J C Bozeman.

Ballston Spa

577. Ballston Spa, Naval Nuclear Power Training Unit
NPTU Ballston Spa
PO Box 300
Ballston Spa, NY 12020-0300
518-884-1260; FAX 518-884-1843
Profile
BRANCH: Navy.
LOCATION: 10 mi from Saratoga Springs, NY, 8 mi from Ballston Spa, 42 mi NE of Scotia, NY, near town of West Milton, approx 3 mi from NY Rte 29. *County:* Saratoga.
MAJOR UNITS: Naval Nuclear Power Training Unit.
BASE HISTORY: Department of Energy facility operated by Lockheed Martin to train Navy personnel in safe operation and maintenance of nuclear reactors.
VISITOR ATTRACTIONS: No visitors allowed.
Key Contacts
COMMANDER: CDR D M Baker, Jr.
PUBLIC AFFAIRS: CDR C G Wenz; LTjg J A Wurley (point of contact) 518-884-1850.
Personnel and Expenditures
ACTIVE DUTY PERSONNEL: 1100
DEPENDENTS: 560
Services
Housing: Family units None. *Commissary:* Yes; *Exchange:* Retail store; Barber shop; Military clothing store; Convenience store; Located 30 mi S. *Child Care/Capacities:* Home day care program. *Schools:* No on-base schools. *Medical Facilities:* Navy branch clinic located 8 mi away.

Bronx

578. Bronx Naval & Marine Corps Reserve Center
MCRC Ft Schuyler
4 Pennyfield Ave, Ft Schuyler
Bronx, NY 10465-4196
718-892-0312, 892-7568; FAX 718-892-9464
Profile
BRANCH: Naval Reserve; Marine Corps Reserve.
LOCATION: *County:* Bronx.
MAJOR UNITS: REDCOM FOUR Activity; HQ, 6th Communications Bn; HQ Co, 6th Communications Bn; Communications Support Co, 6th Communications Bn.
Key Contacts
COMMANDER: CDR W A Gustafson.

Brooklyn

579. Brooklyn Coast Guard Air Station
CGAS Brooklyn
Floyd Bennett Field
Brooklyn, NY 11234-7097
718-615-2409; FAX 718-615-2411
Profile
BRANCH: Coast Guard; Naval Reserve; Marine Corps Reserve.
SIZE AND LOCATION: 400 acres. On Jamaica Bay 6 mi across from JFK IAP; off I-278 at Flatbush Ave. *County:* Kings.
MAJOR UNITS: Coast Guard Air Station, Brooklyn; NY Police Dept Aviation; Naval Reserve Center, Brooklyn; Marine Corps Reserve Center, Brooklyn; Armed Forces Reserve Center, Brooklyn.
BASE HISTORY: 1938, established at New York Municipal Airport, Floyd Bennett Field, on property granted to federal government by Mayor LaGuardia. Noted for early work with helicopters & 1st helicopter training school. 1943, all Allied helicopter pilots trained here. Developed early rescue equipment including rescue hoist.
VISITOR ATTRACTIONS: Tours (contact PAO).
Key Contacts
COMMANDER: CDR Michael Wallace, 718-615-2499, FAX 718-615-2483.
PUBLIC AFFAIRS: LT John Brenner, 718-615-2405, FAX 718-615-2411.
Personnel and Expenditures
ACTIVE DUTY PERSONNEL: 100
Services
Housing: Unaccompanied enlisted quarters 40; Mobile home units 10. *Exchange:* Retail store; Barber shop; Dry cleaners; Food shop; Furniture store; Military clothing store; Convenience store; Beauty shop; Laundromat. *Child Care/Capacities:* No day care facilities. *Schools:* No on-base schools. *Medical Facilities:* Medical clinic. *Recreational Facilities:* Pool; Fitness center/ Weight room; Softball field; Auto shop; Craft shop; Picnic area; Consolidated club.

580. Brooklyn Coast Guard Supply Center
SUPCEN Brooklyn
830 Third Ave
Brooklyn, NY 11232-1596
718-965-5091

OFFICER-OF-THE-DAY: Customer Service
Branch 718-965-5386

Profile

BRANCH: Coast Guard.

SIZE AND LOCATION: 2 warehouse buildings. In Brooklyn on corner of Third Ave and
30th St; 1 mi W of Hamilton (3rd) Ave Exit
of US-278, Brooklyn-Queens Expy. *County:*
Kings.

MAJOR UNITS: Coast Guard Electronics/Gen-
eral Materiel Inventory Control Point (E/
GICP).

BASE HISTORY: 1921, established as US
Army base, 58th St, Brooklyn. 1930, command moved to present location. 1942, "Coast
Guard Store" relocated to Jersey City, NJ, until 1955, when it returned to present location.
1950, designated Coast Guard Supply Center.
Today, base serves as an inventory control
point, warehousing, light industrial facility.
Open only during working hours, 0630-1700,
weekdays.

Key Contacts

COMMANDER: 718-965-5234.
PROCUREMENT: 718-965-5757.
TRANSPORTATION: 718-965-5793.
PERSONNEL/COMMUNITY ACTIVITIES:
718-965-5734.

Personnel and Expenditures

ACTIVE DUTY PERSONNEL: 130
CIVILIAN PERSONNEL: 130
CONTRACT EXPENDITURE: $2 mil

581. New York Area Command & Fort Hamilton

NYAC & Ft Hamilton
101st St & Fort Hamilton Pky
Brooklyn, NY 11252-5330
718-630-4101; FAX 718-630-4439; DSN
232-4101; DSN FAX 323-4439
OFFICER-OF-THE-DAY: Staff Duty Officer (after
4pm); 718-630-4565

Profile

BRANCH: Army.

SIZE AND LOCATION: 177 acres. Residential
area; SW tip of Brooklyn Borough at base of
Verrazano-Narrows Bridge; approx 8 mi to
midtown NYC; approx 8 mi to JFK and LGA
airports. *County:* Kings.

MAJOR UNITS: New York City Recruiting Bn;
Military Entrance Processing Station;
Ainsworth Army Medical Clinic; 77th AR-
COM Ernie Pyle USAR; 8th Medical Bri-
gade; 1179th Deployment Support Brigade.

BASE HISTORY: June 1826, cornerstone laid
(20th Century fort named after first Secretary
of Treasury, Alexander Hamilton). Robert E
Lee served as post engineer. During Civil
War, fort federal prison for captured confeder-
ates. Abner Doubleday commander during
first months of war. During WWI & WWII
fort served as embarkation & separation center. Original fort is Officers Club; one of few
Army saluting stations with salutes fired by
Ceremonial Platoon for visiting warships; provides facilities and support for Army and
DOD in NY metro area, more than 300 reserve and NG units; only active Army post in
NY metro area. Forts Wadsworth, Totten, &
Bellmore Maintenance Support Facility are
sub-installations. Ft Hamilton provides 26th
Army Band & honor guards for patriotic
events.

VISITOR ATTRACTIONS: Harbor Defense
Museum, part of original fort.

Key Contacts

COMMANDER: LTC Donald J McGhee,
718-630-4706, FAX 718-630-4709, DSN
232-4706.
PUBLIC AFFAIRS: Concetta E Pinto,
718-630-4820, FAX 718-630-4439, DSN
232-4820, PINTOC@dix-emh1-army.mil..
TRANSPORTATION: Dina Piacenti,
718-630-4077, FAX 718-630-4217, DSN
232-4077, DSN FAX 232-4217.
PERSONNEL/COMMUNITY ACTIVITIES:
Stephanie Ataman, 718-630-4040, FAX
718-630-4613, DSN 232-4040.

Personnel and Expenditures

ACTIVE DUTY PERSONNEL: 289
DEPENDENTS: 863
CIVILIAN PERSONNEL: 200

Services

Housing: Family units 442; Unaccompanied enlisted quarters 58; Duplex units 2; Townhouse
units 15; Barracks spaces 32. *Temporary Housing:* VOQ units 24; VEQ units 22; Unaccompanied officer/Enlisted quarters 30; Guesthouse
units 42; Transient quarters 25. *Commissary:*
Yes; *Exchange:* Retail store; Barber shop; Dry
cleaners; Service station; Military clothing store;
Convenience store; Beauty shop; Credit union;
ATM; Post office; Fast food; Thrift shop; Class
VI; Garden center. *Child Care/Capacities:* Day
care center capacity 72, 6wks-4yrs; Home day
care program; Summer day camp; Before & after school programs. *Schools:* No on-base
schools. *Base Library:* Yes. *Medical Facilities:*
Medical clinic; Pharmacy; Veterinary services
once every 3 months. *Recreational Facilities:*
Bowling center; Movie theater; Pool; Gym; Recreation center; Tennis courts; Fitness center/
Weight room; Softball field; Football field; Auto
shop; Craft shop; Youth center; Picnic area;
Community club.

Buffalo

582. Buffalo Coast Guard Group

1 Fuhrmann Blvd
Buffalo, NY 14203-3189
716-843-9502, 843-9561
OFFICER-OF-THE-DAY: 716-846-4152

Profile

BRANCH: Coast Guard.

SIZE AND LOCATION: 10 acres. City of Buffalo; N end of Fuhrmann Blvd. *County:* Erie.

MAJOR UNITS: Coast Guard Station, Buffalo;
Marine Safety Office, Buffalo; Electronic
Support Det, Buffalo; Coast Guard Reserve
Group, Buffalo.

VISITOR ATTRACTIONS: Buffalo lighthouse.

Key Contacts

PUBLIC AFFAIRS: 716-846-4184.
PROCUREMENT: 716-846-5823.
TRANSPORTATION: 716-846-5823.

Personnel and Expenditures

ACTIVE DUTY PERSONNEL: 75
CIVILIAN PERSONNEL: 2

Services

Housing: Dormitory spaces 8. *Exchange:* Retail
store. *Recreational Facilities:* Tennis courts;
Softball field; Football field; Basketball.

583. Buffalo Naval & Marine Corps Reserve Center

NMCRC
3 Porter Ave
Buffalo, NY 14201-1096
716-883-1016, 883-1046; FAX 716-883-2170;
DSN 1-800-737-8762, ext 695

Profile

BRANCH: Naval Reserve; Marine Corps Reserve.

LOCATION: *County:* Erie.

MAJOR UNITS: REDCOM ONE Activity; I
Co, 3rd Bn, 25th Marine Regiment.

Key Contacts

COMMANDER: CDR L G Neuwirth.

584. US Army Corps of Engineers, Buffalo District

CELRB
1776 Niagara St
Buffalo, NY 14207-3199
716-879-4200; FAX 716-879-4195
Internet: http://www.ncb.usace.army.mil/

Profile

BRANCH: Army.

SIZE AND LOCATION: 6 acres. From NY
State Thruway, Niagara Exit in Buffalo at NY
Rte 198, Dann St; also at Black Rock Lock on
Niagara River. *County:* Erie.

MAJOR UNITS: Corps of Engineers, Buffalo
District.

BASE HISTORY: 1824, Corps began serving
lower lakes region. 1857, Buffalo District began. District boundaries have changed some-
what over the years, but there has been a Buffalo District since mid-19th century. District
stretches from St Lawrence Valley in northern NY to lowlands W of Toledo, OH. Part of
North Central Division. Performs civil works
construction.

VISITOR ATTRACTIONS: Locks.

Key Contacts

COMMANDER: Col Michael J Conrad Jr.
PUBLIC AFFAIRS: John E Derbyshire.

Personnel and Expenditures

ACTIVE DUTY PERSONNEL: 3
CIVILIAN PERSONNEL: 350

Services *Base Library:* Yes. *Recreational Facilities:* Horseshoe pits.

Fort Drum

585. Fort Drum

HQ, 10th Mountain Div (Light Infantry) & Ft
Drum
Fort Drum, NY 13602-5000
315-772-6900; FAX 315-772-5809; DSN
341-6900
Internet: http://www.drum.army.mil
OFFICER-OF-THE-DAY: 315-772-5647, DSN
341-5647

Profile

BRANCH: Army.

SIZE AND LOCATION: 107,265 acres. Off of I-
81, Exit 48; approx 75 mi N of Syracuse and
30 mi S of Canadian border. Approx 12 mi
from Watertown. *County:* Jefferson.

MAJOR UNITS: 10th Mountain Division (Light
Infantry).

BASE HISTORY: Named for Lt Gen Hugh A
Drum, Commander of First Army during

early years of WWII. Training facility for Army National Guard and Reserve units.
VISITOR ATTRACTIONS: Close to Thousand Islands resort/ski areas.

Key Contacts
COMMANDER: Maj Gen Lawson W Magruder, 10000 10th Mtn Div Dr, Ft Drum, NY 13602-5007, 315-772-5565, FAX 315-772-5165, DSN 341-5565, MagruderL@drum-emh5.army.mil 341-5565.
PUBLIC AFFAIRS: Maj Robert D Saxon, Public Affairs Office, 10000 10th Mtn Div Dr, Ft Drum 13602-5028, 315-772-5461, FAX 315-772-8295, DSN 341-5461, afzs-pao@drum-emh4.army.mil.
PROCUREMENT: Bruce Ferguson, 315-772-6515, FAX 315-772-8277, DSN 341-6515, afzs-doc@drum-emh4.army.mil.
TRANSPORTATION: Ms Ann Coleman, 315-772-8232, FAX 315-772-3451, DSN 341-8232, SMPT.colemana@drum-emh1.army.mil.
PERSONNEL/COMMUNITY ACTIVITIES: William Steinhauer, 315-772-5685, FAX 315-772-0481, DSN 341-5685, afzs-pa@drum-emh4.army.mil.

Personnel and Expenditures
ACTIVE DUTY PERSONNEL: 10,100
DEPENDENTS: 13,500
CIVILIAN PERSONNEL: 2800
MILITARY PAYROLL EXPENDITURE: $247.5 mil
CONTRACT EXPENDITURE: $61 mil

Services
Housing: Family units 4272; Unaccompanied officer quarters; Unaccompanied enlisted quarters; Barracks spaces; RV/Camper sites. *Temporary Housing:* VOQ units; Inn/Hotel 100 rooms. *Commissary:* Yes; *Exchange:* Retail store; Barber shop; Dry cleaners; Food shop; Florist; Bank; Service station; Furniture store; Bakery; Military clothing store; Convenience store; Beauty shop; Laundromat; Credit union. *Child Care/Capacities:* Day care center capacity 430, 6wks-12yrs; Home day care program; Latch key program; Summer day camp. *Schools:* No on-base schools. *Base Library:* Yes. *Medical Facilities:* Medical clinic; Dental clinic; Pharmacy; Veterinary services; Ambulatory health care center. *Recreational Facilities:* Bowling center; Movie theater; Pool; Gym; Tennis courts; Racquetball court; Fitness center/Weight room; Softball field; Football field; Auto shop; Craft shop; Officers club; NCO club; Camping; Fishing/Hunting; Enlisted club; Youth center; Picnic area; Skeet range; Outdoor recreation equipment rental; Outdoor swimming area.

Fort Tilden

586. Fort Tilden (USAR)
Fort Tilden, NY 11695-0513
718-945-4900
Profile
BRANCH: Army Reserve.
SIZE AND LOCATION: 9 acres. 5 mi W of Rockaway, NY; 1 mi E of Breezy Point Retirement Community; JFK IAP 15 mi; 2.5 mi from Exit 11 S Belt Pkwy; 12 mi from Ft Hamilton, NY. *County:* Kings.
MAJOR UNITS: 449th Maintenance Co; 766th Supply & Service Co; 695th Maintenance Bn.

BASE HISTORY: Formerly a Nike missile base with two 16" gun emplacements for coastal defense during WWII.
Key Contacts
COMMANDER: Capt Richard M Garkand, 718-945-4900.
PUBLIC AFFAIRS: 718-352-5657.
PROCUREMENT: 609-562-3456.

Frankfort

587. Frankfort Naval Reserve Center
201 3rd Ave
Frankfort, NY 13340-1419
315-894-8296, 894-6156; FAX 315-894-6213
Profile
BRANCH: Naval Reserve.
LOCATION: NE central NY; 10 mi ESE of Utica. *County:* Herkimer.
MAJOR UNITS: REDCOM ONE Activity.
Key Contacts
COMMANDER: LCDR P L Joseph.

Garden City

588. 1st Marine Corps District Headquarters
1st MCD (Branch)
605 Stewart Ave
Garden City, NY 11530-4703
516-228-5640; FAX 516-228-5794
Profile
BRANCH: Marine Corps.
SIZE AND LOCATION: 4 acres. On Long Island, NY in heart of Garden City; 35 mi E of NYC; 30 mi E of JFK IAP & LaGuardia AP. *County:* Nassau.
MAJOR UNITS: Inspector-Instructor 2nd Bn 25th Marines; Defense Contract Management Agency.
BASE HISTORY: First MCD (Marine Corps District) spread over 159,000 sq mi. Bldg formerly owned by Atlantic & Pacific Tea Co.
Key Contacts
COMMANDER: Col A D Blice.
PUBLIC AFFAIRS: Capt Bentley.
Services *Commissary:* Yes; *Exchange: Child Care/Capacities: Base Library:* Yes. *Recreational Facilities:* Gym; Clubs combined.

Glens Falls

589. Glens Falls Naval Reserve Center
NRC Glens Falls
2 Parker St
Glens Falls, NY 12801-2285
518-792-6368, 792-0807; FAX 518-745-5847
Profile
BRANCH: Naval Reserve.
LOCATION: *County:* Warren.
MAJOR UNITS: REDCOM ONE Activity.
Key Contacts
COMMANDER: LCDR Russell E Dorrell III.
Personnel and Expenditures
ACTIVE DUTY PERSONNEL: 6; 156 reservists

Horseheads

590. Horseheads Naval Reserve Center
NAVRESCEN Horseheads
3126 Lake Rd
Horseheads, NY 14845-3103
607-732-7950, 732-8938; FAX 607-732-0269
Profile
BRANCH: Naval Reserve.
SIZE AND LOCATION: 0.5 acre. Near Big Flats & Elmira, NY. 1 mi S of Hwy 17. Near Elmira/Corning Regional Airport. *County:* Chemung.
MAJOR UNITS: REDCOM ONE Activity.
BASE HISTORY: Colocated with Cpt R D Allen Army Reserve Training Center built in 1956.
VISITOR ATTRACTIONS: Mark Twain Museum; Soaring Air Museum.
Key Contacts
COMMANDER: LCDR Mark A Moore.
Personnel and Expenditures
ACTIVE DUTY PERSONNEL: 11; 200 reservists
Services *Base Library:* Yes.

Lake Seneca

591. Seneca Lake Sonar Test Facility
NUSC, Det Seneca Lake
Lake Seneca, NY 14441
Profile
BRANCH: Navy.
LOCATION: Finger Lakes region of NY. *County:* Yates; Seneca.
MAJOR UNITS: Naval Undersea Warfare Center Det; Sonar Test Facility Seneca Lake.
BASE HISTORY: Conducts testing & evaluation of equipment from single-element transducers to complex sonar arrays. Detachment of Naval Undersea Warfare Center HQ, Newport, RI, 401-841-2182.

Latham

592. Adjutant General/Commander of New York
330 Old Niskayuna Rd
Latham, NY 12110-2224
518-786-4502; FAX 518-786-4325
Profile
BRANCH: Army National Guard.
MAJOR UNITS: New York National Guard.
Key Contacts
COMMANDER: Maj Gen John H Fenimore V.

Mattydale

593. Syracuse Naval & Marine Corps Reserve Center
5803 E Molly Rd
Mattydale, NY 13211-1999
Mailing Address
PO Box 36

Syracuse, NY 13211-0036
315-455-2441, 455-2442; FAX 315-454-4327
Profile
BRANCH: Naval Reserve; Marine Corps Reserve.
LOCATION: In N Syracuse, near junct of I-90 & I81. *County:* Onondaga.
MAJOR UNITS: REDCOM ONE Activity; B Co, 8th Tank Bn.
Key Contacts
COMMANDER: LCDR G J Haben.

New York

594. Fort Totten
643 Park Ave
New York, NY 11359
718-352-5700; DSN 456-0700
Profile
BRANCH: Army Reserve.
LOCATION: Flushing, Queens at Throgs Neck Bridge off of Cross Island Expy. *County:* Queens.
MAJOR UNITS: 77th Infantry Division (RTU); 1174th Transportation Terminal Bn.
BASE HISTORY: 1967, 77th USARCOM, "Statue of Liberty" Division, 1 of 5 Army Reserve Commands in 1st Army and 1 of 20 in continental US formed at Ft Wadsworth. 1968, moved to Ft Totten. With assigned strength of 15,000 citizen-soldiers, largest Army Reserve Command. Under jurisdiction of Ft Hamilton, NY.
VISITOR ATTRACTIONS: Tours of Old Fort Totten.
Key Contacts
COMMANDER: Col John W Pershing.
PUBLIC AFFAIRS: 718-352-5657, DSN 456-0657.
Services *Exchange:* Retail store; Barber shop. *Child Care/Capacities:* Day care center. *Recreational Facilities:* Pool; Gym; Tennis courts; Fitness center/Weight room; Softball field.

595. Governors Island Coast Guard Support Center
Bldg 140, Box 5, Governors Island
New York, NY 10004
Profile
BRANCH: Coast Guard.
SIZE AND LOCATION: 175 acres. On Governors Island off S tip of Manhattan. *County:* Kings.
BASE HISTORY: Island currently in caretaker status with island plus 3 mil sq ft. of offices, apartments, and historic forts empty; final disposition of property due by 2002.
FUTURE CLOSURE/REALIGNMENT: Center in caretaker status.
Personnel and Expenditures
ACTIVE DUTY PERSONNEL: 60
Services
Housing: Family units 714; Unaccompanied enlisted quarters 145; BAQ units 470; Student units, 250. *Temporary Housing:* VIP units 2.

596. Navy Office of Information, East
605 Third Ave, 14 Fl
New York, NY 10158-0180
212-801-0031; FAX 212-801-0034
Profile
BRANCH: Navy.
MAJOR UNITS: Navy Office of Information, East.
BASE HISTORY: Serves DE, MD, NJ, NY, & PA. Also liaison with publishing & television industry in NYC area.

597. US Army Corps of Engineers, New York District
26 Federal Plaza
New York, NY 10278-0090
212-264-0100
Internet: http://www.nan.usace.army.mil/
Profile
BRANCH: Army.
LOCATION: Jacob K Javits Federal Bldg.
MAJOR UNITS: Corps of Engineers, New York District.
BASE HISTORY: The Cradle of the Corps. One of 4 districts in North Atlantic Division. 1776, Rufus Putnam named Chief Engineer by President Washington. 1802, Corps established at West Point; until 1866, Superintendent also Chief of Engineers. Early 1900s, New York Corps formally organized into 3 districts. 1938, districts merged into present organization. Mission: military construction & civil works.
Key Contacts
PUBLIC AFFAIRS: Peter H Shugert, Peter.H. Shugert@usace.army.mil.

598. US Army Corps of Engineers, North Atlantic Division
CENAD
90 Church St
New York, NY 10007-2979
212-264-7101; FAX 212-264-9498
Internet: http://www.usace.army.mil/nad/nad. htm
Profile
BRANCH: Army.
SIZE AND LOCATION: Offices only. In Federal Post Office Bldg in NYC financial district. *County:* New York.
MAJOR UNITS: Corps of Engineers, North Atlantic Division.
BASE HISTORY: Oversees five subordinate districts: NY, PA, MD, VA, & MA. Performs military & civil works construction.
Key Contacts
COMMANDER: Maj Gen Milton Hunter.
PUBLIC AFFAIRS: David Lipsky, CENAD-PA, 212-264-7500.

Newburgh

599. Stewart Air National Guard Base
Stewart ANGB
One Militia Way
Newburgh, NY 12550-5043
914-563-2000; DSN 636-2000
Internet: http://132.24.33.177
OFFICER-OF-THE-DAY: 914-563-2286, DSN 636-2286
Profile
BRANCH: Marine Corps; Air National Guard.
SIZE AND LOCATION: 250 acres. Entrance on Rte 17K, 1 mi from intersection of I-84 & I-87; 4 mi W of Newburgh, adj to Stewart IAP and Stewart Army Subpost of US Military Academy; 60 mi N of NYC. *County:* Orange.
MAJOR UNITS: 105th Airlift Wing; Marine Air Transport Refueler Group (VMGR-452); Armed Forces Health Clinic; Marine Aircraft Group 49, Det B (MAG-49); Marine Air Logistics Squadron 49 (MALS-49) MAG-49.
BASE HISTORY: Named for Lachlan Stewart, Scottish sea captain 1850-70s. 1941, made part of West Point and dedicated as "Wings of West Point." 1947, became AFB. 1949, became air defense base. 1960s, redesignated Air Force and Air Force Academy Aircrew and Examining Center. 1970, released back to civilian control. Early 80s, ANG base built & 100th relocated to Stewart from Westchester. Currently nation's 2nd largest airport in total area.
VISITOR ATTRACTIONS: Historic Mid-Hudson Valley; West Point Military Academy.
Key Contacts
COMMANDER: Col Thomas P Maguire, Jr; 914-563-2001, DSN 636-2001.
PUBLIC AFFAIRS: Trish Heikkila, Public Affairs Manager, 914-563-2031, FAX 914-563-2013, DSN 636-2031, theikkila@ nyswf.ang.af.mil.
PROCUREMENT: SMSgt Carolyn Melber, 914-563-2831, DSN 636-2831.
TRANSPORTATION: MSgt Gregory Sullivan, 914-563-2839, DSN 636-2839.
PERSONNEL/COMMUNITY ACTIVITIES: Capt Edward Kenny, Director of Personnel, 914-563-2011, FAX 914-563-2013; Maj Ron LoPorto, Director of Community Initiatives, 914-563-2018, DSN 636-2018 636-2011.
Personnel and Expenditures
ACTIVE DUTY PERSONNEL: 550
CIVILIAN PERSONNEL: 400
MILITARY PAYROLL EXPENDITURE: $30 mil
Services *Exchange:* Retail store; Barber shop; Dry cleaners; Bank. *Child Care/Capacities:* Day care center. *Base Library:* Yes. *Medical Facilities:* Medical clinic; Dental clinic; Major hospital at West Point. *Recreational Facilities:* Bowling center; Pool; Gym; Tennis courts; Racquetball court; Softball field; Auto shop; Craft shop; Officers club; Enlisted club; Support activities and all on-base housing provided by US Military Academy and Stewart Army Subpost.

Niagara Falls

600. Niagara Falls Air Reserve Station
914 AW
914th Airlift Wing
Niagara Falls, NY 14304-5000
716-236-2000; FAX 716-236-6349; DSN 238-2000
Profile
BRANCH: Air Force Reserve.
SIZE AND LOCATION: 987 acres. 6 mi E of Niagara Falls, adj to Niagara Falls IAP. *County:* Niagara.
MAJOR UNITS: 914th Airlift Wing; 328th Airlift Squadron; 70th Aeromedical Evacuation Unit; 30th Aerial Port Squadron; 914th Logistics Group; 914th Support Group; 107th Air Refueling Wing, ANG.
BASE HISTORY: 1963, activated as 914th Troop Carrier Group (Medium) at Niagara

Falls IAP and assigned to 512th Troop Carrier Wing (Medium). 328th Troop Carrier Squadron assigned to newly activated group. Active duty Oct-Nov 1962 (Cuban Missile Crisis). 1967, redesignated Tactical Airlift Group. 1971, assumed command Niagara Falls Air Reserve Base. Flew C-130A Hercules transport until 1986, when it converted to C-130E, currently flying C-130H, was assigned to 22nd Air Force, 1990-91, assigned to AMC, and called to active duty in Operation Desert Shield/Storm.

VISITOR ATTRACTIONS: Bldg 800—display dedicated to Desert Shield/Storm; Niagra Falls.

Key Contacts
COMMANDER: Col C Von Berge, USAFR, Attn: Wing Commander/CC, 716-236-2121, DSN 238-2121.
PUBLIC AFFAIRS: Neil E Nolf, Attn: Public Affairs Office/PA, Bldg 800 Kirkbridge Dr, 716-236-2136, DSN 238-2136.
PROCUREMENT: Dennis Pasiak, Contracting Office/LGC, 716-236-2177, DSN 238-2177.
TRANSPORTATION: Bob Arndt, Transportation Officer/LGTM.
PERSONNEL/COMMUNITY ACTIVITIES: See Public Affairs Office.

Personnel and Expenditures
ACTIVE DUTY PERSONNEL: 60; 2277 Reservists
CIVILIAN PERSONNEL: 738
MILITARY PAYROLL EXPENDITURE: $50 mil
CONTRACT EXPENDITURE: $20 mil

Services
Housing: Barracks spaces 4. *Temporary Housing:* VIP units 3; VOQ units 1. *Exchange:* Retail store; Military clothing store; Convenience store; Credit union. *Schools:* No on-base schools. *Medical Facilities:* Medical clinic. *Recreational Facilities:* Bowling center; Gym; Recreation center; Fitness center/Weight room; Softball field; Falcon club, all ranks.

Peekskill

601. Camp Smith
Rte 202
Peekskill, NY 10566-5000
914-734-7654; FAX 914-734-7376; DSN 589-7654
Internet: http://www.dmna.state.ny.us/map/
OFFICER-OF-THE-DAY: Command Post, 914-734-7993, DSN 589-7993
Profile
BRANCH: Joint Service Installation; Army National Guard.
SIZE AND LOCATION: 1970 acres. In NW corner of Westchester Co on Rte 202 & Rte 6; 1 mi from Peekskill; 8 mi from USMA, West Point; 40 mi N of NTC; situated in NY highlands along Hudson River. *County:* Westchester.
MAJOR UNITS: State Area Readiness Command-NY, Det 2, HQ; 53rd Troop Command (Det 1, HQ, STARC-NY); 1st Bn 105th Infantry, Co A; 199th Band; Combined Maintenance Shop A; Organizational Maintenance Shop 16; Organizational Maintenance Shop 20; 106th Regimental Training Institute; Peekskill Warehouse.
BASE HISTORY: 1882, established; first encampment. 1885, site purchased. 1926, named

for Alfred E Smith, NY Governor. 1977, NG garrison detachment formed. Base serves weekend training needs of local, state, & USAR; ranges used daily for marksmanship programs for small arms. Occasionally houses military transients in BOQ, if room. No families unless justified to post commander. Occasionally supports boy/girl scout troops in transit. Camp classified as Collective Training Area & Annual Training site for battalion sized units. Terrain restricts camp to light infantry, signal & maintenance units.
VISITOR ATTRACTIONS: Views of Bear Mountain Park & Hudson River; Appalachian Trail.
Key Contacts
COMMANDER: Post Commander, 914-734-7654, FAX 914-734-7376, DSN 589-7654; Facility Manager 914-734-7429, DSN 589-7429.
PROCUREMENT: Supply, 914-734-7392, DSN 589-7392.
PERSONNEL/COMMUNITY ACTIVITIES: Director of Personnel, 914-734-7361, FAX 914-734-7394, DSN 589-7361.
Personnel and Expenditures
ACTIVE DUTY PERSONNEL: 5
CIVILIAN PERSONNEL: 190
Services
Housing: Unaccompanied officer quarters 4; Barracks spaces 1680; Dormitory spaces; All temporary 30 day maximum, no weekends. *Temporary Housing:* VIP/VOQ/VEQ weekdays only; BOQ/BAQ weekends if not scheduled for troops. *Medical Facilities:* Infirmary. *Recreational Facilities:* Gym; Softball field; Officers club; NCO club; Camping; Youth center.

Rochester

602. Combined Support Maintenance Shop C/US Property & Fiscal Office—NY
CSMS-C/USP&FO-NY
Shop C, Rochester Warehouse
1500 E Henrietta Rd
Rochester, NY 14623-3181
716-424-2165, 424-3457; FAX 716-292-1623
OFFICER-OF-THE-DAY: 716-424-2165
Profile
BRANCH: Army National Guard.
SIZE AND LOCATION: 8 acres. 3 mi S of Rochester in Henrietta, NY; near Exit 14 of I-390, just N of intersection of E Henrietta Rd and Jefferson Rd. *County:* Monroe.
MAJOR UNITS: US Property & Fiscal Office-NY; ARL-SS Rochester Warehouse; Combined Support Maintenance Shop C; NY ARNG-Class IX.
BASE HISTORY: 1959, built as a supply support facility for NY Army NG, handling supplies such as service stock & repair parts. Currently used as transportation terminal, repair parts, warehouse, & direct support maintenance activity.
Key Contacts
TRANSPORTATION: ARL-SS Warehouse Supervisor, 716-424-3457, FAX 716-424-6036.
Personnel and Expenditures
ACTIVE DUTY PERSONNEL: 8
CIVILIAN PERSONNEL: 56

Services
Housing: None. *Child Care/Capacities:* No day care facilities. *Schools:* No on-base schools. *Medical Facilities:* No medical facilities.

603. Rochester Naval & Marine Corps Reserve Center
N&MCRTC Rochester
439 Paul Rd
Rochester, NY 14624-4790
716-247-6858, 247-6859, 247-7902; FAX 716-247-2014
Profile
BRANCH: Naval Reserve; Marine Corps Reserve.
LOCATION: *County:* Monroe.
MAJOR UNITS: REDCOM ONE Activity; HQ, 8th Tank Bn; HQ & Service Co, 8th Tank Bn.
Key Contacts
COMMANDER: LCDR S Vazquez.

Rome

604. Northeast Air Defense Sector
NEADS
305 Burhanna Rd
Rome, NY 13441-4507
MEADS: HQ, 315-334-6515, DSN 587-6515; MEA, 315-334-2119, DSN 587-2119
Internet: http://www.dmna.state.ny.us/ang/neads.html
Profile
BRANCH: Air National Guard.
SIZE AND LOCATION: 5836 acres. In Rome, NY; NY State Thruway, I-90, provides access. Traveling W, Exit 31 at Utica, follow Rte 49 W, or Exit 32 and Rte 233 N. Traveling E, Exit 33 to Rte 365 E; signs will lead to Skyline Gate. By air, use Handcock IAP at Syracuse, about 45 mi, or Oneida County 6 mi; NEADS, 305 Burhanna Rd, Rome, NY 13441-4507; MEA, 678 Perimeter Rd, Rome, NY 13441-4507. *County:* Oneida.
MAJOR UNITS: Northeast Air Defense Sector (NEADS); Minimal Essential Airfield (MEA); Rome Laboratories; Defense Finance and Accounting Service, Rome.
BASE HISTORY: Feb 1942, operations began. 13 name changes. 1948, named for Army Air Force pilot LTC Townsend E Griffiss, Buffalo native & first American flyer killed in European operations, WWII. Fighter Interceptor Group (FIG) first flying unit assigned. Air Materiel Command, later Air Force Logistics Command, host until 1951; Air Research & Development Command took over with Watson Laboratories, Rome Air Development Center. 1954, returned to Air Materiel Command. 1983, HQ 24th North American Defense Region. 1987, mission shifted to reserve forces. Mission of 416th BMW immediate & sustained, long-range strategic bombardment & aerial refueling. 1996, Griffiss AFB closed; made Air National Guard facility.
Services
Housing: None. *Exchange:* Barber shop; Dry cleaners; Food shop; Florist; Service station; Military clothing store; Convenience store; Beauty shop; Credit union; Class VI. *Child Care/Capacities: Medical Facilities:* Medical clinic.

Romulus

605. Seneca Army Depot Activity
SEDA
5786 State Rte 96
Romulus, NY 14541-5001
607-869-1110; FAX 607-869-1241; DSN
489-5110
Internet: http://147.217.15.5/rm/iocfact/seda.
htm
Profile
BRANCH: Army.
SIZE AND LOCATION: 10,600 acres. On NY
Rte 96 & 96A; 16 mi SE of Geneva, NY; 55
mi SE of Rochester; 50 mi SW of Syracuse;
35 mi N of Ithaca; 17 mi S of NY State Thru-
way. *County:* Seneca.
MAJOR UNITS: Seneca Army Depot Activity;
Coast Guard LORAN-C Transmitting Station;
Army Test, Maintenance, and Diagnostic
Equipment Support Operations; Defense Reu-
tilization & Marketing Office, Romulus
Branch.
BASE HISTORY: 1941, broke established records for speed of construction. 1956, expansion included Sampson AFB; development of
special weapons site (North Depot Activity).
1963, transferred from Chief of Ordnance to
Army Supply & Maintenance Command; renamed Seneca Army Depot. 1966, reassigned
to Army Materiel Command (later DAR-
COM, then AMC again). 1976, DESCOM activated with command & control over all
DARCOM depots. 1993, downgraded to depot activity under Tobyhanna Army Depot,
with major Reduction in Force (RIF). Current
missions: receives, stores, & ships conventional ammunition (including ammo demilitarization) & provides general supply, including
hazardous materials.
FUTURE CLOSURE/REALIGNMENT: BRAC
95, slated for closure, Sep 2000.
Key Contacts
COMMANDER: LTC Donald C Olson,
607-869-1206, FAX 607-869-1296, DSN
489-5206, DSN FAX 489-5296, siose-co @
ria-emh2.army.mil; Bruce W Johnson,
Civilian Executive, 607-869-1771, DSN
489-5771.
PUBLIC AFFAIRS: 607-869-1235, DSN
489-5235.
Personnel and Expenditures
ACTIVE DUTY PERSONNEL: 2
CIVILIAN PERSONNEL: 146
MILITARY PAYROLL EXPENDITURE: $10.4
mil (civilian/military)
CONTRACT EXPENDITURE: $10.5 mil
Services
Housing: Family units 180; Barracks spaces
450; Mobile home units 19; RV/Camper sites 3.
Medical Facilities: Medical clinic. *Recreational
Facilities:* Bowling center; Movie theater; Pool;
Gym; Recreation center; Tennis courts; Racquet-
ball court; Fitness center/Weight room; Softball
field; Football field; Auto shop; Craft shop; Offi-
cers club; NCO club; Camping; Fishing/Hunt-
ing.

Roslyn

606. Roslyn Station, Air National Guard
209 Harbor Hill Rd
Roslyn, NY 11576-2399
516-299-5201; DSN 456-5201
Internet: http://www.dmna.state.ny.us/ang/274.
html
Profile
BRANCH: Air National Guard.
SIZE AND LOCATION: 50.3 acres. Off Rte
495 (Long Island Expy), Clen Cove Rd exit;
27 mi E of New York City, on W end of Long
Island. *County:* Nassau; Suffolk.
MAJOR UNITS: 71st Regiment, 1st Bn, Det 2
(NYANG); 213th Engineer Installation
Squadron; 274th Combat Communications
Squadron.
FUTURE CLOSURE/REALIGNMENT: Major
closure by Sep 2000, contingent upon BRAC
requirement for sale of property at fair market
value.
Key Contacts
COMMANDER: Station Supervisor,
516-299-5212, DSN 456-5212.

Scotia

607. Schenectady County Airport, Air National Guard Base
1 Air National Guard Rd
Scotia, NY 12302-9752
518-786-4502; DSN 974-9210
Profile
BRANCH: Air National Guard.
SIZE AND LOCATION: 106 acres. Adj to
Schenectady Co Airport in town of Scotia; 2
mi N of Schenectady, off State Rte 50, 3 mi
from I-890; on S bank of Mohawk River; 15
mi from Albany Airport. *County:* Schenec-
tady.
MAJOR UNITS: 109th Airlift Wing (ANG).
BASE HISTORY: 1948, organized as 139th
Fighter Squadron. 1960, transitioned to heavy
transport aircraft. Mission: resupply remote
radar sites in Greenland; provide support to
Arctic & Antarctic operations as directed by
Air Mobility Command & Air National
Guard, including National Science Founda-
tion research in remote Arctic areas. Only to-
tal Air Force unit with aircraft equipped with
skis.
VISITOR ATTRACTIONS: Empire State
Aerosciences Museum.
Personnel and Expenditures
ACTIVE DUTY PERSONNEL: 1136 Guard
CIVILIAN PERSONNEL: 281
MILITARY PAYROLL EXPENDITURE: $22.1
mil
Services *Medical Facilities:* Dispensary; *Rec-
reational Facilities:* NCO club.

608. Scotia Naval Administrative Unit
Amsterdam Rd #1
Scotia, NY 12302-9460
518-370-0352
Profile
BRANCH: Navy.

LOCATION: 3 mi W of Schenectady, NY, on
Rte 5. *County:* Schenectady.
MAJOR UNITS: Navy Recruiting Area 1; Per-
sonnel Support Det.
Personnel and Expenditures
ACTIVE DUTY PERSONNEL: 2500
DEPENDENTS: 3000
Services *Commissary:* Yes; *Exchange:* Small
exchange. *Medical Facilities:* Medical clinic;
Dental clinic.

Syracuse

609. Defense Contract Management Command, Syracuse
615 Erie Blvd W
Syracuse, NY 13204
315-448-7817, FAX 315-448-7914
Internet: http://www.dcmc.dcrb.dla.mil/
Cassites/Syracuse/Index.htm
Profile
BRANCH: Defense Logistics Agency.
LOCATION: *County:* Onondaga.
MAJOR UNITS: Defense Contract Management
Command, Syracuse.
Key Contacts
COMMANDER: LTC Michael Padgett.

610. Syracuse Hancock IAP, Air National Guard Base
Syracuse, NY 13211-7099
315-454-6100; DSN 489-9100
Profile
BRANCH: Air National Guard.
SIZE AND LOCATION: 371 acres. 5 mi NE of
Syracuse, Exit 27, off I-81. *County:* Onon-
daga.
MAJOR UNITS: 174th Fighter Wing (ANG);
Base Operations, Hancock ANGB; 152nd
Tactical Control Group; 108th Tactical Con-
trol Squadron (ANG); 113th Tactical Control
Squadron (ANG).
BASE HISTORY: 174th TFW: 1947, organized
as 138th Fighter Squadron. Fighter unit for
most of its history; assigned to Tactical Air
Command (brief period with Air Defense
Command). Tactical Control Group: 1948, or-
ganized as 152nd Aircraft Control & Warning
Group, White Plains, NY. 1962, moved to
Hancock Field.
Personnel and Expenditures
ACTIVE DUTY PERSONNEL: 1058 Guard
CIVILIAN PERSONNEL: 343
MILITARY PAYROLL EXPENDITURE: $26.2
mil
Services *Medical Facilities:* Dispensary.

Watertown

611. Watertown Naval Reserve Center
NAVRESCEN Watertown
327 Mullin St
Watertown, NY 13601
Mailing Address
PO Box 247
Watertown, NY 13601-0247
315-782-1851; FAX 315-782-2350

E-mail: watertown@cnsrf.navy.mil
Profile
BRANCH: Naval Reserve.
SIZE AND LOCATION: 2 acres. In downtown Watertown; approx 70 mi from Syracuse Airport. *County:* Jefferson.
MAJOR UNITS: REDCOM ONE Activity; Naval Weapons Station Det 8 (NR); Naval Hospital Portsmouth Det (NR); NMCB 27 Det (NR).
BASE HISTORY: One of the oldest reserve centers.
Key Contacts
COMMANDER: LCDR P L Joseph.
PUBLIC AFFAIRS: RMCS(SW) T R Cramer.
Personnel and Expenditures
ACTIVE DUTY PERSONNEL: 6; 120 reservists
Services *Base Library:* Yes. *Recreational Facilities:* Fitness center/Weight room; Picnic area.

Watervliet

612. Watervliet Arsenal
WVA
Watervliet, NY 12189-4050
518-266-5111; DSN 974-5111
Profile
BRANCH: Army.
SIZE AND LOCATION: 140 acres. 7 mi N of Albany, NY, across Hudson River from Troy, NY, 6 mi from Albany Co. Airport. *County:* Albany.
MAJOR UNITS: Watervliet Arsenal; Benet Laboratories.
VISITOR ATTRACTIONS: Watervliet Arsenal Museum; History of cannon development; Site of Erie Canal; 19th-century manufacturing buildings; Arsenal on National Historic Register.
Key Contacts
COMMANDER: Col John C Rickman, 518-266-4294, DSN 974-4294.
PUBLIC AFFAIRS: John Swantek, 518-266-5090, 266-5418, DSN 974-5090, 974-5418.
Personnel and Expenditures
ACTIVE DUTY PERSONNEL: 3
DEPENDENTS: 48 (military & dependents residing at base)
CIVILIAN PERSONNEL: 1300
CONTRACT EXPENDITURE: $100 mil
Services
Housing: Family units 24. *Exchange:* Retail store. *Base Library:* Yes. *Medical Facilities:* Medical clinic. *Recreational Facilities:* Pool; Gym; Golf course; Tennis courts; Racquetball court; Fitness center/Weight room; Softball field; Craft shop; Officers club.

West Point

613. United States Military Academy
USMA/West Point
West Point, NY 10996-5000
914-938-4011; DSN 688-4011
Internet: http://www.usma.edu/
OFFICER-OF-THE-DAY: 914-938-3500, DSN 688-3500

Profile
BRANCH: Army.
SIZE AND LOCATION: 16,625 acres. Approx 56 mi N of New York City. NY Thruway N, Exit 16, follow US-6 E to Rte 293, signs to Academy marked; Stewart Airport approx 15 mi N in Newburgh, NY. *County:* Orange.
MAJOR UNITS: Corps of Cadets.
BASE HISTORY: Since 1802, West Point & US Military Academy have become synonymous titles. Nation's oldest service academy operated at historic site of nation's oldest military post in continuous operation. 1778, permanent garrison of Revolutionary troops stationed here on Hudson River. Mar 16, 1802, marks birth of Military Academy; opened with 10 cadets. US Corps of Cadets, approx 4400, organized as brigade of four regiments. Cadets members of Regular Army; receive about half of basic pay of 2nd Lt; pay for uniforms, textbooks, & incidentals; quarters, rations, & medical care provided. Training includes field & classroom instruction in military skills, intensive physical education program, and practical & classroom training in leadership. Academic year, formal military instruction limited to 2 hours per week; devoted primarily to theory & classroom work; practical, field-type military training conducted in summer.
VISITOR ATTRACTIONS: West Point Museum (Pershing Center, oldest Army museum, 1854); West Point Gift Shop; Michie Football Stadium; Quarter 100; The Plains (Parade Grounds); Trophy Point; Washington Hall; Cadet Chapel (world's largest church organ); Dress Parades (dates & times change by season, for info 914-938-2638); New Visitors Information Center.
Key Contacts
COMMANDER: Lt Gen Daniel W Christman, Superintendent, 914-938-2610, DSN 688-2610, yd9745@trotter.usma.edu; Brig Gen John P Abizaid, Commandant of Cadets.
PUBLIC AFFAIRS: LTC Maureen Lebeouf, ATTN: MAPO, 914-938-3808, DSN 688-3808.
TRANSPORTATION: ATTN: MALO-DOL, 914-938-4449, DSN 688-4449.
PERSONNEL/COMMUNITY ACTIVITIES: Director of Community & Family Activities, ATTN: MAPA, 914-938-2103, DSN 688-2103.
Personnel and Expenditures
ACTIVE DUTY PERSONNEL: 1612; cadets 4400
DEPENDENTS: 3752
CIVILIAN PERSONNEL: 2063
Services
Housing: Family units 960; Unaccompanied officer quarters 80; Barracks spaces 323; Data for both West Point & Army Garrison. *Temporary Housing:* VIP units (West Point Hotel Thayer, 914-446-4731; suites 8; rooms 196; 5-Star Inn 52 rooms). *Commissary:* Yes; *Exchange:* Retail store; Barber shop; Dry cleaners; Food shop; Florist; Service station; Bookstore; Military clothing store; Convenience store; Beauty shop. *Child Care/Capacities:* Day care center capacity 158; Home day care program; Before and after school care. *Schools:* Preschool/Kindergarten; Elementary; College courses. *Base Library:* Yes. *Medical Facilities:* See West Point Army Garrison. *Recreational Facilities:* See West Point Army Garrison.

614. West Point, Army Garrison
West Point, NY 10996
Internet: http://www.usma.edu/Garrison/
Profile
BRANCH: Army.
SIZE AND LOCATION: 16,625 acres. Approx 56 mi N of NYC. NY Thruway N, Exit 16, follow US-6 E to Rte 293, follow signs to Academy/Garrison. Stewart Airport approx 15 mi N in Newburgh, NY. *County:* Orange.
MAJOR UNITS: Military Academy, West Point; Corps of Cadets; Army Garrison, West Point; Keller Army Community Hospital; 1st Bn, 1st Infantry Regiment; Army Band, West Point; Provost Marshal, West Point; West Point School.
BASE HISTORY: 1778, established as Revolutionary War fortress (oldest active garrison in Army). 1802, home to Military Academy (see separate entry). Garrison provides professional environment to support Military Academy.
VISITOR ATTRACTIONS: See United States Military Academy.
Key Contacts
COMMANDER: Col R P Kane, Garrison Commander.
Personnel and Expenditures
ACTIVE DUTY PERSONNEL: 28,000 (total military & civilian)
Services
Housing: See United States Military Academy, West Point. *Base Library:* Yes. *Medical Facilities:* Hospital 65 beds; Medical clinic; Dental clinic; Dispensary; Pharmacy; Veterinary services. *Recreational Facilities:* Bowling center; Movie theater; Pool; Gym; Recreation center; Golf course; Stables; Tennis courts; Racquetball court; Skating rink; Fitness center/Weight room; Softball field; Football field; Auto shop; Craft shop; Officers club; Camping; Fishing/Hunting; Youth center; Picnic area; Skeet range; Water sports; Playground; Snow sports; Equipment rental.

Westhampton Beach

615. Francis S Gabreski Airport (ANG Base)
Gabreski Airport
106th Rescue Wing
150 Old Riverhead Rd
Westhampton Beach, NY 11978-1294
516-288-7400; FAX 516-288-7619; DSN 456-7400; DSN FAX 456-7619
Internet: http://www.infoshop.com/106rescue
Profile
BRANCH: Air National Guard.
SIZE AND LOCATION: 70 acres. 90 mi E of NYC; within corporate limits of Westhampton Beach, on Long Island, off State Rte 31. *County:* Suffolk.
MAJOR UNITS: 106th Rescue Wing (ARG); 102nd Rescue Squadron.
BASE HISTORY: Formerly Suffolk County Airport, 106th ARG's mission is combat rescue. Peacetime mission is to perform life-saving rescues and provide overwater escort for presidential flights, rescue support for manned spaceflight missions, and fighter escort for travel to and from Europe. 102nd Rescue

Squadron is the oldest ANG unit. Originally formed in 1908 by the NY National Guard.

Key Contacts

COMMANDER: Col Bobby Brittain, 516-288-7400, DSN 456-7400.

PUBLIC AFFAIRS: Maj James Finkle, 516-288-7601, DSN 456-7601, jfinkle@nyfok.ang.af.mil.

PROCUREMENT: LTC James Scuttina, 516-288-7497.

PERSONNEL/COMMUNITY ACTIVITIES: Maj William McArdel, 516-288-7451, DSN 456-7451.

Personnel and Expenditures

ACTIVE DUTY PERSONNEL: 1168 reservists

MILITARY PAYROLL EXPENDITURE: $17 mil

CONTRACT EXPENDITURE: $4.4 mil

Services

Housing: None. *Temporary Housing:* None. *Child Care/Capacities:* No day care facilities. *Schools:* No on-base schools. *Medical Facilities:* Dental clinic.

North Carolina

Asheville

616. Asheville Naval Reserve Center
NRC Asheville
721 Merrimon Ave
Asheville, NC 28732
704-253-4441; FAX 704-252-0104
E-mail: intille@cnrf.nola.navy.mil
Profile
BRANCH: Naval Reserve.
LOCATION: *County:* Buncombe.
MAJOR UNITS: REDCOM SIX Activity.
Key Contacts
COMMANDER: LCDR William J Intille.

Butner

617. Camp Butner
Butner, NC 27509
919-251-7300
Profile
BRANCH: Army National Guard.
SIZE AND LOCATION: 4750.39 acres. N-central North Carolina. *County:* Granville; Person; Durham.
MAJOR UNITS: Camp Butner (ARNG).
BASE HISTORY: 1942, training facility & hospital. Named for Maj Gen Henry Wolfe Butner, NC native. WWII, "Lighting" Division trained; POW stockade; support for 40,000 troops. 1945, closed. 1947, purchased by state for John Umstead Hospital for mentally retarded, "The Colony," later Butner Training School, then Murdoch School, later Murdoch Center. Federal Correctional Complex added later.

Camp Lejeune

618. Camp Lejeune Marine Corps Base
MCB Camp Lejeune
Camp Lejeune, NC 28542
Mailing Address
PSC Box 20004
Camp Lejeune, NC 28542-0004
910-451-1113; DSN 484-1113

Internet: http://www.usmc.mil
OFFICER-OF-THE-DAY: 910-451-5520, DSN 484-5520
Profile
BRANCH: Marine Corps.
SIZE AND LOCATION: 192,000 acres. Off Hwy 24, E of Jacksonville, NC; Albert Ellis Airport approx 15 mi from main gate. *County:* Onslow.
MAJOR UNITS: II Marine Expeditionary Force (MEF); 2nd Marine Division; 2nd Force Service Support Group (REIN); 2nd Surveillance, Reconnaissance & Intelligence Group; Marine Corps Base, Camp Lejeune; Naval Hospital, Camp Lejeune; Naval Dental Center, Camp Lejeune.
BASE HISTORY: 1930s, selection board decided on New River area of NC; ideal location for new Marine training base. 1941, construction of Marine Barracks, New River. 1942, renamed for 13th Commandant of Marine Corps, Lt Gen John A Lejeune. Camp Lejeune/New River complex, known as "The World's Most Complete Amphibious Training Base." Largest concentration of Marines & Sailors. Camp Geiger & Camp Johnson are included in data.
VISITOR ATTRACTIONS: Beirut Memorial; Grenada Memorial.
Key Contacts
PUBLIC AFFAIRS: Joint Public Affairs Office, 910-451-5655, FAX 910-451-5882, DSN 484-5655.
PROCUREMENT: Contracting Officer, 910-451-5520, DSN 484-5520.
TRANSPORTATION: 910-451-5608, DSN 484-5508.
PERSONNEL/COMMUNITY ACTIVITIES: See Public Affairs Officer.
Personnel and Expenditures
ACTIVE DUTY PERSONNEL: 38,480
DEPENDENTS: 29,900
CIVILIAN PERSONNEL: 4350
Services
Housing: Family units 4453; Unaccompanied enlisted quarters 19; BAQ units 233; RV/Camper sites 112; Trailer spaces 187. *Temporary Housing:* VOQ units 71; VEQ units (Senior NCO) 21; Lodge units 90; Transient quarters 1392. *Commissary:* Yes; *Exchange:* Retail store; Barber shop; Dry cleaners; Food shop; Florist; Bank; Service station; Furniture store; Bakery; Bookstore; Military clothing store; Convenience store; Beauty shop; Credit union; ATM; Optical store; Post office; Fast food; Video rentals; Four seasons; Thrift shop; Travel agency; Class VI;

Shoe repair; Computer store; Garden center; Tailor/Alterations; Laundry; Cafeteria; Photo store. *Child Care/Capacities:* Day care center capacity 326, 6 wks-12yrs; Home day care program; Summer day camp; Before & after school programs. *Schools:* Preschool/Kindergarten; Elementary; Intermediate/Junior high; High school; College courses; Adult education. *Base Library:* Yes. *Medical Facilities:* Hospital 206 beds; Medical clinic; Dental clinic; Dispensary; Pharmacy; Veterinary services. *Recreational Facilities:* Bowling center; Movie theater; Pool; Gym; Recreation center; Golf course; Stables; Tennis courts; Racquetball court; Fitness center/Weight room; Softball field; Football field; Auto shop; Craft shop; Officers club; NCO club; Camping; Fishing/Hunting; Enlisted club; Youth center; Picnic area; Skeet range; Water sports; Playground; Community club; Rod & Gun club; Boating; Archery.

Charlotte

619. 145th Airlift Wing
145 AW
5225 Morris Field Dr
Charlotte, NC 28208-5797
704-391-4100; FAX 704-391-4196; DSN 583-9210
Profile
BRANCH: Air National Guard.
SIZE AND LOCATION: 100 acres. At Charlotte/Douglas IAP; off Billy Graham Pky. Approx 5 mi from US 77; 3 mi from US 85. *County:* Mecklenburg.
MAJOR UNITS: North Carolina Air National Guard, HQ; 145th Airlift Wing, HQ; 145th Civil Engineering Squadron; 145th Services Flight; 145th Mission Support; 145th Communications Flight; 145th Maintenance Squadron; 145th Aerial Port Squadron; 145th Logistics Squadron; 145th Security Police Squadron; 145th Medical Squadron.
BASE HISTORY: 1948, NC ANG established. 1950-52, called to active duty for Korean War. 1964, designated 145th Air Transport Group. 1971, assigned to Tactical Air Command. 1990, squadron activated to support Operation Desert Shield/Storm. 1993, received new C-130H Hercules; was first ANG unit to provide C-130 airlift support for Operation Southern Watch in Saudi Arabia.
VISITOR ATTRACTIONS: Base hours: 7:30-4:00.

Key Contacts
COMMANDER: Col Samuel A Coleman, 704-391-4174, DSN 583-9174.
PUBLIC AFFAIRS: Capt Christy Rowzee, 704-391-4141, DSN 583-9141.

Personnel and Expenditures
ACTIVE DUTY PERSONNEL: 1550 (including reservists)
DEPENDENTS: 0
CIVILIAN PERSONNEL: 35
MILITARY PAYROLL EXPENDITURE: $10.9 mil
CONTRACT EXPENDITURE: $25 mil+

Services
Housing: None. *Temporary Housing:* None. *Child Care/Capacities:* No day care facilities. *Schools:* No on-base schools. *Medical Facilities:* Medical clinic; Dental clinic. *Recreational Facilities:* Fitness center/Weight room; Consolidated club.

620. Charlotte Naval & Marine Corps Reserve Center
6115 N Hills Circle
Charlotte, NC 28213-6256
704-598-0447, 598-0523; FAX 704-598-5257

Profile
BRANCH: Naval Reserve; Marine Corps Reserve.
SIZE: Offices only. *County:* Mecklenburg.
MAJOR UNITS: REDCOM SIX Activity; HQ & Service Co, 4th Maintenance Bn.

Key Contacts
COMMANDER: LCDR V E Fredericks.

Cherry Point

621. Cherry Point Marine Corps Air Station
MCAS Cherry Point
PSC Box 8003
Cherry Point, NC 28533-0003
919-466-2811; DSN 582-2811
OFFICER-OF-THE-DAY: 919-466-5236, DSN 582-5236

Profile
BRANCH: Marine Corps.
SIZE AND LOCATION: 13,164 acres (plus 15,746 acres support location). Midway between New Bern & Morehead City, NC. Main gate off NC Hwy 101, connects with US-70. Adj to city of Havelock & Craven County Regional Airport, New Bern. *County:* Craven.
MAJOR UNITS: 2nd Marine Aircraft Wing (MAW); Marine Aircraft Group 14 (MAG-14); Marine Wing Support Group 27; Marine Air Control Group 28; 2nd Marine Aircraft Wing Band; Naval Aviation Depot; Naval Hospital; Combat Service Support, Det 21; Fleet Aviation Specialized Operational Training Group, Atlantic (FASO); Defense Logistics Agency; Mid-Atlantic Electronic Warfare Range (MAEWR); Tactical Aircrew Combat Training System (TACTS).
BASE HISTORY: 1941, clearing of site began with extensive drainage and malaria control work. 1942, air station commissioned as Cunningham Field, for Marine Corps' first aviator, Lt Alfred A Cunningham. 1946, 2nd Marine Aircraft Wing replaced 9th MAW. 1950, became more active with reservists reporting

for duty, schooling, refresher courses, and training. Currently, world's largest Marine Corps Air Station and best all-weather jet base.

Key Contacts
COMMANDER: Maj Gen George M Karamarkovich, 919-466-2847, DSN 582-2847.
PUBLIC AFFAIRS: Capt Jeffrey L Blau, PSC Box 8013, MCAS, Cherry Point, NC 28533-0013, 919-466-4241, DSN 582-4241.
PROCUREMENT: Kathy Rogers, 919-466-3446, DSN 582-3446.
TRANSPORTATION: Jerome Brown, 919-466-4309, DSN 582-4455.
PERSONNEL/COMMUNITY ACTIVITIES: Ann Hall, 919-466-2197, DSN 582-2197.

Personnel and Expenditures
ACTIVE DUTY PERSONNEL: 8258
DEPENDENTS: 37,037
CIVILIAN PERSONNEL: 6120
MILITARY PAYROLL EXPENDITURE: $567.3 mil
CONTRACT EXPENDITURE: $160 mil

Services
Housing: Family units 2764; Senior NCO units 132; Junior NCO units 3368; Mobile home units 76. *Temporary Housing:* VIP units 4 units; Unaccompanied officer/Enlisted quarters 52; Guesthouse units 1; Transient quarters 242; *Commissary:* Yes; *Exchange:* Retail store; Barber shop; Dry cleaners; Food shop; Florist; Bank; Service station; Military clothing store; Convenience store; Laundromat; Credit union; ATM; Post office; Fast food; Thrift shop; Travel agency; Tailor/Alterations; Laundry. *Child Care/Capacities:* Day care center; Home day care program. *Schools:* No on-base schools. *Base Library:* Yes. *Medical Facilities:* Hospital 23; Pharmacy; Veterinary services. *Recreational Facilities:* Bowling center; Movie theater; Pool; Gym; Golf course; Stables; Tennis courts; Racquetball court; Fitness center/Weight room; Softball field; Football field; Auto shop; Craft shop; Officers club; Camping; Fishing/Hunting; Youth center; Picnic area; Water sports; Senior NCO club.

Elizabeth City

622. Coast Guard Aircraft Repair & Supply Center
AR&SC
Elizabeth City, NC 27909-5001
919-335-6191
OFFICER-OF-THE-DAY: 919-335-6289

Profile
BRANCH: Coast Guard.
SIZE AND LOCATION: 55 acres. Follow Hwy 34 from US-17 S; approx 6 mi E of Elizabeth City, NC. *County:* Pasquotank.
MAJOR UNITS: Coast Guard Aircraft Repair & Supply Center.
BASE HISTORY: 1946, established along Pasquotank River as tenant activity of Coast Guard Support Center, Elizabeth City, NC. AR & SC originally envisioned as central supply activity & overhaul unit for Coast Guard aviation. Currently, responsible for overhaul, major repair, modification of aircraft & aeronautical equipment, technical assistance including field repair team visits & engineering studies prototypes, kit designs, & installation.

Key Contacts
COMMANDER: 919-335-6191.
PUBLIC AFFAIRS: 919-335-6292.
PROCUREMENT: 919-335-6436.
TRANSPORTATION: See CG Support Center, Elizabeth City, NC.

Personnel and Expenditures
ACTIVE DUTY PERSONNEL: 150
CIVILIAN PERSONNEL: 475

Services
Housing: See Elizabeth City Coast Guard Support Center. *Exchange:* Retail store; Barber shop; Bank; Service station. *Base Library:* Yes. *Medical Facilities:* Medical clinic; Dental clinic. *Recreational Facilities:* Pool; Gym; Tennis courts; Softball field; Football field; Officers club; NCO club; Fishing/Hunting.

623. Elizabeth City Coast Guard Support Center
USCG SUPRTCEN Elizabeth City Support Center
USCG Support Center
Elizabeth City, NC 27909
919-335-6224; FAX 919-335-6230

Profile
BRANCH: Coast Guard.
SIZE AND LOCATION: 800 acres. Follow Hwy 34 (Weeksville Rd) from US-17 S; approx 4 mi SE of Elizabeth City, NC. *County:* Pasquotank.
MAJOR UNITS: Aircraft Repair & Supply Center, Elizabeth City; Coast Guard Aviation Technical Training Center; Coast Guard Station, Elizabeth City; Coast Guard Air Station, Elizabeth City; Electronic Support Det, Elizabeth City; National Strike Force Coordination Center.
BASE HISTORY: 1946, begun as USCG Aircraft Repair & Supply Base, subunit of Air Station. 1964, Air Base established. 1978, Air Base redesignated Support Center.

Key Contacts
COMMANDER: Capt Gregory H Magee, 919-335-6537, FAX 919-335-6230.
PUBLIC AFFAIRS: CDR James B Crawford, 919-335-6535, FAX 919-335-6230.
PERSONNEL/COMMUNITY ACTIVITIES: 919-335-6482.

Personnel and Expenditures
ACTIVE DUTY PERSONNEL: 87 active duty & reservists
CIVILIAN PERSONNEL: 50

Services
Housing: Family housing off base. *Temporary Housing:* Extremely limited, except for USCG personnel TAD/PCS. *Exchange:* Retail store; Barber shop; Bank; Service station; Military clothing store; Convenience store; Beauty shop; Credit union; Small exchange. *Child Care/Capacities:* No day care facilities. *Schools:* No on-base schools. *Medical Facilities:* Medical clinic; Dental clinic; Pharmacy. *Recreational Facilities:* Pool; Gym; Recreation center; Tennis courts; Racquetball court; Fitness center/Weight room; Softball field; Football field; Auto shop; Officers club; Camping; Fishing/Hunting; Enlisted club; Picnic area; Water sports; Playground; Community club; All ranks club.

Fort Bragg

624. Fort Bragg
Ft Bragg
XVIII Airborne Corps and Fort Bragg
Fort Bragg, NC 28307
910-396-0011; DSN 236-0011
Internet: http://www.bragg.army.mil/
OFFICER-OF-THE-DAY: 910-396-6100, DSN
396-6100

Profile
BRANCH: Army.
SIZE AND LOCATION: 142,330 acres (92,000
acres used for training). On NC Rte 24, approx 10 mi NW of Fayetteville, NC; 50 mi S
of Raleigh, NC. *County:* Cumberland;
Harnett; Hoke; Moore.
MAJOR UNITS: 82nd Airborne Division; 1st
Corps Support Command; Army Special Operations Command; XVIII Airborne Corps;
16th Military Police Brigade; 18th Aviation
Brigade; 18th Corps Finance Group; 18th Per-
sonnel Group; 20th Engineer Brigade; 35th
Signal Brigade; 44th Medical Brigade; 525th
Military Intelligence Brigade; Army JFK Spe-
cial Warfare Center and School; Army Spe-
cial Forces Command; Army Civil Affairs
and Psychological Operations Command; 2nd
Judicial Circuit; 10th Military Police Bn
(ABN); 18th Weather Squadron; 297th Mili-
tary Police Bn; 902nd Military Intelligence
Group; Grounds Intelligence Support Activity
(CONUS); Joint Special Operations Com-
mand; National Imagery and Mapping
Agency (NIMA); Readiness Group, Bragg;
TMDE Support Center (MICOM); Army 1st
Region, Army Cadet Command; Army Audit
Agency, Ft Bragg Field Office; Army Dental
Activity, Ft Bragg; Army Parachute Team
(FORSCOM) (Golden Knights); Womack
Army Medical Center; 3rd Infantry Division
(Mechanized); 10th Mountain Division (L);
101st Airborne Division (Air Assault); XVIII
Airborne Corps Artillery; 2nd Armored Cav-
alry Regiment; 108th Air Defense Artillery
Brigade; Dragon Brigade.
BASE HISTORY: 1918, designated as Camp
Bragg, field artillery site, named for Confeder-
ate Gen Braxton Bragg, artillery officer &
North Carolinian. 1922, made permanent
Army post; redesignated Ft Bragg. 1934, first
military parachute jump. 1942, all five WWII
airborne divisions trained in Ft Bragg-Camp
Mackall area. Nearby Camp Mackall, established 1943, major training facility until 1948.
1946, 82nd Airborne assigned to fort. 1951,
XVIII Airborne Corps reactivated (only Airborne Corp in USA); became known as
"Home of the Airborne." 1952, Psychological
Warfare Center (Special Operations Command) established; HQ for special forces.
1973, came under Army Forces Command
HQ, Ft McPherson, GA. Ft Bragg & neighboring Pope AFB form one of world's largest
military complexes.
VISITOR ATTRACTIONS: 82nd Airborne Division Museum; JFK Special Warfare Museum.

Key Contacts
COMMANDER: Commander, XVIII Airborne
Corps & Ft Bragg, 910-396-6100, DSN
396-6100.

PUBLIC AFFAIRS: ATTN: AFZA-PAO, Ft
Bragg, 910-396-2122, 396-5600, pao-corps@
bbs.bragg.army.mil.
PROCUREMENT: ATTN: AFZA-DC, Ft
Bragg, 910-396-2703, DSN 396-2703.
TRANSPORTATION: ATTN: AFZA-DL, Ft
Bragg, 910-396-5212, DSN 396-5212.
PERSONNEL/COMMUNITY ACTIVITIES:
ATTN: AFZA-PA, Ft Bragg, 910-396-2407,
DSN 396-2407.

Personnel and Expenditures
ACTIVE DUTY PERSONNEL: 45,000; Guard
& Reserve 47,000
DEPENDENTS: 74,000
CIVILIAN PERSONNEL: 8500
MILITARY PAYROLL EXPENDITURE: $1.21 bil
CONTRACT EXPENDITURE: $235.3 mil

Services
Housing: Family units 4756; plus 250 leased off
post; Unaccompanied officer quarters 148; Duplex units 966; Townhouse units 2868; Barracks
spaces 18,186; Senior NCO units 32. *Temporary
Housing:* VIP units 3; Guesthouse units 119;
Guest cottages 14; VOQ, VEQ, VAQ, BOQ,
BAQ, 547. *Commissary:* Yes; *Exchange:* Retail
store; Barber shop; Dry cleaners; Food shop; Flo-
rist; Bank; Service station; Bakery. *Child Care/
Capacities:* Day care center; Home day care pro-
gram. *Schools:* Preschool/Kindergarten; Elemen-
tary; Intermediate/Junior high. *Base Library:*
Yes. *Medical Facilities:* Hospital 310 beds;
Medical clinic; Dental clinic. *Recreational Fa-
cilities:* Bowling center; Movie theater; Pool;
Gym; Recreation center; Golf course; Stables;
Tennis courts; Racquetball court; Skating rink;
Fitness center/Weight room; Softball field; Foot-
ball field; Auto shop; Craft shop; Officers club;
NCO club; Camping; Fishing/Hunting.

Goldsboro

625. Seymour Johnson Air Force Base
SJAFB
1510 Wright Brothers Ave
Goldsboro, NC 27531-2468
919-736-5400; FAX 919-736-6654; DSN
488-1110; DSN FAX 488-6654
E-mail: pa@wg4.seymourjohnson.af.mil In-
ternet:http://www.seymourjohnson.af.mil

Profile
BRANCH: Air Force.
SIZE AND LOCATION: 3233 acres; Dare
County Bomb Range 46,604 acres. Right off
Hwy 70, in corporate limits of Goldsboro,
NC; approx 26 mi W of Kinston, NC Airport;
approx 60 mi SE of Raleigh, NC. *County:*
Wayne.
MAJOR UNITS: 4th Fighter Wing (ACC);
916th Air Refueling Group (AFRES); Air
Force Office of Special Investigations; Area
Defense Counsel; Defense Investigative
Agency; Defense Reutilization & Marketing
Office; Corps of Engineers; Air Force Audit
Agency; 372nd Training Squadron, Det 1
(AETC); Air Combat Command (ACC) Train-
ing Support Squadron, Det 15.
BASE HISTORY: 1942, Seymour Johnson Field
activated as HQ, Technical School, Army Air
Forces Technical Training Command; named
for Navy Lt Seymour Andrew Johnson, na-
tive of Goldsboro, killed in aircraft crash.
1943, Provisional Overseas Replacement

Training Center added to prepare troops for
overseas duty; Aviation Cadet Pre-Training
School established for basic military training
of cadets. Near end of WWII, designated Central Assembly Station for processing and training troops that were reassigned. 1945, Army
Air Force Separation Center established.
1946-52, inactive. 1952, city transferred base
to federal government. 1956, Seymour
Johnson AFB reactivated as TAC base. 1957,
4th Fighter-Day Wing (redesignated 4th
TFW) replaced 83rd Fighter-Day Wing.
1992, 4th Wing merged with 68th Air Refueling Wing to become 4th Wing. F15E Strike
Eagles, KC-10 Extenders, and T-38s. 1995,
KC-10s & T-38s departed; F15E formal training unit assigned to base, renamed 4th Fighter
Wing.

Key Contacts
COMMANDER: Brig Gen Randall K Bigum,
Wing Commander, 4WG/CC, 1510 Wright
Ave, Ste 100, 27531-2468, 919-736-6481,
FAX 919-736-6929, DSN 488-6481.
PUBLIC AFFAIRS: Capt Brenda Campbell,
919-736-6352, FAX 919-736-6654, DSN
488-6352.
TRANSPORTATION: 4th TRNS/CC, 1215
Pope St, 919-736-5237, DSN 488-5237.
PERSONNEL/COMMUNITY ACTIVITIES:
4th SPTG/CC, 1540 Wright Ave,
919-736-5766, DSN 488-5766, DSN FAX
488-5627.

Personnel and Expenditures
ACTIVE DUTY PERSONNEL: 5175
DEPENDENTS: 3793
CIVILIAN PERSONNEL: 1248
MILITARY PAYROLL EXPENDITURE: $210
mil (incl civilians)
CONTRACT EXPENDITURE: $33.8 mil

Services
Housing: Family units 1698; BAQ units 1698;
Duplex units 1512; Dormitory spaces 1109, 658
rooms; Senior NCO units 198; Junior NCO units
1346; Trailer spaces 45; *Temporary Housing:*
VOQ units 43; VAQ units 39; Guesthouse units
29; Senior Officer suites 10. *Commissary:* Yes;
Exchange: Retail store; Barber shop; Dry clean-
ers; Florist; Bank; Service station; Military cloth-
ing store; Convenience store; Beauty shop;
Credit union; ATM; Optical store; Post office;
Fast food; Video rentals; Thrift shop; Class VI;
Tailor/Alterations. *Child Care/Capacities:* Day
care center capacity 148, 6mos-5yrs; waiting
list, hourly care, Give Parents a Break Program.
Schools: No on-base schools. *Base Library:* Yes.
Medical Facilities: Hospital 20; Dental clinic;
Pharmacy; Veterinary services. *Recreational Fa-
cilities:* Bowling center; Movie theater; Pool;
Gym; Recreation center; Golf course; Tennis
courts; Racquetball court; Fitness center/Weight
room; Softball field; Football field; Auto shop;
Craft shop; Officers club; NCO club; Camping;
Enlisted club; Youth center; Picnic area; Skeet
range; Playground.

Greensboro

626. Greensboro Naval & Marine Corps Reserve Readiness Center
NAVMARCORESCEN Greensboro
Triad Armed Forces Reserve Center, Greensboro; AFRC Greensboro
7838 McCloud Rd
Greensboro, NC 27409-9634
910-668-0053; FAX 910-668-2898
Profile
BRANCH: Naval Reserve; Marine Corps Reserve.
SIZE AND LOCATION: 12 acres. 4.7 mi from Greensboro Intl Airport, near jun of I-40 & Rt 68, outside Greensboro City limits; On I-40 use exit 210 to Rt 68 N, turn left on Triad Ctr Dr, left on Thatcher Rd, right on McCloud Rd. *County:* Guilford.
MAJOR UNITS: REDCOM SIX Activity; I & I Staff (USMC); Communications Co, HQ & Service Bn; Det 1, Electrical Maintenance Co, 4th Maintenance Bn; 312th Field Hospital (Army); AS-39 Land 407 (NR); SECGRU Greensboro (NR); NAVAIRTERM Norfolk 307 (NR); NAVHOSP CHASN 807 (NR); CLANTFLT Det 307 (NR); FLTSUPTRA 1007 (NR); RNMCB 24 Det 0824 (NR); RNCFSU 3 Det C (NR); VOLTRAUNIT 0706 (NR); NAVHOSP CHASN P0725 (NR); PSD SOEUR Support Unit (NR); MASC PIER OPS 3 (NR); COMNAVSURFLANT Det 202 (NR); NAVBASE Norfolk 0702 (NR).
Key Contacts
COMMANDER: CDR Ronald L Smith, 910-668-3125, FAX 910-668-2898.
Personnel and Expenditures
ACTIVE DUTY PERSONNEL: 21; 400 reservists (Navy); 15; 300 reservists (Marines); 9; 378 reservists (Army)
Services *Recreational Facilities:* Weight room.

Jacksonville

627. New River Marine Corps Air Station
MCAS New River
PSC Box 21002
Jacksonville, NC 28545-1002
910-451-6568, 451-1113; DSN 484-1717
Internet: http://www.onslow.com/
OFFICER-OF-THE-DAY: 919-451-6524, DSN 484-6524
Profile
BRANCH: Marine Corps.
SIZE AND LOCATION: 2772 acres (incl 560 acres wetlands). Adj to Hwy US-17, 3 mi S of Jacksonville, NC. *County:* Onslow.
MAJOR UNITS: Marine Corps Air Station, New River; Marine Aircraft Group 29 (MAG-29); Marine Aircraft Group 26 (MAG-26); Marine Wing Support Squadron 272.
BASE HISTORY: 1944, initially commissioned as Peterfield Point. End of WWII, closed. 1951, reactivated as air facility. Under concurrent jurisdiction of station outlying field at Camp Davis, Holly Ridge. 1954, MAG-26 first helicopter group assigned. 1968, redesignated Air Station. 1972, airfield named

McCutcheon Field for Gen Keith Barr McCutcheon. As part of major reorganization, Marine Helicopter Training Group-40 deactivated; MAG-29 activated. Since 1974, many support functions, including transportation & maintenance, consolidated with & under control of Camp Lejeune. Participated in peacekeeping forces in Lebanon, invasion of Grenada, & Operation Desert Storm.
VISITOR ATTRACTIONS: Last UH-34 "Sea Horse" helicopter, used in Vietnam War, on display at main gate.
Key Contacts
COMMANDER: Col David Anderson, 910-451-6305.
PUBLIC AFFAIRS: SSgt P R Redmond, 910-451-6160.
Personnel and Expenditures
ACTIVE DUTY PERSONNEL: 6000
DEPENDENTS: 2200
CIVILIAN PERSONNEL: 130
Services
Housing: Family units 4060; Unaccompanied officer quarters 74; Unaccompanied enlisted quarters 1516; BAQ units; Duplex units; Townhouse units; Dormitory spaces; Junior NCO units 51; Mobile home units. *Temporary Housing:* VIP units 6; VOQ units 73; VEQ units 5; Unaccompanied officer/Enlisted quarters 44; Transient quarters. *Commissary:* Yes; *Exchange:* Retail store; Barber shop; Dry cleaners; Food shop; Florist; Bank; Service station. *Child Care/Capacities:* Day care center capacity 100; Home day care program. *Schools:* Preschool/Kindergarten; Elementary; *Base Library:* Yes. *Medical Facilities:* Medical clinic; Dental clinic. *Recreational Facilities:* Bowling center; Movie theater; Pool; Gym; Tennis courts; Racquetball court; Fitness center/Weight room; Softball field; Football field; Auto shop; Craft shop; Officers club; NCO club; Camping; Fishing/Hunting; Marina.

Kure Beach

628. Fort Fisher Air Force Recreation Area
FFAFRA
118 Riverfront Rd
Kure Beach, NC 28449
910-458-6723; FAX 910-458-6298; DSN 488-8781
E-mail: ffafra@mail.wilmington.net Internet: http://caro-kure.wilmington.net/ffafra/index.htm
Profile
BRANCH: Air Force.
SIZE AND LOCATION: 58 acres. On Pleasure Island, between Cape Fear River & Atlantic Ocean, 17 mi S of Wilmington, NC on Hwy US-421. *County:* New Hanover.
MAJOR UNITS: Fort Fisher Air Force Recreation Area; 4th Services Squadron.
BASE HISTORY: 1862, S tip of Pleasure Island fortified by Confederacy. Fort kept Wilmington Port secure until last month of Civil War. 1955, 701st Radar Squadron established at Ft Fisher AF Station. 1988, deactivated; converted to outdoor recreation area, now operated by Seymour Johnson AFB, NC. Nonsummer months used for as on-site NC National Guard Training site.
VISITOR ATTRACTIONS: NC Military History Museum. Off base: Ft Fisher Civil War

Museum; Battleship *North Carolina*; NC Aquarium at Ft Fisher; Beach activities; Several area golf courses; Special off-season rates in effect from Nov 1 thru Mar 31. Reservations: 910-458-6549.
Key Contacts
COMMANDER: Robert M Hayes, Site Director; Kenneth W Tyler, 919-736-6678, FAX 919-736-6570, DSN 488-6678, SVR@vkag.afsv.af.mil.
Personnel and Expenditures
ACTIVE DUTY PERSONNEL: All NAF
CIVILIAN PERSONNEL: 65 summer, 30 winter
Services *Temporary Housing:* Guest cottages 26; Lodge units 21; Mobile home units 6; RV/Camper sites 15; Lodge suites 16; Executive rooms 6; Executive suites 2; Farm Camp Area; Tent Camping. *Exchange:* Convenience store; Gift shop; Kennel; Restaurants. *Child Care/Capacities:* No day care facilities; Summer resident camp. *Schools:* No on-base schools. *Medical Facilities:* No medical facilities. *Recreational Facilities:* Pool; Gym; Recreation center; Tennis courts; Fitness center/Weight room; Softball field; Camping; Fishing/Hunting; Picnic area; Water sports; Playground; Hot tubs; Boat ramp.

Pope AFB

629. Pope Air Force Base
259 Maynard St
Pope AFB, NC 28308-5000
910-394-1110; DSN 424-1110
Internet: http://www.pope.af.mil/
Profile
BRANCH: Air Force.
SIZE AND LOCATION: 1885.5 acres. Adj to Ft Bragg; 12 mi NW of Fayetteville, NC; From I-95 S, Business I-95/US-310 exit into Fayetteville, then right on NC-24 (Bragg Blvd) to Ft Bragg & Pope AFB; From I-95 N, Business I-95/US-301 exit into Fayetteville, left on Owen Dr to All American Expy to Reilly Rd Exit, to Reilly Rd Gate. *County:* Cumberland.
MAJOR UNITS: 43rd Airlift Wing; 18th Air Support Operations Group (ACC); 21st Special Tactics Squadron (AFSOC); 23rd Fighter Group (ACC); 24th Special Tactics Squadron (AFSOC); 373rd Training Squadron, Det 2 (AETC); Combat Control School; Joint Special Operations Command; 43rd Operations Group; 43rd Logistics Group; 43rd Support Group; 43rd Medical Group; 43rd Comptroller Squadron; 2nd Airlift Squadron; 41st Airlift Squadron; 43rd Aeromedical Evacuation Squadron; 74th Fighter Squadron; 75th Fighter Squadron.
BASE HISTORY: 1918, Pope Field began flights. 1919, Pope Field established (one of oldest installations in Air Force); named after 1st Lt Harley Halbert Pope, killed in air crash near Fayetteville. 1927, Maj Carl Spaatz developed concept of aerial bombing. WWII, air & ground crews trained for troop carrier & aerial resupply duty. Korean War, 464th Troop Carrier Wing moved in; runways expanded. Vietnam War, 317th TAW pioneered development of Adverse Weather Aerial Delivery System (AWADS). 1971, 464th Troop inactivated; 317th Airlift Wing established. 1975, Pope transferred from TAC to MAC; US Airlift Center established. 1983, provided

bulk of Air Force effort in Grenada; served as primary staging site for operation. 1988, supported deployment of troops to Honduras. 1989, supported Operation Just Cause in Panama. 1990-91, transported troops to Operation Desert Shield/Storm. 1992, 317th Airlift Wing inactivated; 23rd Wing "Flying Tigers" activated under the Air Combat Command, one of two wings built from ground up.

VISITOR ATTRACTIONS: Closed to public.

Key Contacts

COMMANDER: Col David L Johnson, 43rd Airlift Wing.

PUBLIC AFFAIRS: Capt Travis, 43 AW/PA, 259 Maynard ST, 910-394-4183, DSN 424-4183, 43aw.pa@pope.af.mil.

Personnel and Expenditures

ACTIVE DUTY PERSONNEL: 5300

DEPENDENTS: 5530

CIVILIAN PERSONNEL: 340

Services

Housing: Family units Officer 90; Enlisted 370; Unaccompanied enlisted quarters 1200; *Temporary Housing:* VIP units 13; VOQ units 140; VAQ units 112; Lodge units 8. *Commissary:* Yes; *Exchange:* Barber shop; Dry cleaners; Food shop; Bank; Service station; Military clothing store; Convenience store; Credit union; Commissary shared with Ft Bragg. *Child Care/Capacities:* Day care center capacity 150, 6mo-10yrs; Home day care program; Summer day camp; Youth center before & after school. *Schools:* Elementary. *Base Library:* Yes. *Medical Facilities:* Medical clinic; Dental clinic; Pharmacy. *Recreational Facilities:* Fitness center/Weight room; Golf course; Tennis courts; Bowling center; Picnic area; Auto shop; Youth center.

Raleigh

630. Adjutant General of North Carolina

4105 Reedy Creek Rd

Raleigh, NC 27607-6410

919-664-6101; FAX 919-664-6400

Profile

BRANCH: Army National Guard.

MAJOR UNITS: North Carolina National Guard.

Key Contacts

COMMANDER: Maj Gen Gerald A Rudisill Jr.

631. Raleigh Naval & Marine Corps Reserve Center

NAVMARCORESCEN Raleigh; NMCRTC Raleigh

2725 Western Blvd

Raleigh, NC 27606-2127

919-834-6461, 834-5931; FAX 919-839-8947

Profile

BRANCH: Naval Reserve; Marine Corps Reserve.

SIZE AND LOCATION: 5.74 acres. Across from NC State Univ on Western Blvd which runs approx 2 mi off Exit US-1 (Raleigh Beltline). *County:* Wake.

MAJOR UNITS: REDCOM SIX Activity; SASSY Management Unit (SMU), Supply Co, 4th Supply Bn.

Key Contacts

COMMANDER: CDR A Briggs.

Personnel and Expenditures

ACTIVE DUTY PERSONNEL: 16

Research Triangle Park

632. Army Research Office

ARO

4300 S Miami Blvd

Research Triangle Park, NC 27709-2211

Mailing Address

PO Box 12211

Research Triangle Park, NC 27709-2211

919-549-4201; 919-549-4310; DSN 832-4298

Internet: http://www.aro.ncren.net

Profile

BRANCH: Army.

SIZE AND LOCATION: 1 acre. Off I-40 at 4300 S Miami Blvd, Exit 282; approx 14 mi equidistant from Raleigh, Durham, & Chapel Hill, NC; approx 5 mi E to Raleigh-Durham IAP. *County:* Durham.

MAJOR UNITS: Army Research Office.

BASE HISTORY: 1951, evolved from Army Office of Ordnance Research (OOR); Class II military installation established at Duke University. 1958, Research & Development Field Office, Ft Belvoir, redesignated Army Research Office (ARO); moved to Arlington Hall Station, Arlington, VA. 1961, OOR transferred from Chief of Ordnance to Chief of Research & Development, redesignated Army Research Office-Durham (AROD). AROD expanded to monitor programs in physical sciences Army-wide. 1973, ARO in Arlington discontinued; Office-Durham designated Army Research Office (ARO). 1974, ARO transferred to AMC as separate reporting activity. 1975, ARO moved from Duke to Research Triangle Park. 1984, ARO moved to present location. 1985, emergence of Army Laboratory Command (LABCOM).

Key Contacts

COMMANDER: Dr Gerald J Iafrate, Office Director, 919-549-4201, FAX 919-549-4348, DSN 832-4203.

PUBLIC AFFAIRS: Dr Roger Cannon, 919-549-4278, FAX 919-549-4288, DSN 832-4278.

PROCUREMENT: Larry Travis, 919-549-4271, DSN 832-4271, DSN FAX 832-4388.

TRANSPORTATION: Ms Rene Kirkwood, 919-549-4341, FAX 919-547-7701, DSN 832-4341.

PERSONNEL/COMMUNITY ACTIVITIES: Ms Sarah Evans, Director of Personnel, 919-549-4296, FAX 919-549-4382, DSN 832-4382.

Personnel and Expenditures

ACTIVE DUTY PERSONNEL: 2

DEPENDENTS: 0

CIVILIAN PERSONNEL: 115

Services

Housing: None, offices only. *Base Library:* Yes.

Southport

633. Military Ocean Terminal, Sunny Point

597th USA TTG

Sunny Point

597th USA Transportation Terminal Group

Southport, NC 28461-5000

910-457-8000; FAX 910-457-8416; DSN 488-8000; DSN FAX 488-8416

Profile

BRANCH: Army.

SIZE AND LOCATION: 16,000 acres. 5 mi N of Southport, NC, at junction of NC Rte 87/133. *County:* Brunswick; New Hanover.

MAJOR UNITS: 597th Army Transportation Terminal Group; 1205th TRO Bn, Det 1; Military Sealift Command Office; 1303rd Major Port Command.

BASE HISTORY: 1955, activated; major modifications completed 1982 for container movement & handling. Three wharfs with two berths each; approx 100 mi of rail track, 50 mi of paved roads, & 195,500 sq ft of building space. Provides worldwide transshipment of DOD ammunition, explosives, & other dangerous cargo. Only DOD terminal equipped to handle containerized ammunition. Terminal commander supervises deployment/redeployment of joint forces through NC state ports of Wilmington & Morehead City.

VISITOR ATTRACTIONS: Closed to public except for official business.

Key Contacts

COMMANDER: Col Michael J Toal, 910-457-8556, DSN 488-8556, toalm@bayonne-emh3.army.mil.

PUBLIC AFFAIRS: Beverly W Brown, 910-457-8230, DSN 488-8230, brown@bayonne-emh3.army.mil.

Personnel and Expenditures

ACTIVE DUTY PERSONNEL: 10

CIVILIAN PERSONNEL: 227

Services

Housing: Family units 5. *Medical Facilities:* Occupational health clinic. *Recreational Facilities:* Fitness center/Weight room; Softball field; Rod & Gun club.

Wilmington

634. US Army Corps of Engineers, Wilmington District

69 Darlington

Wilmington, NC 28403-1398

910-251-4645

Internet: http://www.saw.usace.mil/

Profile

BRANCH: Army.

LOCATION: *County:* New Hanover.

MAJOR UNITS: Corps of Engineers, Wilmington District.

BASE HISTORY: 1884, Corps office established at Cape Fear. Serves NC & S-central VA. Operates 4 field offices: Asheville, Raleigh, Washington, & Wilmington, NC.

Key Contacts

COMMANDER: Col Terry R Youngbluth.

635. Wilmington (NC) Naval & Marine Corps Reserve Center
Armed Forces Reserve Center
2144 W Lakeshore Dr
Wilmington, NC 28401-7297

910-762-9676, 762-9677; FAX 910-762-9422

Profile

BRANCH: Naval Reserve; Marine Corps Reserve.

LOCATION: In SE North Carolina. *County:* New Hanover.

MAJOR UNITS: REDCOM SIX Activity; 2nd Longshoreman Plt, 3rd Beach & Terminal Operations Co, 4th Landing Support Bn.

Key Contacts

COMMANDER: LCDR D Pullen.

North Dakota

Bismarck

636. Adjutant General of North Dakota
PO Box 5511
Bismarck, ND 58502-5511
701-224-5102; FAX 701-224-5180
Profile
BRANCH: Army National Guard.
MAJOR UNITS: North Dakota National Guard.
Key Contacts
COMMANDER: Maj Gen Keith D Bjerke.

Cavalier AS

637. Cavalier Air Station
Cavalier AS
10 SWS, HCR 3, Box 260
Cavalier AS, ND 58220-9314
701-993-3292; FAX 701-993-3284; DSN
330-3292; DSN FAX 330-3284
OFFICER-OF-THE-DAY: MWOC Crew
    Commander, 701-993-3292, FAX
    701-993-3206, DSN 330-3292
Profile
BRANCH: Air Force.
SIZE AND LOCATION: 278 acres. In NE ND,
    approx 15 mi W of Cavalier on Hwy 5; 95 mi
    NW of Grand Forks, ND. *County:* Pembina.
MAJOR UNITS: 10th Space Warning Squadron.
BASE HISTORY: Originally served as the ac-
    quisition radar portion of only operational
    anti-ballistic missile system, SAFEGUARD.
    1976, all components of SAFEGUARD com-
    plex, with exception of PARCS radar, deacti-
    vated, due to 1972 Anti-Ballistic Missile
    Treaty. 1977, unit turned over to Air Force
    and began passing tactical warning and attack
    assessment data to Cheyenne Mountain. 1979,
    unit transferred to SAC. 1983, unit joined Air
    Force Space Command, as Detachment 5, 1st
    Space Wing. 1986, redesignated as 10th Mis-
    sile Warning Squadron, 1st Space Wing.
    1992, redesignated 10th Space Warning
    Squadron, 21st Space Wing (Peterson AFB,
    CO). Operationally part of North American
    Air Defense Command (NORAD). Site
    leased from Army through 5-year renewable
    lease. Primary mission is to provide warning
    and attack characterization of submarine
    launched ballistic missiles and ICBMs. Also
    responsible for tracking, reporting, and identi-
    fying space objects.
VISITOR ATTRACTIONS: Site of Perimeter
    Acquisition Radar portion of deactivated Safe-
    guard Complex.
Key Contacts
COMMANDER: LTC Donald T Kidd,
    701-993-3297, DSN 330-3297,
    6su-10sws/cc@spacelan.af.mil.
PUBLIC AFFAIRS: Capt Scott D Jacobs,
    701-993-3292, FAX 701-993-3206, DSN
    330-3292, 6su-10sws/do@spacelan.af.mil.
TRANSPORTATION: Maj Dave Hollenga,
    Operations Officer, 701-3693, DSN
    330-3693, DSN FAX 330-3206,
    6su-10sws/do@spacelan.af.mil.
Personnel and Expenditures
ACTIVE DUTY PERSONNEL: 28
DEPENDENTS: 40
CIVILIAN PERSONNEL: 125
Services
Housing: Family units 12; Unaccompanied offi-
cer quarters 11; Unaccompanied enlisted quar-
ters 14. *Temporary Housing:* VIP units 14. *Ex-
change:* Convenience store. *Child Care/Capaci-
ties:* No day care facilities. *Schools:* No on-base
schools. *Base Library:* Yes. *Medical Facilities:*
No medical facilities. *Recreational Facilities:*
Bowling center; Gym; Recreation center; Tennis
courts; Racquetball court; Fitness center/Weight
room; Softball field; Auto shop; Picnic area;
Playground; Community club.

Devils Lake

638. Camp Gilbert C Grafton
Cp Grafton
RR 5, Box 278A
Devils Lake, ND 58301-9235
701-662-0200; FAX 701-662-0376; DSN
344-5226
Profile
BRANCH: Army National Guard.
SIZE AND LOCATION: 2100 acres (main
    camp); 10,000 acres (Camp Grafton South). 6
    mi S of Devils Lake, ND, on Hwy ND-20.
    County: Ramsey (Camp Grafton North);
    Eddy (Camp Grafton South, field training
    only).
MAJOR UNITS: 3662nd Maintenance Co;
    136th Quartermasters Bn; 164th Regiment Re-
    gional Training Institute, HQ; HQ & HQ Det
    (ND ARNG).
BASE HISTORY: Late 1800s, set aside & desig-
    nated Fort Totten Military Wood Reservation
    by federal government. Later abandoned by
    War Department; transferred to ND as Rock
    Island Military Reservation. 1892, first ND
    NG encampment. After WWI, named Camp
    Grafton in honor of LTC Gilbert C Grafton of
    ND ARNG, who died in France during WWI.
    Today, Annual Training Site.
VISITOR ATTRACTIONS: Military Museum
    (small); Edwards House (repository for state
    military history).
Key Contacts
COMMANDER: Col Eugene Orson,
    701-662-0211, DSN 344-5226, ext 211.
PUBLIC AFFAIRS: Capt Patrick Richards, Box
    5511, Bismarck, ND 58502-5511,
    701-224-5106, DSN 344-5106.
Personnel and Expenditures
ACTIVE DUTY PERSONNEL: 2; Guard 300
CIVILIAN PERSONNEL: 140
Services
Housing: Barracks spaces 720; Dormitory
spaces 80; Mobile home units 19; RV/Camper
sites 10; Huts 198. *Temporary Housing:* VIP
units 2; Dormitory units 80; Mobile home units
19. *Exchange:* Retail store; Food shop; Laundromat. *Child Care/Capacities:* No day care facilities. *Schools:* No on-base schools. *Medical Facilities:* Medical clinic; Dispensary 6 beds; Pharmacy; Open only during annual training. *Recreational Facilities:* Movie theater; Gym; Recreation center; Tennis courts; Fitness center/Weight
room; Softball field; Officers club; NCO club;
Camping; Enlisted club; Picnic area; Fishing;
Service club.

Fargo

639. Fargo Naval Reserve Center
Armed Forces Reserve Center
3920 31st St N, Ste B
Fargo, ND 58102-6206
701-232-3689; FAX 701-241-9895
Profile
BRANCH: Naval Reserve.
LOCATION: *County:* Cass.
MAJOR UNITS: REDCOM SIXTEEN Activity.
Key Contacts
COMMANDER: CDR J R Havlik.

640. Hector IAP, Air National Guard Base

119FG, 1400 28th Ave N
Fargo, ND 58105-5536
701-237-6030; DSN 362-8110

Profile
BRANCH: Air National Guard.
SIZE AND LOCATION: 209 acres. On NW edge of Fargo, ND; just N of corner of 19th Ave N and Univ Dr N. *County:* Cass.
MAJOR UNITS: 119th Fighter Interceptor Wing (ANG).
BASE HISTORY: 1947, organized. Assigned F-51 tactical aircraft during Korean War & Air Defense mission early 1950s. 1954, assigned first jet fighter, F-94. 1959, assigned F-89J with nuclear weapons. Since then the "Happy Hooligans" progressed from F-102, F-101B, to present F-4D. 1990, received F-16s.

Personnel and Expenditures
ACTIVE DUTY PERSONNEL: 1029 Guard
CIVILIAN PERSONNEL: 327
MILITARY PAYROLL EXPENDITURE: $54.1 mil

Services *Temporary Housing:* VIP units 1. *Exchange:* Retail store. *Medical Facilities:* Medical clinic. *Recreational Facilities:* Fitness center/Weight room; Softball field; Officers club; NCO club.

Grand Forks AFB

641. Grand Forks Air Force Base

GFAFB
460 Steen Blvd
Grand Forks AFB, ND 58205
Mailing Address
226 Steen Blvd
Grand Forks AFB, ND 58205-6219
701-747-5016; FAX 701-747-5022; DSN 88-362-5016; DSN FAX 88-362-5022
Internet: http://www.gf.af.mil
OFFICER-OF-THE-DAY: 701-747-6711, FAX 701-747-6804, DSN 88-362-6711

Profile
BRANCH: Air Force.
SIZE AND LOCATION: 5418 acres. 15 mi W of Grand Forks, off Hwy 2. *County:* Grand Forks.
MAJOR UNITS: 319th Air Refueling Wing; 321st Missile Group; 319th Support Group; 319th Operations Group; 319th Logistics Group; 319th Medical Group; Area Defense Counsel; Air Force Office of Special Investigations, Det 320; Ogden AFB Material Command (Rivet Mile); Defense Reutilization & Marketing Office; Defense Investigative Service.
BASE HISTORY: 1956, construction of Air Defense Command (ADC) base. 1960, operations started with 18th FIS. 1963, SAC assumed control. 1964, home of first Minuteman II Wing. 1970, under operational control of 15th Air Force. 1988, a number of organizational changes; 42nd Air Division, 8th Air Force, took operational control. 1991, 319th Bombardment Wing host. 1992, base transferred to Air Combat Command (ACC) 319th Wing became 319th Bomb Wing. 1993, redesignated 319th Air Refueling Wing, Air Mobility Command. Mission air refueling & airlift operations.

FUTURE CLOSURE/REALIGNMENT: 321st Missile Group in process of realigning. All 150 Minuteman III missiles shipped to Malmstrom AFB, MT, by Sep 1998.
VISITOR ATTRACTIONS: Heritage Park (military aircraft), Avenue of Flags & POW/MIA Memorial (all at front gate).

Key Contacts
COMMANDER: Brig Gen Select James A Hawkins, 460 Steen Blvd, 701-747-4150, DSN 88-362-4150.
PUBLIC AFFAIRS: Capt Byron Spencer, 226 Steen Blvd, 701-747-5016, FAX 701-747-5022, DSN 88-362-5022, spencerb@gf.af.mil.
PROCUREMENT: 319th Contracting Squadron Commander, 701-747-5260, FAX 701-747-4215, DSN 88-362-5260.
TRANSPORTATION: 319th Transportation Squadron Commander, 701-747-3477, FAX 701-747-6968, DSN 88-362-3477.
PERSONNEL/COMMUNITY ACTIVITIES: 319th Services Squadron Commander, 701-747-3258, FAX 701-747-3221, DSN 88-362-3258.

Personnel and Expenditures
ACTIVE DUTY PERSONNEL: 4750
DEPENDENTS: 6800
CIVILIAN PERSONNEL: 350

Services
Housing: Family units; BAQ units; Duplex units; Townhouse units; Dormitory spaces; Senior NCO units; Junior NCO units; Mobile home units 9; RV/Camper sites. *Temporary Housing:* VIP units; VOQ units; VAQ units; BAQ units; Dormitory units; Transient quarters; TLF; TLQ. *Commissary:* Yes; *Exchange:* Retail store; Barber shop; Dry cleaners; Food shop; Florist; Bank; Service station; Furniture store; Military clothing store; Convenience store; Beauty shop; Credit union; ATM; Optical store; Post office; Fast food; Video rentals; Thrift shop; Travel agency; Class VI; Tailor/Alterations; Laundry; Cafeteria. *Child Care/Capacities:* Day care center capacity 144; Home day care program; Before & after school programs. *Schools:* Preschool/Kindergarten; Elementary; Intermediate/Junior high. *Base Library:* Yes. *Medical Facilities:* Hospital 20; Medical clinic; Dental clinic; Pharmacy; Veterinary services. *Recreational Facilities:* Bowling center; Movie theater; Pool; Gym; Recreation center; Golf course; Stables; Tennis courts; Racquetball court; Skating rink; Fitness center/Weight room; Softball field; Auto shop; Craft shop; Officers club; Camping; Enlisted club; Youth center; Skeet range; Playground.

Minot AFB

642. Minot Air Force Base

5 BW/PA, 201 Summit Dr, Ste 105
Minot AFB, ND 58705-5000
701-723-1110; DSN 453-1110
Internet: http://www.minot.af.mil
OFFICER-OF-THE-DAY: 701-723-3102, DSN 453-3102

Profile
BRANCH: Air Force.
SIZE AND LOCATION: 5049 acres; 8,500 acres for missile sites. 13 mi N of Minot, ND, on US-83. *County:* Ward.

MAJOR UNITS: 5th Bomb Wing; 91st Missile Wing (AFSPC); 5th Comptroller Squadron; 5th Operations Group; 23rd Bomb Squadron; 5th Logistics Group; 5th Support Group; 5th Medical Group; 91st Operations Group; 91st Logistics Group; Air Force Office of Special Investigations, Det 228; Defense Accounting Office; 372nd Training Squadron, Det 8A; Air Force Audit Agency; Defense Reutilization & Marketing Office; Defense Investigative Service; HQ USAF Area Defense Counsel.
BASE HISTORY: 1957, opened as Air Defense Command installation; 4136th Strategic Wing first SAC unit provided aerial refueling for northern air defense operations. 1962, site selected for Minuteman I ICBM complex; 4136th Strategic Wing deactivated; 455th Strategic Missile Wing & 450th Bombardment Wings (BMW) activated. 1968, 91st Strategic Missile Wing replaced 455th SMW; 5th BMW replaced 450th BMW. 1970, 91st Strategic Missile Wing (SMW) converted to Minuteman III ICBM. 1988, 5th BMW received air launched Cruise missile. 1990s, deployed forces to Middle East. 5th Bomb Wing made host. 1991, alert status ended after 35 continuous years. 1993, Advanced Cruise Missiles activated. 1994, final KC-135 left Minot. 1996, Minuteman III upgraded.
VISITOR ATTRACTIONS: Ft Lincoln State Park; Lake Metigoshe State Park; International Peace Garden; Lake Sakakawea State Park; Turtle River State Park; Icelandic State Park; Lewis and Clark State Park; Theodore Roosevelt National Park; Bottineau Winter Park; North Dakota State Fair.

Key Contacts
COMMANDER: 5 BW/CC, 701-723-3115, DSN 453-3115.
PUBLIC AFFAIRS: 5 BW/PA, 701-723-6212, DSN 453-6212.
PROCUREMENT: 5 CONS/CC, 701-723-4186, DSN 453-4186.
TRANSPORTATION: 5 TRANS/CC, 701-723-2288, DSN 453-2288.

Personnel and Expenditures
ACTIVE DUTY PERSONNEL: 4620
DEPENDENTS: 6326
CIVILIAN PERSONNEL: 589
MILITARY PAYROLL EXPENDITURE: $143.2 mil
CONTRACT EXPENDITURE: $46.1 mil

Services
Housing: Family units 2447; Unaccompanied officer quarters 22 units; Dormitory spaces 1302; Senior NCO units 255; Junior NCO units 1766. *Temporary Housing:* VOQ units 39; VAQ units 32; Transient quarters 39. *Commissary:* Yes; *Exchange:* Retail store; Barber shop; Dry cleaners; Food shop; Florist; Bank; Service station; Furniture store; Bakery; Military clothing store; Convenience store; Beauty shop; Credit union; ATM; Optical store; Post office; Fast food; Video rentals; Thrift shop; Travel agency; Class VI; Computer store; Garden center; Tailor/Alterations; Photo store. *Child Care/Capacities:* Day care center capacity 292, 6wks-9yrs; Home day care program; Summer day camp; Before & after school programs. *Schools:* Preschool/Kindergarten; Elementary; Intermediate/Junior high; College courses. *Base Library:* Yes. *Medical Facilities:* Hospital 25; Medical clinic; Dental clinic; Pharmacy; Veterinary services. *Recreational Facilities:* Bowling center; Movie thea-

ter; Pool; Gym; Recreation center; Golf course; Stables; Tennis courts; Racquetball court; Skat-ing rink; Fitness center/Weight room; Softball field; Football field; Auto shop; Craft shop; Offi-cers club; Camping; Enlisted club; Youth center; Picnic area; Skeet range; Playground.

Ohio

Akron

643. Akron Naval & Marine Corps Reserve Center
800 Dan St
Akron, OH 44310-3986
330-376-9054, 376-9722; FAX 330-376-9966
Profile
BRANCH: Naval Reserve; Marine Corps Reserve.
LOCATION: *County:* Summit.
MAJOR UNITS: REDCOM THIRTEEN Activity; Co K, 3rd Bn, 25th Marine Regiment.
Key Contacts
COMMANDER: LCDR P F Sargent.

Bratenahl

644. Defense Contract Management Command, Cleveland
DCMC Cleveland
555 E 88th St
Bratenahl, OH 44108-1068
216-522-5444
Internet: http://www.dcro.dls.mil/
Profile
BRANCH: Defense Logistics Agency.
LOCATION: In Admiral Kidd Center on shore of Lake Erie, 5 mi E of downtown. *County:* Cuyahoga.
MAJOR UNITS: Defense Contract Management Command, Cleveland.
BASE HISTORY: Site originally private residences. 1950s, site of NIKE missile base. 1971, NIKE base inactivated. 1971-73, Bratenahl High School. 1973, Adm Kidd Ctr constructed for Navy Automatic Data Processing facility. 1995, data center disestablished by BRAC; DCMC renovates building. 1996, reopened. Currently manages 8400 contracts with 500 contractors.
Key Contacts
COMMANDER: Col Joseph Paddock, jpaddock@dcrb.dla.mil.

Cincinnati

645. Cincinnati Naval & Marine Corps Reserve Center
NAVMARCORESCEN Cincinnati
3190 Gilbert Ave
Cincinnati, OH 45207-1498
513-221-0138; FAX 513-221-1078
Profile
BRANCH: Naval Reserve; Marine Corps Reserve.
SIZE AND LOCATION: 3 acres. Corner of Victory Pkwy & Gilbert Ave. *County:* Hamilton.
MAJOR UNITS: REDCOM THIRTEEN Activity; Reserve I & I (USMC); 4th Marine Division, Communications Co, HQ Bn, 4th.
BASE HISTORY: 1890, unofficially established as 51st Fleet Reserves. 1946, unit commissioned. 1950, center opened. 1983, current center commissioned.
Key Contacts
COMMANDER: LCDR Guy E Dunan.
Personnel and Expenditures
ACTIVE DUTY PERSONNEL: 13; 250 reservists
Services *Recreational Facilities:* Fitness center.

646. Defense Contract Management Command, GE Aircraft Engines Cincinnati
DCMC GEAE
1 Neumann Way, Mail Drop N-1
Cincinnati, OH 45215-6303
513-243-6015; FAX 513-243-7615
Internet: http://33.19.101.198/DCMCGEAE/index.htm
Profile
BRANCH: Defense Logistics Agency.
MAJOR UNITS: Defense Contract Management Command, GE Aircraft Engines Cincinnati.
Key Contacts
COMMANDER: Col David L Mastin, USAF.

647. US Army Corps of Engineers, Great Lakes & Ohio River Division
CELRD
550 Main St
Cincinnati, OH 45202-2215
Mailing Address
PO Box 1159
Cincinnati, OH 45201-1159
513-684-3002; FAX 513-684-3800
Internet: http://www.usace.army.mil/ord/
Profile
BRANCH: Army.
SIZE AND LOCATION: Offices only. Downtown Cincinnati in John Weld Peck Federal Bldg. *County:* Hamilton.
MAJOR UNITS: Corps of Engineers, Great Lakes & Ohio River Division.
BASE HISTORY: One of 8 division offices; 4 subordinate districts at: Huntington, WV, Louisville, KY, Nashville, TN, & Pittsburgh, PA. Performs military & civil works construction.
Key Contacts
COMMANDER: Brig Gen Hans A Van Winkle, Commander, 513-684-3002.
PUBLIC AFFAIRS: Donna Strachn, 513-684-3010.
PROCUREMENT: Michael Lee, 513-684-3048.
PERSONNEL/COMMUNITY ACTIVITIES: William D St John, Human Resources, 513-684-2822.
Personnel and Expenditures
ACTIVE DUTY PERSONNEL: 3
CIVILIAN PERSONNEL: 225
Services *Child Care/Capacities:* Day care center. *Medical Facilities:* Medical clinic. *Recreational Facilities:* Fitness center/Weight room.

Cleveland

648. 9th Coast Guard District Headquarters
CCGD9
1240 E 9th St
Cleveland, OH 44199
216-902-6038; FAX 216-902-6044
E-mail: dnine1@gwis.com Internet:http://www.dot.gov/dotinfo/uscg/d9/uscgd9.html
Profile
BRANCH: Coast Guard.
SIZE AND LOCATION: Offices only. In downtown Cleveland at E 9th St & Lakeside Ave; from I-90, N on E 9th to Lakeside. *County:* Cuyahoga.
MAJOR UNITS: 9th Coast Guard District HQ; Integrated Support Command, Cleveland; Electronics Systems Support Unit, Cleveland; Naval Engineering Support Unit, Cleveland; Civil Engineering Unit, Cleveland.
Key Contacts
COMMANDER: RADM J F McGowan, 216-902-6001, FAX 216-902-6018.

PUBLIC AFFAIRS: Lt T N Thomson, 216-902-6020, FAX 216-902-6018, dnine1@gwis.com.

Personnel and Expenditures
ACTIVE DUTY PERSONNEL: 70; 20 reservists
CIVILIAN PERSONNEL: 17
Services *Exchange:* Retail store; Dry cleaners; Florist; Military clothing store; Convenience store; Credit union. *Recreational Facilities:* Coast Guard club.

649. Cleveland Naval Reserve Center
NRC Cleveland
1089 E 9th St
Cleveland, OH 44114-1091
216-771-0844; FAX 216-0806
Profile
BRANCH: Naval Reserve.
LOCATION: Downtown Cleveland. *County:* Cuyahoga.
MAJOR UNITS: REDCOM THIRTEEN Activity.
VISITOR ATTRACTIONS: USS *Cod* (WWII submarine), *Mather* (Great Lakes Ship), and Rock 'n' Roll Hall of Fame adj to center.
Key Contacts
COMMANDER: CAPT W J Ferenczy.
PUBLIC AFFAIRS: LCDR M D Phillips, markfilip@aol.com.
Personnel and Expenditures
ACTIVE DUTY PERSONNEL: 500 reservists
Services *Recreational Facilities:* All hands club.

650. Defense Finance and Accounting Service, Cleveland Center
DFAS-CL
1240 E 9th St
Cleveland, OH 44199
216-522-5620; FAX 216-522-5805; DSN 580-5620; DSN FAX 580-5805
Internet: http://www.dfas.mil
OFFICER-OF-THE-DAY: 216-522-5620, DSN 580-5620
Profile
BRANCH: DOD.
SIZE AND LOCATION: 35 acres. Downtown Cleveland, Anthony J Celebrezze Federal Bldg, two blocks from lakefront/inner harbor foot of 9th St. Adj to Cleveland Stadium & Burke Lakefront Airport. Main computer facility, Consolidated Data Center, 4 mi E on Rte 90 in village of Bratenahl, OH. *County:* Cuyahoga.
MAJOR UNITS: Defense Finance and Accounting Service, Cleveland.
BASE HISTORY: Navy Finance Center & predecessor, Field Branch, Bureau of Supplies & Accounts, in Cleveland since 1942. Primary mission to plan, design, develop, implement, & manage Navy-wide pay systems for active duty, retired, & reserve personnel. Isaac Campbell Kidd Computer Center, Bratenahl, OH, located on site formerly occupied by Nike missile facility. 1974, Navy Finance Center; "Bratenahl Annex" became home to Navy Finance Center's communications facility & mainframe computer operations. 1991, moved from Navy to DFAS control. Occupies several sites including North Point Office Complex, Bingham Building &

Anthony J Celebrezze Federal Bldg. Center also responsible for six remote sites: Charleston, Honolulu, Norfolk, Oakland, Pensacola, and San Diego.
Key Contacts
COMMANDER: Phyllis A Hudson, Director, 216-522-5511, FAX 216-522-6055, DSN 580-5511.
PUBLIC AFFAIRS: Zanell L Osowski, 216-522-5620, DSN 580-5620, zosowski@cleveland.dfas.mil.
PROCUREMENT: 216-522-6845, DSN 580-6845.
Personnel and Expenditures
ACTIVE DUTY PERSONNEL: 12
CIVILIAN PERSONNEL: 1636
Services *Child Care/Capacities:* Day care center capacity 70. *Base Library:* Yes. *Medical Facilities:* Medical clinic. *Recreational Facilities:* Gym; Fitness center by lease with downtown health club.

Columbus

651. Adjutant General of Ohio
2825 W Dublin Granville Rd
Columbus, OH 43235-2789
614-889-7070; FAX 614-889-7074
Profile
BRANCH: Army National Guard.
MAJOR UNITS: Ohio National Guard.
Key Contacts
COMMANDER: Maj Gen Richard C Alexander.

652. Columbus Naval & Marine Corps Readiness Center
85 N Yearling Rd
Columbus, OH 43213-1392
614-235-2630, 235-3179, 235-2265; FAX 614-235-0714; DSN 850-2933
Profile
BRANCH: Naval Reserve; Marine Corps Reserve.
LOCATION: *County:* Franklin.
MAJOR UNITS: REDCOM THIRTEEN Activity; Co L, 3rd Bn, 25th Marine Regiment.
Key Contacts
COMMANDER: CDR S R Newton.

653. Defense Finance and Accounting Service
4280 E 5th Ave
Columbus, OH 43214-1879
Customer Service Resource Center
800-756-4571
Internet: http://www.dfas.mil/agency/centers/dfasco/index.htm
Profile
BRANCH: DOD.
SIZE AND LOCATION: 420 acres. In AF Plant #85, 6 mi from Columbus. *County:* Franklin.
MAJOR UNITS: Defense Finance and Accounting Service, Columbus.
BASE HISTORY: 1988, established as part of Defense Logistics Agency. 1991, consolidated and reorganized. 1999, moving into new facility next to DSCC Operating Center.
Key Contacts
COMMANDER: Charles R Coffee, Director, 614-693-6701.

PUBLIC AFFAIRS: 614-693-6605.
Personnel and Expenditures
ACTIVE DUTY PERSONNEL: 3269 (military & civilian)

654. Defense Supply Center, Columbus
DSCC
3990 E Broad St
Columbus, OH 43216-5000
614-692-8702; DSN 850-8702
Internet: http://www.dscc.dla.mil/DSCC_Info.html
Profile
BRANCH: Defense Logistics Agency.
SIZE AND LOCATION: 570 acres. On US-16, Broad St, approx 7 mi E-NE of downtown Columbus. *County:* Franklin.
MAJOR UNITS: Defense Supply Center, Columbus; Systems Design Center (DSDC); Defense Contract Management Command (DCMC); Defense Reutilization & Marketing Service Operation East (DRMS); Defense Reutilization & Marketing Office, Columbus (DRMO); Civilian Personnel Support Office (DCPSO); Defense Industrial Security Clearance Office (DISCO); Air Force Occupational Medicine Clinic, Columbus (SGPOC); 83rd Army Reserve Command (ARCOM); Directorate for Industrial Security Clearance Review (DSICR); Defense Criminal Investigative Service (DCIS); Defense Megacenter, Columbus (DSIO); Defense Printing Service; Military Retiree Activities Program (RAO); HQ, 1st Brigade, 2nd ROTC Region, Army Cadet Command (ATOB); Defense Finance and Accounting Service, Columbus (DFAS-CO).
BASE HISTORY: 1918, established as Columbus Quartermaster Reserve Depot, charged with routing materiel for overseas shipment. 1930s, became district headquarters for Civilian Conservation Corps; military function diminished. 1942, Quartermaster General assumed responsibility of Columbus Quartermaster Depot; world's largest military supply installation; some warehouses turned into secured barracks for POWs. During Korean War, activated. 1962, assigned to Army Supply & Maintenance Command. 1963, became Defense Construction Supply Center (later Defense Logistics Agency). 1996, current name (merged with Defense Electronics Supply Center, Dayton); largest supplier of weapon systems spare parts.
Key Contacts
COMMANDER: Brig Gen Paul L Bielowica.
PUBLIC AFFAIRS: 614-692-2328, DSN 850-2328.
Personnel and Expenditures
ACTIVE DUTY PERSONNEL: 40
CIVILIAN PERSONNEL: 3000
CONTRACT EXPENDITURE: $1.84 bil (annual sales)
Services *Temporary Housing:* VOQ units 1; Guesthouse units 2; Guest cottages 1. *Child Care/Capacities:* Day care center. *Medical Facilities:* Medical clinic. *Recreational Facilities:* Gym; Recreation center; Golf course; Tennis courts; Racquetball court; Fitness center/Weight room; Softball field; Officers club; NCO club.

655. Rickenbacker IAP, Air National Guard Base

Columbus, OH 43217-5887
614-492-4223; DSN 950-8211

Profile

BRANCH: Air National Guard.
SIZE AND LOCATION: 2200 acres. 13 mi S-SW of Columbus; 4 mi S of I-270 at Exit 49, Alum Creek Dr, at intersection of Alum Creek Dr and State Rte 317. *County:* Franklin; Pickaway.
MAJOR UNITS: 121st Air Refueling Wing (ANG); Naval Air Reserve; Naval Construction Bn (USNR).
BASE HISTORY: 1942, began as Lockbourne Army Air Base, known as nation's Southwest Training Center; first used for Army Air Force Glider Pilot Training School; replaced by B-17 school. 1943, class of Women Air Force Service Pilots (WASP) trained as engineering test pilots. Following WWII, developed & tested equipment for all-weather flight operations. 1947, 332nd Fighter Group & 477th Composite Group formed 332nd Fighter Wing, Air Force's first all-black operational flying unit, one of first units to commence total integration in Air Force. 1949, Lockbourne deactivated; operational control turned over to NG. 1951, Lockbourne reactivated; became SAC aerial refueling & aircrew training facility. 301st BMW host until 1964, when redesignated 301st Air Refueling Wing (ARW). 1974, Lockbourne AFB officially renamed Rickenbacker AFB for Capt Edward "Eddie" Rickenbacker, Ace of Aces of WWI, a Columbus native. 1979, included in President Carter's base closing program; 301st ARW deactivated. 1980, transferred to OH ANG. 1986, 121st TFW OH ANG host. 1988, joined by 160th Air Refueling Group; together operate as Consolidated Operating Support staff.
VISITOR ATTRACTIONS: Aircraft on static display, F-100, F-84F, F-84E, T-33; Base tour of major air command units, TAC, SAC, MAC.

Personnel and Expenditures

ACTIVE DUTY PERSONNEL: 1353 Guard
CIVILIAN PERSONNEL: 441
MILITARY PAYROLL EXPENDITURE: $32.9 mil

Services

Housing: Unaccompanied officer quarters; Unaccompanied enlisted quarters; BAQ units; Above for joint use for approx 300 bed spaces for military units AFRES. *Temporary Housing:* Unaccompanied officer/Enlisted quarters; BAQ units; BEQ units; Above for joint use for approx 300 bed spaces for military units AFRES. *Exchange:* Retail store; Barber shop; Dry cleaners; Service station. *Medical Facilities:* First aid station for military units only. *Recreational Facilities:* Pool; Gym; Tennis courts; Racquetball court; Fitness center/Weight room; Softball field; Consolidated club.

Dayton

656. Dayton Naval & Marine Corps Reserve Readiness Center

Armed Forces Reserve Center

410 N Gettysburg Ave
Dayton, OH 45417-1797
937-268-1664, 268-1665, 268-9629; FAX 513-268-7455

Profile

BRANCH: Naval Reserve; Marine Corps Reserve.
LOCATION: *County:* Montgomery.
MAJOR UNITS: REDCOM THIRTEEN Activity; Military Police Plt, 1st Military Police Co, HQ & Service Co, 4th FSSG.

Key Contacts

COMMANDER: Lt J P Sarafolean II.

657. Defense Contract Management Command, International

DCMC International

200 Hamilton St
Dayton, OH 45444-5410
513-296-6684; FAX 513-296-6809; DSN 986-6684

Profile

BRANCH: Defense Logistics Agency.
LOCATION: *County:* Montgomery.
MAJOR UNITS: Defense Contract Management Command International.

Lima

658. Lima Army Tank Plant

LATP

Defense Contract Management Command, General Dynamics Lima

1155 Buckeye Rd
Lima, OH 45804-1898
419-221-9500; FAX 419-221-9600

Profile

BRANCH: Army; Defense Logistics Agency.
SIZE AND LOCATION: 369.2 acres. 5 mi from downtown Lima, OH; mid-way off I-75 between Dayton & Toledo. From I-75, Exit 120, Fort Shawnee and Breese Rd, W on Breese Rd to first stoplight, right onto S Dixie Hwy, S on Dixie for 2 mi to first light, left onto Buckeye Rd, facility approx 0.5 mi on left. Nearest military support installation Wright-Patterson AFB, Dayton, 78 mi S. *County:* Allen.
MAJOR UNITS: Tank Automotive Command (TACOM); General Dynamics Land Systems (operating contractor); Army Upgrade Tank Program; Corps of Engineers, Louisville District.
BASE HISTORY: 1942, constructed to produce centrifugally cast gun tubes; improved technique discovered before facility completed; General Motors Corp operated facility as Lima Tank Depot. 1943, used for intermediate depot by Army Ordnance Corps. During WWII, depot processed over 40 types of combat vehicles. 1945, became Class III Ordnance Depot; thousands of combat vehicles placed in storage until Korean War. After Korean War, became inactive, renamed Lima

Army Modification Center. 1959, inactive status. 1961, began storing Industrial Plant Equipment & records holding area for several commands. 1976-79, received, inspected, & processed 12,400 M880 1.5-ton commercial trucks. 1976, chosen as initial production site for XM-1 tank (M-1 Abrams Tank). Chrysler Corp, Defense Division awarded contract. 1979, renamed Lima Army Tank Center. 1982, General Dynamics Land Systems bought out Chrysler Defense, including tank center; renamed Lima Army Tank Plant. 1985, last M1 built & production of M1A1 Abrams tank began; M1A2 only item currently produced. 1990, Defense Logistics Agency, Defense Contract Management Command, took over all contract administrative services. Production of Army Upgrade Tanks to continue to 2001.
VISITOR ATTRACTIONS: Secure installation, visitors must be approved; briefings & plant tour visits must be authorized.

Key Contacts

COMMANDER: LTC Alvin J Leonard, (Army, Quartermaster Corps), 419-221-9501, FAX 419-221-9600, brq1498@dcrb.dla.mil.

Personnel and Expenditures

ACTIVE DUTY PERSONNEL: 4
CIVILIAN PERSONNEL: 59

Services *Recreational Facilities:* Softball field; Fishing/Hunting; Picnic area.

Mansfield

659. Mansfield Lahm Airport, Air National Guard Base

1947 Harrington Memorial Dr
Mansfield, OH 44903-0179
419-521-0100; DSN 696-6210

Profile

BRANCH: Air National Guard.
SIZE AND LOCATION: 224 acres. 3 mi N of Mansfield, on State Rte 13. *County:* Richland.
MAJOR UNITS: 179th Airlift Wing (ANG).
BASE HISTORY: 1948, founded & named for aviation pioneer Brig Gen Frank P Lahm. 1976, first flew F-51D Mustang final conversion to C-130.

Key Contacts

COMMANDER: Col Warren J Drouhard Jr, 419-521-0179, DSN 696-6179.

Personnel and Expenditures

ACTIVE DUTY PERSONNEL: 911 Guard
CIVILIAN PERSONNEL: 247
MILITARY PAYROLL EXPENDITURE: $16.1 mil

Services

Housing: None. *Exchange:* Retail store. *Medical Facilities:* Dispensary.

Newton Falls

660. Ohio National Guard, Unit Training Equipment Site #1

UTES #1

1488 Newton Falls Portage Rd
Newton Falls, OH 44444-9519
330-872-0055; FAX 330-872-0055

Profile
BRANCH: Army National Guard.
SIZE AND LOCATION: 920 acres. 2 mi W of Ohio Tpke, Exit 14, off Rte 5. Approx 20 mi from Youngstown or Ravenna, OH. Nearest airport 30 mi. *County:* Trumbull.
MAJOR UNITS: 107th Armored Cavalry.
BASE HISTORY: Established to provide maintenance support for OH Army NG units; weekend training.
Key Contacts
COMMANDER: SFC Leroy A Caranci.
Personnel and Expenditures
CIVILIAN PERSONNEL: 12
Services
Housing: None.

North Canton

661. Army Aviation Support Facility #1
AASF #1
5989 Airport Dr, NW
North Canton, OH 44720-1483
330-966-4880; FAX 330-966-7699
E-mail: aasf1oh@oh-ngnet.army.mil
Profile
BRANCH: Army National Guard.
SIZE AND LOCATION: 92 acres. Just off I-77 at Akron-Canton Airport; 10 mi to Akron & 6 mi to Canton, OH. *County:* Stark.
MAJOR UNITS: 107th Medical Co (AA); Det 1, Co D, 137th AVIM; Co D 1-137th AHB; Co E 1-137th AHB.
BASE HISTORY: Fall 1986, flight facility completed. Consists of over 63,000 sq ft of office/hangar space & helicopter maintenance shops. 1988, new armory constructed for HQ aviation, ground squadron, & aircraft maintenance company.
Key Contacts
COMMANDER: Col Thomas P Luczynski.
Personnel and Expenditures
ACTIVE DUTY PERSONNEL: 44
DEPENDENTS: 0
CIVILIAN PERSONNEL: 1
Services
Housing: None. *Temporary Housing:* 1 bunkroom w/10 bunks. *Child Care/Capacities:* No day care facilities. *Schools:* No on-base schools; *Medical Facilities:* No medical facilities.

Perrysburg

662. Toledo Naval & Marine Corps Reserve Center
NAVMARCORESCEN Toledo
28828 Glenwood Rd
Perrysburg, OH 43551-3014
419-666-3444; FAX 419-666-6606
E-mail: tdco@rc13post.rc13.org
Profile
BRANCH: Naval Reserve; Marine Corps Reserve.
SIZE AND LOCATION: 13 acres. E SE of Perrysburg, OH. 3/4 mi N of junct of SR795 & Glenwood Rd. *County:* Wood.
MAJOR UNITS: REDCOM THIRTEEN Activity; 4MD 1/24 W (NR); MIUW Det 201; PHIB CB 2 DET 205 (NR); NMCB 26 Det

1226; NAVHOSP GLAKES 1613 (NR); VOLTRAUNIT 0517 (NR); Weapons Co, 1st Bn, 24th Marine Regiment.
Key Contacts
COMMANDER: LCDR Michael D Herman.
Personnel and Expenditures
ACTIVE DUTY PERSONNEL: 27; 420 reservists

Port Clinton

663. Camp Perry Training Site
Camp Perry
1000 Lawrence Rd
Port Clinton, OH 43452-9578
419-635-4101; FAX 419-635-4191; DSN 346-4101; DSN FAX 346-4191
E-mail: cpperyoh@oh-ngnet.army.mil Internet: http://www.campperry.org
Profile
BRANCH: Army National Guard.
SIZE AND LOCATION: 648 acres. On Lake Erie at State Rte 2 & 358, approx 5 mi W of Port Clinton; nearest air service, Toledo, 45 mi NW, Cleveland, 60 mi SE. *County:* Ottawa.
MAJOR UNITS: State Area Readiness Command, Det 2; 213th Maintenance Co; Organizational Maintenance Shop 10; 200th Red Horse Civil Engineering Squadron (OH Air NG); Unit Training Equipment Shop 2; Port Security Unit 309 (USCGR); Port Security Unit Training Det (USCG).
BASE HISTORY: 1906, land purchased for rifle range & camp. 1907, National Rifle Matches first held. 1908, named after Commodore Oliver Hazard Perry, who defeated British at Battle of Lake Erie. WWII, used as reception center; POW camp for German & Italian prisoners. Today, daily use by non-military agencies; weekend use by military units; and, home of National Rifle & Pistol Matches.
VISITOR ATTRACTIONS: Static display of military equipment; White sand beach on Lake Erie; Gratitude Train (gift from France in 1949); WWII POW huts.
Key Contacts
COMMANDER: LTC Dean W Brown, Facility Manager, 419-635-4101, DSN 346-4101, DSN FAX 346-4191, cpts@campperry.net.
Personnel and Expenditures
ACTIVE DUTY PERSONNEL: 4, reservists/guard 480
CIVILIAN PERSONNEL: 120
Services
Housing: Family units 6; Unaccompanied officer quarters 50; Unaccompanied enlisted quarters 300; Barracks spaces 4; Senior NCO units 10; Trailer spaces 10; RV/Camper sites 20. *Temporary Housing:* VOQ units 6; VEQ units 6; Guest cottages 30; Apartment units 1; Transient quarters 300. *Exchange:* Retail store; Barber shop; Convenience store; Laundromat; *Child Care/Capacities:* No day care facilities. *Schools:* No on-base schools. *Medical Facilities:* Medical clinic. *Recreational Facilities:* Movie theater; Recreation center; Tennis courts; Fitness center/Weight room; Softball field; Camping; Fishing/Hunting; Picnic area; Skeet range; Water sports; Playground; Beach.

Springfield

664. Springfield Municipal Airport Air National Guard Base
178th FW, ANG, 706 Regula Ave
Springfield, OH 45501
937-327-2100; FAX 937-327-2331; DSN 346-2100
Internet: http://www.178fw.ohang.ang.af.mil
Profile
BRANCH: Air National Guard.
SIZE AND LOCATION: 113 acres. 5 mi S of Springfield, off US-68, between Rte 68 & 72. *County:* Clark.
MAJOR UNITS: 178th Fighter Wing (ANG); 251st Combat Communications Group (ANG); 269th Combat Communications (ANG).
Key Contacts
PUBLIC AFFAIRS: Capt Ann-Maria Coghlin, 937-327-2321, DSN 346-2321, acoghlin@ohsgh.ang.af.mil.
Personnel and Expenditures
ACTIVE DUTY PERSONNEL: 1106 (guardsmen)
CIVILIAN PERSONNEL: 231
Services
Housing: None. *Child Care/Capacities:* No day care facilities. *Schools:* No on-base schools. *Medical Facilities:* Dispensary.

Swanton

665. Toledo Express Airport, Air National Guard Base
2660 S Eber Rd
Swanton, OH 43558
419-868-4078; DSN 580-4078
Profile
BRANCH: Air National Guard.
SIZE AND LOCATION: 114 acres. Adj to Toledo Express Airport, Swanton, OH, approx 14 mi W of Toledo, OH. *County:* Lucas.
MAJOR UNITS: 180th Fighter Wing (ANG).
BASE HISTORY: 1955, unit moves in as 112th Fighter Interceptor Squadron. 1958, became Tactical Fighter Squadron. 1961, activated for Berlin Crisis. 1962, became part of 180th Tactical Fighter Group. 1989, took part in Operation Just Cause in Panama. 1991, provided volunteers for Operations Desert Shield/Storm. 1992, designated 180th Fighter Group, equipped with F-16s.
Personnel and Expenditures
ACTIVE DUTY PERSONNEL: 1023 Guard
CIVILIAN PERSONNEL: 321
MILITARY PAYROLL EXPENDITURE: $24.9 mil
Services *Exchange:* Retail store. *Medical Facilities:* Medical clinic; Dental clinic.

Vienna

666. Youngstown-Warren Regional Airport, Air Reserve Station
Y/WRA-ARS
King-Graves Rd
Vienna, OH 44473-0910
330-392-1000; DSN 346-1000

Profile

BRANCH: Air Force Reserve.

SIZE AND LOCATION: 236 acres. 16 mi N of Youngstown, between State Rte 46 and 193. *County:* Trumbull.

MAJOR UNITS: 910th Airlift Wing (AFRC); 757th Airlift Squadron; 773rd Airlift Squadron; 76th Aerial Port Squadron; Naval Reserve Readiness Command, Region 5; Marine Corps Reserve Center, Youngstown.

BASE HISTORY: 1952, constructed as an active duty installation. 1961, base turned over to Air Force Reserve. Small facility used for local proficiency flights only.

Personnel and Expenditures

ACTIVE DUTY PERSONNEL: 27; Reserve 1566

CIVILIAN PERSONNEL: 450

MILITARY PAYROLL EXPENDITURE: $26.5 mil

Services

Housing: None. *Temporary Housing:* Billeting for Active Duty/Reservists on orders only 76; No Space-A flights; No PAX service. *Exchange:* Convenience store. *Recreational Facilities:* Gym.

Wright-Patterson AFB

667. Wright-Patterson Air Force Base

Wright-Patterson AFB, OH 45433-5417
937-257-1110; DSN 787-1110

Internet: http://www.wpafb.af.mil

Profile

BRANCH: Air Force.

SIZE AND LOCATION: 8145 acres. 10 mi NE of Dayton, OH, off State Rte 444. *County:* Greene; Montgomery.

MAJOR UNITS: Air Force Materiel Command, HQ (AFMC); Air Force Research Laboratory (AFRL); Wright Laboratory; Crew Systems Directorate, Armstrong Laboratory; Aeronautical Systems Center (ASC); 88th Air Base Wing; Wright-Patterson Medical Center; Air Force Institute of Technology; 445th Airlift Wing (AFRES); National Air Intelligence Center (NAIC); US Air Force Museum; Joint Logistics Systems Center; Major Shared Resource Center; Simulation & Analysis Facility.

BASE HISTORY: 1917, established as McCook Field. 1924, renamed Wilbur Wright Field. 1931, renamed Patterson Field, for Lt Frank Patterson, who was killed in airplane crash. 1948, designated Wright-Patterson. Largest, most diverse & organizationally complex base in AF. Missions range from logistics management, research & development, education, flight operations, & many other defense related activities.

VISITOR ATTRACTIONS: Air Force Museum (largest & oldest aviation museum), open every day 9-5, free admission. Aviation Heritage National Historic Park.

Key Contacts

COMMANDER: Lt Gen Kenneth E Eickmann, Commander, ASC (host); Gen George T Babbitt, AFMC, 4375 Chidlaw Rd, Ste 6, 45433.

PUBLIC AFFAIRS: Ronald Fry, ASC/PA, 937-257-6307, FAX 937-257-2558, DSN 787-6307, DSN FAX 787-2558, ascpa@wpafb.af.mil.

Personnel and Expenditures

ACTIVE DUTY PERSONNEL: 7100; Reserve 2071

DEPENDENTS: 11,000

CIVILIAN PERSONNEL: 15,000

MILITARY PAYROLL EXPENDITURE: $1.2 bil

Services

Housing: Family units 2365; Dormitory spaces 300; Trailer spaces 80. *Temporary Housing:* VIP units 32; VOQ units 606; VAQ units 115; Transient quarters 40. *Commissary:* Yes; *Exchange:* Retail store; Barber shop; Dry cleaners; Food shop; Florist; Bank; Service station; Furniture store; Bakery; Bookstore; Military clothing store; Convenience store; Beauty shop; Laundromat; Credit union; ATM; Optical store; Post office; Fast food; Video rentals; Four seasons; Thrift shop; Travel agency; Class VI; Shoe repair; Computer store; Garden center; Tailor/Alterations; Laundry; Cafeteria; Photo store. *Child Care/Capacities:* Day care center capacity 410; Home day care program; Before & after school programs. *Schools:* Preschool/Kindergarten. *Base Library:* Yes. *Medical Facilities:* Hospital 301 beds. *Recreational Facilities:* Bowling center; Movie theater; Pool; Gym; Recreation center; Golf course; Stables; Tennis courts; Racquetball court; Fitness center/Weight room; Auto shop; Craft shop; Officers club; NCO club; Camping; Fishing/Hunting; Rod & Gun club; Hunting lodge; Aero club; Family camping area; Park, 65 acres; Lakes, 4.

Oklahoma

Altus AFB

668. Altus Air Force Base
AAFB
97th AMW
Altus AFB, OK 73523-5067
405-482-8100; FAX 405-481-5966; DSN
866-1110
Internet: http://www.lts.aetc.af.mil/
OFFICER-OF-THE-DAY: 405-482-8100, DSN
866-8100

Profile
BRANCH: Air Force.
SIZE AND LOCATION: 3500 acres. In corporate city limits of Altus; 120 mi SW of Oklahoma City; 55 mi W of Lawton, OK; Hwys 62 & 283 run through city. *County:* Jackson.
MAJOR UNITS: 97th Air Mobility Wing; 97th Support Group; 97th Operations Group; 97th Medical Group; 97th Logistics Group; 55th Air Refueling Squadron; 56th Airlift Squadron; 57th Airlift Squadron; 58th Airlift Squadron.
BASE HISTORY: 1942, base established. 1943, opened; mission to train multi-engine aircraft pilots for European Theater. 1945, deactivated. 1953, reactivated under TAC, then SAC. 1960s, operated 12 Atlas ICBM sites in southwestern OK. 1965, deactivated. 1967, became MAC's Airlift Training Center. 1990, during Operations Desert Shield/Storm served as aerial port of debarkation for Ft Sill. 1992, 97th Air Mobility Wing formed from 443rd Airlift Wing and 340th Air Refueling Wing. 1993, 97th AMW from Air Mobility Command to Air Education & Training Command, 19th Air Force. 1994, transfer of KC-135 from Castle AFB begun; 55th Air Refueling Sq activated.
VISITOR ATTRACTIONS: Static displays of C-47, C-118, and C-45 aircraft; Museum of Western Prairie in Altus; Quartz Mt State Park, 15 mi N of base.

Key Contacts
COMMANDER: Col Christopher A Kelly, 100 Inez Blvd, Suite, 73523-5067, 405-481-5097, DSN 866-5097.
PUBLIC AFFAIRS: M Borg, 97th AMW, 100 Inez Blvd, Suite 2, 73523-5067, 405-481-7229, DSN 866-7229, borgm@ltsgate1.lts.aetc.af.mil.
PROCUREMENT: 97th Contracting Squadron; 205 S 6th St, Bldg 318, 73523-5117, 405-481-7320, DSN 866-7320.

TRANSPORTATION: 97th Transportation Squadron, 6th St, Bldg 352, 73523-5117, 405-481-6309, DSN 866-6309.
PERSONNEL/COMMUNITY ACTIVITIES: 97th Mission Support Squadron, 300 N 1st St, 73523-5000, 405-481-7343, DSN 866-7343.

Personnel and Expenditures
ACTIVE DUTY PERSONNEL: 3500; 300-400 students
DEPENDENTS: 5000
CIVILIAN PERSONNEL: 900

Services
Housing: Family units Officer 150; Enlisted 650; Unaccompanied enlisted quarters 580; Dormitory spaces 600; Senior NCO units 98; Junior NCO units 559; RV/Camper sites 5. *Temporary Housing:* VIP units 6; VOQ units 285; VEQ units 296; Guesthouse units 2; Dormitory units 267; Transient quarters 10. *Commissary:* Yes; *Exchange:* Retail store; Barber shop; Dry cleaners; Food shop; Florist; Bank; Service station; Bakery; Military clothing store; Convenience store; Beauty shop; Credit union. *Child Care/Capacities:* Day care center capacity 135, 6mo-10yrs; Home day care program; Enrichment before/after-school programs. *Schools:* Preschool/Kindergarten; Elementary. *Base Library:* Yes. *Medical Facilities:* Hospital 15 beds. *Recreational Facilities:* Bowling center; Movie theater; Pool; Gym; Recreation center; Golf course; Tennis courts; Racquetball court; Fitness center/Weight room; Softball field; Auto shop; Craft shop; Officers club; NCO club; Camping; Fishing/Hunting; Enlisted club; Youth center; Picnic area; Skeet range; Water sports; Playground; Camping/Fishing 18 mi N of base.

Braggs

669. Camp Gruber, Army National Guard Training Site
ARNG TNG Site CG
Camp Gruber Training Site (CGTS)
State Hwy 10, 20 mi SE of Muskogee
Braggs, OK 74423-0029
Mailing Address
PO Box 29
Braggs, OK 74423-0029
918-487-6001; FAX 918-487-6009
OFFICER-OF-THE-DAY: 918-487-6044
Profile
BRANCH: Army National Guard.

SIZE AND LOCATION: 66,000 acres (including hunting area). Approx 20 mi SE of Muskogee, OK, on State Hwy 10, 15 mi N of Webbers Falls/Gore. Davis Field is 5 mi S of Muskogee on US-64; I-40 approx 20 mi S of Camp; Hwy 69 approx 25 mi W; Hwy 62 approx 12 mi N; and Tahlequah, OK approx 32 mi NE on Hwy 62. *County:* Muskogee; Cherokee.
MAJOR UNITS: HQ State Area Readiness Command (CGTS) Det 3; Unit Training Equipment Site (UTES) #1; Oklahoma Maintenance Shop (OMS) #3.
BASE HISTORY: 1942, opened with a 3,000-man German POW camp; major training facility for 42nd Rainbow, 88th Blue Devil, & 86th Black Hawk Divisions activated here. 1947, deactivated & little used until 1968 when OK ANG started annual training. 1987, established as home of National Guard Air Assault School; Today, Class A Training Facility, used by Army & Air National Guard, Army Reserves, Naval & Marine Corps Reserves, active components from all branches, & local/state law enforcement agencies. Facilities: ranges for small arms, rifles, pistols, machine guns, LAWs, grenades, M203s, Modified Record Fire, ambush, and TOW; MOUT course; Air Assault obstacle course; personnel & equipment drop zones; water landing course; & barge docking facility. Davis Field, capable of handling aircraft up to Galaxy C-5; port on Arkansas River capable of accommodating barge traffic.
VISITOR ATTRACTIONS: WWII exhibits; WWII POW Camp memorabilia.

Key Contacts
COMMANDER: Col Larry N Cluck, 918-487-6004.
PUBLIC AFFAIRS: CW3 Ronald G Petty, 918-487-6222.
PROCUREMENT: See Public Affairs Officer.
TRANSPORTATION: CW2 Thomas A Suddut, 918-487-6066.
PERSONNEL/COMMUNITY ACTIVITIES: LTC Dale L Painter, 918-487-6003.

Personnel and Expenditures
ACTIVE DUTY PERSONNEL: 7
DEPENDENTS: 0
CIVILIAN PERSONNEL: 55
MILITARY PAYROLL EXPENDITURE: $0.3 mil
CONTRACT EXPENDITURE: $8 mil

Services
Housing: Barracks spaces 3000; Mobile home units 15; Trailer spaces 22; RV/Camper sites 12.

Temporary Housing: VOQ units 76; VEQ units 100; Lodge units 1; Mobile home units 14; Transient quarters 40. *Exchange:* Military clothing store; Convenience store; Laundromat. *Child Care/Capacities:* No day care facilities. *Schools:* No on-base schools. *Medical Facilities:* No medical facilities. *Recreational Facilities:* Fitness center/Weight room; Softball field; Picnic area; Lake; Golf driving range.

Broken Arrow

670. Tulsa Naval & Marine Corps Reserve Center
Armed Forces Reserve Center
1101 N 6th St, Ste 5
Broken Arrow, OK 74012-2041
918-251-2908, 258-7577; FAX 918-251-6684
Profile
BRANCH: Naval Reserve; Marine Corps Reserve.
LOCATION: In NE Oklahoma, approx 14 mi SE of Tulsa. *County:* Tulsa.
MAJOR UNITS: REDCOM ELEVEN Activity; Anti-Tank (TOW) Co, 4th Tank Bn.
Key Contacts
COMMANDER: LCDR P A Sharp.

Fort Sill

671. Fort Sill
Army Field Artillery Center & Fort Sill
Fort Sill, OK 73503-5000
405-442-8111; DSN 639-7090
Internet: http://sil-ww.army.mil/
Profile
BRANCH: Army.
SIZE AND LOCATION: 94,220 acres. Approx 70 mi S of Oklahoma City on H E Bailey Tpke (I-44); 5 mi N of Lawton. *County:* Comanche.
MAJOR UNITS: Army Field Artillery Training Center; Army Field Artillery School; III Corps Artillery; 95th Adjutant General Bn (Reception); Army Noncommissioned Officers Academy, Ft Sill; 82nd Medical Co; Depth and Simultaneous Attack Battle Lab; Marine Corps Field Artillery.
BASE HISTORY: 1869, established by Gen Phillip Sheridan as frontier post for pacifying Comanche & Kiowa Indian tribes of Southern Great Plains. 1911, School of Fire of Field Artillery (today, Army Field Artillery School) established. Trains more than 15,000 officers & enlisted students annually. III Corps Artillery Army's largest, most diverse field artillery organization; three brigades combatready. Fire Support Test Directorate (formerly Field Artillery Board) oldest test agency in Army. Verification/inspection site for INF Treaty.
VISITOR ATTRACTIONS: Fort Sill Museum; Geronimo's Grave Site; Artillery and Military History exhibits in Commissary Store House.
Key Contacts
PUBLIC AFFAIRS: ATZR-A, 405-442-2521.
PERSONNEL/COMMUNITY ACTIVITIES: Community Services, 405-442-4357.

Personnel and Expenditures
ACTIVE DUTY PERSONNEL: 17,045; Reserve 1725
DEPENDENTS: 32,440
CIVILIAN PERSONNEL: 2546
Services
Housing: Family units 1415; Unaccompanied officer quarters 100; Unaccompanied enlisted quarters 8; RV/Camper sites 64; Campground tent sites 9. *Temporary Housing:* VIP units 26; VOQ units 660; VEQ units 100; Guesthouse units 75; Transient quarters 870. *Commissary:* Yes; *Exchange:* Retail store; Barber shop; Dry cleaners; Food shop; Florist; Bank; Service station; Beauty shop. *Child Care/Capacities:* Day care center capacity 300; Home day care program; Summer day camp. *Schools:* Preschool/Kindergarten; Elementary. *Base Library:* Yes. *Medical Facilities:* Hospital 116 beds; Medical clinic; Dental clinic. *Recreational Facilities:* Bowling center; Movie theater; Pool; Gym; Recreation center; Golf course; Stables; Tennis courts; Racquetball court; Fitness center/Weight room; Softball field; Football field; Auto shop; Craft shop; Officers club; NCO club; Camping; Fishing/Hunting.

Lawton

672. Keathley Army Reserve Center
900 NW Cache Rd
Lawton, OK 73507-5400
405-355-5500
Internet: http://sill-www.army.mil/95div/1bde.htm
Profile
BRANCH: Army Reserve.
LOCATION: George D Keathley Army Reserve Center; 80 mi SW of Oklahoma City. *County:* Comanche.
MAJOR UNITS: 1st Brigade, 95th Division (IT)(USAR).
BASE HISTORY: Only Field Artillery asset in Army reserve.

McAlester

673. McAlester Army Ammunition Plant
MCAAP
McAlester, OK 74501
918-421-2011; DSN 956-6011
Internet: http://mcalestr-http://www.army.mil/
OFFICER-OF-THE-DAY: 918-421-2642, DSN 956-6642
Profile
BRANCH: Army.
SIZE AND LOCATION: 44,964 acres. Approx 9 mi S of McAlester, OK, adj to Savanna, OK on Hwy 69; approx 6 mi S of McAlester Municipal Airport; 5 mi S of intersection of Hwy 69 and Indian Nations Tpke. *County:* Pittsburg.
MAJOR UNITS: McAlester Army Ammunition Plant; Naval Surface Warfare Center, Indian Head Division Det, McAlester; Army Test, Measurement, and Diagnostic Support Center, McAlester; Defense Reutilization & Marketing Office; Army Health Clinic, McAlester.

BASE HISTORY: 1943, commissioned as McAlester Naval Ammunition Depot. 1977, transferred to Army Materiel Command's single manager for conventional ammunition. Currently, 2nd largest installation of this type in US. Government-Owned, Government-Operated; produces, stores, issues, & receives conventional ammunition for all military branches. Premier bomb-loading facility for DOD; only Plastic Bonded Explosive bombloading facility in US.
VISITOR ATTRACTIONS: Wildlife tours.
Key Contacts
COMMANDER: Col David A Hafele, SIOMC-CO, 1 C Tree Rd, McAlester, OK 74501-9002, 918-421-2211, FAX 918-421-3581, DSN 956-6211, DSN FAX 956-7581, co@mcalestr-emh1.army.mil.
PUBLIC AFFAIRS: 918-421-2591, DSN 956-6591, pa@mcalestr-emh1.army.mil.
Personnel and Expenditures
ACTIVE DUTY PERSONNEL: 2
CIVILIAN PERSONNEL: 890
MILITARY PAYROLL EXPENDITURE: $44.4 mil
CONTRACT EXPENDITURE: $6.8 mil
Services
Housing: Family units 18; Unaccompanied officer quarters 18; Barracks spaces 81; RV/Camper sites 1. *Temporary Housing:* Unaccompanied officer/Enlisted quarters 12. *Exchange:* Retail store; Food shop; Bank. *Child Care/Capacities:* Day care center capacity 42; Before & after school programs. *Schools:* No on-base schools. *Medical Facilities:* Medical clinic. *Recreational Facilities:* Bowling center; Pool; Gym; Recreation center; Stables; Tennis courts; Racquetball court; Fitness center/Weight room; Softball field; Auto shop; Craft shop; Camping; Fishing/Hunting; Youth center; Enlisted club Lakeview Community Club (military & civilian).

Oklahoma City

674. Adjutant General of Oklahoma
3501 Military Circle NE
Oklahoma City, OK 73111-4398
405-425-8201; FAX 405-425-8289
Profile
BRANCH: Army National Guard.
MAJOR UNITS: Oklahoma National Guard.
Key Contacts
COMMANDER: Maj Gen Stephen P Cortight.

675. Coast Guard Institute
5900 SW 64th St
Oklahoma City, OK 73169-6990
Mailing Address
5900 SW 64th St, Rm 235
Oklahoma City, OK 73169-6990
405-954-1028; FAX 405-954-7249
E-mail: uscg-irm@mmacmail.jccb.gov Internet: http://www.dot.gov/dotinfo/uscg/hq/cgi/
Profile
BRANCH: Coast Guard.
LOCATION: In Mike Monroney Aeronautical Center; approx 10 mi SW of downtown Oklahoma City; 1 mi W of Will Roger's World Airport. *County:* Oklahoma.
MAJOR UNITS: Coast Guard Institute; Coast Guard Mike Monroney Aeronautical Center.

BASE HISTORY: 1928, established to provide correspondence course training; originally located at Marine Corps Institute in Washington, DC. 1929, moved to Ft Trumbull, Groton, CT. 1942, moved to Coast Guard Training Station, Avery Point, Groton, CT. 1967, relocated to present location as part of Dept of Transportation. Mission today to coordinate the submission & distribution of 120 correspondence courses & 196 competitive examinations.

Key Contacts

COMMANDER: Capt Mark Jorgensen, 405-954-1028.
PUBLIC AFFAIRS: Ltjg Brad Wilson, 405-954-7275.
PROCUREMENT: SK1 Andrew Jepson, 405-954-7254.
PERSONNEL/COMMUNITY ACTIVITIES: See Public Affairs Officer.

Personnel and Expenditures

ACTIVE DUTY PERSONNEL: 21
DEPENDENTS: 0
CIVILIAN PERSONNEL: 8

Services

Housing: None. *Child Care/Capacities:* No day care facilities. *Schools:* No on-base schools. *Medical Facilities:* No medical facilities. *Recreational Facilities:* None.

676. Oklahoma City Naval & Marine Corps Reserve Readiness Center

5316 S Douglas Blvd
Oklahoma City, OK 73150-9702
405-733-2674, 733-1052, 737-7885, 737-5316;
FAX 405-736-6281; DSN 339-2743

Profile

BRANCH: Naval Reserve; Marine Corps Reserve.
LOCATION: *County:* Oklahoma.
MAJOR UNITS: REDCOM ELEVEN Activity; Battery F, 2nd Bn, 14th Marine Regiment.

Key Contacts

COMMANDER: CDR I G Williams.

677. Will Rogers World Airport, Air National Guard Base

Oklahoma City, OK 73169-5000
405-686-5210; DSN 940-8210

Profile

BRANCH: Air National Guard.
SIZE AND LOCATION: 133 acres. 7 mi SW of Oklahoma City, off I-44. *County:* Oklahoma; Cleveland.
MAJOR UNITS: 137th Airlift Wing (ANG).

Personnel and Expenditures

ACTIVE DUTY PERSONNEL: 2577 Guard
CIVILIAN PERSONNEL: 370
MILITARY PAYROLL EXPENDITURE: $21.3 mil

Tinker AFB

678. Tinker Air Force Base

3001 Staff Dr
Tinker AFB, OK 73145-5990
405-732-7321; DSN 884-1110
OFFICER-OF-THE-DAY: 405-734-2191, DSN 884-2191

Profile

BRANCH: Air Force.
SIZE AND LOCATION: 4800 acres. 9 mi SE of Oklahoma City off I-40; use Tinker Gate off Air Depot Blvd. *County:* Oklahoma.
MAJOR UNITS: Oklahoma City Air Logistics Center; 72nd Air Base Wing; Navy Strategic Communications Wing 1; 552nd Air Control Wing; Communications Systems Center; 507th Wing; Defense Distribution Depot, Oklahoma City.
BASE HISTORY: 1942, named for Maj Gen Clarence L Tinker, Oklahoman killed on Wake Island. 1943, Douglas Aircraft began production of cargo planes immediately E of base. WWII, Tinker workers repaired B-17 & B-24 bombers; outfitted B-29 bombers for combat. Following WWII, expanded to include Douglas facility, named Oklahoma City Air Materiel Area (OCAMA). Materiel support for Korean War. 1960s, supported Berlin Crisis, Cuban Missile Crisis, and logistics support for B-52 bombers in Vietnam. 1967, designated inland aerial port of embarkation for Southeast Asia. 1974, renamed Oklahoma City Air Logistics Center (OC-ALC). 1980s, B-1 bomber added to management responsibilities.
VISITOR ATTRACTIONS: Heritage Park Museum.

Key Contacts

COMMANDER: Col Robert Smolen, 72 ABW, 405-734-2101, DSN 884-2101.
PUBLIC AFFAIRS: Eugene R Pickett, 3001 Staff Dr, Ste 1AG78A, 73145-3010, 405-739-2026, DSN 339-2026; DSN FAX 339-2882.
PROCUREMENT: John Blair, 3001 Staff Dr, Ste 1AG76A, 73145-3010, 405-739-3900, DSN 339-3900.
TRANSPORTATION: Eddie Allen, 72 ABW/LGTV, 405-734-3438, DSN 884-3438.
PERSONNEL/COMMUNITY ACTIVITIES: LTC Larry Spencer, 3001 Staff Dr, Ste 1AH190B, 73145-3010, 405-739-2856, DSN 339-2856.

Personnel and Expenditures

ACTIVE DUTY PERSONNEL: 7534
CIVILIAN PERSONNEL: 10,999
MILITARY PAYROLL EXPENDITURE: $806 mil
CONTRACT EXPENDITURE: $2.4 bil

Services

Housing: Family units 730; RV/Camper sites 29; Tent spaces 5. *Temporary Housing:* VIP units 10; VOQ units 120; VAQ units 49; Apartment units 39; Dormitory units 1140; Transient quarters 5. *Commissary:* Yes; *Exchange:* Retail store; Barber shop; Dry cleaners; Food shop; Florist; Bank; Service station; Furniture store; Bakery; Bookstore; Military clothing store; Convenience store; Beauty shop; Laundromat; Credit union; ATM; Optical store; Post office; Fast food; Video rentals; Four seasons; Thrift shop; Travel agency; Class VI; Shoe repair; Computer store; Garden center; Tailor/Alterations; Laundry; Cafeteria; Photo store; Jewelry/watch sales/repair. *Child Care/Capacities:* Day care center capacity 308, 6wks-5yrs; Home day care program; Summer day camp. *Schools:* Elementary. *Base Library:* Yes. *Medical Facilities:* Hospital 30; Medical clinic; Dental clinic; Dispensary; Pharmacy; Veterinary services. *Recreational Facilities:* Bowling center; Movie theater; Pool; Gym; Recreation center; Golf course; Stables; Tennis courts; Racquetball court; Fitness center/Weight room; Softball field; Football field; Auto shop; Craft shop; Officers club; NCO club; Camping; Fishing/Hunting; Enlisted club; Youth center; Picnic area; Skeet range; Playground; Rod & Gun club; Equipment rental; South 40 Recreation Area with 29 RV sites.

Tulsa

679. Tulsa IAP, Air National Guard Base

4200 N 93rd E Ave
Tulsa, OK 74115-1699
918-832-8300; DSN 956-5210

Profile

BRANCH: Air National Guard.
SIZE AND LOCATION: 82 acres. Off Gilcrease Dr, N from I-244 within corporate limits of Tulsa; Hwy 169 & 46th St N. *County:* Tulsa.
MAJOR UNITS: 138th Fighter Wing (ANG); 219th Electronic Installation Squadron.
BASE HISTORY: 1940, organized as OK ANG first flying unit. 1941, federally recognized as 125th Observation Squadron. WWII, attached to 77th Observation Group & 76th Tactical Reconnaissance Group. 1945, redesignated as 125th Fighter Squadron. 1947, redesignated as 125th Fighter Bomber Squadron. 1950-52, activated. 1960, redesignated 125th Air Transport Squadron. 1972, converted to 125th Tactical Fighter Wing. 1973, activated as part of 138th Tactical Fighter Group. 1993, converted to F-16C.

Personnel and Expenditures

ACTIVE DUTY PERSONNEL: 1190 Guard
CIVILIAN PERSONNEL: 321
MILITARY PAYROLL EXPENDITURE: $23.1 mil

680. US Army Corps of Engineers, Tulsa District

CESWT
1645 South 101 East Ave
Tulsa, OK 74128-4629

Mailing Address

PO Box 61
Tulsa, OK 74121-0061
918-669-7201; FAX 918-669-7207
Internet: http://www.swt.usace.army.mil/

Profile

BRANCH: Army.
SIZE: Offices only. *County:* Tulsa.
MAJOR UNITS: Corps of Engineers, Tulsa District.
BASE HISTORY: 1939, founded to provide engineering support for flood control. 1970, McClellan-Kerr Arkansas River Navigation System ready. 1989, became Design Center for Hazardous, Toxic, & Radiological Waste program, Southwestern Division area. Currently, supplies engineering, scientific & construction management expertise for civil works, military construction, & environmental restoration.

Key Contacts

COMMANDER: Col Timothy L Sanford, District Engineer, 918-669-7201.
PUBLIC AFFAIRS: Ross Adkins, Chief, CESWT-PA.
PROCUREMENT: CESWT-CT-P, 918-669-7277.

Personnel and Expenditures
ACTIVE DUTY PERSONNEL: 5
CIVILIAN PERSONNEL: 850
Services *Base Library:* Yes. *Recreational Facilities:* Camping and fishing at all 38 lake projects in OK, northern TX, and southern KS.

Vance AFB

681. Vance Air Force Base
VAFB
PO Box 5000
Vance AFB, OK 73705-5000
580-213-7111; DSN 448-7110
Internet: http://www.vnc.aetc.af.mil
OFFICER-OF-THE-DAY: Command Post,
   580-213-7384, DSN 448-7384

Profile
BRANCH: Air Force.
SIZE AND LOCATION: 4394 acres (incl Kegelman Auxiliary Field, 1285 acres, Jet OK). 2 mi S of Enid, OK on US-81; US-64 runs E & W through city; Woodring Municipal Airport, city airport; Vance 80 mi N-NW of Oklahoma City. *County:* Garfield.
MAJOR UNITS: 71st Flying Training Wing; 19th Air Force; Air Education and Training Command; 71st Operations Group; 71st Medical Group; 71st Support Group; 8th Flying Training Squadron; 25th Flying Training Squadron; 32nd Flying Training Squadron; 5th Flying Training Flight (AFRC).
BASE HISTORY: 1941, Enid Army Air Field established. 1947, deactivated. 1948, reactivated as Enid AFB. 1949, renamed for LTC Leon Robert Vance Jr, WWII hero & Medal of Honor recipient. 1961, converted to consolidated pilot training base. 1972, Northrop Worldwide Aircraft Services, Inc assumed support contract from Serv Air, Inc; 71st FTW activated; northernmost pilot training base in Air Training Command. 1987, began fixed wing qualification training program. 1996, began training Navy & Marine Corps pilots.
VISITOR ATTRACTIONS: Base tours, static aircraft displays, flightline; Undergraduate Pilot Training (UPT) program.

Key Contacts
COMMANDER: Col David J Mumaug, 71 FTW Commander.
PUBLIC AFFAIRS: Capt Tadd Sholtis, 71 FTW/PA, 246 Brown Pky, Ste 120, 73705-5028, 580-213-7476, FAX 580-213-6376 73705-5016, 405-249-7476, DSN 940-7476.

Personnel and Expenditures
ACTIVE DUTY PERSONNEL: 695; Student pilots 330
DEPENDENTS: 1400
CIVILIAN PERSONNEL: 205; Northrop Worldwide Aircraft Services, 1200
MILITARY PAYROLL EXPENDITURE: $34.7 mil
CONTRACT EXPENDITURE: $10.6 mil
Services
Housing: Family units 230; Senior NCO units 18; Junior NCO units 80. *Temporary Housing:* VOQ units 34; Dormitory units 266; Unaccompanied Officers' Quarters 230; Temporary lodging facilities 10. *Commissary:* Yes; *Exchange:* Retail store; Barber shop; Dry cleaners; Florist; Bank; Service station; Military clothing store; Convenience store; Beauty shop; Credit union. *Child Care/Capacities:* Day care center capacity 56, 1yr-11yrs; *Schools:* Public elementary school outside main gate. *Base Library:* Yes. *Medical Facilities:* Medical clinic; Dental clinic; Pharmacy; Veterinary services. *Recreational Facilities:* Bowling center; Pool; Gym; Tennis courts; Racquetball court; Fitness center/Weight room; Softball field; Auto shop; Craft shop; Officers club; NCO club; Youth center; Picnic area; Playground; Driving range.

Oregon

Boardman

682. Boardman Naval Weapons Systems Training Facility
NWSTF Boardman
Boardman Range
Bombing Range Rd
Boardman, OR 97818-0319
Mailing Address
PO Box 319
Boardman, OR 97818-0319
541-481-2565; FAX 541-481-2187; DSN 820-3328
E-mail: etcscott@juno.com
Profile
BRANCH: Navy.
SIZE AND LOCATION: 47,000 acres. NE Oregon desert; 3 mi S of Columbia River; off I-84, 180 mi E of Portland, OR; 185 mi SW of Spokane, WA; 360 mi from NAS Whidbey Island; 6 mi S of Boardman, OR. *County:* Morrow.
BASE HISTORY: Supports stationary & mobile targets to provide simulated combat release conditions essential to maintain fleet air wing combat readiness.
VISITOR ATTRACTIONS: Oregon Trail crosses SE corner; Well Spring.
Key Contacts
COMMANDER: LCDR Robert M Purdom, Officer in Charge, 541-481-2565, DSN 820-3328, rmpurdom@juno.com.
PUBLIC AFFAIRS: See NAS Whidbey Island, WA.
Personnel and Expenditures
ACTIVE DUTY PERSONNEL: 10
Services
Housing: at Umatilla Army Depot 22 mi E. *Exchange:* at Fairchild AFB 180 mi away. *Recreational Facilities:* Volleyball court; Horseshoe pit.

Central Point

683. Central Point Naval Reserve Center
3070 Ross Lane
Central Point, OR 97502-1399
541-772-2566, 772-7633; FAX 541-772-3815
Profile
BRANCH: Naval Reserve.
LOCATION: *County:* Jackson.

MAJOR UNITS: REDCOM TWENTY-TWO Activity.
Key Contacts
COMMANDER: LCDR H L Zick.

Clackamas

684. Camp Withycombe
10101 SE Clackamas Rd
Clackamas, OR 97015-9191
503-557-5368
Profile
BRANCH: Army National Guard.
LOCATION: 20 mi from Portland; off I-205, at intersection of Hwy 224 & SE Evelyn, turn N follow road approx 0.25 mi. *County:* Clackamas.
MAJOR UNITS: Camp Withycombe (ARNG).
VISITOR ATTRACTIONS: Oregon Military Museum (Fri-Sat, 1pm-4pm & by appointment, free, 503-557-5359, Maj(ret) Stephan C McGeorge, Director).

Services *Base Library:* Yes.

Eugene

685. Eugene Naval & Marine Corps Reserve Center
N&MCRTC Eugene
1520 W 13th Ave
Eugene, OR 97402-3899
541-342-1887, 484-6342; FAX 541-683-5669
Profile
BRANCH: Naval Reserve; Marine Corps Reserve.
LOCATION: *County:* Lane.
MAJOR UNITS: REDCOM TWENTY-TWO Activity; Bridge Co B, 6th Engineer Support Bn.
Key Contacts
COMMANDER: CDR R B Robinson.

Hermiston

686. Umatilla Chemical Depot
UMCD
Hermiston, OR 97838-9544
541-564-8632; DSN 790-8632

OFFICER-OF-THE-DAY: 541-564-5279, DSN 790-5279
Profile
BRANCH: Army.
SIZE AND LOCATION: 19,729 acres. In High Desert in NE OR, 7 mi W of Hermiston; along main line of Union Pacific Railroad; at intersections of I-82 and I-84, Exit 177; approx 175 mi E of Portland; 35-40 mi to Pasco, WA Airport & Pendleton, OR Airport. *County:* Umatilla; Morrow.
MAJOR UNITS: Army Chemical Depot; Army Occupational Health Clinic.
BASE HISTORY: 1940, site selected for new arsenal. 1941, constructed as Umatilla Army Depot (UMD) for Territorial Indian tribe. Following WWII, huge stocks of munitions returned from overseas routed to UMD for renovation, maintenance, & storage; unserviceable ammunition demilitarized; reusable parts salvaged. Similar activities repeated for Korean War, Vietnam War & Desert Storm. 1996, changed to present name; sole mission safe & secure storage of chemical munitions.
FUTURE CLOSURE/REALIGNMENT: Slated for closure once chemicals destroyed; currently mandated disposal date, Dec 2004.
VISITOR ATTRACTIONS: Closed to public.
Key Contacts
COMMANDER: LTC Martin Jacoby, Office of the Commander, 541-564-5200, FAX 541-564-5370, DSN 790-5200.
PUBLIC AFFAIRS: Donna K Fuzi, 541-564-5312, DSN 790-5312, DSN FAX 790-5395, umcdpao@oregontrail.net.
TRANSPORTATION: Richard Edwards, 541-564-5221, DSN 790-5221, DSN FAX 790-5340.

Personnel and Expenditures
ACTIVE DUTY PERSONNEL: 2
DEPENDENTS: 1
CIVILIAN PERSONNEL: 150
Services
Housing: Family units 7; Unaccompanied enlisted quarters 13. *Temporary Housing.* None. *Exchange:* None. *Child Care/Capacities:* No day care facilities. *Schools:* No on-base schools. *Medical Facilities:* Medical clinic. *Recreational Facilities:* Pool; Recreation center; Stables (self-help); Tennis courts; Racquetball court; Fitness center/Weight room; Playground; Basketball; Area bordered by Columbia River with variety of recreation.

Klamath Falls

687. Kingsley Field Air National Guard Base
Kingsley Field
222 Arnold Ave, Suite 40
Klamath Falls, OR 97603
541-885-6350; FAX 541-885-6187; DSN
830-6350; DSN FAX 830-6187
Internet: http://www.orang-klmt.ang.af.mil/
homepage/kingsley.htm
Profile
BRANCH: Air National Guard.
SIZE AND LOCATION: 405 acres. At Klamath
Falls IAP in S central Oregon; E of Hwy 97,
20 mi N of CA border. 285 mi S of Portland;
300 mi N of San Francisco; 265 mi W of
Reno, NV. *County:* Klamath.
MAJOR UNITS: 173rd Fighter Wing; 114th
Tactical Fighter Training Squadron; 270th
ATC Squadron; 104th TCS/OLAA.
BASE HISTORY: Named in honor of Lt David
R Kingsley, bombardier killed in raids on
Ploesti, Romania, 1944. WWII, Naval Air Sta-
tion. 1946, deactivated. 1956, 408th Fighter
Group activated. 1957-1970, operated by
408th FW, 4788th ABG, & 827th ADG.
1979, realigned from HQ ADCOM to HQ
TAC; all active units removed; remained alert
detachment for air defense. 1992, 114th Tacti-
cal Fighter Training Squadron redesignated
114th Fighter Squadron under air Combat
Command. 1993, became part of Air Education Training Command. 1995, Guard assumed control of airport tower from FAA;
Air Traffic Control Squadron established.
1996, unit redesignated 173rd Fighter Wing
with 114th Fighter Squadron retained as flying component.
VISITOR ATTRACTIONS: Air park with F-4C
Phantom & F16-A Fighting Falcon.
Key Contacts
COMMANDER: Col Billy J Cox,
541-885-6301, DSN 830-6301, DSN FAX
830-6187, COXB@orang\klmt.ang.af.mil..
PUBLIC AFFAIRS: 1Lt Vince Walters,
541-885-6301, DSN 830-6301, DSN FAX
830-6187, WATERSV@orang-klmt.ang.af.
mil. (Guard Drill Weekends only).
Personnel and Expenditures
ACTIVE DUTY PERSONNEL: 404 guardsmen
DEPENDENTS: 0
CIVILIAN PERSONNEL: 52
Services *Recreational Facilities:* Movie thea-
ter; Gym; Fitness center/Weight room; Skeet
range; All ranks club.

Portland

688. Portland Naval & Marine Corps Reserve Readiness Center
NAVMARCORESCEN Portland
Reserve Center, Portland
6735 N Basin Ave
Portland, OR 97217-3993
503-285-4566; FAX 503-735-1788
Profile
BRANCH: Naval Reserve; Marine Corps Re-
serve.
SIZE AND LOCATION: 20 acres. Swan Island,
city of Portland. *County:* Multnomah.

MAJOR UNITS: REDCOM TWENTY-TWO
Activity; 4th FSSG, 6th Engineers (NR); In-
shore Boat Unit 13; Combat Service Support
Element-41; HQ & Service Co, 6th Engineer
Support Bn; 6th Engineer Support Bn.
Key Contacts
COMMANDER: LCDR Theresa M Kelsay,
USNR, 503-285-4566, ext 510, FAX
503-735-1788; Capt K W Miller, USMCR.
PUBLIC AFFAIRS: LCDR Jeff Davisson,
USNR (SELRES).
Personnel and Expenditures
ACTIVE DUTY PERSONNEL: 22; 650 reserv-
ists
Services *Base Library:* Yes. *Recreational Fa-
cilities:* Gym.

689. US Army Corps of Engineers, Northwestern Division
CENWD
220 NW 8th Ave
Portland, OR 97209-3589
Mailing Address
PO Box 2870
Portland, OR 97208-2870
503-808-3710; FAX 503-808-3713
Internet: http://www.nwd.usace.army.mil
Profile
BRANCH: Army.
SIZE AND LOCATION: Offices only. In down-
town Portland. *County:* Multnomah.
MAJOR UNITS: Corps of Engineers, Northwest-
ern Division.
BASE HISTORY: Oversees 5 district offices:
Seattle & Walla Walla, WA; Portland, OR;
Kansas City, MO; & Omaha, NE. Performs
military & civil works construction and mili-
tary & civil works real estate.
Key Contacts
COMMANDER: Brig Gen Robert H Griffin,
Division Engineer.
Services *Base Library:* Yes.

690. US Army Corps of Engineers, Portland District
CENWP
333 SW 1st Ave, 10th FL
Portland, OR 97204-3495
Mailing Address
PO Box 2946
Portland, OR 97208-2946
503-808-4510; FAX 503-808-4515
Internet: http://www.nwp.usace.army.mil/
Profile
BRANCH: Army.
SIZE AND LOCATION: Offices only. In city of
Portland. *County:* Multnomah.
MAJOR UNITS: Corps of Engineers, Portland
District.
BASE HISTORY: One of the largest, most di-
versified programs of any district in Corps.
Mission to protect & develop water resources
of 79,405 sq mi in western & central Oregon,
& 8740 sq mi in southwestern WA. Major re-
sponsibilities include providing safe entrance
to coastal/inland harbors & generating hydroelectric power for region at Bonneville, The
Dalles, & John Day dams on Columbia River.
Lake projects in Willamette & Rogue River
valleys provide flood control, hydropower,
recreation, & improved water quality for areas downstream. Only Corps' district with responsibilities relating to active volcano, Mt St

Helens. Performs civil works construction &
civil works real estate.
Key Contacts
COMMANDER: Col Robert T Slusar.
PUBLIC AFFAIRS: Diana C Brimhall.
Personnel and Expenditures
ACTIVE DUTY PERSONNEL: 3
CIVILIAN PERSONNEL: 1185
Services *Base Library:* Yes.

Portland IAP

691. Portland Air National Guard Base
PANG
Oregon Air National Guard, 142FW
6801 NE Cornfoot Rd
Portland IAP, OR 97218-2797
503-335-4104; DSN 638-4104
Profile
BRANCH: Air National Guard.
SIZE AND LOCATION: 246 acres. Within cor-
porate limits of Portland, between I-205 & I-5
along Columbia River; attached to S side of
Portland IAP. *County:* Multnomah.
MAJOR UNITS: 142nd Fighter Wing (ANG);
Oregon Air National Guard, Headquarters;
123rd Weather Flight (ANG); 218th Field Ar-
tillery, 2nd Bn, Headquarters (ARNG); 244th
Combat Communications Squadron (ANG);
272nd Combat Communications Squadron
(ANG); 939th Rescue Wing (AFRES); Ore-
gon Wing (CAP); OL A 366th Communica-
tions Squadron; 83rd Aerial Port Squadron
(AFRES).
BASE HISTORY: 1939, Portland Air Base
opened and served as active duty Army Air
Corps base; built in conjunction with Portland
IAP. 1940, home of OR ANG 123rd Observa-
tion Squadron, one of first ANG units. 1963,
property turned over to OR ANG.
VISITOR ATTRACTIONS: Aircraft memorial
(F-101 & F-4); Base Chapel (built in 1939)
National Historic Site.
Key Contacts
COMMANDER: LTC Bruce A Marshall,
503-335-5000, DSN 638-5000.
PUBLIC AFFAIRS: Mona Spenst Jordan,
503-335-4104, DSN 638-4104.
Personnel and Expenditures
ACTIVE DUTY PERSONNEL: 1402 reservists
CIVILIAN PERSONNEL: 548
MILITARY PAYROLL EXPENDITURE: $17.2
mil
Services *Exchange:* Barber shop; Credit union;
Mini BX. *Medical Facilities:* Medical clinic.
Recreational Facilities: Recreation center; Fit-
ness center/Weight room; Softball field; Picnic
area; Playground; All ranks club.

Salem

692. Camp Rilea, Oregon National Guard Training Site
Camp Rilea
1776 Military Way
Salem, OR 97309-5047
Mailing Address
PO Box 14350
Salem, OR 97309-5047

503-861-4000; DSN 355-3972

Profile

BRANCH: Army National Guard.

SIZE AND LOCATION: 2000 acres (plus 400,000 acres available). Immediately W of US-101 between Astoria and Seaside; 90 mi W of Portland. *County:* Marion.

MAJOR UNITS: State Area Readiness Command HQ, Det 3 (ARNG); 442nd Engineer Det (Utilities); 1249th Engineer Bn, Co D; 116th Tactical Control Squadron.

BASE HISTORY: 1927, state-owned training site founded; originally called Camp Clatsop. Prior to WWII, used as mobilization site for 249th Coast Artillery. June 21, 1942, fired on by Japanese submarine. 1959, name changed for Maj Gen Thomas E Rilea, Oregon Adj Gen, 1941-59. 1975, major revitalization.

Key Contacts

COMMANDER: Maj Gen Raymond F Rees, 503-945-3991.

PUBLIC AFFAIRS: Capt Dan McCabe, 503-945-3917.

PROCUREMENT: Billeting Info & Supply, 503-861-4051.

Personnel and Expenditures

ACTIVE DUTY PERSONNEL: 72

Services

Housing: Barracks spaces 800; RV/Camper sites 10; Troop hutments 600. *Temporary Housing:* VOQ 7; Huts for rental individual/family. *Exchange:* Laundry. *Medical Facilities:* Dispensary. *Recreational Facilities:* Movie theater; Gym; Recreation center; Fishing/Hunting; Water sports; Part of Neacoxie Lake complex; Beach.

693. Salem Naval & Marine Corps Reserve Center

NMCRC Salem

1015 Airport Rd, SE
Salem, OR 97301-5097
503-399-5886, 588-8394; FAX 503-588-5899

Profile

BRANCH: Naval Reserve; Marine Corps Reserve.

LOCATION: *County:* Marion.

MAJOR UNITS: REDCOM TWENTY-TWO Activity; Engineer Co, 6th Engineer Support Bn.

Key Contacts

COMMANDER: CDR R B Robinson.

Pennsylvania

Allentown

694. Lehigh Valley Naval & Marine Corps Reserve Center
1400 Postal Dr
Allentown, PA 18103-9503
610-264-8823, 264-8843; FAX 610-264-1169
Profile
BRANCH: Naval Reserve; Marine Corps Reserve.
LOCATION: *County:* Lehigh.
MAJOR UNITS: REDCOM FOUR Activity; Motor Transport Maintenance Co; Det 2, Communications Co, HQ & Service Co; Motor Transport Maintenance Section, Motor Transport Co, 4th Maintenance Bn.
Key Contacts
COMMANDER: Lt A Haynes.

Annville

695. Adjutant General of Pennsylvania
Dept of Military Affairs, Fort Indiantown Gap
Annville, PA 17003-5002
717-861-8500, 861-8501; FAX 717-861-8314
Profile
BRANCH: Army National Guard.
MAJOR UNITS: Pennsylvania National Guard.
Key Contacts
COMMANDER: Maj Gen James W MacVay.

696. Fort Indiantown Gap
FTIG
1 Garrison Rd
Annville, PA 17003-5000
717-861-2000; FAX 717-861-2036; DSN 491-2000; DSN FAX 491-2036
Internet: http://www.indgap.army.mil
OFFICER-OF-THE-DAY: 717-861-2160, DSN 491-2160, DSN FAX 491-2627
Profile
BRANCH: Army.
SIZE AND LOCATION: 18,000 acres. Approx 20 mi NE of Harrisburg, PA, Exit 29, I-81. *County:* Lebanon; Dauphin.
MAJOR UNITS: Pennsylvania Department of Military & Veterans Affairs; Army Readiness Group; Eastern ARNG Aviation Training Site; 756th Explosive Ordnance Disposal; Equipment Concentration Site 24; Army Reserve Center.

BASE HISTORY: Named for Indian communities that flourished in area; as defense measure, many forts and blockhouses built; Swatara Ft, located N of present site. 1930, PA NG used Mt Gretna as training area for field training for horse cavalry. WWII, used as staging area for NY Port of Embarkation & later as separation center. 1946, inactivated. 1951-53, reactivated as 5th Infantry Division. 1953-57, under PA Military District. 1957-68, XXI US Army Corps administered Army Reserve program (PA, MD, DE, VA, and DC). 1968, mission transferred to First Army, Ft George G Meade, MD. Site used as resettlement camp (1975, 22,228 Vietnamese & Cambodian refugees; 1980, 19,094 Cubans). Oct 1983, became Subpost of Ft Meade, MD. Oct 1993, became subpost of Ft Drum, NY. Mission: training Army Reserve & National Guardsmen; Ft Indiantown Gap leased by federal government from PA State.
FUTURE CLOSURE/REALIGNMENT: Closure scheduled to be completed by Oct 1998.
VISITOR ATTRACTIONS: Hunting and fishing with post permit.
Key Contacts
COMMANDER: LTC Thomas A Allmon, 717-861-2666, DSN 491-2666, DSN FAX 491-2036, cdr0s@indgap-emh1.army.mil.
PUBLIC AFFAIRS: John C Blanda, 717-861-2193, DSN 491-2193, DSN FAX 491-2231, pao@indgap-emh1.army.mil.
PROCUREMENT: William H Potters, 717-861-2191, DSN 491-2191, DSN FAX 491-2423, doc@indgap-emh1.army.mil.
TRANSPORTATION: William Sypher (Acting), 717-861-2311, FAX 717-861-2337, DSN 491-2311 dol@indgap-emh1.army.mil.
PERSONNEL/COMMUNITY ACTIVITIES: Ms Claudia Berwager, Director of Community Activities (Acting), 717-861-2060, 717-861-2337, DSN 491-2060, dpca01@indgap-emh1.army.mil.
Personnel and Expenditures
ACTIVE DUTY PERSONNEL: 2
DEPENDENTS: 4
CIVILIAN PERSONNEL: 206
CONTRACT EXPENDITURE: $7 mil
Services
Housing: Family units 5. *Temporary Housing:* Guest cottages 12; VOQ/VEQ 700; Suites 25. *Exchange:* Retail store; Barber shop; Dry cleaners; Food shop; Bank; Service station; Bookstore; Military clothing store; Convenience store; Laundromat; Credit union; ATM; Class VI; Cafeteria.

Child Care/Capacities: Day care center capacity 45, 4mos-6yrs; Summer day camp; Before & after school programs School age child care SAC Program. *Schools:* No on-base schools. *Base Library:* Yes. *Medical Facilities:* Medical clinic; Dental clinic; Dispensary; Veterinary services. *Recreational Facilities:* Bowling center; Pool; Gym; Tennis courts; Racquetball court; Fitness center/Weight room; Softball field; Auto shop; NCO club; Camping; Fishing/Hunting; Picnic area; Water sports; Playground; Community club.

Avoca

697. Avoca Naval Reserve Center
1200 Navy Way Rd
Avoca, PA 18641-2299
717-457-8430; FAX 717-457-4042
Profile
BRANCH: Naval Reserve.
LOCATION: Approx 7 mi SW of Scranton. *County:* Luzerne.
MAJOR UNITS: REDCOM FOUR Activity.
Key Contacts
COMMANDER: LCDR J Steinbronn.

Carlisle Barracks

698. Carlisle Barracks
Army Garrison
Carlisle Barracks, PA 17013-5002
717-245-3232; DSN 242-3232
Internet: http://carlisle-www.army.mil/
Profile
BRANCH: Army.
SIZE AND LOCATION: 403 acres. Approx 18 mi W of Harrisburg, PA on US-11. Maingate on Ashburn Dr 2 mi off Exit 16 of PA Tpke. *County:* Cumberland.
MAJOR UNITS: Army War College; Military History Institute; Center for Strategic Leadership; Army Physical Fitness Research Institute; Strategic Studies Institute; Army Garrison, Carlisle Barracks; Knowledge Engineering Group (KEG); Dunham Army Health Clinic; Dunham Army Dental Clinic; Allegheny Regional Veterinary Command.
BASE HISTORY: Second oldest active military post in US, established May 30, 1757. French & Indian War, served as supply base & jump-

ing-off point to West. 1777, site of Ordnance Magazine; first American Artillery School. 1794, Whiskey Rebellion, President Washington's troops assembled; Cavalry School of Practice established. 1879, transferred to Dept of Interior as Indian School. 1918, Army reclaimed post for hospital, Medical Field Service School. 1946-51, temporary home of School of Government of Occupied Area, Adjutant General's School, Army Chaplain School, Military Police School, Army Security Agency School, & Army Information School (later Armed Forces Information School). 1951, Army War College established. Main post 217 acres; detached areas, Stanwix Area (family housing) and Farm 2 (golf course, heliport, and stables). Training & Doctrine Command installation.

VISITOR ATTRACTIONS: Omar N Bradley Museum; Hessian Powder Magazine Museum; Indian Cemetery; Military History Institute; Indian Industrial School Sites; Revolutionary War Forge; Schools Monument; Army War College Alumni Weekend (May each year).

Key Contacts
COMMANDER: 717-245-3232, DSN 242-3232.
PUBLIC AFFAIRS: 717-245-4101, DSN 242-4101, AWCCI@carlisle-emh2.army.mil.
PROCUREMENT: Director of Contracting, ATZE-DOC, Carlisle Barracks, PA 17013-5002, 717-245-3953, DSN 242-3953.
TRANSPORTATION: ATZE DIS-L-T, Carlisle Barracks, PA 17013-5002, 717-245-3172, DSN 242-3172.
PERSONNEL/COMMUNITY ACTIVITIES: ATZE-PA, Carlisle Barracks, PA 17013-5002, 717-245-4332, DSN 242-4332.

Personnel and Expenditures
ACTIVE DUTY PERSONNEL: 651; Students 300
DEPENDENTS: 93,000 (50 mi radius)
CIVILIAN PERSONNEL: 800

Services
Housing: Family units 321; Unaccompanied officer quarters 3; Unaccompanied enlisted quarters 55; BAQ units 18; Duplex units 101; Townhouse units 50; Barracks spaces 63; Senior NCO units 25; Junior NCO units 68. *Temporary Housing:* Guesthouse units 2. *Commissary:* Yes; *Exchange:* Retail store; Barber shop; Dry cleaners; Food shop; Bank; Service station; Convenience store; Bookstore; Beauty shop; Credit union; Optical store; Fast food; Thrift shop; Class VI; Garden center; Tailor/Alterations; Laundry; Candy/Ice cream. *Child Care/Capacities:* Day care center capacity 52, 6wks-5 yrs; Home day care program; Latch key program. *Schools:* Preschool/Kindergarten; *Base Library:* Yes. *Medical Facilities:* Medical clinic; Dental clinic; Veterinary services. *Recreational Facilities:* Bowling center; Movie theater; Pool; Gym; Recreation center (squash); Golf course; Stables; Tennis courts; Racquetball court; Fitness center/Weight room; Softball field; Football field; Auto shop; Craft shop; Officers club; NCO club; Youth center; Riding & Hunt club; Ski club; ITT; Outdoor recreation center.

Chambersburg

699. Letterkenny Army Depot
LEAD
1 Overcash Ave
Chambersburg, PA 17201-4150
717-267-8111; FAX 717-267-9724; DSN 570-8111; DSN FAX 570-9724
E-mail: alky@letterkenn-emh1.army.mil Internet:http://www/letterkenny.army.mil

Profile
BRANCH: Army.
SIZE AND LOCATION: 19,300 acres. In S central PA, about 5 mi N of Chambersburg; 8 mi SW of Shippensburg. Off I-81, use Exit 5 & 6 (Chambersburg) & 8 (Scotland). Air service provided through Hagerstown Regional & Harrisburg IAP. Hagerstown 25 mi; Harrisburg 50 mi. *County:* Franklin.
MAJOR UNITS: Army IOC Industrial Logistics System Center; Army Test, Measurement, Diagnostic Equipment (TMDE) Support, Region 1; TMDE Support System; Defense Reutilization & Marketing Office; USAMC Management Engineer Activity; Defense Megacenter, Chambersburg.
BASE HISTORY: Sep 1942, received 1st shipment of ammunition. 1948, depot began reworking guns, fire control equipment, & combat & general service vehicles. Korean War, construction boom. 1950s, overhauled Nike ground-to-air missile components. 1960s, developed automatic data processing systems for Army depots. Vietnam period, rebuilt artillery recoil mechanisms & stored/maintained Air Force missiles. 1976, established Major Item Supply Management Agency; later, Army Depot System Command headquartered here. 1980-90, modernization projects, automatic storage & retrieval; Paladin, Patriot, & Hawk maintenance work. 1993, named tactical missile maintenance center for all DOD.

Key Contacts
COMMANDER: Col Thomas W Resau, 717-267-8300, FAX 717-267-9724; DSN 570-8306.
PUBLIC AFFAIRS: Daniel Gallagher, 717-267-5102, FAX 717-267-9724; DSN 570-5102, ALKYCA@letterkenn-Emh1.army.mil.
PROCUREMENT: Richard Rector, SIOLE-KO, 717-267-9711, FAX 717-267-9834, DSN 570-9711, alkypa@leterkenn-Emh1.army.mil.
TRANSPORTATION: SDSLE-TT, 717-267-9017, DSN 570-9017.
PERSONNEL/COMMUNITY ACTIVITIES: John L Izzi, SIOLE-RM, 717-267-8404, FAX 717-267-8253, DSN 570-8404, alkyrm@letterkenn-Emh1.army.mil; Garry L Gontz, Base Transition Coordinator, 717-267-9815; Bryan Hoke, BRAC Environmental Coordinator, 717-267-9836.

Personnel and Expenditures
ACTIVE DUTY PERSONNEL: 14
DEPENDENTS: 14 (families)
CIVILIAN PERSONNEL: 2707 (including tenants)
CONTRACT EXPENDITURE: $12.2 mil (local procurement)

Services
Housing: Family units 6; Duplex units 4; Barracks spaces 8.

Temporary Housing: VIP units 1; VOQ units 2; Guesthouse units 3. *Exchange:* Barber shop; Credit union; Travel agency. *Child Care/Capacities:* Day care center capacity 60, 6mos-12yrs; Latch key program; Summer day camp. *Schools:* No on-base schools. *Medical Facilities:* Medical clinic. *Recreational Facilities:* Pool; Gym; Golf course; Tennis courts; Racquetball court; Fitness center/Weight room; Softball field; Camping; Fishing/Hunting; Picnic area; Skeet range; Playground; Community club; Rod & Gun club.

Coraopolis

700. Pittsburgh International Airport Air National Guard Base
PA ANG
300 Tanker Rd
Coraopolis, PA 15108-4800
412-474-7359; DSN 277-7359

Profile
BRANCH: Air National Guard.
SIZE AND LOCATION: 179 acres. SE portion of Pittsburgh IAP; 13 mi N of Golden Triangle of Pittsburgh; AFRS has separate facility at this location. *County:* Allegheny.
MAJOR UNITS: 171st Air Refueling Wing (ANG).
BASE HISTORY: 1947, PA ANG organized as 53rd Fighter Wing at Harrisburg State Airport (later transferred to Pittsburgh Airport). 1949, 112th Fighter Group granted federal recognition at Greater Pittsburgh Airport. 1968, 171st Aeromedical Airlift Wing called to active duty to support 375th Wing. 1972, redesignated 171st ARW. 1990, activated for Operations Desert Shield/Storm refueling missions. 1992, 171st Air Refueling Wing (ARW) came under Air Mobility Command (AMC). Currently, one of largest air refueling organizations.

Personnel and Expenditures
ACTIVE DUTY PERSONNEL: 1397 Guard
CIVILIAN PERSONNEL: 421
MILITARY PAYROLL EXPENDITURE: $24.9 mil

Services *Exchange:* Retail store. *Schools:* College courses. *Medical Facilities:* No medical facilities. *Recreational Facilities:* Fitness center/Weight room.

701. Pittsburgh IAP, Air Reserve Station
316 Defense Ave
Coraopolis, PA 15108-4403
412-474-8000; DSN 277-8000

Profile
BRANCH: Air Force Reserve.
SIZE AND LOCATION: 115 acres. 15 mi N of Pittsburgh on Business Rte 60, at Pittsburgh IAP; ANG has separate facilities at this location. *County:* Allegheny.
MAJOR UNITS: 911th Airlift Wing; 911th Mission Support Flight; 911th Morale, Welfare, and Recreation and Services Flight; 911th Operations Support Flight; 911th Communications Squadron; 911th Civil Engineering Squadron; 911th Medical Squadron; 911th Maintenance Squadron; 911th Logistics Squadron; 911th Security Police Squadron; 32nd Mobile Aerial Port Squadron; 33rd

Aeromedical Evacuation Squadron; 758th Airlift Squadron.

BASE HISTORY: Since 1943, Pittsburgh IAP has hosted a number of active duty & reserve flying units. 1963, 911th Troop Carrier Group activated. 1967, redesignated Military Airlift Group. 1972, redesignated Tactical Airlift Group. 1992, renamed 911th Airlift Group (AG). Mission: to organize, recruit & train AF Reserve personnel to provide airlift of airborne forces. During mobilization 911th AG would become part of Air Combat Command.

Personnel and Expenditures
ACTIVE DUTY PERSONNEL: 1080 Reservists
CIVILIAN PERSONNEL: 222
MILITARY PAYROLL EXPENDITURE: $32.7 mil

Services *Temporary Housing:* VOQ units 24; VAQ units 230. *Exchange:* Retail store; Credit union. *Child Care/Capacities:* No day care facilities. *Schools:* No on-base schools. *Medical Facilities:* No medical facilities. *Recreational Facilities:* Gym; Racquetball court; Fitness center/Weight room; Softball field; Consolidated club.

Ebensburg

702. Ebensburg Naval & Marine Corps Reserve Center
NAVMARCORESCEN Ebensburg PA
261 Industrial Park Rd
Ebensburg, PA 15931-8955
814-472-5083; FAX 814-472-6361
E-mail: ebenburg@cnsrf.navy.mil
Profile
BRANCH: Naval Reserve; Marine Corps Reserve.
SIZE AND LOCATION: 8.5 acres. Within Cambria Co Industrial Park near intersection of SR219 & SR22. *County:* Cambria.
MAJOR UNITS: REDCOM FOUR Activity; NMCB 23 Det 0523; Fleet Hospital 500 CBTZ Det O; PHIB CB 2 Det 405 (NR); AD Det 4 (NR); 2nd Platoon Truck Co (USMC); HQ Bn 4th Marine Division (USMC).
BASE HISTORY: Established July 5, 1946, Johnstown, PA. Armory opened 1947. 1982, present reserve center constructed.
Key Contacts
COMMANDER: LCDR John G Esarey, 814-472-5083, FAX 814-472-6361.
PUBLIC AFFAIRS: PH2 Brunner.
Personnel and Expenditures
ACTIVE DUTY PERSONNEL: 340 reservists
Services *Base Library:* Yes. *Recreational Facilities:* Fitness center/Weight room; Picnic area; Volleyball court; horseshoe pits.

Erie

703. Erie Naval & Marine Corps Reserve Center
NAVMARCORESCEN Erie
Armed Forces Reserve Center
3838 Old French Rd
Erie, PA 16504-2098
814-866-3073; FAX 814-864-8749

Profile
BRANCH: Naval Reserve; Marine Corps Reserve.
SIZE AND LOCATION: 1.8 acres. 3 mi off Rte 90, Exit 7. *County:* Erie.
MAJOR UNITS: REDCOM ONE Activity; Co H, 2nd Bn, 25th Marine Regiment.
Key Contacts
COMMANDER: LCDR Drew G Flavell.
Personnel and Expenditures
ACTIVE DUTY PERSONNEL: 45; 590 reservists
Services *Recreational Facilities:* Fitness center/Weight room.

Harrisburg

704. Harrisburg Naval & Marine Corps Reserve Center
NAVMARESCEN Harrisburg
2991 N Second St
Harrisburg, PA 17110-1298
717-255-8069; FAX 717-234-4567; DSN 430-4753, 430-4766
E-mail: harris@cnsrf.navy.mil
Profile
BRANCH: Naval Reserve; Marine Corps Reserve.
SIZE AND LOCATION: 4 acres. In downtown Harrisburg; 1.5 mi from I-81 on Susquahana River. *County:* Dauphin.
MAJOR UNITS: REDCOM FOUR Activity; Co H, 2nd Bn, 25th Marine Regiment.
Key Contacts
COMMANDER: LCDR John E Coster, Jr.
PUBLIC AFFAIRS: JO2 Snyder.
Personnel and Expenditures
ACTIVE DUTY PERSONNEL: 10; 300 reservists
Services *Base Library:* Yes. *Recreational Facilities:* Fitness center/Weight room; Softball field.

Lester

705. Naval Facilities Engineering Command, Northern Division
10 Industrial Hwy, MS#82
Lester, PA 19113-2090
FAX 610-595-0611
Profile
BRANCH: Navy.
BASE HISTORY: Component of Atlantic Division (LANTDIV) of Naval Facilities Engineering Command (NAVFACENGCOM); performs engineering functions for Naval bases in NE US.
Key Contacts
COMMANDER: CDR W P Fogarty, 610-595-0600, DSN 443-0600.
PUBLIC AFFAIRS: Elaine McNeil, PAO, Naval Facilities Engineering Command, 703-325-0310.
PROCUREMENT: CDR D J Stewart, Contracts Department, 610-595-0641, DSN 443-0641.

Mechanicsburg

706. Mechanicsburg Navy Inventory Control Point
NAVICP Mechanicsburg
5450 Carlisle Pike
Mechanicsburg, PA 17055-0788
717-790-2000; DSN 430-2000
Internet: http://www.fmso.navy.mil/NAVICP/
Profile
BRANCH: Navy.
SIZE AND LOCATION: 825 acres. On US-11; US-15 & 11 cross approx 3 mi to E at Camp Hill, PA; Harrisburg 8 mi E; Harrisburg IAP 18 mi E; from I-81, Rte 581 Exit, take Carlisle Pike/NAVICP exit on right, follow across to North Gate. *County:* Cumberland.
MAJOR UNITS: Navy Fleet Materiel Support Office; Defense Depot, Mechanicsburg; Naval Sea Logistics Support Engineering Center; Personnel Support Activity Det, Mechanicsburg; Defense Publications and Printing Service Det Office.
BASE HISTORY: July 16, 1945, established as master control center for ships parts under Naval Supply Depot Mechanicsburg. 1953, commissioned as independent command as inventory manager of hull and machinery & diesel engine parts. July 1970, decommissioned. Installation changed to Navy Ships Parts Control Center; later renamed NAVICP. Mission: provide program support functions, including inventory management.
Key Contacts
COMMANDER: RADM Keith Lippert, Code 00, 717-790-3701, DSN 430-3701; Sandra Leggieri, Vice Commande.
PUBLIC AFFAIRS: Denise Deon, 215-697-5570, DSN 442-5570.
PROCUREMENT: Robert Barnhart, Deputy Contracting Directorate, 717-790-2774, DSN 430-2774.
PERSONNEL/COMMUNITY ACTIVITIES: John J Windish, Human Resources Directorate, 717-790-3358.
Personnel and Expenditures
ACTIVE DUTY PERSONNEL: 140
CIVILIAN PERSONNEL: 6000
Services
Housing: Family units 92. *Exchange:* Retail store; Barber shop; Bank; Credit union. *Child Care/Capacities:* Day care center. *Medical Facilities:* Dispensary; Pharmacy. *Recreational Facilities:* Bowling center; Pool; Gym; Golf course; Tennis courts; Racquetball court; Fitness center/Weight room; Softball field; Auto shop; Officers club; Playground.

707. Naval Supply Systems Command
NAVSUP
5450 Carlisle Pike
Mechanicsburg, PA 17055-0791
Mailing Address
PO Box 2050
Mechanicsburg, PA 17055
Internet: http://www.navsup.navy.mil/
Profile
BRANCH: Navy.
LOCATION: S-central PA across Susquehanna River from Harrisburg; from I-81 & I-83, take Rte 581 to front gate; from I-76, traveling

west, exit at Carlisle; traveling east, exit at Harrisburg. *County:* Cumberland.

MAJOR UNITS: Naval Supply Systems Command; Naval Inventory Control Point; Navy Head of Contracting Activity; Navy Field Contracting System; Navy Exchange Service Command; Fleet Material Support Office; Navy Petroleum Office; Navy Transportation Office; Fleet Support Services; Navy Security Assistance Office; Fleet Hospital Program Office; Hazardous Material Afloat Program.

BASE HISTORY: Navy's professional staff corps responsible for supply phases of naval logistics. Since 1795, supplied Navy with items essential to operation of ships, facilities; later aircraft & missiles. 1997, relocated to PA from Arlington, VA.

Key Contacts
COMMANDER: RADM Hickman, Commander, Navy Supply Systems Command & Chief of Supply corps.
PUBLIC AFFAIRS: Liz Van Wye, 717-790-1543, DSN 430-1543, liz_van_wye@navsup.navy.mil.

Personnel and Expenditures
CONTRACT EXPENDITURE: $6.2 bil
Services *Base Library:* Yes.

Middletown

708. Harrisburg IAP Air National Guard Base
HIAP
193rd SOW, 81 Constellation Ct
Middletown, PA 17057-5086
717-948-2201; FAX 717-948-9548; DSN 430-9201; DSN FAX 430-9548
E-mail: 193SOW@pamdt.ang.af.mil
Profile
BRANCH: Air National Guard.
SIZE AND LOCATION: 39 acres. Approx 8 mi SE of Harrisburg, PA; S of I-76, off State Rte 230, on Harrisburgh IAP. *County:* Dauphin.
MAJOR UNITS: 193rd Special Operations Wing; 193rd Support Group; 193rd Operations Group; 193rd Logistics Group.
Key Contacts
COMMANDER: Col E Thomas Kuhn, 717-948-2201, FAX 717-948-2490, DSN 430-2201, DSN FAX 430-9490, EKuhn@ pamdt.ang.af.mil.
PUBLIC AFFAIRS: Maj Kathleen M B Roth, 717-948-2311, FAX 717-948-2490, DSN 430-9581.
Personnel and Expenditures
ACTIVE DUTY PERSONNEL: 300; 800 reservists
DEPENDENTS: 0
CIVILIAN PERSONNEL: 300
Services *Recreational Facilities:* Fitness center/ Weight room; All ranks club.

New Cumberland

709. Defense Distribution Region East
DDRE
New Cumberland, PA 17070-5001
717-770-7401; FAX 717-770-7180; DSN 977-7401

OFFICER-OF-THE-DAY: 717-770-6270, DSN 977-6270
Profile
BRANCH: Defense Logistics Agency.
SIZE AND LOCATION: 850 acres. Foothills of Cumberland Mountains 5 mi S of Harrisburg, 4 mi from intersection of US-83 and PA Tpke (I-76). *County:* York.
MAJOR UNITS: Defense Distribution Region East (DDRE); Administrative Support Center East (ASCE); Defense Distribution Depot, Susquehanna; Army Logistics Evaluation Agency; Army Security Assistance Command; Army Petroleum Center; Military Entrance Processing Station; 315th Engineer Group; 318th Air Force Recruiting Squadron; Marine Corps Recruiting Station; Army Recruiting Bn; Navy Recruiting.
BASE HISTORY: 1917, built by Corps of Engineers as Marsh Run Storage Depot; later redesignated Army Reserve Depot for storage of Quartermaster, Signal, Ordnance, Medical, Engineer, and Chemical Warfare items. Jan 1948, became separate installation under Quartermaster General. Reorganized several times since. Part of Army Materiel Command (AMC), responsible for insuring weapon, equipment, and logistics readiness of Army. 1991, DDRE established with consolidation of Defense Depot Mechanicsburg and New Cumberland Army Depot. Responsible for receiving, storing, issuing and shipping DOD-owned commodities (medical material, clothing and textiles, subsistence, industrial construction, electronics, general items) to all branches of armed forces, other Federal agencies, and some foreign governments. Installation currently has 4 mil sq ft of covered and 2 mil sq ft of uncovered space. Manages all defense depots E of Mississippi River.
FUTURE CLOSURE/REALIGNMENT: Site of new Defense Distribution Center; transition begun Oct 1997, completion scheduled Oct 1999.
Key Contacts
COMMANDER: Brig Gen Kenneth L Privratsky, USA; DDRE-D, 717-770-7401, DSN 977-7401.
PUBLIC AFFAIRS: Keith G Beebe, DDRE-DB, 717-770-6223, DSN 977-6223.
PROCUREMENT: Pat Ebersole, DDRE-P, 717-770-7186, DSN 977-7186.
TRANSPORTATION: Ron Holland, DDRE-TO, 717-770-4757, DSN 977-4757.
PERSONNEL/COMMUNITY ACTIVITIES: Paul Okum, DDRE-K, 717-770-6112, DSN 977-6112.
Personnel and Expenditures
ACTIVE DUTY PERSONNEL: 19 (plus personnel from other activities)
DEPENDENTS: 340
CIVILIAN PERSONNEL: 3200
MILITARY PAYROLL EXPENDITURE: $121.2 mil (military & civilian)
CONTRACT EXPENDITURE: $32.5 mil
Services
Housing: Family units 143; Unaccompanied enlisted quarters 26; Duplex units 40; Townhouse units 93; Senior NCO units 24; Junior NCO units 93; Detached units 10. *Temporary Housing:* VOQ units 18; Unaccompanied officer/Enlisted quarters 4. *Commissary:* Yes; *Exchange:* Bank; Service station; Credit union; Thrift shop; Class VI; Airline ticket office.

Child Care/Capacities: Day care center capacity 93, infant-5yrs; Latch key program. *Schools:* No on-base schools. *Medical Facilities:* Medical clinic. *Recreational Facilities:* Bowling center; Movie theater; Pool; Gym; Golf course; Tennis courts; Racquetball court; Fitness center/Weight room; Softball field; Auto shop; Craft shop; Fishing/Hunting.

North Versailles

710. Pittsburgh Naval & Marine Corps Reserve Readiness Center
625 E Pittsburgh-McKeesport Blvd
North Versailles, PA 15137-2209
412-673-0816, 672-3472; FAX 412-673-1381
Profile
BRANCH: Naval Reserve; Marine Corps Reserve.
LOCATION: SE of Pittsburgh. *County:* Allegheny.
MAJOR UNITS: REDCOM FOUR Activity; Collecting & Clearing Co D, 4th Medical Bn; Military Police Co B.
Key Contacts
COMMANDER: CDR J Webster II.

Oakdale

711. Charles E Kelly Support Facility
CEKSF Oakdale
Kelly Support Facility
6 Lobaugh St
Oakdale, PA 15071-5000
412-693-1845; FAX 412-693-2631
Profile
BRANCH: Army.
SIZE AND LOCATION: 201 acres. 13 mi W of Pittsburgh; 12 mi from Greater Pittsburgh IAP. *County:* Allegheny.
MAJOR UNITS: 99th Regional Support Command; Training Support Bn, Pittsburgh; Defense Commissary Agency; Army/Air Force Exchange System; FAA, Oakdale; GSA, Fleet Management Center.
BASE HISTORY: 1961, HQ, Army Support Detachment, Oakdale moved from South Park, county park of Allegheny County, PA, to present location; site first occupied by 18th Artillery Group & 662nd Radar Squadron (USAF). 1962, FAA assumed radar mission from USAF. 1974, Army Support Detachment & FAA remaining activities at Oakdale; land released to Dept of Interior for Legacy of Parks program. 1977, FORSCOM implements one-post concept, deactivating HQ, Army Support Detachment; post redesignated as Oakdale Support Element; remaining support activities transferred to existing Directorships, Ft Indiantown Gap, Annville, PA. 1983, Oakdale Support Element became subinstallation of Ft George G Meade, MD. 1987, received current name.
Key Contacts
COMMANDER: Chester E Wolicki, Deputy Garrison Commander, 412-693-1845, FAX 412-693-2631, cwolicki@pulsenet.com.
PUBLIC AFFAIRS: See Commander.

Personnel and Expenditures
ACTIVE DUTY PERSONNEL: 120
CIVILIAN PERSONNEL: 150
Services *Commissary:* Yes; *Exchange:* Retail store; Barber shop; MCSS; Personal items. *Recreational Facilities:* Gym; Fitness center/Weight room; Picnic area; Community club.

Philadelphia

712. 305th Aerial Port Squadron, Detachment 1 (AMC)
AMC
Terminal D, Philadelphia IAP
Philadelphia, PA 19153-3701
215-897-5600; FAX 215-897-5647; DSN
443-5600; DSN FAX 443-5647
Profile
BRANCH: Air Force.
SIZE AND LOCATION: 3 acres. At Philadelphia IAP, in SW Philadelphia, directly off I-95, Located near AMC processing center. *County:* Philadelphia.
MAJOR UNITS: 305th Aerial Port Squadron, Det 1 (AMC).
BASE HISTORY: Provides services required to process, move, and receive DOD air transportation and eligible passengers using DOD owned, controlled, or procured air transportation. Detachment located at commercial airport assigned to APS, which is attached to Air Wing (AW). This detachment reports to 438th APS, McGuire AFB, NJ. Prior to civilian contracting, staffed entirely by Air Force personnel. Services: interline baggage from connecting domestic flights; transportation to & from Bayonne, NJ; USO facilities; VIP passenger facility; contracts with local hotels to provide lodges for distressed passengers; transportation to Ft Dix, McGuire AFB, & Dover AFB.
Key Contacts
COMMANDER: SMSgt Randy J Finney, Det Chief, 215-897-5640, FAX 215-897-5647, DSN 443-5640.
Personnel and Expenditures
ACTIVE DUTY PERSONNEL: 14
DEPENDENTS: 0
CIVILIAN PERSONNEL: 4 DOD, 20 contractor

713. Industrial Analysis Support Office
IASO
200 S 20th St, Bldg 6, 2nd Fl, Pole 34B
Philadelphia, PA 19145
215-737-3397; DSN 444-3397
Internet: http://131.86.27.21/
Profile
BRANCH: Defense Logistics Agency.
SIZE AND LOCATION: Offices only. Follow I-95N to Broad St exit in Philadelphia, left on Shunk St, left on 21st St to DPSC Bldg.
MAJOR UNITS: Space, Missile, Electronics, Computers, & Ammunition Team; Operations Team; Land, Sea, Air, Simulators & Combat Support Operations Team; Information & Management Support Team; Military Operations Team.
BASE HISTORY: 1992, founded to assess & support military major weapons acquisition, logistics, & readiness programs by performing integrated industrial capability analyses.

Key Contacts
COMMANDER: William V Ennis, Director.

714. Philadelphia Coast Guard Marine Safety Office & Group
MSO/GROUP Philadelphia
1 Washington Ave
Philadelphia, PA 19147-4395
215-271-4800; FAX 215-271-4899
E-mail: CGphila1@op.net Internet:http://www.dot.gov/dotinfo/uscg/d5/msophily/philly.htm
OFFICER-OF-THE-DAY: 215-271-4884
Profile
BRANCH: Coast Guard.
SIZE AND LOCATION: 3 acres. At intersection of Washington & Delaware Ave approx 1 mi N of Walt Whitman Bridge; Columbus Blvd/Washington Ave exit off I-95; approx 10 mi from Philadelphia IAP. *County:* Philadelphia.
MAJOR UNITS: Marine Safety Office, Philadelphia; Coast Guard Group, Philadelphia; USCGC *Red Wood*; USCGC *Capstan*; USCGC *Cleat*; Aids to Navigation (ANT) Team, Philadelphia.
BASE HISTORY: June 7, 1988, commissioned with merger of Marine Inspection Office, Philadelphia and Base Gloucester City, NJ. Combined all Coast Guard assets and missions under a single command. Co-located with tenant marine units of Philadelphia Police and Fire Departments. Search and rescue from falls in Trenton, NJ, in N to Ship John Shoal light in S and tributaries of Delaware River.
Key Contacts
COMMANDER: Capt John E Veentjer, 215-271-4803.
PUBLIC AFFAIRS: LTjg Cari M Savarese.
PROCUREMENT: CWO2 Monty Holcombe, 215-271-4810.
Personnel and Expenditures
ACTIVE DUTY PERSONNEL: 130
DEPENDENTS: 0
CIVILIAN PERSONNEL: 2
MILITARY PAYROLL EXPENDITURE: $5 mil
CONTRACT EXPENDITURE: $500,000
Services
Housing: Barracks spaces 10. *Temporary Housing:* Transient quarters 1. *Exchange:* Convenience store. *Child Care/Capacities:* No day care facilities. *Schools:* No on-base schools. *Medical Facilities:* No medical facilities. *Recreational Facilities:* Fitness center/Weight room; Recreational equipment; Movie rentals.

715. Philadelphia Defense Personnel Support Center
DPSC Philadelphia
2800 S 20th Street
Philadelphia, PA 19101-8419
215-737-2411; DSN 444-2411
Internet: http://www.dpsc.dla.mil
Profile
BRANCH: DOD; Defense Logistics Agency.
SIZE AND LOCATION: 86 acres. In S Philadelphia, right off I-76, 3 mi from airport, 6 mi from downtown. *County:* Delaware.
MAJOR UNITS: Defense Personnel Support Center, Philadelphia; Office of Commander Subsistence Field Activities and Director, Subsistence; Directorate of Clothing and Textiles; Defense Contract Management District

Mid-Atlantic; Directorate of Medical Materiel; Directorate of Manufacturing; Office of Telecommunications and Informations Systems.
BASE HISTORY: 1800, began as Philadelphia Arsenal, warehouse for supplies and ammunition. 1941, expansion with new warehouses, today's HQ building, and clothing factory. 1965, Defense Personnel Support Center established when Defense Subsistence Supply of Chicago and Defense Medical Supply of Brooklyn consolidated with Clothing and Textiles Supply Center in Philadelphia. Buys food, clothing, textiles, medicines, and medical equipment for members of Army, Navy, Air Force, Marines, and Coast Guard.
FUTURE CLOSURE/REALIGNMENT: No later than Jul 2, 1999: to be relocated at Aviation Supply Office compound in North Philadelphia; Defense Clothing Factory to be closed and personnel supporting flag mission to be relocated.
VISITOR ATTRACTIONS: Flag room.
Key Contacts
COMMANDER: Brig Gen Hawthorne L Proctor, 215-952-2300, DSN 444-2300.
PUBLIC AFFAIRS: 215-737-2311, DSN 444-2311; Defense Contract Management District, 215-737-5490.
PROCUREMENT: 215-952-2600, DSN 444-2600.
TRANSPORTATION: 215-952-2651, DSN 444-2651.
PERSONNEL/COMMUNITY ACTIVITIES: 215-952-2320, DSN 444-2320.
Personnel and Expenditures
ACTIVE DUTY PERSONNEL: 150
CIVILIAN PERSONNEL: 8000
Services *Temporary Housing:* Apartment units 4. *Exchange:* Barber shop; Food shop. *Base Library:* Yes. *Medical Facilities:* Medical clinic. *Recreational Facilities:* Bowling center; Gym; Recreation center; Racquetball court; Fitness center/Weight room; Auto shop; Officers club.

716. Philadelphia, Naval Inventory Control Point
NAVICP Philadelphia
700 Robbins Ave
Philadelphia, PA 19111-5098
215-697-2000; DSN 442-2000
Internet: http://www.fmso.navy.mil/NAVICP/
Profile
BRANCH: Navy.
SIZE AND LOCATION: 137 acres. NE Philadelphia, 15 mi N of Philadelphia IAP; from I-95N exit at Bridge St, merge into Harbison Ave, left on Levick St, left on Oxford Ave, NAVICP on right; from I-95S, exit at 73 (Cottman Ave), left on US 1S (Roosevelt Blvd), right onto Levick St, left onto Oxford Ave, NAVICP on right. *County:* Philadelphia.
MAJOR UNITS: Naval Inventory Control Point Philadelphia.
Key Contacts
COMMANDER: Sandra Leggieri, Vice Commander, 215-697-2103, DSN 442-2103.
PUBLIC AFFAIRS: Denise Deon, 215-697-5570, DSN 442-5570.
PERSONNEL/COMMUNITY ACTIVITIES: Michael J Abbott, Human Resources Department, 215-697-2633, DSN 442-2633.
Personnel and Expenditures
ACTIVE DUTY PERSONNEL: 150

CIVILIAN PERSONNEL: 6500
Services
Housing: Family units 15 total. *Temporary Housing:* VIP units 1. *Exchange:* Convenience store. *Medical Facilities:* Medical clinic. *Recreational Facilities:* Pool; Gym; Tennis courts; Fitness center/Weight room; Softball field; Football field; Craft shop; Officers club.

717. US Army Corps of Engineers, Philadelphia District

100 Penn Square E
Philadelphia, PA 19107-3390
215-656-6516; FAX 215-656-6820
Internet: http://www.nap.usace.army.mil/
Profile
BRANCH: Army.
LOCATION: *County:* Philadelphia.
MAJOR UNITS: Corps of Engineers, Philadelphia District; Corps of Engineers, Marine Design Center.
BASE HISTORY: 1866, established to manage water resources. District covers 13,000 sq mi Delaware River Basin & Atlantic coasts of NJ (S from Manasquan Inlet) & DE.
Key Contacts
COMMANDER: LTC Robert B Keyser.
PUBLIC AFFAIRS: Richard Chlan, 215-656-6515, CENAP-PA.
Personnel and Expenditures
ACTIVE DUTY PERSONNEL: 570 (military & civilian)
CONTRACT EXPENDITURE: $200 mil (total program)

Pittsburgh

718. US Army Corps of Engineers, Pittsburgh District

CELRP
1000 Liberty Ave, Rm 1817
Pittsburgh, PA 15222-4186
412-395-7500; FAX 412-644-4093; DSN 242-3185
Internet: http://www.lrp.usace.army.mil
Profile
BRANCH: Army.
SIZE AND LOCATION: Offices only. In William S Moorhead Federal Bldg downtown Pittsburgh. *County:* Allegheny.
MAJOR UNITS: Corps of Engineers, Pittsburgh District.
BASE HISTORY: 1868, began service. District's missions are flood control, navigation, water supply, water quality, hydropower, recreation, wildlife management, wetlands regulation & disaster assistance. District encompasses 26,000 sq mi, portions of PA, WV, OH, MD, NY. Known as Headwaters District because it includes upper 127 miles of Ohio River & drainage basins of Allegheny & Monongahela rivers. Performs civil works construction & real estate.
VISITOR ATTRACTIONS: District has 16 reservoirs and 23 locks and dams with camp sites and recreational facilities (hunting, fishing, picnicking, hiking, & boating) open to the public.
Key Contacts
COMMANDER: Col Stephen B Massey, District Engineer, 412-395-7103.

PUBLIC AFFAIRS: Richard V Dowling, 412-395-7501, rdowling@smtp.lrp.usace.army.mil.
PROCUREMENT: George Reule, 412-395-7474.
TRANSPORTATION: Jim Edinger, Operations & Readiness Division, 412-395-7140.
PERSONNEL/COMMUNITY ACTIVITIES: Lisa A Eberly, Human Resources, 412-395-7482.
Personnel and Expenditures
ACTIVE DUTY PERSONNEL: 2
DEPENDENTS: 0
CIVILIAN PERSONNEL: 900
Services *Child Care/Capacities:* Day care center In Federal Bldg.

Reading

719. Reading Naval & Marine Corps Reserve Center

NMCRC Reading
615 Kenhorst Blvd
Reading, PA 19611-1717
215-378-5175, 378-0164
E-mail: reading@cnsrf.navy.mil
Profile
BRANCH: Naval Reserve; Marine Corps Reserve.
SIZE AND LOCATION: 7 acres. In Reading. *County:* Berks.
MAJOR UNITS: REDCOM FOUR Activity; Navy Recruiting; Battery I, 3rd BN, 14th Marine Regiment; plus 11 drilling reserve units.
Key Contacts
COMMANDER: LCDR Dale E Drake.
Personnel and Expenditures
ACTIVE DUTY PERSONNEL: 160 USNR; 125 Marine Forces Reserve
Services *Base Library:* Yes. *Recreational Facilities:* Gym; Fitness center/Weight room.

Scranton

720. Scranton Army Ammunition Plant

SAAP
156 Cedar Ave
Scranton, PA 18505-1138
717-342-7801; DSN 247-1350
Profile
BRANCH: Army.
SIZE AND LOCATION: 15.3 acres. Downtown Scranton, PA. From airport, I-81 N to Exit 53 (Central Scranton Expy), 1st exit onto Cedar Ave; right at stop sign, Scranton AAP on left. *County:* Lacawana.
BASE HISTORY: 1951, established; converted 50-year-old, privately owned, railroad maintenance facility to production plant for metal parts used in large caliber artillery projectiles. 1953, began manufacturing projectiles pursuant to GOCO agreement between Army and US Hoffman Machinery Co. 1962, contract awarded to current operator, Chamberlain Manufacturing Co.
Personnel and Expenditures
ACTIVE DUTY PERSONNEL: 0
CIVILIAN PERSONNEL: 9 DOD; 257 contractors

Services *Medical Facilities:* Industrial medical clinic with nurse on duty.

Tobyhanna

721. Tobyhanna Army Depot

TYAD
11 Hap Arnold Blvd
Tobyhanna, PA 18466-5076
717-895-7308; FAX 717-895-7868; DSN 795-7308; DSN FAX 795-7868
Internet: http://www.tobyhanna.army.mil
OFFICER-OF-THE-DAY: 717-895-7550, 717-895-7550, DSN 795-7550, DSN FAX 795-7556
Profile
BRANCH: Army.
SIZE AND LOCATION: 1293 acres. Heart of Pocono Mountains, NE PA, Exit 7 off I-380 approx 20 mi SE of Scranton, PA; Scranton/Wilkes-Barre Airport approx 30 mi. *County:* Monroe.
MAJOR UNITS: Army District Test, Management, and Diagnostic Equipment Support Center; Army Materiel Command Packaging Storage and Containerization Center; Defense Distribution Depot, Tobyhanna; Joint Visual Information Activity; Medical Maintenance Operations Division-Pennsylvania; Defense Reutilization and Marketing Office; Army Health Clinic; Defense Commissary Agency; Post Exchange; US Army Corps of Engineers, Baltimore District-Northeast Resident Office; Carlisle Barracks Veterinary Service; High Tech Regional Training Center; Monroe County Memorial, Army Reserve Center.
BASE HISTORY: 1913, Reservation used as Army and NG artillery training site; known as Camp Summerall, Camp Tobyhanna, and Tobyhanna Artillery Target Range. WWI, used as ambulance and tank training center. 1919-32, reverted to field artillery training site. Late 1930s, served as Civilian Conservation Corps processing center. 1938-41, West Point cadets trained at site. WWII, anti-aircraft training site, storage depot for Normandy invasion gliders, POW camp for German prisoners, and hospital built. Post WWII, turned over to state for conservation and recreation. Proposed site for United Nations HQ. 1953, Corps of Engineers opened Signal Corps Depot. 1962, renamed Tobyhanna Army Depot. 1990, provided extensive support to Operation Desert Shield/Storm. Today, largest full-service communications and electronics maintenance facility in DOD.
VISITOR ATTRACTIONS: Various military equipment displays; Tours available by appointment.
Key Contacts
COMMANDER: Col Robert A Benson, ATTN: SDSTO-C, 717-895-7201, 717-895-6061, DSN 795-7201, SIOTY-C@Tobyhanna-emhl.army.mil.
PUBLIC AFFAIRS: Kevin M Toolan, ATTN: SDSTO-UA, 717-895-6552, FAX 717-895-7868, DSN 795-6552, ktoolan@Tobyhanna.emh3.army.mil.
PROCUREMENT: Thomas A Garubba, ATTN: SDSTO-K, 717-895-7232, FAX 895-6794, DSN 795-7232, DSN FAX 795-6794, tgarubba@Tobyhanna-emh3.army.mil.

TRANSPORTATION: Dennis Barnum, ATTN: DDDT-P, 717-895-7270, FAX 717-895-6151, DSN 795-7270, DSN FAX 795-6151, dbarnum@Tobyhanna-emh3.army.mil.
PERSONNEL/COMMUNITY ACTIVITIES: Walter Dorosky, ATTN: SDSTO-Z, 717-895-8150, DSN 795-8150, DSN FAX 795-7419, wdorosky@Tobyhanna-emh3. army.mil.

Personnel and Expenditures
ACTIVE DUTY PERSONNEL: 102
DEPENDENTS: 78
CIVILIAN PERSONNEL: 3150
MILITARY PAYROLL EXPENDITURE: $2.7 mil
CONTRACT EXPENDITURE: $16 mil

Services
Housing: Family units 42; Unaccompanied enlisted quarters 9; Duplex units 2; Barracks spaces 20; *Temporary Housing:* Guest cottages 4; *Commissary:* Yes; *Exchange:* Retail store; Barber shop; Food shop; Service station; Credit union; ATM; Travel agency; Class VI; Cafeteria. *Child Care/Capacities:* Home day care program; Latch key program; Summer day camp; Before & after school programs; Supplemental care & services. *Schools:* No on-base schools. *Base Library:* Yes. *Medical Facilities:* Medical clinic; Pharmacy; Veterinary services. *Recreational Facilities:* Pool; Gym; Tennis courts; Racquetball court; Fitness center/Weight room; Softball field; Auto shop; Craft shop; Fishing/Hunting; Youth center; Picnic area; Playground; Community club; Snow sports; Barney's Lake; Equipment rental; Basketball; Volleyball; Car wash.

Williamsport

722. Williamsport Naval & Marine Corps Reserve Center
NAVRESCEN Williamsport PA
1307 Grove St
Williamsport, PA 17701-2423
717-323-7991; FAX 717-323-4312
Profile
BRANCH: Naval Reserve; Marine Corps Reserve.

SIZE AND LOCATION: 2-3 acres. In Williamsport about 2 mi from I-80, 6 mi from Lycoming County IAP. *County:* Lycoming.
MAJOR UNITS: REDCOM FOUR Activity; NH Bethesda 1306 (NR); NMCB 21 Det 0921; VTU 0416G.
Key Contacts
COMMANDER: LCDR John A Kauderman.
Personnel and Expenditures
ACTIVE DUTY PERSONNEL: 5; 95 reservists
Services *Recreational Facilities:* Fitness center/Weight room.

Willow Grove

723. Willow Grove Naval Air Station (JRB)
NAS Willow Grove
Box 21
Willow Grove, PA 19090-5021
215-443-1776; 215-443-6017; DSN 991-1776
OFFICER-OF-THE-DAY: 215-443-6054, 443-6000, DSN 991-6404
Profile
BRANCH: Naval Reserve; Joint Reserve Base.
SIZE AND LOCATION: 1100 acres. In town of Hatboro, 3 mi N of PA Tpke Exit 27, Rte 611; 25 mi N of Philadelphia at Horsham off I-276. *County:* Montgomery; Bucks.
MAJOR UNITS: Naval Air Station, Willow Grove; Fleet Logistics Support Squadron 52 (VR-52); Helicopter Antisubmarine Squadron Light 94 (HSL-94); Patrol Squadron 64 (VP-64); Patrol Squadron 66 (VP-66); Marine Aircraft Group-49 (MAG-49); 79th Army Reserve Command; 97th Army Reserve Command; Reserve Antisubmarine Warfare Training Center (RESASWTRACEN); 913th Tactical Airlift Group; 111th Pennsylvania Air National Guard.
VISITOR ATTRACTIONS: Antique aircraft display; Tours (Thurs/Fri, 10am by appointment).
Key Contacts
COMMANDER: 215-443-6051, DSN 991-6051.
PUBLIC AFFAIRS: 215-443-1776, DSN 991-1776.

Personnel and Expenditures
ACTIVE DUTY PERSONNEL: 1700
CIVILIAN PERSONNEL: 1000
Services
Housing: Family units 6; Unaccompanied enlisted quarters; Base housing 8 mi from base at Naval Air Development Center, Warminister, PA. *Temporary Housing:* Unaccompanied officer/Enlisted quarters; BEQ. *Exchange:* Barber shop; Dry cleaners; Military clothing store; Convenience store; Credit union. *Child Care/Capacities:* Day care center capacity 45-50, 6wks-6yrs. *Base Library:* Yes. *Medical Facilities:* Medical clinic; Dental clinic; Pharmacy. *Recreational Facilities:* Bowling center; Movie theater; Pool; Gym; Racquetball court; Fitness center/Weight room; Softball field; Football field; Auto shop; Officers club; Enlisted club; Picnic area; Playground.

Wyoming

724. Wyoming Aerial Port (AFRES)
92 APS
1160 Wyoming Ave
Wyoming, PA 18644-1348
717-288-5427; DSN 991-1290
Profile
BRANCH: Air Force Reserve.
SIZE AND LOCATION: 2 acres. In town of Wyoming, on US-11; 10 mi from I-81 and 10 mi from PA Tpke. *County:* Luzerne.
MAJOR UNITS: 92nd Aerial Port Squadron (AFRES).
BASE HISTORY: 1960, Air Force Reserve Center constructed with 2 buildings & C-130A fuselage training aid; part of 512th AW, Dover AFB, DE.
Key Contacts
COMMANDER: LTC Kenneth P Johnson, USAFR.
PUBLIC AFFAIRS: TSgt Peter Shuleski.
PROCUREMENT: MSgt David Hodges.
Personnel and Expenditures
ACTIVE DUTY PERSONNEL: 2
CIVILIAN PERSONNEL: 2

Rhode Island

Cranston

725. Adjutant General of Rhode Island
645 New London Ave
Cranston, RI 02920-3097
401-457-4102; FAX 401-457-4338
Profile
BRANCH: Army National Guard.
MAJOR UNITS: Rhode Island National Guard.
Key Contacts
COMMANDER: Maj Gen Reginald
Centracchio.

Newport

726. Naval Education and Training Center, Newport
NETC Newport
61 Capodanno Dr
Newport, RI 02841-1513
401-841-3538; FAX 401-841-2265; DSN
948-3538; DSN AFX 948-2265
E-mail: NETC-NEP.011@smtp.cnet.navy.mil
Internet:http://www.cnet.navy.mil/newport/
netc.htm
OFFICER-OF-THE-DAY: 401-841-3456, DSN
948-3456
Profile
BRANCH: Navy.
SIZE AND LOCATION: 1200 acres. Off Rte
138 off-ramp from Newport Bridge; approx
30 mi from Providence Airport. *County:* Newport.
MAJOR UNITS: Defense Automated Printing
Service; Defense Fuel Support Point,
Melville, Allied Management; Defense Investigative Service, Investigative RA (D11NP);
Explosive Ordnance Disposal Mobile Unit 2
Det Newport; Fleet Industrial Supply Center
Norfolk, Newport Det; General Support-Motor Transport Co, 6 Motor Transport Bn; Marine Corps Det, Newport; Naval Academy
Preparatory School; Naval & Marine Corps
Reserve Readiness Center; Naval Audit Site;
Naval Computer and Telecommunications
Area Master Station, Atlantic Det; Naval
Command, Control, and Ocean Surveillance
Center, In-Service Engineering; Naval Criminal Investigative Service; Naval Dental Center, Newport; Naval Branch Dental Clinic,
Newport; Naval Education and Training Center; Naval Hospital Newport; Naval Justice
School; Naval Legal Service Office Det; Naval Reserve Readiness Command, Region
One; Naval Training Meteorology & Oceanography Det, Newport; Naval Undersea Warfare Center HQ; Naval Undersea Warfare
Center Division; Naval War College; Naval
Band, Newport; Navy Exchange Newport;
Newport Defense Commissary Agency,
Northeast Region; Office of Naval Intelligence Det; Patent Counsel, Naval Undersea
Warfare Center; Personnel Support Activity
Det, Newport; Personnel Support Det Newport; Surface Warfare Officers School Command; USCGC *Lewis* (WLM-551); USCGC
Juniper (WLB-201); USCGC *Willow* (WLB-
202).
BASE HISTORY: During Civil War, Naval
Academy moved to Newport. 1869-1951 experimental torpedo station established at Goat
Island, replaced by Naval Underwater Ordnance Station. 1883, 1st recruit training station established at Coasters Harbor Island.
1884, Naval War College established. 1913,
Navy acquired Government Landing in downtown Newport. 1940, Coddington Cove established as Supply Station, & Melville as PT-
Boat Training Center & Net Depot. 1941, Air
Station became operational & Advanced Base
Depot formed at Davisville (later Construction Battalion Center). 1946, Naval complex
in Bay area consolidated as US Naval Base.
1952, Naval Training Station, Newport transferred to Bainbridge, MD. 1973, Quonset
Point Naval Air Station closed; drawdown of
facilities at Davisville; active fleet moved
from Newport.
VISITOR ATTRACTIONS: Naval War College Museum.
Key Contacts
COMMANDER: Capt Ronald C Bogle.
PUBLIC AFFAIRS: David Sanders.
PROCUREMENT: CDR Aubrey Lane, SC,
USN, 401-841-3037, FAX 401-841-7144,
DSN 948-3037.
TRANSPORTATION: Norman Agostinho,
401-841-3670, DSN 948-3670.
Personnel and Expenditures
ACTIVE DUTY PERSONNEL: 3500
CIVILIAN PERSONNEL: 4200
MILITARY PAYROLL EXPENDITURE: $184 mil
CONTRACT EXPENDITURE: $475 mil
Services
Housing: Family units 1300; Mobile home units
52. *Temporary Housing:* VIP units 2; Lodge
units 60.

Commissary: Yes; *Exchange:* Retail store; Barber shop; Dry cleaners; Food shop; Florist;
Bank; Service station; Convenience store;
Beauty shop; Credit union; ATM; Optical store;
Post office; Fast food; Thrift shop; Tailor/Alterations; Personalized services; Watch repair; TV
rentals; Wine & spirits shop. *Child Care/Capacities:* Home day care program; Summer day
camp. *Schools:* College courses. *Base Library:*
Yes. *Medical Facilities:* Hospital; Medical
clinic; Dental clinic; Pharmacy; *Recreational Facilities:* Bowling center; Pool (indoor); Gym;
Recreation center; Tennis courts; Racquetball
court; Fitness center/Weight room; Softball
field; Football field; Auto shop; Officers club;
Camping; Enlisted club; Picnic area; Playground; CPO lounge; Gear rental; Storage lot;
Soccer field; Marina; Ticket connection.

727. Region One, Naval Reserve Readiness Command
REDCOM 1
344 Easton St
Newport, RI 02841-1515
401-841-3981; DSN 948-3981
Internet: http://redcom1.cnrf.nola.navy.mil/
Profile
BRANCH: Naval Reserve.
MAJOR UNITS: Naval Reserve Readiness Command, Region 1.
BASE HISTORY: Administers 19 Naval & Marine Corps Reserve Centers with 6,000 Reservists.
Key Contacts
COMMANDER: Capt James J Quinn,
401-841-4460, DSN 948-4460.

North Kingstown

728. Quonset State Airport, Air National Guard Base
1 Belver Ave
North Kingstown, RI 02852-7507
401-886-1200; DSN 476-3210
Profile
BRANCH: Air National Guard.
SIZE AND LOCATION: 79 acres. In town of
North Kingstown at Quonset State Airport; 25
mi S of Providence; take I-95 to Rte 4, North
Kingstown Exit to Develsfoot Rd, access road
to Belver Rd, base on left. *County:* Washington.
MAJOR UNITS: 143rd Airlift Wing (ANG).

BASE HISTORY: 1948, RI ANG organized as 152nd Fighter Squadron. 1948-55, variously designated as Fighter, Fighter Interceptor, Fighter Bomber, & Interceptor Squadron. 1955, expanded to Group as 143rd Air Resupply Group; later 143rd Troop Carrier Group. 1975, redesignated 143rd Tactical Airlift Group. 1980, moved from T F Green Airport, Warwick, to current location.
VISITOR ATTRACTIONS: Quonset Air Museum.

Key Contacts
COMMANDER: Brig Gen Joseph N Waller.

Personnel and Expenditures
ACTIVE DUTY PERSONNEL: 1362 Guard

CIVILIAN PERSONNEL: 339
MILITARY PAYROLL EXPENDITURE: $21.4 mil

Providence

729. Providence Naval & Marine Corps Reserve Center
AFRC
1 Narragansett St
Providence, RI 02905-4233
401-941-9262, 941-1540; FAX 401-941-3561

Profile
BRANCH: Naval Reserve; Marine Corps Reserve.
LOCATION: *County:* Providence.
MAJOR UNITS: REDCOM ONE Activity; General Support Motor Transport Co, 6th Motor Transport Bn.

Key Contacts
COMMANDER: CDR J E Pereira.

South Carolina

Beaufort

730. Beaufort Marine Corps Air Station
MCAS Beaufort
PO Box 55001
Beaufort, SC 29904-5001
803-522-7100; DSN 832-7100
Internet: http://204.223.60.4/welcome.htm
OFFICER-OF-THE-DAY: 803-522-7121, DSN 832-7121

Profile
BRANCH: Marine Corps.
SIZE AND LOCATION: 6900 acres (incl Laurel Bay family housing area 1100 acres); Townsend Bombing Range, McIntosh County, GA 5200 acres. Approx 4 mi N of Beaufort, SC, on Hwy 21; 8 mi from Marine Corps Recruit Depot Parris Island; 70 mi SW of Charleston, SC. *County:* Beaufort.
MAJOR UNITS: Marine Corps Air Station, Beaufort; Marine Aircraft Group 31; Marine Wing Support Group 273; Marine Air Control Squadron 2; Combat Service Support Det 23; Marine Fighter Attack Squadron 115; Marine Fighter Attack Squadron 122; Marine Fighter Attack Squadron 224; Marine Fighter Attack Squadron 251; Marine Fighter Attack Squadron 312; Marine Fighter Attack Squadron 332; Marine Fighter Attack Squadron 451; Marine Fighter Attack Squadron 533.
BASE HISTORY: Location of Tidewater Hospital, Scott Crop Dusting Service, Busbee Pike Flying Service, Blue Channel Freezer Plant & several plantations, before becoming airfield. 1943, Naval Auxiliary Air Station commissioned. During WWII, operated antisubmarine patrols. 1946, deactivated. 1956, reactivated as Marine Corps Auxiliary Airfield. 1960, redesignated MCAS, named Merritt Field for Maj Gen Lewie Merritt, SC native. MCAS base of operations for seven aircraft squadrons which deploy to the Far East on aircraft carriers; also operates family housing area 4 mi W of base, Laurel Bay.

Key Contacts
COMMANDER: Col Larry D Staak, 803-522-7158, DSN 832-7158.
PUBLIC AFFAIRS: CWO4 TR Bennett, 803-522-7201, DSN 832-7201.
PROCUREMENT: Debbie Foss, 803-522-7845, DSN 832-7845.
TRANSPORTATION: 803-522-7507, DSN 832-7507.

Personnel and Expenditures
ACTIVE DUTY PERSONNEL: 3800
DEPENDENTS: 5456
CIVILIAN PERSONNEL: 700
MILITARY PAYROLL EXPENDITURE: $117 mil

Services
Housing: Family units 1100; Senior NCO units 1643; Barracks spaces 238 rooms, newly constructed; RV/Camper sites 157 spaces. *Temporary Housing:* Unaccompanied officer/Enlisted quarters 119; Transient quarters 156. *Exchange:* Retail store; Barber shop; Dry cleaners; Food shop; Bank; Service station. *Child Care/Capacities:* Day care center capacity 230. *Schools:* Preschool/Kindergarten; Elementary; High school. *Base Library:* Yes. *Medical Facilities:* Medical clinic; Dental clinic. *Recreational Facilities:* Bowling center; Movie theater; Pool; Gym; Recreation center; Tennis courts; Racquetball court; Fitness center/Weight room; Softball field; Football field; Auto shop; Officers club; NCO club; Fishing/Hunting; Youth center; Hobby shop; Recreational issue facility; Jogging trail.

731. Beaufort Naval Hospital
Jean Ribaut Rd
Beaufort, SC 29902-6148
803-525-5600; DSN 832-5600
OFFICER-OF-THE-DAY: 803-525-5400, 525-5401, emergency room

Profile
BRANCH: Navy.
SIZE AND LOCATION: 24 acres. On Beaufort River approx halfway between MCAS Beaufort & USMC Recruit Depot, Parris Island. *County:* Beaufort.
MAJOR UNITS: Naval Hospital Beaufort.
BASE HISTORY: Modern, small- to medium-sized Navy hospitals; provides medical care for all active duty, retired military personnel & dependents in SE SC & NE GA; serves as Medical Command for MCAS Beaufort & Parris Island MC Recruit Depot.

Personnel and Expenditures
ACTIVE DUTY PERSONNEL: 420
CIVILIAN PERSONNEL: 186

Services
Housing: Family units 53 (11 at Laurel Bay); BAQ units 3. *Exchange:* Retail store; Barber shop; Service station; Convenience store; Optical store; Snacks. *Child Care/Capacities:* No day care facilities. *Schools:* No on-base schools. *Base Library:* Yes. *Medical Facilities:* Hospital 207 beds; Dental clinic. *Recreational Facilities:* Pool; Recreation center; Tennis courts; Softball field; Auto shop; Picnic area; Playground; Recreational services; Volleyball; Equipment rental.

Charleston

732. Charleston Coast Guard Group
GRU Chasn
Base Charleston
196 Tradd St
Charleston, SC 29401-1899
803-724-7600
Internet: http://www.awod.com/gallery/uscg

Profile
BRANCH: Coast Guard.
SIZE AND LOCATION: 8.5 acres. In southernmost part of city of Charleston. *County:* Charleston.
MAJOR UNITS: Coast Guard Group, Charleston; Coast Guard Base, Charleston; Coast Guard Station, Charleston; USCGC *Madrona*; USCGC *Metompkin*; USCGC *Rambler*; US Coast Guard Marine Safety Office; Coast Guard Reserve Group, Charleston; Coast Guard Auxiliary Flotilla 12-8; Electronic Support Det, Charleston; Marine Safety Office, Charleston; Coast Guard Reserve Group; Coast Guard Forces, Charleston.
BASE HISTORY: 1914, US Lighthouse Service purchased "Dunkins Sawmill" for buoy depot. 1915, Navy established remote, wireless unit here and US Weather Service contracted to use radio tower for storm warning signals. 1930, Lighthouse Service merged with and became part of Coast Guard. WWII, base under operational control of Sixth Naval District. Mission: buoy repair and logistical supply for visiting and assigned vessels. WWII to today, industrial buoy depot and host to various vessels. 1974, added search and rescue responsibilities and general law enforcement duties to existing functions.
VISITOR ATTRACTIONS: Located in historic Charleston.

Key Contacts
COMMANDER: CDR Mason K Brown, 803-724-7612; FAX 803-724-7652.
PUBLIC AFFAIRS: LTjg Mike DaPonte, 803-724-7621, FAX 803-720-7741, M. Daponte/Gruchasn@internet.uscg.mil.
PROCUREMENT: 803-724-7604.
TRANSPORTATION: Charles Bennet, 803-724-7605.

PERSONNEL/COMMUNITY ACTIVITIES:
See Public Affairs Officer.
Personnel and Expenditures
ACTIVE DUTY PERSONNEL: 200+
CIVILIAN PERSONNEL: 20+
Services
Housing: Barracks spaces. *Temporary Housing:*
BAQ units 4. *Exchange:* Retail store; Barber
shop; Dry cleaners; Military clothing store; Convenience store. *Medical Facilities:* Medical
clinic. *Recreational Facilities:* NCO club; Boating.

733. Charleston, Naval & Marine Corps Reserve Readiness Center

4500 Leeds Ave, Ste 401
Charleston, SC 29405-8521
803-743-8620, 743-8635; FAX 803-743-8632;
DSN 563-8625
Profile
BRANCH: Naval Reserve; Marine Corps Reserve.
LOCATION: *County:* Charleston.
MAJOR UNITS: Naval Reserve Readiness Center, Charleston; Marine Corps Reserve Readiness Center, Charleston.
Key Contacts
COMMANDER: CDR D L Brown.

734. Charleston, Naval Weapons Station

Charleston, SC 29408
803-743-4111; DSN 563-4111
Internet: http://www.noclant.navy.mil/charles/
index.html
Profile
BRANCH: Navy.
SIZE AND LOCATION: 17,221 acres. Along
Cooper River, 6 mi N of Charleston off I-26.
County: Charleston; Berkeley.
MAJOR UNITS: Naval Weapons Station, Charleston; NISE East Calibration Laboratory;
Strategic Maintenance Complex; Maritime
Prepositioning Force Program; Naval Reserve, Charleston; Strategic Mobility Logistics Base (ARMY SMLB); Nuclear Power
Training Unit; Propulsion Training Facility;
Naval Consolidated Brig; 1304th Military
Traffic Management Command; Major Port
Command.
BASE HISTORY: 1941, established. 1967, chartered as Navy Industrial Funded Activity.
1991, transitioned to Defense Business Operating Funded Activity.
VISITOR ATTRACTIONS: NISE East Laboratory tours (contact Bradley Woode, 803-764-7854, woodeb@niseeast.nosc.mil).
Key Contacts
COMMANDER: Capt T B Stark.
PUBLIC AFFAIRS: Glenn Cox, 803-764-7601,
DSN 794-7601.
Personnel and Expenditures
ACTIVE DUTY PERSONNEL: 187; Tenants
5147 (military & civilian)
DEPENDENTS: 9573
CIVILIAN PERSONNEL: 1217
MILITARY PAYROLL EXPENDITURE: $94 mil
Services
Housing: Family units 2765; Dormitory spaces;
RV/Camper sites 6. *Temporary Housing:* Unaccompanied officer/Enlisted quarters 227; Lodge
units 45; Mobile home units 60. *Commissary:*
Yes; *Exchange:* Retail store; Barber shop; Convenience store; Garden center.

Child Care/Capacities: Day care center capacity
282; Home day care program. *Schools:* No on-base schools. *Medical Facilities:* Hospital See
Charleston Naval Hospital. *Recreational Facilities:* Bowling center; Movie theater; Pool; Gym;
Golf course; Tennis courts; Racquetball court;
Fitness center/Weight room; Auto shop; Craft
shop; Camping; Youth center; Picnic area; Boating; Lake Moultrie recreation area, 40 mi N.

735. Naval Facilities Engineering Command, Southern Division

2155 Eagle Dr
Charleston, SC 29406-4804
Mailing Address
PO Box 190010
North Charleston, SC 29419-9010
Internet: http://web.infoave.net/~southdiv/
Profile
BRANCH: Navy.
LOCATION: Exit 211B from I-26E, to East
Aviation Ave, left at light on Rivers Ave
(west), 1 mi past Post Office, take left after
light onto Eagle Drive, parking lot on first
left. *County:* Charleston.
MAJOR UNITS: Naval Facilities Engineering
Command, Southern Division.
Key Contacts
COMMANDER: Capt Leonard P Scullion.
PUBLIC AFFAIRS: 803-820-5771, DSN
583-5771.

736. US Army Corps of Engineers, Charleston District

CESAC
334 Meeting St
Charleston, SC 29403-6479
Mailing Address
PO Box 919
Charleston, SC 29402-0919
803-727-4229; FAX 803-727-4356
Internet: http://www.sac.usace.army.mil/
Profile
BRANCH: Army.
SIZE AND LOCATION: Offices only. In city of
Charleston. *County:* Charleston.
MAJOR UNITS: Corps of Engineers, Charleston District.
BASE HISTORY: 1895, District's first project
(stabilize erosion around Charleston) finished.
Today, responsible for maintaining 210 mi of
Atlantic Intracoastal Waterway, 7 small harbors, & ports of Charleston, Georgetown, Port
Royal. Performs civil works construction.
Key Contacts
COMMANDER: LTC Thomas F Julich, District
Engineer, 803-727-4344.
PUBLIC AFFAIRS: David A Rich,
803-727-4201.
PROCUREMENT: Christy Watts,
803-727-4204.
Personnel and Expenditures
ACTIVE DUTY PERSONNEL: 3
CIVILIAN PERSONNEL: 190

Charleston AFB

737. Charleston Air Force Base

437th Airlift Wing, 102 E Hill Blvd, Bldg 1600
Charleston AFB, SC 29404-5154
803-566-6000; DSN 673-2100

Profile
BRANCH: Air Force.
SIZE AND LOCATION: 6200 acres. 10 mi NW
of Charleston, SC in city of North Charleston;
shares runway with Charleston IAP; terminal
on opposite side of runway. *County:* Charleston.
MAJOR UNITS: 437th Airlift Wing (AMC);
315th Airlift Wing (Associate) (AFRES);
437th Support Group; 437th Medical Squadron; 437th Operations Group; 437th Logistics
Group; Aerial Port Squadron; 437th Civil Engineering Squadron; 1361st Audiovisual
Squadron, Det 7; Office of Special Investigations, Det 310; Area Defense Counsel; Air
Force Audit Agency Area Audit Office; Defense Courier Service; Military Air Traffic
Coordination Unit; Army Assistance Office;
Defense Commissary Agency; 107th Fighter
Interceptor Group, Det 1; 1st Combat Camera
Squadron; Field Training Det 317; Office of
Special Investigations, Det 719; Site Activation Task Force, Det 17.
BASE HISTORY: 1919, airfield established.
1942, Army Air Corps took control of field,
but civilian use of runways still allowed; base
used as training site for combat and ground
crews for B-17 Flying Fortress and B-24 Liberator aircraft, under First Air Force. 1943, reassigned to Air Transport Command and
trained transport crews. After WWII, closed
and returned to city. 1952, Charleston and Air
Force agreed to establish troop carrier base
and joint use of runways. 1985, new civilian
terminal completed. 1993, first wing to receive C-17 Globemaster III aircraft. One of 3
AMC aerial ports on Atlantic coast.
VISITOR ATTRACTIONS: Fort Sumter.
Key Contacts
COMMANDER: Brig Gen Thomas R
Mikolajcik; Wing Commander, Bldg
1600SE, 437 AW/CC, 803-566-3201, DSN
673-3201.
PUBLIC AFFAIRS: Capt Rick Sanford; Rm
223, 803-566-5608, DSN 673-5608.
PROCUREMENT: Maj Brice C Moore; Chief
of Supply, 101 W Stewart St, 803-566-4902,
DSN 673-4902.
TRANSPORTATION: LTC Charles D Jolly;
201 N Graves Ave.
Personnel and Expenditures
ACTIVE DUTY PERSONNEL: 4200 (plus
2800 reservists)
CIVILIAN PERSONNEL: 1500
Services
Housing: Family units 977; 75-unit trailer park.
Temporary Housing: The Charleston House,
416 spaces. *Commissary:* Yes; *Exchange:* Retail
store; Barber shop; Dry cleaners; Food shop; Florist; Bank; Service station; Military clothing
store; Convenience store; Beauty shop. *Child
Care/Capacities:* Day care center capacity 125,
6mo-5yrs; Home day care program; Summer
day camp. *Schools:* College courses. *Base Library:* Yes. *Medical Facilities:* Medical clinic;
Dental clinic; Pharmacy; Veterinary services;
Naval Regional Medical Center, 10 mi away.
Recreational Facilities: Bowling center; Movie
theater; Pool; Gym; Recreation center; Golf
course; Tennis courts; Racquetball court; Fitness
center/Weight room; Softball field; Football
field; Auto shop; Craft shop; Officers club; NCO
club; Camping; Enlisted club; Youth center; Picnic area; Skeet range; Playground; Rod & gun
club; Aero club.

Columbia

738. Adjutant General of South Carolina

#1 National Guard Rd
Columbia, SC 29201-4766
803-806-4217; FAX 803-806-4499
Profile
BRANCH: Army National Guard.
MAJOR UNITS: South Carolina National Guard.
Key Contacts
COMMANDER: Maj Gen Stanhope S Spears.

739. Columbia Naval & Marine Corps Reserve Center

NRC Columbia
513 Pickens St
Columbia, SC 29201-4198
803-799-3412; FAX 803-765-1412
E-mail: nrjhl@navtap.navy.mil
Profile
BRANCH: Naval Reserve; Marine Corps Reserve.
SIZE AND LOCATION: 2.11 acres. In the Univ of SC campus area in downtown Columbia corner of Pickens & Blossom Sts. *County:* Richland.
MAJOR UNITS: REDCOM EIGHT Activity.
BASE HISTORY: 1946, activated as Naval Reserve Training Center Columbia. 1953, 89th Special Infantry Co (USMC) activated and added to center. 1991, independent Marine Corps facility constructed near Ft Jackson and center returned to Naval only facility. Presently home of 10 Naval Reserve units.
Key Contacts
COMMANDER: LCDR Hudspeth.
PUBLIC AFFAIRS: PN2 Jeff Louden.
Personnel and Expenditures
ACTIVE DUTY PERSONNEL: 330 reservists
Services *Base Library:* Yes. *Recreational Facilities:* Fitness center/Weight room; Basketball court.

740. Fort Jackson

USATC-FJ; Ft Jackson
US Army Training Center
HQ US Army Training Center
Columbia, SC 29207-5060
803-751-7611, 7612; FAX 803-751-2722; DSN 734-7611; DSN FAX 734-7414
OFFICER-OF-THE-DAY: 803-751-7611, DSN 734-7611, DSN FAX 734-7414
Profile
BRANCH: Army.
SIZE AND LOCATION: 52,301 acres. In central SC, adj to city of Columbia on E. From Atlanta, I-20 through Augusta to Columbia; from Knoxville, Hwy 25 to I-40, then Hwy 26 to Columbia; from Fayetteville, NC, I-95 until it joins I-20 to Columbia. *County:* Richland.
MAJOR UNITS: Army Training Center Command; 1st Basic Training Brigade; 4th Training Brigade; 120th Adjutant General BN (Reception); Drill Sergeant School; 282nd Army Band; Army Criminal Investigation Division; 902nd Military Intelligence Group; 48th Explosive Ordnance Disposal Unit; 12th Judge Advocate General Det; Moncrief Army Community Hospital.

BASE HISTORY: 1917, Sixth National Cantonment, Company E, 1st Regiment, SC Infantry first unit at Camp Jackson, named for Maj Gen Andrew Jackson, native of SC and president of US. Troops trained here were part of American Expeditionary Forces in WWI. 1917, first all-black regiment of WWI, 1st Provisional Infantry Regiment (Colored), organized. Birthplace of Army unit patch, beginning with 81st "Wildcat" Division. 1925-39, reverted to Cantonment Lands Commission and used by SC NG for training exercises. 1940, 8th Division reactivated at Camp Jackson, designated Ft Jackson, and organized under federal control as Infantry Training Center. WWII, "Old Hickory" Division trained. 1973, first all-female brigade, 5th Basic Training Brigade, established (deactivated 1977 with total integration of forces) & Fort Jackson designated US Army Training Center. 1988, initial entry training implemented with hands-on skill development.
FUTURE CLOSURE/REALIGNMENT: 1998, Single Soldiers Housing Complex Polygraph Institute to close.
VISITOR ATTRACTIONS: Ft Jackson Museum; Finance Corps Museum; Adjutant General Museum; Andrew Jackson statue sculptured by Felix De Welder; Independence Day Torchlight Tattoo.
Key Contacts
COMMANDER: Maj Gen John Allen Van Alstyne, 803-751-7611, DSN FAX 734-7414.
PUBLIC AFFAIRS: ATTN: ATZJ-PAO, 803-751-7650, DSN 734-6719; FAX 734-2722.
PROCUREMENT: Director of Contracting, ATTN: ATZJ-DOC; 803-751-5231, DSN 734-5231.
TRANSPORTATION: ATTN: ATZJ-DLT, 803-751-7696, DSN 734-7696.
PERSONNEL/COMMUNITY ACTIVITIES: ATTN: ATZJ-DPCA, 803-751-7538, DSN 734-7538.
Personnel and Expenditures
ACTIVE DUTY PERSONNEL: 12,077
DEPENDENTS: 7348
CIVILIAN PERSONNEL: 4329
MILITARY PAYROLL EXPENDITURE: $256.2 mil
CONTRACT EXPENDITURE: $13.7 mil
Services
Housing: Family units 1270; Unaccompanied officer quarters 22; Unaccompanied enlisted quarters 76; Barracks spaces 743. *Temporary Housing:* VIP units 7; VOQ units 148; VEQ units 12; Unaccompanied officer/Enlisted quarters 62; Guesthouse units 140. *Commissary:* Yes; *Exchange:* Retail store; Barber shop; Dry cleaners; Food shop; Florist; Bank; Service station; Military clothing store; Convenience store; Beauty shop; Laundromat; Credit union; ATM; Optical store; Post office; Fast food; Video rentals; Four seasons; Thrift shop; Travel agency; Class VI; Shoe repair; Garden center; Tailor/Alterations; Laundry; Photo store; Toys; Garden center; Pharmacy. *Child Care/Capacities:* Day care center capacity 400; Home day care program; Before & after school programs. *Schools:* Preschool/Kindergarten; Elementary; College courses. *Base Library:* Yes. *Medical Facilities:* Hospital; Medical clinic; Dental clinic; Pharmacy; Veterinary services. *Recreational Facilities:* Bowling center; Movie theater; Pool; Gym; Recreation cen-

ter; Golf course; Tennis courts; Racquetball court; Fitness center/Weight room; Softball field; Auto shop; Craft shop; Officers club; NCO club; Camping; Fishing/Hunting; Youth center; Picnic area; Playground; Alpine lodge; Video rental; Boy Scouts; Girl Scouts; SATO; Do-it-yourself center.

Eastover

741. McEntire Air National Guard Station

McEntire ANGS
10313 Garner's Ferry Rd
Eastover, SC 29044-9690
803-776-5121; FAX 803-695-6465; DSN 583-8200; DSN FAX 583-8465
E-mail: cwesley@scmmt.ang.af.mil
Profile
BRANCH: Air National Guard.
SIZE AND LOCATION: 2300 acres. On SC State Hwy 378 (Garner's Ferry Rd), between Sumter & Columbia; 12 mi E of Columbia. *County:* Richland.
MAJOR UNITS: 169th Fighter Wing (ANG); 240th Combat Communications Squadron; 151st Army Aviation 1st Bn (SC ANG).
BASE HISTORY: WWII, built as Marine Corps flying training facility. 1946, became Congaree Air National Guard Base. 1961, named for Brig Gen Barnie B McEntire Jr, SC ANG's first general officer, killed in F-104 accident. 1992, 169th changed from Tactical Fighter Group to Fighter Group. 1995, renamed 169th Fighter Wing. 1997, part of 169th FW deployed to Qatar in support of Operation Southern Watch, 1st for ANG unit.
Key Contacts
COMMANDER: 803-695-6200, DSN 583-8200.
PUBLIC AFFAIRS: Maj Les Carroll, Stop 19, 803-695-6208, DSN 583-8208, LCARROLL@scmmt.ang.af.mil; Maj Fred Monk, Stop 34.
Personnel and Expenditures
ACTIVE DUTY PERSONNEL: 300; 1000 reservists
DEPENDENTS: 0
CIVILIAN PERSONNEL: 50
MILITARY PAYROLL EXPENDITURE: $12 mil
Services
Housing: None. *Exchange:* Convenience store; Credit union; Drill weekends only. *Child Care/ Capacities:* No day care facilities. *Schools:* No on-base schools. *Medical Facilities:* Medical clinic. *Recreational Facilities:* All ranks club.

Goose Creek

742. Charleston Naval Weapons Station

NWS Charleston
Goose Creek, SC 29445-8601
803-764-4094; DSN 794-4094
Internet: http://www.nolcant.navy.mil/charles/overview.htm
OFFICER-OF-THE-DAY: 803-764-7901, DSN 794-7901
Profile
BRANCH: Navy.
SIZE AND LOCATION: 17,221 acres.

Approx 25 mi from Charleston, SC; Exit 203 off of I-26, US-78 to US-52, to SC-37 (Red Bank Rd) to main gate. Approx 17 mi from Charleston IAP. *County:* Berkeley; Charleston.
MAJOR UNITS: Naval Weapons Station, Charleston.
BASE HISTORY: 1941, established. 1967, chartered as Navy Industrial Funded Activity. 1991, transitioned to Defense Business Operating Funded Activity. Provides materiel & technical support for ammunition, assigned weapons & weapons systems; operates an explosive ordnance outloading facility; manages Navy family housing for Charleston area.

Key Contacts
COMMANDER: Capt T B Stark, 803-764-7886, DSN 794-7886.
PROCUREMENT: 803-764-7721, DSN 794-7721.
TRANSPORTATION: 803-764-7991, DSN 794-7991.
PERSONNEL/COMMUNITY ACTIVITIES: 803-764-7601, DSN 794-7601.

Personnel and Expenditures
ACTIVE DUTY PERSONNEL: 187; tenant military & civilian 5147
DEPENDENTS: 9573
CIVILIAN PERSONNEL: 1007
MILITARY PAYROLL EXPENDITURE: $94 mil (total budet)

Services
Housing: Family units 2675; Mobile home units 60 pads. *Commissary:* Yes; *Exchange:* Retail store; Barber shop; Service station. *Child Care/ Capacities:* Day care center. *Schools:* Elementary; Intermediate/Junior high. *Base Library:* Yes. *Medical Facilities:* Medical clinic; Dental clinic. *Recreational Facilities:* Bowling center; Movie theater; Pool; Gym; Recreation center; Golf course; Stables; Tennis courts; Racquetball court; Fitness center/Weight room; Softball field; Auto shop; Officers club; NCO club; Fishing/Hunting.

743. Combat Equipment Group-Army, HQ
103 Guidance Rd
Goose Creek, SC 29445-6060
803-764-4428; FAX 803-764-4430
Profile
BRANCH: Army.
LOCATION: *County:* Berkeley.
MAJOR UNITS: Combat Equipment Group, Army, HQ; Combat Equipment Base-Afloat, HQ.
Key Contacts
COMMANDER: Col Dale R Granger 803-764-4428, DSN 794-6101, SIOSM@ msa.nwschs.sea/6.navy.mil.

Greenville

744. Greenville Naval & Marine Corps Reserve Center
Donaldson Center
669 Perimeter Rd
Greenville, SC 29605-5452
864-277-9775, 299-9693; FAX 864-277-9794
Profile
BRANCH: Naval Reserve; Marine Corps Reserve.

LOCATION: *County:* Greenville.
MAJOR UNITS: REDCOM EIGHT Activity; Ammunition Co, 4th Supply Bn.
Key Contacts
COMMANDER: CDR S Hagins.

North Auxiliary Airfield

745. North Auxiliary Airfield
North Field; Operating Location Alpha
Rte 2, Box 141
North Auxiliary Airfield, SC 29152
803-247-2241; FAX 803-247-2105
Profile
BRANCH: Air Force.
SIZE AND LOCATION: 2270 acres. Approx 35 mi S of Columbia, SC, between North and Orangeburg, SC; off US-321/178. *County:* Orangeburg.
MAJOR UNITS: 437th Civil Engineering Squadron; 437th Military Airlift Wing.
BASE HISTORY: Built during WWII as fighter dispersal base. 1950s, B-29 bomber & test base. 1960s-70s, under Shaw AFB. Currently, controlled by Charleston AFB. Mission: Special Operations Low-Level (SOLL II) nighttime missions, aircrew proficiency training (air drops), & forward deployment site (training).
VISITOR ATTRACTIONS: Open-house 1st Sat in Sept.
Key Contacts
COMMANDER: MSgt Williams.
Personnel and Expenditures
ACTIVE DUTY PERSONNEL: 10
CIVILIAN PERSONNEL: 0
Services
Housing: RV/Camper sites 2. *Temporary Housing:* None. *Child Care/Capacities:* No day care facilities. *Schools:* No on-base schools. *Medical Facilities:* No medical facilities. *Recreational Facilities:* Camping; Fishing/Hunting.

North Charleston

746. Charleston Naval Hospital
3600 Rivers Ave
North Charleston, SC 29405-7769
803-743-7000; DSN 563-7000
Profile
BRANCH: Navy.
LOCATION: *County:* Charleston.
MAJOR UNITS: Naval Hospital Charleston.
Personnel and Expenditures
ACTIVE DUTY PERSONNEL: 450
CIVILIAN PERSONNEL: 350
Services
Housing: Unaccompanied enlisted quarters 64; See Charleston Naval Weapons Station. *Exchange:* See Charleston Naval Weapons Station. *Child Care/Capacities:* See Charleston Naval Weapons Station. *Schools:* No on-base schools. *Medical Facilities:* Hospital 40 beds. *Recreational Facilities:* See Charleston Naval Weapons Station.

Parris Island

747. Parris Island Marine Corps Recruit Depot/Eastern Recruiting Region
MCRD Parris Island
PO Box 19001
Parris Island, SC 29905-9001
803-525-2111; DSN 832-1110
Internet: http://www.parrisisland.com/
OFFICER-OF-THE-DAY: 803-525-3712, DSN 832-3712
Profile
BRANCH: Marine Corps.
SIZE AND LOCATION: 7132 acres. On SC 802 adjacent to Port Royal, 5 mi from Beaufort, SC; 45 mi N of Savannah, GA; 70 mi S of Charleston, SC; I-95 to SC exit 33, right on Rte 280 (which turns into Rte 802) follow signs. *County:* Beaufort.
MAJOR UNITS: Marine Corps Recruit Depot; Marine Corps Eastern Recruiting Region; 1st Recruit Training Bn; 2nd Recruit Training Bn; 3rd Recruit Training Bn; 4th Recruit Training Bn; Support Bn; Weapons and Field Training Bn; Drill Instructor School; 6th Marine Corps District, HQ.
BASE HISTORY: Island named after Englishman, Alexander Parris, purchased island 1715. 1891, first Marine Corps post at Parris Island; security detachment attached to Naval Station, Port Royal. 1891-WWI, military buildings & homes constructed (Parris Island Historic District, on National Register of Historic Places). 1909, Marine Officers' School established. 1911, recruit depot started for enlisted Marines. Prior to 1929 causeway, all transportation by boat from Port Royal. 1949, battalion (now 4th Recruit Training Battalion), activated for training women Marine recruits.
VISITOR ATTRACTIONS: Parris Island open for visitors daily, 6am-6pm; Parris Island Museum (free, 10am-4:30pm, daily except holidays, 803-525-2951); Historic tours (every Sat-Wed, 1pm, 803-525-3650); Recruit graduation parades (Fri); Douglas Visitor's Center (provides maps, brochures, place to relax, receptionist on duty, M-W&F 7:30am-5pm, Thur 7:30am-7pm, Sat-Sun-holidays 11am-4pm, 803-525-3650); 16th century French/ Spanish historical site & monuments.
Key Contacts
COMMANDER: Brig Gen James R Battaglini, 803-525-2535; Col Steven J Tomisek.
PUBLIC AFFAIRS: Maj R S Lang, 803-525-3276.
PROCUREMENT: Capt J F Wade, Contracts & Purchasing, 803-525-2141, DSN 832-2141.
TRANSPORTATION: 803-525-3483, DSN 832-3483.
PERSONNEL/COMMUNITY ACTIVITIES: Family Services Center, 803-525-3791, DSN 832-3791.
Personnel and Expenditures
ACTIVE DUTY PERSONNEL: 2050 (plus 3000 recruits)
DEPENDENTS: 3500
CIVILIAN PERSONNEL: 800
Services
Housing: Family units 231; Mobile home units 125 spaces; Bachelor spaces 550; Additional family housing provided by MCAS Beaufort at Laurel Bay, 13 mi.

Temporary Housing: Transient quarters 1; Temporary lodging facility with efficiencies 30 rooms; Osprey Inn 18 rooms. *Commissary:* Yes; *Exchange:* Retail store; Barber shop; Dry cleaners; Food shop; Bank; Service station; Military clothing store; Convenience store; Beauty shop; Credit union; Ice cream shop; Cobbler shop; Post office; Western Union. *Child Care/Capacities:* Day care center capacity 89; Home day care program. *Schools:* Elementary schools in off-base housing area. *Base Library:* Yes. *Medical Facilities:* Medical clinic; Dental clinic; Veterinary services; Beaufort Naval Hospital, 5 mi away. *Recreational Facilities:* Bowling center; Movie theater; Pool; Gym; Recreation center; Golf course; Tennis courts; Racquetball court; Fitness center/Weight room; Softball field; Football field; Auto shop; Craft shop; Officers club; NCO club; Enlisted club; Youth center; Picnic area; Water sports; Playground; Marina; Stables at MCAS Beaufort; Wildlife observation area; Fishing.

Plum Branch

748. Clarks Hill Training Site

RR 1, Box 139G
Plum Branch, SC 29845-9716
864-443-2507

Profile

BRANCH: Army National Guard.
LOCATION: In W-central South Carolina; off US 221 & SC 28. *County:* McCormick.
MAJOR UNITS: Clarks Hill Training Site (ARNG).

Shaw AFB

749. Shaw Air Force Base

517 Lance Ave
Shaw AFB, SC 29152-5041
803-668-3621; 668-3816; FAX 803-668-2276; DSN 965-3621
OFFICER-OF-THE-DAY: 803-668-2850, DSN 965-2850

Profile

BRANCH: Air Force.
SIZE AND LOCATION: 11,746 acres. Off US-76/378, 10 mi W of Sumter, SC; approx 40 mi E of Columbia, SC. *County:* Sumter.
MAJOR UNITS: 363rd Fighter Wing; 9th Air Force, HQ; 609th Air Operations Group; 682nd Air Support Squadron; 337th Air Force Recruiting Squadron, Det 307; 371st Field Training Squadron; Air Force Office of Special Investigations, Det 212; 20th Area Defense Counsel, Det QD; Defense Investigative Service; Defense Commissary Agency; Air Force Audit Agency.
BASE HISTORY: 1941, activated as Shaw Field; named for 1st Lt Ervin D Shaw, Sumter County native shot down in WWI; small basic flying school established. After WWII, transferred to TAC. 1948, redesignated Shaw AFB. 1951, 363rd FW (then 363rd TRW) became host unit and continues today. Cuban Missile Crisis, helped identify Russian missiles in Cuba. 1985, transition to F-16CS fighters. 1990, first operational F-16 squadron in Operation Desert Shield/Storm. 1992, first F-16 air-to-air kill in Air Force history.
VISITOR ATTRACTIONS: Static aircraft: RB-66, RF-101, RF-4C, and OV-2.

Key Contacts

COMMANDER: Col Daniel P Leaf, 20 FW/CC, 517 Lance Ave, Shaw AFB, SC 29152-5041, 803-668-3630, FAX 803-668-2276, DSN 965-3630.
PUBLIC AFFAIRS: Capt Laurent J Fox, 20 FW/PA, 517 Lance Ave, Ste 106, Shaw AFB, SC, 29152-5041, 803-668-3621, FAX 803-668-2276, DSN 965-3621.
PROCUREMENT: LTC Laura A Huff, Contracting Officer, 20 CONS/CC, 803-668-2434, DSN 965-2434.
TRANSPORTATION: Commander, 20 Trans/CC, 803-668-3412, DSN 965-3412.
PERSONNEL/COMMUNITY ACTIVITIES: LTC Nancy A Lee, 20 MSS/CC, 803-668-2324, DSN 965-2324.

Personnel and Expenditures

ACTIVE DUTY PERSONNEL: 5800
DEPENDENTS: 12,000
CIVILIAN PERSONNEL: 1002
MILITARY PAYROLL EXPENDITURE: $178 mil

Services

Housing: Family units 1704. *Temporary Housing:* VIP units 4; VOQ units 84; VAQ units 40; Dormitory units 17; Transient quarters 40. *Commissary:* Yes; *Exchange:* Barber shop; Dry cleaners; Food shop; Florist; Bank; Service station. *Child Care/Capacities:* Day care center capacity 150. *Base Library:* Yes. *Medical Facilities:* Hospital 30; Dental clinic; Veterinary services. *Recreational Facilities:* Bowling center; Movie theater; Pool; Gym; Recreation center; Golf course; Tennis courts; Racquetball court; Fitness center/Weight room; Softball field; Football field; Auto shop; Craft shop; Officers club; NCO club; Camping; Fishing/Hunting; Picnic area; Aero club; Recreation supply; Rod & Gun club; Wateree Recreation Area, off Hwy 97, 10 mi past Camden, SC.

South Dakota

Ellsworth AFB

750. Ellsworth Air Force Base
EAFB
1958 Scott Dr, Ste 1
Ellsworth AFB, SD 57706-4710
605-385-5056; FAX 605-385-4668; DSN
385-5056; DSN FAX 675-4668
E-mail: Plainsman@28bw.af.mil Internet:http://
www.ellsworth.af.mil
Profile
BRANCH: Air Force.
SIZE AND LOCATION: 5282 acres. 12 mi E of
Rapid City, SD, 1 mi N of I-90, Exit 66.
County: Meade; Pennington.
MAJOR UNITS: 28th Bomb Wing; 28th Operations Support Group; 77th Bomb Squadron;
37th Bomb Squadron; 28th Logistics Group;
28th Logistics Support Squadron; 28th Maintenance Squadron; 28th Transportation Squadron; 28th Supply Squadron; 28th Civil Engineer Squadron; 28th Medical Group; 28th
Support Group; 28th Mission Support Squadron; 28th Contracting Squadron; 28th Communications Squadron; 28th Comptroller
Squadron; 28th Services Squadron; 28th Security Forces Squadron; Airman Leadership
School; Air Force Office of Special Investigations, Det 1302; Air Force Audit Agency Det;
Defense Reutilization and Marketing Service;
372nd Training Squadron, Det 8; US Air
Force Weapons School, Det 4; Test & Evaluation Group, Det 2.
BASE HISTORY: 1942, activated as Rapid City
Army Air Force Base, training B-17 bomber
crews. 1946-47, temporary inactive status.
1947, reactivated, part of 15th Air Force.
1948, renamed Weaver AFB, for Brig Gen
Walter R Weaver, pioneer in AF; renamed
again Rapid City AFB, in response to public
opinion; declared permanent installation.
1953, President Eisenhower dedicated base in
honor of Brig Gen Richard E Ellsworth, commander of 28th SRW, killed in RB-36 crash.
1960, 850th Strategic Missile Squadron with
Titan I missile activated. 1962, 44th Strategic
Missile Wing formed with Minuteman I.
1958-71, served as 821st Aerospace Division
HQ. 1988, HQ for 12th Air Division. 1992,
units transferred from SAC to Air Combat
Command; 28th Wing redesignated 28th
Bomb Wing. 1994, missile complex completely shut down. 1997, 77th Bomb Squadron, recently inactivated, returns to active
status.

VISITOR ATTRACTIONS: South Dakota Air
& Space Museum. Area attractions: Badlands
National Park; Mount Rushmore; Fort Meade
Museum; Crazy Horse Mountain; Wall Drug;
Custer State Park; Wind Cave; Black Hills.
Key Contacts
COMMANDER: Col William M Fraser III,
605-385-2801, DSN 675-2801.
PUBLIC AFFAIRS: Maj Louise Lund-Vaa,
605-385-5056, FAX 605-385-4668, DSN
675-5056, DSN FAX 675-4668, lundvaa@
bw28.ellsworth.af.mil.
Personnel and Expenditures
ACTIVE DUTY PERSONNEL: 3000
DEPENDENTS: 6500
CIVILIAN PERSONNEL: 461
MILITARY PAYROLL EXPENDITURE: $100.8
mil
Services
Housing: Family units 2036; Dormitory spaces
748; Senior NCO units 234; Junior NCO units
1582; RV/Camper sites 36; Officer housing 220.
Temporary Housing: VIP units 2 units; VOQ
units 126; VEQ units 57; Lodge units 30; Tent
spaces 15. *Commissary:* Yes; *Exchange:* Retail
store; Barber shop; Dry cleaners; Food shop; Florist; Bank; Service station; Bakery; Military
clothing store; Convenience store; Beauty shop;
Credit union; ATM; Optical store; Fast food;
Video rentals; Four seasons; Thrift shop; Travel
agency; Class VI. *Child Care/Capacities:* Day
care center capacity 104, 6mo-10yrs; Home day
care program; Latch key program; Summer day
camp; Before & after school programs. *Schools:*
College courses. *Base Library:* Yes. *Medical Facilities:* Hospital 15; Medical clinic; Dental
clinic; Pharmacy; Veterinary services. *Recreational Facilities:* Bowling center; Movie theater;
Pool; Gym; Recreation center; Golf course; Stables; Tennis courts; Racquetball court; Fitness
center/Weight room; Softball field; Auto shop;
Craft shop; Camping; Fishing/Hunting; Youth
center; Picnic area; Skeet range; Playground;
Community club; Consolidated club.

Fort Meade

751. Fort Meade Military Reservation
113 Comanche Rd
Fort Meade, SD 57741
605-347-2511
Profile
BRANCH: Army National Guard.

SIZE AND LOCATION: 250 acres. In SW SD,
2 mi E of Sturgis, SD, off I-90, on Hwy 34.
County: Meade.
MAJOR UNITS: South Dakota ARNG.
BASE HISTORY: 1878, founded as military
post; number of different units assigned, including glider detachment. 1944, turned over
to Veterans Administration. All old buildings
on register of historic places. Currently, SD
NG using buildings for training site; buildings
restored; used for classrooms, barracks, & administration.
VISITOR ATTRACTIONS: Museum.

Mitchell

752. Mitchell National Guard Complex
PO Box 610
Mitchell, SD 57301-0610
605-995-1671, 605-995-2671
Profile
BRANCH: Army National Guard.
SIZE AND LOCATION: 25 acres. 4 mi N of
Mitchell, SD, on Hwy 37 at Mitchell Munici-
pal Airport Industrial Park. *County:* Davison.
MAJOR UNITS: 665th Maintenance Co; 147th
Field Artillery, Battery A, 1st Bn; 147th
Army Band; Combined Support Maintenance
Shop 1; Organizational Maintenance Shop 5.
BASE HISTORY: Area former WWII air base.
1950, original shop built. Since 1950, facility
was Combined Support Maintenance Shop 1
(CSMS 1). Since 1956, Armory & Organiza-
tional Maintenance Shop 1. Presently, outdoor baffled rifle range serving units in 70 mi
radius, equipment cold storage, & vehicle
storage buildings; responsible for majority of
maintenance of SD ARNG equipment.
Services
Housing: None. *Recreational Facilities:* Fitness
center/Weight room.

Rapid City

753. Camp Rapid
2823 W Main St
Rapid City, SD 57702-8186
605-399-6200; FAX 605-399-6677; DSN
747-8200

E-mail: Sd-SMTP.army.mil Internet:http://
www.sd-smtp.army.mil
OFFICER-OF-THE-DAY: 605-399-1444

Profile

BRANCH: Army National Guard.

SIZE AND LOCATION: 84 acres. In western portion of Rapid City; approx 15 mi W of Ellsworth AFB. *County:* Pennington.

MAJOR UNITS: State Area Command, HQ; South Dakota NG.

BASE HISTORY: 1933, established on 84 acres of Rapid City Indian School land. 1950, Secretary of Interior transferred 673 acres of Sioux Sanatorium property for SD NG (West Camp Rapid). 1962, 90 acres of West Camp David deeded to Rapid City School District No 1 for a high school. 1963, NG designated 22 acres for Rapid City NG Armory. Currently, Camp Rapid is a state-owned, federally supported training site, consisting of cantonment area for troop housing logistics and training facilities. West Camp Rapid provides training in field. Used by units of SD Army NG, Army reserve forces, Ellsworth AFB, units of active Army and Office of Adjutant General, and support facilities of SD Army NG.

Key Contacts

COMMANDER: Maj Gen Harold J Sykora, 605-399-6702, DSN 747-8702.

PUBLIC AFFAIRS: Maj Ted Johnson, 605-399-6721, DSN 747-8721, FAX 747-8264.

PROCUREMENT: Capt Don Hollis, 605-399-6664, DSN 747-8664.

TRANSPORTATION: Capt Tim Moran, 605-399-6796, DSN 747-8796.

PERSONNEL/COMMUNITY ACTIVITIES: Col Dennis Pike, 605-399-6710, DSN 747-8710.

Personnel and Expenditures

ACTIVE DUTY PERSONNEL: 50

CIVILIAN PERSONNEL: 170

MILITARY PAYROLL EXPENDITURE: $15.8 mil

CONTRACT EXPENDITURE: $1.5 mil

Services

Housing: Barracks spaces 570. *Temporary Housing:* Unaccompanied officer/Enlisted quarters 34. *Exchange:* Limited retail only during two-week annual training. *Medical Facilities:* Dispensary; Only during two-week annual training period. *Recreational Facilities:* Tennis courts; Fitness center/Weight room; Softball field.

Sioux Falls

754. Sioux Falls Naval Reserve Center

NAVRESCEN Sioux Falls
1800 W Russell St
Sioux Falls, SD 57104-1393
605-336-2402; FAX 605-334-3690
E-mail: NRCSXF@ideasign.com

Profile

BRANCH: Naval Reserve.

SIZE AND LOCATION: 1 acre. In Sioux Falls, 10 min from Sioux Falls regional airport; adj to I-29; 5 min from I-90. *County:* Minnehaha.

MAJOR UNITS: REDCOM SIXTEEN Activity; Fleet Hospital 500 CBTZ 23 Det Q; RNCMB 15, Det 0715; FISC Yokosuka Det 116 (NR); Destroyer Squadron 24 (NR).

Key Contacts

COMMANDER: CDR James M Nugent.

Personnel and Expenditures

ACTIVE DUTY PERSONNEL: 8; 1222 reservists

Services *Base Library:* Yes.

755. South Dakota Air National Guard Base

SDANG; Joe Foss Field
Foss Field
1201 W Algonquin St
Sioux Falls, SD 57104-0264
Mailing Address
BOX 5044
Sioux Falls, SD 57177-5044
605-988-5700; FAX 605-988-5764; DSN 939-7000

Profile

BRANCH: Air National Guard.

SIZE AND LOCATION: 166 acres. NW corner of Sioux Falls, between I-29 and I-229; just S of I-90, at Airport Industrial Park, corner of Industrial Ave & Algonquin St. *County:* Minnehaha.

MAJOR UNITS: South Dakota Air National Guard, HQ; 114th Fighter Wing (ANG).

BASE HISTORY: 1946, Foss Field named for Brig Gen Joseph J Foss, WWII ace, former governor of SD, founder of SD ANG; federal recognition of 175th Fighter Squadron. 1951-52, active duty. 1989-90, combat duty as part of Operation Just Cause in Panama. 1992, redesignated 114th Fighter Group; first operational unit to fly F-16C Fighting Falcon.

Key Contacts

COMMANDER: Col Thomas J Lien, TLIEN@sdfsd.ang.af.mil.

PUBLIC AFFAIRS: 1Lt Kristin Miller, 605-988-5709, KMILLER@sdfsd.ang.af.mil.

Personnel and Expenditures

ACTIVE DUTY PERSONNEL: 1004 Guard

CIVILIAN PERSONNEL: 247

MILITARY PAYROLL EXPENDITURE: $19.5 mil

Services

Housing: None. *Exchange:* Convenience store; Credit union. *Recreational Facilities:* Fitness center/Weight room; Softball field; All ranks club.

Tennessee

Arnold Air Force Base

756. Arnold Engineering Development Center
AEDC
AEDC/PA, 100 Kindel Dr, Suite B213
Arnold Air Force Base, TN 37389
615-454-5586; FAX 615-454-6720; DSN 340-5586
Internet: http://info.arnold.af.mil/aedc/fact/aedc.html
Profile
BRANCH: Air Force.
SIZE AND LOCATION: 40,000 acres. Off I-24, 65 mi S of Nashville; 12 mi from Manchester, Tullahoma, & Winchester. *County:* Coffee; Franklin.
MAJOR UNITS: Arnold Engineering Development Center (AEDC).
BASE HISTORY: Part of Air Force Materiel Command Test Facility, named for Gen Henry H "Hap" Arnold, Commanding General of Army Air Forces during WWII; responsible for concept of engineering development center. 1950, construction begun at old Camp Forrest. Major divisions: Engine Test Facility, von Karman Gas Dynamics Facility, & Propulsion Wind Tunnel. 1951, AEDC Mission established to support development of aerospace systems by testing hardware in aerodynamic, propulsion, & space test facilities that simulate flight conditions.
VISITOR ATTRACTIONS: Woods Reservoir, boating, fishing, picnic areas.
Key Contacts
COMMANDER: Col Robert W Chedister, AEDC/CC, Suite A303, 37389-1303, 615-454-4222, DSN 340-4222.
PUBLIC AFFAIRS: Capt Steven Doub, 615-454-5586.
PROCUREMENT: Temple Bowling IV, 615-454-4419.
Personnel and Expenditures
ACTIVE DUTY PERSONNEL: 150
DEPENDENTS: 75
CIVILIAN PERSONNEL: 3800
Services
Housing: Family units 40. *Temporary Housing:* VOQ units 40. *Commissary:* Yes; *Exchange:* Retail store; Bank. *Medical Facilities:* Medical clinic (part-time facilities only); Dental clinic. *Recreational Facilities:* Recreation center; Golf course; Softball field; Auto shop; Craft shop; Of-
ficers club; NCO club; Camping; Fishing/Hunting; Picnic area; Marina.

Bristol

757. Defense Contract Management Office Raytheon
DCMO Raytheon Bristol
100 Vance Tank Rd
Bristol, TN 37620-5698
423-652-5000; FAX 423-652-5017
Profile
BRANCH: Defense Logistics Agency.
SIZE AND LOCATION: 99.9 acres. In S Bristol, 7 mi S of I-81; 15 mi from Tri-City Airport. *County:* Sullivan.
MAJOR UNITS: Defense Contract Management Office, Raytheon.
BASE HISTORY: 1952-53, constructed. 1954, manufacturing operations begun by Sperry Farragut Corp. 1957, Raytheon Co took over. Base is a GOCO industrial production facility with capabilities in research & development, design engineering & testing associated with manufacture of advanced weapons systems, and fabrication & assembly of missiles. Formerly named Naval Weapons Industrial Reserve Plant.
Key Contacts
COMMANDER: Jay Bliestein, Plant Manager.
Personnel and Expenditures
ACTIVE DUTY PERSONNEL: 1
CIVILIAN PERSONNEL: 25
Services
Housing: None.

Chattanooga

758. Chattanooga Naval & Marine Corps Reserve Center
N&MCRC Chattanooga; NAVMAR-CORESCEN Chattanooga
4051 Amnicola Hwy
Chattanooga, TN 37406-1008
423-698-8955, 698-8957; FAX 423-698-8958
Profile
BRANCH: Naval Reserve; Marine Corps Reserve.
SIZE AND LOCATION: 9.11 acres. Downtown Chattanooga on N side of river between Market & Walnut St bridges. *County:* Hamilton.

MAJOR UNITS: REDCOM NINE Activity; Naval Reserve Voluntary Training Unit (VOL-TRAUNIT) 0802; Naval Reserve CHEM-RADTECHLANT 108; Naval Reserve, Naval Shipyard NORVA 308; Naval Reserve, USS *Yosemite* (AD-19); Naval Reserve Naval Hospital, Jacksonville, Det 208; Naval Reserve, Weapon Station Charleston 908; Naval Reserve Guarded Missile Frigate Support Unit (FFG SUPPU 0)108; Naval Mobile Construction Bn 24, Det 1224; Naval Reserve MAC-G; Battery M, 4th Bn, 14th Marine Regiment.
BASE HISTORY: 1954, constructed; 5 buildings (26,686 sq ft) for mobilization, training, administrative support & recruiting.
Key Contacts
COMMANDER: Capt P A Young.
Personnel and Expenditures
ACTIVE DUTY PERSONNEL: 24; 325 drilling personnel
Services *Medical Facilities:* No medical facilities. *Recreational Facilities:* Fitness center/Weight room; Picnic area; Volleyball court.

759. Volunteer Army Ammunition Plant
VAAP
PO Box 22607
Chattanooga, TN 37422-2607
423-855-7100; FAX 423-855-7205; DSN 760-9100; DSN FAX 760-9205
Profile
BRANCH: Army.
SIZE AND LOCATION: 6600 acres. VAAP approx 12 mi NE of Chattanooga, TN. I-75 N, Exit 7B W, facility on State Hwy 317, approx 2 mi from exit. *County:* Hamilton.
BASE HISTORY: 1941-43, constructed; originally Volunteer Ordnance Works. Following WWII, shut down and placed on stand-by status. Rehabilitated for Korean War and produced TNT until placed on standby status, 1957. 1965, activated to produce TNT for Vietnam War. 1970, gradual phasedown started. 1977, put on inactive status. Presently has several contractors, leasees & tenants.
Key Contacts
COMMANDER: James E Fry, Commander's Representative, 423-855-7109, DSN 760-9109.
Personnel and Expenditures
CIVILIAN PERSONNEL: 100

Kingsport

760. Holston Army Ammunition Plant
HSAAP; Holston AAP
Kingsport, TN 37660-9982
423-578-6000; FAX 423-578-6326; DSN 748-6000
OFFICER-OF-THE-DAY: Security Officer, 423-278-6281, DSN 748-6281
Profile
BRANCH: Army.
SIZE AND LOCATION: 6000 acres. In Kingsport, TN, on Hwy 11-W. *County:* Sullivan.
MAJOR UNITS: Holston Defense Corp.
BASE HISTORY: 1942, constructed; originally Holston Ordnance Works, a GOCO facility. Mission is manufacture of military explosives. Current operating contractor, Holston Defense Corp.
Key Contacts
COMMANDER: 423-578-6241, DSN 748-6241.
PROCUREMENT: 423-578-6296, DSN 748-6296.
TRANSPORTATION: 423-578-6280, DSN 748-6280.
PERSONNEL/COMMUNITY ACTIVITIES: 423-578-6285, DSN 748-6285.
Personnel and Expenditures
ACTIVE DUTY PERSONNEL: 2
CIVILIAN PERSONNEL: 20

Knoxville

761. Knoxville Naval & Marine Corps Reserve Center
2101 Alcoa Hwy
Knoxville, TN 37920-2231
423-971-4709, 971-4803; FAX 423-637-3950; DSN 697-8001
Profile
BRANCH: Naval Reserve; Marine Corps Reserve.
LOCATION: *County:* Knox.
MAJOR UNITS: REDCOM NINE Activity; Co A, 4th Medical Bn; Co D, 4th Combat Engineer Bn.
Key Contacts
COMMANDER: Lt P G Metzler.

762. McGee Tyson Airport, Air National Guard Base
Knoxville, TN 37901
615-985-3200; DSN 266-8200
Profile
BRANCH: Air National Guard.
SIZE AND LOCATION: 271 acres. 10 mi SW of Knoxville, off US-129. *County:* Knox.
MAJOR UNITS: 134th Air Refueling Wing (ANG); 228th Combat Communications Squadron; I G Brown Professional Military Education Center (ANG).
Personnel and Expenditures
ACTIVE DUTY PERSONNEL: 1056 Guard
CIVILIAN PERSONNEL: 371
MILITARY PAYROLL EXPENDITURE: $29.4 mil
Services *Medical Facilities:* Dispensary.

Memphis

763. Memphis Detachment, Large Cavitation Channel
2700 Channel Ave
Memphis, TN 38113-0428
901-947-3117
Internet: http://www50.dt.navy.mil/org/
Profile
BRANCH: Navy.
MAJOR UNITS: Large Cavitation Channel, Memphis Det.
BASE HISTORY: Detachment of Naval Surface Warfare Center, Carderock Division.
Key Contacts
COMMANDER: David M Foster, Director, 901-947-3117, ext 104; FAX 901-948-9816, fosterd@dt.navy.mil.

764. Memphis IAP, Air National Guard Base
2815 Democrat Rd
Memphis, TN 38181-0026
901-541-7111; DSN 966-8210
Profile
BRANCH: Air National Guard.
SIZE AND LOCATION: 103 acres. Near junction of I-55 and I-240; 10 mi S of Memphis, exit 24 off I-240, at Memphis IAP. *County:* Shelby.
MAJOR UNITS: 164th Airlift Wing (ANG).
BASE HISTORY: 1946, activated.
Personnel and Expenditures
ACTIVE DUTY PERSONNEL: 1023 Guard
CIVILIAN PERSONNEL: 280
MILITARY PAYROLL EXPENDITURE: $20.1 mil
Services
Housing: None. *Exchange:* Convenience store. *Medical Facilities:* Medical clinic. *Recreational Facilities:* Community club.

765. US Army Corps of Engineers, Memphis District
CEMUM
167 N Main St, Rm B202
Memphis, TN 38103-1894
800-317-4156; FAX 901-544-3786
E-mail: cemvm-pa@smtp.1mm.usace.army.mil
    Internet:http://www.lmm.usace.army.mil/
Profile
BRANCH: Army.
SIZE AND LOCATION: Offices only; Shipyard 157 acres. HQs in downtown Memphis in Clifford Davis Federal Bldg, corner of Front & Poplar Sts; 10 mi to airport, off I-40; Ensley Engineer Yard (shipyard) 5 mi S of Memphis on McKellar Lake; Other Field Offices in Wynne, AR, & Caruthersville, MO. *County:* Shelby.
MAJOR UNITS: Corps of Engineers, Memphis District; Shipyard, Ensley Engineer Yard; Field Office, Wynne, AR; Field Office, Caruthersville, MO.
BASE HISTORY: 1876, established. Since 1882, has performed flood control & navigation works in 25,000 sq mi of Lower Mississippi River Valley to keep channel open for navigation on 355 mi of Mississippi River between Cairo, IL, & Rosedale, MS. Detailed account can be found in *A Century on the Mississippi: A History of the Memphis District*

Army Corps of Engineers 1876-1981, 1986, by Floyd M Clay. Performs civil works construction.
Key Contacts
COMMANDER: Col Gregory G Bean, District Engineer, 901-544-3223, FAX 901-544-3628, celmm-de@smtp.1mm.usace.army.mil.
PUBLIC AFFAIRS: Robert Anderson, 901-544-3360, 901-544-3786, andersob@smtp.1mm.usace.army.mil.
PROCUREMENT: Steve Shankle, Contracting Division Chief, 901-544-3118.
TRANSPORTATION: Steve Beasley, 901-544-3384.
PERSONNEL/COMMUNITY ACTIVITIES: Charles D Gibson, Human Resources Management Office Chief, 901-544-3105.
Personnel and Expenditures
ACTIVE DUTY PERSONNEL: 3
CIVILIAN PERSONNEL: 475
Services *Base Library:* Yes.

Milan

766. Milan Army Ammunition Plant
MLAAP
Milan Arsenal
2280 Hwy 104 W
Milan, TN 38358-3176
Mailing Address
MLAAP
Milan, TN 38006-3176
901-686-6087; FAX 901-686-6077; DSN 966-6087; DSN FAX 966-6077
E-mail: MILAN-AAP@ria-emh2.army.mil
OFFICER-OF-THE-DAY: 901-686-6784, DSN 966-6784, DSN FAX 966-6077
Profile
BRANCH: Army.
SIZE AND LOCATION: 22,500 acres. Adj to E boundary of Milan, TN, approx 100 mi E/NE of Memphis via I-40 & US-45. *County:* Gibson; Carroll.
MAJOR UNITS: Corps of Engineers; Defense Contract Audit Agency.
BASE HISTORY: 1941-42, Milan Ordnance Depot constructed; operated by government personnel. 1943, merged with Wolf Creek Ordnance Plant, operated by Procter & Gamble Defense Corp. 1945, redesignated Milan Arsenal. 1945-53, deactivated. 1954, designated permanent installation. 1957, Harvey Aluminum Sales Inc became operating contractor; Arsenal placed in inactive status. 1960, activated. 1963, given present name. 1969, Martin Marietta Inc acquired Harvey Aluminum Sales & operates plant. Current operating contractor: General Dynamic Ordnance Systems, Inc.
Key Contacts
COMMANDER: LTC Billy J Dowdy, DOWDYB@ria-emh2.army.mil.
PUBLIC AFFAIRS: Cooper Stephens, 901-686-6611, DSN 966-6611, DSN FAX 966-6619, CSTEPHEN@ria-emh2.army.mil 966-6251.
PROCUREMENT: Lawrence E Smith, Administrative Contracting Officer, 901-686-6244, DSN 966-6246, DSN FAX 966-6077, LSMITH@ria-emh2.army.mil.

TRANSPORTATION: Bruce S Laird, 901-686-6895, DSN 966-6895, DSN FAX 966-6077, BLAIRD@ria-emh2.army.mil.
PERSONNEL/COMMUNITY ACTIVITIES: Patricia Moore, 901-686-6249, DSN 966-6249, DSN FAX 966-6077, PMOORE@ria-emh2.army.mil.

Personnel and Expenditures
ACTIVE DUTY PERSONNEL: 2
CIVILIAN PERSONNEL: 26

Services
Housing: Family units 32. *Temporary Housing:* None. *Medical Facilities:* Medical clinic. *Recreational Facilities:* Picnic area.

Millington

767. Bureau of Naval Personnel Detachment, Memphis
BUPERS, Memphis
5820 Navy Rd
Millington, TN 38053-2781
FAX 901-874-5035; DSN FAX 882-5035
Internet: http://www.navy.mil/homepages/bupers/det/detpage.html

Profile
BRANCH: Navy.
LOCATION: In Millington, just N of Memphis. *County:* Shelby.
MAJOR UNITS: Bureau of Naval Personnel Det, Memphis; Naval Manpower and Analysis Center; Morale, Welfare, & Recreation Division (BUPERS); Network Control Center (BUPERS).
BASE HISTORY: 1995, established. 1999, Naval Personnel Research and Development Center to be established.

Key Contacts
COMMANDER: RADM John T Natter; CDR G G Brown Jr, Deputy 901-874-6426.

768. Memphis Naval Reserve Readiness Center
7800 3rd Ave, Bldg 5-241
Millington, TN 38054-5048
901-874-5550; FAX 901-874-7598; DSN 882-5550
Internet: http://www.ncts.navy.mil/homepages/navresfor/navsurf/redcom09.html

Profile
BRANCH: Naval Reserve.

LOCATION: N of Memphis. *County:* Shelby.
MAJOR UNITS: REDCOM NINE Activity.

Key Contacts
COMMANDER: Capt. C Laporte.

Nashville

769. Adjutant General of Tennessee
Houston Barracks, PO Box 41502
Nashville, TN 37204-1501
615-313-3001; FAX 615-313-3129

Profile
BRANCH: Army National Guard.
MAJOR UNITS: Tennessee National Guard.

Key Contacts
COMMANDER: Maj Gen Jackie D Wood.

770. Nashville IAP, ANG Base
Berry Field ANG Base
240 Knapp Blvd
Nashville, TN 37217-2538
615-399-5401; FAX 615-399-5508; DSN 778-6201
E-mail: BerryField@tnbna.ang.af.mil. Internet: http://132.46.29.16/

Profile
BRANCH: Air National Guard.
SIZE AND LOCATION: 85 acres. Approx 15 mi SE of Nashville at junction of Murfreesboro Rd & Donelson Pike. *County:* Davidson.
MAJOR UNITS: 105th Airlift Squadron.
BASE HISTORY: 1935, after a series of moves, TN ANG as the 105th Aero Squadron moved to present location (named later in honor of Col Harry S Berry, state WPA administrator). 1940, called to federal duty. 1946, made part of 54th Fighter Wing. 1950, formed 118th Composite Wing. 1951, activated; remained in Nashville as part of Air Defense Command. 1956-61, reformed as 118th Photo Reconnaissance Squadron and Wing. 1961, changed to Military Airlift Command. 1990, designation changed to present name under the Airlift Mobility Command.

Key Contacts
COMMANDER: Brig Gen George Wilson, 615-399-5401, DSN 778-6201, GWilson@TNBNA.ANG.AF.MIL.

PUBLIC AFFAIRS: LTC Larry Burriss, 615-399-5532, LBurriss@TNBNA.ANG.AF.MIL.

Personnel and Expenditures
ACTIVE DUTY PERSONNEL: 62; 1130 RESERVISTS
CIVILIAN PERSONNEL: 230

Services *Recreational Facilities:* Fitness center/Weight room; Picnic area.

771. Nashville Naval Reserve Center
1515 Davidson St
Nashville, TN 37206-3199
615-228-6894, 228-6895; FAX 615-228-7549

Profile
BRANCH: Naval Reserve.
LOCATION: *County:* Davidson.
MAJOR UNITS: REDCOM NINE Activity.

Key Contacts
COMMANDER: CDR R D Thomas.

772. US Army Corps of Engineers, Nashville District
CELRN
110 9th Ave S
Nashville, TN 37203-3863
Mailing Address
PO Box 1070
Nashville, TN 37202-1070
615-736-7161; FAX 615-736-2052
Internet: http://www.orn.usace.army.mil/

Profile
BRANCH: Army.
LOCATION: In John Weld Peck Federal Office Bldg, downtown Nashville. *County:* Davidson.
MAJOR UNITS: Corps of Engineers, Nashville District.
BASE HISTORY: Covers 7 states, over 59,000 sq mi. Performs civil works construction.
VISITOR ATTRACTIONS: Only operating gristmill at Lake Cumberland.

Key Contacts
COMMANDER: LTC Christopher J Young.
PUBLIC AFFAIRS: Edward M Evans, edward.m.evans@usace.army.mil.

Personnel and Expenditures
ACTIVE DUTY PERSONNEL: 4
CIVILIAN PERSONNEL: 450; 450 in field offices

Services *Base Library:* Yes.

Texas

Abilene

773. Dyess Air Force Base
Dyess; DAFB
650 Second St
Abilene, TX 79607-1960
915-696-3113; DSN 461-3113
Internet: http://www.dyess.af.mil
Profile
BRANCH: Air Force.
SIZE AND LOCATION: 6405 acres. On W of Abilene; bordered by city of Tye; Hwy 80 runs through Abilene and joins DUB Wright Blvd on W, Dyess on right of DUB Wright Blvd; 9 mi from Abilene Municipal Airport. *County:* Taylor.
MAJOR UNITS: 7th Bomb Wing; 317th Airlift Group.
BASE HISTORY: 1852, first military base established, only used a few years, Ft Phantom. WWII, established Camp Barkeley, which became Army training camp for recruits; Army Air Corps cadets learned to fly light aircraft at Tye Army Field. Following WWII, both installations closed; Tye Army Field sold to city of Abilene; site used by TX NG as training facility. 1953, ground broken for SAC base, originally Abilene AFB. 1956, dedicated and renamed for LTC William Edwin Dyess. 1993, 96th Wing and 463rd Airlift Wing merged into 7th Wing. 1997, 7th Wing became 7th Bomb Wing under ACC & C-130s separated to 317th Airlift Group under AMC.
VISITOR ATTRACTIONS: Linear Air Park, static display of aircraft from WWII to Desert Storm.
Key Contacts
COMMANDER: Col (Brig Gen Sel) Michael McMahan, 915-696-2121, DSN 461-2121.
PUBLIC AFFAIRS: Maj John Boyle, 915-696-2864, DSN 461-2864, DSN FAX 461-2866, pastaff@wg7.dyess.af.mil.
PROCUREMENT: 915-696-3368, DSN 461-3368.
TRANSPORTATION: 690 Ave F, 915-696-5018, DSN 461-5018.
Personnel and Expenditures
ACTIVE DUTY PERSONNEL: 5032
DEPENDENTS: 7304
CIVILIAN PERSONNEL: 419
MILITARY PAYROLL EXPENDITURE: $127.7 mil
CONTRACT EXPENDITURE: $54.1 mil

Services
Housing: Family units 1190; Dormitory spaces 854. *Temporary Housing:* VOQ units 81; VAQ units 43; Apartment units 40. *Commissary:* Yes; *Exchange:* Retail store; Barber shop; Dry cleaners; Food shop; Florist; Bank; Service station; Military clothing store; Convenience store; Beauty shop; Laundromat; Credit union. *Child Care/Capacities:* Day care center capacity 124, 6 wks-10yrs; Home day care program; Summer day camp. *Schools:* No on-base schools. *Base Library:* Yes. *Medical Facilities:* Hospital 20; Medical clinic; Dental clinic; Dispensary; Pharmacy; Veterinary services. *Recreational Facilities:* Bowling center; Movie theater; Pool; Gym; Golf course; Stables; Tennis courts; Racquetball court; Fitness center/Weight room; Softball field; Football field; Auto shop; Craft shop; Officers club; Enlisted club; Youth center; Picnic area; Playground; Community club; Health club.

Alice

774. Orange Grove, Naval Auxiliary Landing Field
NALFOG
RR 3, Box 410
Alice, TX 78332-9315
512-595-6140; FAX 512-664-7201; DSN 861-6140
Profile
BRANCH: Navy.
LOCATION: 46 mi NW of NAS Kingsville, TX; near Orange Grove, 14 mi N of Alice, TX on US-281. *County:* Jim Wells.
MAJOR UNITS: Naval Auxiliary Landing Field, Orange Grove.
BASE HISTORY: Operates under an officer-in-charge to provide mirror landing facilities for 3 training squadrons out of NAS Kingsville; small installation, consisting of 2 8,000-foot runways, air traffic control center, fuel farm, & crash crew.
Key Contacts
COMMANDER: Officer-in-Charge.
Personnel and Expenditures
ACTIVE DUTY PERSONNEL: 43
Services
Housing: None. *Medical Facilities:* Corpsman on duty during operating hours. *Recreational Facilities:* Limited hunting/fishing for DOD personnel.

Amarillo

775. Amarillo Naval & Marine Corps Reserve Center
N&MCRC Amarillo
2500 Tee Anchor Blvd
Amarillo, TX 79104-2499
806-372-5589, 376-5946; FAX 806-372-4710
Profile
BRANCH: Naval Reserve; Marine Corps Reserve.
LOCATION: *County:* Potter; Randall.
MAJOR UNITS: REDCOM ELEVEN Activity; TOW Scout Plt, HQ & Service Co, 4th Tank Bn.
Key Contacts
COMMANDER: CDR D J Conner.

Austin

776. Austin Naval & Marine Corps Reserve Center
Armed Forces Reserve Center
4601 Fairview Dr
Austin, TX 78731-5398
512-458-4154, 467-2317, 458-4075; FAX 512-452-9059; DSN 954-5001
Profile
BRANCH: Naval Reserve; Marine Corps Reserve.
LOCATION: *County:* Travis.
MAJOR UNITS: REDCOM ELEVEN Activity; Weapons Co, 1st Bn, 23rd Marine Regiment.
Key Contacts
COMMANDER: CDR A M Clark.

777. Camp Mabry
2210 W 35th St
Austin, TX 78763
Mailing Address
PO Box 5218
Austin, TX 78763-5218
512-465-5001; DSN 954-5001
OFFICER-OF-THE-DAY: 512-465-5001, DSN 954-5001
Profile
BRANCH: Joint Service Installation.
SIZE AND LOCATION: 375 acres. In W Austin at intersection of Loop 1 & 35th St. *County:* Travis.

MAJOR UNITS: Texas Army National Guard, HQ; Texas Air National Guard, HQ; Texas State Guard; 49th Armored Division; 71st Troop Command of Texas ANG; US Property and Fiscal Office for Texas; Texas National Guard Academy.

BASE HISTORY: 1882, original tract donated to state of TX for establishing permanent encampment for TX Volunteer Guard. 1898, named for Brig Gen Woodford H Mabry, Adjutant Gen of TX. 1915, arsenal constructed; on parade field, Teddy Roosevelt once broke wild mustangs, Jenny biplanes landed, citizen-soldiers trained, and TX State Exposition held. WWI and WWII, portions used as active military installation by federal government. Also occupied at various times by Department of Public Safety, Texas Rangers, and State Board of Control.

VISITOR ATTRACTIONS: Texas Military Forces Museum; Texas Guard all-faiths chapel with stained glass windows depicting 10 Battle Flags of TX; static displays of military equipment; Statue of Audie Murphy, Medal of Honor winner.

Key Contacts
COMMANDER: Brig Gen Daniel James, III, Adjutant Gen of TX, 512-465-5006, DSN 954-5006.
PUBLIC AFFAIRS: LTC Ed S Komandosky, 512-465-5059, DSN 954-5059.
PROCUREMENT: Col James West.
TRANSPORTATION: Col Clifford Barkley.
PERSONNEL/COMMUNITY ACTIVITIES: Col Dennis Haire.

Personnel and Expenditures
ACTIVE DUTY PERSONNEL: 300
DEPENDENTS: 10
CIVILIAN PERSONNEL: 400
MILITARY PAYROLL EXPENDITURE: $10 mil
Services
Housing: Unaccompanied enlisted quarters 300; Barracks spaces 300; Senior NCO units 10. *Temporary Housing:* VOQ units 6; Unaccompanied officer/Enlisted quarters 10. *Exchange:* Retail store; Barber shop; Dry cleaners; Convenience store; Beauty shop; Credit union; ATM; Fast food; Travel agency; Class VI; Cafeteria. *Child Care/Capacities:* No day care facilities. *Schools:* College courses. *Medical Facilities:* Dispensary. *Recreational Facilities:* Gym; Fitness center/Weight room; Fishing/Hunting; Picnic area; Running track.

Bastrop

778. Camp Swift Training Site
Camp Swift
RR 7, Box 757X
Bastrop, TX 78602
512-321-2497; FAX 512-321-1419
Profile
BRANCH: Army National Guard.
SIZE AND LOCATION: 11,740 acres. On E side of TX Hwy 95 about half-way between towns of Elgin and Bastrop; 35 mi E of Austin. *County:* Bastrop.
MAJOR UNITS: Camp Swift Training Site HQ; Unit Training Equipment Site 3; 386th Engineer Bn, Co A.
BASE HISTORY: 1942, activated as training base for Army. 1946, leased to TX National Guard. Also used for federal prison & Boy Scout camp.
Key Contacts
COMMANDER: Facility Manager.
PUBLIC AFFAIRS: LTC Ed S Komandosky; PO Box 5218, Austin, TX 78763, 512-465-5059.
Personnel and Expenditures
ACTIVE DUTY PERSONNEL: 3
CIVILIAN PERSONNEL: 28

Corpus Christi

779. Corpus Christi Army Depot
CCAD
308 Crecy St
Corpus Christi, TX 78419-5260
512-939-3626; FAX 512-939-2312; DSN 861-3626
E-mail: sioccpa@corpus-chr-emh2.army.mil Internet:http://ccad-http://www.army.mil
Profile
BRANCH: Army.
SIZE AND LOCATION: 154 acres. On Corpus Christi Naval Air Station; on Corpus Christi Bay & Intercoastal Waterway, 5.5 mi from Gulf of Mexico. *County:* Nueces.
MAJOR UNITS: US Customs Service; Mine Warfare Command; Marine Corps Reserve Training; Corpus Christi Army Depot.
BASE HISTORY: 1940s-1959, NAS operated aircraft overhaul & repair facility on site. 1961, Army Aeronautical Depot Maintenance Center began operations. 1974, renamed Corpus Christi Army Depot. 1992, Defense Logistics Agency took over receipt, storage, & issue supply functions. Currently, world's largest helicopter repair & overhaul facility.
Key Contacts
COMMANDER: Col Dennis A Williamson, 512-939-3771, FAX 512-939-3039, DSN 861-3771, sioccco@corpus-chr-emh2.army. mil.
PUBLIC AFFAIRS: Ralph Yoder, 512-3627, FAX 512-939-2312, DSN 861-3627, ryoder@ corpus-chr-emh2.amry.mil.
PROCUREMENT: Claude Adams, 512-939-3913, FAX 512-939-1126, DSN 861-3913, sioccaq@corpus-chr-emh2.army. mil.
PERSONNEL/COMMUNITY ACTIVITIES: Connie Nelson, 512-939-2775, FAX 512-939-2700, DSN 861-2775, sioccp@ corpus-chr-emh2.army.mil.
Personnel and Expenditures
ACTIVE DUTY PERSONNEL: 14
DEPENDENTS: 0
CIVILIAN PERSONNEL: 3144
MILITARY PAYROLL EXPENDITURE: $162.2 mil (military & civilian)
Services
Housing: See Corpus Christi NAS. *Commissary:* Yes; *Exchange:* Retail store; Class VI. *Base Library:* Yes. *Medical Facilities:* Dispensary. *Recreational Facilities:* Lake; Fitness trail; Community club; Also see Corpus Christi NAS.

780. Corpus Christi Naval Air Station
NASCORPC
11001 D St, Suite 143
Corpus Christi, TX 78419-5021
512-939-2383; FAX 512-939-3402; DSN 861-2383
OFFICER-OF-THE-DAY: 512-939-2383, DSN 861-2383
Profile
BRANCH: Navy.
SIZE AND LOCATION: 4400 acres. 18 mi from downtown Corpus Christi. *County:* Nueces.
MAJOR UNITS: Naval Air Station, Corpus Christi; Mine Warfare Command; Corpus Christi Army Depot (CCAD); Coast Guard Air Station Corpus Christi; Marine Aviation Training Support Command (MATSG); Chief of Naval Air Training (CNATRA); Training Air Wing Four; Training Squadron 27 (VT-27); Training Squadron 28 (VT-28); Naval Reserve Center, Corpus Christi.
BASE HISTORY: Naval Auxiliary Landing Field Waldron part of NAS Corpus Christi.
VISITOR ATTRACTIONS: Public tour every Wed at 1:00 pm departing from North Gate (Ocean Dr).
Key Contacts
COMMANDER: 512-939-2332, DSN 861-2332.
PUBLIC AFFAIRS: 512-939-2674, DSN 861-2568.
Personnel and Expenditures
ACTIVE DUTY PERSONNEL: 1700
DEPENDENTS: 4800
CIVILIAN PERSONNEL: 5000
MILITARY PAYROLL EXPENDITURE: $236 mil
CONTRACT EXPENDITURE: $43.5 mil
Services
Housing: Family units 439; Unaccompanied enlisted quarters 471; BAQ units 329; Senior NCO units 8; Mobile home units 28; Trailer spaces 28; RV/Camper sites 24 RV, 8 Camp; Leased apts 100. *Temporary Housing:* Lodge units 22. *Commissary:* Yes; *Exchange:* Retail store; Barber shop; Food shop; Florist; Bank; Service station; Military clothing store; Convenience store; Beauty shop; Laundromat; Credit union; ATM; Optical store; Post office; Fast food; Thrift shop; Travel agency; Garden center; Tailor/Alterations; SATO Travel. *Child Care/Capacities:* Day care center capacity 72, 6wks-5yrs. *Schools:* Preschool/Kindergarten. *Base Library:* Yes. *Medical Facilities:* Hospital 20 beds; Dental clinic; Pharmacy; Veterinary services. *Recreational Facilities:* Bowling center; Movie theater; Pool; Gym; Recreation center; Golf course; Tennis courts; Racquetball court; Fitness center/Weight room; Softball field; Football field; Auto shop; Craft shop; Officers club; Camping; Fishing/Hunting; Enlisted club; Youth center; Picnic area; Water sports; Playground; Rod & Gun club.

781. Corpus Christi Naval Hospital
NAVHOSP Corpus Christi
10651 E St
Corpus Christi, TX 78419-5131
512-939-2688, 939-2994; FAX 512-939-5131; DSN 861-2688, 861-2994; DSN FAX 861-2975
Internet: http://192.101.131.150/
OFFICER-OF-THE-DAY: 512-939-2688, DSN 861-2688, DSN FAX 861-2975

Profile
BRANCH: Navy.
SIZE AND LOCATION: 32.2 acres. 10 mi from downtown Corpus Christi; 3 mi from I-37; 18 mi from airport; 10 mi from USS *Lexington* Museum. *County:* Nueces.
MAJOR UNITS: Naval Hospital Corpus Christi.
Key Contacts
COMMANDER: Capt Nancy J Lescavage, 512-939-2685, 939-2686, DSN 861-2685, DSN FAX 861-2975, CCH1NJL@cch10. med.navy.mil.
PUBLIC AFFAIRS: LTjg Chad E Roe, 512-939-3811, DSN 861-3811, DSN FAX 861-2975, CCH1CER@cch10.med.navy.mil.
PROCUREMENT: Lt Desmond J McMullan, 512-939-2215, DSN 861-2215, DSN FAX 861-3759, CCH1DJM@cch10.med.navy. mil.
TRANSPORTATION: Lt Donna R Kimball, 512-939-3211, DSN 861-3103, DSN FAX 861-3297, CC1DRK@cch10.med.navy.mil.
PERSONNEL/COMMUNITY ACTIVITIES: CDR Desider P Zubritzky, 512-939-2684, DSN 861-2684, DSN FAX 861-2975, CCH1DPZ@cch10.med.navy.mil.
Personnel and Expenditures
ACTIVE DUTY PERSONNEL: 295
DEPENDENTS: 124
CIVILIAN PERSONNEL: 95
MILITARY PAYROLL EXPENDITURE: $25 mil
CONTRACT EXPENDITURE: $5 mil
Services
Housing: Family units 439; Unaccompanied enlisted quarters 471; BAQ units 329; Mobile home units 28; Trailer spaces 28; RV/Camper sites RV 24; Camper 8; leased apartments 100. *Temporary Housing:* Lodge units 22. *Commissary:* Yes; *Exchange:* Retail store; Barber shop; Food shop; Florist; Bank; Service station; Military clothing store; Convenience store; Beauty shop; Laundromat; Credit union; ATM; Optical store; Post office; Fast food; Thrift shop; Travel agency; Garden center; Tailor/Alterations; SATO Travel Office. *Child Care/Capacities:* Day care center capacity 72, 6wks-5yrs; *Schools:* Preschool/Kindergarten. *Base Library:* Yes. *Medical Facilities:* Hospital 20; Dental clinic; Pharmacy; Veterinary services. *Recreational Facilities:* Bowling center; Movie theater; Pool; Gym; Recreation center; Golf course; Tennis courts; Racquetball court; Fitness center/Weight room; Softball field; Football field; Auto shop; Craft shop; Officers club; Camping; Fishing/Hunting; Enlisted club; Youth center; Picnic area; Water sports; Playground; Rod & Gun club.

782. Naval Reserve Center, Corpus Christi
1430 Dimmitt Dr, Ste 140
Corpus Christi, TX 78419-5121
512-939-2241; FAX 512-939-9507; DSN 861-2241
Profile
BRANCH: Naval Reserve.
LOCATION: *County:* Nueces.
MAJOR UNITS: Naval Reserve Center, Corpus Christi.
Key Contacts
COMMANDER: LCDR J F Carlson.

Dallas

783. Dallas Naval Air Station
NAS Dallas
818100 W Jefferson Blvd
Dallas, TX 75211-9501
214-266-6111; FAX 214-266-6207; DSN 874-6111
Profile
BRANCH: Navy; Air National Guard; Marine Corps Reserve.
SIZE AND LOCATION: 840 acres. 13 mi W of Dallas, in Grand Prairie; I-30 W, Loop 12 Exit, Loop 12 S to Jefferson Ave/Blvd W Exit off Loop 12 S, NAS on left clearly marked. *County:* Dallas; Tarrant.
MAJOR UNITS: Naval Air Station, Dallas; 14th Marines; 136th Tactical Wing (TX ANG); Commander, Naval Reserve Center (Dallas); Commander, Naval Reserve Readiness Command, Region 11 (REDCOM 11); Reserve Intelligence Programs Office Six (RIPO Six); Naval Mobile Construction Bn (NMCB 22); Army National Guard, Dallas.
BASE HISTORY: 1941, commissioned to provide training of aircrews & aviation ground support personnel; test site for aircraft manufactured at adjacent North American aviation plant; training facility for Army Air Corps during WWII. Following WWII, assigned to Naval Air Reserve. AF converted Hemsley Field to TX ANG. NAS under operational & administrative command of Commander Naval Air Reserve Force, New Orleans, LA; 1 of 15 major aviation reserve activities located throughout US.
FUTURE CLOSURE/REALIGNMENT: Scheduled for closure Sep 1998. 14th Marines & 136th Tactical Airlift Wing (Texas ANG) scheduled to move by Sep 1998.

784. Dallas NAS, Air National Guard Base
818100 W Jefferson Blvd
Dallas, TX 75211
214-269-3206
Profile
BRANCH: Air National Guard.
SIZE AND LOCATION: 49 acres. On Dallas Naval Air Station. *County:* Dallas.
MAJOR UNITS: 136th Tactical Airlift Wing (ANG).
FUTURE CLOSURE/REALIGNMENT: Scheduled to move to Naval Air Station Joint Reserve Base Fort Worth by Sep 1998.

785. Hensley Field Texas Air National Guard Base
8150 W Jefferson Blvd
Dallas, TX 75211-9570
972-269-3202; FAX 972-269-3330; DSN 874-3202
E-mail: RWILSON@txnbe.ang.af.mil
Profile
BRANCH: Air National Guard.
SIZE AND LOCATION: 49 acres. Bordering Dallas Naval Air Station in Grand Prairie, TX; 15 mi SW of Dallas-Forth Worth IAP. *County:* Dallas.
MAJOR UNITS: 136th Airlift Wing (AMC); 136th Mission Support Squadron; 531st Air Force Band; 136th Maintenance Squadron; 136th Mobile Aerial Port Squadron; 136th

Communications Squadron; 136th Civil Engineering Squadron; 181st Weather Flight; 136th Security Police Squadron; 136th Aircraft Generation Squadron; 136th Medical Support Squadron.
BASE HISTORY: 1960, moved in from Love Field, Dallas. 1965, Wing reorganized under TAC. 1976, transferred to Strategic Air Command; received Distinguished Flying Unit Award. 1978, redesignated 136th Tactical Airlift Wing, Military Airlift Command. 1983, ANG Unit of the Year. 1989, participated in Operation Just Cause, Panama. 1990, 136th MAPS called to active duty for Operation Desert Shield/Storm. 1992, redesignated 136th Airlift Wing, Air Mobility Command.
FUTURE CLOSURE/REALIGNMENT: 136th Airlift Wing to relocate to Fort Worth Joint Reserve Base at NAS Fort Worth, 1998.
Key Contacts
COMMANDER: Col Rowland R. Wilson, 972-269-3200, FAX 972-269-3330, DSN 874-3200, RWilson@txnbe.ang.af.mil.
PUBLIC AFFAIRS: Maj Celso Martinez, 972-930-8210, FAX 972-930-8245, CMartinez@txnbe.ang.af.mil.
PERSONNEL/COMMUNITY ACTIVITIES: Capt Amy Fisher, 972-269-3231, FAX 972-269-3330, DSN 874-3231, AAsher@ txnbe.ang.af.mil.
Personnel and Expenditures
ACTIVE DUTY PERSONNEL: 60

786. Navy Office of Information, Southwest
1114 Commerce St, Ste 811
Dallas, TX 75242
214-767-2553; FAX 214-767-4792
Profile
BRANCH: Navy.
MAJOR UNITS: Navy Office of Information, Southwest.
BASE HISTORY: Serves AR, CO, KS, LA, MO, NM, OK, TX, & WY.

787. Region Eleven, Naval Reserve Readiness Command
REDCOM 11
8100 W Jefferson Blvd, NAS Bldg 11
Dallas, TX 75211-9502
972-266-6530, 266-6807; DSN 874-6530
Internet: http://www.navy.mil/homepages/ navresfor/redcom11.html
Profile
BRANCH: Naval Reserve.
MAJOR UNITS: Naval Reserve Readiness Command, Region 11.
BASE HISTORY: Overseas, 6000 Reservists. Scheduled to move to NAS Fort Worth, Joint Reserve Base, 1998.
Key Contacts
COMMANDER: Capt U L Nolen.

788. US Army Corps of Engineers, Southwestern District
CESWD
1114 Commerce St, Santa Fe Bldg, Rm 404
Dallas, TX 75242-0216
214-767-2502; FAX 214-767-6499
Internet: http://www.swt.usace.army.mil/
Profile
BRANCH: Army.
SIZE AND LOCATION: Offices only.

In downtown Dallas. *County:* Dallas.

MAJOR UNITS: Corps of Engineers, Southwestern District.

BASE HISTORY: 1937, established to oversee projects on Arkansas, White, Black, North & South Canadian Rivers in Southwest; initially included Conchas (later Caddoa) District & Little Rock District. Began functioning in Little Rock, AR. 1941, Galveston District transferred to Southwestern, adding most of TX, parts of LA, CO, & NM. WWII, turned to military construction. 1941, moved to Dallas. 1950-55, special study of Arkansas, White, & Red River basins, known as AWRBIAC. 1958, full-scale survey of water in TX. 1980s, reviewing & approving designs, plans, & specifications for hydroelectric plants at its water projects. Work on traditional dam & reservoir projects is drawing to close. Five district offices: Galveston & Fort Worth, TX; Little Rock, AR; Tulsa, OK; & Albuquerque, NM; geotechnical laboratory in Dallas. Performs military & civil works construction.

Key Contacts

COMMANDER: Brig Gen Henry S Miller Jr, 214-767-2502.

PUBLIC AFFAIRS: Lu Christie, Chief, 214-767-2510, LU.CHRISTIE@SWD01. USACE.ARMY.MIL.

PROCUREMENT: John Brigance, Director of Contracting, 214-767-2476.

PERSONNEL/COMMUNITY ACTIVITIES: Jerry Sosebee, Director, 817-978-2200.

Personnel and Expenditures

CIVILIAN PERSONNEL: 4100

El Paso

789. El Paso Naval & Marine Corps Reserve Readiness Center

NMCRC El Paso

4810 Pollard St
El Paso, TX 79930-6898
915-565-3993, 566-8698; FAX 915-562-1526; DSN 978-6950

Profile

BRANCH: Naval Reserve; Marine Corps Reserve.

LOCATION: *County:* El Paso.

MAJOR UNITS: REDCOM ELEVEN Activity; Battery N, 5th Bn, 14th Marine Regiment.

Key Contacts

COMMANDER: LCDR C M Saylor.

790. Fort Bliss

USADACEN & Ft Bliss

HQ, USADACEN & Ft Bliss, Bldg 2
El Paso, TX 79916-5000
915-568-2121; FAX 915-568-2995; DSN 978-2121

OFFICER-OF-THE-DAY: Staff Duty Officer

Profile

BRANCH: Army.

SIZE AND LOCATION: 1,119,722 acres. Borders on El Paso City, along US-54; 2 mi W of El Paso IAP off I-10 on Patriot Freeway on US-54. *County:* El Paso.

MAJOR UNITS: Army Sergeants Major Academy; 11th Air Defense Artillery Brigade; 70th Ordnance Bn; 3rd Armored Cavalry Regiment; 6th Air Defense Artillery Brigade; 7th Ranger Bn; Air Defense Artillery School;

William Beaumont Army Medical Clinic; 1st Combined Arms Support Bn; German Air Force Training Command; 35th Air Defense Artillery Brigade; 204th Military Intelligence Bn.

BASE HISTORY: 1849, troops establish post in what is now downtown El Paso. 1853, Military Post of El Paso established. 1854, renamed Ft Bliss in honor of William Wallace Smith Bliss, veteran of Florida Indian War & Mexican War & Adj Gen of Western Division. 1868, the Rio Grande forced relocation of Fort, renamed Camp Concordia. 1877, Ft Bliss abandoned. 1879, new post established. 1890, railroad construction forced a move to current location; began training infantry then moved to cavalry units until 1940s. Post WWI, original Briggs Field constructed (later Briggs AFB). 1940, Antiaircraft Training Center established. 1943, cavalry units ended; Women's Auxiliary Army Corps (WACS) arrived. 1945, first Antiaircraft & Guided Missile Battalion activated. 1990, every unit at Ft Bliss deployed personnel to Operations Desert Shield/Storm, including Patriot missile system.

VISITOR ATTRACTIONS: Air Defense Artillery Museum; 3rd Armored Cavalry Regiment Museum; Army Museum of the Noncommissioned Officer; Fort Bliss Museum; Bliss Monument; Memorial Circle; Japanese Gardens; Pershing House; Building 2 HQ; Bradley Tree; Replica Museum.

Key Contacts

COMMANDER: Maj Gen John H Little; Post Commander, ATTN: ATZC-CG, 915-568-3898, 568-3401, DSN 978-3898, 978-3401.

PUBLIC AFFAIRS: Jean Offutt; ATTN: ATZC-CGP-CI, Bldg 15, 915-568-4505, 568-4601, DSN 978-4505, 978-4601.

PROCUREMENT: Pat Gill; ATTN: ATZC-DOC Bldg 2021, 915-568-5150, DSN 978-5150.

TRANSPORTATION: Mr Stewart; ATTN: ATZC-ISL-T, Bldg 504A, 915-568-3433, DSN 978-3433.

PERSONNEL/COMMUNITY ACTIVITIES: A A Cole Jr; ATTN: ATZC-CA, 915-568-3500, DSN 978-3500.

Personnel and Expenditures

ACTIVE DUTY PERSONNEL: 11,642
DEPENDENTS: 8476
CIVILIAN PERSONNEL: 7469
MILITARY PAYROLL EXPENDITURE: $402.5 mil
CONTRACT EXPENDITURE: $63.5 mil

Services

Housing: Family units 3640; Unaccompanied officer quarters 32; Unaccompanied enlisted quarters 240; BAQ units; Barracks spaces; Senior NCO units; Junior NCO units; RV/Camper sites 73; Housing referral office: 915-568-2898. *Temporary Housing:* VIP units 4; VOQ units 634; VEQ units 384; Unaccompanied officer/Enlisted quarters 116; Guesthouse units 154; Guest cottages 32; Transient quarters; Ft Bliss Inn 103 rooms. *Commissary:* Yes; *Exchange:* Retail store; Barber shop; Dry cleaners; Food shop; Florist; Bank; Service station; Furniture store; Bakery; Bookstore; Military clothing store; Convenience store; Beauty shop; Laundromat; Credit union; ATM; Post office; Fast food; Video rentals; Four seasons; Thrift shop; Travel agency; Class VI; Shoe repair; Computer store;

Garden center; Tailor/Alterations; Laundry; Cafeteria; Photo store; *Child Care/Capacities:* Day care center 5yrs-12yrs; Home day care program; Summer day camp; Before & after school programs. *Schools:* Preschool/Kindergarten; Elementary; Intermediate/Junior high. *Base Library:* Yes. *Medical Facilities:* Hospital 200; Medical clinic; Dental clinic; Dispensary; Pharmacy; Veterinary services. *Recreational Facilities:* Bowling center; Movie theater; Pool; Gym; Recreation center; Golf course; Stables; Tennis courts; Racquetball court; Skating rink; Fitness center/Weight room; Softball field; Football field; Auto shop; Craft shop; Officers club; NCO club; Camping; Fishing/Hunting; Enlisted club; Youth center; Picnic area; Skeet range; Water sports; Playground.

Eldorado

791. Eldorado Air Force Station

EAFS

8th Space Warning Squadron, PO Drawer X
Eldorado, TX 76936-5000
915-654-4273; FAX 915-654-4287; DSN 477-4273

Profile

BRANCH: Air Force.

SIZE AND LOCATION: 120 acres. Host support from Goodfellow AFB, including housing; 35 mi S of San Angelo on Hwy 277; 250 mi SW of Dallas. *County:* Tom Green.

MAJOR UNITS: 8th Space Warning Squadron.

BASE HISTORY: 1986, activated as 8th Missile Warning Squadron. 1992, redesignated 8th Space Warning Squadron. Primary mission to provide warning and attack assessment of sea-launched ballistic missiles or intercontinental missiles through the Phased Array Warning System.

VISITOR ATTRACTIONS: Priority "A" resource; site is restricted area. No individual tours.

Key Contacts

COMMANDER: LTC Timothy J Kelly.

PUBLIC AFFAIRS: MSgt Steve E Heil; 915-654-4248, DSN 477-4248.

PROCUREMENT: Maj Frank E Levesque; 915-654-4263, DSN 477-4263.

TRANSPORTATION: Capt Mark Kramer; 915-654-4288, DSN 477-4288.

Personnel and Expenditures

ACTIVE DUTY PERSONNEL: 100

Services

Housing: See Goodfellow AFB, TX. *Recreational Facilities:* Gym.

Fort Hood

792. Fort Hood

Fort Hood, TX 76544
254-287-1110; DSN 737-2131
Internet: http://www.hood-pao.army.mil/

Profile

BRANCH: Army.

SIZE AND LOCATION: 217,337 acres. In hill and lake country of central TX, approx 60 mi NE of Austin; 50 mi SW of Waco; adj to Killeen, TX on Rte 190. *County:* Coryell; Bell.

MAJOR UNITS: 1st Cavalry Division; 4th Infantry Division (Mechanized); III Corps, HQ Command; 3rd Personnel Group; 3rd Signal Brigade; 3rd Air Support Operations Group (USAF); 13th Corps Support Command (COSCOM); 13th Finance Brigade; 21st Cavalry Brigade (Air Combat); 89th Military Police; 504th Military Intelligence Brigade; Test and Experimentation Command (TEXCOM).

BASE HISTORY: 1942, South Camp Hood constructed; North Camp Hood, 17 miles N, established shortly after founding of cantonment area; named for Confederate Gen John Bell Hood, Civil War commander of Hood's Texas Brigade. 1951, South Camp Hood designated Ft Hood, permanent installation. North Camp Hood became North Ft Hood; training facilities used for summer training of Army Reserve NG units. 1947, West Fort Hood, originally Killeen Base, constructed. 1952, AF facility established. 1952-69, variously named Killeen Base & Robert Gray AFB, named after Capt Robert M Gray, WWII Army Air Corps pilot from Killeen, TX; under Defense Atomic Support Agency, manned by Army, Navy, & Air Force personnel. 1969, Robert Gray Army Air Field became part of Ft Hood with Hood Army Airfield (HAAF), fully instrumented airfield (3,000 acres) capable of handling largest aircraft & FAA-approved helicopter instrument airfield (773 acres), exclusively for rotary wing aircraft. Both restricted areas for security reasons. 2 paved, non-instrumented airstrips used for training at North Ft Hood: Longhorn & Shorthorn Strips summer training sites for NG & Reserve aviation units. Only post capable of stationing & training two armored divisions.

VISITOR ATTRACTIONS: 2nd Armored Division Museum; 1st Cavalry Museum (both open 9am-3:30pm M-F, Noon-3:30pm Sat, Sun, holidays; closed Christmas, New Year's, Thanksgiving, & Easter).

Key Contacts
COMMANDER: Lt Gen Thomas A Schwartz, III Corps.
PUBLIC AFFAIRS: III Corps.

Personnel and Expenditures
ACTIVE DUTY PERSONNEL: 43,995
DEPENDENTS: 60,918
CIVILIAN PERSONNEL: 8909

Services
Housing: Family units 5558; Unaccompanied officer quarters 278; Unaccompanied enlisted quarters 24,000; Junior NCO units 500; RV/Camper sites 64. *Temporary Housing:* VIP units 10; VOQ units 410; VEQ units 32; BAQ units; Guesthouse units 123; General officer guesthouse 1; Junior enlisted guest quarters rooms 48; Campground cottages 10. *Commissary:* Yes; *Exchange.* Retail store; Barber shop; Dry cleaners; Food shop; Service station; Military clothing store; Convenience store; Four seasons; Fast food; Video rentals; Class VI; Shoe repair; Computer store; Garden center; Laundry; Ice cream; Snacks; Car rental. *Child Care/Capacities:* Day care center capacity 785; Home day care program. *Schools:* Preschool/Kindergarten; Elementary; Intermediate/Junior high. *Base Library:* Yes. *Medical Facilities:* Hospital 264 beds; Medical clinic; Dental clinic; Veterinary services. *Recreational Facilities:* Bowling center; Movie theater; Pool; Gym; Recreation center; Golf course; Tennis courts; Racquetball court;

Skating rink; Fitness center/Weight room; Softball field; Football field; Auto shop; Craft shop; Officers club; NCO club; Camping; Fishing/Hunting; Youth center; Picnic area; Rod & Gun club; Golf driving range; Equipment checkout center; Marina; Field house; Belton Lake Outdoor Recreation Area (BLORA) camper spaces.

Fort Sam Houston

793. Camp Bullis Training Site
Cp Bullis
Bldg 5000
Fort Sam Houston, TX 78234-5000
210-221-1211
Profile
BRANCH: Army.
SIZE AND LOCATION: 28,000 acres. Approx 17 mi NW of Ft Sam Houston, in Texas Hill Country; accessible from I-10, Military Hwy, and Blanco Rd. *County:* Bexar.
MAJOR UNITS: Camp Bullis Training Site.
BASE HISTORY: Training facility for all services & many federal agencies; sub-installation of Ft Sam Houston. Divided into 20 separate training areas; supports 23 firing ranges.
Key Contacts
COMMANDER: LTC Kenneth Wade, 210-221-7611.
PUBLIC AFFAIRS: Philip Rudinger, 210-221-1151.
PROCUREMENT: Lawrence Roberts, 210-221-5930.
Personnel and Expenditures
CIVILIAN PERSONNEL: 37
Services
Housing: Family units 4. *Exchange:* Class C retail store. *Medical Facilities:* Medical clinic.

794. Fort Sam Houston
FSH, TX
Fort Sam Houston, TX 78234-5000
210-221-1211; DSN 471-1110
Internet: http://www.samhou-usag.army.mil/
OFFICER-OF-THE-DAY: 210-221-3810, 221-3105, DSN 471-3810, 471-3105
Profile
BRANCH: Army.
SIZE AND LOCATION: 3000 acres. Adj to downtown San Antonio; City bus lines cross post in all directions. No gates or checkpoints on major thoroughfares. Airport approx 10 min away; Immediate access from IH-37 at N Braufels Ave. *County:* Bexar.
MAJOR UNITS: Army Medical Command; Army Medical Department Center & School; 5th Army, HQ; Health Services Command; Academy of Health Sciences; 5th Recruiting Brigade; Brooke Army Medical Center; Camp Bullis; Army Garrison, Ft Sam Houston; Army Audit Agency, SW Region; ISR Institute of Surgical Research; Army TMDE Activity 4055; 1110th Signal Bn; 137th Ordnance Det; 41st Combat Support Hospital; 596th Ordnance Det; 902nd Military Intelligence Det; Navy Det, Ft Sam Houston.
BASE HISTORY: Garrison can loosely trace origins back to first troops in San Antonio, 1870; troops housed in rented buildings around Alamo & Arsenal areas of downtown; HQ located where Gunter Hotel now stands at Houston & St Marys streets; most cavalry sent to

protect settlers & wagon trains. Mission of Ft Sam Houston passed from supplying frontier outposts as Quartermaster Depot to providing medical training.
VISITOR ATTRACTIONS: Post Museum; Medical Museum; Quadrangle; Quadrangle Gift Shoppe; Post on Grayline tour.
Key Contacts
COMMANDER: Col J Michael Hardesty, Garrison Commander, ATTN: AFZG-CO, 210-221-0905, FAX 210-221-1744, DSN 471-0905, Col_J_Michael_Hardesty@ smtplink.medcom.amedd.arm y.mil.
PUBLIC AFFAIRS: 210-221-0015.
Personnel and Expenditures
ACTIVE DUTY PERSONNEL: 12,700
DEPENDENTS: 2500
CIVILIAN PERSONNEL: 5800
Services
Housing: Family units 1169; Barracks spaces 7546. *Temporary Housing:* Unaccompanied officer/Enlisted quarters 506; Guesthouse units 28. *Commissary:* Yes; *Exchange:* Retail store; Barber shop; Dry cleaners; Food shop; Florist; Bank; Service station; Furniture store. *Child Care/Capacities:* Day care center capacity 250; Home day care program. *Schools:* Preschool/Kindergarten; Elementary; Intermediate/Junior high; High school. *Base Library:* Yes. *Medical Facilities:* Hospital 470 beds; Medical clinic; Dental clinic; Veterinary services; USAF Medical Ctr also available, 20 min away at Lackland AFB. *Recreational Facilities:* Bowling center; Movie theater; Pool; Gym; Recreation center; Golf course; Stables; Tennis courts; Racquetball court; Softball field; Football field; Auto shop; Craft shop; Officers club; NCO club; Canyon Lake Travel Camp/Recreation Area with camping and fishing, 50 mi NW.

Fort Worth

795. Defense Plant Representative Office, Air Force Plant No 4
DPRO/GD
PO Box 371, General Dynamics Fort Worth Division
Fort Worth, TX 76101-0371
817-763-4422; FAX 817-737-7814; DSN 838-5422
Profile
BRANCH: Defense Logistics Agency.
SIZE AND LOCATION: 300 acres. Adj to Carswell AFB, 10 mi from downtown Fort Worth. *County:* Tarrant.
MAJOR UNITS: Defense Plant Representative; Air Force Institute of Technology-Education with Industry; Air Force Office of Special Investigations, Det 1058; Air Force Systems Command/Central Technical Order Control Unit; 6510th CRS (OL-AA/JTF); Air Force Systems Command/Joint Test Force; Defense Contract Audit Agency; Tactical Air Command Logistics Liaison Office; Air Force Electronic Warfare Evaluation Simulator; Resident Integrated Logistics Support Activity.
BASE HISTORY: 1941, construction began on Air Force Plant No 4, one of largest aircraft plants in world. WWII, 3034 B-24s assembled here. Subsequent production resulted in more than 7166 aircraft deliveries.

Key Contacts

COMMANDER: Richard See; Commander.
PUBLIC AFFAIRS: DCMDS-DX, 805 Walker St, Marietta, GA 30060-2789, 404-590-2904, DSN 697-2904.

796. Fort Worth, Naval Air Station, Joint Reserve Base

NAS JRB Fort Worth
1510 Chennault Ave
Fort Worth, TX 76127-6200
817-782-5000; FAX 817-782-7722; DSN 739-8000; DSN FAX 739-7722
E-mail: naspao@flash.net Internet:http://www.afres.af.mil/units/301fw/base\nas_jrb/htm

Profile

BRANCH: Joint Service Installation.
SIZE AND LOCATION: 1803 acres. 8 mi NW of downtown Fort Worth; 35 mi E of Dallas; 25 mi E of Dallas-Fort Worth IAP. *County:* Tarrant.
MAJOR UNITS: 10th Air Force (AFRES); 301st Fighter Wing (AFRES); Marine Aircraft Group 41 (MAG 41); Marine Fighter Attack Squadron 112 (VMFA 112); Marine Aerial Refueller Transport Squadron (VMGR 234); Marine Aviation Logistics Squadron (MALS 41); Fighter Squadron 201 (VF 201); Commander, Fleet Logistics Support Wing; Fleet Logistics Support Squadron 59 (VR 59); 14th Marines; 136th Tactical Airlift Wing (TX ANG); Commander, Naval Reserve Intelligence Command; 9th Naval Construction Regiment.
BASE HISTORY: On the site of former Carswell AFB. 1941, known as Tarrant Field Airdrome serving Consolidated Vultee Aircraft Corp. 1942, Fort Worth Army Air Field; variety of aircraft produced at Air Force Plant 4. 1948, renamed Carswell AFB to honor Maj Horace Seaver Carswell Jr, Medal of Honor recipient. Early Strategic Air Command base as 7th Bomb Wing. 1991-92, AF reorganization & consolidation; SAC disestablished. 1993, made Air Reserve base with 301st Fighter Wing. 1994, established as first joint reserve base; Navy made host unit; relocation in stages.

Key Contacts

COMMANDER: Capt Dale A Lewelling, USNR, 817-782-7600, FAX 817-782-7722, DSN 739-7600.
PUBLIC AFFAIRS: JOC Dave Marr, 817-782-7815, FAX 817-782-7722, DSN 739-7815, naspao@flash.net.

Personnel and Expenditures

ACTIVE DUTY PERSONNEL: 2500; Reserve 6000
CIVILIAN PERSONNEL: 1100
Services *Base Library:* Yes. *Recreational Facilities:* Bowling center; Pool; Gym; Golf course; Tennis courts; Racquetball court; Fitness center/Weight room; Softball field; Football field; Auto shop; Picnic area; Consolidated club; Marina.

797. US Army Corps of Engineers, Fort Worth District

819 Taylor St
Fort Worth, TX 76102-0300
Mailing Address
PO Box 17300
Fort Worth, TX 76102-0300

Internet: http://www.swf.usace.army.mil/
Profile
BRANCH: Army.
LOCATION: In Federal Bldg downtown. *County:* Tarrant.
MAJOR UNITS: Corps of Engineers, Fort Worth District.
BASE HISTORY: 1950, district established. Responsible for water resources development in two-thirds of TX; military design & construction in TX and parts of LA and NM; total 410,000 sq mi.

Key Contacts

COMMANDER: Col Peter T Madsen.
PUBLIC AFFAIRS: Ronald Ruffennach, 817-978-3395.

Personnel and Expenditures

CIVILIAN PERSONNEL: 1150

Galveston

798. Galveston Coast Guard Base

PO Box 1912
Galveston, TX 77553-1912
409-766-5633, 766-5696
OFFICER-OF-THE-DAY: 409-766-5641
Profile
BRANCH: Coast Guard.
SIZE AND LOCATION: 100 acres. Eastern end of Galveston Island next to Galveston-Boliver Ferry Terminal; 50 mi from Houston via I-45S. *County:* Galveston.
MAJOR UNITS: Coast Guard Group, Galveston; Coast Guard Station, Galveston; USCGC *Clamp*; USCGC *Dauntless*; USCGC *Papaw*; USCGC *Point Spencer*; USCGC *Hatchet*; Aids to Navigation (ANT) Team, Galveston; Electronic Support Det, Galveston.
BASE HISTORY: 1938, established at current location, Ft Point. Controls units operating from Marsh Island, LA, to Matagorda, TX; primary missions include search & rescue, aids to navigation & maritime law enforcement; group provides operational guidance, administrative support, materiel & technical support for 10 sub-units, including Coast Guard cutters, Aids to Navigation Team at Sabine & Coast Guard stations at Freeport and Sabine.

Key Contacts

COMMANDER: 409-766-5601.
PUBLIC AFFAIRS: 409-766-5603.
PROCUREMENT: 409-766-5610.
PERSONNEL/COMMUNITY ACTIVITIES: 409-766-5604.

Personnel and Expenditures

ACTIVE DUTY PERSONNEL: 130
CIVILIAN PERSONNEL: 20
Services *Temporary Housing:* Transient quarters 10. *Exchange:* Retail store; Military clothing store. *Medical Facilities:* Dental clinic. *Recreational Facilities:* Tennis courts; Fitness center/Weight room; Enlisted club.

799. US Army Corps of Engineers, Galveston District

CESWG
2000 Fort Point Rd, Jadwin Bldg
Galveston, TX 77550
Mailing Address
PO Box 1229

Galveston, TX 77553-1229
409-766-3001; FAX 409-766-3951
Internet: http://www.usace.army.mil/swg/
Profile
BRANCH: Army.
SIZE AND LOCATION: 53 acres. On Galveston Island next to ferry landing; approx 75 mi S of Houston. *County:* Galveston.
MAJOR UNITS: Corps of Engineers, Galveston District.
BASE HISTORY: 1880, District founded. Today, oversees flood control, navigation, and civil works projects along Texas coast from Brownsville to the Louisiana River and inland some 100 mi, covering 50,000 sq mi. Performs civil works construction & military real estate.
VISITOR ATTRACTIONS: Exhibits & history of Galveston District on walls of Jadwin Bldg. Overlooks Galveston/Houston Ship Channels.

Key Contacts

COMMANDER: Col Eric R Potts, 409-766-3001.
PUBLIC AFFAIRS: Kenneth B Bonham, 409-766-3004.
PROCUREMENT: Tom Benero, 409-766-3850.
TRANSPORTATION: Larry Duneway, 409-766-3839.

Personnel and Expenditures

ACTIVE DUTY PERSONNEL: 4
CIVILIAN PERSONNEL: 400
CONTRACT EXPENDITURE: $65.1 mil
Services
Housing: None.

Garland

800. Garland Air National Guard Station

Garland ANG Station
PO Box 461635
Garland, TX 75046-1635
214-494-7221; DSN 874-7221
Profile
BRANCH: Air National Guard.
SIZE AND LOCATION: 2 acres. Center of Garland, TX, in NE Dallas County. *County:* Dallas.
MAJOR UNITS: 254th Combat Communications Group, HQ; 221st Combat Communications Squadron.
BASE HISTORY: 1952, 254th Combat Communications Group evolved from small squadron organized as 221st Radio Relay Squadron. 1968, redesignated 221st Mobile Communications Squadron. Following reassignments, designated 254th Combat Communications Group. First Guard unit to lead combat communications unit in Joint Chiefs of Staff-directed joint exercise.
VISITOR ATTRACTIONS: Hall of Flags; Hall of Honor.

Key Contacts

COMMANDER: LTC Paul W Richards, 221st CCS, 214-494-7221, DSN 874-7221; Col Allen R Dehnert, 254th CCG, 972-494-7254, DSN 874-7254.

Personnel and Expenditures

ACTIVE DUTY PERSONNEL: 5
CIVILIAN PERSONNEL: 2

Services *Recreational Facilities:* Fitness center/ Weight room.

Goodfellow AFB

801. Goodfellow Air Force Base
GAFB
184 Ft Lancaster Ave, Ste J
Goodfellow AFB, TX 76908-4410
Mailing Address
17 TRW/PA, 184 Ft Lancaster Ave, Ste J
Goodfellow AFB, TX 76908-4410
915-654-3876; 915-654-5414; DSN 477-3876;
DSN FAX 477-5414
E-mail: webmaster@comlan.gdf.aetc.af.mil Internet:http://www.gdf.aetc.af.mil
Profile
BRANCH: Air Force.
SIZE AND LOCATION: 1119 acres. Just E of San Angelo, TX on US-87. *County:* Tom Green.
MAJOR UNITS: 17th Training Wing; 17th Support Group; 17th Training Group; 17th Medical Group; 344th Military Intelligence Bn; Naval Technical Training Center Det; Marine Corps Det; Goodfellow NCO Academy.
BASE HISTORY: 1941, established & named after Lt John J Goodfellow Jr, native of San Angelo killed in plane crash in WWI. For most of its history served as pilot training site, except 1958-78, when used by Security Service (later Electronic Security Command).
Key Contacts
COMMANDER: Col Kelvin R Coppock, 915-654-5402, DSN 477-5402, DSN FAX 477-5414.
PUBLIC AFFAIRS: Maj (Select) R Nicholas Carter, 915-654-3877, DSN 477-3877, DSN FAX 477-5414.
Personnel and Expenditures
ACTIVE DUTY PERSONNEL: 1700; 1900 students
DEPENDENTS: 2900
CIVILIAN PERSONNEL: 620
Services
Housing: Family units 99; BAQ units 520; BOQ/ VOQ units 36. *Temporary Housing:* VIP units 4; VOQ units 36; VAQ units 618; Transient quarters 12; TDY reservations only. *Commissary:* Yes; *Exchange:* Barber shop; Food shop; Service station; Convenience store; Beauty shop; Optical store; Toys. *Child Care/Capacities:* Day care center capacity 69; Home day care program. *Schools:* No on-base schools. *Medical Facilities:* Medical clinic; Veterinary services. *Recreational Facilities:* Bowling center; Movie theater; Pool; Gym; Recreation center; Golf course; Stables; Tennis courts; Racquetball court; Fitness center/Weight room; Auto shop; Craft shop; Fishing/Hunting; Youth center (activities); Skeet range; Consolidated club; Aero club; Lake Nasworth recreation camp, 10 mi SW.

Harlingen

802. Harlingen Naval Reserve Center
1300 Teege Ave
Harlingen, TX 78550-5363
210-425-0404; FAX 425-3104
Profile
BRANCH: Naval Reserve.
LOCATION: *County:* Cameron.
MAJOR UNITS: REDCOM ELEVEN Activity.
Key Contacts
COMMANDER: LCDR L Hill Jr.

Houston

803. Ellington Field, Air National Guard Base
14657 Sneider St
Houston, TX 77034-5586
713-929-2110; DSN 954-2110
Profile
BRANCH: Air National Guard.
SIZE AND LOCATION: 214 acres. 17 mi SE of Houston; I-45 from Houston to Ellington Field Exit, field 1 mi E. *County:* Harris.
MAJOR UNITS: 147th Fighter Wing (ANG); Coast Guard Air Station, Houston; NASA Flight Operations.
BASE HISTORY: 1923-27, 111th Aero Squadron at Ellington Field; named for Lt Eric L Ellington, pilot killed in 1913. 1945, redesignated 111th Fighter Squadron, returned to Ellington following WWII duty. 1950-52, called to active duty as 136th Fighter Group, Langley AFB, VA. First ANG Wing mobilized since WWII, into combat as intact unit, & to down a MIG-15. 1952, returned to Hobby Field, TX. 1956, redesignated 111th Fighter Interceptor Squadron returned to Ellington AFB. 1957-61, operated ANG Jet Instrument School. 1958, 147th FIG formed to support the 111th FIS. 1970-76, served as training center for all ANG interceptors. 1976, 147th FIG took control of Ellington AFB for transition to State of TX. 1984, Ellington Field taken over by City of Houston. 1988, 147th FIG assigned to 144th Fighter Interceptor Wing, 1st Air Force, Fresno, CA. 1992, redesignated 147th Fighter Group & 111th Fighter Squadron.
VISITOR ATTRACTIONS: Johnson Space Flight Center; Astro World theme park; Astrodome.
Personnel and Expenditures
ACTIVE DUTY PERSONNEL: 1013 Guard
CIVILIAN PERSONNEL: 349
MILITARY PAYROLL EXPENDITURE: $30.1 mil
Services *Recreational Facilities:* NCO club; SATO; Adjacent to public golf course and driving range.

804. Houston Coast Guard Air Station
1178 Ellington Field
Houston, TX 77034-5569
281-481-0025; FAX 281-481-9628; DSN 954-2100
Profile
BRANCH: Coast Guard; Joint Service Installation.
LOCATION: 17 mi SE of Houston; I-45 from Houston to Ellington Field Exit, E for 2.5 mi to field. *County:* Harris.
MAJOR UNITS: Coast Guard Air Station, Houston; Texas Air National Guard; Army Air Guard; NASA.

VISITOR ATTRACTIONS: Johnson Space Flight Center, Astro World theme park, and Astrodome nearby.
Key Contacts
COMMANDER: CDR A Halvorson.
PUBLIC AFFAIRS: Lt K O'Dell.
Services *Exchange:* Retail store. *Medical Facilities:* Pharmacy. *Recreational Facilities:* NCO club; SATO; Adjacent to public golf course and driving range.

805. Houston Naval & Marine Corps Reserve Readiness Center
1902 Old Spanish Trail
Houston, TX 77054-2097
713-795-5201, 796-1261; FAX 713-795-5733
Profile
BRANCH: Naval Reserve; Marine Corps Reserve.
LOCATION: *County:* Harris.
MAJOR UNITS: REDCOM ELEVEN Activity; HQ, 1st Bn, 23rd Marine Regiment; HQ & Service Co, 1st Bn, 23rd Marine Regiment; Co A, 1st Bn, 23rd Marine Regiment; HQ Det 6 (Rein), 4th Marine Division.
Key Contacts
COMMANDER: Capt B J Dean.

Ingleside

806. Ingleside Naval Station
NAVSTA Ingleside
Mine Warfare Center of Excellence
1455 Ticonderoga, Ste W210
Ingleside, TX 78362-5001
512-776-4200; FAX 512-776-4203; DSN 776-4200; DSN FAX 776-4203
Profile
BRANCH: Navy.
SIZE AND LOCATION: 483 acres. Off FM 1069; approx 20 mi from downtown Corpus Christi. *County:* San Patricio.
MAJOR UNITS: Naval Station, Ingleside; Shore Intermediate Maintenance Facility; Mine Warfare Training Center; Mine Countermeasures Squadron 1; Mine Countermeasures Squadron 2; Personnel Support Det; Regional Support Group, Ingleside; USO of South Texas; Avenger Class Mine Countermeasures Ships (12); Osprey Class Coastal Mine Hunters (9); *USS Inchon* (MCS-12).
VISITOR ATTRACTIONS: Public tours every Tue (1:30pm, no charge).
Key Contacts
COMMANDER: Capt Donald E Peters, 512-776-4712, FAX 512-776-4203, DSN 776-4712.
PUBLIC AFFAIRS: Lt Ingrid Mueller, 512-776-4206, FAX 512-776-4651, DSN 776-4206.
PROCUREMENT: Cheri Burnett, 512-776-4501, FAX 512-776-5590, DSN 776-4501.
Personnel and Expenditures
ACTIVE DUTY PERSONNEL: 3309
DEPENDENTS: 0
CIVILIAN PERSONNEL: 194
MILITARY PAYROLL EXPENDITURE: $61 mil
CONTRACT EXPENDITURE: $14.7 mil
Services
Housing: Unaccompanied enlisted quarters 260.
Temporary Housing: None.

Exchange: Retail store; Barber shop; Military clothing store; ATM; Post office; Video rentals; Thrift shop; Family service center; Galley. *Child Care/Capacities:* No day care facilities. *Schools:* College courses. *Medical Facilities:* Medical clinic; Dental clinic; Pharmacy. *Recreational Facilities:* Pool; Gym; Tennis courts; Racquetball court; Fitness center/Weight room; Softball field; Football field; Auto shop; USO.

Kelly AFB

807. Kelly Air Force Base
SA-ALC/PA, 807 Bruckner Dr
Kelly AFB, TX 78241-5842
210-925-1110; DSN 945-1110
Internet: http://www.kelly-afb.org/

Profile
BRANCH: Air Force.
SIZE AND LOCATION: 52,000 acres. 5 mi SW of downtown San Antonio; S of Hwy 90; off Loop 13. *County:* Bexar.
MAJOR UNITS: San Antonio Air Logistics Center; 76th Air Base Wing; Air Intelligence Agency, HQ; 433rd Airlift Wing (AFRES); 149th Fighter Group (TX ANG); Air Force News Agency, HQ; Defense Depot Distribution Station, San Antonio; Air Education & Training Command; Inter-American Air Forces Academy; 4th Aeromedical Staging Flight; Air Force Audit Agency, Kelly Office; Air Force Element, Det 12, Joint Cryptologic Center; OL-AE, MSG (Software Development Agency); 412th Logistics Support Squadron; 838th Engineering Squadron; 307th Red Horse (AFRES); Defense Courier Service; Defense Contract Audit Agency; Defense Commissary Agency, Midwest Region; Defense Investigative Service; Defense Information Systems Agency, Defense Megacenter San Antonio; Army Field Station, San Antonio; Corps of Engineers, San Antonio Area Office; Naval Inventory Control Point; Air Force Office of Special Investigations, Det 107.
BASE HISTORY: 1917, first aircraft from 3rd Aero Squadron at South San Antonio Aviation Camp; became Camp Kelly, then Kelly Field, named for Lt George E M Kelly, first American military aviator killed in military plane crash. WWI, served as reception & testing center for new recruits, training center for mechanics, chauffeurs, engineering & supply officers, and cooks & bakers. 1917, Aviation General Supply Depot moved from San Antonio. Kelly unofficially divided into two adjoining fields: Kelly Number 1, original site, warehouses, supply functions, & recruit training; Kelly Number 2, to N, site of flying training. 1921, Aviation Repair Depot moved from Dallas to Kelly Number 1, to form San Antonio Air Intermediate Depot. 1922, Air Service Advanced Flying School opened at Kelly Number 2. 1925, field officially divided: Kelly Number 1 became Duncan Field; Number 2 retained Kelly name. Kelly hosted 1924 National Elimination Balloon Race, 1926 Pan American Goodwill Flight, & filming of silent movie "Wings." 1943, bases reunited as Kelly Field; transferred to Air Service Command. WWII, developed into industrial complex; acquired Normoyle Ordnance Depot, known today as East Kelly.

1946, logistics depot defined as separate facility called San Antonio Air Materiel Area (SA-ALC, 1974). 1948, became Kelly AFB. Today, logistics center operates independently within Kelly AFB. Kelly also provides refueling facilities for space shuttle's "piggy-back" mother ship.
FUTURE CLOSURE/REALIGNMENT: BRAC 95: scheduled for realignment by Jul 2001.
VISITOR ATTRACTIONS: Veterans Monument; static display of aircraft.

Key Contacts
COMMANDER: Maj Gen James S Childress, Commander SA-ALC, 100 Moorman St, Ste 1, 78241-5808, 210-925-6914, DSN 945-6914.
PUBLIC AFFAIRS: SA-ALC/PA, 807 Buckner Dr, STE 1, 78241-5842, 210-925-7951, DSN 945-7951, pa@www.kelly-afb.org.
PROCUREMENT: 143 Billy Mitchell Rd, Ste 1, 78241-6014, 210-925-4679, DSN 945-4679.
TRANSPORTATION: 59 Billy Mitchell Rd, 78241-6011, 210-925-4418, DSN 945-4679.
PERSONNEL/COMMUNITY ACTIVITIES: 143 Billy Mitchell Rd, Ste 2, 78241-6015, 210-925-6741, DSN 945-6741.

Personnel and Expenditures
ACTIVE DUTY PERSONNEL: 5400; Guard/Reserve 4300
CIVILIAN PERSONNEL: 14,600

Services
Housing: Family units 430; BAQ units 625; RV/Camper sites 32. *Temporary Housing:* VOQ units 51; VAQ units 120. *Commissary:* Yes; *Exchange:* Retail store; Dry cleaners; Bank; Service station; Convenience store; Credit union. *Child Care/Capacities:* Day care center capacity 200. *Schools:* College courses. *Base Library:* Yes. *Medical Facilities:* Medical clinic; Dental clinic; Dispensary; Pharmacy. *Recreational Facilities:* Bowling center; Pool; Gym; Golf course; Tennis courts; Racquetball court; Fitness center/Weight room; Softball field; Football field; Auto shop; Craft shop; Officers club; NCO club; Youth center; Picnic area; Playground; Jogging; Aero Club; Sports equipment rental; Lindbergh Park, 32 acres; Laguna Shores recreational area at Corpus Christi NAS; Flying K Recreational Ranch, 5 mi W of Marble Falls, TX.

Kingsville

808. Kingsville Naval Air Station
NAS KingsvilleD
Kingsville, TX 78363-5000
512-516-6136; DSN 861-6136

Profile
BRANCH: Navy.
SIZE AND LOCATION: 3986 acres. 40 mi SW of Corpus Christi, TX, in Kingsville off Rte 77. *County:* Kleberg.
MAJOR UNITS: Commander, Training Air Wing 2 (CTWII); Training Squadron 21 (VT-21); Training Squadron 22 (VT-22); Naval Auxiliary Landing Field, Orange Grove (NALFOG); McMullen Target Site (near Freer, TX); Naval Training Meteorology Oceanography Command Det Kingsville (NTMOD); Naval Air Mobile Mine Assembly Unit 15 (MOMAU-15); Seabee Division.
BASE HISTORY: 1942, established to house 4 P-4 squadrons and training base for fighter

and bomber tactics, gunnery school for combat aircrews, and later temporary basic training center for overflow from Naval Training Center, Great Lakes, IL. Following WWII, caretaker status; leased to Texas A & I University, Kingsville, for agricultural station. 1951, reopened as Naval Auxiliary Station. 1968, redesignated NAS. 1986, airfield named for Vice Adm Alva D Bernhard, founder of station. 1992, VT-21 established as first T-45 (Navy's newest jet) squadron.

Key Contacts
PUBLIC AFFAIRS: JOCM(SW) Mark S Malinowski, 512-516-6146, nask-00@navdafgw.navy.mil; BQ Officer, Lt Stephen Dininger.

Personnel and Expenditures
ACTIVE DUTY PERSONNEL: 786
DEPENDENTS: 750
CIVILIAN PERSONNEL: 442 government employees; 600 contract workers

Services
Housing: Family units 242; Unaccompanied officer quarters 159; Unaccompanied enlisted quarters 402. *Temporary Housing:* VIP units 3; VOQ units 10; VEQ units 14; Guesthouse units 8; Transient quarters 19. *Commissary:* Yes; *Exchange:* Retail store; Barber shop; Dry cleaners; Florist; Service station; Military clothing store; Convenience store; Beauty shop; Credit union; Class VI. *Child Care/Capacities:* Day care center capacity 70; Home day care program; Summer day camp. *Base Library:* Yes. *Medical Facilities:* Medical clinic; Dental clinic; Dispensary; Pharmacy; Veterinary services. *Recreational Facilities:* Bowling center; Movie theater; Pool; Gym; Recreation center; Golf course; Stables; Tennis courts; Racquetball court; Softball field; Football field; Auto shop; Craft shop; Officers club; NCO club; Camping; Fishing/Hunting; Picnic area; Skeet range; Equipment rental; Rod & Gun club; ITT.

Lackland AFB

809. Lackland Air Force Base
1701 Kenly Ave
Lackland AFB, TX 78236-5110
210-671-1110; DSN 473-1110
E-mail: publicaf@smtp.lak.aetc.af.mil Internet: http://www.lak.aetc.af.mil
OFFICER-OF-THE-DAY: 210-671-4225, DSN 473-4225

Profile
BRANCH: Air Force.
SIZE AND LOCATION: 6783 acres. 8 mi SW of San Antonio, adj to Kelly AFB; at intersections of US-90 & Military Dr, near Loop 410 W; approx 20 mi W of San Antonio IAP. *County:* Bexar.
MAJOR UNITS: 37th Training Wing (host); 37th Training Group; 737th Training Group; Defense Language Institute English Language Center; Inter-American Air Forces Academy; 59th Medical Wing; 820th Security Forces Group; Force Protection Battlelab.
BASE HISTORY: 1941, construction began; designated Air Corps Replacement Training Center with mission to produce potential Army Air Corps pilots; named for Brig Gen Frank D Lackland, pioneer of military flying.

FUTURE CLOSURE/REALIGNMENT: BRAC 95, anticipate mission gains from realignment of Kelly AFB by 2001.

VISITOR ATTRACTIONS: Basic Military Training graduation on Lackland Parade Ground (Fri, 9am); History and Traditions Museum; Security Police Museum; Military Training Instructor Monument; Aircraft static display on parade grounds.

Key Contacts
COMMANDER: Brig Gen (select) Barry W Barksdale, 210-671-3337, DSN 473-3337.
PUBLIC AFFAIRS: Maj Carla Sylvester, 1701 Kenly Ave, Ste 220, 210-671-2907, DSN 473-2907, DSN FAX 473-2022.
PROCUREMENT: LTC Stephen Smith, 210-671-1700, DSN 473-1700.
TRANSPORTATION: LTC Don King, 210-671-2855, DSN 473-2855.

Personnel and Expenditures
ACTIVE DUTY PERSONNEL: 6268
DEPENDENTS: 1750
CIVILIAN PERSONNEL: 4245
MILITARY PAYROLL EXPENDITURE: $458.5 mil
CONTRACT EXPENDITURE: $22 mil

Services
Housing: Family units 720; Dormitory spaces 709. *Temporary Housing:* VIP units 49 units; VOQ units 325; VEQ units 1665; Temporary lodging 158. *Commissary:* Yes; *Exchange:* Retail store; Barber shop; Dry cleaners; Food shop; Florist; Bank; Service station; Military clothing store; Convenience store; Beauty shop; Credit union; ATM; Optical store; Post office; Fast food; Video rentals; Four seasons; Thrift shop; Travel agency; Class VI; Garden center; Cafeteria. *Child Care/Capacities:* Day care center capacity 108, 3yrs-5yrs; Home day care program; Summer day camp; Before & after school programs. *Schools:* Preschool/Kindergarten; Elementary; Intermediate/Junior high; High school. *Base Library:* Yes. *Medical Facilities:* Hospital 290 beds; Dental clinic; Pharmacy; Veterinary services. *Recreational Facilities:* Bowling center; Movie theater; Pool; Gym; Recreation center; Golf course; Stables; Tennis courts; Racquetball court; Fitness center/Weight room; Softball field; Football field; Auto shop; Craft shop; Youth center; Picnic area; Skeet range; Playground; Consolidated club; Rod & Gun club; Camping/Fishing at Medina Lake facility.

Laughlin AFB

810. Laughlin Air Force Base
LAFB
47th Flying Training Wing
Laughlin AFB, TX 78843
Mailing Address
561 Liberty Dr, Ste 3
Laughlin AFB, TX 78843-5227
210-298-5988, DSN 732-5988
E-mail: @laugate1.lau.aetc.af.mil Internet:http://www.lau.aetc.af.mil/

Profile
BRANCH: Air Force.
SIZE AND LOCATION: 4194 acres. On perimeter of Del Rio, TX; 150 mi due W of San Antonio on Hwy 90. *County:* Val Verde.
MAJOR UNITS: 47th Flying Training Wing; 85th Flying Training Squadron (FTS); 87th Flying Training Squadron (FTS); 47th Civil

Engineer Squadron; 47th Mission Support Squadron; 47th Security Police Squadron; 47th Operations Group; 47th Operations Support Squadron; Laughlin Civil Service Aircraft Maintenance (LCSAM); 47th Medical Group; 47th Contracting Squadron; 47th Communications Squadron; Defense Investigative Service; Air Force Office of Special Investigations, Det 410; Defense Reutilization and Marketing Office; 86th Flying Training Squadron; 47th Support Group; 47th Services Division; 47th Supply Flight; 47th Transportation Flight; 47th Aerospace Medicine Squadron; 47th Medical Operations Squadron; 47th Medical Support Squadron; 47th Dental Flight.
BASE HISTORY: 1942, activated as Laughlin Army Air Field, named for 1st Lt Jack T Laughlin, Del Rio native killed in WWII; primarily a pilot training base. Following WWII, closed until reactivated in 1952 as jet fighter training base and transition to basic gunnery training. 1957, became part of SAC. 1962, U-2s discovered Soviet missile sites in Cuba. 1962, Air Training Command took control; returned to pilot training mission.

Key Contacts
COMMANDER: Col Gary A Wingerberger.
PUBLIC AFFAIRS: Capt Tania L Daniels, 47 FTW/PA, danielst@laugate1.lau.aetc.af.mil.
PROCUREMENT: Maj Wally Ruiz, 210-298-5116, DSN 732-5116, DSN FAX 732-4178, 732-5993.
TRANSPORTATION: Capt Joel Peterson, 210-298-5857, DSN 732-5857.
PERSONNEL/COMMUNITY ACTIVITIES: Ron Scharven, Director of Community Activities, 210-298-5988, DSN 732-5988, DSN FAX 732-5047.

Personnel and Expenditures
ACTIVE DUTY PERSONNEL: 1232
DEPENDENTS: 1020
CIVILIAN PERSONNEL: 1705
MILITARY PAYROLL EXPENDITURE: $31.97 mil
CONTRACT EXPENDITURE: $12.98 mil

Services
Housing: Family units 603; Unaccompanied officer quarters 221; Unaccompanied enlisted quarters 604; Mobile home units 54; RV/Camper sites 24. *Temporary Housing:* Transient quarters 22. *Commissary:* Yes; *Exchange:* Retail store; Barber shop; Dry cleaners; Food shop; Service station. *Child Care/Capacities:* Day care center capacity 100. *Schools:* No on-base schools. *Base Library:* Yes. *Medical Facilities:* Medical clinic; Dental clinic. *Recreational Facilities:* Bowling center; Movie theater; Pool; Gym; Recreation center; Golf course; Stables; Tennis courts; Racquetball court; Fitness center/Weight room; Softball field; Football field; Auto shop; Craft shop; Officers club; NCO club; Camping; Water sports; Recreational facilities at Lake Amistad Reservoir.

Lubbock

811. Lubbock Naval & Marine Corps Reserve Center
301 E Regis St, Ste 1118
Lubbock, TX 79403-1118
806-765-6657; FAX 806-765-9683; DSN 838-1110

Profile
BRANCH: Naval Reserve; Marine Corps Reserve.
LOCATION: *County:* Lubbock.
MAJOR UNITS: REDCOM ELEVEN Activity; Direct Support Motor Transport Co B, 6th Motor Transport Bn.
Key Contacts
COMMANDER: Lt C A Shawn.

Marshall

812. Longhorn Army Ammunition Plant
LHAAP
PO Box 11029
Marshall, TX 75671-1059
903-679-3181; DSN 956-2010

Profile
BRANCH: Army.
SIZE AND LOCATION: 8493 acres. Approx 1 mi off State Hwy 43; 13 mi from Marshall, TX; 3.5 mi W of LA-TX border; served by Greater Shreveport Regional Airport. *County:* Harrison.
BASE HISTORY: 1941, designated as Longhorn Ordnance Works until 1963; established to support mobilization requirements for WWII. 1941-46, operated by Monsanto Chemical Co; Plant 1 produced over 400 mil pounds of TNT flake, and Plant 2 was under construction 1945, designed to produce solid rocket fuel. 1945-52, standby and GOGO status. 1952, active status; operated by Universal Match Corp. 1955, Plant 3, designated to produce solid propellant rocket motors, operated by Thiokol Corp (later Morton Thiokol, Inc). GOCO plant, managed by operating contractor but under command of Army Armament, Munitions, and Chemical Command (AMCCOM). Current workload includes loading, assembly, and pack-out of illuminating munitions, infrared flares, signals, and simulators.
Key Contacts
COMMANDER: 903-679-2100, DSN 956-2100.
PUBLIC AFFAIRS: 903-679-2228, DSN 956-2228.
Personnel and Expenditures
ACTIVE DUTY PERSONNEL: 2
CIVILIAN PERSONNEL: 887
Services *Base Library:* Yes. *Medical Facilities:* Contractor operated dispensary. *Recreational Facilities:* Picnic area for employees.

Orange

813. Orange Naval Reserve Center
905 Pier Rd
Orange, TX 77630-5289
Mailing Address
Box 8001
Orange, TX 77631-8001
409-883-6795; FAX 409-883-8285

Profile
BRANCH: Naval Reserve.
LOCATION: *County:* Orange.
MAJOR UNITS: REDCOM ELEVEN Activity.
Key Contacts
COMMANDER: LCDR N R Bond.

Randolph AFB

814. Randolph Air Force Base
RAFB
1 Washington Circle, Ste 4
Randolph AFB, TX 78150-5000
210-652-4410; 210-652-5412; DSN 487-4410
Internet: http://www.randolph.af.mil; http://
www.rnd.aetc.af.mil/main.htm
Profile
BRANCH: Air Force.
SIZE AND LOCATION: 5003 acres. 17 mi NE
of San Antonio; in small community of Uni-
versal City, TX. Main gate at intersection of
Farm Rd 78 & Pat Booker Rd. *County:*
Bexar.
MAJOR UNITS: Air Education and Training
Command, HQ; Air Force Personnel Center;
12th Flying Training Wing; Air Force Recruit-
ing Service; 19th Air Force, HQ; Air Force
Center for Quality and Management Innova-
tion; Air Force Services Agency; Air Force
Occupational Measurement Squadron; 12th
Logistics Group; 12th Medical Group; 12th
Operations Group; 12th Support Group; 12th
Comptroller Squadron; 3rd Flying Training
Squadron; 99th Flying Training Squadron;
559th Flying Training Squadron; 560th Fly-
ing Training Squadron; 562nd Flying Train-
ing Squadron; 332nd Airlift Flight (AMC);
Aeronautical Systems Center (SATAF); Air
Force Office of Special Investigations, Det
401; Air Force ROTC Southwest Region; 4th
Field Investigations Regiment, HQ; Marine
Aerial Navigation School; Naval Civilian Per-
sonnel Data Systems Center; 2nd German Air
Force Training Squadron, USA.
BASE HISTORY: 1930, dedicated, partially
completed; nicknamed "West Point of the
Air"; named for Capt William Millican Ran-
dolph, native Texan & former adjutant of Ad-
vanced Flying School, Kelly Field. 1931, Air
Corps Primary Flying School trained cadets
& regular Army officers. 1943, trained instructor pilots; briefly, B-29 crews. Following
WWII, series of different training programs:
primary & basic pilot training; B-29, C-119,
B-57 crews, & helicopters. 1958-71, pilot
training returned. 1971-present, home of Air
Force Pilot Instructor Training program.
VISITOR ATTRACTIONS: "Showplace of the
Air Force." Buildings Spanish Colonial design, accented by arches & red tile roofs. Hun-
dreds of tall oak trees dot landscape. Bldg
100, "The Taj Mahal," listed in National Reg-
istry of Historic Places; Randolph Air Park,
with 7 historic aircraft used in pilot training;
Hangar 12; Atterberry Hall, dedicated to Col
Ed Atterberry, former POW who died in cap-
tivity; Freedom Hall dedicated to repatriation
of shot-down USAF pilots; Missing Man
Monument; Air Heritage Park.
Key Contacts
COMMANDER: Gen Lloyd "Fig" Newton,
Commander, HQ AETC, Ste 01,
78150-4559, 210-652-3510, DSN 487-3510;
Maj Gen Kurt B Anderson, Commander,
19th Air Force; Col Richard A Mentemeyer,
Commander 12th Flying Training Wing.
PUBLIC AFFAIRS: Col Patrick C Mullaney,
100 H ST, STe 3, 78150-4330, 210-652-3946,
DSN 487-3946; Air Force Personnel Center,
PAO, 550 C St W, Ste 43, 78150-4745,
210-652-6141, DSN 487-6141.

Personnel and Expenditures
ACTIVE DUTY PERSONNEL: 5200
DEPENDENTS: 9960
CIVILIAN PERSONNEL: 5900
Services
Housing: Family units 1019; Unaccompanied en-
listed quarters 348; Dormitory spaces; RV/
Camper sites Tent spaces 40; Shelters 11; Trail-
ers 9. *Temporary Housing:* VIP units 80; VOQ
units 280; VEQ units 173; Guesthouse units 30.
Commissary: Yes; *Exchange:* Retail store; Bar-
ber shop; Dry cleaners; Food shop; Florist;
Bank; Service station; Military clothing store;
Convenience store; Beauty shop; Credit union.
Child Care/Capacities: Day care center capacity
135, 6mo-5yrs; Home day care program; Latch
key program; Summer day camp. *Schools:* Pre-
school/Kindergarten; Elementary; Intermediate/
Junior high; High school; College courses. *Base
Library:* Yes. *Medical Facilities:* Medical clinic;
Dental clinic; Pharmacy; Veterinary services.
Recreational Facilities: Bowling center; Movie
theater; Pool; Gym; Recreation center; Golf
course; Stables; Racquetball court; Fitness cen-
ter/Weight room; Softball field; Football field;
Auto shop; Craft shop; Officers club; NCO club;
Enlisted club; Youth center; Picnic area; Skeet
range; Playground.

San Antonio

815. Brooks Air Force Base
2510 Kennedy Circle
San Antonio, TX 78235
Mailing Address
HSC/PA, 2510 Kennedy Circle, Ste 220
Brooks AFB, TX 78235-5120
210-536-1110; DSN 240-1110
Profile
BRANCH: Air Force.
SIZE AND LOCATION: 1310 acres. In SE part
of San Antonio at corner of I-37 & Military
Dr; approx 20 mi from San Antonio IAP.
County: Bexar.
MAJOR UNITS: Human Systems Center; Armstrong Laboratory; Air Force School of Aerospace Medicine; 70th Support Group; 70th
Services Squadron; 70th Civil Engineering
Squadron; 70th Security Police Squadron;
70th Medical Squadron; 70th Training Squadron; 70th Communications Squadron (CS);
70th Air Base Group; Air Force Office of Special Investigations, Det 1008; Air Force Medical Support Agency.
BASE HISTORY: Originally Gosport Field,
name derived from flight instruction system
used. 1917, Army named site Kelly Field No
5. 1918, renamed Brooks Field for Cadet Sidney J Brooks Jr, native of San Antonio killed
in training flight. 1919, pilot instructor school
closed and Balloon & Airship School opened
for pilots & ground crew members. 1922, series of mishaps closed school. 1922-31, became Primary Flying School of Army Air
Corps; School of Aviation Medicine moved
from Mitchell Field, NY. 1929, site of
world's first successful mass parachute drop.
1930s, center of aerial observation activity.
1931, both schools transferred to newly constructed Randolph Field. 1940, school for
combat observers established. 1943, home for
training pilots in B-25 bomber. 1950s, trans-
formed from flying training center to modern

medical research and development center &
education center. 1959, School of Aviation
Medicine returned and HQ, Aerospace Medical Center established. 1960, last plane took
off Brooks' runway. 1961, school's title
changed to School of Aerospace Medicine.
1963, President Kennedy dedicated 4 build-
ings, last official act before assassination in
Dallas. Researchers study man's interaction
with aerospace environment. 1992, Human
Systems Division (HSD) renamed Human
Systems Center (HSC) as part of restructuring
of new Air Force Materiel Command.
VISITOR ATTRACTIONS: Air Force Museum
of Flight Medicine; Hangar 9 (oldest Air
Force hangar); Edward H White II Museum;
Sidney J Brooks Jr Memorial Park; Schriever
Heritage Park.
Key Contacts
COMMANDER: Brig Gen Robert P Belihar,
HSC Commander; Col Klaus B Bartels, 70th
Air Base Group Commander.
PUBLIC AFFAIRS: Maj Erin Campbell,
HSC/PA, 210-536-3234, DSN 240-3234,
DSN FAX 240-3235.
Personnel and Expenditures
ACTIVE DUTY PERSONNEL: 1590
CIVILIAN PERSONNEL: 1580
Services
Housing: Duplex units 150; Dormitory spaces
71; Single officers live off base; Capehart single
units 20. *Temporary Housing:* VIP units 6; VOQ
units 160; VAQ units 136; Transient quarters 8.
Commissary: Yes; *Exchange:* Retail store; Bar-
ber shop; Dry cleaners; Bank; Service station;
Convenience store; Beauty shop; Credit union;
Optical store; Video rentals; Thrift shop; Laun-
dry; Snacks; Fabric care. *Child Care/Capacities:*
Day care center. *Base Library:* Yes. *Medical Facilities:* Medical clinic; Dental clinic; Pharmacy;
Veterinary services. *Recreational Facilities:*
Bowling center; Movie theater; Pool; Gym; Recreation center; Golf course; Stables; Tennis
courts; Racquetball court; Fitness center/Weight
room; Softball field; Auto shop; Craft shop;
Youth center; Picnic area; Playground; Recreational supply; Ticket sales.

816. San Antonio Naval & Marine Corps Reserve Center
NMCRC San Antonio
3837 Binz-Englemann Rd, Bldg 3620 Ft Sam
Houston
San Antonio, TX 78219-2296
210-225-2997, 223-1584; FAX 210-225-3082
Profile
BRANCH: Naval Reserve; Marine Corps Re-
serve.
LOCATION: *County:* Bexar.
MAJOR UNITS: REDCOM ELEVEN Activity;
HQ & Service Co, 4th Reconnaissance Bn;
Co A, 4th Reconnaissance Bn; Co C, 4th Re-
connaissance Bn.
Key Contacts
COMMANDER: CDR J A Ottum.

Sheppard AFB

817. Sheppard Air Force Base
Sheppard AFB, TX 76311-2943
940-676-2511; DSN 736-2511

Internet: http://www.spd.aetc.af.mil/
OFFICER-OF-THE-DAY: 940-676-2621
Profile
BRANCH: Air Force.
SIZE AND LOCATION: 5406 acres. In N-central TX, 4 mi N of Wichita Falls off Rte 281; 12 mi S of OK border. *County:* Wichita.
MAJOR UNITS: 82nd Training Wing; 80th Flying Training Wing; Euro-NATO Joint Jet Pilot Training; 82nd Training Group; 782nd Training Group; 882nd Training Group; 982nd Training Group; 82nd Support Group; 82nd Medical Group; 82nd Logistics Group; 80th Operations Support Squadron; 88th Flying Training Squadron; 89th Flying Training Squadron; 90th Flying Training Squadron.
BASE HISTORY: 1941, opened, named for Senator Morris Sheppard, chairman of Senate Military Affairs Committee. WWII, conducted training for pilots & mechanics. 1946-48, deactivated. Conducts technical, health care, & flying training.
Key Contacts
COMMANDER: Brig Gen Scott C Bergren, 82 TRW Commander.
PUBLIC AFFAIRS: 940-676-2732, pa@spd.aetc.af.mil.
Personnel and Expenditures
ACTIVE DUTY PERSONNEL: 5300
DEPENDENTS: 6400
CIVILIAN PERSONNEL: 2400
Services
Housing: Family units 200; Senior NCO units 1087. *Temporary Housing:* VIP units 18; VOQ units 112; VAQ units 1269; Apartment units 50. *Commissary:* Yes; *Exchange:* Retail store; Barber shop; Dry cleaners; Food shop; Bank; Service station; Military clothing store; Convenience store; Beauty shop; Credit union; Four seasons; Class VI; Laundry; Snacks; Jewelry/watch sales/repair. *Child Care/Capacities:* Day care center capacity 115. *Schools:* Elementary. *Base Library:* Yes. *Medical Facilities:* Hospital 160 beds. *Recreational Facilities:* Bowling center; Movie theater; Pool; Gym; Recreation center; Golf course; Stables; Tennis courts; Racquetball court; Fitness center/Weight room; Softball field; Football field; Auto shop; Craft shop; Officers club; NCO club; Camping; Fishing/Hunting; Picnic area; Skeet range; Amusement center; Running track; Aero club; MWR supply; Gun club; Lake Texoma Recreation Annex, 356

acre site 120 mi E of base on TX side of lake, 940-676-2876.

Texarkana

818. Red River Army Depot
RRAD
Texarkana, TX 75507-5000
214-334-2141; DSN 829-2141
Profile
BRANCH: Army.
SIZE AND LOCATION: 19,081 acres; Camp Stanley 4000 acres. In NE TX, approx 18 mi W of Texarkana, TX; I-30, Exit 206 leads into main entrance. *County:* Bowie.
MAJOR UNITS: Red River Army Depot; Defense Distribution Depot, Red River; School of Engineering and Logistics (AMC); Camp Stanley Storage Activity.
BASE HISTORY: 1941, activated as ammunition storage site. Since 1991, supply activities responsibility of Defense Distribution Depot Red River (DLA). Currently, one of Army's largest depots in terms of workload and personnel; part of Army Industrial Operations Command & responsible for maintenance & ammunition; center for maintenance of Bradley Fighting Vehicle, Multiple Launch Rocket System (MLRS), & other light tracked vehicles; also serves as training site for Reserve and NG troops. Also operates Camp Stanley, located NW of San Antonio (25800 Ralph Fair Rd, Boerne, TX 78006-4800). Separate activity responsible for receipt, storage, maintenance, testing, and issue of ordnance items.
FUTURE CLOSURE/REALIGNMENT: Scheduled for major realignment by Sep 98.
Key Contacts
PUBLIC AFFAIRS: Cecil A Green.
Personnel and Expenditures
ACTIVE DUTY PERSONNEL: 10
CIVILIAN PERSONNEL: 1717
MILITARY PAYROLL EXPENDITURE: $91 mil (including civilians)
CONTRACT EXPENDITURE: $10 mil
Services
Housing: Unaccompanied officer quarters; Unaccompanied enlisted quarters.

Exchange: Retail store; Credit union. *Recreational Facilities:* Pool; Gym; Golf course; Tennis courts; Racquetball court; Fitness center/Weight room; Softball field; Camping; Fishing/Hunting; Youth center; Picnic area; Water sports; Playground; Community club; Manmade lake.

Tyler

819. Tyler Naval Reserve Center
NAVRESCEN Tyler
NRC Tyler
1818 N Confederate Ave
Tyler, TX 75702-3128
903-592-3351; FAX 903-597-0147
E-mail: TYLER@CNSRF.NAVY.MIL
Profile
BRANCH: Naval Reserve.
SIZE AND LOCATION: 1 acre. 140 mi from JRB Fort Worth. *County:* Smith.
MAJOR UNITS: REDCOM ELEVEN Activity; DESRON 31 (NR); NMCB 28, Det 1628; NF FH-500 CBTZ 21 Det L.
Key Contacts
COMMANDER: LCDR Rodelio Laco Jr.
PUBLIC AFFAIRS: BMC, CMC Thomas I Blair.
Personnel and Expenditures
ACTIVE DUTY PERSONNEL: 7; 178 reservists

Waco

820. Waco Naval & Marine Corps Reserve Center
2100 N New Rd
Waco, TX 76707-1097
817-776-1841, 772-5571; FAX 817-776-4493
Profile
BRANCH: Naval Reserve; Marine Corps Reserve.
LOCATION: *County:* McLennan.
MAJOR UNITS: REDCOM ELEVEN Activity; Ordnance Maintenance Co(-), 4th Maintenance Bn.
Key Contacts
COMMANDER: Lt Craig.

Utah

Draper

821. Adjutant General of Utah
12953 S Minuteman Dr
Draper, UT 84020-1776
801-576-3900; FAX 801-576-3575
Profile
BRANCH: Army National Guard.
MAJOR UNITS: Utah National Guard.
Key Contacts
COMMANDER: Maj Gen James M Miller.

Dugway

822. Dugway Proving Ground
DPG
ATTN: STEDP-PA
Dugway, UT 84022-5000
801-831-3757; FAX 801-831-3758; DSN
789-3757
Profile
BRANCH: Army.
SIZE AND LOCATION: 798,855 acres. 85 mi
W of Salt Lake City and Salt Lake City Air-
port by I-80; 37 mi S of I-80. Tooele, UT,
nearest city, 37 mi NE via Johnson's Pass.
County: Tooele.
MAJOR UNITS: Support Troops, HQ.
BASE HISTORY: 1942, officially activated on
land withdrawn from public domain with incendiary bombs, chemical weapons, and
modified agents as spray, disseminated from
aircraft, and pioneer work on mortars. 1943,
biological warfare and testing facilities established. 1945, part of Wendover Bombing
Range transferred to proving ground. After
WWII, combined with Deseret Chemical Depot to form Dugway Deseret Command, later
renamed Western Chemical Center and
placed on stand-by basis. 1950, resumed active status with additional 279,000 acres.
1954, confirmed as permanent installation.
1968, Ft Douglas-based Deseret Test Center
and Dugway Proving Ground combined as
Deseret Test Center. 1969, discontinued biological warfare testing. 1973, received present
name from nearby Dugway Mountains. Now
aligned under Army's Test and Evaluation
Command (TECOM), HQ Aberdeen Proving
Ground, MD, subordinate command of Army
Materiel Command, HQ Alexandria, VA. Cur-
rently testing battlefield smokes and obscur-
ants.
VISITOR ATTRACTIONS: Visitors wel-
comed; Lincoln Memorial Bridge, part of first
transcontinental highway on National Regis-
ter of Historic Places; Pony Express site at
Simpson Springs.
Key Contacts
COMMANDER: Col John A Como, ATTN:
STEDP-CO, 801-831-3701, DSN 789-3701.
PUBLIC AFFAIRS: Melanie Moore.
PROCUREMENT: Robert Andrus, ATTN:
STEDP-DOC, 801-831-2102, DSN
789-2102.
TRANSPORTATION: Samuel Liddiard,
ATTN: STEDP-DOL-T, 801-831-2131, DSN
789-2131.
PERSONNEL/COMMUNITY ACTIVITIES:
Donald Bash, ATTN: STEDP-CA,
801-831-2181, DSN 789-2181.
Personnel and Expenditures
ACTIVE DUTY PERSONNEL: 60
DEPENDENTS: 1000
CIVILIAN PERSONNEL: 513
Services
Housing: Family units 661. *Commissary:* Yes;
Exchange: Retail store; Barber shop; Dry clean-
ers; Bank; Service station; Military clothing
store; Convenience store; Beauty shop; Credit
union; Video rentals; Thrift shop; Class VI.
Child Care/Capacities: Day care center capacity
132; Home day care program; Latch key program. *Schools:* Preschool/Kindergarten; Elementary; Intermediate/Junior high; High school; College courses. *Base Library:* Yes. *Medical Facilities:* Medical clinic; Dispensary; Pharmacy; Veterinary services. *Recreational Facilities:* Bowling center; Movie theater; Pool; Gym; Recreation center; Golf course; Stables; Tennis courts;
Racquetball court; Fitness center/Weight room;
Softball field; Football field; Auto shop; Craft
shop; Fishing/Hunting; Youth center; Skeet
range; Playground; Community club.

Hill AFB

823. Defense Non-Tactical Generator & Rail Equipment Center
DGRC
6233 Aspen Ave, Bldg 1701
Hill AFB, UT 84056
801-777-5913; FAX 801-777-5916; DSN
777-5913; DSN FAX 777-5916
E-mail: arringto@oodis01.hill.af.mil Internet:
http://www.tooele.army.mil/dgrc.htm
Profile
BRANCH: Army.
LOCATION: At Hill AFB, Ogden, UT; 32 mi N
of Salt Lake City Airport. *County:* Tooele;
Davis.
BASE HISTORY: 1942, Transportation Depot
Maintenance Division Shops built for Odgen
Arsenal. 1944, became Class II installation;
maintenance of all Army (later Air Force) rail-
road stock west of Mississippi. 1954, deacti-
vated. 1956, became section of Utah General
Depot. 1964, renamed Rail Equipment Divi-
sion under Tooele Army Depot with Depot
changed to Defense Supply Agency activity.
1994, took current name. Only rail overhaul
shop in DOD; part of Tooele Army Depot.
Key Contacts
COMMANDER: SDSTE-CO, Tooele Army
Depot, Tooele, UT 84074, 801-833-2211,
DSN 790-2211.
PUBLIC AFFAIRS: SDSTE-PAO, Tooele
Army Depot, Tooele, UT 84074,
801-833-3216, DSN 790-3216.
PROCUREMENT: Director of Contracting,
SDSTE-CD, Tooele Army Depot, Tooele,
UT 84074, 801-833-2616, DSN 790-2616.
TRANSPORTATION: Tooele Army Depot,
Tooele, UT 84074, 801-833-2914, DSN
790-2914.
PERSONNEL/COMMUNITY ACTIVITIES:
SDSTE-PC, Tooele Army Depot, Tooele, UT
84074, 801-833-2412, DSN 790-2412.

824. Hill Air Force Base
Ogden Air Logistics Center
Hill AFB, UT 84056
801-777-7221; DSN 777-1110
Internet: http://www.hill.af.mil/
OFFICER-OF-THE-DAY: Command Post,
801-777-2310
Profile
BRANCH: Air Force.
SIZE AND LOCATION: 6666 acres; 962,100
acres including Test Range. Approx 5 mi S of
Ogden; 30 mi N of Salt Lake City, off I-15.
County: Davis.
MAJOR UNITS: Ogden Air Logistics Center;
388th Fighter Wing; 514th Flight Test Squad-
ron; 75th Air Base Wing; 75th Communica-
tions Squadron; 75th Civil Engineer Group;
75th Medical Group; 75th Operations Support
Squadron; Utah Test and Training Range; De-

fense Megacenter, Ogden; 367th Training Support Squadron.

BASE HISTORY: Begun as Ogden Air Depot. 1939, Hill Field named for Maj Ployer P Hill, died piloting original model of B-17. During WWII, aircraft rehabilitation major activity; crews of 509th Composite Group practiced bombing runs over Wendover Range from Hill in preparation for Hiroshima & Nagasaki missions. 1948, became Hill AFB. Following WWII, became storage & deposition site for airplanes & support equipment. 1955, Ogden Arsenal property, now West Area of Hill AFB, added. 1959, single assembly & recycling point for Minuteman missiles. 1974, Ogden Air Materiel Area became Ogden Air Logistics Center.

VISITOR ATTRACTIONS: Hill AFB Heritage Museum & Aerospace Park.

Key Contacts
COMMANDER: Maj Gen Richard H Roellig, ALC.
PUBLIC AFFAIRS: 801-777-3200, 388th FW; SSgt James Rush, 801-777-2310.

Personnel and Expenditures
ACTIVE DUTY PERSONNEL: 4700
DEPENDENTS: 10,000
CIVILIAN PERSONNEL: 9800

Services
Housing: Family units 1145; Duplex units 500; Dormitory spaces 1605. *Temporary Housing:* VIP units 14; VOQ units 107; VAQ units 120; Transient quarters 45; TDY reservations only. *Commissary:* Yes; *Exchange:* Retail store; Barber shop; Dry cleaners; Food shop; Florist; Bank; Service station; Furniture store; Military clothing store; Convenience store; Beauty shop; Credit union; Tailor; Optical shop; Class VI; Thrift shop. *Child Care/Capacities:* Day care center capacity 132. *Schools:* No on-base schools. *Base Library:* Yes. *Medical Facilities:* Hospital 30 beds; Medical clinic; Dental clinic; Veterinary services. *Recreational Facilities:* Bowling center; Movie theater; Pool; Gym; Recreation center; Golf course; Stables; Tennis courts; Racquetball court; Fitness center/Weight room; Auto shop; Craft shop; Officers club; NCO club; Camping; Fishing/Hunting; Youth center; Skeet range; Amusement center; Aero club; Skiing; MWR supply/sports loan; Centennial Park; SATO.

825. Utah Test and Training Range
UTTR
6067 Boxelder Lane
Hill AFB, UT 84056-5811
FAX 801-777-6209; DSN 777-6209
Profile
BRANCH: Air Force.
SIZE AND LOCATION: 1.8 mil acres. 48 mi (105 mi by road) W of Hill AFB; 18 mi N of Utah exit 62 off I-80. *County:* Tooele.
MAJOR UNITS: 388th Range Squadron; 299th Range Control Squadron; 729th Air Control Squadron.
BASE HISTORY: Range equipped with radar, telemetry, scoring, ACMI, communications & mission control centers, & threat systems to provide full-scale air combat maneuvering environment. Air Logistics Command, Air Combat Command, & Air Force Materiel Command (AFMC) routinely conduct operational exercises. UTTR capable of receiving real-time data & providing mission control function for missions being conducted from West-

ern Space & Missile Center at Vandenberg AFB or Edwards AFB. In addition, serves as test site for manned & unmanned aircraft programs & site for storage & testing of conventional munitions. Also provides facilities for combat units of ACC, AFMC, Navy, Marines, & Army Aviation.
VISITOR ATTRACTIONS: No public access.
Key Contacts
COMMANDER: Col Ronald E Fly, 388th Fighter Wing.
PUBLIC AFFAIRS: 388th Fighter Wing, 801-777-5201 (Hill AFB).
Personnel and Expenditures
ACTIVE DUTY PERSONNEL: 70

Magna

826. Program Management Office, Strategic Systems Programs Detachment
PMOSSP Det Magna
Box 157
Magna, UT 84044-0157
FAX 801-251-2307
E-mail: SPLBOO@SSP.NAVY.MIL
OFFICER-OF-THE-DAY: 801-250-5911
Profile
BRANCH: Navy.
SIZE AND LOCATION: Tenant Command on private contractors facility. 20 mi from Salt Lake IAP; 5000 S, 8400 W (Salt Lake City). *County:* Salt Lake.
MAJOR UNITS: Program Management Office Strategic Systems Programs Det.
BASE HISTORY: NAVPBRO office within Alliant Tech Systems Inc Complex; mission to monitor DOD contracts and rocket motor production, quality assurance, and shipping at Alliant Missile, Ordnance and Space Rocket Motor Plant, Magna; Officer in Charge (OIC) is cognizant over operation of Naval Industrial Reserve Ordnance Plant (NIROP), government land maintained and operated by Alliant.
Key Contacts
COMMANDER: Officer in Charge, 801-251-4102.
PUBLIC AFFAIRS: Technical Director, 801-251-4188.
Personnel and Expenditures
ACTIVE DUTY PERSONNEL: 2
CIVILIAN PERSONNEL: 16
Services
Housing: None. *Temporary Housing:* None. *Child Care/Capacities:* No day care facilities. *Schools:* No on-base schools. *Medical Facilities:* No medical facilities.

Riverton

827. Camp W G Williams
UT-AGCW
Camp Williams
17800 Camp Williams Rd
Riverton, UT 84065-4999
801-576-3950; FAX 801-576-3834; DSN 766-3950; DSN FAX 766-3834
Profile
BRANCH: Army National Guard.
SIZE AND LOCATION: 28,000 acres.

Approx 26 mi S of Salt Lake City, off UT Hwy 68. *County:* Salt Lake; Utah.
MAJOR UNITS: Det 2, UT STARC (Army Garrison); 140th Regiment (Regional Training Institute); 1/19 Special Forces Bn; 117th Engineer Det; 120th Quartermaster Det; Unit Training Equipment Site (UTES); Organizational Maintenance Shop 8; Joint Language Training Center (JLTC); Lone Peak Facility (UT Dept. of Corrections).
BASE HISTORY: 1854, land used for encampments; 1914, made Federal Military Reservation; 1927, state bought land. 1928, named for Brig Gen W G Williams. WWII, major training site for Ft Douglas. 1944, declared surplus. Today, used all year with 4-5 annual training periods; Category A installation. UT NG also has facility at Dugway Proving Ground, operated by Commander of Camp Williams.
VISITOR ATTRACTIONS: Museum; Pony Express historical marker; Jordan River Parkway; Veterans Cemetary.
Key Contacts
COMMANDER: Maj Ted H Frandsen, Training Site Manager, 801-576-3727, FAX 801-576-3834, DSN 766-3727.
PUBLIC AFFAIRS: CW4 Robert V Sheriff, 801-576-3978, FAX 801-576-3834, DSN 766-3978.
PROCUREMENT: Maj David A Robinson, 801-576-3720, FAX 801-576-3834, DSN 766-3720.
Personnel and Expenditures
ACTIVE DUTY PERSONNEL: 300
DEPENDENTS: 0
CIVILIAN PERSONNEL: 85
MILITARY PAYROLL EXPENDITURE: $9 mil
CONTRACT EXPENDITURE: $2.5 mil
Services
Housing: None. *Temporary Housing:* VOQ units 74; VEQ units 150; VAQ units 174; Guesthouse units 8; Apartment units 2; Dormitory units capacity 1100. *Exchange:* Barber shop; Dry cleaners; Convenience store; Laundromat; Fast food; Video rentals; Laundry; Contract cafe. *Child Care/Capacities:* No day care facilities. *Schools:* No on-base schools. *Medical Facilities:* Medical clinic. *Recreational Facilities:* Pool; Fitness center/Weight room; Softball field; Officers club; NCO club; Enlisted club; Biathalon course & range.

Salt Lake City

828. Salt Lake City IAP, Air National Guard Base
Salt Lake City, UT 84116
801-595-2200; DSN 924-9200
Profile
BRANCH: Air National Guard.
SIZE AND LOCATION: 135 acres. 3 mi W of Salt Lake City, off I-215. *County:* Salt Lake.
MAJOR UNITS: 151st Air Refueling Wing (ANG); 169th Electronic Security Squadron (ANG); 130th Engineering Installation Squadron (ANG); 109th Tactical Control Flight (ANG).
Personnel and Expenditures
ACTIVE DUTY PERSONNEL: 1371 Guard
CIVILIAN PERSONNEL: 443
MILITARY PAYROLL EXPENDITURE: $27.2 mil

Services *Medical Facilities:* Dispensary.

829. Salt Lake City Naval & Marine Corps Reserve Center
NAVMARCORESCEN Salt Lake City
116 Pollock Rd
Salt Lake City, UT 84113-5010
801-584-4201; FAX 801-584-4058

Profile

BRANCH: Naval Reserve; Marine Corps Reserve.

SIZE AND LOCATION: 3 acres. Fort Douglas Armed Forces Reserve Center, near Univ of Utah, downtown. *County:* Salt Lake.

MAJOR UNITS: REDCOM TWENTY-TWO Activity; Co F (-), 2nd Bn, 23rd Marine Regiment.

VISITOR ATTRACTIONS: Ft Douglas historical landmark.

Key Contacts

COMMANDER: Capt Robert W Micken, 801-584-4200.

PUBLIC AFFAIRS: YNC(AW) Ronnie E Manning, 801-584-4201, FAX 801-584-4058.

Personnel and Expenditures

ACTIVE DUTY PERSONNEL: 22; 400 reservists

Services *Recreational Facilities:* Gym; Fitness center/Weight room; Softball field.

Tooele

830. Tooele Army Depot
TEAD
Main Depot Rd, Bldg 510
Tooele, UT 84074-5000

Mailing Address
ATTN: SIOTE-CO
Tooele, UT 84074-5000
801-833-2211; FAX 801-833-2810; DSN 790-2211; DSN FAX 790-2810
E-mail: cdrsec@tooele-emh1.army.mil Internet: http://www.tead.army.mil/history.htm
OFFICER-OF-THE-DAY: 801-833-2304, DSN 790-2304

Profile

BRANCH: Army.

SIZE AND LOCATION: North Area 25,172.55 acres; South Area 19,364 acres. North Area adj to Tooele, UT; South Area in desert valley 15 mi S of main HQs. *County:* Tooele.

MAJOR UNITS: Army Test Measurement Diagnostic Equipment Center; Co C, 4th Light Armored Reconnaissance Bn, 4th Marine Division; UT National Guard; DOD Print Service; 62nd Ordnance Co (EOD).

BASE HISTORY: 1942, construction of Tooele Ordnance Depot began; administrative area included hospital, POW camp, troop barracks, housing facilities, and storage depot for Chemical Corps toxins 15 mi S in Rush Valley (Deseret Chemical Warfare Depot); mission to store vehicles, small arms, and fire control equipment; later, maintenance shop and shops to rebuild, modify, and reclaim 75mm howitzer motor carriages and artillery pieces established. 1956, Ammunition Equipment Directorate began. 1961, assimilation of Deseret Depot Activity. 1962, name changed to Tooele Army Depot. 1977, CAMDS mission added. Command expanded to include 4 additional depot activities: Umatilla, 1973; Ft Wingate, Navajo, and Pueblo in 1975. Depot (North Area) mission currently retains only conventional ammunition storage & maintenance & demilitarization. South Area realigned with CBDCOM as Deseret Chemical Depot.

Key Contacts

COMMANDER: LTC Mark R Henscheid, comdr@tooele-emh1.army.mil.

PUBLIC AFFAIRS: Kathy R Anderson, SIOTE-PA, 801-833-2211, DSN 790-2211, DSN FAX 790-2810, cdrsec@tooele-emh1.army.mil.

PROCUREMENT: Mike Newton, 801-833-2616, DSN 790-2616, DSN FAX 790-3468, siotecd@tooele-emh1.army.mil.

TRANSPORTATION: Don Hamilton, 801-833-2916, DSN 790-2916, DSN FAX 790-3093, sioteao@tooele-emh1.army.mil.

PERSONNEL/COMMUNITY ACTIVITIES: Berdett Rogers, 801-833-3118, DSN 790-3118, DSN FAX 790-2096, sioters@tooele-emh1.army.mil.

Personnel and Expenditures

ACTIVE DUTY PERSONNEL: 6
CIVILIAN PERSONNEL: 657
MILITARY PAYROLL EXPENDITURE: $38.2 mil
CONTRACT EXPENDITURE: $4.5 mil

Services

Housing: Family units 5; Unaccompanied officer quarters 8; Barracks spaces 14; Wherry housing 25. *Temporary Housing:* VIP units 2; VOQ units 2. *Exchange:* Convenience store; Credit union; Travel agency; Class VI; Laundry. *Child Care/Capacities:* No day care facilities. *Medical Facilities:* Medical clinic. *Recreational Facilities:* Pool; Gym; Recreation center; Stables; Racquetball court; Fitness center/Weight room; Softball field; Craft shop; Camping; Picnic area; Skeet range; Playground; Community club; Golf driving range; Rifle/Pistol range; Archery range.

Vermont

Burlington IAP

831. Burlington IAP, Air National Guard Base
Burlington IAP, VT 05401
802-660-5215; DSN 220-5210

Profile
BRANCH: Air National Guard.
SIZE AND LOCATION: 240 acres. Adj to Burlington IAP; 3 mi E of Burlington. *County:* Chittenden.
MAJOR UNITS: 158th Fighter Wing (ANG).
BASE HISTORY: 1946, organized Burlington Municipal Airport as 134th Fighter Squadron, first air unit in VT. 1951, activated Korean War unit, assigned to Eastern Air Defense Commander until Oct 1952. 1960, became part of Air Defense Runway Alert program; reorganized as 158th Fighter Group under Air Force Air Defense Command. 1973, became Defense Systems Evaluation Group. 1982, became 158th TFG.
VISITOR ATTRACTIONS: Static display of aircraft.

Key Contacts
PUBLIC AFFAIRS: Green Mountain Armory, Camp Johnson, Colchester, VT 05446, 802-864-1246, DSN 636-3246.

Personnel and Expenditures
ACTIVE DUTY PERSONNEL: 310 full time; 986 Guard
MILITARY PAYROLL EXPENDITURE: $23.6 mil

Services *Medical Facilities:* Medical clinic. *Recreational Facilities:* NCO club.

Colchester

832. Adjutant General of Vermont
Camp Johnson
Green Mountain Armory, Camp Johnson
Colchester, VT 05446-3004
802-654-0124; FAX 802-654-0425

Profile
BRANCH: Army National Guard.
LOCATION: N of Burlngton, off I-89 in Wineoski (Colchester PO address).
MAJOR UNITS: Vermont National Guard; Camp Johnson; 40th Army Band (ANG).

Key Contacts
COMMANDER: MajGen Martha T Rainville.
PUBLIC AFFAIRS: Maj Lloyd Goodrow, 802-654-0246.

Jericho

833. Ethan Allen Firing Range
EAFR
RR 1, Box 57
Jericho, VT 05465
802-899-7005; FAX 802-899-1063; DSN 636-3111

Profile
BRANCH: Army National Guard.
SIZE AND LOCATION: 11,219 acres. Approx 15 mi E of Burlington, VT, off Rte 15; served by Burlington IAP. *County:* Chittenden.
MAJOR UNITS: 172nd Infantry, 3rd Det, HQ (MTN); ARNG Mountain Warfare School; State Area Readiness Command-VT, Det 2, HQ.
BASE HISTORY: 1926, 6000 acres acquired for artillery range. 1941, expanded. 1952, ownership transferred to AF. 1965, transferred to Army. AMC is current agent for Army. Currently, serves as test facility for General Electric (GOCO) & training site for VT NG.

Key Contacts
COMMANDER: Col Alan L Nye.
PUBLIC AFFAIRS: Maj Lloyd Goodrow, GMA, Bldg #5, Camp Johnson, Colchester, VT 05446-3004.

Personnel and Expenditures
ACTIVE DUTY PERSONNEL: 0
DEPENDENTS: 0
CIVILIAN PERSONNEL: 12
CONTRACT EXPENDITURE: $0.6 mil

Services
Housing: Unaccompanied enlisted quarters 13; Barracks spaces 600. *Exchange:* Convenience store. *Child Care/Capacities:* No day care facilities. *Schools:* No on-base schools. *Medical Facilities:* No medical facilities. *Recreational Facilities:* Fitness center/Weight room.

White River Junction

834. White River Junction Naval Reserve Center
5 Holiday Inn Dr
White River Junction, VT 05001-2049
802-295-0500; FAX 802-295-5552
Internet: http://redcom1.cnrf.nola.navy.mil/wrj

Profile
BRANCH: Naval Reserve.
LOCATION: 9 mi NNE of Woodstock, VT. *County:* Windsor.
MAJOR UNITS: Destroyer Tender, Det 3 (NR); Naval Shipyard Portsmouth, NH 302 (NR); NH Bethesda 1206 (NR); Naval Mobile Construction Bn 27, Det 0927 (NMCB); Volunteer Training Unit 0267 (NR).
BASE HISTORY: 1947, property leased to Navy for reserve unit; LCI 799 (ship) delivered. 1949, new Training Center dedicated.

Key Contacts
COMMANDER: LCDR Michael L Merwin

Virginia

Alexandria

835. Army Communications-Electronics Command Acquisition Center
CECOM AC
2461 Eisenhower Ave, Hoffman I
Alexandria, VA 22331-0700
703-325-9760
Internet: http://issaa-www1.army.mil/

Profile
BRANCH: Army.
SIZE AND LOCATION: Offices only. In Alexandria, VA, just off I-95 (Telegraphh Rd exit) N of 495 intersection. *County:* Alexandria, City of.
MAJOR UNITS: Army Communications-Electronics Command Acquisition Center.
BASE HISTORY: 1996, Army Information Systems Selection and Acquisition Agency (ISSAA) name changed to CECOM Acquisition Center, Washington. Army's acquisition agency for information systems, hardware, software, & services.

Key Contacts
COMMANDER: Edward G Elgart, Director, 703-325-9760.
PUBLIC AFFAIRS: Helen Garamone, 703-325-9762.

Personnel and Expenditures
ACTIVE DUTY PERSONNEL: 100 (military & civilian)

836. Army Materiel Command Headquarters
AMC
5001 Eisenhower Ave
Alexandria, VA 22333-5001
703-274-8010
Internet: http://www.amc.citi.net

Profile
BRANCH: Army.
SIZE AND LOCATION: Offices only. Just off Capital Beltway, I-495/I-95 at Telegraph Rd exit. *County:* City of Alexandria.
MAJOR UNITS: Army Materiel Command Headquarters.

Key Contacts
COMMANDER: Gen Johnny E Wilson.
PUBLIC AFFAIRS: Tansill R Johnson, 703-671-0120, amcpa@alexandria-emh1.army.mil.

837. Coast Guard Telecommunication & Information Systems Command
TISCOM
7323 Telegraph Rd
Alexandria, VA 22315-3999
703-313-5400; FAX 703-313-5449

Profile
BRANCH: Coast Guard.
SIZE AND LOCATION: 200 acres. 5 mi S from Telegraph Rd Exit of I-95/495; 8 mi NE of Ft Belvoir on Telegraph Rd. *County:* Fairfax.
MAJOR UNITS: Coast Guard Telecommunications and Information Systems Command; Coast Guard Ceremonial Honor Guard; Coast Guard Navigation Center (NAVCEN).
BASE HISTORY: Land once part of George Washington's estate, Mount Vernon. 1939, USGC radio station, NMH, "Voice of the Commandant," move from nearby Fort Hunt Reservation; Electronic Engineering Laboratory established to test submarine cables & grind crystals. 1965, Honor Guard moved from Coast Guard Yard as major activity. 1976, radio station disestablished; unit renamed Coast Guard Station, Alexandria. 1988, renamed USCG Information Systems Center. 1993, current name. Current mission: USCG communications & computer test & development center; provide honor guard.

Key Contacts
COMMANDER: Capt C I Pearson, 703-313-5700, tiscomCO@tiscom.uscg.mil.
PUBLIC AFFAIRS: Executive Officer, 703-313-5430, FAX 703-313-5449, tiscomXO@tiscom.uscg.mil.

Personnel and Expenditures
ACTIVE DUTY PERSONNEL: 250
CIVILIAN PERSONNEL: 40

Services
Housing: None. *Exchange:* Barber shop; Convenience store; Small store, USCG uniforms only. *Child Care/Capacities:* No day care facilities. *Schools:* No on-base schools. *Medical Facilities:* Dispensary. *Recreational Facilities:* Tennis courts; Fitness center/Weight room; Softball field; Auto shop; Picnic area; Playground; Consolidated club.

838. Naval Facilities Engineering Command Headquarters
NAVFAC; NAVFACENGCOM
200 Stovall St, Ste 12517
Alexandria, VA 22332-2300
703-325-0310; DSN 221-0310
Internet: http://www.navy.mil/homepages/navfac/
OFFICER-OF-THE-DAY: 703-325-0400, DSN 221-0400

Profile
BRANCH: Navy.
SIZE AND LOCATION: Offices only. Near intersection of Telegraph Rd & Duke St (Rte 236) in Alexandria, VA, in Hoffman complex, 10th through 12th floors, directly across from Eisenhower Metro (subway) station. *County:* City of Alexandria.
MAJOR UNITS: Naval Facilities Engineering Command, HQ.
BASE HISTORY: 1942, Board of Navy Commissioners replaced by Bureau Systems & Bureau of Yards & Docks; charged with responsibility for building & maintaining Navy's shore establishment. 1966, reorganized as Naval Facilities Engineering Command. Currently provides, manages, & maintains public works, family housing & public utilities for the Navy; acquires & disposes of Navy real estate; program manager for Navy bachelor quarters; technical, engineering & program management support to expedite realignment & closure of naval bases; physical work done through subordinate commands, Engineering Field Divisions, Engineering Field Activities, Construction Battalion Centers, & Naval Facilities Engineering Service Center.

Key Contacts
COMMANDER: RADM David J Nash, CEC, 703-325-0400, DSN 221-0400.
PUBLIC AFFAIRS: Elaine McNeil, Code 00D, 703-325-0310, DSN 221-0310, elmcneil@hq.navfac.navy.mil.
PROCUREMENT: 703-325-8577, DSN 221-8577.
TRANSPORTATION: 703-325-8185, DSN 221-8185.
PERSONNEL/COMMUNITY ACTIVITIES: 703-325-8542, DSN 221-8542.

Personnel and Expenditures
ACTIVE DUTY PERSONNEL: 465 military & civilians
DEPENDENTS: 0
CONTRACT EXPENDITURE: $3.1 bil

Services *Base Library:* Yes. *Recreational Facilities:* Gym.

839. US Army Corps of Engineers, Center for Public Works
7701 Telegraph Rd
Alexandria, VA 22315-3862
Internet: http://www.usacpw.belvoir.army.mil/
cpw.htm
Profile
BRANCH: Army.
LOCATION: *County:* Fairfax.
MAJOR UNITS: Army Center for Public Works; 249th Engineer Bn.
BASE HISTORY: A field Operating Agency of the Corps of Engineers. Mission: provide public works guidance, support, & services to Army installations around the world.
Key Contacts
COMMANDER: Edward T Watling, Director, 703-428-6300, FAX 703-428-7926, DSN 328-6300.
PUBLIC AFFAIRS: Betty Fancis, 703-428-7000; Penny Schmitt, Chief, Customer Relations Office, 703-428-6933, FAX 703-428-7926, penny.schmitt@cpw01. usace.army.mil.

840. US Army Corps of Engineers, Topographic Engineering Center
TEC
7701 Telegraph Rd
Alexandria, VA 22315-3864
703-428-6634
Internet: http://www.tec.army.mil/
Profile
BRANCH: Army.
SIZE AND LOCATION: Offices only. Bldg 2592, The Cude Bldg. *County:* Fairfax.
MAJOR UNITS: Corps of Engineers, Topographic Engineering Center.
BASE HISTORY: One of 4 laboratories of the US Army Corps of Engineers.
Key Contacts
PUBLIC AFFAIRS: 703-428-6634.

841. US Army Corps of Engineers, Water Resources Support Center
7701 Telegraph Rd, Casey Bldg
Alexandria, VA 22315-3868
Internet: http://www.wrc-ndc.usace.army.mil/
Profile
BRANCH: Army.
SIZE: Offices only. *County:* Fairfax.
MAJOR UNITS: Corps of Engineers, Water Resources Support Center.

Arlington

842. Army National Guard Readiness Center
ARNGRC
Arlington Hall; Readiness Center
111 S George Mason Dr
Arlington, VA 22204-1382
703-607-7010; DSN 327-7010
Internet: http://www-ngb5.ngb.army.mil
Profile
BRANCH: Army National Guard.
SIZE AND LOCATION: 15 acres. Just S of Rte 50 on S George Mason Dr; 10 min from Pentagon. *County:* Arlington.

MAJOR UNITS: Army National Guard Readiness Center.
BASE HISTORY: Occupies part of site of former Arlington Hall Station.
Key Contacts
COMMANDER: LTC Harold W Billingsly, 703-607-7042, FAX 703-607-7087, DSN 327-7042, BillingslyH@arngrc-emh2.army. mil.
PUBLIC AFFAIRS: National Guard Bureau, The Pentagon, Washington, DC 20310-2500, 703-695-0421.
Personnel and Expenditures
ACTIVE DUTY PERSONNEL: 850 guard/active
DEPENDENTS: 0
CIVILIAN PERSONNEL: 200

843. Bureau of Naval Personnel
BUPERS
FOB #2, Navy Annex
Arlington, VA
Mailing Address
Bureau of Naval Personnel
Washington, DC 20370-5000
703-545-6700
Internet: http://www.navy.mil/homepages/
bupers/
Profile
BRANCH: Navy.
LOCATION: Near Pentagon at E end of Columbia Pike. *County:* Arlington.
MAJOR UNITS: Bureau of Naval Personnel.
BASE HISTORY: Navy personnel matters handled by Secretary of War until establishment of Navy Department, 1798. 1815, Secretary of Navy took control of personnel. 1861, Office of Detail & Bureau of Equipment & Recruiting created. 1942, renamed Bureau of Naval Personnel. 1982, renamed Naval Military Personnel Command. 1991, revered to Bureau of Naval Personnel, BUPERS. 1998, scheduled for relocation to Naval Support Activity, Memphis, TN.
FUTURE CLOSURE/REALIGNMENT: To relocate to Naval Support Activity, Memphis by Sep 1998.
Key Contacts
COMMANDER: VADM Daniel T Oliver, Chief of Naval Personnel, 703-614-1101.
PUBLIC AFFAIRS: CDR T McCreary, Director, Public Affairs, 703-614-2000.

844. Defense Finance and Accounting Service, Headquarters
DFAS-HQ
1931 Jefferson Davis Hwy
Arlington, VA 22240-5291
703-607-2716; FAX 703-607-2829; DSN 327-2716
Internet: http://www.dfas.mil/
Profile
BRANCH: DOD.
SIZE AND LOCATION: Offices only. Off Rte 1, in Crystal City Mall, Bldg 3, approx 0.5 mi from National Airport; at Crystal Mall 3, floors 2-5. *County:* Arlington.
MAJOR UNITS: Defense Finance and Accounting Service, HQ.
BASE HISTORY: 1991, activated as accounting firm of DOD to improve overall effectiveness of DOD financial management through consolidation, standardization, & integration of finance & accounting procedures, operations,

& systems. Other major centers Cleveland, Columbus, Denver, Indianapolis, & Kansas City. Approx 300 Defense Accounting Offices on DOD installations (including small European liaison office & Pacific) report to these 5 centers. Approx 3.7 million military personnel, 2 million retirees & annuitants, 250,000 DOD civilians, & 5 million contractor invoices receive their pay from DFAS.
Key Contacts
COMMANDER: Gary W Amlin, Agency Director (Acting) 703-607-2616, DSN 327-2616.
PUBLIC AFFAIRS: Catherine Ferguson.
PERSONNEL/COMMUNITY ACTIVITIES: Steve Freeman, Director of Personnel, 703-607-0690, DSN 327-0690.
Personnel and Expenditures
ACTIVE DUTY PERSONNEL: 15
CIVILIAN PERSONNEL: 250

845. Defense Information Systems Agency
701 S Courthouse Rd, Code D04
Arlington, VA 22204-2199
703-607-6436
Profile
BRANCH: DOD.
SIZE AND LOCATION: Offices only. Off Columbia Pike. *County:* Arlington.
MAJOR UNITS: Defense Information Systems Agency.

846. Defense National Stockpile Center
1745 Jefferson Davis Hwy, Suite 100, Crystal Square Bldg 4
Arlington, VA 22202
703-274-6135
Profile
BRANCH: Defense Logistics Agency.
SIZE AND LOCATION: Offices only. Approx 1 mi from Washington National Airport. *County:* Arlington.
BASE HISTORY: Manages the stockpile of 90 strategic materials.

847. Fort Myer
204 Lee Ave
Arlington, VA 22211-5050
703-545-6700; DSN 227-0101
Internet: http://www.myer.army.mil/
Profile
BRANCH: Army.
SIZE AND LOCATION: 256 acres. Off US-50 & Rte 27 in Arlington, VA. Post adj to Arlington National Cemetery; min from I-395; 15 min from National Airport. *County:* Arlington.
MAJOR UNITS: Army Band (Pershing's Own); 3rd Infantry Regiment (The Old Guard); Army Garrison, HQ; Co Special Activities, HQ; MDW Military Police Co; Co Army Garrison, HQ; 1101st Signal Brigade; Andrew Rader Medical Clinic; Army Criminal Investigation Command, Washington District; Army Engineering Activity, Capital Area; Army Chorus.
BASE HISTORY: Site formerly owned by Martha Custis Washington's son, John Parke Custis; called Arlington Heights. Later owned by Custis' granddaughter, Mary Ann Randolph, who married Robert E Lee who rescued estate from financial ruin. 1861, confis-

cated by federal government. 1864, bought by government for property taxes; part what is now Arlington National Cemetery; remainder Ft Whipple. Signal Corps took over by late 1860s. Brig Gen Albert J Myer, after whom fort was renamed, Army's first Chief Signal Officer & Commander, Ft Whipple. 1887, Gen Philip H Sheridan transferred communications unit; assigned cavalry. As many as 1500 horses stabled. Sep 1908, 1st military test flight of aircraft made from parade grounds by Orville Wright. On second flight, Lt Thomas Selfridge killed. Since early 1900s, known as "Home of the Generals." Most buildings built from 1895-1905; historic landmarks. Quarters Number One official residence of Chief of Staff of Army since 1899. WWII, served as inprocessing & outprocessing station. 1942, Army School of Music established. 1948, 3rd Infantry Regiment, oldest regular infantry regiment, reactivated; assigned to Ft Myer & Ft McNair. Ft Myer falls under jurisdiction of commanding general, USA Military District of Washington, Ft McNair. Post commander serves as Garrison Commander. Also see Military District of Washington.

VISITOR ATTRACTIONS: 3rd Infantry Museum; 3rd Infantry Caisson Platoon Stables; Summerall Field (burial site of Black Jack); Arlington National Cemetery; Tomb of the Unknowns; Whipple Field; Quarters One, & many other buildings on National Historic Register.

Key Contacts
COMMANDER: Col Owen C Powell Jr.
PUBLIC AFFAIRS: 703-696-1400; Also see Military District of Washington, 202-685-2892.

Personnel and Expenditures
ACTIVE DUTY PERSONNEL: 2400
DEPENDENTS: 420
CIVILIAN PERSONNEL: 671

Services
Housing: Family units 180; Barracks spaces 2461. *Temporary Housing:* VIP units 18 uits; VOQ units 5 units; Transient quarters 56. *Commissary:* Yes; *Exchange:* Retail store; Barber shop; Dry cleaners; Food shop; Florist; Bank; Service station; Beauty shop; Clothing store; Optical shop; Shoe repair. *Child Care/Capacities:* Day care center capacity 76; Home day care program. *Schools:* No on-base schools. *Base Library:* Yes. *Medical Facilities:* Medical clinic; Dental clinic; Veterinary services; Rader Clinic, one of Army's largest ambulatory health care facility. *Recreational Facilities:* Bowling center; Movie theater; Pool; Gym; Recreation center; Tennis courts; Racquetball court; Fitness/ Weight room; Softball field; Football field; Auto shop; Craft shop; Officers club; NCO club; Equipment checkout.

848. Henderson Hall, HQ USMC
Henderson Hall
1555 S Southgate Rd
Arlington, VA 22214-5003
703-614-2014; 703-545-6700; FAX
703-979-0972, 486-9251; DSN 224-2013
Profile
BRANCH: Marine Corps.
SIZE AND LOCATION: 21 acres. 2 mi S of Pentagon off Columbia Pike, adj to Ft Myer and Arlington National Cemetery. *County:* Arlington.

MAJOR UNITS: HQ Bn, HQ US Marine Corps.
Key Contacts
COMMANDER: Col Lief Larson, 703-614-1625.
PUBLIC AFFAIRS: Capt Stephen Oster, 703-614-8958.
PROCUREMENT: SSgt Jose Pagan, 703-614-1555.
Personnel and Expenditures
ACTIVE DUTY PERSONNEL: 500
Services
Housing: At Fort Myer, Fort Belvoir, & Bolling AFB. *Exchange:* Retail store; Barber shop; Dry cleaners; Food shop; Florist; Bakery; Garden center; Mall; 7 day store. *Child Care/Capacities:* No day care facilities. *Schools:* No on-base schools. *Medical Facilities:* Dispensaries at Ft Myer & Navy Annex; Other care at Bethesda National Naval Medical Center, MD and Andrews AFB, MD. *Recreational Facilities:* Pool; Gym; Tennis courts; Racquetball court; Fitness center/Weight room;

849. Naval Sea Systems Command, HQ
NAVSEA
2531 Jefferson Davis Hwy
Arlington, VA 22242-5160
Internet: http://www.navsea.navy.mil/
Profile
BRANCH: Navy.
SIZE AND LOCATION: Offices only. In Crystal City along Rte 1. *County:* Arlington.
MAJOR UNITS: Naval Sea Systems Command, HQ.
BASE HISTORY: Navy Department's central activity for designing, engineering, integrating, building, procuring naval ships, shipboard weapons, & combat systems. NAVSEA employs over 63,000 military & civilian personnel at 50 field activities, 104 detachments, 105 on-site offices, HQ. Largest of Navy Systems Commands.
FUTURE CLOSURE/REALIGNMENT: Relocating to Washington Navy Yard by 2001.
Key Contacts
PUBLIC AFFAIRS: 703-602-6920.
Personnel and Expenditures
ACTIVE DUTY PERSONNEL: 3968
CONTRACT EXPENDITURE: $14.8 bil (total budget)

850. Navy Recruiting Command
4015 Wilson Blvd
Arlington, VA 22203
1-800-USA-NAVY
Profile
BRANCH: Navy.
SIZE AND LOCATION: Offices only. Just across Washington, DC, Key Bridge. *County:* Arlington.
MAJOR UNITS: Navy Recruiting Command.
Services
Housing: None.

851. Office of Naval Research
ONR
800 N Quincy St, Code 25
Arlington, VA 22217-5660
703-696-5031, 696-2579
Internet: http://www.onr.navy.mil/onr/
Profile
BRANCH: Navy.

SIZE AND LOCATION: Offices. In Ballston Tower I; take I-66 E to N Fairfax Dr exit (exit 71) approx 0.5 mi right onto N Quincy St; I-66 W to Glebe Rd S (exit 71), left on Glebe Rd, 3rd stop light, onto Fairfax Dr, 0.5 mi right onto N Quincy St. *County:* Arlington.
MAJOR UNITS: Office of Naval Research.
BASE HISTORY: Coordinates, executes, & promotes science & technology programs of Navy & Marine Corps through universities, government laboratories, & other organizations.
Key Contacts
COMMANDER: RADM Paul G Gaffney II.

852. The Pentagon
Arlington, VA 22211
Mailing Address
Washington, DC 20301
703-545-6700; FAX 703-695-4299
Internet: http://www.defenselink.mil/pubs/ pentagon/index.html
Profile
BRANCH: DOD.
SIZE AND LOCATION: 583 acres; Bldg 29 acres. Adj to Arlington National Cemetery and Ft Myer; exits off I-395 and I-66. *County:* Arlington.
MAJOR UNITS: Secretary of Defense; Chairman of the Joint Chiefs of Staff; Secretary of the Army; Secretary of the Navy; Secretary of the Air Force; Commandant of the Marine Corps; Office of the Chief, Army Reserve; Air Force Command Center.
BASE HISTORY: Original site swampy area into which over 40,000 concrete piles & tons of sand & gravel were added. Building constructed in 16 months, completed 1943. One of world's largest office buildings, 3,705,793 sq ft (twice size of Merchandise Mart, Chicago); 3 times floor space of Empire State Building. A city in itself, building includes 17.5 miles of corridors; 7 minute walk between any 2 points in building; consolidated 17 buildings of War Department. DOD managed by civilian Secretary of Defense, appointed by President. Highest ranking military position, Chairman, Joint Chiefs of Staff. Undergoing 14 year, $1.1 bil renovation; some offices temporarily moved to Crystal City & Rosslyn, VA.
VISITOR ATTRACTIONS: Daily tours (M-F except federal holidays): walk-in 9:30-3:30 every half hour for 90 min; group tours, reservations required 2 weeks in advance through Director, Pentagon Tours, Rm 1E776, 1400 Defense Pentagon, Washington, DC 20301-1400, FAX 703-614-1642, tourschd@pa-gate.pa.osd.mil, or on line.
Key Contacts
COMMANDER: Secretary of Defense.
PUBLIC AFFAIRS: Fort McNair, HQ, Military District of Washington, Washington, DC 20319-5050, 202-475-0856, DSN 335-0856.
Personnel and Expenditures
ACTIVE DUTY PERSONNEL: 11,500
DEPENDENTS: 0
CIVILIAN PERSONNEL: 11,500
Services
Housing: None. *Exchange:* Mall. *Schools:* No on-base schools. *Base Library:* Yes. *Medical Facilities:* Medical clinic; Dental clinic. *Recreational Facilities:* Gym; Racquetball court; Fitness center/Weight room; Restaurant; 2 cafeterias; 6 snack bars; 1 outdoor snack bar.

853. Washington, DC, Coast Guard Air Station
USCG AIRSTA WASH
National Airport, Hangar 6
Arlington, VA
Mailing Address
National Airport, Hangar 6
Washington, DC 20001-4964
703-603-7050; FAX 703-603-7081; DSN
703-332-5951
OFFICER-OF-THE-DAY: 703-603-7050, FAX
703-603-7019, DSN 332-5951

Profile
BRANCH: Coast Guard.
LOCATION: At Washington National Airport,
Arlington, VA. *County:* Arlington.
MAJOR UNITS: Coast Guard Air Station,
Washington, DC.
BASE HISTORY: Facility supports 1 aircraft
for USCG Command & Control purposes.

Key Contacts
COMMANDER: CDR Ronald L Rutledge.
PUBLIC AFFAIRS: Commandant (G-CP),
USCG, 2100 2nd St, SW, Washington, DC,
20593-0001, 202-267-1933.
PROCUREMENT: SK2 Floyd R Mallett,
703-603-7050, ext 322, FAX 703-603-7081,
DSN 332-5951.
TRANSPORTATION: See Procurement
Officer.

Personnel and Expenditures
ACTIVE DUTY PERSONNEL: 16
DEPENDENTS: 0
CIVILIAN PERSONNEL: 0

Services *Recreational Facilities:* Fitness center/
Weight room.

Blackstone

854. Fort Pickett, Maneuver Training Center
Army National Guard
Blackstone, VA 23824-5000
804-292-2722; FAX 804-292-2409; DSN
438-2722

Profile
BRANCH: Army National Guard.
SIZE AND LOCATION: 46,000 acres. 1 mi
from Blackstone, VA; 40 mi SW of Peters-
burg; from US 460, W of Petersburg, take Ft
Pickett exit, follow signs, main entrance on
State Rte 40; Richmond IAP 60 mi. *County:*
Nottoway; Brunswick; Dinwiddie; Lunen-
burg.
MAJOR UNITS: ANG Maneuver Training Cen-
ter, Fort Pickett.
BASE HISTORY: 1942, established and named
for Maj Gen George Pickett. Oct 1997, opera-
tional control transferred to Virginia National
Guard.

Key Contacts
PUBLIC AFFAIRS: 804-292-7522.

Services
Housing: Family units; Trailer spaces; RV/
Camper sites. *Temporary Housing:* VIP units;
VOQ units; VEQ units. *Exchange:* Retail store;
Service station. *Child Care/Capacities:* No day
care facilities. *Schools:* No on-base schools.
Medical Facilities: Medical clinic. *Recreational
Facilities:* Bowling center; Movie theater; Pool;
Gym; Recreation center; Tennis courts; Racquet-
ball court; Fitness center/Weight room; Softball

field; Auto shop; Craft shop; Camping; Fishing/
Hunting; Picnic area; Community club; Thrift
shop.

Bowling Green

855. Fort A P Hill
Bowling Green, VA 22427
804-633-8710

Profile
BRANCH: Army.
SIZE AND LOCATION: 75,944 acres (plus 111
acres of leased land). Approx 10 mi SE of
Fredericksburg, VA; 2 mi E of Bowling
Green, VA on Rte 301; midway between
Richmond & Washington, DC. Leased area
located along Rappahannock River & used
for float bridge training site. *County:*
Caroline.
MAJOR UNITS: Army Communications-Elec-
tronics Command Center for Night Vision
and Electro-Optics Directorate; 20th Special
Forces (General Purposes, Airborne) Det A,
3rd Bn (VA ARNG); Sea-Air Land Team
Two (SEAL, Amphibious Force, Navy Atlan-
tic Fleet); Leadership Academy, 80th Train-
ing Support Brigade, 80th Division; Corps of
Engineers, Norfolk District; 4th Brigade, 78th
Training Division; 299th Engineer Co; Army
Health Clinic, Ft AP Hill.
BASE HISTORY: 1940, site recommended for
national training area. 1941, Fort A P Hill es-
tablished; maneuver area for II Army Corps
& National Guard. 1942, staging area for Gen
Patton's Task Force A preparing for invasion
of Morocco. 1944, field training for Officer
Candidate School for Forts Lee, Eustis, and
Belvoir. Korean War, major staging area for
European units. Vietnam War, center for En-
gineer Officer Candidate School, Ft Belvoir.
Formerly a subpost of Ft Lee, VA. Currently,
sub-installation of Ft Belvoir, VA; part of
Military District of Washington. Hosted Boy
Scouts of America National Jamboree in
1981, 1985, 1989, 1993, & 1997.
VISITOR ATTRACTIONS: Liberty Church
(built in 1850); site of National Boy Scout
Jamboree.

Key Contacts
COMMANDER: LTC Bruce L Hopkins, Acting
Commander.

Personnel and Expenditures
ACTIVE DUTY PERSONNEL: 45
CIVILIAN PERSONNEL: 185 (plus 100 sea-
sonal)

Services
Housing: Family units 25; Duplex units; Trailer
spaces 10; RV/Camper sites 48; Housing units
28. *Temporary Housing:* VOQ units 3; Guesthouse units 6 rooms, 3 suites; Unaccompanied
officer/Enlisted quarters units 46. *Exchange:*
Small exchange; Full services at nearby
Dahlgren Naval Station, Ft Belvoir, or Quantico
Marine Corps Base. *Child Care/Capacities:*
Home day care program. *Medical Facilities:*
Medical clinic. *Recreational Facilities:* Bowling
center; Movie theater; Pool; Gym; Tennis
courts; Fitness center/Weight room; Softball
field; Auto shop; Craft shop; Camping; Fishing/
Hunting; Skeet range; Youth center; Community
club; Skiing; Lakeside cabins; Camp Opechan-
canough with 24 camp sites.

Chesapeake

856. Coast Guard Finance Center
USCG FINCEN
1430A Kristina Way
Chesapeake, VA 23326
757-523-6700; FAX 757-523-6717
Internet: http://www.dot.gov/dotinfo/uscg/hq/
fincen/finhome.htm

Profile
BRANCH: Coast Guard.
SIZE AND LOCATION: Offices only. Green-
brier section of Chesapeake; 20 min from Nor-
folk IAP, off I-64E. *County:* City of
Chesapeake.
MAJOR UNITS: Coast Guard Finance Center;
Coast Guard Training Quota Management
Center.

Key Contacts
COMMANDER: Capt R D Reck, 757-523-6704.
PUBLIC AFFAIRS: Lt A T Martin,
757-523-6706.
PROCUREMENT: CWO S K Phifer,
757-523-6708, FAX 757-523-6717.

Personnel and Expenditures
ACTIVE DUTY PERSONNEL: 48
CIVILIAN PERSONNEL: 255

Services
Housing: None. *Temporary Housing:* None. *Exchange:* Credit union; Satellite exchange. *Child
Care/Capacities:* No day care facilities.
Schools: No on-base schools. *Medical Facilities:* No medical facilities. *Recreational Facilities:* Fitness center/Weight room; Sand volleyball.

857. Fentres Naval Auxiliary Landing Field
NALF Fentress
2500 Lockheed Ave
Chesapeake, VA 23322-1213
757-433-2259; DSN 433-2259

Profile
BRANCH: Navy.
SIZE AND LOCATION: 3500 acres. 10 mi SW
of NAS Oceana in Chesapeake, VA; on Rte
64, Indian River Rd. *County:* City of
Chesapeake.
MAJOR UNITS: Naval Auxiliary Landing
Field, Fentres.
BASE HISTORY: WWII, erected as airfield
training facility. Mission converted to field
carrier landing practice for pilot training prior
to shipboard landings (average number of total operations ranges from 80,000-100,000 annually); secondary function as emergency recovery field for NAS Oceana. Under operational control of NAS Oceana.

Key Contacts
COMMANDER: Officer-in-Charge.
PUBLIC AFFAIRS: Naval Air Station Oceana,
757-433-3131.

Services
Housing: Unaccompanied enlisted quarters 12.
Child Care/Capacities: No day care facilities.
Schools: No on-base schools. *Medical Facilities:* No medical facilities. *Recreational Facilities:* Pool; Fitness center/Weight room; Auto
shop.

858. Northwest Naval Security Group Activity
NAVSECGRUACT
1320 Northwest Blvd, Ste 100
Chesapeake, VA 23322-4094
757-421-8000
Profile
BRANCH: Navy.
SIZE AND LOCATION: 4500 acres. In city of Chesapeake, near Rte 125 & 337. *County:* City of Chesapeake.
MAJOR UNITS: Naval Security Group Activity, Northwest; Navy Communications Area Master Station Satellite Communications Atlantic Facility; North Atlantic Treaty Organization Satellite Communications Facility; Coast Guard Communication Station; Electronic Warfare Operational Programming Facility; Fleet Surveillance Support Command; Marine Corps Security Force Training Center.
BASE HISTORY: Situated on wooded farm and swamp lands; all Naval Security Group operational elements located at Northwest except for COMSEC Material Issuing Office (CMIO) and a division of Signal Security Department, both located on Naval Base, Norfolk.
Key Contacts
COMMANDER: Capt S Peyronel, 757-421-8200.
PUBLIC AFFAIRS: R R Barrera, 757-421-8328.
PROCUREMENT: Lt Terrell, Contracting, 757-421-8287.
Personnel and Expenditures
ACTIVE DUTY PERSONNEL: 1400
Services
Housing: Family units; Unaccompanied officer quarters; Unaccompanied enlisted quarters; Mobile home units. *Exchange:* Retail store; Credit union. *Medical Facilities:* Medical clinic; Dental clinic. *Recreational Facilities:* Bowling center; Pool; Gym; Tennis courts; Racquetball court; Fitness center/Weight room; Softball field; NCO club; Camping; Fishing/Hunting; Youth center; Picnic area; Water sports; Archery range.

Dahlgren

859. Dahlgren Division, Naval Surface Warfare Center
NSWCDD
Code C05
Dahlgren, VA 22448-5000
703-663-8291; DSN 249-8291
E-mail: c05@nswc.navy.mil Internet:http://www.nswc.navy.mil/
OFFICER-OF-THE-DAY: 703-663-8291, DSN 249-8291
Profile
BRANCH: Navy.
SIZE AND LOCATION: 4300 acres. From Fredericksburg, VA, 28 mi, Rte 3 E, left on Rte 206 at King George to Dahlgren. From Richmond, VA, I-95 to Rte 208, Carmel Church Exit, to Rte 301 N, right on Rte 206 to Dahlgren. From Washington, DC, I-95 S to Rte 5, Waldorf, MD, Exit, S to Rte 301 S, across Harry W Nice Bridge, left on Rte 206 to Dahlgren. *County:* King George.
MAJOR UNITS: Naval Surface Warfare Center, Dahlgren Division; Naval Space Command;

Naval Space Surveillance Center; AEGIS Missile System Training Center.
BASE HISTORY: 1918, established as Naval Proving Ground; named for RADM John A Dahlgren, father of modern naval ordnance; moved from Indian Head facility to use 90,000 yard Potomac River range to test naval guns & ammunition. Post WWII, added R&D. 1959, renamed Naval Weapons Laboratory. Today, gun line & 20 mile down river range still used for projectile testing. Primarily civilian organization with military commander & civilian executive director. Three main sites: Dahlgren, VA; White Oak, MD; and CSS Panama City, FL. Field test facilities at Ft Monroe, VA; Ft Lauderdale, FL; and Wallops Island, VA.
VISITOR ATTRACTIONS: During special events, such as Armed Forces Day & 4th of July, public invited to tour, watch gun firings (up to 16" guns) & view exhibits. Area located near sports & recreational activities with Potomac River, Blue Ridge Mountains, Chesapeake Bay & Atlantic Ocean within easy driving distance. Many historical sites associated with Colonial America, American Revolution & Civil War nearby.
Key Contacts
COMMANDER: Capt John C Overton, 703-663-8101, DSN 249-8101.
PUBLIC AFFAIRS: 703-663-8154, DSN 249-8154.
PROCUREMENT: 703-663-8391, DSN 249-8391.
TRANSPORTATION: 703-663-8251, DSN 249-8251.
PERSONNEL/COMMUNITY ACTIVITIES: Family Service Center, 703-663-1839, DSN 249-8216.
Personnel and Expenditures
ACTIVE DUTY PERSONNEL: 700; 100 Reservists
DEPENDENTS: 1300
CIVILIAN PERSONNEL: 3400
Services
Housing: Family units 154; Unaccompanied officer quarters 24 units; Unaccompanied enlisted quarters 198. *Temporary Housing:* VIP units 2 suites; VOQ units 36; VEQ units 53; Transient quarters 4. *Commissary:* Yes; *Exchange:* Barber shop; Dry cleaners; Food shop; Bank. *Child Care/Capacities:* Day care center capacity 82; Home day care program. *Schools:* Preschool/Kindergarten; Elementary; Intermediate/Junior high. *Base Library:* Yes. *Medical Facilities:* Medical clinic; Dental clinic. *Recreational Facilities:* Bowling center; Movie theater; Pool; Gym; Recreation center; Golf course; Tennis courts; Racquetball court; Fitness center/Weight room; Softball field; Craft shop; Officers club; NCO club; Camping; Fishing/Hunting.

Fairfax

860. National Imagery & Mapping Agency
NIMA
8613 Lee Hwy
Fairfax, VA 22031-2139
703-275-5545, 275-8409; FAX 703-275-8561; DSN 235-5545; DSN FAX 235-8561

Internet: http://www.nima.mil
Profile
BRANCH: DOD.
SIZE AND LOCATION: Offices only. Just outside Capital Beltway, I-495. *County:* Fairfax.
MAJOR UNITS: Production Center, St Louis, MO; Production Center, Bethesda, MD; Production Center, Washington, DC; Production Center, Reston Center, Reston, VA; Defense Mapping College, Ft Belvoir, VA.
BASE HISTORY: 1972, established with consolidation of mapping activities; organized into HQ, Fairfax, VA, and 5 components. 1996, established as NIMA.
VISITOR ATTRACTIONS: Generally closed to public.
Key Contacts
COMMANDER: R ADM J J Dantone, Jr, 703-275-5900, FAX 275-8596, DSN 235-5900.
PUBLIC AFFAIRS: Laura B Snow, Director, Congressional & Public Liaison, 703-275-5545, FAX 703-275-8561, DSN 235-5545 Washington, DC 20315-0030, 202-227-2032.
Personnel and Expenditures
ACTIVE DUTY PERSONNEL: 500
CIVILIAN PERSONNEL: 8500
Services *Recreational Facilities:* Fitness center/Weight room.

Falls Church

861. Military Traffic Management Command, HQ
HQMTMC
5611 Columbia Pike
Falls Church, VA 22041-5050
800-756-6862
Internet: http://mtmc.army.mil/hq.htm
Profile
BRANCH: Army.
SIZE AND LOCATION: Office only. Approx 5 mi W of Pentagon; Nassif Bldg. *County:* Fairfax.
MAJOR UNITS: Military Traffic Management Command, HQ.
Key Contacts
COMMANDER: Col Donald Lamb, Director.

Fort Belvoir

862. Army Criminal Investigation Command
6010 6th St, Bldg 1465
Fort Belvoir, VA 22060-5506
703-806-0400
Profile
BRANCH: Army.
SIZE AND LOCATION: See Fort Belvoir. On Fort Belvoir. *County:* Fairfax.
MAJOR UNITS: Army Criminal Investigation Command.
BASE HISTORY: 1995, moved to Fort Belvoir.
Key Contacts
COMMANDER: Brig Gen Daniel A Doherty.
PUBLIC AFFAIRS: John P Boyce, 703-806-0373.

863. Belvoir Research, Development & Engineering Center

Belvoir RD&E Center
10115 Gridley Rd, Ste 228
Fort Belvoir, VA 22060-5849
703-704-2247; FAX 703-704-2258; DSN
654-2247

Profile
BRANCH: Army.
SIZE AND LOCATION: 240 acres. At Ft Belvoir, approx 15 mi S of Washington, DC. *County:* Fairfax.
MAJOR UNITS: Belvoir Research, Development, and Engineering Center.
BASE HISTORY: Supports Combat Support & Combat Service Support missions of Army. Also provides for all ground equipment fuels & lubricants for DOD. Provides equipment for Training & Doctrine Command Schools, & other project managers. Oversees GOCO Belvoir Fuels & Lubricants Research Facility, Southwest Research Institute, San Antonio, TX.

Key Contacts
COMMANDER: Lynwood M Rabon Jr, PIPE Division Chief.
PERSONNEL/COMMUNITY ACTIVITIES: Perky Thomas, Personnel Officer, 703-704-2872.

Personnel and Expenditures
ACTIVE DUTY PERSONNEL: 900 (military & civilian)

Services
Housing: See Ft Belvoir.

864. Davison Army Airfield

Davison AAF
8926 Gavin Rd
Fort Belvoir, VA 22060
703-656-7662
Internet: http://www.mdw.army.mil/fs-i14.htm

Profile
BRANCH: Army.
LOCATION: At Ft Belvoir off Rte 1 near I-95, on State Rte 617; 15 mi S of Washington, DC. *County:* Fairfax.
MAJOR UNITS: 12th Aviation Bn; Operations Airlift Command; District of Columbia National Guard Aviation Det; Research & Development Activity (night-vision & electronic sensing).
BASE HISTORY: Opened 1952, as part of Ft Belvoir's Engineering School, named in honor of Brig Gen Donald A Davison, WWII aviator. 1954, assigned to Military District of Washington. Army's only "Priority Air Transport" command, providing transportation to military & government organizations in National Capital Region. Supports White House, Congress, DOD, foreign heads of state on visits, 3rd US Infantry tactical missions, & DC ARNG, trains reservists, & conducts Air Assault Training course for Military District of Washington. Runway at Davison, Pentagon heliport, Ft Meade airfield, Andrews AFB. Executive flight detachment flew Presidents from Eisenhower to Ford (1957-76).

Key Contacts
PUBLIC AFFAIRS: Military District of Washington, Ft McNair, 202-685-2892; Fort Belvoir, 703-805-2402.

Services
Housing: See Ft Belvoir.

865. Defense Logistics Agency, HQ

DLA
8725 John J Kingman Rd
Fort Belvoir, VA 22060
Internet: http://www.dla.mil/

Profile
BRANCH: Defense Logistics Agency.
LOCATION: On Ft Belvoir; take US Rte 1 S, right onto Woodlawn Rd, second traffic light, left onto Kingman Rd, visitors use Main Gate. *County:* Fairfax.
MAJOR UNITS: Defense Logistics Agency, HQ; Defense Logistics Services Center; Defense National Stockpile; Defense Reutilization and Marketing Service; Systems Design Center; Defense Automated and Printing Support Center.
BASE HISTORY: 1952, Joint Army-Navy-Air Force Support Center established. 1954-56, commodity-manager agencies established. 1961, consolidation into Defense Supply Agency (DSA). 1965, supply centers consolidated. 1977, renamed DLA. 1979, responsible for disposal of surplus materiel. 1988, assumed management of stockpile of strategic materials. A combat support agency; provides materiel & supplies to military services; supports acquisition of weapons & other equipment. Manages supply centers in Columbus, OH; Ft Belvoir; Richmond, VA & Philadelphia, PA. Manages 90% of military supply items.
VISITOR ATTRACTIONS: Ft Belvoir an open base; DLA, HQ Complex, controlled access.

Key Contacts
COMMANDER: Lt Gen Henry T Glisson, USA.
PUBLIC AFFAIRS: Sharon Gavin, 8725 John J Kingman Rd, Ste 2533, Ft Belvoir, VA 22060-6221, 703-767-6200.

Services
Housing: See Ft Belvoir.

866. Fort Belvoir

US Army Garrison & Ft Belvoir
Fort Belvoir, VA 22060-5932
703-805-5001; FAX 703-805-3151; DSN 655-5001
Internet: http://www.belvoir.amy.mil/
OFFICER-OF-THE-DAY: Staff Duty Officer, 703-806-3012, DSN 655-3012

Profile
BRANCH: Army.
SIZE AND LOCATION: 8656 acres. In N VA on peninsula just below Mount Vernon, approx 35 minutes SE of Washington, DC. Enter main gate from Richmond Hwy, Rte 1. 20 minutes from National Airport. Borders city of Alexandria; 8 min from I-95. *County:* Fairfax.
MAJOR UNITS: Army Garrison, Ft Belvoir; Army Intelligence & Security Command; Army Criminal Investigation Command, HQ; Defense Mapping School; Defense Systems Management College; 310th Theater Army Area Command; 29th Infantry Division (Light), HQ (VA ARNG); Army Information Systems Software Center; Belvoir Research, Development and Engineering Center; Night Vision & Electronic Sensors Directorate; Army Operational Support Airlift Command; Army Management Staff College; 57th Ordnance Det, Explosive Ordnance Disposal; 610th Ordnance Bn; Defense Logistics Agency, HQ; *Soldiers* Magazine; Institute of Heraldry; Soldier Show (Army Community & Family Support Center); 902nd Military Intelligence Group.
BASE HISTORY: Original tract acquired for use of District of Columbia. 1912, transferred to War Dept to establish rifle range & summer camp. 1915, engineering troops from Washington Barracks, establish Camp Belvoir. 1917, Camp A A Humphreys opened to train Army engineers. 1918, designated training center for engineers. 1922, made permanent post, Ft Humphreys. 1935, became Ft Belvoir, named after mansion built on property by Col Fairfax in 1741, home of Army Engineer School. 1988, transferred from TRADOC's Army Engineer School (moved to Ft Leonard Wood) to part of Military District of Washington (MDW). 1990, served as mobilization station for Operations Desert Shield/ Storm.
VISITOR ATTRACTIONS: Accotink Bay Wildlife Refuge (1460 acres); Jackson Miles Abbott Wetland Refuge (150 acres); Belvoir Manor/Fairfax grave historic site.

Key Contacts
COMMANDER: Col Michael Lepper, Garrison Commander, 703-805-2052, DSN 655-2052.
PUBLIC AFFAIRS: Becky Wriggle, Bldg 269, Rm 201, 703-805-2402, DSN 655-2402; MDW 202-685-2892, kukoskip@belvoir. army.mil.
PROCUREMENT: Director of Contracting, Bldg 732, Stop 75, 703-805-3354, DSN 655-3354.
TRANSPORTATION: Chief, Movements Branch, Bldg 630, Stop 80B, 703-805-2576, DSN 655-2576.
PERSONNEL/COMMUNITY ACTIVITIES: Bldg 498, Stop 11, 703-805-2532, DSN 655-2532.

Personnel and Expenditures
ACTIVE DUTY PERSONNEL: 4300; Reservists 80; Guard 50
DEPENDENTS: 4720
CIVILIAN PERSONNEL: 14,400

Services
Housing: Family units 2089; Unaccompanied officer quarters 10; Unaccompanied enlisted quarters 646; Senior NCO units 8. *Temporary Housing:* VIP units 9; VOQ units 455; VEQ units 25. *Commissary:* Yes; *Exchange:* Retail store; Barber shop; Dry cleaners; Food shop; Florist; Bank; Service station; Furniture store; Bakery; Military clothing store; Convenience store; Beauty shop; Laundromat; Credit union; Optical store; Video rentals; Shoe repair; Tailor/Alterations; Laundry; 1hr Photo; Watch repair; Self-help center; Computer center. *Child Care/Capacities:* Day care center 2 centers, total capacity 540, 6wks-6yrs; Home day care program; Latch key program. *Schools:* Preschool/Kindergarten; Elementary; College courses. *Base Library:* Yes. *Medical Facilities:* Hospital 68 beds; Medical clinic; Dental clinic; Pharmacy; Veterinary services. *Recreational Facilities:* Bowling center; Movie theater; Pool Indoor & Outdoor; Gym; Recreation center; Golf course 9-hole & 18 hole; Tennis courts; Racquetball court; Fitness center/Weight room 4 facilities; Softball field; Football field; Auto shop; Craft shop; Officers club; NCO club; Camping; Fishing/Hunting; Enlisted club; Youth center; Picnic area; Skeet range; Water sports; Playground; Community club; Marina; Sosa Community Recreation Center.

867. Humphreys Engineer Center
HECSA
7701 Telegraph Rd
Fort Belvoir, VA 22315-3860
703-428-6214; FAX 703-428-6188
Internet: http://www.hecsa.usace.army.mil/
hecexmis.htm

Profile
BRANCH: Army.
SIZE AND LOCATION: 583 acres. On Ft
Belvoir; 6 mi from US-1; 6 mi from I-95; 8
mi S of Capital Beltway, I-495. *County:* Fairfax.
MAJOR UNITS: Humphreys Engineer Center
Support Activity; Corps of Engineers, Field
Operating Agency.
BASE HISTORY: 1973, developed on Ft
Belvoir by Army Corps of Engineers. 1980,
land transferred from former Kingman Complex; located contiguous to, but not part of, Ft
Belvoir. 1982, formally designated in honor
of Maj Gen Andrew Atkinson Humphreys
(1810-1883).

Key Contacts
COMMANDER: John J Quinn, Jr, Director,
703-428-6169.
PUBLIC AFFAIRS: Debra J Flowers,
703-428-6077, Debra.J.Flowers@hq01.usace.
army.mil.

Personnel and Expenditures
ACTIVE DUTY PERSONNEL: 200
CIVILIAN PERSONNEL: 1145
Services *Exchange:* Credit union; See Ft
Belvoir for other services. *Base Library:* Yes.
Recreational Facilities: Fitness center/Weight
room; Softball field; SATO.

Fort Eustis

868. Army Transportation Center & Fort Eustis
USATC Fort Eustis
c/o Bldg 210
Fort Eustis, VA 23604-5015
757-878-5251; DSN 927-5251
OFFICER-OF-THE-DAY: 757-878-5050, DSN
927-5050

Profile
BRANCH: Army.
SIZE AND LOCATION: 8228 acres; Training
1226 acres; Ranges 175 acres; Airfield 349
acres. On W side of Newport News on Mulberry Island; on Exit 250A, on I-64 E or W,
& W on Fort Eustins Blvd. *County:* City of
Newport News.
MAJOR UNITS: Army Transportation Center;
Army Transportation School; Deployment
Process Modernization Office; 8th Transportation Brigade; Noncommissioned Officer
Academy; 7th Transportation Group (Composite); Army Aviation Logistics School;
Army Training Support Center; Reserve Component Enclave (13 US Army Reserve Units);
Equipment Concentration Site 93; Defense
Military Pay Office; Aviation Applied Technology Directorate; Military Traffic Management Command Transportation Engineering
Agency; Army Medical Department Activity;
Army Dental Activity; Defense Commissary
Agency; TRADOC Contracting Activity;
Army & Air Force Exchange Service; Army
Materiel Command Logistics Assistance Of-

fice; Army Test, Measurement & Diagnostic
Equipment Support Center; Army Aviation &
Troop Command, Eastern Inspection Region;
TRADOC System Manager for Tactical
Wheeled Vehicle Modernization; TRADOC
Tactical Wheeled Requirements Management
Office; Civilian Personnel Advisory Center
(CPAC); Defense Printing Service Det Office; 99th Army Reserve Command Aviation
Support Facility, Eustis; 12th MP Det (Criminal Investigation Division); Det 13, 1st
Weather Group (USAF); US Coast Guard
Port Security Unit 305; Marine Corps Liaison
Office; Dept of Transportation, James River
Reserve Fleet; Army Transportation Museum;
362nd Training Squadron, Det 1 (USAF).
BASE HISTORY: 1914, Ft Story began as installation. 1918, Mulberry Island purchased
for Coast Artillery Training Center, named
for Brevet Brig Gen Abraham Eustis, artillery
officer. 1947, became principal training post,
Army Transportation Corps. 1948, transferred
to Transportation Corps. 1950, Transportation
Center established. Felker Army Airfield was
Army's 1st military heliport; remains only
Army heliport with at least one of every
Army helicopter in active Army. 1964,
McDonald Army Community Hospital
opened with major outpatient clinic added in
1976. 1986, Transportation Corps Regiment
established.
VISITOR ATTRACTIONS: Army Transportation Museum; James River Reserve Fleet (anchored opposite post).

Key Contacts
COMMANDER: Maj Gen Daniel G Brown,
757-878-4802, DSN 286-4802.
PUBLIC AFFAIRS: Ronald A Johnson, Bldg
213, 757-878-4920, FAX 757-878-3585,
DSN 927-4920.
PROCUREMENT: Mrs E Van Lieu,
757-878-2808, FAX 757-878-2715, DSN
927-2808.
TRANSPORTATION: George Hart, Director,
Regional Directorate of Logistics,
757-878-5874, FAX 757-878-0331, DSN
927-5874.
PERSONNEL/COMMUNITY ACTIVITIES:
Bill Franssen, 757-878-3102, DSN 927-3102.

Personnel and Expenditures
ACTIVE DUTY PERSONNEL: 8848
DEPENDENTS: 2955
CIVILIAN PERSONNEL: 4096
MILITARY PAYROLL EXPENDITURE: $226.2
mil
CONTRACT EXPENDITURE: $88.2 mil
Services
Housing: Family units 953; Barracks spaces
3537; Trailer spaces 64; *Temporary Housing:*
VIP units 7; VOQ units 236; VEQ units 302;
VAQ units; Guesthouse units 7; Transient quarters 30. *Commissary:* Yes; *Exchange:* Retail
store; Barber shop; Dry cleaners; Food shop; Florist; Bank; Service station; Bakery; Bookstore;
Military clothing store; Convenience store;
Beauty shop; Laundromat; Credit union; ATM;
Optical store; Post office; Fast food; Video rentals; Thrift shop; Travel agency; Shoe repair; Garden center; Tailor/Alterations; Laundry; Photo
store. *Child Care/Capacities:* Day care center capacity 175, 6mos-5yrs; Home day care program;
Latch key program; Summer day camp; Before
& after school programs. *Schools:* College/University; No on-base schools. *Base Library:* Yes.

Medical Facilities: Hospital 35 beds; Medical
clinic; Dental clinic; Pharmacy; Veterinary services. *Recreational Facilities:* Bowling center;
Movie theater; Pool; Gym; Recreation center;
Golf course; Stables; Tennis courts; Racquetball
court; Fitness center/Weight room; Softball
field; Football field; Auto shop; Fishing/Hunting; Enlisted club; Youth center; Picnic area;
Skeet range; Water sports; Playground; All
ranks club; Consolidated club; Rod & Gun club;
Soccer field; ITT.

Fort Lee

869. Fort Lee
Combined Arms Support Command, 3901 A
Ave
Fort Lee, VA 23801-1802
804-539-3000; DSN 687-3000
OFFICER-OF-THE-DAY: 804-734-7993, DSN
687-7993

Profile
BRANCH: Army.
SIZE AND LOCATION: 5575 acres. 22 mi S of
Richmond and 35 mi from Richmond IAP.
Surrounding cities: Petersburg, Colonial
Heights, Hopewell. I-95 runs to W of post
and I-85 begins in nearby Petersburg. *County:*
Prince George.
MAJOR UNITS: Quartermaster Center and
School; Army Combined Arms Support Command; 23rd Quartermaster Brigade; Army Logistics Management College; Defense Commissary Agency; Readiness Group, Lee;
Gerow Army Reserve Center; Army Information Systems Software Development Center.
BASE HISTORY: 1917, first Camp Lee selected as state mobilization camp and later division training camp; named for Gen Robert
E Lee, Confederate Civil War commander.
After WWI, Camp Lee taken over by state
and designated game preserve. Later, portions
incorporated into National Military Park of
Petersburg. 1940, construction of another
Camp Lee on site of earlier installation. 1941,
Quartermaster Replacement Training Center
(QMRTC) started operation; also home of
Medical Replacement Training Center
(MRTC), later relocated to Camp Pickett;
QMRTC redesignated as Army Service
Forces Training Center; Quartermaster
School transferred to Camp Lee and full program of courses conducted, including Officer
Candidate School. 1950, redesignated as Ft
Lee. 1962, became Class 1 military installation under Second Army; school, part of Continental Army Command service school system, served as home of Quartermaster Corps
and Corps Historian. 1963, Camp Pickett and
Camp A P Hill established as sub-installations of Ft Lee. 1973, came under Army
Training and Doctrine Command.
VISITOR ATTRACTIONS: Quartermaster Museum located on A Ave just inside main gate.

Key Contacts
PROCUREMENT: Director of Contracting,
Bldg 7124, 804-734-1068, DSN 687-1068.
TRANSPORTATION: Bldg T-1105,
804-765-1630, DSN 539-1630.
PERSONNEL/COMMUNITY ACTIVITIES:
Bldg 80244320, 804-734-6969, DSN
687-6969; Community Activities, Bldg
12001, 804-734-6388, DSN 687-6388.

Personnel and Expenditures
ACTIVE DUTY PERSONNEL: 3016
DEPENDENTS: 5105
CIVILIAN PERSONNEL: 3063
Services
Housing: Family units 1273; Barracks spaces 6211. *Temporary Housing:* VIP units 16; VOQ units 461; Unaccompanied officer/Enlisted quarters 44; Guesthouse units 47; Transient quarters 521. *Commissary:* Yes; *Exchange:* Retail store; Barber shop; Dry cleaners; Food shop; Florist; Bank; Service station; Bookstore. *Child Care/Capacities:* Day care center capacity 110; Home day care program. *Schools:* No on-base schools. *Medical Facilities:* Medical clinic; Dental clinic. *Recreational Facilities:* Bowling center; Pool; Gym; Recreation center; Golf course; Stables; Tennis courts; Racquetball court; Fitness center/Weight room; Softball field; Football field; Auto shop; Craft shop; Officers club; NCO club; Camping; Skeet range; Track; Playhouse.

Fort Monroe

870. Fort Monroe
Fort Monroe, VA 23651-6000
757-727-1110; FAX 757-727-3521; DSN 680-1110
Internet: http://www-tradoc.monroe.army/monroe
OFFICER-OF-THE-DAY: 757-727-3241, DSN 680-3241
Profile
BRANCH: Army.
SIZE AND LOCATION: 1068 acres. Adj to city of Hampton, 1 mi E of I-64; 17 mi SE of Newport News/Williamsburg IAP; 17 mi NW of Norfolk IAP. *County:* City of Hampton.
MAJOR UNITS: TRADOC HQ; ROTC Cadet Command HQ; Naval Surface Warfare Center, Dahlgren Division Det.
BASE HISTORY: 1819, formed as irregular polygon with 7 fronts and 7 bastions; largest stone fort in US. Nicknamed "Gibraltar of the Chesapeake," one of few federal military installations in South not to fall to Confederate forces at outbreak of Civil War. WWII, HQ for Harbor Defenses of Chesapeake Bay. Later, HQ for US Ground Forces. Third oldest continuously operating fort in US. Only active Army post with a moat.
VISITOR ATTRACTIONS: Casemate Museum; Chamberlin Hotel; Tours; Fort registered National Landmark.
Key Contacts
COMMANDER: Col Michael D Rochelle, ATZG-CO, 757-727-3241, DSN 680-3241.
PUBLIC AFFAIRS: Camille Meyers, ATZG-PAO, 23651-6035, 757-727-3206, DSN 680- 3206.
PROCUREMENT: Lee Layton, Director of Peninsula Contracting, Bldg 2746, Ft Eustis, VA 23604, 757-878-2808, DSN 927-2808.
TRANSPORTATION: Robert E Sahms, ATZG-ISL, 757-727-2101, DSN 680-2101.
PERSONNEL/COMMUNITY ACTIVITIES: Paul Heilman, Community & Family Activities; ATZG-PA, 757-727-3737, DSN 680-3737.
Personnel and Expenditures
ACTIVE DUTY PERSONNEL: 879
DEPENDENTS: 852
CIVILIAN PERSONNEL: 1817

MILITARY PAYROLL EXPENDITURE: $65 mil
CONTRACT EXPENDITURE: $64 mil
Services
Housing: Family units 187; Unaccompanied enlisted quarters 106; RV/Camper sites 13. *Temporary Housing:* Visiting quarters 18. *Commissary:* Yes; *Exchange:* Retail store; Barber shop; Dry cleaners; Food shop; Bank; Service station; Furniture store; Military clothing store; Convenience store; Beauty shop; Credit union; Optical shop; Alteration shop. *Child Care/Capacities:* Day care center 2 centers: capacity 90, 6wks-6yrs; capacity 30, 6wks-8yrs; Home day care program; Summer day camp. *Schools:* College courses. *Base Library:* Yes. *Medical Facilities:* Medical clinic; Dental clinic; Pharmacy; Veterinary services. *Recreational Facilities:* Bowling center; Movie theater; Pool; Tennis courts; Racquetball court; Fitness center/Weight room; Softball field; Football field; Auto shop; Craft shop; Officers club; Camping; Fishing/Hunting; Youth center; Picnic area; Water sports; Playground; Marina; Outdoor recreation equipment checkout center; Information, Tour & Registration Office.

Fort Story

871. Fort Story
HQ
Fort Story, VA 23459-5061
757-878-5251
OFFICER-OF-THE-DAY: 757-422-7454, DSN 438-7454
Profile
BRANCH: Army.
SIZE AND LOCATION: 1451 acres. On Cape Henry off Atlantic Ave, I-60; 3 mi N of Virginia Beach; from I-64, across Hampton Roads to US 13, right onto Shore Drive E to Ft Story. *County:* City of Virginia Beach.
MAJOR UNITS: Post HQ, Ft Story; 7th Transportation Group, 11th Transportation Bn; Fort Story Community Clinic; Army Transportation School Rough Terrain Container; I Co, 71st Transportation Bn, 8th Transportation Brigade; Army Element, School of Music; 80th Division (IT), 1st Bn, 318th Regiment, 1st Brigade (USAR); 18th Field Hospital (HUH), 99th Regional Support Command (Oakland, PA)(USAR); 680th Transportation Co (USAR); 377th Engineer Co (USAR); Branch Maintenance Activity (USAR); Combined Service Support Program School, Atlantic; Navy Explosive Ordnance Disposal Training & Evaluation Unit Two; Navy Mobile Dive and Salvage Unit TWO, Det 506; Naval Undersea Warfare Center; Naval Sea Combat Systems Engineering Station; Navy Public Works; Marine Corps Expeditionary Warfare Training Group, Atlantic, Amphibious Reconnaissance School; Coast Guard, Cape Henry Light Station; Shipboard Electronic Systems Evaluation Facility; 789th Medical Det (USAR).
BASE HISTORY: 1914, commonwealth of VA gave land to federal government to build fortifications; fort named after Gen John Patton Story, coastal artilleryman. WWI, integrated into Coast Defense of Chesapeake Bay including Ft Monroe (HQ) & Ft Wool. 1925, designated Harbor Defense Command. 1941, following inactivity, extensive development. 1944, transition from heavily fortified coast

artillery garrison to convalescent hospital for returning veterans. 1946, hospital closed; amphibious training began. 1961, declared permanent installation. 1962, redesignated Class I sub-installation of Ft Eustis.
VISITOR ATTRACTIONS: Old Cape Henry Lighthouse; Jamestown Landing Site; Get visitor's pass at gate to see historic sites.
Key Contacts
COMMANDER: LTC Ronald Newton, 757-422-7101, DSN 438-7101.
PUBLIC AFFAIRS: Olivia C Alfriend, 757-422-7755.
PROCUREMENT: Edna VanLiew, 757-878-2808.
Personnel and Expenditures
ACTIVE DUTY PERSONNEL: 2040
DEPENDENTS: 1740
CIVILIAN PERSONNEL: 260
Services
Housing: Family units 164; Unaccompanied officer quarters; Unaccompanied enlisted quarters; Barracks spaces; RV/Camper sites. *Temporary Housing:* VIP units; VOQ units; VEQ units; Guest cottages. *Commissary:* Yes; *Exchange:* Retail store; Barber shop; Dry cleaners; Food shop; Bank; Service station; Military clothing store; Convenience store; Credit union; Thrift shop; Class VI; Tailor/Alterations. *Child Care/Capacities:* Day care center capacity 60, 13 mo-6yrs; Home day care program; Latch key program. *Schools:* No on-base schools. *Base Library:* Yes. *Medical Facilities:* Medical clinic; Dental clinic; Pharmacy; Veterinary services. *Recreational Facilities:* Bowling center; Movie theater; Gym; Recreation center; Tennis courts; Racquetball court; Fitness center/Weight room; Softball field; Football field; Auto shop; Camping; Fishing/Hunting; Youth center; Picnic area; Playground; Ft Story club; Soccer; Go-cart track; Beach.

Langley AFB

872. Langley Air Force Base
Langley AFB
Langley AFB, VA 23665-2292
757-764-5615; DSN 574-1110
Internet: http://www.langley.af.mil/
Profile
BRANCH: Air Force.
SIZE AND LOCATION: 511 acres. 3 mi N of city of Hampton; I-64 exit 265-C, north on LaSalle Ave, to main gate. *County:* City of Hampton.
MAJOR UNITS: Air Combat Command; 1st Fighter Wing; 1st Operations Group; 1st Logistics Group; 1st Support Group; 1st Medical Group.
BASE HISTORY: Langley AFB makes a claim to being oldest continuously active air base in US. 1916, Army, Navy, & National Advisory Committee for Aeronautics agreed to construct facility for government sponsored aviation research & development center and purchased land for Aviation Experimental Station & Proving Ground. 1917, officially named Langley Field for Samuel Pierpont Langley, former Secretary of Smithsonian Institute & pioneer in American aviation. 1920s, used by Brig Gen William "Billy" Mitchell to demonstrate use of airplanes as offensive weapons against ships anchored in

Chesapeake Bay; conducted experiments with lighter-than-air machines, part of Langley still called LTA area. 1935, General HQ Air Force. WWII, antisubmarine operations. Following WWII, HQs TAC established. 1965-75, home for a number of MAC units. 1976, 1st TFW arrived.
VISITOR ATTRACTIONS: A closed base; visitors must have sponsor on base to enter.

Key Contacts
COMMANDER: Brig Gen Theodore W Lay II, 1st Fighter Wing; Gen Richard E Hawley, ACC;.
PUBLIC AFFAIRS: Vic Johnson, 1st FW/PA, 159 Sweeney Blvd, Ste 100, 23665-2292, 757-764-2018, FAX 757-764-3475, johnsov@fw1.langley.af.mil.

Personnel and Expenditures
ACTIVE DUTY PERSONNEL: 8985; Reserve 300
DEPENDENTS: 13,000
CIVILIAN PERSONNEL: 2256

Services
Housing: Family units Officer 380; Enlisted 1200; Unaccompanied enlisted quarters 1000; Duplex units 14; Senior NCO units 1604; Junior NCO units; Family housing also available at Bether Manor 5 mi from base. *Temporary Housing:* VIP units 25; VOQ units 78; VEQ units 215; Lodge units 100. *Commissary:* Yes; *Exchange:* Retail store; Barber shop; Dry cleaners; Food shop; Florist; Bank; Service station; Military clothing store; Convenience store; Beauty shop; Credit union; Video rentals; Thrift shop; Tailor/Alterations; Laundry; Ice cream; Snacks; Contruction materials. *Child Care/Capacities:* Day care center capacity 353; Home day care program. *Schools:* Elementary. *Base Library:* Yes. *Medical Facilities:* Hospital 50 beds; Medical clinic; Dental clinic; Veterinary services. *Recreational Facilities:* Bowling center; Movie theater; Pool; Gym; Recreation center; Golf course (driving range); Stables; Tennis courts; Racquetball court; Fitness center/Weight room; Softball field; Auto shop; Craft shop; Officers club; NCO club; Fishing/Hunting; Youth center; Skeet range; Marina; Big Bethel Recreation Area; Tickets & Tour; Jr Rifle Club; MWR supply; Yacht club; Aero club.

Newport News

873. Newport News Supervisor of Shipbuilding, Conversion and Repair
SUPSHIPNN
Newport News, VA 23607-2787
757-380-4122
Profile
BRANCH: Navy.
SIZE AND LOCATION: Offices only. Within shipyard, Newport News; from I-64, take I-664 to exit 5, cross Warwick Blvd & Huntington Ave, right on Washington Ave. *County:* City of Newport News.
MAJOR UNITS: Supervisor of Shipbuilding, Newport News.
BASE HISTORY: SUPSHIPNN oversees contractors building of aircraft carriers & submarines.

Key Contacts
PUBLIC AFFAIRS: Capt Kevin Perkins, 757-380-3687.
Personnel and Expenditures
ACTIVE DUTY PERSONNEL: 81
CIVILIAN PERSONNEL: 366
Services *Exchange:* Retail store; Barber shop.

874. Transportation Engineering Agency, MTMC
MTMC TEA
720 Thimble Shoals Blvd, Ste 130
Newport News, VA 23606-2574
Internet: http://144.100.189.52/tea.htm
Profile
BRANCH: Army.
SIZE AND LOCATION: Office only. From I-64, take exit 258-A, Rte 17 S, at first traffic light right onto Diligence Dr, at second traffic light right onto Thimble Shoals Blvd, just past next traffic light look for Thimble Shoals Business Center on left. *County:* City of Newport News.
MAJOR UNITS: Transportation Engineering Agency, MTMC.
BASE HISTORY: Part of the Military Traffic Management Command (MTMC).

Norfolk

875. Armed Forces Staff College
AFSC
7800 Hampton Blvd
Norfolk, VA 23511-1702
757-444-5431; FAX 757-444-5120; DSN 564-5431
Profile
BRANCH: Joint Service Installation.
SIZE AND LOCATION: 30 acres. On grounds of Norfolk Naval Base; 15 min from Norfolk IAP. *County:* City of Norfolk.
MAJOR UNITS: Armed Forces Staff College.
BASE HISTORY: 1946, established at site of WWII Naval Receiving Station; 1981 incorporated into National Defense University, a joint intermediate-level college under Joint Chiefs of Staff to prepare selected mid-career officers for joint and combined staff duty. Primary Academic Programs: the Joint and Combined Staff Officer School, 12-week program taught 4 times a year to 850 officers; the Senior Program, recently expanded to 12 weeks with 90 officers attending; and the Joint Command, Control, Information, and Warfare School, with 390 students. Navy has responsibility for fiscal and logistic support of college through Commanding Officer, Naval Administrative Command. Commandant (0-7 level) position rotates among the 4 services.
Key Contacts
COMMANDER: Brig Gen William R Looney, III.
PUBLIC AFFAIRS: Ken Fritz, 757-444-5431.
Personnel and Expenditures
ACTIVE DUTY PERSONNEL: 170
CIVILIAN PERSONNEL: 136
MILITARY PAYROLL EXPENDITURE: $10.7 mil
CONTRACT EXPENDITURE: $1.5 mil
Services
Housing: Family units 110; Unaccompanied officer quarters 100.

Exchange: Barber shop; Dry cleaners; Convenience store. *Child Care/Capacities:* Day care center capacity 76, 6wks-5yrs. *Schools:* No on-base schools. *Base Library:* Yes. *Medical Facilities:* No medical facilities. *Recreational Facilities:* Gym; Tennis courts; Racquetball court; Fitness center/Weight room; Softball field; Officers club; Youth center; Playground;

876. Army Corps of Engineers, Norfolk District
NAO
803 Front St
Norfolk, VA 23510
757-441-7562 (Library)
Internet: http://155.78.30.111/
Profile
BRANCH: Army.
LOCATION: Waterfield Bldg overlooking Elizabeth River. *County:* City of Norfolk.
MAJOR UNITS: Corps of Engineers, Norfolk District.
BASE HISTORY: 1923, District established at Fort Norfolk. 1983, moved next door to Waterfield Bldg. One of four districts in North Atlantic Division. Mission encompasses most of state of VA.
Key Contacts
COMMANDER: Col Robert H Readrdon Jr, 757-441-7601.
PUBLIC AFFAIRS: William E Brown, 757-441-7264.
Personnel and Expenditures
ACTIVE DUTY PERSONNEL: 6
CIVILIAN PERSONNEL: 325

877. Camp Elmore
1468 Ingram St
Norfolk, VA 23551
757-889-1644
Profile
BRANCH: Marine Corps.
SIZE AND LOCATION: 4 acres. Adj to Norfolk Naval Base; off Terminal Blvd. *County:* City of Norfolk.
MAJOR UNITS: HQ & Service Bn; Fleet Marine Force, Atlantic (FMFLANT), HQ.
BASE HISTORY: 1950s, established; named after recipient of Navy Cross. One of the smallest Marine Corps facilities.
Key Contacts
COMMANDER: Lt Gen C Wilhelm, 757-889-1543.
Personnel and Expenditures
ACTIVE DUTY PERSONNEL: 600
CIVILIAN PERSONNEL: 5
Services *Exchange:* Retail store; Barber shop; Dry cleaners; Food shop; Service station. *Recreational Facilities:* Gym.

878. Fleet Industrial Supply Center
FISC
1968 Gilbert St
Norfolk, VA 23511-3392
757-444-2585; FAX 757-445-8690; DSN 564-2585
OFFICER-OF-THE-DAY: 757-444-2530
Profile
BRANCH: Navy.
SIZE AND LOCATION: 2873 acres. Majority on Naval Station, Norfolk; fuel facilities in Portsmouth, VA, additional storage/recrea-

tion facility (Cheatham Annex) near Williamsburg, VA. *County:* City of Norfolk.

MAJOR UNITS: Fleet & Industrial Supply Center.

BASE HISTORY: Headquartered on Naval Station, Norfolk, FISC is Navy's oldest & largest supply center. 1919, commissioned as Navy Supply Station. 1927, designated Naval Supply Depot. 1948, consolidated as Naval Supply Center, Norfolk. 1993, current name with mission to reduce fleet operating costs & provide services to Atlantic Fleet ships homeported in Norfolk, Second Fleet ships in Atlantic, and Sixth Fleet in Mediterranean. Also supports Middle East Force Force ships in Persian Gulf & Indian Ocean. Support also provided to shore activities worldwide; facilities include Craney Island & Yorktown fuel terminals, main complex on Naval Station, Norfolk, South Annex located off base, & Cheatham Annex near Williamsburg, VA.

Key Contacts
COMMANDER: Capt Mark Young, 757-444-3401, DSN 564-3401.

PUBLIC AFFAIRS: Robert Anderson, 757-444-2585, FAX 757-445-8690, DSN 564-2585.

PROCUREMENT: CDR Mike Colesar, 757-444-2554, DSN 564-2554.

PERSONNEL/COMMUNITY ACTIVITIES: Shedrick Byrd, 757-444-3150, DSN 564-3150.

Personnel and Expenditures
ACTIVE DUTY PERSONNEL: 82; Naval Reservists 600

CIVILIAN PERSONNEL: 3400

MILITARY PAYROLL EXPENDITURE: $64 mil

CONTRACT EXPENDITURE: $5 bil

Services
Housing: See Norfolk Naval Base Complex. *Exchange:* See Norfolk Naval Base Complex. *Base Library:* Yes.

879. Fleet Training Center, Norfolk
FTC Norfolk
9549 Bainbridge Ave
Norfolk, VA 23511-2594
757-444-0000

Profile
BRANCH: Navy.

LOCATION: On Naval Station, Norfolk. *County:* City of Norfolk.

MAJOR UNITS: Fleet Training Center, Norfolk; Fleet Training Command.

BASE HISTORY: A fleet, shore-based activity, under command of Commander, Training Command, US Atlantic Fleet, providing practical, operational, & maintenance training in shipboard operations; training officers & enlisted people in advanced and/or specialized courses; & providing reactivation or precommissioning training. 65,000 students taught annually in 198 courses.

Key Contacts
PUBLIC AFFAIRS: Naval Station, Norfolk, Public Affairs Ctr X-18, Norfolk, VA 23511-6199.

Personnel and Expenditures
ACTIVE DUTY PERSONNEL: 608

CIVILIAN PERSONNEL: 25

880. Little Creek, Naval Amphibious Base
NAVPHIBASE; NAVPHIBASELCREEK
2600 Tarawa Court, #107
Norfolk, VA 23521-3229
757-464-7385; DSN 680-7385

Profile
BRANCH: Navy.

SIZE AND LOCATION: 2120 acres. At extreme NW corner of Virginia Beach along Shore Dr, Rte 60; 2 mi W of Chesapeake Bay Bridge-Tunnel off I-60; from I-64 E to Northhampton Blvd to Independence Blvd, follow signs to base. *County:* City of Norfolk; City of Virginia Beach.

MAJOR UNITS: Naval Amphibious Base, Little Creek; Amphibious Group 2; Expeditionary Warfare Training Group Atlantic; Navy Special Warfare Group 2; Naval Beach Group 2; Beach Master Unit 2; Assault Craft Unit 2; Assault Craft Unit 4; Armed Forces School of Music.

BASE HISTORY: Grew out of 4 bases constructed during WWII—Amphibious Training Base, Naval Frontier Base, and Camps Bradford & Shelton. Consisted of 3 annexes, named for former owners: Shelton on E, Bradford in center, & Whitehurst on W. 1945, established as base. 1946, designated permanent base. Largest amphibious base. Operates Radio Island, Morehead City, NC, as embarkation & debarkation area for USMC Camp Lejeune. Also leases 3200 acres at Gate Riverline Training Facility, NC.

VISITOR ATTRACTIONS: Amphibious Training Demonstrator; Ship tours.

Key Contacts
COMMANDER: Capt Leroy A Brown, 757-464-7231.

PUBLIC AFFAIRS: Barbara Jennings, 757-464-7923.

PROCUREMENT: Melvin J Rayman Jr, Contracting, 757-464-7430.

Personnel and Expenditures
ACTIVE DUTY PERSONNEL: 12,450

DEPENDENTS: 7000

CIVILIAN PERSONNEL: 1950

Services
Housing: Family units 1000; Unaccompanied officer quarters 1; Unaccompanied enlisted quarters 36; RV/Camper sites 34. *Temporary Housing:* VIP units 2; VOQ units 225; VEQ units 425; Unaccompanied officer/Enlisted quarters 79; Naval Lodge Units (15 day max occupancy) 90. *Commissary:* Yes; *Exchange:* Retail store; Barber shop; Dry cleaners; Food shop; Florist; Bank; Service station; Furniture store; Bookstore; Convenience store; Beauty shop; Credit union; Optical store; Class VI; Shoe repair; Ice cream store; Photo studio; Frame shop; Jewelry/watch sales/repair; Wood shop; Camera shop; Home entertainment center; Engraving services; Sound shop; Photo finishing; Country store. *Child Care/Capacities:* Day care center capacity 180; Home day care program; Before & after school care. *Schools:* Preschool/Kindergarten. *Base Library:* Yes. *Medical Facilities:* Medical clinic; Dental clinic; Portsmouth Naval Medical Center. *Recreational Facilities:* Bowling center; Pool; Gym; Recreation center; Golf course (and Pro shop); Tennis courts (and Pro shop); Racquetball court; Fitness center/Weight room; Softball field; Football field; Auto shop; Craft shop; Officers club; NCO club; Fishing/Hunting (No

hunting); Youth center (and teen center); Picnic area; Water sports; ITT office; Sailing center; Beaches and boat piers; Storage lot for recreational vehicles; Boat/Camper shop; Rugby field; Amusement center; Full-service campground.

881. Naval Facilities Engineering Command, Atlantic Division
LANTNAVFACENGCOM LANTDIV
1510 Gilbert St
Norfolk, VA 23511-2699
757-322-8122; FAX 757-322-8124; DSN 262-8122; DSN FAX 262-8124
E-mail: @efdlant.navfac.navy.mil Internet:http://www.efdlant.navfac.navy.mil

Profile
BRANCH: Navy.

SIZE AND LOCATION: Tenant of Norfolk Naval Base. On Norfolk Naval base, 8 mi W of Norfolk IAP via I-64 & I-564.. *County:* City of Norfolk.

MAJOR UNITS: Naval Facilities Engineering Command, Atlantic Division.

BASE HISTORY: Atlantic Division one of 6 Engineering Field Divisions of Naval Facilities Engineering Command (NAVFAC), established 1942, as agent of Bureau of Yards & Docks to decentralize & expedite Bureau actions in Atlantic area. WWII, supported actions in Africa & chain of advance bases from Iceland to Brazil. Today, plans, designs, & constructs shore facilities for Navy & Marine Corps on geographic basis. Atlantic Division HQ in Norfolk provides centralized financial services, in-depth engineering, design & planning support for other components; serves VA, WV, NC, Atlantic, & Caribbean (LANTOPS). Engineering Field Division, North, in Philadelphia, serves Northeastern US. Engineering Field Activity, Chesapeake, in Washington, DC, serves northern VA, MD, & DC. Engineering Field Activity, Mediterranean, in Naples, Italy, serves Europe. Other locations include Iceland, the Caribbean, Africa, & Mediterranean Area.

Key Contacts
COMMANDER: RADM Michael W Shelton, CEC, USN, Commander, DSN FAX 322-8219.

PUBLIC AFFAIRS: John E Peters, 757-322-8005, FAX 757-322-8187, DSN 262-8005, petersje@efdlant.navfac.nav.mil.

PROCUREMENT: David Lamoureux, 757-322-8220, FAX 757-322-8225, DSN 262-8220, lamourda@efdlant.navfac.navy.mil.

Personnel and Expenditures
ACTIVE DUTY PERSONNEL: 800 (military & civilian)

CONTRACT EXPENDITURE: $600 mil

Services
Housing: See Norfolk Naval Base Complex.

882. Norfolk Naval Air Station
NAS, Norfolk
9420 Third Ave
Norfolk, VA 23511-2118
757-444-0000; FAX 757-445-9216; DSN 565-6647
OFFICER-OF-THE-DAY: 757-444-8047, DSN 564-8047

Profile
BRANCH: Navy.

SIZE AND LOCATION: 1950 acres. Approx 5 mi N of downtown Norfolk; bounded on N & W by James & Elizabeth Rivers; on E by Chesapeake Bay; off I-64 in Norfolk on Norfolk Naval Base; 5 mi from Norfolk IAP. *County:* City of Norfolk.

MAJOR UNITS: Naval Air Station, Norfolk; Naval Air Force, Atlantic Fleet; Naval Safety Center; Carrier Airborne Early Warning Wing, Atlantic; Helicopter Sea Control Wing, Atlantic.

BASE HISTORY: 1918, commissioned on historic site of 1907 Jamestown Exhibition. Initially, NAS provided support for operational & experimental flights; grew into major sea plane base, training pilots & crews. During WWI & WWII, provided antisubmarine patrols in mid-Atlantic. Home to 20 aircraft squadrons; part of Norfolk Naval Base Complex.

Key Contacts

COMMANDER: Capt Ronald E Keyes, 757-444-8595, DSN 564-8595.

PUBLIC AFFAIRS: Ltjg J M Jayme, 757-444-2650.

PROCUREMENT: Dale Staley, 757-444-7676, DSN 564-7676.

TRANSPORTATION: 757-444-3063, DSN 564-3063.

Personnel and Expenditures

ACTIVE DUTY PERSONNEL: 9155
DEPENDENTS: 253
CIVILIAN PERSONNEL: 7176

Services

Housing: Family units 37; Unaccompanied officer quarters Bldgs, 2; Unaccompanied enlisted quarters Bldgs, 6. *Temporary Housing:* See Norfolk Naval Station. *Exchange:* Barber shop; Dry cleaners; Food shop; Florist; Service station; Convenience store; Beauty shop; Credit union. *Child Care/Capacities:* No day care facilities. *Schools:* See Norfolk Naval base Complex. *Medical Facilities:* See Norfolk Naval Base Complex. *Recreational Facilities:* Bowling center; Pool; Gym; Tennis courts; Fitness center/Weight room; Softball field; Auto shop; Picnic area; Playground; All hands club; Breezy Park Recreation Area.

883. Norfolk Naval & Marine Corps Reserve Readiness Center

7690 Shore Dr, Ste 100
Norfolk, VA 23521-3298
757-464-8009; FAX 757-363-4021; DSN 864-8009

Profile

BRANCH: Naval Reserve; Marine Corps Reserve.

LOCATION: *County:* City of Norfolk.

MAJOR UNITS: Naval Reserve Readiness Center, Norfolk; Marine Corps Readiness Center, Norfolk.

Key Contacts

COMMANDER: Capt H Peterson.

884. Norfolk Naval Aviation Depot

NADep
1126 Pocahontas St
Norfolk, VA 23511-2195
757-444-8233; FAX 757-444-3599; DSN 564-8233

Profile

BRANCH: Navy.
SIZE AND LOCATION: 172 acres.

On Norfolk Naval Air Station; at juncture of I-64 & I-564 directly across from Hampton Roads Bridge Tunnel. *County:* City of Norfolk.

MAJOR UNITS: Naval Aviation Depot, Norfolk.

BASE HISTORY: Since 1917, mission to perform depot-level maintenance, engineering, and logistic management in support of tactical naval aviation. Largest tenant command at NAS Norfolk; largest industrial employer in Norfolk. Aircraft inducted at NADEP for Standard Depot Level Maintenance, damage repair, & major modifications. One of two depots for repair & maintenance of air-launched missiles for Navy, Air Force, & NATO countries.

Key Contacts

COMMANDER: 757-444-8444, DSN 564-8444.

PUBLIC AFFAIRS: Bldg V-28, 23511-2195, 757-444-8233, DSN 564-8233.

Personnel and Expenditures

ACTIVE DUTY PERSONNEL: 33
CIVILIAN PERSONNEL: 3500

Services

Housing: See Norfolk Naval Station.

885. Norfolk Naval Base Complex

1530 Gilbert St, Ste 2200
Norfolk, VA 23511-2797
757-444-0001; DSN 564-0000

Profile

BRANCH: Navy.

SIZE AND LOCATION: 3327 acres. Sewell's Point area of Norfolk off I-64E. Take right onto I-564 interchange, left onto Hampton Blvd. *County:* City of Norfolk.

MAJOR UNITS: Commander, Naval Base Norfolk, Headquarters; Naval Aviation Depot; Naval Station, Norfolk; Naval Air Station, Norfolk; Commander-in-Chief, Atlantic (also Supreme Allied Commander, Atlantic SACLANT); Commander-in-Chief, Atlantic Fleet; Commander, Naval Surface Force, Atlantic; Commander, Submarine Force, Atlantic; Commanding General, Fleet Marine Force, Atlantic; Commander, Second Fleet; US Navy Recreation Park; Naval Computer and Telecommunications Area Master Station.

BASE HISTORY: Situated near site of battle of *Monitor* and *Merrimack*, world's largest naval complex; HQ Commander, Naval Base, Norfolk; includes Navy's largest supply center, Naval Aviation Depot (second largest employer in VA), Naval Station, and NAS, Norfolk. Also part of Naval Base complex HQ for Commander-in-Chief, Atlantic/Supreme Allied Commander, Atlantic, North Atlantic Treaty Organization (NATO) command (under command of 4-star admirals who oversee defense of entire Atlantic area). Homeport for about 156 ships, 50 aircraft squadrons, and 252 shore activities.

VISITOR ATTRACTIONS: Daily bus tours; Weekend ship tours (757-444-7955); Hampton Roads Naval Museum.

Key Contacts

PUBLIC AFFAIRS: JOC Lamar Raker, 757-322-2853, FAX 757-444-6007.

Personnel and Expenditures

ACTIVE DUTY PERSONNEL: 58,460; 4179 reservists
DEPENDENTS: 129,000
CIVILIAN PERSONNEL: 14,570

Services

Housing: Family units Officer 437; Enlisted 3390; BAQ units 375; Townhouse units 225; Barracks spaces 1730; Unaccompanied units, officer 489; enlisted 1849; also see Norfolk Navy Public Works Center. *Temporary Housing:* VOQ units 371; Lodge units 294; Officer: distinguished visitor units, 32; Enlisted: VIP rooms 7, enlisted units 1104; Reservations: on orders SATO 1-800-5769327; Naval Station, officer 757-402-7006, enlisted 757-444-3523/25; NAS officer/enlisted 757-444-4667; Navy Lodge 757-489-2656, 1-800-NAVY-INN. *Commissary:* Yes; *Exchange:* Retail store; Barber shop; Dry cleaners; Food shop; Service station; Beauty shop; Credit union; Tailor/Alterations; Laundry; Mall; 5 mini-marts; Sporting goods; Hardware; Toys; Jewelry/watch sales/repair. *Child Care/Capacities:* Day care center capacity 288, 6am-6pm, M-F; Home day care program capacity 330-390. *Schools:* No on-base schools; In Norfolk. *Base Library:* Yes. *Medical Facilities:* Medical clinic 7 branches; Dental clinic 7 branches; Portsmouth Naval Medical Center; Tricare available. *Recreational Facilities:* Bowling center; Movie theater; Pool; Gym; Recreation center; Golf course; Tennis courts; Auto shop; Craft shop; Officers club; NCO club; Fishing/Hunting; Enlisted club; Picnic area; Single Sailor program; ITT; Recreational club.

886. Norfolk Naval Station

NS Norfolk
1653 Morris St
Norfolk, VA 23511-2895
757-444-0000

Profile

BRANCH: Navy.

SIZE AND LOCATION: 1950 acres. Bounded on N & W by James & Elizabeth Rivers & on E by Chesapeake Bay; off I-64 in Norfolk; Part of Norfolk Naval Base Complex. *County:* City of Norfolk.

MAJOR UNITS: Naval Station, Norfolk; Naval Training Station; Transient Personnel Unit; Armed Forces Staff College; Naval Facilities Engineering Command, Atlantic Division; Norfolk Fleet Training Center; Training Command, Atlantic Fleet; Navy Supply Center; Navy Public Works Center, Norfolk; Surface Force, Atlantic.

BASE HISTORY: 1917, Naval Operating Base constructed on historic site of 1907 Jamestown Exhibition; Fifth Naval District HQ, naval training center, naval air station, naval hospital, & submarine station established. Late 1930s-early 1940s, additional construction. 1942, recruit training ended. 1945, name changed to present name. 1946, Naval Station made separate command under military command of Commandant (later Commander), Naval Base. Homeport for more than 90 ships.

VISITOR ATTRACTIONS: Ship tours; Hampton Roads Naval Museum.

Key Contacts

COMMANDER: Capt John Petrie, 757-322-2302.

PUBLIC AFFAIRS: Lt A Scerfey, 757-445-9923.

PROCUREMENT: Sybil Custer, Contracting, 757-322-7642.

Services

Housing: Family units 5989; Trailer spaces 195 (homesites); Waiting list 2-30 months.

Temporary Housing: Navy Lodge units (each, 15 day max occupancy), 90; Naval Base, 7811 Hampton Blvd, Norfolk, VA 23505, 804-489-2656; Naval Amphibious Base, Little Creek, Norfolk, VA 23521, 804-464-6215. *Commissary:* Yes; *Exchange:* See Norfolk Naval Complex. *Child Care/Capacities:* Day care center. *Base Library:* Yes. *Medical Facilities:* Portsmouth Naval Hospital. *Recreational Facilities:* Bowling center; Movie theater; Pool; Recreation center; Golf course; Auto shop; Officers club; NCO club; Fishing/Hunting; Sailing.

887. Norfolk Navy Public Works Center
PWC Norfolk
9742 Maryland Ave
Norfolk, VA 23511-3095
757-444-7141; FAX 757-444-4889; DSN 564-7141; DSN FAX 564-7141
Internet: http://www.norfolk.navy.mil/pwc
Profile
BRANCH: Navy.
LOCATION: On Norfolk Naval Station. *County:* City of Norfolk.
MAJOR UNITS: Navy Public Works Center.
BASE HISTORY: 1948, Navy's 1st center to consolidate public works functions for naval base; opened under control of Bureau of Yards & Docks, Commander, Naval Operating Base, Norfolk. 1991, Defense Management Review Decision (967) consolidated services of PWC. 1993, Hampton Roads area consolidated: Naval Base, Norfolk; Naval Amphibious Base, Little Creek; Naval Air Station, Oceana; Fleet Combat Training Center, Dam Neck; Norfolk Naval Shipyard; & Naval Medical Center, Portsmouth. 1996, expanded to include Naval Weapons Station, Yorktown; PWC Det, Philadelphia transferred in from PWC San Francisco Bay. Currently, largest of 10 Navy PWCs; provide facilities maintenance, transportation, engineering, utilities, & environmental support; under Commander, Naval Base, Norfolk.
Personnel and Expenditures
ACTIVE DUTY PERSONNEL: 17
CIVILIAN PERSONNEL: 3700

888. Training Command, US Atlantic Fleet
Naval Station Norfolk
Norfolk, VA 23511-6597
757-444-0000
Profile
BRANCH: Navy.
LOCATION: On Naval Station, Norfolk. *County:* City of Norfolk.
MAJOR UNITS: Training Command, US Atlantic Fleet.
BASE HISTORY: Conducts more than 550 courses, ranging from fire fighting to celestial navigation.
Key Contacts
PUBLIC AFFAIRS: Naval Station, Norfolk, Public Affairs Ctr X-18, Norfolk, VA 23511-6199.

889. United States Atlantic Command
USACOM
1562 Mitscher Ave, Ste 200
Norfolk, VA 23551
757-322-6555; FAX 757-322-6561
Profile
BRANCH: Navy.
SIZE AND LOCATION: Offices only. On Naval Station, Norfolk. *County:* City of Norfolk.
MAJOR UNITS: US Atlantic Command.
BASE HISTORY: 1993, created by revision of Unified Command Plan. Mission: to integrate military capabilities of all forces based in continental US through USAF Air Combat Command, Army Forces Command, USMC Marine Forces Atlantic, and USN Atlantic Fleet. Commander in Chief of US Atlantic Command also serves as NATO's Supreme Allied Commander, Atlantic.
Key Contacts
COMMANDER: Adm Harold W Gehman Jr.
PERSONNEL/COMMUNITY ACTIVITIES: Col John Radke, USA, Dir of Personnel & Manpower.

Portsmouth

890. Atlantic Area & Fifth Coast Guard District HQ
CCGD5
431 Crawford St
Portsmouth, VA 23704-5004
757-398-6272; FAX 757-398-6238
Internet: http://www.dot.gov/dotinfo/uscg/uscglant.html
OFFICER-OF-THE-DAY: 757-398-6391
Profile
BRANCH: Coast Guard.
SIZE AND LOCATION: Offices only. In historic waterfront area of downtown Portsmouth, overlooks Elizabeth River near Portsmouth's Portside area; across from Norfolk Shipyards & Norfolk Waterside area. *County:* City of Portsmouth.
MAJOR UNITS: US Coast Guard Atlantic Area & Fifth District HQ; Coast Guard Tactical Law Enforcement Team, Portsmouth; Investigative Services, Chesapeake Region; Coast Guard Reserve Unit CNCWGRU Atlantic.
BASE HISTORY: 1996, Atlantic Area & Maritime Defense Zone Atlantic commands merged with Fifth Coast Guard District Command. New command manages operations throughout Atlantic Ocean, Caribbean, Gulf of Mexico, Great Lakes, US inland rivers in 40 states and borders on 29 foreign countries. Performs maritime safety, law enforcement, marine environmental protection & national defense functions. The Fifth District covers all or parts of 6 states from NJ to NC/SC border. Service facilities are available from Coast Guard Support Center, 400 Coast Guard Blvd, Portsmouth, VA 23703-2199.
Key Contacts
COMMANDER: VADM Roger T Rufe, Jr.
PUBLIC AFFAIRS: LCDR Fitzgerald, 757-398-6275.
Personnel and Expenditures
ACTIVE DUTY PERSONNEL: 340 (Coast Guard, Reserves, Auxiliarists, civilians, Navy)

891. Norfolk Naval Shipyard, Portsmouth
NNSY
1 Norfolk Naval Shipyard
Portsmouth, VA 23709-5000
757-396-3000; DSN 961-3000
OFFICER-OF-THE-DAY: 757-396-8615, DSN 961-8615
Profile
BRANCH: Navy.
SIZE AND LOCATION: 1294 acres. On Elizabeth River in Portsmouth; 1 mi from I-264W; main gate at Effington St & Portsmouth Blvd; Norfolk IAP 15 min away; units also located in Berkley area of Norfolk & Chesapeake. *County:* City of Portsmouth; City of Norfolk; City of Chesapeake.
MAJOR UNITS: Norfolk Naval Shipyard; Supervisor of Shipbuilding, Conversion, and Repair, Portsmouth; Naval Electronic Systems Engineering Center.
BASE HISTORY: Navy's oldest shipyard. 1767, established by British; known as Gosport; taken over by Virginia during the American Revolution. 1794, leased by Navy. 1801, purchased by Federal government as Gosport Navy Yard. 1833, Dry Dock One, first in Western Hemisphere, opened. 1889-1942, 6 graving docks added; responsible for a number of firsts: converted USS *Merrimack* into first ironclad, CSS *Virginia*, 1862; built first battleship commissioned by Navy (USS *Texas*); built first platform for first plane flight from ship; converted a collier into first aircraft carrier (USS *Langley*), 1922. 1939-45, built 101 ships, from landing craft to aircraft carriers. 1983-88, repaired & returned 96 ships to fleet operations, more than any other shipyard. Now largest shipyard in the world specializing in repairing, overhauling, & modernizing warships.
VISITOR ATTRACTIONS: Portsmouth Naval Shipyard Museum.
Key Contacts
COMMANDER: Capt Timothy E Scheib, 757-396-9333, DSN 961-9333.
PUBLIC AFFAIRS: Stephen Milner, Code 1160, 757-396-9550, DSN 961-9550.
PROCUREMENT: CDR Mark Kennedy, 757-396-8800, DSN 961-8800.
PERSONNEL/COMMUNITY ACTIVITIES: Human Resources Office, 757-396-5726, DSN 961-5726.
Personnel and Expenditures
ACTIVE DUTY PERSONNEL: 150 (Sailors aboard ships under repair 5000)
CIVILIAN PERSONNEL: 7000
Services
Housing: Family units 282; Unaccompanied officer quarters 80; Unaccompanied enlisted quarters 1435; Townhouse units 8. *Temporary Housing:* See Norfolk Naval Base Complex. *Commissary:* Yes; *Exchange:* Barber shop; Food shop; Florist; Service station; Military clothing store; Laundromat; Credit union. *Child Care/Capacities:* Day care center capacity 57, infant-5 yrs. *Schools:* No on-base schools. *Medical Facilities:* Medical clinic; Dental clinic; Dispensary; Pharmacy, Portsmouth Naval Medical Center. *Recreational Facilities:* Bowling center; Pool; Gym; Recreation center; Tennis courts; Racquetball court; Fitness center/Weight room; Softball field; Auto shop; Basketball courts; Handball courts; Consolidated club.

892. Portsmouth Naval Hospital
NRMC Portsmouth
Portsmouth, VA 23708-2197
757-953-5000; DSN 564-0111

Profile
BRANCH: Navy.
SIZE AND LOCATION: 110 acres. In city of Portsmouth off I-264. *County:* City of Portsmouth.
MAJOR UNITS: Naval Medical Command, Mid-Atlantic Region.
BASE HISTORY: 1827, cornerstone laid; oldest and second largest Navy hospital in US. 1830, first patients admitted. 1960, modern 15-story addition built. Hospital is a teaching hospital with comprehensive range of emergency, outpatient, and inpatient health care services. 1998, new facility due for completion.

Personnel and Expenditures
ACTIVE DUTY PERSONNEL: 2234

Services
Housing: Family units 2234; Unaccompanied enlisted quarters 19. *Temporary Housing:* Guesthouse units. *Exchange:* Credit union. *Child Care/Capacities:* No day care facilities. *Schools:* No on-base schools. *Base Library:* Yes. *Medical Facilities:* Hospital 500 beds; Dental clinic. *Recreational Facilities:* Bowling center; Movie theater; Pool; Gym; Recreation center (pool tables); Softball field; NCO club; Picnic area.

893. Portsmouth Supervisor of Shipbuilding, Conversion and Repair
SupShip Portsmouth VA
PO Box 215
Portsmouth, VA 23705-0215
757-396-3579
OFFICER-OF-THE-DAY: 757-396-3736, DSN 961-3736

Profile
BRANCH: Navy.
LOCATION: On banks of S branch of Elizabeth River opposite Norfolk, VA. Immediate access to I-64, I-264, US-13, US-17. Serviced by Norfolk Airport approx 10 mi away. *County:* City of Portsmouth.
MAJOR UNITS: Supervisor of Shipbuilding, Conversion, and Repair, Portsmouth.
BASE HISTORY: 1947, Commander, Norfolk Naval Shipyard designated as Industrial Manager, USN, Fifth Naval District. 1951, Office of Industrial Manager established independently of shipyard. 1967, Industrial Manager redesignated Supervisor of Shipbuilding, Conversion and Repair, USN Fifth Naval District. 1975, Command title changed to current title. 1985, NAVSEA established detachment, Colts Neck, NJ, Charleston, SC, & Vallejo, CA. Also see Norfolk Naval Shipyard.

Personnel and Expenditures
ACTIVE DUTY PERSONNEL: 23
CIVILIAN PERSONNEL: 561

Services *Commissary:* Yes; *Exchange:* Retail store; Barber shop; Dry cleaners; Food shop; Florist; Service station. *Child Care/Capacities:* Day care center capacity 40. *Medical Facilities:* Medical clinic; Dental clinic. *Recreational Facilities:* Bowling center; Movie theater; Pool; Gym; Recreation center; Tennis courts; Racquetball court; Fitness center/Weight room; Softball field; Football field; Auto shop; NCO club.

894. Shore Intermediate Maintenance Activity
SIMA
St Julien's Creek Annex
Portsmouth, VA 23709
757-396-0117; DSN 961-0117
OFFICER-OF-THE-DAY: 757-396-0117, DSN 961-0117

Profile
BRANCH: Navy.
SIZE AND LOCATION: 50 acres. On Victory Blvd between George Washington Hwy and NNSY. *County:* City of Portsmouth.
MAJOR UNITS: Shore Intermediate Maintenance Activity, Portsmouth.
BASE HISTORY: SIMA is a tenant command of Norfolk Naval Shipyard and uses its facilities.

Key Contacts
COMMANDER: 757-396-0120, DSN 961-0120.
PUBLIC AFFAIRS: 757-396-0145, DSN 961-0145.

Personnel and Expenditures
ACTIVE DUTY PERSONNEL: 320
CIVILIAN PERSONNEL: 7

Services *Commissary:* Yes; *Exchange:* Retail store; Barber shop; Dry cleaners; Food shop; Florist; Service station. *Child Care/Capacities:* Day care center. *Medical Facilities:* Medical clinic; Dental clinic. *Recreational Facilities:* Bowling center; Pool; Gym; Recreation center; Tennis courts; Racquetball court; Fitness center/Weight room; Softball field; Auto shop; Camping; Fishing/Hunting.

Quantico

895. Quantico Marine Corps Combat Development Command
MCCDC, Quantico
Quantico
3250 Catilin Ave
Quantico, VA 22134-5001
703-784-1212; FAX 703-784-3527; DSN 278-1212
Internet: http://ismo-www1.mqg.usmc.mil
OFFICER-OF-THE-DAY: 703-784-2707, DSN 278-2707

Profile
BRANCH: Marine Corps.
SIZE AND LOCATION: 60,000 acres. Approx 30 mi S of Washington, DC, on I-95 or Rte 1; surrounds town of Quantico, VA, on three sides with Potomac River running adj to base. *County:* Stafford; Prince William; Fauquier.
MAJOR UNITS: Marine Corps Base, Quantico; Marine Corps Combat Development Command; Marine Air-Ground Task Force Warfighting Center; Marine Corps Intelligence Activity; Staff Noncommissioned Officers Academy; Officers Candidates School; The Basic School, Camp Barrett; Marine Corps University; Amphibious Warfare School; Communication Officers School; Command & Control Systems School; Command and Staff College; Computer Sciences School; Weapons Training Bn; HQ & Service Bn; Security Bn; Marine Corps Air Facility Quantico; Quantico Marine Corps Band; Range Control; Marine Helicopter Squadron 1 (HMX-1); Marine Security Guard Bn; Marine Corps Systems Command; Marine Corps Op-

erational Test and Evaluation Activity; Morale, Welfare and Recreation Support Activity; Naval Investigative Service; Marine Corps Association; Federal Bureau of Investigation Academy; Co D, 4th Light Armored Reconnaissance Bn (MARFORRES).
BASE HISTORY: 1917, first Marines arrive at Quantico, which means *by the large stream;* thousands trained during WWI, including 4th Marine Brigade. 1920, Marine Corps Schools founded. 1935-41, tactical units became Fleet Marine Force and developed amphibious warfare techniques used during WWII. Air facility and HMX-1 continue to aid in development, training and education, and support of president. 1968, redesignated as Marine Corps Development and Education Command (MCDEC), forerunner of today's MCCDC, created Nov 10, 1987.
VISITOR ATTRACTIONS: Marine Corps Air Ground Museum.

Key Contacts
PUBLIC AFFAIRS: Public Affairs Office, MCCDC, Quantico, VA 22134-5001, 703-784-2741, 784-2742, 784-3341, DSN 278-2741, 278-2742, 278-3341.

Personnel and Expenditures
ACTIVE DUTY PERSONNEL: 7000
DEPENDENTS: 9250
CIVILIAN PERSONNEL: 1120

Services
Housing: Family units 2030; Unaccompanied enlisted quarters 860; BAQ units 4782; RV/Camper sites 31. *Temporary Housing:* VIP units 3; Crossroads Inn, 100 rooms. *Commissary:* Yes; *Exchange:* Retail store; Barber shop; Dry cleaners; Food shop; Florist; Bank; Service station; Bakery; Credit union; 7 day store. *Child Care/Capacities:* Day care center; Home day care program. *Schools:* Preschool/Kindergarten; Elementary; Intermediate/Junior high; High school; Northern VA Community College; Univ of Denver, Park College; Univ of VA. *Base Library:* Yes. *Medical Facilities:* Medical clinic; Dental clinic; Branch clinics: TBS, OCS, and Camp Usher; Seasonal—open during officer candidate training. *Recreational Facilities:* Bowling center; Movie theater; Pool; Gym; Golf course; Stables; Tennis courts; Racquetball court; Fitness center/Weight room; Softball field; Football field; Auto shop; Officers club; NCO club; Camping; Fishing/Hunting.

Radford

896. Radford Army Ammunition Plant
RAAP
PO Box 2
Radford, VA 24141-0099
703-639-8611; FAX 703-639-7789, DSN 931-8611

Profile
BRANCH: Army.
SIZE AND LOCATION: Radford: 4080 acres; New River Unit: 2821 acres. Radford Unit: near city of Radford & town of Blacksburg, N of I-81; 47 mi from Roanoke; 108 mi NE from Bristol, TN. New River Unit: just outside city of Dublin, VA, off US-11. *County:* Montgomery; Pulaski.
MAJOR UNITS: Army Armament, Munitions and Chemical Command (AMCCOM).

BASE HISTORY: 1940, construction began on site where Byron McDonald made gunpowder for Revolutionary War, named Radford Ordnance Works. Became first GOCO facility. After WWII, standby status. Korean War, reactivated and has remained in operation since. Divided between two sites: Radford Unit, which handles all manufacturing operations, producing explosives and propellants, and New River Unit, a propellant storage site.

VISITOR ATTRACTIONS: Museum.

Key Contacts
COMMANDER: LTC Paul E Wojciechowski, 703-639-8711, DSN 931-8711.
PUBLIC AFFAIRS: Howard R Angel.
PROCUREMENT: Don Evans, 703-639-7388, DSN 931-7388.
TRANSPORTATION: Iris Williams, 703-639-8602, DSN 931-7388.
PERSONNEL/COMMUNITY ACTIVITIES: See Public Affairs Officer.

Personnel and Expenditures
ACTIVE DUTY PERSONNEL: 2
CIVILIAN PERSONNEL: 1195

Services
Housing: Family units 20. *Temporary Housing:* BAQ units.

Richmond

897. Adjutant General of Virginia
600 E Broad St
Richmond, VA 23219-1832
804-775-9102; FAX 804-775-9338; DSN 953-2107

Profile
BRANCH: Air National Guard; Army National Guard.
MAJOR UNITS: Virginia National Guard.

Key Contacts
COMMANDER: Maj Gen Carroll Thackston.

898. Defense Supply Center, Richmond
8000 Jefferson Davis Hwy
Richmond, VA 23297-5100
804-275-3209; FAX 804-279-6084; DSN 695-3209

Profile
BRANCH: Defense Logistics Agency.
SIZE AND LOCATION: 355 acres. 12 mi S of Richmond, VA; 14 mi N of Petersburg on US-1 and US-301; easily accessible from Richmond-Petersburg Tpke (I-95) via Exits 67 or 64; 14 mi from Richmond IAP using I-64. *County:* Chesterfield.
MAJOR UNITS: Defense Distribution Depot, Richmond; Defense Reutilization and Marketing Office; Defense Security Institute (DSI); Defense Logistics Agency Operations Research Office (DORO); Defense Logistics Agency Operations Support Office (DOSO); Defense Logistics Agency Performance Standards Support Office (DPSSO); Defense Printing Reprographic Facility (DPS-RF); Army Recruiting Bn Richmond; Defense Criminal Investigative Service (DCIS); Defense Contract Management Office; Army Corps of Engineers, Central Virginia Area Office, DSCR Project Office; Defense Education Supplies Procurement Office.

BASE HISTORY: Occupies one of oldest inhabited parcels of land in US. Early 1600s settled by colonists who ventured upriver from Jamestown. 1942, activated as Richmond General Depot (later Richmond Armed Service Forces Depot, Richmond Quartermaster Depot, & Military General Supply Agency). WWII, 2500 German POWs housed. 1962, received present name upon activation of Defense Supply Agency as parent command. 1960, processed up to 48 million sandbags a month. 1977, headquarters became Defense Logistics Agency, extension of supply systems of individual services. Mission: management of military general supplies for Armed Services worldwide; also major procurement & supply responsibility for school & library materials for overseas military dependents & service libraries.

VISITOR ATTRACTIONS: Bellwood Officer's Club on Virginia and National Register of Historic Landmarks.

Key Contacts
COMMANDER: Frank B Lotts, 804-279-3801, DSN 695-3801.

Personnel and Expenditures
ACTIVE DUTY PERSONNEL: 40
DEPENDENTS: 42
CIVILIAN PERSONNEL: 3600
MILITARY PAYROLL EXPENDITURE: $800 mil

Services
Housing: Family units 5; Unaccompanied officer quarters 6. *Temporary Housing:* VOQ units 6. *Commissary:* Yes; *Exchange:* Barber shop; Furniture store. *Child Care/Capacities:* No day care facilities. *Schools:* No on-base schools. *Medical Facilities:* Medical clinic. *Recreational Facilities:* Pool; Gym; Tennis courts; Fitness center/Weight room; Softball field; Officers club.

899. Richmond Naval & Marine Corps Reserve Center
6000 Strathmore Rd
Richmond, VA 23234-4999
804-271-6096, 275-7906; FAX 804-271-8598

Profile
BRANCH: Naval Reserve; Marine Corps Reserve.
LOCATION: *County:* City of Richmond.
MAJOR UNITS: REDCOM SIX Activity; Co B, 4th Combat Engineer Bn.

Key Contacts
COMMANDER: LCDR W H Jacob.

Roanoke

900. Roanoke Naval & Marine Corps Reserve Center
5301 Barns Ave, NW
Roanoke, VA 24019-3899
540-563-9723; FAX 540-563-0711

Profile
BRANCH: Naval Reserve; Marine Corps Reserve.
LOCATION: *County:* City of Roanoke.
MAJOR UNITS: REDCOM SIX Activity; Co B, 4th Combat Engineer Bn.

Key Contacts
COMMANDER: LCDR M E Donahue.

Sandston

901. Richmond IAP Air National Guard Base
50 Falcon Rd
Sandston, VA 23150-2524
804-236-6000; FAX 804-236-6935; DSN 864-6000

Profile
BRANCH: Air National Guard.
SIZE AND LOCATION: 143 acres. 7 mi E of Richmond directly adj to Richmond IAP; 2 mi SW of intersection of I-64 and I-295; access from VA Hwy 60 and 33. *County:* Henrico.
MAJOR UNITS: State Headquarters, VA ANG; 192nd Fighter Wing; 200th Weather Flight.
BASE HISTORY: Unit can trace lineage to 328th Fighter Squadron, one of top Army Air Force fighter units of WWII. 1947, 328th redesignated 149th Tactical Fighter Squadron, assigned to VA ANG, and located at Byrd Field with federal recognition. 1951, called to active duty; served 21 months in Korea and other overseas areas. 1953, reorganized into 149th Bombardment Squadron. 1958, redesignated Tactical Fighter Squadron. 1961-62, activated for Berlin Crisis. 1963, redesignated 192nd Tactical Fighter Group. 1987, AF Outstanding Unit Award. 1991, first ANG unit to upgrade to F-16C/D. 1993-94, deployed to Incirlik AB, Turkey for Operation Provide Comfort II; patrolled Iraq no-fly zone. Feb 1996, redeployed to Incirlik AB, Turkey to patrol no-fly zone. Apr 1996, became reconnaissance capable with portable pod on F-16C airframe. May 1996, deployed to Aviano AB, Italy to fly reconnaissance over Bosnia.

Key Contacts
COMMANDER: Col Robert O Seifert.
PUBLIC AFFAIRS: Capt D D Magaldi.

Personnel and Expenditures
ACTIVE DUTY PERSONNEL: 74; 992 guard
CIVILIAN PERSONNEL: 246
MILITARY PAYROLL EXPENDITURE: $18.5 mil

Virginia Beach

902. Dam Neck, Fleet Combat Training Center, Atlantic
FCTCLANT, Dam Neck
1912 Regulus Ave
Virginia Beach, VA 23461-2098
757-433-6234; FAX 757-433-6775; DSN 433-6234
Internet: http://www.cnet.navy.mil/tralant/fctcl

Profile
BRANCH: Navy.
SIZE AND LOCATION: 1171 acres. Approx 5 mi S of downtown resort area of Virginia Beach; From I-64, I-44E to Virginia Beach, S on Birdneck Rd to Gen Booth Blvd, S on Gen Booth Blvd to Dam Neck Rd, follow to main gate. *County:* City of Virginia Beach.
MAJOR UNITS: Fleet Combat Training Center, Atlantic; Fleet Combat Direction Systems Support Activity; Missiles School; Tactical Training Group, Atlantic; Navy & Marine Corps Intelligence Training Center; Naval Surface Warfare Center, Port Hueneme, East

Coast Division; Naval Ocean Processing Facility; Joint Targeting School; Fleet Composite Squadron, Det 6; Navy Education & Training Management Support Activity; Commander Undersea Surveillance; Navy Special Warfare Development Group; Marine Air Control Squadron 24; Personnel Support Det; Public Works Center, Virginia Beach Site.

BASE HISTORY: Built on site of 19th-century Coast Guard lifesaving station. 1941, established as Anti-Aircraft Training & Test Center (Anti-Aircraft Range) to provide live firing range to train fleet gunnery crews. One of few Navy commands with all-military police force. Smallest naval base in Tidewater area. Only half of facility used due to wetlands. Has only open ocean gunline in US. Mission to provide training in operation & employment of specified tactical combat direction & control systems in naval warfare; support operational commanders in evaluation, development & analysis of naval warfare doctrines & tactics; and provide training in maintenance of specified equipment.

VISITOR ATTRACTIONS: Federal game preserve; Trained Sailor Statue; Gallery Plaza with two original twin 40 guns from battleship USS *Missouri*; open to DOD personnel only.

Key Contacts
COMMANDER: Capt Robert T Murphy, 757-433-6542.
PUBLIC AFFAIRS: Robin Holland, 757-433-6595.
PROCUREMENT: Mike Coyle, contracting, 757-433-6790.

Personnel and Expenditures
ACTIVE DUTY PERSONNEL: 2566
DEPENDENTS: 62
CIVILIAN PERSONNEL: 839

Services
Housing: Family units Officer 19; *Temporary Housing:* VIP units 10; VOQ units 159; VEQ units 394; Transient quarters 2100. *Exchange:* Retail store; Barber shop; Dry cleaners; Service station; Military clothing store; Convenience store; Laundromat; Credit union; Commissary at Oceana NAS. *Child Care/Capacities:* Day care center capacity 120; No day care facilities. *Schools:* No on-base schools. *Base Library:* Yes. *Medical Facilities:* Dental clinic; Dispensary. *Recreational Facilities:* Bowling center; Movie theater; Pool; Gym; Tennis courts; Racquetball court; Fitness center/Weight room; Softball field; Football field; Auto shop; Fishing/Hunting; Equipment gear rental; Jogging trail; Beach with cabanas.

903. Oceana Naval Air Station
NAS Oceana
Virginia Beach, VA 23460-5120
757-433-2366; FAX 757-433-3156; DSN 433-2366
OFFICER-OF-THE-DAY: 757-433-2366, DSN 433-2366

Profile
BRANCH: Navy.
SIZE AND LOCATION: 6000 acres. Within city limits of Virginia Beach; approx 3 mi S of resort area off I-264; 25 mi E of Norfolk Naval Base Complex; Take I-64 E to exit 44, Norfolk-Virginia Beach Expressway, exit at NAS Oceana, follow signs. *County:* City of Virginia Beach.

MAJOR UNITS: Commander, Carrier Wing One; Commander, Carrier Wing Three; Commander, Carrier Wing Seven; Commander, Carrier Wing Eight; Commander, Carrier Wing Seventeen; Commander, Fighter Wing, US Atlantic Fleet; Fighter Squadron 2; Fighter Squadron 11; Fighter Squadron 14; Fighter Squadron 31; Fighter Squadron 32; Fighter Squadron 41; Fighter Squadron 101; Fighter Squadron 102; Fighter Squadron 103; Fighter Squadron 211; Fighter Squadron 143; Fighter Squadron 213; Fleet Composite Squadron 12; Fleet Area Control & Surveillance Facility, Virginia Capes; Naval Air Maintenance Training Group Dets; Fleet Aviation Specialized Operational Training Group, Atlantic Fleet; Naval Construction Bn Unit 415; Naval Oceanography Command Det; Fleet Imaging Center, Atlantic; Naval Auxiliary Landing Field, Fentress.

BASE HISTORY: 1940, commissioned as auxiliary airfield. 1943, changed to Naval Auxiliary Air Station. 1952, designated NAS. 1953, designated all-weather air station. 1957, designated Master Jet Base with longest runways in Tidewater region. Largest employer in Virginia Beach area. Current mission to insure readiness of F-14 Tomcats for Atlantic Fleet. All F-14s, except 1 squadron in Japan, are at NAS Oceana.

VISITOR ATTRACTIONS: Atlantic beach resorts.

Key Contacts
COMMANDER: Capt Eric Benson, 757-433-2922, DSN 433-2922.
PUBLIC AFFAIRS: Troy R Snead, 757-433-3131, DSN 433-3131, tsnead@series2000.com.
PROCUREMENT: CDR John Martin, 757-433-2297, DSN 433-2397.
TRANSPORTATION: John Althizer, 757-433-2250, DSN 433-2250.
PERSONNEL/COMMUNITY ACTIVITIES: Jim Lytle, 757-433-2560, DSN 433-2560.

Personnel and Expenditures
ACTIVE DUTY PERSONNEL: 6714
DEPENDENTS: 11,500
CIVILIAN PERSONNEL: 1765
MILITARY PAYROLL EXPENDITURE: $354 mil
CONTRACT EXPENDITURE: $156 mil

Services
Housing: Family units 1094; Unaccompanied enlisted quarters 2500; Junior NCO units 24. *Temporary Housing:* Unaccompanied officer/Enlisted quarters 200. *Commissary:* Yes; *Exchange:* Retail store; Barber shop; Dry cleaners; Food shop; Florist; Bank; Service station; Bakery; Bookstore; Military clothing store; Convenience store; Laundromat; Credit union; Optical store; Video rentals; Class VI; Personal services center; Jewelry sales and repair. *Child Care/Capacities:* Day care center capacity 50. *Schools:* No on-base schools. *Base Library:* Yes. *Medical Facilities:* Medical clinic; Dental clinic; Dispensary; Pharmacy. *Recreational Facilities:* Gym; Golf course; Stables; Skeet range; Gear locker checkout.

904. State Military Reservation, Camp Pendleton
SMR Camp Pendleton
Camp Pendleton
PO Box 9
Virginia Beach, VA 23458-0009
757-491-5140

Profile
BRANCH: Army National Guard.
SIZE AND LOCATION: 390 acres. Just S of Rudee Inlet in Virginia Beach; adj to US Fleet Anti-Air Warfare Training Center; off Atlantic Ave, extension of I-60 S. *County:* City of Virginia Beach.
MAJOR UNITS: Virginia National Guard.
BASE HISTORY: 1887, roots at National Encampment held at Camp Fitz Lee, Montgomery County & NC; training moved to State Fair Grounds, Richmond. 1904, 71st Infantry first paid camp at Ocean View. 1908-12, funds appropriated, land purchased, & site opened as State Rifle Range. WWI, known as US Navy Rifle Range. 1920, reverted to state control. 1928, renamed State Military Reservation & Camp, named for each current governor. 1930s, used by units from Reserves, Regular Army, Navy, Marine Corps, Coast Guard, VA State Police & by aviators (used parade ground as emergency landing field). 1940, Army redesignated SMR as Camp Pendleton for Civil War general, VA native (name that continued in popular use to present but ceased to be official with state control, 1946). Trained & billeted coastal artillery units; later served as boot camp. Following WWII, site of annual amphibious exercises including Naval Academy & West Point. 1948, ARNG resumed summer training. 1950s, little use except for instruction & meetings. 1960s, rehabilitation & annual training by 107th Artillery Brigade. 1970-80s, period of rebirth. Today, a Major Training Area (MTA), Category D site, capable of supporting 900 personnel.

Key Contacts
COMMANDER: LTC T E Mendenhall, Training Site Commander, 757-491-5140.
PUBLIC AFFAIRS: Office of the Adjutant General of Virginia, 501 E Franklin St, Richmond, VA 23219-2317.

Personnel and Expenditures
ACTIVE DUTY PERSONNEL: 3
CIVILIAN PERSONNEL: 20

Services
Housing: Unaccompanied enlisted quarters; BAQ units; Dormitory spaces 1780. *Temporary Housing:* VIP units; Unaccompanied officer/Enlisted quarters; Guest cottages; Trailers. *Exchange:* Barber shop; PX shoppette at Ft Story. *Schools:* No on-base schools. *Medical Facilities:* Dispensary. *Recreational Facilities:* Exercise room; Sauna; Beach; Lake Christine.

Wallops Island

905. AEGIS Combat Systems Center
ACSC
Commander
Wallops Island, VA 23337
Internet: http://www.nswc.navy.mil/homepages/aegis/

Profile
BRANCH: Navy.
LOCATION: Tenant on Wallops Flight Facility of NASA. Coastal site: on Wallops Island approx 10 mi S of HQ. HQ, BOQ, combined dining facility, & Navy family housing units on mainland W of Chincoteague, VA. 157 mi

from Washington, DC; 125 mi from Annapolis, MD; 110 mi from Norfolk, VA; 200 mi from NSWC Dahlgren, VA. *County:* Accomac.

MAJOR UNITS: AEGIS Combat Systems Center; AEGIS Training Unit, Det (ATU); Integrated Ship Defense Systems Engineering Center (ISDSEC).

BASE HISTORY: 1980, formal arrangements for Navy use of Wallops Island; leased Bldg Z-41. 1996, new bldg for testing shipboard systems.

Key Contacts

COMMANDER: CDR Richard W White, 757-824-2272, FAX 757-824-2043.

PROCUREMENT: Robert Warren, Supply Management, 757-824-1200.

Personnel and Expenditures

ACTIVE DUTY PERSONNEL: 106

CIVILIAN PERSONNEL: contractors 165; civil service 42

Services

Housing: Unaccompanied officer quarters 16 rooms; Unaccompanied enlisted quarters 66 rooms.

Williamsburg

906. Camp Peary

Hawtree Landing Rd
Williamsburg, VA 23188
757-221-8623

Profile

BRANCH: DOD.

SIZE AND LOCATION: 10,000 acres. Off I-64 Camp Peary Exit, Rte 143; just E of Williamsburg, along York River. *County:* York.

MAJOR UNITS: Armed Forces Experimental Training Activity.

BASE HISTORY: WWII, established as training base for Navy Seabees. 1951, transferred to CIA; redesignated Armed Forces Experimental Training Activity.

VISITOR ATTRACTIONS: Closed to the public.

Key Contacts

PUBLIC AFFAIRS: 757-229-2121; Army Public Affairs Office, The Pentagon, 202-694-0739.

PROCUREMENT: 1100 Executive Dr.

907. Fleet & Industrial Supply Center, Cheatham Annex

NSC CAX
108 Sanda Ave
Williamsburg, VA 23185-5830
757-887-7108, 887-7109; FAX 757-888-0833; DSN 953-7108, 953-7109
Internet: http://mintaka.spawar.navy.mil/nr/ cnsr/iuwg2/
OFFICER-OF-THE-DAY: Duty Desk, 757-887-7383, FAX 757-887-8833

Profile

BRANCH: Navy.

SIZE AND LOCATION: 1579 acres. On York River approx 5 mi outside of Williamsburg on Rte 199, approx 2 mi off of I-64, exit 242-B. *County:* York.

MAJOR UNITS: Fleet & Industrial Supply Center, Cheatham Annex; Naval Inshore Undersea Warfare Group 2; Naval Reserve Force, Cheatham Annex; Navy Cargo Handling and Port Group; Army Veterinarian Food Inspection Office.

BASE HISTORY: Built on site of munitions plant named for Russell S Penniman, inventor of ammonia dynamite. Following WWI, plant all but disappeared, returning to farm land. A number of old buildings still stand, in use as Ranger's Field Office & Paint Storage. Old-timers still refer to area as Penniman. 1943, Naval Supply Depot named for Rear Adm Joseph Johnston Cheatham, former Chief of Bureau of Supplies & Accounts.

Key Contacts

COMMANDER: Capt G "Skip" Giessing, COMNAVIUWGRU TWO, 757-887-7383, ext 20, DSN 953-7383, ext 200.

PROCUREMENT: CDR Rob Beck, Supply Officer, 757-887-7383 ext 270.

Personnel and Expenditures

ACTIVE DUTY PERSONNEL: 502

DEPENDENTS: 30

CIVILIAN PERSONNEL: 432

Services

Housing: Family units 13; Unaccompanied enlisted quarters 112; RV/Camper sites 19; Chiefs Quarters 6. *Temporary Housing:* VIP units 2; Guesthouse units 8. *Exchange:* Retail store; Barber shop; Service station. *Recreational Facilities:* Bowling center; Pool; Gym; Golf course; Tennis courts; Softball field; Camping; Fishing/Hunting.

Winchester

908. US Army Corps of Engineers, Transatlantic Programs Center

201 Prince Frederick Dr
Winchester, VA 22602-1450

Mailing Address
PO Box 2250
Winchester, VA 22604-1450
540-665-4023; FAX 540-665-4023; DSN 265-4023
Internet: http://144.3.144.33/

Profile

BRANCH: Army.

LOCATION: *County:* Frederick.

MAJOR UNITS: Corps of Engineers, Transatlantic Programs Center.

Key Contacts

COMMANDER: LTC Nicholas J Kolar Jr, Acting Commander, 540-665-3601, Nicholas. J.Kolar.LTC@usace.army.mil.

PUBLIC AFFAIRS: Hoan F Kibler, Chief, 540-665-4085, joan.f.kibler@usace.army. mil.

Yorktown

909. Yorktown Coast Guard Reserve Training Center

USCG RESTRACEN Yorktown; RTC Yorktown
Box 21
Yorktown, VA 23690-5000
757-898-2212

Profile

BRANCH: Coast Guard.

LOCATION: 2 mi S of Yorktown on Rte 238; 15 mi from Newport News; from I-64 take exit 258 onto Rte 17 to Yorktown, right on Colonial Pky Rd to Moore House Rd to Hamilton Rd. *County:* York.

MAJOR UNITS: Coast Guard Reserve Training Unit; Training & Technical Assistance Center; Coast Guard International Training Division; USCGC *Morro Bay.*

Personnel and Expenditures

ACTIVE DUTY PERSONNEL: 406

DEPENDENTS: 850

CIVILIAN PERSONNEL: 48

Services

Housing: Student housing. *Temporary Housing:* Unaccompanied officer/Enlisted quarters. *Exchange:* Small exchange. *Child Care/Capacities:* No day care facilities. *Schools:* No on-base schools. *Medical Facilities:* Dispensary. *Recreational Facilities:* Bowling center; Movie theater; Pool; Gym; Tennis courts; Racquetball court; Fitness center/Weight room.

910. Yorktown Naval Weapons Station

WPNSTA YORKTOWN
PO Drawer 160
Yorktown, VA 23691-0160
757-887-4000; DSN 953-4000
Internet: http://www.noclant.navy.mil/ yorktown/command.htm
OFFICER-OF-THE-DAY: 757-887-4545, DSN 953-4545

Profile

BRANCH: Navy.

SIZE AND LOCATION: 10,654 acres. Exit 247 off I-64, approx 5 mi S of Williamsburg, VA, on border of Newport News, VA; From I-64, take exit 250-B, left on Jefferson Ave to base on right. *County:* York; City of Newport News.

MAJOR UNITS: Naval Weapons Station, Yorktown; Allied Command Atlantic Communications Logistics Depot; Explosive Ordnance Disposal Mobile Unit 2; Marine Corps Security Force Co; NIS Resident Agency; Naval Air Warfare Center, Weapons Division Det; Naval Ophthalmic Support and Training Activity; NAVSEA RASO Det; Naval Surface Warfare Center, Indian Head Det; Navy Publications and Printing Service Center; Navy Regional Branch Medical Clinic; Navy Regional Branch Dental Clinic; Navy Submarine Torpedo Facility; Navy Exchange; Personnel Support Activity Det; Commissary Store.

BASE HISTORY: 1918, established as Naval Mine Depot to support laying of 100,000-mine North Sea barrage in WWI; at that time, world's largest naval reservation, covering about 20 sq mi. During WWII, developed mines, depth charges, & new ordnance devices. 1953, Skiffes Creek Annex commissioned with Guided Missile Service Unit No 211. 1956, Naval Mine Engineering Facility (later Naval Mine Warfare Engineering Activity) established for mines & depth charges. 1958, name changed to US Naval Weapons Station. Mission to store, maintain, & provide ordnance for Atlantic Fleet. 1983, reorganized as Naval Mine Warfare Engineering Activity.

VISITOR ATTRACTIONS: Lee House, circa 1650; closed base, must have sponsor to enter.

Key Contacts

COMMANDER: Capt Stanley A Denham, 757-887-4141, FAX 757-887-4596, sdenham@noclant.navy.mil.

PUBLIC AFFAIRS: 757-887-4444, DSN
953-4444.

Personnel and Expenditures
ACTIVE DUTY PERSONNEL: 238
DEPENDENTS: 4060
CIVILIAN PERSONNEL: 864

Services

Housing: Family units 470; Trailer spaces 40.
Commissary: Yes; *Exchange:* Retail store; Barber shop; Service station; Military clothing store; Convenience store; Credit union. *Child Care/Capacities:* Day care center capacity 104; Home day care program. *Schools:* No on-base schools. *Base Library:* Yes.

Medical Facilities: Medical clinic; Dental clinic.
Recreational Facilities: Bowling center; Pool; Gym; Golf course; Stables; Tennis courts; Racquetball court; Fitness center/Weight room; Softball field; Football field; Auto shop; Craft shop; Officers club; NCO club; Camping; Fishing/Hunting; Enlisted club; Youth center; Picnic area.

Washington

Arlington

911. Jim Creek Naval Radio Station (T)

NAVRASTA (T) Jim Creek
21027 Jim Creek Rd
Arlington, WA 98223-8599
425-304-5315; FAX 425-304-5306; DSN
727-5315; DSN FAX 727-5306
E-mail: Kiel-KrohnTD@NCTS-PUGET.nsb.
navy.mil
OFFICER-OF-THE-DAY: 425-304-5314, DSN
727-5314

Profile
BRANCH: Navy.
SIZE AND LOCATION: 4899 acres. Approx 60
mi NE of Seattle North Cascades foothills;
from Everett N on I-15 approx 10 mi to Exit
208 (Arlington), right on SR 530, 7 mi to
mile marker 25, next right on Jim Creek Rd, 7
mi to end of road. *County:* Snohomish.
MAJOR UNITS: Naval Radio Station, Jim
Creek; Jim Creek Regional Outdoor Recreation Area.
BASE HISTORY: 1953, activated as low frequency (VLF) site; later added function as Pacific Northwest Regional Outdoor Recreation
Center.
VISITOR ATTRACTIONS: Campsites/outdoor
recreational facilities (reservations 1-800-734-
1123).

Key Contacts
COMMANDER: LCDR Cheryl D Blake,
425-304-5301, DSN 727-5301, BlakeCD@
NCTS-PUGET.nsb.navy.mil.
PROCUREMENT: 425-304-5312, DSN
727-5312.
TRANSPORTATION: Lt Trent L Carmichael,
Facilities Manager, 425-304-5302, DSN
727-5302, CarmichaelTL@NCTS-PUGET.
nsb.navy.mil.

Personnel and Expenditures
ACTIVE DUTY PERSONNEL: 7
DEPENDENTS: 11
CIVILIAN PERSONNEL: 50

Services
Housing: Family units 4; RV/Camper sites RV
pads 2, No-hookup sites, 22. *Temporary Housing:* VIP units 1. *Child Care/Capacities:* No day
care facilities. *Schools:* No on-base schools.
Medical Facilities: No medical facilities. *Recreational Facilities:* Gym; Fitness center/Weight
room; Softball field; Camping; Fishing/Hunting;
Playground; Paint ball; Picnic shelters; Canoe
rentals; Ski trails; Conference facilities; Meeting
spaces.

Bellevue

912. Defense Contract Management Command, Seattle

DCMC Seattle
3009 112th Ave NE
Bellevue, WA 98004-8019
206-889-7300; FAX 206-889-7252; DSN
972-7300
Internet: http://www.dcmdw.dla.mil/seaao/
seattle.htm

Profile
BRANCH: Defense Logistics Agency.
LOCATION: Near shore of Lake Washington.
County: King.
MAJOR UNITS: Defense Contract Management
Command, Seattle.

Key Contacts
COMMANDER: LTC Gregory S Miller,
gregory_ltc_miller@seaao.dcmdw.dla.mil.

Bremerton

913. Bremerton Naval Hospital

NAVHOSPBREM
Boone Rd
Bremerton, WA 98312-1898
360-479-6600; 1-800-422-1383; FAX
360-478-9476; DSN 439-6600; DSN FAX
439-9476
Internet: http://nh_bremerton.med.navy.mil
OFFICER-OF-THE-DAY: 360-792-9857 (pager)

Profile
BRANCH: Navy.
SIZE AND LOCATION: 49 acres. 4 mi N of
Bremerton on Rte 3. *County:* Kitsap.
MAJOR UNITS: Naval Hospital, Bremerton.
BASE HISTORY: A stand-alone hospital with
no base facilities. Community based acute
care & obstetrical hospital. Branch medical
clinics at Puget Sound Naval Shipyard, Submarine Base Bangor, Keyport Undersea Warfare Engineering Station, & Everett Naval Station. Public health & preventive medicine
services provided to Naval & Marine Corps
activities throughout the Pacific Northwest.
VISITOR ATTRACTIONS: Medical library for
staff use only.

Key Contacts
COMMANDER: Capt Gregg S Parker,
360-478-9239, FAX 360-478-9476, DSN
439-9239, DSN FAX 439-9476.
PUBLIC AFFAIRS: Judith A Robertson,
360-478-9368, FAX 360-478-9476, DSN
439-9368, DSN FAX 439-9476, robertso@
brm10.med.navy.mil.
PROCUREMENT: Lt Rollins, 360-478-9576,
DSN 439-9576, mrollins@brm10.med.navy.
mil.
PERSONNEL/COMMUNITY ACTIVITIES:
CDR R Becker, Director for Administration,
360-478-9210, DSN 439-9210.

Personnel and Expenditures
ACTIVE DUTY PERSONNEL: 732
DEPENDENTS: 0
CIVILIAN PERSONNEL: 372
CONTRACT EXPENDITURE: $60.7 mil

Services
Housing: Unaccompanied enlisted quarters 134.
Temporary Housing: None. *Exchange:* Convenience store; Dining hall for patients, visitors,
guests, staff. *Child Care/Capacities:* Children's
waiting room for temporary drop-off during parent appointments; other child care at Bangor
NSB. *Schools:* No on-base schools. *Base Library:* Yes. *Medical Facilities:* Hospital 60;
Pharmacy. *Recreational Facilities:* Fitness cen-
ter/Weight room; Softball field; Track.

914. Puget Sound Naval Shipyard

1400 Farragut Ave
Bremerton, WA 98314-5001
360-476-3711; DSN 439-3711; FISC:
360-476-7300; FAX 360-476-0768
Internet: http://www.puget.fisc.navy.mil/

Profile
BRANCH: Navy.
SIZE AND LOCATION: 1393 acres. 60 mi W
of Seattle on Rte 3 & Rte 16 in Bremerton.
County: Kitsap.
MAJOR UNITS: Naval Shipyard, Puget Sound;
Fleet & Industrial Supply Center, Puget
Sound; USS *Camden*; USS *Sacramento*; USS
Ranier; USS *California*; USS *Arkansas*;
Navy Fuel Depot, Manchester.
BASE HISTORY: Repairs, overhauls, & main-
tains Navy ships. Only Navy shipyard that re-
moves defueled reactor compartments from
decommissioned nuclear submarines. Fuel De-
partment, Manchester, largest underground
storage facility in continental US.

Key Contacts
COMMANDER: Capt Dale E Baugh,
360-476-3161.
PUBLIC AFFAIRS: John Gordon,
360-476-7111.
PROCUREMENT: CDR Keith Marchbanks,
360-476-2801.
Personnel and Expenditures
ACTIVE DUTY PERSONNEL: 11,800
DEPENDENTS: 18,550
CIVILIAN PERSONNEL: 8900
CONTRACT EXPENDITURE: $200 mil
Services
Housing: Family units 1090; Unaccompanied officer quarters 4; Unaccompanied enlisted quarters 320; Barracks spaces 2500. *Temporary Housing:* VIP units 4; VOQ units 71; VEQ units 1455; Transient quarters 6. *Commissary:* Yes; *Exchange:* Retail store; Convenience store. *Child Care/Capacities:* Day care center capacity 133; Home day care program. *Schools:* No on-base schools. *Medical Facilities:* Bremerton Naval Hospital nearby. *Recreational Facilities:* Bowling center; Pool; Gym; Tennis courts; Fitness center/Weight room; Softball field; Football field; Auto shop; Craft shop; Community club; Park on lake.

Cheney

915. Four Lakes Communications Station
12414 Andrus Rd
Cheney, WA 99004-9659
DSN 323-8526
Profile
BRANCH: Air National Guard.
SIZE AND LOCATION: 10 acres. 13 mi SW of Spokane, WA; 3.5 mi N of Cheney, WA; 7 mi W of Fairchild AFB, WA. *County:* Spokane.
MAJOR UNITS: 256th CBCS.
BASE HISTORY: 1955, originally built as home for Army Nike Missile Battery, to protect Fairchild AFB. 1961, closed; property transferred to Air Force; leased to ANG, known as Four Lakes Communications Station; first ANG occupants of "The Hill" were HQ 252nd Mobile Communications Groups & Squadron. 1971, 105th Tactical Control Squadron (later 105th ACS) maintains, equips, & trains a mobile air radar control & warning post.
Services
Housing: None.

Everett

916. Everett Naval Reserve Center
2220 W Marine View Dr
Everett, WA 98201-2600
206-304-4777, 304-4764; FAX 206-304-4776;
DSN 727-4777
Profile
BRANCH: Naval Reserve.
LOCATION: *County:* Snohomish.
MAJOR UNITS: REDCOM TWENTY-TWO Activity.
Key Contacts
COMMANDER: LCDR M T Maddock.

917. Everett Naval Station
2000 W Marine View Dr
Everett, WA 98207-0002
Internet: http://www.naswi.navy.mil/everett/
OFFICER-OF-THE-DAY: 206-304-3366; DSN 727-3366
Profile
BRANCH: Navy.
LOCATION: *County:* Snohomish.
MAJOR UNITS: Naval Station Everett; USS *Abraham Lincoln* (CVN 72); USS *Ingraham* (FFG 61); USS *Ford* (FFG 54); USS *Paul F Foster* (DD 964); USS *David R Ray* (DD 971); USS *Callaghan* (DDG 994); USS *Chandler* (DDG 996).
BASE HISTORY: 1983, proposed as part of Strategic Homeport concept. 1984, site selected. 1986-87, construction. 1992, carrier pier opened. 1994, official dedication. 1993-95, Family Support Complex, Smokey Point construction. Navy's newest facility; provides operational support to Carrier Battle Group.
Key Contacts
PUBLIC AFFAIRS: 206-304-3201, 304-3688, DSN 727-3201, 727-3688.
Services
Housing: Unaccompanied officer quarters; Unaccompanied enlisted quarters; Smokey Point Complex, Marysville, WA. *Commissary:* Yes; *Exchange:* Retail store; Optical store; Video rentals; Florist; Barber shop; Beauty shop; Dry cleaners; Thrift shop; Laundry; Photo store; Fast food; Service station; Military clothing store; Tailor/Alterations; Laundromat; Food shop; Bank; ATM; Exchange at Family Support Complex Smokey Point. *Child Care/Capacities:* Day care center. *Medical Facilities:* Medical clinic; Dental clinic. *Recreational Facilities:* Auto shop; Craft shop; Recreation center; Outdoor gear issue; Pacific Beach Resort.

918. Region Twenty-Two, Naval Reserve Readiness Command
REDCOM 22
2000 W Marine View Dr, NAS Everett
Everett, WA 98207-2600
206-304-1871; DSN 727-1871
Internet: http://www.rc22.navy.mil/
Profile
BRANCH: Naval Reserve.
MAJOR UNITS: Naval Reserve Readiness Command, Region 22.
BASE HISTORY: Oversees 22 Reserve Centers with 8500 Reservists.
Key Contacts
COMMANDER: Capt Bell, 206-304-3338, FAX 206-304-3257, DSN 727-3338.
PUBLIC AFFAIRS: JO2 Webster, 206-304-3107, DSN 727-3107.

Fairchild AFB

919. Fairchild Air Force Base
FAFB
Fairchild AFB, WA 99011-5000
509-247-1212; DSN 657-1212
Internet: http://www.fairchild.af.mil
OFFICER-OF-THE-DAY: 509-247-2566, DSN 657-2566
Profile
BRANCH: Air Force.
SIZE AND LOCATION: 4223 acres.

Approx 12 mi W of Spokane, WA, on US-2, in community of Airway Heights. *County:* Spokane.
MAJOR UNITS: 92nd Air Refueling Wing; 92nd Operations Group; 92nd Support Group; 92nd Medical Group; 92nd Logistics Group; Air Force Survival School; 336th Training Group; 36th Rescue Flight; 2nd Support Squadron; 141st Air Refueling Wing (WA ANG); Air Force Office of Special Investigations, Det 322.
BASE HISTORY: 1942, opened on donated land as Spokane Army Air Depot; site chosen partly because of strategic defense location 300 miles inland behind mountain range. 1950, renamed for Gen Muir S Fairchild, native of Bellingham, WA. 1992, became Air Combat Command base.
VISITOR ATTRACTIONS: Air Force History Museum.
Key Contacts
COMMANDER: Brig Gen Paul W Essex, 92 ARW/CC, 509-247-2113, DSN 657-2113.
PUBLIC AFFAIRS: 92 ARW/PA, 509-247-5704, DSN 657-5704.
Personnel and Expenditures
ACTIVE DUTY PERSONNEL: 4000; Guard 1200
DEPENDENTS: 6000
CIVILIAN PERSONNEL: 840
Services
Housing: Unaccompanied officer quarters 221; Senior NCO units 1359. *Temporary Housing:* VIP units 2; VOQ units 126; VAQ units 121; Transient quarters 8. *Commissary:* Yes; *Exchange:* Retail store; Barber shop; Dry cleaners; Food shop; Florist; Bank; Service station; Bakery; Video rental. *Child Care/Capacities:* Day care center capacity 135; Home day care program. *Schools:* Elementary. *Base Library:* Yes. *Medical Facilities:* Hospital 40 beds; Medical clinic; Dental clinic. *Recreational Facilities:* Bowling center; Movie theater; Pool; Gym; Recreation center; Tennis courts; Racquetball court; Skating rink; Fitness center/Weight room; Softball field; Football field; Auto shop; Craft shop; Officers club; NCO club.

Fort Lawton

920. Fort Lawton, 70th Regional Support Command
70th RSC
4575 36th Ave W
Fort Lawton, WA 98199-5000
Mailing Address
4575 36th Ave W
Seattle, WA 98199-5000
206-281-3019; FAX 206-281-3093
Profile
BRANCH: Army Reserve.
SIZE AND LOCATION: 75 acres. Approx 5 mi NW of downtown Seattle in Magnolia Community area; approx 17 mi N of Seattle-Tacoma IAP; adj to Discovery Park, operated by city of Seattle. From airport, I-5 N to Mercer St Exit, right on Fairview Ave N, left on Valley St, right on Westlake Ave N, continue onto Nickerson, left on W Emerson, right on Gilman, right on 36th W. *County:* King.
MAJOR UNITS: 70th Regional Support Command; 174th Corps Support Group.

VISITOR ATTRACTIONS: Next to Discovery Park.

Key Contacts

COMMANDER: MajGen Craig Bambrough, RSC Commander.

PUBLIC AFFAIRS: LTC Allan Havrilla (drill weekends); Pam Briola (full time deputy PAO) ATTN: AFRC-CWA-PA, FAX 206-281-3093, briolap@ftlawton.uu.holonet. net.

PERSONNEL/COMMUNITY ACTIVITIES: Pat Leonard, Customer Service Office (ID cards, military vehicle registration, referral & information) 206-281-3299, 1-800-347-2735, FAX 206-281-3594.

Personnel and Expenditures

ACTIVE DUTY PERSONNEL: 85
DEPENDENTS: 0
CIVILIAN PERSONNEL: 180
MILITARY PAYROLL EXPENDITURE: $4.6 mil
CONTRACT EXPENDITURE: $5.3 mil

Services

Housing: None. *Child Care/Capacities:* No day care facilities. *Schools:* No on-base schools. *Medical Facilities:* No medical facilities.

Fort Lewis

921. Fort Lewis

PO Box 339500
Fort Lewis, WA 98433-9500
253-967-1110; DSN 357-1110
Internet: http://www.lewis.army.mil

Profile

BRANCH: Army.

SIZE AND LOCATION: 86,176 acres. 10 mi S of Tacoma, WA; I-5 Exit 120. *County:* Pierce.

MAJOR UNITS: I Corps; Army Garrison, Ft Lewis; 1st Personnel Group; 1st Brigade, 25th Infantry Division (L); 1st Military Police Brigade (P); 1st Air Support Operations Group; 201st Military Intelligence Brigade; 3rd Brigade, 2nd Infantry Division; 555th Engineer Group; 593rd CSG; 62nd Medical Group; Noncommissioned Officer Academy, Ft Lewis; Vancouver Barracks; Yakima Training Center; 1st Special Forces Group; 2nd Bn, 75th Ranger Regiment; 66th CBT Aviation Brigade; 311th COSCOM (FWD); 902nd Military Intelligence Group; 142nd Signal Brigade (FWD); 5th Army West; HQ 6th Military Police Group (CID); 22nd Military Police Det (CID); 7th Brigade, 104th Infantry Division (Reserve); 95th Maintenance Co; Naval Reserve Training Center; Marine Corps Reserve Training Center; TRADOC Region G; TMDE Support Center; Army Reserve NCO Academy; Washington OSA Flight Det; Madigan Army Medical Center.

BASE HISTORY: 1917, began as Camp Lewis; land donated to federal government; named after Meriwether Lewis of Lewis & Clark expedition. 1926, permanent barracks constructed. 1927, became Ft Lewis, full-fledged Army post. During WWII, IX Corps & 3rd & 41st Divisions trained at Ft Lewis/Camp Murray. 1943, POW camp established. 1944, redesignated as Army Service Forces Training Center, training medics & engineers. Following WWII, separation center & basic training center for overseas occupation troops. During Korean War, trained US & Canadian troops.

Since 1954, home to various divisions, 2nd, 3rd, 4th, 33rd, 40th, 41st, 44th, 71st, & 96th. Since 1981, home of newly reorganized I Corps.

VISITOR ATTRACTIONS: Ft Lewis Museum.

Key Contacts

COMMANDER: Lt Gen George A Crocker, I Corps Commander; Col Edward P Egan, Garrison Commander, 253-967-0005, FAX 253-967-0623, DSN 357-0005, egane@lewis-ems1.army.mil.

PROCUREMENT: Director of Contracting, HQ Ft Lewis, WA 98466-5000, 253-967-2151, DSN 357-2151.

TRANSPORTATION: Joint Personal Property Shipping Office, HQ Ft Lewis, WA 98466-5000, 253-967-5744, DSN 357-5744.

PERSONNEL/COMMUNITY ACTIVITIES: HQ Ft Lewis, WA 98466-5000, 253-967-6681, DSN 357-6681.

Personnel and Expenditures

ACTIVE DUTY PERSONNEL: 20,000
DEPENDENTS: 22,120
CIVILIAN PERSONNEL: 5400

Services

Housing: Family units 3509; Unaccompanied officer quarters 30; Senior NCO units 87. *Temporary Housing:* VIP units 5; VOQ units 16; Guesthouse units 8; Guest cottages 18; All ranks facility 30. *Commissary:* Yes; *Exchange:* Retail store; Barber shop; Dry cleaners; Food shop; Florist; Bank; Service station; Furniture store; Bakery; Bookstore; Military clothing store; Convenience store; Beauty shop; Laundromat; Credit union. *Child Care/Capacities:* Day care center; Home day care program; Latch key program; Summer day camp. *Schools:* Preschool/Kindergarten; Elementary. *Base Library:* Yes. *Medical Facilities:* Hospital 364 beds; Medical clinic; Dental clinic; Pharmacy; Veterinary services. *Recreational Facilities:* Bowling center; Movie theater; Pool; Gym; Recreation center; Golf course; Stables; Tennis courts; Racquetball court; Skating rink; Fitness center/Weight room; Softball field; Auto shop; Craft shop; Officers club; NCO club; Camping; Fishing/Hunting; Enlisted club; Youth center; Picnic area; Skeet range; Water sports; Playground; Flying & parachuting clubs.

Keyport

922. Keyport Division, Naval Undersea Warfare Center

NUWC, Keyport
610 Dowell St
Keyport, WA 98345-7610
360-396-2699; DSN 744-2699
Internet: http://www.nuwc.navy.mil/hq/keyport.html

Profile

BRANCH: Navy.

SIZE AND LOCATION: 250 acres. 12 mi N of Bremerton & Puget Sound Naval Shipyard; 5 mi E of Submarine Base, Bangor, on State Hwy 308. *County:* Kitsap.

MAJOR UNITS: Naval Undersea Warfare Center, Keyport Division; Arctic Submarine Lab.

BASE HISTORY: 1914, Pacific Coast Torpedo Station commissioned. 1930, name changed to Naval Torpedo Station (NTS). 1950, NTS & Naval Ammunition Depot (NAD), Bangor merged to become Naval Ordnance Depot,

Puget Sound. 1970, NAD Bangor disestablished & residual functions transferred to NTS. 1974, Hawaii detachment established. 1976, Social, Hawthorne, & Indian Island Detachment established. 1978, renamed Naval Undersea Warfare Engineering Station. 1992, renamed to current name; Indian Island Detachment transferred to Naval Weapons Station, Seal Beach.

VISITOR ATTRACTIONS: Naval Undersea Museum (360-396-4148).

Key Contacts

COMMANDER: RADM John F Shipway.

PUBLIC AFFAIRS: NUWC PAO, 1176 Howell St, Newport, RI 02841, 401-841-3611.

Personnel and Expenditures

ACTIVE DUTY PERSONNEL: 260
DEPENDENTS: 105
CIVILIAN PERSONNEL: 3200

Services

Housing: Family units 25; Unaccompanied enlisted quarters 1; Senior NCO units 1; Junior NCO units 13. *Exchange:* Retail store; Food shop; Credit union. *Base Library:* Yes. *Medical Facilities:* Medical clinic. *Recreational Facilities:* Gym; Tennis courts; Softball field; Auto shop; Craft shop; All hands club; Wood hobby shop.

McChord AFB

923. McChord Air Force Base

62nd Airlift Wing (AMC)
McChord AFB, WA 98438-1109
Mailing Address
100 Main St, Ste 1050
McCord AFB, WA 98438-1109
253-984-1910; FAX 253-984-5025; DSN 984-1110
Internet: http://www.mccord.af.mil

Profile

BRANCH: Air Force.

SIZE AND LOCATION: 4535 acres. 3 mi S of Tacoma, WA; I-5 passes approx 0.5 mi away. *County:* Pierce.

MAJOR UNITS: 62nd Airlift Wing (Host); 446th Airlift Wing (Reserve); Western Air Defense Sector; 22nd Special Tactics Squadron.

BASE HISTORY: 1920s-30s, Tacoma Pierce County Airport occupied site of McChord Field. 1938, airfield deeded to federal government. 1940, dedicated as McChord Field, named for Col William C McChord, who was killed in bomber crash in VA in 1937. 1941, British crews trained on British Fortress I versions of Flying Fortress bombers. During WWII, McChord trained fliers; participated in 1942 Doolittle bombing raid on Tokyo. 1944, massive overhaul center established to refurbish fighters. Postwar, became major airlift center. 1947, 62nd Troop Carrier Group & Wing came to McChord. 1950, became part of Air Defense Command's 25th Air Division. 1960s-early 1970s, major port for equipment & troops during Vietnam War. 1968, transferred to MAC. 1992, became part of Air Mobility Command (AMC).

VISITOR ATTRACTIONS: McChord Air Museum.

Key Contacts

COMMANDER: Col Duncan J McNabb, 62 AW/CC, 253-984-2621.

PUBLIC AFFAIRS: Capt Adriane B Wood, 62
AW/PA.
Personnel and Expenditures
ACTIVE DUTY PERSONNEL: 3800
DEPENDENTS: 2000
CIVILIAN PERSONNEL: 2100
MILITARY PAYROLL EXPENDITURE: $158.9
mil
CONTRACT EXPENDITURE: $7.6 mil
Services
Housing: Family units 981; Dormitory spaces
1488; RV 18 full hook up, 18 water & electric-
ity; unlimited parking. *Temporary Housing:* VIP
units units 22; VOQ units 47; Apartment units
12; Transient quarters 200. *Commissary:* Yes;
Exchange: Retail store; Barber shop; Dry clean-
ers; Food shop; Florist; Bank; Service station;
Furniture store; Bakery; Military clothing store;
Convenience store; Beauty shop; Credit union;
ATM; Optical store; Post office; Fast food;
Video rentals; Thrift shop; Travel agency; Class
VI; Computer store; Garden center; Tailor/Al-
terations; Photo store. *Child Care/Capacities:*
Day care center capacity 218; Hourly daycare &
drop-in care on space available basis. *Schools:*
Preschool/Kindergarten; Elementary; College
courses. *Base Library:* Yes. *Medical Facilities:*
Medical clinic; Dental clinic; Pharmacy; Veterinary services; Madigan Army Medical Center, 4
mi away. *Recreational Facilities:* Bowling center; Pool; Gym; Golf course; Stables; Tennis
courts; Racquetball court; Fitness center/Weight
room; Softball field; Football field; Auto shop;
Craft shop; Camping; Fishing/Hunting; Youth
center; Picnic area; Skeet range; Consolidated
club; Rod & Gun club; Horseshoe pits.

Oak Harbor

924. Whidbey Island Naval Air Station
NAS Whidbey Island
1155 W Lexington
Oak Harbor, WA 98278-5700
360-257-2211; DSN 820-0111
Internet: http://www.naswi.navy.mil/
Profile
BRANCH: Navy.
SIZE AND LOCATION: Ault Field 4362 acres;
Seaplane Base 2793 acres. In middle of Puget
Sound, 80 mi NW of Seattle. Oak Harbor 2
mi from NAS. Driving: I-5 N, Anacortes/
Whidbey Exit 230, W on Hwy 20 follow
signs to Oak Harbor/Whidbey Island. Ferry N
of Seattle at Mukilteo, Mukilteo Exit on I-5 in
Everett area; ferry crosses on hourly basis to
S Whidbey, 45 min drive to NAS. *County:* Is-
land.
MAJOR UNITS: Naval Air Station, Whidbey Is-
land; Antisubmarine Warfare Communica-
tions Center, Det Whidbey Island; Patrol
Wing 10; Electronic Combat Wing, Pacific
Fleet; Electronic Combat Weapon School; Ex-
plosive Ordnance Disposal Mobile Unit 17;
Fleet Aviation Specialized Operational Train-
ing Group, Pacific; Marine Aviation Training
Support Group; NAMTRAGRUDET Widbey
Island; Naval Air Reserve, Whidbey Island;
Naval Oceanographic Processing Facility;
Northwest Regional Naval Intelligence Cen-
ter; Naval Security Group Activity, Whidbey
Island; Naval Hospital Oak Harbor; Tactical
Electronic Warfare Squadron 131; Electronic

Warfare Squadron 135; Electronic Warfare
Squadron 137; Electronic Warfare Squadron
139; Electronic Warfare Squadron 141; Patrol
Squadron One; Fleet Air Reconnaissance
Squadron One; Fleet Imaging Command,
Whidbey Island; 27th Fighter Wing, OL-A;
Explosive Ordnance Disposal Mobile Unit
11; Construction Bn Unit 417.
BASE HISTORY: 1942, commissioned on largest island in continental US. 1943, field designated Ault Field for CDR William B Ault,
missing in Battle of Coral Sea. Originally
used for seaplane patrol operations, rocket firing training, torpedo overhaul, and recruit &
petty officer training. End of WWII-1949, reduced operating status. Today, home of all
Navy electronic warfare squadrons flying EA-
6B "Prowler" carrier-based tactical jamming
aircraft; W coast training & operations center
for A-6 "Intruder" attack bomber squadrons;
and Naval & Marine Air Reserve training activities center, Northwest. Composed of 2
bases 5 mi apart: Seaplane Base & NAS,
known as Ault Field. NAS contains most of
station's military activities. Seaplane Base located on E shore at edge of Oak Harbor. Also
under jurisdiction of NAS is Outlying Field,
Coupeville; Boardman Bombing Range,
Boardman OR; and, Radar Bomb Scoring
Unit, Spokane, WA.
Key Contacts
COMMANDER: Larry J Munns, Bldg 2644,
360-257-2037, DSN 820-2037, munnsj@
naswi.navy.mil.
PUBLIC AFFAIRS: Bldg 385, 360-257-2286,
DSN 820-2286.
Personnel and Expenditures
ACTIVE DUTY PERSONNEL: 7930; Reserv-
ists 330
DEPENDENTS: 12,680
CIVILIAN PERSONNEL: 2200
Services
Housing: Family units 1550; Unaccompanied of-
ficer quarters 15; Unaccompanied enlisted quar-
ters 1080; *Temporary Housing:* VIP units 6;
VOQ units /Enlisted 192; Lodge units 23; Campground RV spaces 42; Tent spaces 4. *Commissary:* Yes; *Exchange:* Retail store; Barber shop;
Dry cleaners; Food shop; Florist; Bank; Service
station; Furniture store; Bakery; Bookstore; Military clothing store; Convenience store; Beauty
shop; Laundromat; Credit union. *Child Care/Ca-
pacities:* Day care center capacity 80; Home day
care program. *Schools:* No on-base schools.
Base Library: Yes. *Medical Facilities:* Hospital
25; Dental clinic. *Recreational Facilities:* Bowling center; Movie theater; Gym; Recreation center; Golf course; Tennis courts; Racquetball
court; Fitness center/Weight room; Softball
field; Football field; Auto shop; Craft shop; Officers club; NCO club; Camping; Fishing/Hunt-
ing; Archery; Motorcross.

Pacific Beach

925. Pacific Beach Resort & Conference Center
Pacific Beach
Pacific Beach, WA 98571
Mailing Address
Ocean Gateway, Bldg 47/Code 60
Puget Sound NS, WA 98115-5014
1-800-626-4414; 360-276-8192

Profile
BRANCH: Navy.
SIZE AND LOCATION: 53 acres. On W coast
of WA, 150 mi SW of Seattle; reached by
highways connecting to I-5 from Seattle and
Portland; from US-101 Coastal Hwy and US-
12 from Yakima. *County:* Grays Harbor.
MAJOR UNITS: Pacific Beach Resort.
BASE HISTORY: Operated expressly for active
duty military community; retired military personnel and DOD civilians welcome on space-
available basis; reservations must be made in
advance 1-888-463-6697.
Services
Housing: RV/Camper sites 43. *Temporary Housing:* Cabins 28; Suites 4. *Recreational Facilities:* Fishing/Hunting; Beach; Hiking.

Port Angeles

926. Port Angeles Coast Guard Air Station/Group
USCG Port Angeles
EDIZ Hook
Port Angeles, WA 98362
Mailing Address
USCG AIRSTA/GROUP
Port Angles, WA 98362-0159
360-457-2226; FAX 360-457-2229; DSN
744-6431
OFFICER-OF-THE-DAY: 360-457-2226
Profile
BRANCH: Coast Guard.
LOCATION: On N Olympic Peninsula; approx
75 mi W of Seattle on Hwy 101; due S across
Straits of Juan de Fuca from Victoria, BC.
County: Clallam.
MAJOR UNITS: Coast Guard Group, Port Ange-
les; Coast Guard Air Station, Port Angeles;
USCGC *Cuttyhunk*; Electronic Support Unit
Det, Port Angeles.
VISITOR ATTRACTIONS: Small museum of
USCG historical items.
Key Contacts
COMMANDER: Capt Phil Volk, 360-457-2206.
PUBLIC AFFAIRS: Lt Matthew Rother,
360-457-2227.
Personnel and Expenditures
ACTIVE DUTY PERSONNEL: 220
DEPENDENTS: 0
CIVILIAN PERSONNEL: 15
Services
Housing: None. *Temporary Housing:* Transient
quarters 2. *Exchange:* Retail store; Barber shop;
Military clothing store. *Child Care/Capacities:*
No day care facilities. *Schools:* No on-base
schools. *Medical Facilities:* Medical clinic; Den-
tal clinic; Pharmacy. *Recreational Facilities:* Fit-
ness center/Weight room; Fishing/Hunting; Pic-
nic area; All ranks club; Morale equipment
locker.

Port Hadlock

927. Port Hadlock, Naval Ordnance Center, Pacific Division Detachment
NOCPACDIV DET PORT HADLOCK
100 Indian Island Annex Rd
Port Hadlock, WA 98339-9723

360-385-5201

Profile

BRANCH: Navy.

SIZE AND LOCATION: 2716 acres. On Puget Sound in NE portion of Olympic Peninsula; 35 mi NW of SUBASE Bangor; 9 mi from Jefferson IAP; W on Rte 104, approx 18 mi from Hood Canal Bridge; Bounded on E by Marrowstone Island & on W by Hadlock; 11 mi to NW by land & Port Townsend 2 mi (by water). *County:* Jefferson.

MAJOR UNITS: Naval Ordnance Center, Pacific Division Det, Port Hadlock.

BASE HISTORY: 1939, bought for stowing ammunition & arming area for aircraft at NAS, Seattle. 1939-early 1940s, constructed. 1959, reduced activity status; used for storage. 1979, reactivated as Detachment of Naval Undersea Warfare Engineering Station, Keyport. Today, only explosive outloading facility in Pacific Northwest.

Key Contacts

COMMANDER: CDR Philip G Beieri, 360-379-5827.

PUBLIC AFFAIRS: Danny R Johnson, Seal Beach NWS, 562-626-7215.

Personnel and Expenditures

ACTIVE DUTY PERSONNEL: 23

CIVILIAN PERSONNEL: 91

Services

Housing: Family units 14; Barracks spaces 17; RV/Camper sites. *Exchange:* Retail store. *Base Library:* Yes. *Medical Facilities:* Medical clinic. *Recreational Facilities:* Bowling center; Gym; Racquetball court; Fitness center/Weight room; Softball field; Fishing/Hunting; Enlisted club; Picnic area; Playground.

Seattle

928. 13th Coast Guard District Office

CCGD13

915 Second Ave

Seattle, WA 98174-1067

206-220-7237

Profile

BRANCH: Coast Guard.

SIZE AND LOCATION: Offices only. In Jackson Federal Bldg, downtown Seattle. *County:* King.

MAJOR UNITS: 13th Coast Guard District Office, Seattle; Coast Guard Liaison Officer, Seattle; Maritime Defense Command 13; Composite Naval Coastal Warfare Unit 113; Coast Guard Administrative Law Judge; Investigative Services, Seattle; Coast Guard FD & CC Pacific.

Personnel and Expenditures

ACTIVE DUTY PERSONNEL: 153

CIVILIAN PERSONNEL: 50

Services *Exchange:* At Pier 36 Coast Guard Complex, 0.5 mi away. *Recreational Facilities:* At Pier 36 Coast Guard Complex, 0.5 mi away.

929. Seattle Coast Guard Integrated Support Command

USCG ISC Seattle

1519 Alaskan Way S

Seattle, WA 98134-1192

206-217-6400

OFFICER-OF-THE-DAY: 206-217-6410, FAX 206-217-6412

Profile

BRANCH: Coast Guard.

SIZE AND LOCATION: 11 acres. In downtown Seattle at waterfront Pier 36; approx 10 mi from Seattle-Tacoma Airport & North Annex on Lake Washington Ship Canal. From N: follow I-5 S to exit 164, stay right, at light take right onto 4th Ave S, take next right onto Royal Brougham Way, follow to end, take left onto Alaskan Way S, Pier 36 0.25 mi on right. From S, follow I-5 N to exit 164, follow above directions. From E, take I-90 W until it ends, follow signs for Kingdome, follow above directions. *County:* King.

MAJOR UNITS: Coast Guard Group, Seattle; Coast Guard Station, Seattle; Marine Safety Office, Seattle; Vessel Traffic Service, Puget Sound; Naval Engineering Support Unit, Seattle; Electronic Systems Support Unit, Seattle; USCGC *Polar Sea*; USCGC *Polar Star*; USCGC *Mellon*; USCGC *Midgett*; USCGC *Mariposa*; USCGC *Bayberry*; Integrated Support Command, Seattle; Aids to Navigation (ANT) Team, Puget Sound; Coast Guard Reserve Unit CNCWU 113; Coast Guard Forces, Seattle; Armory Det, Seattle; Coast Guard Reserve Center; Coast Guard Regional Reserve Personnel Office; Marine Safety Office, Puget Sound.

BASE HISTORY: 1926, Pier 36 built by Pacific Steamship Terminal Co. 1940, Pier 36 acquired for Port of Embarkation. 1941, Pier 37 constructed to expand port facilities. 1960, occupied by Army Corps of Engineers; used as district HQ. 1966, Coast Guard acquired site. 1976, commissioned to provide services & support to 13th Coast Guard District commands in Seattle area; home to numerous vessels & various commands. 1996, recommissioned ISC Seattle with expanded support activities; host to 6 ships & 8 shore-based units. Responsibilities include moorage & port services for floating units, office & work space for shore-based commands, personnel & pay support services, logistics support, & transient personnel administration.

VISITOR ATTRACTIONS: Polar class ice breakers; 378 ft cutters; Coast Guard Museum; Tours of MSO & VTS facilities.

Key Contacts

COMMANDER: Capt D Gary Beck, 206-217-6400, FAX 206-217-6639.

PUBLIC AFFAIRS: Ltjg Lisa Schulz, 206-217-6408, FAX 206-217-6634.

PROCUREMENT: LCDR Jim Wierzbicki, 206-217-6421.

PERSONNEL/COMMUNITY ACTIVITIES: CWO Steve Walsh, 206-217-6407, FAX 206-217-6639.

Personnel and Expenditures

ACTIVE DUTY PERSONNEL: 1000

CIVILIAN PERSONNEL: 25

Services *Temporary Housing:* Transient quarters 46; *Exchange:* Retail store; *Child Care/Capacities:* No day care facilities. *Schools:* No on-base schools. *Medical Facilities:* Medical clinic; Dental clinic; Pharmacy. *Recreational Facilities:* Gym; Tennis courts; Racquetball court; Fitness center/Weight room;

930. Seattle Naval Reserve Readiness Center

NRC Seattle

860 Terry Ave N

Seattle, WA 98109-4391

206-623-6970; FAX 206-526-3149; DSN 941-3348; DSN FAX 941-3149

Profile

BRANCH: Naval Reserve.

SIZE AND LOCATION: 5.4 acres. In downtown Seattle at S end of Lake Union. *County:* King.

MAJOR UNITS: REDCOM TWENTY-TWO Activity; Naval Reserve Center, Seattle; IBU-11; IBU-12.

Key Contacts

COMMANDER: Capt M W Heath.

Personnel and Expenditures

ACTIVE DUTY PERSONNEL: 330 reservists

Services *Recreational Facilities:* Fitness center/Weight room.

931. US Army Corps of Engineers, Seattle District

4735 E Marginal Way S

Seattle, WA 98134-2385

Mailing Address

PO Box 3755

Seattle, WA 98124-3755

206-764-6958

Internet: http://www.nps.usace.army.mil/

Profile

BRANCH: Army.

LOCATION: *County:* King.

MAJOR UNITS: Corps of Engineers, Seattle District.

Key Contacts

COMMANDER: LTC James M Rigsby, District Engineer; David G Harris, Chief, 206-764-6958.

PUBLIC AFFAIRS: Diane M Lake, 206-764-6957; Patricia C Graesser, 206-764-3760; Gerry M Arbios, 206-764-3751.

Silverdale

932. Bangor Naval Submarine Base

SUBASE Bangor

1100 Hunley Rd

Silverdale, WA 98315-1199

360-396-4800; FAX 360-396-6032; DSN 744-4800

Internet: http://www.subase.nsb.navy.mil

OFFICER-OF-THE-DAY: 360-396-4800, DSN 744-4800

Profile

BRANCH: Navy.

SIZE AND LOCATION: 7000 acres. On W side of Puget Sound, on Hood Canal, approx 1 hr drive from Seattle/Tacoma area; 0.25 mi off State Hwy 3; 7 mi N of Bremerton. *County:* Kitsap.

MAJOR UNITS: Commander, Naval Base Seattle; Commander, Submarine Group 9; Submarine Squadron 17; Trident Training Facility; Trident Refit Facility; Strategic Weapons Facility, Pacific; Marine Corps Security Force Co, Bangor.

BASE HISTORY: 1942, commissioned as Naval Ammunition Depot, Bangor Annex; Pacific Coast transshipment point for ammunition and explosives. 1963, Polaris Missile Facility, Pacific established. 1974, redesignated Strategic Weapons Facility, Pacific; work began at Bangor support site. 1977, commissioned Naval Submarine Base, Bangor. 1981, base fully operational with arrival of first Trident submarine, USS *Ohio*.

VISITOR ATTRACTIONS: Naval Undersea Museum at Naval Undersea Warfare Center, Keyport (3 mi from Main Gate).

Key Contacts
COMMANDER: Capt Mike Landers, 360-396-4949, FAX 360-396-6032, DSN 744-4949.
PUBLIC AFFAIRS: Paul W Taylor, Code 005, 360-396-4843, FAX 360-396-7127, DSN 744-4843, paul.taylor@subase.nsb.navy.mil.
PROCUREMENT: Supply Officer, Code N6A, 360-396-4550, 360-396-4146, DSN 744-4550.
TRANSPORTATION: Annette Kensmoe, Code 822, 360-396-5660, DSN 744-5660.
PERSONNEL/COMMUNITY ACTIVITIES: Diane Vanderwerf, Code 1, 360-396-4775, DSN 744-4775.

Personnel and Expenditures
ACTIVE DUTY PERSONNEL: 5500
DEPENDENTS: 3000
CIVILIAN PERSONNEL: 5300
MILITARY PAYROLL EXPENDITURE: $85.8 mil
CONTRACT EXPENDITURE: $18 mil

Services
Housing: Family units 1319; Unaccompanied enlisted quarters 534. *Temporary Housing:* VIP units 1; Unaccompanied officer/Enlisted quarters 66. *Commissary:* Yes; *Exchange:* Barber shop; Dry cleaners; Food shop; Florist; Bank; Service station; Furniture store; Bakery; Military clothing store; Convenience store; Beauty shop; Credit union; ATM; Optical store; Post office; Fast food; Thrift shop; Travel agency; Computer store; Garden center; Tailor/Alterations; Laundry; Photo store. *Child Care/Capacities:* Day care center capacity 104; Home day care program; Latch key program; Summer day camp. *Schools:* College courses; 2 elementary schools located on border of base. *Base Library:* Yes. *Medical Facilities:* Medical clinic; Dental clinic; Pharmacy; Veterinary services. *Recreational Facilities:* Bowling center; Movie theater; Pool; Gym; Recreation center; Tennis courts; Racquetball court; Fitness center/Weight room; Softball field; Auto shop; Craft shop; Fishing/Hunting; Enlisted club; Picnic area; Consolidated club.

933. Naval Computer and Telecommunications Station, Puget Sound
1008 Harder Rd, Ste 105
Silverdale, WA 98315-1099
360-396-6756
Internet: http://www.ncts-puget.navy.mil
Profile
BRANCH: Navy.
SIZE AND LOCATION: On Naval Submarine Base, Bangor. 12 mi N of Bremerton, WA, on Naval Submarine Base, Bangor. *County:* Kitsap.
MAJOR UNITS: Naval Computer and Telecommunications Station, Puget Sound.
Key Contacts
COMMANDER: CDR Sharon A Stanley, 360-396-6756, DSN 744-6756.

PROCUREMENT: Supply Dept, 360-396-4355.
Services
Housing: See Bangor Naval Submarine Base.

Spokane

934. Spokane Naval & Marine Corps Reserve Readiness Center
NO. 5101 Assembly St
Spokane, WA 99205-6199
509-327-3346, 326-3476; FAX 509-326-8257; DSN 657-5852, 657-5854
Profile
BRANCH: Naval Reserve; Marine Corps Reserve.
LOCATION: In city of Spokane. *County:* Spokane.
MAJOR UNITS: REDCOM TWENTY-TWO Activity; Navy Radar Bomb Scoring Unit-Spokane (RBSU); Battery A, 1st Bn, 14th Marine Regiment.
BASE HISTORY: Unit's state-of-the-art AN/TSQ-151 "no drop" bomb scoring system; 1 of 2 used by Navy (other in Mediterranean). Provides electronic scoring of simulated bombing missions on actual urban targets for aircraft based at NAS Whidbey Island. Commissary, exchange facilities, medical/dental care, & quarters provided by Fairchild AFB, approx 15 mi away.
Key Contacts
COMMANDER: CDR T F Fessell Jr.

Tacoma

935. Adjutant General of Washington
Camp Murray, Bldg 1
Tacoma, WA 98430-5000
253-512-8000; FAX 253-512-8497
Profile
BRANCH: Army National Guard.
MAJOR UNITS: Washington National Guard.
Key Contacts
COMMANDER: Maj Gen Gregory P Barlow.

936. Madigan Army Medical Center
MAMC
9040 Reid St
Tacoma, WA 98431-5000
253-968-1110; FAX 253-968-3270; DSN 782-1110; DSN FAX 782-3270
Internet: http://www.mamc.amedd.army.mil
Profile
BRANCH: Army.
SIZE AND LOCATION: 120 acres. Adj to Fort Lewis, WA; Exit 122 from I-5, S of Tacoma, WA. *County:* Pierce.
MAJOR UNITS: Western Regional Medical Command.
BASE HISTORY: WWI, established as Ft Lewis Station Hospital. 1944, became Madigan General Hospital, named for Col Patrick Sarsfield Madigan, assistant to Surgeon General, US Army from 1940-43, known as Father of Army Neuropsychiatry. 1973, redesignated Madigan Army Medical Center & assigned to Army Health Services Command, Ft Sam Houston, TX. Responsibilities include Army, Navy, and Air Force installations in WA, OR,

MT, ID, and AK; 8 troop clinics & 21 aid stations at Ft Lewis; and, health clinics at Yakima Firing Center & Umatilla, OR. 1992, new facility dedicated; one of the newest DOD medical centers. Largest & busiest military hospital on West Coast. Center provides training, research, & logistical support; equipped with latest computer radiology & monitoring/informatics technology.
Key Contacts
COMMANDER: Brig Gen George Brown.
PUBLIC AFFAIRS: Michael G Meines, MCHJ-PAO, 253-968-1901, DSN 782-1901, DSN FAX 782-3270, Michael_Meines@smtplink.mamc.amedd.army.mil.
Personnel and Expenditures
ACTIVE DUTY PERSONNEL: 1400
DEPENDENTS: 0
CIVILIAN PERSONNEL: 1400
MILITARY PAYROLL EXPENDITURE: $92 mil
Services *Temporary Housing:* Unaccompanied officer/Enlisted quarters; BAQ units; Guesthouse units 10. *Exchange:* Retail store; Barber shop; Florist; Service station; Convenience store; ATM; Optical store; Post office; Cafeteria. *Child Care/Capacities:* No day care facilities. *Schools:* No on-base schools. *Base Library:* Yes. *Medical Facilities:* Hospital 256 beds; expandable to 622; Medical clinic; Dental clinic; Pharmacy; Veterinary services. *Recreational Facilities:* Pool; Gym; Racquetball court; Fitness center/Weight room; Picnic area.

937. Tacoma Naval & Marine Corps Reserve Center
NAVMARCORCEN Tacoma; NMCRC Tacoma
1100 Alexander Ave
Tacoma, WA 98421-4198
253-383-3577; FAX 253-383-3579
Profile
BRANCH: Naval Reserve; Marine Corps Reserve.
LOCATION: *County:* Pierce.
MAJOR UNITS: REDCOM TWENTY-TWO Activity; I & I Unit (USMC); Bulk Fuel Co B, 6th Engineer Support Bn.
Key Contacts
COMMANDER: Lt David V Badzik.
PROCUREMENT: Chief Allen Church.

Vancouver

938. Vancouver Barracks
VB
The Barracks
638 Hathaway Rd
Vancouver, WA 98661-3846
360-694-7550; FAX 360-750-0129
Profile
BRANCH: Army.
SIZE AND LOCATION: 3872 acres (52 acres downtown, 3820 Camp Bonneville). 1 block from downtown Vancouver, WA; Exit 1C off I-5 to Fort Vancouver Way. *County:* Clark.
MAJOR UNITS: 104th Infantry Division (TNG)(Reserve); 70th Army Reserve Command (70th RSC); 396th Combat Support Hospital; 222nd Judge Advocate General, Det; Area Maintenance Support Activity #82; Maintenance Activity #10 (WANG); 146th Field Artillery, 2nd Bn (WANG).

BASE HISTORY: 1849, established following Treaty of 1846, which provided for fort within sight of British Ft Vancouver. Main outpost in NW until Camp Lewis established. 1937-38, commanded by George C Marshall.

FUTURE CLOSURE/REALIGNMENT: Camp Bonneville Range Complex (18 mi away) used for light infantry & weapons firing training, scheduled for closure/realignment by Nov 2000.

VISITOR ATTRACTIONS: Adj to Officers Row (22 restored officer's quarters dating to mid-1800s, including Gen George C Marshall's quarters); Pearson Air Park Museum; British Fort Vancouver (active 1824-1849).

Key Contacts
COMMANDER: LTC Robert K Knight, 360-694-7555, FAX 360-750-019.
PUBLIC AFFAIRS: Steve Hartung, 360-694-7555, FAX 360-750-0129.
PROCUREMENT: Bob Berncopf, 360-694-7555, 360-696-3151.
TRANSPORTATION: SFC Nilsen.

Personnel and Expenditures
ACTIVE DUTY PERSONNEL: 10
DEPENDENTS: 64
CIVILIAN PERSONNEL: 4
MILITARY PAYROLL EXPENDITURE: $329,000
CONTRACT EXPENDITURE: See Ft Lewis, WA

Services
Housing: Family units 16; Unaccompanied enlisted quarters 5. *Exchange:* Retail store; Barber shop; Convenience store. *Child Care/Capacities:* No day care facilities. *Schools:* No on-base schools; Clark College nearby. *Medical Facilities:* No medical facilities. *Recreational Facilities:* Gym; Fitness center/Weight room; Playground.

Walla Walla

939. US Army Corps of Engineers, Walla Walla District
CENWW
201 N Third Ave
Walla Walla, WA 99362-1876
509-527-7700; FAX 509-527-7804
Internet: http://www.npw.usace.army.mil/

Profile
BRANCH: Army.
SIZE AND LOCATION: Offices only. In downtown Walla Walla. *County:* Walla Walla.
MAJOR UNITS: Corps of Engineers, Walla Walla District.
BASE HISTORY: 1948, District established; linked directly to development of water resource projects on Columbia & lower Snake rivers. 1995, moved from City-County Airport to current location. District generally follows Snake River drainage, includes more than 115,000 sq mi in 6 states: WA, OR, ID, WY, & small portions of NV and UT. Operates and maintains 8 projects in WA, OR, and

ID. Part of the North Pacific Division; performs civil works construction & civil works real estate.

Key Contacts
COMMANDER: LTC Donald R Curtis Jr, 509-522-6506.
PUBLIC AFFAIRS: Duane "Dutch" Meier, Chief, 509-522-6658, duane.dutch.meier@usace.army.mil.
PROCUREMENT: Jackie Anderson, Contracting Officer, 509-522-6801.
TRANSPORTATION: Logistics Chief, 509-522-6429.
PERSONNEL/COMMUNITY ACTIVITIES: Glen Houk, Chief, Human Resources Office, 509-522-6741.

Personnel and Expenditures
ACTIVE DUTY PERSONNEL: 4
CIVILIAN PERSONNEL: 650
Services *Base Library:* Yes.

Yakima

940. Washington Army National Guard Mobilization and Training Equipment Site
MATES
1211 Firing Center Rd
Yakima, WA 98901-9347
509-575-2602; DSN 638-3261

Profile
BRANCH: Army National Guard.
SIZE AND LOCATION: 20 acres. 10 mi N of Yakima off of I-82, Firing Center Exit, E approx 1.5 mi. *County:* Yakima.
MAJOR UNITS: Mobilization and Training Equipment Site (MATES) (WA ANG).
BASE HISTORY: Tenant facility on Yakima Firing Center; Guard equipment pool & maintenance facility.

Key Contacts
COMMANDER: Chief Hamilton.
PUBLIC AFFAIRS: Camp Murray, Tacoma, WA 98430-5000, 253-512-8481.

Personnel and Expenditures
ACTIVE DUTY PERSONNEL: 0; Guard 124
CIVILIAN PERSONNEL: 2
Services *Exchange:* Through Yakima Firing Center.

941. Yakima Training Center
YTC
HQ
Yakima, WA 98901-9399
509-577-3205; FAX 509-577-3556; DSN 638-3205; DSN FAX 638-3556
E-mail: afzh-yt@lewis-emh3.army.mil
OFFICER-OF-THE-DAY: 509-577-3215, DSN 638-3215, DSN FAX 638-3162

Profile
BRANCH: Army.
SIZE AND LOCATION: 320,000 acres.

In S central WA, approx 10 mi from Yakima; 130 mi from Seattle; Exit 26 off I-82. *County:* Yakima.
MAJOR UNITS: Army Garrison, Co A; 704th Military Police, B Co; 53rd Explosive Ordnance Disposal; 1115th Signal Bn; 54th Medivac; 737th TRANS; DPCA, HQ; Mobilization and Training Equipment Site (MATES).
BASE HISTORY: Just before WWII, Army leased land for what was to become Yakima Anti-Aircraft Artillery Range. 1941, used for both range firing & small unit tests. 1942, first camp constructed on Umtanum Ridge, 13 mi NE of present cantonment area. 1942-43, Yakima Firing Center constructed on present site. 1946-47, use greatly curtailed and approx 60,000 acres returned to original owners. 1949-50, used for summer training of WA NG units. 1951, Army expanded facility for training requirements. 1955, 10 ranges named for Yakima Valley war heroes: William H Perkins, Merl H Todd, Frank R Goulet, James Russell, Dolph Barnett Jr, Winfield M Black, Joseph H Carvo, Herbert E Lane, Jack J Pendleton, and James B Kinyon. 1965-72, used by Reservists and Guardsmen for weekend & summer camp training; with activation of 9th Infantry Division, Center became training center for Ft Lewis. 1977-78, used as test site for Improved TOW Vehicle (ITV); terrain ideal for artillery, tank, mortar, recoilless weapons, & small arms training exercises.

Key Contacts
COMMANDER: LTC Richard N Helfer, 509-577-3206, DSN 638-3206, DSN FAX 638-3556.
PUBLIC AFFAIRS: Kenneth D Cooper, ATTN: AFZH-Y-DPCA, 509-577-3201, DSN 638-3201, DSN FAX 638-3201.
PROCUREMENT: Dennis Sant, 509-577-3224, DSN 638-3224, DSN FAX 638-3224.
TRANSPORTATION: See Procurement Officer.
PERSONNEL/COMMUNITY ACTIVITIES: See Public Affairs Officer.

Personnel and Expenditures
ACTIVE DUTY PERSONNEL: 116
DEPENDENTS: 200
CIVILIAN PERSONNEL: 101
Services
Housing: Unaccompanied officer quarters 1; Unaccompanied enlisted quarters; Barracks spaces; Senior NCO units; Junior NCO units. *Temporary Housing:* BAQ units; Guesthouse units 1. *Exchange:* Barber shop; Military clothing store; Convenience store; ATM; Post office. *Child Care/Capacities:* No day care facilities. *Schools:* No on-base schools. *Base Library:* Yes. *Medical Facilities:* Medical clinic; Pharmacy. *Recreational Facilities:* Gym; Recreation center; Tennis courts; Racquetball court; Fitness center/Weight room; Softball field; Football field; Auto shop; Craft shop; Fishing/Hunting; All ranks club.

West Virginia

Charleston

942. Adjutant General of West Virginia
1703 Coonskin Dr
Charleston, WV 25311-1085
304-341-6316, 341-6318; FAX 304-341-6466
Profile
BRANCH: Army National Guard.
MAJOR UNITS: West Virginia National Guard.
Key Contacts
COMMANDER: Maj Gen Allen E Tackett.

943. Charleston Naval & Marine Corps Reserve Center
Armed Forces Reserve Center
105 Lakeview Dr
Charleston, WV 25313-14877
304-776-2307, 776-4807, 776-7543; FAX 304-776-5119
Profile
BRANCH: Naval Reserve; Marine Corps Reserve.
LOCATION: W central WV. *County:* Kanawha.
MAJOR UNITS: REDCOM SIX Activity; Co A, 4th Combat Engineer Bn.
Key Contacts
COMMANDER: LCDR D R Kennetz.

944. Yeager Airport, Air National Guard Base
1679 Coonskin Dr
Charleston, WV 25311-5000
304-341-6126; DSN 366-6210
Profile
BRANCH: Air National Guard.
SIZE AND LOCATION: 269 acres. 4 mi NE of Charleston, off US-119. *County:* Kanawha.
MAJOR UNITS: 130th Airlift Wing (ANG); West Virginia ANG, HQ.
BASE HISTORY: 1946, 130th AG reactivated; allotted to WV ANG as 167th Fighter Squadron at Kanawha Airport. Following Korean War mobilization, returned as 167th Fighter-Bomber Squadron; because runway too short for jets, squadron left. 1955, new unit formed, 130th Troop Carrier Squadron. 1960, became 130th Air Commando Group, later 130th Special Operations Group. 1975, renamed 130th Tactical Airlift Group, part of Military Airlift Command. 1985, airport renamed in honor of Brig Gen "Chuck" Yeager. 1992, 130th TAG renamed 130th AG under command of the Air Mobility Command (AMC).
Key Contacts
COMMANDER: 304-341-6131, DSN 366-6131.
PUBLIC AFFAIRS: 304-341-6129, DSN 366-6129.
Personnel and Expenditures
ACTIVE DUTY PERSONNEL: 903 Guard
CIVILIAN PERSONNEL: 243
MILITARY PAYROLL EXPENDITURE: $15.5 mil
Services *Exchange:* Retail store. *Medical Facilities:* Dispensary.

Huntington

945. Huntington Naval Reserve Center
841 Jackson Ave
Huntington, WV 25704-2595
304-523-7471, 523-7472; FAX 529-2735
Profile
BRANCH: Naval Reserve.
LOCATION: *County:* Cabell.
MAJOR UNITS: REDCOM SIX Activity.
Key Contacts
COMMANDER: LCDR D Kennetz.

946. US Army Corps of Engineers, Huntington District
CELRH
502 Eighth St
Huntington, WV 25701-2070
304-529-5211; 304-529-5253 (after 4:45pm ET)
Profile
BRANCH: Army.
MAJOR UNITS: Corps of Engineers, Huntington District.
BASE HISTORY: Administers civil works in 45,000 sq mi area of OH, KY, WV, VA, & NC in Ohio River drainage basin. Part of Great Lakes and Ohio River Division.
Key Contacts
COMMANDER: Col Dana Robertson, 304-529-5395.
PUBLIC AFFAIRS: Steve Wright, 304-529-5453, Stevew@mail.orh.usace.army.mil.
PERSONNEL/COMMUNITY ACTIVITIES: 304-529-5662.

Kingwood

947. Camp Dawson
Army Training Site, 240 Army Rd
Kingwood, WV 26537-1092
304-329-4331; FAX 304-341-6591; DSN 366-6552; DSN FAX 366-6591
E-mail: CampDawson@aol.com
OFFICER-OF-THE-DAY: 304-329-4334, DSN 366-6552; DSN FAX 366-6591
Profile
BRANCH: Army National Guard.
SIZE AND LOCATION: 8000 acres. Served by nearby airports, Morgantown, WV, approx 30 mi NW; Clarksburg, WV, approx 45 mi SW; and Elkins, WV, approx 60 mi S. Major highways serving area: US-48, US-50, and US-219. Routes into Camp Dawson: WV State Rte 7, 26, and 72. *County:* Preston.
MAJOR UNITS: HQ WV State Area Readiness Command, Det 3; 19th Special Forces Group, Co C, 2nd Bn (A); 19th Special Forces Group, Det 1, Support Co (A); 201st Field Artillery, Service Battery; 229th Engineer Det; Organizational Maintenance Shop 4; Special Operations Forces Equipment Pool; WV Mountaineer Challenge Academy.
BASE HISTORY: Regional "major training area" for many types of units from all branches of Armed Forces. Nestled in WV hills, offers unique terrain and serenity. Ideal site for conferences and most types of management training; also offers rugged mountainous regions for readiness training.
VISITOR ATTRACTIONS: Within driving distance of many historic sites & resort areas.
Key Contacts
COMMANDER: LTC Larry A Brown, Training Site Manager & Commander, 304-329-4334, DSN 366-6552, DSN FAX 366-6591, CampDawson@aol.com.
PROCUREMENT: CW2 James W Buseman, 304-329-4458, DSN 366-6552, ATSLog@aol.com.
TRANSPORTATION: See Procurement Officer.
Personnel and Expenditures
ACTIVE DUTY PERSONNEL: 11 AGR, 21 technicians
DEPENDENTS: 0
CIVILIAN PERSONNEL: 42
MILITARY PAYROLL EXPENDITURE: $8 mil
CONTRACT EXPENDITURE: $0.5 mil

Services

Housing: Unaccompanied officer quarters 5; Unaccompanied enlisted quarters 152 beds; Barracks spaces 800 beds. *Temporary Housing:* VIP units 1. *Exchange:* Retail store; Military clothing store. *Child Care/Capacities:* No day care facilities. *Schools:* No on-base schools. *Medical Facilities:* No medical facilities. *Recreational Facilities:* Gym; Golf course; Tennis courts; Fitness center/Weight room; Softball field; Football field; Fishing/Hunting; Picnic area; Soccer field; Running track.

Martinsburg

948. Eastern West Virginia Regional Airport, Air National Guard Base

Shepherd Field
222 Saber Jet Blvd
Martinsburg, WV 25401-7704
304-267-5100; DSN 242-9210

Profile

BRANCH: Air National Guard.
SIZE AND LOCATION: 420 acres. 4 mi S of Martinsburg. *County:* Berkeley.
MAJOR UNITS: 167th Airlift Wing (ANG).

Personnel and Expenditures

ACTIVE DUTY PERSONNEL: 1191 Guard
CIVILIAN PERSONNEL: 282
MILITARY PAYROLL EXPENDITURE: $18.3 mil

Services *Medical Facilities:* Dispensary.

Moundsville

949. Moundsville Naval & Marine Corps Reserve Center

1600 Lafayette Ave
Moundsville, WV 26041-2347
304-843-1553, 843-1759; FAX 304-845-0371

Profile

BRANCH: Naval Reserve; Marine Corps Reserve.
LOCATION: In N WV, in panhandle on Ohio R. *County:* Marshall.
MAJOR UNITS: REDCOM FOUR Activity; Weapons Co, 3rd Bn, 25th Marine Regiment.

Key Contacts

COMMANDER: LCDR G Daly.

Sugar Grove

950. Sugar Grove Naval Security Group Activity

NAVSECGRUACT Sugar Grove; NSGA Sugar Grove
State Rte 21
Sugar Grove, WV 26815-9700
304-249-6304; FAX 304-249-6334
OFFICER-OF-THE-DAY: 304-249-6310

Profile

BRANCH: Navy.
SIZE AND LOCATION: 160 acres (main base); 600 acres (operation site). 5 mi S of Brandywine, WV, on State Rte 21; approx 35 mi W of Harrisonburg, VA, on US Rte 33 to Brandywine. *County:* Pendleton.
MAJOR UNITS: Naval Security Group Activity.
BASE HISTORY: 1955, established as radio receiving station. 1956, 60-ft antenna completed. 1962, radio telescope project terminated. 1963, site utilized as radio receiving station. 1968, 150-ft parabolic antenna completed. 1969, NRS commissioned. 1992, NRS closed; Naval Security Group Activity established.

Key Contacts

COMMANDER: CDR Keith W Ludwig, 304-249-6308.
PUBLIC AFFAIRS: Senior Chief Steven B Tait, 304-249-6305.
PROCUREMENT: Lt Jeffrey M Morrison, 304-249-6370.
TRANSPORTATION: LT William Timberlake; 304-249-6342.
PERSONNEL/COMMUNITY ACTIVITIES: Vacant.

Personnel and Expenditures

ACTIVE DUTY PERSONNEL: 185
DEPENDENTS: 400
CIVILIAN PERSONNEL: 70

Services

Housing: Family units 59; Unaccompanied enlisted quarters 30. *Temporary Housing:* Guest cottages 6. *Exchange:* Barber shop; Food shop; Military clothing store; Convenience store. *Child Care/Capacities:* Home day care program. *Schools:* College courses. *Base Library:* Yes. *Medical Facilities:* Medical clinic. *Recreational Facilities:* Bowling center; Pool; Gym; Tennis courts; Racquetball court; Fitness center/Weight room; Softball field; Auto shop; Youth center; Picnic area.

Wisconsin

Baraboo

951. Badger Army Ammunition Plant
BAAP
1 Badger Rd
Baraboo, WI 53913-5000
608-356-5525; DSN 280-9600
Profile
BRANCH: Army.
SIZE AND LOCATION: 7400 acres. On US-12, 8 mi S of Baraboo, WI; 6 mi N of Prairie du Sac/Sauk City; 38 mi NW of Madison, WI. *County:* Sauk.
MAJOR UNITS: Badger Army Ammunition Plant.
Key Contacts
COMMANDER: Commander's Representative, David Fordham.
Personnel and Expenditures
ACTIVE DUTY PERSONNEL: 5
CIVILIAN PERSONNEL: 100
Services *Base Library:* Yes.

Camp Douglas

952. Hardwood Air-to-Ground Weapons Range
Camp Douglas, WI 54618
Mailing Address
c/o Volk Field ANGB, 100 Independence Dr
Camp Douglas, WI 54618-5001
608-565-2884
Profile
BRANCH: Air National Guard.
SIZE AND LOCATION: 7680 acres. N of Necedah, WI, near town of Finley. *County:* Juneau.
BASE HISTORY: 1954, federal government leased Volk Field from WI State as permanent air training site; work began on air-to-ground range. 1955, initial construction completed; range used to meet variety of missions, from tactical fighter units to specialized weapons systems testing, such as "Strike Eagle" F-15 field testing. Today, used by units from all over Midwest, including all flying units deployed to Volk Field. Class A range: manned, scoring capability from ground, & Range Control Officer on ground who controls aircraft using range. Munitions employed are all inert or practice ordnance.

Also capable of night bombing & providing simulated threats to aircrews.
VISITOR ATTRACTIONS: Visits to range in operation can be arranged, call 608-565-2884; Open house held every other year.
Key Contacts
PUBLIC AFFAIRS: See Volk Field Air National Guard Base.

953. Volk Field Air National Guard Base
Volk Field
100 Independence Dr
Camp Douglas, WI 54618-5001
608-427-1200; FAX 608-427-1399; DSN 946-3200; DSN FAX 946-3399
Profile
BRANCH: Air National Guard.
SIZE AND LOCATION: 2336 acres; plus 7929 acres Hardwood Range. 0.5 mi N of village of Camp Douglas; 85 mi NE of Madison on I-90/94, Camp Douglas Exit; 55 mi SE of Lacrosse on I-90 & I-90/94 Camp Douglas Exit. *County:* Juneau.
MAJOR UNITS: Combat Readiness Training Center (CRTC); 128th Air Control Squadron (ACS); Hardwood Air-to-Ground Weapons Range (Detached).
BASE HISTORY: 1888, land purchased for rifle range. 1903, camp expanded to 800 acres for use by NG. 1927, named Camp Williams, for LTC Charles R Williams, Chief Quartermaster of post, 1917-1926. 1935-36, first hard-surfaced runways constructed. 1947, Army NG training at Camp McCoy & ANG squadron at Camp Williams. 1954, federal government leased field as permanent air training site. 1957, name changed to present name for 1st Lt Jerome A Volk, first WI ANG pilot killed in Korean War. Today, year-round training of ANG & military units of all branches. Designated as Air Mobility Command aerial port of embarkation for Ft McCoy; used extensively during 1991 Operation Desert Shield/Storm.
VISITOR ATTRACTIONS: Wisconsin National Guard Museum; Static display of ANG aircraft; Hardwood Range, Finley, WI, Tue-Sat, call 608-565-2884 for operational hours recording.
Key Contacts
COMMANDER: Col James A McMurry, 128th ACS, 608-427-1200, DSN 946-3200, DSN FAX 946-3399, JMCMURRY@WIMSN. ANG.AF.MIL.

PUBLIC AFFAIRS: Fred G LeSavage, 608-427-1202, DSN 946-3202, DSN FAX 946-3399, flesavate@wimsn.ang.af.mil.
PROCUREMENT: LTC Thomas Reis, 608-427-1231, DSN 946-3231.
TRANSPORTATION: See Procurement Officer.
PERSONNEL/COMMUNITY ACTIVITIES: See Public Affairs Officer.
Personnel and Expenditures
ACTIVE DUTY PERSONNEL: 89; 117 reservists
DEPENDENTS: 0
CIVILIAN PERSONNEL: 86
MILITARY PAYROLL EXPENDITURE: $25 mil (payroll/contracts)
Services
Housing: None. *Temporary Housing:* None. *Exchange:* Convenience store; TLA, recreational commissary, main BX available at Ft McCoy, 25 mi NW (608-388-2107, DSN 280-2107). *Child Care/Capacities:* No day care facilities. *Schools:* College courses. *Medical Facilities:* No medical facilities. *Recreational Facilities:* Softball field; Consolidated club.

Fort McCoy

954. Fort McCoy
FMC
100 E Headquarters Rd
Fort McCoy, WI 54656-5263
608-388-2222; FAX 608-388-4237; DSN 280-1110; DSN FAX 280-4237
Internet: http://www.mccoy.army.mil
OFFICER-OF-THE-DAY: 608-388-2216, DSN 280-2216, DSN FAX 280-4111
Profile
BRANCH: Army.
SIZE AND LOCATION: 60,000 acres. In W-central WI, between Sparta & Tomah. Hwy 16, 21, I-90 & I-94 provide easy access to reservation; nearest commercial airport 35 mi W, LaCrosse, WI. *County:* Monroe.
MAJOR UNITS: Army Reserve Readiness Training Center; Regional Training Site, Medical; Army Readiness Group; Regional Training Site, Maintenance; Naval Mobile Construction Bn 25 (NMCB-25); 88th Ordnance Co; Equipment Concentration Site 67; Mobilization and Training Equipment Site (MATES); Wisconsin Military Academy.
BASE HISTORY: 1909, founded, on what is known today as "south post"; northern half,

maneuver camp named Camp Emory Upton set up; artillery camp, known as Camp Robinson, set up in south. 1923-25, training stopped; redesignated Sparta Ordnance Depot; mission changed to handling, shipping, & storage of explosives. 1925, transferred to Dept of Agriculture. 1926, reestablished; named for Maj Gen Robert Bruce McCoy, prominent local resident. 1933-35, served as supply base for Civilian Conservation Corps (CCC). 1935, put on standby status. 1940, chosen as site for Second Army maneuvers. 1942, "new camp," today's cantonment area, begun. WWII, used as POW & relocation camp for European & Japanese prisoners, & Japanese-Americans relocated from West Coast. Nation's 1st ordnance regiment, 301st, organized here. 1943, hospital built along with induction & basic training center for Army nurses; Limited Service School established to train physically handicapped soldiers. 1945, discharge center; induction center; then, on inactive status except summer training camps. 1950, reactivated with Fifth Army units. 1953, deactivated again. 1955, Wisconsin State Patrol Academy established. 1966-68, Jobs Corps Training Center established. 1971, Mobilization & Training Equipment Site (MATES) established. 1973, designated Forces Command installation. 1974, renamed Ft McCoy. 1980, 15,000 Cubans, relocated here. Only installation to have its own insignia. 1987, operational control to Army NG. 1988, Sparta-Ft McCoy Airport, a civilian/military facility, dedicated. 1990s, played major role in mobilization for Operations Desert Shield/Storm; assumed missions transferred from Ft Sheridan & Ft Benjamin Harrison; major new construction. Only active Army installation in 14-state area.

VISITOR ATTRACTIONS: Ft McCoy History Center with Museum, WWII Commemorative Area, & Equipment Park.

Key Contacts
COMMANDER: Col Harold K Miller Jr, 608-388-3001, DSN 280-3001, DSN FAX 280-4168.
PUBLIC AFFAIRS: Marv Clark, ATTN: AFZR-XO-PA, 608-388-4209, DSN 280-4209, DSN FAX 280-3749.
PROCUREMENT: Gary Friedl, ATTN: AFZR-DC, 608-388-3818, DSN 280-3818, DSN FAX 280-3349.
TRANSPORTATION: William Kasten, ATTN: AFZR-DLT, 608-388-3714, DSN 280-3714, DSN FAX 280-2077.
PERSONNEL/COMMUNITY ACTIVITIES: Thomas Nemmers, ATTN: AFZR-PA, 608-388-2201, DSN 280-2201, DSN FAX 280-3743.

Personnel and Expenditures
ACTIVE DUTY PERSONNEL: 286
DEPENDENTS: 47
CIVILIAN PERSONNEL: 2219
MILITARY PAYROLL EXPENDITURE: $11 mil
CONTRACT EXPENDITURE: $43 mil

Services
Housing: Family units 96; Unaccompanied officer quarters 12; Unaccompanied enlisted quarters 73; Barracks spaces 14,550; Trailer spaces 16; *Temporary Housing:* VEQ units 543; Guesthouse units 5; Transient quarters 653. *Commissary:* Yes; *Exchange:* Barber shop; Service station; Military clothing store; Convenience store; Laundromat; Credit union; ATM; Post office;

Fast food; Video rentals; Thrift shop; Travel agency; Class VI; Tailor/Alterations; Cafeteria; Car rental. *Child Care/Capacities:* Day care center capacity 58, 6wks-5yrs; Home day care program; Summer day camp. *Schools:* No on-base schools. *Base Library:* Yes. *Medical Facilities:* Medical clinic; Dental clinic; Pharmacy. *Recreational Facilities:* Bowling center; Movie theater; Pool; Gym; Recreation center; Tennis courts; Racquetball court; Fitness center/Weight room; Softball field; Auto shop; Craft shop; Camping; Fishing/Hunting; Youth center; Picnic area; Water sports; Playground; Consolidated club; Rod & Gun club; Ski hill operation with tow bar, tubing run, & heated chalet with snack bar & rental equipment.

Green Bay

955. Green Bay Naval & Marine Corps Reserve Center
NMCRC Green Bay
2949 Ramada Way
Green Bay, WI 54304-5799
414-336-2444, 336-2083; FAX 414-336-5854
Profile
BRANCH: Naval Reserve; Marine Corps Reserve.
LOCATION: *County:* Brown.
MAJOR UNITS: REDCOM SIXTEEN Activity; Det B, Marine Wing Support Squadron 471 (MWSS-471); Det F, 4th FSSG.
Key Contacts
COMMANDER: Lt J Knuth.

La Crosse

956. La Crosse Naval Reserve Center
2226 Green Bay St
La Crosse, WI 54601-5961
608-788-2565; FAX 608-788-2557
Profile
BRANCH: Naval Reserve.
LOCATION: *County:* La Crosse.
MAJOR UNITS: REDCOM SIXTEEN Activity.
Key Contacts
COMMANDER: LCDR J G Gray.

Madison

957. Madison Naval & Marine Corps Reserve Center
AFRC Madison
1430 Wright St
Madison, WI 53704-4192
608-249-0129; FAX 608-249-0385
Profile
BRANCH: Naval Reserve; Marine Corps Reserve.
LOCATION: *County:* Dane.
MAJOR UNITS: REDCOM SIXTEEN Activity; Co G, 2nd Bn, 24th Marine Regiment.
Key Contacts
COMMANDER: LCDR Stephen P Carmichael.

958. Truax Field Air National Guard Base
Truax Field
3110 Mitchell St
Madison, WI 53704-2591
608-245-4502; FAX 608-245-4450; DSN 724-8502; DSN FAX 724-4450
Profile
BRANCH: Air National Guard.
SIZE AND LOCATION: 156 acres. In Madison, adj to Dane County Regional Airport, off E Washington Ave (Hwy 151); Hwy 51N intersection with Hwy 151. *County:* Dane.
MAJOR UNITS: 115th Fighter Wing; 115th Operations Group; 176th Fighter Squadron; 115th Operations Support Flight; 115th Logistics Group; 115th Aircraft Generation Squadron; 115th Maintenance Squadron; 115th Logistics Support Flight; 115th Logistics Squadron; 115th Support Group; 115th Civil Engineer Squadron; 115th Security Police Squadron; 115th Mission Support Flight; 115th Services Flight; 115th Communications Flight; 115th Medical Squadron.
BASE HISTORY: 1948, established as 176th Fighter Squadron. 1951, Korean War, active duty. 1956, reorganized as 128th Air Defense Wing. 1974, transferred from Aerospace Command to TAC as 128th Tactical Fighter Wing. 1996, reorganized as 115th Fighter Wing.
Key Contacts
COMMANDER: Brig Gen Fred R Sloan, 608-245-4503, DSN 724-8503.
PUBLIC AFFAIRS: Maj Dave Olson, 608-245-4339, DSN 724-4339, PAFFAIRS@ WIMSN.ANG.AF.MIL.
PROCUREMENT: SMSgt Dave Marcum, 608-245-4548, DSN 724-8548, DMARCUM@WIMSN.ANG.AF.MIL.
TRANSPORTATION: 2Lt Gary Pelletier.
Personnel and Expenditures
ACTIVE DUTY PERSONNEL: 1467
CIVILIAN PERSONNEL: 59
MILITARY PAYROLL EXPENDITURE: $21.8 mil
CONTRACT EXPENDITURE: $1.5 mil
Services *Exchange:* Retail store; Military clothing store; Credit union. *Medical Facilities:* Medical clinic; Dental clinic; Optometric Clinic. *Recreational Facilities:* Softball field; All ranks club.

959. Wisconsin National Guard, Office of the Adjutant General
2400 Wright St
Madison, WI 53708
Mailing Address
PO Box 8111
Madison, WI 53708-8111
608-242-3000; FAX 608-242-3111; DSN 724-3000; DSN FAX 724-3111
Profile
BRANCH: Air National Guard; Army National Guard.
SIZE: Offices only. *County:* Dane.
MAJOR UNITS: Wisconsin Army National Guard, HQ; Wisconsin Air National Guard, HQ.
Key Contacts
COMMANDER: Maj Gen James G Blaney.
PUBLIC AFFAIRS: LTC Tim Donovan, 608-242-3050, DSN 724-3050, DSN FAX 724-3051, donovt@wi-ang.ngb.army.mil.

Milwaukee

960. 84th Division (IT) HQ

4828 W Silver Spring Dr
Milwaukee, WI 53218-3498
414-438-6141, 438-6143; FAX 414-438-6101
Internet: http://160.136.109.3/84th/wisconsin. htm

Profile
BRANCH: Army Reserve.
SIZE AND LOCATION: 70 acres. In N-central Milwaukee; between Rte 181 & I-43; near Havenwoods Park. *County:* Milwaukee.
MAJOR UNITS: 84th Division (IT) HQ; 84th Division (IT) Retention Office; 84th Division Band; 5th Brigade, 84th Division; 7th Brigade, 84th Division; Drill Sergeant School; 1/334th Bn.
BASE HISTORY: Formerly a Nike air defense site; consists of helipad, tank simulation center, & outdoor training areas. Provides: guidance & training in personnel retention & recruiting; Basic Combat Training to new recruits.
VISITOR ATTRACTIONS: Half of complex turned over to establishment of Havenwoods Environmental Awareness Center.

Key Contacts
COMMANDER: MajGen Joseph A Scheinkoenig.

Personnel and Expenditures
ACTIVE DUTY PERSONNEL: Guard 4137 (authorized); Active Guard Reserve 119
CIVILIAN PERSONNEL: 65

Services *Exchange:* Retail store; Branch BX of Ft Sheridan.

961. Milwaukee Coast Guard Base/ Group

USCG Base Milwaukee
2420 S Lincoln Memorial Dr
Milwaukee, WI 53207-1997
414-747-7100; FAX 414-747-7108
OFFICER-OF-THE-DAY: 414-747-7181

Profile
BRANCH: Coast Guard.
SIZE AND LOCATION: 4 acres. 3 mi S of downtown Milwaukee on Lakefront, at S end of Hoan Bridge via I-794E. *County:* Milwaukee.
MAJOR UNITS: Coast Guard Group, Milwaukee; Marine Safety Office, Milwaukee; Coast Guard Station, Milwaukee; Coast Guard Base, Milwaukee; Electronic Support Det, Milwaukee; Navy Reserve Training Center; Marine Corps Reserve Training Center; Coast Guard Reserve Group, Milwaukee.
BASE HISTORY: 1877-1970, Coast Guard station operated at McKinley Park. 1968, present base constructed. Responsible for conducting & coordinating rescue operations, boating safety, law enforcement, marine safety, commercial vessel inspections, ice breaking, & aids to navigation on Lake Michigan. Open 0700-1600 daily; duty officer present all other times.

Key Contacts
COMMANDER: CDR Edward J Gleason.
PUBLIC AFFAIRS: LT T Gasser.

Personnel and Expenditures
ACTIVE DUTY PERSONNEL: 95
DEPENDENTS: 0
CIVILIAN PERSONNEL: 5

Services
Housing: Unaccompanied enlisted quarters. *Exchange:* Small exchange. *Base Library:* Yes. *Medical Facilities:* Corpsman for active duty personnel only. *Recreational Facilities:* Fitness center/Weight room; Basketball court; Volleyball; Horsehoe pit; Manages Rawley Pt, Lighthouse recreation cottage (reservations: 414-747-7120).

962. Milwaukee Naval & Marine Corps Reserve Center

2401 S Lincoln Memorial Dr
Milwaukee, WI 53207-1999
414-744-9764; FAX 414-744-2258

E-mail: MILWAUK@CNSRF.NAVY.MIL

Profile
BRANCH: Naval Reserve; Marine Corps Reserve.
LOCATION: *County:* Milwaukee.
MAJOR UNITS: REDCOM SIXTEEN Activity; MIUW 213; CO F, 2nd Bn, 24th Marine Regiment.

Key Contacts
COMMANDER: CDR M W Robison.

Personnel and Expenditures
ACTIVE DUTY PERSONNEL: 350 reservists

963. Mitchell Field Air National Guard Base

Mitchell Field
1835 E Grange Ave
Milwaukee, WI 53207
414-747-4405; FAX 414-747-4491; DSN 580-8405; DSN FAX 580-8412

Profile
BRANCH: Air National Guard.
SIZE AND LOCATION: ANG 111 acres; AFRC 103 acres. 7 mi S of Milwaukee, E side of Mitchell IAP; ANG & AFRC in separate facilities. *County:* Milwaukee.
MAJOR UNITS: 128th Air Refueling Wing (ANG); 440th Airlift Wing (AFRC).
BASE HISTORY: June 25, 1947, formed. Korean War, served 21 months of active duty. Aug 1961, redesignated from Fighter Group to Refueling Group (TAC). Oct 1976, reassigned to SAC.

Key Contacts
COMMANDER: Col John Cozad.

Personnel and Expenditures
ACTIVE DUTY PERSONNEL: 897 Guard; 1300 Reservists
CIVILIAN PERSONNEL: ANG 282; Reservist technicians/civilians 350
MILITARY PAYROLL EXPENDITURE: $18.8 mil ANG; $23 mil AFRC

Services *Commissary:* Yes; *Exchange:* Credit union. *Medical Facilities:* Medical clinic; Dental clinic. *Recreational Facilities:* All ranks club.

Wyoming

Cheyenne

964. Adjutant General of Wyoming
5500 Bishop Blvd
Cheyenne, WY 82009-3320
307-772-5234; FAX 307-772-5010
Profile
BRANCH: Army National Guard.
MAJOR UNITS: Wyoming National Guard.
Key Contacts
COMMANDER: Maj Gen Edmond W
Boenisch.

965. Cheyenne Municipal Airport, Air National Guard Base
Cheyenne, WY 82001
307-772-6201; DSN 943-6201
Profile
BRANCH: Air National Guard.
SIZE AND LOCATION: 70 acres. Within corporate limits of Cheyenne. *County:* Laramie.
MAJOR UNITS: 153rd Airlift Wing (ANG).
Personnel and Expenditures
ACTIVE DUTY PERSONNEL: 974 Guard
CIVILIAN PERSONNEL: 249
MILITARY PAYROLL EXPENDITURE: $14.8 mil

966. Cheyenne Naval Reserve Center
NAVRESCEN Cheyenne
4700 Ocean Loop
Cheyenne, WY 82009-5604
307-772-2221, 772-2224; FAX 307-772-2225
E-mail: nrcchey@sisna.com
Profile
BRANCH: Naval Reserve; Marine Corps Reserve.
SIZE AND LOCATION: 3 acres. In city residential area. *County:* Laramie.
MAJOR UNITS: NMCB 17 Det 0317; NWS CON EOT Det 10; FH 500 CBTZ23 O; ABFC A4 Admin FAC-4; Marine Air Control Squadron 23 (MACS-23), MACG-48.
Key Contacts
COMMANDER: LCDR Steven J Klister, Commanding Officer.
Personnel and Expenditures
ACTIVE DUTY PERSONNEL: 180 navy & marine reservists

F E Warren AFB

967. Francis E Warren Air Force Base
F E Warren AFB
5305 Randall Ave
F E Warren AFB, WY 82005-2271
307-773-1110; FAX 307-773-2074; DSN 481-1110; DSN FAX 481-2074
Internet: http://www.warren.af.mil
OFFICER-OF-THE-DAY: 307-773-3921, FAX 307-773-2257, DSN 481-3971
Profile
BRANCH: Air Force.
SIZE AND LOCATION: 5866 acres. Immediately adj & W of Cheyenne, WY; 2 mi N of I-80 & adj to I-25. *County:* Laramie.
MAJOR UNITS: 20th Air Force; 90th Missile Wing, HQ (Air Force Space Command).
BASE HISTORY: Oldest continuously active Air Force base. On active duty since 1867, when Fort D A Russell, largest old cavalry post, established. 1885, Ft Russell made permanent post & rebuilt. 1930, presidential decree changed name to Ft Francis E Warren, for Senator/Governor Warren, Congressional Medal of Honor winner in Civil War. WWII, Quartermaster Training Center, Women's Auxiliary Army Corps, Transportation Corps, & POW camp. 1947, Army relinquished jurisdiction to AF with 463rd AFB, Aviation Engineer School. 1948, School redesignated AF Technical School under Air Training Command. 1949, designated Francis E Warren AFB (no runway), with aircraft stationed at Cheyenne Municipal Airport. 1957, first operational ICBM base. 1959, became SAC base. 1984, Peacekeeper support facilities added. 1986, became part of US Strategic Triad. 1992, Air Combat Command activated. 1993, Air Force Space Command activated & HQ 20th Air Force host.
VISITOR ATTRACTIONS: Warren Historical Association Museum (base history from 1800s to 1947); Reunion Center (Warren's Air Force history, 1947-present); National Historic Site.
Key Contacts
COMMANDER: Col Robert P Summers, 307-773-2005, 481-2005.
PUBLIC AFFAIRS: Capt Kathleen Cook, 90 MW/PA, 307-773-3381, DSN 481-3381, DSN FAX 481-2074, cook.kathleen@warren.af.mil.
PROCUREMENT: Maj Michael Swankoski, 307-773-3535, FAX 307-773-3964, DSN 481-3535, Swankoski.michael@warren.af.mil.
TRANSPORTATION: Maj Gary Pond, 307-773-3083, FAX 307-773-2004, DSN 481-3083, Pond.gary@warren.af.mil.
PERSONNEL/COMMUNITY ACTIVITIES: Maj Ann Borgmann, 307-773-4251, FAX 307-773-3212, DSN 481-4251, Borgmann.ann@warren.af.mil.
Personnel and Expenditures
ACTIVE DUTY PERSONNEL: 3506
DEPENDENTS: 1990
CIVILIAN PERSONNEL: 568
MILITARY PAYROLL EXPENDITURE: $102 mil
CONTRACT EXPENDITURE: $69 mil
Services
Housing: Family units 831; Barracks spaces 1310; RV/Camper sites 51. *Temporary Housing:* VIP units 3; VOQ units 30; Transient quarters 18. *Commissary:* Yes; *Exchange:* Retail store; Barber shop; Dry cleaners; Food shop; Florist; Bank; Service station; Bakery; Military clothing store; Convenience store; Beauty shop; Credit union; ATM; Optical store; Post office; Fast food; Video rentals; Thrift shop; Travel agency; Class VI. *Child Care/Capacities:* Day care center capacity 138, 6mo-12yrs; Home day care program; Summer day camp. *Schools:* Preschool/Kindergarten; College courses. *Base Library:* Yes. *Medical Facilities:* Hospital 40; Medical clinic; Dental clinic; Dispensary; Pharmacy; Veterinary services. *Recreational Facilities:* Bowling center; Movie theater; Pool; Gym; Recreation center; Golf course; Stables; Tennis courts; Racquetball court; Fitness center/Weight room; Softball field; Auto shop; Craft shop; Camping; Fishing/Hunting; Youth center; Picnic area; Playground; Consolidated club.

Guernsey

968. R L Esmay Training Center
Camp Guernsey; Camp Guernsey Annual Training Site
South Dakota St, Bldg 015
Guernsey, WY 82214
Mailing Address
PO Box 399
Guernsey, WY 82214-0399
307-836-2823; FAX 307-772-5751; DSN 772-5786; DSN FAX 772-5751

Profile

BRANCH: Army National Guard.

SIZE AND LOCATION: 34,000 acres. In SE WY on North Platte River between Wheatland & Torrington, elevation 4338 ft. Adj to town of Guernsey on Hwy 26 not far from I-25; approx 30 mi from NE border & approx 100 mi N of CO border. *County:* Platte.

MAJOR UNITS: Wyoming Army National Guard Training Site; State Area Readiness Command, Det 2; Wyoming Regional Training Institute.

BASE HISTORY: Originally, WY ANG used Pole Mountain, on Ft Warren Military Reservation, for annual training. 1938-39, summer camp site moved; Camp Guernsey became training center. WWII, active Army training center. Post WWII, deactivated, used as state maintenance site. 1950s, WY NG reactivated camp; used yearly ever since for NG training. Training Center named for Lt Gen Rhodolph L Esmay. 1980s, night land navigation course, air operations building, USPFO, & maintenance shop built; includes 25,000-acre artillery firing range. Airstrip at E edge of main camp. 1990s, automated ranges, 5500-ft lighted runway (C-130 capable & shared with Town of Guernsey), Tisa air operations, control tower, & fire hall complex.

VISITOR ATTRACTIONS: In heart of Wyoming's Oregon Trail area with Ft Laramie National Historic Site about 13 mi E; Guernsey State Park/Reservoir; Oregon Trail ruts; Register Cliff.

Key Contacts

COMMANDER: Col Joseph E Michaels, 307-836-2823, FAX 307-772-5751, DSN 943-5702.

PUBLIC AFFAIRS: Maj Norman E Boese, 307-836-2823, FAX 307-772-5751, DSN 943-5799.

Personnel and Expenditures

ACTIVE DUTY PERSONNEL: 2; Reserve 61
CIVILIAN PERSONNEL: 80

Services

Housing: Barracks spaces 1367; Trailer spaces 9; RV/Camper sites 40. *Temporary Housing:* VIP units 1; VOQ units 10; Unaccompanied officer/Enlisted quarters 365. *Exchange:* Retail store; Military clothing store; Convenience store. *Medical Facilities:* Dispensary. *Recreational Facilities:* Recreation center; Fitness center/Weight room; Softball field; Officers club; NCO club; Camping; Fishing/Hunting; Enlisted club; Picnic area.

Pinedale

969. Pinedale Seismic Research Facility

Pinedale, WY 82941

Internet: http://www.aftac.gov/dets/489/det489.html

Profile

BRANCH: Air Force.

LOCATION: 6 mi E of Boulder, WY; 18 mi SE of Pinedale, WY; just W of Continental Divide. *County:* Sublette.

MAJOR UNITS: Air Force Technical Applications Center, Det 489.

BASE HISTORY: Data supplied to National Data Center at AFTAC, HQ, Patrick AFB.

Key Contacts

PUBLIC AFFAIRS: MSgt Rene Uzee, 407-494-9915, DSN 854-9915, ruzee@aftac.gov.

Profiles of U.S. Military Bases Overseas

Australia

Joint Defense Facility Nurrungar

970. Joint Defense Facility Nurrungar

5SWS, Unit 11014
APO AP, 96552
DSN 640-1350, ext 300, 730-1350, ext 300;
FAX ext 387
OFFICER-OF-THE-DAY: Duty Officer DSN
  730-1350, ext 312

Profile
BRANCH: Air Force.
SIZE AND LOCATION: 1 acre. Approx 8 mi
  from Woomera.
MAJOR UNITS: 5th Space Warning Squadron.
BASE HISTORY: Space-age listening post with
  space-based surveillance system providing
  space warning. Mission to track missile &
  space launches.

Services
Housing: Family units Houses 89; Apartments
27. *Temporary Housing:* None. *Exchange:* Retail store; Post office; Class VI; Service station.
Child Care/Capacities: No day care facilities;
Home day care program. *Schools:* No on-base
schools. *Base Library:* Yes. *Medical Facilities:*
Limited facilities. *Recreational Facilities:* Bowling center; Movie theater; Pool; Golf course;
Tennis courts; Fitness center/Weight room;
Craft shop; Youth center; Community club; Recreation checkout.

Joint Geological and Geophysical Research Station

971. Joint Geological and Geophysical Research Station
APO, AP 96548

Internet: http://www.aftac.gov/dets/421/det421.
  html
Profile
BRANCH: Air Force.
LOCATION: In Central Australia; at Alice
  Springs.
MAJOR UNITS: Air Force Technical Applications Center, Det 421.
BASE HISTORY: 1955, established. 1965, began monitoring 1963 Limited Test Ban
  Treaty. Monitors & records natural & man-made seismic disturbances to monitor nuclear
  test ban treaties. Also acts as Air Mobility
  Command representative for Central Australia.
Key Contacts
PUBLIC AFFAIRS: MSgt Rene Uzee,
  407-494-9915, DSN 854-9915, ruzee@aftac.
  gov.

Bahamas

Naval Undersea Warfare Center, Detachment, Atlantic Undersea Test & Evaluation Center

972. Naval Undersea Warfare Center, Detachment, Atlantic Undersea Test & Evaluation Center
NUWC DET AUTEC
PSC 1012
FPO, AA 34058-9998
561-655-5155; FAX 561-655-5155, ext 5695;
DSN 483-7390; DSN FAX 483-7390, ext 5695

Profile
BRANCH: Navy.
SIZE AND LOCATION: 1 sq mi. On E seaboard in middle of chief island of W group of
Bahamas, 1 mi S of Fresh Creek; area known
as "Tongue of the Ocean" (TOTO); locally
called Andros Island. *Locality:* Andros Island.
MAJOR UNITS: Naval Undersea Warfare Center, Det.
BASE HISTORY: 1963, agreement negotiated
with UK granted permission to establish AUTEC. 1963-67, construction. 1967, commissioned. Mission to provide deep-water test facility for precision tracking of submarines,
surface ships, aircraft, & associated weaponry.
Key Contacts
COMMANDER: CDR D C Schmitz,
  561-655-5155, ext 5123, DSN 483-7390,ext
  5123, DSN FAX 483-7390, ext 5695.
PUBLIC AFFAIRS: CWO2 M H Sanders,
  561-655-5155, ext 5124, DSN 483-7390, ext
  5124, sanders@wpb.nuwc.navy.mil.
PROCUREMENT: Lt F Bobo, 561-832-7354,
  FAX 561-832-7395, DSN 483-7354, bobo@
  wpb.nuwc.navy.mil.
TRANSPORTATION: See Procurement
  Officer.

PERSONNEL/COMMUNITY ACTIVITIES:
  See Public Affairs Officer.
Personnel and Expenditures
ACTIVE DUTY PERSONNEL: 18
DEPENDENTS: 24
CIVILIAN PERSONNEL: 400
Services
Housing: Family units 63; Duplex units 60; Barracks spaces 162; Triplex 180. *Temporary Housing:* Unaccompanied officer/Enlisted quarters
76; Transient quarters 74; Concrete block homes
177. *Exchange:* Retail store; Barber shop; Food
shop; Service station; Beauty shop; Laundromat;
Post office; Fast food; Video rentals; Laundry.
Child Care/Capacities: Day care center capacity
20, 2-5yrs. *Schools:* One school K-12. *Base Library:* Yes. *Medical Facilities:* Medical clinic;
Pharmacy; Veterinary services Once a month.
Recreational Facilities: Recreation center; Tennis courts; Racquetball court; Fitness center/
Weight room; Softball field; Auto shop; Craft
shop; Picnic area; Water sports; Playground;
Community club; Consolidated club; Fishing.

Bahrain

Administrative Support Unit, South West Asia

973. Administrative Support Unit, South West Asia
ASU SWA
PSC 451, Box 95
FPO, AE 09834-2800
011-973-724-224; FAX 011-973-724-210; DSN 318-439-4224; DSN FAX 318-439-4224
E-mail: fsc5230@dhahran-emh1.army.mil

Profile
BRANCH: Navy.
SIZE AND LOCATION: 23.5 acres. In northeast section of the island of Bahrain. *Locality:* City of Manama, Juffair (Subdivision).
MAJOR UNITS: Naval Forces Central Command (COMUSNAVCENT); Defense Courier Service; Defense Fuel Middle East; Military Sealift Command Office, Southwest Asia; Helicopter Support Squadron 2, Det 2 (HC-2); Helicopter Support Squadron 4, Det 1 (HC-4); Fleet Logistics Support Squadron 50 (VRC-50); Naval Regional Contracting Center, Bahrain; Ship Repair Unit Det Bahrain; 11th Signal Brigade (USA); Defense Mapping Agency Representative; Explosive Ordnance Disposal, Det Bahrain; Maritime Liaison Officer, Bahrain; Navy Broadcasting Service, Det Bahrain; Naval Criminal Investigative Service, Bahrain.
BASE HISTORY: 1935, British Navy established HMS Juffair in area. 1950, USN leased office space. 1971, British withdrew after treaty expired; USN took over part of area as Administrative Support Unit Bahrain. 1992, renamed current name. Mission to support ships through remote sites throughout Commander US Naval Forces Central Command (COMUSNAVCENT) Area.

Key Contacts
COMMANDER: 011-973-724-220, DSN 318-439-4220.
PUBLIC AFFAIRS: Administration, 011-973-724-290, DSN 318-439-4224.

Personnel and Expenditures
ACTIVE DUTY PERSONNEL: 580
DEPENDENTS: 380
CIVILIAN PERSONNEL: 180

Services
Housing: All off-base housing. *Temporary Housing:* CBQ Combined Quarters 33 (for active duty on orders); Contract rooms in town for active duty 689; Space available for retired personnel. *Exchange:* Barber shop; Dry cleaners; Food shop; Convenience store; Beauty shop; Laundromat; No cash transactions. *Child Care/Capacities:* Day care center capacity 27, 6wks-6yrs; Summer day camp. *Schools:* Preschool/Kindergarten; Elementary; Intermediate/Junior high; High school. *Base Library:* Yes. *Medical Facilities:* Medical clinic; Dental clinic; Dispensary; Pharmacy; Hospital rooms in town. *Recreational Facilities:* Bowling center; Movie theater; Pool; Gym; Recreation center; Racquetball court; Fitness center/Weight room; Officers club; NCO club; Camping; Fishing/Hunting; Enlisted club; Picnic area; Playground.

Belgium

16th Combat Equipment Company

974. 16th Combat Equipment Company
Unit 21901
APO, AE 09713-1901

Profile
BRANCH: Army.
LOCATION: Leutsestraat 3690, Zutendaal.
MAJOR UNITS: 16th Combat Engineering Co.

Key Contacts
COMMANDER: Maj John Davis, Commander/Site Manager, 011-003289353143, FAX 011-003289357480, davisjm@cege.schinnen.army.mil.
Services *Exchange:* PX.

80th Area Support Group

975. 80th Area Support Group
APO, AE 09724

Profile
BRANCH: Army.
LOCATION: No one post but various locations in & around Brussels.
MAJOR UNITS: 80th Area Support Group; Bettembourg Site; Chievres Airbase; Daumerie Caserne; Everberg Armed Forces Network (AFN) Facility; Grobbendonk Site; Olen Storage Facility; Sanem Site; Supreme Headquarters Allied Powers Europe (SHAPE) HQ; Zutendaal Site; 39th Signal Bn; Brussels American School; Defense Contract Management Area Operations, Brussels; DODDS, Superintendent's Office; NATO Communications and Information Systems Agency; NATO HQ; Army Education Center, Chievres.

Key Contacts
COMMANDER: Col Taylor, 011-68-27-1300, DSN 361-1300, 361-5406.
PUBLIC AFFAIRS: CMR 451, APO AE 09708, 011-32-6827-5111, DSN 361-1110.

Personnel and Expenditures
ACTIVE DUTY PERSONNEL: 315
DEPENDENTS: 1300
CIVILIAN PERSONNEL: 460

Services
Housing: None. *Exchange:* Convenience store. *Child Care/Capacities:* No day care facilities. *Schools:* No on-base schools. *Base Library:* Yes. *Medical Facilities:* Medical clinic; Dental clinic. *Recreational Facilities:* Fitness center/Weight room; Recreation center; Craft shop; Auto shop; Tennis courts.

Chievres Air Base

976. Chievres Air Base
APO, AE 09708

Profile
BRANCH: Army.
LOCATION: Just SW of Brussels.
MAJOR UNITS: Chievres Air Base; 886th Communications Squadron, OL-B, Kester/Flobecq; 886th Communications Squadron, OL-A, Pruem; 80th ASG, Directorate of Public Works; Daumerie Kaserne.

Key Contacts
PUBLIC AFFAIRS: 80th ASG, CMR 451, APO AE 09708, 011-32-3827-5111, DSN 361-1110.

Services *Temporary Housing:* Hotel Raymond, 27 Blvd Charles Quint, 7000 Mons, Rooms 67 (011-32-65-32-75-01; DSN 361-5248). *Commissary:* Yes; *Exchange:* PX. *Recreational Facilities:* Officers club.

Kleine Brogel Air Base

977. Kleine Brogel Air Base
Unit 21903
APO, AE 09713
0032-11-51-2406; FAX 0032-11-63-4883; DSN 361-1110
E-mail: 52munss.kleinebrogel@spangdahlem.af.mil Internet:http://www.spangdahlem.af.mil/org/52munss/index.htm
Profile
BRANCH: Air Force.
LOCATION: 60 mi NE of Brussels IAP; 60 mi E of Antwerp; 40 mi N of Liege; 15 mi S of Eindhoven; 16 mi from Netherlands border.
MAJOR UNITS: 52nd Munitions Support Squadron.
BASE HISTORY: 1962, Detachment 0600, 306th Munitions Maintenance Squadron, acti-

vated to support 10th Wing Tactical; first American military unit in Belgium since WWII. 1996, current designation. Mission: receive, store, & maintain munitions.
Personnel and Expenditures
ACTIVE DUTY PERSONNEL: 121
DEPENDENTS: 250
Services
Housing: None. *Temporary Housing:* None. *Exchange:* Barber shop; Beauty shop; Convenience store; Snack bar; Dining facilities; Commissary at Schinnen, Netherlands, 40 mi. *Child Care/Capacities:* No day care facilities. *Schools:* No on-base schools; College courses. *Base Library:* Yes. *Medical Facilities:* Dispensary. *Recreational Facilities:* Movie theater; Gym; Recreation center; Racquetball court; Fitness center/Weight room; Softball field; Football field; Playground; Soccer field; MWR recreational supply.

Northern Law Center

978. Northern Law Center
Bldg B.P. 13
APO, AE 09708
011-32-065-44-4910; DSN 423-4910, 423-4868
E-mail: aerja@email.shape.army.mil Internet: http://147.35.210.53/Aerja/NLC.htm
Profile
BRANCH: Army.
LOCATION: Mons, in SW Belgium. *Locality:* Hainaut Province.
MAJOR UNITS: Northern Law Center.
Key Contacts
COMMANDER: LTC Natalie L Griffin, Law Center Judge Advocate.

Canada

22nd Wing

979. 22nd Wing
CFB North Bay
APO, AE 09732-5000

DSN 628-2660
Profile
BRANCH: Air Force.
LOCATION: In SE Ontario at North Bay, on NE shore of Lake Nipissing. *Locality:* Nipissing District, Ontario.

MAJOR UNITS: 22nd Wing.
Key Contacts
PUBLIC AFFAIRS: See Langley AFB, 1. sheppard@langley.af.mil.

China

Ship Support Office, American Consulate General, Hong Kong

980. Ship Support Office, American Consulate General, Hong Kong
SHIP SUPPORT OFFICE; SSO
No 1 Long King St, Fenwick Pier, Wan Chai
FPO, AP, Hong Kong
Mailing Address
PSC 464 Box 20
FPO AP, 96552-2200
852-2802-7866; FAX 852-2511-3703
Profile
BRANCH: Navy.
LOCATION: At Fleet Landing, Fenwick Pier. *Locality:* Wan Chai District.

MAJOR UNITS: Navy Contracting Office (USNCD).
BASE HISTORY: 1951, Central Purchasing Office for non-appropriated fund activities established. 1954, Navy Purchasing Branch (NPB) established. 1967, NPB became department of Naval Supply Depot Yokosuka. 1991, 5-year lease for Fenwick Pier to accommodate USN facilities. 1994, new facility opened. 1997, renamed from Navy Contracting Department, Hong Kong.
Key Contacts
COMMANDER: LCDR S R Shapro, SC, Officer in Charge, 852-2802-7866, srshapro@hk.super.net.
PUBLIC AFFAIRS: Lt A C Ehlers, Asst Officer in Charge, 852-2802-9380, FAX 852-2511-3703, aehlers@hk.super.net.
PROCUREMENT: Ms A Kong, Contracting Officer, 852-2802-9699, konga@hk.super.net.

TRANSPORTATION: Fleet Services Officer, 852-2802-8977.
Personnel and Expenditures
ACTIVE DUTY PERSONNEL: 7
CIVILIAN PERSONNEL: 9
MILITARY PAYROLL EXPENDITURE: $200,000
CONTRACT EXPENDITURE: $10 mil
Services
Housing: None. *Temporary Housing:* None. *Exchange:* Retail store; Barber shop; Furniture store; Bookstore; Beauty shop; Credit union; Optical store; Post office; Fast food; Tailor/Alterations; Laundry; Arcade shops (with guaranteed genuine items); Video/CD store; Oriental carpet store; Jewelry store; Gift shop; Chinaware store; Silverware store; Shoemaker; Sporting goods shop; Leather goods store; Money exchange. *Child Care/Capacities:* No day care facilities. *Schools:* No on-base schools. *Base Library:* Yes. *Medical Facilities:* No medical facilities. *Recreational Facilities:* Recreation center; Servicemen's Guides Association; American Women's Association; Game room; MWR section.

Cuba

Guantanamo Bay, Naval Base

981. Guantanamo Bay, Naval Base
Gitmo
Naval Base 82312, Box 32
FPO, AE 09596-0120
011-53-99-2279; DSN 564-4063-2279
OFFICER-OF-THE-DAY: Command Post
011-53-99-4708, 4453

Profile
BRANCH: Navy.
SIZE AND LOCATION: 36 sq mi. On SE coast of Cuba; 200 air mi from Miami. *Locality:* Oriente Province.
MAJOR UNITS: Naval Station, Guantanamo Bay; Naval Hospital Guantanamo Bay; Marine Barracks, Guantanamo Bay; Naval Security Group Activity, Guantanamo Bay.

BASE HISTORY: 1898, Naval Squadron (first combined arms expeditionary force formed by the Corps) established advanced base to support campaign against Santiago. Marine presence continuous since then. WWII, mission expanded to include external security. 1953, Ground Defense Force established to defend Base until reinforcements arrive. 1994, housed refugee population including over 14,000 Haitians & 16,000 Cubans. No access to Cuban community; base totally self-sufficient.

Key Contacts
COMMANDER: 011-5399-2648, FAX 011-5399-3237.
TRANSPORTATION: 011-53-99-4417.

Personnel and Expenditures
ACTIVE DUTY PERSONNEL: 1400
CIVILIAN PERSONNEL: 640

Services
Housing: Unaccompanied officer quarters; Unaccompanied enlisted quarters; Total units 1091. *Temporary Housing:* Lodge units. *Commissary:* Yes; *Exchange:* Retail store; Barber shop; Dry cleaners; Food shop; Florist; Bank; Service station; Furniture store; Bakery; Military clothing store; Convenience store; Beauty shop; Laundromat; Credit union; Video rentals. *Child Care/Capacities:* Day care center new born to school age; Home day care program. *Schools:* College courses. *Base Library:* Yes. *Medical Facilities:* Hospital 6 beds; Dental clinic; Pharmacy; Veterinary services. *Recreational Facilities:* Bowling center; Movie theater; Pool; Gym; Recreation center; Golf course; Stables; Tennis courts; Racquetball court; Fitness center/Weight room; Softball field; Auto shop; Craft shop; Officers club; NCO club; Enlisted club; Picnic area; Water sports; Playground; Fishing; Marina; SATO.

Diego Garcia

Diego Garcia, Naval Support Facility

982. Diego Garcia, Naval Support Facility
US NAVSUPPFAC; NSF Diego Garcia
PSC 466, Box 2
FPO, AP 96595-0002
DSN 370-4112, 370-3800
E-mail: RVAGLE@NCTSDG.NAVY.MIL Internet:http://www.andersen.af.mil/gsus.htm

Profile
BRANCH: Navy.
LOCATION: Largest of 52 islands forming Chagos Archipelago in central Indian Ocean, just below equator. *Locality:* British Indian Ocean Territory.
MAJOR UNITS: Naval Support Facility, Diego Garcia; Naval Computer and Telecommunications Station, Diego Garcia; Navy Maritime Prepositioning Ships Squadron 2; Military Sealift Command Unit, Diego Garcia; Marine Corps Security Force Co, Diego Garcia; Naval Pacific Meteorology and Oceanography Det, Diego Garcia; Naval Media Center Det, Diego Garcia; Navy Personnel Support Det Activity, Diego Garcia; Naval Mobile Construction Bn Seabee Det; Patrol Squadron, Diego Garcia; Patrol Wing One, Det; 18th Space Surveillance Squadron, Det 4; 750th Space Group, Det 8; Naval Criminal Investigative Service Resident Unit; Air Movement Center, Diego Garcia; 18th Space Surveillance Squadron, Det 2.
BASE HISTORY: 1966, agreement signed with UK for joint operation. 1986, base fully operational. 1990, only US Navy base launching offensive air operations during Operation Desert Shield/Storm.
VISITOR ATTRACTIONS: No visitors allowed.

Key Contacts
COMMANDER: DSN 370-4001.

Personnel and Expenditures
ACTIVE DUTY PERSONNEL: 2000
CIVILIAN PERSONNEL: 1000

Services
Housing: Unaccompanied officer quarters; Unaccompanied enlisted quarters; Senior NCO units. *Temporary Housing:* VIP units Bob Hope Suite, 1; Transient quarters 3. *Exchange:* Barber shop; Bookstore; Convenience store; Laundromat; Credit union; Pacific Stars & Stripes. *Child Care/Capacities:* No day care facilities. *Schools:* College courses. *Base Library:* Yes. *Medical Facilities:* Combined medical/dental with pharmacy. *Recreational Facilities:* Bowling center; Movie theater; Pool; Gym; Tennis courts; Racquetball court; Fitness center/Weight room; Softball field; Football field; Officers club; NCO club; Enlisted club; Skeet range; Water sports; Fishing; Snorkeling.

Egypt

Cairo West AFB

983. Cairo West AFB
APO, AE 09878
Profile
BRANCH: Air Force.
MAJOR UNITS: 9th Air Expeditionary Support Group.
Key Contacts
PUBLIC AFFAIRS: SSgt Dee Ann Poole, 9th AEW.
Personnel and Expenditures
ACTIVE DUTY PERSONNEL: Army 14; Air Force 11

Cario (East)

984. Cario (East)
APO, AE 09868
AMC Office: 011-0020-2-357-3212; FAX 011-0020-2-279-1290; DSN 312-725-1456, ext 3212
Profile
BRANCH: Air Force.

LOCATION: At Cairo International Airport.
MAJOR UNITS: 621st AMSG, OL-B.
Key Contacts
COMMANDER: OL Chief,
011-0020-2-376-8366.

Multinational Force and Observers

985. Multinational Force and Observers
USAE-MFO
APO, AE 09832
972-7-281801; FAX 972-7-281801, ext 4037
Profile
BRANCH: Multinational Base.
SIZE AND LOCATION: 25 acres. On Sinai Peninsula. North Camp, 40 mi from El'Arish at el Gorah; 150 mi from Cairo; 100 mi from Tel Aviv, Israel. South Camp, near Sharm el Sheikh, on S tip of Sinai Peninsula overlooks Red Sea. *Locality:* Sinai.
MAJOR UNITS: 1st US Support Bn.
BASE HISTORY: 1973, built by Israel after Yom Kippur War. 1979, abandoned by treaty; created by 1978 Camp David Accords. MFO

independent, non-UN peacekeeping mission. North Camp site of Force Commander's HQ; provides logistical & operational needs. South Camp smaller. MFO additionally operates approx 30 remote operational sites.
VISITOR ATTRACTIONS: Visitors must be sponsored & approved by HQ, Rome.
Key Contacts
COMMANDER: ext 2195.
PUBLIC AFFAIRS: ext 3125, murphy@main. aquanet.co.il.
Personnel and Expenditures
ACTIVE DUTY PERSONNEL: North Camp 400; South Camp 650
DEPENDENTS: 15
CIVILIAN PERSONNEL: 550
Services
Housing: Duplex units 20; Barracks spaces 500; Mobile home units 60. *Temporary Housing:* VIP units 2; Apartment units 6. *Exchange:* Retail store; Barber shop; Dry cleaners; Bank; Beauty shop; Travel service. *Child Care/Capacities:* No day care facilities. *Schools:* College courses. *Base Library:* Yes. *Medical Facilities:* Medical clinic; Dental clinic. *Recreational Facilities:* Movie theater; Pool; Gym; Tennis courts; Racquetball court; Fitness center/Weight room; Softball field; Football field; Officers club; NCO club; Enlisted club.

France

Istres Air Base

986. Istres Air Base
16 EOG
APO, AE 09791-9075
Internet: http://www.fas.org/irp/agency/usaf/acc/12af/9rw/ol-fr/index.html
Profile
BRANCH: Air Force.

LOCATION: 125 CNES Flight Test Center, Le Tube, France.
MAJOR UNITS: Operating Location France (OL-FR); 16th Expeditionary Operations Group; 507th Air Refueling Wing.
BASE HISTORY: Pilots from 99th RS rotate to support 9th RW various operating locations. U-2 pilots fly military reconnaissance missions, humanitarian, search & rescue, & environmental missions. 1995, operations move from RAF Fairford. 1997, KC-135 Stratotankers transferred from Pisa due to reduced oper-

ating space; support peacekeeping effort in Bosnia.
Key Contacts
COMMANDER: Col Charles Stallworth, 16th Air Expeditionary Wing.
PUBLIC AFFAIRS: Mitch Chandran, PA, 507th ARW, 7435 Reserve Rd, Ste 7, Tinker AFB, OK 73145-8726, 405-734-3078, DSN 884-3078.
Personnel and Expenditures
ACTIVE DUTY PERSONNEL: 150

Germany

6th Area Support Group, Garmish

987. 6th Area Support Group, Garmish
APO, AE 09053
Profile
BRANCH: Army.
LOCATION: In foothills of Bavarian Alps near Oberammergau. *Locality:* Bavaria.
MAJOR UNITS: Sheridan Barracks; Artillery Kaserne; Garmish Family Housing; Osterfelderstrasse Housing; Armed Forces Recreation Center, Garmish; George C Marshall European Center for Security Studies; Breitenau Kaserne.
Services *Temporary Housing:* 2 hotels; Ski lodge. *Recreational Facilities:* Skating rink; Golf course; Armed Forces Recreation Center; Sports program; Skiing; White water rafting.

6th Area Support Group, Stuttgart

988. 6th Area Support Group, Stuttgart
Unit 23203
APO, AE 09263
011-49-631-413-7601; FAX
011-49-631-413-8019; DSN 484-7601
Internet: http://147.35.210.53/crominfo.htm
Profile
BRANCH: Army.
SIZE AND LOCATION: 1 acre. In W-central Germany, just E of Kaiserslautern on Hwy B-37; just S of Autobahn A6. *Locality:* Rhineland-Pfalz.
MAJOR UNITS: 6th Area Support Group; Böblingen Family Housing; Böblingen Range; Böblingen Training Area; Echterdingen Airfield; Friolzheim Communication Facility; Kefurt Family Housing; Craig Village Family Housing; Kelley Barracks; Möhringen Family Housing; Panzer Kaserne; Patch Barracks; Robinson Barracks; Robinson-Grendadier Family Housing; Steuben Family Housing; Weicht Village Family Housing; Stuttgart Administration Facility; Weilimdorf Warehouse.
BASE HISTORY: WWII, German Kaserne. 1974, 21st TAACOM established.
Personnel and Expenditures
ACTIVE DUTY PERSONNEL: 500
CIVILIAN PERSONNEL: 450
Services *Exchange:* Barber shop; Convenience store; Snack bar. *Child Care/Capacities:* No day care facilities. *Schools:* No on-base schools. *Medical Facilities:* No medical facilities. *Recreational Facilities:* None.

67th Combat Support Hospital/ USAMEDDAC

989. 67th Combat Support Hospital/USAMEDDAC
67th CSH/USAMEDDAC
Würzburg Hospital
APO, AE 09244
011-49-931-804-3953; FAX
011-49-931-804-3859; DSN 350-3953; DSN FAX 350-3859
E-mail: @wuerzburg.smtplink.amedd.army.mil
OFFICER-OF-THE-DAY: 011-49-931-889-3861, DSN 350-3861, DSN FAX 350-3859
Profile
BRANCH: Army.
SIZE AND LOCATION: 10 acres. N side of Würzburg, near Leighton Barracks; 1.5 mi from city center. *Locality:* Franconia, Upper Bavaria.
MAJOR UNITS: 67th Combat Support Hospital; 1st Infantry Division, HQ; 101st Military Intelligence.
BASE HISTORY: 1935-37, built as 300-bed hospital. 1975, 67th Evacuation Hospital reactivated at Würzburg; renamed 67th Combat Support Hospital.
Key Contacts
COMMANDER: Col Holly Doyne.
PUBLIC AFFAIRS: 1Lt Timothy Valentine.
Personnel and Expenditures
ACTIVE DUTY PERSONNEL: 600
DEPENDENTS: 1000
CIVILIAN PERSONNEL: 500
Services *Commissary:* Yes; *Exchange:* Retail store; Barber shop; Dry cleaners; Food shop; Florist; Bank; Service station; Furniture store; Bakery; Bookstore; Military clothing store; Convenience store; Beauty shop; Laundromat; Credit union; ATM; Optical store; Post office; Fast food; Video rentals; Four seasons; Thrift shop; Travel agency; Class VI; Shoe repair; Computer store; Tailor/Alterations; Laundry. *Child Care/Capacities:* Day care center; Home day care program. *Medical Facilities:* Hospital.

98th Area Support Group

990. 98th Area Support Group
Unit 26622
APO, AE 09244
011-49-931-889-7103
Profile
BRANCH: Army.

LOCATION: Leighton Barracks in central Germany; in Main River Valley, approx 70 mi SE of Frankfurt. *Locality:* Lower Franconia, Bavaria.
MAJOR UNITS: 98th Area Support Group; Leighton Barracks; Faulenberg Kaserne; 101st Military Intelligence Bn; 106th Finance Support Command; 1st Infantry Division, HQ; 1st Military Police Co; 67th Combat Support Hospital; 817th ASOS (USAF); Area Support Team Würzburg; Breitsol Communication Station; Steinbachtal Ammunition Area; Würzburg Hospital; Würzburg Supply Point; Würzburg Training Areas.
BASE HISTORY: Built for German Air Force. 1945, occupied by US forces. Leighton Barracks, named for Cpt John A Leighton, killed in action, 1944. 1996, 1st Infantry Division moved in.
Key Contacts
COMMANDER: Col Williamson, 98th ASG, DSN 350-1300.
PUBLIC AFFAIRS: 011-49-931-2964-113, DSN 350-113.
Personnel and Expenditures
ACTIVE DUTY PERSONNEL: 9500
DEPENDENTS: 8000
Services *Commissary:* Yes; *Exchange:* Convenience store; Fast food; Service station; Bank; Credit union; PX. *Child Care/Capacities:* Day care center. *Medical Facilities:* Hospital. *Recreational Facilities:* Youth center; Movie theater.

100th Area Support Group

991. 100th Area Support Group
Unit 21830
APO, AE 09114
011-49-9641-3281; DSN 475-8370, 475-6249
Internet: http://www.grafenwoehr.army.mil/asgtop.htm
Profile
BRANCH: Army.
LOCATION: Approx 10 mi SE of Bayreuth. *Locality:* Bavaria.
MAJOR UNITS: 100th Area Support Group; Grafenwöhr Army Training Area; 886th Communications Squadron, OL-D, Grafenwöhr; Grafenwöhr Army Airfield; 7th Army Training Command; 409th Base Support Bn; East Camp Grafenwöhr.
BASE HISTORY: 1976, 7th Army Training Command established. Comprises Grafenwöhr & Hohenfels Training Areas, Combined Arms Training Center (Vilseck) & Training Support Activity, Europe (Roedelheim).
Key Contacts
COMMANDER: Col Philip D Coker, 100th ASG, DSN 475-1300.

PUBLIC AFFAIRS: 100th ASG, 011-49-964183-113, DSN 475-113, 7ATCPAO@hq.7atc.army.mil.

Personnel and Expenditures
ACTIVE DUTY PERSONNEL: 15,000 (military & civilian)
DEPENDENTS: 9500

Services *Commissary:* Yes; *Exchange:* Convenience store; PX. *Base Library:* Yes. *Medical Facilities:* Medical clinic; Dental clinic. *Recreational Facilities:* Bowling center; Movie theater; Pool; Gym; Recreation center; Golf course; Tennis courts; Racquetball court; Fitness center/ Weight room; Softball field; Auto shop; Football field; Craft shop; Officers club; Enlisted club; Youth center; Picnic area.

221st Base Support Battalion

992. 221st Base Support Battalion
CMR 430
APO, AE 09096
011-49-611-705-1500

Profile
BRANCH: Army.
LOCATION: On Rhine River, 20 mi W of Frankfurt. *Locality:* Hesse.
MAJOR UNITS. 221st Base Support Bn; McCully Barracks; AAFES, HQ; American Forces Network; Criminal Investigation Division (CID) Wiesbaden; Northern Europe Veterinary Det; Science & Technology Center; TMDE Support Center; Army Engineer Transatlantic; 205th Military Intelligence Brigade; 1st Military Intelligence Bn; 302nd Military Intelligence Bn; 12th Aviation Brigade; 3rd Corps Support Command (COSCOM); 39th Finance Det; 317th Weather Squadron, Det 6; Amelia Earhardt Hotel; American Arms Hotel; Aukamm Housing Area; Crestview Housing Area; Hainerberg Housing; Kastel Housing Area; Kastel Storage Facility; Rheinblick Recreation Annex; Wiesbaden Air Base; Wiesbaden Service Annex; Wiesbaden Small Arms Range; Mainz Area Support Team; Azbill Barracks; Dr Martin Luther King Village; Finthen Airfield; Finthen Family Housing; Fintherlandstrasse Family Housing; Lee Barracks; Mainz Repair and Upkeep Area; Uhlerborn Housing Area; Wackernheim-Schwabenwäldchen Training Area.

Key Contacts
COMMANDER: McCully Barracks, Installation Commander, DSN 334-4851.

Personnel and Expenditures
ACTIVE DUTY PERSONNEL: 3400
DEPENDENTS: 7500
CIVILIAN PERSONNEL: 2200

223rd Base Support Battalion

993. 223rd Base Support Battalion
CMR 431
APO, AE 09175
001-49-6151-69-1500, 1510; FAX 011-49-6151-69-6115; DSN 348-1500, 348-1510

Profile
BRANCH: Army.
MAJOR UNITS: 223rd Base Support Bn; 66th Military Intelligence Bn; 94th Air Defense Artillery; 413th Signal Co; 22nd Signal Brigade; 32nd Signal Bn; 440th Signal Bn; 165th Military Intelligence Bn; 596th Maintenance Bn; 41st Field Artillery Bn; 1/27th Field Artillery Bn; 77th Maintenance Co; Adjutant General Publications and Training Aids Center; Bensheim Maintenance and Supply Facility; Cambrai Fritsch Kaserne; Darmstadt Training Center; Egelsbach Transmitter Facility; Ernst Ludwig Kaserne; Frankfurt AFN Station; Frankfurt Mortuary; Griesheim Airfield; Jefferson Village Family Housing; Kelley Barracks; Langen Terrace Family Housing; Lincoln Village Family Housing; Melibokus Radio Relay Station; Messel Small Arms Range; Nathan Hale Quartermaster Area; Rhein Main Air Base; Rodelheim Ordnance Facility; St Barbara Village Family Housing; Weisskirchen AFN Transmittal Facility; Babenhausen Kaserne; Aschaffenburg Community.

Services *Commissary:* Yes;

280th Base Support Battalion

994. 280th Base Support Battalion
CMR 457
APO, AE 09033
Community Operations Center (24 hours)
011-49-354-6708; DSN 354-6708
Internet: http://www.per.hqusareur.army.mil/odcsper/cfsd/schwein.htm

Profile
BRANCH: Army.
LOCATION: In Schweinfurt, N of Würzburg, along banks of Main River; 99 mi E of Frankfurt; 72 mi NW of Nürnberg. *Locality:* Franconia.
MAJOR UNITS: 280th Base Support Bn; 1st Infantry Division, 2nd Brigade; 1/18 Infantry Bn; 1/26 Infantry Bn; 1/77 Armor Bn; 299th Support Bn; 1/4 Cavalry; 1/7 Field Artillery; 9th Engineers; 106th Finance; 38th Personnel Service Bn, B Det; 566th Postal Commander; 560th Military Police; 212th Military Police; 1st Military Police, Platoon; Askren Manor Family Housing; Conn Barracks; Daley Village Family Housing; Ledward Barracks; Massbach Quick Reaction Site; Rottershausen Ammunition Storage Area; Schweinfurt Training Areas; Sulzheim Training Area.
BASE HISTORY: Schweinfurt Military Community, "The Big Red One," makes up 280th BSB attached to 98th ASG, Würzburg; consists of two barracks (kasernes), Conn & Ledward. 1996, from 3rd Infantry Division to 1st Infantry Division. Conn Barracks: 1936, constructed; Luftwaffe training post for Stuka dive bombers. 1945, seized by 42nd Division, 7th US Army. 1948, transferred from Air Corps to Army; renamed for 2Lt Orville B Conn Jr, first WWII casualty of 6th Cavalry Group. Ledward Barracks: 1936, constructed as Panzer Kaserne. 1945, refugee camp & US Consulate offices. Renamed in honor of LTC William J Ledward, killed in action in Italy 1944. 1948, Army took control.

Personnel and Expenditures
ACTIVE DUTY PERSONNEL: 4400
DEPENDENTS: 5532
CIVILIAN PERSONNEL: 800

Services
Housing: Family units 2452; Unaccompanied officer quarters 74; Barracks spaces; Senior NCO units 162; Junior NCO units 1416; Askren Manor housing area. *Temporary Housing:* Transient quarters Bradley Inn Guest House 52 rooms. *Commissary:* Yes; *Exchange:* Retail store; Barber shop; Dry cleaners; Food shop; Florist; Bank; Service station; Furniture store; Bakery; Bookstore; Military clothing store; Convenience store; Beauty shop; Laundromat; Credit union; ATM; Optical store; Post office; Fast food; Video rentals; Four seasons; Thrift shop; Travel agency; Class VI; Shoe repair; Computer store; Garden center; Tailor/Alterations; Laundry; Cafeteria; Photo store; . *Child Care/Capacities:* Day care center capacity 100, 6wks-5yrs; Home day care program; Latch key program; Before & after school programs; Summer day camp. *Schools:* Elementary; Intermediate/Junior high; High school; College courses. *Base Library:* Yes. *Medical Facilities:* Medical clinic; Dental clinic; Dispensary; Pharmacy; Veterinary services. *Recreational Facilities:* Bowling center; Movie theater; Pool; Gym; Recreation center; Golf course; Tennis courts; Racquetball court; Fitness center/Weight room; Softball field; Football field; Auto shop; Craft shop; Officers club; NCO club; Camping; Enlisted club; Youth center; Picnic area; Playground; MWR.

282nd Base Support Battalion

995. 282nd Base Support Battalion
Unit 28216
APO, AE 09173
DSN 466-2861; DSN FAX 466-2035

Profile
BRANCH: Army.
SIZE AND LOCATION: 40,000 acres. Approx 45 mi SW of Grafenwoehr; 60 mi from Czech Republic. *Locality:* Palatinate District, Bavaria.
MAJOR UNITS: 282nd Base Support Bn; Amberg Family Housing; Brandhof Radio Relay Site; Dambach Family Housing; Darby Kaserne; Frechetsfeld Radio Site; Freihölser Training Area; Hohenfels Combat Maneuver Training Center; Johnson Barracks; Kalb Family Housing; Pioneer Kaserne; Pond Barracks; Regensburg Family Housing; Reinwarzhofen Radio Relay Facility; 69th Signal Bn; 94th Engineers, A Co; 106th Finance; 58th Aviation, E Co; 536th Military Police Platoon; 731st General Dispensary.
BASE HISTORY: 1937, training area established. WWII, used to house POWs. 1945, occupied by US troops; used to house Displaced Persons. 1946-51, German refugee farmers settled. 1951, area requisitioned for US Army training area. 1960, German army began training at Camp Poellenricht. Largest maneuver area available to US troops in Europe.

Personnel and Expenditures
ACTIVE DUTY PERSONNEL: 6000

Services *Commissary:* Yes; *Exchange:* Bank; Service station; Convenience store; Credit union; Fast food; PX. *Recreational Facilities:* Movie theater.

293rd Base Support Battalion

996. 293rd Base Support Battalion
APO, AE 09086

Profile
BRANCH: Army.
LOCATION: In SW Germany; Sullivan, Taylor, & Funari Barracks, Benjamin Franklin Village housing & shopping area within walking distance of one another in Mannheim suburb of Kaefertal. Spinelli Barracks 10 min SE. Coleman Barracks off Autobahn A6 at Sandhofen. Turley Barracks approx 5 mi from center of Mannheim. Thomas Jefferson Village housing in city of Worms, 30-45 min away. Friedsrichfeld depot off Autobahn A565 toward Heidelberg. *Locality:* Baden-Württemberg.
MAJOR UNITS: 293rd Base Support Bn; Benjamin Franklin Village Family Housing; Coleman Barracks; Dannenfels Communication Station; De La Police Kaserne; Edigheim Beacon Site; Frankenthal; Friedrichsfeld Quartermaster Service Center; Friedrichfeld Storage Area; Funari Barracks; Grunstadt AAFES Facility; Grunstadt Communication Station; Kerzenheim Communication Facility; Lampertheim Training Area; Leistadt Communication Facility Hill 460; Lohnsfeld Communication Station; Mannheim Class III Point; Quirnheim Missile Station; Rheinau Coal Point D-1; Spinelli Barracks; Sullivan Barracks; Taylor Barracks; Taukkunen Barracks; Thomas Jefferson Village Family Housing; Turley Barracks; Weierhof; Worms Quartermaster Area; Worms Repair and Upkeep Area.
Services *Schools:* College courses.

414th Base Support Battalion

997. 414th Base Support Battalion
Unit 20193
APO, AE 09165
DSN 322-1300

Profile
BRANCH: Army.
LOCATION: 11 mi E of Frankfurt am Main. *Locality:* Hessen.
MAJOR UNITS: 104th Area Support Group; 414th Base Support Bn; Pioneer Kaserne; Büdingen Area Support Team; Fliegerhorst Airfield Kaserne; Hanau Army Airfield; 1st Armor Division, 4th Brigade; 1-501st Aviation; 2-501st Aviation; 127th Aviation Support Bn; 3/58th Aviation; 617th Weather Det; 5/7 Air Defense Artillery; 19th Maintenance Co; 18th Corps Support Bn; 16th Corps Support Group; 26th Quartermaster; 27th Transportation Bn; 39th Finance; 55th Postal; 71st Ordnance Co; 135th Communications Squadron, Det; 110th Medical Det (VETS); 13th Medical Det; 133rd Medical Det; 22nd Medi-

cal Det; 709th Military Police Bn; 127th Military Police Co; 560th Military Police Co; 130th Engineer Brigade; 38th Engineer Co; 502nd Engineer Co; 261st Signal Co; 149th Maintenance Co; 521st Maintenance Co; 485th CORPS Support Bn; 1/1 Cavalry; 69th Chemical Co; Argonner Kaserne; Campo Pond Training Area; Cardwell Village Family Housing; New Argonner Family Housing; Pioneer Village Family Housing; Wolfgang Kaserne; Yorkhof Kaserne; Armstrong Barracks; Armstrong Village Family Housing; Büdingen Ammunition Area; Büdingen Army Heliport; Coleman Village Family Housing; Tiergarten Training Area.
BASE HISTORY: 1991, Hanau Military Community redesignated 414th BSB. 1938, Pioneer Kaserne built; German Railroad Recruiting & Training Battalions. 1944-45, damaged by Allied bombardment.
Key Contacts
COMMANDER: Col Glover, 104th ASG, DSN 322-1300.
PUBLIC AFFAIRS: 104th ASG, CMR 470, 011-49-618188-113, DSN 322-113.
Personnel and Expenditures
ACTIVE DUTY PERSONNEL: 700
DEPENDENTS: 7
CIVILIAN PERSONNEL: 785
Services *Commissary:* Yes; *Exchange:* Convenience store; Fast food; Service station; Bank; Credit union; Post office; Cafeteria; PX. *Child Care/Capacities:* Day care center capacity 380; Home day care program. *Medical Facilities:* Hospital; Medical clinic; Dental clinic; Veterinary services. *Recreational Facilities:* Movie theater.

Anderson Barracks

998. Anderson Barracks
410th BSB, Dexheim AST, Unit 24308
APO, AE
06133-69-852, FAX 06133-69-827; DSN 334-5852
E-mail: actubkdast1@email.badkreuznach.army.mil

Profile
BRANCH: Army.
LOCATION: In W-central Germany, in Dexheim; 17 mi from Mainz; 30 mi from Frankfurt IAP; 24 mi from Bad Kreuznach. *Locality:* Rheinland-Pfalz.
MAJOR UNITS: 501st Military Intelligence Bn; 123rd Main Support Bn; 20th Medical Det; 133rd Dental Det; Anderson Barracks; Camp Oppenheim Training Area; Dexheim Family Housing.
BASE HISTORY: Named for TSgt 4c Ameth Anderson, WWII hero.
VISITOR ATTRACTIONS: Nestled in Rhein wine country; Oppenheim & Nierstein historic towns.
Key Contacts
COMMANDER: Dr James J Hearn, Community Management Officer; LTC John Hall, Installation Coordinator.
PUBLIC AFFAIRS: Frau Mair Klein, 410th BSB, ATTN: PAO, 0671-609-7373, DSN 490-7373, DSN FAX 490-7392.
TRANSPORTATION: SFC Turner, DSN 334-5741.

PERSONNEL/COMMUNITY ACTIVITIES: Ms Elaine DurdenHunter, 410th BSB, 06133-69-776, DSN 334-5776.
Personnel and Expenditures
ACTIVE DUTY PERSONNEL: 950
DEPENDENTS: 350
CIVILIAN PERSONNEL: 50
Services
Housing: Family units 166; Duplex units 48; Barracks spaces 850; Leased housing 70. *Temporary Housing:* None. *Commissary:* Yes; *Exchange:* Retail store; Barber shop; Dry cleaners; Food shop; Bank; Furniture store; Laundromat; ATM; Post office; Fast food; Video rentals; Thrift shop; Class VI; Laundry. *Child Care/Capacities:* Day care center capacity 87, 6mos-12yrs; Home day care program; Latch key program; Summer day camp; Before & after school programs. *Schools:* Preschool/Kindergarten; Elementary; College courses. *Base Library:* Yes. *Medical Facilities:* Medical clinic; Dental clinic; Dispensary; Pharmacy; Veterinary services once a month. *Recreational Facilities:* Bowling center; Movie theater 1 day/week; Gym; Tennis courts; Racquetball court; Fitness center/Weight room; Softball field; Football field; Auto shop; Youth center; Picnic area; Playground; Consolidated club.

Augsburg Military Community

999. Augsburg Military Community
AST Augsburg
APO, AE 09178
0821-540-6666; DSN 435-6666
OFFICER-OF-THE-DAY: 0821-540-6166, DSN 435-6166

Profile
BRANCH: Army.
LOCATION: In S Germany, in Augsburg; 43 mi W of Munich; 70 mi S of Nürnberg; 80 mi E of Stuttgart. *Locality:* Bavaria, Swabia.
MAJOR UNITS: 66th Military Intelligence Group; Bad Aibling Station; Bonstetten Radio Relay Facility; Centerville Family Housing; Cramerton Family Housing; Deuringen Training Area; Frasdorf Operations Area; Fryar Circle Family Housing; Gablingen Kaserne; Hohenstadt Radio Relay Station; Lechfeld Training Area; Munich AFN Facility; Sheridan Kaserne; Sullivan Heights Family Housing; Quartermaster Kaserne.
BASE HISTORY: Subordinate to 6th Area Support Group, Stuttgart.
FUTURE CLOSURE/REALIGNMENT: Presently in a draw-down mode. Scheduled for closure Sep 1998.
Key Contacts
COMMANDER: Norman H Marcus.
PUBLIC AFFAIRS: Karin Johnson.
Services
Housing: Family units 190; Duplex units. *Temporary Housing:* Guesthouse units. *Commissary:* Yes; *Exchange:* Retail store; Barber shop; Dry cleaners; Food shop; Bank; Service station; Convenience store; Beauty shop; Credit union. *Child Care/Capacities:* Day care center 6wks-5yrs; Home day care program; Latch key program. *Schools:* Preschool/Kindergarten; Elementary; High school; College courses. *Base Library:* Yes.

Medical Facilities: Medical clinic; Dental clinic; Veterinary services. *Recreational Facilities:* Bowling center; Movie theater; Gym; Recreation center; Golf course; Football field; Auto shop; Craft shop; Enlisted club; Youth center; Consolidated club; Community counseling center; Equipment rental; Video rental; Outdoor recreation center; Community theater.

Babenhausen Area Support Team

1000. Babenhausen Area Support Team
AST
APO, AE 09089
Profile
BRANCH: Army.
LOCATION: See 233rd Base Support Battalion.
MAJOR UNITS: Babenhausen Kaserne; Babenhausen Area Support Team; Aschaffenburg Family Housing; Aschaffenburg Training Area; Babenhausen Family Housing; Münster Ammunition Depot.

Bamberg Military Community

1001. Bamberg Military Community
Warner Barracks
Unit 27535
APO, AE 09139-7535
011-49-951-300-8820; DSN 469-8820
Internet: http://155.155.230.10/OldHome.htm
OFFICER-OF-THE-DAY: Duty Officer, 011-49-951-300-7509, DSN 469-7509
Profile
BRANCH: Army.
SIZE AND LOCATION: 3347 acres. In S-central Germany, N of Nürnberg; approx 2.5 hours driving time to Frankfurt IAP and Munich IAP. *Locality:* Bavaria, Upper Franconia.
MAJOR UNITS: 279th Base Support Bn; Warner Barracks; 1/6 Field Artillery Bn; 82nd Engineer Bn; 201st Forward Support Bn, B Co; 5/2 Air Defense Artillery; 1st Infantry Division Engineer Brigade; 1st Infantry Division, Divarty; 16th Engineer Brigade; 630th Military Police Co; 566th Postal Co; 106th Finance Bn, Det B; 188th General Dispensary; 38th Personnel Services Bn, Det B; 1st Infantry Division Marne Band; 301st Support Group; 317th Maintenance; 71st Ordnance Co; 25th Field Artillery, B Battery; 33rd Field Artillery, A Battery; 793rd Military Police Bn; 71st Combat Support Bn; 30th Movement Control Team; 316th Support (Reserves); 7th Command Support Group; 262nd Military Police Det; 200th Bulk Petroleum Accounting Activity; 240th Quartermaster Supply Co; 345th Support Center (Reserves); Bamberg Airfield; Flynn Family Housing Area; Flynn Training Area; Warner Barracks Family Housing.
BASE HISTORY: 1891, Warner Kaserne, then Lagarde Kaserne, built by Royal Bavarian Government as cavalry garrison. WWI-WWII, almost every branch of German Army stationed. 1928, airfield added. Post WWII, renamed in honor of Medal of Honor recipient Corp Henry F Warner, killed in action in Belgium; HQ for Constabulary command in S Germany. 1970-91, Bamberg designated community. 1991, drawdown of troops begun; redesignated Base Support Battalion under Area Support Group, Nürnberg. 1993, joined 98th Area Support Group; later, 279th Base Support Battalion.
Personnel and Expenditures
ACTIVE DUTY PERSONNEL: 3060; Reserve 46
DEPENDENTS: 3730
CIVILIAN PERSONNEL: 500
Services
Housing: Family units 1500; Unaccompanied officer quarters 17; Unaccompanied enlisted quarters 50; Barracks spaces; Senior NCO units; Junior NCO units. *Temporary Housing:* Guesthouse units; Transient quarters 1. *Commissary:* Yes; *Exchange:* Retail store; Barber shop; Dry cleaners; Food shop; Bank; Service station; Furniture store; Bookstore; Military clothing store; Convenience store; Beauty shop; Laundromat; Credit union; Fast food. *Child Care/Capacities:* Day care center; Home day care program. *Schools:* Preschool/Kindergarten; Elementary; High school; College courses; Education Center. *Base Library:* Yes. *Medical Facilities:* Dental clinic; Dispensary; German city hospital. *Recreational Facilities:* Bowling center; Movie theater; Gym; Recreation center; Golf course; Tennis courts; Racquetball court; Skating rink; Fitness center/Weight room; Softball field; Football field; Auto shop; Craft shop; NCO club; Fishing/Hunting; Youth center; Picnic area; Skeet range; Playground.

Barton Barracks, Ansbach

1002. Barton Barracks, Ansbach
235th BSB, Unit 28614
APO, AE 09177
0981-183-1600; FAX 0981-183-815; DSN 468-1600
OFFICER-OF-THE-DAY: DSN 468-7637, 468-7643
Profile
BRANCH: Army.
LOCATION: In S Germany, in Ansbach off Autobahn 6; Nürnberg/Fürth Community approx 45 min. *Locality:* Bavaria, Middle Franconia.
MAJOR UNITS: 235th Base Support Bn, HQ; 615th Military Police; 55th PSL; Finance Co, Det B; 193rd Military Police Customs; Barton Barracks; Bleidorn Family Housing; Heideneim Radio Relay Site; Shipton Kaserne.
BASE HISTORY: Formerly known as Ansbach Military Community.
Key Contacts
COMMANDER: LTC Chamberlin, 235th BSB, 0981-183-1500, 0981-183-1510, DSN 468-1500, 468-1510.
PUBLIC AFFAIRS: Mrs Frauka E Davis.
PROCUREMENT: Mr Rose, 0781-183-1540, DSN 468-1540.
TRANSPORTATION: Mr Weber.

PERSONNEL/COMMUNITY ACTIVITIES: Ms Esters, 0981-183-1550, DSN 468-1550.
Personnel and Expenditures
ACTIVE DUTY PERSONNEL: 5574
Services
Housing: Family units; Unaccompanied enlisted quarters; Barracks spaces; Dormitory spaces; Senior NCO units. *Temporary Housing:* Guesthouse units. *Commissary:* Yes; *Exchange:* Retail store; Barber shop; Dry cleaners; Food shop; Bank; Furniture store; Bookstore; Military clothing store; Convenience store; Beauty shop; Laundromat; Credit union. *Child Care/Capacities:* Day care center; Home day care program; Summer day camp. *Schools:* Preschool/Kindergarten; Elementary; Intermediate/Junior high; High school. *Base Library:* Yes. *Medical Facilities:* Medical clinic; Dental clinic; Pharmacy. *Recreational Facilities:* Bowling center; Movie theater; Pool (German); Gym; Recreation center; Golf course (German); Tennis courts; Racquetball court; Fitness center/Weight room; Softball field; Football field; Auto shop; Craft shop; Officers club; NCO club; Enlisted club; Youth center; Photo; Ceramics.

Baumholder Military Community, H.D. Smith Barracks

1003. Baumholder Military Community, H.D. Smith Barracks
222d BSB, Unit 23746
APO, AE 09034
DSN 485-1500, DSN FAX 485-7415
OFFICER-OF-THE-DAY: 06783-6-7533, DSN 485-7533
Profile
BRANCH: Army.
SIZE AND LOCATION: 25,000 acres. 35 mi NW of Kaiserlautern; Autobahn A62 exit at Freisen, L348 to Baumholder; nearby towns Birkenfeld and Idar-Oberstein, approx 10 mi; Frankfurt IAP 2.5 hours driving distance. *Locality:* Rhineland-Pfalz.
MAJOR UNITS: 222nd Base Support Bn; 1st Armored Division Artillery; 2nd Brigade, 40th Engineer Combat Bn; 8th Finance Support; 29th Medical Det; 64th Medical Det (Veterinary); 464th Medical Det (Dental); 90th Postal (2nd PLT); 92nd Military Police Co; 90th Personnel Service Bn; 47th Support Bn; 102nd Signal Bn; Baumholder Airfield; Baumholder Family Housing; Baumholder Hospital; Baumholder Quartermaster Area; Birkenfeld Housing Facility; Idar Oberstein Family Housing; Nahbollenbach Storage Area; Neubrücke Hospital; Smith Barracks; Strassburg Kaserne; Wetzel Family Housing; Wetzel Kaserne.
BASE HISTORY: 1937, post constructed as part of German rearmament. 1945, surrendered to American forces. 1945-51, occupied by French units. H.D. Smith Barracks, commonly called Baumholder, currently home for largest concentration of combat soldiers outside US. Consists of main post and subcommunity of Strassburg (40th Engineers). Baumholder also parent installation for several remote sites.

VISITOR ATTRACTIONS: 1st Armored Division Museum

Key Contacts

COMMANDER: LTC Peter F Porcelli, Box 3, 06783-6-1500, DSN 485-1600.

PUBLIC AFFAIRS: Madeleine Dwoiakowski, Box 32, 06783-6-1600, DSN 485-1600.

PROCUREMENT: Ronnie Crews, Box 17, 06783-6-7209, DSN 484-7209.

TRANSPORTATION: Herbert Wobito, Box 17, 06783-6-7193, DSN 485-7193.

PERSONNEL/COMMUNITY ACTIVITIES: Mike Duday, Box 18, 06783-6-1550, DSN 485-1550.

Personnel and Expenditures

ACTIVE DUTY PERSONNEL: 5526

DEPENDENTS: 5444

CIVILIAN PERSONNEL: 725

MILITARY PAYROLL EXPENDITURE: $28.9 mil

CONTRACT EXPENDITURE: $14.1 mil

Services

Housing: Unaccompanied officer quarters 106; Barracks spaces 4557; Senior NCO units 78. *Temporary Housing:* VIP units 2; Guesthouse units 25; Apartment units 3. *Commissary:* Yes; *Exchange:* Retail store; Barber shop; Dry cleaners; Food shop; Florist; Bank; Service station; Bakery; Bookstore; Military clothing store; Convenience store; Beauty shop; Laundromat; Credit union. *Child Care/Capacities:* Day care center capacity 350, 6wks-12yrs; Home day care program; Latch key program; Summer day camp; Supplemental programs & services; Short term on-site care; Sure start/head start. *Schools:* Preschool/Kindergarten; Elementary; Intermediate/Junior high; High school; College courses; Univ of Maryland. *Base Library:* Yes. *Medical Facilities:* Dental clinic; Dispensary; Pharmacy; Veterinary services; 2nd General Hospital, Landstuhl, 40 min away. *Recreational Facilities:* Bowling center; Movie theater; Pool; Gym; Recreation center; Golf course; Tennis courts; Racquetball court; Fitness center/Weight room; Softball field; Football field; Auto shop; Craft shop; Officers club; NCO club; Camping; Fishing/Hunting; Youth center; Picnic area; Skeet range; Playground; Consolidated club; Rod & Gun club; Major sports; Video club.

Bitburg Annex

1004. Bitburg Annex

APO, AE 09137

DSN 452-1110 (Spangdahlem AB)

Profile

BRANCH: Air Force.

SIZE AND LOCATION: 1735 acres. W-central Germany; 25 mi from Luxembourg border; adj to SE section of Bitburg; 135 mi W of Rhein-Main AB. *Locality:* Rhineland-Pfalz.

MAJOR UNITS: 52nd Fighter Wing (Support); 52nd Medical Group.

BASE HISTORY: 1950, 36th Fighter Wing. 1957, 525th Fighter-Interceptor Squadron host. 1958, Wing redesignated Tactical Fighter Wing. 1959, assigned to 17th Air Force. 1991, redesignated back to 36th Fighter Wing. 1992, Wing reorganized. 1994, Bitburg Air Base closed; Annex remained open without air operations.

Services

Housing: Family units 1200; Dormitory spaces.

Temporary Housing: VIP units 2; VOQ units 32; VAQ units 190. *Commissary:* Yes; *Exchange:* Barber shop; Dry cleaners; Food shop; Bank; Service station; Furniture shop; Bakery; Bookstore; Military clothing store; Convenience store; Beauty shop; Laundromat; Credit union; Class VI; Thrift shop; BX. *Schools:* High school. *Base Library:* Yes. *Medical Facilities:* Hospital. *Recreational Facilities:* Bowling center; Movie theater; Gym; Recreation center; Tennis courts; Racquetball court; Fitness center/Weight room; Softball field; Football field; Auto shop; Craft shop; Officers club; NCO club; Youth center; Skeet range; Playground; Rod & Gun club.

Campbell Barracks

1005. Campbell Barracks

OCHAP, Unit 29351

APO, AE 09014

Profile

BRANCH: Army.

LOCATION: Take A-5 from Frankfurt IAP to A656, Exit 656 to Scholss, turn right at Bahnof, turn right on to Romer Strasse, Barracks on left.

MAJOR UNITS: US Army Europe (USAREUR), HQ; 7th Army, HQ; USAREUR Office of the Chaplain.

Key Contacts

COMMANDER: Chaplain (Col) David Hicks, USAREUR Chaplain, hicksd@hq.hqusareur. army.mil.

PUBLIC AFFAIRS: USAREUR 011-49-6221-57-1110, DSN 370-1110.

Coleman Barracks

1006. Coleman Barracks

293rd BSB

APO, AE 09025

011-49-0621-779-5198; DSN 382-5198, 382-5397

Profile

BRANCH: Army.

LOCATION: See Mannheim Military Community. *Locality:* Baden-Württemberg.

MAJOR UNITS: 70th Transportation Bn; European Confinement Facility; 2nd Bn, 502nd Aviation Regiment; 617th Air Force ASOS; 18th Military Brigade; 28th Transportation Bn; 9th Military Police Det; 560th Military Police Co; Coleman Army Airfield.

BASE HISTORY: 1938-39, Fliegerhorst Kaserne airfield for fighters & bombers. After WWII, named for LTC Wilson D Coleman, recipient of Distinguished Service Cross. One of busiest airfields, USAREUR.

Services *Exchange:* Barber shop; Food shop; Bank; Military clothing store; Convenience store; Class VI; Tailor/Alterations. *Schools:* College courses. *Base Library:* Yes. *Medical Facilities:* Medical clinic; Dental clinic. *Recreational Facilities:* Bowling center; Movie theater; Gym; Recreation center; Racquetball court; Fitness center/Weight room; NCO club; Enlisted club; Photo lab; Aero club.

Friedberg Area Support Team

1007. Friedberg Area Support Team

APO, AE 09074

011-49-6031-81-3528; DSN 324-3528; DSN FAX 324-3156

Profile

BRANCH: Army.

LOCATION: Near Usa River, approx 15 mi N of Frankfurt. *Locality:* Hesse.

MAJOR UNITS: 1st Armored Brigade; Ray Barracks; Alvin York Village Family Housing; Friedberg Training and Storage Area; McArthur Place Family Housing; 1st Bn, 37th Armor Division; 2nd Bn, 37th Armor Division; 501st Forward Support Bn; 1st Bn, 36th Infantry Division; 55th Postal Co.

BASE HISTORY: 1900, Ray Barracks built as Wattrum Kaserne; used in WWI & WWII. WWI, housed captured Russian, French, & English officers. 1945, occupied by US troops; named for 1st Lt Bernard J Ray, Medal of Honor recipient. Elvis Presley served at Ray.

Key Contacts

COMMANDER: 011-49-6031-81-3801, DSN 324-3801.

Personnel and Expenditures

ACTIVE DUTY PERSONNEL: 3500

DEPENDENTS: 2200

CIVILIAN PERSONNEL: 45

Services *Commissary:* Yes; *Exchange:* Convenience store; Service station; Bank; Credit union; Fast food; PX. *Recreational Facilities:* Movie theater; Youth center.

Funari Barracks

1008. Funari Barracks

APO, AE 09056

011-49-621-730-4000; DSN 380-4000

Internet: http://www.mannheim.army.mil/mainpg.htm

Profile

BRANCH: Army.

LOCATION: In W-central Germany, 20 mi from Worms; 10 mi from Heidelberg. *Locality:* Rhineland-Pfalz.

MAJOR UNITS: Mannheim Military Community; 5th Signal Command.

BASE HISTORY: 1897, Kaserne 118 built. During WWII, renamed Kemmel Kaserne. Following WWII, renamed Foch Kaserne. 1956 renamed for SSgt Ernest Taukkunen, recipient of Distinguished Service Cross. 1967-74, home of US Theater Army Support Command, Europe. 1974, home of US Army Strategic Communications Command, Europe, later redesignated HQ, 5th Signal Command, subordinate of US Army Information Systems Command, Ft Huachuca, AZ.

Key Contacts

COMMANDER: Brig Gen Robert L Nabors.

PUBLIC AFFAIRS: 011-49-621-730-5024; DSN 380-5024.

Services *Exchange:* Barber shop. *Schools:* College courses. *Base Library:* Yes. *Recreational Facilities:* Bowling center; Movie theater; Auto shop; Craft shop; NCO club; Enlisted club; Photo lab; Performing arts center; USO Center.

Germersheim Sub-Community

1009. Germersheim Sub-Community

APO, AE 09095
07274-58-508, 58-617; FAX 07274-58-844;
DSN 378-3508, 378-3617

Profile

BRANCH: Army.

SIZE AND LOCATION: 450 acres. On W bank of Rhine River, between Karlsruhe (22 mi) & Heidelberg (25 mi). *Locality:* Baden-Württemberg.

MAJOR UNITS: 411th Base Support Bn; Germersheim Army Depot; Germersheim Rail Transportation Office Facility; Gerszewski Barracks.

BASE HISTORY: 1951, Ordnance Vehicle Park established for handling WWII surplus vehicles; site of German training ground. 1951-82, organization & command changes; mission remained to receive, store, maintain, & issue major items of equipment & general supplies. 1982, General Support Center Germersheim. 1990, Germersheim Area Support Team (former Germersheim Military Sub-Community) transferred to 291st Base Support Battalion, Karlsruhe; redesignated Germersheim Sub-Community.

Personnel and Expenditures

ACTIVE DUTY PERSONNEL: 25
DEPENDENTS: 40
CIVILIAN PERSONNEL: 500

Services *Exchange:* Retail store; Barber shop; Bank. *Child Care/Capacities:* Day care in Karlsruhe. *Schools:* Schools in Karlsruhe. *Base Library:* Yes. *Medical Facilities:* Located in Karlsruhe or Heidelberg. *Recreational Facilities:* Bowling center; Gym; Racquetball court; Craft shop; NCO club.

Giebelstadt Army Airfield

1010. Giebelstadt Army Airfield

GAAF; Giebelstadt AAF
CMR 408
APO, AE 09182-9998
011-49-9334-8114; DSN 352-7323, 352-7454
OFFICER-OF-THE-DAY: 011-49-9-334-87296, DSN 352-7296

Profile

BRANCH: Army.

SIZE AND LOCATION: 633 acres. In S-central Germany; part of community of Giebelstadt; at Autobahn B-19 between Würzburg (12.5 mi) and Bad Mergentheim (22 mi); airport at Frankfurt (80 mi); nearest Autobahn approach 10 mi N. *Locality:* Bavaria, Lower Franconia.

MAJOR UNITS: 159th Aviation Regiment, 5th Bn, A Co; 159th Aviation Regiment, 6th Bn, C Co; Embrey-Riddle Aeronautical University, Giebelstadt; 7th Weather Station, Det 10; 886th Communications Squadron, OL-C.

BASE HISTORY: 1936, airfield built for German Luftwaffe. 1941-45, development of ME-262 jet aircraft. 1945, captured by US 12th Armored Division. 1946-48, used as USAF fighter (P-80) & Air Command bomber base (B-29). 1950-56, aircraft control & warning installation. 1956-58, USAF reconnaissance base (U-2); Capt Gary Powers started flight from here. 1959, German Air Force took over installation. 1976, US Army aviation base.

Key Contacts

COMMANDER: 011-49-9334-8-7441, DSN 352-7441.
PUBLIC AFFAIRS: 011-49-9334-8-7367, DSN 352-7367.

Services

Housing: None. *Temporary Housing:* None. *Exchange:* Retail store; Barber shop; Dry cleaners; Food shop; Florist; Bank; Bookstore; Convenience store; Laundromat. *Child Care/Capacities:* Latch key program; Summer day camp. *Schools:* No on-base schools. *Medical Facilities:* Medical clinic; Dental clinic; Pharmacy. *Recreational Facilities:* Bowling center; Movie theater; Pool; Gym; Tennis courts; Racquetball court; Fitness center/Weight room; Softball field; Football field; Auto shop; Officers club; NCO club; Enlisted club; Youth center; Playground.

Heidelberg Military Community

1011. Heidelberg Military Community

26th ASG, Unit 29237
APO, AE 09102
011-49-6221-57-6860; DSN 370-6494, 370-6860, 370-6050

Profile

BRANCH: Army.

LOCATION: 55 mi S of Frankfurt along Necker River. *Locality:* Baden-Württemberg.

MAJOR UNITS: 26th Area Support Group; 411th Base Support Bn; Campbell Barracks; Edingen Radio Receiver Facility; Germersheim Army Depot; Germersheim Rail Transportation Office Facility; Gerszewski Barracks; Hammond Barracks; Heidelberg AFN Relay Facility; Heidelberg Army Airfield; Heidelberg Community Support Center; Heidelberg Hospital; Kilbourne Kaserne; Königstuhl Radio Relay Station; Mark Twain Village Family Housing; Neureut Kaserne; Oftersheim Small Arms Range; Patton Barracks; Patrick Henry Village Family Housing; Schwetzingen Training Area; Stem Kaserne; Stocksberg Communication Station; Tompkins Barracks; Waldstadt AFN Facility; US Army Europe, HQ; 7th Army, HQ; V Corps, HQ; Allied Land Forces Central Europe, HQ; US Medical Activity, HQ Co; 30th Medical Brigade; 1st Personnel Command; 7th Army Reserve Command Europe; Army Materiel Command Europe; 266th Theater Finance Command; 207th Aviation Co.

BASE HISTORY: Community encompasses over 12 separate installations in & around Heidelberg. Shopping center complex within walking distance of Campbell & Patton Barracks.

Key Contacts

COMMANDER: Col Brown, 26th ASG, DSN 373-1300, 373-1310.
PUBLIC AFFAIRS: 011-49-6221-57-113, DSN 370-113.

Services *Commissary:* Yes; *Exchange:* Convenience store; Fast food; Credit union; Bank; PX. *Recreational Facilities:* Bowling center; Golf course.

Johnson Barracks

1012. Johnson Barracks

71st Corps Support Battalion, Unit 27925
APO, AE 09222
49-0911-700-7517; 700-7384; FAX
49-0911-700-7295; DSN 460-7517, 460-7384

Profile

BRANCH: Army.

SIZE AND LOCATION: 131 acres. In S Germany, approx 30 min SW of Nürnberg; 2 min from Autobahn 73; 10 min from access Autobahns 6 & 9. *Locality:* Bavaria, Middle Franconia.

MAJOR UNITS: 71st Corps Support Bn, Headquarters and Headquarters Det; 240th Quartermaster Supply Co; 317th Maintenance Co; 1st Transportation Co (Medium); 11th Transportation Co (Heavy Equipment Transport); 127th Postal Co.

BASE HISTORY: 1913-14, constructed as quarters for 21st German Infantry Regiment. 1920-34, used as low-income housing. 1933-35, Panzer Abwehr Abteilung 17 moved in and added food service depot. 1945, taken over by US Army, named after Pvt Eldon H Johnson, 15th Infantry, 3rd Infantry Division.

Key Contacts

COMMANDER: LTC Douglas Stephensen.
PUBLIC AFFAIRS: Lt Kevin Terrell; 0911-700-7526, DSN 460-7526.
PROCUREMENT: Lt Rick Jones; 0911-700-7518, DSN 460-7518.
TRANSPORTATION: Lt William Duda; 0911-700-7518, 700-7501, DSN 460-7518, 460-7501.
PERSONNEL/COMMUNITY ACTIVITIES: Daryll Clay; 416th BSB, Unit 27933, APO AE 09222, 0911-96-0023.

Personnel and Expenditures

ACTIVE DUTY PERSONNEL: 450
CIVILIAN PERSONNEL: 117

Services

Housing: Barracks spaces 187. *Temporary Housing:* Dormitory units 5. *Exchange:* Barber shop; Automated teller machine. *Child Care/Capacities:* Kalb Day Care 5 min drive away. *Schools:* Schools in Kalb. *Medical Facilities:* No medical facilities; Medical treatment facility 8 min from installation. *Recreational Facilities:* Bowling center; Pool; Recreation center; Tennis courts; Racquetball court; Fitness center/Weight room; Softball field.

Kaiserslautern Military Community

1013. Kaiserslautern Military Community
ATTN: AEUSG-K-ACS, Unit 23152
APO, AE 09227-5000
011-49-0631-536-1110; DSN 483-1110
Internet: http://147.35.210.53/Kmc/install.htm
Profile
BRANCH: Army; Air Force.
SIZE AND LOCATION: 300 acres. In SW Germany; 80 mi SW of Frankfurt. *Locality:* Rhineland-Pfalz.
MAJOR UNITS: 415th Base Support Bn; 21st Theater Army Area Command (TAACOM); 29th Area Support Group; Breitenwald Training Area; Kaiserslautern East Community Facility; Daenner Kaserne; Eselsfürth Quartermaster Facility; Hill 365 Radio Relay Facility; Kaiserslautern Army Depot; Kaiserslautern Equipment Support Center; Kleber Kaserne; Landstuhl Hospital; Miesau Ammunition Depot; Panzer Kaserne; Pulaski Barracks; Ramstein Air Base; Rhine Ordnance Barracks; Sambach AFN Facility; Vogelweh Cantonment; Kapaun Air Station.
BASE HISTORY: Largest overseas military community. Combined Army-Air Force community.
Key Contacts
COMMANDER: LTC Alejandro L Champin, 415th BSB.
Personnel and Expenditures
ACTIVE DUTY PERSONNEL: 4500
DEPENDENTS: 4800
CIVILIAN PERSONNEL: 2500
Services
Housing: Family units 481; One main housing office responsible for 8 housing areas at Ramstein, Landstuhl, Vogelweh, & Sembach. *Commissary:* Yes; *Exchange:* Barber shop; Beauty shop; Credit union; Bank; Florist; Service station; Four seasons; Laundry; Dry cleaners; Photo store; Optical store; Furniture store; Food shop; Fast food; Bakery; Convenience store; Military clothing store; Class VI; Video rentals; Post office; Shoe repair; Computer store; Tailor/Alterations; Retail store. *Child Care/Capacities:* Day care center; Home day care program; Child development center. *Schools:* Preschool/Kindergarten; Elementary; Intermediate/Junior high; High school; College courses. *Base Library:* Yes. *Medical Facilities:* Medical clinic; Dental clinic; Dispensary; Pharmacy; Veterinary services; Hospital at Landstuhl. *Recreational Facilities:* Bowling center; Movie theater; Pool; Gym; Recreation center; Golf course; Tennis courts; Racquetball court; Fitness center/Weight room; Softball field; Football field; Auto shop; Craft shop; Officers club; NCO club; Enlisted club; Youth center; Skeet range; Rod & Gun club; Community club; Consolidated club; All ranks club; Outdoor recreation; Roller rink.

Kapaun Air Station

1014. Kapaun Air Station
APO, AE 09021
Profile
BRANCH: Army.

LOCATION: 7 mi from Ramstein AB; SW part of Germany. *Locality:* Rheinland-Pfalz.
MAJOR UNITS: Kapaun Air Station; 3rd Space Communications Squadron.
Key Contacts
COMMANDER: LTC Bradley D Duty, 3rd SCS.
Services
Housing: Facilities available at Vogelweh military housing area. *Commissary:* Yes; *Exchange:* Service station; Post office. *Schools:* College courses. *Recreational Facilities:* Bowling center.

Katterbach Air Field/ Kaserne

1015. Katterbach Air Field/Kaserne
4th Avn Bd
APO, AE 09250
0981-183-1600; FAX 0981-183-815; DSN 468-1600
Profile
BRANCH: Army.
LOCATION: In S Germany, 2.5 mi outside of Ansbach on B14. *Locality:* Bavaria, Middle Franconia.
MAJOR UNITS: 4th Aviation Brigade; 3rd Infantry Division; 886th Communications Squadron, OL-E.
Services
Housing: Family units; Unaccompanied enlisted quarters; Barracks spaces; Dormitory spaces; Senior NCO units. *Commissary:* Yes; *Exchange:* Retail store; Barber shop; Dry cleaners; Food shop; Bank; Furniture store; Bookstore; Military clothing store; Convenience store; Beauty shop; Laundromat; Credit union; Tailor shop; Optical shop; Fast food; Four seasons. *Child Care/Capacities:* Day care center; Home day care program; Summer day camp. *Schools:* Preschool/Kindergarten; Elementary; Intermediate/Junior high; High school. *Base Library:* Yes. *Medical Facilities:* Medical clinic; Dental clinic; Pharmacy. *Recreational Facilities:* Bowling center; Movie theater; Gym; Recreation center; Tennis courts; Racquetball court; Fitness center/Weight room; Softball field; Football field; Auto shop; Craft shop; Officers club; NCO club; Enlisted club; Youth center.

Kisling NCO Academy

1016. Kisling NCO Academy
Unit 3345, Box 570
APO, AE 09094-3345
Internet: http://www.usafe.af.mil/bases/ramstein/kncoa/right.htm
Profile
BRANCH: Air Force.
LOCATION: On Kapaun Air Station, Kaiserslautern Military Community; approx 6 mi from Ramstein AB; just off German Hwy B-40. *Locality:* Vogelweh.
MAJOR UNITS: NCO Academy, Kisling.
BASE HISTORY: 1976, Command Leadership & Management Center expanded into USAFE NCO Academy. 1978, accredited by Southern Association of Colleges & Schools. 1986, renamed in honor of CMSgt Richard D Kisling.

Key Contacts
COMMANDER: CMSgt Vickie C Mauldin, Commandant.
PUBLIC AFFAIRS: MSgt Steve R Owens, Information Management.
Services
Housing: Dormitory spaces. *Exchange:* Convenience store. *Base Library:* Yes.

Kitzingen Military Community

1017. Kitzingen Military Community
417th BSB, Unit 26137
APO, AE 09031
Community Manager 011-49-09321-702-400, DSN 355-2400; Harvey, 011-49-09321-305-509, DSN 355-8509; Larson, 011-49-09321-702-377, DSN 355-2377
Internet: http://www.per.hqusareur.army.mil/odcsper/cfsd/kitzingen/install.htm
Profile
BRANCH: Army.
SIZE AND LOCATION: 644,940 acres (including local training area). In SE Germany, 94 mi E of Frankfurt, approx 8 mi from intersection of Autobahn 3 and Autobahn 7; overlooking town of Kitzingen. *Locality:* Bavaria, Lower Franconia.
MAJOR UNITS: Harvey Barracks; Kitzingen Family Housing; Kitzingen Training Areas; Larson Barracks; Schwanberg Defense Communication Site; 417th Base Support Bn; 147th Maintenance Co; 38th Personnel Services Bn, Det A; 3rd Air Defense Artillery, 4th Bn; 121st Signal Bn; 17th Signal Bn; 42nd Medical Co; 701st MSB; 12th Chemical Co; 212th Military Police Co.
BASE HISTORY: Larson Barracks: 1938, opened as German air defense site (Flak Kaserne). 1945, turned over to US. 1945-47, camp for displaced persons. 1947-52, collection point for German Army trucks to be overhauled. 1962, renamed in honor of Capt Stanley E Larson, awarded distinguished service cross for bravery, Anzio, Italy. Harvey Barracks: 1917, built as training school for pilots. 1933, airfield; trained civilian personnel for Luftwaffe; dive bomber squadrons & pursuit pilots trained; first jets stationed. 1947-49, called Kitzingen Training Center. 1951, renamed for Capt James R Harvey, killed in Normandy invasion.
VISITOR ATTRACTIONS: Larson golf course; "I Strike Gardens" unique soldier-donated park featuring historic combat vehicles; dedicated to principles of noncommissioned officer corps.
Key Contacts
COMMANDER: 417th BSB, 011-49-09321-305-1500, DSN 355-1500.
Personnel and Expenditures
ACTIVE DUTY PERSONNEL: 3660
DEPENDENTS: 3860
CIVILIAN PERSONNEL: 200
Services
Housing: Family units 683; Barracks spaces 1509; Senior NCO units 334; Junior NCO units 99. *Temporary Housing:* Lodge units Woodland Inn. *Commissary:* Yes; *Exchange:* Retail store; Barber shop; Dry cleaners; Bank; Service sta-

tion; Bookstore; Military clothing store; Convenience store; Beauty shop; Laundromat; Fast food; Tailor/Alterations; Pick-Up Point service store; PX. *Child Care/Capacities:* Day care center capacity 122; Home day care program; Latch key program; Summer day camp. *Schools:* Elementary; College courses. *Base Library:* Yes. *Medical Facilities:* Medical clinic; Dental clinic; Pharmacy; Hospital near Leighton Barracks. *Recreational Facilities:* Bowling center; Movie theater; Pool; Gym; Golf course; Tennis courts; Racquetball court; Fitness center/Weight room; Softball field; Auto shop; Youth center; Playground; All grades community club.

Kleber Kaserne

1018. Kleber Kaserne
37 TRANSCOM
APO, AE 09067
E-mail: alexandr%37trancom@taacom.kaiserslautern.army.mil Internet:http://147.35.202.56/37trans/37home.htm
Profile
BRANCH: Army.
LOCATION: See Kaiserslautern Military Community.
MAJOR UNITS: 37th Transportation Command; 6966th Transportation TTT.
BASE HISTORY: Former French Kaserne, named after Napoleonic Era French General Kleber.
VISITOR ATTRACTIONS: 37th Transportation Command Truck Museum
Key Contacts
COMMANDER: Col Wolf.

Kleber Kaserne (Kaiserslautern Law Center)

1019. Kleber Kaserne (Kaiserslautern Law Center)
Bldg 3212
APO, AE 09263
011-49-0631-411-8858; DSN 483-8858, 483-8860
E-mail: aerja-lc@server.kaiserslautern.army.mil Internet:http://147.35.210.53/Aerja/klc.htm
Profile
BRANCH: Army.
MAJOR UNITS: Kaiserslautern Law Center.
Key Contacts
COMMANDER: Maj Alan Cook, Law Center Judge Advocate.

Landstuhl Regional Medical Center

1020. Landstuhl Regional Medical Center
LRMC
Kirchberg
Landstuhl,
Mailing Address
CMR 402 09180

49-6371-86-8105; FAX 0049-6371-86-8585; DSN 486-7181; DSN FAX 486-8829
Internet: http://www.lrmc.amedd.army.mil
OFFICER-OF-THE-DAY: 0049-6371-86-8107, DSN 486-8107
Profile
BRANCH: Air Force; Army.
SIZE AND LOCATION: 74 acres. In W-central Germany, approx 90 mi S of Frankfurt; 5 mi from Kaiserslautern; 45 mi N of French border; 3 mi S of Ramstein AB. *Locality:* Rhineland-Pfalz.
MAJOR UNITS: CHPPM; 2336th Medical Co; 181st Signal Bn, DCS Landstuhl; C Co-1st SATCON; 464th Medical Co; Dental Command, Europe; Regional Medical Command, Europe; 18th Aeromedical Staging Facility.
BASE HISTORY: Some buildings on site of former Hitler Schule. 1951, took operational control of local hospital; construction began for American-run hospital. 1952, area of Kirchberg Kaserne designated Wilson Barracks, after Cpl Alfred Wilson, medic killed in WWII. 1953, hospital dedicated under 320th General Hospital. 1954, 2nd General Hospital activated. 1980, treated Marines injured in aborted rescue of American hostages in Iran. 1983, treated Marines injured in Lebanon bombing. 1986, treated soldiers injured in Berlin disco bombing. 1988, treated injuries of Ramstein Air Show disaster. 1990s, repatriation center for casualties of Operations Desert Shield & Desert Storm, Rwanda, & Balkan region. 1994, 2nd General Hospital deactivated and renamed LRMC. Largest American-run medical center outside USA. Provides primary care, hospitalization, & treatment for European Theater.
VISITOR ATTRACTIONS: Medieval Castle.
Key Contacts
COMMANDER: Brig Gen Kevin C Kiley, Post Commander, DSN 486-8105, DSN FAX 486-8585.
PUBLIC AFFAIRS: Marie L Shaw, LARMC, CMR 402, Box 1696, 0049-6371-86-8144, DSN 486-7181, DSN FAX 486-8829, MarieShaw@smtplink.lrmc.amedd.army.mil.
PROCUREMENT: Col Kaufmann, 0049-6371-86-7304, DSN 486-7304.
Personnel and Expenditures
ACTIVE DUTY PERSONNEL: 1500
DEPENDENTS: 1700
CIVILIAN PERSONNEL: 350
MILITARY PAYROLL EXPENDITURE: $40 mil
CONTRACT EXPENDITURE: $25 mil
Services
Housing: Family units 250; Barracks spaces 300; Junior NCO units 50. *Temporary Housing:* None. *Exchange:* Barber shop; Dry cleaners; Florist; Bank; Bookstore; Convenience store; Beauty shop; Laundromat; Video rentals; Thrift shop; Class VI; Tailor/Alterations. *Child Care/Capacities:* Day care center capacity 72, 6wks-12yrs; Home day care program. *Schools:* Preschool/Kindergarten; Elementary; Intermediate/Junior high. *Base Library:* Yes. *Medical Facilities:* Hospital 180 beds, expandable to 500; Dental clinic. *Recreational Facilities:* Bowling center; Gym; Tennis courts; Racquetball court; Fitness center/Weight room; Softball field; Football field; Auto shop; Youth center; Picnic area; Playground.

Oberammergau

1021. NATO School (SHAPE)
Am Rainenbichl 54
Oberammergau, 82487
Mailing Address
Unit 24503
APO AE, 09172-4251
08822-6051, ext 350, 321; FAX 088822-7368; DSN 440-2802
E-mail: lewis@natoschool-shape.de Internet: http://www.natoschool-shape.de
Profile
BRANCH: Joint Service Installation.
LOCATION: In S Germany, in Oberammergau, 42 mi SSW of Munich, 12 mi N of Garmisch. *Locality:* Bavaria, Upper Bavaria.
BASE HISTORY: 1953, began as Special Weapons Branch of US Army School. 1966, redesignated NATO Weapons Systems Department under control of Supreme Allied Commander Europe. 1973, became NATO Weapons System School and assigned to US European Command as joint service activity. 1975, received present name. Mission: training military and civilian personnel who serve the Atlantic Alliance through 29 courses with 5500 students each year.
Key Contacts
COMMANDER: Col Lloyd W Buchanan, Jr, buchanan@natoschool-shape.de.
PUBLIC AFFAIRS: Capt James C Lewis.
Personnel and Expenditures
ACTIVE DUTY PERSONNEL: 103 (US civilian & military)
Services *Exchange:* Convenience store; Video rentals. *Child Care/Capacities:* No day care facilities. *Schools:* No on-base schools. *Base Library:* Yes. *Medical Facilities:* No medical facilities. *Recreational Facilities:* Recreation center.

Patton Barracks

1022. Patton Barracks
APO, AE 09102
Profile
BRANCH: Army.
LOCATION: See Heidelberg Military Community.
MAJOR UNITS: 26th Area Support Group; 411th Base Support Bn; Heidelberg Education Center.
Key Contacts
PUBLIC AFFAIRS: 26th ASG, Unit 29237, 011-49-6221-57-113, DSN 370-113; Education Center, 011-49-6221-176176, DSN 373-6176, DSN FAX 373-6632.

Ramstein Air Base

1023. Ramstein Air Base
Unit 3325
APO, AE 09094
DSN 480-1110
Internet: http://www.usafe.af.mil/bases/ramstein/ramstein.htm
Profile
BRANCH: Air Force.

LOCATION: Part of Kaiserslautern Military Community (KMC); 7.5 mi W of Kaiserslautern; 1.5 mi E of Ramstein; 2 mi W of Landstuhl; 85 mi SW of Rhein-Main AB. *Locality:* Rhineland-Pfalz.

MAJOR UNITS: 86th Airlift Wing; 86th Services Squadron; 37th Airlift Squadron; Staff Judge Advocate, Ramstein; 86th Security Forces Squadron; 86th Supply Squadron; 86th Medical Group; 86th Operations Squadron; 86th Mission Support Squadron; Area Defense Counsel, Ramstein; NCO Academy, Ramstein; Airman Leadership School, Ramstein; 86th Maintenance Squadron; Kapaun Air Station; Einsiedlerhof Air Station; Sembach Annex; Vogelweh Military Complex; USAF Europe, HQ; Allied Air Forces Central Europe (NATO HQ); Air Mobility Command, Ramstein; Air Education and Training Command, Ramstein; 76th Airlift Squadron; 621st Air Mobility Support Group; 623rd Air Mobility Support Squadron; 1st Combat Communications Squadron; 24th Air Operations Squadron; 32nd Air Operations Group; Air Operations Squadron, Ramstein; C2 Systems Flight; HQ USAFE/CSS; HQ USAFE/DP; HQ USAFE/LG; Intelligence Systems Flight; USAFE Command Surgeon; USAFE Contracting Squadron.

BASE HISTORY: 1994, changed from fighter/airlift mission to airlift. Largest NATO air base in Europe.

Key Contacts

COMMANDER: Brig Gen John W Brooks, 86th AW & Kaiserslautern Military Community commander.

PUBLIC AFFAIRS: Unit 3050, Box 120, APO AE 09094-0120, 011-49-6371-47-6559, DSN 480-6559, usafepai@usafe25.ramstein.af.mil.

PERSONNEL/COMMUNITY ACTIVITIES: Col Doyle Brown.

Personnel and Expenditures

ACTIVE DUTY PERSONNEL: 8979
DEPENDENTS: 11,000
CIVILIAN PERSONNEL: 1172

Services

Housing: Family units 770; Unaccompanied officer quarters 1158; Unaccompanied enlisted quarters 4740; Dormitory spaces 2000; Senior NCO units 660. *Temporary Housing:* VOQ units 320; VAQ units 446; Unaccompanied officer/Enlisted quarters 117; Transient quarters Prime Kinght facility. *Commissary:* Yes; *Exchange:* Retail store; Barber shop; Bank; Service station; Military clothing store; Convenience store; Beauty shop; Credit union; Optical store; Fast food; Bakery; ATM; Furniture store; Florist; Food shop. *Child Care/Capacities:* Day care center 6wks-6yrs. *Schools:* Preschool/Kindergarten; Elementary; Intermediate/Junior high; High school; College courses. *Base Library:* Yes. *Medical Facilities:* Medical clinic; Dental clinic; Landstuhl Regional Medical Center nearby. *Recreational Facilities:* Bowling center; Movie theater; Gym; Recreation center; Golf course; Craft shop; Officers club; Enlisted club; Youth center; Photo club; ITT; USO; Community activities center.

Ray Barracks

1024. Ray Barracks

Unit 21105
APO, AE 09074
011-49-6031-81-3801; DSN 324-3801
Profile
BRANCH: Army.
LOCATION: Friedberg, Germany. *Locality:* Hessen.
MAJOR UNITS: 414th Base Support Bn; 1st Brigade, 37th Armor Division; 2nd Brigade, 37th Armor Division; 501st Forward Support Bn; 1st Bn, 36th Infantry; 55th PSB, Det C; 55th Postal Co.
Key Contacts
COMMANDER: DSN 324-3801.
Services
Housing: Barracks spaces. *Medical Facilities:* Dental clinic. *Recreational Facilities:* Bowling center.

Rhein-Main Air Base

1025. Rhein-Main Air Base

Unit 7420, Box 130
APO, AE 09097-0130
49-069-699-1110; FAX 49-069-699-6893; DSN 330-1110
Internet: http://mobility.ramstein.af.mil/~621AMSG/c2/rhein_main.htm
Profile
BRANCH: Air Force.
SIZE AND LOCATION: 970 acres. In S-central Germany, 5 mi S of Frankfurt; adj to Frankfurt IAP; shares civilian runways. *Locality:* Hessen.
MAJOR UNITS: 469th Air Base Group (USAFE); 37th Airlift Squadron; 362nd Airlift Group; On-Site Inspection Agency Europe; Army 21st Replacement Bn; Defense Courier Service; 626th Air Mobility Support Squadron; 886th Communications Squadron, OL-F.
BASE HISTORY: 1936, Rhein-Main Airport began operations. Pre-WWII, base of operations for Graf Zeppelin & Hindenburg. WWII, Luftwaffe base in 1940 & 1944-45. 1948, supported Berlin Airlift. 1975-92, only Military Airlift Command base in Europe. 1992, returned to US Air Force Europe base. 1980-90s, point of return for released international hostages, evacuees; staging base for humanitarian airlift operations. 1992, home for Operation Provide Hope, relief effort to Commonwealth of Independent States & Operation Provide Promise in Bosnia-Herzegovina. 1993, 435th Airlift Wing placed under USAFE, Ramstein AB, Germany. Mission: contingency support moving cargo, equipment, & personnel throughout Europe. Gateway to Europe via commercial contract aircraft.
VISITOR ATTRACTIONS: Berlin Airlift Memorial.
Services
Housing: Family units; Unaccompanied officer quarters; Unaccompanied enlisted quarters; BAQ units; Dormitory spaces. *Temporary Housing:* VOQ units; VAQ units; Transient quarters; *Commissary:* Yes; *Exchange:* Retail store; Barber shop; Dry cleaners; Food shop; Florist;

Bank; Service station; Bakery; Bookstore; Military clothing store; Convenience store; Beauty shop; Laundromat; Credit union; Fast food; Four seasons; Class VI; *Child Care/Capacities:* Day care center; Home day care program. *Schools:* Preschool/Kindergarten; Elementary; Intermediate/Junior high; College courses. *Base Library:* Yes. *Medical Facilities:* Medical clinic; Dental clinic; Pharmacy. *Recreational Facilities:* Bowling center; Movie theater; Gym; Recreation center; Tennis courts; Racquetball court; Skating rink; Fitness center/Weight room; Softball field; Football field; Auto shop; Craft shop; Officers club; NCO club; Camping; Enlisted club; Youth center; Picnic area; Skeet range; Playground; Rod & gun club; Sports center.

Rheinau

1026. Army Postal Group Europe

Unit 29301
APO, AE
Rheinau, 09186
DSN 379-7837, 379-7643; DSN FAX 379-6365
Profile
BRANCH: Army.
SIZE AND LOCATION: 10 acres. In SW Germany, in city of Rheinau, near Heidelberg. *Locality:* Baden-Württemberg.
MAJOR UNITS: Mail Service Branch Postal Inspection & Audit Division.
Key Contacts
COMMANDER: Postal Battalion Europe, DSN 379-6141, 379-6131.
PUBLIC AFFAIRS: DSN 379-7643, 379-7837.
Personnel and Expenditures
ACTIVE DUTY PERSONNEL: 15
CIVILIAN PERSONNEL: 15

Rose Barracks

1027. Rose Barracks

53rd ASG, Unit 23408
APO, AE 09252
011-49-9662-83-2305; DSN 476-2305
Internet: http://www.grafenwoehr.army.mil/afn/409.htm
Profile
BRANCH: Army.
SIZE AND LOCATION: 2184 acres. In W-central Germany, approx 60 mi SW of Frankfurt IAP & Rhein-Main Air Base; approx 70 mi N of Heidelberg (HQ, USAREUR); approx 100 mi E of French & Luxembourg border. *Locality:* Rheinland-Pfalz.
MAJOR UNITS: 410th Base Support Bn; 7th Combined Arms Training Center; 2nd Bn, 2nd Infantry; 201st Support Bn; 1st Bn, 63rd Artillery Regiment; 2nd Bn, 63rd Artillery Regiment; 94th Engineers Bn; 1st Military Police, 3rd Platoon; 3rd Brigade, 1st Infantry Division; 561st Medical Co; 3rd Bn, 1st Field Artillery Regiment; 529th Ordnance; 3rd Bn, 58th Aviation Regiment; 317th Maintenance; 536th Military Police; 67th Signal Regiment; 535th Engineers; 817th Air Force, Det 1, ASOS; 617th Communications Squadron; Bad Kreuznach Airfield; Bad Kreuznach Family Housing; Bad Kreuznach Hospital; George C Marshall Kaserne; Mörsfeld Stor-

age Point; Rheingrafenstein Training & Storage Area; Rose Barracks.

BASE HISTORY: 1945, US Army took over Hindenburg Kaserne from German Army; French Army relieved Americans, renamed HQ Marshal Foch Kaserne. 1951, 2nd Armored Division took over Kaserne, renamed Maurice Rose Kaserne, in honor of Maj Gen Maurice Rose, WWII hero. 1957-91, home of 8th Infantry Division (Mechanized). 1991, redesignated 1st Armored Division.

Key Contacts

COMMANDER: LTC Lester C Jauron, commander409th@email.grafenwoehr.army. mil.

PUBLIC AFFAIRS: Bill Yankers.

Personnel and Expenditures

ACTIVE DUTY PERSONNEL: 9000 (permanent residents)

Services

Housing: Family units 1050; Unaccompanied officer quarters 52; Unaccompanied enlisted quarters 32; Duplex units 6; Townhouse units 100; Senior NCO units 118; Junior NCO units 132. *Temporary Housing:* VOQ units 3; Guesthouse units 31. *Commissary:* Yes; *Exchange:* Retail store; Barber shop; Dry cleaners; Food shop; Florist; Bank; Bookstore; Military clothing store; Convenience store; Beauty shop; Laundromat; Credit union. *Child Care/Capacities:* Day care center capacity 199, infant-12yrs; Home day care program; Latch key program; Summer day camp; Hourly care spaces. *Schools:* Preschool/ Kindergarten; Elementary; Intermediate/Junior high; High school; College courses. *Base Library:* Yes. *Medical Facilities:* Medical clinic; Dental clinic; Dispensary; Pharmacy; Veterinary services. *Recreational Facilities:* Bowling center; Movie theater; Gym; Tennis courts; Racquetball court; Fitness center/Weight room; Softball field; Football field; Auto shop; Camping; Youth center; Picnic area; Playground; All ranks club.

Rose Barracks, Vilseck

1028. Rose Barracks, Vilseck

HQ 409 BSB, Bldg 305, Unit 28038
APO, AE 09112
0149-966-283-1500; FAX 0149-966-283-2821;
DSN 476-1500, 476-1510; DSN FAX 476-2821
E-mail: commander409th@email.grafenwoehr.
army.mil Internet:http://www.grafenwoehr.
army.mil

Profile

BRANCH: Army.

SIZE AND LOCATION: 2184 acres. Approx 45 mi NE of Nuremberg; 77 mi N of Regensburg; 148 mi N of Munich; approx 197 mi to Heidelberg; 12.5 mi SW of Grafenwöhr Training Area. *Locality:* Sulzbach; Rosenburg.

MAJOR UNITS: 409th Support Bn; 1st Infantry Division, 3rd Brigade; 2nd Bn, 2nd Infantry Division; 1st Bn, 63rd Armor Division; 2nd Bn, 63rd Armor Division; 94th Engineer Bn; 201st Support Bn; 5/29th Ordnance Det; South Camp Vilseck.

BASE HISTORY: 1936-38, camp constructed by German army; WWII training area. 1945, occupied by 90th Infantry Division, 3rd US Army. 1946, assembly point for Polish & Ukrainian displaced persons. 1947-48, proc-

essing station for Jewish displaced persons & German refugees from Russian occupied territories. 1949, made Constabulary Tank Training Center. 1950, redesignated European Command Tank Training Center, later 7th Army Tank Training Center. 1952, South Camp designated Rose Barracks, honoring Maj Gen Maurice Rose, WWII Commander of 3rd Armored Division. 1971, Combined Arms School redesignated 7th Army Combined Arms Training Center. 1992, inactivation of Combined Arms Training Center & activation of 281st Base Support Battalion. Grafenwöhr, Vilseck & Hohenfels make up 100th ASG with 409th BSB covering Vilseck & Grafenwöhr and 282nd BSB covering Hohenfels.

Key Contacts

COMMANDER: 0149-966-283-1500, DSN 476-1500, 476-1510, DSN FAX 476-2821.

PUBLIC AFFAIRS: William Yankers, HQ 409th BSB, Bldg 305.

PERSONNEL/COMMUNITY ACTIVITIES: Ms Kim Mills, Chief, Community & Family Activities, 0149-9662-2629, DSN 476-2629, aettvsbl@email.grafenwoehr.army.mil.

Personnel and Expenditures

ACTIVE DUTY PERSONNEL: 3289
DEPENDENTS: 5863
CIVILIAN PERSONNEL: 964

Services

Housing: Family units 1512; Unaccompanied officer quarters 44; Unaccompanied enlisted quarters 84; Barracks spaces 2068; Junior NCO units 196; RV/Camper sites; Private rentals/government leased housing 1107. *Temporary Housing:* Apartment units 20; Transient quarters 212. *Commissary:* Yes; *Exchange:* Retail store; Barber shop; Dry cleaners; Food shop; Florist; Bank; Service station; Furniture store; Bakery; Bookstore; Military clothing store; Convenience store; Beauty shop; Laundromat; Credit union; ATM; Optical store; Post office; Fast food; Video rentals; Four seasons; Thrift shop; Travel agency; Class VI; Computer store; Garden center; Tailor/Alterations; Laundry; Cafeteria; Photo store; *Child Care/Capacities:* Day care center capacity 303, 6wks-16yrs; Home day care program; Summer day camp; Before & after school programs. *Schools:* Preschool/Kindergarten; Elementary; Intermediate/Junior high; High school; College/University; College courses. *Medical Facilities:* Medical clinic; Dental clinic; Dispensary; Veterinary services; Outpatient care only. *Recreational Facilities:* Bowling center; Movie theater; Gym; Recreation center; Tennis courts; Racquetball court; Fitness center/Weight room; Softball field; Football field; Auto shop; Craft shop; Camping; Fishing/Hunting; Youth center; Picnic area; Playground; Community club.

Sembach Air Base

1029. Sembach Air Base

Unit 4080, Box 95
APO, AE 09142
DSN 496-1110 (Ramstein operator)
Internet: http://www.sembach.af.mil/

Profile

BRANCH: Air Force.

LOCATION: In W-central Germany, off A-6, 10 mi E of Kaiserslautern; 14 mi from Ram-

stein AFB; approx 65 mi SW of Rhein-Main AB. *Locality:* Rheinland-Pfalz.

MAJOR UNITS: 86th Airlift Wing, Ramstein Air Base Annex; 886th Communications Squadron; 569th Security Police.

BASE HISTORY: 1995, administrative side of Semabach AB made annex of Ramstein AB; flightline operations ended & returned to German government.

Key Contacts

COMMANDER: Maj Gary W Klabunde, 886th CS, 011-49-496-7410, DSN 496-7553.

Services

Housing: Family units; Dormitory spaces; Apartments 489. *Temporary Housing:* Transient quarters 17 apartments. *Commissary:* Yes; *Exchange:* Barber shop; Dry cleaners; Food shop; Bank; Service station; Bookstore; Military clothing store; Convenience store; Beauty shop; Laundromat; Credit union; Post office; Four seasons; Class VI. *Child Care/Capacities:* Day care center. *Schools:* Preschool/Kindergarten; Elementary; Intermediate/Junior high. *Base Library:* Yes. *Medical Facilities:* Medical clinic. *Recreational Facilities:* Bowling center; Movie theater; Gym; Recreation center; Tennis courts; Racquetball court; Fitness center/Weight room; Softball field; Football field; Auto shop; Craft shop; Youth center; Skeet range; Playground; Consolidated club.

Spangdahlem Air Base

1030. Spangdahlem Air Base

Unit 3680, Box 220
APO, AE 09126-5000
49-06565-61-6012; DSN 452-6012
Internet: http://www.spangdahlem.af.mil/

Profile

BRANCH: Air Force.

LOCATION: In western Germany; approx 9 mi from Bitburg AB; 45 min from Luxembourg border; 125 mi W of Rhein-Main. *Locality:* Eifel Region.

MAJOR UNITS: 52nd Fighter Wing; 22rd Fighter Squadron; 23rd Fighter Squadron; 53rd Fighter Squadron; 81st Fighter Squadron; 52nd Operations Group; 52nd Support Group; 52nd Logistics Group; 52nd Medical Group; 52nd Fighter Wing Staff.

BASE HISTORY: 52nd Fighter Wing roots in 52nd Pursuit Group (interceptor) Selfridge Field, MI, 1941. WWII, combat operations out of UK & Mediterranean. Post WWII, inactivated at Drew Field, FL; reactivated & deactivated several times; finally activated as 52nd Fighter Group at Suffolk County AFB, NY. 1971, 52nd TFW established at Spangdahlem. 1990, major deployment for Operations Desert Shield/Storm. 1991, Wing detachments deployed in Saudi Arabia for Operations Desert Calm & Southern Watch, along with Turkey for Operation Provide Comfort. 1993, 81st Fighter Squadron inactivated; March 1994, 53rd Fighter Squadron (F-15C) activated; core base with largest fighter operation in Europe; Bitburg Annex added. Responsible for more than 80 geographically separated units including: Volkel Air Base, The Netherlands; Buechel Munitions Storage, Germany; Geilenkirchen Air Base, Germany; Kalkar Air Base, Germany; Pruem Air Station, Germany.

VISITOR ATTRACTIONS: Located in historic Eifel region of Germany with many attractions: rolling hills & valleys with scenic forests, quaint villages, lakes, extinct volcanic craters, & Mosel wine producing region.

Key Contacts
COMMANDER: Wing Commander, 52 FW/CC, 49-656561-6001, DSN 452-6001.
PUBLIC AFFAIRS: 52nd FW/PA.

Personnel and Expenditures
ACTIVE DUTY PERSONNEL: 4350
DEPENDENTS: 5100
CIVILIAN PERSONNEL: 600

Services
Housing: Family units 568; Dormitory spaces. *Temporary Housing:* VOQ units 45; VAQ units 96; Unaccompanied officer/Enlisted quarters; Dormitory units; Transient quarters. *Commissary:* Yes; *Exchange:* Retail store; Barber shop; Food shop; Florist; Bank; Service station; Bakery; Bookstore; Military clothing store; Convenience store; Beauty shop; Credit union; Fast food; Video rentals; Four seasons; Class VI; Auto parts store; Sports store. *Child Care/Capacities:* Day care center 6mo-12yrs; Home day care program. *Schools:* Preschool/Kindergarten; Elementary; Intermediate/Junior high; College courses; High school at Bitburg. *Base Library:* Yes. *Medical Facilities:* Medical clinic; Dental clinic; Bitburg AB hospital, 9 mi away. *Recreational Facilities:* Bowling center; Movie theater; Gym; Recreation center; Golf course; Tennis courts; Racquetball court; Fitness center/Weight room; Softball field; Football field; Auto shop; Craft shop; Officers club; NCO club; Youth center; Equipment checkout; Video arcade; ITT office.

Stars and Stripes Kaserne

1031. Stars and Stripes Kaserne
ESES
Unit 29480
APO, AE 09211
E-mail: papers@mail.estripes.ods.mil
OFFICER-OF-THE-DAY: Director, Newspaper Operations, NF-5, 011-49-6155-601-202, FAX 011-49-6155-601-389 DSN 348-8202

Profile
BRANCH: Joint Service Installation.
SIZE AND LOCATION: 72 acres. In S-central Germany, in Griesheim outside Darmstadt, approx 17 mi S of Frankfurt-am-Main. *Locality:* Hessen.
MAJOR UNITS: European Stars & Stripes.
BASE HISTORY: *Stars and Stripes* goes back to the US Civil War; during WWII, first edition printed in London. 1945, first newspaper printed in Pfungstadt, Germany. 1946, moved to Altdorf, Bavaria; took over presses of *Der Sturmer*, Nazi newspaper; later returned to Pfungstadt. 1949, moved to present location, former Luftwaffe training field in Griesheim, outskirts of Darmstadt. Newspaper a Nonappropriated Fund Instrumentality with full-time civilian staff augmented by small contingent of professional military journalists; authorized, unofficial newspaper published under the authority of DOD.
VISITOR ATTRACTIONS: Griesheim Airfield.

Key Contacts
COMMANDER: Col Robert N Mirelson, US Army.
PUBLIC AFFAIRS: Brian Brooks, Editor, NF-5, 011-49-6155-601-214, DSN 348-8214.
PROCUREMENT: Comptroller, NF-5, 011-49-6155-601-219, DSN 348-8219.
TRANSPORTATION: Director, Support Services, NF-5, 011-49-6155-601-364, DSN 348-8364.
PERSONNEL/COMMUNITY ACTIVITIES: NF-4, 011-49-6155-601-390, DSN 348-8390.

Personnel and Expenditures
ACTIVE DUTY PERSONNEL: 18
CIVILIAN PERSONNEL: 225

Services
Housing: None. *Child Care/Capacities:* No day care facilities. *Schools:* No on-base schools. *Medical Facilities:* No medical facilities. *Recreational Facilities:* Tennis courts; Fitness center/Weight room; Softball field; Picnic area; Playground; All ranks club.

Storck Barracks, Illesheim

1032. Storck Barracks, Illesheim
11th Avn Bde
APO, AE 09177
0981-183-1600; FAX 0981-183-815; DSN 468-1600

Profile
BRANCH: Army.
LOCATION: In S Germany, just outside of Ansbach on Autobahn 6. *Locality:* Bavaria, Middle Franconia.
MAJOR UNITS: 11th Aviation Brigade; Oberdachstetten Training Area; Storck Barracks.

Services
Housing: Family units; Unaccompanied enlisted quarters; Barracks spaces; Dormitory spaces; Senior NCO units. *Commissary:* Yes; *Exchange:* Retail store; Barber shop; Dry cleaners; Food shop; Bank; Service station; Furniture store; Bookstore; Military clothing store; Convenience store; Beauty shop; Laundromat; Credit union. *Child Care/Capacities:* Day care center; Home day care program; Summer day camp. *Schools:* Preschool/Kindergarten; Elementary; Intermediate/Junior high; High school. *Base Library:* Yes. *Medical Facilities:* Medical clinic; Dental clinic; Pharmacy. *Recreational Facilities:* Bowling center; Movie theater; Gym; Recreation center; Tennis courts; Racquetball court; Fitness center/Weight room; Softball field; Football field; Auto shop; Craft shop; Officers club; NCO club; Enlisted club; Youth center; Skeet range.

Sullivan Barracks

1033. Sullivan Barracks
293rd BSB
APO, AE 09183
011-49-0621-730-6125; DSN 380-6119

Profile
BRANCH: Army.
LOCATION: See Mannheim Military Community. *Locality:* Baden-Württemberg.

MAJOR UNITS: 51st Maintenance Bn; 414th Signal Co; 510th Personnel Services Bn; 208th Finance Bn; 574th Maintenance Co.
BASE HISTORY: 1936-38, Falk Kaserne built as Air Force Anti-Aircraft-Artillery Officer Candidate School. 1945-47, served as POW camp; renamed for PFC George F Sullivan, Silver Star recipient.
Services *Exchange:* Food shop; Military clothing store; Pizza shop. *Schools:* College courses. *Base Library:* Yes. *Recreational Facilities:* Gym; Racquetball court; Fitness center/Weight room.

Taylor Barracks

1034. Taylor Barracks
Southern Law Center (Mannheim)
Unit 29901, Box 19
APO, AE 09086
DSN 380-1500

Profile
BRANCH: Army.
LOCATION: See Mannheim Military Community. *Locality:* Baden-Württemberg.
MAJOR UNITS: 293rd Base Support Bn; 181st Transportation Bn; 2nd Signal Brigade; Office of USAREUR Provost Marshal; 95th Military Police Bn; Allied Military Force, Land, HQ; 5th Signal Command; 7th Signal Brigade; 272nd Military Police Co; USAREUR Vehicle Registry; Office of Staff Judge Advocate, Mannheim; Mannheim Law Center.
BASE HISTORY: 1939-40, Taylor Barracks built as Searchlight Kaserne. 1945, renamed in honor of Silver Star recipient PFC Cecil V Taylor. 1990, Mannheim US Military Community Activity (USMCA) consolidated with USMCA-Worms as 293rd Base Support Battalion & 26th Area Support Group (ASG) in 1991.

Key Contacts
COMMANDER: LTC Smothers.

Services *Base Library:* Yes. *Medical Facilities:* Dispensary; Veterinary services. *Recreational Facilities:* Bowling center; Movie theater; Gym; Tennis courts; Racquetball court; Fitness center/Weight room; Softball field; Football field; Auto shop; Craft shop; Officers club; NCO club; Enlisted club; Youth center; Picnic area.

Tompkins Barracks

1035. Tompkins Barracks
Unit 29056
APO, AE 09081
011-49-6202-80-7696, DSN 379-7696, 379-6220

Profile
BRANCH: Army.
LOCATION: See Heidelberg Military Community.
MAJOR UNITS: Army Education Center, Tompkins Barracks.

USAFE Air Postal Squadron, Det 1

1036. USAFE Air Postal Squadron, Det 1
Det 1, USAFE AIRPS/CCF
Bldg 441
APO, AE 09060
DSN 330-6007
Internet: http://www.usafe.af.mil/bases/rhein/airps/index.htm

Profile
BRANCH: Air Force.
LOCATION: DOD Aerial Mail Terminal (AMT) at Frankfurt Main Flughafen Airport.
MAJOR UNITS: USAFE Air Postal Squadron, Det 1.

Key Contacts
COMMANDER: Vernaon Yowell, Postal Superintendent.
PUBLIC AFFAIRS: AB Marisa Cheek, Information Manager.
PERSONNEL/COMMUNITY ACTIVITIES: Wendy Goetz.

Wiesbaden

1037. US Army Corps of Engineers, Transatlantic Programs Center, Europe
CMR 410, Box 1
APO, AE
Wiesbaden, 09096
Internet: http://www.tae.usace.army.mil/

Profile
BRANCH: Army.
LOCATION: In Wiesbaden, Germany.
MAJOR UNITS: Corps of Engineers, Transatlantic Programs Center.
BASE HISTORY: Provides engineering services to US military & federal agencies in Europe & Asia.

Key Contacts
PUBLIC AFFAIRS: Marnah Woken, CETAE-PA, 011-49-611-816-2782, Marnah.L.Woken@usace.army.mil.

Personnel and Expenditures
ACTIVE DUTY PERSONNEL: 300 (military & civilians)

Würzburg

1038. Faulenberg Kaserne
98th ASG, Unit 26622
APO, AE
Würzburg, 09244

OFFICER-OF-THE-DAY: DSN 350-7291
Profile
BRANCH: Army.
LOCATION: In S Germany, on German Federal Hwy B-8, E side of Würzburg. *Locality:* Bavaria, Lower Franconia.
MAJOR UNITS: 98th Area Support Group, Headquarters; 98th Support Group, Headquarters and Headquarters Co.
BASE HISTORY: Built 1876-79, housed German 2nd Field Artillery Regiment and later 9th Bavarian Infantry Regiment. WWII, unit of 2nd Panzer Division stationed here. 1991, Aschaffenburg, Schweinfurt, and Great Würzburg combined to form the first Area Support Group under US Army Europe Community Plan. Now home to 98th Area Support Group.

Key Contacts
COMMANDER: DSN 350-1300.
PUBLIC AFFAIRS: DSN 350-1400.
PERSONNEL/COMMUNITY ACTIVITIES: DSN 350-1350.

Services
Housing: Barracks spaces. *Temporary Housing:* None. *Exchange:* Snack bar. *Schools:* No on-base schools. *Medical Facilities:* No medical facilities. *Recreational Facilities:* Basketball.

Greece

Araxos Air Base

1039. Araxos Air Base
The Axe
Unit 7230
APO, AE 09843
30-693-51902, ext 2192; DSN 314-631-2192
E-mail: 731munss-cce@smtpgate.aviano.af.mil
Internet:http://www.aviano.af.mil/organizations/araxos/

Profile
BRANCH: Air Force.
LOCATION: Approx 20 mi W of Patra; approx 6 mi from Kato Achaia; split between Diaspora, "The Det," (administrative & support facilities near town of Kalamaki) & 5mi E, the Aerodrome (operations center near Araxos).
MAJOR UNITS: 731st Munitions Support Squadron.
BASE HISTORY: 1962, mission established. 1972, 7061st MUNSS activated. 1993-6, various reorganizations; redesignated as 731st MUNSS. Primary mission: provide munitions & weapons to 116th Combat Wing, Hellenic Air Force.

Personnel and Expenditures
ACTIVE DUTY PERSONNEL: 130
DEPENDENTS: 0

Services
Housing: Dormitory spaces for enlisted; prefabricated housing for officers. *Temporary Housing:* No transient military quarters. *Exchange:* Post office; BX with limited merchandise; Video rentals; Vehicle rental. *Child Care/Capacities:* No day care facilities. *Schools:* College courses. *Base Library:* Yes. *Medical Facilities:* Independent Duty Medical Technicians; All other treatment at Aviano AB, Italy. *Recreational Facilities:* Bowling center; Tennis courts; Racquetball court; Fitness center/Weight room; Softball field; Recreational checkout; Recreational lounge with bar & grill; Basketball & volleyball courts.

Souda Bay, Naval Support Activity

1040. Souda Bay, Naval Support Activity
NAVSUPPACT Souda Bay
PSC 814
FPO, AE 09865
011-30-8211-66200-1110; DSN 266-1110

Internet: http://mobility.ramstein.af.mil/~621AMSG/c2/souda.htm
OFFICER-OF-THE-DAY: Base Operations, DSN 266-1269
Profile
BRANCH: Navy.
SIZE AND LOCATION: 110 acres. On Greek AFB, 3 mi from Chania Airport, on Akroteri Peninsula on NW side of island; 15 mi from port city of Souda. *Locality:* Canea Department, Crete.
MAJOR UNITS: 621St AMSG, OL-A, Det 2; Naval European Meteorology and Oceanography Det, Souda Bay.
BASE HISTORY: 1948, USS *Tallahatchie County* (AVB 2) first single US fleet unit operating at Souda Bay in support of 6th Fleet. 1969, US Naval Detachment commissioned. Mission: provide support base for US Naval Forces in Mediterranean. Detachment of Naval Air Facility Sigonella, Sicily, under control of Commander Fleet Air, Mediterranean, Naples. 1980, present Activity established. Currently operates as operating base, air station, & weapons station.
VISITOR ATTRACTIONS: Duty classified as isolated (unaccompanied); entrance to Activity controlled by Greek AF.

Key Contacts
COMMANDER: 011-30-8211-66200-1231; DSN 266-1232.

Personnel and Expenditures
ACTIVE DUTY PERSONNEL: 550
CIVILIAN PERSONNEL: 95

Services
Housing: Billeting not available; transient aircrews FAX DSN 266-1251. *Commissary:* Yes; *Exchange:* Retail store; Dry cleaners; Food shop; Laundromat; Navy exchange.

Child Care/Capacities: No day care facilities. *Schools:* No on-base schools. *Medical Facilities:* Medical clinic. *Recreational Facilities:* Pool; Gym; Tennis courts; Racquetball court; Fitness center/Weight room; All hands club.

Greenland

Thule Air Base

1041. Thule Air Base
Unit 82501
APO, AE 09704-5000
DSN 834-1211 (ask for Thule operator)
Profile
BRANCH: Air Force.
SIZE AND LOCATION: 406 sq mi defense area; main base 5 sq mi. On NW coast 700 mi N of Arctic Circle; 947 mi from North Pole; Moriussaq, nearest permanent settlement, 20 mi W; Qaanaaq, district capital, 90 mi N; 2185 mi from New York City. *Locality:* Greenland.
MAJOR UNITS: 12th Space Warning Squadron; 750th Space Group, Det 3.
BASE HISTORY: 1951-53, constructed as SAC bomber base. 1960-65, Army deployed 4 Nike missile units. 1965-77, fighter-interceptor squadron deployed. 1982, Air Force Space Command base (AFSPC).
VISITOR ATTRACTIONS: No visitors.
Key Contacts
COMMANDER: PAO, 21st Space Wing, Peterson AFB, Co 80914-1294, 719-556-4696.

Personnel and Expenditures
ACTIVE DUTY PERSONNEL: 125
CIVILIAN PERSONNEL: 1000
Services
Housing: Dormitory spaces; Senior NCO units. *Temporary Housing:* Dormitory units; Billeting. *Exchange:* Retail store; Barber shop; Dry cleaners. *Child Care/Capacities:* No day care facilities. *Schools:* No on-base schools. *Base Library:* Yes. *Medical Facilities:* Hospital 6 beds; Pharmacy. *Recreational Facilities:* Bowling center; Gym; Recreation center; Fitness center/Weight room; Consolidated club.

Guam

Adjutant General of Guam

1042. Adjutant General of Guam
Fort Juan Muna, 622 E Harmon Industrial Park Rd
Tamuning, 96911-4421
011-671-475-0801; FAX 011-671-477-9317
Profile
BRANCH: Army National Guard.
MAJOR UNITS: Guam National Guard.
Key Contacts
COMMANDER: Brig Gen Benny M Paulino.

Andersen Air Force Base

1043. Andersen Air Force Base
AAFB
Unit 14003, Box 25
APO, AP 96543-5000
671-366-1110; FAX 671-366-6060; DSN 366-1110
Internet: http://www.andersen.af.mil/
Profile
BRANCH: Air Force.
SIZE AND LOCATION: 22,456 acres. In N Guam, in Yigo; 14 mi NE of Agana; on Route 1/Marine Dr. *Locality:* Guam.

MAJOR UNITS: 13th Air Force; 36th Air Base Wing; 634th Air Mobility Support Squadron; Naval Combat Helicopter Support Unit 5; 613th Air Operations Squadron; 613th Air Support Squadron; 613th Air Communications Squadron; 613th Air Intelligence Flight; 36th Operations Support Squadron; 36th Logistics Group; 36th Medical Group; 36th Support Group; 750th Space Group, Det 5 (AFSPC); Area Defense Counsel, Det QD7H; Air Force Office of Special Investigations, Guam; 692nd Intelligence Group, Det 1 (AIA); Guam Air National Guard; 44th Aerial Port Squadron (AFRC); Defense Courier Service Station, Guam.
BASE HISTORY: 1944, construction started by 854th Airfield Construction Battalion. 1945, operations began. 1947, designated North Guam Air Force Base. 1949, renamed in honor of Brig Gen James Roy Andersen, chief of staff of Harmon Field, Guam. Korean War, supported rotational bomber deployments. Vietnam War, conducted Arc Light Operations. 1972, site of most massive buildup of air power in history with 150 B-52s. 1989, changed from SAC to Pacific Air Forces with 633rd Air Base Wing.
VISITOR ATTRACTIONS: Arc Light Memorial Park; Heritage Room Museum.
Key Contacts
COMMANDER: Col William W Hodges, 36th ABW.
PUBLIC AFFAIRS: 36th ABW/PA, Unit 14003, Box 25, APO AP 96543, 671-366-4202, DSN 366-4202.

Personnel and Expenditures
ACTIVE DUTY PERSONNEL: 2472
CIVILIAN PERSONNEL: 584
Services
Housing: Family units 1389; Dormitory spaces 1200. *Temporary Housing:* Unaccompanied officer/Enlisted quarters 30. *Commissary:* Yes; *Exchange:* Retail store; Barber shop; Dry cleaners; Food shop; Florist; Bank; Service station; Furniture store; Bakery; Bookstore; Military clothing store; Convenience store; Beauty shop; Laundromat; Credit union; Four seasons; Class VI; Gift shop; Toyland. *Child Care/Capacities:* Day care center; *Schools:* Preschool/Kindergarten; Elementary; Intermediate/Junior high; High school; College courses. *Base Library:* Yes. *Medical Facilities:* Medical clinic; Dental clinic; Pharmacy; Veterinary services. *Recreational Facilities:* Bowling center; Movie theater; Pool; Gym; Recreation center; Golf course; Tennis courts; Racquetball court; Fitness center/Weight room; Softball field; Football field; Auto shop; Craft shop; Officers club; NCO club; Camping; Fishing/Hunting; Youth center; Water sports; Playground; AMC terminal; Activity center; SATO.

Guam Naval Magazine

1044. Guam Naval Magazine
c/o COMNAVMAR
FPO, AP 96536

Profile
BRANCH: Navy.
LOCATION: In S-central Guam approx 26.5 mi from Andersen AFB.
MAJOR UNITS: Naval Magazine, Guam.
Services *Recreational Facilities:* Fresh water fishing; Hunting.

Guam US Naval Hospital

1045. Guam US Naval Hospital
USNAVHOSP GU
PSC 490
FPO, AP 96538-1600
671-344-9340, 671-344-9352; FAX 671-344-9746; DSN 344-9746
Profile
BRANCH: Navy.
SIZE AND LOCATION: 111.79 acres. In the central part of island. Guam IAP is approx 6 mi away. Hospital on Rte 7, approx 2 mi inland from Agana and Philippine Sea. *Locality:* Agana Heights.
MAJOR UNITS: Naval Hospital Guam.
BASE HISTORY: 1901, Marie Schroeder Hospital established. 1909, US Naval Hospital, Island of Guam, Mariana built. 1941-44, Japanese forces occupied Guam. 1944, Fleet Hospital 103 built on "hospital point" in Agana. 1954, present hospital commissioned. During Vietnam War, capacity increased to 823 beds. Branch clinics at Naval Station, Naval Computer & Telecommunications Area Master Station, & Naval Air Station.
VISITOR ATTRACTIONS: Commanding & Executive Officer's houses built in 1944, occupied by Naval Governor when Guam was under USN Administration.
Key Contacts
COMMANDER: 671-344-9234, DSN 344-9234.
PUBLIC AFFAIRS: 671-344-9462, DSN 344-9462.
Personnel and Expenditures
ACTIVE DUTY PERSONNEL: 467
DEPENDENTS: 188
CIVILIAN PERSONNEL: 223

MILITARY PAYROLL EXPENDITURE: $21.1 mil
CONTRACT EXPENDITURE: $263,000
Services
Housing: Family units 71; Unaccompanied enlisted quarters 44; Senior NCO units 4. *Temporary Housing:* Unaccompanied officer/Enlisted quarters 18; Transient quarters 1. *Exchange:* Barber shop; Dry cleaners; Food shop; Service station; Convenience store; Laundromat. *Child Care/Capacities:* Day care center capacity 54, 6 wks-5yrs; *Schools:* College courses. *Base Library:* Yes. *Medical Facilities:* Hospital 55 beds, potential to expand to 442 in emergency. *Recreational Facilities:* Pool; Tennis courts; Softball field; Weight room; Volleyball court; Recreation center.

Naval Computer & Telecommunications Area Master Station, WESTPAC

1046. Naval Computer & Telecommunications Area Master Station, WESTPAC
NCTAMS WESTPAC
PSC 455, Box 101
FPO, AP 96540
671-339-7133
Internet: http://www.guam.navy.mil/nctams.htm
Profile
BRANCH: Navy.
MAJOR UNITS: Naval Computer and Telecommunications Area Master Station WESTPAC.
Services *Exchange:* Barber shop; Convenience store. *Child Care/Capacities:* Day care center. *Schools:* College courses. *Base Library:* Yes. *Recreational Facilities:* Pool; Gym; Tennis courts; Softball field; Water sports; Playground; Beach; Mini golf; Par golf.

Naval Station, Guam

1047. Naval Station, Guam
FPO, AP 96540
671-339-7133
Internet: http://www.guam.navy.mil/nglink.htm
Profile
BRANCH: Navy.
LOCATION: On W coast of central Guam at Orote Point. *Locality:* Guam.
MAJOR UNITS: Commander, Naval Forces Marianas; Commander, Maritime Prepositioning Ship's Squadron; Explosive Ordnance Disposal Mobile Unit 5, Det Guam; Helicopter Support Squadron 5; METOC; Military Sealift Command, Western Pacific; Naval Hospital Guam; Naval Computer and Telecommunications Area Master Station (NCTAMS-Guam); Navy Reserve, Guam; Public Works Center, Guam; USS *Frank Cable*.
BASE HISTORY: Site of official War Dog Cemetery, dedicated Jul 1994.
Key Contacts
COMMANDER: RADM Martin Janczak; Lt Lowell, Flag Lieutenant, 671-339-3200, N002@guam.navy.mil.
PUBLIC AFFAIRS: Lt Gai, N01PA@guam.navy.mil, 671-339-2115; Dave Furlong, N01PA2@guam.navy.mil, 671-339-7113.
Personnel and Expenditures
ACTIVE DUTY PERSONNEL: 8700
DEPENDENTS: 7500
CIVILIAN PERSONNEL: 6500
Services *Temporary Housing:* Unaccompanied officer/Enlisted quarters. *Commissary:* Yes; *Exchange:* Retail store; Barber shop; Dry cleaners; Food shop; Service station; Furniture store; Bookstore; Convenience store; Beauty shop; Laundromat; Fast food; Toy store; Class VI; Appliances; Car rental; Garden shop. *Child Care/Capacities:* Day care center. *Schools:* College courses. *Base Library:* Yes. *Medical Facilities:* Medical clinic; Dental clinic; Dispensary; Veterinary services. *Recreational Facilities:* Bowling center; Movie theater; Pool; Gym; Tennis courts; Softball field; Auto shop; Craft shop; Officers club; NCO club; Enlisted club; Youth center; Sumay Cove Marina; Gab Gab Beach; Game room; SATO.

Honduras

Joint Task Force— Bravo

1048. Joint Task Force—Bravo
Soto Cano AB
APO, AA 34042
DSN 449-4416, 449-4253
Profile
BRANCH: Air Force; Army; Joint Service Installation.

LOCATION: Remote airfield in S central Honduras; 60 mi W of Tegucigalpa; 10 mi from Comayagua. *Locality:* Comayagua Department.
MAJOR UNITS: ARFOR (Army Forces); AFFOR (Air Force Forces); MEDEL (Medical Element); Joint Security Force; 228th Aviation Regiment, 4th Bn (Camp Pickett); Military Intelligence Bn.
BASE HISTORY: Aug 1984, established at Soto Cano AB, home of Honduran Air Force Academy. Third in-country headquarters for command of US forces in Honduras: JTF-11 & JTF-Alpha. Under operational control of

US Southern Command, Quarry Heights, Panama. Mission: to exercise operational control of all US military forces in Central America; act as Commander in Chief, US Southern Command's directive authority in logistics; plan & support joint exercises & contingency missions; conduct search, air, and rescue missions; & assist Honduran government in counter-drug action.
Key Contacts
COMMANDER: COL Joseph Prasek, USA; LTC Dave Janik, USAF, DSN 449-4107.
PUBLIC AFFAIRS: DSN 449-4150.

Personnel and Expenditures
ACTIVE DUTY PERSONNEL: 500
Services
Housing: C-Huts.

Exchange: Retail store; Barber shop; Food shop; Military clothing store; Convenience store; Laundromat; Fast food. *Child Care/Capacities:* No day care facilities. *Schools:* College courses. *Base Library:* Yes.

Medical Facilities: Medical clinic; Dental clinic; Pharmacy; Veterinary services. *Recreational Facilities:* Movie theater; Pool; Recreation center; Tennis courts; Racquetball court; Fitness center/ Weight room; Softball field; Football field; Craft shop; Picnic area; Open ranks club.

Iceland

Keflavik

1049. Kaflavik Naval Air Station
PSC 1003, Box 8
FPO, AE
Keflavik, 09728-0308
011-354-425-3206 (Hospital); DSN 450-3206
Internet: http://www.nctskef.navy.mil/nas/
Profile
BRANCH: Navy.

LOCATION: Part of NATO base, Iceland.
MAJOR UNITS: Naval Air Station, Keflavik, Iceland.
Key Contacts
COMMANDER: Capt Allen A Efraimson.
PUBLIC AFFAIRS: CDR David R Willis.
Services
Housing: Unaccompanied enlisted quarters rooms 70; Senior NCO units rooms 130; Junior NCO units rooms 103; Unaccompanied officer

quarters suites 26; Apartment style bldgs; limited off base housing. *Commissary:* Yes; *Exchange:* Post office. *Child Care/Capacities:* Day care center capacity 144, 6wks-4yrs; Half-day care, capacity 72, 3-4 yrs. *Schools:* Elementary; Intermediate/Junior high; High school. *Medical Facilities:* Hospital; Dental clinic.

Italy

22nd Area Support Group

1050. 22nd Area Support Group
Unit 31401, Box 80
APO, AE 09630
011-39-444-51-7111; DSN 634-1110
Profile
BRANCH: Army.
LOCATION: At Caserma Ederle in Vincenza. *Locality:* Veneto.
MAJOR UNITS: Allied Land Forces Southern Europe; Southern European Task Force; 22nd Area Support Group.
BASE HISTORY: 1951, unit established. Subordinate to Allied Forces, Southern Europe, Naples. Includes German, Greek, Italian, Portuguese, Turkish, US personnel, & French military representative. Historically called Palazzo Carli. US personnel work at either Palazzo Carli, Palazzo Pianell or WEST STAR, Allied Land Forces, Southern Europe war HQ (about 15 mi from Verona); rely on Caserma Ederle for many facilities & services.
Services *Exchange:* Stocks only basic items; other available at Ederle commissary. *Schools:* Preschool/Kindergarten; Elementary; College courses; High school at Ederle. *Base Library:* Yes. *Recreational Facilities:* Bowling center; Pool; Tennis courts; Fitness center/Weight room; Softball field; Football field; Youth center; Video clubs; Community center; Basketball; Track; Volleyball; Handball.

Aviano Air Base

1051. Aviano Air Base
Unit 6140, Box 0100
APO, AE 09601
039-434-667555; FAX 039-434-667083; DSN 632-7555; DSN FAX 632-7083
E-mail: pa@smtpgate.aviano.af.mil Internet: http://www.aviano.af.mil
OFFICER-OF-THE-DAY: 039-434-667673, DSN 632-7673
Profile
BRANCH: Air Force.
SIZE AND LOCATION: 1467 acres. Base divided into five main areas in & around town of Aviano; 1 hour from Marco Polo Airport, Venice (NE); 20 min from Pordenone. *Locality:* Veneto Region; Pordenone Province.
MAJOR UNITS: 31st Fighter Wing; 555th Fighter Sq; 510th Fighter Sq; 16th Air Force; 603rd Air Control Sq; 31st Support Group, HQ; 31st Operations Group; 31st Logistics Group; 31st Support Group; E Co, 502nd Regiment (Army); 31st Medical Group; 621st Air Mobility Support Group, Det 3.
BASE HISTORY: Italian Air Force Base officially known as Aeroporto Pagliano e Gori. Area 1 & 2 in Aviano: 31st Support Group, HQ & most facilities; Area 3, Base Civil Engineer area with Transportation & Communications squadrons; Area 600, 16th Air Force; Flightline, 3 mi from Aviano.
Key Contacts
COMMANDER: Brig Gen Timothy A Peppe, 039-434-664700, DSN 632-4700.
PUBLIC AFFAIRS: Capt Tracy O'Grady-Walsh, 039-434-667555, DSN

632-7555, FAX 632-7083, ogradyt@ smtpgate.aviano.af.mil.
PROCUREMENT: Col Worthey Brisco, 039-434-667209, DSN 632-7209.
TRANSPORTATION: LtC Larry Stephens, 039-434-667532, DSN 632-7532.
PERSONNEL/COMMUNITY ACTIVITIES: Col Lee Meador, 31st Support Group, Commander, 039-434-667613, DSN 632-7613.
Personnel and Expenditures
ACTIVE DUTY PERSONNEL: 3427; 956 TDY
DEPENDENTS: 4000
CIVILIAN PERSONNEL: 1200
MILITARY PAYROLL EXPENDITURE: $121.9 mil
CONTRACT EXPENDITURE: $49.2 mil
Services
Housing: Dormitory spaces 1104. *Temporary Housing:* VIP units suites 5; VOQ units 17; VEQ units 12; Lodge units Mountain View Lodge. *Commissary:* Yes; *Exchange:* Barber shop; Dry cleaners; Food shop; Florist; Bank; Furniture store; Bakery; Bookstore; Military clothing store; Convenience store; Beauty shop; Laundromat; Credit union; ATM; Optical store; Post office; Fast food; Video rentals; Four seasons; Thrift shop; Travel agency; Class VI; Computer store; Tailor/Alterations; Laundry; Photo store; CD Store. *Child Care/Capacities:* Day care center capacity 150, 6wks to kindergarten; Summer day camp; Before & after school programs. *Schools:* Preschool/Kindergarten; Elementary; Intermediate/Junior high; High school; College courses. *Base Library:* Yes. *Medical Facilities:* Medical clinic; Dental clinic; Pharmacy; Veterinary services. *Recreational Facilities:* Bowling center; Movie theater; Pool; Gym; Rec-

reation center; Golf course; Tennis courts; Racquetball court; Fitness center/Weight room; Softball field; Auto shop; Craft shop; Officers club; Enlisted club; Youth center; Picnic area; Playground; Consolidated club.

Camp Darby, Livorno Military Community

1052. Camp Darby, Livorno Military Community
Unit 31301
APO, AE 09613
011-39-50-54-7111
Internet: http://www.livorno.army.mil/mwr/index.htm
OFFICER-OF-THE-DAY: Duty Officer, 011-39-50-54-7057
Profile
BRANCH: Army.
LOCATION: On NW coast of Italy between Livorno and Pisa; a few miles from Tyrrhenain Sea. *Locality:* Tuscany.
MAJOR UNITS: Southern European Task Force, HQ; Southern European Task Force Infantry Brigade; 22nd Area Support Group; 31st Munitions Squadron (USAFE); 31st Civil Engineering Squadron; 31st Maintenance Squadron; 509th Signal Bn.
BASE HISTORY: 1951, established as logistical support base for liberation forces in Austria; named for Brig Gen William O Darby, Vice Commander of 10th Mountain Division in WWII.
Key Contacts
PUBLIC AFFAIRS: Sgt John Valceanu.
Personnel and Expenditures
ACTIVE DUTY PERSONNEL: 13,000 military community total
Services
Housing: Barracks spaces; Housing units 375. *Temporary Housing:* VIP units 2; Apartment units 6; Lodge units Casa Toscana rooms 24. *Commissary:* Yes; *Exchange:* Retail store; Barber shop; Bank; Food shop; Beauty shop; Fast food; Class VI; Credit union; Four seasons; Service station; Laundromat; Military clothing store; Post office; Laundry; Convenience store; Photo store; Tailor/Alterations; Thrift shop; Video rentals; Auto parts store; Ice Cream; AAFES mall; Car rental; Car sales; Jewelry shop; Toyland; Gift service market; ITT; Photo Lab; Self-service supply center. *Child Care/Capacities:* Day care center. *Schools:* Preschool/Kindergarten; Elementary; Intermediate/Junior high; High school; College courses. *Base Library:* Yes. *Medical Facilities:* Medical clinic; Dental clinic. *Recreational Facilities:* Bowling center; Movie theater; Pool; Gym; Tennis courts; Fitness center/Weight room; Softball field; Football field; Auto shop; Craft shop; Water sports; Community club; Amusement center; Campgrounds at Sea Pines Lodge (with spaces for trailers and tents); American Beach at Tirrenia (10 min from post).

Ghedi Air Base

1053. Ghedi Air Base
31 MUNSS
31 MUNSS, PSC 57, Box 1
APO, AE 09610
39-30-901-608; 0434-66-4657; DSN 632-7424, DSN FAX 632-4657
Profile
BRANCH: Air Force.
LOCATION: In N Italy on Autostrada A-4; 60 mi E of Milan, 6 mi E of Brescia. *Locality:* Province of Lombardy.
MAJOR UNITS: 31st Munitions Support Squadron.
BASE HISTORY: 1951, 6th STORMO Italian Air Force Wing moved to Ghedi AFB. 1963, 401st Munitions Support Squadron established as Detachment 1200 of 722nd Munitions Maintenance Group. 1993, became 401 MUNNS. 1996, redesignated 31 MUNNS. Mission: to receive, store, maintain, and provide reliable weapons to 154th Fighter Bomber Squadron of 6th STORMO.
VISITOR ATTRACTIONS: Italian military installation not open to general public.
Key Contacts
COMMANDER: LTC Don L Harper, 39-30-903-2926, DSN 632-7424, DSN FAX 632-4657, 831munss-cc@swtpgate.aviano.af.mil.
PUBLIC AFFAIRS: Lt Kevin P Wilson, 39-30-904-2720, DSN 632-7424, DSN FAX 632-4657, 831munns-im@swtpgate.aviano.af.mil.
PROCUREMENT: Maj Frederick Dinsmore, 39-30-904-2720, DSN 632-7424, DSN FAX 632-4657, dinsmorf@swtpgate.aviano.af.mil.
TRANSPORTATION: Capt Blake Sibly, 39-30-904-2741, DSN 632-7424, DSN FAX 632-4657, 831munns-im@swtpgate.aviano.af.mil.
PERSONNEL/COMMUNITY ACTIVITIES: MSgt Doswell, 30-30-904-2720, DSN 632-7424, DSN FAX 632-4657, 831munns-im@swtpgate.aviano.af.mil.
Personnel and Expenditures
ACTIVE DUTY PERSONNEL: 130
DEPENDENTS: 140
CIVILIAN PERSONNEL: 11
Services
Housing: BAQ units 36. *Temporary Housing:* None. *Exchange:* Barber shop; Dry cleaners; Bank; Convenience store; Laundromat; ATM; Post office; Video rentals. *Child Care/Capacities:* No day care facilities. *Schools:* DODDS schools in Verona & Vicenza. *Base Library:* Yes. *Medical Facilities:* Medical clinic Active duty only. *Recreational Facilities:* Pool; Tennis courts; Racquetball court; Fitness center/Weight room; Softball field; Picnic area; Playground; Community club; Italian Officer's club/NCO club.

La Maddalena Navy Support Office

1054. La Maddalena Navy Support Office
NAVSUPPO LA MADDALENA IT
PSC 816
FPO, AE 09612
011-39-0789-798427; DSN 623-8427; FAX DSN 623-8334
OFFICER-OF-THE-DAY: Security Dispatch, DSN 623-8244
Profile
BRANCH: Navy.
LOCATION: On island off NE tip of Sardinia in Straits of Bonifacio, 15 min ferry ride from Palau, Sardinia; nearest airport Olbia, 45 min car ride from Palau; N on Emerald Coast. *Locality:* Sardinia.
MAJOR UNITS: Navy Support Office, La Maddalena; USS *Simon Lake* (AS-33); Commander, Submarine Squadron 22.
BASE HISTORY: 1972, Italian government granted US Navy "homeport" at La Maddalena. Additional facilities located at Palau on Sardinia (community center, game room, & library) & Santo Stefano Island (commissary, small exchange, gym, & bowling alley).
VISITOR ATTRACTIONS: Area popular vacation spot, Jul & Aug.
Key Contacts
COMMANDER: DSN 623-8427.
PUBLIC AFFAIRS: DSN 623-8261.
Personnel and Expenditures
ACTIVE DUTY PERSONNEL: 1564
DEPENDENTS: 1146
CIVILIAN PERSONNEL: 312
Services
Housing: Family units 38; Unaccompanied enlisted quarters 91. *Commissary:* Yes; *Exchange:* Credit union; Video rentals; Small Exchange. *Child Care/Capacities:* Day care center capacity 40, 3mo-6yrs; Home day care program; Summer day camp. *Schools:* Preschool/Kindergarten; Elementary; College courses. *Base Library:* Yes. *Medical Facilities:* Medical clinic; Dental clinic. *Recreational Facilities:* Movie theater; Pool; Gym; Recreation center; Tennis courts; Racquetball court; Fitness center/Weight room; Softball field; Auto shop; Craft shop; Enlisted club; Youth center; Water sports; Marina; ITT office.

Naples (Capodichino) Naval Support Activity

1055. Naples (Capodichino) Naval Support Activity
NAVSUPPACT
NSA Naples
PSC 817, Box 40
FPO, AE 09622
081-568-5856; 314-626-5856
Internet: http://www.naples.navy.mil
OFFICER-OF-THE-DAY: DSN 626-5547
Profile
BRANCH: Navy.
LOCATION: At Capodichino Air Field on Nisida Island; support facilities under construction at Gricignano. *Locality:* Campania.

MAJOR UNITS: Commander Allied Forces Southern Europe (CINCSOUTH); Allied Naval Forces Southern Europe (NAVSOUTH); Marine Corps Security Force Co, Naples; OL-B, Det 2, 621st Air Mobility Support Group.

BASE HISTORY: NSA Naples provides administrative & logistical support to over 100 tenant commands & activities throughout the Mediterranean region, including forces assigned to NATO & Sixth Fleet.

Key Contacts
COMMANDER: Capt J Coyne, PSC 817, Box 1.
PUBLIC AFFAIRS: Lt Jeff Gordon, DSN 626-5110, gordonj@nsanaples.navy.mil.

Services *Commissary:* Yes; *Exchange:* Retail store; Barber shop; Dry cleaners; Food shop; Florist; Bank; Furniture store; Bakery; Bookstore; Military clothing store; Convenience store; Beauty shop; Laundromat; Credit union; ATM; Optical store; Post office; Fast food; Video rentals; Thrift shop; Travel agency; Computer store; Tailor/Alterations; Laundry; Photo store. *Child Care/Capacities:* Day care center; Home day care program; Summer day camp; Before & after school programs. *Schools:* Elementary; Intermediate/Junior high; High school; College courses. *Base Library:* Yes. *Medical Facilities:* Hospital; Dental clinic; Pharmacy; Veterinary services. *Recreational Facilities:* Movie theater; Pool; Gym; Recreation center; Golf course; Tennis courts; Racquetball court; Fitness center/Weight room; Softball field; Football field; Auto shop; Camping; Enlisted club; Youth center; Picnic area; Playground.

Naval Computer & Telecommunications Area Master Station MED, Naples

1056. Naval Computer & Telecommunications Area Master Station MED, Naples
NCTAMS Med
PSC 822, Box 1000
FPO, AE 09621-7000
39-81-568-3402; DSN 626-3402
E-mail: NCTAMS@naples.navy.mil
Profile
BRANCH: Navy.
LOCATION: At Capodichino.
MAJOR UNITS: Naval Computer and Telecommunications Area Master Station MED, Naples; Joint Fleet Telecommunications Operations Center (JFTOC).
BASE HISTORY: 1963, established on AFSOUTH Post, Bagnoli; provided communications for Naples area. 1968, expanded mission to include fleet support; renamed Naval Communications Station, Italy. 1974, Naval Communication Processing & Routing System activated. 1976, redesignated NAVCAM MED. 1991, redesignated NCTAMS-MED; added ADP systems. Four sites in Naples: satellite receiver site at Lago Patria, NTCCs Agnano & Capodichino, & HQ at Bagnoli. Largest military command in Naples area. 1993, NCTAMS-MED Detachment Rota, Spain es-

tablished. 1997, moving from Agnano, Bldg 70, & AFSOUTH, Bldg Q to Capodichino.
Key Contacts
PUBLIC AFFAIRS: DSN 314-625-6043.
Personnel and Expenditures
ACTIVE DUTY PERSONNEL: 400 (four sites, military & civilian)

Naval Regional Contracting Center

1057. Naval Regional Contracting Center
NRCC Naples
PSC 810, Box 50
FPO, AE 09619-3700
39-81-724-4117; FAX 39-81-724-4735; DSN 314-625-4117; DSN 314-625-4735FAX
Internet: http://www.naples.navy.mil/nrcc/
Profile
BRANCH: Navy.
LOCATION: At Via Scarfoglio, 21A, 80078 Agano-Pozzouli, Napoli-Italia; near Naval Support Activity, Naples.
MAJOR UNITS: Naval Regional Contracting Center.
BASE HISTORY: Shore activity under Commander, Naval Supply Systems Command (NAVSUP). Branch detachments in London & Dubai, UAE. Mission to provide contract support for Navy & Navy ships in Europe, Africa, & SW Asia.
Personnel and Expenditures
ACTIVE DUTY PERSONNEL: 11 (combined staff)
CIVILIAN PERSONNEL: 92

San Vito dei Normanni

1058. San Vito dei Normanni Air Station
120 Unit 6230
APO, AE
San Vito dei Normanni, 09601-3120
Profile
BRANCH: Air Force.
SIZE AND LOCATION: 320 acres. Approx 7 mi W NW of port city of Brindisi in the "heel" of Italy. *Locality:* Apulia region, Brindisi Province.
MAJOR UNITS: Operation Joint Endeavor.
BASE HISTORY: 1978, 7275th ABG took over as host when AF took operational control of base; support functions provided by 6917th Electronic Security Group. 1993, 7275th ABG restructured into 775th ABG. 1997, operational support for Joint Endeavor. Scheduled for closure following operation.
Services
Housing: Family units 150; Dormitory spaces. *Temporary Housing:* VIP units 3; VOQ units 10; VAQ units 35; Transient quarters 30. *Commissary:* Yes; *Exchange:* Retail store; Barber shop; Dry cleaners; Food shop; Florist; Bank; Service station; Furniture store; Bookstore; Military clothing store; Convenience store; Beauty shop; Laundromat; Credit union; Four seasons; Class VI.

Child Care/Capacities: Day care center; Home day care program. *Schools:* Preschool/Kindergarten; Elementary; Intermediate/Junior high; High school; College courses. *Base Library:* Yes. *Medical Facilities:* Medical clinic; Dental clinic; Pharmacy. *Recreational Facilities:* Bowling center; Movie theater; Pool; Gym; Recreation center; Golf course; Tennis courts; Racquetball court; Fitness center/Weight room; Softball field; Football field; Auto shop; Craft shop; Officers club; NCO club; Enlisted club; Youth center; Picnic area; Playground; SATO; Dive club.

Sigonella Naval Air Station

1059. Sigonella Naval Air Station
NAS SIG
PSC 812, Box 1000
FPO, AE 09627
011-39-95-86-5440; FAX 011-39-95-86-6933; DSN 624-5440, 624-5330; DSN FAX 624-6933
Internet: http://www.sicily.navy.mil
Profile
BRANCH: Navy.
SIZE AND LOCATION: 225 acres. On E coast of Sicily, accessible from A-19 or IT-417; 10 mi SW of Catania, Sicily, & Fontana Rosa IAP; divided into two sections (15 min apart) NAS I (housing, shopping, recreation) and NAS II (military operations and offices). *Locality:* Catania Province, Sicily.
MAJOR UNITS: Helicopter Combat Support Squadron 4 (HC-4); Patrol Squadron (PATRON SIG); Fleet Logistic Support Squadron 40 (VRC-40); American Forces Network, Naples; Naval Mobile Construction Bn Det; Naval Computer & Telecommunications Station; Naval Hospital Sigonella; Explosive Ordnance Disposal Mobile Unit 8 (EODMU EIGHT); Commander, Helicopter Antisubmarine Light Wing, US Atlantic Fleet, Det Sigonella; Mobile Mine Assembly Group, Det 5; Naval Aviation Engineering Service Unit; Naval European Meteorology and Oceanography Det; Naval Mobile Construction Bn, Camp Olson Sigonella; Tactical Support Center; Army Veterinary Activity; 401st Fighter Wing, Aviano AB; Defense Mapping Agency; Commander Task Group 68.6; Marine Corps Security Force Co; 621st Air Mobility Support Group, Det 2.
BASE HISTORY: 1959, commissioned as Naval Air Facility at site of former Italian Air Base. 1960s, jointly developed by NATO & US to relieve crowded Hal Far Air Facility, Malta. 1970s, increased fleet support. 1981, designated NAS. Reports to Commander in Chief, US Naval Forces Europe (CINCUSNAVEUR) through Commander, Fleet Air Mediterranean (COMFAIRMED). Facility comprises two separate bases, NAS I (former US Naval Base) & II. NAS I provides personnel support services: housing, medical, dental, commissary, exchange, and dependents' school. NAS II is operational base & primary tenant at NATO Maritime Airfield Sigonella, with Italian Air Force as host. NAS II host to over 40 tenant commands & activities; 1100-acre communications transmitter site near Niscemi (approx 65 mi SW of NAS II) also part of complex; Pachino Target Range (on SE tip

of Sicily) operated by Operations Department; NATO pier & fuel facility at Augusta Bay (35 mi SE) coordinated by Sigonella Supply Department.

Key Contacts
COMMANDER: Capt W J Tyson III, 39-95-86-5251, dsn 624-5251, 624-5252.
PUBLIC AFFAIRS: Lt Cappy Surette, PSC 812, Box 3020, 39-95-86-5440, 39-95-86-5330, DSN 624-5440, 624-5330 pao@nassig.sicily.navy.mil.
PROCUREMENT: LCDR Eric Glaser, Comptroller, Box 3230, 39-95-86-5711, DSN 624-5711.
TRANSPORTATION: Public Works Officer, Box 3200, 39-95-86-5771, DSN 624-5771.
PERSONNEL/COMMUNITY ACTIVITIES: Mick McAndrews, Morale, Welfare, & Recreation Dir, Box 3390, 39-95-86-5271, DSN 624-5721.

Personnel and Expenditures
ACTIVE DUTY PERSONNEL: 2800
DEPENDENTS: 3100
CIVILIAN PERSONNEL: 200 US; 690 local nationals
MILITARY PAYROLL EXPENDITURE: $140 mil
CONTRACT EXPENDITURE: $5.2 mil

Services
Housing: Family units 98; Unaccompanied enlisted quarters 3 bldgs; Barracks spaces 1000; several government leased housing complexes available; waiting list 18-24 months. *Temporary Housing:* VIP units 16; Unaccompanied officer/Enlisted quarters 42; Lodge units 50 on base; Due to overcrowding, temporary lodging units difficult to get, members on orders placed in local hotels. *Commissary:* Yes; *Exchange:* Retail store; Barber shop; Dry cleaners; Florist; Bank; Furniture store; Bookstore; Military clothing store; Convenience store; Beauty shop; Laundromat; Credit union; ATM; Optical store; Post office; Fast food; Video rentals; Thrift shop; Travel agency; Shoe repair; Garden center; Tailor/Alterations; Laundry; Photo store; Minimall; Auto accessories; Repair parts; Hardware; Appliances; Gifts; Personalized services center. *Child Care/Capacities:* Day care center capacity 32, infant-12yrs; Home day care program; Summer day camp. *Schools:* Preschool/Kindergarten; Elementary; Intermediate/Junior high; High school; College courses; *Base Library:* Yes. *Medical Facilities:* Hospital 17 beds; Medical clinic; Dental clinic; Dispensary; Pharmacy; Veterinary services.

Recreational Facilities: Bowling center; Movie theater; Pool; Gym; Recreation center; Tennis courts; Racquetball court; Fitness center/Weight room; Softball field; Football field; Auto shop; Officers club under renovation; NCO club; Camping; Enlisted club; Youth center; Water sports; Playground; Community club; All ranks club; Non-alcoholic club; Aerobics; Karate; Italian classes; Equipment rental; Basketball; Reacquetball; Sauna; ITT; Travel agent; Sports shop.

Vincenza

1060. Caserma Ederle/Vicenza Military Community
HQ USASETAF
HQ, 22D ASG, Unit 31401, Box 10
APO, AE
Vincenza, 09630
444-51-1110; DSN 634-1110

Profile
BRANCH: Army.
LOCATION: In Vicenza in NE Italy, 40 mi NW of Venice; exit autostrada at Vicenza Est, follow signs for Caserma Ederle US Army. *Locality:* Veneto Province.
MAJOR UNITS: Army Southern European Task Force; 1st Bn, 508th Infantry (ABCT); USASETAF Lion Brigade; Combat Support Bn; 22nd Area Support Group; 8th Area Support Team (Livorno); 509th Signal Bn; 13th Military Police Co; 510th Personnel Services Co; 208th Finance Bn, Det D; 24th Quartermaster Det; 6th Aviation Co; 14th Transportation Bn; US Army Health Clinic, Vicenza; Southern Europe Veterinary Det; US Army Dental Clinic, Vicenza; Aviano Air Base; Camp Ederle; Dal Molin Airfield; Longare Communication Site; San Gottardo Signal Site; Vicenza Basic Load Storage Area; Vicenza Family Housing.
BASE HISTORY: 1955, activated upon withdrawal of US forces from Austria at Camp Darby. 1956, moved to Caserma Passalacqua, Verona. 1965, moved to Caserma Ederle, Vicenza. Major subordinate command of US Army, Europe. 1972, assumed command of US Army artillery groups in Greece and Turkey. Today, Southern European Task Force supports the European Command with its only conventional Rapid Reaction Force (Air-

borne), and a joint task force headquarters which are deployable within 72 hours; plans & conducts joint warfighting or stability operations in the European Command area; enhances regional stability by providing host nation liaison for any operations conducted in Italy and provides fully deployable core of a joint task force oriented on stability operations.

Key Contacts
COMMANDER: Maj Gen E P Smith, 444-51-8306; DSN 634-8306.
PUBLIC AFFAIRS: Maj John Robinson, 444-51-7866; DSN 634-7866; Jon Fleshman, 444-51-7000, DSN 634-7000.
PROCUREMENT: Joseph E Harris, Regional Contracting Office, Vicenza, Via Casone, 8-36040 Torri Di Quartesolo-(VI), 444-51-3907, DSN 634-3907.
TRANSPORTATION: Col Henry S Alcott, 444-51-7704; DSN 634-7704.
PERSONNEL/COMMUNITY ACTIVITIES: LTC Daniel P Sacks, 444-51-7701; DSN 634-7701.

Personnel and Expenditures
ACTIVE DUTY PERSONNEL: 3300
DEPENDENTS: 4951
CIVILIAN PERSONNEL: 2100

Services
Housing: Unaccompanied enlisted quarters; Barracks spaces; Dormitory spaces. *Temporary Housing:* Guesthouse units. *Commissary:* Yes; *Exchange:* Barber shop; Dry cleaners; Bank; Furniture store; Bookstore; Military clothing store; Convenience store; Beauty shop; Laundromat; Credit union; Clothing PX; Four seasons; Class VI; Food mall; Car rental; Tailor shop; Gift shop; Optical shop. *Child Care/Capacities:* Day care center 6mo-13yrs; Home day care program; Latch key program; Summer day camp. *Schools:* Preschool/Kindergarten; Elementary; Intermediate/Junior high; High school; College courses. *Base Library:* Yes. *Medical Facilities:* Medical clinic; Dental clinic; Pharmacy; Veterinary services. *Recreational Facilities:* Bowling center; Movie theater; Pool; Gym; Recreation center; Tennis courts; Racquetball court; Fitness center/Weight room; Softball field; Football field; Auto shop; Craft shop; Camping; Youth center; Picnic area; Playground; Clubs (2); Community center; Basketball; Volleyball; Sauna.

Japan

35th Supply & Service Battalion

1061. 35th Supply & Service Battalion
Unit 45008, Log Opns Div
APO, AP 96343-0071
DSN FAX 263-4257

Profile
BRANCH: Army.
LOCATION: At Camp Zama.
MAJOR UNITS: 35th Supply & Service Bn.
Key Contacts
COMMANDER: Bob Williams, Chief of Storage, 011-81-3117-63-4515, DSN 268-4515, williamr.logops@zama-emh2.army.mil.

Army Corps of Engineers, Japan District

1062. Army Corps of Engineers, Japan District
Unit 45006
APO, AP 96343-5006

011-81-3117-63-3575; 0462-51-1570 (off base in Japan); DSN 263-3575
Internet: http://www.poj.usace.army/

Profile
BRANCH: Army.
SIZE AND LOCATION: Offices only. At Camp Zama with field offices at: Misawa Air Base, Atsugi NAF, Yokota AB, Yokosuka NB, Iwakuni MCAS, Sasebo NB, Kadena AB, & Ojana Compound (Camp Butler), Okinawa.
MAJOR UNITS: Corps of Engineers, Japan District.
BASE HISTORY: 1972, began operations. Mission: execute MILCON & Japanese funded construction programs as DOD design & construction agent for all US forces in Japan; support US installations through engineering services, design & construction management; and, respond to contingencies throughout the Pacific.

Key Contacts
COMMANDER: Col Jonathan A Jacobsen, Commander & District Engineer.
PUBLIC AFFAIRS: Doug MaKitten, doug.s.makitten@poj.usace.army.mil.

Personnel and Expenditures
ACTIVE DUTY PERSONNEL: 200

Atsugi Naval Air Facility

1063. Atsugi Naval Air Facility
FPO, AP 96306
011-467-78-2664; FAX 011-467-78-2664; DSN 315-264-3201
Internet: http://www.ncts.navy.mil/homepages/comnavfor-japan/atsugi.htm
OFFICER-OF-THE-DAY: 011-462-51-1520

Profile
BRANCH: Navy.
LOCATION: 22.5 mi SW of Tokyo; 10 mi from Yokohama; at Sagamiohtsuka train station; in Ayase City.
MAJOR UNITS: Carrier Wing Five; HSL-51; VF-154; VFA-27; VFA-192; VFA-195; VAQ-136; VAW-115; VS-21; HS-14; VRC-30; VQ-5.
BASE HISTORY: 1945, Gen MacArthur landed at Atsugi Airdrome, Japanese Imperial Navy facility; under Army control; virtual disuse except 8th US Army Replacement Training Center. 1950, NAS Atsugi commissioned; Patrol Squadron Six first unit. 1950-54, major construction; additional units, including Marine Aircraft Group 11, East Camp, now Japanese park; Commander Fleet Air Japan, Commander Naval Air Bases Japan, & Commander Fleet Air Western Pacific. 1965, MAG-11 transferred to MCAS Iwakuni. 1971, designated NAF; administrative control transferred to Japanese Maritime Self-Defense Force. 1991, fleet carrier landing practice moved to Iwo Jima. Largest Naval air facility in Pacific.

Key Contacts
COMMANDER: Capt Frank Sweigart.
PUBLIC AFFAIRS: Pam Warnken, P-Warnke@emh.atsugi.navy.mil.

Personnel and Expenditures
ACTIVE DUTY PERSONNEL: 8000 total personnel

Services
Housing: Unaccompanied officer quarters; Unaccompanied enlisted quarters; Housing also at Kamiseya Communication Station. *Temporary Housing:* Unaccompanied officer/Enlisted quarters; Lodge units 30; Transient quarters. *Commissary:* Yes; *Exchange:* Retail store; Barber shop; Dry cleaners; Florist; Bank; Service station; Furniture store; Bookstore; Military clothing store; Convenience store; Beauty shop; Laundromat; Credit union; Four Seasons; Fast food; Optical shop; Class VI; Video rentals; Flower shop; New car sales; Personal services; Watch/Jewelry repair. *Child Care/Capacities:* Day care center. *Schools:* Preschool/Kindergarten; Elementary; College courses; Grades 7-12 at Camp Zama Army Base, 7 mi). *Base Library:* Yes. *Medical Facilities:* Hospital; Medical clinic; Dental clinic. *Recreational Facilities:* Bowling center; Movie theater; Pool; Gym; Recreation center; Golf course; Tennis courts; Racquetball court; Skating rink; Softball field; Football field; Auto shop; Craft shop; Officers club; Enlisted club; Youth center; Picnic area; Skeet range; Community Center; Golf driving range; Flying club; Gear issue; SATO; Tours office; Tama Getaway (13 min away): stables, wooded area, miniature golf, golf course, camping, cabins.

Camp Smedley D Butler, MCB

1064. Camp Smedley D Butler, MCB
MCB Camp S D Butler
Unit 35001
FPO, AP 96373-5001
011-81-611-745-7421; FAX 011-81-745-3803; DSN 645-7421; DSN FAX 645-3803
Internet: http://www.okr.usmc.mil
OFFICER-OF-THE-DAY: DSN 645-7218; 645-2644

Profile
BRANCH: Marine Corps.
LOCATION: On Camp Foster in S-central Okinawa between Guadalcanal & Nebraska roads. *Locality:* Okinawa Prefecture.
MAJOR UNITS: Marine Corps Base, Camp Smedley D Butler; 1st Marine Aircraft Wing.
BASE HISTORY: 1955, Marine Corps Base located at Camp Tengan. Named in honor of Maj Gen Smedley D Butler, Medal of Honor recipient. Today, consists of separate camps spread from Camp Kinser in S-Cent Okinawa to Camp Gonsalves in Northern Training Area & Camp Fuji in mainland Japan. Camp Butler provides training facilities, logistics, & limited administrative support for Fleet Marine Forces units on Okinawa, including maintenance & scheduling of firing ranges.
VISITOR ATTRACTIONS: War Memorials scattered throughout island.

Key Contacts
PUBLIC AFFAIRS: Maj D K Carpenter, 011-81-611-745-7421, FAX 011-81-611-745-3803, DSN 645-7421.

Services
Housing: See Camp Foster. *Commissary:* Yes; *Exchange:* Barber shop; Dry cleaners; Convenience store; Laundry; Snack bar. *Base Library:* Yes. *Medical Facilities:* Dental clinic; Dispensary. *Recreational Facilities:* See Camp Foster.

Camp Courtney

1065. Camp Courtney
FPO, AP 96377
011-81-6117-622-1131
Internet: http://www.okr.usmc.mil/okinawa/courtney.htm

Profile
BRANCH: Marine Corps.
SIZE AND LOCATION: 451,210 acres (with Camp SD Butler). On E coast of central Okinawa directly off Rte 75. *Locality:* Okinawa Prefecture.
MAJOR UNITS: III Marine Expeditionary Force; III Marine Amphibious Force; III Marine Amphibious Force Command Center HQ; 9th Marine Amphibious Brigade; 3rd Marine Division, Landing Force 7th Fleet; Western Pacific Marine Corps HQ; 31st Marine Expeditionary Unit; 7th Communications Bn; 3rd Force Service Support Group.
BASE HISTORY: 1971, resettled on Okinawa as Marine Amphibious Force. 1988, redesignated III MEF. Under jurisdiction of Camp Smedley D Butler Marine Corps Base.

Key Contacts
COMMANDER: Lt Gen Frank Libutti, II Marine Expeditionary Force & Commander Marine Corps Bases Japan.

Personnel and Expenditures
ACTIVE DUTY PERSONNEL: 25,000 (III MEF, Japan/Hawaii)

Services
Housing: Barracks spaces; 4-plex; 6-plex; 8-plex; apartments; Family housing at nearby Camp McTureous. *Temporary Housing:* Lodge units Courtney Lodge; Temporary lodging facility. *Commissary:* Yes; *Exchange:* Barber shop; Dry cleaners; Food shop; Bank; Service station; Furniture store; Bookstore; Convenience store; Beauty shop; Laundromat; Credit union; Optical store; Fast food; Class VI; Shoe repair; Tailor/Alterations; Ice cream shop; New car sales; Jewelry store. *Child Care/Capacities:* Day care center capacity 188, 6wks-12yrs; Before/after school program. *Schools:* College courses. *Base Library:* Yes. *Medical Facilities:* Medical clinic; Dental clinic. *Recreational Facilities:* Bowling center; Movie theater; Pool; Gym; Fitness center/ Weight room; Football field; Craft shop; Officers club; NCO club; Enlisted club; Youth center; Skeet range; Water sports; Scuba center; Handball; Video tape rental.

Camp Foster

1066. Camp Foster
See Camp Smedley D Butler MCB
FPO, AP 96379
81-611-7-401113
Internet: http://www.okr.usnc.mil/okinawa.butler.htm

Profile
BRANCH: Marine Corps.
LOCATION: Overlooking East China Sea approx 5 mi S of Kadena AB at intersection of Hwys 330, 81, and 58. *Locality:* Okinawa Prefecture.
MAJOR UNITS: Headquarters and Service Bn; Marine Corps Base; 3rd Support Bn; 12th Marine Regiment; Marine Wing Headquarters

Squadron 1; III Marine Expeditionary Force Band.

Key Contacts

COMMANDER: Maj Ben Owens, Operations Officer, owensb@okinawa.usmc.mil.

PUBLIC AFFAIRS: GySgt Alfred Briggs, Bldg 1, DSN 645-7423, biggs_jra@okinawa.usmc. mil.

Services

Housing: Family units; Duplex units; Barracks spaces; Quadraplexes; Apartment units. *Commissary:* Yes; *Exchange:* Retail store; Barber shop; Dry cleaners; Food shop; Florist; Bank; Service station; Furniture store; Bookstore; Military clothing store; Convenience store; Beauty shop; Laundromat; Credit union; Appliance repair; Alterations; Audio accessories; Ice cream shop; Fast food; Optical shop; Class VI; Shoe repair; New car sales. *Child Care/Capacities:* Day care center capacity 252, 6wks-12yrs; Before & after school program. *Schools:* Elementary; High school; College courses. *Base Library:* Yes. *Medical Facilities:* Medical clinic; Dental clinic. *Recreational Facilities:* Bowling center; Movie theater; Pool; Gym; Golf course; Tennis courts; Racquetball court; Fitness center/Weight room; Softball field; Football field; Auto shop; Craft shop; Officers club; NCO club; Enlisted club; Youth center; Picnic area; Water sports; Scuba center; MARS station; Slot machines; Basketball; Sauna; Pistol range; Sports gear checkout; Volleyball; Driving range.

Camp Hansen

1067. Camp Hansen
FPO, AP 96384
011-81-6117-622-1131
Internet: http://dns1.iimef.usmc.mil/7comm/ hansen.html

Profile

BRANCH: Marine Corps.

LOCATION: In central Okinawa between Hwy 329 & Okinawa Expressway; Approx 20 mi N of Camp Foster; S of Camp Schwab; 1 mi inland. *Locality:* Okinawa Prefecture.

MAJOR UNITS: III Marine Division; 3rd Force Service Support Group; 9th Marine Regiment; 3rd Combat Engineer Bn; 9th Engineer Support Bn; 3rd Medical Bn; III Marine Expeditionary Force, HQ & Service Bn; 7th Communications Bn; SNCO Battle Skills Course; Combat Squad Leaders Course; Counter-Terrorism School; Noncommissioned Officer Academy, Okinawa; Sergeants School, Okinawa; Joint Forces Brig, Okinawa; 31st Marine Expeditionary Unit (SOC).

Key Contacts

COMMANDER: Major Pleis, HQ Staff.

PUBLIC AFFAIRS: Capt M A McClelland, 011-81-722-7662, DSN 622-7662, DSN FAX 622-7510.

TRANSPORTATION: Lt Tsung, 7th Comm Bn.

Services

Housing: Unaccompanied officer quarters; Unaccompanied enlisted quarters; Barracks spaces. *Exchange:* Fast food; Barber shop; Tailor/Alterations; Shoe repair; Laundry; Dry cleaners; Food shop; Bank; Service station; Laundromat; Credit union; Class VI; Retail store. *Schools:* College courses. *Base Library:* Yes. *Medical Facilities:* Medical clinic; Dental clinic; Dispensary. *Recreational Facilities:* Movie theater; Officers

club; NCO club; Enlisted club; Bowling center; Fitness center/Weight room; Softball field; Tennis courts; Racquetball court; Gym; Craft shop; Picnic area; Kin Red Beach; Kin Blue Beach; Swimming; Sports complex.

Camp Kinser

1068. Camp Kinser
Unit 38404
FPO, AP 96604-8404
011-81-6117-640-1113; DSN 640-2505, 640-3600
Internet: http://www.okr.usmc.mil/okinawa/ kinser.htm

Profile

BRANCH: Marine Corps.

SIZE AND LOCATION: 763 acres. On southernmost part of Okinawa; near Urasoe City, 5 mi N of Naha Airport; 12 mi S of Kadena AB off Hwy 58. *Locality:* Prefecture of Okinawa.

MAJOR UNITS: 3rd Force Service Support Group, HQ & Service Bn; 3rd Marine Expeditionary Force; 3rd Supply Bn; 3rd Maintenance Bn; 10th Army Support Group, Det; 3rd Force Service Support Group, HQ.

BASE HISTORY: Under jurisdiction of Camp Smedley D Butler MCB.

VISITOR ATTRACTIONS: Air Force Cemetery

Personnel and Expenditures

ACTIVE DUTY PERSONNEL: 2460
DEPENDENTS: 2600

Services

Housing: Unaccompanied officer quarters; Unaccompanied enlisted quarters; Townhouse units 100; Barracks spaces; Senior NCO units; Apartments. *Commissary:* Yes; *Exchange:* Retail store; Barber shop; Dry cleaners; Food shop; Florist; Bank; Service station; Furniture store; Bakery; Bookstore; Military clothing store; Convenience store; Beauty shop; Laundromat; Credit union; Alterations; Ice cream shop; Optical shop; Class VI; Fast food; Shoe repair; Car dealer; Car rental; Jewelry shop; Special services. *Child Care/Capacities:* Day care center capacity 145, 6wks-12yrs; Before/after school program. *Schools:* Preschool/Kindergarten; Elementary; College courses. *Base Library:* Yes. *Medical Facilities:* Medical clinic; Dental clinic. *Recreational Facilities:* Bowling center; Movie theater; Pool; Gym; Recreation center; Tennis courts; Racquetball court; Fitness center/Weight room; Softball field; Football field; Auto shop; Officers club; NCO club; Enlisted club; Youth center; Picnic area; Playground; Basketball; Sauna; Gear issue; MARS station; MWR office; Scuba locker; USO.

Camp Lester

1069. Camp Lester
FPO, AP 96362
Internet: http://www.okr.usmc.mil/okinawa/ lester.htm

Profile

BRANCH: Marine Corps.

LOCATION: Between Camp Foster & Kadena AB off Hwy 58. *Locality:* Okinawa Prefecture.

MAJOR UNITS: AAFES, Okinawa, HQ; Naval Hospital Okinawa.

Key Contacts

PUBLIC AFFAIRS: DSN 645-7703.

Services

Housing: Family units; Duplex units; Barracks spaces. *Temporary Housing:* Lodge units Kuwae Lodge. *Exchange:* Convenience store; Furniture store; Tailor/Alterations; Laundry; Dry cleaners; Shoe repair; Laundromat; Barber shop; Beauty shop; Post office; Food shop; Florist; Bank; Snack bar; Exchange; Gift shop. *Schools:* Preschool/Kindergarten; Intermediate/Junior high. *Medical Facilities:* Hospital Naval Hospital Okinawa (also known as Camp Kuwae); Medical clinic; Dental clinic. *Recreational Facilities:* Tennis courts; Softball field; Football field; Youth center; Bowling center; Movie theater; Gym; Picnic area; Minature golf.

Camp Schwab

1070. Camp Schwab
FPO, AP 96388
011-81-6117-622-1131
Internet: http://www.okr.usmc.mil/okinawa/ schwab.htm

Profile

BRANCH: Marine Corps.

LOCATION: NE coast of Okinawa overlooking Pacific Ocean; along Hwy 329; northernmost base on island; adj to Henoko village. *Locality:* Okinawa Prefecture.

MAJOR UNITS: 4th Marine Regiment.

BASE HISTORY: Training base; tours of duty 6 months-1 year, unaccompanied.

Personnel and Expenditures

ACTIVE DUTY PERSONNEL: 4000

Services

Housing: Unaccompanied officer quarters; Unaccompanied enlisted quarters; Barracks spaces. *Exchange:* Fast food; Service station; Bank; Credit union; Class VI; Barber shop; Military clothing store; Post office; Food shop; Convenience store; Laundromat; Tailor/Alterations; Shoe repair; PX. *Child Care/Capacities:* No day care facilities. *Schools:* No on-base schools. *Base Library:* Yes. *Medical Facilities:* Medical clinic; Dental clinic. *Recreational Facilities:* Movie theater; Bowling center; All ranks club; Gym; Softball field; Pool; USO; Scuba center; Ourawan Beach.

Camp Zama

1071. Camp Zama
Unit 45006
APO, AP 96343-5006
81-311-763-8500; FAX 81-311-763-7554; DSN 315-3151

Profile

BRANCH: Army.

SIZE AND LOCATION: 2265.7 acres. On island of Honshu; 35 mi SW of Tokyo; surrounded by towns of Zama & Sagamihara; divided into South Camp and North Camp by railway. *Locality:* Kanagawa Prefecture.

MAJOR UNITS: 17th Area Support Group; 9th Corps, US Army Japan, HQ; 17th Area Support Group, HQ; 500th Military Intelligence Brigade; Defense Investigative Service; Dental Activity Japan; Engineer District Japan; Medical Department Activity Japan; United Nations Command (Rear), HQ; Army Special Security Det; Army Criminal Investigation Command; Army and Air Force Exchange Service, Camp Zama; Defense Commissary Agency, Camp Zama; Sagami General Depot; 78th Army Signal Bn; Kastner Army Airfield; US Army Finance and Accounting Office.

BASE HISTORY: Site of former Rikugun Shikan Gakko, Japanese Imperial Military Academy, built 1937. 1945, 1st Cavalry Division took control; named 4th Replacement Depot (later Camp Zama); served as stopover for soldiers awaiting transportation to & from Far East. 1953, US Army Headquarters moved from Yokohama. Korean War, used as staging area for troops. Vietnam War, used as medical center, recreation area, & supply center. 1971, Japanese units returned as part of joint use facility. Post won Chief of Staff of the Army's Communities of Excellence award for overseas posts in 1988, runner-up 1991 & 1992, finalist 1993/94.

Key Contacts

COMMANDER: Col David R Booze, 001-81-3117-63-3661, FAX 011-81-3117-63-3388, DSN 263-3661, boozed@zama-emh2.army.mil.

PUBLIC AFFAIRS: Unit 45005, APO AP 96343-0054, 011-81-3117-63-3151, DSN 263-3151.

Personnel and Expenditures

ACTIVE DUTY PERSONNEL: 1059
DEPENDENTS: 1722
CIVILIAN PERSONNEL: 5000

Services

Housing: Family units (single) 107; Unaccompanied officer quarters 164; Unaccompanied enlisted quarters 64; Duplex units 138; Townhouse units; Barracks spaces 518; Dormitory spaces 77; Chapel Hill & Sagamihara Family Housing areas: Quadraplexes 127; Hi-rise 1; Apartment bldg 1. *Temporary Housing:* VIP units 12 units; VOQ units 45; VEQ units 21; Guesthouse units 75; Apartment units 2; Received lodging operation of year award, 1992. *Commissary:* Yes; *Exchange:* Retail store; Barber shop; Food shop; Florist; Bank; Service station; Furniture store; Bookstore; Military clothing store; Convenience store; Beauty shop; Credit union; Optical store; Four seasons; Class VI; Shoe repair; Tailor/Alterations; Watch repair. *Child Care/Capacities:* Day care center capacity 305, 6wks-5yrs; Home day care program; Latch key program; Summer day camp. *Schools:* Preschool/Kindergarten; Elementary; Intermediate/Junior high; High school; College courses. *Base Library:* Yes. *Medical Facilities:* Medical clinic; Dental clinic; Dispensary; Pharmacy; Veterinary services. *Recreational Facilities:* Bowling center; Movie theater; Pool; Gym; Recreation center; Golf course (award winning); Stables; Tennis courts; Racquetball court; Skating rink; Fitness center/Weight room; Softball field; Football field; Auto shop; Craft shop; Camping; Fishing/Hunting; Youth center; Picnic area; Skeet range; Playground; Community club; Basketball; Sauna; Golf driving range; ITT; MARS station; Theater workshop; Outdoor recreation equipment rental; Tama Getaway (13 min away): wooded area, miniature golf, camping, cabins.

Futenma, Marine Corps Air Station

1072. Futenma, Marine Corps Air Station

FPO, AP 96372
011-81-6117-622-1131
Internet: http://www.okr.usmc.mil/okinawa/futenma.htm

Profile

BRANCH: Marine Corps; United Nations.
SIZE AND LOCATION: 1188 acres. 3 mi S of Camp Foster off Hwy 58 in S-central Okinawa; center of Ginowan City. *Locality:* Okinawa Prefecture.
MAJOR UNITS: 1st Marine Aircraft Wing; 36th Marine Air Wing; Marine Aircraft Group 36; Marine Aviation Logistics Squadron 36; Marine Aerial Refueler Transport Squadron 152; Marine Medium Helicopter Squadron 265; Marine Air Control Group 18; Marine Air Support Squadron 2; Marine Tactical Control Squadron 18; Marine Air Control Squadron 4; 1st Stinger Battery; Marine Wing Support Squadron 172.
BASE HISTORY: Under jurisdiction of Camp Smedley D Butler MCB.
FUTURE CLOSURE/REALIGNMENT: Agreement with Japan for floating helicopter base off island Dec 1996 under negotiation. Base scheduled to close 2003.

Key Contacts

PUBLIC AFFAIRS: Maj DK Carpenter, Consolidated PAO, Camp S D Butler, FPO AP 96373-5001, 011-81-611-745-7421.

Services

Housing: Unaccompanied officer quarters; Unaccompanied enlisted quarters; Barracks spaces. *Exchange:* Barber shop; Dry cleaners; Food shop; Bank; Service station; Military clothing store; Credit union; ATM; Video rentals; Shoe repair; Tailor/Alterations; Ice cream shop; Snack bar; Car rental; Watch repair; New car sales; Car wash. *Schools:* No on-base schools. *Base Library:* Yes. *Medical Facilities:* Medical clinic; Dental clinic; Dispensary. *Recreational Facilities:* Bowling center; Movie theater; Pool; Gym; Tennis courts; Racquetball court; Fitness center/Weight room; Softball field; Football field; Officers club; NCO club; Enlisted club; Consolidated club; Basketball; Sports gear checkout; Volleyball; USO; SCUBA training program.

Iwakuni Marine Corps Air Station

1073. Iwakuni Marine Corps Air Station

MCAS Iwakuni

PCS 561, Box 1868
FPO, AP 96310-0029
Internet: http://www.iwakuni.usmc.mil/

Profile

BRANCH: Marine Corps.
SIZE AND LOCATION: 1359 acres. At the SW end of Honshu Island; in Nishiki delta of reclaimed land at mouth of Monzen River; 30 mi S of Hiroshima; 600 mi S of Tokyo. *Locality:* Yamaguchi Prefecture.

MAJOR UNITS: Marine Air Group 12; Marine Aviation Logistics Squadron 12; Marine Wing Support Squadron 171; Combat Service Support Det 36; Marine Fighter Attack Squadron 212; 11th Dental Clinic; Fleet Air Wing 31; 1st Marine Aircraft Wing Det; Naval Hospital Yokosuka, Branch Clinic.
BASE HISTORY: 1940, Japanese naval air station activated. 1943, became branch of Naval Academy on Etajima Island. 1945-48, occupied by various Allied military forces. 1948, designated Royal Australian AFB. 1950, USAF base for combat operations against North Korea. 1958-62, went from USMC to USAF, to USN, & back to USMC. 1962, designated USMC Air Station. Only Marine Corps base on mainland of Japan.
VISITOR ATTRACTIONS: Zero Hanger (WWII) with plane; Bldg 360 (Yamamoto's HQs).

Key Contacts

COMMANDER: Col Robert S Melton, 011-81-827-21-4211.
PUBLIC AFFAIRS: Capt T Lyman, 011-81-6117-53-5551, FAX 011-81-827-21-4181, DSN 253-5554.

Personnel and Expenditures

ACTIVE DUTY PERSONNEL: 4200
DEPENDENTS: 1147
CIVILIAN PERSONNEL: 173 (US); 4544 (Japanese Nationals)

Services

Housing: Family units 479; Unaccompanied officer quarters 400; Unaccompanied enlisted quarters 850; Townhouse units 303; Barracks spaces 900; Midrises 176. *Temporary Housing:* VIP units 2; VOQ units 10; VEQ units 10; Unaccompanied officer/Enlisted quarters 88; BAQ units 135; Guesthouse units 24; Apartment units 24. *Commissary:* Yes; *Exchange:* Barber shop; Dry cleaners; Food shop; Florist; Bank; Service station; Furniture store; Bookstore; Military clothing store; Convenience store; Beauty shop; Laundromat; Credit union. *Child Care/Capacities:* Day care center infant-5yrs; Home day care program; Summer day camp; Hourly care 6wks-12yrs. *Schools:* Preschool/Kindergarten; Elementary; High school; College courses. *Base Library:* Yes. *Medical Facilities:* Medical clinic; Dental clinic; Pharmacy; Veterinary services. *Recreational Facilities:* Bowling center; Movie theater; Pool; Gym; Recreation center; Golf course; Tennis courts; Racquetball court; Skating rink; Fitness center/Weight room; Softball field; Football field; Auto shop; Craft shop; Officers club; NCO club; Enlisted club; Youth center; Playground; MARS station; MWR services; SATO.

Kadena Air Base

1074. Kadena Air Base

Unit 5141, Box 30
APO, AP 96368-5141
011-81-6117-34-1509; FAX 011-81-6117-34-2344; DSN 315-634-1509; DSN FAX 315-634-2344
Internet: http://www.kadena.af.mil

Profile

BRANCH: Air Force.
SIZE AND LOCATION: 5000 acres; Kesaji 142 acres; Camp Hansen 12,718.7 acres.

In S-central Okinawa just off Hwy 58; 15 mi N of Naha. *Locality:* Okinawa Prefecture.
MAJOR UNITS: 18th Wing; 18th Operations Group; 18th Logistics Group; 18th Support Group; 18th Civil Engineer Group; 18th Medical Group; 353rd Special Operations Group; Commander, Fleet Activities, Okinawa (COMFLRACT); Support Center Pacific, Det 15; 633rd Air Mobility Support Squadron; 390th Intelligence Squadron; 82nd Reconnaissance Squadron; Armstrong Laboratory, Det 3.
BASE HISTORY: 1945, Japanese constructed small airfield, Yara Hikojo, near village of Kadena. Aug 1945, taken by US forces; made fighter base. 316th Bombardment Wing original host unit. Since then, hosted by 19th Bombardment Group, 307th Bombardment Group, 18th Fighter-Bomber Wing, 20th Air Force, 313th Air Division, & now 18th Wing in 1991. Currently largest USAF base in the Far East. Geographically separated units: Kesaji, Coast Guard LORAN-C Station; Camp Hanson, shooting range & training facility.
VISITOR ATTRACTIONS: Okinawa Recreation Area; Chibawa Recreation Area; USO; Kadena Marina.

Key Contacts
COMMANDER: Brig Gen John R Baker.
PUBLIC AFFAIRS: Maj Ed Memi, 011-81-6117-34-4502, DSN 315-634-4502, memie @emh.kadena.af.mil.

Personnel and Expenditures
ACTIVE DUTY PERSONNEL: 7000
DEPENDENTS: 10,500
CIVILIAN PERSONNEL: 4480

Services
Housing: Family units 1543; Unaccompanied officer quarters 274; Unaccompanied enlisted quarters 2487; Duplex units 1064; Townhouse units 3707; Dormitory spaces 2487; Senior NCO units 1555; Tower Apartments 1808. *Temporary Housing:* VIP units units 29; VOQ units 301; VAQ units 274; Guesthouse units 3; Dormitory units 2761; TLF 122. *Commissary:* Yes; *Exchange:* Barber shop; Dry cleaners; Food shop; Florist; Bank; Service station; Bakery; Bookstore; Military clothing store; Convenience store; Beauty shop; Credit union; ATM; Optical store; Post office; Fast food; Video rentals; Four seasons; Travel agency; Class VI; Shoe repair; Computer store; Garden center; Tailor/Alterations; Laundry; Cafeteria; Photo store. *Child Care/Capacities:* Day care center capacity 450, 6 wks-4 yrs; Home day care program; Latch key program; Summer day camp; Before & after school programs. *Schools:* Preschool/Kindergarten; Elementary; Intermediate/Junior high; High school; College courses. *Base Library:* Yes. *Medical Facilities:* Medical clinic; Dental clinic; Veterinary services. *Recreational Facilities:* Bowling center; Movie theater; Pool; Gym; Recreation center; Golf course; Tennis courts; Racquetball court; Fitness center/Weight room; Softball field; Football field; Auto shop; Craft shop; Officers club; NCO club; Enlisted club; Youth center; Picnic area; Water sports; Playground; Roller blade rink; Women's gym; Basketball; Volleyball; Kennels; Community activities center; Mini-golf; Equipment checkout; SATO; Okuma Recreation Area (120 acres, DSN 634-4322).

Kadena Naval Air Facility

1075. Kadena Naval Air Facility
PSC 480
FPO, AP 96370
011-81-6117-34-8232; FAX 011-81-6117-34-8227; DSN 634-8232
OFFICER-OF-THE-DAY: 011-81-6117-32-7653; DSN 632-7653

Profile
BRANCH: Navy.
SIZE AND LOCATION: 525 acres. On Kadena AFB, adj to Kadena Town. *Locality:* Okinawa Prefecture.
MAJOR UNITS: Commander, Fleet Activities Okinawa (COMFLEACT); Commander Naval Forces Japan Det; Patrol Wing 1, Det; Task Force 72.2; Mobile Mine Assembly Group, Det 10; Naval Oceanography Command Det, Okinawa; Naval Security Group Activity, Hanza; Navy Personnel Support Activity, Det Okinawa; White Beach Port Facility; Weapons Department, Tengan Pier; Port Services, Kin Red Pier; Awase Transmitter Facility; Camp Marvin B Shields.
BASE HISTORY: 1951, US Naval Air Facility, Naha reactivated; commissioned. 1957, Commander Fleet Activities, Ryukyus commissioned to provide coordination & logistical support to all non-aviation naval activities in Ryukyus. 1972, two commands consolidated as Commander, Fleet Activities Okinawa. 1976, relocated to Kadena Air Base.

Key Contacts
COMMANDER: Capt Richard Weyrick.

Services
Housing: Unaccompanied officer quarters Units, 141; Unaccompanied enlisted quarters 734. *Exchange:* All facilities available from Kadena AFB. *Base Library:* Yes.

Misawa Air Base

1076. Misawa Air Base
Unit 5009
APO, AP 96319-5009
011-81-176-53-5181; DSN 226-1110 (base operator)
Internet: http://www.misawa.af.mil/docs/baseinfo.htm

Profile
BRANCH: Joint Service Installation.
SIZE AND LOCATION: 3865 acres; Ripsaw Range 1884 acres; Wakkanai Air Station 2 acres. On NE shore of Honshu Island; 400 mi N of Tokyo; adj to Misawa City on shore of Lake Ogawara. *Locality:* Aomori Prefecture.
MAJOR UNITS: 35th Fighter Wing; 35th Communications Squadron.
BASE HISTORY: 1945, 32nd Army Engineering Construction Group rebuilt base. 1946, 49th Fighter Group, first US air unit. Only combined, joint service installation in Western Pacific.

Personnel and Expenditures
ACTIVE DUTY PERSONNEL: 15,628 (total population)

Services
Housing: Family units 2174; Dormitory spaces 3286.

Temporary Housing: Transient quarters 56. *Commissary:* Yes; *Exchange:* Retail store; Barber shop; Dry cleaners; Food shop; Florist; Bank; Service station; Furniture store; Bakery; Bookstore; Military clothing store; Convenience store; Beauty shop; Credit union; ATM; Optical store; Post office; Fast food; Video rentals; Thrift shop; Travel agency; Class VI; Computer store; Tailor/Alterations; Laundry; Cafeteria; Photo store. *Child Care/Capacities:* Day care center; Home day care program; Latch key program; Summer day camp; Before & after school programs. *Schools:* Preschool/Kindergarten; Elementary; Intermediate/Junior high; High school; College courses. *Base Library:* Yes. *Medical Facilities:* Hospital; Medical clinic; Dental clinic; Pharmacy; Veterinary services. *Recreational Facilities:* Bowling center; Movie theater; Pool; Gym; Recreation center; Golf course; Tennis courts; Racquetball court; Fitness center/Weight room; Softball field; Football field; Auto shop; Craft shop; Officers club; Camping; Enlisted club; Youth center; Picnic area; Skeet range; Water sports; Playground; Rod & Gun club; Fishing.

Misawa, Naval Air Facility

1077. Misawa, Naval Air Facility
Unit 5009
FPO, AP 96319-5009
011-81-176-53-5181; DSN 226-1110
Internet: http://www.ncts.navy.mil/homepages/comnavfor-japan/misawa.htm

Profile
BRANCH: Joint Service Installation.
LOCATION: On Misawa Air Base, E of Lake Ogawara on Honshu Island; 400 mi S to Tokyo. *Locality:* Aomori Prefecture.
MAJOR UNITS: Naval Air Facility, Misawa.

Key Contacts
COMMANDER: Capt Keith J Denman, USN.

Services
Housing: See Misawa AB. *Exchange:* See Misawa AB. *Schools:* College courses.

New Sanno Hotel, US Naval Joint Services Activity

1078. New Sanno Hotel, US Naval Joint Services Activity
Unit 45003
APO, AP 95337-5003
03-3440-7871; DSN 229-8111
E-mail: navjntse@zama-emh1.army.mil Internet:http://www.ncts.navy.mil/homepages/comnavfor-japan/general.htm

Profile
BRANCH: Navy.
LOCATION: In central downtown Tokyo.
MAJOR UNITS: New Sanno Hotel, Japan.
VISITOR ATTRACTIONS: Reservation requests require deposit (Reservation Department).

Services *Temporary Housing:* 149 rooms; open to I.D. card holders & their guests; rates based on rank. *Exchange:* Retail store; Dry cleaners; Florist; Bank; Bookstore; Beauty shop; Navy exchange; General store; Concessions; Snack bar; Japanese restaurant; Continental dining; Cocktail lounge. *Recreational Facilities:* Pool; Tour & travel desk; APO, Pack 'N' Wrap, gift wrapping; Luggage transport & storage; Exercise room; Video game room; TV.

Pacific Stars and Stripes

1079. Pacific Stars and Stripes
PS&S
Unit 45002
APO, AP 96337-5002
03-3404-9428; FAX 03-3408-8936; DSN 229-3121; DSN FAX 229-3132
Internet: http://www.pstripes.com/about.html
Profile
BRANCH: DOD.
LOCATION: 23-17, Roppongi 7-chrome, Minato-ku, Tokyo 106, Japan.
MAJOR UNITS: Pacific Stars & Stripes.
BASE HISTORY: Began publishing in Honolulu just prior to end of WWII. 1945, first issue printed in Tokyo. An authorized, unofficial publication of DOD. Editorial content controlled by civilian editor. Field bureaus: Guam, PO Box 20178, GMF, Barrigada, Guam 96921, 671-477-1069, FAX 671-349-6238, DSN 349-6136; Okinawa, Camp Foster, FPO AP 96373, 0988-93-2702, DSN 645-3807, DSN FAX 645-9165; Korea, Yongsan Army Garrison, APO AP 96205-0423, 82-2-7914-8194, DSN 724-8180, DSN FAX 724-8194; & Washington, DC.
Key Contacts
COMMANDER: Col Kenneth R Boerum, USAF, Commander/Publisher, 03-3404-9428, DSN 229-3121; Allan R Andrews, Editor.

Sasebo, US Fleet Activities

1080. Sasebo, US Fleet Activities
COMFLEACT Sasebo JA
CFAS
PSC 476, Box 1
FPO, AP 96322-1100
011-81-0956-24-6111 (ask for extension); DSN 252-3029 (Public Affairs Office); FAX 252-3204
Internet: http://www.cfas.navy.mil
OFFICER-OF-THE-DAY: Duty Officer, 001-81-0956-24-6111, ext 3311
Profile
BRANCH: Navy.
SIZE AND LOCATION: 1,000 acres. On Kyushu Island in S Japan; approx 600 mi SW of Tokyo; 30 mi NW of Nagasaki. *Locality:* Kyushu.
MAJOR UNITS: Commander Amphibious Squadron 11; USS *Belleau Wood* (LHA 3); USS *Dubuque* (LPD 8); USS *Fort McHenry* (LSD 43); USS *Germantown* (LSD 42); USS *Guardian* (MCM 5); USS *Patriot* (MCM 7);

Ship Repair Facility Det; Fleet Industrial Supply Center Det; Branch Medical Clinic, Sasebo; Naval Dental Branch Clinic, Sasebo; Afloat Training Group Det; Marine Barracks, Japan, Sasebo Det; Naval Mobile Construction Bn Det; Personnel Support Activity Det.
BASE HISTORY: Sasebo important naval base since 1883 when LCDR Heihachiro Togo nominated village to become base for Imperial Japanese Navy. 1945, Marine Corps Fifth Division landed. 1946, US Fleet Activities established. Korean War, base main launching point for UN & US forces. Post War, Japanese Self-Defense Forces formed; used Sasebo homeport; US Fleet Activities supported US Seventh Fleet. 1970s, Sasebo became Naval Ordnance Facility; fleet visits dwindled. 1980, returned to US Fleet Activities & Seventh Fleet.
VISITOR ATTRACTIONS: CFAS Museum.
Key Contacts
COMMANDER: Capt Bruce Dunscombe.
PUBLIC AFFAIRS: Lt George Minick, c00b@fas.navy.mil.
Personnel and Expenditures
ACTIVE DUTY PERSONNEL: 2788
DEPENDENTS: 2264
CIVILIAN PERSONNEL: 183
Services
Housing: Family units Sasebo, 156; Hario Village 488; Unaccompanied officer quarters; Unaccompanied enlisted quarters. *Temporary Housing:* Unaccompanied officer/Enlisted quarters; Lodge units; BEQ. *Commissary:* Yes; *Exchange:* Retail store; Barber shop; Dry cleaners; Food shop; Florist; Bank; Service station; Furniture store; Bakery; Bookstore; Military clothing store; Convenience store; Beauty shop; Laundromat; Credit union; ATM; Four seasons; Fast food; Video rentals; Tailor/Alterations; Garage; New car sales; Rental car; Minimart; Personalized services. *Child Care/Capacities:* Day care center 6wks-6yrs; Home day care program; Summer day camp; Before & after school programs. *Schools:* Preschool/Kindergarten; Elementary; Intermediate/Junior high; High school; College courses. *Base Library:* Yes. *Medical Facilities:* Medical clinic; Dental clinic; Pharmacy; Veterinary services. *Recreational Facilities:* Bowling center; Movie theater; Pool; Gym; Recreation center; Tennis courts; Racquetball court; Fitness center/Weight room; Softball field; Football field; Auto shop; Craft shop; Officers club; NCO club; Youth center; Picnic area; Water sports; Playground; Golf simulator; Nimitz Park Recreation Area; Gear issue; Volleyball; Basketball; Sauna; Community center; Sailing center; Single Sailor/Marine Programming/Center; Commercial travel office; CPO club; All hands nightclub & restaurants.

Tokyo

1081. Asian Office of Aerospace Research & Development
AOARD
Hardy Barracks
7-23 Roppongi, Minato-ku
Tokyo,
Mailing Address
Unit 45002 96337-5002
81-3-5410-4409; FAX 81-3-5410-4407; DSN 315-229-3212; DSN FAX 315-229-3133

E-mail: aoard@aoard.yokota.af.mil Internet: http://www.nmjc.org/aoard/aoardt.html
Profile
BRANCH: Air Force; Army; Navy.
SIZE AND LOCATION: Offices. In downtown Tokyo, in Akasaka Press Center complex, Bldg 1, also known as Hardy Barracks. *Locality:* Tokyo Prefecture.
MAJOR UNITS: Asian Office of Aerospace Research & Development; Office of Naval Research Asian Office; Army Research Office—Far East.
BASE HISTORY: 1992, established by Air Force Office of Scientific Research (AFOSR); part of Air Force Material Command (AFMC).

Torii Station

1082. Torii Station
APAJ-GOC; 10 ASG
10th ASG, Unit 35115
APO, AP 96376-5115
011-81-6117-44-4730; DSN 644-4678; DSN FAX 644-4798
Internet: http://www.okr.usmc.mil/okinawa/torii.htm
Profile
BRANCH: Army.
SIZE AND LOCATION: 50 acres. On East China Sea coast, on Okinawa Rte Six in village of Yomitan; approx 1 hr N from Naha IAP; approx 15 min from Kadena AB. *Locality:* Yomitan, Okinawa Prefecture.
MAJOR UNITS: 10th Area Support Group; Army Space Command MSQ-114 Det; 1st Special Forces Group, 1st Bn (Airborne); 349th Signal Co (58th Signal Bn); 500th Military Intelligence Det; 505th Quartermaster Bn; 58th Signal Bn; 1315th Medium Port Command; Army Veterinary Services; Army Broadcasting Det; Army Test, Measurement, Diagnostic, and Equipment Det-Okinawa; Pacific Stars & Stripes; Marine Corps Det.
BASE HISTORY: 1986, US Army Garrison, Okinawa, redesignated as 10th Area Support Group (Provisional). 1987, provisional dropped; 10th ASG HQ transferred to present location at Torii Station.
VISITOR ATTRACTIONS: Torii Beach (all ranks, all services).
Key Contacts
COMMANDER: Col G Bishop, ATTN: APAJ-GOC, 011-81-6117-44-4439, DSN 644-4434, DSN FAX, bishopg@torii-emh1.army.mil 644-4997.
PUBLIC AFFAIRS: Kimberly Prato, Bldg 236, ATTN: APAJ-GO-XO(PAO), DSN 644-4730, DSN FAX 644-4798, pratok@torii-emh2.army.mil.
PROCUREMENT: CWO3 Rickey McIntyre, ATTN: APAJ-GO-LPB, DSN 644-4247.
TRANSPORTATION: Mr Bagby, ATTN: APAJ-GO-L, 011-81-6117-44-4327, DSN 644-4327.
PERSONNEL/COMMUNITY ACTIVITIES: John Senatore, Installation Coordinator, ATTN: APAJ-GO-DCFA, 011-81-6117-44-4343, DSN 644-4343, DSN FAX 644-4678, senatore@torii-emh1.army.mil.
Personnel and Expenditures
ACTIVE DUTY PERSONNEL: 890

DEPENDENTS: None
CIVILIAN PERSONNEL: 149 US; 722 local nationals
Services
Housing: Unaccompanied officer quarters 30; Unaccompanied enlisted quarters; Barracks spaces. *Exchange:* Barber shop; Dry cleaners; Food shop; Bank; Service station; Convenience store; Credit union; ATM; Post office; Fast food; Video rentals; Travel agency; Tailor/Alterations; Laundry; Shoe repair; Personal services. *Child Care/Capacities:* No day care facilities. *Schools:* No on-base schools. *Base Library:* Yes. *Medical Facilities:* Medical clinic; Dental clinic; Veterinary services. *Recreational Facilities:* Bowling center; Movie theater; Pool; Gym; Recreation center; Racquetball court; Fitness center/Weight room; Softball field; Craft shop; Camping; Picnic area; Water sports; Playground; Community club; Consolidated club; Fishing; Outdoor recreation facility: Torii Beach with camping, scuba shop, snack bar, water slide, & equipment rentals.

Yokosuka, Fleet Activities

1083. Yokosuka, Fleet Activities
CFAY
PSC 472, Box 1
FPO, AP 96348-1100
011-81-045-661-4101; FAX
011-81-045-661-4818; DSN 242-4101; DSN FAX 242-4818
E-mail: C1300@CFAY-emh.yoko.mrms.navy.mil Internet:http://www.ncts.navy.mil/homepages/comnavfor-japan/cfay.htm
OFFICER-OF-THE-DAY: Quarterdeck, 011-81-045-661-4111
Profile
BRANCH: Navy.
SIZE AND LOCATION: 568 acres. 18 mi S of Yokohama; 43 mi S of Tokyo; on Miura peninsula in Kanto Plain region of Pacific Coast in Central Honshu. *Locality:* Naka-Ku; Kanagawa-Ken.
MAJOR UNITS: Yokosuka Naval Base; Fleet Activities Yokosuka; Military Sealift Command, Far East; 1316th Medium Port Command; Fleet Mail Center, Yokohama; US Naval Forces, Japan; US Seventh Fleet; Volunteer Training Unit 3005.
BASE HISTORY: 1867, racetrack & grandstands built in Negishi. WWII, Japanese Navy constructed printing plant; later Australian POW camp. 1945-53, occupied by US Army Corps of Engineers. 1952, COMNAVFE moved from HQ Tokyo. 1959, turned over to USN as Navy's first overseas housing activity. 1983, all land except "grandstands" returned to Japan. Mission: provides, maintains, & operates base facilities & services in support of US forces in Yokohama area.
VISITOR ATTRACTIONS: Historic Japanese grandstands.
Key Contacts
COMMANDER: Capt William D Lynch; RADM Michael D Haskins, Commander, US Naval Forces, Japan, PSC 473 BOX 12, FPO AP 96349-0051, 011-81-311-743-7600, DSN 311-243-7600.

PUBLIC AFFAIRS: YNC(SW) Jack L Taylor, C1300A@cfay-emh.yoko.mrms.navy.mil; CNFJ 011-81-311-743-7614, DSN 311-243-7614, cnfjpao@ctf74.ctf74.navy.mil.
Personnel and Expenditures
ACTIVE DUTY PERSONNEL: 9388
DEPENDENTS: 8342
CIVILIAN PERSONNEL: 6746
CONTRACT EXPENDITURE: $1 mil
Services
Housing: Family units 405; Unaccompanied officer quarters Units 28; Unaccompanied enlisted quarters 32; Negishi Bachelor Quarters 105 (permanently assigned/transient). *Temporary Housing:* VIP units 1. *Commissary:* Yes; *Exchange:* Retail store; Barber shop; Food shop; Bank; Service station; Bookstore; Convenience store; Beauty shop; Laundromat; ATM; Post office; Fast food; Video rentals; Laundry; Credit union; One of the largest Navy exchanges in the world; Car rentals; Car sales. *Child Care/Capacities:* Day care center capacity 30, 6wks-8yrs; Home day care program; Latch key program; Summer day camp. *Schools:* Preschool/Kindergarten; Elementary; High school. *Base Library:* Yes. *Medical Facilities:* Medical clinic; Dental clinic. *Recreational Facilities:* Bowling center; Movie theater; Pool; Gym; Recreation center; Tennis courts; Fitness center/Weight room; Softball field; Youth center; Playground; Community club; Consolidated club; Berkey Field Sports Complex; Basketball; Golf driving range.

Yokosuka, US Naval Hospital

1084. Yokosuka, US Naval Hospital
PSC 475, Box 1
FPO, AP 96350-1600
Internet: http://www.nhyoko.med.navy.mil/
Profile
BRANCH: Navy.
LOCATION: On Naval Station Yokosuka.
MAJOR UNITS: Naval Hospital Yokosuka.
Key Contacts
COMMANDER: yok1wbd@yok10.med.navy.mil.
PUBLIC AFFAIRS: Lt Leslie A Moore, Chief Information Officer, 011-81-311-743-8244; 011-81-311-743-7194.
Services
Housing: See Yokosuka Fleet Activities. *Exchange:* See Yokosuka Fleet Activities. *Medical Facilities:* Hospital.

Yokota Air Base

1085. Yokota Air Base
Yokota
374th Airlift Wing, Unit 5078
APO, AP 96328-5078
011-81-311-755-7203, (within Japan 011-81-0425-52-2511+ext); FAX 011-311-554-867; DSN 225-7338; DSN FAX 225-4867

E-mail: wingpa@emh.yokota.af.mil Internet: http://www.yokota.af.mil
OFFICER-OF-THE-DAY: 81-3117-55-2536 (Command Post, ask for duty officer to be paged), DSN 225-2536
Profile
BRANCH: Air Force.
SIZE AND LOCATION: 1750 acres. 35 mi W of Tokyo. *Locality:* Akishima, Fussa, Hamura, Mizuho, Musashi-Murayama, & Tachikawa municipalities.
MAJOR UNITS: 374th Airlift Wing; US Forces Japan; 5th Air Force; 603rd Air Mobility Support Squadron; FEN; Air Force Broadcasting Service; Army/Air Force Exchange Service; Defense Commissary Agency; DODDS; Defense Special Representative Japan (DSRJ); On-Site Inspection Agency (OSIA).
BASE HISTORY: 1938, base opened as Tama Army Air Base, primary Japanese flight test center; little damage during war; remained operational. 1945, US operations began; renamed after small village previously located in NE corner of base. Today, primary US military port on mainland Japan; home to 3 HQ units. 1992, 174th Airlift Wing activated, only airlift wing in Far East; provides airlift support to all DOD agencies; movement of passengers, cargo, & mail throughout Pacific with regular scheduled missions to South Korea, Micronesia, Guam, & Thailand.
VISITOR ATTRACTIONS: Historical walking tours.
Key Contacts
COMMANDER: Col Alan J Briding, 374 AW/CC, Unit 5078, APO AP 96328-5078, 011-81-3117-55-3741, DSN 225-3741, FAX 225-5910 225-3741.
PUBLIC AFFAIRS: Capt Edwina Walton, 011-81-3117-55-7203, DSN 225-7203, DSN FAX 225-4867, waltone@emh.yokota.af.mil.
PERSONNEL/COMMUNITY ACTIVITIES: Ms Sayoko Ichikawa, 011-81-3117-55-7409, DSN 225-7409, DSN FAX 225-4867, ichikaws@emh.yokota.af.mil.
Personnel and Expenditures
ACTIVE DUTY PERSONNEL: 3743 Air Force
DEPENDENTS: 4414 Air Force; 202 DoDD Schools; 264 NAF; 562 AAFES
CIVILIAN PERSONNEL: 263; local nationals 1869
MILITARY PAYROLL EXPENDITURE: $291 mil
CONTRACT EXPENDITURE: $415 mil
Services
Housing: Apartment towers/Garden apartments: Officers 557, enlisted 17,452; Dorms: Officer 2 units, capacity 184, enlisted 8 units, capacity 732. *Temporary Housing:* VOQ units 7, capacity 221; VAQ units 4, capacity 202. *Commissary:* Yes; *Exchange:* Retail store; Barber shop; Dry cleaners; Florist; Bank; Service station; Furniture store; Bakery; Bookstore; Military clothing store; Convenience store; Beauty shop; Laundromat; Credit union; ATM; Optical store; Post office; Fast food; Video rentals; Four seasons; Thrift shop; Travel agency; Class VI; Computer store; Garden center; Tailor/Alterations; Laundry; Cafeteria; Photo store; Audio zone; Bazaar-Concessions; Car rentals; Car sales; Electronic repair; Toyland. *Child Care/Capacities:* Day care center 5mos-10yrs; Home day care program; Summer day camp; Before & after school programs. *Schools:* Preschool/Kindergarten; Elementary; Intermediate/Junior high; High school; College/University; College courses.

Base Library: Yes. *Medical Facilities:* Hospital 25 beds; Medical clinic; Dental clinic; Pharmacy; Veterinary services; Aeromedical Staging Flight.

Recreational Facilities: Bowling center; Movie theater; Pool; Gym; Recreation center; Golf course; Stables; Tennis courts; Racquetball court; Fitness center/Weight room; Softball field; Football field; Auto shop; Craft shop; Officers club; NCO club; Camping; Youth center; Picnic area; Playground; Rod & Gun club; Nanatorium (therapeutic pool).

Johnston Atoll

Army Chemical Activity Pacific

1086. Army Chemical Activity Pacific
APO, AP 96558-0008
808-621-3044; FAX 808-622-3827; DSN 315-441-2411; DSN FAX 315-441-2039
E-mail: administrator@usacap.ja.dswa.mil Internet:http://www.ja.dswa.mic; http://www.usarpac.army.mil/docs/usacap.htm
OFFICER-OF-THE-DAY: 808-621-3044, ext 5006, DSN 315-441-5006
Profile
BRANCH: Army.
SIZE AND LOCATION: 624 acres. In Pacific Ocean, 825 mi W-SW of Hawaii. *Locality:* Johnston Island.
MAJOR UNITS: Army Chemical Activity, Pacific; Field Command, Johnston Atoll; Program Manager Chemical Demilitarization; Johnston Atoll Chemical Agent Disposal System.

BASE HISTORY: 1971, relocation of chemical munitions from Okinawa to Johnston Island by 267th Chemical Co. 1983, redesignated Johnston Island Chemical Activity. 1985, reorganized as US Army Chemical Activity, Western Command. 1990, renamed US Army Chemical Activity, Pacific; Operation "Steel Box" brought retrograde munitions from Federal Republic of Germany. Mission: to provide integrated command & management of all Army activities on Johnston Island; administration for Johnston Atoll Chemical Disposal System project; responsible for receipt, issue, & disposal of toxic chemical munitions. Estimates call for remaining stockpile munitions to be destroyed by end of 1999, followed by facility closure & site remediation operations.
Key Contacts
COMMANDER: Col Dick Savage, USAF, FCJ, 808-621-3044, ext 3005, FAX 808-422-6905, DSN 315-441-3005, savaged@ja.dswa.mil.
PUBLIC AFFAIRS: Cpt Greg Blake, HHD, USACAP, 808-621-3044, ext 2411, FAX 808-622-3827, DSN 315-441-2411, Blakeg@usacap.ja.dswa.mil.
PROCUREMENT: Dave Shogren, 808-621-3044, ext 3306, DSN 315-441-3306, Shogrend@usacap.ja.dswa.mil.
TRANSPORTATION: Donnie Sims, 808-621-2764, DSN 315-441-2764, Simsd@usacap.ja.dswa.mil.
Personnel and Expenditures
ACTIVE DUTY PERSONNEL: 300
DEPENDENTS: 0
CIVILIAN PERSONNEL: 1100
Services *Exchange:* Barber shop; Beauty shop; Post office; Cafeteria. *Child Care/Capacities:* No day care facilities. *Schools:* No on-base schools. *Base Library:* Yes. *Medical Facilities:* Medical clinic; Dental clinic. *Recreational Facilities:* Bowling center; Movie theater; Pool; Gym; Golf course; Tennis courts; Racquetball court; Fitness center/Weight room; Softball field; Craft shop; Water sports; Consolidated club.

Korea, Republic of

6005th Air Postal Squadron, OL-D, Det 1

1087. 6005th Air Postal Squadron, OL-D, Det 1
APO, AP 96276-9998
DSN 723-7882, 723-6589
Profile
BRANCH: Air Force.
SIZE AND LOCATION: 100 acres. At Kimpo IAP; 15 mi from Seoul. *Locality:* Seoul.
MAJOR UNITS: 6005th Air Postal Squadron, Operating Location D, Det 1.
Personnel and Expenditures
ACTIVE DUTY PERSONNEL: 20
CIVILIAN PERSONNEL: 9
Services
Housing: None.

Camp Carroll

1088. Camp Carroll
USAMSC-K
Unit 15476
APO, AP 96260-5476
DSN 765-7489
Internet: http://143.138.250.38/co.htm
Profile
BRANCH: Army.
SIZE AND LOCATION: 489.2 acres. In SE South Korea; S of Waegwan; 20 mi NW of Taegu.
MAJOR UNITS: USA Materiel Support Center-Korea; 20th Support Group; 2nd Maintenance Co; 5th PMU; 6th Ordnance Bn; 16th MEDLOG Bn; 23rd Chemical Bn; 57th Military Police Co; 168th Medical Bn; 307th Signal Bn; 665th Medical Co; Combat Equipment Base-NE Asia.
Key Contacts
COMMANDER: Col Donald E Plater, DSN 765-7495, DSN FAX 765-8525, platerd@usfk.korea.army.mil.
PUBLIC AFFAIRS: Mr. Kai, Chief, DSN 765-8821, eanc-msc-i@emh6.korea.army.mil.
Personnel and Expenditures
ACTIVE DUTY PERSONNEL: 1044
CIVILIAN PERSONNEL: 83
Services *Commissary:* Yes; *Exchange:* Post office; Bank; Credit union. *Schools:* College courses; No on-base schools. *Medical Facilities:* Medical clinic. *Recreational Facilities:* Fitness center/Weight room; Bowling center.

Camp Casey

1089. Camp Casey
Unit 15543
APO, AP 96224-0543
011-82-351-869-2277; FAX 869-1629; DSN 315-730-1629
Internet: http://www-2id.korea.army.mil/camps/casey.htm
OFFICER-OF-THE-DAY: Staff Duty Officer, 011-82-351-869-3343, DSN 315-730-3343

Profile

BRANCH: Army.

SIZE AND LOCATION: 3487.3 acres. Approx 40 mi from Seoul; near city of Tongduchon; divided into East & West Casey; just S of DMZ. *Locality:* Kyonggi Province.

MAJOR UNITS: 2nd Infantry Division, 1st Brigade, HQ; 1st Brigade, 72nd Armor; 2nd Bn, 72nd Armor; 1st Bn, 503rd Infantry; 9th Infantry, 2nd Bn; 702nd Main Support Bn; 302nd Forward Support Bn; 4th Chemical Co; 122nd Signal Bn, HQ; 122nd Signal Bn, A Co; 122nd Signal Bn, B Co; 1st Bn, 15th Field Artillery; 5th Bn, 5th Air Defense Artillery, C Co; 2nd Military Police Co; 509th Personnel Services Bn; 177th Finance Bn.

BASE HISTORY: 1965, 2nd Infantry returned to Korea to maintain forces along Demilitarized Zone (DMZ). Occupies sector along main highway from Panmunjon to Seoul; principal American ground combat element of US 8th Army, under control of Combined Field Army (ROK/US). Two guardposts, Collier and Ouellette, located within DMZ. Only infantry division in US Army with both infantry & mechanized infantry units.

VISITOR ATTRACTIONS: Museum.

Personnel and Expenditures

ACTIVE DUTY PERSONNEL: 6300
CIVILIAN PERSONNEL: 2500

Services

Housing: Barracks spaces; Dormitory spaces; Senior NCO units; All personnel live on post; most serve 1-year unaccompanied tour. *Commissary:* Yes; *Exchange:* Barber shop; Dry cleaners; Food shop; Florist; Bank; Service station; Bookstore; Convenience store; Beauty shop; Laundromat; Credit union; Class VI; Tailor/Alterations; PX; Burger bar; Airline Ticket Office; Pizza delivery. *Child Care/Capacities:* No day care facilities. *Schools:* College courses; No on-base schools. *Base Library:* Yes. *Medical Facilities:* Medical clinic; Dental clinic; Dispensary; Pharmacy. *Recreational Facilities:* Bowling center; Pool; Gym; Recreation center; Golf course; Tennis courts; Racquetball court; Fitness center/Weight room; Softball field; Football field; Craft shop; Officers club; NCO club; Enlisted club; Picnic area; Playground.

Camp Castle

1090. Camp Castle

APO, AP
Internet: http://www-2id.korea.army.mil/camps/castle.htm
OFFICER-OF-THE-DAY: Duty Officer, 011-82-351-869-3214, DSN 315-730-3214

Profile

BRANCH: Army.

SIZE AND LOCATION: 48.6 acres. Within walking distance of Camp Casey; near Tongduchon; 40 mi from Seoul.

MAJOR UNITS: 2nd Engineer Bn.

BASE HISTORY: Provide engineering support for 2nd Infantry Division.

Personnel and Expenditures

ACTIVE DUTY PERSONNEL: 500
CIVILIAN PERSONNEL: 130

Services

Housing: All personnel live on post; most serve 1-year unaccompanied tour. *Exchange:* Laundry; PX; Snack bar.

Recreational Facilities: Gym; Racquetball court; Tennis courts; NCO club; Enlisted club; Basketball court.

Camp Colbern

1091. Camp Colbern

APO, AP 96205
Internet: http://www-1sig.korea.army.mil/304th.htm

Profile

BRANCH: Army.

LOCATION: In Hanam-shi; 25 mi SE of Yongsan Army Garrison; small camp S of Seoul.

MAJOR UNITS: 304th Signal Bn, HQ; 304th Signal Bn, C Co.

BASE HISTORY: Mission to provide tactical communications.

Key Contacts

COMMANDER: Capt Kristina M Heise.

Services *Schools:* College courses; No on-base schools.

Camp Edwards

1092. Camp Edwards

Unit 15561
APO, AP 96251-5561
Internet: http://www-2id.korea.army.mil/camps/edwards.htm
OFFICER-OF-THE-DAY: Duty Officer, 011-82-348-50-5786; DSN 315-734-5786

Profile

BRANCH: Army.

SIZE AND LOCATION: 61.5 acres. Approx 1 mi from Kumchon, 5 mi S of DMZ; 14 mi N of Seoul; on MSR-1, Western Corridor. *Locality:* Yono-Te-Ri, Paju-Gun.

MAJOR UNITS: 82nd Engineering Co (CSE).

BASE HISTORY: Isolated remote site named for SFC Junior Edwards, Medal of Honor recipient, Korean War. Provides Combat Engineer Support for 2nd Infantry Division.

Personnel and Expenditures

ACTIVE DUTY PERSONNEL: 275
DEPENDENTS: 0
CIVILIAN PERSONNEL: 125

Services

Housing: Barracks spaces 250; Senior NCO units 40; Unaccompanied officer quarters spaces 12; Unaccompanied enlisted quarters spaces 8; All personnel live in on-post quarters. *Exchange:* Retail store; Barber shop; Dry cleaners; Military clothing store; Beauty shop; Tailor/Alterations; PX. *Child Care/Capacities:* No day care facilities. *Schools:* No on-base schools. *Base Library:* Yes. *Medical Facilities:* Medical clinic; Dental clinic. *Recreational Facilities:* Movie theater; Pool; Gym; Recreation center; Tennis courts; Racquetball court; Fitness center/Weight room; Softball field; All ranks club.

Camp Essayons

1093. Camp Essayons

Unit 15404
APO, AP 96257-5404

Internet: http://www-2id.korea.army.mil/camps/essayons.htm
OFFICER-OF-THE-DAY: Staff Duty Officer; 011-82-351-870-6637; DSN 315-732-6637

Profile

BRANCH: Army.

LOCATION: Near Camps Red Cloud & Stanley & Uijongbu City; 20 mi from Seoul.

MAJOR UNITS: 102nd Military Intelligence Bn.

BASE HISTORY: Provides military intelligence support for 2nd Infantry Division.

Personnel and Expenditures

ACTIVE DUTY PERSONNEL: 450
CIVILIAN PERSONNEL: 135

Services

Housing: All personnel live on post; most serve 1-year unaccompanied tours. *Exchange:* Barber shop; Shoe repair; Tailor/Alterations; PX; Pizza delivery; Snack bar. *Base Library:* Yes. *Recreational Facilities:* Recreation center; Gym; Bowling center; Tennis courts; Pool; Craft shop; NCO club; Enlisted club; Basketball.

Camp Garry Owen

1094. Camp Garry Owen

APO, AE
Internet: http://www-2id.korea.army.mil/camps/owen.htm

Profile

BRANCH: Army.

SIZE AND LOCATION: 64.3 acres. Near Camp Howze; 1.5 mi from Munsan; 26.5 mi from Seoul.

MAJOR UNITS: 7th Cavalry HQ, 4th Squadron; 7th Cavalry, 4th Squadron, A Troop; 7th Cavalry, 4th Squadron, B Troop; 7th Cavalry, 4th Squadron, C Troop.

BASE HISTORY: Provide cavalry support for 2nd Infantry Division. Formerly named Camp Pelham.

Personnel and Expenditures

ACTIVE DUTY PERSONNEL: 650
CIVILIAN PERSONNEL: 130

Services

Housing: All personnel live on post; most serve 1-year unaccompanied tours. *Exchange:* Tailor/Alterations; PX; Snack bar; Airline ticket office. *Schools:* College courses; No on-base schools. *Base Library:* Yes. *Recreational Facilities:* Recreation center; Gym; Pool; Tennis courts; Craft shop; Basketball.

Camp George

1095. Camp George

APO, AP 96212

Profile

BRANCH: Army.

SIZE AND LOCATION: 16 acres. 0.5 mi from Camp Henry. *Locality:* Kyong-sang-buk-do Province.

MAJOR UNITS: 19th Theater Army Area Command.

BASE HISTORY: Named after PFC Charles George, Medal of Honor recipient.

Services

Housing: Family units. *Child Care/Capacities:* Child development center.

Schools: Preschool/Kindergarten; Elementary; Intermediate/Junior high; High school. *Recreational Facilities:* Outdoor recreation area.

Camp Giant

1096. Camp Giant
APO, AP
Internet: http://www-2id.korea.army.mil/camps/
    giant/.htm
Profile
BRANCH: Army.
SIZE AND LOCATION: 23.9 acres. Near Camp
    Howze & Munsan; 25 mi from Seoul.
MAJOR UNITS: 1st Bn, 506th Infantry, A Co.
Personnel and Expenditures
ACTIVE DUTY PERSONNEL: 150
CIVILIAN PERSONNEL: 400
Services
Housing: All personnel live on post; most serve
1-year unaccompanied tour. *Exchange:* Barber
shop; Laundry; PX. *Recreational Facilities:*
Mini-gym.

Camp Greaves

1097. Camp Greaves
APO, AP
Internet: http://www-2id.korea.army.mil/camps/
    greaves.htm
Profile
BRANCH: Army.
SIZE AND LOCATION: 58.5 acres. Near Camp
    Howze; 1.5 mi from DMZ; 38 mi to Seoul.
MAJOR UNITS: 1st Bn, 506th Infantry.
Personnel and Expenditures
ACTIVE DUTY PERSONNEL: 700
CIVILIAN PERSONNEL: 30
Services
Housing: All personnel live on post; most serve
1-year unaccompanied tour. *Exchange:* Barber
shop; Tailor/Alterations; Laundry; PX; Burger
bar. *Schools:* College courses; No on-base
schools. *Base Library:* Yes. *Medical Facilities:*
Dental clinic. *Recreational Facilities:* Recreation center; Gym; Bowling center; Pool; Tennis
courts; Racquetball court; Craft shop; Officers
club; NCO club; Enlisted club.

Camp Henry

1098. Camp Henry
Unit 15494
APO, AP 96218-5494
011-822-7913-1110; FAX 011-82-53-470-7785;
DSN 723-1110
Internet: http://143.138.5.196/36thjava.htm
Profile
BRANCH: Army.
SIZE AND LOCATION: 51 acres. In SE South
    Korea in city of Taegu; 107 mi N NW of
    Pusan; 200 mi S of Seoul. *Locality:* Kyong-
    sang-buk-do Province.
MAJOR UNITS: 20th Area Support Group; 6th
    Support Center; 728th Military Police Bn;
    36th Signal Bn.
BASE HISTORY: 1921, built by Japanese
    Army, HQ for Gen Minami. Named after Lt
    Frederick Henry, Medal of Honor recipient.

Performs direct support supply, service, &
maintenance for units in Area IV.
Services
Housing: Duplex units 86; Townhouse units.
Temporary Housing: VIP units 4. *Exchange:*
Barber shop; Dry cleaners; Food shop; Beauty
shop; Laundromat; Red Cross. *Schools:* College
courses; No on-base schools. *Base Library:* Yes.
Recreational Facilities: Gym; Recreation center;
Tennis courts; Racquetball court; Fitness center/
Weight room; Softball field; Football field; Auto
shop; NCO club; Enlisted club; Youth center;
Playground; Combined club; Teen club.

Camp Hialeah

1099. Camp Hialeah
Unit 15181
APO, AP 96259-0270
DSN 763-7469; DSN FAX 763-3904
E-mail: EANC-TP-P@emh5.korea.army.mil In-
    ternet:http://143.138.5.196/74th.htm
OFFICER-OF-THE-DAY: DSN 763-3656
Profile
BRANCH: Army.
SIZE AND LOCATION: 143 acres. In SE Ko-
    rea, approx 5 mi N of Pusan. *Locality:* Pusan
    Province.
MAJOR UNITS: 20th Support Group, Pusan;
    4th Quartermaster Det; 552nd Military Police
    Co; 74th Signal Co; 72nd Ordnance Co; HSC,
    16th Medical Bn, Area Support; 25th Trans,
    2nd MCR; 106th Medical Det (Vet); 665th
    Medical Co (Dental); HHC, 1st Signal Bde,
    CLSCK.
BASE HISTORY: Main area once owned by
    Cho Sun Racing Association as horse racing
    stadium. 1945, first US troops in camp; used
    by American Consulate & United Nations un-
    til 1950. Principal terminal for supplies as
    8069th US Replacement Depot. 1953, used
    by troops of Korean Communications Zone.
    1954-84, series of reorganizations: Pusan
    Military Post, Pusan Sub Area Command,
    Pusan Area Command, Pusan Base Com-
    mand, 2nd Transportation Group, Pusan Sup-
    port Activity, & US Army Garrison, Pusan.
    1984, 34th Support Group activated. 1990,
    20th Support Group took over. 74th Signal
    Co operates & maintains all Army Fixed De-
    fense Communications Systems & base com-
    munications in Pusan, Changsan, Chinhae &
    Cheju Island; maintains operations sites at
    Pulmosan, Brooklyn, Changsan Microwave
    relay sites; Pusan Telecommunications Cen-
    ter, Pusan DSN, Pusan Outside Plant &
    Masan & Kimhae Fiber Optics repeater sta-
    tions.
Key Contacts
COMMANDER: LTC Steve T Wilberger.
PUBLIC AFFAIRS: I-uk Kim, Community
    Relations Officer, DSN 763-7469.
TRANSPORTATION: Ronald L Walton, DSN
    763-7640.
PERSONNEL/COMMUNITY ACTIVITIES: F
    W Morris, Chief, Admin Service Div, DSN
    763-7479, EANC-TP-P@emh5.korea.army.
    mil; SGM James D Puppke, Community
    Activities, DSN 763-3773.
Personnel and Expenditures
ACTIVE DUTY PERSONNEL: 510
DEPENDENTS: 415
CIVILIAN PERSONNEL: 136

Services
Housing: Family units 59; Unaccompanied officer quarters 28; Unaccompanied enlisted quarters 49. *Temporary Housing:* VIP units 1. *Commissary:* Yes; *Exchange:* Barber shop; Food
shop; Florist; Bank; Military clothing store; Convenience store; Beauty shop; Laundromat; Post
office; Fast food; Video rentals. *Child Care/Ca-
pacities:* Day care center 1yr-12yrs; After-
school programs. *Schools:* Preschool/Kindergar-
ten; Elementary; Intermediate/Junior high; High
school; College courses. *Base Library:* Yes.
Medical Facilities: Dental clinic; Dispensary;
Pharmacy; Veterinary services. *Recreational Facilities:* Bowling center; Movie theater; Pool;
Gym; Recreation center; Tennis courts; Racquetball court; Fitness center/Weight room; Softball
field; Football field; Craft shop; Youth center;
Community club.

Camp Hovey

1100. Camp Hovey
APO, AP 96224
Internet: http://www-2id.korea.army.mil/camps/
    hovey.htm
OFFICER-OF-THE-DAY: Duty Officer,
    011-82-351-5061; DSN 315-730-5061
Profile
BRANCH: Army.
SIZE AND LOCATION: 3928.4 acres. Approx
    41 mi N of Seoul; 1 mi from Tongduchon;
    just SW of Camp Casey. *Locality:* Kyonggi
    Province.
MAJOR UNITS: 2nd Infantry Division, 2nd Bri-
    gade HQ; 9th Infantry, 1st Bn; 5th Bn, 5th
    Air Defense Artillery, B Co; 2nd Forward
    Support Bn; 503rd Infantry, 1st Bn, C Co;
    17th Field Artillery, 2nd Bn; Long Range Sur-
    veillance Det.
Personnel and Expenditures
ACTIVE DUTY PERSONNEL: 2500
DEPENDENTS: 0
CIVILIAN PERSONNEL: 105
Services
Housing: All soldiers live on post; most serve 1-
year unaccompanied tour. *Temporary Housing:*
None. *Exchange:* Barber shop; Bank; Military
clothing store; Convenience store; Tailor/Altera-
tions; Exchange; Fast food; Minimall. *Schools:*
College courses; No on-base schools. *Base Li-
brary:* Yes. *Recreational Facilities:* Bowling
center; Movie theater; Pool; Gym; Recreation
center; Craft shop; Officers club; NCO club; Enlisted club.

Camp Howze

1101. Camp Howze
Unit 15529
APO, AP 96251-5529
Internet: http://www-2id.korea.army.mil/camps/
    howze.htm
OFFICER-OF-THE-DAY: Staff Duty Officer,
    011-82-348-940-5252, DSN 315-734-5252,
    734-5081
Profile
BRANCH: Army.
SIZE AND LOCATION: 148.9 acres.

Hub of Munsan area; at Hongilchon City; 3 mi from Kumchon; 14 mi from Seoul; 5 mi S of DMZ.
MAJOR UNITS: Assistant Division Commander (Maneuver), Camp Howze; Engineer Brigade HQ, Camp Howze; 44th Engineer Bn.
BASE HISTORY: Provides engineer support for 2nd Infantry Division.
Personnel and Expenditures
ACTIVE DUTY PERSONNEL: 450
CIVILIAN PERSONNEL: 250
Services
Housing: All personnel live on post; most serve 1-year unaccompanied tour. *Exchange:* Barber shop; Tailor/Alterations; PX; Airline ticket office; Burger bar. *Schools:* College courses; No on-base schools. *Base Library:* Yes. *Recreational Facilities:* Recreation center; Gym; Bowling center; Tennis courts; Officers club; NCO club; Enlisted club; Craft shop; Pool; Basketball.

Camp Humphreys

1102. Camp Humphreys
Unit 15716
APO, AP 96271-0716
Internet: http://www.aafes.com/Bases/Camp_Humphreys/gm.htm
OFFICER-OF-THE-DAY: 011-82-333-690-6133, DSN 753-6133; Command Post 011-82-333-690-6222, DSN 753-6222
Profile
BRANCH: Army.
SIZE AND LOCATION: 1351 acres. In W South Korea; S of Pyongtaek; near Anjung-ri; 25 mi S Osan; 52 mi SW of Seoul.
MAJOR UNITS: 23rd Support Group; 194th Maintenance Bn; 8th Army Confinement Facility; Katusa Training Academy.
BASE HISTORY: Largest & busiest Army airfield, OCONUS.
Key Contacts
COMMANDER: Col Michael Kobbe, Garrison Commander, DSN 315-753-6108, eanc-hg-co@korea.emh5.army.mil.
Personnel and Expenditures
ACTIVE DUTY PERSONNEL: 3812
CIVILIAN PERSONNEL: 67
Services
Housing: All personnel live on post; most serve 1-year unaccompanied tour. *Commissary:* Yes; *Exchange:* Barber shop; Beauty shop; Video rentals; Fast food; Class VI; Food shop; Four seasons; Laundromat; Military clothing store; Post office; Convenience store; Tailor/Alterations; Service station; Mini-mall; Exchange (small). *Child Care/Capacities:* No day care facilities. *Schools:* College courses; No on-base schools. *Base Library:* Yes. *Medical Facilities:* Dental clinic. *Recreational Facilities:* Bowling center; Movie theater; Gym; Recreation center; Auto shop; Craft shop; Officers club; NCO club; Enlisted club; Tour & travel office; Mini-arcade.

Camp LaGuardia

1103. Camp LaGuardia
APO, AE
Internet: http://www-2id.korea.army.mil/camps/laguardia.htm
OFFICER-OF-THE-DAY: Staff Duty Officer, 011-82-351-870-6522, DSN 315-732-6522
Profile
BRANCH: Army.
SIZE AND LOCATION: 33.8 acres. Near Camps Red Cloud & Stanley & Uijongbu; 20 mi from Seoul.
MAJOR UNITS: 50th Engineer Co.
BASE HISTORY: Provides engineering support for 2nd Infantry Division.
Personnel and Expenditures
ACTIVE DUTY PERSONNEL: 170
CIVILIAN PERSONNEL: 80
Services
Housing: All personnel live on post; most serve 1-year unaccompanied tour. *Exchange:* Barber shop; PX. *Recreational Facilities:* Tennis courts; Gym; NCO club; Enlisted club; Basketball.

Camp Long

1104. Camp Long
APO, AP 96297-0246
011-82-721-3335; FAX 721-3555
Internet: http://www.aftac.gov/sets/452/det452.html
Profile
BRANCH: Army.
SIZE AND LOCATION: 82 acres. In suburb of Taejang; approx 180 mi ESE of Seoul; 50 mi S of DMZ. *Locality:* Kangwon-bo Province.
MAJOR UNITS: Combat Support Coordination Team 1; 304th Signal Bn, B Co; 6th Bn, 538th Ordnance Co; 61st Maintenance Co; 501st Aviation Bn, Det 5; 275th Signal Site; 51st Military Police Co; 665th Dental Clinic; 218th Medical Clinic.
BASE HISTORY: 1970, Camp Long organized to support tenant units at R-401 Airfield; named in honor of Sgt Charles R Long, Medal of Honor recipient, killed near Wonju in Korean War. Unit assigned to 20th General Support Group under operational control of Commanding General, FROKA Detachment, Korean Military Advisory Group. 1978, reassigned to 19th Support Command, Commander, Camp Page. 1987, Camp Long & Page under Command of 501st Corps Support Group.
Personnel and Expenditures
ACTIVE DUTY PERSONNEL: 500
CIVILIAN PERSONNEL: 500
Services
Housing: All personnel live on post; most serve 1-year unaccompanied tour. *Exchange:* Retail store; Barber shop; Dry cleaners; Bank. *Schools:* College courses; No on-base schools. *Base Library:* Yes. *Medical Facilities:* Dental clinic; Dispensary; Pharmacy. *Recreational Facilities:* Bowling center; Gym; Recreation center; Tennis courts; Racquetball court; Fitness center/Weight room; Softball field; Football field; Craft shop; Officers club; NCO club; Enlisted club; Playground.

Camp MacNab (Cheju Do)

1105. Camp MacNab (Cheju Do)
Unit 15031
APO, AP 96220-5031
011-82-53-470-7132; FAX 011-82-53-470-7404; DSN 314-768-7132
E-mail: eanc-t-cdr@emh5.korea.army.mil
Profile
BRANCH: Army.
LOCATION: On SW corner of island of Cheju-Do, just N of Mosulpo; 70 mi S of W coast of Korea. *Locality:* Island of Cheju.
MAJOR UNITS: 20th Area Support Group; Cheju-Do Training Center.
BASE HISTORY: 1950-53, Camp founded; named after Col Alexander J MacNab, member of Korean Military Advisors Group during Korean War. 1950-60, Army training base. 1960, compound turned over to Detachment 4, 51st Air Base Wing, USAF; operated as airfield. 1973, became joint ROK Air Force & US Army compound. 1975, 8th Army established Cheju-Do Training Center. Today, training in military mountaineering & Australian-style rappelling.
VISITOR ATTRACTIONS: Semi-tropical island with beautiful beaches.
Personnel and Expenditures
ACTIVE DUTY PERSONNEL: 20
CIVILIAN PERSONNEL: 30
Services
Housing: Barracks spaces 23; Mobile home units 1. *Temporary Housing:* MWR guest rooms 7. *Exchange:* Convenience store. *Child Care/Capacities:* No day care facilities. *Schools:* No on-base schools. *Base Library:* Yes. *Medical Facilities:* Dispensary. *Recreational Facilities:* Gym; Recreation center; Tennis courts; Racquetball court; Fitness center/Weight room; Fishing/Hunting; Skeet range; Water sports; All ranks club.

Camp Mobile

1106. Camp Mobile
APO, AP
Internet: http://www-2id.korea.army.mil/camps/mobile.htm
OFFICER-OF-THE-DAY: Staff Duty Officer, 011-82-351-869-4208, DSN 315-730-4208
Profile
BRANCH: Army.
SIZE AND LOCATION: 30.8 acres. Near Tongduchon; 40 mi from Seoul.
MAJOR UNITS: Warrior Replacement Co.
BASE HISTORY: In-processing center for 2nd Infantry Division.
Personnel and Expenditures
ACTIVE DUTY PERSONNEL: Changes daily with new arrivals
CIVILIAN PERSONNEL: 100
Services
Housing: All personnel live on post; most serve 1-year unaccompanied tours. *Exchange:* Barber shop; Laundry; PX. *Recreational Facilities:* Racquetball court; Tennis courts; NCO club; Enlisted club; Basketball.

Camp Nimble

1107. Camp Nimble
APO, AP
Internet: http://www-2id.korea.army.mil/camps/
nimble.htm
OFFICER-OF-THE-DAY: Duty Officer,
011-82-351-869-3565, DSN 315-730-3565

Profile
BRANCH: Army.
SIZE AND LOCATION: 14 acres. Near Camps
Casey & Mobile; near Tongduchon; 40 mi
from Seoul.
MAJOR UNITS: 702nd Main Support Bn, A
Co; 702nd Main Support Bn, B Co.
BASE HISTORY: Provides combat support for
2nd Infantry Division.

Personnel and Expenditures
ACTIVE DUTY PERSONNEL: 330
CIVILIAN PERSONNEL: 20

Services
Housing: All personnel live on post; most serve
1-year unaccompanied tour. *Exchange:* Barber
shop; Laundry; PX. *Recreational Facilities:*
Pool; Gym; Racquetball court; Tennis courts;
NCO club; Enlisted club; Basketball court.

Camp Page

1108. Camp Page
Unit 15002
APO, AP 96208-0252
Internet: http://www-2id.korea.army.mil/camps/
page.htm
OFFICER-OF-THE-DAY: Staff Duty Officer,
011-82-361-59-5410, DSN 315-721-5410

Profile
BRANCH: Army.
SIZE AND LOCATION: 157.2 acres. In N-cen-
tral South Korea; near Chunchon City; 48 mi
from Seoul. *Locality:* Kangwon Province.
MAJOR UNITS: Area I (East); 1st Bn, 2nd
Aviation.
BASE HISTORY: Provides aviation support for
2nd Infantry Division.

Key Contacts
COMMANDER: Col Tom B Foulk III, Garrison
Commander, 011-49-823-6159-502, DSN
721-5025, eanc-yg-cp-co@emh5.korea.army.
mil.

Personnel and Expenditures
ACTIVE DUTY PERSONNEL: 700
CIVILIAN PERSONNEL: 650

Services
Housing: All personnel live on post; most serve
1-year unaccompanied tour. *Exchange:* Barber
shop; Convenience store; Tailor/Alterations;
Class VI; PX; Burger bar; Airline ticket office;
Pizza delivery. *Schools:* College courses; No on-
base schools. *Base Library:* Yes. *Recreational
Facilities:* Recreation center; Pool; Tennis
courts; Craft shop; Community club; Basketball.

Camp Red Cloud

1109. Camp Red Cloud
Unit 15707
APO, AP 96258-0707

Internet: http://www-2id.korea.army.mil/camps/
redcloud.htm
OFFICER-OF-THE-DAY: Staff Duty Officer,
011-82-351-870-8948, DSN 315-732-8948

Profile
BRANCH: Army.
SIZE AND LOCATION: 169.7 acres. In NW
South Korea; near city of Uijongbu; 20 mi
from Seoul.
MAJOR UNITS: 2nd Infantry Division, HQ;
122nd Signal Bn, HQ; 122nd Signal Bn, C
Co; 122nd Signal Bn, D Co; Area I (West) &
Camp Red Cloud; 501st Corps Support
Group; 8th Ordnance Det.
BASE HISTORY: Provides installation manage-
ment & base operations support for Camp
Red Cloud, Camp Stanley, Camp Page, Camp
Essayons, Camp Kyle, Camp Sears, Camp
Jackson, Camp LaGuardia, Camp Falling
Water, & Camp Kwangsari.

Key Contacts
COMMANDER: LTC George A Latham II,
DSN 732-6046, enac-yg-cdr@emh5.korea.
army.mil.

Personnel and Expenditures
ACTIVE DUTY PERSONNEL: 1200
CIVILIAN PERSONNEL: 400

Services
Housing: All personnel live on post; most serve
1-year unaccompanied tour. *Exchange:* Convenience store; Service station; Retail store; Beauty
shop; Fast food; Tailor/Alterations; Class VI;
PX; Airline Ticket Office; Pizza delivery.
Schools: College courses; No on-base schools.
Base Library: Yes. *Recreational Facilities:* Recreation center; Golf course; Bowling center;
Pool; Tennis courts; Gym; Craft shop; NCO
club; Enlisted club; Basketball; Community
club.

Camp Sears

1110. Camp Sears
APO, AP
Internet: http://www-2id.koea.amry.mil/camps/
sears.htm
OFFICER-OF-THE-DAY: Duty Officer,
011-82-351-870-7695, DSN 315-732-7695

Profile
BRANCH: Army.
SIZE AND LOCATION: 31.9 acres. Near
Camps Red Cloud & Stanley; 1.5 mi from Ui-
jongbu; 21.5 mi from Seoul.
MAJOR UNITS: 702nd Main Support Bn, E Co.
BASE HISTORY: Provides combat service sup-
port for 2nd Infantry Division.

Personnel and Expenditures
ACTIVE DUTY PERSONNEL: 150
CIVILIAN PERSONNEL: 40

Services
Housing: All personnel live on post; most serve
1-year unaccompanied tours. *Exchange:* Barber
shop; Laundry; PX. *Recreational Facilities:*
Pool; Tennis courts; NCO club; Enlisted club;
Gym; Football field; Basketball court.

Camp Stanley

1111. Camp Stanley
Unit 15435
APO, AP 96257-0481

Internet: http://www-2id.korea.army.mil/camps/
stanley.htm
OFFICER-OF-THE-DAY: Duty Officer,
011-82-351-5351, DSN 315-732-5351

Profile
BRANCH: Army.
SIZE AND LOCATION: 419.8 acres. Bordering
Hwy 43, 17 mi from Seoul (2 hr drive), 3 mi
SE of downtown Uijongbu; NE of Surak
Mountain between Uijongbu Correctional Fa-
cility & village of Kosan-Dong. *Locality:*
Sosan-dong.
MAJOR UNITS: 2nd Infantry, Division Artil-
lery HQ; 6th Bn, 37th Field Artillery; 26th
Field Artillery, F Battery; 38th Field Artillery
A Battery; Aviation Brigade HQ; 2nd Bn, 2nd
Aviation; 5th Bn, 5th Air Defense Artillery,
HQ Battery; 5th Bn, 5th Air Defense Artil-
lery, D Battery; 702nd Maintenance Bn, D
Co.
BASE HISTORY: Post Korean War armistice,
area around Camp Stanley made temporary
HQ 11th Engineer Company. 1956, 36th Engi-
neer Group occupied area. 1957, Korean gov-
ernment apportioned area for permanent com-
pound. 1959, named for first commander Col
Stanley. Provides artillery & aviation support
for 2nd Infantry Division.

Key Contacts
COMMANDER: 011-82-351-870-5928, DSN
732-5928.

Personnel and Expenditures
ACTIVE DUTY PERSONNEL: 2200
DEPENDENTS: 0 (Dependent restricted area)
CIVILIAN PERSONNEL: 500

Services
Housing: Unaccompanied officer quarters Units
212; Senior NCO units 152; Most personnel live
on post. *Temporary Housing:* VIP units 1; Transient quarters 52. *Commissary:* Yes; *Exchange:*
Retail store; Barber shop; Dry cleaners; Food
shop; Bank; Bookstore; Military clothing store;
Convenience store; Laundromat; Tailor/Altera-
tions; Fast food; SATO. *Schools:* College
courses; No on-base schools. *Base Library:* Yes.
Medical Facilities: Medical clinic; Dental clinic.
Recreational Facilities: Bowling center; Movie
theater; Pool; Gym; Recreation center; Tennis
courts; Fitness center/Weight room; Softball
field; Football field; Craft shop; All ranks club;
Community club.

Camp Stanton

1112. Camp Stanton
APO, AP
Internet: http://www-2id.korea.army/camps/
stanton.htm

Profile
BRANCH: Army.
SIZE AND LOCATION: 67.4 acres. Near Camp
Howze; 1 mi from Tonggo-ri; 13.5 mi from
Seoul.
MAJOR UNITS: 7th Cavalry, 4th Squadron
(Air).
BASE HISTORY: Provides cavalry support for
2nd Infantry Division.

Personnel and Expenditures
ACTIVE DUTY PERSONNEL: 200
DEPENDENTS: 0
CIVILIAN PERSONNEL: 80

Services

Housing: All personnel live on base; most for 1-year unaccompanied tour. *Exchange:* Fast food; Tailor/Alterations; Convenience store; Class VI; Service station; Barber shop; Beauty shop; Airline ticket office; Pizza delivery. *Base Library:* Yes. *Recreational Facilities:* Recreation center; Gym; Tennis courts; NCO club; Enlisted club; Craft shop; Portable swimming pool.

Camp Walker

1113. Camp Walker
Unit 15026
APO, AE 96218-0183
011-82-53-470-4936; FAX
011-82-53-470-4761; DSN 315-764-4936
OFFICER-OF-THE-DAY: MP Desk, DSN
764-4141

Profile

BRANCH: Army.

SIZE AND LOCATION: 190 acres. In Taegu, Korea; 2 mi from Camp Henry. *Locality:* Kyong-sang-buk-do Province.

MAJOR UNITS: 36th Signal Bn, HQ; 19th Theater Army Area Command.

BASE HISTORY: 1921, opened as firing range for Japanese Army. 1974, 36th Signal Bn activated. Provides administrative & logistical for command group & staff. N end of camp operations use & airfield; central area recreational use & golf course; W-Central area family housing; E-Central portion community facilities. Named after Lt Gen Walton A Walker, Commander, American Ground Forces, Korea, killed in Jeep accident, 1950.

Key Contacts

COMMANDER: LTC Jane F Maliszewski.

Services

Housing: Family units; Unaccompanied officer quarters. *Commissary:* Yes; *Exchange:* Service station; Credit union; Military clothing store; Post office; PX. *Medical Facilities:* Dispensary; Dental clinic; Veterinary services; Emergency room. *Recreational Facilities:* Gym; Golf course; Community club; Sport support facility; Tour & Travel center.

Chinhae Fleet Activities

1114. Chinhae Fleet Activities
CFAC
PSC 479
FPO, AP 96269-1100
011-82-553-40-5310; DSN 315-762-5310; DSN FAX 315-762-5308
Internet: http://144.59.63.170/

Profile

BRANCH: Navy.

SIZE AND LOCATION: 84 acres. Approx 35 mi W of Pusan on S coast of Korea; adj to Korea, Republic of (ROK) Navy Base; 25 mi S of DMZ. *Locality:* Kyongsang Nam Do Province.

MAJOR UNITS: Commander, Naval Forces Korea (COMNAVFORKOREA); Commander, United Nations Command Naval Component; Commander, Republic of Korea/US Forces

Korea Combined Forces; Commander, Combat Coordination Group Korea.

BASE HISTORY: Late 19th century, Chinhae established as naval base by Russians; occupied by Japanese after Russo-Japanese War. WWII, Japanese support base; Air Academy established. Today, home of ROK Naval Academy; homeport of ROK Navy. 1952, US Naval Advisory Group established. 1969, reorganized to Fleet Detachment Naval Section, Joint US Military Advisory Group-Korea. 1972, became Chinhae Facility, US Naval Forces, Korea. 1987, following other reorganizations, realigned under Commander, Naval Surface Force Pacific.

Key Contacts

COMMANDER: RADM Richard W Mayo; Capt Daivd P Austin, Chief of Staff.

Personnel and Expenditures

ACTIVE DUTY PERSONNEL: 90
DEPENDENTS: 100
CIVILIAN PERSONNEL: 129 (US & Korean)

Services

Housing: Family units 50; Barracks spaces 19; BEQ/BOQ 60. *Temporary Housing:* VIP units 1; Dormitory units 6; Transient quarters 60. *Commissary:* Yes; *Exchange:* Post office; ATM. *Child Care/Capacities:* No day care facilities; Youth center activities. *Schools:* Elementary; *Base Library:* Yes. *Medical Facilities:* Medical clinic. *Recreational Facilities:* Fitness center/Weight room; Gym; Bowling center; Pool; Youth center; All hands club.

K-16 (Army Airfield)

1115. K-16 (Army Airfield)
Unit 15238, Box 10
APO, AP 96205-0011
82-342-720-6319; FAX 82-342-720-6527; DSN 741-6319
OFFICER-OF-THE-DAY: DSN 741-6617

Profile

BRANCH: Army.

SIZE AND LOCATION: 165 acres. In Song Nam City on S boundary of Seoul; near Camp Colbern. *Locality:* Kyonggi Do.

MAJOR UNITS: 1st Bn, 501st Aviation, Co A; 8th US Army Simulated Flight Training Facility; 595th Maintenance Co (DS/GS); 8th US Army Milk Plant.

BASE HISTORY: Originally located on Youido Island in Seoul. 1971, moved to present location as part of Seoul Master Planning Commission; US Forces Korea granted exclusive use of 55 acres & joint use of 110 acres. 1977, Simulated Flight Training Facility opened. 1982, Installation Support Activity formed for base operations. 1984, 377th Medical Company (Air Ambulance) moved in. 1985, milk plant opened; provides milk for forces on Korean Peninsula. 1986, Flying Club moved to Camp Humphreys. Area II installation under 34th Area Support Group.

Key Contacts

COMMANDER: Col William J Elder; 17th Aviation Brigade, APO AP 96205-0043; DSN 723-350.

PUBLIC AFFAIRS: MSG John C Collins; DSN 741-6411.

Personnel and Expenditures

ACTIVE DUTY PERSONNEL: 400
CIVILIAN PERSONNEL: 300

Services

Housing: Unaccompanied officer quarters 48; Unaccompanied enlisted quarters 10; Barracks spaces 350. *Exchange:* Retail store; Barber shop; Dry cleaners; Bank; Laundromat. *Child Care/Capacities:* No day care facilities. *Schools:* College courses; No on-base schools. *Medical Facilities:* Dispensary. *Recreational Facilities:* Pool; Gym; Recreation center; Tennis courts; Racquetball court; Fitness center/Weight room; Softball field; Officers club; NCO club; Enlisted club; Picnic area.

Kimpo Military Mail Terminal

1116. Kimpo Military Mail Terminal
Kimpo MMT
66th AG Co (Postal), 1st Plt, Unit 15368
APO, AP 96201-9998
DSN 723-3838

Profile

BRANCH: Air Force; Army.

SIZE AND LOCATION: 1.9 acres. At Kimpo Airport; off Hwy 88 Olympic.

MAJOR UNITS: 66th AG Co (Postal), 1st Plt.

BASE HISTORY: Unit may relocate to New IAP, Inchon, Korea in 2000.

Key Contacts

COMMANDER: 1Lt Stephen R Esther.
PUBLIC AFFAIRS: 2Lt Joseph M DeSalvo.

Personnel and Expenditures

ACTIVE DUTY PERSONNEL: 19
CIVILIAN PERSONNEL: 14

Services

Housing: None. *Child Care/Capacities:* No day care facilities. *Schools:* No on-base schools. *Medical Facilities:* No medical facilities.

Kunsan Air Base

1117. Kunsan Air Base
Unit 2090
APO, AP 96264-2090
82-654-470-4705; FAX 782-4517; DSN 782-4705
Internet: http://www.kusan.af.mil/

Profile

BRANCH: Air Force.

LOCATION: 7 mi W of Kunsan City on W coast of peninsula near Kum River estuary. *Locality:* Chollabuk-do Province.

MAJOR UNITS: 8th Fighter Wing; 35th Fighter Squadron; 80th Fighter Squadron; 8th Support Group; 8th Medical Group; 8th Logistics Group; 8th Operations Group; 25th Transportation Bn (Army); 1/43 Air Defense Artillery, E Battery; 1/43 Air Defense Artillery, F Battery.

BASE HISTORY: 1938, built as fighter-interceptor base by Japanese. 1945, home of US Military Assistance Advisory Group. 1949, turned over to Republic of Korea. 1950, occupied by North Korean forces; recaptured & occupied by 5th Air Force. 1954-71, operated by 6175th Air Base Wing. 1971-74, operated by 3rd Tactical Fighter Wing. 1974, under 8th Tactical Fighter Wing, now 8th Fighter Wing, "Wolf Pack."

Key Contacts
COMMANDER: Col Mark A Welsh, III.
PUBLIC AFFAIRS: 1Lt Sam Highley.
TRANSPORTATION: Billeting, DSN 782-4604.
Personnel and Expenditures
ACTIVE DUTY PERSONNEL: 2657
CIVILIAN PERSONNEL: 38 (US civilians); 766 (Korean Nationals)
Services
Housing: Unaccompanied officer quarters; Unaccompanied enlisted quarters; BAQ units; Barracks spaces; Dormitory spaces; Senior NCO units; Junior NCO units. *Temporary Housing:* VIP units; VOQ units; VEQ units; VAQ units; Unaccompanied officer/Enlisted quarters; BAQ units; Dormitory units. *Commissary:* Yes; *Exchange:* Retail store; Barber shop; Dry cleaners; Food shop; Florist; Bank; Service station; Bookstore; Military clothing store; Convenience store; Beauty shop; Laundromat. *Child Care/Capacities:* No day care facilities. *Schools:* College courses; No on-base schools. *Base Library:* Yes. *Medical Facilities:* Hospital 8 beds; Dental clinic; Primary Care; Emergency Room; Physical Therapy; Counselling services. *Recreational Facilities:* Bowling center; Movie theater; Pool; Gym; Recreation center; Golf course; Tennis courts; Racquetball court; Fitness center/Weight room; Softball field; Craft shop; Consolidated club.

Osan Air Base

1118. Osan Air Base
Unit 2067
APO, AP 96278-2067
Internet: http://www.osan.af.mil/
Profile
BRANCH: Air Force.
SIZE AND LOCATION: 1674 acres. 38 mi S of Seoul, adj to Songtan Si; 48 mi from N Korea. *Locality:* Kyonggi Province.
MAJOR UNITS: 7th Air Force, HQ; 607th Air Operations Group; 607th Air Support Operations Group; 51st Fighter Wing; 51st Communications Squadron; 51st Service Squadron; 51st Medical Group; 51st Mission Support Squadron; 631st Air Mobility Support Squadron.
BASE HISTORY: 1952, base opened as "K-55" with 18th Fighter Bomber Wing. 1956, designated Osan AB, after village (now city of Songtan) scene of first fighting between US & North Korean forces, July 1950. Only American base in Korea built from scratch. 1954-55, HQ, 5th Air Force. 1957, 58th Air Base Group host unit. 1971, 51st Air Base Wing took over support responsibilities. 1974, redesignated 51st Composite Wing. 1982, redesignated 51st Tactical Fighter Wing. 1992, redesignated 51st Fighter Wing.
VISITOR ATTRACTIONS: Hill 180 Monument (Korean War battle memorial).
Key Contacts
COMMANDER: Lt Gen Joseph E Hurd, Commander 7th AF; Brig Gen Paul R Dordal, Commander, 51st FW.
Personnel and Expenditures
ACTIVE DUTY PERSONNEL: 5766
DEPENDENTS: 1440
CIVILIAN PERSONNEL: 986

Services
Housing: Family units 287; Unaccompanied officer quarters 300; Unaccompanied enlisted quarters; Dormitory spaces 200; Senior NCO units 317; Additional housing at Sochong Village, USAF & Mustang Valley Village. *Temporary Housing:* VIP units 18; VOQ units 70; VAQ units 400; BAQ units; Osan Inn. *Commissary:* Yes; *Exchange:* Retail store; Barber shop; Dry cleaners; Food shop; Florist; Bank; Service station; Bookstore; Military clothing store; Convenience store; Beauty shop; Laundromat; Credit union; Four seasons; Class VI; Shopping arcade. *Child Care/Capacities:* Day care center capacity 66, 6mo-6yrs; Part-day preschool program. *Schools:* Preschool/Kindergarten; Elementary; Intermediate/Junior high; College courses. *Base Library:* Yes. *Medical Facilities:* Hospital 30 beds; Dental clinic; Pharmacy; Veterinary services. *Recreational Facilities:* Bowling center; Movie theater; Pool; Gym; Recreation center; Golf course; Tennis courts; Racquetball court; Fitness center/Weight room; Softball field; Football field; Auto shop; Craft shop; Officers club; NCO club; Enlisted club; Youth center; Picnic area; Aero club; MAC terminal; Military Affiliate Radio System (MARS) station; USO.

Pusan Storage Facility

1119. Pusan Storage Facility
EANC-MSC-P
Unit 15183
APO, AP 96259-0272
DSN 763-7800; DSN FAX 763-7789
Internet: http://143.138.250.38/pb_psf.htm
Profile
BRANCH: Army.
MAJOR UNITS: Pusan Storage Facility.
Key Contacts
COMMANDER: LTC Steve T Wilberger, DSN 763-7799.
PUBLIC AFFAIRS: Information Mgr, DSN 765-3929.
PROCUREMENT: Logistics Sys Spt Br, DSN 763-3614.

US Army Corps of Engineers, Far East District

1120. US Army Corps of Engineers, Far East District
USAEDFE
USAEDFE, Unit 15546
APO, AP 96205-0610
011-822-270-7489
Internet: http://www.pod.usace.army.mil/org/fed/quick.html
Profile
BRANCH: Army.
LOCATION: Korean local address: Post Office #100-195, Ulchiro 5 GA, Choonggu, Seoul, Korea, US Army Engineer Compound. *Locality:* Seoul.
MAJOR UNITS: Corps of Engineers, Far East District.
BASE HISTORY: Activated June 1957. Operating component of Army Engineer Division,

Pacific Ocean. Responsible for designing projects, administrating contracts for architectural & engineering services, construction, & maintenance & repair in support of US forces Korea. Resident offices at Osan AB, Camp Henry, & Uijongbu.
Key Contacts
COMMANDER: Col James L Hickey.
PUBLIC AFFAIRS: Stephanie Scott, Steph. Scott@POF01.usace.army.mil.
Personnel and Expenditures
ACTIVE DUTY PERSONNEL: 250 (active duty, civilians, Korean Nationals)

Yongsan Army Garrison

1121. Yongsan Army Garrison
Unit 15333
APO, AP 96205
Profile
BRANCH: Army.
SIZE AND LOCATION: 1389.9 acres (includes Yongsan, Camp Colbern, K-16, Market Area, Camp Mercer Area, and Camp Coiner). In downtown Seoul; divided into Main Post & South Post by Hannam-No Hwy. *Locality:* Seoul.
MAJOR UNITS: 34th Area Support Group & Area II; 227th Maintenance Bn; Combined Forces Command, HQ; 8th Army; US-ROK Combined Forces Command; 121st Evacuation Hospital; United Nations Command; US Forces Korea.
VISITOR ATTRACTIONS: Dragon Hill Recreation Center: TDY rate; other special discount rates based on rank; Recreation Dept, Unit 15335, APO AP 96205-0427, 790-0016, DSN 738-2222, FAX CONUS 011-822-790-1576.
Key Contacts
COMMANDER: Col John D Kennedy, ATTN: EANC-SA-CDR, DSN 738-7441, FAX 011-82-2791-83021, eanc-sa-cdr@emh5. korea.army.mil.
Services
Housing: Hunnam Village housing area. *Temporary Housing:* Lodge units Dragon Hill 299 rooms. *Commissary:* Yes; *Exchange:* Retail store; Barber shop; Food shop; Bank; Service station; Furniture store; Bookstore; Military clothing store; Convenience store; Beauty shop; Laundromat; Credit union; Fast food; Video rentals; Four seasons; Class VI; Largest exchange in Korea with shopping arcade, ice cream shop, bicycle shop, sports store. *Child Care/Capacities:* Day care center; Latch key program. *Schools:* Elementary; High school; College courses. *Base Library:* Yes. *Medical Facilities:* Hospital; Medical clinic; Dental clinic; Veterinary services. *Recreational Facilities:* Bowling center; Movie theater; Pool; Racquetball court; Fitness center/Weight room; Auto shop; Craft shop; Officers club; NCO club; Enlisted club; Youth center; Picnic area; Community club; All ranks club; Tour & Travel center; Navy club; Field house; Basketball; Equipment issue; Performing arts center; Pet kennel.

Zoeckler Station

1122. Zoeckler Station
CDR, 751st MI Bn
APO, AP 96271-0162
DSN 753-3090; DSN FAX 753-3237
OFFICER-OF-THE-DAY: Capt Rupinen, DSN
753-3350

Profile
BRANCH: Army.
SIZE AND LOCATION: 140 acres. 60 mi S of
Seoul; 19 mi N of Cheonan; 5 mi SW of
Pyong Tack. *Locality:* Kyongi Do.
MAJOR UNITS: 751st Military Intelligence Bn;
3rd Military Intelligence Bn; 532nd Military
Intelligence Bn, B Co; INSCOM Support Ele-
ment; Mission Support Activity Korea, Con-
figuration Management Office & Installation
Team Pacific; 501st Signal Co, Det; Telecom-
munications Center, Zoeckler Station.
BASE HISTORY: 1971, established as US
Army Security Agency Field Station; took
over mission from previous Army Security
Agency units. Named for LTC Zoeckler, station's first commanding officer. 1977, redesignated US Army Field Station Korea.

Key Contacts
COMMANDER: LTC Charles S Lewis.
PUBLIC AFFAIRS: Capt Jon Ross, DSN
753-3234.
PROCUREMENT: Capt Jim Llotz, DSN
753-3217.
TRANSPORTATION: See Procurement
Officer.

PERSONNEL/COMMUNITY ACTIVITIES:
See Public Affairs Officer.
Personnel and Expenditures
ACTIVE DUTY PERSONNEL: 371
CIVILIAN PERSONNEL: 68
Services
Housing: Barracks spaces; Senior NCO units;
Junior NCO units; Unaccompanied officer quar-
ters unit. *Exchange:* Barber shop; Dry cleaners;
Convenience store; ATM; Tailor/Alterations;
PX. *Child Care/Capacities:* No day care facili-
ties. *Schools:* Korean language training facility.
Base Library: Yes. *Medical Facilities:* No medi-
cal facilities. *Recreational Facilities:* Pool;
Gym; Tennis courts; Racquetball court; Fitness
center/Weight room; Softball field; Craft shop;
Picnic area; All ranks club.

Luxembourg

23rd Combat Equipment Company

1123. 23rd Combat Equipment Company
CEC 23
APO, AE 09054

FAX 011-35-251-520791
Profile
BRANCH: Army.
LOCATION: Bettembourg, Luxembourg.
MAJOR UNITS: 23rd Combat Equipment Co;
CEB-North.

Key Contacts
COMMANDER: Keith Mostofi, CEA,
011-35-251-895509, mostofik@cege.
schinnen.army.mil.

Marshall Islands

Kwajalein Missile Range

1124. Kwajalein Missile Range
Box 26
APO, AP 96555

Profile
BRANCH: Army.
SIZE AND LOCATION: 1400 acres. On Kwajalein Atoll, Republic of the Marshall Islands;
2415 mi SW of Pearl Harbor.
MAJOR UNITS: Kwajalein Missile Range.
BASE HISTORY: Provides missile testing, sen-
sor system research, developmental testing &
support for space operations for DOD, Army
Space & Strategic Defense Command.
Key Contacts
COMMANDER: Col Scott B Cottrell,
805-355-1401, FAX 805-355-1410, DSN
315-254-1401, cottrells@ssdck-usassdc.
army.mil.

Netherlands

18th Combat Equipment Company

1125. 18th Combat Equipment Company
18 CEC
APO, AE 09703
FAX 011-31-45-5645059; DSN FAX 3635059

Profile
BRANCH: Army.
LOCATION: Kranenpool 16443 VA Brunssum;
in SE Netherlands, 11 mi NE of Maastricht.
Locality: Limburg Province.
MAJOR UNITS: 18th Combat Equipment Co.
Key Contacts
COMMANDER: C David, 011-31-45-5645072,
DSN 3635072, davidc@cege.schinnen.army.
mil; G Severens, Site Manager,
011-31-45-5645167, DSN 3635167,
severeng@cege.schinnen.army.mil.

19th Combat Equipment Company

1126. 19th Combat Equipment Company
Unit 21607
APO, AE 09703
Profile
BRANCH: Army.
LOCATION: Vriezenveen, in E Netherlands; N of Almelo. *Locality:* Overijssel Province.
MAJOR UNITS: 19th Combat Equipment Co.
Key Contacts
COMMANDER: Maj Lonzel Lakey, 011-0546-576655, FAX 011-0546-573599, lakeyl@cege.schinnen.army.mil.

254th Base Support Battalion

1127. 254th Base Support Battalion
Shinnen Army Base
254th BSB, Unit 21602
APO, AE 09703
011-31-46-443-7512; DSN 360-7512
OFFICER-OF-THE-DAY: DSN 360-7591, 360-7113
Profile
BRANCH: Army.
LOCATION: Between Germany & Belgium. *Locality:* Limburg.
MAJOR UNITS: 254th Base Support Bn; Eygelshoven Reserve Storage Area; Geilenkirchen Airbase; Grefrath Kaserne; Herongen Storage Area; Rotterdam Administration Facility; Schinnen Army Base; Windberg Barracks; AFCENT, Brunssum; 18th Combat Equipment Co, Brunssum; 19th Combat Equipment Co, Vriezenveen; 20th Combat Equipment Co, Coevorden; 22nd Combat Equipment Co, Eygelshoven; 18th Military Intelligence, Maastricht; 532nd Signal Co, Maastricht; Combat Equipment Bn NW, Coevorden; HQ, CEG-E, Kerkrade; 1318th Military Transportation Management Command, Rotterdam; HQ, ARCC, Moenchengladbach.
BASE HISTORY: 1971, Schinnen Mine compound leased for AFCENT SUPACT from Fountainbleau, France. 1981, AFCENT SUPACT separated from NATO SHAPE; made full community under 21st TAACOM. 1982, realigned under Rheinberg Community. 1990, Rheinberg closed; Schinnen Military Community assumed responsibility. 1993, Schinnen Military Community redesignated Base Support Battalion. Area Support Group responsibilities transferred to 80th ASG, Mons, Belgium.

Key Contacts
COMMANDER: LTC Zacharzuk, 011-31-46-443-1500, DSN 360-1510.
Personnel and Expenditures
ACTIVE DUTY PERSONNEL: 2500
DEPENDENTS: 3880
CIVILIAN PERSONNEL: 620
Services *Commissary:* Yes; *Exchange:* Bank; Barber shop; Beauty shop; Convenience store; Post office; Dry cleaners. *Recreational Facilities:* Officers club; NCO club.

Combat Equipment Group-Europe, HQ

1128. Combat Equipment Group-Europe, HQ
CEG-E, HQ
Unit 21615
APO, AE 09703
DSN FAX 314-363-8160
Profile
BRANCH: Army.
LOCATION: Kerkrade, Netherlands.
MAJOR UNITS: Combat Equipment Group, Europe, HQ.
Key Contacts
COMMANDER: Steve Pineo, 011-31-045-567-7364, DSN 314-363-7364, pineos@cegeexch.cege.army.mil.

Military Traffic Management Command, Europe

1129. Military Traffic Management Command, Europe
MTMC Europe
Lylantse Plein 1
2908 LH Capelle aan den IJssel,
Internet: http://144.100.189.52/eur.htm
Profile
BRANCH: Army.
MAJOR UNITS: Military Traffic Management Command, Europe.

Netherlands Law Center

1130. Netherlands Law Center
APO, AE 09703
011-31-045-563-6204; DSN 364-6204, 364-6213

E-mail: aerja@email.netherlands.army.mil Internet:http://147.35.210.53/Aerja/NeLC.htm
Profile
BRANCH: Army.
LOCATION: In Brunssum, 11 mi NE of Maastricht. *Locality:* Limburg Province.
MAJOR UNITS: Netherlands Law Center.
Key Contacts
COMMANDER: Maj B Don Perritt Jr, Law Center Judge Advocate.

Volkel Air Base

1131. Volkel Air Base
752nd MUNSS, Unit 6790
APO AE, 09717-6790
011-31-4132-77218 (CONUS); FAX 011-31-4132-72417
E-mail: 752munss@smtplink.sembach.af.mil Internet:http://www.spangdahlem.af.mil/org/volkel/home.htm
OFFICER-OF-THE-DAY: Command Post, 011-31-4132-73986; DSN 360-7006
Profile
BRANCH: Air Force.
LOCATION: Outside town of Uden in SE Netherlands; 85 mi S of Amsterdam; near Eindhoven & Nijmegen.
MAJOR UNITS: 752nd Munitions Support Squadron.
BASE HISTORY: 1941, Volkel Air Base established by German occupation forces. 1944, destroyed by German forces; occupied by British squadron. 1945, training base for Dutch marines. 1950, turned over to Royal Netherlands Air Force. 1960s, American presence established as part of NATO forces. Mission to provide safe reliable munitions.
Key Contacts
COMMANDER: 011-31-4132-78315.
Personnel and Expenditures
ACTIVE DUTY PERSONNEL: 120
Services
Housing: Family units none on or off base for accompanied personnel; Dormitory spaces. *Exchange:* Video rentals; Class VI; Commissary at Schinnen Army Post. *Child Care/Capacities:* No day care facilities. *Schools:* Elementary; College courses. *Base Library:* Yes. *Medical Facilities:* Medical aid station with Independent Duty Medical Technicians in Dutch clinic. *Recreational Facilities:* Fitness center/Weight room; Playground; Consolidated club; Equipment checkout; Recreation longue; basketball court.

Norway

426th Air Base Squadron

1132. 426th Air Base Squadron
426 ABS
Sola Sea
Unit 6655
APO, AE 09706-6655

47-51-64-1431; FAX 47-51-64-1434; DSN
224-1431; DSN FAX 224-1434
Profile
BRANCH: Air Force.
LOCATION: In Stravanger, Norway.
MAJOR UNITS: 426th Air Base Squadron;
NATO HQ North.

BASE HISTORY: 1994, 724th Air Base Squadron relocated from Oslo, Norway; renamed 426th ABS.
Key Contacts
COMMANDER: LTC David Wetleson.
PUBLIC AFFAIRS: TSgt James Bertling,
bertlinj@sola-sea.af.mil.

Panama

Fort Clayton

1133. Fort Clayton
USARSO
Unit 7116, SOCO, PSC 4, Box 205
APO, AA 34004
011-507-287-3007; FAX 011-507-87-6246;
DSN 313-287-4109
Internet: http://www.army.mil/USARSO/
default.htm
Profile
BRANCH: Army.
LOCATION: On NW edge of Panama City, on
Gaillard Hwy, bordering E bank of Panama
Canal, approx 5 mi from Pacific terminus of
Canal; near Miraflores Locks. Tocumen IAP
approx 18 mi E; Howard AFB on W bank of
Canal approx 10 mi W. *Locality:* Panama
Province.
MAJOR UNITS: 1st Bn, 228th Aviation Regiment; 245th Area Support Bn; Army Garrison, Ft Clayton; 518th Engineer Bn; 202nd
Military Intelligence Brigade; 56th Signal Brigade; 160th Special Operations Aviation Regiment, D Co; 7th Special Forces Group, 3rd
Bn, Co C; 5th Bn, 87th Infantry Bn; Jungle
Operations Training Bn; Criminal Investigation Command, Panama; Exercise Support
Command; 1st Corps Support Command; 41st
Area Support Group; 142nd Medical Bn;
193rd Support Bn; Southern Command Network; Army Tropic Test Center.
BASE HISTORY: 1920-22, constructed; named
for Col Bertram T Clayton, planner of Panama Canal. 1963, Caribbean Command redesignated US Southern Command; Army component became US Army Forces Southern
Command (USARSO). 1974, USARSO deactivated; 193rd Infantry Brigade (Canal Zone)
reorganized as installation of US Army
Forces Command & Army component of US
Southern Command. 1979, brigade became
193rd Infantry Brigade (Panama). 1986, US
Army South reactivated. 1994, 193rd Infantry

inactivated. Housing, community, & support
services maintained at Cocoli, Ft Amador,
Quarry Heights, Corozal Subpost, Curundu
Subpost, and Ft Espinar.
FUTURE CLOSURE/REALIGNMENT: To be
closed by 2000 per Panama Canal Treaty.
Key Contacts
COMMANDER: 011-507-287-6715, FAX
011-507-287-5017, DSN 313-287-6715.
PUBLIC AFFAIRS: J Curtain,
011-507-287-3007, DSN 313-287-4109,
jcurtain@usarso-lan1.army.mil.
Personnel and Expenditures
ACTIVE DUTY PERSONNEL: 8500
DEPENDENTS: 9600
CIVILIAN PERSONNEL: 2400
Services *Commissary:* Yes; *Exchange:* Retail
store; Barber shop; Dry cleaners; Food shop;
Bank; Service station; Furniture store; Bookstore; Military clothing store; Convenience
store; Beauty shop; Laundromat. *Child Care/Capacities:* Day care center; Home day care program; Latch key program; Summer day camp.
Schools: Preschool/Kindergarten; Elementary;
College courses. *Base Library:* Yes. *Medical Facilities:* Hospital; Medical clinic; Dental clinic;
Dispensary; Pharmacy; Veterinary services. *Recreational Facilities:* Bowling center; Movie theater; Pool; Gym; Recreation center; Stables;
Tennis courts; Racquetball court; Fitness center/
Weight room; Softball field; Craft shop; NCO
club; Youth center; Picnic area; Playground;
Nearby golf course, fishing, beach/water sports,
Officers club, and Enlisted club.

Fort Davis

1134. Fort Davis
Unit 1503
APO, AA 34005-5000
Profile
BRANCH: Army.
SIZE AND LOCATION: 4325 acres.

Near Gatun Locks on Atlantic side.
MAJOR UNITS: 5th Bn, 87th Infantry; 7th Special Forces Group, 3rd Bn, Co C (Airborne);
549th Military Police Co; 1097th Army Boat
Co.
Services *Base Library:* Yes.

Fort Sherman

1135. Fort Sherman
USAJOTC
Unit 1505
APO, AA 34005
DSN 289-6111, 289-6113
Profile
BRANCH: Army.
SIZE AND LOCATION: 23,400 acres. Between
Limon Bay and Chagres River at Atlantic entrance to Canal. *Locality:* Colon.
MAJOR UNITS: Jungle Operations Training
Bn.
BASE HISTORY: 1911, named in honor of
Civil War Gen William Tecumseh Sherman.
1914, began operations. Original mission to
provide defense for Atlantic port of Cristobal
and Gatun Locks. 1946-48, used to billet
troops assigned to Caribbean side of isthmus.
1951, jungle training operations began and
continued with 7437th Army Unit, 44rd Infantry. 1956, 20th Infantry Regiment activated;
reorganized as 1st Battle Group, 20th Infantry. 1963, operated as Jungle Operations Committee under Army School of the Americas,
Ft Gulick, Canal Zone. 1968, current US
Army Jungle Operations Training Center
(JOTC) established. 1970, placed under operational control of 8th Special Forces Group
(Airborne). 1975, made independent major
subordinate command under 193rd Infantry
Brigade. 1987, JOTC became Forces Command Training Center.

FUTURE CLOSURE/REALIGNMENT: Scheduled to close Dec 1999 per Panama Canal Treaty.
VISITOR ATTRACTIONS: Fort San Lorenzo (Spanish, 1597); abandoned WWI/II coastal artillery batteries.

Key Contacts
COMMANDER: LTC James C Hiett; DSN 289-6208, 289-6210.

Personnel and Expenditures
ACTIVE DUTY PERSONNEL: 1100
DEPENDENTS: 163
CIVILIAN PERSONNEL: 15

Services
Housing: Family units 67; Unaccompanied enlisted quarters 54; Barracks spaces 73. *Temporary Housing:* VIP units 2; Guest cottages 2. *Exchange:* Barber shop; Convenience store. *Child Care/Capacities:* Day care center capacity 25, 3-7yrs. *Schools:* No on-base schools. *Base Library:* Yes. *Medical Facilities:* Medical clinic. *Recreational Facilities:* Movie theater; Gym; Recreation center; Racquetball court; Fitness center/Weight room; Softball field; NCO club; Water sports; Playground.

Howard Air Force Base

1136. Howard Air Force Base
24th Wing
APO, AA 34001-5000
Internet: http://www.howard.af.mil/

Profile
BRANCH: Air Force.
SIZE AND LOCATION: 14,121 acres. On the Pacific side of the Panama Canal.
MAJOR UNITS: Air Force Southern Air Forces; 24th Wing; 24th Operations Group; 310th Airlift Squadron; 24th Air Support Operations Squadron; 24th Weather Squadron; 24th Operations Support Squadron; 24th Communications Squadron; 24th Services Squadron; 24th Air Postal Squadron; 24th Logistics Group; 24th Contracting Squadron; 24th Supply Squadron; 24th Transportation Squadron; 24th Logistics Support Flight; 640th Air Mobility Support Squadron; Standardization & Evaluation Division (OGV); Coronet Oak (AFRES); Coronet Nighthawk (ANG); 612th Theater Air Group.
BASE HISTORY: 1928, established as Bruja Point Military Reservation. 1939-41, renamed Bruja Point Air Base; later named for Maj Charles Harold Howard, pioneer in Air Service-Air Corps operations in Canal Zone. 1950, inactivated; base turned over to Army. 1962, flight operations ended at Albrook; Howard returned to USAF. 1963, redesignated USAF Southern Command. 1976, Command inactivated; reported to Tactical Air

Command. 1989, became 830th Air Division. 1991, redesignated Air Forces Panama. 1992, 24th Wing activated as senior AF organization in Panama.
FUTURE CLOSURE/REALIGNMENT: Scheduled to close Dec 1999 per Panal Canal Treaty.

Key Contacts
COMMANDER: Col Trebon, DSN 284-9781.
PUBLIC AFFAIRS: Capt Murk, DSN 284-5554.

Personnel and Expenditures
ACTIVE DUTY PERSONNEL: 2100
DEPENDENTS: 3000
CIVILIAN PERSONNEL: US 400; Panamaian 800

Services
Housing: Unaccompanied officer quarters; Dormitory spaces; Senior NCO units. *Commissary:* Yes; *Exchange:* Bookstore; Convenience store; Food shop; Service station; Video rentals; Cafeteria; BX; Mall. *Child Care/Capacities:* Day care center 6mos-10yrs; Home day care program; Before & after school programs. *Schools:* Preschool/Kindergarten; Elementary; Intermediate/Junior high; High school; College courses. *Base Library:* Yes. *Medical Facilities:* Medical clinic; Dental clinic. *Recreational Facilities:* Bowling center; Movie theater; Pool; Gym; Golf course; Stables; Fitness center/Weight room; Softball field; Auto shop; Craft shop; Enlisted club; NCO club; Officers club; Youth center; Community actiivites center; Scuba diving; Horseback riding; Hiking; Fishing; Recreational rental.

Panama Canal Naval Station

1137. Panama Canal Naval Station
NAVSTA Panama Canal
Rodman Naval Station
Unit 6249
FPO, AA 34061-6249
011-507-283-6315; FAX 507-283-4236; DSN 313-283-6315
E-mail: ntns4@navtap.navy.mil Internet:http://www.ncts.navy.mil/homepages/NAVSTA-Panama/Default.htm

Profile
BRANCH: Navy.
SIZE AND LOCATION: 3619.47 acres; 786 acre Farfan Communications Activity; 150 acre Marine Barracks; 807 acres Arraijan Tank Farm; Summit; Galeta Island; Coco Solo Submarine Base. On Pacific side of Isthmus of Panama; 5 min from Howard AFB; 60 min from IAP; 15 min from center of Panama City.
MAJOR UNITS: Naval Station, Panama Canal; Military Sealift Command; Special Boat Unit

26; Naval Special Warfare Unit 8; Marine Corps Security Force Co; Inter-American Naval Telecommunications Network; Naval Criminal Investigative Service Resident Agency; Naval Small Craft Instruction & Technical Training School; Personnel Support Activity Det, Panama; Arraijan Tank Farm.
BASE HISTORY: Also known as Rodman Naval Station. 1937-43, construction of waterfront & piers at Rodman. 1976, 15th Naval District disestablished; Naval Station Panama Canal established. 1993, Commanding Officer, Naval Station Panama Canal combined with Officer-in-Charge of Commander in Chief, Atlantic Fleet Detachment South to form Commander, Naval Forces Panama. 1994, Operation Safe Haven; 4 temporary camps built; 9000 Cuban migrants housed. 1995, last migrant departed.
FUTURE CLOSURE/REALIGNMENT: All military bases in Republic of Panama will cease operation Dec 1999 in compliance with Panama Canal Treaty.
VISITOR ATTRACTIONS: Hosts many local trips and excursions.

Key Contacts
COMMANDER: Capt Linda Long, DSN 283-3300.
PUBLIC AFFAIRS: Unit 6251, FPO AA 34061-6251, 507-283-4314, DSN 283-4314, 283-4301.
PROCUREMENT: Supply & Fiscal Officer, 507-283-4412, DSN 283-4412.
TRANSPORTATION: Public Works Officer, 507-283-3400, DSN 283-3400.
PERSONNEL/COMMUNITY ACTIVITIES: Morale, Welfare & Recreation Officer, 507-283-4315, DSN 283-4315.

Personnel and Expenditures
ACTIVE DUTY PERSONNEL: 850
DEPENDENTS: 800
CIVILIAN PERSONNEL: 500

Services
Housing: Family units 235; Unaccompanied enlisted quarters 84 rooms; BAQ units 26; Duplex units 57; Barracks spaces 156; Dormitory spaces 26; Senior NCO units 36; Junior NCO units 143. *Temporary Housing:* VOQ units 4; Unaccompanied officer/Enlisted quarters 21; BAQ units 42; Guesthouse units 2; Apartment units 7; Dormitory units 17; Transient quarters 56. *Commissary:* Yes; *Exchange:* Retail store; Barber shop; Dry cleaners; Food shop; Furniture store; Military clothing store; Convenience store. *Child Care/Capacities:* No day care facilities. *Schools:* No on-base schools. *Medical Facilities:* Dental clinic; Dispensary. *Recreational Facilities:* Pool; Gym; Golf course; Tennis courts; Fitness center/Weight room; Softball field; NCO club; Camping; Fishing/Hunting; Enlisted club; Skeet range; Water sports; Playground; Marina; ITT.

Portugal

Lajes Field

1138. Lajes Field
Unit 7710
APO, AE 09720-5000
011-351-95-52101; FAX 011-351-95-58119
Internet: http://www.lajes.af.mil/65thabw.html
Profile
BRANCH: Joint Service Installation.
LOCATION: On NE tip of Terceira Island; 2200 mi E of New York; 850 mi W of Lisbon, Portugal; operated in conjunction with Air Base 4, Portuguese Authority. *Locality:* Azores.
MAJOR UNITS: 65th Air Base Wing; 65th Communications Squadron; 65th Medical Group; 65th Support Group; 65th Contracting Squadron; 65th Transportation Squadron; 65th Comptroller Flight; US Forces Azores Joint Staff; Air Force Office of Special Investigations, Det 250; 1324th Medium Port Command (Army); Naval Security Group Activity, Lajes; Air Force European Broadcasting Squadron, Det 3; Azores Air Command (Portuguese); Naval Air Facility, Lajes; 629th Air Mobility Support Squadron.
BASE HISTORY: 1943, activated with British construction of airfield; US personnel stationed. 1944, US Military Transport Command (later Military Airlift Command) began occupancy. 1953, US Forces Azores Command organized as Unified Command under Command-in-Chief Atlantic.1977, MAC became specified command. 1992, redesignated Air Mobility Command. 1993, converted from AMC to Air Combat Command.
VISITOR ATTRACTIONS: Air Base 4 Museum; Heritage City.
Key Contacts
COMMANDER: Col Rodney Gibson.
PUBLIC AFFAIRS: SSgt Rosaire Bushey, 65th ABW/PA, DSN 535-2369.
Personnel and Expenditures
ACTIVE DUTY PERSONNEL: 1500
DEPENDENTS: 1000
Services *Commissary:* Yes; *Exchange:* Retail store; Barber shop; Dry cleaners; Food shop; Florist; Service station; Military clothing store; Convenience store; Beauty shop; Credit union. *Child Care/Capacities:* Day care center; Home day care program; Latch key program. *Schools:* Preschool/Kindergarten; Elementary; High school. *Base Library:* Yes. *Medical Facilities:* Hospital; Dental clinic. *Recreational Facilities:* Bowling center; Movie theater; Pool; Gym; Recreation center; Golf course; Tennis courts; Racquetball court; Fitness center/Weight room; Softball field; Football field; Auto shop; Craft shop; Camping; Fishing/Hunting; Youth center; Water sports; Playground; Consolidated club; Community center.

Puerto Rico

Adjutant General of Puerto Rico

1139. Adjutant General of Puerto Rico
PO Box 3786
San Juan, 00904-3786
787-724-1295; FAX 787-723-6360
Profile
BRANCH: Army National Guard.
MAJOR UNITS: Puerto Rico National Guard.
Key Contacts
COMMANDER: Maj Gen Emilio Diaz-Colon.

Camp Santiago

1140. Camp Santiago
PO Box 1166
Salinas, 00751-1166
809-824-3110, ext 241
Profile
BRANCH: Army National Guard.
SIZE AND LOCATION: 11,925.46 acres. S Puerto Rico, 2 mi from Salinas; 25 mi from Ponce. *Locality:* Guayama District.
MAJOR UNITS: 201st Evacuation Hospital; HQ & HQ Det Training Site; 156th Det ANG.
BASE HISTORY: Terrain includes steep mountain slopes over one-third of area. Unimproved roads provide access to training area. 3 battalion-size units can conduct non-live fire exercises simultaneously.
VISITOR ATTRACTIONS: Puerto Rican Militia Museum.
Key Contacts
PUBLIC AFFAIRS: Puerto Rico National Guard, Box 3786, San Juan, PR 00902, 809-824-1474.
Personnel and Expenditures
CIVILIAN PERSONNEL: 135
Services
Housing: Unaccompanied enlisted quarters; BAQ units; Barracks spaces; Senior NCO units; Junior NCO units. *Temporary Housing:* VIP units 7; Unaccompanied officer/Enlisted quarters 280; Apartment units 16; Transient quarters Billets 3720. *Exchange:* Convenience store; Laundromat. *Child Care/Capacities:* No day care facilities. *Schools:* No on-base schools. *Medical Facilities:* Troop medical clinic, IDT/AT only. *Recreational Facilities:* Movie theater; Pool; Recreation center; Tennis courts; Softball field; Officers club; NCO club; Enlisted club.

Fort Buchanan Army Garrison

1141. Fort Buchanan Army Garrison
Bldg 399, Chrisman Rd
Fort Buchanan, 00934-5000
Internet: http://buch376.buchanan.army.mil
OFFICER-OF-THE-DAY: MP 787-273-3337, 740-3337
Profile
BRANCH: Army.
SIZE AND LOCATION: 476 acres. Six mi SW of San Juan. From Luis Munoz Marina IAP, take Hwy 26W toward Myamon to Hwy 22 to Fort Buchanan sign. *Locality:* San Juan Municipality.
MAJOR UNITS: 65th Army Reserve Command; Buchanan CS/CSS Bn; Criminal Investigations Division; Defense Military Pay Office; Military Entrance Processing Station; Military Traffic Management Command; Senior Army Advisor PR ANG; Antilles Consolidated School System.
BASE HISTORY: 1923, Camp Buchanan established S of San Juan Bay. 1926-30, used as maneuver training area and range by Regular Army, National Guard, and Citizens Military Training Camp. 1940, designated Fort Buchanan. WWII, housed depot for Army Antilles Dept. Post-WWII, reduced from 4500 acres to present size; used as supply and replacement

depot. 1966, post closed, came under Navy control. 1971, Rodriguez Army Hospital inactivated; fort returned to Army control under 3rd Army. 1973, reorganized as Army Garrison under HQ FORSCOM. Currently, only active Army post in Caribbean Basin area. Mission: mobilization readiness, deployment of 15,000 Reserve Component soldiers in PR and US Virgin Islands, and support DOD Caribbean operations. 1997, became US Army South (USARSO) installation.

Key Contacts

COMMANDER: Col Brad M Beasley, Garrison Cmdr, 787-273-3340, DSN 740-3340; Brig Gen P E Lima, 65th Army Research Command, 787-273-2191, DSN 740-2191.

PUBLIC AFFAIRS: J Pagan, Bldg 399, SOFB-PO, 787-273-3999, DSN 740-3000.

PROCUREMENT: V Cosme, Supply Officer, 787-273-3970, DSN 740-3254.

TRANSPORTATION: J Miranda 787-273-3254, DSN 740-3254.

Services

Housing: Family units Buchanan Heights 98 units (enlisted); Coconut Grove 141 units (senior enlisted/company grade); Coqui Gardens 91 apt units (enlisted/company grade); Las Colinas 31 units (field grade officers); Barracks spaces. *Temporary Housing:* Guesthouse units; Transient quarters None. *Exchange:* Retail store; Barber shop; Bank; Service station; Furniture store; Military clothing store; Convenience store; Credit union; ATM; Class VI; Toyland. *Child Care/Capacities:* Day care center for children 1-12 yrs; Home day care program. *Schools:* Elementary; Intermediate/Junior high; High school. *Base Library:* Yes. *Medical Facilities:* Medical clinic; Dental clinic; Pharmacy; Veterinary services. *Recreational Facilities:* Bowling center; Pool; Golf course (9 holes); Racquetball court; Fitness center/Weight room; Auto shop; Youth center; Community club; Water park with pool; Equipment rental; Golf pro shop.

Roosevelt Roads Naval Reserve Center

1142. Roosevelt Roads Naval Reserve Center

Bldg 78
Ceiba, 00735
Mailing Address
PSC 1008, Box 3937
FPO AA, 34051
787-865-3573, 865-4300, 865-4070; FAX 787-865-3003; DSN 831-4836, 831-4300, 831-4070

Profile

BRANCH: Naval Reserve.

MAJOR UNITS: Naval Reserve Center, Roosevelt Roads.

Key Contacts

COMMANDER: CDR H T Krumm Jr.

Roosevelt Roads Naval Station

1143. Roosevelt Roads Naval Station

NAVSTA Roosevelt Roads
PSC 1008, Box 3001
FPO, AA 34051-0001
809-865-4018, 865-4022; FAX 865-4976; DSN 831-4022
OFFICER-OF-THE-DAY: 767-865-4311, 865-4307, DSN 831-4311

Profile

BRANCH: Navy.

SIZE AND LOCATION: 31,000 acres (8,600 acres on E tip of Puerto Rico; 22,400 acres on Vieques Island, 7.5 mi SE). On far E coast of Puerto Rico; approx 50 mi from San Juan; Base borders town of Fajardo on N, Ceiba in center, Naguabo to S. *Locality:* Ceiba.

MAJOR UNITS: Naval Station, Roosevelt Roads; Western Hemisphere Group (WESTHEMGRU); Caribbean Area Coordinator; Commander South Atlantic Force (USCOMSOLANT); Atlantic Fleet Weapons Training Facility (AFWTF); Naval Hospital; Naval Dental Center; Fleet Composite Squadron Eight (VC-8); Naval Computer and Telecommunications Station; Naval Mobile Construction Bn; Naval Special Warfare Unit 4 (NSWU-4); Personal Support Activity Det (PSD); Resident Officer in Charge of Construction (ROICC); Naval Warfare Assessment Center; Naval Atlantic Meteorology & Oceanography Det; Naval Media Center; Naval Legal Services Office (NLSO); Mobile Diving Salvage Unit TWO Det; Explosive Ordnance Disposal (EOD); Fleet Imaging Facilities Det Atlantic; Army Reserve Center; Naval Reserve Center; Marine Corps Reserve Center; US Coast Guard Patrol Boat Support Det; Naval Criminal Investigative Service; Antilles Consolidated Schools.

BASE HISTORY: 1940, construction ordered by Pres Roosevelt. 1943, commissioned as US Naval Operations Base; served as training facility and base for ships and aircraft. After WWII, closed 7 times. 1955, base became guided-missile training center; redesignated Naval Station. Army's Fort Bundy comprises southern portion of NS. Today, base is used for training & service to fleet. No ships homeported here; facilities for military ships in transit; over 1000 ships use facilities annually. Island of Vieques is mainly Marine encampment with beaches for landing sites for amphibious training & ship-to-shore shelling. Roosevelt Roads is largest naval station in the world by area.

Key Contacts

COMMANDER: Capt Keith W Martello, 787-865-4444, DSN 831-4444.

PUBLIC AFFAIRS: LCpl J M Goodwin, DSN 831-3191, 831-4430.

PROCUREMENT: PSC 1008, Box 3002, 767-865-4433, DSN 831-4433.

TRANSPORTATION: PSC 1008, Box 3021, 767-865-4049.

PERSONNEL/COMMUNITY ACTIVITIES: PSC 1008, Box 3015, 787-865-4355, FAX 787-865-2075, DSN 831-4355.

Personnel and Expenditures

ACTIVE DUTY PERSONNEL: 3000

DEPENDENTS: 2500; 7990 retired military

CIVILIAN PERSONNEL: 3850

MILITARY PAYROLL EXPENDITURE: $15.6 mil

CONTRACT EXPENDITURE: $25.5 mil

Services

Housing: Family units 930; Unaccompanied enlisted quarters 10 bldgs. *Temporary Housing:* Lodge units 120 (info 1-800-NAVY-INN, 787-865-8282). *Commissary:* Yes; *Exchange:* Retail store; Barber shop; Dry cleaners; Food shop; Florist; Service station; Military clothing store; Convenience store; Beauty shop; Laundromat; ATM; Optical store; Post office; Fast food; Video rentals; Computer store; Garden center; Photo store; Appliance/TV sales; Toys; Gift shop; Electronic game room; Car rental; Appliance rentals. *Child Care/Capacities:* Day care center capacity 75, newborn-5yrs; new facility for 250 opens 9/94; Home day care program; Latch key program; Summer day camp. *Schools:* Preschool/Kindergarten; Elementary; Intermediate/Junior high; High school; College courses. *Base Library:* Yes. *Medical Facilities:* Hospital; Dental clinic; Veterinary services. *Recreational Facilities:* Bowling center; Movie theater; Pool; Gym; Recreation center; Golf course; Stables; Tennis courts; Racquetball court; Fitness center/Weight room; Softball field; Football field; Auto shop; Officers club; NCO club; Enlisted club; Youth center; Picnic area; Water sports; Playground; Fishing; Scuba club; Flying club.

Sabana Seca, US Naval Security Group Activity

1144. Sabana Seca, US Naval Security Group Activity

NSGA Sabana Seca; USNSGA Sabana Seca
Bldg 1
Toa Baja, 00952
Mailing Address
Bldg 1
FPO AA, 34053-1000
787-261-8300; FAX 787-784-4633
OFFICER-OF-THE-DAY: 787-261-8300

Profile

BRANCH: Navy.

SIZE AND LOCATION: 2300 acres. N coast; 14 mi W of San Juan; 40 min from San Juan IAP. *Locality:* Toa Baja.

MAJOR UNITS: Naval Security Group Activity; Defense Contract Management Area Office; Personnel Support Det; Marine Corps Security Co, Puerto Rico; Branch Medical Clinic, Sabana Seca; Branch Dental Clinic, Sabana Seca.

BASE HISTORY: WWII, land bought for ammunition depot. Post WWII, depot turned over to Army. 1951, Navy transferred in from San Juan IAP. 1952, US Naval Radio Station established. 1971, current Activity established.

VISITOR ATTRACTIONS: Stevenson Place, original plantation home.

Key Contacts

COMMANDER: CDR Bruce L Drake.

PUBLIC AFFAIRS: Lt Ivy Hamchett.

PROCUREMENT: Ltjg Early Grady.

TRANSPORTATION: Lt Scott Hinton.

PERSONNEL/COMMUNITY ACTIVITIES:
See Public Affairs Officer.
Personnel and Expenditures
ACTIVE DUTY PERSONNEL: 247
DEPENDENTS: 182
CIVILIAN PERSONNEL: 152
MILITARY PAYROLL EXPENDITURE: $1.7 mil
CONTRACT EXPENDITURE: $1.3 mil

Services
Housing: Family units 43; Unaccompanied officer quarters 5; Unaccompanied enlisted quarters 52; Duplex units 98; Dormitory spaces 118; Senior NCO units 3. *Temporary Housing:* VIP units 1. *Exchange:* Retail store; Barber shop; Dry cleaners; Service station; Convenience store; Laundromat.

Child Care/Capacities: Day care center capacity 25, 6wks-4yrs; Home day care program.
Schools: College courses; No on-base schools.
Base Library: Yes. *Medical Facilities:* Medical clinic; Dental clinic; Dispensary. *Recreational Facilities:* Bowling center; Pool; Gym; Tennis courts; Racquetball court; Fitness center/Weight room; Softball field 2; Auto shop; Officers club; Enlisted club; Youth center; Picnic area; Playground.

Saudi Arabia

Eskan Village

1145. Eskan Village
APO, AE 09881
E-mail: webmaster@eskan.swablack.af.mil Internet:http://www.eskan.swablack.af.mil/home2.htm
Profile
BRANCH: Air Force.
LOCATION: Near Riyadh, Saudi Arabia.
MAJOR UNITS: 4409th Air Base Group; 4409th Air Base Group Staff; 4409th Civil Engineering Squadron; 4409th Communications Squadron; 4409th Logistics Squadron; 4409th Security Forces Squadron; 4409th Support Squadron; Air Force Office of Special Investigations, Det 243; Joint Task Force, Southwest Asia; Offices of the Program Manager for Security Assistance with the Saudi Arabian National Guard; Joint Rear Area Coordinator (JRAC); Defense Contract Management Command, Saudi Arabia; Army Forces Central Command-Saudi Arabia; United States Military Training Mission; Friendly Forces Coordination Cell.
BASE HISTORY: Provided by the Saudi Arabian government as housing area for US Armed Forces.
Key Contacts
COMMANDER: Col Randolph L Cagle.
Services
Housing: Villas 836; Highrise towers 37.

Commissary: Yes; *Exchange:* Barber shop; Dry cleaners; Military clothing store; Post office; Video rentals; Tailor/Alterations; Laundry; Snack food; Restaurant; Ice cream shop; Pizza parlor. *Schools:* College courses. *Base Library:* Yes. *Recreational Facilities:* Pool; Fitness center/Weight room; Softball field; Village pub with billiards, table tennis, volleyball, darts, snacks; miniature golf; Sports equipment checkout.

Prince Sultan Air Base

1146. Prince Sultan Air Base
Unit 70404, Box 4
APO AE, 09882
011-966-01-498-5173; DSN (Non-tactical) 318-434-0000 DSN (Tactical) 318-222-4100 DSN
E-mail: 4404hqscca@psab.aorcentraf.af.mil Internet:http://www.aorcentaf.af.mil/4404th.htm
OFFICER-OF-THE-DAY: Command Post, DSN 434-6705
Profile
BRANCH: Air Force.
LOCATION: Al Kharj, Saudi Arabia; SE of Riyadh.
MAJOR UNITS: 4404th Wing (P); 4404th Operations Group; 4407th Reconnaissance Squadron; 4408th Air Refueling Squadron;

4410th Airlift Squadron; 4410th Rescue Squadron; 4404th Logistics Group; 4404th Support Group; 4404th Medical Group; 4416th Intelligence Squadron; Det 1, 621st Air Mobility Support Group (AMSG)(AMC); 1621st Air Mobility Support Squadron (AMSS)(P); 57th Med-Evac Det; Team Alpha, Task Force 1-7 ADA (Patriot).
BASE HISTORY: 1994, 4404th Wing moved from Dhahran. Enforces the no-fly zone in Iraq, deters Iraqi aggression, protects UN forces, & prepares to conduct offensive operations, if needed.
Key Contacts
COMMANDER: Brig Gen Bentley B Rayburn.
PUBLIC AFFAIRS: 011-966-01-498-5173, ext. 7833/7252, DSN 318-434-7833/7252, 4404wgpa@psab.aorcentaf.af.mil.
Personnel and Expenditures
ACTIVE DUTY PERSONNEL: 4500 (in six locations)
Services
Housing: Tent city. *Exchange:* Retail store; Barber shop; Dry cleaners; Laundromat; Post office; Fast food; Video rentals; Tailor/Alterations; Laundry; Gift shop. *Recreational Facilities:* Pool; Fitness center/Weight room; Softball field; Officers club; Enlisted club; Video checkout; Volleyball courts; Basketball courts.

Singapore

Logistics Group Western Pacific

1147. Logistics Group Western Pacific
COMLOG WESTPAC
FPO, AP 96534
011-65-750-2421; FAX 011-65-750-2469; DSN 325-2421, 325-2308

Internet: http://www.andersen.af.mil/gsus.htm
OFFICER-OF-THE-DAY: COMLOG WESTPAC, 011-65-724-2387; NRCC, 011-65-722-8691, 497th FTS, 011-65-824-2961
Profile
BRANCH: Navy.
SIZE AND LOCATION: Converted warehouse. In N-central part of island. *Locality:* Singapore.
MAJOR UNITS: Logistics Group Western Pacific; Naval Regional Contracting Center, Western Pacific; 497th Fighter Training

Squadron (USAF); 497th Tactical Fighter Wing/MSM (USAF).
Key Contacts
COMMANDER: Commander, Logistics Group Western Pacific, 011-65-750-2441, 750-2442, DSN 325-2441, 325-2442; Commanding Officer, Naval Regional Contracting Center, PSC 470, Box 2100, FPO AP 96534-2100, 011-65-750-2515, DSN 325-2515; Commanding Officer, 497th FTS/CC, PSC 470, Box 2300, FPO AP

96534-2300, 011-65-750-2316, DSN
325-2316.
Personnel and Expenditures
ACTIVE DUTY PERSONNEL: 135
DEPENDENTS: 200
CIVILIAN PERSONNEL: 25

Services
Housing: Family units 50; Duplex units 42;
flats, 52; Housing owned by government of Singapore & not considered military housing. *Temporary Housing:* Transient quarters 36 with 214
beds; primarily for TAD USAF exercise partici-
pants, used by others on available basis. *Exchange:* Convenience store; Credit union; Small
exchange.

Child Care/Capacities: No day care facilities.
Schools: College courses. *Base Library:* Yes.
Medical Facilities: Medical clinic; Dental clinic.
Recreational Facilities: Gym; Fitness center/
Weight room; Softball field; Youth center; Playground; All hands club; Sand volleyball; Fleet
laundromat; Fleet post office; All facilities available locally, more facilities scheduled to be
built.

Spain

Moron Air Base

1148. Moron Air Base
PSC 62
APO, AE 09643
Internet: http://www.moron.af.mil/
Profile
BRANCH: Air Force.
LOCATION: In S Spain approx 35 mi SE of
Sevilla; 75 mi NE of Rota Naval Station.
MAJOR UNITS: 496th Security Forces Flight;
496th Air Base Squadron; NASA Transoce-
anic Abort Landing Site.
BASE HISTORY: 1951-53, negotiations for
bases in Spain conducted. 1957, 3973rd Air
Base Group activated. 1958, B-47s assigned
for Reflex operations. 1960, base officially under USAF command. 1966, mission transferred from SAC to USAFE; communications
support of fair weather flying operations.
1969, mission changed to Standby Dispersal
Base. 1971, redesignated to modified caretaker status. 1983, host to multiple exercises.
1984, selected by NASA for Transoceanic
Abort Landing site for space shuttle. 1990-91,
supported Desert Shield & Desert Storm.
1993, 7120th ABF redesignated 712th ABF.
1994, picked up regional responsibility with
drawdown of units at Torrejon, Spain, San
Vito AS, Italy, & Iraklion AS, Greece; 712th
ABF became 496th ABS under 616th Regional Support Group, Aviano Air Base, Italy. In NATO terms base remains standby;
austerely manned with no permanently assigned operational tactical forces. No USAF
aircraft stationed at base; squadron provides
oversight of contractor personnel. Base
shared with 21st Ala (wing), Spanish Air
Force.
Key Contacts
COMMANDER: LTC Ian P O'Connell.
Services
Housing: Family units 36; Dormitory spaces .
978. *Temporary Housing:* Transient quarters;
Hotel 82 guests: 4 VIP suites, 10 singles, 36 double bedrooms. *Exchange:* Barber shop; Service
station; Convenience store; Beauty shop; Post of-
fice; Class VI; Dining facility; Snack bar; Gift
shop; Commissary at Rota Naval Station. *Child
Care/Capacities:* No day care facilities.
Schools: Elementary; High school at Rota Naval
Station. *Base Library:* Yes. *Medical Facilities:*
Aid station. *Recreational Facilities:* Bowling
center; Pool; Recreation center; Tennis courts;
Racquetball court; Fitness center/Weight room;

Softball field; Auto shop; Craft shop; Youth center; Community club; Volleyball court; Running
track; Soccer field; Additional facilities at Rota
Naval Station.

Rota Naval Station

1149. Rota Naval Station
NAVSTA Rota
PSC 819, Box 1
FPO, AE 09645-1000
011-3456-82-1680; FAX 011-3456-82-1740;
DSN 727-1680; DSN FAX 727-1740
Internet: http://www.rota.navy.mil
OFFICER-OF-THE-DAY: Command Duty Officer,
011-34-5682-2222, DSN 727-2222
Profile
BRANCH: Navy.
SIZE AND LOCATION: 60,000 acres. On SW
coast of Spain, south of Seville on Hwy NIV;
across bay from Cadiz on Spain's Base Naval
de Rota. *Locality:* Andalucia.
MAJOR UNITS: Commander, US Naval Activi-
ties, Spain; Chief Staff Officer, US Naval Ac-
tivities, Spain; Antisubmarine Warfare Operations Center (ASWOC); Aeromedical Safety
Unit; Marine Support Bn; Cryptologic Sup-
port Group; Commander, Task Force 63, Det
ROTA; Explosive Ordnance Disposal, Group
2, Det ROTA; Fleet Imaging Center Atlantic;
Fleet Ocean Surveillance Information Facility; Naval Hospital; Marine Corps Security
Force Co; Naval Aviation Engineering Serv-
ice Unit; Naval Air Maintenance Training
Group, Det ROTA; Navy Calibration Laboratory; Navy Broadcasting Service Det, ROTA;
Naval Computer and Telecommunications
Station; Naval Investigative Service; Naval
Mobile Construction Bn; Commander, Con-
struction Bn Atlantic Det, Europe; Naval
Oceanography Command Center; Naval Re-
connaissance Support Activity; Fleet Recon-
naissance Squadron 2 (VQ-2); Fleet Logistic
Support Squadron 22 (VR-22); Air Mobility
Command Liaison (USAF); Military Traffic
Management Command; Defense Reutiliza-
tion Management Office; Aviation Intermedi-
ate Maintenance Department (AIMD); Naval
Security Group Activity; NEMOC (Weather);
NCTAMS; 625th Air Mobility Support
Squadron.
BASE HISTORY: 1953, construction began.
1989, new 8-yr agreement of cooperation
went into effect. Spanish Base used jointly by

US & Spain; remains under Spanish flag,
commanded by Spanish RADM. Spanish
Navy responsible for external security. American facilities, with 42 tenant commands, support US 6th Fleet in Mediterranean with fuel
oil, ammunition, & spare parts.
VISITOR ATTRACTIONS: Spanish base;
those not on orders (not leave) cannot access
commissary/exchange facilities.
Key Contacts
COMMANDER: Capt Bruce T Stuckert,
011-34-5682-2440, DSN 727-2440.
PUBLIC AFFAIRS: Ltjg Daniel Hetlage,
011-34-5682-1680, DSN 727-1680, DSN
FAX 727-1021, dhetlage@navsta-rota.navy.
mil; Cpl P D Rubinberak, Navy Broadcast
Service, Det Rota, Box 27, DSN 227-2122.
PERSONNEL/COMMUNITY ACTIVITIES:
Steve Endres.
Personnel and Expenditures
ACTIVE DUTY PERSONNEL: 3100
DEPENDENTS: 3300
CIVILIAN PERSONNEL: 600
MILITARY PAYROLL EXPENDITURE: $70.7
mil
CONTRACT EXPENDITURE: $57.3 mil
Services
Housing: Family units 300; Duplex units 486.
Temporary Housing: VOQ units 35; VEQ units
136; Unaccompanied officer/Enlisted quarters
65; Lodge units 48; Transient quarters 100; DV
suites 8; 0-6 suites 12; E-7 & above, suites 11.
Commissary: Yes; *Exchange:* Retail store; Bar-
ber shop; Dry cleaners; Food shop; Florist; Serv-
ice station; Furniture store; Bakery; Bookstore;
Military clothing store; Convenience store;
Beauty shop; Laundromat; Credit union; ATM;
Optical store; Post office; Video rentals; Four
seasons; Thrift shop; Travel agency; Shoe repair; Computer store; Garden center; Tailor/Al-
terations; Laundry; Cafeteria; Photo store;
Baskin Robbins ice cream; Drive-in deli; All limited to use by base personnel. *Child Care/Ca-
pacities:* Day care center capacity 105, 3mos-
6yrs; Home day care program; Summer day
camp; Before & after school programs. *Schools:*
Preschool/Kindergarten; Elementary; Intermedi-
ate/Junior high; High school; College courses.
Base Library: Yes. *Medical Facilities:* Hospital
52 beds; Medical clinic; Dental clinic; Pharmacy; Veterinary services. *Recreational Facilities:* Bowling center; Movie theater; Pool; Gym;
Recreation center; Golf course; Stables; Tennis
courts; Racquetball court; Fitness center/Weight
room; Softball field; Football field; Auto shop;
Craft shop; Fishing/Hunting; Youth center; Pic-

nic area; Water sports; Playground; Consolidated club; Rod & Gun club; Morale, Welfare, & Recreation; ITT; SATO; Kennel Klub; Pizza Villa; Market Street Grill.

Thailand

Air Force Technical Applications Center, Det 415

1150. Air Force Technical Applications Center, Det 415
APO, AP 96547

Internet: http://www.aftac.gov/dets/415/det415. html
Profile
BRANCH: Air Force.
LOCATION: In northern Thailand. *Locality:* Chiang Mai Province.
MAJOR UNITS: Air Force Technical Applications Center, Det 415.
BASE HISTORY: 1962, activated; seismic station supporting compliance of nuclear test ban treaties. 1976, USAF personnel replaced by Royal Thai Navy. 1977, Equipment Location 415, established with two USAF advisors. 1980, renamed present name. Data sent to AF Technical Applications Center, Patrick AFB.
Key Contacts
PUBLIC AFFAIRS: MSgt Rene Uzee, 407-494-9915, DSN 854-9915, ruzee@aftac. gov.
Personnel and Expenditures
ACTIVE DUTY PERSONNEL: 4

Turkey

Balikesir Air Field

1151. Balikesir Air Field
39 MUNSS Balikesir
39th MUNSS, Unit 6860
APO, AE 09816-6860
FAX 011-266-243175; DSN 675-1110, request Balikesir Operator, ext 137
Profile
BRANCH: Air Force.
LOCATION: 10 mi from Balikesir; 110 mi from Izmir. *Locality:* Balikesir Province.
MAJOR UNITS: 39th Munitions Support Squadron; Secure Communications Branch; Security Police Branch; Maintenance Branch; Command and Control Branch; Support Branch.
BASE HISTORY: 1968, US site on Turkish Air Force 9th Main Jet Base activated as Tuslog Detachment 194. 1968, reorganized as Detachment 1, 41st TACG, Cigli AB, Turkey. 1972, designated as 7391st Munitions Support Squadron (MUNSS). 1993, redesignated 39th MUNSS. Mission: custodial agent of US resources assigned to NATO in support of Turkish AF.
Key Contacts
COMMANDER: LTC Scott W Berry; ext 121.
PUBLIC AFFAIRS: A1C Thomas E Haerr.
TRANSPORTATION: SSgt Kevin D Rushing; ext 161.
PERSONNEL/COMMUNITY ACTIVITIES: TSgt Scott Gannaway; ext 142.
Personnel and Expenditures
ACTIVE DUTY PERSONNEL: 105
CIVILIAN PERSONNEL: 7
Services
Housing: Dormitory spaces. *Temporary Housing:* Transient quarters 2. *Exchange:* Convenience store. *Child Care/Capacities:* No day care facilities. *Schools:* College courses. *Base Library:* Yes. *Medical Facilities:* Medical Technicians. *Recreational Facilities:* Bowling center; Pool; Gym; Recreation center; Tennis courts; Racquetball court; Fitness center/Weight room; Softball field; Camping; Fishing/Hunting; All ranks club.

Incirlick Air Base

1152. Incirlick Air Base
Unit 7090
APO, AE 09824-5000
AMCC, DSN 676-6837, DSN FAX 676-3654; ATOC, DSN 676-6811; MACC DSN 676-6464
Internet: http://www.incirlik.af.mil/
OFFICER-OF-THE-DAY: BaseOperations, DSN 676-6156
Profile
BRANCH: Air Force.
SIZE AND LOCATION: 3323 acres. In S Turkey, approx 10 mi NE of Adana; 0.5 mi N of A-6; 25 mi from Mediterranean Sea. *Locality:* Adana Province.
MAJOR UNITS: 39th Wing; 39th Medical Group; 39th Operations Group; 39th Logistics Group; 39th Support Group; 39th Accounting and Finance Squadron; 39th Security Police Squadron; 628th Air Mobility Support Squadron; 628th Air Mobility Command and Control Squadron; 628th Aerial Port Services Squadron; 628th Air Mobility Maintenance Squadron; 7440th Wing (Provisional); Operation Northern Watch; 32nd Air Force Station (AFS); Air Force Office of Special Investigations, Det 52 FIS.
BASE HISTORY: 1951, construction began. 1954, Adana AB; later Incirlik ("fig orchard") Common Defense Installation; 7216th Air Base Squadron; first American personnel. 1955, SAC operation at base. 1960, U-2 flight of Francis Gary Powers originated. Support base for training rotational fighter aircraft. 1966, responsibility changed to Torrejon AB, Spain. 1975-78, NATO use only; name shortened to Incirlik Installation. Under Weapons Training Detachment Program, hosts fighter squadrons, USAF Europe & US for combined exercises with Turkish, USAF, & NATO aircrews. 1991, supported Operations Desert Shield/Storm. 1992, hub of Operation Provide Comfort for Kurdish refugees. 1993, 39th TACG redesignated 39th Wing.
Key Contacts
COMMANDER: Col Scott Gration, 39th Wing, DSN 676-6346.
PUBLIC AFFAIRS: Jesse Hall, 011-90-322-316-6060, DSN 676-6060, jesse. ha..@incirlik.af.mil.
Personnel and Expenditures
ACTIVE DUTY PERSONNEL: 2800
DEPENDENTS: 2000
CIVILIAN PERSONNEL: 2100
Services
Housing: Family units 950; Dormitory spaces 828; Senior NCO units 80. *Temporary Housing:* VOQ units 229; VAQ units 426; Unaccompanied officer/Enlisted quarters 60; BAQ units 922; Guesthouse units 16; Transient quarters Limited; Prime Knight 24 rooms. *Commissary:* Yes; *Exchange:* Food shop; Military clothing store; ATM; Fast food; Video rentals; Class VI; Exchange; Turkish BX; Sports store; Music store. *Child Care/Capacities:* Day care center; Home day care program; Summer day camp. *Schools:* Preschool/Kindergarten; Elementary; Intermediate/Junior high; High school. *Medical Facilities:* Hospital 20 beds. *Recreational Facilities:* Bowling center; Movie theater; Pool; Gym; Recreation center; Golf course; Stables; Tennis courts; Racquetball court; Fitness center/Weight room; Softball field; Football field; Auto shop; Craft shop; Officers club; NCO club; Enlisted

club; Youth center; Skeet range; Playground; Consolidated club.

Izmir Air Station

1153. Izmir Air Station
425 ABS
Unit 6870, Box 120
APO, AE 09821
90-232-484-5360; FAX 90-232-489-6252; DSN 675-3332; DSN FAX 675-3372
Profile
BRANCH: Air Force.
LOCATION: In Izmir, seaport city at head of Gulf of Izmir in W Turkey; 300 mi S of Istanbul. *Locality:* Izmir Province.
MAJOR UNITS: 425th Air Base Squadron; 6th Allied Tactical Air Force; Allied Land Forces Southeastern Europe; Izmir AS.
BASE HISTORY: 1955, activated as 7266th Support Squadron to support Allied Land Forces SE Europe; NATO principal subordinate command. 1959, moved to Cigli Air Base, 15 mi N of Izmir, merged with 7231st Combat Support Group. 1966, became 41st Tactical Group. 1970, facilities turned over to Turkish AF; 41st TG inactivated; 7241st Support Squadron moved to Izmir. 1970-73, moved to Incirlik AB. 1973-80, 7241st changed to air base squadron; redesignated air base group. 1993, redesignated 741st ABS. 1994, assumed current name. No real base, all offices within metropolitan community; no air operations.

VISITOR ATTRACTIONS: Ancient ruins within 50 mi: Epheses & Bergama.
Key Contacts
COMMANDER: Col John E Kuconis.
PUBLIC AFFAIRS: Capt Sean McKenna, mckennas@mailgate.izmir.af.mil.
TRANSPORTATION: Robert Crumpton, DSN 675-3262.
Personnel and Expenditures
ACTIVE DUTY PERSONNEL: 600
DEPENDENTS: 900
CIVILIAN PERSONNEL: 50
CONTRACT EXPENDITURE: $12 mil
Services
Housing: None. *Temporary Housing:* Grand Mercure Hotel 60 rms. *Commissary:* Yes; *Exchange:* Retail store; Barber shop; Dry cleaners; Food shop; Florist; Service station; Military clothing store; Convenience store; Beauty shop; Laundromat; Optical store; Post office; Fast food; Video rentals; Thrift shop; Travel agency; Class VI; Tailor/Alterations; Cafeteria. *Child Care/Capacities:* Day care center capacity 49, newborn-5yrs; Summer day camp; Before & after school programs. *Schools:* Preschool/Kindergarten; Elementary; Intermediate/Junior high; High school; College courses. *Base Library:* Yes. *Medical Facilities:* Medical clinic; Dental clinic; Pharmacy; Veterinary services. *Recreational Facilities:* Pool; Gym; Tennis courts; Racquetball court; Fitness center/Weight room; Softball field; Officers club; NCO club; Youth center; Water sports; Playground.

Vecihi Akin Garrison

1154. Vecihi Akin Garrison
HQ LSE Unit 6895, Box 4000
APO, AE 09821
011-90-232-4484848, ext 2005, 2007, 2008; FAX 011-90-232-4484495
E-mail: lse01@egenet.com.tr Internet:http://www2.egenet.comtr/~lse01/
Profile
BRANCH: NATO.
LOCATION: Near Izmir, at Sirinyer, Turkey.
MAJOR UNITS: Land Forces Southeastern Europe (LANDSOUTHEAST); 6th Allied Tactical Air Force; Joint Signal Group; Allied Naval Forces Southern Europe (NAVSOUTH), Representative; Naval Striking and Support Forces Southern Europe (STRIKFORSOUTH), Representative.
BASE HISTORY: Site dates back to late 1800s as Christian training school. 1891, called American Boys School; later, American High School for Boys & American Collegiate Institute. 1934, school transferred to Beirut; used by Turkish Ministry of Education as teacher training school. 1952, LANDSOUTHEAST established as Sirinyer Garrison. Mar 1996, renamed General Vecihi Akin Garrison; NATO principal subordinate command, comparable to HQ of army group. Commanded by Turkish Army General, assisted by American Maj Gen as Deputy.
Key Contacts
COMMANDER: Maj Gen Reginal Graham Clemmons, Deputy Commander.

United Kingdom

424nd Air Base Squadron, RAF Fairford

1155. 424nd Air Base Squadron, RAF Fairford
Fairford RAF Base Glos GL7 4DL
Mailing Address
424 ABS, Unit 4820, PSC 36
APO AE, 09456
011-01285-714000; FAX 011-01285-714012; DSN 247-4000
E-mail: 424ABS.Fairford.af.mil Internet:http://100ARW.mildenhall.af.mil
Profile
BRANCH: Air Force.
SIZE AND LOCATION: 1200 acres. RAF Fairford, GLOS, GL7, 4DL (civilian address); 2 mi from market town of Fairford in the Cotswolds. 15 mi from Swindon; 1-hr drive from London. *Locality:* Gloucestershire.
MAJOR UNITS: 424th Air Base Squadron; 424th Civil Engineering Squadron; 424th Communications Squadron; 424th Services Squadron; 424th Logistics Squadron; 424th Plans & Programs Squadron.

BASE HISTORY: 1944, RAF base opened. WWII, participated in D-Day & Arnhem operations. 1950, jointly occupied by USAF (7507th ABS) & RAF. 1964, base transferred back to RAF control. 1969, became British Airline Company Concorde Flight Test Center. 1977, resumed reserve role. 1979, USAF (7020th ABG) returned. 1985, International Air Tattoo held. 1990, 7020th ABS (now 720th ABS) activated. Supported operation Desert Shield/Storm. 1993, International Air Tattoo again held.
Key Contacts
COMMANDER: LTC Francis J Robinson Jr, 011-01285-714200, DSN 247-4200, DSN FAX 247-4012, Robinson@424abs.fairford.af.mil.
PUBLIC AFFAIRS: Capt Mike Roth, 011-01285-714229, DSN 247-4229, DSN FAX 247-4222, RothM@424abs.fairford.af.mil.
PROCUREMENT: Capt Gary Cochran, 011-01285-4568, DSN 247-4568, DSN FAX 247-4012, CochranG@424abs.fairford.af.mil.
TRANSPORTATION: MSgt Jackson, 011-01285-714059, DSN 247-4059, DSN FAX 247-4059, 424ABS/LGT@424abs.fairford.af.mil.

Personnel and Expenditures
ACTIVE DUTY PERSONNEL: 180
DEPENDENTS: 400
CIVILIAN PERSONNEL: 273
CONTRACT EXPENDITURE: $12 mil
Services
Housing: Family units 106; Dormitory spaces 120; Senior NCO units 2. *Temporary Housing:* VOQ units 55. *Commissary:* Yes; *Exchange:* Retail store; Barber shop; Dry cleaners; Food shop; Bank; Service station; Convenience store; Beauty shop; Laundromat; ATM; Post office; Video rentals; Four seasons; Thrift shop; Class VI. *Child Care/Capacities:* Day care facility under construction. *Schools:* No on-base schools. *Base Library:* Yes. *Medical Facilities:* Medical Aid Station for active duty only. *Recreational Facilities:* Bowling center; Movie theater; Gym; Recreation center; Racquetball court; Fitness center/Weight room; Softball field; Football field; Auto shop; Craft shop; Fishing/Hunting; Youth center; Playground; Community club; All ranks club.

Alconbury RAF Base

1156. Alconbury RAF Base

423 ABS/DPF, Bldg 578
Huntingdon, CAMBS, RAF Alconbury PE17
  5DA
Mailing Address
423 ABS/DPF, Unit 5585, Box 100
APO AE, 09470
01480-822174; FAX 1480-823557; DSN
  268-2174
Internet: http://www.molesworth.af.mil/
  site4645.htm
OFFICER-OF-THE-DAY: 01480-4237; DSN
  314-268-4237
Profile
BRANCH: Air Force.
SIZE AND LOCATION: 2146 acres. 60 mi N of
  London on A-1/A-604 motorways; 3 mi NE
  of Huntingdon; near town of Little Stukeley;
  25 mi N of RAF Chicksands; 15 mi NW of
  Cambridge; 54 mi from London. *Locality:*
  Huntingdon, Cambridgeshire.
MAJOR UNITS: US Air Forces in Europe
  (USAFE); US European Command; 423rd
  Air Base Squadron.
BASE HISTORY: 1938, satellite base for Royal
  Air Force (RAF) Upwood. 1942, home to US
  93rd Bomber Group (Heavy). 1943, home to
  92nd Bomber Group (Heavy); later 482nd
  Bomber Group (Heavy). 1946, returned to
  RAF; various US Army Air Corps tenants.
  1951, 3rd US Air Force took control of base;
  59th Air Depot Wing activated. 1950s, sev-
  eral administrative support units stationed at
  Alconbury. 1959, 10th Tactical Reconnais-
  sance Wing arrived. 1982, 17th Reconnais-
  sance Wing (SAC) activated. 1987, 10th Tac-
  tical Reconnaissance Wing redesignated 10th
  Tactical Fighter Wing. 1991, 17th Reconnais-
  sance Wing inactivated with 95th Reconnais-
  sance Squadron remaining. 1993, 10th TFW
  redesignated 10th Air Base Wing. Currently,
  423rd ABW host.
Key Contacts
COMMANDER: LTC Gerald B Evans, 423
  ABS.
Personnel and Expenditures
ACTIVE DUTY PERSONNEL: 1200 (Tri-base
  area); retirees 320
DEPENDENTS: 2500
CIVILIAN PERSONNEL: 80
MILITARY PAYROLL EXPENDITURE: $68 mil
CONTRACT EXPENDITURE: $10 mil
Services
Housing: Family units 373; Unaccompanied officer quarters 6; Unaccompanied enlisted quarters
  89; Dormitory spaces 1524; Senior NCO units
  113; Junior NCO units 416. *Temporary Hous-
  ing:* VOQ units 46; VEQ units 130; Lodge units
  Spartan Inn; Stukeley Inn. *Commissary:* Yes; *Exchange:* Retail store; Barber shop; Dry cleaners;
  Food shop; Florist; Bank; Service station; Furniture store; Bakery; Bookstore; Military clothing
  store; Convenience store; Beauty shop; Laundromat; Credit union; Fast food; Class VI; Ice
  cream store; Concessions; Mini-mall; SATO-
  OS. *Child Care/Capacities:* Day care center;
  Home day care program. *Schools:* Preschool/
  Kindergarten; Elementary; Intermediate/Junior
  high; High school; College courses. *Base Library:* Yes. *Medical Facilities:* Medical clinic;
  Dental clinic; Pharmacy; Outpatient medical

services provided by 10th Medical Squadron at
RAF Upwood. *Recreational Facilities:* Bowling
center; Movie theater; Gym; Recreation center;
Tennis courts; Racquetball court; Fitness center/
Weight room; Softball field; Football field; Auto
shop; Craft shop; Officers club; NCO club;
Youth center; Picnic area; Skeet range; Play-
ground; SATO.

Croughton RAF Base

1157. Croughton RAF Base

Unit 5855
APO, AE 09494
DSN 314-236-8000
Internet: http://www.usafe.af.mil/bases/crough/
  crough/htm; http://www.usafe.af.mil/usafes.
  htm
Profile
BRANCH: Air Force.
SIZE AND LOCATION: 694 acres. 3 mi from
  Bracley; 10 mi NE of Bicester; 25 mi SW of
  Stratford-Upon-Avon; 22 mi N of Oxford.
MAJOR UNITS: 422nd Air Base Squadron;
  Communications & Information Flight, RAF
  Croughton; Operating Location Alpha, RAF
  Barford St John.
BASE HISTORY: 1930s, three farms consoli-
  dated to form RAF Brackley. 1940, renamed
  RAF Crougton. WWII, heavy bombing base;
  bomber conversion base. 1943, Glider Pilot
  Training Unit. RAF Barford St John high fre-
  quency transmitter site. 1950, USAFE estab-
  lished HF airways station detachment, 1969th
  Communications Service; major US military
  communications sites in Europe. 1961, designated 2130th Communications Squadron.
  1972, renamed 2130th Communications
  Group; later deactivated; combined with RAF
  Upper Heyford. 1983, 2130th Communications Squadron reactivated. 1986, redesignated 2130th Communications Group. 1993,
  redesignated 630th Communications Squadron. 1994, renamed 603rd Communications
  Squadron. 1996, deactivated; unit redesig-
  nated 422 Air Base Squadron under 100th air
  Refueling Wing, RAF Mildenhall. RAF Bar-
  ford St John designated Operating Location
  Alpha (OL-A), 422nd Air Base Squadron (22
  mi away, near Bloxham, Oxfordshire).
Key Contacts
COMMANDER: LTC John M Langlois, DSN
  314-236-8207.
PUBLIC AFFAIRS: Pamela Robbins, DSN
  236-8426, robbinsp@croughton.af.mil.
Personnel and Expenditures
ACTIVE DUTY PERSONNEL: 400; British
  Milinstry of Defense 109
CIVILIAN PERSONNEL: 109
Services
Housing: Family units 71; Dormitory spaces.
Temporary Housing: Lodge units Shepard's
Rest Inn rooms 16; Transient quarters Houses 6.
Exchange: Dry cleaners; Computer store; Tailor/
Alterations; Convenience store; Service station;
Barber shop; Beauty shop; Food shop; Post of-
fice; ATM; Credit union; Bank. *Child Care/Ca-
pacities:* Day care center. *Schools:* Elementary;
College courses. *Medical Facilities:* Dental
clinic; Veterinary services; Medical Air Station.
Recreational Facilities: Consolidated club; Fit-
ness center/Weight room; Bowling center; Auto

shop; Craft shop; Outdoor recreation services;
Community center.

Feltwell RAF Base

1158. Feltwell RAF Base

Unit 3375
APO, AE 09461
011-44-01638-52-7168, 7170; DSN 226-7168,
DSN FAX 226-7171
Internet: http://www.lakenheath.af.mil/afnews.
  htm
Profile
BRANCH: Air Force.
LOCATION: On B-1112, 12 mi NW of Thet-
  ford; 80 mi from London. *Locality:* Norfolk.
MAJOR UNITS: 48th Fighter Wing; Air Force
  News Agency, OL-A, Det 4; 5th Space Sur-
  veillance Squadron.
BASE HISTORY: Provides news coverage for
  RAF Lakenheath & RAF Mildenhall commu-
  nities & units around UK. 5th Space Surveil-
  lance Squadron operates a Deep Space Track-
  ing System site.
Key Contacts
PUBLIC AFFAIRS: Capt Patrick Ryder, 48th
  Fighter Wing.

Fylingdales-Moor RAF Base

1159. Fylingdales-Moor RAF Base

PSC 52
APO, AE 09496
Profile
BRANCH: Air Force.
LOCATION: In N England. *Locality:* York-
  shire.
MAJOR UNITS: 21st OG/USAFLO.
BASE HISTORY: One of 3 Ballistic Missile
  Early Warning System sites. Operated by
  RAF.
Key Contacts
COMMANDER: Maj J Stone, USAF Liaison
  Officer; RAF Squadron Leader Morman P
  Reeve, Space Warning Squadron.
Personnel and Expenditures
ACTIVE DUTY PERSONNEL: 1

Hythe Depot Activity

1160. Hythe Depot Activity

Unit 8145, PSC 33, Box 10
APO, AE 09447-5360
Profile
BRANCH: Army.
LOCATION: In SE England, on Strait of Dover,
  10 mi WSW of Dover. *Locality:* Kent Bor-
  ough.
MAJOR UNITS: Hythe Depot Activity.
Key Contacts
COMMANDER: Ivan Hampton, CEA,
  011-44-703-20-3466, DSN 243-3466,
  ihampton@letterkenn-emh1.army.mil.

Lakenheath RAF Base

1161. Lakenheath RAF Base
Unit 5210, Box 215
APO, AE 09464-0215
011-44-01638-522151; FAX
011-44-01638-525637
Internet: http://www.lakenheath.af.mil/
Profile
BRANCH: Air Force.
SIZE AND LOCATION: 2000 acres. Approx 80 mi from London on A-1065; NW corner of Suffolk; bordering on village of Lakenheath; 30 mi NE of Cambridge; 75 mi from London. Local address: 48FW/PA, RAF Lakenheath, Brandon, Suffolk IP27 9PN. *Locality:* East Anglia, Suffolk County.
MAJOR UNITS: US Air Forces in Europe (USAFE); 48th Fighter Wing; 48th Medical Group.
BASE HISTORY: 1941, RAF Lakenheath opens as satellite of RAF Mildenhall. 1943, made independent station. 1944-47, equipment depot; master diversion airfield. 1948, 2nd Bombardment Group assigned to support Berlin Airlift. 1959-present, converted from SAC base to USAF, Europe fighter base. 1991, augmenting Operation Provide Comfort, Bosnia-Herzegovina. Largest USAF operated base in UK. Mission to train for & conduct air operations in support of NATO. Known as the "Statue of Liberty" Wing (only wing with both numerical & descriptive designation).
Key Contacts
COMMANDER: Col Douglas J Richardson.
PUBLIC AFFAIRS: 48th FW, 011-44-441638-522151, FAX 011-44-441638-525637, 48fw.pa@ lakenheath.af.mil.
Personnel and Expenditures
ACTIVE DUTY PERSONNEL: 4750
DEPENDENTS: 6900
CIVILIAN PERSONNEL: 1300
Services
Housing: Family units 2089. *Temporary Housing:* Dormitory units. *Commissary:* Yes; *Exchange:* Retail store; Barber shop; Dry cleaners; Food shop; Bank; Service station; Furniture store; Bakery; Bookstore; Military clothing store; Convenience store; Beauty shop; Credit union; Optical store; Video rentals; Four seasons; Class VI; Ice cream shop. *Child Care/Capacities:* Day care center capacity 262, 6mo-11yrs, no reservations; Home day care program; Before & after school programs; Summer day camp. *Schools:* Preschool/Kindergarten; Elementary; Intermediate/Junior high; High school; College courses; Schools serve RAF Lakenheath, Feltwell, & Mildenhall; Before & after school programs. *Base Library:* Yes. *Medical Facilities:* Hospital 70 beds; Medical clinic; Dental clinic; Hospital central departure point for all aeromedical evacuation to Germany & US; Veterinary services at RAF Feltwell. *Recreational Facilities:* Bowling center; Movie theater; Pool (Only USAF indoor, heated pool); Gym; Recreation center; Golf course (Only USAF course in UK); Tennis courts; Racquetball court; Skating rink (Only military roller rink in UK); Fitness center/Weight room; Softball field; Football field; Auto shop; Craft shop; Officers club; Fishing/Hunting; Youth center; Skeet range 4500 acre area; All ranks club; Rod & Gun club; Aero club; Community center; ITT office; Activity center; Video rentals; SATO.

London

1162. Army Research, Development & Standardization Group, UK
USARDSG
Edison House, 223 Old Marylebone Rd
London, NW1 5TH
Mailing Address
PSC 802, Box 15
FPO AE, 09499-1500
011-44-171-514-4906; FAX
011-44-171-723-6112
Profile
BRANCH: Army.
LOCATION: Edison House, London.
MAJOR UNITS: Army Research, Development & Standardization Group UK.
Key Contacts
COMMANDER: LTC Thomas J Kindel.

1163. European Office of Aerospace Research & Development
EOARD
Edison House, 223/231 Old Marylebone Rd
London, NW1 5TH
Mailing Address
PSC 802, Box 14
APO AE, 09499-0200
011-44-171-514-4950; FAX
011-44-171-514-4960
Profile
BRANCH: Air Force.
LOCATION: Edison House, London.
MAJOR UNITS: European Office of Aerospace Research & Development.
Key Contacts
COMMANDER: LTC Don McGillen.

1164. Office of Naval Research Europe
ONREUR
Edison House, 223/231 Old Marylebone Rd
London, NW1 5TH
Mailing Address
PSC 802, Box 39
FPO AE, 09499-0700
011-44-171-514-4516; FAX
011-44-171-723-6359
Internet: http://www.ehis.navy.mil/
Profile
BRANCH: Navy.
LOCATION: Edison House, London.
MAJOR UNITS: Office of Naval Research Europe.
Key Contacts
COMMANDER: CDR Albert L Raithel III.

1165. Research & Development Liaison Office London (USAF)
RDLL
223/231 Old Marylebone Rd
London, NW1 5TH
Mailing Address
PSC 802, Box 19
FPO AE, 09499-0100
011-44-171-514-4668; FAX
011-44-171-514-4928
Profile
BRANCH: Air Force.
LOCATION: Edison House, London.
MAJOR UNITS: Research & Development Liaison Office London (USAF).
Key Contacts
COMMANDER: LTC Jonathan B Sumner.

Menwith Hill

1166. Menwith Hill
APO, AE 09648
011-0423-770421; FAX 011-441-423-77-7982
Profile
BRANCH: DOD.
LOCATION: Off A-59 & B-6451, 7 mi W of Harrogate; 20 mi N of Bradford; 220 mi from London. *Locality:* North Yorkshire.
MAJOR UNITS: Communications Relay Station.

Mildenhall RAF Base

1167. Mildenhall RAF Base
Team Mildenhall
RAF Mildenhall, Bury St Edmunds
Suffolk, 1P28 8NF
Mailing Address
100th ARW, Unit 4890, Box 190
APO AE, 09459-5000
011-44-1638-543000; DSN 314-238-3000
Internet: http://www.mildenhall.af.mil
Profile
BRANCH: Air Force.
SIZE AND LOCATION: 1144 acres. Approx 2 mi W of Mildenhall Village on A-1101; approx 80 mi NE of London; approx 30 mi NE of Cambridge. *Locality:* East Anglia; Suffolk County; Forest Heath District.
MAJOR UNITS: 100th Air Refueling Wing; 351st Air Refueling Squadron; European Tanker Task Force; HQ, 3rd Air Force; 352nd Special Operations Group; 627th Air Mobility Support Squadron; 488th Intelligence Squadron; 95th Reconnaissance Squadron; Naval Air Facility.
BASE HISTORY: 1934, RAF base opened as one of the largest bases under British Bomber Command. Site of Royal Aero Club's Mildenhall-to-Melbourne, Australia, air Race. WWII, primary RAF base. Post WWII, caretaker status. 1948, activated for Berlin Blockade. 1966, assumed US European Command Post function with 513th Troop Carrier Wing. 1972, 3rd USAF. 1991, command post inactivated. 1992, 100th ARW activated (originated as 100th Bombardment Group at Orlando AB, FL, in 1942. WWII, deployed to RAF Station Thorpe Abbott. 1956, reactivated at Portsmouth AFB, NH. 1950s-1990s, series of activations, moves, & redesignations); host unit & tanker support for European Theater.
Key Contacts
COMMANDER: Col Jeffrey B Kohler, DSN FAX 238-2101.
PUBLIC AFFAIRS: 100th ARW/PA, 011-44-1638-542654, DSN 238-2654, DSN FAX 238-2101.

Personnel and Expenditures
ACTIVE DUTY PERSONNEL: 4000
DEPENDENTS: 4100
CIVILIAN PERSONNEL: 500
MILITARY PAYROLL EXPENDITURE: $95.5 mil
CONTRACT EXPENDITURE: $17.9 mil
Services
Housing: Family units 2178 units through RAF Lakenheath; Dormitory spaces 576. *Temporary Housing:* VOQ units 46; VAQ units 163; Lodge units 41; Aircrew 153. *Commissary:* Yes; *Exchange:* Retail store; Barber shop; Dry cleaners; Food shop; Bank; Service station; Bookstore; Convenience store; Beauty shop; Laundromat; Credit union; ATM; Post office; Fast food; Video rentals; Four seasons; Thrift shop; Travel agency; Class VI; Laundry; Alterations; Main exchange at RAF Lakenheath. *Child Care/Capacities:* Day care center Capacity 67, 6wks-5yrs; Home day care program; Summer day camp; Before & after school programs. *Schools:* College courses; DOD schools operated through Lakenheath/Feltwell Complex. *Base Library:* Yes. *Medical Facilities:* Dental clinic; Flight Surgeons Office; Hospital facilities at RAF Lakenheath; Veterinary services at RAF Feltwell. *Recreational Facilities:* Bowling center; Movie theater; Recreation center; Tennis courts; Racquetball court; Fitness center/Weight room; Softball field; Auto shop; Craft shop; Officers club; NCO club; Enlisted club; Youth center; Picnic area.

Molesworth RAF Base

1168. Molesworth RAF Base
423 ABS/DPF, Bldg 578, RAF Alconbury
Huntingdon, PE17 5DA
Mailing Address
423 ABS/DPF, Unit 5585, Box 100
APO AE, 09470
FAX 011-01480-823557
Internet: http://www.molesworth.af.mil/site4645.htm
OFFICER-OF-THE-DAY: DSN 268-2546
Profile
BRANCH: Air Force.
LOCATION: On motorway A-14 near Old Western; 11 mi NW of Huntingdon; 14 mi W of RAF Alconbury. *Locality:* Old Weston.
MAJOR UNITS: Joint Analysis Center (USEUCOM JAC); National Imagery and Mapping Agency (NIMA); Defense Reutilization & Marketing Office.
BASE HISTORY: 1940, bomber base for RAF. 1942, US 15th Bombardment Squadron arrived (1st American bombing operations of WWII); replaced by 303rd Bombardment Group. 1945, RAF regained possession of base. 1946, airbase closed. 1951, reopened for Air Force use. 1954, 582nd Air Resupply Group arrived. 1956, 482nd Troop Carrier Squadron replaced 582nd Air Refueling Group. 1957-1985, used as military family housing annex; base reverted to RAF. 1986, 303rd Tactical Missile Wing (TMW) activated. 1989, 303rd TMW inactivated under Intermediate-range Nuclear Forces Treaty. 1991, Joint Operations Center began operations.
Key Contacts
COMMANDER: Col Philip Marcum, JAC.
Personnel and Expenditures
ACTIVE DUTY PERSONNEL: 400
DEPENDENTS: 600
CIVILIAN PERSONNEL: 55
Services
Housing: Family units 40; See RAF Alconbury. *Exchange:* Convenience store. *Schools:* See RAF Alconbury. *Medical Facilities:* Medical Aid Station.

Upwood RAF Base

1169. Upwood RAF Base
423 ABS/DPF, Bldg 578, RAF Alconbury
Huntingdon CAMBS, PE17 5DA
Mailing Address
423 ABS/DPF, Unit 5585, Box 100
APO AE, 09470
011-01480-824506
Profile
BRANCH: Navy.
LOCATION: Off B-1040, SW of Ramsey; 80 mi from London; 14 mi from RAF Alconbury. *Locality:* Cambridgeshire.
MAJOR UNITS: 10th Fighter Wing Clinic; 608th Contingency Hospital; 7028th School Squadron (NCO Academy); 423rd OL-A Medical Facility.
Key Contacts
COMMANDER: 011-01480-4800; DSN 268-4800.

Services
Housing: Housing for DOD enlisted military families 28 units. *Medical Facilities:* Medical clinic; Dental clinic; Provides primary care for RAF Alconbury, Molesworth, & Upwood; aditional facilities at RAF Lakenheath, 48 mi E.

West Ruislip RAF Base

1170. West Ruislip RAF Base
COMNAVACTUK
PSC 802, Box 60
FPO, AE 09499-1000
011-44-171-514-4500
Profile
BRANCH: Navy.
LOCATION: Not a base, but 4 locations: RAF Base approx 10 mi from Heathrow Airport, take J4A at M4 right onto A4, turn off onto A437, at Hayes go onto A312, bear left onto B455, turn left onto A4180; In Westminster, Navy HQ Building, 7 N Audley St, caddy-corner from US Embassy. *Locality:* Central London, Borough of Westminster; Greater London, Borough of Hillingdon.
MAJOR UNITS: Commander-in-Chief, US Naval Forces Europe; Commander, Naval Activities, UK (COMNAVACTUK); Marine Corps Security Force Co, London; Defense Fuel Office, UK.
BASE HISTORY: Mission of Commander Naval Activities United Kingdom: act as ISIC for designated commands, support tenant activities and US government personnel in Greater London, and perform as area coordinator for US Naval activities and deployed units in UK & N Europe.
Personnel and Expenditures
ACTIVE DUTY PERSONNEL: 600
DEPENDENTS: 1300
CIVILIAN PERSONNEL: 350
Services
Housing: Family units. *Exchange:* Retail store; Barber shop; Food shop; Bank; Service station; Bookstore; Thrift shop; Personal services; Gift shop; New car sales. *Child Care/Capacities:* Day care center. *Schools:* Elementary; High school; College courses. *Medical Facilities:* Veterinary services. *Recreational Facilities:* Movie theater; Tennis courts; Racquetball court; Fitness center/Weight room; Softball field; Auto shop; Craft shop; Community club; Basketball; All hands club.

Virgin Islands

Adjutant General of the Virgin Islands

1171. Adjutant General of the Virgin Islands
4031 La Grande Princess, Lot 1B
St Croix, VI 00820-4353
809-772-7711; FAX 809-778-3282
Profile
BRANCH: Army National Guard.
MAJOR UNITS: Virgin Islands National Guard.
Key Contacts
COMMANDER: Maj Gen Jean A Romney.

Wake Island

Wake Island Missile Launch Facility

1172. Wake Island Missile Launch Facility

APO, AP 96518
808-422-5212 (Hickham AFB)

Profile

BRANCH: Army.

SIZE AND LOCATION: 1826 acres. 2458 mi W of Hawaii; 1591 mi E of Guam; 1140 mi N of Kwajalein Atoll. *Locality:* Wake Island.

MAJOR UNITS: Missile Launch Facility, Wake Island; Marine Attack Squadron 211.

BASE HISTORY: Originally named San Francisco by Spanish explorer Alvaro de Mon- dana, later renamed after Capt Samuel Wake, British captain, who visited in 1776. Uninhab- ited due to lack of fresh water. 1899, claimed by US. 1934, under US Navy control. 1941, US Navy began building base. 1942-45, occu- pied by Japanese. 1945-47, under US military control. 1947-72, under Federal Aviation Ad- ministration control. 1972, Wake Island AFB. 1994, transferred to Army. 1996, under high- level caretaker status. Mission: support contin- gency deployments; service transiting air- craft; serve as emergency landing field; pro- vide petroleum, oils, and lubricants storage; & support DOD & civil tenants under Hick- ham AFB, HI.

VISITOR ATTRACTIONS: Island is historic landmark; Bird sanctuary; Ruins of Pan Am buildings.

Key Contacts

COMMANDER: Under ISABW, Hickam AFB, HI.

Personnel and Expenditures

ACTIVE DUTY PERSONNEL: 40
CIVILIAN PERSONNEL: 160

Services

Housing: Family units 1; Duplex units 3; Dormi- tory spaces 346. *Temporary Housing:* Dormitory units 344. *Exchange:* Barber shop; Bank; Bak- ery; Convenience store; Laundromat. *Child Care/Capacities:* No day care facilities. *Schools:* No on-base schools. *Base Library:* Yes. *Medical Facilities:* Dispensary. *Recreational Fa- cilities:* Bowling center; Golf course; Tennis courts; Fitness center/Weight room; Softball field; Football field; Fishing/Hunting; Picnic area; Community club.

Appendixes

Appendix I

1995 BASE CLOSURES AND REALIGNMENTS

Major Base Closures—Army

Fort McClellan, Alabama
Fort Chaffee, Arkansas
Oakland Army Base, California
Fitzsimons Army Medical Center, Colorado
Savanna Army Depot Activity, Illinois
Fort Holabird, Maryland
Fort Richie, Maryland
Bayonne Military Ocean Terminal, New Jersey
Seneca Army Depot, New York
Fort Indiantown Gap, Pennsylvania
Fort Pickett, Virginia

Major Base Closures—Navy

Naval Air Facility, Adak, Alaska
Fleet Industrial Supply Center, Oakland, California
Naval Shipyard, Long Beach, California
Ship Repair Facility, Guam
Naval Air Warfare Center, Aircraft Division Detachment, Indianapolis, Indiana
Naval Air Warfare Center, Aircraft Division Detachment, Louisville, Kentucky
Naval Surface Warfare Center, Dahlgren Division Detachment, White Oak, Maryland
Naval Air Station, South Weymouth, Massachusetts
Naval Air Warfare Center, Aircraft Division, Warminster, Pennsylvania

Major Base Closures—Air Force

McClellan AFB, California
Ontario IAP Air Guard Station, California
Roslyn Air Guard Station, New York [Closure contingent upon Commission requirement for sale of property at fair market value.]

Bergstrom Air Reserve Base, Texas
Reese Air Force Base, Texas

Major Base Closures—Defense Logistics Agency

Defense Distribution Depot Memphis, Tennessee
Defense Distribution Depot Ogden, Utah

Major Base Realignments—Army

Fort Greely, Alaska
Fort Hunter Liggett, California
Sierra Army Depot, California
Fort Meade, Maryland
Detroit Arsenal, Michigan
Fort Dix, New Jersey
Charles E. Kelly Support Center, Pennsylvania
Letterkenny Army Depot, Pennsylvania
Fort Buchanan, Puerto Rico
Red River Army Depot, Texas
Fort Lee, Virginia

Major Base Realignments—Navy

Naval Air Station, Key West, Florida
Naval Activities, Guam
Naval Air Station, Corpus Christi, Texas
Naval Undersea Warfare Center, Keyport, Washington

Major Base Realignments—Air Force

Onizuka Air Station, California
Eglin Air Force Base, Florida
Malmstrom Air Force Base, Montana
Grand Forks Air Force Base, North Dakota
Kelly Air Force Base, Texas
Hill Air Force Base, Utah

Appendix II

BASE CLOSURE AND REALIGNMENT SCHEDULES* AS OF SEPTEMBER 30, 1997

BRAC Round 1995

BASE/INSTALLATION	ACTION	DATE
Air Force		
McClellan Air Force Base, CA	Major Closure	Jul 2001
Onizuka Air Station, CA	Major Realignment	Sep 2000
Ontario IAP, Air Guard Station, CA	Major Closure	Sep 1998
Eglin Air Force Base, FL	Minor Realignment	Sep 1998
Malmstrom Air Force Base, MT	Major Realignment	Jul 2001
Grand Forks Air Force Base	Major Realignment	Sep 1998
Real-Time Digitally Controlled Analyzer Processor Activity, NY	Minor Closure/Realignment	Sep 1997
Roslyn Air Guard Station, NY	Major Closure #1	Sep 2000
Bergstrom Air Reserve Base, TX	Closed	Sep 1997
Kelly Air Force Base, TX	Major Realignment	Jul 2001
Reese Air Force Base, TX	Closed	Sep 1997
Hill Air Force Base, UT	Minor Realignment	Sep 1997
Army		
Fort Greely, AK	Major Realignment	Jul 2001
Fort McClellan, AL	Major Closure	Sep 1999
Fort Chaffee, AR	Closed	Sep 1997
Branch U.S. Disciplinary Barracks, CA	Minor Closure/Realignment	Sep 1998
East Fort Baker, CA	Minor Closure/Realignment #2	Sep 1999
Fort Hunter Liggett, CA	Major Realignment	Sep 1999
Oakland Army Base, CA	Major Closure	Jul 2001
Rio Vista Army Reserve Center, CA	Closed	Jan 1996
Sierra Army Depot, CA	Major Realignment	Jul 2001
Fitzsimons Army Medical Center, CO	Major Closure	Sep 1999
Stratford Army Engine Plant, CT	Minor Closure/Realignment	Dec 1997
Big Coppitt Key, FL	Closed	Jan 1996
Savanna Army Depot Activity, IL	Major Closure	Sep 2000
Hingham Cohasset, MA	Closed	Sep 1998**
Sudbury Training Annex, MA	Closed	Nov 1998**
Concepts Analysis Agency, MD	Minor Closure/Realignment	Jun 1999

* Information in this appendix was obtained from the Defense Base Closure and Realignment Commission (BRAC). Installations are listed alphabetically by
  BRAC round, service, and state. Evolving circumstances subject all of the projected dates to change. See end of Appendix II for explanations of #s.
** Closed ahead of schedule

Fort Holabird, MD	Closed	Jul 1996
Fort Meade, MD	Minor Realignment	Sep 1997
Fort Richie, MD	Major Closure	Sep 1998
Publications Distribution Center Baltimore, MD	Closed	Jul 1997
Detroit Arsenal, MI	Major Realignment #3	Sep 1999
Aviation-Troop Command, MO	Major Closure/Realignment	Dec 1997
Fort Missoula, MT	Minor Closure/Realignment	Sep 1998
Recreation Center #2, NC	Closed	Jan 1996
Bayonne Military Ocean Terminal, NJ	Major Closure	Jul 2001
Camp Kilmer, NJ	Minor Closure/Realignment	Sep 1997
Camp Pedricktown, NJ	Minor Closure/Realignment	Nov 2000
Fort Dix, NJ	Major Realignment	Sep 1997
Bellmore Logistics Activity, NY	Closed	Sep 1997
Fort Totten, NY	Minor Closure/Realignment	Oct 1997
Seneca Army Depot, NY	Major Closure	Sep 2000
Charles E. Kelly Support Center, PA	Major Realignment	Oct 2000
Fort Indiantown Gap, PA	Major Closure	Oct 1998
Letterkenny Army Depot, PA	Major Realignment	Sep 2000
Fort Buchanan, PR	Major Realignment	Jun 2000
Red River Army Depot, TX	Major Realignment	Sep 1998
Fort Lee, VA	Minor Realignment	Sep 1997
Fort Pickett, VA	Closed	Sep 1997
Information Systems Software Command (ISSC), VA	Minor Closure/Realignment	Sep 2000
Camp Bonneville, WA	Minor Closure/Realignment	Nov 2000

Defense Investigative Service (DIS)

Investigations Control and Automation Directorate, MD	Minor Closure/Realignment	Jul 2001

Defense Logistics Agency

Defense Distribution Depot McClellan, CA	Minor Closure/Realignment	Jul 2001
Defense Contract Management District South, GA	Closed	Jun 1996
Defense Contract Management Command International, OH	Closed	Jun 1996
Defense Distribution Depot Columbus, OH	Minor Closure/Realignment	Sep 1997
Defense Distribution Depot Letterkenny, PA	Minor Closure/Realignment	Sep 1998
Defense Industrial Supply Center, PA	Minor Closure/Realignment	Jul 1999
Defense Distribution Depot Memphis, TN	Closed	Sep 1997
Defense Distribution Depot San Antonio, TX	Minor Closure/Realignment	Jul 2001
Defense Distribution Depot Ogden, UT	Closed	Sep 1997

Navy

Naval Air Facility Adak, AK	Closed	Mar 1997
Naval Reserve Center Huntsville, AL	Closed	Sep 1996
Fleet Industrial Supply Center Oakland, CA	Major Closure	Sep 1998
Naval Command, Control and Ocean Surveillance Center, ISW, CA	Minor Closure/Realignment	Sep 1997
Naval Personnel Research and Development Center, CA	Minor Closure/Realignment	Dec 1999
Naval Reserve Center Pomona, CA	Closed	Nov 1995
Naval Reserve Center Santa Ana, CA	Closed	Dec 1995
Naval Reserve Center Stockton, CA	Closed	Sep 1996
Naval Shipyard Long Beach, CA	Closed	Sep 1997
Supervisor of Shipbuilding, Conversion and Repair, CA	Major Realignment	Sep 1996
Naval Undersea Warfare Center-Newport Division, New London Det, CT	Closed	Mar 1997
Naval Air Station Key West, FL	Major Realignment	Sep 1997
Naval Research Laboratory, Underwater Sound Reference Detachment, FL	Minor Closure/Realignment	Sep 1997

Fleet and Industrial Supply Center, Guam	Minor Closure/Realignment	Sep 1997
Naval Activities Guam	Major Realignment	Sep 2000
Public Works Center Guam	Minor Closure/Realignment	Sep 1999
Ship Repair Facility Guam	Closed	Sep 1997
Naval Air Warfare Center, Aircraft Division Detachment Indianapolis, IN	Closed #4	Sep 1997
Naval Air Reserve Center Olathe, KS	Closed	Sep 1996
Naval Air Warfare Center, Aircraft Division Louisville, KY	Closed #5	Sep 1997
Naval Biodynamics Laboratory, LA	Minor Closure/Realignment	Sep 1996
Naval Reserve Readiness Command New Orleans (Region 10), LA	Closed	Dec 1996
Naval Air Station South Weymouth, MA	Closed	Sep 1997
Naval Medical Research Institute (Tri-Service Project Reliance), MD	Minor Closure/Realignment	Feb 1999
Naval Surface Warfare Center, Carderock Division Detachment, MD	Minor Closure/Realignment	Dec 1999
Naval Surface Warfare Center, Dahlgren Division Detachment White Oak, MD	Closed	Jul 1997
Naval Reserve Center Cadillac, MI	Closed	May 1996
Naval Reserve Center Staten Island, NY	Closed	Dec 1995
Naval Air Technical Services Facility Philadelphia, PA	Minor Closure/Realignment	Jan 1999
Naval Air Warfare Center, Aircraft Division Warminster, PA	Closed	Mar 1997
Naval Air Warfare Center, Aircraft Division, Open Water Test Facility, PA	Minor Closure/Realignment	Mar 1997
Naval Aviation Engineering Support Unit Philadelphia, PA	Minor Closure/Realignment	Jan 1999
Naval Command, Control and Ocean Surveillance Center, Research, Development, Testing, and Engineering Division, PA	Minor Closure/Realignment	Mar 1997
Fleet and Industrial Supply Center Charleston, SC	Minor Closure/Realignment	Apr 1996
Naval Reserve Readiness Command Charleston (Region 7), SC	Closed	Dec 1996
Naval Air Station Corpus Christi, TX	Major Realignment	Jun 1996
Naval Reserve Center Laredo, TX	Closed	Dec 1995
Naval Command, Control and Ocean Surveillance Center, In-Service Engineering East Coast Detachment, Norfolk, VA	Minor Closure/Realignment	Sep 1998
Naval Information Systems Management Center Arlington, VA	Minor Closure/Realignment	Sep 1998
Naval Management Systems Support Office Chesapeake, VA	Minor Closure/Realignment	Sep 1999
Naval Undersea Warfare Center Keyport, WA	Major Realignment	Sep 1996
Naval Reserve Center Sheboygan, WI	Closed	Dec 1995

BRAC Round 1993

BASE/INSTALLATION	ACTION	DATE

Air Force

March Air Force Base, CA	Major Realignment	Mar 1996
Homestead Air Force Base, FL	Closed	Mar 1994
O'Hare IAP Air Reserve Station, IL	Major Closure #6	Jun 1999
K.I. Sawyer Air Force Base, MI	Closed	Sep 1995
Griffiss Air Force Base, NY	Major Realignment	Sep 1995
Plattsburgh Air Force Base, NY	Closed	Sep 1995
Gentile Air Force Station, OH	Major Closure #7	Dec 1996
Newark Air Force Base, OH	Closed #8	Sep 1996

Army

Anniston Army Depot, AL	Major Realignment	Sep 1997
Fort Monmouth, NJ	Major Realignment	Jun 1998
Letterkenny Army Depot, PA	Major Realignment	Dec 1997

Toole Army Depot, UT	Major Realignment	Sep 1995
Fort Belvoir, VA	Major Realignment	Sep 1996
Vint Hill Farms, VA	Closed	Sep 1997

Defense Information Systems Agency (DISA) Data Center Consolidation

Data Processing Centers

Facilities Systems Office Port Hueneme, CA	Minor Closure/Realignment	Mar 1997
Fleet Industrial Support Center San Diego, CA	Minor Closure/Realignment	Nov 1994
Marine Corps Air Station El Toro, CA	Minor Closure/Realignment	Jun 1994
Naval Air Warfare Center, Weapons Division, China Lake, CA	Minor Closure/Realignment	May 1996
Naval Air Warfare Center, Weapons Division, Point Mugu, CA	Minor Closure/Realignment	Oct 1993
Naval Command, Control & Ocean Surveillance Center San Diego, CA	Minor Closure/Realignment	Sep 1993
Navy Regional Data Automation Center, San Francisco, CA	Minor Closure/Realignment	May 1995
Region Automated Services Center Camp Pendleton, CA	Minor Closure/Realignment	Jul 1995
Bureau of Naval Personnel, DC	Minor Closure/Realignment	Mar 1995
Naval Computer & Telecommunications Station Washington, DC	Minor Closure/Realignment	Aug 1995
Naval Air Station Key West, FL	Minor Closure/Realignment	Sep 1997
Naval Air Station Mayport, FL	Minor Closure/Realignment	Sep 1997
Naval Computer & Telecommunications Station Pensacola, FL	Minor Closure/Realignment	Nov 1995
Trident Refit Facility Kings Bay, GA	Minor Closure/Realignment	May 1997
Naval Computer & Telecommunications Area Master Station EASTPAC, HI	Minor Closure/Realignment	Jul 1995
Naval Supply Center Pearl Harbor, HI	Minor Closure/Realignment	Feb 1997
Information Processing Center Indianapolis, IN	Minor Closure/Realignment	Jan 1995
Enlisted Personnel Management Center, LA	Minor Closure/Realignment	Apr 1995
Naval Computer & Telecommunications Station New Orleans, LA	Minor Closure/Realignment	Jul 1995
Naval Air Warfare Center, Aircraft Division, Patuxent River, MD	Minor Closure/Realignment	Aug 1993
Naval Air Station Brunswick, ME	Minor Closure/Realignment	Sep 1997
Information Processing Center Battle Creek, MI	Minor Closure/Realignment	Jul 1996
Information Processing Center Kansas City, MO	Minor Closure/Realignment	Feb 1995
Marine Corps Air Station Cherry Point, NC	Minor Closure/Realignment	Jun 1996
Regional Automated Services Center Camp Lejeune, NC	Minor Closure/Realignment	May 1995
Defense Information Technology Service Organization Columbus Annex, OH	Minor Closure/Realignment	Jul 1994
RMBA Cleveland, OH	Minor Closure/Realignment	Aug 1995
Aviation Supply Office, PA	Minor Closure/Realignment	Sep 1994
Information Processing Center Philadelphia, PA	Minor Closure/Realignment	Mar 1995
Naval Supply Center Charleston, SC	Minor Closure/Realignment	Sep 1994
Air Force Military Personnel Center, TX	Minor Closure/Realignment	Aug 1995
Computer Service Center, TX	Minor Closure/Realignment	Jul 1995
Navy Data Automation Facility Corpus Christi, TX	Minor Closure/Realignment	Jan 1994
Information Processing Center Ogden, UT	Minor Closure/Realignment	Jan 1995
7th Communications Group, Pentagon, VA	Minor Closure/Realignment	Oct 1994
Information Processing Center Richmond, VA	Minor Closure/Realignment	Oct 1995
Naval Air Station Oceana, VA	Minor Closure/Realignment	Sep 1997
Naval Computer & Telecommunications Area Master Station Atlantic, VA	Minor Closure/Realignment	Dec 1994
Naval Supply Center Norfolk, VA	Minor Closure/Realignment	Jan 1997
Navy Recruiting Command, VA	Minor Closure/Realignment	Aug 1994
Naval Air Station Whidbey Island, WA	Minor Closure/Realignment	Jan 1997
Naval Supply Center Puget Sound, WA	Minor Closure/Realignment	May 1995
Trident Refit Facility Bangor, WA	Minor Closure/Realignment	May 1997

Defense Logistics Agency

Defense Contract Management District West, CA	Minor Closure/Realignment	Jul 1999

Defense Distribution Depot Oakland, CA	Closed	Mar 1997
Defense Distribution Depot Pensacola, FL	Closed	Sep 1996
Defense Contract Management District North Central, IL	Closed	Jul 1994
Defense Electronics Supply Center, OH	Closed	Jun 1996
Defense Contract Management District Mid-Atlantic, PA	Closed	Jul 1994
Defense Logistics Agency Clothing Factory, PA	Closed	Sep 1994
Defense Personnel Support Center, PA	Major Closure	Jul 1999
Defense Distribution Depot Charleston, SC	Closed	Sep 1995
Defense Distribution Depot Tooele, UT	Closed	Sep 1995

Navy

Naval Reserve Center Gadsen, AL	Closed	Jun 1994
Naval Reserve Center Montgomery, AL	Closed	Mar 1994
Naval Station Mobile, AL	Closed	Jun 1994
Naval Reserve Center Fayetteville, AR	Closed	Apr 1994
Naval Reserve Center Fort Smith, AR	Closed	Jul 1994
Marine Corps Air Station El Toro, CA	Major Closure	Jul 1999
Marine Corps Logistics Base Barstow, CA	Major Realignment	Sep 1996
Naval Air Station Alameda, CA	Closed	Apr 1997
Naval Aviation Depot Alameda, CA	Closed	Sep 1996
Naval Civil Engineering Laboratory, CA	Closed	Jun 1996
Naval Facilities Engineering Command,Western Engineering Field Division, CA	Closed	Oct 1994
Naval Hospital Oakland, CA	Closed	Sep 1996
Naval Reserve Center Pacific Grove, CA	Closed	Jul 1994
Naval Shipyard Mare Island, CA	Closed	Mar 1996
Naval Station Treasure Island, CA	Major Closure	Sep 1997
Naval Training Center San Diego, CA	Major Closure	Apr 1997
Naval Weapons Station Seal Beach, CA	Major Realignment	Sep 1996
Planning, Estimating, Repair and Alterations (Surface) Pacific, CA	Minor Closure/Realignment	Aug 1996
Public Works Center San Francisco, CA	Minor Closure/Realignment	Apr 1997
Naval Electronic Security Systems Engineering Center, DC	Closed	Sep 1995
Office of the Deputy Chief of Staff (I&L) USMC, DC	Minor Closure/Realignment	Jun 1999
Office of the Deputy Chief of Staff (Manpower & Reserve Affairs), DC	Minor Closure/Realignment	Feb 1999
Security Group Command, Station and Detachment Potomac, DC	Closed	Sep 1995
Naval Air Station Cecil Field, FL	Major Closure	Sep 1999
Naval Aviation Depot Pensacola, FL	Closed	Mar 1996
Naval Hospital Orlando, FL	Closed	Jun 1995
Naval Supply Center Pensacola, FL	Closed	Sept 1995
Naval Training Center Orlando, FL	Major Closure	Apr 1999
Naval Reserve Center Macon, GA	Closed	Jul 1994
Naval Air Station Agana, GU	Closed	Mar 1995
Naval Air Station Barbers Point, HI	Major Closure	Jul 1999
Naval Air Station Glenview, IL	Closed	Sep 1995
Naval Reserve Center Terre Haute, IN	Closed	Mar 1994
Navy/Marine Corps Reserve Center Fort Wayne, IN	Closed	Oct 1994
Naval Readiness Command Olathe (Region 18), KS	Closed	Sep 1994
Naval Reserve Center Hutchinson, KS	Closed	Jul 1994
Naval Reserve Center Monroe, LA	Closed	Apr 1994
Naval Reserve Facility Alexandria, LA	Closed	Apr 1994
Naval Air Facility Midway Island	Closed	Sep 1993
Naval Reserve Center Chicopee, MA	Closed	Oct 1994
Naval Reserve Center Bedford, MA	Closed	Apr 1994
Naval Reserve Center Pittsfield, MA	Closed	Jul 1994
Naval Reserve Center Quincy, MA	Reestablished - BRAC 95 redirect	

Navy/Marine Corps Reserve Center Lawrence, MA	Closed	Mar 1995
Naval Electronics Systems Engineering Center St Inigoes, MD	Closed	Sep 1997
Naval Surface Warfare Center (Dahlgren) White Oak Detachment, MD	Major Realignment	Jul 1997
Navy Radio Transmission Facility Annapolis, MD	Minor Closure/Realignment	Sep 1996
Sea Automated Data Systems Activity, MD	Closed	May 1996
Naval Air Facility Detroit, MI	Closed	Apr 1994
Naval Reserve Center Joplin, MO	Closed	Jul 1994
Naval Reserve Center St Joseph, MO	Closed	Jul 1994
Naval Reserve Center Great Falls, MT	Minor Closure/Realignment	Sep 1998
Naval Reserve Center Missoula, MT	Minor Closure/Realignment	Sep 1998
Submarine Maintenance, Engineering, Planning and Procurement Ports, NH	Minor Closure/Realignment	Jun 1998
Naval Air Warfare Center-Aircraft Division Trenton, NJ	Minor Closure/Realignment	Dec 1998
Naval Reserve Center Atlantic City, NJ	Closed	Dec 1993
Naval Reserve Center Perth Amboy, NJ	Closed	Jul 1994
DoD Family Housing Office Niagara Falls, NY	Closed	Oct 1995
Naval Readiness Command Scotia (Region 2), NY	Closed	Sep 1994
Naval Reserve Center Jamestown, NY	Closed	Jul 1994
Naval Reserve Center Poughkeepsie, NY	Closed	Jul 1994
Naval Station Staten Island, NY	Closed	Aug 1994
Naval Readiness Command Ravenna (Region 5), OH	Closed	Sept 1994
Joint Armed Services Aviation Facility, PA	Minor Closure/Realignment	Never Opened
Naval Reserve Center Altoona, PA	Closed	Jul 1994
Planning, Estimating, Repair and Alterations (Surface) Atlantic (HQ), PA	Closed	Aug 1996
Naval Education and Training Center Newport, RI	Major Realignment	Jun 1994
Naval Shipyard Charleston, SC	Closed	Apr 1996
Naval Station Charleston, SC	Closed	Apr 1996
Naval Supply Center Charleston, SC	Minor Closure/Realignment	Apr 1996
Naval Air Station Memphis, TN	Major Realignment	Sep 1997
Naval Reserve Center Kingsport, TN	Closed	Jul 1994
Naval Reserve Center Memphis, TN	Closed	Feb 1994
Naval Air Station Dallas, TX	Major Closure	Sep 1998
Naval Reserve Facility Midland, TX	Closed	Feb 1994
Navy/Marine Corps Reserve Center Abilene, TX	Closed	Apr 1994
Naval Reserve Center Ogden, UT	Closed	Sep 1997
Bureau of Navy Personnel, VA	Minor Closure/Realignment	Sep 1998
Marine Corps Systems Command, VA	Minor Closure/Realignment	Jun 1999
Naval Air Facility Martinsburg, WV	Minor Closure/Realignment	Never Opened
Naval Air Systems Command, VA	Minor Closure/Realignment	Sep 1997
Naval Aviation Depot Norfolk, VA	Closed	Mar 1997
Naval Electronics Systems Engineering Center Portsmouth, VA	Minor Closure/Realignment	Sep 1998
Naval Facilities Engineering Command, VA	Minor Closure/Realignment	Sep 1998
Navy Recruiting Command, VA	Minor Closure/Realignment	Sep 1998
Naval Reserve Center Parkersburg, WV	Closed	Jul 1994
Naval Reserve Center Staunton, VA	Closed	Jul 1994
Naval Sea Systems Command, VA	Minor Closure/Realignment	Sep 2001
Naval Supply Systems Command, VA	Minor Closure/Realignment	Sep 1996
Naval Surface Warfare Center Port Hueneme Virginia Beach Detachment, VA	Minor Closure/Realignment	Sep 1996
Naval Undersea Warfare Center, Norfolk Detachment, VA	Minor Closure/Realignment	Sep 1995
Naval Radio Transmission Facility Driver, VA	Closed	Nov 1994
Office of Naval Research, VA	BRAC 95 redirect - remain in place	
Planning, Estimating, Repair and Alterations (Surface) Atlantic, VA	Closed	Aug 1996
Space and Naval Warfare Systems Command, VA	Minor Closure/Realignment	Sep 1997
Strategic Systems Program Office, VA	Minor Closure/Realignment	Aug 1998
Tactical Support Office, VA	Minor Closure/Realignment	Sep 1998

Planning, Estimating, Repair and Alterations (CV) Bremerton, WA	Minor Closure/Realignment	Jul 1999

BRAC Round 1991

BASE/INSTALLATION	ACTION	DATE

Air Force

Eaker Air Force Base, AR	Closed	Dec 1992
Williams Air Force Base, AZ	Closed	Sep 1993
Castle Air Force Base, CA	Closed	Sep 1995
Lowry Air Force Base, CO	Closed	Sep 1994
MacDill Air Force Base, FL	Major Realignment	Mar 1994
Grissom Air Force Base, IN	Closed	Sep 1994
England Air Force Base, LA	Closed	Dec 1992
Loring Air Force Base, ME	Closed	Sep 1994
Wurtsmith Air Force Base, MI	Closed	Jun 1993
Richards-Gebaur Air Reserve Station, MO	Closed	Sep 1994
Rickenbacker Air Guard Base, OH	Closed	Sep 1994
Myrtle Beach Air Force Base, SC	Closed	Mar 1993
Bergstrom Air Force Base (Active Component) TX	Closed	Sep 1993
Carswell Air Force Base, TX	Closed	Sep 1993

Army

Aeromedical Research Laboratory (Tri-Service Project Reliance), AL	Minor Closure/Realignment	Sep 1994
Redstone Arsenal, AL	Major Realignment	Aug 1994
Fort Chaffee, AR	Major Realignment	Sep 1993
Fort Ord, CA	Closed	Sep 1994
Letterman LAIR (Tri-Service Project Reliance Study), CA	Minor Closure/Realignment	Sep 1993
Sacramento Army Depot, CA	Closed	Mar 1995
Army Institute of Dental Research (Tri-Service Project Reliance), DC	Minor Closure/Realignment	Jul 1997
Walter Reed Army Institute of Research, DC	Minor Closure/Realignment	Sep 1993
Rock Island Arsenal, IL	Major Realignment	Aug 1995
Fort Benjamin Harrison, IN	Closed	Sep 1995
Fort Polk, LA	Major Realignment	Feb 1994
Army Materials Technology Laboratory, MA	Minor Closure/Realignment	Sep 1995
Fort Devens, MA	Major Closure	Mar 1996
Army Materials Technology Laboratory-Structures Element, MD	Minor Closure/Realignment	Sep 1993
Biomedical Research Development Laboratory (BRAC 95 Redirect), MD	Minor Closure/Realignment	Sep 1996
Harry Diamond Laboratories Adelphi, MD	Major Realignment	Sep 1994
Ground Vehicle Propulsion Research, MI	Minor Closure/Realignment	Sep 1993
Aviation Systems Command/Troop Support Command, MO	Minor Closure/Realignment	Sep 1993
Electronic Technology Device Laboratory, NJ	Minor Closure/Realignment	Sep 1997
Fort Dix (Redirect), NJ	Major Realignment	Jun 1997
Picatinny Arsenal, NJ	Major Realignment	Aug 1994
Atmospheric Science Laboratory, NM	Minor Closure/Realignment	Sep 1997
Army Research Institute for Behavioral and Social Sciences, VA	Minor Closure/Realignment	Jul 1997
Belvoir Research and Development Center, VA	Minor Closure/Realignment	Sep 1995
Center for Night Vision and Electro-Optics, VA	Minor Closure/Realignment	Sep 1997
Harry Diamond Army Research Laboratory, VA	Closed	Sep 1994

Navy

Fleet Combat Direction Systems Support Activity San Diego, CA	Minor Closure/Realignment	Apr 1992

ICSTF San Diego, CA	Minor Closure/Realignment	Jul 1993
Marine Corps Air Station Tustin, CA	Major Closure	Jul 1999
Naval Air Station Moffett Field, CA	Closed	Jul 1994
Naval Electronic Systems Engineering Center, San Diego, CA	Closed	Oct 1994
Naval Electronic Systems Engineering Center, Vallejo, CA	Closed	Sep 1995
Naval Hospital Long Beach, CA	Closed	Mar 1994
Naval Station Long Beach, CA	Closed	Sep 1994
Naval Station Treasure Island (Hunter Point Annex), CA	Closed	Apr 1994
Naval Weapons Center China Lake, CA	Major Realignment	Jan 1992
Naval Space Systems Activity Los Angeles, CA	Closed	Oct 1992
Pacific Missile Test Center, CA	Major Realignment	Jan 1992
Naval Underwater Systems Center Detachment New London, CT	Minor Closure/Realignment	Nov 1996
Naval Coastal Systems Center, FL	Major Realignment	Oct 1992
Naval Ocean Systems Center Detachment Kanehoe, HI	Closed	Sep 1993
Naval Air Warfare Center Indianapolis, IN	Minor Closure/Realignment	Sep 1992
Naval Weapons Support Center Crane, IN	Major Realignment	Oct 1994
Naval Ordnance Station Louisville, KY	Major Realignment	May 1994
Naval Air Facility Midway Island	Minor Closure/Realignment	Sep 1993
David Taylor Research Center Detachment Annapolis, MD	Minor Closure/Realignment	Jun 1997
Naval Ordnance Station Indian Head, MD	Major Realignment	Jan 1992
Naval Surface Warfare Center Detachment White Oak, MD	Minor Closure/Realignment	Jul 1997
Naval Air Engineering Center, NJ	Major Realignment	Oct 1993
Naval Air Propulsion Center, NJ	Major Realignment	Jul 1997
Naval Weapons Evaluation Facility Albuquerque, NM	Closed	Sep 1993
Naval Air Development Center Warminster, PA	Minor Closure/Realignment	Mar 1997
Naval Shipyard Philadelphia, PA	Closed	Sep 1996
Naval Station Philadelphia, PA	Closed	Jan 1996
Construction Battalion Center, RI	Closed	Apr 1994
Trident Command and Control System Maintenance Activity Newport, RI	Minor Closure/Realignment	Oct 1993
Naval Air Station Chase Field, TX	Closed	Feb 1993
Naval Mine Warefare Engineering Activity Yorktown, VA	Closed	Oct 1995
Naval Sea Combat Systems Engineering Station Norfolk, VA	Minor Closure/Realignment	Jan 1993
Naval Station Puget Sound (Sand Point), WA	Closed	Sep 1995
Naval Undersea Warfare Engineering Station, WA	Major Realignment	Jan 1992

BRAC Round 1988

BASE/INSTALLATION	ACTION	DATE

Air Force

George Air Force Base, CA	Closed	Dec 1992
Mather Air Force Base, CA	Closed	Sep 1993
Norton Air Force Base, CA	Closed	Mar 1994
Chanute Air Force Base, IL	Closed	Sep 1993
Pease Air Force Base, NH	Closed	Mar 1991

Army

53 Stand Alone Family Housing Areas	Minor Closure/Realignment	Oct 1994
Alabama Ammunition Plant, AL	Closed	May 1992
Coosa River Annex, AL	Closed	Sep 1992
Navajo Depot Activity, AZ	Closed	Sep 1993
Hamilton Army Airfield, CA	Closed	Sep 1994
Presidio of San Francisco (BRAC 93 Redirect), CA	Major Closure	Sep 1994
Bennett Army National Guard, CO	Closed	Jan 1989
Pueblo Army Depot, CO	Major Realignment	#9

Cape St George, FL	Closed	Feb 1988
Kapalama Military Reservation Phase III, HI	Closed	Sep 1993
Fort Des Moines, IA	Minor Closure/Realignment	Sep 1994
Fort Sheridan, IL	Closed	May 1993
Indiana Army Ammunition Plant (Partial), IN	Minor Closure/Realignment	Aug 1993
Jefferson Proving Ground, IN	Closed	Sep 1994
Lexington Army Depot, KY	Closed	Sep 1995
New Orleans Military Ocean Terminal, LA	Closed	Dec 1994
Army Materials Technology Laboratory, MA	Closed	Sep 1995
Fort Devens, MA (Includes Forts Huachuca, Holabird and Meade)	Major Realignment	Sep 1995
Former Nike Site, Aberdeen Proving Ground, MD	Closed	Sep 1993
Fort Meade, MD (Training areas and Tipton Army Airfield)	Closed	Sep 1995
US Army Reserve Center Gaithersburg, MD	Minor Closure/Realignment	Jan 1989
Pontiac Storage Facility, MI	Closed	Oct 1992
Nike Kansas City 30, MO	Closed	Feb 1988
Fort Dix, NJ	Major Realignment	Sep 1995
Fort Wingate Ammunition Storage Depot, NM	Closed	Jan 1993
Umatilla Army Depot, OR	Closed	Sep 1994
Tacony Warehouse, PA	Closed	Sep 1992
Fort Douglas, UT	Closed	Nov 1991
Cameron Station, VA	Closed	Sep 1995
Defense Mapping Agency Herndon, VA	Closed	Oct 1993

Navy

Naval Station San Francisco, CA (Hunters Point Annex)	Minor Closure/Realignment	Never Opened
Salton Sea Test Bed, CA	Closed	Oct 1993
Naval Reserve Center Miami, FL	Minor Closure/Realignment	Sep 1991
Naval Station Lake Charles, LA	Major Closure	Never Opened
Naval Station New York (Brooklyn), NY	Closed	May 1993
Naval Hospital Philadelphia, PA	Closed	Apr 1993
Naval Station Galveston, TX	Major Closure	Never Opened
Naval Station Puget Sound (Sand Point), WA	Major Realignment	Sep 1995

#1 Closure contingent upon Commission requirement for sale of property at fair market value.
#2 Land to be conveyed to the Golden Gate National Recreation Area.
#3 Tank Plant closed (Dec 1996).
#4 Privatized Mar 1997.
#5 Privatized Aug 1996.
#6 Contingent upon City of Chicago's compliance with Commission recommendations.
#7 Defense Electronics Supply Center closed Dec 1996.
#8 Privatized.
#9 Contingent upon completion of chemical demilitarization mission.

Indexes

Alphabetical Listing of Bases

Note: Numbers refer to entry numbers

United States

1st Coast Guard District, Boston, MA, 431

8th Coast Guard District, New Orleans, LA, 380

9th Coast Guard District Headquarters, Cleveland, OH, 648

9th Marine Corps District, Shawnee Mission, KS, 358

13th Coast Guard District Office, Seattle, WA, 928

17th Coast Guard District, Juneau, AK, 29

18th Cavalry, 1st Squadron, HQ, Ontario, CA, 92

32nd St Naval Station, San Diego, CA, 122

84th Division (IT) HQ, Milwaukee, WI, 960

99th Electronic Combat Range Group, Forsyth, MT, 518

99th Range Support Squadron, OL-B, La Junta, CO, 155

101st ARW/MEANG, Bangor, ME, 393

106th Rescue Wing, Westhampton Beach, NY, 615

120th Fighter Wing, Great Falls, MT, 521

145th Airlift Wing, Charlotte, NC, 619

190th Air Guard, Topeka, KS, 361

261CBCS, Van Nuys, CA, 140

305th Aerial Port Squadron, Detachment 1 (AMC), Philadelphia, PA, 712

Aberdeen Proving Ground, Aberdeen Proving Ground, MD, 404

Adelphi Laboratory Center, Army Research Laboratory, Adelphi, MD, 405

Adelphi Naval Reserve Center, Adelphi, MD, 406

Adjutant General of Alabama, Montgomery, AL, 13

Adjutant General of Alaska, Fort Richardson, AK, 26

Adjutant General of Arizona, Phoenix, AZ, 39

Adjutant General of Arkansas, North Little Rock, AR, 51

Adjutant General of California, Sacramento, CA, 105

Adjutant General of Colorado, Englewood, CO, 150

Adjutant General of Connecticut, Hartford, CT, 159

Adjutant General of Delaware, Wilmington, DE, 168

Adjutant General of Florida, Saint Augustine, FL, 228

Adjutant General of Georgia, Atlanta, GA, 241

Adjutant General of Illinois, Springfield, IL, 319

Adjutant General of Indiana, Indianapolis, IN, 332

Adjutant General of Iowa, Johnston, IA, 345

Adjutant General of Kansas, Topeka, KS, 359

Adjutant General of Kentucky, Frankfort, KY, 367

Adjutant General of Louisiana, New Orleans, LA, 381

Adjutant General of Maine, Augusta, ME, 391

Adjutant General of Maryland, Baltimore, MD, 412

Adjutant General of Massachusetts, Reading, MA, 443

Adjutant General of Michigan, Lansing, MI, 459

Adjutant General of Minnesota, Saint Paul, MN, 475

Adjutant General of Mississippi, Jackson, MS, 484

Adjutant General of Missouri, Jefferson City, MO, 503

Adjutant General of Montana, Helena, MT, 522

Adjutant General of Nebraska, Lincoln, NE, 527

Adjutant General of New Hampshire, Concord, NH, 547

Adjutant General of New Jersey, Trenton, NJ, 565

Adjutant General/Commander of New York, Latham, NY, 592

Adjutant General of North Carolina, Raleigh, NC, 630

Adjutant General of North Dakota, Bismarck, ND, 636

Adjutant General of Ohio, Columbus, OH, 651

Adjutant General of Oklahoma, Oklahoma City, OK, 674

Adjutant General of Pennsylvania, Annville, PA, 695

Adjutant General of Rhode Island, Cranston, RI, 725

Adjutant General of South Carolina, Columbia, SC, 738

Adjutant General of Tennessee, Nashville, TN, 769

Adjutant General of Utah, Draper, UT, 821

Adjutant General of Vermont, Colchester, VT, 832

Adjutant General of Virginia, Richmond, VA, 897

Adjutant General of Washington, Tacoma, WA, 935

Adjutant General of West Virginia, Charleston, WV, 942

Adjutant General of Wyoming, Cheyenne, WY, 964

Adjutant Genral of Idaho, Boise, ID, 294

AEGIS Combat Systems Center, Wallops Island, VA, 905

Afloat Training Group, Western Pacific, Pearl Harbor, HI, 281

AFRC, Providence, RI, 729

AFRC Greensboro, Greensboro, NC, 626

Air Force Reserve Command Personnel Center, Denver, CO, 148

Air Station San Diego, San Diego, CA, 117

Aircrew Training Research Division, Armstrong Laboratory, Mesa, AZ, 38

Akron Naval & Marine Corps Reserve Center, Akron, OH, 643

Alameda Coast Guard Integrated Support Command, Alameda, CA, 54

Alameda Naval & Marine Corps Reserve Readiness Center, Alameda, CA, 55

Albany Marine Corps Logistics Base, Albany, GA, 239

Albany Naval & Marine Corps Reserve Readiness Center, Albany, NY, 575

Albuquerque Naval & Marine Corps Reserve Center, Albuquerque, NM, 568

Alpena Combat Readiness Training Center, Alpena, MI, 449

Alternate Joint Communications Center/ Site R, Fort Ritchie, MD, 423

Altus Air Force Base, Altus AFB, OK, 668

Amarillo Naval & Marine Corps Reserve Center, Amarillo, TX, 775

Amityville Naval & Marine Corps Reserve Center, Amityville, NY, 576

Anacostia Naval Station, Washington, DC, 171

Anchorage Naval Reserve Center, Anchorage, AK, 18

Andrews Air Force Base, Andrews AFB, MD, 407

ANG Armory, Ontario, CA, 92

Annapolis Naval Station, Annapolis, MD, 409

Anniston Army Depot, Anniston, AL, 1

Arlington Hall, Arlington, VA, 842

Armament Research, Development, and Engineering Center, US Army TACOM, Picatinny Arsenal, NJ, 562

Armed Forces Institute of Pathology, Washington, DC, 172

Armed Forces Reserve Center, Fresno, CA, 71

Armed Forces Reserve Center, Pocatello, ID, 299

Armed Forces Reserve Center, Cedar Rapids, IA, 341

Armed Forces Reserve Center, Saginaw, MI, 461

Armed Forces Reserve Center, Amityville, NY, 576

Armed Forces Reserve Center, Wilmington, NC, 635

Armed Forces Reserve Center, Fargo, ND, 639

Armed Forces Reserve Center, Dayton, OH, 656

Armed Forces Reserve Center, Broken Arrow, OK, 670

Armed Forces Reserve Center, Erie, PA, 703

Armed Forces Reserve Center, Austin, TX, 776

Armed Forces Reserve Center, Charleston, WV, 943

Armed Forces Staff College, Norfolk, VA, 875

Army Armor Center & Fort Knox, Fort Knox, KY, 366

Army Aviation Support Facility, Winder, GA, 264

Army Aviation Support Facility #1, North Canton, OH, 661

Army Cold Regions Research & Engineering Laboratory, Hanover, NH, 548

Army Communications-Electronics Command Acquisition Center, Alexandria, VA, 835

Army Corps of Engineers, Louisville District, Louisville, KY, 369

Army Corps of Engineers, Norfolk District, Norfolk, VA, 876

Army Criminal Investigation Command, Fort Belvoir, VA, 862

Army Engineering & Support Center, Huntsville, AL, 7

Army Materiel Command Headquarters, Alexandria, VA, 836

Army National Guard Readiness Center, Arlington, VA, 842

Army Research Office, Research Triangle Park, NC, 632

Army Reserve Personnel Center, Saint Louis, MO, 510

Army Signal Center & Fort Gordon, Fort Gordon, GA, 249

Army Soldier Systems Command, Natick, MA, 441

Army Tank-Automotive & Armaments Command, Warren, MI, 466

Army Transportation Center & Fort Eustis, Fort Eustis, VA, 868

Arnold Engineering Development Center, Arnold Air Force Base, TN, 756

Arsenal, Commerce City, CO, 147

Asheville Naval Reserve Center, Asheville, NC, 616

Atlanta Naval Air Station, Marietta, GA, 254

Atlanta Naval & Marine Corps Reserve Readiness Center, Dobbins AFB, GA, 246

Atlantic Area & Fifth Coast Guard District HQ, Portsmouth, VA, 890

Atlantic City Airport, Air National Guard Base, Pleasantville, NJ, 563

Auburn Range, Auburn, ME, 390

Augusta Naval & Marine Corps Reserve Center, Augusta, GA, 244

Austin Naval & Marine Corps Reserve Center, Austin, TX, 776

Avoca Naval Reserve Center, Avoca, PA, 697

Badger Army Ammunition Plant, Baraboo, WI, 951

Bakersfield Naval & Marine Corps Reserve Center, Bakersfield, CA, 56

Ballston Spa, Naval Nuclear Power Training Unit, Ballston Spa, NY, 577

Baltimore Naval Reserve Readiness Center, Baltimore, MD, 413

Bangor IAP Air National Guard Base, Bangor, ME, 393

Bangor Naval Reserve Center, Bangor, ME, 394

Bangor Naval Submarine Base, Silverdale, WA, 932

Barbers Point Naval Air Station, Barbers Point, HI, 265

Barksdale Air Force Base, Barksdale AFB, LA, 374

Barnes Municipal Airport, Air National Guard Base, Westfield, MA, 446

The Barracks, Vancouver, WA, 938

Barstow, Marine Corps Logistics Base, Barstow, CA, 57

Base Charleston, Charleston, SC, 732

Bath Supervisor of Shipbuilding, Conversion and Repair, Bath, ME, 395

Baton Rouge Naval & Marine Corps Reserve Center, Baton Rouge, LA, 375

Battle Creek Naval & Marine Corps Reserve Center, Battle Creek, MI, 450

Bayonne Military Ocean Terminal, Bayonne, NJ, 552

Beale Air Force Base, Beale AFB, CA, 58

Beaufort Marine Corps Air Station, Beaufort, SC, 730

Beaufort Naval Hospital, Beaufort, SC, 731

Bellows, Waimanalo, HI, 291

Bellows Air Force Station, Waimanalo, HI, 291

Belvoir Research, Development & Engineering Center, Fort Belvoir, VA, 863

Berry Field ANG Base, Nashville, TN, 770

Bessemer Naval & Marine Corps Reserve Readiness Center, Bessemer, AL, 3

Billings Naval & Marine Corps Reserve Center, Billings, MT, 517

Birmingham Airport, Air National Guard Base, Birmingham, AL, 4

Blount Island Command, Jacksonville, FL, 201

Blue Grass Army Depot, Richmond, KY, 373

Boardman Naval Weapons Systems Training Facility, Boardman, OR, 682

Boardman Range, Boardman, OR, 682

Boise Air Terminal, Air National Guard Base, Boise, ID, 295

Boise Naval & Marine Corps Reserve Center, Boise, ID, 296

Bolling Air Force Base, Washington, DC, 173

Boston Coast Guard Reserve Center, Boston, MA, 432

Bradley IAP Air National Guard Base, Windsor Locks, CT, 166

Bremerton Naval Hospital, Bremerton, WA, 913

Bronx Naval & Marine Corps Reserve Center, Bronx, NY, 578

Brooklyn Coast Guard Air Station, Brooklyn, NY, 579

Brooklyn Coast Guard Supply Center, Brooklyn, NY, 580

Brooks Air Force Base, San Antonio, TX, 815

Brunswick Naval Air Station, Brunswick, ME, 396

Buckley Air National Guard Base, Aurora, CO, 142

Buffalo Coast Guard Group, Buffalo, NY, 582

Buffalo Naval & Marine Corps Reserve Center, Buffalo, NY, 583

Bureau of Naval Personnel, Arlington, VA, 843

Bureau of Naval Personnel Detachment, Memphis, Millington, TN, 767

Burlington IAP, Air National Guard Base, Burlington IAP, VT, 831

Callendar Field, New Orleans, LA, 383

Calumet Naval Reserve Facility, Calumet, MI, 454

Camp Ashland, Ashland, NE, 525

Camp Atterbury, Edinburgh, IN, 325

Camp Beauregard, Pineville, LA, 388

Camp Blanding Training Site, Starke, FL, 232

Camp Bullis Training Site, Fort Sam Houston, TX, 793

Camp Butner, Butner, NC, 617

Camp Carroll, Fort Richardson, AK, 26

Camp Clark, Nevada, MO, 508

Camp Curtis Guild, Reading, MA, 444

Camp Dawson, Kingwood, WV, 947

Camp Dodge Iowa, Johnston, IA, 346

Camp Elmore, Norfolk, VA, 877

Camp George West, Golden, CO, 154

Camp Gilbert C Grafton, Devils Lake, ND, 638

Camp Grayling, Grayling, MI, 458

Camp Grayling Maneuver Training Center, Grayling, MI, 458

Camp Gruber, Army National Guard Training Site, Braggs, OK, 669

Camp Gruber Training Site (CGTS), Braggs, OK, 669

Camp Guernsey, Guernsey, WY, 968

Camp Guernsey Annual Training Site, Guernsey, WY, 968

Camp Johnson, Colchester, VT, 832

Camp Keyes, Augusta, ME, 392

Camp Lejeune Marine Corps Base, Camp Lejeune, NC, 618

Camp Lincoln, Springfield, IL, 320

Camp Mabry, Austin, TX, 777

Camp McCain Training Site, Elliott, MS, 480

Camp Navajo, Bellemont, AZ, 34

Camp Parks, Dublin, CA, 62

Camp Peary, Williamsburg, VA, 906

Camp Pendleton, Virginia Beach, VA, 904

Camp Pendleton Marine Corps Base, Oceanside, CA, 91

Camp Perry Training Site, Port Clinton, OH, 663

Camp Rapid, Rapid City, SD, 753

Camp Rilea, Salem, OR, 692

Camp Rilea, Oregon National Guard Training Site, Salem, OR, 692

Camp Ripley, Little Falls, MN, 470

Camp Roberts, Paso Robles, CA, 95

Camp Robinson, North Little Rock, AR, 52

Camp Joseph T Robinson, North Little Rock, AR, 52

Camp Rowland, Niantic, CT, 163

Camp San Luis Obispo, San Luis Obispo, CA, 130

Camp Shelby Training Site, Camp Shelby, MS, 478

Camp Smith, Peekskill, NY, 601

Camp H M Smith, Camp Smith, HI, 266

Camp Swift Training Site, Bastrop, TX, 778

Camp Villere, Slidell, LA, 389

Camp Williams, Riverton, UT, 827

Camp W G Williams, Riverton, UT, 827

Camp Withycombe, Clackamas, OR, 684

Cannon Air Force Base, Cannon AFB, NM, 570

Cape Canaveral Air Force Station, Cocoa Beach, FL, 194

Cape Cod Coast Guard Air Station, Cape Cod, MA, 436

Cape Girardeau Naval Reserve Center, Cape Girardeau, MO, 500

Cape May Coast Guard Training Center, Cape May, NJ, 553

Capital Municipal Airport, Air National Guard Base, Springfield, IL, 321

Carderock Division, Naval Surface Warfare Center, West Bethesda, MD, 429

Carlisle Barracks, Carlisle Barracks, PA, 698

Caswell Range, Caribou, ME, 398

Catoosa Area Training Center, Tunnel Hill, GA, 263

Cavalier Air Station, Cavalier AS, ND, 637

Cecil Field Naval Air Station, Jacksonville, FL, 202

Cecil Field Naval Air Station, Detachment Astor, Astor, FL, 190

Cedar Rapids Naval Reserve Center, Cedar Rapids, IA, 341

Central Point Naval Reserve Center, Central Point, OR, 683

Charleston Air Force Base, Charleston AFB, SC, 737

Charleston Coast Guard Group, Charleston, SC, 732

Charleston Naval & Marine Corps Reserve Center, Charleston, WV, 943

Charleston, Naval & Marine Corps Reserve Readiness Center, Charleston, SC, 733

Charleston Naval Hospital, North Charleston, SC, 746

Charleston, Naval Weapons Station, Charleston, SC, 734

Charleston Naval Weapons Station, Goose Creek, SC, 742

Charlotte Naval & Marine Corps Reserve Center, Charlotte, NC, 620

Chattanooga Naval & Marine Corps Reserve Center, Chattanooga, TN, 758

Cheltenham Naval Communication Detachment, Cheltenham, MD, 418

Cherry Point Marine Corps Air Station, Cherry Point, NC, 621

Cheyenne Mountain Air Force Station, Colorado Springs, CO, 145

Cheyenne Municipal Airport, Air National Guard Base, Cheyenne, WY, 965

Cheyenne Naval Reserve Center, Cheyenne, WY, 966

China Lake Naval Air Weapons Station, China Lake, CA, 60

Cincinnati Naval & Marine Corps Reserve Center, Cincinnati, OH, 645

Clarks Hill Training Site, Plum Branch, SC, 748

Clear Air Force Station, AK, 22

Clearwater Coast Guard Air Station, Clearwater, FL, 192

Cleveland Naval Reserve Center, Cleveland, OH, 649

Coast Guard Academy, New London, CT, 161

Coast Guard Aircraft Repair & Supply Center, Elizabeth City, NC, 622

Coast Guard Communication Station Pacific, San Francisco, Point Reyes Station, CA, 99

Coast Guard Communication Station Pacific, Transmitter Site, Point Reyes Station, CA, 100

Coast Guard Finance Center, Chesapeake, VA, 856

Coast Guard Headquarters, Washington, DC, 174

Coast Guard Human Resources Service & Information Center, Topeka, KS, 360

Coast Guard Institute, Oklahoma City, OK, 675

Coast Guard Island, Alameda, CA, 54

Coast Guard Pacific Strike Team, Novato, CA, 87

Coast Guard Telecommunication & Information Systems Command, Alexandria, VA, 837

Columbia Naval & Marine Corps Reserve Center, Columbia, SC, 739

Columbus Air Force Base, Columbus AFB, MS, 479

Columbus Naval & Marine Corps Readiness Center, Columbus, OH, 652

Columbus Naval Reserve Center, Columbus, GA, 245

Combat Equipment Group-Army, HQ, Goose Creek, SC, 743

Combined Support Maintenance Shop C/ US Property & Fiscal Office—NY, Rochester, NY, 602

Commanding General, DC National Guard, Washington, DC, 175

Concord Naval Weapons Station, Concord, CA, 61

Cornhusker Army Ammunition Plant, Grand Island, NE, 526

Coronado Naval Amphibious Base, San Diego, CA, 109

Corps of Engineers/Huntsville, Huntsville, AL, 7

Corpus Christi Army Depot, Corpus Christi, TX, 779

Corpus Christi Naval Air Station, Corpus Christi, TX, 780

Corpus Christi Naval Hospital, Corpus Christi, TX, 781

Corry Station Naval Technical Training Center, Pensacola, FL, 222

Cortez Coast Guard Station, Cortez, FL, 195

Crane Division, Naval Surface Warfare Center, Crane, IN, 324

Jim Creek Naval Radio Station (T), Arlington, WA, 911

CRREL, Hanover, NH, 548

Cudjoe Key Air Force Station, Summerland Key, FL, 233

Cumberland Naval Reserve Center, Cumberland, MD, 419

Curtis Bay Coast Guard Yard, Curtis Bay, MD, 420

Cutler Naval Computer & Telecommunications Station, Cutler, ME, 399

Dahlgren Division, Naval Surface Warfare Center, Dahlgren, VA, 859

Dallas Naval Air Station, Dallas, TX, 783

Dallas NAS, Air National Guard Base, Dallas, TX, 784

Dam Neck, Fleet Combat Training Center, Atlantic, Virginia Beach, VA, 902

Dannelly Field Air National Guard Base, Montgomery, AL, 14

Davis-Monthan Air Force Base, Tucson, AZ, 42

Davison Army Airfield, Fort Belvoir, VA, 864

Dayton Naval & Marine Corps Reserve Readiness Center, Dayton, OH, 656

DC Armory, Washington, DC, 176

Decatur Naval Reserve Center, Decatur, IL, 305

Defense Contract Management Command, Clearwater, Saint Petersburg, FL, 229

Defense Contract Management Command, Cleveland, Bratenahl, OH, 644

Defense Contract Management Command, General Dynamics Lima, Lima, OH, 658

Defense Contract Management Command, GE Aircraft Engines Cincinnati, Cincinnati, OH, 646

Defense Contract Management Command, Hughes Los Angeles, Los Angeles, CA, 75

Defense Contract Management Command, Indianapolis, Indianapolis, IN, 333

Defense Contract Management Command, Indianapolis, HDC, Fort Wayne, IN, 327

Defense Contract Management Command, Indianapolis-South Bend, South Bend, IN, 337

Defense Contract Management Command, International, Dayton, OH, 657

Defense Contract Management Command, Lockheed Martin, Marietta, Marietta, GA, 255

Defense Contract Management Command, PLAS, Chicago, IL, 301

Defense Contract Management Command, San Diego, San Diego, CA, 110

Defense Contract Management Command, Seattle, Bellevue, WA, 912

Defense Contract Management Command, Stratford, Stratford, CT, 165

Defense Contract Management Command, Syracuse, Syracuse, NY, 609

Defense Contract Management Command, Wichita, Wichita, KS, 363

Defense Contract Management District Northeast, Boston, MA, 433

Defense Contract Management District South, Marietta, GA, 256

Defense Contract Management District West, El Segundo, CA, 66

Defense Contract Management Office Raytheon, Bristol, TN, 757

Defense Distribution Region East, New Cumberland, PA, 709

Defense Distribution Region West, Stockton, CA, 134

Defense Finance and Accounting Service, Columbus, OH, 653

Defense Finance and Accounting Service Center, Kansas City, Kansas City, MO, 504

Defense Finance and Accounting Service, Cleveland Center, Cleveland, OH, 650

Defense Finance and Accounting Service, Denver Center, Denver, CO, 149

Defense Finance and Accounting Service, Headquarters, Arlington, VA, 844

Defense Finance and Accounting Service, Indianapolis Center, Indianapolis, IN, 334

Defense Industrial Plant Equipment Facility, Atchison, KS, 351

Defense Information Systems Agency, Arlington, VA, 845

Defense Logistics Agency, HQ, Fort Belvoir, VA, 865

Defense Logistics Services Center, Battle Creek, MI, 451

Defense National Stockpile Center, Arlington, VA, 846

Defense Non-Tactical Generator & Rail Equipment Center, Hill AFB, UT, 823

Defense Plant Representative Office, Air Force Plant No 4, Fort Worth, TX, 795

Defense Reutilization and Marketing Service, Battle Creek, MI, 452

Defense Supply Center, Columbus, Columbus, OH, 654

Defense Supply Center, Richmond, Richmond, VA, 898

Denver Naval Reserve Readiness Center, Aurora, CO, 143

Department of Defense Housing Facility, Novato, CA, 88

The Depot, Granite City, IL, 307

Des Moines IAP, Air National Guard Base, Des Moines, IA, 342

Des Moines Naval & Marine Corps Reserve Center, Des Moines, IA, 343

Detroit Arsenal, Warren, MI, 466

Detroit Coast Guard Group/Base, Detroit, MI, 455

Detroit Naval Reserve Readiness Center, Selfridge ANG Base, MI, 463

Devens Reserve Forces Training Center, Devens, MA, 439

District of Columbia National Guard, HQ, Washington, DC, 176

Dobbins Air Reserve Base, Marietta, GA, 257

Donaldson Center, Greenville, SC, 744

Dover Air Force Base, Dover AFB, DE, 167

Dubuque Naval Reserve Center, Dubuque, IA, 344

Dugway Proving Ground, Dugway, UT, 822

Duluth IAP Air National Guard Base, Duluth, MN, 468

Duluth Naval Reserve Center, Duluth, MN, 469

Dyess Air Force Base, Abilene, TX, 773

Eareckson Air Force Station, AK, 23

Earle Naval Weapons Station, Colts Neck, NJ, 554

Eastern West Virginia Regional Airport, Air National Guard Base, Martinsburg, WV, 948

Ebensburg Naval & Marine Corps Reserve Center, Ebensburg, PA, 702

Edwards Air Force Base, Edwards AFB, CA, 63

Eglin Air Force Base, Fort Walton Beach, FL, 197

Egmont Key Coast Guard Light Station, Saint Petersburg, FL, 230

Eielson Air Force Base, Eielson AFB, AK, 24

El Centro Naval Air Facility, El Centro, CA, 64

El Paso Naval & Marine Corps Reserve Readiness Center, El Paso, TX, 789

El Toro Marine Corps Air Station, Santa Ana, CA, 132

Eldorado Air Force Station, Eldorado, TX, 791

Elizabeth City Coast Guard Support Center, Elizabeth City, NC, 623

Ellington Field, Air National Guard Base, Houston, TX, 803

Ellsworth Air Force Base, Ellsworth AFB, SD, 750

Elmendorf Air Force Base, Anchorage, AK, 19

Encino Naval & Marine Corps Reserve Center, Encino, CA, 67

Engineer Corps, Detroit, Detroit, MI, 456

Erie Naval & Marine Corps Reserve Center, Erie, PA, 703

R L Esmay Training Center, Guernsey, WY, 968

Ethan Allen Firing Range, Jericho, VT, 833

Eugene Naval & Marine Corps Reserve Center, Eugene, OR, 685

Evansville Naval & Marine Corps Reserve Center, Evansville, IN, 326

Everett Naval Reserve Center, Everett, WA, 916

Everett Naval Station, Everett, WA, 917

Fairchild Air Force Base, Fairchild AFB, WA, 919

Falcon Air Force Base, Falcon AFB, CO, 151

Fallbrook Naval Ordnance Center, Pacific Division, Fallbrook, CA, 68

Fallon Naval Air Station, Fallon, NV, 535

Fargo Naval Reserve Center, Fargo, ND, 639

Fentres Naval Auxiliary Landing Field, Chesapeake, VA, 857

1st Marine Corps District Headquarters, Garden City, NY, 588

Fitzsimons Army Medical Center, Aurora, CO, 144

Fleet and Industrial Supply Center, Jacksonville, FL, 203

Fleet & Industrial Supply Center, Cheatham Annex, Williamsburg, VA, 907

Fleet Antisubmarine Warfare Training Center, Pacific, San Diego, CA, 111

Fleet Combat Training Center, Pacific, San Diego, CA, 112

Fleet Industrial Supply Center, Norfolk, VA, 878

Fleet Training Center, Norfolk, Norfolk, VA, 879

Forbes Field Air National Guard Base, Topeka, KS, 361

Forest Park Naval Reserve Center, Forest Park, IL, 306

Fort Belvoir, Fort Belvoir, VA, 866

Fort Benning, Fort Benning, GA, 248

Fort Bliss, El Paso, TX, 790

Fort Bragg, Fort Bragg, NC, 624

Fort Campbell, Fort Campbell, KY, 365

Fort Carson and 4th Infantry Division (Mechanized), Fort Carson, CO, 152

Mobile Coast Guard Group/Station, Mobile, AL, 10

Mobile Naval & Marine Corps Reserve Center, Mobile, AL, 11

Montana Air National Guard, Great Falls, MT, 521

Montgomery Marine Corps Reserve Center, Montgomery, AL, 15

Moody Air Force Base, Moody AFB, GA, 258

Moundsville Naval & Marine Corps Reserve Center, Moundsville, WV, 949

Mountain Home Air Force Base, Mountain Home AFB, ID, 298

Nashville IAP, ANG Base, Nashville, TN, 770

Nashville Naval Reserve Center, Nashville, TN, 771

Natick Labs, Natick, MA, 441

National Imagery & Mapping Agency, Fairfax, VA, 860

National Imagery & Mapping Agency, Dissemination Division, Bethesda, MD, 416

National Imagery and Mapping Agency, Saint Louis, Saint Louis, MO, 511

National Naval Medical Center, Bethesda, MD, 417

Naval Air Warfare Center, Aircraft Division, Trenton, NJ, 566

Naval Air Warfare Center, Training Systems Division, Orlando, FL, 216

Naval Coastal Systems Station, Panama City, FL, 219

Naval Computer & Telecommunications Area Master Station, Eastern Pacific, Wahiawa, HI, 288

Naval Computer and Telecommunications Station, Puget Sound, Silverdale, WA, 933

Naval District Washington, Washington Navy Yard, Washington, DC, 180

Naval Education and Training Center, Newport, Newport, RI, 726

Naval Education and Training Professional Development and Technology Center, Pensacola, FL, 223

Naval Facilities Engineering Command, Atlantic Division, Norfolk, VA, 881

Naval Facilities Engineering Command Headquarters, Alexandria, VA, 838

Naval Facilities Engineering Command, Northern Division, Lester, PA, 705

Naval Facilities Engineering Command, Southern Division, Charleston, SC, 735

Naval Facilities Engineering Service Center, Port Hueneme, CA, 102

Naval Health Research Center, San Diego, CA, 114

Naval Medical Command, Bureau of Medicine & Surgery, Washington, DC, 181

Naval Meteorology and Oceanography Command, Stennis Space Center, MS, 493

Naval Postgraduate School, Monterey, CA, 83

Naval Research Laboratory, Washington, DC, 182

Naval Research Laboratory, Marine Meteorology Division, Monterey, CA, 84

Naval Research Laboratory, Stennis Space Center, Stennis Space Center, MS, 494

Naval Reserve Center, Corpus Christi, Corpus Christi, TX, 782

Naval Sea Systems Command, HQ, Arlington, VA, 849

Naval Security Station, Washington, DC, 183

Naval Supply Systems Command, Mechanicsburg, PA, 707

Naval Surface Warfare Center, Carderock Division, Annapolis Detachment, Annapolis, MD, 410

Naval Undersea Warfare Center, New London, CT, 162

Naval Warfare Assessment Division, Norco, CA, 86

Navy Clothing and Textile Research Facility, Natick, MA, 442

Navy Office of Information, East, New York, NY, 596

Navy Office of Information, Midwest, Chicago, IL, 302

Navy Office of Information, New England, Boston, MA, 434

Navy Office of Information, Southeast, Atlanta, GA, 242

Navy Office of Information, Southwest, Dallas, TX, 786

Navy Office of Information, West, Los Angeles, CA, 78

Navy Recruiting Command, Arlington, VA, 850

Navy Recruiting District New England, Boston, MA, 435

Navy Supply Corps School, Athens, GA, 240

Nellis Air Force Base, Nellis AFB, NV, 541

Nevada Army National Guard, Fallon, Fallon, NV, 536

Nevada National Guard Headquarters, Carson City, NV, 534

Nevada National Guard Henderson, Henderson, NV, 538

Nevada National Guard Las Vegas, Las Vegas, NV, 540

New Boston Air Station, New Boston AS, NH, 549

New Castle County Airport, Air National Guard Base, Wilmington, DE, 169

New Haven Naval & Marine Corps Reserve Center, New Haven, CT, 160

New London Naval Submarine Base, Groton, CT, 158

New Mexico National Guard State Headquarters, Santa Fe, NM, 573

New Orleans Naval Air Station Joint Reserve Base, Air Force Reserve, New Orleans, LA, 383

New Orleans Naval Air Station Joint Reserve Base, Naval Air Station, New Orleans, LA, 384

New Orleans Naval & Marine Corps Reserve Readiness Center, New Orleans, LA, 385

New Orleans Naval Support Activity, New Orleans, LA, 386

New River Marine Corps Air Station, Jacksonville, NC, 627

New York Area Command & Fort Hamilton, Brooklyn, NY, 581

Newport News Supervisor of Shipbuilding, Conversion and Repair, Newport News, VA, 873

Niagara Falls Air Reserve Station, Niagara Falls, NY, 600

Nickell Barracks Training Center, Salina, KS, 357

N&MCRC San Jose, San Jose, CA, 129

NMCRC Billings, Billings, MT, 517

Norfolk Naval Air Station, Norfolk, VA, 882

Norfolk Naval & Marine Corps Reserve Readiness Center, Norfolk, VA, 883

Norfolk Naval Aviation Depot, Norfolk, VA, 884

Norfolk Naval Base Complex, Norfolk, VA, 885

Norfolk Naval Shipyard, Portsmouth, Portsmouth, VA, 891

Norfolk Naval Station, Norfolk, VA, 886

Norfolk Navy Public Works Center, Norfolk, VA, 887

North Auxiliary Airfield, North Auxiliary Airfield, SC, 745

North Field, North Auxiliary Airfield, SC, 745

North Island Naval Air Station, San Diego, CA, 115

Northeast Air Defense Sector, Rome, NY, 604

Northwest Naval Security Group Activity, Chesapeake, VA, 858

NRC Adelphi, Adelphi, MD, 406

NRC Lexington, Lexington, KY, 368

NRC Tyler, Tyler, TX, 819

NSS, Washington, DC, 183

Oakland Army Base, Oakland, CA, 90

Oceana Naval Air Station, Virginia Beach, VA, 903

Office of Naval Research, Arlington, VA, 851

Offutt Air Force Base, Offutt AFB, NE, 530

O'Hare International Airport Air Reserve Station, O'Hare IAP ARS, IL, 311

Ohio National Guard, Unit Training Equipment Site #1, Newton Falls, OH, 660

Oklahoma City Naval & Marine Corps Reserve Readiness Center, Oklahoma City, OK, 676

Old Fort Benjamin Harrison, Indianapolis, IN, 336

Omaha Naval & Marine Corps Reserve Center, Omaha, NE, 531

Onizuka Air Station, Sunnyvale, CA, 136

Ontario Air National Guard Station, Ontario, CA, 93

Operating Location Alpha, North Auxiliary Airfield, SC, 745

Operating Location Alpha Bravo South East Air Defense Sector, Old Town, FL, 214

Orange Grove, Naval Auxiliary Landing Field, Alice, TX, 774

Orange Naval Reserve Center, Orange, TX, 813

Oregon Air National Guard, 142FW, Portland IAP, OR, 691

Orlando Naval & Marine Corps Reserve Readiness Center, Orlando, FL, 217

Orlando, Naval Training Center, Orlando, FL, 218

Pacific Beach Resort & Conference Center, Pacific Beach, WA, 925

Pacific Missile Range Facility, Kekaha, HI, 279

Papago Military Reservation, Phoenix, AZ, 39

Parks Reserve Forces Training Area, Dublin, CA, 62

Parris Island Marine Corps Recruit Depot/ Eastern Recruiting Region, Parris Island, SC, 747

Pascagoula Naval Station, Pascagoula, MS, 490

Pascagoula, Supervisor of Shipbuilding, Conversion and Repair, Pascagoula, MS, 491

Patrick Air Force Base, Patrick AFB, FL, 221

Patuxent River, Naval Air Station, Patuxent River, MD, 427

PAX River, Patuxent River, MD, 427

Pearl Harbor Naval Complex, Pearl Harbor, HI, 283

Pearl Harbor Naval Submarine Base, Pearl Harbor, HI, 284

Pearl Harbor Navy Public Works Center, Pearl Harbor, HI, 285

Pease Air National Guard Base, Pease ANGB, NH, 550

Pensacola Coast Guard Station, Pensacola, FL, 224

Pensacola Naval Air Station, Pensacola, FL, 225

Pensacola Naval Hospital, Pensacola, FL, 226

Pensacola Naval Reserve Center, Pensacola, FL, 227

The Pentagon, Arlington, VA, 852

Peoria Naval & Marine Corps Reserve Center, Peoria, IL, 313

Petaluma Coast Guard Training Center, Petaluma, CA, 96

Peterson Air Force Base, Peterson AFB, CO, 156

Phelps Collins ANG, Alpena, MI, 449

Philadelphia Coast Guard Marine Safety Office & Group, Philadelphia, PA, 714

Philadelphia Defense Personnel Support Center, Philadelphia, PA, 715

Philadelphia, Naval Inventory Control Point, Philadelphia, PA, 716

Phoenix Naval & Marine Corps Reserve Readiness Center, Phoenix, AZ, 40

Picatinny Arsenal, Picatinny Arsenal, NJ, 562

Pickel Meadows, Bridgeport, CA, 59

Pillar Point Air Force Station, El Granada, CA, 65

Pine Bluff Arsenal, Pine Bluff, AR, 53

Pinedale Seismic Research Facility, Pinedale, WY, 969

Pittsburgh International Airport Air National Guard Base, Coraopolis, PA, 700

Pittsburgh IAP, Air Reserve Station, Coraopolis, PA, 701

Pittsburgh Naval & Marine Corps Reserve Readiness Center, North Versailles, PA, 710

Plainville Naval & Marine Corps Reserve Center, Plainville, CT, 164

Pocatello Naval Reserve Facility, Pocatello, ID, 299

Pohakuloa Training Area, Hilo, HI, 272

Point Arena Air Force Station, Point Arena AFS, CA, 97

Point Mugu, Naval Air Weapons Station, Point Mugu, CA, 98

Pomona Naval Industrial Reserve Ordnance Plant, Pomona, CA, 101

Pope Air Force Base, Pope AFB, NC, 629

Port Angeles Coast Guard Air Station/ Group, Port Angeles, WA, 926

Port Hadlock, Naval Ordnance Center, Pacific Division Detachment, Port Hadlock, WA, 927

Port Hueneme Division, Naval Surface Warfare Center, Port Hueneme, CA, 103

Port Hueneme, Naval Construction Battalion Center, Port Hueneme, CA, 104

Portland Air National Guard Base, Portland IAP, OR, 691

Portland Naval & Marine Corps Reserve Readiness Center, Portland, OR, 688

Portland Naval Reserve Readiness Center, Portland, ME, 400

Portsmouth Naval Hospital, Portsmouth, VA, 892

Portsmouth Naval Shipyard, Portsmouth, NH, 551

Portsmouth Supervisor of Shipbuilding, Conversion and Repair, Portsmouth, VA, 893

Presidio of Monterey, Monterey, CA, 85

The Price Center, Granite City, IL, 307

Charles Melvin Price Army Support Center, Granite City, IL, 307

Production Flight Test Installation, Air Force Plant 42, Palmdale, CA, 94

Program Management Office, Strategic Systems Programs Detachment, Magna, UT, 826

Providence Naval & Marine Corps Reserve Center, Providence, RI, 729

Pueblo Chemical Depot, Pueblo, CO, 157

Puget Sound Naval Shipyard, Bremerton, WA, 914

Quantico, Quantico, VA, 895

Quantico Marine Corps Combat Development Command, Quantico, VA, 895

Quonset State Airport, Air National Guard Base, North Kingstown, RI, 728

Radford Army Ammunition Plant, Radford, VA, 896

Raleigh Naval & Marine Corps Reserve Center, Raleigh, NC, 631

Randolph Air Force Base, Randolph AFB, TX, 814

Readiness Center, Arlington, VA, 842

Reading Naval & Marine Corps Reserve Center, Reading, PA, 719

Recruit Training Command Great Lakes, Great Lakes, IL, 309

Red River Army Depot, Texarkana, TX, 818

Redstone Arsenal, Redstone Arsenal, AL, 16

Region One, Naval Reserve Readiness Command, Newport, RI, 727

Region Four, Naval Reserve Readiness Command, Fort Dix, NJ, 556

Region Six, Naval Reserve Readiness Command, Washington, DC, 184

Region Eight, Naval Reserve Readiness Command, Jacksonville, FL, 207

Region Eleven, Naval Reserve Readiness Command, Dallas, TX, 787

Region Thirteen, Naval Reserve Readiness Command, Great Lakes, IL, 310

Region Sixteen, Naval Reserve Readiness Command, Minneapolis, MN, 473

Region Nineteen, Naval Reserve Readiness Command, San Diego, CA, 116

Region Twenty-Two, Naval Reserve Readiness Command, Everett, WA, 918

Reno Naval & Marine Corps Reserve Center, Reno, NV, 542

Reno Nevada Army National Guard Armory, Reno, NV, 543

Reno/Tahoe IAP, Air National Guard Base, Reno, NV, 544

Reserve Base, Fort Chaffee, Fort Smith, AR, 48

Reserve Center, Phoenix, AZ, 40

Reserve Center, Honolulu, HI, 276

Reserve Center, Portland, Portland, OR, 688

Richmond IAP Air National Guard Base, Sandston, VA, 901

Richmond Naval & Marine Corps Reserve Center, Richmond, VA, 899

Rickenbacker IAP, Air National Guard Base, Columbus, OH, 655

Roanoke Naval & Marine Corps Reserve Center, Roanoke, VA, 900

Robins Air Force Base, Robins AFB, GA, 259

Rochester Naval & Marine Corps Reserve Center, Rochester, NY, 603

The Rock, Little Rock AFB, AR, 50

Rock Island Arsenal, Rock Island, IL, 314

Rock Island Naval & Marine Corps Reserve Center, Rock Island, IL, 315

Rocky Mountain Arsenal, Commerce City, CO, 147

Rosecrans Memorial Airport, Air National Guard Base, Saint Joseph, MO, 509

Roslyn Station, Air National Guard, Roslyn, NY, 606

Sacramento Naval & Marine Corps Reserve Readiness Center, Sacramento, CA, 106

Saginaw Naval & Marine Corps Reserve Center, Saginaw, MI, 461

Saint Louis Army Publications Distribution Center, Saint Louis, MO, 512

Saint Louis Coast Guard Base, Saint Louis, MO, 513

Saint Louis Naval & Marine Corps Reserve Center, Bridgeton, MO, 499

St Paul Naval & Marine Corps Reserve Center, Saint Paul, MN, 476

St Petersburg Coast Guard Group/Station, Saint Petersburg, FL, 231

St Petersburg Naval Reserve Center, Clearwater, FL, 193

Salem Naval & Marine Corps Reserve Center, Salem, OR, 693

Salt Lake City IAP, Air National Guard Base, Salt Lake City, UT, 828

Salt Lake City Naval & Marine Corps Reserve Center, Salt Lake City, UT, 829

San Antonio Naval & Marine Corps Reserve Center, San Antonio, TX, 816

San Bruno Naval & Marine Corps Reserve Center, San Bruno, CA, 108

San Diego Coast Guard Activities, San Diego, CA, 117

San Diego Fleet and Industrial Supply Center, San Diego, CA, 118

San Diego Marine Corps Recruit Depot, San Diego, CA, 119

San Diego Naval & Marine Corps Reserve Center, San Diego, CA, 120

San Diego Naval Medical Center, San Diego, CA, 121

San Diego Naval Station, San Diego, CA, 122

San Diego Naval Submarine Base, San Diego, CA, 123

San Francisco Coast Guard Air Station, San Francisco, CA, 125

San Francisco Coast Guard Group, San Francisco, CA, 126

San Jose Naval & Marine Corps Reserve Center, San Jose, CA, 129

San Pedro Coast Guard Support Center, San Pedro, CA, 131

Santa Clara, Naval Air Reserve, Moffett Federal Airfield, CA, 82

Saufley Field, Pensacola, FL, 223

Sault Ste Marie Coast Guard Group, Sault Ste Marie, MI, 462

Savanna Army Depot Activity, Savanna, IL, 317

Savannah IAP Air National Guard Base, Garden City, GA, 251

Savannah Naval & Marine Corps Reserve Center, Savannah, GA, 261

Schenectady County Airport, Air National Guard Base, Scotia, NY, 607

Schofield Barracks, Schofield Barracks, HI, 286

Scotia Naval Administrative Unit, Scotia, NY, 608

Scott Air Force Base, Scott AFB, IL, 318

Scranton Army Ammunition Plant, Scranton, PA, 720

Sea Girt, Sea Girt, NJ, 564

Sea Girt National Guard Training Center, Sea Girt, NJ, 564

Seal Beach Naval Weapons Station, Seal Beach, CA, 133

Seattle Coast Guard Integrated Support Command, Seattle, WA, 929

Seattle Naval Reserve Readiness Center, Seattle, WA, 930

Selfridge Air National Guard Base, Selfridge ANG Base, MI, 464

Seneca Army Depot Activity, Romulus, NY, 605

Seneca Lake Sonar Test Facility, Lake Seneca, NY, 591

Sepulveda Air National Guard Station, Van Nuys, CA, 140

Seymour Johnson Air Force Base, Goldsboro, NC, 625

Shaw Air Force Base, Shaw AFB, SC, 749

Shepherd Field, Martinsburg, WV, 948

Sheppard Air Force Base, Sheppard AFB, TX, 817

Shop C, Rochester Warehouse, Rochester, NY, 602

Shore Intermediate Maintenance Activity, Portsmouth, VA, 894

Shreveport Naval & Marine Corps Reserve Center, Bossier City, LA, 376

Sierra Army Depot, Herlong, CA, 73

Sioux City Naval Reserve Center, Sioux City, IA, 349

Sioux Falls Naval Reserve Center, Sioux Falls, SD, 754

Sioux Gateway Airport, Air National Guard Base, Sergeant Bluff, IA, 348

Sky Harbor IAP, Air National Guard Base, Phoenix, AZ, 41

Soldiers Home, Washington, DC, 187

Solomons, Navy Recreation Center, Solomons, MD, 428

South Bend Naval & Marine Corps Reserve Center, South Bend, IN, 338

South Dakota Air National Guard Base, Sioux Falls, SD, 755

South Portland Air National Guard Station, South Portland, ME, 401

Southwest Harbor Coast Guard Group, Southwest Harbor, ME, 402

Space & Naval Warfare Systems Command, San Diego, CA, 124

SPAWAR, San Diego, CA, 124

Spokane Naval & Marine Corps Reserve Readiness Center, Spokane, WA, 934

Springfield Municipal Airport Air National Guard Base, Springfield, OH, 664

Springfield Naval & Marine Corps Reserve Center, Springfield, MO, 515

St Francis Barracks, Saint Augustine, FL, 228

Standiford Field Air National Guard Base, Louisville, KY, 372

State Military Reservation, Camp Pendleton, Virginia Beach, VA, 904

State of Hawaii, Department of Defense HQ, Honolulu, HI, 277

Stead Training Center, Reno, NV, 545

Stewart Air National Guard Base, Newburgh, NY, 599

Stockton Naval Communications Station, Stockton, CA, 135

Sugar Grove Naval Security Group Activity, Sugar Grove, WV, 950

Sumpter Smith ANG Base, Birmingham, AL, 4

Sunny Point, Southport, NC, 633

Support Center, Elizabeth City, NC, 623

Syracuse Hancock IAP, Air National Guard Base, Syracuse, NY, 610

Syracuse Naval & Marine Corps Reserve Center, Mattydale, NY, 593

Tacoma Naval & Marine Corps Reserve Center, Tacoma, WA, 937

Tallahassee Naval & Marine Corps Reserve Center, Tallahassee, FL, 234

Tampa Coast Guard Marine Safety Office, Tampa, FL, 235

Tampa Naval Reserve Center, Tampa, FL, 236

Tatalina Air Force Station, McGrath, AK, 33

David Taylor Model Basin (DTMB), West Bethesda, MD, 429

Terre Haute Marine Corps Reserve Center, Terre Haute, IN, 340

Allen C Thompson Air National Guard Base, Jackson, MS, 486

Thompson Field, Jackson, MS, 486

Tinker Air Force Base, Tinker AFB, OK, 678

Tobyhanna Army Depot, Tobyhanna, PA, 721

Toledo Express Airport, Air National Guard Base, Swanton, OH, 665

Toledo Naval & Marine Corps Reserve Center, Perrysburg, OH, 662

Tooele Army Depot, Tooele, UT, 830

Topeka Naval & Marine Corps Reserve Center, Topeka, KS, 362

Training Command, US Atlantic Fleet, Norfolk, VA, 888

Transpoint, Washington, DC, 174

Transportation Engineering Agency, MTMC, Newport News, VA, 874

Traverse City Coast Guard Air Station, Traverse City, MI, 465

Travis, Travis AFB, CA, 137

Travis Air Force Base, Travis AFB, CA, 137

Travis Field ANGB, Garden City, GA, 251

Triad Armed Forces Reserve Center, Greensboro, Greensboro, NC, 626

Tripler Army Medical Center, Tripler AMC, HI, 287

Truax Field Air National Guard Base, Madison, WI, 958

Tucson IAP, Air National Guard Base, Tucson, AZ, 43

Tucson Naval & Marine Corps Reserve Center, Tucson, AZ, 44

Tulsa IAP, Air National Guard Base, Tulsa, OK, 679

Tulsa Naval & Marine Corps Reserve Center, Broken Arrow, OK, 670

Tuscaloosa Armed Forces Reserve Center, Tuscaloosa, AL, 17

Tustin Marine Corps Air Station, Tustin, CA, 138

Twentynine Palms Marine Corps Air Ground Combat Center, Twentynine Palms, CA, 139

Twin Cities Army Ammunition Plant, Arden Hills, MN, 467

Twin Cities, Fort Snelling, Saint Paul, MN, 476

Tyler Naval Reserve Center, Tyler, TX, 819

Tyndall Air Force Base, Panama City, FL, 220

Umatilla Chemical Depot, Hermiston, OR, 686

US Air Force Academy, Colorado Springs, CO, 146

US Army Corps of Engineers, Galveston District, Galveston, TX, 799

US Army Corps of Engineers, New York District, New York, NY, 597

US Army Corps of Engineers, Alaska District, Anchorage, AK, 21

US Army Corps of Engineers, Albuquerque District, Albuquerque, NM, 569

US Army Corps of Engineers, Baltimore District, Baltimore, MD, 415

US Army Corps of Engineers, Buffalo District, Buffalo, NY, 584

US Army Corps of Engineers, Center for Public Works, Alexandria, VA, 839

US Army Corps of Engineers, Charleston District, Charleston, SC, 736

US Army Corps of Engineers, Chicago District, Chicago, IL, 303

US Army Corps of Engineers, Construction Engineering Research Laboratories, Champaign, IL, 300

US Army Corps of Engineers, Detroit District, Detroit, MI, 456

US Army Corps of Engineers, Fort Worth District, Fort Worth, TX, 797

US Army Corps of Engineers, Great Lakes & Ohio River Division, Cincinnati, OH, 647

US Army Corps of Engineers, Great Lakes Regional Office, Chicago, IL, 304

US Army Corps of Engineers, Headquarters, Washington, DC, 185

US Army Corps of Engineers, Honolulu District, Fort Shafter, HI, 268

US Army Corps of Engineers, Huntington District, Huntington, WV, 946

US Army Corps of Engineers, Jacksonville District, Jacksonville, FL, 208

US Army Corps of Engineers, Kansas City District, Kansas City, MO, 506

US Army Corps of Engineers, Little Rock District, Little Rock, AR, 49

US Army Corps of Engineers, Los Angeles District, Los Angeles, CA, 79

US Army Corps of Engineers, Memphis District, Memphis, TN, 765

US Army Corps of Engineers, Mississippi Valley Division/Mississippi River Commission, Vicksburg, MS, 495

US Army Corps of Engineers, Missouri River Regional Office, Omaha, NE, 532

US Army Corps of Engineers, Mobile District, Mobile, AL, 12

US Army Corps of Engineers, Nashville District, Nashville, TN, 772

US Army Corps of Engineers, New England District, Waltham, MA, 445

US Army Corps of Engineers, New Orleans District, New Orleans, LA, 387

US Army Corps of Engineers, North Atlantic Division, New York, NY, 598

US Army Corps of Engineers, Northwestern Division, Portland, OR, 689

US Army Corps of Engineers, Omaha District, Omaha, NE, 533

US Army Corps of Engineers, Pacific Ocean Division, Fort Shafter, HI, 269

US Army Corps of Engineers, Philadelphia District, Philadelphia, PA, 717

US Army Corps of Engineers, Pittsburgh District, Pittsburgh, PA, 718

US Army Corps of Engineers, Portland District, Portland, OR, 690

US Army Corps of Engineers, Rock Island District, Rock Island, IL, 316

US Army Corps of Engineers, Sacramento District, Sacramento, CA, 107

US Army Corps of Engineers, St Louis District, Saint Louis, MO, 514

US Army Corps of Engineers, St Paul District, Saint Paul, MN, 477

US Army Corps of Engineers, San Francisco District, San Francisco, CA, 127

US Army Corps of Engineers, Savannah District, Savannah, GA, 262

US Army Corps of Engineers, Seattle District, Seattle, WA, 931

US Army Corps of Engineers, South Atlantic Division, Atlanta, GA, 243

US Army Corps of Engineers, South Pacific Division, San Francisco, CA, 128

US Army Corps of Engineers, Southwestern District, Dallas, TX, 788

US Army Corps of Engineers, Topographic Engineering Center, Alexandria, VA, 840

US Army Corps of Engineers, Transatlantic Programs Center, Winchester, VA, 908

US Army Corps of Engineers, Tulsa District, Tulsa, OK, 680

US Army Corp of Engineers, Vicksburg District, Vicksburg, MS, 496

US Army Corps of Engineers, Walla Walla District, Walla Walla, WA, 939

US Army Corps of Engineers, Water Resources Support Center, Alexandria, VA, 841

US Army Corps of Engineers, Waterways Experiment Station, Vicksburg, MS, 497

US Army Corps of Engineers, Wilmington District, Wilmington, NC, 634

United States Atlantic Command, Norfolk, VA, 889

United States Military Academy, West Point, NY, 613

United States Naval Academy, Annapolis, MD, 411

US Naval Home, Gulfport, MS, 483

US Naval Observatory, Washington, DC, 186

US Soldiers' and Airmen's Home, Washington, DC, 187

US Army Training Center, Columbia, SC, 740

US Southern Command, Miami, FL, 211

Utah Test and Training Range, Hill AFB, UT, 825

Vance Air Force Base, Vance AFB, OK, 681

Vancouver Barracks, Vancouver, WA, 938

Vandenberg Air Force Base, Vandenberg AFB, CA, 141

Volk Field Air National Guard Base, Camp Douglas, WI, 953

Volunteer Army Ammunition Plant, Chattanooga, TN, 759

Waco Naval & Marine Corps Reserve Center, Waco, TX, 820

Waianae Army Recreation Center, Waianae, HI, 290

Walter Reed Army Medical Center, Washington, DC, 188

Francis E Warren Air Force Base, F E Warren AFB, WY, 967

Washington Army National Guard Mobilization and Training Equipment Site, Yakima, WA, 940

Washington, DC, Coast Guard Air Station, Arlington, VA, 853

Washington, DC, Naval Air Facility, Andrews AFB, MD, 408

Washington, Naval Station, Washington, DC, 189

Waterloo Marine Corps Reserve Center, Waterloo, IA, 350

Watertown Naval Reserve Center, Watertown, NY, 611

Watervliet Arsenal, Watervliet, NY, 612

WES, Vicksburg, MS, 497

West Palm Beach Naval & Marine Corps Reserve Center, West Palm Beach, FL, 237

West Point, Army Garrison, West Point, NY, 614

West Trenton Marine Corps Reserve Center, West Trenton, NJ, 567

Western Mobilization & Training Complex, Paso Robles, CA, 95

Westover Air Reserve Base, Chicopee, MA, 438

Wheeler Army Airfield, Wheeler Army Airfield, HI, 293

Whidbey Island Naval Air Station, Oak Harbor, WA, 924

White River Junction Naval Reserve Center, White River Junction, VT, 834

White Sands, White Sands Missile Range, NM, 574

White Sands Missile Range, White Sands Missile Range, NM, 574

Whiteman Air Force Base, Whiteman AFB, MO, 516

Whiting Field, Milton, FL, 213

Whiting Field Naval Air Station, Milton, FL, 213

Wichita Naval & Marine Corps Reserve Center, Wichita, KS, 364

Will Rogers World Airport, Air National Guard Base, Oklahoma City, OK, 677
Williamsport Naval & Marine Corps Reserve Center, Williamsport, PA, 722
Willow Grove Naval Air Station (JRB), Willow Grove, PA, 723
Wilmington (DE) Naval & Marine Corps Reserve Center, Wilmington, DE, 170
Wilmington (NC) Naval & Marine Corps Reserve Center, Wilmington, NC, 635
Winter Harbor Naval Security Group Activity, Winter Harbor, ME, 403
Wisconsin National Guard, Office of the Adjutant General, Madison, WI, 959
Woods Hole Coast Guard Group, Woods Hole, MA, 447
Worcester Naval & Marine Corps Reserve Center, Worcester, MA, 448
Wright-Patterson Air Force Base, Wright-Patterson AFB, OH, 667
Wyoming Aerial Port (AFRES), Wyoming, PA, 724
Yakima Training Center, Yakima, WA, 941
Yankeetown Coast Guard Station, Yankeetown, FL, 238
YBI (Yerba Buena Island), San Francisco, CA, 126
Yeager Airport, Air National Guard Base, Charleston, WV, 944
Yorktown Coast Guard Reserve Training Center, Yorktown, VA, 909
Yorktown Naval Weapons Station, Yorktown, VA, 910
Youngstown-Warren Regional Airport, Air Reserve Station, Vienna, OH, 666
Yuma Marine Corps Air Station, Yuma, AZ, 45
Yuma Proving Ground, Yuma, AZ, 46

Outside United States

6th Area Support Group, Garmish, Germany, 987
6th Area Support Group, Stuttgart, Germany, 988
16th Combat Equipment Company, Belgium, 974
18th Combat Equipment Company, Netherlands, 1125
19th Combat Equipment Company, Netherlands, 1126
22nd Area Support Group, Italy, 1050
22nd Wing, Canada, 979
23rd Combat Equipment Company, Luxembourg, 1123
35th Supply & Service Battalion, Japan, 1061
67th Combat Support Hospital/ USAMEDDAC, Germany, 989
80th Area Support Group, Belgium, 975
98th Area Support Group, Germany, 990
100th Area Support Group, Germany, 991
221st Base Support Battalion, Germany, 992
223rd Base Support Battalion, Germany, 993
254th Base Support Battalion, Netherlands, 1127

280th Base Support Battalion, Germany, 994
282nd Base Support Battalion, Germany, 995
293rd Base Support Battalion, Germany, 996
414th Base Support Battalion, Germany, 997
424nd Air Base Squadron, RAF Fairford, United Kingdom, 1155
426th Air Base Squadron, Norway, 1132
6005th Air Postal Squadron, OL-D, Det 1, Korea, Republic of, 1087
Adjutant General of Guam, Guam, 1042
Adjutant General of Puerto Rico, Puerto Rico, 1139
Adjutant General of the Virgin Islands, VI, Virgin Islands, 1171
Administrative Support Unit, South West Asia, Bahrain, 973
Air Force Technical Applications Center, Det 415, Thailand, 1150
Alconbury RAF Base, United Kingdom, 1156
Andersen Air Force Base, Guam, 1043
Anderson Barracks, Germany, 998
Araxos Air Base, Greece, 1039
Army Chemical Activity Pacific, Johnston Atoll, 1086
Army Corps of Engineers, Japan District, Japan, 1062
Army Postal Group Europe, Rheinau, Germany, 1026
Army Research, Development & Standardization Group, UK, London, United Kingdom, 1162
Asian Office of Aerospace Research & Development, Tokyo, Japan, 1081
Atsugi Naval Air Facility, Japan, 1063
Augsburg Military Community, Germany, 999
Aviano Air Base, Italy, 1051
The Axe, Greece, 1039
Babenhausen Area Support Team, Germany, 1000
Balikesir Air Field, Turkey, 1151
Bamberg Military Community, Germany, 1001
Barton Barracks, Ansbach, Germany, 1002
Baumholder Military Community, H.D. Smith Barracks, Germany, 1003
Bitburg Annex, Germany, 1004
Cairo West AFB, Egypt, 983
Camp Smedley D Butler, MCB, Japan, 1064
Camp Carroll, Korea, Republic of, 1088
Camp Casey, Korea, Republic of, 1089
Camp Castle, Korea, Republic of, 1090
Camp Colbern, Korea, Republic of, 1091
Camp Courtney, Japan, 1065
Camp Darby, Livorno Military Community, Italy, 1052
Camp Edwards, Korea, Republic of, 1092
Camp Essayons, Korea, Republic of, 1093
Camp Foster, Japan, 1066
Camp Garry Owen, Korea, Republic of, 1094
Camp George, Korea, Republic of, 1095
Camp Giant, Korea, Republic of, 1096

Camp Greaves, Korea, Republic of, 1097
Camp Hansen, Japan, 1067
Camp Henry, Korea, Republic of, 1098
Camp Hialeah, Korea, Republic of, 1099
Camp Hovey, Korea, Republic of, 1100
Camp Howze, Korea, Republic of, 1101
Camp Humphreys, Korea, Republic of, 1102
Camp Kinser, Japan, 1068
Camp LaGuardia, Korea, Republic of, 1103
Camp Lester, Japan, 1069
Camp Long, Korea, Republic of, 1104
Camp MacNab (Cheju Do), Korea, Republic of, 1105
Camp Mobile, Korea, Republic of, 1106
Camp Nimble, Korea, Republic of, 1107
Camp Page, Korea, Republic of, 1108
Camp Red Cloud, Korea, Republic of, 1109
Camp Santiago, Puerto Rico, 1140
Camp Schwab, Japan, 1070
Camp Sears, Korea, Republic of, 1110
Camp Stanley, Korea, Republic of, 1111
Camp Stanton, Korea, Republic of, 1112
Camp Walker, Korea, Republic of, 1113
Camp Zama, Japan, 1071
Campbell Barracks, Germany, 1005
Cario (East), Egypt, 984
Caserma Ederle/Vicenza Military Community, Vincenza, Italy, 1060
CFAS, Japan, 1080
Chievres Air Base, Belgium, 976
Chinhae Fleet Activities, Korea, Republic of, 1114
Coleman Barracks, Germany, 1006
Combat Equipment Group-Europe, HQ, Netherlands, 1128
Croughton RAF Base, United Kingdom, 1157
Diego Garcia, Naval Support Facility, Diego Garcia, 982
Eskan Village, Saudi Arabia, 1145
European Office of Aerospace Research & Development, London, United Kingdom, 1163
Faulenberg Kaserne, Würzburg, Germany, 1038
Feltwell RAF Base, United Kingdom, 1158
Fort Buchanan Army Garrison, Puerto Rico, 1141
Fort Clayton, Panama, 1133
Fort Davis, Panama, 1134
Fort Sherman, Panama, 1135
Friedberg Area Support Team, Germany, 1007
Funari Barracks, Germany, 1008
Futenma, Marine Corps Air Station, Japan, 1072
Fylingdales-Moor RAF Base, United Kingdom, 1159
Germersheim Sub-Community, Germany, 1009
Ghedi Air Base, Italy, 1053
Giebelstadt Army Airfield, Germany, 1010
Gitmo, Cuba, 981
Guam Naval Magazine, Guam, 1044
Guam US Naval Hospital, Guam, 1045
Guantanamo Bay, Naval Base, Cuba, 981
Hardy Barracks, Tokyo, Japan, 1081

Branch of Service Index

Note: Numbers refer to entry numbers.

United States

Air Force

Alabama
Gunter Annex, Gunter, 6
Maxwell Air Force Base, Maxwell AFB, 8

Alaska
Clear Air Force Station, 22
Eareckson Air Force Station, 23
Eielson Air Force Base, Eielson AFB, 24
Elmendorf Air Force Base, Anchorage, 19
King Salmon Airport, 31
Tatalina Air Force Station, McGrath, 33

Arizona
Aircrew Training Research Division, Armstrong
  Laboratory, Mesa, 38
Davis-Monthan Air Force Base, Tucson, 42
Gila Bend Auxiliary Air Field, Gila Bend, 36
Luke Air Force Base, Luke AFB, 37

Arkansas
Little Rock Air Force Base, Little Rock AFB, 50

California
Beale Air Force Base, Beale AFB, 58
Edwards Air Force Base, Edwards AFB, 63
Los Angeles Air Force Base, Los Angeles, 76
McClellan Air Force Base, McClellan AFB, 81
Onizuka Air Station, Sunnyvale, 136
Pillar Point Air Force Station, El Granada, 65
Point Arena Air Force Station, Point Arena
  AFS, 97
Production Flight Test Installation, Air Force
  Plant 42, Palmdale, 94
Travis Air Force Base, Travis AFB, 137
Vandenberg Air Force Base, Vandenberg AFB,
  141

Colorado
99th Range Support Squadron, OL-B, La Junta,
  155
Air Force Reserve Command Personnel Center,
  Denver, 148
Falcon Air Force Base, Falcon AFB, 151
Peterson Air Force Base, Peterson AFB, 156
US Air Force Academy, Colorado Springs, 146

Delaware
Dover Air Force Base, Dover AFB, 167

District of Columbia
Bolling Air Force Base, Washington, 173

Florida
Cape Canaveral Air Force Station, Cocoa Beach,
  194
Cudjoe Key Air Force Station, Summerland
  Key, 233
Eglin Air Force Base, Fort Walton Beach, 197
Hurlburt Field, Hurlburt Field, 200

MacDill Air Force Base, MacDill AFB, 209
Operating Location Alpha Bravo South East Air
  Defense Sector, Old Town, 214
Patrick Air Force Base, Patrick AFB, 221
Tyndall Air Force Base, Panama City, 220

Georgia
Moody Air Force Base, Moody AFB, 258
Robins Air Force Base, Robins AFB, 259

Hawaii
Bellows Air Force Station, Waimanalo, 291
Fort Kamehameha, Honolulu, 274
Hickam Air Force Base, Hickam AFB, 271
Maui Space Surveillance Complex, Kihei, 280

Idaho
Mountain Home Air Force Base, Mountain
  Home AFB, 298

Illinois
Scott Air Force Base, Scott AFB, 318

Kansas
McConnell Air Force Base, McConnell AFB,
  354

Louisiana
Barksdale Air Force Base, Barksdale AFB, 374

Maryland
Andrews Air Force Base, Andrews AFB, 407

Massachusetts
Hanscom Air Force Base, Bedford, 430
Massachusetts Military Reservation/Otis Air Na-
  tional Guard Base, Cape Cod, 437

Mississippi
Columbus Air Force Base, Columbus AFB, 479
Keesler Air Force Base, Keesler AFB, 487

Missouri
Whiteman Air Force Base, Whiteman AFB, 516

Montana
99th Electronic Combat Range Group, Forsyth,
  518
Malmstrom Air Force Base, Great Falls, 520

Nebraska
Offutt Air Force Base, Offutt AFB, 530

Nevada
Nellis Air Force Base, Nellis AFB, 541

New Hampshire
New Boston Air Station, New Boston AS, 549

New Jersey
Gibbsboro Air Force Station, Gibbsboro, 558
McGuire Air Force Base, McGuire AFB, 561

New Mexico
Cannon Air Force Base, Cannon AFB, 570
Holloman Air Force Base, Holloman AFB, 571
Kirtland Air Force Base, Kirtland AFB, 572

North Carolina
Fort Fisher Air Force Recreation Area, Kure
  Beach, 628
Pope Air Force Base, Pope AFB, 629
Seymour Johnson Air Force Base, Goldsboro,
  625

North Dakota
Cavalier Air Station, Cavalier AS, 637
Grand Forks Air Force Base, Grand Forks AFB,
  641
Minot Air Force Base, Minot AFB, 642

Ohio
Wright-Patterson Air Force Base, Wright-Patterson AFB, 667

Oklahoma
Altus Air Force Base, Altus AFB, 668
Tinker Air Force Base, Tinker AFB, 678
Vance Air Force Base, Vance AFB, 681

Pennsylvania
305th Aerial Port Squadron, Detachment 1
  (AMC), Philadelphia, 712

South Carolina
Charleston Air Force Base, Charleston AFB, 737
North Auxiliary Airfield, North Auxiliary Air-
  field, 745
Shaw Air Force Base, Shaw AFB, 749

South Dakota
Ellsworth Air Force Base, Ellsworth AFB, 750

Tennessee
Arnold Engineering Development Center, Arnold Air Force Base, 756

Texas
Brooks Air Force Base, San Antonio, 815
Dyess Air Force Base, Abilene, 773
Eldorado Air Force Station, Eldorado, 791
Goodfellow Air Force Base, Goodfellow AFB,
  801
Kelly Air Force Base, Kelly AFB, 807
Lackland Air Force Base, Lackland AFB, 809
Laughlin Air Force Base, Laughlin AFB, 810
Randolph Air Force Base, Randolph AFB, 814
Sheppard Air Force Base, Sheppard AFB, 817

Utah
Hill Air Force Base, Hill AFB, 824
Utah Test and Training Range, Hill AFB, 825

Virginia
Langley Air Force Base, Langley AFB, 872

Washington
Fairchild Air Force Base, Fairchild AFB, 919
McChord Air Force Base, McChord AFB, 923

Wyoming
Pinedale Seismic Research Facility, Pinedale,
  969

Francis E Warren Air Force Base, F E Warren AFB, 967

Air Force Reserve

California
March Air Reserve Base, March ARB, 80
Onizuka Air Station, Sunnyvale, 136
Travis Air Force Base, Travis AFB, 137

Colorado
Cheyenne Mountain Air Force Station, Colorado Springs, 145

Delaware
Dover Air Force Base, Dover AFB, 167

Florida
Homestead Air Reserve Base, Homestead ARB, 199

Georgia
Dobbins Air Reserve Base, Marietta, 257

Illinois
O'Hare International Airport Air Reserve Station, O'Hare IAP ARS, 311

Indiana
Grissom Air Reserve Base, Grissom ARB, 331

Louisiana
New Orleans Naval Air Station Joint Reserve Base, Air Force Reserve, New Orleans, 383

Massachusetts
Westover Air Reserve Base, Chicopee, 438

Minnesota
Minneapolis-Saint Paul IAP, Air National Guard Base/ARS, Minneapolis-Saint Paul IAP, 474

New York
Niagara Falls Air Reserve Station, Niagara Falls, 600

Ohio
Youngstown-Warren Regional Airport, Air Reserve Station, Vienna, 666

Pennsylvania
Pittsburgh IAP, Air Reserve Station, Coraopolis, 701
Wyoming Aerial Port (AFRES), Wyoming, 724

Air National Guard

Alabama
Birmingham Airport, Air National Guard Base, Birmingham, 4
Dannelly Field Air National Guard Base, Montgomery, 14

Alaska
Kulis Air National Guard Base, Anchorage, 20

Arizona
Sky Harbor IAP, Air National Guard Base, Phoenix, 41
Tucson IAP, Air National Guard Base, Tucson, 43

Arkansas
Fort Smith Municipal Airport, Air National Guard Base, Fort Smith, 47

California
Fresno Air National Guard Base, Fresno Air Terminal, 72
Ontario Air National Guard Station, Ontario, 93
Sepulveda Air National Guard Station, Van Nuys, 140

Colorado
Buckley Air National Guard Base, Aurora, 142

Connecticut
Bradley IAP Air National Guard Base, Windsor Locks, 166

Delaware
New Castle County Airport, Air National Guard Base, Wilmington, 169

District of Columbia
District of Columbia National Guard, HQ, Washington, 176

Florida
Jacksonville IAP, Air National Guard Base, Jacksonville, 204

Georgia
Dobbins Air Reserve Base, Marietta, 257
Savannah IAP Air National Guard Base, Garden City, 251

Hawaii
Fort Kamehameha, Honolulu, 274
Kokee Air Force Station, Waimea, 292
State of Hawaii, Department of Defense HQ, Honolulu, 277

Illinois
Camp Lincoln, Springfield, 320
Capital Municipal Airport, Air National Guard Base, Springfield, 321
Greater Peoria Regional Airport Air National Guard Base, Peoria, 312

Indiana
Fort Wayne IAP, Air National Guard Base, Fort Wayne, 328
Hulman Regional Airport, Air National Guard Base, Terre Haute, 339

Iowa
Camp Dodge Iowa, Johnston, 346
Des Moines IAP, Air National Guard Base, Des Moines, 342
Sioux Gateway Airport, Air National Guard Base, Sergeant Bluff, 348

Kansas
Forbes Field Air National Guard Base, Topeka, 361

Kentucky
Standiford Field Air National Guard Base, Louisville, 372

Louisiana
Camp Beauregard, Pineville, 388
Hammond Air National Guard Station, Hammond, 378
Jackson Barracks, New Orleans, 382

Maine
Bangor IAP Air National Guard Base, Bangor, 393
Camp Keyes, Augusta, 392
South Portland Air National Guard Station, South Portland, 401

Maryland
Martin State Airport, Air National Guard Base, Baltimore, 414

Massachusetts
Barnes Municipal Airport, Air National Guard Base, Westfield, 446
Massachusetts Military Reservation/Otis Air National Guard Base, Cape Cod, 437

Michigan
Alpena Combat Readiness Training Center, Alpena, 449
Camp Grayling Maneuver Training Center, Grayling, 458
W K Kellogg Airport, Air National Guard Base, Battle Creek, 453
Selfridge Air National Guard Base, Selfridge ANG Base, 464

Minnesota
Duluth IAP Air National Guard Base, Duluth, 468
Minneapolis-Saint Paul IAP, Air National Guard Base/ARS, Minneapolis-Saint Paul IAP, 474

Mississippi
Gulfport-Biloxi Regional Airport, Air National Guard Base, Gulfport, 481
Key Field, Air National Guard Base, Meridian, 488
Allen C Thompson Air National Guard Base, Jackson, 486

Missouri
Lambert Field Air National Guard Base, Bridgeton, 498
Rosecrans Memorial Airport, Air National Guard Base, Saint Joseph, 509

Montana
Montana Air National Guard, Great Falls, 521

Nebraska
Lincoln Air National Guard Base, Lincoln, 528

Nevada
Nevada National Guard Headquarters, Carson City, 534
Reno/Tahoe IAP, Air National Guard Base, Reno, 544

New Hampshire
Pease Air National Guard Base, Pease ANGB, 550

New Jersey
Atlantic City Airport, Air National Guard Base, Pleasantville, 563

New Mexico
New Mexico National Guard State Headquarters, Santa Fe, 573

New York
Francis S Gabreski Airport (ANG Base), Westhampton Beach, 615
Northeast Air Defense Sector, Rome, 604
Roslyn Station, Air National Guard, Roslyn, 606
Schenectady County Airport, Air National Guard Base, Scotia, 607
Stewart Air National Guard Base, Newburgh, 599
Syracuse Hancock IAP, Air National Guard Base, Syracuse, 610

North Carolina
145th Airlift Wing, Charlotte, 619

North Dakota
Hector IAP, Air National Guard Base, Fargo, 640

Ohio
Mansfield Lahm Airport, Air National Guard Base, Mansfield, 659
Rickenbacker IAP, Air National Guard Base, Columbus, 655
Springfield Municipal Airport Air National Guard Base, Springfield, 664
Toledo Express Airport, Air National Guard Base, Swanton, 665

Oklahoma
Tulsa IAP, Air National Guard Base, Tulsa, 679
Will Rogers World Airport, Air National Guard Base, Oklahoma City, 677

Oregon
Kingsley Field Air National Guard Base, Klamath Falls, 687
Portland Air National Guard Base, Portland IAP, 691

Pennsylvania
Harrisburg IAP Air National Guard Base, Middletown, 708
Pittsburgh International Airport Air National Guard Base, Coraopolis, 700

Rhode Island
Quonset State Airport, Air National Guard Base, North Kingstown, 728

Nevada
Hawthorne Army Depot, Hawthorne, 537

New Hampshire
Army Cold Regions Research & Engineering Laboratory, Hanover, 548

New Jersey
Armament Research, Development, and Engineering Center, US Army TACOM, Picatinny Arsenal, 562
Bayonne Military Ocean Terminal, Bayonne, 552
Fort Dix, Fort Dix, 555
Fort Monmouth, Fort Monmouth, 557

New Mexico
US Army Corps of Engineers, Albuquerque District, Albuquerque, 569
White Sands Missile Range, White Sands Missile Range, 574

New York
Fort Drum, Fort Drum, 585
New York Area Command & Fort Hamilton, Brooklyn, 581
Seneca Army Depot Activity, Romulus, 605
US Army Corps of Engineers, New York District, New York, 597
US Army Corps of Engineers, Buffalo District, Buffalo, 584
US Army Corps of Engineers, North Atlantic Division, New York, 598
United States Military Academy, West Point, 613
Watervliet Arsenal, Watervliet, 612
West Point, Army Garrison, West Point, 614

North Carolina
Army Research Office, Research Triangle Park, 632
Fort Bragg, Fort Bragg, 624
Military Ocean Terminal, Sunny Point, Southport, 633
US Army Corps of Engineers, Wilmington District, Wilmington, 634

Ohio
Lima Army Tank Plant, Lima, 658
US Army Corps of Engineers, Great Lakes & Ohio River Division, Cincinnati, 647

Oklahoma
Fort Sill, Fort Sill, 671
McAlester Army Ammunition Plant, McAlester, 673
US Army Corps of Engineers, Tulsa District, Tulsa, 680

Oregon
Umatilla Chemical Depot, Hermiston, 686
US Army Corps of Engineers, Northwestern Division, Portland, 689
US Army Corps of Engineers, Portland District, Portland, 690

Pennsylvania
Carlisle Barracks, Carlisle Barracks, 698
Fort Indiantown Gap, Annville, 696
Charles E Kelly Support Facility, Oakdale, 711
Letterkenny Army Depot, Chambersburg, 699
Scranton Army Ammunition Plant, Scranton, 720
Tobyhanna Army Depot, Tobyhanna, 721
US Army Corps of Engineers, Philadelphia District, Philadelphia, 717
US Army Corps of Engineers, Pittsburgh District, Pittsburgh, 718

South Carolina
Combat Equipment Group-Army, HQ, Goose Creek, 743
Fort Jackson, Columbia, 740
US Army Corps of Engineers, Charleston District, Charleston, 736

Tennessee
Holston Army Ammunition Plant, Kingsport, 760
Milan Army Ammunition Plant, Milan, 766

US Army Corps of Engineers, Memphis District, Memphis, 765
US Army Corps of Engineers, Nashville District, Nashville, 772
Volunteer Army Ammunition Plant, Chattanooga, 759

Texas
Camp Bullis Training Site, Fort Sam Houston, 793
Corpus Christi Army Depot, Corpus Christi, 779
Fort Bliss, El Paso, 790
Fort Hood, Fort Hood, 792
Fort Sam Houston, Fort Sam Houston, 794
Longhorn Army Ammunition Plant, Marshall, 812
Red River Army Depot, Texarkana, 818
US Army Corps of Engineers, Galveston District, Galveston, 799
US Army Corps of Engineers, Fort Worth District, Fort Worth, 797
US Army Corps of Engineers, Southwestern District, Dallas, 788

Utah
Defense Non-Tactical Generator & Rail Equipment Center, Hill AFB, 823
Dugway Proving Ground, Dugway, 822
Tooele Army Depot, Tooele, 830

Virginia
Army Communications-Electronics Command Acquisition Center, Alexandria, 835
Army Corps of Engineers, Norfolk District, Norfolk, 876
Army Criminal Investigation Command, Fort Belvoir, 862
Army Materiel Command Headquarters, Alexandria, 836
Army Transportation Center & Fort Eustis, Fort Eustis, 868
Belvoir Research, Development & Engineering Center, Fort Belvoir, 863
Davison Army Airfield, Fort Belvoir, 864
Fort A P Hill, Bowling Green, 855
Fort Belvoir, Fort Belvoir, 866
Fort Lee, Fort Lee, 869
Fort Monroe, Fort Monroe, 870
Fort Myer, Arlington, 847
Fort Story, Fort Story, 871
Humphreys Engineer Center, Fort Belvoir, 867
Military Traffic Management Command, HQ, Falls Church, 861
Radford Army Ammunition Plant, Radford, 896
Transportation Engineering Agency, MTMC, Newport News, 874
US Army Corps of Engineers, Center for Public Works, Alexandria, 839
US Army Corps of Engineers, Topographic Engineering Center, Alexandria, 840
US Army Corps of Engineers, Transatlantic Programs Center, Winchester, 908
US Army Corps of Engineers, Water Resources Support Center, Alexandria, 841

Washington
Fort Lewis, Fort Lewis, 921
Madigan Army Medical Center, Tacoma, 936
US Army Corps of Engineers, Seattle District, Seattle, 931
US Army Corps of Engineers, Walla Walla District, Walla Walla, 939
Vancouver Barracks, Vancouver, 938
Yakima Training Center, Yakima, 941

West Virginia
US Army Corps of Engineers, Huntington District, Huntington, 946

Wisconsin
Badger Army Ammunition Plant, Baraboo, 951
Fort McCoy, Fort McCoy, 954

Army National Guard

Alabama
Adjutant General of Alabama, Montgomery, 13

Alaska
Adjutant General of Alaska, Fort Richardson, 26

Arizona
Adjutant General of Arizona, Phoenix, 39
Camp Navajo, Bellemont, 34

Arkansas
Adjutant General of Arkansas, North Little Rock, 51
Camp Joseph T Robinson, North Little Rock, 52

California
18th Cavalry, 1st Squadron, HQ, Ontario, 92
Adjutant General of California, Sacramento, 105
Camp San Luis Obispo, San Luis Obispo, 130
Western Mobilization & Training Complex, Paso Robles, 95

Colorado
Adjutant General of Colorado, Englewood, 150
Camp George West, Golden, 154

Connecticut
Adjutant General of Connecticut, Hartford, 159
Camp Rowland, Niantic, 163

Delaware
Adjutant General of Delaware, Wilmington, 168
New Castle County Airport, Air National Guard Base, Wilmington, 169

District of Columbia
Commanding General, DC National Guard, Washington, 175
District of Columbia National Guard, HQ, Washington, 176

Florida
Adjutant General of Florida, Saint Augustine, 228
Camp Blanding Training Site, Starke, 232

Georgia
Adjutant General of Georgia, Atlanta, 241
Army Aviation Support Facility, Winder, 264
Catoosa Area Training Center, Tunnel Hill, 263

Hawaii
State of Hawaii, Department of Defense HQ, Honolulu, 277

Idaho
Adjutant Genral of Idaho, Boise, 294

Illinois
Adjutant General of Illinois, Springfield, 319
Camp Lincoln, Springfield, 320

Indiana
Adjutant General of Indiana, Indianapolis, 332
Camp Atterbury, Edinburgh, 325

Iowa
Adjutant General of Iowa, Johnston, 345
Camp Dodge Iowa, Johnston, 346

Kansas
Adjutant General of Kansas, Topeka, 359
Nickell Barracks Training Center, Salina, 357

Kentucky
Adjutant General of Kentucky, Frankfort, 367

Louisiana
Adjutant General of Louisiana, New Orleans, 381
Camp Beauregard, Pineville, 388
Camp Villere, Slidell, 389
Jackson Barracks, New Orleans, 382

Maine
Adjutant General of Maine, Augusta, 391
Auburn Range, Auburn, 390
Camp Keyes, Augusta, 392
Caswell Range, Caribou, 398
Hollis Plaines, Buxton, 397

Maryland
Adjutant General of Maryland, Baltimore, 412
Gunpowder Military Reservation, Glen Arm, 425

Michigan

Selfridge Air National Guard Base, Selfridge
ANG Base, 464

New York

Camp Smith, Peekskill, 601

Texas

Camp Mabry, Austin, 777
Fort Worth, Naval Air Station, Joint Reserve
Base, Fort Worth, 796
Houston Coast Guard Air Station, Houston, 804

Virginia

Armed Forces Staff College, Norfolk, 875

Marine Corps

Arizona

Yuma Marine Corps Air Station, Yuma, 45

California

Barstow, Marine Corps Logistics Base, Barstow,
57
Camp Pendleton Marine Corps Base, Oceanside,
91
El Toro Marine Corps Air Station, Santa Ana,
132
Marine Corps Mountain Warfare Training Cen-
ter, Bridgeport, 59
Miramar Marine Corps Air Station, San Diego,
113
San Diego Marine Corps Recruit Depot, San Di-
ego, 119
Tustin Marine Corps Air Station, Tustin, 138
Twentynine Palms Marine Corps Air Ground
Combat Center, Twentynine Palms, 139

District of Columbia

Marine Barracks Washington DC, Washington,
178

Florida

Blount Island Command, Jacksonville, 201

Georgia

Albany Marine Corps Logistics Base, Albany,
239

Hawaii

Camp H M Smith, Camp Smith, 266
Kaneohe Bay Marine Corps Base, Kaneohe Bay,
278
Marine Barracks, Hawaii, Pearl Harbor, 282

Kansas

9th Marine Corps District, Shawnee Mission, 358
Marine Corps Reserve Support Center, Overland
Park, 355

New York

1st Marine Corps District Headquarters, Garden
City, 588
Stewart Air National Guard Base, Newburgh,
599

North Carolina

Camp Lejeune Marine Corps Base, Camp Leje-
une, 618
Cherry Point Marine Corps Air Station, Cherry
Point, 621
New River Marine Corps Air Station, Jackson-
ville, 627

South Carolina

Beaufort Marine Corps Air Station, Beaufort,
730
Parris Island Marine Corps Recruit Depot/East-
ern Recruiting Region, Parris Island, 747

Virginia

Camp Elmore, Norfolk, 877
Henderson Hall, HQ USMC, Arlington, 848
Quantico Marine Corps Combat Development
Command, Quantico, 895

Marine Corps Reserve

Alabama

Bessemer Naval & Marine Corps Reserve Readi-
ness Center, Bessemer, 3
Mobile Naval & Marine Corps Reserve Center,
Mobile, 11
Montgomery Marine Corps Reserve Center,
Montgomery, 15

Arizona

Phoenix Naval & Marine Corps Reserve Readi-
ness Center, Phoenix, 40
Tucson Naval & Marine Corps Reserve Center,
Tucson, 44

California

Alameda Naval & Marine Corps Reserve Readi-
ness Center, Alameda, 55
Bakersfield Naval & Marine Corps Reserve Cen-
ter, Bakersfield, 56
Encino Naval & Marine Corps Reserve Center,
Encino, 67
Los Angeles Naval & Marine Corps Reserve
Center, Los Angeles, 77
Sacramento Naval & Marine Corps Reserve
Readiness Center, Sacramento, 106
San Bruno Naval & Marine Corps Reserve Cen-
ter, San Bruno, 108
San Diego Naval & Marine Corps Reserve Cen-
ter, San Diego, 120
San Jose Naval & Marine Corps Reserve Center,
San Jose, 129

Connecticut

New Haven Naval & Marine Corps Reserve Center, New Haven, 160
Plainville Naval & Marine Corps Reserve Center, Plainville, 164

Delaware

Wilmington (DE) Naval & Marine Corps Reserve Center, Wilmington, 170

Florida

Miami Naval & Marine Corps Reserve Readiness Center, Hialeah, 198
Orlando Naval & Marine Corps Reserve Readiness Center, Orlando, 217
Tallahassee Naval & Marine Corps Reserve Center, Tallahassee, 234
West Palm Beach Naval & Marine Corps Reserve Center, West Palm Beach, 237

Georgia

Atlanta Naval Air Station, Marietta, 254
Atlanta Naval & Marine Corps Reserve Readi-
ness Center, Dobbins AFB, 246
Augusta Naval & Marine Corps Reserve Center,
Augusta, 244
Savannah Naval & Marine Corps Reserve Cen-
ter, Savannah, 261

Hawaii

Honolulu Naval & Marine Corps Reserve Readiness Center, Honolulu, 276

Idaho

Boise Naval & Marine Corps Reserve Center,
Boise, 296

Illinois

Peoria Naval & Marine Corps Reserve Center,
Peoria, 313
Rock Island Naval & Marine Corps Reserve
Center, Rock Island, 315

Indiana

Evansville Naval & Marine Corps Reserve Cen-
ter, Evansville, 326
Fort Wayne Marine Corps Reserve Center, Fort
Wayne, 329
Gary Naval & Marine Corps Reserve Center,
Gary, 330
Indianapolis Naval & Marine Corps Reserve
Readiness Center, Indianapolis, 335
South Bend Naval & Marine Corps Reserve Cen-
ter, South Bend, 338

Terre Haute Marine Corps Reserve Center, Terre
Haute, 340

Iowa

Des Moines Naval & Marine Corps Reserve
Center, Des Moines, 343
Waterloo Marine Corps Reserve Center, Water-
loo, 350

Kansas

Topeka Naval & Marine Corps Reserve Center,
Topeka, 362
Wichita Naval & Marine Corps Reserve Center,
Wichita, 364

Louisiana

Baton Rouge Naval & Marine Corps Reserve
Center, Baton Rouge, 375
New Orleans Naval & Marine Corps Reserve
Readiness Center, New Orleans, 385
Shreveport Naval & Marine Corps Reserve Cen-
ter, Bossier City, 376

Massachusetts

Lawrence Marine Corps Reserve Center,
Lawrence, 440
Massachusetts Military Reservation/Otis Air Na-
tional Guard Base, Cape Cod, 437
Worcester Naval & Marine Corps Reserve Cen-
ter, Worcester, 448

Michigan

Battle Creek Naval & Marine Corps Reserve
Center, Battle Creek, 450
Grand Rapids Naval & Marine Corps Reserve
Center, Grand Rapids, 457
Lansing Naval & Marine Corps Reserve Center,
Lansing, 460
Saginaw Naval & Marine Corps Reserve Center,
Saginaw, 461

Minnesota

Minneapolis Naval Air Reserve Center, Minnea-
polis, 472
St Paul Naval & Marine Corps Reserve Center,
Saint Paul, 476

Missouri

Saint Louis Naval & Marine Corps Reserve Center, Bridgeton, 499
Springfield Naval & Marine Corps Reserve Center, Springfield, 515

Montana

Billings Naval & Marine Corps Reserve Center,
Billings, 517

Nebraska

Omaha Naval & Marine Corps Reserve Center,
Omaha, 531

Nevada

Las Vegas Naval & Marine Corps Reserve Cen-
ter, Las Vegas, 539
Reno Naval & Marine Corps Reserve Center,
Reno, 542

New Hampshire

Manchester Naval & Marine Corps Reserve Center, Bedford, 546

New Jersey

West Trenton Marine Corps Reserve Center,
West Trenton, 567

New Mexico

Albuquerque Naval & Marine Corps Reserve
Center, Albuquerque, 568

New York

Albany Naval & Marine Corps Reserve Readi-
ness Center, Albany, 575
Amityville Naval & Marine Corps Reserve Cen-
ter, Amityville, 576
Bronx Naval & Marine Corps Reserve Center,
Bronx, 578
Brooklyn Coast Guard Air Station, Brooklyn,
579
Buffalo Naval & Marine Corps Reserve Center,
Buffalo, 583

Rochester Naval & Marine Corps Reserve Center, Rochester, 603
Syracuse Naval & Marine Corps Reserve Center, Mattydale, 593

North Carolina

Charlotte Naval & Marine Corps Reserve Center, Charlotte, 620
Greensboro Naval & Marine Corps Reserve Readiness Center, Greensboro, 626
Raleigh Naval & Marine Corps Reserve Center, Raleigh, 631
Wilmington (NC) Naval & Marine Corps Reserve Center, Wilmington, 635

Ohio

Akron Naval & Marine Corps Reserve Center, Akron, 643
Cincinnati Naval & Marine Corps Reserve Center, Cincinnati, 645
Columbus Naval & Marine Corps Readiness Center, Columbus, 652
Dayton Naval & Marine Corps Reserve Readiness Center, Dayton, 656
Toledo Naval & Marine Corps Reserve Center, Perrysburg, 662

Oklahoma

Oklahoma City Naval & Marine Corps Reserve Readiness Center, Oklahoma City, 676
Tulsa Naval & Marine Corps Reserve Center, Broken Arrow, 670

Oregon

Eugene Naval & Marine Corps Reserve Center, Eugene, 685
Portland Naval & Marine Corps Reserve Readiness Center, Portland, 688
Salem Naval & Marine Corps Reserve Center, Salem, 693

Pennsylvania

Ebensburg Naval & Marine Corps Reserve Center, Ebensburg, 702
Erie Naval & Marine Corps Reserve Center, Erie, 703
Harrisburg Naval & Marine Corps Reserve Center, Harrisburg, 704
Lehigh Valley Naval & Marine Corps Reserve Center, Allentown, 694
Pittsburgh Naval & Marine Corps Reserve Readiness Center, North Versailles, 710
Reading Naval & Marine Corps Reserve Center, Reading, 719
Williamsport Naval & Marine Corps Reserve Center, Williamsport, 722

Rhode Island

Providence Naval & Marine Corps Reserve Center, Providence, 729

South Carolina

Charleston, Naval & Marine Corps Reserve Readiness Center, Charleston, 733
Columbia Naval & Marine Corps Reserve Center, Columbia, 739
Greenville Naval & Marine Corps Reserve Center, Greenville, 744

Tennessee

Chattanooga Naval & Marine Corps Reserve Center, Chattanooga, 758
Knoxville Naval & Marine Corps Reserve Center, Knoxville, 761

Texas

Amarillo Naval & Marine Corps Reserve Center, Amarillo, 775
Austin Naval & Marine Corps Reserve Center, Austin, 776
Dallas Naval Air Station, Dallas, 783
El Paso Naval & Marine Corps Reserve Readiness Center, El Paso, 789
Houston Naval & Marine Corps Reserve Readiness Center, Houston, 805
Lubbock Naval & Marine Corps Reserve Center, Lubbock, 811
San Antonio Naval & Marine Corps Reserve Center, San Antonio, 816

Waco Naval & Marine Corps Reserve Center, Waco, 820

Utah

Salt Lake City Naval & Marine Corps Reserve Center, Salt Lake City, 829

Virginia

Norfolk Naval & Marine Corps Reserve Readiness Center, Norfolk, 883
Richmond Naval & Marine Corps Reserve Center, Richmond, 899
Roanoke Naval & Marine Corps Reserve Center, Roanoke, 900

Washington

Spokane Naval & Marine Corps Reserve Readiness Center, Spokane, 934
Tacoma Naval & Marine Corps Reserve Center, Tacoma, 937

West Virginia

Charleston Naval & Marine Corps Reserve Center, Charleston, 943
Moundsville Naval & Marine Corps Reserve Center, Moundsville, 949

Wisconsin

Green Bay Naval & Marine Corps Reserve Center, Green Bay, 955
Madison Naval & Marine Corps Reserve Center, Madison, 957
Milwaukee Naval & Marine Corps Reserve Center, Milwaukee, 962

Wyoming

Cheyenne Naval Reserve Center, Cheyenne, 966

Naval Reserve

Alabama

Bessemer Naval & Marine Corps Reserve Readiness Center, Bessemer, 3
Mobile Naval & Marine Corps Reserve Center, Mobile, 11

Alaska

Anchorage Naval Reserve Center, Anchorage, 18

Arizona

Phoenix Naval & Marine Corps Reserve Readiness Center, Phoenix, 40
Tucson Naval & Marine Corps Reserve Center, Tucson, 44

California

Alameda Naval & Marine Corps Reserve Readiness Center, Alameda, 55
Bakersfield Naval & Marine Corps Reserve Center, Bakersfield, 56
Encino Naval & Marine Corps Reserve Center, Encino, 67
Fresno Naval Reserve Center, Fresno, 71
Los Angeles Naval & Marine Corps Reserve Center, Los Angeles, 77
Onizuka Air Station, Sunnyvale, 136
Region Nineteen, Naval Reserve Readiness Command, San Diego, 116
Sacramento Naval & Marine Corps Reserve Readiness Center, Sacramento, 106
San Bruno Naval & Marine Corps Reserve Center, San Bruno, 108
San Diego Naval & Marine Corps Reserve Center, San Diego, 120
San Jose Naval & Marine Corps Reserve Center, San Jose, 129
Santa Clara, Naval Air Reserve, Moffett Federal Airfield, 82

Colorado

Denver Naval Reserve Readiness Center, Aurora, 143
Fort Carson Naval Reserve Center, Fort Carson, 153

Connecticut

New Haven Naval & Marine Corps Reserve Center, New Haven, 160

Plainville Naval & Marine Corps Reserve Center, Plainville, 164

Delaware

Wilmington (DE) Naval & Marine Corps Reserve Center, Wilmington, 170

District of Columbia

Region Six, Naval Reserve Readiness Command, Washington, 184

Florida

Miami Naval & Marine Corps Reserve Readiness Center, Hialeah, 198
Orlando Naval & Marine Corps Reserve Readiness Center, Orlando, 217
Pensacola Naval Reserve Center, Pensacola, 227
Region Eight, Naval Reserve Readiness Command, Jacksonville, 207
St Petersburg Naval Reserve Center, Clearwater, 193
Tallahassee Naval & Marine Corps Reserve Center, Tallahassee, 234
Tampa Naval Reserve Center, Tampa, 236
West Palm Beach Naval & Marine Corps Reserve Center, West Palm Beach, 237

Georgia

Atlanta Naval Air Station, Marietta, 254
Atlanta Naval & Marine Corps Reserve Readiness Center, Dobbins AFB, 246
Augusta Naval & Marine Corps Reserve Center, Augusta, 244
Columbus Naval Reserve Center, Columbus, 245
Savannah Naval & Marine Corps Reserve Center, Savannah, 261

Hawaii

Honolulu Naval & Marine Corps Reserve Readiness Center, Honolulu, 276

Idaho

Boise Naval & Marine Corps Reserve Center, Boise, 296
Pocatello Naval Reserve Facility, Pocatello, 299

Illinois

Decatur Naval Reserve Center, Decatur, 305
Forest Park Naval Reserve Center, Forest Park, 306
Peoria Naval & Marine Corps Reserve Center, Peoria, 313
Region Thirteen, Naval Reserve Readiness Command, Great Lakes, 310
Rock Island Naval & Marine Corps Reserve Center, Rock Island, 315

Indiana

Evansville Naval & Marine Corps Reserve Center, Evansville, 326
Gary Naval & Marine Corps Reserve Center, Gary, 330
Indianapolis Naval & Marine Corps Reserve Readiness Center, Indianapolis, 335
South Bend Naval & Marine Corps Reserve Center, South Bend, 338

Iowa

Cedar Rapids Naval Reserve Center, Cedar Rapids, 341
Des Moines Naval & Marine Corps Reserve Center, Des Moines, 343
Dubuque Naval Reserve Center, Dubuque, 344
Sioux City Naval Reserve Center, Sioux City, 349

Kansas

Topeka Naval & Marine Corps Reserve Center, Topeka, 362
Wichita Naval & Marine Corps Reserve Center, Wichita, 364

Kentucky

Lexington Naval Reserve Center, Lexington, 368
Louisville Naval Reserve Center, Louisville, 371

Louisiana

Baton Rouge Naval & Marine Corps Reserve Center, Baton Rouge, 375

Madison Naval & Marine Corps Reserve Center, Madison, 957

Milwaukee Naval & Marine Corps Reserve Center, Milwaukee, 962

Wyoming

Cheyenne Naval Reserve Center, Cheyenne, 966

Navy

California

China Lake Naval Air Weapons Station, China Lake, 60

Concord Naval Weapons Station, Concord, 61

Coronado Naval Amphibious Base, San Diego, 109

Department of Defense Housing Facility, Novato, 88

El Centro Naval Air Facility, El Centro, 64

Fallbrook Naval Ordnance Center, Pacific Division, Fallbrook, 68

Fleet Antisubmarine Warfare Training Center, Pacific, San Diego, 111

Fleet Combat Training Center, Pacific, San Diego, 112

Lemoore Naval Air Station, Lemoore, 74

Naval Facilities Engineering Service Center, Port Hueneme, 102

Naval Health Research Center, San Diego, 114

Naval Postgraduate School, Monterey, 83

Naval Research Laboratory, Marine Meteorology Division, Monterey, 84

Naval Warfare Assessment Division, Norco, 86

Navy Office of Information, West, Los Angeles, 78

North Island Naval Air Station, San Diego, 115

Point Mugu, Naval Air Weapons Station, Point Mugu, 98

Pomona Naval Industrial Reserve Ordnance Plant, Pomona, 101

Port Hueneme Division, Naval Surface Warfare Center, Port Hueneme, 103

Port Hueneme, Naval Construction Battalion Center, Port Hueneme, 104

San Diego Fleet and Industrial Supply Center, San Diego, 118

San Diego Naval Medical Center, San Diego, 121

San Diego Naval Station, San Diego, 122

San Diego Naval Submarine Base, San Diego, 123

Seal Beach Naval Weapons Station, Seal Beach, 133

Space & Naval Warfare Systems Command, San Diego, 124

Stockton Naval Communications Station, Stockton, 135

Connecticut

Naval Undersea Warfare Center, New London, 162

New London Naval Submarine Base, Groton, 158

District of Columbia

Anacostia Naval Station, Washington, 171

Naval District Washington, Washington Navy Yard, Washington, 180

Naval Medical Command, Bureau of Medicine & Surgery, Washington, 181

Naval Research Laboratory, Washington, 182

Naval Security Station, Washington, 183

US Naval Observatory, Washington, 186

Washington, Naval Station, Washington, 189

Florida

Cecil Field Naval Air Station, Jacksonville, 202

Cecil Field Naval Air Station, Detachment Astor, Astor, 190

Corry Station Naval Technical Training Center, Pensacola, 222

Fleet and Industrial Supply Center, Jacksonville, 203

Jacksonville Naval Air Station, Jacksonville, 205

Jacksonville Naval Hospital, Jacksonville, 206

Key West Naval Air Facility, Boca Chica Key, 191

Mayport Naval Air Station, Mayport, 210

Naval Air Warfare Center, Training Systems Division, Orlando, 216

Naval Coastal Systems Station, Panama City, 219

Naval Education and Training Professional Development and Technology Center, Pensacola, 223

Orlando, Naval Training Center, Orlando, 218

Pensacola Naval Air Station, Pensacola, 225

Pensacola Naval Hospital, Pensacola, 226

Whiting Field Naval Air Station, Milton, 213

Georgia

Kings Bay Naval Submarine Base, Kings Bay, 253

Navy Office of Information, Southeast, Atlanta, 242

Navy Supply Corps School, Athens, 240

Hawaii

Afloat Training Group, Western Pacific, Pearl Harbor, 281

Barbers Point Naval Air Station, Barbers Point, 265

Lualualei Naval Magazine, Waianae, 289

Naval Computer & Telecommunications Area Master Station, Eastern Pacific, Wahiawa, 288

Pacific Missile Range Facility, Kekaha, 279

Pearl Harbor Naval Complex, Pearl Harbor, 283

Pearl Harbor Naval Submarine Base, Pearl Harbor, 284

Pearl Harbor Navy Public Works Center, Pearl Harbor, 285

Idaho

Idaho Falls Naval Nuclear Power Training Unit, Idaho Falls, 297

Illinois

Great Lakes Naval Training Center, Great Lakes, 308

Navy Office of Information, Midwest, Chicago, 302

Recruit Training Command Great Lakes, Great Lakes, 309

Indiana

Crane Division, Naval Surface Warfare Center, Crane, 324

Kentucky

Louisville Naval Ordnance Station, Louisville, 370

Louisiana

New Orleans Naval Air Station Joint Reserve Base, Naval Air Station, New Orleans, 384

Maine

Bath Supervisor of Shipbuilding, Conversion and Repair, Bath, 395

Brunswick Naval Air Station, Brunswick, 396

Cutler Naval Computer & Telecommunications Station, Cutler, 399

Winter Harbor Naval Security Group Activity, Winter Harbor, 403

Maryland

Annapolis Naval Station, Annapolis, 409

Carderock Division, Naval Surface Warfare Center, West Bethesda, 429

Cheltenham Naval Communication Detachment, Cheltenham, 418

Indian Head Division, Naval Surface Warfare Center, Indian Head, 426

National Naval Medical Center, Bethesda, 417

Naval Surface Warfare Center, Carderock Division, Annapolis Detachment, Annapolis, 410

Patuxent River, Naval Air Station, Patuxent River, 427

Solomons, Navy Recreation Center, Solomons, 428

United States Naval Academy, Annapolis, 411

Washington, DC, Naval Air Facility, Andrews AFB, 408

Massachusetts

Navy Clothing and Textile Research Facility, Natick, 442

Navy Office of Information, New England, Boston, 434

Navy Recruiting District New England, Boston, 435

Minnesota

Fridley Naval Industrial Reserve Ordnance Plant, Minneapolis, 471

Mississippi

Gulfport Naval Construction Battalion Center, Gulfport, 482

Meridian Naval Air Station, Meridian, 489

Naval Meteorology and Oceanography Command, Stennis Space Center, 493

Naval Research Laboratory, Stennis Space Center, Stennis Space Center, 494

Pascagoula Naval Station, Pascagoula, 490

Pascagoula, Supervisor of Shipbuilding, Conversion and Repair, Pascagoula, 491

US Naval Home, Gulfport, 483

Nevada

Fallon Naval Air Station, Fallon, 535

New Hampshire

Portsmouth Naval Shipyard, Portsmouth, 551

New Jersey

Earle Naval Weapons Station, Colts Neck, 554

Lakehurst Naval Air Engineering Station, Lakehurst, 560

Naval Air Warfare Center, Aircraft Division, Trenton, 566

New York

Ballston Spa, Naval Nuclear Power Training Unit, Ballston Spa, 577

Navy Office of Information, East, New York, 596

Scotia Naval Administrative Unit, Scotia, 608

Seneca Lake Sonar Test Facility, Lake Seneca, 591

Oregon

Boardman Naval Weapons Systems Training Facility, Boardman, 682

Pennsylvania

Mechanicsburg Navy Inventory Control Point, Mechanicsburg, 706

Naval Facilities Engineering Command, Northern Division, Lester, 705

Naval Supply Systems Command, Mechanicsburg, 707

Philadelphia, Naval Inventory Control Point, Philadelphia, 716

Rhode Island

Naval Education and Training Center, Newport, Newport, 726

South Carolina

Beaufort Naval Hospital, Beaufort, 731

Charleston Naval Hospital, North Charleston, 746

Charleston, Naval Weapons Station, Charleston 734

Charleston Naval Weapons Station, Goose Creek, 742

Naval Facilities Engineering Command, Southern Division, Charleston, 735

Tennessee

Bureau of Naval Personnel Detachment, Memphis, Millington, 767

Memphis Detachment, Large Cavitation Channel, Memphis, 763

Texas

Corpus Christi Naval Air Station, Corpus Christi, 780

Corpus Christi Naval Hospital, Corpus Christi, 781

Dallas Naval Air Station, Dallas, 783

Ingleside Naval Station, Ingleside, 806

Kingsville Naval Air Station, Kingsville, 808
Navy Office of Information, Southwest, Dallas, 786
Orange Grove, Naval Auxiliary Landing Field, Alice, 774

Utah
Program Management Office, Strategic Systems Programs Detachment, Magna, 826

Virginia
AEGIS Combat Systems Center, Wallops Island, 905
Bureau of Naval Personnel, Arlington, 843
Dahlgren Division, Naval Surface Warfare Center, Dahlgren, 859
Dam Neck, Fleet Combat Training Center, Atlantic, Virginia Beach, 902
Fentres Naval Auxiliary Landing Field, Chesapeake, 857
Fleet & Industrial Supply Center, Cheatham Annex, Williamsburg, 907
Fleet Industrial Supply Center, Norfolk, 878
Fleet Training Center, Norfolk, Norfolk, 879
Little Creek, Naval Amphibious Base, Norfolk, 880
Naval Facilities Engineering Command, Atlantic Division, Norfolk, 881
Naval Facilities Engineering Command Headquarters, Alexandria, 838
Naval Sea Systems Command, HQ, Arlington, 849
Navy Recruiting Command, Arlington, 850
Newport News Supervisor of Shipbuilding, Conversion and Repair, Newport News, 873
Norfolk Naval Air Station, Norfolk, 882
Norfolk Naval Aviation Depot, Norfolk, 884
Norfolk Naval Base Complex, Norfolk, 885
Norfolk Naval Shipyard, Portsmouth, Portsmouth, 891
Norfolk Naval Station, Norfolk, 886
Norfolk Navy Public Works Center, Norfolk, 887
Northwest Naval Security Group Activity, Chesapeake, 858
Oceana Naval Air Station, Virginia Beach, 903
Office of Naval Research, Arlington, 851
Portsmouth Naval Hospital, Portsmouth, 892
Portsmouth Supervisor of Shipbuilding, Conversion and Repair, Portsmouth, 893
Shore Intermediate Maintenance Activity, Portsmouth, 894
Training Command, US Atlantic Fleet, Norfolk, 888
United States Atlantic Command, Norfolk, 889
Yorktown Naval Weapons Station, Yorktown, 910

Washington
Bangor Naval Submarine Base, Silverdale, 932
Bremerton Naval Hospital, Bremerton, 913
Jim Creek Naval Radio Station (T), Arlington, 911
Everett Naval Station, Everett, 917
Keyport Division, Naval Undersea Warfare Center, Keyport, 922
Naval Computer and Telecommunications Station, Puget Sound, Silverdale, 933
Pacific Beach Resort & Conference Center, Pacific Beach, 925
Port Hadlock, Naval Ordnance Center, Pacific Division Detachment, Port Hadlock, 927
Puget Sound Naval Shipyard, Bremerton, 914
Whidbey Island Naval Air Station, Oak Harbor, 924

West Virginia
Sugar Grove Naval Security Group Activity, Sugar Grove, 950

Outside United States

Air Force

Australia
Joint Defense Facility Nurrungar, 970

Joint Geological and Geophysical Research Station, 971

Belgium
Kleine Brogel Air Base, 977

Canada
22nd Wing, 979

Egypt
Cairo West AFB, 983
Cario (East), 984

France
Istres Air Base, 986

Germany
Bitburg Annex, 1004
Kaiserslautern Military Community, 1013
Kisling NCO Academy, 1016
Landstuhl Regional Medical Center, 1020
Ramstein Air Base, 1023
Rhein-Main Air Base, 1025
Sembach Air Base, 1029
Spangdahlem Air Base, 1030
USAFE Air Postal Squadron, Det 1, 1036

Greece
Araxos Air Base, 1039

Greenland
Thule Air Base, 1041

Guam
Andersen Air Force Base, 1043

Honduras
Joint Task Force—Bravo, 1048

Italy
Aviano Air Base, 1051
Ghedi Air Base, 1053
San Vito dei Normanni Air Station, San Vito dei Normanni, 1058

Japan
Asian Office of Aerospace Research & Development, Tokyo, 1081
Kadena Air Base, 1074
Yokota Air Base, 1085

Korea, Republic of
6005th Air Postal Squadron, OL-D, Det 1, 1087
Kimpo Military Mail Terminal, 1116
Kunsan Air Base, 1117
Osan Air Base, 1118

Netherlands
Volkel Air Base, 1131

Norway
426th Air Base Squadron, 1132

Panama
Howard Air Force Base, 1136

Saudi Arabia
Eskan Village, 1145
Prince Sultan Air Base, 1146

Spain
Moron Air Base, 1148

Thailand
Air Force Technical Applications Center, Det 415, 1150

Turkey
Balikesir Air Field, 1151
Incirlick Air Base, 1152
Izmir Air Station, 1153

United Kingdom
424nd Air Base Squadron, RAF Fairford, 1155
Alconbury RAF Base, 1156
Croughton RAF Base, 1157
European Office of Aerospace Research & Development, London, 1163
Feltwell RAF Base, 1158
Fylingdales-Moor RAF Base, 1159
Lakenheath RAF Base, 1161

Mildenhall RAF Base, 1167
Molesworth RAF Base, 1168
Research & Development Liaison Office London (USAF), London, 1165

Army

Belgium
16th Combat Equipment Company, 974
80th Area Support Group, 975
Chievres Air Base, 976
Northern Law Center, 978

Germany
6th Area Support Group, Garmish, 987
6th Area Support Group, Stuttgart, 988
67th Combat Support Hospital/USAMEDDAC, 989
98th Area Support Group, 990
100th Area Support Group, 991
221st Base Support Battalion, 992
223rd Base Support Battalion, 993
280th Base Support Battalion, 994
282nd Base Support Battalion, 995
293rd Base Support Battalion, 996
414th Base Support Battalion, 997
Anderson Barracks, 998
Army Postal Group Europe, Rheinau, 1026
Augsburg Military Community, 999
Babenhausen Area Support Team, 1000
Bamberg Military Community, 1001
Barton Barracks, Ansbach, 1002
Baumholder Military Community, H.D. Smith Barracks, 1003
Campbell Barracks, 1005
Coleman Barracks, 1006
Faulenberg Kaserne, Würzburg, 1038
Friedberg Area Support Team, 1007
Funari Barracks, 1008
Germersheim Sub-Community, 1009
Giebelstadt Army Airfield, 1010
Heidelberg Military Community, 1011
Johnson Barracks, 1012
Kaiserslautern Military Community, 1013
Kapaun Air Station, 1014
Katterbach Air Field/Kaserne, 1015
Kitzingen Military Community, 1017
Kleber Kaserne, 1018
Kleber Kaserne (Kaiserslautern Law Center), 1019
Landstuhl Regional Medical Center, 1020
Patton Barracks, 1022
Ray Barracks, 1024
Rose Barracks, 1027
Rose Barracks, Vilseck, 1028
Storck Barracks, Illesheim, 1032
Sullivan Barracks, 1033
Taylor Barracks, 1034
Tompkins Barracks, 1035
US Army Corps of Engineers, Transatlantic Programs Center, Europe, Wiesbaden, 1037

Honduras
Joint Task Force—Bravo, 1048

Italy
22nd Area Support Group, 1050
Camp Darby, Livorno Military Community, 1052
Caserma Ederle/Vicenza Military Community, Vincenza, 1060

Japan
35th Supply & Service Battalion, 1061
Army Corps of Engineers, Japan District, 1062
Asian Office of Aerospace Research & Development, Tokyo, 1081
Camp Zama, 1071
Torii Station, 1082

Johnston Atoll
Army Chemical Activity Pacific, 1086

Korea, Republic of
Camp Carroll, 1088
Camp Casey, 1089
Camp Castle, 1090

State/Country and Branch of Service Index

Note: Numbers refer to entry numbers.

United States

Alabama

Air Force
Gunter Annex, Gunter, 6
Maxwell Air Force Base, Maxwell AFB, 8

Air National Guard
Birmingham Airport, Air National Guard Base,
    Birmingham, 4
Dannelly Field Air National Guard Base,
    Montgomery, 14

Army
Anniston Army Depot, Anniston, 1
Army Engineering & Support Center,
    Huntsville, 7
Fort McClellan, Anniston, 2
Fort Rucker, Fort Rucker, 5
Redstone Arsenal, Redstone Arsenal, 16
Tuscaloosa Armed Forces Reserve Center, Tus-
    caloosa, 17
US Army Corps of Engineers, Mobile District,
    Mobile, 12

Army National Guard
Adjutant General of Alabama, Montgomery, 13

Coast Guard
Mobile Coast Guard Aviation Training Center,
    Mobile, 9
Mobile Coast Guard Group/Station, Mobile, 10

Marine Corps Reserve
Bessemer Naval & Marine Corps Reserve Readi-
    ness Center, Bessemer, 3
Mobile Naval & Marine Corps Reserve Center,
    Mobile, 11
Montgomery Marine Corps Reserve Center,
    Montgomery, 15

Naval Reserve
Bessemer Naval & Marine Corps Reserve Readi-
    ness Center, Bessemer, 3
Mobile Naval & Marine Corps Reserve Center,
    Mobile, 11

Alaska

Air Force
Clear Air Force Station, 22
Eareckson Air Force Station, 23
Eielson Air Force Base, Eielson AFB, 24
Elmendorf Air Force Base, Anchorage, 19
King Salmon Airport, 31
Tatalina Air Force Station, McGrath, 33

Air National Guard
Kulis Air National Guard Base, Anchorage, 20

Army
Fort Greely, Fort Greely, 25
Fort Richardson, Fort Richardson, 27
Fort Wainwright, Fort Wainwright, 28
US Army Corps of Engineers, Alaska District,
    Anchorage, 21

Army National Guard
Adjutant General of Alaska, Fort Richardson, 26

Coast Guard
17th Coast Guard District, Juneau, 29
Ketchikan Coast Guard Station, Ketchikan, 30
Kodiak Coast Guard Integrated Support Com-
    mand, Kodiak, 32

Naval Reserve
Anchorage Naval Reserve Center, Anchorage, 18

Arizona

Air Force
Aircrew Training Research Division, Armstrong
    Laboratory, Mesa, 38
Davis-Monthan Air Force Base, Tucson, 42
Gila Bend Auxiliary Air Field, Gila Bend, 36
Luke Air Force Base, Luke AFB, 37

Air National Guard
Sky Harbor IAP, Air National Guard Base, Phoe-
    nix, 41
Tucson IAP, Air National Guard Base, Tucson,
    43

Army
Fort Huachuca, Fort Huachuca, 35
Yuma Proving Ground, Yuma, 46

Army National Guard
Adjutant General of Arizona, Phoenix, 39
Camp Navajo, Bellemont, 34

Marine Corps
Yuma Marine Corps Air Station, Yuma, 45

Marine Corps Reserve
Phoenix Naval & Marine Corps Reserve Readi-
    ness Center, Phoenix, 40
Tucson Naval & Marine Corps Reserve Center,
    Tucson, 44

Naval Reserve
Phoenix Naval & Marine Corps Reserve Readi-
    ness Center, Phoenix, 40
Tucson Naval & Marine Corps Reserve Center,
    Tucson, 44

Arkansas

Air Force
Little Rock Air Force Base, Little Rock AFB, 50

Air National Guard
Fort Smith Municipal Airport, Air National
    Guard Base, Fort Smith, 47

Army
Pine Bluff Arsenal, Pine Bluff, 53
US Army Corps of Engineers, Little Rock Dis-
    trict, Little Rock, 49

Army National Guard
Adjutant General of Arkansas, North Little
    Rock, 51
Camp Joseph T Robinson, North Little Rock, 52

Army Reserve
Reserve Base, Fort Chaffee, Fort Smith, 48

California

Air Force
Beale Air Force Base, Beale AFB, 58
Edwards Air Force Base, Edwards AFB, 63
Los Angeles Air Force Base, Los Angeles, 76
McClellan Air Force Base, McClellan AFB, 81
Onizuka Air Station, Sunnyvale, 136
Pillar Point Air Force Station, El Granada, 65
Point Arena Air Force Station, Point Arena
    AFS, 97
Production Flight Test Installation, Air Force
    Plant 42, Palmdale, 94
Travis Air Force Base, Travis AFB, 137
Vandenberg Air Force Base, Vandenberg AFB,
    141

Air Force Reserve
March Air Reserve Base, March ARB, 80
Onizuka Air Station, Sunnyvale, 136
Travis Air Force Base, Travis AFB, 137

Air National Guard
Fresno Air National Guard Base, Fresno Air Ter-
    minal, 72
Ontario Air National Guard Station, Ontario, 93
Sepulveda Air National Guard Station, Van
    Nuys, 140

Army
Fort Hunter Liggett, Fort Hunter Liggett, 69
Fort Irwin, National Training Center, Fort Irwin,
    70
Military Traffic Management Command, West-
    ern Area, Oakland, 89
Oakland Army Base, Oakland, 90
Presidio of Monterey, Monterey, 85
Sierra Army Depot, Herlong, 73
US Army Corps of Engineers, Los Angeles Dis-
    trict, Los Angeles, 79
US Army Corps of Engineers, Sacramento Dis-
    trict, Sacramento, 107
US Army Corps of Engineers, San Francisco
    District, San Francisco, 127

US Army Corps of Engineers, South Pacific Division, San Francisco, 128

Army National Guard
18th Cavalry, 1st Squadron, HQ, Ontario, 92
Adjutant General of California, Sacramento, 105
Camp San Luis Obispo, San Luis Obispo, 130
Western Mobilization & Training Complex, Paso Robles, 95

Army Reserve
Fresno Naval Reserve Center, Fresno, 71
Parks Reserve Forces Training Area, Dublin, 62

Coast Guard
Alameda Coast Guard Integrated Support Command, Alameda, 54
Coast Guard Communication Station Pacific, San Francisco, Point Reyes Station, 99
Coast Guard Communication Station Pacific, Transmitter Site, Point Reyes Station, 100
Coast Guard Pacific Strike Team, Novato, 87
Department of Defense Housing Facility, Novato, 88
Petaluma Coast Guard Training Center, Petaluma, 96
San Diego Coast Guard Activities, San Diego, 117
San Francisco Coast Guard Air Station, San Francisco, 125
San Francisco Coast Guard Group, San Francisco, 126
San Pedro Coast Guard Support Center, San Pedro, 131

Defense Logistics Agency
Defense Contract Management Command, Hughes Los Angeles, Los Angeles, 75
Defense Contract Management Command, San Diego, San Diego, 110
Defense Contract Management District West, El Segundo, 66
Defense Distribution Region West, Stockton, 134

DOD
Defense Distribution Region West, Stockton, 134
Department of Defense Housing Facility, Novato, 88

Joint Service Installation
Defense Distribution Region West, Stockton, 134

Marine Corps
Barstow, Marine Corps Logistics Base, Barstow, 57
Camp Pendleton Marine Corps Base, Oceanside, 91
El Toro Marine Corps Air Station, Santa Ana, 132
Marine Corps Mountain Warfare Training Center, Bridgeport, 59
Miramar Marine Corps Air Station, San Diego, 113
San Diego Marine Corps Recruit Depot, San Diego, 119
Tustin Marine Corps Air Station, Tustin, 138
Twentynine Palms Marine Corps Air Ground Combat Center, Twentynine Palms, 139

Marine Corps Reserve
Alameda Naval & Marine Corps Reserve Readiness Center, Alameda, 55
Bakersfield Naval & Marine Corps Reserve Center, Bakersfield, 56
Encino Naval & Marine Corps Reserve Center, Encino, 67
Los Angeles Naval & Marine Corps Reserve Center, Los Angeles, 77
Sacramento Naval & Marine Corps Reserve Readiness Center, Sacramento, 106
San Bruno Naval & Marine Corps Reserve Center, San Bruno, 108
San Diego Naval & Marine Corps Reserve Center, San Diego, 120
San Jose Naval & Marine Corps Reserve Center, San Jose, 129

Naval Reserve
Alameda Naval & Marine Corps Reserve Readiness Center, Alameda, 55

Bakersfield Naval & Marine Corps Reserve Center, Bakersfield, 56
Encino Naval & Marine Corps Reserve Center, Encino, 67
Fresno Naval Reserve Center, Fresno, 71
Los Angeles Naval & Marine Corps Reserve Center, Los Angeles, 77
Onizuka Air Station, Sunnyvale, 136
Region Nineteen, Naval Reserve Readiness Command, San Diego, 116
Sacramento Naval & Marine Corps Reserve Readiness Center, Sacramento, 106
San Bruno Naval & Marine Corps Reserve Center, San Bruno, 108
San Diego Naval & Marine Corps Reserve Center, San Diego, 120
San Jose Naval & Marine Corps Reserve Center, San Jose, 129
Santa Clara, Naval Air Reserve, Moffett Federal Airfield, 82

Navy
China Lake Naval Air Weapons Station, China Lake, 60
Concord Naval Weapons Station, Concord, 61
Coronado Naval Amphibious Base, San Diego, 109
Department of Defense Housing Facility, Novato, 88
El Centro Naval Air Facility, El Centro, 64
Fallbrook Naval Ordnance Center, Pacific Division, Fallbrook, 68
Fleet Antisubmarine Warfare Training Center, Pacific, San Diego, 111
Fleet Combat Training Center, Pacific, San Diego, 112
Lemoore Naval Air Station, Lemoore, 74
Naval Facilities Engineering Service Center, Port Hueneme, 102
Naval Health Research Center, San Diego, 114
Naval Postgraduate School, Monterey, 83
Naval Research Laboratory, Marine Meteorology Division, Monterey, 84
Naval Warfare Assessment Division, Norco, 86
Navy Office of Information, West, Los Angeles, 78
North Island Naval Air Station, San Diego, 115
Point Mugu, Naval Air Weapons Station, Point Mugu, 98
Pomona Naval Industrial Reserve Ordnance Plant, Pomona, 101
Port Hueneme Division, Naval Surface Warfare Center, Port Hueneme, 103
Port Hueneme, Naval Construction Battalion Center, Port Hueneme, 104
San Diego Fleet and Industrial Supply Center, San Diego, 118
San Diego Naval Medical Center, San Diego, 121
San Diego Naval Station, San Diego, 122
San Diego Naval Submarine Base, San Diego, 123
Seal Beach Naval Weapons Station, Seal Beach, 133
Space & Naval Warfare Systems Command, San Diego, 124
Stockton Naval Communications Station, Stockton, 135

Colorado

Air Force
99th Range Support Squadron, OL-B, La Junta, 155
Air Force Reserve Command Personnel Center, Denver, 148
Falcon Air Force Base, Falcon AFB, 151
Peterson Air Force Base, Peterson AFB, 156
US Air Force Academy, Colorado Springs, 146

Air Force Reserve
Cheyenne Mountain Air Force Station, Colorado Springs, 145

Air National Guard
Buckley Air National Guard Base, Aurora, 142

Army
Fitzsimons Army Medical Center, Aurora, 144
Fort Carson and 4th Infantry Division (Mechanized), Fort Carson, 152
Pueblo Chemical Depot, Pueblo, 157
Rocky Mountain Arsenal, Commerce City, 147

Army National Guard
Adjutant General of Colorado, Englewood, 150
Camp George West, Golden, 154

DOD
Defense Finance and Accounting Service, Denver Center, Denver, 149

Joint Service Installation
Buckley Air National Guard Base, Aurora, 142

Naval Reserve
Denver Naval Reserve Readiness Center, Aurora, 143
Fort Carson Naval Reserve Center, Fort Carson, 153

Connecticut

Air National Guard
Bradley IAP Air National Guard Base, Windsor Locks, 166

Army National Guard
Adjutant General of Connecticut, Hartford, 159
Camp Rowland, Niantic, 163

Coast Guard
Coast Guard Academy, New London, 161

Defense Logistics Agency
Defense Contract Management Command, Stratford, Stratford, 165

Marine Corps Reserve
New Haven Naval & Marine Corps Reserve Center, New Haven, 160
Plainville Naval & Marine Corps Reserve Center, Plainville, 164

Naval Reserve
New Haven Naval & Marine Corps Reserve Center, New Haven, 160
Plainville Naval & Marine Corps Reserve Center, Plainville, 164

Navy
Naval Undersea Warfare Center, New London, 162
New London Naval Submarine Base, Groton, 158

Delaware

Air Force
Dover Air Force Base, Dover AFB, 167

Air Force Reserve
Dover Air Force Base, Dover AFB, 167

Air National Guard
New Castle County Airport, Air National Guard Base, Wilmington, 169

Army National Guard
Adjutant General of Delaware, Wilmington, 168
New Castle County Airport, Air National Guard Base, Wilmington, 169

Marine Corps Reserve
Wilmington (DE) Naval & Marine Corps Reserve Center, Wilmington, 170

Naval Reserve
Wilmington (DE) Naval & Marine Corps Reserve Center, Wilmington, 170

District of Columbia

Air Force
Bolling Air Force Base, Washington, 173

Air National Guard
District of Columbia National Guard, HQ, Washington, 176

Navy

Louisville Naval Ordnance Station, Louisville, 370

Louisiana

Air Force

Barksdale Air Force Base, Barksdale AFB, 374

Air Force Reserve

New Orleans Naval Air Station Joint Reserve Base, Air Force Reserve, New Orleans, 383

Air National Guard

Camp Beauregard, Pineville, 388
Hammond Air National Guard Station, Hammond, 378
Jackson Barracks, New Orleans, 382

Army

Fort Polk, Fort Polk, 377
Longhorn/Louisiana Army Ammunition Plant, Minden, 379
US Army Corps of Engineers, New Orleans District, New Orleans, 387

Army National Guard

Adjutant General of Louisiana, New Orleans, 381
Camp Beauregard, Pineville, 388
Camp Villere, Slidell, 389
Jackson Barracks, New Orleans, 382

Coast Guard

8th Coast Guard District, New Orleans, 380

Joint Service Installation

New Orleans Naval Air Station Joint Reserve Base, Naval Air Station, New Orleans, 384

Marine Corps Reserve

Baton Rouge Naval & Marine Corps Reserve Center, Baton Rouge, 375
New Orleans Naval & Marine Corps Reserve Readiness Center, New Orleans, 385
Shreveport Naval & Marine Corps Reserve Center, Bossier City, 376

Naval Reserve

Baton Rouge Naval & Marine Corps Reserve Center, Baton Rouge, 375
New Orleans Naval & Marine Corps Reserve Readiness Center, New Orleans, 385
New Orleans Naval Support Activity, New Orleans, 386
Shreveport Naval & Marine Corps Reserve Center, Bossier City, 376

Navy

New Orleans Naval Air Station Joint Reserve Base, Naval Air Station, New Orleans, 384

Maine

Air National Guard

Bangor IAP Air National Guard Base, Bangor, 393
Camp Keyes, Augusta, 392
South Portland Air National Guard Station, South Portland, 401

Army National Guard

Adjutant General of Maine, Augusta, 391
Auburn Range, Auburn, 390
Camp Keyes, Augusta, 392
Caswell Range, Caribou, 398
Hollis Plaines, Buxton, 397

Coast Guard

Southwest Harbor Coast Guard Group, Southwest Harbor, 402

Naval Reserve

Bangor Naval Reserve Center, Bangor, 394
Portland Naval Reserve Readiness Center, Portland, 400

Navy

Bath Supervisor of Shipbuilding, Conversion and Repair, Bath, 395
Brunswick Naval Air Station, Brunswick, 396

Cutler Naval Computer & Telecommunications Station, Cutler, 399
Winter Harbor Naval Security Group Activity, Winter Harbor, 403

Maryland

Air Force

Andrews Air Force Base, Andrews AFB, 407

Air National Guard

Martin State Airport, Air National Guard Base, Baltimore, 414

Army

Aberdeen Proving Ground, Aberdeen Proving Ground, 404
Adelphi Laboratory Center, Army Research Laboratory, Adelphi, 405
Fort Detrick, Fort Detrick, 421
Fort George G Meade, Fort Meade, 422
Fort Ritchie, Fort Ritchie, 424
US Army Corps of Engineers, Baltimore District, Baltimore, 415

Army National Guard

Adjutant General of Maryland, Baltimore, 412
Gunpowder Military Reservation, Glen Arm, 425

Coast Guard

Curtis Bay Coast Guard Yard, Curtis Bay, 420

DOD

National Imagery & Mapping Agency, Dissemination Division, Bethesda, 416
Patuxent River, Naval Air Station, Patuxent River, 427

Joint Service Installation

Alternate Joint Communications Center/Site R, Fort Ritchie, 423
Washington, DC, Naval Air Facility, Andrews AFB, 408

Naval Reserve

Adelphi Naval Reserve Center, Adelphi, 406
Baltimore Naval Reserve Readiness Center, Baltimore, 413
Cumberland Naval Reserve Center, Cumberland, 419
Washington, DC, Naval Air Facility, Andrews AFB, 408

Navy

Annapolis Naval Station, Annapolis, 409
Carderock Division, Naval Surface Warfare Center, West Bethesda, 429
Cheltenham Naval Communication Detachment, Cheltenham, 418
Indian Head Division, Naval Surface Warfare Center, Indian Head, 426
National Naval Medical Center, Bethesda, 417
Naval Surface Warfare Center, Carderock Division, Annapolis Detachment, Annapolis, 410
Patuxent River, Naval Air Station, Patuxent River, 427
Solomons, Navy Recreation Center, Solomons, 428
United States Naval Academy, Annapolis, 411
Washington, DC, Naval Air Facility, Andrews AFB, 408

Massachusetts

Air Force

Hanscom Air Force Base, Bedford, 430
Massachusetts Military Reservation/Otis Air National Guard Base, Cape Cod, 437

Air Force Reserve

Westover Air Reserve Base, Chicopee, 438

Air National Guard

Barnes Municipal Airport, Air National Guard Base, Westfield, 446
Massachusetts Military Reservation/Otis Air National Guard Base, Cape Cod, 437

Army

Army Soldier Systems Command, Natick, 441
US Army Corps of Engineers, New England District, Waltham, 445

Army National Guard

Adjutant General of Massachusetts, Reading, 443
Camp Curtis Guild, Reading, 444
Massachusetts Military Reservation/Otis Air National Guard Base, Cape Cod, 437

Army Reserve

Devens Reserve Forces Training Center, Devens, 439

Coast Guard

1st Coast Guard District, Boston, 431
Boston Coast Guard Reserve Center, Boston, 432
Cape Cod Coast Guard Air Station, Cape Cod, 436
Massachusetts Military Reservation/Otis Air National Guard Base, Cape Cod, 437
Woods Hole Coast Guard Group, Woods Hole, 447

Defense Logistics Agency

Defense Contract Management District Northeast, Boston, 433

Marine Corps Reserve

Lawrence Marine Corps Reserve Center, Lawrence, 440
Massachusetts Military Reservation/Otis Air National Guard Base, Cape Cod, 437
Worcester Naval & Marine Corps Reserve Center, Worcester, 448

Naval Reserve

Worcester Naval & Marine Corps Reserve Center, Worcester, 448

Navy

Navy Clothing and Textile Research Facility, Natick, 442
Navy Office of Information, New England, Boston, 434
Navy Recruiting District New England, Boston, 435

Michigan

Air National Guard

Alpena Combat Readiness Training Center, Alpena, 449
Camp Grayling Maneuver Training Center, Grayling, 458
W K Kellogg Airport, Air National Guard Base, Battle Creek, 453
Selfridge Air National Guard Base, Selfridge ANG Base, 464

Army

Army Tank-Automotive & Armaments Command, Warren, 466
US Army Corps of Engineers, Detroit District, Detroit, 456

Army National Guard

Adjutant General of Michigan, Lansing, 459
Camp Grayling Maneuver Training Center, Grayling, 458

Army Reserve

Selfridge Air National Guard Base, Selfridge ANG Base, 464

Coast Guard

Detroit Coast Guard Group/Base, Detroit, 455
Sault Ste Marie Coast Guard Group, Sault Ste Marie, 462
Selfridge Air National Guard Base, Selfridge ANG Base, 464
Traverse City Coast Guard Air Station, Traverse City, 465

Defense Logistics Agency

Defense Logistics Services Center, Battle Creek, 451
Defense Reutilization and Marketing Service, Battle Creek, 452

Joint Service Installation

Selfridge Air National Guard Base, Selfridge ANG Base, 464

Marine Corps Reserve

Battle Creek Naval & Marine Corps Reserve Center, Battle Creek, 450

Grand Rapids Naval & Marine Corps Reserve Center, Grand Rapids, 457
Lansing Naval & Marine Corps Reserve Center, Lansing, 460
Saginaw Naval & Marine Corps Reserve Center, Saginaw, 461

Naval Reserve
Battle Creek Naval & Marine Corps Reserve Center, Battle Creek, 450
Calumet Naval Reserve Facility, Calumet, 454
Detroit Naval Reserve Readiness Center, Selfridge ANG Base, 463
Grand Rapids Naval & Marine Corps Reserve Center, Grand Rapids, 457
Lansing Naval & Marine Corps Reserve Center, Lansing, 460
Saginaw Naval & Marine Corps Reserve Center, Saginaw, 461
Selfridge Air National Guard Base, Selfridge ANG Base, 464

Minnesota

Air Force Reserve
Minneapolis-Saint Paul IAP, Air National Guard Base/ARS, Minneapolis-Saint Paul IAP, 474

Air National Guard
Duluth IAP Air National Guard Base, Duluth, 468
Minneapolis-Saint Paul IAP, Air National Guard Base/ARS, Minneapolis-Saint Paul IAP, 474

Army
Twin Cities Army Ammunition Plant, Arden Hills, 467
US Army Corps of Engineers, St Paul District, Saint Paul, 477

Army National Guard
Adjutant General of Minnesota, Saint Paul, 475
Camp Ripley, Little Falls, 470

Marine Corps Reserve
Minneapolis Naval Air Reserve Center, Minneapolis, 472
St Paul Naval & Marine Corps Reserve Center, Saint Paul, 476

Naval Reserve
Duluth Naval Reserve Center, Duluth, 469
Minneapolis Naval Air Reserve Center, Minneapolis, 472
Region Sixteen, Naval Reserve Readiness Command, Minneapolis, 473
St Paul Naval & Marine Corps Reserve Center, Saint Paul, 476

Navy
Fridley Naval Industrial Reserve Ordnance Plant, Minneapolis, 471

Mississippi

Air Force
Columbus Air Force Base, Columbus AFB, 479
Keesler Air Force Base, Keesler AFB, 487

Air National Guard
Gulfport-Biloxi Regional Airport, Air National Guard Base, Gulfport, 481
Key Field, Air National Guard Base, Meridian, 488
Allen C Thompson Air National Guard Base, Jackson, 486

Army
Mississippi Army Ammunition Plant, Stennis Space Center, 492
US Army Corps of Engineers, Mississippi Valley Division/Mississippi River Commission, Vicksburg, 495
US Army Corp of Engineers, Vicksburg District, Vicksburg, 496
US Army Corps of Engineers, Waterways Experiment Station, Vicksburg, 497

Army National Guard
Adjutant General of Mississippi, Jackson, 484
Camp McCain Training Site, Elliott, 480

Camp Shelby Training Site, Camp Shelby, 478

Naval Reserve
Jackson Naval Reserve Center, Jackson, 485

Navy
Gulfport Naval Construction Battalion Center, Gulfport, 482
Meridian Naval Air Station, Meridian, 489
Naval Meteorology and Oceanography Command, Stennis Space Center, 493
Naval Research Laboratory, Stennis Space Center, Stennis Space Center, 494
Pascagoula Naval Station, Pascagoula, 490
Pascagoula, Supervisor of Shipbuilding, Conversion and Repair, Pascagoula, 491
US Naval Home, Gulfport, 483

Missouri

Air Force
Whiteman Air Force Base, Whiteman AFB, 516

Air National Guard
Lambert Field Air National Guard Base, Bridgeton, 498
Rosecrans Memorial Airport, Air National Guard Base, Saint Joseph, 509

Army
Army Reserve Personnel Center, Saint Louis, 510
Fort Leonard Wood, Fort Leonard Wood, 501
Lake City Army Ammunition Plant, Independence, 502
Saint Louis Army Publications Distribution Center, Saint Louis, 512
US Army Corps of Engineers, Kansas City District, Kansas City, 506
US Army Corps of Engineers, St Louis District, Saint Louis, 514

Army National Guard
Adjutant General of Missouri, Jefferson City, 503
Camp Clark, Nevada, 508
Fort Crowder, Neosho, 507

Army Reserve
Army Reserve Personnel Center, Saint Louis, 510

Coast Guard
Saint Louis Coast Guard Base, Saint Louis, 513

DOD
Defense Finance and Accounting Service Center, Kansas City, Kansas City, 504
National Imagery and Mapping Agency, Saint Louis, Saint Louis, 511

Marine Corps Reserve
Saint Louis Naval & Marine Corps Reserve Center, Bridgeton, 499
Springfield Naval & Marine Corps Reserve Center, Springfield, 515

Naval Reserve
Cape Girardeau Naval Reserve Center, Cape Girardeau, 500
Kansas City Naval Reserve Readiness Center, Kansas City, 505
Saint Louis Naval & Marine Corps Reserve Center, Bridgeton, 499
Springfield Naval & Marine Corps Reserve Center, Springfield, 515

Montana

Air Force
99th Electronic Combat Range Group, Forsyth, 518
Malmstrom Air Force Base, Great Falls, 520

Air National Guard
Montana Air National Guard, Great Falls, 521

Army National Guard
Adjutant General of Montana, Helena, 522
Fort William Henry Harrison, Helena, 523

Marine Corps Reserve
Billings Naval & Marine Corps Reserve Center, Billings, 517

Naval Reserve
Billings Naval & Marine Corps Reserve Center, Billings, 517
Great Falls Naval Reserve Center, Great Falls, 519
Missoula Naval Reserve Center, Missoula, 524

Nebraska

Air Force
Offutt Air Force Base, Offutt AFB, 530

Air National Guard
Lincoln Air National Guard Base, Lincoln, 528

Army
Cornhusker Army Ammunition Plant, Grand Island, 526
US Army Corps of Engineers, Missouri River Regional Office, Omaha, 532
US Army Corps of Engineers, Omaha District, Omaha, 533

Army National Guard
Adjutant General of Nebraska, Lincoln, 527
Camp Ashland, Ashland, 525

Marine Corps Reserve
Omaha Naval & Marine Corps Reserve Center, Omaha, 531

Naval Reserve
Lincoln Naval Reserve Center, Lincoln, 529
Omaha Naval & Marine Corps Reserve Center, Omaha, 531

Nevada

Air Force
Nellis Air Force Base, Nellis AFB, 541

Air National Guard
Nevada National Guard Headquarters, Carson City, 534
Reno/Tahoe IAP, Air National Guard Base, Reno, 544

Army
Hawthorne Army Depot, Hawthorne, 537

Army National Guard
Nevada Army National Guard, Fallon, Fallon, 536
Nevada National Guard Headquarters, Carson City, 534
Nevada National Guard Henderson, Henderson, 538
Nevada National Guard Las Vegas, Las Vegas, 540
Reno Nevada Army National Guard Armory, Reno, 543
Stead Training Center, Reno, 545

Marine Corps Reserve
Las Vegas Naval & Marine Corps Reserve Center, Las Vegas, 539
Reno Naval & Marine Corps Reserve Center, Reno, 542

Naval Reserve
Las Vegas Naval & Marine Corps Reserve Center, Las Vegas, 539
Reno Naval & Marine Corps Reserve Center, Reno, 542

Navy
Fallon Naval Air Station, Fallon, 535

New Hampshire

Air Force
New Boston Air Station, New Boston AS, 549

Air National Guard
Pease Air National Guard Base, Pease ANGB, 550

Grand Forks Air Force Base, Grand Forks AFB, 641

Minot Air Force Base, Minot AFB, 642

Air National Guard

Hector IAP, Air National Guard Base, Fargo, 640

Army National Guard

Adjutant General of North Dakota, Bismarck, 636

Camp Gilbert C Grafton, Devils Lake, 638

Naval Reserve

Fargo Naval Reserve Center, Fargo, 639

Ohio

Air Force

Wright-Patterson Air Force Base, Wright-Patterson AFB, 667

Air Force Reserve

Youngstown-Warren Regional Airport, Air Reserve Station, Vienna, 666

Air National Guard

Mansfield Lahm Airport, Air National Guard Base, Mansfield, 659

Rickenbacker IAP, Air National Guard Base, Columbus, 655

Springfield Municipal Airport Air National Guard Base, Springfield, 664

Toledo Express Airport, Air National Guard Base, Swanton, 665

Army

Lima Army Tank Plant, Lima, 658

US Army Corps of Engineers, Great Lakes & Ohio River Division, Cincinnati, 647

Army National Guard

Adjutant General of Ohio, Columbus, 651

Army Aviation Support Facility #1, North Canton, 661

Camp Perry Training Site, Port Clinton, 663

Ohio National Guard, Unit Training Equipment Site #1, Newton Falls, 660

Coast Guard

9th Coast Guard District Headquarters, Cleveland, 648

Defense Logistics Agency

Defense Contract Management Command, Cleveland, Bratenahl, 644

Defense Contract Management Command, GE Aircraft Engines Cincinnati, Cincinnati, 646

Defense Contract Management Command, International, Dayton, 657

Defense Supply Center, Columbus, Columbus, 654

Lima Army Tank Plant, Lima, 658

DOD

Defense Finance and Accounting Service, Columbus, 653

Defense Finance and Accounting Service, Cleveland Center, Cleveland, 650

Marine Corps Reserve

Akron Naval & Marine Corps Reserve Center, Akron, 643

Cincinnati Naval & Marine Corps Reserve Center, Cincinnati, 645

Columbus Naval & Marine Corps Readiness Center, Columbus, 652

Dayton Naval & Marine Corps Reserve Readiness Center, Dayton, 656

Toledo Naval & Marine Corps Reserve Center, Perrysburg, 662

Naval Reserve

Akron Naval & Marine Corps Reserve Center, Akron, 643

Cincinnati Naval & Marine Corps Reserve Center, Cincinnati, 645

Cleveland Naval Reserve Center, Cleveland, 649

Columbus Naval & Marine Corps Readiness Center, Columbus, 652

Dayton Naval & Marine Corps Reserve Readiness Center, Dayton, 656

Toledo Naval & Marine Corps Reserve Center, Perrysburg, 662

Oklahoma

Air Force

Altus Air Force Base, Altus AFB, 668

Tinker Air Force Base, Tinker AFB, 678

Vance Air Force Base, Vance AFB, 681

Air National Guard

Tulsa IAP, Air National Guard Base, Tulsa, 679

Will Rogers World Airport, Air National Guard Base, Oklahoma City, 677

Army

Fort Sill, Fort Sill, 671

McAlester Army Ammunition Plant, McAlester, 673

US Army Corps of Engineers, Tulsa District, Tulsa, 680

Army National Guard

Adjutant General of Oklahoma, Oklahoma City, 674

Camp Gruber, Army National Guard Training Site, Braggs, 669

Army Reserve

Keathley Army Reserve Center, Lawton, 672

Coast Guard

Coast Guard Institute, Oklahoma City, 675

Marine Corps Reserve

Oklahoma City Naval & Marine Corps Reserve Readiness Center, Oklahoma City, 676

Tulsa Naval & Marine Corps Reserve Center, Broken Arrow, 670

Naval Reserve

Oklahoma City Naval & Marine Corps Reserve Readiness Center, Oklahoma City, 676

Tulsa Naval & Marine Corps Reserve Center, Broken Arrow, 670

Oregon

Air National Guard

Kingsley Field Air National Guard Base, Klamath Falls, 687

Portland Air National Guard Base, Portland IAP, 691

Army

Umatilla Chemical Depot, Hermiston, 686

US Army Corps of Engineers, Northwestern Division, Portland, 689

US Army Corps of Engineers, Portland District, Portland, 690

Army National Guard

Camp Rilea, Oregon National Guard Training Site, Salem, 692

Camp Withycombe, Clackamas, 684

Marine Corps Reserve

Eugene Naval & Marine Corps Reserve Center, Eugene, 685

Portland Naval & Marine Corps Reserve Readiness Center, Portland, 688

Salem Naval & Marine Corps Reserve Center, Salem, 693

Naval Reserve

Central Point Naval Reserve Center, Central Point, 683

Eugene Naval & Marine Corps Reserve Center, Eugene, 685

Portland Naval & Marine Corps Reserve Readiness Center, Portland, 688

Salem Naval & Marine Corps Reserve Center, Salem, 693

Navy

Boardman Naval Weapons Systems Training Facility, Boardman, 682

Pennsylvania

Air Force

305th Aerial Port Squadron, Detachment 1 (AMC), Philadelphia, 712

Air Force Reserve

Pittsburgh IAP, Air Reserve Station, Coraopolis, 701

Wyoming Aerial Port (AFRES), Wyoming, 724

Air National Guard

Harrisburg IAP Air National Guard Base, Middletown, 708

Pittsburgh International Airport Air National Guard Base, Coraopolis, 700

Army

Carlisle Barracks, Carlisle Barracks, 698

Fort Indiantown Gap, Annville, 696

Charles E Kelly Support Facility, Oakdale, 711

Letterkenny Army Depot, Chambersburg, 699

Scranton Army Ammunition Plant, Scranton, 720

Tobyhanna Army Depot, Tobyhanna, 721

US Army Corps of Engineers, Philadelphia District, Philadelphia, 717

US Army Corps of Engineers, Pittsburgh District, Pittsburgh, 718

Army National Guard

Adjutant General of Pennsylvania, Annville, 695

Coast Guard

Philadelphia Coast Guard Marine Safety Office & Group, Philadelphia, 714

Defense Logistics Agency

Defense Distribution Region East, New Cumberland, 709

Industrial Analysis Support Office, Philadelphia, 713

Philadelphia Defense Personnel Support Center, Philadelphia, 715

DOD

Philadelphia Defense Personnel Support Center, Philadelphia, 715

Joint Reserve Base

Willow Grove Naval Air Station (JRB), Willow Grove, 723

Marine Corps Reserve

Ebensburg Naval & Marine Corps Reserve Center, Ebensburg, 702

Erie Naval & Marine Corps Reserve Center, Erie, 703

Harrisburg Naval & Marine Corps Reserve Center, Harrisburg, 704

Lehigh Valley Naval & Marine Corps Reserve Center, Allentown, 694

Pittsburgh Naval & Marine Corps Reserve Readiness Center, North Versailles, 710

Reading Naval & Marine Corps Reserve Center, Reading, 719

Williamsport Naval & Marine Corps Reserve Center, Williamsport, 722

Naval Reserve

Avoca Naval Reserve Center, Avoca, 697

Ebensburg Naval & Marine Corps Reserve Center, Ebensburg, 702

Erie Naval & Marine Corps Reserve Center, Erie, 703

Harrisburg Naval & Marine Corps Reserve Center, Harrisburg, 704

Lehigh Valley Naval & Marine Corps Reserve Center, Allentown, 694

Pittsburgh Naval & Marine Corps Reserve Readiness Center, North Versailles, 710

Reading Naval & Marine Corps Reserve Center, Reading, 719

Williamsport Naval & Marine Corps Reserve Center, Williamsport, 722

Willow Grove Naval Air Station (JRB), Willow Grove, 723

Navy

Mechanicsburg Navy Inventory Control Point, Mechanicsburg, 706

Naval Facilities Engineering Command, Northern Division, Lester, 705

Naval Supply Systems Command, Mechanicsburg, 707
Philadelphia, Naval Inventory Control Point, Philadelphia, 716

Rhode Island

Air National Guard
Quonset State Airport, Air National Guard Base, North Kingstown, 728

Army National Guard
Adjutant General of Rhode Island, Cranston, 725

Marine Corps Reserve
Providence Naval & Marine Corps Reserve Center, Providence, 729

Naval Reserve
Providence Naval & Marine Corps Reserve Center, Providence, 729
Region One, Naval Reserve Readiness Command, Newport, 727

Navy
Naval Education and Training Center, Newport, Newport, 726

South Carolina

Air Force
Charleston Air Force Base, Charleston AFB, 737
North Auxiliary Airfield, North Auxiliary Airfield, 745
Shaw Air Force Base, Shaw AFB, 749

Air National Guard
McEntire Air National Guard Station, Eastover, 741

Army
Combat Equipment Group-Army, HQ, Goose Creek, 743
Fort Jackson, Columbia, 740
US Army Corps of Engineers, Charleston District, Charleston, 736

Army National Guard
Adjutant General of South Carolina, Columbia, 738
Clarks Hill Training Site, Plum Branch, 748

Coast Guard
Charleston Coast Guard Group, Charleston, 732

Marine Corps
Beaufort Marine Corps Air Station, Beaufort, 730
Parris Island Marine Corps Recruit Depot/Eastern Recruiting Region, Parris Island, 747

Marine Corps Reserve
Charleston, Naval & Marine Corps Reserve Readiness Center, Charleston, 733
Columbia Naval & Marine Corps Reserve Center, Columbia, 739
Greenville Naval & Marine Corps Reserve Center, Greenville, 744

Naval Reserve
Charleston, Naval & Marine Corps Reserve Readiness Center, Charleston, 733
Columbia Naval & Marine Corps Reserve Center, Columbia, 739
Greenville Naval & Marine Corps Reserve Center, Greenville, 744

Navy
Beaufort Naval Hospital, Beaufort, 731
Charleston Naval Hospital, North Charleston, 746
Charleston, Naval Weapons Station, Charleston, 734
Charleston Naval Weapons Station, Goose Creek, 742
Naval Facilities Engineering Command, Southern Division, Charleston, 735

South Dakota

Air Force
Ellsworth Air Force Base, Ellsworth AFB, 750

Air National Guard
South Dakota Air National Guard Base, Sioux Falls, 755

Army National Guard
Camp Rapid, Rapid City, 753
Fort Meade Military Reservation, Fort Meade, 751
Mitchell National Guard Complex, Mitchell, 752

Naval Reserve
Sioux Falls Naval Reserve Center, Sioux Falls, 754

Tennessee

Air Force
Arnold Engineering Development Center, Arnold Air Force Base, 756

Air National Guard
McGee Tyson Airport, Air National Guard Base, Knoxville, 762
Memphis IAP, Air National Guard Base, Memphis, 764
Nashville IAP, ANG Base, Nashville, 770

Army
Holston Army Ammunition Plant, Kingsport, 760
Milan Army Ammunition Plant, Milan, 766
US Army Corps of Engineers, Memphis District, Memphis, 765
US Army Corps of Engineers, Nashville District, Nashville, 772
Volunteer Army Ammunition Plant, Chattanooga, 759

Army National Guard
Adjutant General of Tennessee, Nashville, 769

Defense Logistics Agency
Defense Contract Management Office Raytheon, Bristol, 757

Marine Corps Reserve
Chattanooga Naval & Marine Corps Reserve Center, Chattanooga, 758
Knoxville Naval & Marine Corps Reserve Center, Knoxville, 761

Naval Reserve
Chattanooga Naval & Marine Corps Reserve Center, Chattanooga, 758
Knoxville Naval & Marine Corps Reserve Center, Knoxville, 761
Memphis Naval Reserve Readiness Center, Millington, 768
Nashville Naval Reserve Center, Nashville, 771

Navy
Bureau of Naval Personnel Detachment, Memphis, Millington, 767
Memphis Detachment, Large Cavitation Channel, Memphis, 763

Texas

Air Force
Brooks Air Force Base, San Antonio, 815
Dyess Air Force Base, Abilene, 773
Eldorado Air Force Station, Eldorado, 791
Goodfellow Air Force Base, Goodfellow AFB, 801
Kelly Air Force Base, Kelly AFB, 807
Lackland Air Force Base, Lackland AFB, 809
Laughlin Air Force Base, Laughlin AFB, 810
Randolph Air Force Base, Randolph AFB, 814
Sheppard Air Force Base, Sheppard AFB, 817

Air National Guard
Dallas Naval Air Station, Dallas, 783
Dallas NAS, Air National Guard Base, Dallas, 784
Ellington Field, Air National Guard Base, Houston, 803
Garland Air National Guard Station, Garland, 800
Hensley Field Texas Air National Guard Base, Dallas, 785

Army
Camp Bullis Training Site, Fort Sam Houston, 793
Corpus Christi Army Depot, Corpus Christi, 779
Fort Bliss, El Paso, 790
Fort Hood, Fort Hood, 792
Fort Sam Houston, Fort Sam Houston, 794
Longhorn Army Ammunition Plant, Marshall, 812
Red River Army Depot, Texarkana, 818
US Army Corps of Engineers, Galveston District, Galveston, 799
US Army Corps of Engineers, Fort Worth District, Fort Worth, 797
US Army Corps of Engineers, Southwestern District, Dallas, 788

Army National Guard
Camp Swift Training Site, Bastrop, 778

Coast Guard
Galveston Coast Guard Base, Galveston, 798
Houston Coast Guard Air Station, Houston, 804

Defense Logistics Agency
Defense Plant Representative Office, Air Force Plant No 4, Fort Worth, 795

Joint Service Installation
Camp Mabry, Austin, 777
Fort Worth, Naval Air Station, Joint Reserve Base, Fort Worth, 796
Houston Coast Guard Air Station, Houston, 804

Marine Corps Reserve
Amarillo Naval & Marine Corps Reserve Center, Amarillo, 775
Austin Naval & Marine Corps Reserve Center, Austin, 776
Dallas Naval Air Station, Dallas, 783
El Paso Naval & Marine Corps Reserve Readiness Center, El Paso, 789
Houston Naval & Marine Corps Reserve Readiness Center, Houston, 805
Lubbock Naval & Marine Corps Reserve Center, Lubbock, 811
San Antonio Naval & Marine Corps Reserve Center, San Antonio, 816
Waco Naval & Marine Corps Reserve Center, Waco, 820

Naval Reserve
Amarillo Naval & Marine Corps Reserve Center, Amarillo, 775
Austin Naval & Marine Corps Reserve Center, Austin, 776
El Paso Naval & Marine Corps Reserve Readiness Center, El Paso, 789
Harlingen Naval Reserve Center, Harlingen, 802
Houston Naval & Marine Corps Reserve Readiness Center, Houston, 805
Lubbock Naval & Marine Corps Reserve Center, Lubbock, 811
Naval Reserve Center, Corpus Christi, Corpus Christi, 782
Orange Naval Reserve Center, Orange, 813
Region Eleven, Naval Reserve Readiness Command, Dallas, 787
San Antonio Naval & Marine Corps Reserve Center, San Antonio, 816
Tyler Naval Reserve Center, Tyler, 819
Waco Naval & Marine Corps Reserve Center, Waco, 820

Navy
Corpus Christi Naval Air Station, Corpus Christi, 780
Corpus Christi Naval Hospital, Corpus Christi, 781
Dallas Naval Air Station, Dallas, 783
Ingleside Naval Station, Ingleside, 806
Kingsville Naval Air Station, Kingsville, 808
Navy Office of Information, Southwest, Dallas, 786
Orange Grove, Naval Auxiliary Landing Field, Alice, 774

Army
Joint Task Force—Bravo, 1048

Joint Service Installation
Joint Task Force—Bravo, 1048

Iceland

Navy
Kaflavik Naval Air Station, Keflavik, 1049

Italy

Air Force
Aviano Air Base, 1051
Ghedi Air Base, 1053
San Vito dei Normanni Air Station, San Vito dei
    Normanni, 1058

Army
22nd Area Support Group, 1050
Camp Darby, Livorno Military Community, 1052
Caserma Ederle/Vicenza Military Community,
    Vincenza, 1060

Navy
La Maddalena Navy Support Office, 1054
Naples (Capodichino) Naval Support Activity,
    1055
Naval Computer & Telecommunications Area
    Master Station MED, Naples, 1056
Naval Regional Contracting Center, 1057
Sigonella Naval Air Station, 1059

Japan

Air Force
Asian Office of Aerospace Research & Develop-
    ment, Tokyo, 1081
Kadena Air Base, 1074
Yokota Air Base, 1085

Army
35th Supply & Service Battalion, 1061
Army Corps of Engineers, Japan District, 1062
Asian Office of Aerospace Research & Develop-
    ment, Tokyo, 1081
Camp Zama, 1071
Torii Station, 1082

DOD
Pacific Stars and Stripes, 1079

Joint Service Installation
Misawa Air Base, 1076
Misawa, Naval Air Facility, 1077

Marine Corps
Camp Smedley D Butler, MCB, 1064
Camp Courtney, 1065
Camp Foster, 1066
Camp Hansen, 1067
Camp Kinser, 1068
Camp Lester, 1069
Camp Schwab, 1070
Futenma, Marine Corps Air Station, 1072
Iwakuni Marine Corps Air Station, 1073

Navy
Asian Office of Aerospace Research & Develop-
    ment, Tokyo, 1081
Atsugi Naval Air Facility, 1063
Kadena Naval Air Facility, 1075
New Sanno Hotel, US Naval Joint Services Ac-
    tivity, 1078
Sasebo, US Fleet Activities, 1080
Yokosuka, Fleet Activities, 1083
Yokosuka, US Naval Hospital, 1084

United Nations
Futenma, Marine Corps Air Station, 1072

Johnston Atoll

Army
Army Chemical Activity Pacific, 1086

Korea, Republic of

Air Force
6005th Air Postal Squadron, OL-D, Det 1, 1087
Kimpo Military Mail Terminal, 1116

Kunsan Air Base, 1117
Osan Air Base, 1118

Army
Camp Carroll, 1088
Camp Casey, 1089
Camp Castle, 1090
Camp Colbern, 1091
Camp Edwards, 1092
Camp Essayons, 1093
Camp Garry Owen, 1094
Camp George, 1095
Camp Giant, 1096
Camp Greaves, 1097
Camp Henry, 1098
Camp Hialeah, 1099
Camp Hovey, 1100
Camp Howze, 1101
Camp Humphreys, 1102
Camp LaGuardia, 1103
Camp Long, 1104
Camp MacNab (Cheju Do), 1105
Camp Mobile, 1106
Camp Nimble, 1107
Camp Page, 1108
Camp Red Cloud, 1109
Camp Sears, 1110
Camp Stanley, 1111
Camp Stanton, 1112
Camp Walker, 1113
K-16 (Army Airfield), 1115
Kimpo Military Mail Terminal, 1116
Pusan Storage Facility, 1119
US Army Corps of Engineers, Far East District,
    1120
Yongsan Army Garrison, 1121
Zoeckler Station, 1122

Navy
Chinhae Fleet Activities, 1114

Luxembourg

Army
23rd Combat Equipment Company, 1123

Marshall Islands

Army
Kwajalein Missile Range, 1124

Netherlands

Air Force
Volkel Air Base, 1131

Army
18th Combat Equipment Company, 1125
19th Combat Equipment Company, 1126
254th Base Support Battalion, 1127
Combat Equipment Group-Europe, HQ, 1128
Military Traffic Management Command,
    Europe, 1129
Netherlands Law Center, 1130

Norway

Air Force
426th Air Base Squadron, 1132

Panama

Air Force
Howard Air Force Base, 1136

Army
Fort Clayton, 1133
Fort Davis, 1134
Fort Sherman, 1135

Navy
Panama Canal Naval Station, 1137

Portugal

Joint Service Installation
Lajes Field, 1138

Puerto Rico

Army
Fort Buchanan Army Garrison, 1141

Army National Guard
Adjutant General of Puerto Rico, 1139
Camp Santiago, 1140

Naval Reserve
Roosevelt Roads Naval Reserve Center, 1142

Navy
Roosevelt Roads Naval Station, 1143
Sabana Seca, US Naval Security Group Activity, 1144

Saudi Arabia

Air Force
Eskan Village, 1145
Prince Sultan Air Base, 1146

Singapore

Navy
Logistics Group Western Pacific, 1147

Spain

Air Force
Moron Air Base, 1148

Navy
Rota Naval Station, 1149

Thailand

Air Force
Air Force Technical Applications Center, Det
    415, 1150

Turkey

Air Force
Balikesir Air Field, 1151
Incirlick Air Base, 1152
Izmir Air Station, 1153

NATO
Vecihi Akin Garrison, 1154

United Kingdom

Air Force
424nd Air Base Squadron, RAF Fairford, 1155
Alconbury RAF Base, 1156
Croughton RAF Base, 1157
European Office of Aerospace Research & De-
    velopment, London, 1163
Feltwell RAF Base, 1158
Fylingdales-Moor RAF Base, 1159
Lakenheath RAF Base, 1161
Mildenhall RAF Base, 1167
Molesworth RAF Base, 1168
Research & Development Liaison Office Lon-
    don (USAF), London, 1165

Army
Army Research, Development & Stand-
    ardization Group, UK, London, 1162
Hythe Depot Activity, 1160

DOD
Menwith Hill, 1166

Navy
Office of Naval Research Europe, London, 1164
Upwood RAF Base, 1169
West Ruislip RAF Base, 1170

Virgin Islands

Army National Guard
Adjutant General of the Virgin Islands, 1171

Wake Island

Army
Wake Island Missile Launch Facility, 1172

Alphabetical Listing of Units

Note: Numbers refer to entry numbers.

Units whose names begin with numbers are listed first in ascending numeric order. Units whose names begin with words are listed alphabetically immediately following the numeric units. Units are listed as reported by each base.

1/1 Cavalry
414th Base Support Battalion, Germany, 997

1/4 Cavalry
280th Base Support Battalion, Germany, 994

1/6 Field Artillery Bn
Bamberg Military Community, Germany, 1001

1/7 Field Artillery
280th Base Support Battalion, Germany, 994

1/18 Infantry Bn
280th Base Support Battalion, Germany, 994

1/19 Special Forces Bn
Camp W G Williams, Riverton, UT, 827

1/26 Infantry Bn
280th Base Support Battalion, Germany, 994

1/27th Field Artillery Bn
223rd Base Support Battalion, Germany, 993

1/43 Air Defense Artillery, E Battery
Kunsan Air Base, Korea, Republic of, 1117

1/43 Air Defense Artillery, F Battery
Kunsan Air Base, Korea, Republic of, 1117

1/77 Armor Bn
280th Base Support Battalion, Germany, 994

Co D 1-137th AHB
Army Aviation Support Facility #1, North Canton, OH, 661

Co E 1-137th AHB
Army Aviation Support Facility #1, North Canton, OH, 661

1/334th Bn
84th Division (IT) HQ, Milwaukee, WI, 960

1-501st Aviation
414th Base Support Battalion, Germany, 997

1st Air Force
Tyndall Air Force Base, Panama City, FL, 220

1st Air Support Operations Group
Fort Lewis, Fort Lewis, WA, 921

1st Armor Division, 3rd Brigade
Fort Riley, Fort Riley, KS, 353

1st Armor Division, 4th Brigade
414th Base Support Battalion, Germany, 997

1st Armor Training Brigade
Army Armor Center & Fort Knox, Fort Knox, KY, 366

1st Armored Brigade
Friedberg Area Support Team, Germany, 1007

1st Armored Division Artillery
Baumholder Military Community, H.D. Smith Barracks, Germany, 1003

1st Army-East, HQ
Fort George G Meade, Fort Meade, MD, 422

1st Aviation Brigade
Fort Rucker, Fort Rucker, AL, 5

1st Basic Training Brigade
Fort Jackson, Columbia, SC, 740

1st Bn, 1st Infantry Regiment
West Point, Army Garrison, West Point, NY, 614

HQ, 1st Brigade, 2nd ROTC Region, Army Cadet Command (ATOB)
Defense Supply Center, Columbus, Columbus, OH, 654

1st Cavalry Division
Fort Hood, Fort Hood, TX, 792

First Coast Guard District
1st Coast Guard District, Boston, MA, 431

1st Combat Camera Squadron
Charleston Air Force Base, Charleston AFB, SC, 737

1st Combat Communications Squadron
Ramstein Air Base, Germany, 1023

1st Combat Evaluation Group, Strategic Air Command, Det 8
Blue Grass Army Depot, Richmond, KY, 373

1st Combined Arms Support Bn
Fort Bliss, El Paso, TX, 790

1st Corps Support Command
Fort Bragg, Fort Bragg, NC, 624
Fort Clayton, Panama, 1133

1st Engineer Brigade
Fort Leonard Wood, Fort Leonard Wood, MO, 501

3rd Bn, 1st Field Artillery Regiment
Rose Barracks, Germany, 1027

1st Fighter Squadron
Tyndall Air Force Base, Panama City, FL, 220

1st Fighter Wing
Langley Air Force Base, Langley AFB, VA, 872

1st Force Service Support Group (1st FSSG)
Camp Pendleton Marine Corps Base, Oceanside, CA, 91

1st FWD, Co B, Det 1
Nevada National Guard Las Vegas, Las Vegas, NV, 540

1st German Air Force
Holloman Air Force Base, Holloman AFB, NM, 571

2nd Bn, 1st Infantry
Fort Wainwright, Fort Wainwright, AK, 28

1st Brigade, 1st Infantry Division (MECH)
Fort Riley, Fort Riley, KS, 353

1st Infantry Division, 2nd Brigade
280th Base Support Battalion, Germany, 994

3rd Brigade, 1st Infantry Division
Rose Barracks, Germany, 1027
Rose Barracks, Vilseck, Germany, 1028

1st Infantry Division, Divarty
Bamberg Military Community, Germany, 1001

1st Infantry Division Engineer Brigade
Bamberg Military Community, Germany, 1001

1st Infantry Division, HQ
67th Combat Support Hospital/USAMEDDAC, Germany, 989
98th Area Support Group, Germany, 990

1st Infantry Division Marne Band
Bamberg Military Community, Germany, 1001

1st Light Antiaircraft Missile Bn
Yuma Marine Corps Air Station, Yuma, AZ, 45

1st Logistics Group
Langley Air Force Base, Langley AFB, VA, 872

1st Marine Aircraft Wing
Camp Smedley D Butler, MCB, Japan, 1064
Futenma, Marine Corps Air Station, Japan, 1072

1st Marine Aircraft Wing, Aviation Support Element
Kaneohe Bay Marine Corps Base, Kaneohe Bay, HI, 278

1st Marine Aircraft Wing Det
Iwakuni Marine Corps Air Station, Japan, 1073

1st Marine Division
Camp Pendleton Marine Corps Base, Oceanside, CA, 91

1st Marine Expeditionary Force (I MEF)
Camp Pendleton Marine Corps Base, Oceanside, CA, 91

1st Medical Group
Langley Air Force Base, Langley AFB, VA, 872

1st Military Intelligence Bn
221st Base Support Battalion, Germany, 992

1st Military Police, 3rd Platoon
Rose Barracks, Germany, 1027

1st Military Police Brigade (P)
Fort Lewis, Fort Lewis, WA, 921

1st Military Police Co
98th Area Support Group, Germany, 990

Military Police Plt, 1st Military Police Co, HQ & Service Co, 4th FSSG
Dayton Naval & Marine Corps Reserve Readiness Center, Dayton, OH, 656

1st Military Police, Platoon
280th Base Support Battalion, Germany, 994

1st Naval Construction Regiment
Port Hueneme, Naval Construction Battalion Center, Port Hueneme, CA, 104

1st Naval Mobile Construction Bn
Gulfport Naval Construction Battalion Center, Gulfport, MS, 482

1st Operations Group
Langley Air Force Base, Langley AFB, VA, 872

1st Personnel Command
Heidelberg Military Community, Germany, 1011

1st Personnel Group
Fort Lewis, Fort Lewis, WA, 921

1st Personnel Services Bn
Fort Riley, Fort Riley, KS, 353

1st Radio Bn
Kaneohe Bay Marine Corps Base, Kaneohe Bay, HI, 278

1st Recruit Training Bn
Parris Island Marine Corps Recruit Depot/ Eastern Recruiting Region, Parris Island, SC, 747

1st Recruiting Brigade
Fort George G Meade, Fort Meade, MD, 422

C Co-1st SATCON
Landstuhl Regional Medical Center, Germany, 1020

HHC, 1st Signal Bde, CLSCK
Camp Hialeah, Korea, Republic of, 1099

1st Space Launch Squadron
Patrick Air Force Base, Patrick AFB, FL, 221

1st Special Forces Group
Fort Lewis, Fort Lewis, WA, 921

1st Special Forces Group, 1st Bn (Airborne)
Torii Station, Japan, 1082

1st Stinger Battery
Futenma, Marine Corps Air Station, Japan, 1072

1st Support Group
Langley Air Force Base, Langley AFB, VA, 872

1st Transportation Co (Medium)
Johnson Barracks, Germany, 1012

1st United Services Credit Union
Concord Naval Weapons Station, Concord, CA, 61

1st US Army, HQ
Fort Gillem, Forest Park, GA, 247

1st US Support Bn
Multinational Force and Observers, Egypt, 985

Det 13, 1st Weather Group (USAF)
Army Transportation Center & Fort Eustis, Fort Eustis, VA, 868

2/25 AVN, B Co
Wheeler Army Airfield, Wheeler Army Airfield, HI, 293

2-501st Aviation
414th Base Support Battalion, Germany, 997

2nd Air Force, HQ
Keesler Air Force Base, Keesler AFB, MS, 487

2nd Airlift Squadron
Pope Air Force Base, Pope AFB, NC, 629

2nd Armored Cavalry Regiment
Fort Bragg, Fort Bragg, NC, 624
Fort Polk, Fort Polk, LA, 377

1st Bn, 2nd Aviation
Camp Page, Korea, Republic of, 1108

2nd Bn, 2nd Aviation
Camp Stanley, Korea, Republic of, 1111

2nd Bomb Wing
Barksdale Air Force Base, Barksdale AFB, LA, 374

2nd Brigade, 40th Engineer Combat Bn
Baumholder Military Community, H.D. Smith Barracks, Germany, 1003

2nd Brigade, ROTC
Fort Dix, Fort Dix, NJ, 555

2nd Coast Guard District Armory
Saint Louis Coast Guard Base, Saint Louis, MO, 513

2nd Engineer Bn
Camp Castle, Korea, Republic of, 1090

2md Fighter Squadron
Tyndall Air Force Base, Panama City, FL, 220

2nd Force Service Support Group (REIN)
Camp Lejeune Marine Corps Base, Camp Lejeune, NC, 618

2nd Forward Support Bn
Camp Hovey, Korea, Republic of, 1100

2nd German Air Force Training Squadron, USA
Randolph Air Force Base, Randolph AFB, TX, 814

2nd Bn, 2nd Infantry
Rose Barracks, Germany, 1027

2nd Infantry Division, 1st Brigade, HQ
Camp Casey, Korea, Republic of, 1089

2nd Bn, 2nd Infantry Division
Rose Barracks, Vilseck, Germany, 1028

2nd Infantry Division, 2nd Brigade HQ
Camp Hovey, Korea, Republic of, 1100

3rd Brigade, 2nd Infantry Division
Fort Lewis, Fort Lewis, WA, 921

2nd Infantry, Division Artillery HQ
Camp Stanley, Korea, Republic of, 1111

2nd Infantry Division, HQ
Camp Red Cloud, Korea, Republic of, 1109

2nd Judicial Circuit
Fort Bragg, Fort Bragg, NC, 624

2nd Maintenance Co
Camp Carroll, Korea, Republic of, 1088

2nd Marine Aircraft Wing (MAW)
Cherry Point Marine Corps Air Station, Cherry Point, NC, 621

2nd Marine Aircraft Wing Band
Cherry Point Marine Corps Air Station, Cherry Point, NC, 621

2nd Marine Division
Camp Lejeune Marine Corps Base, Camp Lejeune, NC, 618

II Marine Expeditionary Force (MEF)
Camp Lejeune Marine Corps Base, Camp Lejeune, NC, 618

2nd Military Police Co
Camp Casey, Korea, Republic of, 1089

2nd Platoon Truck Co (USMC)
Ebensburg Naval & Marine Corps Reserve Center, Ebensburg, PA, 702

2nd Recruit Training Bn
Parris Island Marine Corps Recruit Depot/ Eastern Recruiting Region, Parris Island, SC, 747

2nd Region (ROTC) Army Cadet Command
Army Armor Center & Fort Knox, Fort Knox, KY, 366

2nd Signal Brigade
Taylor Barracks, Germany, 1034

2nd Support Squadron
Fairchild Air Force Base, Fairchild AFB, WA, 919

2nd Surveillance, Reconnaissance & Intelligence Group
Camp Lejeune Marine Corps Base, Camp Lejeune, NC, 618

3/4 CAV, B Troop
Wheeler Army Airfield, Wheeler Army Airfield, HI, 293

3/58th Aviation
414th Base Support Battalion, Germany, 997

HQ, 3rd Air Force
Mildenhall RAF Base, United Kingdom, 1167

3rd Air Support Operations Group (USAF)
Fort Hood, Fort Hood, TX, 792

3rd Airlift Squadron
Dover Air Force Base, Dover AFB, DE, 167

3rd Armored Cavalry Regiment
Fort Bliss, El Paso, TX, 790
Fort Carson and 4th Infantry Division (Mechanized), Fort Carson, CO, 152

3rd Army, HQ
Fort McPherson, Fort McPherson, GA, 250

3rd Beach & Terminal Operations Co, 2nd Longshoreman Plt
Wilmington (DE) Naval & Marine Corps Reserve Center, Wilmington, DE, 170

3rd Bn, 345th Regiment
Army Armor Center & Fort Knox, Fort Knox, KY, 366

Support Co, 3rd Bn
Camp Blanding Training Site, Starke, FL, 232

3rd Combat Engineer Bn
Camp Hansen, Japan, 1067

3rd Component Repair Squadron
Elmendorf Air Force Base, Anchorage, AK, 19

3rd Contracting Squadron
Elmendorf Air Force Base, Anchorage, AK, 19

III Corps Artillery
Fort Sill, Fort Sill, OK, 671

III Corps, HQ Command
Fort Hood, Fort Hood, TX, 792

3rd Corps Support Command (COSCOM)
221st Base Support Battalion, Germany, 992

3rd Equipment Maintenance Squadron
Elmendorf Air Force Base, Anchorage, AK, 19

Commander, 3rd Fleet
Coronado Naval Amphibious Base, San Diego, CA, 109

3rd Flying Training Squadron
Randolph Air Force Base, Randolph AFB, TX, 814

3rd Force Reconnaissance Co (MARFORRES)
Mobile Naval & Marine Corps Reserve Center, Mobile, AL, 11

3rd Force Service Support Group
Camp Courtney, Japan, 1065
Camp Hansen, Japan, 1067

3rd Force Service Support Group, HQ
Camp Kinser, Japan, 1068

3rd Force Service Support Group, HQ & Service Bn
Camp Kinser, Japan, 1068

3rd Infantry, Co A, 1st Bn
Fort Lesley J McNair, Washington, DC, 177

3rd Infantry Division
Katterbach Air Field/Kaserne, Germany, 1015

3rd Brigade, 3rd Infantry Division (Mechanized)
Fort Benning, Fort Benning, GA, 248

3rd Infantry Division (Mechanized)
Fort Bragg, Fort Bragg, NC, 624
Fort Stewart, Hinesville, GA, 252

3rd Infantry Regiment (The Old Guard)
Fort Myer, Arlington, VA, 847

3rd Logistics Group
Elmendorf Air Force Base, Anchorage, AK, 19

3rd Logistics Support Squadron
Elmendorf Air Force Base, Anchorage, AK, 19

3rd Maintenance Bn
Camp Kinser, Japan, 1068

3rd Marine Aircraft Wing
El Toro Marine Corps Air Station, Santa Ana, CA, 132
Miramar Marine Corps Air Station, San Diego, CA, 113

III Marine Amphibious Force
Camp Courtney, Japan, 1065

III Marine Amphibious Force Command Center HQ
Camp Courtney, Japan, 1065

III Marine Division
Camp Hansen, Japan, 1067

3rd Marine Division, Landing Force 7th Fleet
Camp Courtney, Japan, 1065

III Marine Expeditionary Force
Camp Courtney, Japan, 1065
Camp Kinser, Japan, 1068

III Marine Expeditionary Force Band
Camp Foster, Japan, 1066

III Marine Expeditionary Force, HI
Kaneohe Bay Marine Corps Base, Kaneohe Bay, HI, 278

III Marine Expeditionary Force, HQ & Service Bn
Camp Hansen, Japan, 1067

3rd Marine Regiment
Kaneohe Bay Marine Corps Base, Kaneohe Bay, HI, 278
Pohakuloa Training Area, Hilo, HI, 272

3rd Medical Bn
Camp Hansen, Japan, 1067

3rd Medical Group
Elmendorf Air Force Base, Anchorage, AK, 19

3rd Military Intelligence Bn
Zoeckler Station, Korea, Republic of, 1122

3rd Military Police Group, APG Resident Agency
Aberdeen Proving Ground, Aberdeen Proving Ground, MD, 404

CIDC, Ft Benning Dist, 3rd MP Group
Fort Benning, Fort Benning, GA, 248

Commander, Third Naval Construction Brigade
Pearl Harbor Naval Complex, Pearl Harbor, HI, 283

3rd Operations Squadron
Elmendorf Air Force Base, Anchorage, AK, 19

3rd Personnel Group
Fort Hood, Fort Hood, TX, 792

3rd Recruit Training Bn
Parris Island Marine Corps Recruit Depot/ Eastern Recruiting Region, Parris Island, SC, 747

3rd Recruiting Brigade
Army Armor Center & Fort Knox, Fort Knox, KY, 366

3rd Regional Military Police Group (CID)
Fort Dix, Fort Dix, NJ, 555

3rd Regional Training Brigade
Army Armor Center & Fort Knox, Fort Knox, KY, 366

3rd Security Forces Squadron
Elmendorf Air Force Base, Anchorage, AK, 19

3rd Services Squadron
Elmendorf Air Force Base, Anchorage, AK, 19

3rd Signal Brigade
Fort Hood, Fort Hood, TX, 792

3rd Space Communications Squadron
Kapaun Air Station, Germany, 1014

3rd Space Launch Squadron
Patrick Air Force Base, Patrick AFB, FL, 221

3rd Squadron, 17th Cavalry
Fort Wainwright, Fort Wainwright, AK, 28

3rd Supply Bn
Camp Kinser, Japan, 1068

3rd Supply Squadron
Elmendorf Air Force Base, Anchorage, AK, 19

3rd Support Bn
Camp Foster, Japan, 1066

3rd Training Brigade
Fort Leonard Wood, Fort Leonard Wood, MO, 501

3rd Transportation Squadron
Elmendorf Air Force Base, Anchorage, AK, 19

3rd U.S. Infantry (The Old Guard)
Military District of Washington, Washington, DC, 179

4MD 1/24 W (NR)
Toledo Naval & Marine Corps Reserve Center, Perrysburg, OH, 662

4th Aeromedical Staging Flight
Kelly Air Force Base, Kelly AFB, TX, 807

4th Air Force, HQ
McClellan Air Force Base, McClellan AFB, CA, 81

4th Air Naval Gunfire Liaison Co (MARFORRES)
Tallahassee Naval & Marine Corps Reserve Center, Tallahassee, FL, 234
West Palm Beach Naval & Marine Corps Reserve Center, West Palm Beach, FL, 237

4th Aviation Brigade
Katterbach Air Field/Kaserne, Germany, 1015

3rd Air Defense Artillery, 4th Bn
Kitzingen Military Community, Germany, 1017

4th Bn, 11th Field Artillery
Fort Wainwright, Fort Wainwright, AK, 28

4th Bn, 123rd Theater Aviation
Fort Wainwright, Fort Wainwright, AK, 28

4th Brigade, 78th Training Division
Fort A P Hill, Bowling Green, VA, 855

4th Chemical Co
Camp Casey, Korea, Republic of, 1089

4th Combat Camera
March Air Reserve Base, March ARB, CA, 80

Co A, 4th Combat Engineer Bn
Charleston Naval & Marine Corps Reserve Center, Charleston, WV, 943

Co B, 4th Combat Engineer Bn
Richmond Naval & Marine Corps Reserve Center, Richmond, VA, 899
Roanoke Naval & Marine Corps Reserve Center, Roanoke, VA, 900

Co D, 4th Combat Engineer Bn
Knoxville Naval & Marine Corps Reserve Center, Knoxville, TN, 761

4th Field Investigations Regiment, HQ
Randolph Air Force Base, Randolph AFB, TX, 814

4th Fighter Wing (ACC)
Seymour Johnson Air Force Base, Goldsboro, NC, 625

Det, 4th Force Reconnaissance Co (MARFORRES)
Reno Naval & Marine Corps Reserve Center, Reno, NV, 542

4th Force Service Support Group
Fort Wayne Marine Corps Reserve Center, Fort Wayne, IN, 329

Ordnance Contact Team 1, 4th Force Service Support Group (FSSG)
Lawrence Marine Corps Reserve Center, Lawrence, MA, 440

4th Force Service Support Group (USMC) (4FSSG)
Tuscaloosa Armed Forces Reserve Center, Tuscaloosa, AL, 17

Det F, 4th FSSG
Green Bay Naval & Marine Corps Reserve Center, Green Bay, WI, 955
Dayton Naval & Marine Corps Reserve Readiness Center, Dayton, OH, 656

4th Infantry Division, 3rd Brigade (Mechanized)
Fort Carson and 4th Infantry Division (Mechanized), Fort Carson, CO, 152

4th Infantry Division (Mechanized)
Fort Hood, Fort Hood, TX, 792

4th LAAD
Atlanta Naval Air Station, Marietta, GA, 254

1st Longshoreman Plt, 2nd Beach & Terminal Operations Co, 4th Landing Support Bn
Savannah Naval & Marine Corps Reserve Center, Savannah, GA, 261

2nd Longshoreman Plt, 3rd Beach & Terminal Operations Co, 4th Landing Support Bn
Wilmington (NC) Naval & Marine Corps Reserve Center, Wilmington, NC, 635

Co C, 4th Light Armored Reconnaissance Bn, 4th Marine Division
Tooele Army Depot, Tooele, UT, 830

Co D, 4th Light Armored Reconnaissance Bn (MARFORRES)
Quantico Marine Corps Combat Development Command, Quantico, VA, 895

2nd Direct Support Platoon, Motor Transport Maintenance Co, 4th Maintenance Bn
Augusta Naval & Marine Corps Reserve Center, Augusta, GA, 244

4FSSG 4th Maintenance Bn CCB MSE5 (NR)
Augusta Naval & Marine Corps Reserve Center, Augusta, GA, 244

Det 1, Electrical Maintenance Co, 4th Maintenance Bn
Greensboro Naval & Marine Corps Reserve Readiness Center, Greensboro, NC, 626

Maintenance Det A, 4th Maintenance Bn
Minneapolis Naval Air Reserve Center, Minneapolis, MN, 472

HQ & Service Co, 4th Maintenance Bn
Charlotte Naval & Marine Corps Reserve Center, Charlotte, NC, 620

Motor Transport Maintenance Section, Motor Transport Co, 4th Maintenance Bn
Lehigh Valley Naval & Marine Corps Reserve Center, Allentown, PA, 694

Motor Transport Maintenance Co (-), 4th Maintenance Bn
Sacramento Naval & Marine Corps Reserve Readiness Center, Sacramento, CA, 106

Ordnance Maintenance Co(-), 4th Maintenance Bn
Waco Naval & Marine Corps Reserve Center, Waco, TX, 820

4th Marine Aircraft Wing
New Orleans Naval Support Activity, New Orleans, LA, 386

4th Marine Division
New Orleans Naval Support Activity, New Orleans, LA, 386

3rd Bn, 4th Marine Division
Twentynine Palms Marine Corps Air Ground Combat Center, Twentynine Palms, CA, 139

4th Marine Division, Communications Co, HQ Bn, 4th
Cincinnati Naval & Marine Corps Reserve Center, Cincinnati, OH, 645

Military Police Co, HQ Bn, 4th Marine Division
St Paul Naval & Marine Corps Reserve Center, Saint Paul, MN, 476

HQ Det 6 (Rein), 4th Marine Division
Houston Naval & Marine Corps Reserve Readiness Center, Houston, TX, 805

HQ Bn 4th Marine Division (USMC)
Ebensburg Naval & Marine Corps Reserve Center, Ebensburg, PA, 702

4th Marine Regiment
Camp Schwab, Japan, 1070

Co A, 4th Medical Bn
Knoxville Naval & Marine Corps Reserve Center, Knoxville, TN, 761

Collecting & Clearing Co D, 4th Medical Bn
Pittsburgh Naval & Marine Corps Reserve Readiness Center, North Versailles, PA, 710

4th Quartermaster Det
Camp Hialeah, Korea, Republic of, 1099

Co A, 4th Reconnaissance Bn
San Antonio Naval & Marine Corps Reserve Center, San Antonio, TX, 816

4th Reconnaissance Bn, Co B (Marine Corps Reserve)
Billings Naval & Marine Corps Reserve Center, Billings, MT, 517

Co C, 4th Reconnaissance Bn
San Antonio Naval & Marine Corps Reserve Center, San Antonio, TX, 816

D Co, 4th Reconnaissance Bn
Albuquerque Naval & Marine Corps Reserve Center, Albuquerque, NM, 568

E Co, 4th Reconnaissance Bn (USMC Reserve)
Elmendorf Air Force Base, Anchorage, AK, 19

HQ & Service Co, 4th Reconnaissance Bn
San Antonio Naval & Marine Corps Reserve Center, San Antonio, TX, 816

4th Recruit Training Bn
Parris Island Marine Corps Recruit Depot/ Eastern Recruiting Region, Parris Island, SC, 747

4th SCAMP Platoon (MARFORRES)
Mobile Naval & Marine Corps Reserve Center, Mobile, AL, 11

4th Services Squadron
Fort Fisher Air Force Recreation Area, Kure Beach, NC, 628

4th Special Operations Support Command (Prov)
Fort Shafter, Fort Shafter, HI, 267

Ammunition Co, 4th Supply Bn
Greenville Naval & Marine Corps Reserve Center, Greenville, SC, 744

Det 2, Supply Co, 4th Supply Bn
Topeka Naval & Marine Corps Reserve Center, Topeka, KS, 362

SASSY Management Unit (SMU), Supply Co, 4th Supply Bn
Raleigh Naval & Marine Corps Reserve Center, Raleigh, NC, 631

4th Tank Bn
Miramar Marine Corps Air Station, San Diego, CA, 113

Anti-Tank (TOW) Co, 4th Tank Bn
Tulsa Naval & Marine Corps Reserve Center, Broken Arrow, OK, 670

C Co, 4th Tank Bn, 4th Marine Division
Boise Naval & Marine Corps Reserve Center, Boise, ID, 296

4th Tank Bn, Co C (Marine Corps Reserve)
Boise Air Terminal, Air National Guard Base, Boise, ID, 295

TOW Scout Plt, HQ & Service Co, 4th Tank Bn
Amarillo Naval & Marine Corps Reserve Center, Amarillo, TX, 775

4th Training Brigade
Fort Jackson, Columbia, SC, 740

5/2 Air Defense Artillery
Bamberg Military Community, Germany, 1001

5/7 Air Defense Artillery
414th Base Support Battalion, Germany, 997

5/29th Ordnance Det
Rose Barracks, Vilseck, Germany, 1028

5th Bn, 5th Air Defense Artillery, B Co
Camp Hovey, Korea, Republic of, 1100

5th Bn, 5th Air Defense Artillery, C Co
Camp Casey, Korea, Republic of, 1089

5th Bn, 5th Air Defense Artillery, D Battery
Camp Stanley, Korea, Republic of, 1111

5th Bn, 5th Air Defense Artillery, HQ Battery
Camp Stanley, Korea, Republic of, 1111

5th Air Force
Yokota Air Base, Japan, 1085

5th Army, HQ
Fort Sam Houston, Fort Sam Houston, TX, 794

5th Army West
Fort Lewis, Fort Lewis, WA, 921

5th Bomb Wing
Minot Air Force Base, Minot AFB, ND, 642

5th Combat Communications Group
Robins Air Force Base, Robins AFB, GA, 259

5th Comptroller Squadron
Minot Air Force Base, Minot AFB, ND, 642

V Corps, HQ
Heidelberg Military Community, Germany, 1011

5th Engineer Bn (Combat)(Mechanized)
Fort Leonard Wood, Fort Leonard Wood, MO, 501

5th Flying Training Flight (AFRC)
Vance Air Force Base, Vance AFB, OK, 681

5th Logistics Group
Minot Air Force Base, Minot AFB, ND, 642

5th Medical Group
Minot Air Force Base, Minot AFB, ND, 642

5th Operations Group
Minot Air Force Base, Minot AFB, ND, 642

5th PMU
Camp Carroll, Korea, Republic of, 1088

5th Recruiting Brigade
Fort Sam Houston, Fort Sam Houston, TX, 794

5th Signal Command
Funari Barracks, Germany, 1008
Taylor Barracks, Germany, 1034

5th Space Launch Squadron
Patrick Air Force Base, Patrick AFB, FL, 221

5th Space Operations Squadron
Onizuka Air Station, Sunnyvale, CA, 136

5th Space Surveillance Squadron
Feltwell RAF Base, United Kingdom, 1158

5th Space Warning Squadron
Joint Defense Facility Nurrungar, Australia, 970

5th Special Forces Group (Airborne)
Fort Campbell, Fort Campbell, KY, 365

5th Support Group
Minot Air Force Base, Minot AFB, ND, 642

5th Weather Squadron, Det 21
Hunter Army Air Field, Savannah, GA, 260

6th Air Defense Artillery Brigade
Fort Bliss, El Paso, TX, 790

6th Air Refueling Wing
MacDill Air Force Base, MacDill AFB, FL, 209

6th Allied Tactical Air Force
Izmir Air Station, Turkey, 1153
Vecihi Akin Garrison, Turkey, 1154

6th Area NCO Academy
Parks Reserve Forces Training Area, Dublin, CA, 62

6th Area Support Group
6th Area Support Group, Stuttgart, Germany, 988

6th Army Veterinary Food Inspection Det, Tracy Branch
Defense Distribution Region West, Stockton, CA, 134

6th Aviation Co
Caserma Ederle/Vicenza Military Community, Vincenza, Italy, 1060

6th Bn MESS Augmentation
New Mexico National Guard State Headquarters, Santa Fe, NM, 573

HHB, 6th Bn (MUA) 200th ADA
New Mexico National Guard State Headquarters, Santa Fe, NM, 573

A Co, 6th Communications Bn
Amityville Naval & Marine Corps Reserve
Center, Amityville, NY, 576

**Communications Co, 6th
Communications Bn**
Amityville Naval & Marine Corps Reserve
Center, Amityville, NY, 576

**Communications Support Co, 6th
Communications Bn**
Bronx Naval & Marine Corps Reserve Cen-
ter, Bronx, NY, 578

HQ, 6th Communications Bn
Bronx Naval & Marine Corps Reserve Center, Bronx, NY, 578

HQ Co, 6th Communications Bn
Bronx Naval & Marine Corps Reserve Center, Bronx, NY, 578

A Co, 6th Engineer Support Bn
Peoria Naval & Marine Corps Reserve
Center, Peoria, IL, 313

**3rd & 4th Bulk Fuel Platoons, B Co,
6th Engineer Support Bn**
Bakersfield Naval & Marine Corps Reserve Center, Bakersfield, CA, 56

**B Co (REIN), 6th Engineer Support
Bn**
South Bend Naval & Marine Corps Re-
serve Center, South Bend, IN, 338

**Bridge Co A, 6th Engineer Support
Bn**
Battle Creek Naval & Marine Corps Re-
serve Center, Battle Creek, MI, 450

**Bridge Co B, 6th Engineer Support
Bn**
Eugene Naval & Marine Corps Reserve
Center, Eugene, OR, 685

**Bulk Fuel Co A, 6th Engineer
Support Bn**
Tucson Naval & Marine Corps Reserve
Center, Tucson, AZ, 44

**3rd & 4th Plt, Bulk Fuel Co C, 6th
Engineer Support Bn**
Wilmington (DE) Naval & Marine Corps
Reserve Center, Wilmington, DE, 170

**Engineer Co, 6th Engineer Support
Bn**
Salem Naval & Marine Corps Reserve Cen-
ter, Salem, OR, 693

**Engineer Support Co, 6th Engineer
Support Bn**
Battle Creek Naval & Marine Corps Re-
serve Center, Battle Creek, MI, 450
Portland Naval & Marine Corps Reserve
Readiness Center, Portland, OR, 688

**HQ & Service Co, 6th Engineer
Support Bn**
Portland Naval & Marine Corps Reserve
Readiness Center, Portland, OR, 688

4th FSSG, 6th Engineers (NR)
Portland Naval & Marine Corps Reserve
Readiness Center, Portland, OR, 688

**1st Brigade, 6th Infantry Division
(L)**
Fort Richardson, Fort Richardson, AK, 27

**1st Brigade, 6th Infantry Division
(Light)**
Fort Wainwright, Fort Wainwright, AK, 28

6th Marine Corps District, HQ
Parris Island Marine Corps Recruit Depot/
Eastern Recruiting Region, Parris Is-
land, SC, 747

HQ 6th Military Police Group (CID)
Fort Lewis, Fort Lewis, WA, 921

6th Missile Warning Squadron
Massachusetts Military Reservation/Otis
Air National Guard Base, Cape Cod,
MA, 437

**1st Truck Plt, Direct Support Co
A&B, 6th Motor Transport Bn**
New Haven Naval & Marine Corps Re-
serve Center, New Haven, CT, 160

**Direct Support Motor Transport Co
B, 6th Motor Transport Bn**
Lubbock Naval & Marine Corps Reserve
Center, Lubbock, TX, 811

**General Support Motor Transport
Co, 6th Motor Transport Bn**
Providence Naval & Marine Corps Re-
serve Center, Providence, RI, 729

6th Ordnance Bn
Camp Carroll, Korea, Republic of, 1088

6th Space Operations Squadron
Offutt Air Force Base, Offutt AFB, NE,
530

6th Support Center
Camp Henry, Korea, Republic of, 1098

7th Air Force, HQ
Osan Air Base, Korea, Republic of, 1118

**7th Airborne Command & Control
Squadron (ACC)**
Keesler Air Force Base, Keesler AFB, MS,
487

7th Army, HQ
Campbell Barracks, Germany, 1005
Heidelberg Military Community, Ger-
many, 1011

**7th Army Reserve Command
Europe**
Heidelberg Military Community, Ger-
many, 1011

7th Army Training Command
100th Area Support Group, Germany, 991

7th Bomb Wing
Dyess Air Force Base, Abilene, TX, 773

7th Brigade, 84th Division
84th Division (IT) HQ, Milwaukee, WI,
960

7th Cavalry, 4th Squadron, A Troop
Camp Garry Owen, Korea, Republic of,
1094

7th Cavalry, 4th Squadron (Air)
Camp Stanton, Korea, Republic of, 1112

7th Cavalry, 4th Squadron, B Troop
Camp Garry Owen, Korea, Republic of,
1094

7th Cavalry, 4th Squadron, C Troop
Camp Garry Owen, Korea, Republic of,
1094

7th Cavalry HQ, 4th Squadron
Camp Garry Owen, Korea, Republic of,
1094

**7th Combined Arms Training
Center**
Rose Barracks, Germany, 1027

7th Command Support Group
Bamberg Military Community, Germany,
1001

7th Communications Bn
Camp Courtney, Japan, 1065
Camp Hansen, Japan, 1067

7th Fighter Squadron
Holloman Air Force Base, Holloman AFB,
NM, 571

7th Marine Regiment (Reinforced)
Twentynine Palms Marine Corps Air
Ground Combat Center, Twentynine
Palms, CA, 139

7th Naval Mobile Construction Bn
Gulfport Naval Construction Battalion Center, Gulfport, MS, 482

7th Ranger Bn
Fort Bliss, El Paso, TX, 790

7th Signal Brigade
Taylor Barracks, Germany, 1034

**7th Space Operations Squadron
(USAFR)**
Falcon Air Force Base, Falcon AFB, CO,
151

7th Space Warning Squadron
Beale Air Force Base, Beale AFB, CA, 58

**7th Special Forces Group, 3rd Bn,
Co C**
Fort Clayton, Panama, 1133

**7th Special Forces Group, 3rd Bn,
Co C (Airborne)**
Fort Davis, Panama, 1134

**7th Transportation Group, 11th
Transportation Bn**
Fort Story, Fort Story, VA, 871

**7th Transportation Group
(Composite)**
Army Transportation Center & Fort Eustis,
Fort Eustis, VA, 868

7th Weather Station, Det 10
Giebelstadt Army Airfield, Germany, 1010

8th Air Force, HQ
Barksdale Air Force Base, Barksdale AFB,
LA, 374

8th Area Support Team (Livorno)
Caserma Ederle/Vicenza Military Community, Vincenza, Italy, 1060

8th Army
Yongsan Army Garrison, Korea, Republic of, 1121

8th Army Confinement Facility
Camp Humphreys, Korea, Republic of, 1102

8th Coast Guard District
8th Coast Guard District, New Orleans, LA, 380

8th Fighter Squadron
Holloman Air Force Base, Holloman AFB, NM, 571

8th Fighter Wing
Kunsan Air Base, Korea, Republic of, 1117

8th Finance Support
Baumholder Military Community, H.D. Smith Barracks, Germany, 1003

8th Flying Training Squadron
Vance Air Force Base, Vance AFB, OK, 681

8th Logistics Group
Kunsan Air Base, Korea, Republic of, 1117

8th Marine Corps District, Headquarters
New Orleans Naval Support Activity, New Orleans, LA, 386

8th Medical Brigade
New York Area Command & Fort Hamilton, Brooklyn, NY, 581

8th Medical Group
Kunsan Air Base, Korea, Republic of, 1117

8th Operations Group
Kunsan Air Base, Korea, Republic of, 1117

8th Ordnance Det
Camp Red Cloud, Korea, Republic of, 1109

8th Space Warning Squadron
Eldorado Air Force Station, Eldorado, TX, 791

8th Support Group
Kunsan Air Base, Korea, Republic of, 1117

4MD 8 Tank Bn A (NR)
Louisville Naval Reserve Center, Louisville, KY, 371

A Co, 8th Tank Bn (USMC)
Army Armor Center & Fort Knox, Fort Knox, KY, 366

B Co, 8th Tank Bn
Syracuse Naval & Marine Corps Reserve Center, Mattydale, NY, 593

HQ, 8th Tank Bn
Rochester Naval & Marine Corps Reserve Center, Rochester, NY, 603

HQ & Service Co, 8th Tank Bn
Rochester Naval & Marine Corps Reserve Center, Rochester, NY, 603

TOW & Scout Platoons, 8th Tank Bn
Miami Naval & Marine Corps Reserve Readiness Center, Hialeah, FL, 198

8th Transportation Brigade
Army Transportation Center & Fort Eustis, Fort Eustis, VA, 868

I Co, 71st Transportation Bn, 8th Transportation Brigade
Fort Story, Fort Story, VA, 871

8th US Army Milk Plant
K-16 (Army Airfield), Korea, Republic of, 1115

8th US Army Simulated Flight Training Facility
K-16 (Army Airfield), Korea, Republic of, 1115

9th Air Expeditionary Support Group
Cairo West AFB, Egypt, 983

9th Air Force, HQ
Shaw Air Force Base, Shaw AFB, SC, 749

9th Airlift Squadron
Dover Air Force Base, Dover AFB, DE, 167

9th Army Reserve Command
Fort DeRussy, Honolulu, HI, 273

9th Coast Guard District HQ
9th Coast Guard District Headquarters, Cleveland, OH, 648

9th Comptroller Squadron
Beale Air Force Base, Beale AFB, CA, 58

9th Corps, US Army Japan, HQ
Camp Zama, Japan, 1071

9th Engineer Support Bn
Camp Hansen, Japan, 1067

9th Engineers
280th Base Support Battalion, Germany, 994

9th Fighter Squadron
Holloman Air Force Base, Holloman AFB, NM, 571

9th Infantry, 1st Bn
Camp Hovey, Korea, Republic of, 1100

9th Infantry, 2nd Bn
Camp Casey, Korea, Republic of, 1089

9th Logistics Group
Beale Air Force Base, Beale AFB, CA, 58

9th Marine Amphibious Brigade
Camp Courtney, Japan, 1065

9th Marine Corps District, Headquarters Unit
9th Marine Corps District, Shawnee Mission, KS, 358

9th Marine Regiment
Camp Hansen, Japan, 1067

9th Medical Group
Beale Air Force Base, Beale AFB, CA, 58

9th Military Police Det
Coleman Barracks, Germany, 1006

9th Naval Construction Regiment
Fort Worth, Naval Air Station, Joint Reserve Base, Fort Worth, TX, 796

9th Operations Group
Beale Air Force Base, Beale AFB, CA, 58

9th Reconnaissance Wing
Beale Air Force Base, Beale AFB, CA, 58

9th Support Group
Beale Air Force Base, Beale AFB, CA, 58

10th Aeromedical Staging Flight
Andrews Air Force Base, Andrews AFB, MD, 407

10th Air Base Wing
US Air Force Academy, Colorado Springs, CO, 146

10th Air Force (AFRES)
Fort Worth, Naval Air Station, Joint Reserve Base, Fort Worth, TX, 796

10th Area Support Group
Torii Station, Japan, 1082

10th Army Support Group, Det
Camp Kinser, Japan, 1068

10th Fighter Wing Clinic
Upwood RAF Base, United Kingdom, 1169

10th Infantry Regiment
Fort Leonard Wood, Fort Leonard Wood, MO, 501

10th Military Police Bn (ABN)
Fort Bragg, Fort Bragg, NC, 624

10th Mountain Division (L)
Fort Bragg, Fort Bragg, NC, 624
Fort Drum, Fort Drum, NY, 585

10th Space Warning Squadron
Cavalier Air Station, Cavalier AS, ND, 637

10th Special Forces Group
Fort Carson and 4th Infantry Division (Mechanized), Fort Carson, CO, 152

11th Air Defense Artillery Brigade
Fort Bliss, El Paso, TX, 790

11th Air Force
Elmendorf Air Force Base, Anchorage, AK, 19

11th Armored Cavalry Regiment
Fort Irwin, National Training Center, Fort Irwin, CA, 70

11th Aviation Brigade
Storck Barracks, Illesheim, Germany, 1032

11th Chemical Bn
Fort McClellan, Anniston, AL, 2

11th Civil Engineering Squadron
Bolling Air Force Base, Washington, DC, 173

11th Coast Guard District
Alameda Coast Guard Integrated Support Command, Alameda, CA, 54

11th Communications Squadron
Bolling Air Force Base, Washington, DC, 173

Det 2, 11th Contingency Hospital
Barksdale Air Force Base, Barksdale AFB, LA, 374

11th Dental Clinic
Iwakuni Marine Corps Air Station, Japan, 1073

11th Infantry Regiment
Fort Benning, Fort Benning, GA, 248

11th Mission Support Squadron
Bolling Air Force Base, Washington, DC, 173

11th Reconnaissance Squadron
Nellis Air Force Base, Nellis AFB, NV, 541

11th Security Forces Squadron
Bolling Air Force Base, Washington, DC, 173

11th Signal Brigade (USA)
Administrative Support Unit, South West Asia, Bahrain, 973

11th Transportation Co (Heavy Equipment Transport)
Johnson Barracks, Germany, 1012

11th Wing
Bolling Air Force Base, Washington, DC, 173

12th Air Force, HQ
Davis-Monthan Air Force Base, Tucson, AZ, 42

12th Aviation Bn
Davison Army Airfield, Fort Belvoir, VA, 864

12th Aviation Brigade
221st Base Support Battalion, Germany, 992

12th Chemical Co
Kitzingen Military Community, Germany, 1017

12th Comptroller Squadron
Randolph Air Force Base, Randolph AFB, TX, 814

12th Flying Training Wing
Randolph Air Force Base, Randolph AFB, TX, 814

12th Judge Advocate General Det
Fort Jackson, Columbia, SC, 740

12th Logistics Group
Randolph Air Force Base, Randolph AFB, TX, 814

HQ, 12th Marine Corps District
San Diego Marine Corps Recruit Depot, San Diego, CA, 119

12th Marine Regiment
Camp Foster, Japan, 1066

12th Medical Group
Randolph Air Force Base, Randolph AFB, TX, 814

12th MP Det (Criminal Investigation Division)
Army Transportation Center & Fort Eustis, Fort Eustis, VA, 868

12th Operations Group
Randolph Air Force Base, Randolph AFB, TX, 814

12th Space Warning Squadron
Thule Air Base, Greenland, 1041

12th Support Group
Randolph Air Force Base, Randolph AFB, TX, 814

13th Air Force
Andersen Air Force Base, Guam, 1043

13th Coast Guard District Office, Seattle
13th Coast Guard District Office, Seattle, WA, 928

13th Corps Support Command (COSCOM)
Fort Hood, Fort Hood, TX, 792

13th Finance Brigade
Fort Hood, Fort Hood, TX, 792

13th Intelligence Squadron
Beale Air Force Base, Beale AFB, CA, 58

13th Medical Det
414th Base Support Battalion, Germany, 997

13th Military Police Co
Caserma Ederle/Vicenza Military Community, Vincenza, Italy, 1060

13th Ordnance Det
Fort Gillem, Forest Park, GA, 247

13th Space Warning Squadron
Clear Air Force Station, AK, 22

14th Air Force
Vandenberg Air Force Base, Vandenberg AFB, CA, 141

14th Army Band
Fort McClellan, Anniston, AL, 2

14th Flying Training Wing (AETC)
Columbus Air Force Base, Columbus AFB, MS, 479

Battery A, 1st Bn, 14th Marine Regiment
Spokane Naval & Marine Corps Reserve Readiness Center, Spokane, WA, 934

Battery F, 2nd Bn, 14th Marine Regiment
Oklahoma City Naval & Marine Corps Reserve Readiness Center, Oklahoma City, OK, 676

D Battery, 2nd Bn, 14th Marine Regiment
Waterloo Marine Corps Reserve Center, Waterloo, IA, 350

G Battery, 3rd Bn, 14th Marine Regiment
West Trenton Marine Corps Reserve Center, West Trenton, NJ, 567

Battery M, 4th Bn, 14th Marine Regiment
Chattanooga Naval & Marine Corps Reserve Center, Chattanooga, TN, 758

Battery N, 5th Bn, 14th Marine Regiment
El Paso Naval & Marine Corps Reserve Readiness Center, El Paso, TX, 789

HQ Battery, 4th Bn, 14th Marine Regiment
Bessemer Naval & Marine Corps Reserve Readiness Center, Bessemer, AL, 3

HQ Battery, 5th Bn, 14th Marine Regiment
Seal Beach Naval Weapons Station, Seal Beach, CA, 133

L Battery, 4th Bn, 14th Marine Regiment
Bessemer Naval & Marine Corps Reserve Readiness Center, Bessemer, AL, 3

O Battery, 5th Bn, 14th Marine Regiment
Seal Beach Naval Weapons Station, Seal Beach, CA, 133

14th Marines
Dallas Naval Air Station, Dallas, TX, 783
Fort Worth, Naval Air Station, Joint Reserve Base, Fort Worth, TX, 796

14th Medical Group
Columbus Air Force Base, Columbus AFB, MS, 479

14th Operations Group
Columbus Air Force Base, Columbus AFB, MS, 479

14th Support Group
Columbus Air Force Base, Columbus AFB, MS, 479

14th Transportation Bn
Caserma Ederle/Vicenza Military Community, Vincenza, Italy, 1060

15th Air Base Squadron
Wheeler Army Airfield, Wheeler Army Airfield, HI, 293

15th Air Base Wing
Hickam Air Force Base, Hickam AFB, HI, 271

15th Air Force, HQ
Travis Air Force Base, Travis AFB, CA, 137

1st Bn, 15th Field Artillery
Camp Casey, Korea, Republic of, 1089

15th Regimental Signal Brigade
Army Signal Center & Fort Gordon, Fort Gordon, GA, 249

15th SPT6, Det 1
Bellows Air Force Station, Waimanalo, HI, 291

16th Air Force
Aviano Air Base, Italy, 1051

16th Cavalry Regiment
Army Armor Center & Fort Knox, Fort Knox, KY, 366

16th Combat Engineering Co
16th Combat Equipment Company, Belgium, 974

16th Corps Support Group
414th Base Support Battalion, Germany, 997

16th Engineer Brigade
Bamberg Military Community, Germany, 1001

16th Expeditionary Operations Group
Istres Air Base, France, 986

16th MEDLOG Bn
Camp Carroll, Korea, Republic of, 1088

16th Military Police Brigade
Fort Bragg, Fort Bragg, NC, 624

16th Space Surveillance Squadron (SPACECOM)
Eareckson Air Force Station, AK, 23

16th Special Operations Wing (SOW)
Hurlburt Field, Hurlburt Field, FL, 200

17th Air Support Operations Squadron
Fort Benning, Fort Benning, GA, 248

17th Area Support Group
Camp Zama, Japan, 1071

17th Area Support Group, HQ
Camp Zama, Japan, 1071

17th Coast Guard District
17th Coast Guard District, Juneau, AK, 29

17th Field Artillery, 2nd Bn
Camp Hovey, Korea, Republic of, 1100

1st Bn, 17th Infantry
Fort Wainwright, Fort Wainwright, AK, 28

17th Medical Group
Goodfellow Air Force Base, Goodfellow AFB, TX, 801

17th Signal Bn
Kitzingen Military Community, Germany, 1017

17th Support Group
Goodfellow Air Force Base, Goodfellow AFB, TX, 801

17th Training Group
Goodfellow Air Force Base, Goodfellow AFB, TX, 801

17th Training Wing
Goodfellow Air Force Base, Goodfellow AFB, TX, 801

18th Aeromedical Staging Facility
Landstuhl Regional Medical Center, Germany, 1020

18th Air Support Operations Group (ACC)
Pope Air Force Base, Pope AFB, NC, 629

XVIII Airborne Corps
Fort Bragg, Fort Bragg, NC, 624

XVIII Airborne Corps Artillery
Fort Bragg, Fort Bragg, NC, 624

18th Aviation Brigade
Fort Bragg, Fort Bragg, NC, 624

1st Squadron, 18th Cavalry, HQ
18th Cavalry, 1st Squadron, HQ, Ontario, CA, 92

HHT, 1st Squadron, 18th Cavalry
18th Cavalry, 1st Squadron, HQ, Ontario, CA, 92

Troop C, 1st Squadron, 18th Cavalry
18th Cavalry, 1st Squadron, HQ, Ontario, CA, 92

18th Civil Engineer Group
Kadena Air Base, Japan, 1074

18th Combat Equipment Co
18th Combat Equipment Company, Netherlands, 1125

18th Combat Equipment Co, Brunssum
254th Base Support Battalion, Netherlands, 1127

18th Corps Finance Group
Fort Bragg, Fort Bragg, NC, 624

18th Corps Support Bn
414th Base Support Battalion, Germany, 997

18th Field Hospital (HUH), 99th Regional Support Command (Oakland, PA)(USAR)
Fort Story, Fort Story, VA, 871

18th Fighter Squadron
Eielson Air Force Base, Eielson AFB, AK, 24

18th Logistics Group
Kadena Air Base, Japan, 1074

18th Medical Group
Kadena Air Base, Japan, 1074

18th Military Brigade
Coleman Barracks, Germany, 1006

18th Military Intelligence, Maastricht
254th Base Support Battalion, Netherlands, 1127

18th Operations Group
Kadena Air Base, Japan, 1074

18th Personnel Group
Fort Bragg, Fort Bragg, NC, 624

18th Space Surveillance Squadron, Det 2
Diego Garcia, Naval Support Facility, Diego Garcia, 982

18th Space Surveillance Squadron, Det 3
Maui Space Surveillance Complex, Kihei, HI, 280

18th Space Surveillance Squadron, Det 4
Diego Garcia, Naval Support Facility, Diego Garcia, 982

18th Support Group
Kadena Air Base, Japan, 1074

18th Test Flight Squadron
Hurlburt Field, Hurlburt Field, FL, 200

18th Test Squadron
Edwards Air Force Base, Edwards AFB, CA, 63

18th Weather Squadron
Fort Bragg, Fort Bragg, NC, 624

18th Wing
Kadena Air Base, Japan, 1074

19th Air Force
Vance Air Force Base, Vance AFB, OK, 681

19th Air Force, HQ
Randolph Air Force Base, Randolph AFB, TX, 814

19th Air Refueling Group
Robins Air Force Base, Robins AFB, GA, 259

19th Combat Equipment Co
19th Combat Equipment Company, Netherlands, 1126

19th Combat Equipment Co, Vriezenveen
254th Base Support Battalion, Netherlands, 1127

19th Fighter Squadron
Elmendorf Air Force Base, Anchorage, AK, 19

19th Maintenance Co
414th Base Support Battalion, Germany, 997

19th Special Forces Group, Co C, 2nd Bn (A)
Camp Dawson, Kingwood, WV, 947

19th Special Forces Group, Det 1, Support Co (A)
Camp Dawson, Kingwood, WV, 947

19th Theater Army Area Command
Camp George, Korea, Republic of, 1095
Camp Walker, Korea, Republic of, 1113

1st Bn, 149th Armor Division, Co B
Western Mobilization & Training Complex, Paso Robles, CA, 95

1st Marine Aircraft Wing
Kaneohe Bay Marine Corps Base, Kaneohe Bay, HI, 278

20th Air Force
Francis E Warren Air Force Base, F E Warren AFB, WY, 967

20th Area Defense Counsel, Det QD
Shaw Air Force Base, Shaw AFB, SC, 749

20th Area Support Group
Camp Henry, Korea, Republic of, 1098
Camp MacNab (Cheju Do), Korea, Republic of, 1105

20th Combat Equipment Co, Coevorden
254th Base Support Battalion, Netherlands, 1127

20th Engineer Brigade
Fort Bragg, Fort Bragg, NC, 624

20th Medical Det
Anderson Barracks, Germany, 998

20th Naval Construction Regiment
Gulfport Naval Construction Battalion Center, Gulfport, MS, 482

20th Special Forces (General Purposes, Airborne) Det A, 3rd Bn (VA ARNG)
Fort A P Hill, Bowling Green, VA, 855

20th Special Forces Group (Airborne)
Camp Blanding Training Site, Starke, FL, 232

3rd Bn, 20th Special Forces Group (Airborne), HQ & HQ Det
Camp Blanding Training Site, Starke, FL, 232

20th Support Group
Camp Carroll, Korea, Republic of, 1088

20th Support Group, Pusan
Camp Hialeah, Korea, Republic of, 1099

21st Air Force
McGuire Air Force Base, McGuire AFB, NJ, 561

21st Cavalry Brigade (Air Combat)
Fort Hood, Fort Hood, TX, 792

21st OG/USAFLO
Fylingdales-Moor RAF Base, United Kingdom, 1159

21st Space Operations Squadron
Onizuka Air Station, Sunnyvale, CA, 136

21st Space Wing
Peterson Air Force Base, Peterson AFB, CO, 156

21st Special Tactics Squadron (AFSOC)
Pope Air Force Base, Pope AFB, NC, 629

21st Theater Army Area Command (TAACOM)
Kaiserslautern Military Community, Germany, 1013

22nd Air Force, HQ (AFRC)
Dobbins Air Reserve Base, Marietta, GA, 257

22nd Air Refueling Wing
McConnell Air Force Base, McConnell AFB, KS, 354

22nd Area Support Group
22nd Area Support Group, Italy, 1050
Camp Darby, Livorno Military Community, Italy, 1052
Caserma Ederle/Vicenza Military Community, Vincenza, Italy, 1060

22nd Combat Equipment Co, Eygelshoven
254th Base Support Battalion, Netherlands, 1127

22rd Fighter Squadron
Spangdahlem Air Base, Germany, 1030

22nd Medical Det
414th Base Support Battalion, Germany, 997

22nd Military Police Det (CID)
Fort Lewis, Fort Lewis, WA, 921

22nd Signal Brigade
223rd Base Support Battalion, Germany, 993

22nd Special Tactics Squadron
McChord Air Force Base, McChord AFB, WA, 923

22nd Tactical Air Support Squadron
Wheeler Army Airfield, Wheeler Army Airfield, HI, 293

22nd Wing
22nd Wing, Canada, 979

23rd Bomb Squadron
Minot Air Force Base, Minot AFB, ND, 642

23rd Chemical Bn
Camp Carroll, Korea, Republic of, 1088

23rd Combat Equipment Co
23rd Combat Equipment Company, Luxembourg, 1123

23rd Fighter Group (ACC)
Pope Air Force Base, Pope AFB, NC, 629

23rd Fighter Squadron
Spangdahlem Air Base, Germany, 1030

23rd Intelligence Squadron
Patrick Air Force Base, Patrick AFB, FL, 221

HQ, 3rd Bn, 23rd Marine Regiment
New Orleans Naval & Marine Corps Reserve Readiness Center, New Orleans, LA, 385

HQ & Service Co, 3rd Bn, 23rd Marine Regiment
New Orleans Naval & Marine Corps Reserve Readiness Center, New Orleans, LA, 385

B Co, 1st Bn, 23rd Marine Regiment
Shreveport Naval & Marine Corps Reserve Center, Bossier City, LA, 376

Co A, 1st Bn, 23rd Marine Regiment
Houston Naval & Marine Corps Reserve Readiness Center, Houston, TX, 805

HQ, 1st Bn, 23rd Marine Regiment
Houston Naval & Marine Corps Reserve Readiness Center, Houston, TX, 805

HQ & Service Co, 1st Bn, 23rd Marine Regiment
Houston Naval & Marine Corps Reserve Readiness Center, Houston, TX, 805

Weapons Co, 1st Bn, 23rd Marine Regiment
Austin Naval & Marine Corps Reserve Center, Austin, TX, 776

E Co, 2nd Bn, 23rd Marine Regiment
San Bruno Naval & Marine Corps Reserve Center, San Bruno, CA, 108

HQ, 2nd Bn, 23rd Marine Regiment
Encino Naval & Marine Corps Reserve Center, Encino, CA, 67

HQ & Service Co, 2nd Bn, 23rd Marine Regiment
Encino Naval & Marine Corps Reserve Center, Encino, CA, 67

Weapons Co, 2nd Bn, 23rd Marine Regiment
Port Hueneme, Naval Construction Battalion Center, Port Hueneme, CA, 104

L Co, 3rd Bn, 23rd Marine Regiment
Montgomery Marine Corps Reserve Center, Montgomery, AL, 15

Weapons Co, 3rd Bn, 23rd Marine Regiment
Baton Rouge Naval & Marine Corps Reserve Center, Baton Rouge, LA, 375

HQ, 23rd Marine Regiment
San Bruno Naval & Marine Corps Reserve Center, San Bruno, CA, 108

HQ Co, 23rd Marine Regiment
San Bruno Naval & Marine Corps Reserve Center, San Bruno, CA, 108

23rd Quartermaster Brigade
Fort Lee, Fort Lee, VA, 869

23rd Space Operations Squadron
New Boston Air Station, New Boston AS, NH, 549

23rd Support Group
Camp Humphreys, Korea, Republic of, 1102

24th Air Operations Squadron
Ramstein Air Base, Germany, 1023

24th Air Postal Squadron
Howard Air Force Base, Panama, 1136

24th Air Support Operations Squadron
Howard Air Force Base, Panama, 1136

24th Aviation Brigade
Hunter Army Air Field, Savannah, GA, 260

24th Communications Squadron
Howard Air Force Base, Panama, 1136

24th Contracting Squadron
Howard Air Force Base, Panama, 1136

24th Corps Support Group
Fort Stewart, Hinesville, GA, 252

24th Logistics Group
Howard Air Force Base, Panama, 1136

24th Logistics Support Flight
Howard Air Force Base, Panama, 1136

A Co, 1st Bn, 24th Marine Regiment
Grand Rapids Naval & Marine Corps Reserve Center, Grand Rapids, MI, 457

B Co, 1st Bn, 24th Marine Regiment
Saginaw Naval & Marine Corps Reserve Center, Saginaw, MI, 461

C Co, 1st Bn, 24th Marine Regiment
Lansing Naval & Marine Corps Reserve Center, Lansing, MI, 460

Co G, 2nd Bn, 24th Marine Regiment
Madison Naval & Marine Corps Reserve Center, Madison, WI, 957

E Co (-), 2nd Bn, 24th Marine Regiment
Des Moines Naval & Marine Corps Reserve Center, Des Moines, IA, 343

K Co, 3rd Bn, 24th Marine Regiment
Terre Haute Marine Corps Reserve Center, Terre Haute, IN, 340

Weapons Co, 3rd Bn, 24th Marine Regiment
Springfield Naval & Marine Corps Reserve Center, Springfield, MO, 515

HQ, 3rd Bn, 24th Marine Regiment
Saint Louis Naval & Marine Corps Reserve Center, Bridgeton, MO, 499

HQ & Service Co, 3rd Bn, 24th Marine Regiment
Saint Louis Naval & Marine Corps Reserve Center, Bridgeton, MO, 499

24th Operations Group
Howard Air Force Base, Panama, 1136

24th Operations Support Squadron
Howard Air Force Base, Panama, 1136

24th Quartermaster Det
Caserma Ederle/Vicenza Military Community, Vincenza, Italy, 1060

24th Services Squadron
Howard Air Force Base, Panama, 1136

24th Special Tactics Squadron (AFSOC)
Pope Air Force Base, Pope AFB, NC, 629

24th Supply Squadron
Howard Air Force Base, Panama, 1136

24th Transportation Squadron
Howard Air Force Base, Panama, 1136

24th Weather Squadron
Howard Air Force Base, Panama, 1136

24th Wing
Howard Air Force Base, Panama, 1136

25th Field Artillery, B Battery
Bamberg Military Community, Germany, 1001

25th Flying Training Squadron
Vance Air Force Base, Vance AFB, OK, 681

25th Infantry Division (L)
Pohakuloa Training Area, Hilo, HI, 272
Schofield Barracks, Schofield Barracks, HI, 286

1st Brigade, 25th Infantry Division (L)
Fort Lewis, Fort Lewis, WA, 921

25th Infantry Division (L) Aviation Brigade
Wheeler Army Airfield, Wheeler Army Airfield, HI, 293

B Co, 1st Bn, 25th Marine Regiment
Manchester Naval & Marine Corps Reserve Center, Bedford, NH, 546

C Co, 1st Bn, 25th Marine Regiment
Plainville Naval & Marine Corps Reserve Center, Plainville, CT, 164

F Co, 2nd Bn, 25th Marine Regiment
Albany Naval & Marine Corps Reserve Readiness Center, Albany, NY, 575

Co L, 3rd Bn, 25th Marine Regiment
Columbus Naval & Marine Corps Readiness Center, Columbus, OH, 652

I Co, 3rd Bn, 25th Marine Regiment
Buffalo Naval & Marine Corps Reserve Center, Buffalo, NY, 583

Weapons Co, 3rd Bn, 25th Marine Regiment
Moundsville Naval & Marine Corps Reserve Center, Moundsville, WV, 949

Co K, 3rd Bn, 25th Marine Regiment
Akron Naval & Marine Corps Reserve Center, Akron, OH, 643

25th Marine Regiment HQ
Worcester Naval & Marine Corps Reserve Center, Worcester, MA, 448

1st Bn, 25th Marines (Reserves)
Massachusetts Military Reservation/Otis Air National Guard Base, Cape Cod, MA, 437

25th Trans, 2nd MCR
Camp Hialeah, Korea, Republic of, 1099

25th Transportation Bn (Army)
Kunsan Air Base, Korea, Republic of, 1117

26th Area Support Group
Heidelberg Military Community, Germany, 1011
Patton Barracks, Germany, 1022

26th Aviation Brigade
Massachusetts Military Reservation/Otis Air National Guard Base, Cape Cod, MA, 437

26th Field Artillery, F Battery
Camp Stanley, Korea, Republic of, 1111

26th (Yankee) Infantry Division
Cape Cod Coast Guard Air Station, Cape Cod, MA, 436

26th Quartermaster
414th Base Support Battalion, Germany, 997

27th Civil Engineering Squadron
Cannon Air Force Base, Cannon AFB, NM, 570

27th Communications Squadron
Cannon Air Force Base, Cannon AFB, NM, 570

27th Equipment Maintenance Squadron
Cannon Air Force Base, Cannon AFB, NM, 570

27th Fighter Wing
Cannon Air Force Base, Cannon AFB, NM, 570

27th Fighter Wing, OL-A
Whidbey Island Naval Air Station, Oak Harbor, WA, 924

27th Logistics Group
Cannon Air Force Base, Cannon AFB, NM, 570

27th Medical Group
Cannon Air Force Base, Cannon AFB, NM, 570

27th Operations Group
Cannon Air Force Base, Cannon AFB, NM, 570

27th Security Forces Squadron
Cannon Air Force Base, Cannon AFB, NM, 570

27th Support Group
Cannon Air Force Base, Cannon AFB, NM, 570

27th Transportation Bn
414th Base Support Battalion, Germany, 997

28th Bomb Wing
Ellsworth Air Force Base, Ellsworth AFB, SD, 750

28th Civil Engineer Squadron
Ellsworth Air Force Base, Ellsworth AFB, SD, 750

28th Communications Squadron
Ellsworth Air Force Base, Ellsworth AFB, SD, 750

28th Comptroller Squadron
Ellsworth Air Force Base, Ellsworth AFB, SD, 750

28th Contracting Squadron
Ellsworth Air Force Base, Ellsworth AFB, SD, 750

28th Logistics Group
Ellsworth Air Force Base, Ellsworth AFB, SD, 750

28th Logistics Support Squadron
Ellsworth Air Force Base, Ellsworth AFB, SD, 750

28th Maintenance Squadron
Ellsworth Air Force Base, Ellsworth AFB, SD, 750

28th Medical Group
Ellsworth Air Force Base, Ellsworth AFB, SD, 750

28th Mission Support Squadron
Ellsworth Air Force Base, Ellsworth AFB, SD, 750

28th Mobile Aerial Port Squadron
O'Hare International Airport Air Reserve Station, O'Hare IAP ARS, IL, 311

28th Operations Support Group
Ellsworth Air Force Base, Ellsworth AFB, SD, 750

28th Security Forces Squadron
Ellsworth Air Force Base, Ellsworth AFB, SD, 750

28th Services Squadron
Ellsworth Air Force Base, Ellsworth AFB, SD, 750

28th Supply Squadron
Ellsworth Air Force Base, Ellsworth AFB, SD, 750

28th Support Group
Ellsworth Air Force Base, Ellsworth AFB, SD, 750

28th Transportation Bn
Coleman Barracks, Germany, 1006

28th Transportation Squadron
Ellsworth Air Force Base, Ellsworth AFB, SD, 750

29th Air Traffic Services Group, HQ (ANG)
Aberdeen Proving Ground, Aberdeen Proving Ground, MD, 404

29th Area Support Group
Kaiserslautern Military Community, Germany, 1013

29th Brigade (SEP)
Pohakuloa Training Area, Hilo, HI, 272

29th Infantry Division (Light) Aviation Brigade (ANG)
Aberdeen Proving Ground, Aberdeen Proving Ground, MD, 404

29th Infantry Division (Light), HQ (VA ARNG)
Fort Belvoir, Fort Belvoir, VA, 866

29th Infantry Regiment
Fort Benning, Fort Benning, GA, 248

29th Medical Det
Baumholder Military Community, H.D. Smith Barracks, Germany, 1003

29th Training Systems Squadron (OLAB)
Barksdale Air Force Base, Barksdale AFB, LA, 374

30th Aerial Port Squadron
Niagara Falls Air Reserve Station, Niagara Falls, NY, 600

30th Medical Brigade
Heidelberg Military Community, Germany, 1011

30th Movement Control Team
Bamberg Military Community, Germany, 1001

30th Range Squadron
Pacific Missile Range Facility, Kekaha, HI, 279

30th Space Wing
Vandenberg Air Force Base, Vandenberg AFB, CA, 141

31st Civil Engineering Squadron
Camp Darby, Livorno Military Community, Italy, 1052

31st Fighter Wing
Aviano Air Base, Italy, 1051

31st Logistics Group
Aviano Air Base, Italy, 1051

31st Maintenance Squadron
Camp Darby, Livorno Military Community, Italy, 1052

31st Marine Expeditionary Unit
Camp Courtney, Japan, 1065

31st Marine Expeditionary Unit (SOC)
Camp Hansen, Japan, 1067

31st Medical Group
Aviano Air Base, Italy, 1051

31st Munitions Squadron (USAFE)
Camp Darby, Livorno Military Community, Italy, 1052

31st Munitions Support Squadron
Ghedi Air Base, Italy, 1053

31st Naval Construction Regiment HQ
Port Hueneme, Naval Construction Battalion Center, Port Hueneme, CA, 104

31st Operations Group
Aviano Air Base, Italy, 1051

31st Support Group
Aviano Air Base, Italy, 1051

31st Support Group, HQ
Aviano Air Base, Italy, 1051

31st Test & Evaluation Squadron
Edwards Air Force Base, Edwards AFB, CA, 63

32nd Air Force Station (AFS)
Incirlick Air Base, Turkey, 1152

32nd Air Operations Group
Ramstein Air Base, Germany, 1023

32nd Flying Training Squadron
Vance Air Force Base, Vance AFB, OK, 681

32nd Mobile Aerial Port Squadron
Pittsburgh IAP, Air Reserve Station, Coraopolis, PA, 701

32nd Signal Bn
223rd Base Support Battalion, Germany, 993

33rd Aeromedical Evacuation Squadron
Pittsburgh IAP, Air Reserve Station, Coraopolis, PA, 701

33rd Field Artillery, A Battery
Bamberg Military Community, Germany, 1001

33rd Fighter Wing
Eglin Air Force Base, Fort Walton Beach, FL, 197

33rd Interrogator Translator Team (MARFORRES)
Miami Naval & Marine Corps Reserve Readiness Center, Hialeah, FL, 198

34th Area Support Group & Area II
Yongsan Army Garrison, Korea, Republic of, 1121

34th Training Wing (Cadet Wing)
US Air Force Academy, Colorado Springs, CO, 146

35th Air Defense Artillery Brigade
Fort Bliss, El Paso, TX, 790

35th Communications Squadron
Misawa Air Base, Japan, 1076

35th Engineer Bn
Fort Leonard Wood, Fort Leonard Wood, MO, 501

35th Fighter Squadron
Kunsan Air Base, Korea, Republic of, 1117

35th Fighter Wing
Misawa Air Base, Japan, 1076

35th Infantry Division, Headquarters (Mobilized)(ANG)
Fort Leavenworth, Fort Leavenworth, KS, 352

35th Signal Brigade
Fort Bragg, Fort Bragg, NC, 624

35th Supply & Service Bn
35th Supply & Service Battalion, Japan, 1061

36th Aero Patient Staging Squadron
O'Hare International Airport Air Reserve Station, O'Hare IAP ARS, IL, 311

36th Air Base Wing
Andersen Air Force Base, Guam, 1043

36th Engineer Group
Fort Benning, Fort Benning, GA, 248

1st Bn, 36th Infantry
Ray Barracks, Germany, 1024

1st Bn, 36th Infantry Division
Friedberg Area Support Team, Germany, 1007

36th Logistics Group
Andersen Air Force Base, Guam, 1043

36th Marine Air Wing
Futenma, Marine Corps Air Station, Japan, 1072

36th Medical Group
Andersen Air Force Base, Guam, 1043

36th Operations Support Squadron
Andersen Air Force Base, Guam, 1043

36th Rescue Flight
Fairchild Air Force Base, Fairchild AFB, WA, 919

36th Signal Bn
Camp Henry, Korea, Republic of, 1098

36th Signal Bn, HQ
Camp Walker, Korea, Republic of, 1113

36th Support Group
Andersen Air Force Base, Guam, 1043

37th Airlift Squadron
Ramstein Air Base, Germany, 1023
Rhein-Main Air Base, Germany, 1025

1st Bn, 37th Armor Division
Friedberg Area Support Team, Germany, 1007

1st Brigade, 37th Armor Division
Ray Barracks, Germany, 1024

2nd Bn, 37th Armor Division
Friedberg Area Support Team, Germany, 1007

2nd Brigade, 37th Armor Division
Ray Barracks, Germany, 1024

37th Bomb Squadron
Ellsworth Air Force Base, Ellsworth AFB, SD, 750

6th Bn, 37th Field Artillery
Camp Stanley, Korea, Republic of, 1111

37th Flying Training Squadron
Columbus Air Force Base, Columbus AFB, MS, 479

37th Training Group
Lackland Air Force Base, Lackland AFB, TX, 809

37th Training Wing (host)
Lackland Air Force Base, Lackland AFB, TX, 809

37th Transportation Command
Kleber Kaserne, Germany, 1018

38th Air Traffic Control Platoon
Camp Atterbury, Edinburgh, IN, 325

38th Band Division
Old Fort Benjamin Harrison, Indianapolis, IN, 336

38th Engineer Co
414th Base Support Battalion, Germany, 997

38th Field Artillery A Battery
Camp Stanley, Korea, Republic of, 1111

38th Personnel Service Bn, B Det
280th Base Support Battalion, Germany, 994

38th Personnel Services Bn, Det A
Kitzingen Military Community, Germany, 1017

38th Personnel Services Bn, Det B
Bamberg Military Community, Germany, 1001

39th Accounting and Finance Squadron
Incirlick Air Base, Turkey, 1152

39th Finance
414th Base Support Battalion, Germany, 997

39th Finance Det
221st Base Support Battalion, Germany, 992

39th Infantry Brigade
Camp Joseph T Robinson, North Little Rock, AR, 52

39th Intelligence Squadron
Nellis Air Force Base, Nellis AFB, NV, 541

39th Logistics Group
Incirlick Air Base, Turkey, 1152

39th Medical Group
Incirlick Air Base, Turkey, 1152

39th Military Police Co
Jackson Barracks, New Orleans, LA, 382

39th Munitions Support Squadron
Balikesir Air Field, Turkey, 1151

39th Operations Group
Incirlick Air Base, Turkey, 1152

39th Security Police Squadron
Incirlick Air Base, Turkey, 1152

39th Signal Bn
80th Area Support Group, Belgium, 975

39th Support Group
Incirlick Air Base, Turkey, 1152

39th Wing
Incirlick Air Base, Turkey, 1152

40th Army Band (ANG)
Adjutant General of Vermont, Colchester, VT, 832

41st Airlift Squadron
Pope Air Force Base, Pope AFB, NC, 629

41st Area Support Group
Fort Clayton, Panama, 1133

41st Combat Support Hospital
Fort Sam Houston, Fort Sam Houston, TX, 794

41st Engineer Bn
Fort Wainwright, Fort Wainwright, AK, 28

41st Field Artillery Bn
223rd Base Support Battalion, Germany, 993

42nd Air Base Wing
Maxwell Air Force Base, Maxwell AFB, AL, 8

42nd Communications Squadron
Maxwell Air Force Base, Maxwell AFB, AL, 8

42nd Medical Co
Kitzingen Military Community, Germany, 1017

43rd Adjutant General Bn
Fort Leonard Wood, Fort Leonard Wood, MO, 501

43rd Aeromedical Evacuation Squadron
Pope Air Force Base, Pope AFB, NC, 629

43rd Airlift Wing
Pope Air Force Base, Pope AFB, NC, 629

43rd Area Support Group
Fort Carson and 4th Infantry Division (Mechanized), Fort Carson, CO, 152

43rd Comptroller Squadron
Pope Air Force Base, Pope AFB, NC, 629

43rd Logistics Group
Pope Air Force Base, Pope AFB, NC, 629

43rd Medical Group
Pope Air Force Base, Pope AFB, NC, 629

43rd Operations Group
Pope Air Force Base, Pope AFB, NC, 629

43rd Ordnance Det (EOD)
Army Armor Center & Fort Knox, Fort Knox, KY, 366

43rd Support Group
Pope Air Force Base, Pope AFB, NC, 629

44th Aerial Port Squadron (AFRC)
Andersen Air Force Base, Guam, 1043

44th Army Band
New Mexico National Guard State Headquarters, Santa Fe, NM, 573

44th Engineer Bn
Camp Howze, Korea, Republic of, 1101

44th Medical Brigade
Fort Bragg, Fort Bragg, NC, 624

45th Civil Engineer Squadron
Patrick Air Force Base, Patrick AFB, FL, 221

45th Communications Squadron
Patrick Air Force Base, Patrick AFB, FL, 221

45th Corps Support Group (Forward)
Schofield Barracks, Schofield Barracks, HI, 286

45th Logistics Group
Patrick Air Force Base, Patrick AFB, FL, 221

45th Mission Support Squadron
Patrick Air Force Base, Patrick AFB, FL, 221

45th Operations Group
Patrick Air Force Base, Patrick AFB, FL, 221

45th Operations Support Group
Patrick Air Force Base, Patrick AFB, FL, 221

45th Range Squadron
Patrick Air Force Base, Patrick AFB, FL, 221

45th Security Forces Squadron
Patrick Air Force Base, Patrick AFB, FL, 221

45th Services Squadron
Patrick Air Force Base, Patrick AFB, FL, 221

45th Space Wing
Patrick Air Force Base, Patrick AFB, FL, 221

45th Support Group
Patrick Air Force Base, Patrick AFB, FL, 221

45th Weather Squadron
Patrick Air Force Base, Patrick AFB, FL, 221

46th Engineer (Combat) (Heavy), Co D
Fort McClellan, Anniston, AL, 2

46th Support Bn
Fort Wainwright, Fort Wainwright, AK, 28

46th Test Wing
Eglin Air Force Base, Fort Walton Beach, FL, 197

47th Aerospace Medicine Squadron
Laughlin Air Force Base, Laughlin AFB, TX, 810

47th Civil Engineer Squadron
Laughlin Air Force Base, Laughlin AFB, TX, 810

47th Communications Squadron
Laughlin Air Force Base, Laughlin AFB, TX, 810

47th Contracting Squadron
Laughlin Air Force Base, Laughlin AFB, TX, 810

47th Dental Flight
Laughlin Air Force Base, Laughlin AFB, TX, 810

47th Flying Training Wing
Laughlin Air Force Base, Laughlin AFB, TX, 810

47th Medical Group
Laughlin Air Force Base, Laughlin AFB, TX, 810

47th Medical Operations Squadron
Laughlin Air Force Base, Laughlin AFB, TX, 810

47th Medical Support Squadron
Laughlin Air Force Base, Laughlin AFB, TX, 810

47th Mission Support Squadron
Laughlin Air Force Base, Laughlin AFB, TX, 810

47th Operations Group
Laughlin Air Force Base, Laughlin AFB, TX, 810

47th Operations Support Squadron
Laughlin Air Force Base, Laughlin AFB, TX, 810

47th Security Police Squadron
Laughlin Air Force Base, Laughlin AFB, TX, 810

47th Services Division
Laughlin Air Force Base, Laughlin AFB, TX, 810

47th Supply Flight
Laughlin Air Force Base, Laughlin AFB, TX, 810

47th Support Bn
Baumholder Military Community, H.D. Smith Barracks, Germany, 1003

47th Support Group
Laughlin Air Force Base, Laughlin AFB, TX, 810

47th Transportation Flight
Laughlin Air Force Base, Laughlin AFB, TX, 810

48th Explosive Ordnance Disposal Unit
Fort Jackson, Columbia, SC, 740

48th Fighter Wing
Feltwell RAF Base, United Kingdom, 1158
Lakenheath RAF Base, United Kingdom, 1161

48th Flying Training Squadron
Columbus Air Force Base, Columbus AFB, MS, 479

48th Intelligence Squadron
Beale Air Force Base, Beale AFB, CA, 58

48th Medical Group
Lakenheath RAF Base, United Kingdom, 1161

49th Armored Division
Camp Mabry, Austin, TX, 777

49th Bare Base Systems Group
Holloman Air Force Base, Holloman AFB, NM, 571

49th Fighter Wing
Holloman Air Force Base, Holloman AFB, NM, 571

49th Flying Training Squadron
Columbus Air Force Base, Columbus AFB, MS, 479

49th Logistics Group
Holloman Air Force Base, Holloman AFB, NM, 571

49th Medical Group
Holloman Air Force Base, Holloman AFB, NM, 571

49th Operations Group
Holloman Air Force Base, Holloman AFB, NM, 571

49th Support Group
Holloman Air Force Base, Holloman AFB, NM, 571

49th Test Squadron
Barksdale Air Force Base, Barksdale AFB, LA, 374

49th Training Squadron
Holloman Air Force Base, Holloman AFB, NM, 571

50th Engineer Co
Camp LaGuardia, Korea, Republic of, 1103

50th Flying Training Squadron
Columbus Air Force Base, Columbus AFB, MS, 479

50th Logistics Group
Falcon Air Force Base, Falcon AFB, CO, 151

50th Operations Group
Falcon Air Force Base, Falcon AFB, CO, 151

50th Space Wing
Falcon Air Force Base, Falcon AFB, CO, 151

50th Support Group
Falcon Air Force Base, Falcon AFB, CO, 151

51st Communications Squadron
Osan Air Base, Korea, Republic of, 1118

51st Fighter Wing
Osan Air Base, Korea, Republic of, 1118

51st Maintenance Bn
Sullivan Barracks, Germany, 1033

51st Medical Group
Osan Air Base, Korea, Republic of, 1118

51st Military Police Co
Camp Long, Korea, Republic of, 1104

51st Mission Support Squadron
Osan Air Base, Korea, Republic of, 1118

51st Service Squadron
Osan Air Base, Korea, Republic of, 1118

52nd Fighter Wing
Spangdahlem Air Base, Germany, 1030

52nd Fighter Wing Staff
Spangdahlem Air Base, Germany, 1030

52nd Fighter Wing (Support)
Bitburg Annex, Germany, 1004

52nd Logistics Group
Spangdahlem Air Base, Germany, 1030

52nd Medical Group
Bitburg Annex, Germany, 1004
Spangdahlem Air Base, Germany, 1030

52nd Munitions Support Squadron
Kleine Brogel Air Base, Belgium, 977

52nd Operations Group
Spangdahlem Air Base, Germany, 1030

52nd Ordnance Group
Fort Gillem, Forest Park, GA, 247

52nd Support Group
Spangdahlem Air Base, Germany, 1030

53rd Explosive Ordnance Disposal
Yakima Training Center, Yakima, WA, 941

53rd Fighter Squadron
Spangdahlem Air Base, Germany, 1030

53rd Troop Command (Det 1, HQ, STARC-NY)
Camp Smith, Peekskill, NY, 601

53rd Weather Reconnaissance Squadron (Hurricane Hunters)
Keesler Air Force Base, Keesler AFB, MS, 487

53rd Wing
Nellis Air Force Base, Nellis AFB, NV, 541

54th Fighter Squadron
Elmendorf Air Force Base, Anchorage, AK, 19

54th Medivac
Yakima Training Center, Yakima, WA, 941

55th Air Refueling Squadron
Altus Air Force Base, Altus AFB, OK, 668

55th Operation Group, Det 1 (ACC)
Eareckson Air Force Station, AK, 23

55th Postal
414th Base Support Battalion, Germany, 997

55th Postal Co
Friedberg Area Support Team, Germany, 1007
Ray Barracks, Germany, 1024

55th PSB, Det C
Ray Barracks, Germany, 1024

55th PSL
Barton Barracks, Ansbach, Germany, 1002

55th Signal Co (Combat Camera)
Fort George G Meade, Fort Meade, MD, 422

55th Wing
Offutt Air Force Base, Offutt AFB, NE, 530

56th Airlift Squadron
Altus Air Force Base, Altus AFB, OK, 668

56th Fighter Wing
Luke Air Force Base, Luke AFB, AZ, 37

56th Logistics Group
Luke Air Force Base, Luke AFB, AZ, 37

56th Medical Group
Luke Air Force Base, Luke AFB, AZ, 37

56th Operations Group
Luke Air Force Base, Luke AFB, AZ, 37

56th Signal Brigade
Fort Clayton, Panama, 1133

56th Support Group
Luke Air Force Base, Luke AFB, AZ, 37

57th Aircraft Generation Squadron
Nellis Air Force Base, Nellis AFB, NV, 541

57th Airlift Squadron
Altus Air Force Base, Altus AFB, OK, 668

57th Component Repair Squadron
Nellis Air Force Base, Nellis AFB, NV, 541

57th Equipment Maintenance Squadron
Nellis Air Force Base, Nellis AFB, NV, 541

57th Logistics Group
Nellis Air Force Base, Nellis AFB, NV, 541

57th Logistics Support Squadron
Nellis Air Force Base, Nellis AFB, NV, 541

57th Med-Evac Det
Prince Sultan Air Base, Saudi Arabia, 1146

57th Military Police Co
Camp Carroll, Korea, Republic of, 1088

57th Operations Group
Nellis Air Force Base, Nellis AFB, NV, 541

57th Operations Support Squadron
Nellis Air Force Base, Nellis AFB, NV, 541

57th Ordnance Det, Explosive Ordnance Disposal
Fort Belvoir, Fort Belvoir, VA, 866

57th Wing
Nellis Air Force Base, Nellis AFB, NV, 541

Det 5, 57th Wing
Barksdale Air Force Base, Barksdale AFB, LA, 374

58th Airlift Squadron
Altus Air Force Base, Altus AFB, OK, 668

58th Aviation, E Co
282nd Base Support Battalion, Germany, 995

3rd Bn, 58th Aviation Regiment
Rose Barracks, Germany, 1027

58th Signal Bn
Torii Station, Japan, 1082

58th Special Operations Wing
Kirtland Air Force Base, Kirtland AFB, NM, 572

58th Support Squadron
Gila Bend Auxiliary Air Field, Gila Bend, AZ, 36

58th Transportation Bn
Fort Leonard Wood, Fort Leonard Wood, MO, 501

59th Medical Wing
Lackland Air Force Base, Lackland AFB, TX, 809

59th Signal Bn
Fort Richardson, Fort Richardson, AK, 27

60th Air Mobility Wing
Travis Air Force Base, Travis AFB, CA, 137

60th Explosive Ordnance Disposal
Fort Dix, Fort Dix, NJ, 555

61st Air Base Group
Los Angeles Air Force Base, Los Angeles, CA, 76

61st Maintenance Co
Camp Long, Korea, Republic of, 1104

62nd Airlift Wing (Host)
McChord Air Force Base, McChord AFB, WA, 923

62nd Medical Group
Fort Lewis, Fort Lewis, WA, 921

62nd Ordnance Co (EOD)
Tooele Army Depot, Tooele, UT, 830

63rd Aeromedical Evacuation Squadron
O'Hare International Airport Air Reserve Station, O'Hare IAP ARS, IL, 311

1st Bn, 63rd Armor Division
Rose Barracks, Vilseck, Germany, 1028

2nd Bn, 63rd Armor Division
Rose Barracks, Vilseck, Germany, 1028

1st Bn, 63rd Artillery Regiment
Rose Barracks, Germany, 1027

2nd Bn, 63rd Artillery Regiment
Rose Barracks, Germany, 1027

63rd Signal Bn
Army Signal Center & Fort Gordon, Fort Gordon, GA, 249

64th Airlift Squadron
O'Hare International Airport Air Reserve Station, O'Hare IAP ARS, IL, 311

64th Medical Det (Veterinary)
Baumholder Military Community, H.D. Smith Barracks, Germany, 1003

65th Air Base Wing
Lajes Field, Portugal, 1138

65th Army Reserve Command
Fort Buchanan Army Garrison, Puerto Rico, 1141

65th Communications Squadron
Lajes Field, Portugal, 1138

65th Comptroller Flight
Lajes Field, Portugal, 1138

65th Contracting Squadron
Lajes Field, Portugal, 1138

65th Medical Group
Lajes Field, Portugal, 1138

65th Support Group
Lajes Field, Portugal, 1138

65th Transportation Squadron
Lajes Field, Portugal, 1138

66th AG Co (Postal), 1st Plt
Kimpo Military Mail Terminal, Korea, Republic of, 1116

66th CBT Aviation Brigade
Fort Lewis, Fort Lewis, WA, 921

66th Military Intelligence Bn
223rd Base Support Battalion, Germany, 993

66th Military Intelligence Group
Augsburg Military Community, Germany, 999

66th Rescue Squadron
Nellis Air Force Base, Nellis AFB, NV, 541

66th Training Squadron
Eielson Air Force Base, Eielson AFB, AK, 24

67th Combat Support Hospital
67th Combat Support Hospital/USAMED-DAC, Germany, 989
98th Area Support Group, Germany, 990

67th Ordnance Det
Fort Lesley J McNair, Washington, DC, 177

67th Signal Bn
Army Signal Center & Fort Gordon, Fort Gordon, GA, 249

67th Signal Regiment
Rose Barracks, Germany, 1027

Headquarters, 67th Troop Command
Camp Dodge Iowa, Johnston, IA, 346

69th Chemical Co
414th Base Support Battalion, Germany, 997

69th Fighter Squadron
Moody Air Force Base, Moody AFB, GA, 258

69th Signal Bn
282nd Base Support Battalion, Germany, 995

70th Aeromedical Evacuation Unit
Niagara Falls Air Reserve Station, Niagara Falls, NY, 600

70th Air Base Group
Brooks Air Force Base, San Antonio, TX, 815

70th Army Reserve Command (70th RSC)
Vancouver Barracks, Vancouver, WA, 938

70th Civil Engineering Squadron
Brooks Air Force Base, San Antonio, TX, 815

70th Communications Squadron (CS)
Brooks Air Force Base, San Antonio, TX, 815

70th Medical Squadron
Brooks Air Force Base, San Antonio, TX, 815

70th Ordnance Bn
Fort Bliss, El Paso, TX, 790

70th Regional Support Command
Fort Lawton, 70th Regional Support Command, Fort Lawton, WA, 920

70th Security Police Squadron
Brooks Air Force Base, San Antonio, TX, 815

70th Services Squadron
Brooks Air Force Base, San Antonio, TX, 815

70th Support Group
Brooks Air Force Base, San Antonio, TX, 815

70th Training Squadron
Brooks Air Force Base, San Antonio, TX, 815

70th Transportation Bn
Coleman Barracks, Germany, 1006

71st Combat Support Bn
Bamberg Military Community, Germany, 1001

71st Corps Support Bn, Headquarters and Headquarters Det
Johnson Barracks, Germany, 1012

71st Flying Training Wing
Vance Air Force Base, Vance AFB, OK, 681

71st Medical Group
Vance Air Force Base, Vance AFB, OK, 681

71st Operations Group
Vance Air Force Base, Vance AFB, OK, 681

71st Ordnance Co
414th Base Support Battalion, Germany, 997

Bamberg Military Community, Germany, 1001

71st Regiment, 1st Bn, Det 2 (NYANG)
Roslyn Station, Air National Guard, Roslyn, NY, 606

71st Support Group
Vance Air Force Base, Vance AFB, OK, 681

71st Troop Command of Texas ANG
Camp Mabry, Austin, TX, 777

72nd Air Base Wing
Tinker Air Force Base, Tinker AFB, OK, 678

72nd Air Refueling Squadron
Grissom Air Reserve Base, Grissom ARB, IN, 331

1st Brigade, 72nd Armor
Camp Casey, Korea, Republic of, 1089

2nd Bn, 72nd Armor
Camp Casey, Korea, Republic of, 1089

72nd Military Police Co
Nevada National Guard Las Vegas, Las Vegas, NV, 540

72nd Ordnance Co
Camp Hialeah, Korea, Republic of, 1099

73rd Ordnance Bn
Army Signal Center & Fort Gordon, Fort Gordon, GA, 249

74th Air Refueling Squadron
Grissom Air Reserve Base, Grissom ARB, IN, 331

74th Fighter Squadron
Pope Air Force Base, Pope AFB, NC, 629

74th Naval Mobile Construction Bn
Gulfport Naval Construction Battalion Center, Gulfport, MS, 482

74th Signal Co
Camp Hialeah, Korea, Republic of, 1099

74th Troop Command (DC ARNG)
District of Columbia National Guard, HQ, Washington, DC, 176

75th Air Base Wing
Hill Air Force Base, Hill AFB, UT, 824

75th Civil Engineer Group
Hill Air Force Base, Hill AFB, UT, 824

75th Combat Support Hospital (US Army)
Tuscaloosa Armed Forces Reserve Center, Tuscaloosa, AL, 17

75th Communications Squadron
Hill Air Force Base, Hill AFB, UT, 824

75th Fighter Squadron
Pope Air Force Base, Pope AFB, NC, 629

75th Medical Group
Hill Air Force Base, Hill AFB, UT, 824

75th Operations Support Squadron
Hill Air Force Base, Hill AFB, UT, 824

1st Bn, 75th Ranger Division
Fort Stewart, Hinesville, GA, 252

75th Ranger Regiment
Fort Benning, Fort Benning, GA, 248

1st Bn, 75th Ranger Regiment
Hunter Army Air Field, Savannah, GA, 260

2nd Bn, 75th Ranger Regiment
Fort Lewis, Fort Lewis, WA, 921

76th Aerial Port Squadron
Youngstown-Warren Regional Airport, Air Reserve Station, Vienna, OH, 666

76th Air Base Wing
Kelly Air Force Base, Kelly AFB, TX, 807

76th Airlift Squadron
Ramstein Air Base, Germany, 1023

77th ARCOM Ernie Pyle USAR
New York Area Command & Fort Hamilton, Brooklyn, NY, 581

77th Bomb Squadron
Ellsworth Air Force Base, Ellsworth AFB, SD, 750

77th Communications Squadron
McClellan Air Force Base, McClellan AFB, CA, 81

77th Infantry Division (RTU)
Fort Totten, New York, NY, 594

77th Maintenance Co
223rd Base Support Battalion, Germany, 993

78th Air Base Wing
Robins Air Force Base, Robins AFB, GA, 259

78th Army Signal Bn
Camp Zama, Japan, 1071

79th Army Reserve Command
Willow Grove Naval Air Station (JRB), Willow Grove, PA, 723

80th Area Support Group
80th Area Support Group, Belgium, 975

80th ASG, Directorate of Public Works
Chievres Air Base, Belgium, 976

80th Division (IT), 1st Bn, 318th Regiment, 1st Brigade (USAR)
Fort Story, Fort Story, VA, 871

80th Fighter Squadron
Kunsan Air Base, Korea, Republic of, 1117

80th Flying Training Wing
Sheppard Air Force Base, Sheppard AFB, TX, 817

80th Operations Support Squadron
Sheppard Air Force Base, Sheppard AFB, TX, 817

81st Fighter Squadron
Spangdahlem Air Base, Germany, 1030

81st Logistics Group
Keesler Air Force Base, Keesler AFB, MS, 487

81st Medical Group
Keesler Air Force Base, Keesler AFB, MS, 487

81st Regional Support Command
Army Armor Center & Fort Knox, Fort Knox, KY, 366
Fort Gillem, Forest Park, GA, 247

81st Support Group
Keesler Air Force Base, Keesler AFB, MS, 487

81st Technical Training Group
Keesler Air Force Base, Keesler AFB, MS, 487

81st Training Wing
Keesler Air Force Base, Keesler AFB, MS, 487

81st Troop Command, HQ
Camp Atterbury, Edinburgh, IN, 325

82nd Airborne Division
Fort Bragg, Fort Bragg, NC, 624

82nd Engineer Bn
Bamberg Military Community, Germany, 1001

82nd Engineering Co (CSE)
Camp Edwards, Korea, Republic of, 1092

82nd Logistics Group
Sheppard Air Force Base, Sheppard AFB, TX, 817

82nd Medical Co
Fort Riley, Fort Riley, KS, 353
Fort Sill, Fort Sill, OK, 671

82nd Medical Group
Sheppard Air Force Base, Sheppard AFB, TX, 817

82nd Reconnaissance Squadron
Kadena Air Base, Japan, 1074

82nd Support Group
Sheppard Air Force Base, Sheppard AFB, TX, 817

82nd Training Group
Sheppard Air Force Base, Sheppard AFB, TX, 817

82nd Training Wing
Sheppard Air Force Base, Sheppard AFB, TX, 817

83rd Aerial Port Squadron (AFRES)
Portland Air National Guard Base, Portland IAP, OR, 691

83rd Army Reserve Command (ARCOM)
Defense Supply Center, Columbus, Columbus, OH, 654

84th Airlift Flight (AMC)
Peterson Air Force Base, Peterson AFB, CO, 156

84th Division (IT)
Charles Melvin Price Army Support Center, Granite City, IL, 307

5th Brigade, 84th Division
84th Division (IT) HQ, Milwaukee, WI, 960

84th Division Band
84th Division (IT) HQ, Milwaukee, WI, 960

84th Division (IT) HQ
84th Division (IT) HQ, Milwaukee, WI, 960

84th Division (IT) Retention Office
84th Division (IT) HQ, Milwaukee, WI, 960

84th Test Squadron
Tyndall Air Force Base, Panama City, FL, 220

85th Aerial Port Squadron
Hanscom Air Force Base, Bedford, MA, 430

85th Flying Training Squadron (FTS)
Laughlin Air Force Base, Laughlin AFB, TX, 810

86th Airlift Wing
Ramstein Air Base, Germany, 1023

86th Airlift Wing, Ramstein Air Base Annex
Sembach Air Base, Germany, 1029

86th Flying Training Squadron
Laughlin Air Force Base, Laughlin AFB, TX, 810

86th Maintenance Squadron
Ramstein Air Base, Germany, 1023

86th Medical Group
Ramstein Air Base, Germany, 1023

86th Mission Support Squadron
Ramstein Air Base, Germany, 1023

86th Operations Squadron
Ramstein Air Base, Germany, 1023

86th Security Forces Squadron
Ramstein Air Base, Germany, 1023

86th Services Squadron
Ramstein Air Base, Germany, 1023

86th Supply Squadron
Ramstein Air Base, Germany, 1023

3rd Brigade, 87th Division
Camp Shelby Training Site, Camp Shelby, MS, 478

87th Flying Training Squadron (FTS)
Laughlin Air Force Base, Laughlin AFB, TX, 810

5th Bn, 87th Infantry Bn
Fort Clayton, Panama, 1133
Fort Davis, Panama, 1134

87th Troop Command
Camp Joseph T Robinson, North Little Rock, AR, 52

88th Air Base Wing
Wright-Patterson Air Force Base, Wright-Patterson AFB, OH, 667

88th Flying Training Squadron
Sheppard Air Force Base, Sheppard AFB, TX, 817

88th Ordnance Co
Fort McCoy, Fort McCoy, WI, 954

89th Airlift Wing
Andrews Air Force Base, Andrews AFB, MD, 407

89th Explosive Ordnance Disposal Det
Fort Benning, Fort Benning, GA, 248

89th Flying Training Squadron
Sheppard Air Force Base, Sheppard AFB, TX, 817

89th Military Police
Fort Hood, Fort Hood, TX, 792

90th Fighter Squadron
Elmendorf Air Force Base, Anchorage, AK, 19

90th Flying Training Squadron
Sheppard Air Force Base, Sheppard AFB, TX, 817

90th Missile Wing, HQ (Air Force Space Command)
Francis E Warren Air Force Base, F E Warren AFB, WY, 967

90th Personnel Service Bn
Baumholder Military Community, H.D. Smith Barracks, Germany, 1003

90th Postal (2nd PLT)
Baumholder Military Community, H.D. Smith Barracks, Germany, 1003

91st Division (Ex) 1st Brigade
Parks Reserve Forces Training Area, Dublin, CA, 62

91st Division (Ex) Battle Projection Center
Parks Reserve Forces Training Area, Dublin, CA, 62

91st Logistics Group
Minot Air Force Base, Minot AFB, ND, 642

91st Missile Wing (AFSPC)
Minot Air Force Base, Minot AFB, ND, 642

91st Operations Group
Minot Air Force Base, Minot AFB, ND, 642

92nd Aerial Port Squadron (AFRES)
Wyoming Aerial Port (AFRES), Wyoming, PA, 724

92nd Air Refueling Wing
Fairchild Air Force Base, Fairchild AFB, WA, 919

92nd Logistics Group
Fairchild Air Force Base, Fairchild AFB, WA, 919

92nd Medical Group
Fairchild Air Force Base, Fairchild AFB, WA, 919

92nd Military Police Co
Baumholder Military Community, H.D. Smith Barracks, Germany, 1003

92nd Operations Group
Fairchild Air Force Base, Fairchild AFB, WA, 919

92nd Support Group
Fairchild Air Force Base, Fairchild AFB, WA, 919

93rd Air Control Wing
Robins Air Force Base, Robins AFB, GA, 259

93rd Signal Bn
Army Signal Center & Fort Gordon, Fort Gordon, GA, 249

93rd Troop Command
New Mexico National Guard State Headquarters, Santa Fe, NM, 573

94th Air Defense Artillery
223rd Base Support Battalion, Germany, 993

94th Airlift Wing (AFRC)
Dobbins Air Reserve Base, Marietta, GA, 257

94th Engineers, A Co
282nd Base Support Battalion, Germany, 995

94th Engineers Bn
Rose Barracks, Germany, 1027

94th Regional Support Command
Devens Reserve Forces Training Center, Devens, MA, 439

95th Adjutant General Bn (Reception)
Fort Sill, Fort Sill, OK, 671

95th Air Base Wing
Edwards Air Force Base, Edwards AFB, CA, 63

95th Civil Engineering Squadron
Edwards Air Force Base, Edwards AFB, CA, 63

95th Communications-Computer Systems Squadron
Edwards Air Force Base, Edwards AFB, CA, 63

1st Brigade, 95th Division (IT)(USAR)
Keathley Army Reserve Center, Lawton, OK, 672

95th Maintenance Co
Fort Lewis, Fort Lewis, WA, 921

95th Medical Group
Edwards Air Force Base, Edwards AFB, CA, 63

95th Military Police Bn
Taylor Barracks, Germany, 1034

95th Mission Support Squadron
Edwards Air Force Base, Edwards AFB, CA, 63

95th Reconnaissance Squadron
Mildenhall RAF Base, United Kingdom, 1167

95th Security Police
Edwards Air Force Base, Edwards AFB, CA, 63

95th Supply Squadron
Edwards Air Force Base, Edwards AFB, CA, 63

95th Transportation Squadron
Edwards Air Force Base, Edwards AFB, CA, 63

97th Air Mobility Wing
Altus Air Force Base, Altus AFB, OK, 668

97th Army Reserve Command
Willow Grove Naval Air Station (JRB), Willow Grove, PA, 723

97th Logistics Group
Altus Air Force Base, Altus AFB, OK, 668

97th Medical Group
Altus Air Force Base, Altus AFB, OK, 668

97th Operations Group
Altus Air Force Base, Altus AFB, OK, 668

97th Support Group
Altus Air Force Base, Altus AFB, OK, 668

98th Area Support Group
98th Area Support Group, Germany, 990

98th Area Support Group, Headquarters
Faulenberg Kaserne, Würzburg, Germany, 1038

98th Support Brigade Troop Command (ANG)
Adjutant General of Arizona, Phoenix, AZ, 39

98th Support Group, Headquarters and Headquarters Co
Faulenberg Kaserne, Würzburg, Germany, 1038

99th Air Base Wing
Nellis Air Force Base, Nellis AFB, NV, 541

99th Army Reserve Command Aviation Support Facility, Eustis
Army Transportation Center & Fort Eustis, Fort Eustis, VA, 868

99th Civil Engineering Squadron
Nellis Air Force Base, Nellis AFB, NV, 541

99th Communications Squadron
Nellis Air Force Base, Nellis AFB, NV, 541

99th Comptroller Squadron
Nellis Air Force Base, Nellis AFB, NV, 541

99th Contracting Squadron
Nellis Air Force Base, Nellis AFB, NV, 541

99th Electronic Combat Range Group, Det 18
99th Electronic Combat Range Group, Forsyth, MT, 518

99th Flying Training Squadron
Randolph Air Force Base, Randolph AFB, TX, 814

99th Logistics Group
Nellis Air Force Base, Nellis AFB, NV, 541

99th Medical Group
Nellis Air Force Base, Nellis AFB, NV, 541

99th Mission Support Squadron
Nellis Air Force Base, Nellis AFB, NV, 541

99th Range Group
Nellis Air Force Base, Nellis AFB, NV, 541

99th Range Squadron
Nellis Air Force Base, Nellis AFB, NV, 541

99th Range Support Squadron
Nellis Air Force Base, Nellis AFB, NV, 541

99th Range Support Squadron, Operating Location-B (Nellis AFB, NV)
99th Range Support Squadron, OL-B, La Junta, CO, 155

99th Regional Support Command
Charles E Kelly Support Facility, Oakdale, PA, 711

99th Security Forces Squadron
Nellis Air Force Base, Nellis AFB, NV, 541

99th Services Squadron
Nellis Air Force Base, Nellis AFB, NV, 541

99th Supply Squadron
Nellis Air Force Base, Nellis AFB, NV, 541

99th Support Group
Nellis Air Force Base, Nellis AFB, NV, 541

99th Transportation Squadron
Nellis Air Force Base, Nellis AFB, NV, 541

100th Air Refueling Wing
Mildenhall RAF Base, United Kingdom, 1167

100th Area Support Group
100th Area Support Group, Germany, 991

100th Division (Training), 4th Brigade (Training Support)
Army Armor Center & Fort Knox, Fort Knox, KY, 366

101st Air Refueling Wing, HQ
Bangor IAP Air National Guard Base, Bangor, ME, 393

101st Airborne Division (Air Assault)
Fort Bragg, Fort Bragg, NC, 624
Fort Campbell, Fort Campbell, KY, 365

101st Civil Engineering Squadron
Bangor IAP Air National Guard Base, Bangor, ME, 393

101st Consolidated Aircraft Maintenance Squadron
Bangor IAP Air National Guard Base, Bangor, ME, 393

101st Military Intelligence
67th Combat Support Hospital/USAMED-DAC, Germany, 989

101st Military Intelligence Bn
98th Area Support Group, Germany, 990

101st Mission Support Flight
Bangor IAP Air National Guard Base, Bangor, ME, 393

101st Mission Support Squadron
Bangor IAP Air National Guard Base, Bangor, ME, 393

101st Resource Management Squadron
Bangor IAP Air National Guard Base, Bangor, ME, 393

101st Security Police Flight
Bangor IAP Air National Guard Base, Bangor, ME, 393

101st Weather Flight (ANG)
Massachusetts Military Reservation/Otis Air National Guard Base, Cape Cod, MA, 437

102nd Fighter Interceptor Wing (ANG)
Massachusetts Military Reservation/Otis Air National Guard Base, Cape Cod, MA, 437

102nd Fighter Wing
Cape Cod Coast Guard Air Station, Cape Cod, MA, 436

102nd Military Intelligence Bn
Camp Essayons, Korea, Republic of, 1093

102nd Rescue Squadron
Francis S Gabreski Airport (ANG Base), Westhampton Beach, NY, 615

102nd Signal Bn
Baumholder Military Community, H.D. Smith Barracks, Germany, 1003

103rd Military Intelligence Bn
Fort Stewart, Hinesville, GA, 252

103rd Public Affairs Det
Fort William Henry Harrison, Helena, MT, 523

103rd Tactical Fighter Group (ANG)
Bradley IAP Air National Guard Base, Windsor Locks, CT, 166

104th Area Support Group
414th Base Support Battalion, Germany, 997

104th Fighter Wing (ANG)
Barnes Municipal Airport, Air National Guard Base, Westfield, MA, 446

7th Brigade, 104th Infantry Division (Reserve)
Fort Lewis, Fort Lewis, WA, 921

104th Infantry Division (TNG)(Reserve)
Vancouver Barracks, Vancouver, WA, 938

104th TCS/OLAA
Kingsley Field Air National Guard Base, Klamath Falls, OR, 687

105th Airlift Squadron
Nashville IAP, ANG Base, Nashville, TN, 770

105th Airlift Wing
Stewart Air National Guard Base, Newburgh, NY, 599

1st Bn 105th Infantry, Co A
Camp Smith, Peekskill, NY, 601

106th Finance
280th Base Support Battalion, Germany, 994
282nd Base Support Battalion, Germany, 995

106th Finance Bn, Det B
Bamberg Military Community, Germany, 1001

106th Finance Support Command
98th Area Support Group, Germany, 990

106th Medical Det (Vet)
Camp Hialeah, Korea, Republic of, 1099

106th Regimental Training Institute
Camp Smith, Peekskill, NY, 601

106th Rescue Wing (ARG)
Francis S Gabreski Airport (ANG Base), Westhampton Beach, NY, 615

107th Air Refueling Wing, ANG
Niagara Falls Air Reserve Station, Niagara Falls, NY, 600

107th Armored Cavalry
Ohio National Guard, Unit Training Equipment Site #1, Newton Falls, OH, 660

107th Fighter Interceptor Group, Det 1
Charleston Air Force Base, Charleston AFB, SC, 737

107th Medical Co (AA)
Army Aviation Support Facility #1, North Canton, OH, 661

108th Air Defense Artillery Brigade
Fort Bragg, Fort Bragg, NC, 624

108th Air Refueling Wing (ANG)
McGuire Air Force Base, McGuire AFB, NJ, 561

108th Aviation
Adjutant General of Arizona, Phoenix, AZ, 39

108th Tactical Control Squadron (ANG)
Syracuse Hancock IAP, Air National Guard Base, Syracuse, NY, 610

109th Airlift Wing (ANG)
Schenectady County Airport, Air National Guard Base, Scotia, NY, 607

109th Tactical Control Flight (ANG)
Salt Lake City IAP, Air National Guard Base, Salt Lake City, UT, 828

110th Fighter Wing (ANG)
W K Kellogg Airport, Air National Guard Base, Battle Creek, MI, 453

110th Medical Det (VETS)
414th Base Support Battalion, Germany, 997

110th Military Intelligence F Co
Fort Wainwright, Fort Wainwright, AK, 28

110th Resource Management Squadron
W K Kellogg Airport, Air National Guard Base, Battle Creek, MI, 453

110th Weather Flight
Lambert Field Air National Guard Base, Bridgeton, MO, 498

111th Military Intelligence Brigade
Fort Huachuca, Fort Huachuca, AZ, 35

111th Pennsylvania Air National Guard
Willow Grove Naval Air Station (JRB), Willow Grove, PA, 723

113th Army Band (Dragoons)
Army Armor Center & Fort Knox, Fort Knox, KY, 366

113th Aviation Bn, Det 1, HQ & HQ Co
Stead Training Center, Reno, NV, 545

113th Aviation Det 1, Co D
Stead Training Center, Reno, NV, 545

113th Cavalry, Troops A & B, 1st Squadron
Camp Dodge Iowa, Johnston, IA, 346

113th Fighter Wing (DC ANG)
Andrews Air Force Base, Andrews AFB, MD, 407

113th Tactical Control Squadron (ANG)
Syracuse Hancock IAP, Air National Guard Base, Syracuse, NY, 610

114th Combat Communications Squadron
Patrick Air Force Base, Patrick AFB, FL, 221

114th Fighter Wing (ANG)
South Dakota Air National Guard Base, Sioux Falls, SD, 755

114th Tactical Fighter Training Squadron
Kingsley Field Air National Guard Base, Klamath Falls, OR, 687

115th Aircraft Generation Squadron
Truax Field Air National Guard Base, Madison, WI, 958

115th Civil Engineer Squadron
Truax Field Air National Guard Base, Madison, WI, 958

115th Communications Flight
Truax Field Air National Guard Base, Madison, WI, 958

115th Fighter Wing
Truax Field Air National Guard Base, Madison, WI, 958

115th Logistics Group
Truax Field Air National Guard Base, Madison, WI, 958

115th Logistics Squadron
Truax Field Air National Guard Base, Madison, WI, 958

115th Logistics Support Flight
Truax Field Air National Guard Base, Madison, WI, 958

115th Maintenance Squadron
Truax Field Air National Guard Base, Madison, WI, 958

115th Medical Squadron
Truax Field Air National Guard Base, Madison, WI, 958

115th Mission Support Flight
Truax Field Air National Guard Base, Madison, WI, 958

115th Operations Group
Truax Field Air National Guard Base, Madison, WI, 958

115th Operations Support Flight
Truax Field Air National Guard Base, Madison, WI, 958

115th Security Police Squadron
Truax Field Air National Guard Base, Madison, WI, 958

115th Services Flight
Truax Field Air National Guard Base, Madison, WI, 958

115th Support Group
Truax Field Air National Guard Base, Madison, WI, 958

116th Bomb Wing
Robins Air Force Base, Robins AFB, GA, 259

116th Tactical Control Squadron
Camp Rilea, Oregon National Guard Training Site, Salem, OR, 692

117 Air Refueling Wing (ANG)
Birmingham Airport, Air National Guard Base, Birmingham, AL, 4

117th Engineer Det
Camp W G Williams, Riverton, UT, 827

117th Refueling Squadron
Forbes Field Air National Guard Base, Topeka, KS, 361

117th TAC RECON Wing (ANG)
Birmingham Airport, Air National Guard Base, Birmingham, AL, 4

117th Tactical Air Command Control Squadron, Air National Guard
Hunter Army Air Field, Savannah, GA, 260

119th Fighter Interceptor Wing (ANG)
Hector IAP, Air National Guard Base, Fargo, ND, 640

119th Fighter Wing
March Air Reserve Base, March ARB, CA, 80

120th Adjutant General BN (Reception)
Fort Jackson, Columbia, SC, 740

120th Fighter Wing (ANG)
Montana Air National Guard, Great Falls, MT, 521

120th Public Affairs Det
Camp Atterbury, Edinburgh, IN, 325

120th Quartermaster Det
Camp W G Williams, Riverton, UT, 827

121st Air Refueling Wing (ANG)
Rickenbacker IAP, Air National Guard Base, Columbus, OH, 655

121st Evacuation Hospital
Yongsan Army Garrison, Korea, Republic of, 1121

121st Signal Bn
Kitzingen Military Community, Germany, 1017

122nd Fighter Wing (ANG)
Fort Wayne IAP, Air National Guard Base, Fort Wayne, IN, 328

122nd Signal Bn, A Co
Camp Casey, Korea, Republic of, 1089

122nd Signal Bn, B Co
Camp Casey, Korea, Republic of, 1089

122nd Signal Bn, C Co
Camp Red Cloud, Korea, Republic of, 1109

122nd Signal Bn, D Co
Camp Red Cloud, Korea, Republic of, 1109

122nd Signal Bn, HQ
Camp Casey, Korea, Republic of, 1089
Camp Red Cloud, Korea, Republic of, 1109

122nd Smoke Co
Nevada National Guard Las Vegas, Las
Vegas, NV, 540

122nd Weather Flight
Hammond Air National Guard Station,
Hammond, LA, 378

123rd Airlift Wing
Standiford Field Air National Guard Base,
Louisville, KY, 372

123rd Main Support Bn
Anderson Barracks, Germany, 998

123rd Public Affairs Det 1
New Mexico National Guard State Headquarters, Santa Fe, NM, 573

123rd Signal Bn
Fort Stewart, Hinesville, GA, 252

123rd Weather Flight (ANG)
Portland Air National Guard Base, Portland IAP, OR, 691

124th Wing (ANG)
Boise Air Terminal, Air National Guard
Base, Boise, ID, 295

125th Fighter Wing (ANG)
Jacksonville IAP, Air National Guard
Base, Jacksonville, FL, 204

125th Fighter Wing, Det 1 (FL ANG)
Homestead Air Reserve Base, Homestead
ARB, FL, 199

127th Aviation Support Bn
414th Base Support Battalion, Germany,
997

127th Military Police Co
414th Base Support Battalion, Germany,
997

127th Postal Co
Johnson Barracks, Germany, 1012

127th Weather Flight
Forbes Field Air National Guard Base,
Topeka, KS, 361

127th Wing (ANG)
Selfridge Air National Guard Base, Selfridge ANG Base, MI, 464

128th Air Control Squadron (ACS)
Volk Field Air National Guard Base,
Camp Douglas, WI, 953

128th Air Refueling Wing (ANG)
Mitchell Field Air National Guard Base,
Milwaukee, WI, 963

130th Airlift Wing (ANG)
Yeager Airport, Air National Guard Base,
Charleston, WV, 944

130th Engineer Brigade
414th Base Support Battalion, Germany,
997

**130th Engineering Installation
Squadron (ANG)**
Salt Lake City IAP, Air National Guard
Base, Salt Lake City, UT, 828

131st Fighter Wing (ANG)
Lambert Field Air National Guard Base,
Bridgeton, MO, 498

132nd Air Refueling Squadron
Bangor IAP Air National Guard Base, Bangor, ME, 393

132nd Fighter Wing (ANG)
Des Moines IAP, Air National Guard Base,
Des Moines, IA, 342

133rd Airlift Wing (ANG)
Minneapolis-Saint Paul IAP, Air National
Guard Base/ARS, Minneapolis-Saint
Paul IAP, MN, 474

133rd Dental Det
Anderson Barracks, Germany, 998

133rd Medical Det
414th Base Support Battalion, Germany,
997

133rd Naval Mobile Construction Bn
Gulfport Naval Construction Battalion Center, Gulfport, MS, 482

134th Air Refueling Wing (ANG)
McGee Tyson Airport, Air National Guard
Base, Knoxville, TN, 762

**135th Communications Squadron,
Det**
414th Base Support Battalion, Germany,
997

135th Public Affairs Det
Camp Dodge Iowa, Johnston, IA, 346

136th Aircraft Generation Squadron
Hensley Field Texas Air National Guard
Base, Dallas, TX, 785

136th Airlift Wing (AMC)
Hensley Field Texas Air National Guard
Base, Dallas, TX, 785

136th Civil Engineering Squadron
Hensley Field Texas Air National Guard
Base, Dallas, TX, 785

136th Communications Squadron
Hensley Field Texas Air National Guard
Base, Dallas, TX, 785

136th Maintenance Squadron
Hensley Field Texas Air National Guard
Base, Dallas, TX, 785

136th Medical Support Squadron
Hensley Field Texas Air National Guard
Base, Dallas, TX, 785

136th Mission Support Squadron
Hensley Field Texas Air National Guard
Base, Dallas, TX, 785

136th Mobile Aerial Port Squadron
Hensley Field Texas Air National Guard
Base, Dallas, TX, 785

136th Quartermasters Bn
Camp Gilbert C Grafton, Devils Lake, ND,
638

136th Security Police Squadron
Hensley Field Texas Air National Guard
Base, Dallas, TX, 785

136th Tactical Airlift Wing (ANG)
Dallas NAS, Air National Guard Base, Dallas, TX, 784

**136th Tactical Airlift Wing (TX
ANG)**
Fort Worth, Naval Air Station, Joint Re-
serve Base, Fort Worth, TX, 796

136th Tactical Wing (TX ANG)
Dallas Naval Air Station, Dallas, TX, 783

137th Airlift Wing (ANG)
Will Rogers World Airport, Air National
Guard Base, Oklahoma City, OK, 677

Det 1, Co D, 137th AVIM
Army Aviation Support Facility #1, North
Canton, OH, 661

137th Decontamination Co
Nevada National Guard Las Vegas, Las
Vegas, NV, 540

137th Ordnance Det
Fort Sam Houston, Fort Sam Houston, TX,
794

138th Fighter Wing (ANG)
Tulsa IAP, Air National Guard Base,
Tulsa, OK, 679

138th Finance Bn
Camp Atterbury, Edinburgh, IN, 325

138th Finance Bn, HQ
Old Fort Benjamin Harrison, Indianapolis,
IN, 336

139th Airlift Wing (ANG)
Rosecrans Memorial Airport, Air National
Guard Base, Saint Joseph, MO, 509

139th Public Affairs Det
Camp Lincoln, Springfield, IL, 320

**140th Regiment (Regional Training
Institute)**
Camp W G Williams, Riverton, UT, 827

140th Wing (ANG)
Buckley Air National Guard Base, Aurora,
CO, 142

**141st Air Refueling Wing (WA
ANG)**
Fairchild Air Force Base, Fairchild AFB,
WA, 919

141st Field Artillery, 1st Bn
Jackson Barracks, New Orleans, LA, 382

142nd Fighter Wing (ANG)
Portland Air National Guard Base, Portland IAP, OR, 691

142nd Medical Bn
Fort Clayton, Panama, 1133

142nd Signal Brigade (FWD)
Fort Lewis, Fort Lewis, WA, 921

143rd Airlift Wing (ANG)
Quonset State Airport, Air National Guard
Base, North Kingstown, RI, 728

144th Army Band
Camp Lincoln, Springfield, IL, 320

**144th Field Artillery, Headquarters
and Headquarters Bn 2nd Bn,
Det 1**
Nevada National Guard Las Vegas, Las
Vegas, NV, 540

144th Fighter Wing, Headquarters
Fresno Air National Guard Base, Fresno
Air Terminal, CA, 72

144th Logistics Group
Fresno Air National Guard Base, Fresno Air Terminal, CA, 72

144th Medical Squadron
Fresno Air National Guard Base, Fresno Air Terminal, CA, 72

144th Operations Group
Fresno Air National Guard Base, Fresno Air Terminal, CA, 72

144th Support Group
Fresno Air National Guard Base, Fresno Air Terminal, CA, 72

144th Tactical Airlift Squadron
Kulis Air National Guard Base, Anchorage, AK, 20

145th Aerial Port Squadron
145th Airlift Wing, Charlotte, NC, 619

145th Airlift Wing, HQ
145th Airlift Wing, Charlotte, NC, 619

145th Civil Engineering Squadron
145th Airlift Wing, Charlotte, NC, 619

145th Communications Flight
145th Airlift Wing, Charlotte, NC, 619

145th Logistics Squadron
145th Airlift Wing, Charlotte, NC, 619

145th Maintenance Squadron
145th Airlift Wing, Charlotte, NC, 619

145th Medical Squadron
145th Airlift Wing, Charlotte, NC, 619

145th Mission Support
145th Airlift Wing, Charlotte, NC, 619

145th Security Police Squadron
145th Airlift Wing, Charlotte, NC, 619

145th Services Flight
145th Airlift Wing, Charlotte, NC, 619

146th Field Artillery, 2nd Bn (WANG)
Vancouver Barracks, Vancouver, WA, 938

147th Army Band
Mitchell National Guard Complex, Mitchell, SD, 752

147th Field Artillery, Battery A, 1st Bn
Mitchell National Guard Complex, Mitchell, SD, 752

147th Fighter Wing (ANG)
Ellington Field, Air National Guard Base, Houston, TX, 803

147th Maintenance Co
Kitzingen Military Community, Germany, 1017

148th Combat Communications Squadron (ANG)
Ontario Air National Guard Station, Ontario, CA, 93

148th Fighter Wing
Duluth IAP Air National Guard Base, Duluth, MN, 468

148th Fighter Wing, Det 1 (MN ANG)
Tyndall Air Force Base, Panama City, FL, 220

148th Medical Co
Army Aviation Support Facility, Winder, GA, 264

149th Fighter Group (TX ANG)
Kelly Air Force Base, Kelly AFB, TX, 807

149th Maintenance Co
414th Base Support Battalion, Germany, 997

149th Mobile Army Surgical Hospital
Camp Atterbury, Edinburgh, IN, 325

150th Aircraft Control & Warning Flight
Kokee Air Force Station, Waimea, HI, 292

150th Maintenance Co
Nevada National Guard Headquarters, Carson City, NV, 534

150th Maintenance Co, Det 1
Nevada National Guard Las Vegas, Las Vegas, NV, 540

151st Air Refueling Wing (ANG)
Salt Lake City IAP, Air National Guard Base, Salt Lake City, UT, 828

151st Army Aviation 1st Bn (SC ANG)
McEntire Air National Guard Station, Eastover, SC, 741

151st Medical Bn (ARNG)
Dobbins Air Reserve Base, Marietta, GA, 257

152nd Airlift Wing (ANG)
Reno/Tahoe IAP, Air National Guard Base, Reno, NV, 544

152nd Tactical Control Group
Syracuse Hancock IAP, Air National Guard Base, Syracuse, NY, 610

153rd Airlift Wing (ANG)
Cheyenne Municipal Airport, Air National Guard Base, Cheyenne, WY, 965

153rd Field Artillery Brigade (ANG)
Adjutant General of Arizona, Phoenix, AZ, 39

155th Air Refueling Group (ANG)
Lincoln Air National Guard Base, Lincoln, NE, 528

156th Det ANG
Camp Santiago, Puerto Rico, 1140

157th Air Refueling Wing (ANG)
Pease Air National Guard Base, Pease ANGB, NH, 550

1st Bn, 157th Field Artillery, B Battery
Camp George West, Golden, CO, 154

158th Fighter Wing (ANG)
Burlington IAP, Air National Guard Base, Burlington IAP, VT, 831

159th Aviation Regiment, 6th Bn, C Co
Giebelstadt Army Airfield, Germany, 1010

159th Aviation Regiment, 5th Bn, A Co
Giebelstadt Army Airfield, Germany, 1010

159th Fighter Wing (LA ANG)
New Orleans Naval Air Station Joint Reserve Base, Air Force Reserve, New Orleans, LA, 383

159th Infantry (ARNG)
Parks Reserve Forces Training Area, Dublin, CA, 62

159th MASH
Jackson Barracks, New Orleans, LA, 382

159th Tactical Fighter Group (LA ANG)
New Orleans Naval Air Station Joint Reserve Base, Naval Air Station, New Orleans, LA, 384

159th Weather Flight (ANG)
Camp Blanding Training Site, Starke, FL, 232

3rd Bn, 160th Special Operations Aviation Regiment (ABN)
Hunter Army Air Field, Savannah, GA, 260

160th Special Operations Aviation Regiment (Airborne)
Fort Campbell, Fort Campbell, KY, 365

160th Special Operations Aviation Regiment, D Co
Fort Clayton, Panama, 1133

161st Air Refueling Wing (ANG)
Sky Harbor IAP, Air National Guard Base, Phoenix, AZ, 41

162nd Fighter Wing (ANG)
Tucson IAP, Air National Guard Base, Tucson, AZ, 43

163rd Air Refueling Wing
March Air Reserve Base, March ARB, CA, 80

163rd Armored Bn
Fort William Henry Harrison, Helena, MT, 523

164th Airlift Wing (ANG)
Memphis IAP, Air National Guard Base, Memphis, TN, 764

164th Regiment Regional Training Institute, HQ
Camp Gilbert C Grafton, Devils Lake, ND, 638

165th Airlift Squadron
Standiford Field Air National Guard Base, Louisville, KY, 372

165th Airlift Wing (ANG)
Savannah IAP Air National Guard Base, Garden City, GA, 251

165th Military Intelligence Bn
223rd Base Support Battalion, Germany, 993

165th Transportation Bn, HQ and HQ Det
Camp Beauregard, Pineville, LA, 388

166th Airlift Wing (ANG)
New Castle County Airport, Air National Guard Base, Wilmington, DE, 169

167th Airlift Wing (ANG)
Eastern West Virginia Regional Airport, Air National Guard Base, Martinsburg, WV, 948

168th Air Refueling Wing (ANG)
Eielson Air Force Base, Eielson AFB, AK, 24

168th Medical Bn
Camp Carroll, Korea, Republic of, 1088

169th Electronic Security Squadron (ANG)
Salt Lake City IAP, Air National Guard Base, Salt Lake City, UT, 828

169th Engineer Bn
Fort Leonard Wood, Fort Leonard Wood, MO, 501

169th Fighter Wing (ANG)
McEntire Air National Guard Station, Eastover, SC, 741

169th Leadership Regiment
Camp Rowland, Niantic, CT, 163

171st Air Refueling Wing (ANG)
Pittsburgh International Airport Air National Guard Base, Coraopolis, PA, 700

171st CSAB
Army Aviation Support Facility, Winder, GA, 264

172nd Fighter Squadron
W K Kellogg Airport, Air National Guard Base, Battle Creek, MI, 453

172nd Infantry, 3rd Det, HQ (MTN)
Ethan Allen Firing Range, Jericho, VT, 833

172nd Logistics Group (ANG)
Allen C Thompson Air National Guard Base, Jackson, MS, 486

172nd Operations Group (ANG)
Allen C Thompson Air National Guard Base, Jackson, MS, 486

172nd Support Group (ANG)
Allen C Thompson Air National Guard Base, Jackson, MS, 486

172nd Tactical Airlift Group (ANG)
Allen C Thompson Air National Guard Base, Jackson, MS, 486

173rd Civil Engineering Flight
Gulfport-Biloxi Regional Airport, Air National Guard Base, Gulfport, MS, 481

173rd Fighter Wing
Kingsley Field Air National Guard Base, Klamath Falls, OR, 687

174th Corps Support Group
Fort Lawton, 70th Regional Support Command, Fort Lawton, WA, 920

174th Fighter Wing (ANG)
Syracuse Hancock IAP, Air National Guard Base, Syracuse, NY, 610

175th Wing (ANG)
Martin State Airport, Air National Guard Base, Baltimore, MD, 414

176th Composite Group
Kulis Air National Guard Base, Anchorage, AK, 20

176th Fighter Squadron
Truax Field Air National Guard Base, Madison, WI, 958

176th Finance Det
Camp Atterbury, Edinburgh, IN, 325

Old Fort Benjamin Harrison, Indianapolis, IN, 336

176th Medical Squadron
Kulis Air National Guard Base, Anchorage, AK, 20

177th Fighter Wing (ANG)
Atlantic City Airport, Air National Guard Base, Pleasantville, NJ, 563

177th Finance Bn
Camp Casey, Korea, Republic of, 1089

177th Finance Det
Camp Atterbury, Edinburgh, IN, 325
Old Fort Benjamin Harrison, Indianapolis, IN, 336

178th Fighter Wing (ANG)
Springfield Municipal Airport Air National Guard Base, Springfield, OH, 664

178th Finance Det
Camp Atterbury, Edinburgh, IN, 325
Old Fort Benjamin Harrison, Indianapolis, IN, 336

179th Airlift Wing (ANG)
Mansfield Lahm Airport, Air National Guard Base, Mansfield, OH, 659

179th Fighter Squadron
Duluth IAP Air National Guard Base, Duluth, MN, 468

180th Fighter Wing (ANG)
Toledo Express Airport, Air National Guard Base, Swanton, OH, 665

181st Fighter Wing (ANG)
Hulman Regional Airport, Air National Guard Base, Terre Haute, IN, 339

181st Signal Bn, DCS Landstuhl
Landstuhl Regional Medical Center, Germany, 1020

181st Transportation Bn
Taylor Barracks, Germany, 1034

181st Weather Flight
Hensley Field Texas Air National Guard Base, Dallas, TX, 785

182nd Airlift Wing (ANG)
Greater Peoria Regional Airport Air National Guard Base, Peoria, IL, 312

182nd Logistics Group (ANG)
Greater Peoria Regional Airport Air National Guard Base, Peoria, IL, 312

182nd Operations Group (ANG)
Greater Peoria Regional Airport Air National Guard Base, Peoria, IL, 312

182nd Support Group (ANG)
Greater Peoria Regional Airport Air National Guard Base, Peoria, IL, 312

183rd Fighter Wing (ANG)
Capital Municipal Airport, Air National Guard Base, Springfield, IL, 321

184th Bomb Wing (KS ANG)
McConnell Air Force Base, McConnell AFB, KS, 354

184th Fighter Wing (ANG)
Fort Smith Municipal Airport, Air National Guard Base, Fort Smith, AR, 47

185th Fighter Wing (ANG)
Sioux Gateway Airport, Air National Guard Base, Sergeant Bluff, IA, 348

185th Regional Training Institute
Camp Dodge Iowa, Johnston, IA, 346

185th Supply & Service Bn
Camp Dodge Iowa, Johnston, IA, 346

186th Air Refueling Wing (ANG)
Key Field, Air National Guard Base, Meridian, MS, 488

186th Fighter Squadron (ANG)
Montana Air National Guard, Great Falls, MT, 521

187th Fighter Group (ANG)
Dannelly Field Air National Guard Base, Montgomery, AL, 14

188th General Dispensary
Bamberg Military Community, Germany, 1001

189th Airlift Group (ANG)
Little Rock Air Force Base, Little Rock AFB, AR, 50

190th Air Force Clinic
Forbes Field Air National Guard Base, Topeka, KS, 361

190th Air Refueling Group
Forbes Field Air National Guard Base, Topeka, KS, 361

192nd Fighter Wing
Richmond IAP Air National Guard Base, Sandston, VA, 901

193rd Aviation Bn, C Co (ANG)
Wheeler Army Airfield, Wheeler Army Airfield, HI, 293

193rd Logistics Group
Harrisburg IAP Air National Guard Base, Middletown, PA, 708

193rd Military Police Bn
Camp George West, Golden, CO, 154

193rd Military Police Customs
Barton Barracks, Ansbach, Germany, 1002

193rd Operations Group
Harrisburg IAP Air National Guard Base, Middletown, PA, 708

193rd Special Operations Wing
Harrisburg IAP Air National Guard Base, Middletown, PA, 708

193rd Support Bn
Fort Clayton, Panama, 1133

193rd Support Group
Harrisburg IAP Air National Guard Base, Middletown, PA, 708

194th Infantry Det (ABN)
Camp Dodge Iowa, Johnston, IA, 346

194th Maintenance Bn
Camp Humphreys, Korea, Republic of, 1102

198th Army Reserve Hospital
Fort Wainwright, Fort Wainwright, AK, 28

199th Band
Camp Smith, Peekskill, NY, 601

200th Bulk Petroleum Accounting Activity
Bamberg Military Community, Germany, 1001

200th Red Horse Civil Engineering Squadron (OH Air NG)
Camp Perry Training Site, Port Clinton, OH, 663

200th Weather Flight
Richmond IAP Air National Guard Base, Sandston, VA, 901

201st Evacuation Hospital
Camp Santiago, Puerto Rico, 1140

201st Field Artillery, Service Battery
Camp Dawson, Kingwood, WV, 947

201st Forward Support Bn, B Co
Bamberg Military Community, Germany, 1001

201st Military Intelligence Brigade
Fort Lewis, Fort Lewis, WA, 921

201st Support Bn
Rose Barracks, Germany, 1027
Rose Barracks, Vilseck, Germany, 1028

202nd Civil Engineering Squadron (CES), Florida Air National Guard
Camp Blanding Training Site, Starke, FL, 232

202nd Military Intelligence Brigade
Fort Clayton, Panama, 1133

202nd Weather Flight (ANG)
Massachusetts Military Reservation/Otis Air National Guard Base, Cape Cod, MA, 437

203rd Military Intelligence Bn
Aberdeen Proving Ground, Aberdeen Proving Ground, MD, 404

203rd Personnel Service Bn
Fort Wainwright, Fort Wainwright, AK, 28

204th Area Support Group
Jackson Barracks, New Orleans, LA, 382

204th Military Intelligence Bn
Fort Bliss, El Paso, TX, 790

205th Combat Communication Squadron
Standiford Field Air National Guard Base, Louisville, KY, 372

205th Military Intelligence Brigade
221st Base Support Battalion, Germany, 992

207th Aviation Co
Heidelberg Military Community, Germany, 1011

208th Finance Bn
Sullivan Barracks, Germany, 1033

208th Finance Bn, Det D
Caserma Ederle/Vicenza Military Community, Vincenza, Italy, 1060

208th Personnel Det
Camp Rowland, Niantic, CT, 163

208th Regional Training Institute
Fort William Henry Harrison, Helena, MT, 523

210st Air Rescue Squadron
Kulis Air National Guard Base, Anchorage, AK, 20

210th Engineering Installation Squadron (ANG)
Minneapolis-Saint Paul IAP, Air National Guard Base/ARS, Minneapolis-Saint Paul IAP, MN, 474

210th Rescue Squadron, Det 1 (ANG)
Eielson Air Force Base, Eielson AFB, AK, 24

210th Weather Flight
Ontario Air National Guard Station, Ontario, CA, 93

212th Military Police
280th Base Support Battalion, Germany, 994

212th Military Police Co
Kitzingen Military Community, Germany, 1017

HHC, 213 Medical Bde, Health Service Liaison Det
Camp Keyes, Augusta, ME, 392

213th Engineer Installation Squadron
Roslyn Station, Air National Guard, Roslyn, NY, 606

213th Maintenance Co
Camp Perry Training Site, Port Clinton, OH, 663

214th Engineering Installation Squadron
Jackson Barracks, New Orleans, LA, 382

218th Field Artillery, 2nd Bn, Headquarters (ARNG)
Portland Air National Guard Base, Portland IAP, OR, 691

218th Medical Clinic
Camp Long, Korea, Republic of, 1104

219th Electronic Installation Squadron
Tulsa IAP, Air National Guard Base, Tulsa, OK, 679

219th Field Training Det
Dover Air Force Base, Dover AFB, DE, 167

220th Military Police Co
Camp George West, Golden, CO, 154

221st Armor, 1st Bn, Companies B, C, and D
Nevada National Guard Henderson, Henderson, NV, 538

221st Armor, 1st Bn, Det 1, HQ and HQ Co
Nevada Army National Guard, Fallon, Fallon, NV, 536

221st Armor, 1st Bn, Headquarters and Headquarters Co
Nevada National Guard Las Vegas, Las Vegas, NV, 540

221st Base Support Bn
221st Base Support Battalion, Germany, 992

221st Combat Communications Squadron
Garland Air National Guard Station, Garland, TX, 800

221st Ordnance Det
Camp Blanding Training Site, Starke, FL, 232

222nd Base Support Bn
Baumholder Military Community, H.D. Smith Barracks, Germany, 1003

222nd Judge Advocate General, Det
Vancouver Barracks, Vancouver, WA, 938

223rd Base Support Bn
223rd Base Support Battalion, Germany, 993

224th Military Intelligence Bn
Hunter Army Air Field, Savannah, GA, 260

225th Engineer Group (Aviation), Det 1
Camp Beauregard, Pineville, LA, 388

225th Engineer Group, HQ and HQ Co
Camp Beauregard, Pineville, LA, 388

226th Transportation Co
Charles Melvin Price Army Support Center, Granite City, IL, 307

226th Transportation Co (RR Engr)
Charles Melvin Price Army Support Center, Granite City, IL, 307

227th Air Traffic Control Flight (ANG)
Buckley Air National Guard Base, Aurora, CO, 142

227th Maintenance Bn
Yongsan Army Garrison, Korea, Republic of, 1121

1st Bn, 228th Aviation Regiment
Fort Clayton, Panama, 1133

228th Aviation Regiment, 4th Bn (Camp Pickett)
Joint Task Force—Bravo, Honduras, 1048

228th Combat Communications Squadron
McGee Tyson Airport, Air National Guard Base, Knoxville, TN, 762

229th Engineer Det
Camp Dawson, Kingwood, WV, 947

229th Military Intelligence Bn
Presidio of Monterey, Monterey, CA, 85

232nd S & S Bn
Camp Lincoln, Springfield, IL, 320

235th Base Support Bn, HQ
Barton Barracks, Ansbach, Germany, 1002

236th Combat Communications Squadron
Hammond Air National Guard Station, Hammond, LA, 378

237th Air Traffic Control Flight (ANG)
Minneapolis-Saint Paul IAP, Air National Guard Base/ARS, Minneapolis-Saint Paul IAP, MN, 474

238th Combat Communications Squadron (ANG)
Key Field, Air National Guard Base, Meridian, MS, 488

240th Civil Engineering Flight (ANG)
Buckley Air National Guard Base, Aurora, CO, 142

240th Combat Communications Squadron
McEntire Air National Guard Station, Eastover, SC, 741

240th Quartermaster Supply Co
Bamberg Military Community, Germany, 1001
Johnson Barracks, Germany, 1012

243rd Engineering Installations Squadron
South Portland Air National Guard Station, South Portland, ME, 401

244th Aviation Bn, Det 1, Co B
Army Aviation Support Facility, Winder, GA, 264

244th Aviation Brigade, 8th Bn/ 229th Aviation Regiment
Army Armor Center & Fort Knox, Fort Knox, KY, 366

244th Aviation Brigade, Aviation Support Facility Knox
Army Armor Center & Fort Knox, Fort Knox, KY, 366

244th Combat Communications Squadron (ANG)
Portland Air National Guard Base, Portland IAP, OR, 691

245th Area Support Bn
Fort Clayton, Panama, 1133

249th Engineer Bn
US Army Corps of Engineers, Center for Public Works, Alexandria, VA, 839

249th Engineer Bn, B Co, 3rd Plt
Fort Benning, Fort Benning, GA, 248

251st Combat Communications Group (ANG)
Springfield Municipal Airport Air National Guard Base, Springfield, OH, 664

252nd Transportation Unit
Birmingham Airport, Air National Guard Base, Birmingham, AL, 4

254th Base Support Bn
254th Base Support Battalion, Netherlands, 1127

254th Combat Communications Group, HQ
Garland Air National Guard Station, Garland, TX, 800

255th Tactical Control Squadron (ANG)
Gulfport-Biloxi Regional Airport, Air National Guard Base, Gulfport, MS, 481

256th CBCS
Four Lakes Communications Station, Cheney, WA, 915

256th Infantry Brigade, Det (Aviation)
Camp Beauregard, Pineville, LA, 388

260th Military Police Command (DC ARNG)
District of Columbia National Guard, HQ, Washington, DC, 176

260th Quartermaster Bn
Hunter Army Air Field, Savannah, GA, 260

261st CBCS
Sepulveda Air National Guard Station, Van Nuys, CA, 140

261st Signal Co
414th Base Support Battalion, Germany, 997

262nd Military Police Det
Bamberg Military Community, Germany, 1001

265th Combat Communications Squadron
South Portland Air National Guard Station, South Portland, ME, 401

266th Theater Finance Command
Heidelberg Military Community, Germany, 1011

269th Combat Communications (ANG)
Springfield Municipal Airport Air National Guard Base, Springfield, OH, 664

270th ATC Squadron
Kingsley Field Air National Guard Base, Klamath Falls, OR, 687

272nd Combat Communications Squadron (ANG)
Portland Air National Guard Base, Portland IAP, OR, 691

272nd Military Police Co
Taylor Barracks, Germany, 1034

274th Combat Communications Squadron
Roslyn Station, Air National Guard, Roslyn, NY, 606

275th Signal Site
Camp Long, Korea, Republic of, 1104

279th Base Support Bn
Bamberg Military Community, Germany, 1001

280th Base Support Bn
280th Base Support Battalion, Germany, 994

280th MP Det (CID), 3rd MP Group
Army Armor Center & Fort Knox, Fort Knox, KY, 366

Co C, 280th Signal Bn
Camp Rowland, Niantic, CT, 163

282nd Army Band
Fort Jackson, Columbia, SC, 740

282nd Base Support Bn
282nd Base Support Battalion, Germany, 995

293rd Base Support Bn
293rd Base Support Battalion, Germany, 996
Taylor Barracks, Germany, 1034

297th Air Traffic Control Flight (ATCF)
Barbers Point Naval Air Station, Barbers Point, HI, 265

297th Military Police Bn
Fort Bragg, Fort Bragg, NC, 624

299th Engineer Co
Fort A P Hill, Bowling Green, VA, 855

299th Range Control Squadron
Utah Test and Training Range, Hill AFB, UT, 825

299th Support Bn
280th Base Support Battalion, Germany, 994

301st Fighter Wing (AFRES)
Fort Worth, Naval Air Station, Joint Reserve Base, Fort Worth, TX, 796

301st Support Group
Bamberg Military Community, Germany, 1001

302nd Airlift Wing (Reserve)
Peterson Air Force Base, Peterson AFB, CO, 156

302nd Forward Support Bn
Camp Casey, Korea, Republic of, 1089

302nd Military Intelligence Bn
221st Base Support Battalion, Germany, 992

303rd Air Refueling Squadron
March Air Reserve Base, March ARB, CA, 80

304th Signal Bn, C Co
Camp Colbern, Korea, Republic of, 1091

304th Signal Bn, B Co
Camp Long, Korea, Republic of, 1104

304th Signal Bn, HQ
Camp Colbern, Korea, Republic of, 1091

305th Aerial Port Squadron, Det 1 (AMC)
305th Aerial Port Squadron, Detachment 1 (AMC), Philadelphia, PA, 712

305th Air Mobility Wing
McGuire Air Force Base, McGuire AFB, NJ, 561

305th Rescue Squadron (AFRES)
Davis-Monthan Air Force Base, Tucson, AZ, 42

306th Military Intelligence Bn
Fort Huachuca, Fort Huachuca, AZ, 35

307th Red Horse (AFRES)
Kelly Air Force Base, Kelly AFB, TX, 807

Det 1, 307th Red Horse Squadron (AFRES)
Barksdale Air Force Base, Barksdale AFB, LA, 374

307th Signal Bn
Camp Carroll, Korea, Republic of, 1088

307th Transportation Unit
Birmingham Airport, Air National Guard Base, Birmingham, AL, 4

310th Airlift Squadron
Howard Air Force Base, Panama, 1136

310th Theater Army Area Command
Fort Belvoir, Fort Belvoir, VA, 866

311th COSCOM (FWD)
Fort Lewis, Fort Lewis, WA, 921

312th Field Hospital (Army)
Greensboro Naval & Marine Corps Reserve Readiness Center, Greensboro, NC, 626

313th Training Squadron (USAF)
Corry Station Naval Technical Training Center, Pensacola, FL, 222

314th Airlift Wing
Little Rock Air Force Base, Little Rock AFB, AR, 50

314th Logistics Group
Little Rock Air Force Base, Little Rock AFB, AR, 50

314th Medical Group
Little Rock Air Force Base, Little Rock AFB, AR, 50

314th Operations Group
Little Rock Air Force Base, Little Rock AFB, AR, 50

314th Support Group
Little Rock Air Force Base, Little Rock AFB, AR, 50

315th Airlift Wing (Associate) (AFRES)
Charleston Air Force Base, Charleston AFB, SC, 737

315th Engineer Group
Defense Distribution Region East, New Cumberland, PA, 709

316th Support (Reserves)
Bamberg Military Community, Germany, 1001

317th Airlift Group
Dyess Air Force Base, Abilene, TX, 773

317th Maintenance
Bamberg Military Community, Germany, 1001
Rose Barracks, Germany, 1027

317th Maintenance Co
Johnson Barracks, Germany, 1012

317th Weather Squadron, Det 6
221st Base Support Battalion, Germany, 992

318th Air Force Recruiting Squadron
Defense Distribution Region East, New Cumberland, PA, 709

319th Air Refueling Wing
Grand Forks Air Force Base, Grand Forks AFB, ND, 641

319th Logistics Group
Grand Forks Air Force Base, Grand Forks AFB, ND, 641

319th Medical Group
Grand Forks Air Force Base, Grand Forks AFB, ND, 641

319th Operations Group
Grand Forks Air Force Base, Grand Forks AFB, ND, 641

319th Signal Bn, B Co
Parks Reserve Forces Training Area, Dublin, CA, 62

319th Support Group
Grand Forks Air Force Base, Grand Forks AFB, ND, 641

321st Missile Group
Grand Forks Air Force Base, Grand Forks AFB, ND, 641

321st Signal Co
Reno Nevada Army National Guard Armory, Reno, NV, 543

325th Fighter Wing
Tyndall Air Force Base, Panama City, FL, 220

325th Logistics Group
Tyndall Air Force Base, Panama City, FL, 220

325th Medical Group
Tyndall Air Force Base, Panama City, FL, 220

325th Supply Squadron
Tyndall Air Force Base, Panama City, FL, 220

326th Air Division
Wheeler Army Airfield, Wheeler Army Airfield, HI, 293

328th Airlift Squadron
Niagara Falls Air Reserve Station, Niagara Falls, NY, 600

332nd Airlift Flight (AMC)
Randolph Air Force Base, Randolph AFB, TX, 814

333rd USAF Recruiting Squadron
Patrick Air Force Base, Patrick AFB, FL, 221

334th Forward Support Bn, Co C
Camp Dodge Iowa, Johnston, IA, 346

336th Training Group
Fairchild Air Force Base, Fairchild AFB, WA, 919

337th Air Force Recruiting Squadron, Det 307
Shaw Air Force Base, Shaw AFB, SC, 749

341st Missile Wing
Malmstrom Air Force Base, Great Falls, MT, 520

343rd Recruiting Squadron
Offutt Air Force Base, Offutt AFB, NE, 530

343rd Supply Squadron
Moody Air Force Base, Moody AFB, GA, 258

344th Military Intelligence Bn
Goodfellow Air Force Base, Goodfellow AFB, TX, 801

345th Support Center (Reserves)
Bamberg Military Community, Germany, 1001

347th Composite Wing
Moody Air Force Base, Moody AFB, GA, 258

347th Fighter Wing
Moody Air Force Base, Moody AFB, GA, 258

347th Logistics Group
Moody Air Force Base, Moody AFB, GA, 258

347th Medical Group
Moody Air Force Base, Moody AFB, GA, 258

347th Operations Group
Moody Air Force Base, Moody AFB, GA, 258

347th Support Group
Moody Air Force Base, Moody AFB, GA, 258

348th Recruiting Squadron
Little Rock Air Force Base, Little Rock AFB, AR, 50

349th Air Mobility Wing
Travis Air Force Base, Travis AFB, CA, 137

349th Signal Co (58th Signal Bn)
Torii Station, Japan, 1082

351st Air Refueling Squadron
Mildenhall RAF Base, United Kingdom, 1167

352nd Special Operations Group
Mildenhall RAF Base, United Kingdom, 1167

353rd Combat Training Squadron (Cope Thunder)
Eielson Air Force Base, Eielson AFB, AK, 24

353rd Special Operations Group
Kadena Air Base, Japan, 1074

354th Contracting Squadron
Eielson Air Force Base, Eielson AFB, AK, 24

354th Fighter Wing
Eielson Air Force Base, Eielson AFB, AK, 24

354th Fighter Wing Publications Library
Eielson Air Force Base, Eielson AFB, AK, 24

354th Logistics Group
Eielson Air Force Base, Eielson AFB, AK, 24

354th Medical Group
Eielson Air Force Base, Eielson AFB, AK, 24

354th Operations Group
Eielson Air Force Base, Eielson AFB, AK, 24

354th Support Group
Eielson Air Force Base, Eielson AFB, AK, 24

355th Fighter Squadron
Eielson Air Force Base, Eielson AFB, AK, 24

355th Logistics Group
Davis-Monthan Air Force Base, Tucson, AZ, 42

355th Medical Group
Davis-Monthan Air Force Base, Tucson, AZ, 42

355th Operations Group
Davis-Monthan Air Force Base, Tucson, AZ, 42

355th Support Group
Davis-Monthan Air Force Base, Tucson, AZ, 42

335th Training Squadron, Det 1
Hurlburt Field, Hurlburt Field, FL, 200

355th Wing
Davis-Monthan Air Force Base, Tucson, AZ, 42

355th Wing Staff
Davis-Monthan Air Force Base, Tucson, AZ, 42

360th Air Force Recruiting Group
Hanscom Air Force Base, Bedford, MA, 430

362nd Airlift Group
Rhein-Main Air Base, Germany, 1025

362nd Training Squadron, Det 1 (USAF)
Army Transportation Center & Fort Eustis, Fort Eustis, VA, 868

363rd Fighter Wing
Shaw Air Force Base, Shaw AFB, SC, 749

365th Transportation Co (Light Truck)
Fort McClellan, Anniston, AL, 2

366th Wing
Mountain Home Air Force Base, Mountain Home AFB, ID, 298

367th Training Support Squadron
Hill Air Force Base, Hill AFB, UT, 824

371st Field Training Squadron
Shaw Air Force Base, Shaw AFB, SC, 749

372nd Training Squadron, Det 1 (AETC)
Seymour Johnson Air Force Base, Goldsboro, NC, 625

372nd Training Squadron, Det 8
Ellsworth Air Force Base, Ellsworth AFB, SD, 750

372nd Training Squadron, Det 8A
Minot Air Force Base, Minot AFB, ND, 642

373rd Training Squadron, Det 2 (AETC)
Pope Air Force Base, Pope AFB, NC, 629

374th Airlift Wing
Yokota Air Base, Japan, 1085

374th Training Development Squadron
Edwards Air Force Base, Edwards AFB, CA, 63

375th Airlift Wing
Scott Air Force Base, Scott AFB, IL, 318

375th Communications Group
Scott Air Force Base, Scott AFB, IL, 318

375th Logistics Group
Scott Air Force Base, Scott AFB, IL, 318

375th Medical Group
Scott Air Force Base, Scott AFB, IL, 318

375th Operations Group
Scott Air Force Base, Scott AFB, IL, 318

375th Public Affairs
Scott Air Force Base, Scott AFB, IL, 318

375th Supply Hazmat Pharmacy
Scott Air Force Base, Scott AFB, IL, 318

375th Support Group
Scott Air Force Base, Scott AFB, IL, 318

376th Engineer Plt (FF)
Charles Melvin Price Army Support Center, Granite City, IL, 307

377th Air Base Wing
Kirtland Air Force Base, Kirtland AFB, NM, 572

377th Engineer Co (USAR)
Fort Story, Fort Story, VA, 871

381st Intelligence Squadron
Elmendorf Air Force Base, Anchorage, AK, 19

381st Training Group
Vandenberg Air Force Base, Vandenberg AFB, CA, 141

385th Aviation Group, HQ (ANG)
Adjutant General of Arizona, Phoenix, AZ, 39

386th Engineer Bn, Co A
Camp Swift Training Site, Bastrop, TX, 778

388th Fighter Wing
Hill Air Force Base, Hill AFB, UT, 824

388th Range Squadron
Utah Test and Training Range, Hill AFB, UT, 825

389th Engineering Bn (Heavy)(Army)
Dubuque Naval Reserve Center, Dubuque, IA, 344

390th Intelligence Squadron
Kadena Air Base, Japan, 1074

396th Combat Support Hospital
Vancouver Barracks, Vancouver, WA, 938

399th Army Band
Fort Leonard Wood, Fort Leonard Wood, MO, 501

399th Medical Det
Camp Beauregard, Pineville, LA, 388

401st Fighter Wing, Aviano AB
Sigonella Naval Air Station, Italy, 1059

403rd Air Force Reserve
Keesler Air Force Base, Keesler AFB, MS, 487

409th Base Support Bn
100th Area Support Group, Germany, 991

409th Support Bn
Rose Barracks, Vilseck, Germany, 1028

410th Base Support Bn
Rose Barracks, Germany, 1027

411th Base Support Bn
Germersheim Sub-Community, Germany, 1009
Heidelberg Military Community, Germany, 1011
Patton Barracks, Germany, 1022

411th Test Squadron
Edwards Air Force Base, Edwards AFB, CA, 63

412th Aircraft Generation Squadron
Edwards Air Force Base, Edwards AFB, CA, 63

412th Component Repair Squadron
Edwards Air Force Base, Edwards AFB, CA, 63

412th Equipment Maintenance Squadron
Edwards Air Force Base, Edwards AFB, CA, 63

412th Logistics Group
Edwards Air Force Base, Edwards AFB, CA, 63

412th Logistics Support Squadron
Kelly Air Force Base, Kelly AFB, TX, 807

412th Logistics Test Squadron
Edwards Air Force Base, Edwards AFB, CA, 63

412th Operations Support
Edwards Air Force Base, Edwards AFB, CA, 63

412th Test Group
Edwards Air Force Base, Edwards AFB, CA, 63

412th Test Wing
Edwards Air Force Base, Edwards AFB, CA, 63

413rd Test Squadron
Edwards Air Force Base, Edwards AFB, CA, 63

413th Signal Co
223rd Base Support Battalion, Germany, 993

414th Base Support Bn
414th Base Support Battalion, Germany, 997
Ray Barracks, Germany, 1024

414th Signal Co
Sullivan Barracks, Germany, 1033

414th Training Squadron
Nellis Air Force Base, Nellis AFB, NV, 541

415th Base Support Bn
Kaiserslautern Military Community, Germany, 1013

415th Test Squadron
Edwards Air Force Base, Edwards AFB, CA, 63

416th Test Squadron
Edwards Air Force Base, Edwards AFB, CA, 63

417th Base Support Bn
Kitzingen Military Community, Germany, 1017

417th Test Squadron
Edwards Air Force Base, Edwards AFB, CA, 63

418th Test Squadron
Edwards Air Force Base, Edwards AFB, CA, 63

419th Test Squadron
Edwards Air Force Base, Edwards AFB, CA, 63

420th Test Group
Edwards Air Force Base, Edwards AFB, CA, 63

422nd Air Base Squadron
Croughton RAF Base, United Kingdom, 1157

422nd Signal Bn, HQ
Reno Nevada Army National Guard Armory, Reno, NV, 543

422nd Test and Evaluation Squadron
Nellis Air Force Base, Nellis AFB, NV, 541

423rd Air Base Squadron
Alconbury RAF Base, United Kingdom, 1156

423rd OL-A Medical Facility
Upwood RAF Base, United Kingdom, 1169

424th Air Base Squadron
424nd Air Base Squadron, RAF Fairford, United Kingdom, 1155

424th Civil Engineering Squadron
424nd Air Base Squadron, RAF Fairford, United Kingdom, 1155

424th Communications Squadron
424nd Air Base Squadron, RAF Fairford, United Kingdom, 1155

424th Logistics Squadron
424nd Air Base Squadron, RAF Fairford, United Kingdom, 1155

424th Plans & Programs Squadron
424nd Air Base Squadron, RAF Fairford, United Kingdom, 1155

424th Services Squadron
424nd Air Base Squadron, RAF Fairford, United Kingdom, 1155

425th Air Base Squadron
Izmir Air Station, Turkey, 1153

426th Air Base Squadron
426th Air Base Squadron, Norway, 1132

433rd Airlift Wing (AFRES)
Kelly Air Force Base, Kelly AFB, TX, 807

434th Air Refueling Wing (AFRC)
Grissom Air Reserve Base, Grissom ARB, IN, 331

434th Aircraft Generation Squadron
Grissom Air Reserve Base, Grissom ARB, IN, 331

434th Civil Engineering Squadron
Grissom Air Reserve Base, Grissom ARB, IN, 331

434th Communications Squadron
Grissom Air Reserve Base, Grissom ARB, IN, 331

434th Headquarters Squadron
Grissom Air Reserve Base, Grissom ARB, IN, 331

434th Logistics Group
Grissom Air Reserve Base, Grissom ARB, IN, 331

434th Logistics Support Squadron
Grissom Air Reserve Base, Grissom ARB, IN, 331

434th Maintenance Squadron
Grissom Air Reserve Base, Grissom ARB, IN, 331

434th Medical Squadron
Grissom Air Reserve Base, Grissom ARB, IN, 331

434th Mission Support Squadron
Grissom Air Reserve Base, Grissom ARB, IN, 331

434th Operations Group
Grissom Air Reserve Base, Grissom ARB, IN, 331

434th Operations Support Squadron
Grissom Air Reserve Base, Grissom ARB, IN, 331

434th Security Police Squadron
Grissom Air Reserve Base, Grissom ARB, IN, 331

434th Support Group
Grissom Air Reserve Base, Grissom ARB, IN, 331

436th Aerial Port Squadron
Dover Air Force Base, Dover AFB, DE, 167

436th Aerospace Medicine Squadron
Dover Air Force Base, Dover AFB, DE, 167

436th Aircraft Generation Squadron
Dover Air Force Base, Dover AFB, DE, 167

436th Airlift Wing
Dover Air Force Base, Dover AFB, DE, 167

436th Civil Engineer Squadron
Dover Air Force Base, Dover AFB, DE, 167

436th Communications Squadron
Dover Air Force Base, Dover AFB, DE, 167

436th Component Repair Squadron
Dover Air Force Base, Dover AFB, DE, 167

436th Comptroller Squadron
Dover Air Force Base, Dover AFB, DE, 167

436th Contracting Squadron
Dover Air Force Base, Dover AFB, DE, 167

436th Dental Squadron
Dover Air Force Base, Dover AFB, DE, 167

436th Logistics Support Squadron
Dover Air Force Base, Dover AFB, DE, 167

436th Medical Operations Squadron
Dover Air Force Base, Dover AFB, DE, 167

436th Medical Support Squadron
Dover Air Force Base, Dover AFB, DE, 167

436th Operations Support Squadron
Dover Air Force Base, Dover AFB, DE, 167

436th Security Police Squadron
Dover Air Force Base, Dover AFB, DE, 167

436th Services Squadron
Dover Air Force Base, Dover AFB, DE, 167

436th Supply Squadron
Dover Air Force Base, Dover AFB, DE, 167

436th Transportation Squadron
Dover Air Force Base, Dover AFB, DE, 167

437th Airlift Wing (AMC)
Charleston Air Force Base, Charleston AFB, SC, 737

437th Civil Engineering Squadron
Charleston Air Force Base, Charleston AFB, SC, 737
North Auxiliary Airfield, North Auxiliary Airfield, SC, 745

437th Logistics Group
Charleston Air Force Base, Charleston AFB, SC, 737

437th Medical Squadron
Charleston Air Force Base, Charleston AFB, SC, 737

437th Military Airlift Wing
North Auxiliary Airfield, North Auxiliary Airfield, SC, 745

437th Operations Group
Charleston Air Force Base, Charleston AFB, SC, 737

437th Support Group
Charleston Air Force Base, Charleston AFB, SC, 737

439th Airlift Wing
Westover Air Reserve Base, Chicopee, MA, 438

439th Logistics Group
Westover Air Reserve Base, Chicopee, MA, 438

439th Medical Group
Westover Air Reserve Base, Chicopee, MA, 438

439th Operations Group
Westover Air Reserve Base, Chicopee, MA, 438

439th Support Group
Westover Air Reserve Base, Chicopee, MA, 438

440th Airlift Wing (AFRC)
Mitchell Field Air National Guard Base, Milwaukee, WI, 963

440th Signal Bn
223rd Base Support Battalion, Germany, 993

442nd Engineer Det (Utilities)
Camp Rilea, Oregon National Guard Training Site, Salem, OR, 692

442nd Fighter Wing (MO NG)
Whiteman Air Force Base, Whiteman AFB, MO, 516

445th Test Squadron
Edwards Air Force Base, Edwards AFB, CA, 63

446th Airlift Wing (Reserve)
McChord Air Force Base, McChord AFB, WA, 923

449th Maintenance Co
Fort Tilden (USAR), Fort Tilden, NY, 586

452nd Aeromedical Patient Staging Squadron
March Air Reserve Base, March ARB, CA, 80

452nd Air Mobility Wing
March Air Reserve Base, March ARB, CA, 80

452nd Medical Squadron
March Air Reserve Base, March ARB, CA, 80

445th Airlift Wing (AFRES)
Wright-Patterson Air Force Base, Wright-Patterson AFB, OH, 667

459th Airlift Wing (AFRES)
Andrews Air Force Base, Andrews AFB, MD, 407

463rd Airlift Group (AMC)
Little Rock Air Force Base, Little Rock AFB, AR, 50

463rd Military Police Co
Fort Leonard Wood, Fort Leonard Wood, MO, 501

464th Medical Co
Landstuhl Regional Medical Center, Germany, 1020

464th Medical Det (Dental)
Baumholder Military Community, H.D. Smith Barracks, Germany, 1003

469th Air Base Group (USAFE)
Rhein-Main Air Base, Germany, 1025

475th Weapons Evaluation Group
Tyndall Air Force Base, Panama City, FL, 220

482nd Fighter Wing
Homestead Air Reserve Base, Homestead ARB, FL, 199

485th CORPS Support Bn
414th Base Support Battalion, Germany, 997

488th Intelligence Squadron
Mildenhall RAF Base, United Kingdom, 1167

496th Air Base Squadron
Moron Air Base, Spain, 1148

496th Security Forces Flight
Moron Air Base, Spain, 1148

497th Fighter Training Squadron (USAF)
Logistics Group Western Pacific, Singapore, 1147

497th Tactical Fighter Wing/MSM (USAF)
Logistics Group Western Pacific, Singapore, 1147

500th Military Intelligence Brigade
Camp Zama, Japan, 1071

500th Military Intelligence Det
Torii Station, Japan, 1082

1st Bn, 501st Aviation, Co A
K-16 (Army Airfield), Korea, Republic of, 1115

501st Aviation Bn, Det 5
Camp Long, Korea, Republic of, 1104

501st Corps Support Group
Camp Red Cloud, Korea, Republic of, 1109

501st Forward Support Bn
Friedberg Area Support Team, Germany, 1007
Ray Barracks, Germany, 1024

501st Infantry, 1st Bn (Airborne)
Fort Richardson, Fort Richardson, AK, 27

501st Military Intelligence Bn
Anderson Barracks, Germany, 998

501st Range Squadron
Edwards Air Force Base, Edwards AFB, CA, 63

501st Signal Co, Det
Zoeckler Station, Korea, Republic of, 1122

2nd Bn, 502nd Aviation Regiment
Coleman Barracks, Germany, 1006

502nd Engineer Co
414th Base Support Battalion, Germany, 997

E Co, 502nd Regiment (Army)
Aviano Air Base, Italy, 1051

1st Bn, 503rd Infantry
Camp Casey, Korea, Republic of, 1089

503rd Infantry, 1st Bn, C Co
Camp Hovey, Korea, Republic of, 1100

504th Military Intelligence Brigade
Fort Hood, Fort Hood, TX, 792

505th Command and Control Evaluation Group
Hurlburt Field, Hurlburt Field, FL, 200

505th Quartermaster Bn
Torii Station, Japan, 1082

1st Bn, 506th Infantry
Camp Greaves, Korea, Republic of, 1097

1st Bn, 506th Infantry, A Co
Camp Giant, Korea, Republic of, 1096

507th Air Refueling Wing
Istres Air Base, France, 986

507th Signal Co
Fort Greely, Fort Greely, AK, 25

507th Tactical Air Command Air Control Wing, Det 2
Hunter Army Air Field, Savannah, GA, 260

507th Wing
Tinker Air Force Base, Tinker AFB, OK, 678

1st Bn, 508th Infantry (ABCT)
Caserma Ederle/Vicenza Military Community, Vincenza, Italy, 1060

509th Bomb Wing (AFRES)
Whiteman Air Force Base, Whiteman AFB, MO, 516

509th Personnel Services Bn
Camp Casey, Korea, Republic of, 1089

509th Signal Bn
Camp Darby, Livorno Military Community, Italy, 1052
Caserma Ederle/Vicenza Military Community, Vincenza, Italy, 1060

510th Fighter Sq
Aviano Air Base, Italy, 1051

510th Personnel Services Bn
Sullivan Barracks, Germany, 1033

510th Personnel Services Co
Caserma Ederle/Vicenza Military Community, Vincenza, Italy, 1060

512th Airlift Wing (Reserve Associate)
Dover Air Force Base, Dover AFB, DE, 167

513th Military Intelligence Brigade
Army Signal Center & Fort Gordon, Fort Gordon, GA, 249

514th Air Mobility Wing (ASSOC)
McGuire Air Force Base, McGuire AFB, NJ, 561

514th Flight Test Squadron
Hill Air Force Base, Hill AFB, UT, 824

514th Test Squadron
Edwards Air Force Base, Edwards AFB, CA, 63

1st Bn (AD) 515th Regiment
New Mexico National Guard State Headquarters, Santa Fe, NM, 573

2nd Bn, 515th Regiment
New Mexico National Guard State Headquarters, Santa Fe, NM, 573

HQ, 515th Regiment
New Mexico National Guard State Headquarters, Santa Fe, NM, 573

518th Engineer Bn
Fort Clayton, Panama, 1133

519th Military Police Bn
Fort Polk, Fort Polk, LA, 377

520th Theater Army Medical Laboratory
Aberdeen Proving Ground, Aberdeen Proving Ground, MD, 404

521st Maintenance Co
414th Base Support Battalion, Germany, 997

522nd Fighter Squadron
Cannon Air Force Base, Cannon AFB, NM, 570

525th Military Intelligence Brigade
Fort Bragg, Fort Bragg, NC, 624

526th Military Police Det
Fort Greely, Fort Greely, AK, 25

527th Engineer Bn, Co A
Camp Beauregard, Pineville, LA, 388

529th Ordnance
Rose Barracks, Germany, 1027

531st Air Force Band
Hensley Field Texas Air National Guard Base, Dallas, TX, 785

532nd Military Intelligence Bn, B Co
Zoeckler Station, Korea, Republic of, 1122

532nd Signal Co, Maastricht
254th Base Support Battalion, Netherlands, 1127

535th Engineers
Rose Barracks, Germany, 1027

536th Military Police
Rose Barracks, Germany, 1027

536th Military Police Platoon
282nd Base Support Battalion, Germany, 995

6th Bn, 538th Ordnance Co
Camp Long, Korea, Republic of, 1104

541st Maintenance Bn
Fort Riley, Fort Riley, KS, 353

542nd Explosive Ordnance Disposal
Fort Dix, Fort Dix, NJ, 555

545th Test Group
Edwards Air Force Base, Edwards AFB, CA, 63

547th Intelligence Squadron
Nellis Air Force Base, Nellis AFB, NV, 541

547th Ordnance Det (Explosive) Ordnance Disposal Control Center
Fort Gillem, Forest Park, GA, 247

549th Combat Training Squadron
Nellis Air Force Base, Nellis AFB, NV, 541

549th Military Police Co
Fort Davis, Panama, 1134

552nd Air Control Wing
Tinker Air Force Base, Tinker AFB, OK, 678

552nd Military Police Co
Camp Hialeah, Korea, Republic of, 1099

554th Engineer Bn
Fort Leonard Wood, Fort Leonard Wood, MO, 501

555th Fighter Sq
Aviano Air Base, Italy, 1051

557th Flying Training Squadron
US Air Force Academy, Colorado Springs, CO, 146

559th Flying Training Squadron
Randolph Air Force Base, Randolph AFB, TX, 814

559th Quartermaster Bn
Hunter Army Air Field, Savannah, GA, 260

555th Engineer Group
Fort Lewis, Fort Lewis, WA, 921

560th Flying Training Squadron
Randolph Air Force Base, Randolph AFB, TX, 814

560th Military Police
280th Base Support Battalion, Germany, 994

560th Military Police Co
414th Base Support Battalion, Germany, 997
Coleman Barracks, Germany, 1006

561st Medical Co
Rose Barracks, Germany, 1027

562nd Flying Training Squadron
Randolph Air Force Base, Randolph AFB, TX, 814

566th Postal Co
Bamberg Military Community, Germany, 1001

566th Postal Commander
280th Base Support Battalion, Germany, 994

567th Air Force Band (ANG)
Massachusetts Military Reservation/Otis Air National Guard Base, Cape Cod, MA, 437

574th Maintenance Co
Sullivan Barracks, Germany, 1033

577th Engineer Bn
Fort Leonard Wood, Fort Leonard Wood, MO, 501

1st Bn, 509th Parachute Infantry Regiment (JRTC Opposing Force)
Fort Polk, Fort Polk, LA, 377

593rd CSG
Fort Lewis, Fort Lewis, WA, 921

595th Maintenance Co (DS/GS)
K-16 (Army Airfield), Korea, Republic of, 1115

596th Maintenance Bn
223rd Base Support Battalion, Germany, 993

596th Ordnance Det
Fort Sam Houston, Fort Sam Houston, TX, 794

569th Security Police
Sembach Air Base, Germany, 1029

597th Army Transportation Terminal Group
Military Ocean Terminal, Sunny Point, Southport, NC, 633

603rd Air Control Sq
Aviano Air Base, Italy, 1051

603rd Air Mobility Support Squadron
Yokota Air Base, Japan, 1085

607th Air Operations Group
Osan Air Base, Korea, Republic of, 1118

607th Air Support Operations Group
Osan Air Base, Korea, Republic of, 1118

608th Contingency Hospital
Upwood RAF Base, United Kingdom, 1169

609th Air Operations Group
Shaw Air Force Base, Shaw AFB, SC, 749

610th Ordnance Bn
Fort Belvoir, Fort Belvoir, VA, 866

612th Air Operations Group
Beale Air Force Base, Beale AFB, CA, 58

612th Theater Air Group
Howard Air Force Base, Panama, 1136

613th Air Communications Squadron
Andersen Air Force Base, Guam, 1043

613th Air Intelligence Flight
Andersen Air Force Base, Guam, 1043

613th Air Operations Squadron
Andersen Air Force Base, Guam, 1043

613th Air Support Squadron
Andersen Air Force Base, Guam, 1043

615th Military Police
Barton Barracks, Ansbach, Germany, 1002

617th Air Force ASOS
Coleman Barracks, Germany, 1006

617th Communications Squadron
Rose Barracks, Germany, 1027

617th Weather Det
414th Base Support Battalion, Germany, 997

621st Air Mobility Operations Group
McGuire Air Force Base, McGuire AFB, NJ, 561

621st Air Mobility Support Group
Ramstein Air Base, Germany, 1023

Det 1, 621st Air Mobility Support Group (AMSG)(AMC)
Prince Sultan Air Base, Saudi Arabia, 1146

621st Air Mobility Support Group, Det 2
Sigonella Naval Air Station, Italy, 1059

621st Air Mobility Support Group, Det 3
Aviano Air Base, Italy, 1051

OL-B, Det 2, 621st Air Mobility Support Group
Naples (Capodichino) Naval Support Activity, Italy, 1055

621St AMSG, OL-A, Det 2
Souda Bay, Naval Support Activity, Greece, 1040

621st AMSG, OL-B
Cario (East), Egypt, 984

623rd Air Mobility Support Squadron
Ramstein Air Base, Germany, 1023

625th Air Mobility Support Squadron
Rota Naval Station, Spain, 1149

626th Air Mobility Support Squadron
Rhein-Main Air Base, Germany, 1025

627th Air Mobility Support Squadron
Mildenhall RAF Base, United Kingdom, 1167

628th Aerial Port Services Squadron
Incirlick Air Base, Turkey, 1152

628th Air Mobility Command and Control Squadron
Incirlick Air Base, Turkey, 1152

628th Air Mobility Maintenance Squadron
Incirlick Air Base, Turkey, 1152

628th Air Mobility Support Squadron
Incirlick Air Base, Turkey, 1152

629th Air Mobility Support Squadron
Lajes Field, Portugal, 1138

630th Military Police Co
Bamberg Military Community, Germany, 1001

631st Air Mobility Support Squadron
Osan Air Base, Korea, Republic of, 1118

631st Maintenance
Camp Blanding Training Site, Starke, FL, 232

632nd Air Mobility Support Squadron
Elmendorf Air Force Base, Anchorage, AK, 19

633rd Air Mobility Support Squadron
Kadena Air Base, Japan, 1074

634th Air Mobility Support Squadron
Andersen Air Force Base, Guam, 1043

634th FSB, Co C
Camp Lincoln, Springfield, IL, 320

640th Air Mobility Support Squadron
Howard Air Force Base, Panama, 1136

643rd Support Squadron
King Salmon Airport, AK, 31

649th Military Police Co
Camp San Luis Obispo, San Luis Obispo, CA, 130

653rd Engineer Det (Utilities)
Camp Blanding Training Site, Starke, FL, 232

665th Dental Clinic
Camp Long, Korea, Republic of, 1104

665th Maintenance Co
Mitchell National Guard Complex, Mitchell, SD, 752

665th Medical Co
Camp Carroll, Korea, Republic of, 1088

665th Medical Co (Dental)
Camp Hialeah, Korea, Republic of, 1099

673rd Air Base Squadron (PACAF)
Eareckson Air Force Station, AK, 23

680th Transportation Co (USAR)
Fort Story, Fort Story, VA, 871

682nd Air Support Squadron
Shaw Air Force Base, Shaw AFB, SC, 749

692nd Intelligence Group, Det 1 (AIA)
Andersen Air Force Base, Guam, 1043

694th Intelligence Group (USAF)
Fort George G Meade, Fort Meade, MD, 422

695th Maintenance Bn
Fort Tilden (USAR), Fort Tilden, NY, 586

701st Military Police Bn
Fort McClellan, Anniston, AL, 2

701st MSB
Kitzingen Military Community, Germany, 1017

702nd Main Support Bn
Camp Casey, Korea, Republic of, 1089

702nd Main Support Bn, A Co
Camp Nimble, Korea, Republic of, 1107

702nd Main Support Bn, B Co
Camp Nimble, Korea, Republic of, 1107

702nd Main Support Bn, E Co
Camp Sears, Korea, Republic of, 1110

702nd Maintenance Bn, D Co
Camp Stanley, Korea, Republic of, 1111

702nd Ordnance Det
Fort McClellan, Anniston, AL, 2

703rd Military Intelligence Brigade
Schofield Barracks, Schofield Barracks, HI, 286

704th Military Intelligence Brigade
Fort George G Meade, Fort Meade, MD, 422

704th Military Police, B Co
Yakima Training Center, Yakima, WA, 941

704th Ordnance (EOD)
Camp Shelby Training Site, Camp Shelby, MS, 478

709th Military Police Bn
414th Base Support Battalion, Germany, 997

716th Logistics Test Squadron
Edwards Air Force Base, Edwards AFB, CA, 63

717th Medical Co
New Mexico National Guard State Headquarters, Santa Fe, NM, 573

718th Engineer Det
Fort Benning, Fort Benning, GA, 248

720th Special Tactics Group
Hurlburt Field, Hurlburt Field, FL, 200

721st Support Group
Cheyenne Mountain Air Force Station, Colorado Springs, CO, 145

728th Military Police Bn
Camp Henry, Korea, Republic of, 1098

729th Air Control Squadron
Utah Test and Training Range, Hill AFB, UT, 825

729th Airlift Squadron
March Air Reserve Base, March ARB, CA, 80

730th Airlift Squadron
March Air Reserve Base, March ARB, CA, 80

731st General Dispensary
282nd Base Support Battalion, Germany, 995

731st Munitions Support Squadron
Araxos Air Base, Greece, 1039

737th Training Group
Lackland Air Force Base, Lackland AFB, TX, 809

737th TRANS
Yakima Training Center, Yakima, WA, 941

738th Engineering Installation Squadron
Keesler Air Force Base, Keesler AFB, MS, 487

739th Security Police Flight
Westover Air Reserve Base, Chicopee, MA, 438

744th Engineer Det
Camp Lincoln, Springfield, IL, 320

745th Ordnance Det (Explosive Ordnance Disposal)
Camp Grayling Maneuver Training Center, Grayling, MI, 458

750th Communications Squadron
Onizuka Air Station, Sunnyvale, CA, 136

750th Logistic Support Squadron
Onizuka Air Station, Sunnyvale, CA, 136

750th Medical Squadron
Onizuka Air Station, Sunnyvale, CA, 136

750th Mission Support Squadron
Onizuka Air Station, Sunnyvale, CA, 136

750th Space Group
Falcon Air Force Base, Falcon AFB, CO, 151
Onizuka Air Station, Sunnyvale, CA, 136

750th Space Group, Det 3
Thule Air Base, Greenland, 1041

750th Space Group, Det 5 (AFSPC)
Andersen Air Force Base, Guam, 1043

750th Space Group, Det 8
Diego Garcia, Naval Support Facility, Diego Garcia, 982

751st Military Intelligence Bn
Zoeckler Station, Korea, Republic of, 1122

752nd Munitions Support Squadron
Volkel Air Base, Netherlands, 1131

756th Explosive Ordnance Disposal
Fort Indiantown Gap, Annville, PA, 696

757th Airlift Squadron
Youngstown-Warren Regional Airport, Air Reserve Station, Vienna, OH, 666

758th Airlift Squadron
Pittsburgh IAP, Air Reserve Station, Coraopolis, PA, 701

766th Supply & Service Co
Fort Tilden (USAR), Fort Tilden, NY, 586

773rd Airlift Squadron
Youngstown-Warren Regional Airport, Air Reserve Station, Vienna, OH, 666

782nd Training Group
Sheppard Air Force Base, Sheppard AFB, TX, 817

787th Military Police Bn
Fort McClellan, Anniston, AL, 2

789th Medical Det (USAR)
Fort Story, Fort Story, VA, 871

793rd Military Police Bn
Bamberg Military Community, Germany, 1001

813th Engineer Bn (Reserve)
Fort Richardson, Fort Richardson, AK, 27

813th Engineer Combat Bn
Fort Wainwright, Fort Wainwright, AK, 28

817th Air Force, Det 1, ASOS
Rose Barracks, Germany, 1027

817th ASOS (USAF)
98th Area Support Group, Germany, 990

819th Red Horse Squadron
Malmstrom Air Force Base, Great Falls, MT, 520

820th Red Horse Squadron
Nellis Air Force Base, Nellis AFB, NV, 541

820th Security Forces Group
Lackland Air Force Base, Lackland AFB, TX, 809

823rd Civil Engineering Squadron (Red Horse)
Hurlburt Field, Hurlburt Field, FL, 200

838th Engineering Squadron
Kelly Air Force Base, Kelly AFB, TX, 807

838th Transportation Det
Camp Atterbury, Edinburgh, IN, 325

853rd Supply & Service Co
Camp Blanding Training Site, Starke, FL, 232

882nd Training Group
Sheppard Air Force Base, Sheppard AFB, TX, 817

886th Communications Squadron
Sembach Air Base, Germany, 1029

886th Communications Squadron, OL-A, Pruem
Chievres Air Base, Belgium, 976

886th Communications Squadron, OL-B, Kester/Flobecq
Chievres Air Base, Belgium, 976

886th Communications Squadron, OL-C
Giebelstadt Army Airfield, Germany, 1010

886th Communications Squadron, OL-D, Grafenwöhr
100th Area Support Group, Germany, 991

886th Communications Squadron, OL-E
Katterbach Air Field/Kaserne, Germany, 1015

886th Communications Squadron, OL-F
Rhein-Main Air Base, Germany, 1025

896th Munitions Squadron
Nellis Air Force Base, Nellis AFB, NV, 541

902nd Military Intelligence Det
Fort Sam Houston, Fort Sam Houston, TX, 794

902nd Military Intelligence Group
Armament Research, Development, and Engineering Center, US Army TACOM, Picatinny Arsenal, NJ, 562
Fort Belvoir, Fort Belvoir, VA, 866
Fort Bragg, Fort Bragg, NC, 624
Fort Jackson, Columbia, SC, 740
Fort Lewis, Fort Lewis, WA, 921
Fort George G Meade, Fort Meade, MD, 422

902nd Military Intelligence Group, APG Military Intelligence Det
Aberdeen Proving Ground, Aberdeen Proving Ground, MD, 404

Ft Benning Resident Office, 902nd Military Intelligence Group
Fort Benning, Fort Benning, GA, 248

910th Airlift Wing (AFRC)
Youngstown-Warren Regional Airport, Air Reserve Station, Vienna, OH, 666

911th Airlift Wing
Pittsburgh IAP, Air Reserve Station, Coraopolis, PA, 701

911th Civil Engineering Squadron
Pittsburgh IAP, Air Reserve Station, Coraopolis, PA, 701

911th Communications Squadron
Pittsburgh IAP, Air Reserve Station, Coraopolis, PA, 701

911th Logistics Squadron
Pittsburgh IAP, Air Reserve Station, Coraopolis, PA, 701

911th Maintenance Squadron
Pittsburgh IAP, Air Reserve Station, Coraopolis, PA, 701

911th Medical Squadron
Pittsburgh IAP, Air Reserve Station, Coraopolis, PA, 701

911th Mission Support Flight
Pittsburgh IAP, Air Reserve Station, Coraopolis, PA, 701

911th Morale, Welfare, and Recreation and Services Flight
Pittsburgh IAP, Air Reserve Station, Coraopolis, PA, 701

911th Operations Support Flight
Pittsburgh IAP, Air Reserve Station, Coraopolis, PA, 701

911th Security Police Squadron
Pittsburgh IAP, Air Reserve Station, Coraopolis, PA, 701

913th Tactical Airlift Group
Willow Grove Naval Air Station (JRB), Willow Grove, PA, 723

914th Airlift Wing
Niagara Falls Air Reserve Station, Niagara Falls, NY, 600

914th Logistics Group
Niagara Falls Air Reserve Station, Niagara Falls, NY, 600

914th Support Group
Niagara Falls Air Reserve Station, Niagara Falls, NY, 600

916th Air Refueling Group (AFRES)
Seymour Johnson Air Force Base, Goldsboro, NC, 625

917th Wing (AFRES)
Barksdale Air Force Base, Barksdale AFB, LA, 374

920th Rescue Group
Patrick Air Force Base, Patrick AFB, FL, 221

923rd Medical Det
Adjutant General of Arizona, Phoenix, AZ, 39

926th Fighter Wing (AFRC)
New Orleans Naval Air Station Joint Reserve Base, Air Force Reserve, New Orleans, LA, 383

926th Tactical Fighter Group (AFRES)
New Orleans Naval Air Station Joint Reserve Base, Naval Air Station, New Orleans, LA, 384

927th Air Refueling Wing (AFRC)
Selfridge Air National Guard Base, Selfridge ANG Base, MI, 464

928th Airlift Group
O'Hare International Airport Air Reserve Station, O'Hare IAP ARS, IL, 311

928th Civil Engineering Squadron
O'Hare International Airport Air Reserve Station, O'Hare IAP ARS, IL, 311

928th Communication Flight
O'Hare International Airport Air Reserve Station, O'Hare IAP ARS, IL, 311

928th Logistics Group
O'Hare International Airport Air Reserve Station, O'Hare IAP ARS, IL, 311

928th Medical Group
O'Hare International Airport Air Reserve Station, O'Hare IAP ARS, IL, 311

928th Medical Squadron
O'Hare International Airport Air Reserve Station, O'Hare IAP ARS, IL, 311

928th Morale Welfare & Recreation Squadron
O'Hare International Airport Air Reserve Station, O'Hare IAP ARS, IL, 311

928th Operations Group
O'Hare International Airport Air Reserve Station, O'Hare IAP ARS, IL, 311

928th Operations Support Flight
O'Hare International Airport Air Reserve Station, O'Hare IAP ARS, IL, 311

928th Security Police Squadron
O'Hare International Airport Air Reserve Station, O'Hare IAP ARS, IL, 311

928th Support Group
O'Hare International Airport Air Reserve Station, O'Hare IAP ARS, IL, 311

931st Air Refueling Group (AFRES)
McConnell Air Force Base, McConnell AFB, KS, 354

934th Airlift Wing (AFRC)
Minneapolis-Saint Paul IAP, Air National Guard Base/ARS, Minneapolis-Saint Paul IAP, MN, 474

935th Engineer Det
Camp Beauregard, Pineville, LA, 388

936th HOT Mission (Maint)
Charles Melvin Price Army Support Center, Granite City, IL, 307

937th Engineer Group (Combat)
Fort Riley, Fort Riley, KS, 353

939th Rescue Wing (AFRES)
Portland Air National Guard Base, Portland IAP, OR, 691

940th Air Refueling Wing
McClellan Air Force Base, McClellan AFB, CA, 81

940th Air Refueling Wing (AFRES)
Beale Air Force Base, Beale AFB, CA, 58

944th Fighter Wing (AFRC)
Luke Air Force Base, Luke AFB, AZ, 37

982nd Training Group
Sheppard Air Force Base, Sheppard AFB, TX, 817

1015th Adjutant General Co
Camp Atterbury, Edinburgh, IN, 325

1034th Quartermaster Supply Co
Camp Dodge Iowa, Johnston, IA, 346

1049th Engineer Plt (FFTG)
Fort William Henry Harrison, Helena, MT, 523

1071st Maintenance Co
Camp Grayling Maneuver Training Center, Grayling, MI, 458

1079th Garrison Support Unit
Fort Dix, Fort Dix, NJ, 555

1086th Transportation Co, Det 1
Camp Beauregard, Pineville, LA, 388

1097th Army Boat Co
Fort Davis, Panama, 1134

1101st Signal Brigade
Fort Myer, Arlington, VA, 847

1108th Aviation Repair Depot (ARNG)
Gulfport-Biloxi Regional Airport, Air National Guard Base, Gulfport, MS, 481

1108th Signal Brigade
Alternate Joint Communications Center/ Site R, Fort Ritchie, MD, 423
Fort Ritchie, Fort Ritchie, MD, 424

1110th Army Signal Bn
Fort Detrick, Fort Detrick, MD, 421

1110th Signal Bn
Fort Sam Houston, Fort Sam Houston, TX, 794

1111th Signal Bn
Alternate Joint Communications Center/ Site R, Fort Ritchie, MD, 423

1115th Signal Bn
Yakima Training Center, Yakima, WA, 941

1144th Transportation Bn
Camp Lincoln, Springfield, IL, 320

1160th Transportation Co (Heavy Helicopter) GA ANG
Hunter Army Air Field, Savannah, GA, 260

1174th Transportation Terminal Bn
Fort Totten, New York, NY, 594

1179th Deployment Support Brigade
New York Area Command & Fort Hamilton, Brooklyn, NY, 581

1183rd Ordnance TM (MLRS Maintenance)
Camp Grayling Maneuver Training Center, Grayling, MI, 458

1205th TRO Bn, Det 1
Military Ocean Terminal, Sunny Point, Southport, NC, 633

1207th Army Hospital
Fort Benning, Fort Benning, GA, 248

1249th Engineer Bn, Co D
Camp Rilea, Oregon National Guard Training Site, Salem, OR, 692

1255th Medical Co, Det 1
Stead Training Center, Reno, NV, 545

1275th Test & Evaluation Squadron
Edwards Air Force Base, Edwards AFB, CA, 63

1287th Logistical Support Bn
Army Armor Center & Fort Knox, Fort Knox, KY, 366

1301st Major Port Command
Bayonne Military Ocean Terminal, Bayonne, NJ, 552

1302nd Major Port Command (Army)
Oakland Army Base, Oakland, CA, 90

1303rd Major Port Command
Military Ocean Terminal, Sunny Point, Southport, NC, 633

1304th Military Traffic Management Command
Charleston, Naval Weapons Station, Charleston, SC, 734

1313th Engineer Co
Camp Atterbury, Edinburgh, IN, 325

1315th Medium Port Command
Torii Station, Japan, 1082

1316th Medium Port Command
Yokosuka, Fleet Activities, Japan, 1083

1318th Military Transportation Management Command, Rotterdam
254th Base Support Battalion, Netherlands, 1127

1324th Medium Port Command (Army)
Lajes Field, Portugal, 1138

1361st Audiovisual Squadron, Det 7
Charleston Air Force Base, Charleston AFB, SC, 737

1394th Deployment Support Brigade
Camp Pendleton Marine Corps Base, Oceanside, CA, 91

1413th Engineer Det
Camp Atterbury, Edinburgh, IN, 325

1438th Engineering Det (Utilities)
Camp Grayling Maneuver Training Center, Grayling, MI, 458

1438th Transportation Co
Camp Atterbury, Edinburgh, IN, 325

1439th Engineering Det (Fire Fighting)
Camp Grayling Maneuver Training Center, Grayling, MI, 458

1440th Engineering Det (Fire Fighting)
Camp Grayling Maneuver Training Center, Grayling, MI, 458

1621st Air Mobility Support Squadron (AMSS)(P)
Prince Sultan Air Base, Saudi Arabia, 1146

1839th Engineering Installation Group
Keesler Air Force Base, Keesler AFB, MS, 487

1872nd Training Development Squadron
Keesler Air Force Base, Keesler AFB, MS, 487

2014th Information Systems Squadron
Hanscom Air Force Base, Bedford, MA, 430

2145th Garrison Support Unit, Det 11
Fort Benning, Fort Benning, GA, 248

2165th Communications Squadron
Massachusetts Military Reservation/Otis Air National Guard Base, Cape Cod, MA, 437

2336th Medical Co
Landstuhl Regional Medical Center, Germany, 1020

3631st Maintenance Co
New Mexico National Guard State Headquarters, Santa Fe, NM, 573

3637 Maintenance Bn
Camp Lincoln, Springfield, IL, 320

3654th Maintenance Co, Det 3
Camp Dodge Iowa, Johnston, IA, 346

3655th Maintenance Co, Det 1
Camp Dodge Iowa, Johnston, IA, 346

3657th Maintenance Co
Camp Dodge Iowa, Johnston, IA, 346

3662nd Maintenance Co
Camp Gilbert C Grafton, Devils Lake, ND, 638

3669th Maintenance Co
Fort William Henry Harrison, Helena, MT, 523

3671st Heavy Equipment Maintenance Co
Camp Beauregard, Pineville, LA, 388

3673rd Maintenance Co
Jackson Barracks, New Orleans, LA, 382

3673rd Maintenance Co, Det 1
Camp Beauregard, Pineville, LA, 388

4404th Logistics Group
Prince Sultan Air Base, Saudi Arabia, 1146

4404th Medical Group
Prince Sultan Air Base, Saudi Arabia, 1146

4404th Operations Group
Prince Sultan Air Base, Saudi Arabia, 1146

4404th Support Group
Prince Sultan Air Base, Saudi Arabia, 1146

4404th Wing (P)
Prince Sultan Air Base, Saudi Arabia, 1146

4407th Reconnaissance Squadron
Prince Sultan Air Base, Saudi Arabia, 1146

4408th Air Refueling Squadron
Prince Sultan Air Base, Saudi Arabia, 1146

4409th Air Base Group
Eskan Village, Saudi Arabia, 1145

4409th Air Base Group Staff
Eskan Village, Saudi Arabia, 1145

4409th Civil Engineering Squadron
Eskan Village, Saudi Arabia, 1145

4409th Communications Squadron
Eskan Village, Saudi Arabia, 1145

4409th Logistics Squadron
Eskan Village, Saudi Arabia, 1145

4409th Security Forces Squadron
Eskan Village, Saudi Arabia, 1145

4409th Support Squadron
Eskan Village, Saudi Arabia, 1145

4410th Airlift Squadron
Prince Sultan Air Base, Saudi Arabia, 1146

4410th Rescue Squadron
Prince Sultan Air Base, Saudi Arabia, 1146

4416th Intelligence Squadron
Prince Sultan Air Base, Saudi Arabia, 1146

6005th Air Postal Squadron, Operating Location D, Det 1
6005th Air Postal Squadron, OL-D, Det 1, Korea, Republic of, 1087

6010th Aerospace Defense Group
Wheeler Army Airfield, Wheeler Army Airfield, HI, 293

6237th Army Reserve Forces School
Parks Reserve Forces Training Area, Dublin, CA, 62

6510th CRS (OL-AA/JTF)
Defense Plant Representative Office, Air Force Plant No 4, Fort Worth, TX, 795

6949th Electronic Security Squadron
Offutt Air Force Base, Offutt AFB, NE, 530

6966th Transportation TTT
Kleber Kaserne, Germany, 1018

7028th School Squadron (NCO Academy)
Upwood RAF Base, United Kingdom, 1169

7440th Wing (Provisional)
Incirlick Air Base, Turkey, 1152

ABFC A4 Admin FAC-4
Cheyenne Naval Reserve Center, Cheyenne, WY, 966

ABFC NOACT D29A (NR)
Lincoln Naval Reserve Center, Lincoln, NE, 529

Academic Instructor School
Maxwell Air Force Base, Maxwell AFB, AL, 8

Academy of Health Sciences
Fort Sam Houston, Fort Sam Houston, TX, 794

AD-41 Yellowstone Det 16 (NR)
Lexington Naval Reserve Center, Lexington, KY, 368

AD-41 Yellowstone Det 1309 (NR)
Louisville Naval Reserve Center, Louisville, KY, 371

AD 42 Det 9 (NR)
Wichita Naval & Marine Corps Reserve Center, Wichita, KS, 364

AD-42 (NR)
Las Vegas Naval & Marine Corps Reserve Center, Las Vegas, NV, 539

AD-41 Yellowstone Det 0966 (NR)
Cumberland Naval Reserve Center, Cumberland, MD, 419

AD Det 2 (NR)
Evansville Naval & Marine Corps Reserve Center, Evansville, IN, 326

AD Det 4 (NR)
Ebensburg Naval & Marine Corps Reserve Center, Ebensburg, PA, 702

Adjutant General Publications and Training Aids Center
223rd Base Support Battalion, Germany, 993

Administrative Support Center East (ASCE)
Defense Distribution Region East, New Cumberland, PA, 709

Advanced Tactical Information Management System
Point Mugu, Naval Air Weapons Station, Point Mugu, CA, 98

AEGIS Combat Systems Center
AEGIS Combat Systems Center, Wallops Island, VA, 905

AEGIS Combat Systems Det
Port Hueneme Division, Naval Surface Warfare Center, Port Hueneme, CA, 103

AEGIS Missile System Training Center
Dahlgren Division, Naval Surface Warfare Center, Dahlgren, VA, 859

AEGIS Training Unit, Det (ATU)
AEGIS Combat Systems Center, Wallops Island, VA, 905

Aerial Port Squadron
Charleston Air Force Base, Charleston AFB, SC, 737

Aeromedical Safety Unit
Rota Naval Station, Spain, 1149

Aeronautical Systems Center (ASC)
Wright-Patterson Air Force Base, Wright-Patterson AFB, OH, 667

Aeronautical Systems Center (SATAF)
Randolph Air Force Base, Randolph AFB, TX, 814

Aeronautical Systems Division
O'Hare International Airport Air Reserve Station, O'Hare IAP ARS, IL, 311

Aeronautical Systems Division (AFSC) Det 1
Production Flight Test Installation, Air Force Plant 42, Palmdale, CA, 94

Aerospace Maintenance and Regeneration Center (AMARC)
Davis-Monthan Air Force Base, Tucson, AZ, 42

Aerospace Materials Division, NAWCAD
Patuxent River, Naval Air Station, Patuxent River, MD, 427

AFFOR (Air Force Forces)
Joint Task Force—Bravo, Honduras, 1048

Afloat Training Group
Fleet Antisubmarine Warfare Training Center, Pacific, San Diego, CA, 111

Afloat Training Group Det
Sasebo, US Fleet Activities, Japan, 1080

Afloat Training Group, Mayport
Mayport Naval Air Station, Mayport, FL, 210

Afloat Training Group, Western Pacific
Afloat Training Group, Western Pacific, Pearl Harbor, HI, 281

AHC 1-189th Aviation Co A
Fort William Henry Harrison, Helena, MT, 523

AHC 1-189th Aviation Co B
Fort William Henry Harrison, Helena, MT, 523

AHC 1-189th Aviation Co C
Fort William Henry Harrison, Helena, MT, 523

Aids to Navigation (ANT) Team, Cape May
Cape May Coast Guard Training Center, Cape May, NJ, 553

Aids to Navigation (ANT) Team, Curtis Bay
Curtis Bay Coast Guard Yard, Curtis Bay, MD, 420

Aids to Navigation (ANT) Team, Detroit
Detroit Coast Guard Group/Base, Detroit, MI, 455

Aids to Navigation (ANT) Team, Galveston
Galveston Coast Guard Base, Galveston, TX, 798

Aids to Navigation (ANT) Team, Honolulu
Honolulu Coast Guard Base/Station, Honolulu, HI, 275

Aids to Navigation (ANT) Team, Pensacola
Pensacola Coast Guard Station, Pensacola, FL, 224

Aids to Navigation (ANT) Team, Philadelphia
Philadelphia Coast Guard Marine Safety Office & Group, Philadelphia, PA, 714

Aids to Navigation (ANT) Team, St Petersburg
St Petersburg Coast Guard Group/Station, Saint Petersburg, FL, 231

Aids to Navigation (ANT) Team, San Diego
San Diego Coast Guard Activities, San Diego, CA, 117

Aids to Navigation (ANT) Team, San Francisco
San Francisco Coast Guard Group, San Francisco, CA, 126

Aids to Navigation (ANT) Team, San Pedro
San Pedro Coast Guard Support Center, San Pedro, CA, 131

Aids to Navigation (ANT) Team, Sault
Sault Ste Marie Coast Guard Group, Sault Ste Marie, MI, 462

Aids to Navigation (ANT) Team, Puget Sound
Seattle Coast Guard Integrated Support Command, Seattle, WA, 929

Aids to Navigation (ANT) Team, Southwest Harbor
Southwest Harbor Coast Guard Group, Southwest Harbor, ME, 402

Aids to Navigation (ANT) Team, Woods Hole
Woods Hole Coast Guard Group, Woods Hole, MA, 447

Aids to Navigation (ANT) Team, Miami
Miami Beach Coast Guard Group/Station, Miami Beach, FL, 212

Aids to Navigation (ANT) Team, Mobile
Mobile Coast Guard Group/Station, Mobile, AL, 10

Aids to Navigation Training Team
Boston Coast Guard Reserve Center, Boston, MA, 432

Ainsworth Army Medical Clinic
New York Area Command & Fort Hamilton, Brooklyn, NY, 581

Air Combat Command
Langley Air Force Base, Langley AFB, VA, 872

Air Combat Command (ACC) Training Support Squadron, Det 13
Barksdale Air Force Base, Barksdale AFB, LA, 374

Air Combat Command (ACC) Training Support Squadron, Det 15
Seymour Johnson Air Force Base, Goldsboro, NC, 625

Air Combat Command Band
Offutt Air Force Base, Offutt AFB, NE, 530

Air Command and Staff College
Maxwell Air Force Base, Maxwell AFB, AL, 8

Air Defense Artillery School
Fort Bliss, El Paso, TX, 790

Air Defense Operations Center
Cheyenne Mountain Air Force Station, Colorado Springs, CO, 145

Air Education & Training Command
Kelly Air Force Base, Kelly AFB, TX, 807
Tyndall Air Force Base, Panama City, FL, 220
Vance Air Force Base, Vance AFB, OK, 681

Air Education and Training Command, HQ
Randolph Air Force Base, Randolph AFB, TX, 814

Air Education and Training Command, Ramstein
Ramstein Air Base, Germany, 1023

Air Force 23rd Flying Training Flight
Fort Rucker, Fort Rucker, AL, 5

Air Force Academy, HQ
US Air Force Academy, Colorado Springs, CO, 146

Air Force Aerostat Site (Cudjoe Key)
Key West Naval Air Facility, Boca Chica Key, FL, 191

Air Force Air Demonstration Squadron (Thunderbirds)
Nellis Air Force Base, Nellis AFB, NV, 541

Air Force Air Ground Operations School
Fort Rucker, Fort Rucker, AL, 5

Air Force Audit Agency
Minot Air Force Base, Minot AFB, ND, 642
Peterson Air Force Base, Peterson AFB, CO, 156
Seymour Johnson Air Force Base, Goldsboro, NC, 625
Shaw Air Force Base, Shaw AFB, SC, 749

Air Force Audit Agency Area Audit Office
Charleston Air Force Base, Charleston AFB, SC, 737

Air Force Audit Agency Det
Ellsworth Air Force Base, Ellsworth AFB, SD, 750

Air Force Audit Agency, Kelly Office
Kelly Air Force Base, Kelly AFB, TX, 807

Air Force Audit Agency, Los Angeles
Los Angeles Air Force Base, Los Angeles, CA, 76

Air Force Band
Bolling Air Force Base, Washington, DC, 173

Air Force Band of the Pacific
Elmendorf Air Force Base, Anchorage, AK, 19

Air Force Broadcasting Service
Yokota Air Base, Japan, 1085

Air Force C4 Agency (OLB, AFC4A/MB)
Barksdale Air Force Base, Barksdale AFB, LA, 374

Air Force Center for Quality and Management Innovation
Randolph Air Force Base, Randolph AFB, TX, 814

Air Force Chaplain, HQ
Bolling Air Force Base, Washington, DC, 173

US Air Force Civil Air Patrol
Minneapolis-Saint Paul IAP, Air National Guard Base/ARS, Minneapolis-Saint Paul IAP, MN, 474

Air Force Civil Air Patrol Liaison
Dover Air Force Base, Dover AFB, DE, 167

Air Force Civil Engineering Support Agency
Tyndall Air Force Base, Panama City, FL, 220

Air Force Combat Aerial Delivery School
Little Rock Air Force Base, Little Rock AFB, AR, 50

Air Force Command Center
The Pentagon, Arlington, VA, 852

Air Force Command, Control, Communications and Computer Agency
Scott Air Force Base, Scott AFB, IL, 318

Air Force Communications Agency
Scott Air Force Base, Scott AFB, IL, 318

Air Force Development Test Center
Eglin Air Force Base, Fort Walton Beach, FL, 197

Air Force Electronic Warfare Evaluation Simulator
Defense Plant Representative Office, Air Force Plant No 4, Fort Worth, TX, 795

Air Force Element, Det 12, Joint Cryptologic Center
Kelly Air Force Base, Kelly AFB, TX, 807

Air Force Engineering and Technical Services
Elmendorf Air Force Base, Anchorage, AK, 19

Air Force European Broadcasting Squadron, Det 3
Lajes Field, Portugal, 1138

Air Force Flight Test Center
Edwards Air Force Base, Edwards AFB, CA, 63

Air Force Global Weather Center
Offutt Air Force Base, Offutt AFB, NE, 530

Air Force Historian
Bolling Air Force Base, Washington, DC, 173

Air Force Historical Research Agency
Maxwell Air Force Base, Maxwell AFB, AL, 8

Air Force Honor Guard
Bolling Air Force Base, Washington, DC, 173

Air Force Hospital
Dover Air Force Base, Dover AFB, DE, 167

Air Force Inspection Agency
Kirtland Air Force Base, Kirtland AFB, NM, 572

Air Force Institute of Technology
Wright-Patterson Air Force Base, Wright-Patterson AFB, OH, 667

Air Force Institute of Technology-Education with Industry
Defense Plant Representative Office, Air Force Plant No 4, Fort Worth, TX, 795

Air Force Judge Advocate Generals School
Maxwell Air Force Base, Maxwell AFB, AL, 8

US Air Force Judiciary Area Defense Counsel
Dover Air Force Base, Dover AFB, DE, 167

Air Force Materiel Command, HQ (AFMC)
Wright-Patterson Air Force Base, Wright-Patterson AFB, OH, 667

Air Force Medical Support Agency
Brooks Air Force Base, San Antonio, TX, 815

US Air Force Museum
Wright-Patterson Air Force Base, Wright-Patterson AFB, OH, 667

Air Force News Agency, HQ
Kelly Air Force Base, Kelly AFB, TX, 807

Air Force News Agency, OL-A, Det 4
Feltwell RAF Base, United Kingdom, 1158

Air Force Occupational Measurement Squadron
Randolph Air Force Base, Randolph AFB, TX, 814

Air Force Occupational Medicine Clinic, Columbus (SGPOC)
Defense Supply Center, Columbus, Columbus, OH, 654

Air Force Office of Special Investigations
Bolling Air Force Base, Washington, DC, 173
Dover Air Force Base, Dover AFB, DE, 167
Hurlburt Field, Hurlburt Field, FL, 200
Peterson Air Force Base, Peterson AFB, CO, 156
Seymour Johnson Air Force Base, Goldsboro, NC, 625

Air Force Office of Special Investigations, Det 102
Hanscom Air Force Base, Bedford, MA, 430

Air Force Office of Special Investigations, Det 107
Kelly Air Force Base, Kelly AFB, TX, 807

Air Force Office of Special Investigations, Det 110
Los Angeles Air Force Base, Los Angeles, CA, 76

Air Force Office of Special Investigations, Det 212
Shaw Air Force Base, Shaw AFB, SC, 749

Air Force Office of Special Investigations, Det 218
Beale Air Force Base, Beale AFB, CA, 58

Air Force Office of Special Investigations, Det 219
Barksdale Air Force Base, Barksdale AFB, LA, 374

Air Force Office of Special Investigations, Det 228
Minot Air Force Base, Minot AFB, ND, 642

Air Force Office of Special Investigations, Det 243
Eskan Village, Saudi Arabia, 1145

Air Force Office of Special Investigations, Det 250
Lajes Field, Portugal, 1138

Air Force Office of Special Investigations, Det 320
Grand Forks Air Force Base, Grand Forks AFB, ND, 641

Air Force Office of Special Investigations, Det 322
Fairchild Air Force Base, Fairchild AFB, WA, 919

Air Force Office of Special Investigations, Det 401
Randolph Air Force Base, Randolph AFB, TX, 814

Air Force Office of Special Investigations, Det 407
Keesler Air Force Base, Keesler AFB, MS, 487

Air Force Office of Special Investigations, Det 410
Laughlin Air Force Base, Laughlin AFB, TX, 810

Air Force Office of Special Investigations, Det 427
Little Rock Air Force Base, Little Rock AFB, AR, 50

Air Force Office of Special Investigations, Det 1008
Brooks Air Force Base, San Antonio, TX, 815

Air Force Office of Special Investigations, Det 1058
Defense Plant Representative Office, Air Force Plant No 4, Fort Worth, TX, 795

Air Force Office of Special Investigations, Det 1302
Ellsworth Air Force Base, Ellsworth AFB, SD, 750

Air Force Office of Special Investigations, Guam
Andersen Air Force Base, Guam, 1043

Air Force Operational Test and Evaluation Center
Kirtland Air Force Base, Kirtland AFB, NM, 572

Air Force Operational Test and Evaluation Center, Det 5
Edwards Air Force Base, Edwards AFB, CA, 63

Air Force Personnel Center
Randolph Air Force Base, Randolph AFB, TX, 814

US Air Force Port Mortuary
Dover Air Force Base, Dover AFB, DE, 167

Air Force Quality Institute
Maxwell Air Force Base, Maxwell AFB, AL, 8

Air Force Recruiting Service
Randolph Air Force Base, Randolph AFB, TX, 814

Air Force Research Laboratory
Kirtland Air Force Base, Kirtland AFB, NM, 572

Air Force Research Laboratory (AFRL)
Wright-Patterson Air Force Base, Wright-Patterson AFB, OH, 667

Air Force Reserve Command, HQ
Robins Air Force Base, Robins AFB, GA, 259

Air Force ROTC Southwest Region
Randolph Air Force Base, Randolph AFB, TX, 814

Air Force Reuse Center
Gunter Annex, Gunter, AL, 6

Air Force Safety Center
Kirtland Air Force Base, Kirtland AFB, NM, 572

USAF Satellite Management Center, Pacific
Naval Computer & Telecommunications Area Master Station, Eastern Pacific, Wahiawa, HI, 288

Air Force School of Aerospace Medicine
Brooks Air Force Base, San Antonio, TX, 815

Air Force Security Forces Center
Kirtland Air Force Base, Kirtland AFB, NM, 572

Air Force Senior Noncommissioned Officer Academy
Gunter Annex, Gunter, AL, 6

Air Force Services Agency
Randolph Air Force Base, Randolph AFB, TX, 814

Air Force Southern Air Forces
Howard Air Force Base, Panama, 1136

Air Force Space Command
Cheyenne Mountain Air Force Station, Colorado Springs, CO, 145

Air Force Special Operations Command
Hurlburt Field, Hurlburt Field, FL, 200

Air Force Special Operations School
Hurlburt Field, Hurlburt Field, FL, 200

Air Force Surgeon General
Bolling Air Force Base, Washington, DC, 173

Air Force Survival School
Fairchild Air Force Base, Fairchild AFB, WA, 919

Air Force Systems Command/ Central Technical Order Control Unit
Defense Plant Representative Office, Air Force Plant No 4, Fort Worth, TX, 795

Air Force Systems Command/Joint Test Force
Defense Plant Representative Office, Air Force Plant No 4, Fort Worth, TX, 795

Air Force Technical Applications Center
Patrick Air Force Base, Patrick AFB, FL, 221

Air Force Technical Applications Center, Det 415
Air Force Technical Applications Center, Det 415, Thailand, 1150

Air Force Technical Applications Center, Det 460
Eielson Air Force Base, Eielson AFB, AK, 24

Air Force Technical Applications Center, Det 421
Joint Geological and Geophysical Research Station, Australia, 971

Air Force Technical Applications Center, Det 489
Pinedale Seismic Research Facility, Pinedale, WY, 969

Air Force Test Pilot School
Edwards Air Force Base, Edwards AFB, CA, 63

Air Force Water Survival School
Tyndall Air Force Base, Panama City, FL, 220

Air Force Weapons School
Nellis Air Force Base, Nellis AFB, NV, 541

US Air Force Weapons School, Det 4
Ellsworth Air Force Base, Ellsworth AFB, SD, 750

Air Force Weather Service
Scott Air Force Base, Scott AFB, IL, 318

Air Intelligence Agency, HQ
Kelly Air Force Base, Kelly AFB, TX, 807

Air Maneuver Battle Lab
Fort Rucker, Fort Rucker, AL, 5

Air Mobility Command, HQ
Scott Air Force Base, Scott AFB, IL, 318

Air Mobility Command Liaison (USAF)
Rota Naval Station, Spain, 1149

AMC Logistics Assistance Office
Army Armor Center & Fort Knox, Fort Knox, KY, 366

AMC Museum
Dover Air Force Base, Dover AFB, DE, 167

Air Mobility Command, Ramstein
Ramstein Air Base, Germany, 1023

Air Mobility Command Space-A Flight Information
Los Angeles Air Force Base, Los Angeles, CA, 76

Air Mobility Warfare Center
Fort Dix, Fort Dix, NJ, 555
McGuire Air Force Base, McGuire AFB, NJ, 561

Air Movement Center, Diego Garcia
Diego Garcia, Naval Support Facility, Diego Garcia, 982

Air National Guard Readiness Center (ANGRC)
Andrews Air Force Base, Andrews AFB, MD, 407

Air Operations Directorate
White Sands Missile Range, White Sands Missile Range, NM, 574

Air Operations Squadron, Ramstein
Ramstein Air Base, Germany, 1023

Air Test and Evaluation Squadron 1 (VX-1)
Patuxent River, Naval Air Station, Patuxent River, MD, 427

Air Test and Evaluation Squadron, 9th Det
Point Mugu, Naval Air Weapons Station, Point Mugu, CA, 98

Air University
Maxwell Air Force Base, Maxwell AFB, AL, 8

Air University Library
Maxwell Air Force Base, Maxwell AFB, AL, 8

Air War College
Maxwell Air Force Base, Maxwell AFB, AL, 8

Air Warfare Center
Eglin Air Force Base, Fort Walton Beach, FL, 197

Air Warfare Center, HQ
Nellis Air Force Base, Nellis AFB, NV, 541

Air Weather Service, Military Airlift Command
Cheyenne Mountain Air Force Station, Colorado Springs, CO, 145

Air Weather Squadron, Det 5
Keesler Air Force Base, Keesler AFB, MS, 487

Aircraft Repair & Supply Center, Elizabeth City
Elizabeth City Coast Guard Support Center, Elizabeth City, NC, 623

Aircrew Training Research Division
Aircrew Training Research Division, Armstrong Laboratory, Mesa, AZ, 38
Luke Air Force Base, Luke AFB, AZ, 37

Airman Leadership School
Ellsworth Air Force Base, Ellsworth AFB, SD, 750

Airman Leadership School, Ramstein
Ramstein Air Base, Germany, 1023

Alabama National Guard
Adjutant General of Alabama, Montgomery, AL, 13

Alaska National Guard
Adjutant General of Alaska, Fort Richardson, AK, 26
Fort Richardson, Fort Richardson, AK, 27

Alaska Weather Operations Center
Elmendorf Air Force Base, Anchorage, AK, 19

Alaskan Command, HQ
Elmendorf Air Force Base, Anchorage, AK, 19

Allegheny Regional Veterinary Command
Carlisle Barracks, Carlisle Barracks, PA, 698

Allied Air Forces Central Europe (NATO HQ)
Ramstein Air Base, Germany, 1023

Allied Command Atlantic Communications Logistics Depot
Yorktown Naval Weapons Station, Yorktown, VA, 910

AFCENT, Brunssum
254th Base Support Battalion, Netherlands, 1127

Commander Allied Forces Southern Europe (CINCSOUTH)
Naples (Capodichino) Naval Support Activity, Italy, 1055

Allied Land Forces Central Europe, HQ
Heidelberg Military Community, Germany, 1011

Allied Land Forces Southeastern Europe
Izmir Air Station, Turkey, 1153

Allied Land Forces Southern Europe
22nd Area Support Group, Italy, 1050

Allied Liaison Office
Army Armor Center & Fort Knox, Fort Knox, KY, 366

Allied Military Force, Land, HQ
Taylor Barracks, Germany, 1034

Allied Naval Forces Southern Europe (NAVSOUTH)
Naples (Capodichino) Naval Support Activity, Italy, 1055

Allied Naval Forces Southern Europe (NAVSOUTH), Representative
Vecihi Akin Garrison, Turkey, 1154

Alternate National Military Command Center (ANMCC)
Alternate Joint Communications Center/Site R, Fort Ritchie, MD, 423

Alvin York Village Family Housing
Friedberg Area Support Team, Germany, 1007

Amberg Family Housing
282nd Base Support Battalion, Germany, 995

Amelia Earhardt Hotel
221st Base Support Battalion, Germany, 992

American Arms Hotel
221st Base Support Battalion, Germany, 992

American Forces Network
221st Base Support Battalion, Germany, 992

American Forces Network, Naples
Sigonella Naval Air Station, Italy, 1059

Ammunition Demilitarization Support Facility
Pine Bluff Arsenal, Pine Bluff, AR, 53

Ammunition School, Savanna
Savanna Army Depot Activity, Savanna, IL, 317

Amphibious Group 2
Little Creek, Naval Amphibious Base, Norfolk, VA, 880

Amphibious Warfare School
Quantico Marine Corps Combat Development Command, Quantico, VA, 895

AMSA/ECS 30
Parks Reserve Forces Training Area, Dublin, CA, 62

Anderson Barracks
Anderson Barracks, Germany, 998

ANG Field Training Site, Headquarters
Alpena Combat Readiness Training Center, Alpena, MI, 449

Anniston Chemical Activity
Anniston Army Depot, Anniston, AL, 1

Antarctic Development Squadron 6
Point Mugu, Naval Air Weapons Station, Point Mugu, CA, 98

Antilles Consolidated School System
Fort Buchanan Army Garrison, Puerto Rico, 1141

Antilles Consolidated Schools
Roosevelt Roads Naval Station, Puerto Rico, 1143

Antisubmarine Warfare Communications Center, Det Whidbey Island
Whidbey Island Naval Air Station, Oak Harbor, WA, 924

Commander, Antisubmarine Warfare Force, Pacific Fleet
Pearl Harbor Naval Complex, Pearl Harbor, HI, 283

Antisubmarine Warfare Operations Center (ASWOC)
Rota Naval Station, Spain, 1149

Antisubmarine Warfare Operations Center (ASWOC)
North Island Naval Air Station, San Diego, CA, 115

HQ, ARCC, Moenchengladbach
254th Base Support Battalion, Netherlands, 1127

Arctic Submarine Lab
Keyport Division, Naval Undersea Warfare Center, Keyport, WA, 922

Arctic Support Brigade
Fort Richardson, Fort Richardson, AK, 27

Arctic Survival School
Eielson Air Force Base, Eielson AFB, AK, 24

Area I (East)
Camp Page, Korea, Republic of, 1108

Area I (West) & Camp Red Cloud
Camp Red Cloud, Korea, Republic of, 1109

Area Defense Counsel
Seymour Johnson Air Force Base, Goldsboro, NC, 625

Area Defense Counsel
Charleston Air Force Base, Charleston AFB, SC, 737
Edwards Air Force Base, Edwards AFB, CA, 63
Grand Forks Air Force Base, Grand Forks AFB, ND, 641

Area Defense Counsel, Det QD7H
Andersen Air Force Base, Guam, 1043

Area Defense Counsel, Ramstein
Ramstein Air Base, Germany, 1023

Area Maintenance Support Activity #82
Vancouver Barracks, Vancouver, WA, 938

Area Maintenance Support Activity 154G (US Army)
Tuscaloosa Armed Forces Reserve Center, Tuscaloosa, AL, 17

Area Support Team Würzburg
98th Area Support Group, Germany, 990

ARFOR (Army Forces)
Joint Task Force—Bravo, Honduras, 1048

Argonner Kaserne
414th Base Support Battalion, Germany, 997

Arizona National Guard
Adjutant General of Arizona, Phoenix, AZ, 39

Arkansas National Guard
Adjutant General of Arkansas, North Little Rock, AR, 51

Arkansas National Guard, HQ
Camp Joseph T Robinson, North Little Rock, AR, 52

ARL-SS Rochester Warehouse
Combined Support Maintenance Shop C/US Property & Fiscal Office—NY, Rochester, NY, 602

Arlington National Cemetery
Military District of Washington, Washington, DC, 179

Armament & Chemical Acquisition & Logistics Activity
Rock Island Arsenal, Rock Island, IL, 314

Armament Munitions and Chemical Command 10 ROTA 1009 (NR)
Tuscaloosa Armed Forces Reserve Center, Tuscaloosa, AL, 17

Armament Research, Development, and Engineering Center (TACOM-ARDEC)
Armament Research, Development, and Engineering Center, US Army TACOM, Picatinny Arsenal, NJ, 562

Armed Forces Experimental Training Activity
Camp Peary, Williamsburg, VA, 906

Armed Forces Health Clinic
Stewart Air National Guard Base, Newburgh, NY, 599

Armed Forces Institute of Pathology
Armed Forces Institute of Pathology, Washington, DC, 172
Walter Reed Army Medical Center, Washington, DC, 188

Armed Forces Pest Management Board
Walter Reed Army Medical Center, Washington, DC, 188

Armed Forces Radiobiology Research Institute
National Naval Medical Center, Bethesda, MD, 417

Armed Forces Recreation Center
Fort DeRussy, Honolulu, HI, 273

Armed Forces Recreation Center, Garmish
6th Area Support Group, Garmish, Germany, 987

Armed Forces Reserve Center
Stockton Naval Communications Station, Stockton, CA, 135

Armed Forces Reserve Center, Brooklyn
Brooklyn Coast Guard Air Station, Brooklyn, NY, 579

Armed Forces Reserve Center, Westover ARB
Westover Air Reserve Base, Chicopee, MA, 438

Armed Forces Retirement Home (AFRH)
US Naval Home, Gulfport, MS, 483

Armed Forces School of Music
Little Creek, Naval Amphibious Base, Norfolk, VA, 880

Armed Forces Staff College
Armed Forces Staff College, Norfolk, VA, 875
Norfolk Naval Station, Norfolk, VA, 886

Armor Branch Safety Office
Army Armor Center & Fort Knox, Fort Knox, KY, 366

Armory Det, Honolulu
Honolulu Coast Guard Base/Station, Honolulu, HI, 275

Armory Det, Ketchikan
Ketchikan Coast Guard Station, Ketchikan, AK, 30

Armory Det, San Pedro
San Pedro Coast Guard Support Center, San Pedro, CA, 131

Armory Det, Seattle
Seattle Coast Guard Integrated Support Command, Seattle, WA, 929

Armstrong Barracks
414th Base Support Battalion, Germany, 997

Armstrong Laboratories
Tyndall Air Force Base, Panama City, FL, 220

Armstrong Laboratory
Brooks Air Force Base, San Antonio, TX, 815

Armstrong Laboratory, Det 3
Kadena Air Base, Japan, 1074

Armstrong Village Family Housing
414th Base Support Battalion, Germany, 997

Army 1st Region, Army Cadet Command
Fort Bragg, Fort Bragg, NC, 624

Army 2nd Recruiting Brigade
Fort Gillem, Forest Park, GA, 247

Army 21st Replacement Bn
Rhein-Main Air Base, Germany, 1025

Army Aberdeen Test Center
Aberdeen Proving Ground, Aberdeen Proving Ground, MD, 404

Army Aeromedical Center
Fort Rucker, Fort Rucker, AL, 5

Army Aeromedical Research Laboratory
Fort Rucker, Fort Rucker, AL, 5

Army/Air Force Exchange Service
Yokota Air Base, Japan, 1085

AAFES, HQ
221st Base Support Battalion, Germany, 992

AAFES, Okinawa, HQ
Camp Lester, Japan, 1069

Army-Air Force Exchange Service, Western Region Distribution Center
Military Traffic Management Command, Western Area, Oakland, CA, 89

Army/Air Force Exchange System
Charles E Kelly Support Facility, Oakdale, PA, 711

Army Air Guard
Houston Coast Guard Air Station, Houston, TX, 804

Army Traffic Control Activity
Fort Rucker, Fort Rucker, AL, 5

Army Airworthiness Qualification Test Directorate
Edwards Air Force Base, Edwards AFB, CA, 63

HQ, US Army Alaska
Fort Richardson, Fort Richardson, AK, 27

Army & Air Force Exchange Service
Army Armor Center & Fort Knox, Fort Knox, KY, 366
Army Transportation Center & Fort Eustis, Fort Eustis, VA, 868
Dover Air Force Base, Dover AFB, DE, 167

Army and Air Force Exchange Service, Camp Zama
Camp Zama, Japan, 1071

Army & Air Force Exchange System Distribution Center
Fort Gillem, Forest Park, GA, 247

Army Armament and Chemical Acquisition and Logistics Activity (ACALA)
US Army Corps of Engineers, Rock Island District, Rock Island, IL, 316

Army Armament, Munitions and Chemical Command (AMCCOM)
Radford Army Ammunition Plant, Radford, VA, 896

AMCCOM Vault 1
Defense Industrial Plant Equipment Facility, Atchison, KS, 351

AMCCOM Vault 2
Defense Industrial Plant Equipment Facility, Atchison, KS, 351

Army Armor Center & Fort Knox
Army Armor Center & Fort Knox, Fort Knox, KY, 366

Army Armor School, HQ
Army Armor Center & Fort Knox, Fort Knox, KY, 366

Army Assistance Office
Charleston Air Force Base, Charleston AFB, SC, 737

Army Audit Agency, Ft Bragg Field Office
Fort Bragg, Fort Bragg, NC, 624

Army Audit Agency, SW Region
Fort Sam Houston, Fort Sam Houston, TX, 794

Army Aviation and Missile Command
Redstone Arsenal, Redstone Arsenal, AL, 16

Army Aviation & Troop Command, Eastern Inspection Region
Army Transportation Center & Fort Eustis, Fort Eustis, VA, 868

Army Aviation Brigade
Cape Cod Coast Guard Air Station, Cape Cod, MA, 436

Army Aviation Center
Fort Rucker, Fort Rucker, AL, 5

Army Aviation Center Noncommissioned Officer Academy
Fort Rucker, Fort Rucker, AL, 5

Army Aviation Logistics School
Army Transportation Center & Fort Eustis, Fort Eustis, VA, 868
Fort Rucker, Fort Rucker, AL, 5

Army Aviation Support Activity (ANG)
Aberdeen Proving Ground, Aberdeen Proving Ground, MD, 404

Army Aviation Support Facility
Whiteman Air Force Base, Whiteman AFB, MO, 516

Army Aviation Support Facility (ARNG)
Buckley Air National Guard Base, Aurora, CO, 142

Army Aviation Support Group (ARNG)
Massachusetts Military Reservation/Otis Air National Guard Base, Cape Cod, MA, 437

Army Aviation Technical Test Center
Fort Rucker, Fort Rucker, AL, 5

Army Band (Pershing's Own)
Fort Myer, Arlington, VA, 847
Military District of Washington, Washington, DC, 179

Army Band, West Point
West Point, Army Garrison, West Point, NY, 614

Army Broadcasting Det
Torii Station, Japan, 1082

Army Calibration Repair Center
Blue Grass Army Depot, Richmond, KY, 373

Army Center for Health Promotion and Preventive Medicine
Aberdeen Proving Ground, Aberdeen Proving Ground, MD, 404

Army Center for Public Works
US Army Corps of Engineers, Center for Public Works, Alexandria, VA, 839

Army Center of Military History
Anniston Army Depot, Anniston, AL, 1

Army Central Personnel Security Clearance Facility
Fort George G Meade, Fort Meade, MD, 422

Army Chemical Activity, Pacific
Army Chemical Activity Pacific, Johnston Atoll, 1086

Army Chemical & Biological Defense Command
Aberdeen Proving Ground, Aberdeen Proving Ground, MD, 404

Army Chemical Depot
Umatilla Chemical Depot, Hermiston, OR, 686

Army Chemical School
Fort McClellan, Anniston, AL, 2

Army Chorus
Fort Myer, Arlington, VA, 847

Army Civil Affairs and Psychological Operations Command
Fort Bragg, Fort Bragg, NC, 624

Army Claims Service
Fort George G Meade, Fort Meade, MD, 422

Army Cold Regions Research & Engineering Laboratory
Army Cold Regions Research & Engineering Laboratory, Hanover, NH, 548
Fort Wainwright, Fort Wainwright, AK, 28

Army Combined Arms Support Command
Fort Lee, Fort Lee, VA, 869

Army Command Test & Evaluation Coordination
Army Armor Center & Fort Knox, Fort Knox, KY, 366

Army Communications-Electronics Command, Electronics Integration Directorate/Airborne Engineering Evaluation Support Activity
Lakehurst Naval Air Engineering Station, Lakehurst, NJ, 560

Army Communications-Electronics Command Center for Night

Vision and Electro-Optics Directorate
Fort A P Hill, Bowling Green, VA, 855

Army Communications-Electronics Command Acquisition Center
Army Communications-Electronics Command Acquisition Center, Alexandria, VA, 835

Army Communications-Electronics Command (CECOM)
Fort Monmouth, Fort Monmouth, NJ, 557

US Army Corps of Engineers, Baltimore District-Northeast Resident Office
Tobyhanna Army Depot, Tobyhanna, PA, 721

Army Corps of Engineers, Central Virginia Area Office, DSCR Project Office
Defense Supply Center, Richmond, Richmond, VA, 898

Army Corps of Engineers, Ft Rucker
Fort Rucker, Fort Rucker, AL, 5

Pacific Ocean Division, Army Corps of Engineers
Fort Shafter, Fort Shafter, HI, 267

Army Counterintelligence, Army INSCOM, Fort Knox Resident Office, 902nd Military Intelligence Group
Army Armor Center & Fort Knox, Fort Knox, KY, 366

Army Criminal Investigation Command
Army Criminal Investigation Command, Fort Belvoir, VA, 862
Camp Zama, Japan, 1071

Army Criminal Investigation Command, 3rd Region, Field Office
Hunter Army Air Field, Savannah, GA, 260

Army Criminal Investigation Command, HQ
Fort Belvoir, Fort Belvoir, VA, 866

Army Criminal Investigation Command, HQ, Third Region
Fort Gillem, Forest Park, GA, 247

Army Criminal Investigation Command, Washington District
Fort Myer, Arlington, VA, 847

Army Criminal Investigation Division
Fort Jackson, Columbia, SC, 740

Army Criminal Investigation Laboratory-CONUS (Continental US)
Fort Gillem, Forest Park, GA, 247

Army Criminal Investigation Laboratory, HQ
Fort Gillem, Forest Park, GA, 247

Army Dental Activity
Army Signal Center & Fort Gordon, Fort Gordon, GA, 249
Army Transportation Center & Fort Eustis, Fort Eustis, VA, 868
Walter Reed Army Medical Center, Washington, DC, 188

Army Dental Activity, Ft Bragg
Fort Bragg, Fort Bragg, NC, 624

Army Dental Activity, Ft Knox
Army Armor Center & Fort Knox, Fort Knox, KY, 366

US Army Dental Clinic, Vicenza
Caserma Ederle/Vicenza Military Community, Vincenza, Italy, 1060

Army Dental Command, Ft Rucker
Fort Rucker, Fort Rucker, AL, 5

Army Dental Laboratory
Army Signal Center & Fort Gordon, Fort Gordon, GA, 249

Army Depot System Command (DESCOM) Quality Systems and Engineering Center
Blue Grass Army Depot, Richmond, KY, 373

Army District Test, Management, and Diagnostic Equipment Support Center
Tobyhanna Army Depot, Tobyhanna, PA, 721

Army Edgewood Chemical Activity
Aberdeen Proving Ground, Aberdeen Proving Ground, MD, 404

Army Education Center, Chievres
80th Area Support Group, Belgium, 975

Army Education Center, Tompkins Barracks
Tompkins Barracks, Germany, 1035

Army Element, School of Music
Fort Story, Fort Story, VA, 871

Army Engineer Center
Fort Leonard Wood, Fort Leonard Wood, MO, 501

Army Engineer School
Fort Leonard Wood, Fort Leonard Wood, MO, 501

Army Engineer Transatlantic
221st Base Support Battalion, Germany, 992

Army Engineering Activity, Capital Area
Fort Myer, Arlington, VA, 847

Army Engineering & Support Center
Army Engineering & Support Center, Huntsville, AL, 7

Army Environmental Center
Aberdeen Proving Ground, Aberdeen Proving Ground, MD, 404

Army Environmental Hygiene Activity-North
Fort George G Meade, Fort Meade, MD, 422

Army Field Artillery School
Fort Sill, Fort Sill, OK, 671

Army Field Artillery Training Center
Fort Sill, Fort Sill, OK, 671

Army Field Band
Fort George G Meade, Fort Meade, MD, 422

Army Field Station, San Antonio
Kelly Air Force Base, Kelly AFB, TX, 807

US Army Finance and Accounting Office
Camp Zama, Japan, 1071

Army Forces Central Command-Saudi Arabia
Eskan Village, Saudi Arabia, 1145

Army Forces Command, HQ (FORSCOM)
Fort McPherson, Fort McPherson, GA, 250

Army Fuze Management Office (AFMO)
Armament Research, Development, and Engineering Center, US Army TA-COM, Picatinny Arsenal, NJ, 562

Army Garrison, Aberdeen Proving Ground
Aberdeen Proving Ground, Aberdeen Proving Ground, MD, 404

Army Garrison, Bayonne
Bayonne Military Ocean Terminal, Bayonne, NJ, 552

Army Garrison, Carlisle Barracks
Carlisle Barracks, Carlisle Barracks, PA, 698

Army Garrison, Co A
Yakima Training Center, Yakima, WA, 941

Army Garrison, Ft Belvoir
Fort Belvoir, Fort Belvoir, VA, 866

Army Garrison, Ft Clayton
Fort Clayton, Panama, 1133

Army Garrison, Ft Huachuca
Fort Huachuca, Fort Huachuca, AZ, 35

Army Garrison, Ft Leonard Wood
Fort Leonard Wood, Fort Leonard Wood, MO, 501

Army Garrison, Ft Lewis
Fort Lewis, Fort Lewis, WA, 921

Army Garrison, Ft McPherson
Fort McPherson, Fort McPherson, GA, 250

Army Garrison, Ft Meade
Fort George G Meade, Fort Meade, MD, 422

Army Garrison, Ft Polk
Fort Polk, Fort Polk, LA, 377

Army Garrison, Ft Richardson
Fort Richardson, Fort Richardson, AK, 27

Army Garrison, Ft Ritchie
Fort Ritchie, Fort Ritchie, MD, 424

Army Garrison, Ft Sam Houston
Fort Sam Houston, Fort Sam Houston, TX, 794

Army Garrison, Ft Wainwright
Fort Wainwright, Fort Wainwright, AK, 28

Army Garrison, Ft Hunter Liggett
Fort Hunter Liggett, Fort Hunter Liggett, CA, 69

Army Garrison, Hawaii
Schofield Barracks, Schofield Barracks, HI, 286

Army Garrison, HQ
Fort Myer, Arlington, VA, 847

Army Garrison, HQ Co
Fort Greely, Fort Greely, AK, 25

Army Garrison, Oakland Army Base
Oakland Army Base, Oakland, CA, 90

Army Garrison, Picatinny Arsenal
Armament Research, Development, and Engineering Center, US Army TA-COM, Picatinny Arsenal, NJ, 562

Army Garrison, West Point
West Point, Army Garrison, West Point, NY, 614

Army Health Clinic
Tobyhanna Army Depot, Tobyhanna, PA, 721

Army Health Clinic, Ft AP Hill
Fort A P Hill, Bowling Green, VA, 855

Army Health Clinic, McAlester
McAlester Army Ammunition Plant, McAlester, OK, 673

US Army Health Clinic, Vicenza
Caserma Ederle/Vicenza Military Community, Vincenza, Italy, 1060

Army Industrial Engineering Activity
Rock Island Arsenal, Rock Island, IL, 314

Army Infantry Center & School
Fort Benning, Fort Benning, GA, 248

Army Information Systems Command
Hunter Army Air Field, Savannah, GA, 260
Walter Reed Army Medical Center, Washington, DC, 188

Army Information Systems Engineering Command-CONUS
Fort Ritchie, Fort Ritchie, MD, 424

Army Information Systems Software Center
Fort Belvoir, Fort Belvoir, VA, 866

Army Information Systems Software Development Center
Fort Lee, Fort Lee, VA, 869

Army Intelligence & Security Command
Fort Belvoir, Fort Belvoir, VA, 866
Fort George G Meade, Fort Meade, MD, 422

Army Intelligence Center
Fort Huachuca, Fort Huachuca, AZ, 35

Army Intelligence Materiel Activity
Fort George G Meade, Fort Meade, MD, 422

Army Intelligence School
Fort Huachuca, Fort Huachuca, AZ, 35

Army IOC Industrial Logistics System Center
Letterkenny Army Depot, Chambersburg, PA, 699

Army JFK Special Warfare Center and School
Fort Bragg, Fort Bragg, NC, 624

Army Law Enforcement Command
Schofield Barracks, Schofield Barracks, HI, 286

Army Logistics Evaluation Agency
Defense Distribution Region East, New Cumberland, PA, 709

Army Logistics Management College
Fort Lee, Fort Lee, VA, 869

Army Management Career Program Office
Savanna Army Depot Activity, Savanna, IL, 317

Army Management Staff College
Fort Belvoir, Fort Belvoir, VA, 866

Army Marksmanship Unit
Fort Benning, Fort Benning, GA, 248

Army Materiel Command Europe
Heidelberg Military Community, Germany, 1011

Army Materiel Command Headquarters
Army Materiel Command Headquarters, Alexandria, VA, 836

Army Materiel Command Logistics Assistance Office
Army Transportation Center & Fort Eustis, Fort Eustis, VA, 868

Army Materiel Command Packaging Storage and Containerization Center
Tobyhanna Army Depot, Tobyhanna, PA, 721

Army Materiel Command Surety Field Activity, HQ
Aberdeen Proving Ground, Aberdeen Proving Ground, MD, 404

Army Materiel Systems Analysis Activity
Aberdeen Proving Ground, Aberdeen Proving Ground, MD, 404

Army Medical Command
Fort McPherson, Fort McPherson, GA, 250
Fort Sam Houston, Fort Sam Houston, TX, 794

Army Medical Department Activity
Army Transportation Center & Fort Eustis, Fort Eustis, VA, 868
Fort McClellan, Anniston, AL, 2

Army Medical Department Center & School
Fort Sam Houston, Fort Sam Houston, TX, 794

Army Medical Equipment & Optical School
Fitzsimons Army Medical Center, Aurora, CO, 144

Army Medical Material Agency
Defense Distribution Region West, Stockton, CA, 134

Army Medical Research & Materiel Command
Fort Detrick, Fort Detrick, MD, 421

Army Medical Research Institute for the Chemical Defense
Aberdeen Proving Ground, Aberdeen Proving Ground, MD, 404

Army Military District of Washington
Military District of Washington, Washington, DC, 179

Army Military Police School
Fort McClellan, Anniston, AL, 2

Army Natick Research, Development, and Engineering Center
Army Soldier Systems Command, Natick, MA, 441

Army National Guard Aviation Bn
Bradley IAP Air National Guard Base, Windsor Locks, CT, 166

Army National Guard Aviation Co
New Castle County Airport, Air National Guard Base, Wilmington, DE, 169

Army National Guard, Dallas
Dallas Naval Air Station, Dallas, TX, 783

ANG Maneuver Training Center, Fort Pickett
Fort Pickett, Maneuver Training Center, Blackstone, VA, 854

ARNG Mountain Warfare School
Ethan Allen Firing Range, Jericho, VT, 833

Army National Guard Readiness Center
Army National Guard Readiness Center, Arlington, VA, 842

Army Noncommissioned Officers Academy, Ft Sill
Fort Sill, Fort Sill, OK, 671

Army Occupational Health Clinic
Umatilla Chemical Depot, Hermiston, OR, 686

Army Office for Defense Medical Information Systems
Walter Reed Army Medical Center, Washington, DC, 188

Army Operational Support Airlift Command
Fort Belvoir, Fort Belvoir, VA, 866

Army Ordnance Center & School
Aberdeen Proving Ground, Aberdeen Proving Ground, MD, 404

US Army, Pacific (USARPAC)
Fort Shafter, Fort Shafter, HI, 267

Army Parachute Team (FORSCOM) (Golden Knights)
Fort Bragg, Fort Bragg, NC, 624

Army Petroleum Center
Defense Distribution Region East, New Cumberland, PA, 709

Army Physical Disability Agency
Walter Reed Army Medical Center, Washington, DC, 188

Army Physical Fitness Research Institute
Carlisle Barracks, Carlisle Barracks, PA, 698

Army Project Manager for Training Devices (PM TRADE)
Naval Air Warfare Center, Training Systems Division, Orlando, FL, 216

Army Publications Center
Aberdeen Proving Ground, Aberdeen Proving Ground, MD, 404

Army Publications Distribution Center, St Louis
Saint Louis Army Publications Distribution Center, Saint Louis, MO, 512

Army Ranger Training Bn
Eglin Air Force Base, Fort Walton Beach, FL, 197

Army Readiness Group
Fort Indiantown Gap, Annville, PA, 696
Fort McCoy, Fort McCoy, WI, 954

Army Readiness Group, Pacific
Fort Shafter, Fort Shafter, HI, 267

Army Readiness Group Selfridge
Selfridge Air National Guard Base, Selfridge ANG Base, MI, 464

Army Reception Station
Fort McClellan, Anniston, AL, 2

Army Recreation Center
Waianae Army Recreation Center, Waianae, HI, 290

Army Recruiting Bn
Defense Distribution Region East, New Cumberland, PA, 709

Army Recruiting Bn Richmond
Defense Supply Center, Richmond, Richmond, VA, 898

Army Recruiting Command
Army Armor Center & Fort Knox, Fort Knox, KY, 366

Army Recruiting Command HQ Co
Charles Melvin Price Army Support Center, Granite City, IL, 307

Army Research, Development & Standardization Group UK
Army Research, Development & Standardization Group, UK, London, United Kingdom, 1162

US Army Research Institute, Armored Forces Training Research Unit, Fort Knox
Army Armor Center & Fort Knox, Fort Knox, KY, 366

Army Research Institute, Ft Benning
Fort Benning, Fort Benning, GA, 248

Army Research Institute of Environmental Medicine
Army Soldier Systems Command, Natick, MA, 441

Army Research Institute of Infectious Diseases
Fort Detrick, Fort Detrick, MD, 421

Army Research Lab, Fort Knox Field Element
Army Armor Center & Fort Knox, Fort Knox, KY, 366

Army Research Laboratory, Aberdeen Site
Aberdeen Proving Ground, Aberdeen Proving Ground, MD, 404

Army Research Laboratory Battlefield Environments Division & Electronic Warfare Branch
White Sands Missile Range, White Sands Missile Range, NM, 574

Army Research Laboratory, Human Research & Engineering Directorate (ARL, HRED)
Fort Monmouth, Fort Monmouth, NJ, 557

Army Research Office
Army Research Office, Research Triangle Park, NC, 632

Army Research Office—Far East
Asian Office of Aerospace Research & Development, Tokyo, Japan, 1081

Army Reserve Center
Camp Joseph T Robinson, North Little Rock, AR, 52
Dobbins Air Reserve Base, Marietta, GA, 257
Fort Indiantown Gap, Annville, PA, 696
Roosevelt Roads Naval Station, Puerto Rico, 1143

Army Reserve Center, Camp Pendleton
Camp Pendleton Marine Corps Base, Oceanside, CA, 91

Army Reserve Center, Ft Dix
Fort Dix, Fort Dix, NJ, 555

Army Reserve Center, Ft Rucker Regional Flight Center
Fort Rucker, Fort Rucker, AL, 5

Army Reserve Center, Oakland Army Base
Oakland Army Base, Oakland, CA, 90

Army Reserve Command, HQ
Fort McPherson, Fort McPherson, GA, 250

Army Reserve NCO Academy
Fort Dix, Fort Dix, NJ, 555
Fort Lewis, Fort Lewis, WA, 921
Reserve Base, Fort Chaffee, Fort Smith, AR, 48

Army Reserve Personnel Command
Charles Melvin Price Army Support Center, Granite City, IL, 307

Army Reserve Readiness Training Center
Fort McCoy, Fort McCoy, WI, 954

Army Reserve Units
O'Hare International Airport Air Reserve Station, O'Hare IAP ARS, IL, 311

Army Safety School
Fort Rucker, Fort Rucker, AL, 5

Army School of Aviation Medicine
Fort Rucker, Fort Rucker, AL, 5

Army Security Assistance Command
Defense Distribution Region East, New Cumberland, PA, 709

Army Sergeants Major Academy
Fort Bliss, El Paso, TX, 790

Army Signal Center
Army Signal Center & Fort Gordon, Fort Gordon, GA, 249

Army Southeastern Regional Dental Command
Army Signal Center & Fort Gordon, Fort Gordon, GA, 249

Army Southern European Task Force
Caserma Ederle/Vicenza Military Community, Vincenza, Italy, 1060

Army Space and Strategic Defense Command
Redstone Arsenal, Redstone Arsenal, AL, 16

Army Space Command, HQ
Peterson Air Force Base, Peterson AFB, CO, 156

Army Space Command MSQ-114 Det
Torii Station, Japan, 1082

Army Special Forces Command
Fort Bragg, Fort Bragg, NC, 624

Army Special Forces Underwater Operations School
Key West Naval Air Facility, Boca Chica Key, FL, 191

Army Special Operations Command
Fort Bragg, Fort Bragg, NC, 624

Army Special Security Det
Camp Zama, Japan, 1071

Army Special Security Office, Aberdeen
Aberdeen Proving Ground, Aberdeen Proving Ground, MD, 404

Army Support Command, Hawaii (USASCH)
Fort Shafter, Fort Shafter, HI, 267

Army Support Det, Columbus
Army Armor Center & Fort Knox, Fort Knox, KY, 366

Army Tank-Automotive & Armaments Command (TACOM)
Army Tank-Automotive & Armaments Command, Warren, MI, 466

Army Tank Automotive Command Support Activity Selfridge
Selfridge Air National Guard Base, Selfridge ANG Base, MI, 464

Army Technical Escort Unit
Aberdeen Proving Ground, Aberdeen Proving Ground, MD, 404

Army Test and Evaluation Command
Aberdeen Proving Ground, Aberdeen Proving Ground, MD, 404

Army Test, Maintenance, and Diagnostic Equipment Support Operations
Seneca Army Depot Activity, Romulus, NY, 605

Army TMDE Activity 4055
Fort Sam Houston, Fort Sam Houston, TX, 794

Army TMDE Support Center
Aberdeen Proving Ground, Aberdeen Proving Ground, MD, 404
Anniston Army Depot, Anniston, AL, 1
Army Transportation Center & Fort Eustis, Fort Eustis, VA, 868

Army Test, Measurement, Diagnostic Equipment (TMDE) Support, Region 1
Letterkenny Army Depot, Chambersburg, PA, 699

Army Test, Measurement, and Diagnostic Support Center, McAlester
McAlester Army Ammunition Plant, McAlester, OK, 673

Army Test, Measurement, Diagnostic, and Equipment Det-Okinawa
Torii Station, Japan, 1082

Army Test Measurement Diagnostic Equipment Center
Tooele Army Depot, Tooele, UT, 830

Army Test Measuring Diagnostic Equipment Support Activity CONUS, Region 2
Army Armor Center & Fort Knox, Fort Knox, KY, 366

Army Training & Doctrine Command Analysis Center
White Sands Missile Range, White Sands Missile Range, NM, 574

Army Training Brigade
Fort McClellan, Anniston, AL, 2

Army Training Center Command
Fort Jackson, Columbia, SC, 740

Army Training Support Center
Army Transportation Center & Fort Eustis, Fort Eustis, VA, 868

Army Transportation Center
Army Transportation Center & Fort Eustis, Fort Eustis, VA, 868

Army Transportation Museum
Army Transportation Center & Fort Eustis, Fort Eustis, VA, 868

Army Transportation School
Army Transportation Center & Fort Eustis, Fort Eustis, VA, 868

Army Transportation School Rough Terrain Container
Fort Story, Fort Story, VA, 871

Ft Benning Field Office, Region II, US Army Trial Defense Service
Fort Benning, Fort Benning, GA, 248

Army Upgrade Tank Program
Lima Army Tank Plant, Lima, OH, 658

Army Veterinarian Food Inspection Office
Fleet & Industrial Supply Center, Cheatham Annex, Williamsburg, VA, 907

Army Veterinary Activity
Sigonella Naval Air Station, Italy, 1059

Army Veterinary Services
Torii Station, Japan, 1082

Army War College
Carlisle Barracks, Carlisle Barracks, PA, 698

Army War Reserves
Rock Island Arsenal, Rock Island, IL, 314

Arnold Engineering Development Center (AEDC)
Arnold Engineering Development Center, Arnold Air Force Base, TN, 756

Arraijan Tank Farm
Panama Canal Naval Station, Panama, 1137

Artillery Kaserne
6th Area Support Group, Garmish, Germany, 987

AS-33 Simon Lake 3309C (NR)
Lexington Naval Reserve Center, Lexington, KY, 368

AS-39 Land 407 (NR)
Greensboro Naval & Marine Corps Reserve Readiness Center, Greensboro, NC, 626

AS-39 Land Det 309 (NR)
Louisville Naval Reserve Center, Louisville, KY, 371

AS-40 *Cable* Det B
Pocatello Naval Reserve Facility, Pocatello, ID, 299

Aschaffenburg Community
223rd Base Support Battalion, Germany, 993

Aschaffenburg Family Housing
Babenhausen Area Support Team, Germany, 1000

Aschaffenburg Training Area
Babenhausen Area Support Team, Germany, 1000

Asian Office of Aerospace Research & Development
Asian Office of Aerospace Research & Development, Tokyo, Japan, 1081

Askren Manor Family Housing
280th Base Support Battalion, Germany, 994

Assault Craft Unit 2
Little Creek, Naval Amphibious Base, Norfolk, VA, 880

Assault Craft Unit 4
Little Creek, Naval Amphibious Base, Norfolk, VA, 880

Assault Craft Unit 5 (Navy)
Camp Pendleton Marine Corps Base, Oceanside, CA, 91

Assistant Division Commander (Maneuver), Camp Howze
Camp Howze, Korea, Republic of, 1101

Association of the US Army #6102
Presidio of Monterey, Monterey, CA, 85

Atlantic Fleet Weapons Training Facility (AFWTF)
Roosevelt Roads Naval Station, Puerto Rico, 1143

Attack Squadron 205 (VA-205)
Atlanta Naval Air Station, Marietta, GA, 254

Atterbury Reserve Forces Training Area
Camp Atterbury, Edinburgh, IN, 325

Auburn Range (ARNG)
Auburn Range, Auburn, ME, 390

Audio Visual/Photo Office
Corry Station Naval Technical Training Center, Pensacola, FL, 222

Aukamm Housing Area
221st Base Support Battalion, Germany, 992

Avenger Class Mine Countermeasures Ships (12)
Ingleside Naval Station, Ingleside, TX, 806

Aviano Air Base
Caserma Ederle/Vicenza Military Community, Vincenza, Italy, 1060

Aviation Applied Technology Directorate
Army Transportation Center & Fort Eustis, Fort Eustis, VA, 868

Aviation Board of Inspection & Safety
Patuxent River, Naval Air Station, Patuxent River, MD, 427

Aviation Brigade
Fort Stewart, Hinesville, GA, 252

Aviation Brigade HQ
Camp Stanley, Korea, Republic of, 1111

Aviation Flight Facility (ARNG)
Massachusetts Military Reservation/Otis Air National Guard Base, Cape Cod, MA, 437

Aviation Ground Support Element
Twentynine Palms Marine Corps Air Ground Combat Center, Twentynine Palms, CA, 139

Aviation Intermediate Maintenance Department (AIMD)
Rota Naval Station, Spain, 1149

Aviation Support Facility (ANG)
Wheeler Army Airfield, Wheeler Army Airfield, HI, 293

Aviation Support Facility
Birmingham Airport, Air National Guard Base, Birmingham, AL, 4

Aviation Survival Training Center
Lemoore Naval Air Station, Lemoore, CA, 74

Aviation Training Brigade
Fort Rucker, Fort Rucker, AL, 5

Awase Transmitter Facility
Kadena Naval Air Facility, Japan, 1075

Azbill Barracks
221st Base Support Battalion, Germany, 992

Azores Air Command (Portuguese)
Lajes Field, Portugal, 1138

Babenhausen Area Support Team
Babenhausen Area Support Team, Germany, 1000

Babenhausen Family Housing
Babenhausen Area Support Team, Germany, 1000

Babenhausen Kaserne
223rd Base Support Battalion, Germany, 993
Babenhausen Area Support Team, Germany, 1000

Bad Aibling Station
Augsburg Military Community, Germany, 999

Bad Kreuznach Airfield
Rose Barracks, Germany, 1027

Bad Kreuznach Family Housing
Rose Barracks, Germany, 1027

Bad Kreuznach Hospital
Rosc Barracks, Germany, 1027

Badger Army Ammunition Plant
Badger Army Ammunition Plant, Baraboo, WI, 951

Ballistic Missile Early Warning System (BMEWS Site II)
Clear Air Force Station, AK, 22

Ballistic Research Laboratory
Adelphi Laboratory Center, Army Research Laboratory, Adelphi, MD, 405

Bamberg Airfield
Bamberg Military Community, Germany, 1001

Barbers Point Naval Air Station
Pearl Harbor Naval Complex, Pearl Harbor, HI, 283

Barbers Point Squadron Naval Sea Cadet Corps
Pearl Harbor Naval Complex, Pearl Harbor, HI, 283

Barton Barracks
Barton Barracks, Ansbach, Germany, 1002

Base Operations, Hancock ANGB
Syracuse Hancock IAP, Air National Guard Base, Syracuse, NY, 610

Base Support Division
Barstow, Marine Corps Logistics Base, Barstow, CA, 57

The Basic School, Camp Barrett
Quantico Marine Corps Combat Development Command, Quantico, VA, 895

Battery I, 3rd BN, 14th Marine Regiment
Reading Naval & Marine Corps Reserve Center, Reading, PA, 719

Battle Born Brigade
Nevada National Guard Las Vegas, Las Vegas, NV, 540

Battle Command Battle Lab, Huachuca
Fort Huachuca, Fort Huachuca, AZ, 35

Battle Labs
Armament Research, Development, and Engineering Center, US Army TACOM, Picatinny Arsenal, NJ, 562

Battle Projection Center
Fort Dix, Fort Dix, NJ, 555

Baumholder Airfield
Baumholder Military Community, H.D. Smith Barracks, Germany, 1003

Baumholder Family Housing
Baumholder Military Community, H.D. Smith Barracks, Germany, 1003

Baumholder Hospital
Baumholder Military Community, H.D. Smith Barracks, Germany, 1003

Baumholder Quartermaster Area
Baumholder Military Community, H.D. Smith Barracks, Germany, 1003

Beach Master Unit 2
Little Creek, Naval Amphibious Base, Norfolk, VA, 880

William Beaumont Army Medical Clinic
Fort Bliss, El Paso, TX, 790

Bellows Recreation Center
Bellows Air Force Station, Waimanalo, HI, 291

Belvoir Research, Development, and Engineering Center
Belvoir Research, Development & Engineering Center, Fort Belvoir, VA, 863
Fort Belvoir, Fort Belvoir, VA, 866

Benet Laboratories
Watervliet Arsenal, Watervliet, NY, 612

Bensheim Maintenance and Supply Facility
223rd Base Support Battalion, Germany, 993

Bettembourg Site
80th Area Support Group, Belgium, 975

Birkenfeld Housing Facility
Baumholder Military Community, H.D. Smith Barracks, Germany, 1003

Bleidorn Family Housing
Barton Barracks, Ansbach, Germany, 1002

Blount Island Command
Albany Marine Corps Logistics Base, Albany, GA, 239
Blount Island Command, Jacksonville, FL, 201

Böblingen Family Housing
6th Area Support Group, Stuttgart, Germany, 988

Böblingen Range
6th Area Support Group, Stuttgart, Germany, 988

Böblingen Training Area
6th Area Support Group, Stuttgart, Germany, 988

Boeing North American
Production Flight Test Installation, Air Force Plant 42, Palmdale, CA, 94

Bonstetten Radio Relay Facility
Augsburg Military Community, Germany, 999

Borden Institute
Walter Reed Army Medical Center, Washington, DC, 188

Branch Dental Clinic, Sabana Seca
Sabana Seca, US Naval Security Group Activity, Puerto Rico, 1144

Branch Maintenance Activity (USAR)
Fort Story, Fort Story, VA, 871

Branch Medical Clinic
Whiting Field Naval Air Station, Milton, FL, 213

Branch Medical Clinic, Sabana Seca
Sabana Seca, US Naval Security Group Activity, Puerto Rico, 1144

Branch Medical Clinic, Sasebo
Sasebo, US Fleet Activities, Japan, 1080

Branch State Civil Defense, HQ
Camp Beauregard, Pineville, LA, 388

Brandhof Radio Relay Site
282nd Base Support Battalion, Germany, 995

Breitenau Kaserne
6th Area Support Group, Garmish, Germany, 987

Breitenwald Training Area
Kaiserslautern Military Community, Germany, 1013

Breitsol Communication Station
98th Area Support Group, Germany, 990

Brigade of Midshipmen
United States Naval Academy, Annapolis, MD, 411

Brooke Army Medical Center
Fort Sam Houston, Fort Sam Houston, TX, 794

Brussels American School
80th Area Support Group, Belgium, 975

Buchanan CS/CSS Bn
Fort Buchanan Army Garrison, Puerto Rico, 1141

Büdingen Ammunition Area
414th Base Support Battalion, Germany, 997

Büdingen Area Support Team
414th Base Support Battalion, Germany, 997

Büdingen Army Heliport
414th Base Support Battalion, Germany, 997

Bulk Fuel Co B, 6th Engineer Support Bn
Tacoma Naval & Marine Corps Reserve Center, Tacoma, WA, 937

Bulk Fuel Co D, 6th Engineer Support Bn
Phoenix Naval & Marine Corps Reserve Readiness Center, Phoenix, AZ, 40

Bureau of Naval Personnel
Bureau of Naval Personnel, Arlington, VA, 843

Bureau of Naval Personnel Det, Memphis
Bureau of Naval Personnel Detachment, Memphis, Millington, TN, 767

Business Directorate
Carderock Division, Naval Surface Warfare Center, West Bethesda, MD, 429

Business Operations Directorate
Naval Research Laboratory, Washington, DC, 182

C2 Systems Flight
Ramstein Air Base, Germany, 1023

CAG-20
Atlanta Naval Air Station, Marietta, GA, 254

Calibration Lab
Lualualei Naval Magazine, Waianae, HI, 289

California National Guard
Adjutant General of California, Sacramento, CA, 105

Cambrai Fritsch Kaserne
223rd Base Support Battalion, Germany, 993

Camp Ashland (ARNG)
Camp Ashland, Ashland, NE, 525

Camp Bullis
Fort Sam Houston, Fort Sam Houston, TX, 794

Camp Bullis Training Site
Camp Bullis Training Site, Fort Sam Houston, TX, 793

Camp Butner (ARNG)
Camp Butner, Butner, NC, 617

Camp Carroll (ARNG)
Adjutant General of Alaska, Fort Richardson, AK, 26

Camp Clark (ARNG)
Camp Clark, Nevada, MO, 508

Camp Curtis Guild (ARNG)
Camp Curtis Guild, Reading, MA, 444

Camp Ederle
Caserma Ederle/Vicenza Military Community, Vincenza, Italy, 1060

Camp Edwards Army National Guard Training Site
Massachusetts Military Reservation/Otis Air National Guard Base, Cape Cod, MA, 437

Camp Edwards Reserve Training Site (Army)
Cape Cod Coast Guard Air Station, Cape Cod, MA, 436

Camp George West (ARNG)
Camp George West, Golden, CO, 154

Camp Grayling Manuever Training Center
Camp Grayling Maneuver Training Center, Grayling, MI, 458

Camp Johnson
Adjutant General of Vermont, Colchester, VT, 832

Camp La Bonte State Military Reservation
Adjutant General of New Hampshire, Concord, NH, 547

Camp McCain (ARNG)
Camp McCain Training Site, Elliott, MS, 480

Camp Oppenheim Training Area
Anderson Barracks, Germany, 998

Camp Pendleton (NR)
Las Vegas Naval & Marine Corps Reserve Center, Las Vegas, NV, 539

Camp Pike, USAR 90th RSC
Camp Joseph T Robinson, North Little Rock, AR, 52

Camp Ripley (ARNG)
Camp Ripley, Little Falls, MN, 470

Camp Marvin B Shields
Kadena Naval Air Facility, Japan, 1075

Camp H M Smith, HQ & Service Bn
Camp H M Smith, Camp Smith, HI, 266

Camp Stanley Storage Activity
Red River Army Depot, Texarkana, TX, 818

Camp Swift Training Site HQ
Camp Swift Training Site, Bastrop, TX, 778

Camp Villere (ARNG)
Camp Villere, Slidell, LA, 389

Camp Withycombe (ARNG)
Camp Withycombe, Clackamas, OR, 684

Campbell Barracks
Heidelberg Military Community, Germany, 1011

Campo Pond Training Area
414th Base Support Battalion, Germany, 997

Canadian Forces Det
Tyndall Air Force Base, Panama City, FL, 220

Canadian Infantry School
Fort Benning, Fort Benning, GA, 248

Cape Canaveral AFS (AFSC)
Cape Canaveral Air Force Station, Cocoa Beach, FL, 194

Cape Cod Air Force Station
Massachusetts Military Reservation/Otis Air National Guard Base, Cape Cod, MA, 437

Cardwell Village Family Housing
414th Base Support Battalion, Germany, 997

Caribbean Area Coordinator
Roosevelt Roads Naval Station, Puerto Rico, 1143

Caribbean Regional Operating Center (CARIBROC)
Key West Naval Air Facility, Boca Chica Key, FL, 191

Carlisle Barracks Veterinary Service
Tobyhanna Army Depot, Tobyhanna, PA, 721

Carrier Air Wing 2
Lemoore Naval Air Station, Lemoore, CA, 74

Carrier Air Wing 9
Lemoore Naval Air Station, Lemoore, CA, 74

Carrier Air Wing 11
Lemoore Naval Air Station, Lemoore, CA, 74

Carrier Air Wing 14
Lemoore Naval Air Station, Lemoore, CA, 74

Carrier Airborne Early Warning Wing, Atlantic
Norfolk Naval Air Station, Norfolk, VA, 882

Carrier Group 6
Mayport Naval Air Station, Mayport, FL, 210

Commander, Carrier Wing One
Oceana Naval Air Station, Virginia Beach, VA, 903

Commander, Carrier Wing Three
Oceana Naval Air Station, Virginia Beach, VA, 903

Carrier Wing Five
Atsugi Naval Air Facility, Japan, 1063

Commander, Carrier Wing Seven
Oceana Naval Air Station, Virginia Beach, VA, 903

Commander, Carrier Wing Eight
Oceana Naval Air Station, Virginia Beach, VA, 903

Commander, Carrier Wing Seventeen
Oceana Naval Air Station, Virginia Beach, VA, 903

Caswell Range (ARNG)
Caswell Range, Caribou, ME, 398

CB 17 Det 0817 (NR)
Las Vegas Naval & Marine Corps Reserve Center, Las Vegas, NV, 539

CD Det 0918
Pocatello Naval Reserve Facility, Pocatello, ID, 299

CEB-North
23rd Combat Equipment Company, Luxembourg, 1123

Center for Strategic Leadership
Carlisle Barracks, Carlisle Barracks, PA, 698

Centerville Family Housing
Augsburg Military Community, Germany, 999

Central Identification Laboratory, Hawaii
Fort Kamehameha, Honolulu, HI, 274

Central Oil Identification Laboratory, Groton
Coast Guard Academy, New London, CT, 161

Central Test, Measurement, & Diagnostic Equipment (TMDE) Activity
Blue Grass Army Depot, Richmond, KY, 373

CG54 Antietam 5409 (NR)
Lexington Naval Reserve Center, Lexington, KY, 368

Chairman of the Joint Chiefs of Staff
The Pentagon, Arlington, VA, 852

CHB-10 Det D-106 (NR)
Cumberland Naval Reserve Center, Cumberland, MD, 419

Chievres Airbase
80th Area Support Group, Belgium, 975

Cheju-Do Training Center
Camp MacNab (Cheju Do), Korea, Republic of, 1105

Office, Chief of Armor
Army Armor Center & Fort Knox, Fort Knox, KY, 366

Chief of Naval Air Training (CNATRA)
Corpus Christi Naval Air Station, Corpus Christi, TX, 780

Chief of Naval Education & Training
Pensacola Naval Air Station, Pensacola, FL, 225

Chief Staff Officer, US Naval Activities, Spain
Rota Naval Station, Spain, 1149

Chievres Air Base
Chievres Air Base, Belgium, 976

China Lake (NR)
Las Vegas Naval & Marine Corps Reserve Center, Las Vegas, NV, 539

CHPPM
Landstuhl Regional Medical Center, Germany, 1020

Civil Air Patrol
Edwards Air Force Base, Edwards AFB, CA, 63
Hanscom Air Force Base, Bedford, MA, 430
New Orleans Naval Air Station Joint Reserve Base, Air Force Reserve, New Orleans, LA, 383
New Orleans Naval Air Station Joint Reserve Base, Naval Air Station, New Orleans, LA, 384
O'Hare International Airport Air Reserve Station, O'Hare IAP ARS, IL, 311

Civil Air Patrol, HQ
Maxwell Air Force Base, Maxwell AFB, AL, 8

Civil Defense National Warning Center
Cheyenne Mountain Air Force Station, Colorado Springs, CO, 145

Civil Engineering Unit, Cleveland
9th Coast Guard District Headquarters, Cleveland, OH, 648

Civil Engineering Unit, Juneau
17th Coast Guard District, Juneau, AK, 29

Civilian Health & Medical Program for Uniformed Services, HQ (CHAMPUS)
Fitzsimons Army Medical Center, Aurora, CO, 144

Civilian Personnel Advisory Center (CPAC)
Army Transportation Center & Fort Eustis, Fort Eustis, VA, 868

Civilian Personnel Support Office (DCPSO)
Defense Supply Center, Columbus, Columbus, OH, 654

CLANTFLT Det 307 (NR)
Greensboro Naval & Marine Corps Reserve Readiness Center, Greensboro, NC, 626

Clarks Hill Training Site (ARNG)
Clarks Hill Training Site, Plum Branch, SC, 748

Close Combat Armaments Center (CCAC)
Armament Research, Development, and Engineering Center, US Army TACOM, Picatinny Arsenal, NJ, 562

Close Combat Tactical Trainer (CCTT) Project Office
Army Armor Center & Fort Knox, Fort Knox, KY, 366

Clothing & Medical Supplies
Defense Industrial Plant Equipment Facility, Atchison, KS, 351

Clothing Development Division
Navy Clothing and Textile Research Facility, Natick, MA, 442

CNAVEUR (NR)
Omaha Naval & Marine Corps Reserve Center, Omaha, NE, 531

CNRRC Det 1, Zone 9, Station 1
San Diego Naval & Marine Corps Reserve Center, San Diego, CA, 120

Co Army Garrison, HQ
Fort Myer, Arlington, VA, 847

Co F (-), 2nd Bn, 23rd Marine Regiment
Salt Lake City Naval & Marine Corps Reserve Center, Salt Lake City, UT, 829

CO F, 2nd Bn, 24th Marine Regiment
Milwaukee Naval & Marine Corps Reserve Center, Milwaukee, WI, 962

Co H, 2nd Bn, 25th Marine Regiment
Erie Naval & Marine Corps Reserve Center, Erie, PA, 703
Harrisburg Naval & Marine Corps Reserve Center, Harrisburg, PA, 704

Co Special Activities, HQ
Fort Myer, Arlington, VA, 847

Coast Guard Administrative Law Judge
8th Coast Guard District, New Orleans, LA, 380
13th Coast Guard District Office, Seattle, WA, 928
Alameda Coast Guard Integrated Support Command, Alameda, CA, 54

Coast Guard Air Station
Barbers Point Naval Air Station, Barbers Point, HI, 265
Hunter Army Air Field, Savannah, GA, 260

Coast Guard Air Station, Brooklyn
Brooklyn Coast Guard Air Station, Brooklyn, NY, 579

Coast Guard Air Station, Cape Cod
Cape Cod Coast Guard Air Station, Cape Cod, MA, 436
Massachusetts Military Reservation/Otis Air National Guard Base, Cape Cod, MA, 437

Coast Guard Air Station, Cape May
Cape May Coast Guard Training Center, Cape May, NJ, 553

Coast Guard Air Station, Clearwater
Clearwater Coast Guard Air Station, Clearwater, FL, 192

Coast Guard Air Station Corpus Christi
Corpus Christi Naval Air Station, Corpus Christi, TX, 780

Coast Guard Air Station, Detroit
Detroit Coast Guard Group/Base, Detroit, MI, 455

Coast Guard Air Station, Washington, DC
Washington, DC, Coast Guard Air Station, Arlington, VA, 853

Coast Guard Air Station, Elizabeth City
Elizabeth City Coast Guard Support Center, Elizabeth City, NC, 623

Coast Guard Air Station, Houston
Ellington Field, Air National Guard Base, Houston, TX, 803
Houston Coast Guard Air Station, Houston, TX, 804

Coast Guard Air Station, Kodiak
Kodiak Coast Guard Integrated Support Command, Kodiak, AK, 32

Coast Guard Air Station, Miami
Miami Coast Guard Air Station, Opa-Locka, FL, 215

Coast Guard Air Station, New Orleans
New Orleans Naval Air Station Joint Reserve Base, Naval Air Station, New Orleans, LA, 384

Coast Guard Air Station, Port Angeles
Port Angeles Coast Guard Air Station/Group, Port Angeles, WA, 926

Coast Guard Air Station, Sacramento
McClellan Air Force Base, McClellan AFB, CA, 81

Coast Guard Air Station, San Diego
San Diego Coast Guard Activities, San Diego, CA, 117

Coast Guard Air Station, San Francisco
San Francisco Coast Guard Air Station, San Francisco, CA, 125

Coast Guard Air Station, Traverse City
Traverse City Coast Guard Air Station, Traverse City, MI, 465

Coast Guard Aircraft Repair & Supply Center
Coast Guard Aircraft Repair & Supply Center, Elizabeth City, NC, 622

Coast Guard Armory Det, Alameda
Alameda Coast Guard Integrated Support Command, Alameda, CA, 54

US Coast Guard Atlantic Area & Fifth District HQ
Atlantic Area & Fifth Coast Guard District HQ, Portsmouth, VA, 890

Coast Guard Atlantic Strike Team
Fort Dix, Fort Dix, NJ, 555

Coast Guard Auxiliary Flotilla 12-8
Charleston Coast Guard Group, Charleston, SC, 732

Coast Guard Aviation Technical Training Center
Elizabeth City Coast Guard Support Center, Elizabeth City, NC, 623

Coast Guard Aviation Training Center, Mobile
Mobile Coast Guard Aviation Training Center, Mobile, AL, 9

Coast Guard Base, Charleston
Charleston Coast Guard Group, Charleston, SC, 732

Coast Guard Base, Detroit
Detroit Coast Guard Group/Base, Detroit, MI, 455

Coast Guard Base, Honolulu
Honolulu Coast Guard Base/Station, Honolulu, HI, 275

Coast Guard Base, Milwaukee
Milwaukee Coast Guard Base/Group, Milwaukee, WI, 961

Coast Guard Base, Saint Louis
Saint Louis Coast Guard Base, Saint Louis, MO, 513

Coast Guard Base, Sault
Sault Ste Marie Coast Guard Group, Sault Ste Marie, MI, 462

Coast Guard, Cape Henry Light Station
Fort Story, Fort Story, VA, 871

Coast Guard Ceremonial Honor Guard
Coast Guard Telecommunication & Information Systems Command, Alexandria, VA, 837

Coast Guard Communication Station
Northwest Naval Security Group Activity, Chesapeake, VA, 858

US Coast Guard Communication Station, Honolulu
Naval Computer & Telecommunications Area Master Station, Eastern Pacific, Wahiawa, HI, 288

Coast Guard Communication Station, Kodiak
Kodiak Coast Guard Integrated Support Command, Kodiak, AK, 32

Coast Guard Communication Station Pacific San Francisco
Coast Guard Communication Station Pacific, San Francisco, Point Reyes Station, CA, 99

Coast Guard Communication Station Transmitter Site
Coast Guard Communication Station Pacific, Transmitter Site, Point Reyes Station, CA, 100

Coast Guard Director of Auxiliary
Saint Louis Coast Guard Base, Saint Louis, MO, 513

Coast Guard Electronics/General Materiel Inventory Control Point (E/GICP)
Brooklyn Coast Guard Supply Center, Brooklyn, NY, 580

Coast Guard ESD SW Harbor
Southwest Harbor Coast Guard Group, Southwest Harbor, ME, 402

Coast Guard FD & CC Pacific
13th Coast Guard District Office, Seattle, WA, 928

Coast Guard Finance Center
Coast Guard Finance Center, Chesapeake, VA, 856

Coast Guard Forces
Alameda Coast Guard Integrated Support Command, Alameda, CA, 54

Coast Guard Forces, Charleston
Charleston Coast Guard Group, Charleston, SC, 732

Coast Guard Forces, Ketchikan
Ketchikan Coast Guard Station, Ketchikan, AK, 30

Coast Guard Forces, Seattle
Seattle Coast Guard Integrated Support Command, Seattle, WA, 929

Coast Guard Group/Base, Detroit
Selfridge Air National Guard Base, Selfridge ANG Base, MI, 464

Coast Guard Group, Boston
Boston Coast Guard Reserve Center, Boston, MA, 432

Coast Guard Group, Cape May
Cape May Coast Guard Training Center, Cape May, NJ, 553

Coast Guard Group, Charleston
Charleston Coast Guard Group, Charleston, SC, 732

Coast Guard Group, Detroit
Detroit Coast Guard Group/Base, Detroit, MI, 455

Coast Guard Group, Galveston
Galveston Coast Guard Base, Galveston, TX, 798

Coast Guard Group, Honolulu
Honolulu Coast Guard Base/Station, Honolulu, HI, 275

US Coast Guard Group, Key West
Key West Naval Air Facility, Boca Chica Key, FL, 191

Coast Guard Group, Miami
Miami Beach Coast Guard Group/Station, Miami Beach, FL, 212

Coast Guard Group, Milwaukee
Milwaukee Coast Guard Base/Group, Milwaukee, WI, 961

Coast Guard Group, Mobile
Mobile Coast Guard Group/Station, Mobile, AL, 10

Coast Guard Group, Philadelphia
Philadelphia Coast Guard Marine Safety Office & Group, Philadelphia, PA, 714

Coast Guard Group, Port Angeles
Port Angeles Coast Guard Air Station/Group, Port Angeles, WA, 926

Coast Guard Group, St Petersburg
St Petersburg Coast Guard Group/Station, Saint Petersburg, FL, 231

Coast Guard Group, San Diego
San Diego Coast Guard Activities, San Diego, CA, 117

Coast Guard Group, San Francisco
San Francisco Coast Guard Group, San Francisco, CA, 126

Coast Guard Group, Sault
Sault Ste Marie Coast Guard Group, Sault Ste Marie, MI, 462

Coast Guard Group, Seattle
Seattle Coast Guard Integrated Support Command, Seattle, WA, 929

Coast Guard Group, SW Harbor
Southwest Harbor Coast Guard Group, Southwest Harbor, ME, 402

Coast Guard Group, Woods Hole
Woods Hole Coast Guard Group, Woods Hole, MA, 447

Coast Guard Gulf Strike Team
Mobile Coast Guard Aviation Training Center, Mobile, AL, 9

US Coast Guard Health Services Command
Army Soldier Systems Command, Natick, MA, 441

Coast Guard Human Resources Service & Information Center
Coast Guard Human Resources Service & Information Center, Topeka, KS, 360

Coast Guard Institute
Coast Guard Institute, Oklahoma City, OK, 675

Coast Guard International Training Division
Yorktown Coast Guard Reserve Training Center, Yorktown, VA, 909

Coast Guard Liaison Officer, Seattle
13th Coast Guard District Office, Seattle, WA, 928

Coast Guard Liaison, Pensacola
Pensacola Coast Guard Station, Pensacola, FL, 224

Coast Guard LORAN-C Transmitting Station
Seneca Army Depot Activity, Romulus, NY, 605

US Coast Guard Marine Safety Det
Concord Naval Weapons Station, Concord, CA, 61

US Coast Guard Marine Safety Office
Charleston Coast Guard Group, Charleston, SC, 732

Coast Guard Mike Monroney Aeronautical Center
Coast Guard Institute, Oklahoma City, OK, 675

US Coast Guard Naval Engineering Support Unit
Charles Melvin Price Army Support Center, Granite City, IL, 307

Coast Guard Navigation Center (NAVCEN)
Coast Guard Telecommunication & Information Systems Command, Alexandria, VA, 837

Coast Guard Ordnance Support Facility, Cape Cod
Cape Cod Coast Guard Air Station, Cape Cod, MA, 436

Coast Guard Pacific Area HQ
Alameda Coast Guard Integrated Support Command, Alameda, CA, 54

Coast Guard Pacific Area Tactical Law Enforcement Team
San Diego Marine Corps Recruit Depot, San Diego, CA, 119

Coast Guard Pacific Area Training Team
Alameda Coast Guard Integrated Support Command, Alameda, CA, 54

Coast Guard Pacific Strike Team
Coast Guard Pacific Strike Team, Novato, CA, 87
Department of Defense Housing Facility, Novato, CA, 88

US Coast Guard Patrol Boat Support Det
Roosevelt Roads Naval Station, Puerto Rico, 1143

Coast Guard Personnel Command
Coast Guard Headquarters, Washington, DC, 174

US Coast Guard Port Security Unit 305
Army Transportation Center & Fort Eustis, Fort Eustis, VA, 868

Coast Guard Public Affairs Det, Western Alaska
Kodiak Coast Guard Integrated Support Command, Kodiak, AK, 32

Coast Guard Regional Reserve Personnel Office
Seattle Coast Guard Integrated Support Command, Seattle, WA, 929

Coast Guard Reserve Center
Seattle Coast Guard Integrated Support Command, Seattle, WA, 929

Coast Guard Reserve Center, Miami
Miami Beach Coast Guard Group/Station, Miami Beach, FL, 212

Coast Guard Reserve Center, San Francisco
San Francisco Coast Guard Group, San Francisco, CA, 126

Coast Guard Reserve Group
8th Coast Guard District, New Orleans, LA, 380
Alameda Coast Guard Integrated Support Command, Alameda, CA, 54
Charleston Coast Guard Group, Charleston, SC, 732
Coast Guard Headquarters, Washington, DC, 174

Coast Guard Reserve Group, Buffalo
Buffalo Coast Guard Group, Buffalo, NY, 582

Coast Guard Reserve Group, Cape Cod
Cape Cod Coast Guard Air Station, Cape Cod, MA, 436

Coast Guard Reserve Group, Charleston
Charleston Coast Guard Group, Charleston, SC, 732

Coast Guard Reserve Group, Curtis Bay
Curtis Bay Coast Guard Yard, Curtis Bay, MD, 420

Coast Guard Reserve Group, Milwaukee
Milwaukee Coast Guard Base/Group, Milwaukee, WI, 961

Coast Guard Reserve Group, Terminal Island
San Pedro Coast Guard Support Center, San Pedro, CA, 131

Coast Guard Reserve Training Unit
Yorktown Coast Guard Reserve Training Center, Yorktown, VA, 909

Coast Guard Reserve Unit A
Saint Louis Coast Guard Base, Saint Louis, MO, 513

Coast Guard Reserve Unit B
Saint Louis Coast Guard Base, Saint Louis, MO, 513

Coast Guard Reserve Unit CNCWGRU Atlantic
Atlantic Area & Fifth Coast Guard District HQ, Portsmouth, VA, 890

Coast Guard Reserve Unit CNCWU 113
Seattle Coast Guard Integrated Support Command, Seattle, WA, 929

Coast Guard Reserve Unit CNCWU 201
1st Coast Guard District, Boston, MA, 431

Coast Guard Reserve Unit CNCWU 207
Miami Beach Coast Guard Group/Station, Miami Beach, FL, 212

Coast Guard Reserve Unit CNCWU 208
8th Coast Guard District, New Orleans, LA, 380

Coast Guard Small Arms Repair Facility
Crane Division, Naval Surface Warfare Center, Crane, IN, 324

US Coast Guard Station
Naval Coastal Systems Station, Panama City, FL, 219

Coast Guard Station, Boston
Boston Coast Guard Reserve Center, Boston, MA, 432

Coast Guard Station, Buffalo
Buffalo Coast Guard Group, Buffalo, NY, 582

Coast Guard Station, Charleston
Charleston Coast Guard Group, Charleston, SC, 732

Coast Guard Station, Clearwater
Clearwater Coast Guard Air Station, Clearwater, FL, 192

Coast Guard Station, Cortez
Cortez Coast Guard Station, Cortez, FL, 195

Coast Guard Station, Curtis Bay
Curtis Bay Coast Guard Yard, Curtis Bay, MD, 420

Coast Guard Station, Elizabeth City
Elizabeth City Coast Guard Support Center, Elizabeth City, NC, 623

US Coast Guard Station, Ft Myers Beach
Fort Myers Beach Coast Guard Station, Fort Myers Beach, FL, 196

Coast Guard Station, Galveston
Galveston Coast Guard Base, Galveston, TX, 798

Coast Guard Station, Honolulu
Honolulu Coast Guard Base/Station, Honolulu, HI, 275

Coast Guard Station, Ketchikan
Ketchikan Coast Guard Station, Ketchikan, AK, 30

Coast Guard Station, Miami Beach
Miami Beach Coast Guard Group/Station, Miami Beach, FL, 212

Coast Guard Station, Milwaukee
Milwaukee Coast Guard Base/Group, Milwaukee, WI, 961

Coast Guard Station, Mobile
Mobile Coast Guard Group/Station, Mobile, AL, 10

Coast Guard Station, Pensacola
Pensacola Coast Guard Station, Pensacola, FL, 224

Coast Guard Station, St Petersburg
St Petersburg Coast Guard Group/Station, Saint Petersburg, FL, 231

Coast Guard Station, San Diego
San Diego Coast Guard Activities, San Diego, CA, 117

Coast Guard Station, San Francisco
San Francisco Coast Guard Group, San Francisco, CA, 126

Coast Guard Station, San Pedro
San Pedro Coast Guard Support Center, San Pedro, CA, 131

Coast Guard Station, Sault
Sault Ste Marie Coast Guard Group, Sault Ste Marie, MI, 462

Coast Guard Station, Seattle
Seattle Coast Guard Integrated Support Command, Seattle, WA, 929

Coast Guard Station, SW Harbor
Southwest Harbor Coast Guard Group, Southwest Harbor, ME, 402

Coast Guard Station, Woods Hole
Woods Hole Coast Guard Group, Woods Hole, MA, 447

Coast Guard Station, Yankeetown
Yankeetown Coast Guard Station, Yankeetown, FL, 238

Coast Guard Support Center, Kodiak
Kodiak Coast Guard Integrated Support Command, Kodiak, AK, 32

Coast Guard Support Center, San Pedro
San Pedro Coast Guard Support Center, San Pedro, CA, 131

Coast Guard Support Command, HQ
Coast Guard Headquarters, Washington, DC, 174

Coast Guard Tactical Law Enforcement Team
Miami Coast Guard Air Station, Opa-Locka, FL, 215

Coast Guard Tactical Law Enforcement Team, Portsmouth
Atlantic Area & Fifth Coast Guard District HQ, Portsmouth, VA, 890

Coast Guard Telecommunications and Information Systems Command
Coast Guard Telecommunication & Information Systems Command, Alexandria, VA, 837

Coast Guard Training Center, Cape May
Cape May Coast Guard Training Center, Cape May, NJ, 553

Coast Guard Training Center, Petaluma
Petaluma Coast Guard Training Center, Petaluma, CA, 96

Coast Guard Training Quota Management Center
Coast Guard Finance Center, Chesapeake, VA, 856

Coast Guard Yard, Curtis Bay
Curtis Bay Coast Guard Yard, Curtis Bay, MD, 420

Cold Regions Center of Expertise (CRCX)
US Army Corps of Engineers, Alaska District, Anchorage, AK, 21

Cold Regions Test Center
Fort Greely, Fort Greely, AK, 25

Coleman Army Airfield
Coleman Barracks, Germany, 1006

Coleman Barracks
293rd Base Support Battalion, Germany, 996

Coleman Village Family Housing
414th Base Support Battalion, Germany, 997

College for Enlisted Professional Military Education
Gunter Annex, Gunter, AL, 6

College of Aerospace Doctrine, Research and Education
Maxwell Air Force Base, Maxwell AFB, AL, 8

Colorado ANG, HQ
Buckley Air National Guard Base, Aurora, CO, 142

Colorado National Guard
Adjutant General of Colorado, Englewood, CO, 150

Colorado River Patrol
San Diego Coast Guard Activities, San Diego, CA, 117

Combat Camera, Det 9 (1st CTLS)
Andrews Air Force Base, Andrews AFB, MD, 407

Combat Control School
Pope Air Force Base, Pope AFB, NC, 629

Commander, Combat Coordination Group Korea
Chinhae Fleet Activities, Korea, Republic of, 1114

Combat Equipment Base-Afloat, HQ
Combat Equipment Group-Army, HQ, Goose Creek, SC, 743

Combat Equipment Base-NE Asia
Camp Carroll, Korea, Republic of, 1088

Combat Equipment Bn NW, Coevorden
254th Base Support Battalion, Netherlands, 1127

Combat Equipment Group, Army, HQ
Combat Equipment Group-Army, HQ, Goose Creek, SC, 743

Combat Equipment Group, Europe, HQ
Combat Equipment Group-Europe, HQ, Netherlands, 1128

HQ, CEG-E, Kerkrade
254th Base Support Battalion, Netherlands, 1127

Combat Logistics Squadron 2
Earle Naval Weapons Station, Colts Neck, NJ, 554

Combat Readiness Division (FPD)
Fort Dix, Fort Dix, NJ, 555

Combat Readiness Training Center (CRTC)
Volk Field Air National Guard Base, Camp Douglas, WI, 953

Combat Service Support, Det 21
Cherry Point Marine Corps Air Station, Cherry Point, NC, 621

Combat Service Support Det 23
Beaufort Marine Corps Air Station, Beaufort, SC, 730

Combat Service Support Det 36
Iwakuni Marine Corps Air Station, Japan, 1073

Combat Service Support Element-41
Portland Naval & Marine Corps Reserve Readiness Center, Portland, OR, 688

Combat Service Support Group 1
Twentynine Palms Marine Corps Air Ground Combat Center, Twentynine Palms, CA, 139

Combat Service Support Group 3
Kaneohe Bay Marine Corps Base, Kaneohe Bay, HI, 278

Combat Squad Leaders Course
Camp Hansen, Japan, 1067

Combat Support Bn
Caserma Ederle/Vicenza Military Community, Vincenza, Italy, 1060

Combat Support Coordination Team 1
Camp Long, Korea, Republic of, 1104

Combat Systems School
Recruit Training Command Great Lakes, Great Lakes, IL, 309

Combat Weather Facility
Hurlburt Field, Hurlburt Field, FL, 200

Combined Arms and Tactics Directorate
Fort Benning, Fort Benning, GA, 248

Combined Arms Command, US Disciplinary Barracks
Fort Leavenworth, Fort Leavenworth, KS, 352

Combined Forces Command, HQ
Yongsan Army Garrison, Korea, Republic of, 1121

Combined Maintenance Shop A
Camp Smith, Peekskill, NY, 601

Combined Service Support Program School, Atlantic
Fort Story, Fort Story, VA, 871

Combined Support Maintenance Shop
Camp Beauregard, Pineville, LA, 388
Camp Blanding Training Site, Starke, FL, 232

Combined Support Maintenance Shop 1
Mitchell National Guard Complex, Mitchell, SD, 752

Combined Support Maintenance Shop C
Combined Support Maintenance Shop C/US Property & Fiscal Office—NY, Rochester, NY, 602

Command and Control Branch
Balikesir Air Field, Turkey, 1151

Command & Control Systems School
Quantico Marine Corps Combat Development Command, Quantico, VA, 895

Command and General Staff College
Fort Leavenworth, Fort Leavenworth, KS, 352

Command and Staff College
Quantico Marine Corps Combat Development Command, Quantico, VA, 895

Commandant of the Marine Corps
The Pentagon, Arlington, VA, 852

Commander Amphibious Squadron 11
Sasebo, US Fleet Activities, Japan, 1080

Commander, Carrier Group 1
North Island Naval Air Station, San Diego, CA, 115

Commander, Carrier Group 7
North Island Naval Air Station, San Diego, CA, 115

Commander, Construction Bn Atlantic Det, Europe
Rota Naval Station, Spain, 1149

Commander, Fleet Activities, Okinawa (COMFLRACT)
Kadena Air Base, Japan, 1074

Commander, Fleet Logistics Support Wing
Fort Worth, Naval Air Station, Joint Reserve Base, Fort Worth, TX, 796

Commander, Helicopter Antisubmarine Light Wing Pacific
North Island Naval Air Station, San Diego, CA, 115

Commander, Helicopter Antisubmarine Light Wing, US Atlantic Fleet, Det Sigonella
Sigonella Naval Air Station, Italy, 1059

Commander, Helicopter Antisubmarine Wing Pacific
North Island Naval Air Station, San Diego, CA, 115

Commander, Helicopter Tactical Wing Pacific
North Island Naval Air Station, San Diego, CA, 115

Commander, Helicopter Wing Reserve
North Island Naval Air Station, San Diego, CA, 115

Commander-in-Chief, Atlantic (also Supreme Allied Commander, Atlantic SACLANT)
Norfolk Naval Base Complex, Norfolk, VA, 885

Commander-in-Chief, Atlantic Fleet
Norfolk Naval Base Complex, Norfolk, VA, 885

Commander-in-Chief, US Pacific Command
Camp H M Smith, Camp Smith, HI, 266

Commander, Marine Corps Bases Western Area
Miramar Marine Corps Air Station, San Diego, CA, 113

Commander, Marine Reserve Force
New Orleans Naval Support Activity, New Orleans, LA, 386

Commander, Maritime Prepositioning Ship's Squadron
Naval Station, Guam, Guam, 1047

Commander, Naval Activities, UK (COMNAVACTUK)
West Ruislip RAF Base, United Kingdom, 1170

Commander, Naval Air Force, US Pacific Fleet
North Island Naval Air Station, San Diego, CA, 115

Commander, Naval Air Reserve Force
New Orleans Naval Support Activity, New Orleans, LA, 386

Commander, Naval Base Norfolk, Headquarters
Norfolk Naval Base Complex, Norfolk, VA, 885

Commander, Naval Base San Diego, Personnel Support Activity San Diego
San Diego Fleet and Industrial Supply Center, San Diego, CA, 118

Commander, Naval Base Seattle
Bangor Naval Submarine Base, Silverdale, WA, 932

Commander, Naval Forces Marianas
Naval Station, Guam, Guam, 1047

Commander, Naval Reserve Center (Dallas)
Dallas Naval Air Station, Dallas, TX, 783

Commander, Naval Reserve Force
New Orleans Naval Support Activity, New Orleans, LA, 386

Commander, Naval Reserve Intelligence Command
Fort Worth, Naval Air Station, Joint Reserve Base, Fort Worth, TX, 796

Commander, Naval Reserve Readiness Command, Region 11 (REDCOM 11)
Dallas Naval Air Station, Dallas, TX, 783

Commander, Naval Surface Force, Atlantic
Norfolk Naval Base Complex, Norfolk, VA, 885

Commander, Naval Surface Reserve Force
New Orleans Naval Support Activity, New Orleans, LA, 386

Commander, Sea Control Wing Pacific
North Island Naval Air Station, San Diego, CA, 115

Commander, Second Fleet
Norfolk Naval Base Complex, Norfolk, VA, 885

Commander South Atlantic Force (USCOMSOLANT)
Roosevelt Roads Naval Station, Puerto Rico, 1143

Commander, Submarine Force, Atlantic
Norfolk Naval Base Complex, Norfolk, VA, 885

Commander, Submarine Force, US Pacific Fleet (COMSUBPAC)
Pearl Harbor Naval Submarine Base, Pearl Harbor, HI, 284

Commander, Submarine Group 9
Bangor Naval Submarine Base, Silverdale, WA, 932

Commander Submarine Squadron 1 (CSS-1)
Pearl Harbor Naval Submarine Base, Pearl Harbor, HI, 284

Commander Submarine Squadron 3 (CSS-3)
Pearl Harbor Naval Submarine Base, Pearl Harbor, HI, 284

Commander Submarine Squadron 7 (CSS-7)
Pearl Harbor Naval Submarine Base, Pearl Harbor, HI, 284

Commander, Submarine Squadron 22
La Maddalena Navy Support Office, Italy, 1054

Commander, Task Force 63, Det ROTA
Rota Naval Station, Spain, 1149

Commander Task Group 68.6
Sigonella Naval Air Station, Italy, 1059

Commander, Training Wing Six
Pensacola Naval Air Station, Pensacola, FL, 225

Commander, US Naval Activities, Spain
Rota Naval Station, Spain, 1149

Commanding General, Fleet Marine Force, Atlantic
Norfolk Naval Base Complex, Norfolk, VA, 885

Commissary Store
Yorktown Naval Weapons Station, Yorktown, VA, 910

Communication Officers School
Quantico Marine Corps Combat Development Command, Quantico, VA, 895

Communications & Information Flight, RAF Croughton
Croughton RAF Base, United Kingdom, 1157

Det, Communications Co
Indianapolis Naval & Marine Corps Reserve Readiness Center, Indianapolis, IN, 335

Det 1, Communications Co, HQ and Service Bn
Fort Wayne Marine Corps Reserve Center, Fort Wayne, IN, 329

Communications Co, HQ & Service Bn
Greensboro Naval & Marine Corps Reserve Readiness Center, Greensboro, NC, 626

Communications Relay Station
Menwith Hill, United Kingdom, 1166

Communications Security Material System
Naval Security Station, Washington, DC, 183

Communications Systems Center
Tinker Air Force Base, Tinker AFB, OK, 678

Community College of the Air Force
Maxwell Air Force Base, Maxwell AFB, AL, 8

COMNAVSURFLANT Det 202 (NR)
Greensboro Naval & Marine Corps Reserve Readiness Center, Greensboro, NC, 626

COMPHIBRON 8 Det 809 (NR)
Louisville Naval Reserve Center, Louisville, KY, 371

Composite Naval Coastal Warfare Unit 111
Alameda Coast Guard Integrated Support Command, Alameda, CA, 54

Composite Naval Coastal Warfare Unit 113
13th Coast Guard District Office, Seattle, WA, 928

Computer Sciences School
Quantico Marine Corps Combat Development Command, Quantico, VA, 895

Conn Barracks
280th Base Support Battalion, Germany, 994

Connecticut National Guard
Adjutant General of Connecticut, Hartford, CT, 159

Construction Base Unit 412
Kings Bay Naval Submarine Base, Kings Bay, GA, 253

Construction Bn Unit 401
Great Lakes Naval Training Center, Great Lakes, IL, 308

Construction Bn Unit 406
Lemoore Naval Air Station, Lemoore, CA, 74

Construction Bn Unit 417
Whidbey Island Naval Air Station, Oak Harbor, WA, 924

Contracting Directorate
Gunter Annex, Gunter, AL, 6

Contracts Directorate
Albany Marine Corps Logistics Base, Albany, GA, 239

Coronet Nighthawk (ANG)
Howard Air Force Base, Panama, 1136

Coronet Oak (AFRES)
Howard Air Force Base, Panama, 1136

Corporate Information and Computing Center
Adelphi Laboratory Center, Army Research Laboratory, Adelphi, MD, 405

Corporate Information Management Office
Albany Marine Corps Logistics Base, Albany, GA, 239

Corps of Cadets
United States Military Academy, West Point, NY, 613
West Point, Army Garrison, West Point, NY, 614

Corps of Engineers
Edwards Air Force Base, Edwards AFB, CA, 63
Lake City Army Ammunition Plant, Independence, MO, 502
Milan Army Ammunition Plant, Milan, TN, 766
Seymour Johnson Air Force Base, Goldsboro, NC, 625

Corps of Engineers, Aberdeen Field Office
Aberdeen Proving Ground, Aberdeen Proving Ground, MD, 404

Corps of Engineers, Alaska District
US Army Corps of Engineers, Alaska District, Anchorage, AK, 21

Corps of Engineers, Albuquerque District
US Army Corps of Engineers, Albuquerque District, Albuquerque, NM, 569

Corps of Engineers, Baltimore District
US Army Corps of Engineers, Baltimore District, Baltimore, MD, 415

Corps of Engineers, Buffalo District
US Army Corps of Engineers, Buffalo District, Buffalo, NY, 584

Corps of Engineers, Charleston District
US Army Corps of Engineers, Charleston District, Charleston, SC, 736

Corps of Engineers, Chicago District
US Army Corps of Engineers, Chicago District, Chicago, IL, 303

Corps of Engineers, Construction Engineering Research Laboratories
US Army Corps of Engineers, Construction Engineering Research Laboratories, Champaign, IL, 300

Corps of Engineers, Detroit District
US Army Corps of Engineers, Detroit District, Detroit, MI, 456

Corps of Engineers, Far East District
US Army Corps of Engineers, Far East District, Korea, Republic of, 1120

Corps of Engineers, Field Operating Agency
Humphreys Engineer Center, Fort Belvoir, VA, 867

Corps of Engineers, Fort Knox Area Office
Army Armor Center & Fort Knox, Fort Knox, KY, 366

Corps of Engineers, Fort Worth District
US Army Corps of Engineers, Fort Worth District, Fort Worth, TX, 797

Corps of Engineers, Galveston District
US Army Corps of Engineers, Galveston District, Galveston, TX, 799

Corps of Engineers, Great Lakes & Ohio River Division
US Army Corps of Engineers, Great Lakes & Ohio River Division, Cincinnati, OH, 647

Corps of Engineers, Great Lakes Regional Office
US Army Corps of Engineers, Great Lakes Regional Office, Chicago, IL, 304

HQ, Corps of Engineers
US Army Corps of Engineers, Headquarters, Washington, DC, 185

Corps of Engineers, Honolulu District
US Army Corps of Engineers, Honolulu District, Fort Shafter, HI, 268

Corps of Engineers, Huntington District
US Army Corps of Engineers, Huntington District, Huntington, WV, 946

Corps of Engineers, Jacksonville District
US Army Corps of Engineers, Jacksonville District, Jacksonville, FL, 208

Corps of Engineers, Japan District
Army Corps of Engineers, Japan District, Japan, 1062

Corps of Engineers, Kansas City District
US Army Corps of Engineers, Kansas City District, Kansas City, MO, 506

Corps of Engineers, Little Rock District
US Army Corps of Engineers, Little Rock District, Little Rock, AR, 49

Corps of Engineers, Los Angeles District
US Army Corps of Engineers, Los Angeles District, Los Angeles, CA, 79

Corps of Engineers, Louisville District
Army Corps of Engineers, Louisville District, Louisville, KY, 369
Lima Army Tank Plant, Lima, OH, 658

Corps of Engineers, Marine Design Center
US Army Corps of Engineers, Philadelphia District, Philadelphia, PA, 717

Corps of Engineers, Memphis District
US Army Corps of Engineers, Memphis District, Memphis, TN, 765

Corps of Engineers, Mississippi River Commission
US Army Corps of Engineers, Mississippi Valley Division/Mississippi River Commission, Vicksburg, MS, 495

Corps of Engineers, Mississippi Valley Division
US Army Corps of Engineers, Mississippi Valley Division/Mississippi River Commission, Vicksburg, MS, 495

Corps of Engineers, Missouri River Regional Office
US Army Corps of Engineers, Missouri River Regional Office, Omaha, NE, 532

Corps of Engineers, Mobile District
US Army Corps of Engineers, Mobile District, Mobile, AL, 12

Corps of Engineers, Nashville District
US Army Corps of Engineers, Nashville District, Nashville, TN, 772

Corps of Engineers, New England District
US Army Corps of Engineers, New England District, Waltham, MA, 445

Corps of Engineers, New Orleans District
US Army Corps of Engineers, New Orleans District, New Orleans, LA, 387

Corps of Engineers, New York District
US Army Corps of Engineers, New York District, New York, NY, 597

Corps of Engineers, Norfolk District
Army Corps of Engineers, Norfolk District, Norfolk, VA, 876
Fort A P Hill, Bowling Green, VA, 855

Corps of Engineers, North Atlantic Division
US Army Corps of Engineers, North Atlantic Division, New York, NY, 598

Corps of Engineers, Northwestern Division
US Army Corps of Engineers, Northwestern Division, Portland, OR, 689

Corps of Engineers, Omaha District
US Army Corps of Engineers, Omaha District, Omaha, NE, 533

Corps of Engineers, Pacific Ocean Division
US Army Corps of Engineers, Pacific Ocean Division, Fort Shafter, HI, 269

Corps of Engineers, Philadelphia District
US Army Corps of Engineers, Philadelphia District, Philadelphia, PA, 717

Corps of Engineers, Pittsburgh District
US Army Corps of Engineers, Pittsburgh District, Pittsburgh, PA, 718

Corps of Engineers, Portland District
US Army Corps of Engineers, Portland District, Portland, OR, 690

Corps of Engineers, Redstone Arsenal
Redstone Arsenal, Redstone Arsenal, AL, 16

Corps of Engineers, Rock Island
Rock Island Arsenal, Rock Island, IL, 314

Corps of Engineers, Rock Island District
US Army Corps of Engineers, Rock Island District, Rock Island, IL, 316

Corps of Engineers, Sacramento District
US Army Corps of Engineers, Sacramento District, Sacramento, CA, 107

Corps of Engineers, St Louis District
US Army Corps of Engineers, St Louis District, Saint Louis, MO, 514

Corps of Engineers, San Antonio Area Office
Kelly Air Force Base, Kelly AFB, TX, 807

Corps of Engineers, San Francisco District
US Army Corps of Engineers, San Francisco District, San Francisco, CA, 127

Corps of Engineers, Savannah District
Fort Benning, Fort Benning, GA, 248
US Army Corps of Engineers, Savannah District, Savannah, GA, 262

Corps of Engineers, Seattle District
US Army Corps of Engineers, Seattle District, Seattle, WA, 931

Corps of Engineers, South Atlantic Division
US Army Corps of Engineers, South Atlantic Division, Atlanta, GA, 243

Corps of Engineers, South Pacific Division
US Army Corps of Engineers, South Pacific Division, San Francisco, CA, 128

Corps of Engineers, Southwestern District
US Army Corps of Engineers, Southwestern District, Dallas, TX, 788

Corps of Engineers, St Paul District
US Army Corps of Engineers, St Paul District, Saint Paul, MN, 477

Corps of Engineers, Topographic Engineering Center
US Army Corps of Engineers, Topographic Engineering Center, Alexandria, VA, 840

Corps of Engineers, Transatlantic Programs Center
US Army Corps of Engineers, Transatlantic Programs Center, Winchester, VA, 908
US Army Corps of Engineers, Transatlantic Programs Center, Europe, Wiesbaden, Germany, 1037

Corps of Engineers, Tulsa District
US Army Corps of Engineers, Tulsa District, Tulsa, OK, 680

Corps of Engineers, Vicksburg District
US Army Corp of Engineers, Vicksburg District, Vicksburg, MS, 496

Corps of Engineers, Walla Walla District
US Army Corps of Engineers, Walla Walla District, Walla Walla, WA, 939

Corps of Engineers, Water Resources Support Center
US Army Corps of Engineers, Water Resources Support Center, Alexandria, VA, 841

Corps of Engineers, Waterways Experiment Station
US Army Corps of Engineers, Waterways Experiment Station, Vicksburg, MS, 497

Corps of Engineers, Wilmington District
US Army Corps of Engineers, Wilmington District, Wilmington, NC, 634

Corpus Christi Army Depot
Corpus Christi Army Depot, Corpus Christi, TX, 779

Corpus Christi Army Depot (CCAD)
Corpus Christi Naval Air Station, Corpus Christi, TX, 780

Counter-Terrorism School
Camp Hansen, Japan, 1067

Craig Village Family Housing
6th Area Support Group, Stuttgart, Germany, 988

Cramerton Family Housing
Augsburg Military Community, Germany, 999

Crane Army Ammunition Activity
Crane Division, Naval Surface Warfare Center, Crane, IN, 324

Crestview Housing Area
221st Base Support Battalion, Germany, 992

Crew Systems Directorate, Armstrong Laboratory
Wright-Patterson Air Force Base, Wright-Patterson AFB, OH, 667

Criminal Investigation Division (CID) Wiesbaden
221st Base Support Battalion, Germany, 992

Criminal Investigation Command, Panama
Fort Clayton, Panama, 1133

Criminal Investigations Division
Fort Buchanan Army Garrison, Puerto Rico, 1141

Cruiser-Destroyer Group 12
Mayport Naval Air Station, Mayport, FL, 210

Cryptologic Support Group
Rota Naval Station, Spain, 1149

CSMS
Camp Shelby Training Site, Camp Shelby, MS, 478

US Customs Service
North Island Naval Air Station, San Diego, CA, 115

Customs Service, Air Operations Branch, New Orleans
New Orleans Naval Air Station Joint Reserve Base, Naval Air Station, New Orleans, LA, 384

Daenner Kaserne
Kaiserslautern Military Community, Germany, 1013

Dal Molin Airfield
Caserma Ederle/Vicenza Military Community, Vincenza, Italy, 1060

Daley Village Family Housing
280th Base Support Battalion, Germany, 994

Dambach Family Housing
282nd Base Support Battalion, Germany, 995

Dannenfels Communication Station
293rd Base Support Battalion, Germany, 996

Darby Kaserne
282nd Base Support Battalion, Germany, 995

DARCOM Logistics Asst Office
Hunter Army Air Field, Savannah, GA, 260

Darmstadt Training Center
223rd Base Support Battalion, Germany, 993

Daumerie Caserne
80th Area Support Group, Belgium, 975

Daumerie Kaserne
Chievres Air Base, Belgium, 976

De La Police Kaserne
293rd Base Support Battalion, Germany, 996

Dean of the Faculty
US Air Force Academy, Colorado Springs, CO, 146

Defense Accounting Office
Army Armor Center & Fort Knox, Fort Knox, KY, 366
Minot Air Force Base, Minot AFB, ND, 642

Defense Accounting Office, Cleveland Center
Great Lakes Naval Training Center, Great Lakes, IL, 308

Defense Activity for Non-traditional Education Support (DANTES)
Naval Education and Training Professional Development and Technology Center, Pensacola, FL, 223

Defense Ammunition Center, Savanna
Savanna Army Depot Activity, Savanna, IL, 317

Defense Ammunition Logistics Activity (DALA)
Armament Research, Development, and Engineering Center, US Army TACOM, Picatinny Arsenal, NJ, 562

Defense Automated and Printing Support Center
Defense Logistics Agency, HQ, Fort Belvoir, VA, 865

Defense Automated Printing Service
Naval Education and Training Center, Newport, Newport, RI, 726

Defense Commissary Agency
Army Transportation Center & Fort Eustis, Fort Eustis, VA, 868
Charleston Air Force Base, Charleston AFB, SC, 737
Fort Lee, Fort Lee, VA, 869
Charles E Kelly Support Facility, Oakdale, PA, 711
Shaw Air Force Base, Shaw AFB, SC, 749
Tobyhanna Army Depot, Tobyhanna, PA, 721
Yokota Air Base, Japan, 1085

Defense Commissary Agency, Annapolis
Annapolis Naval Station, Annapolis, MD, 409

Defense Commissary Agency, Camp Zama
Camp Zama, Japan, 1071

Defense Commissary Agency, Midwest Region
Kelly Air Force Base, Kelly AFB, TX, 807

Defense Commissary Agency, Northeast Region HQ
Fort George G Meade, Fort Meade, MD, 422

Defense Commissary Agency (SO/ BAR)
Barksdale Air Force Base, Barksdale AFB, LA, 374

Defense Contract Audit Agency

Defense Contract Management Command, Lockheed Martin, Marietta, Marietta, GA, 255

Defense Plant Representative Office, Air Force Plant No 4, Fort Worth, TX, 795

Kelly Air Force Base, Kelly AFB, TX, 807

Lake City Army Ammunition Plant, Independence, MO, 502

Los Angeles Air Force Base, Los Angeles, CA, 76

Milan Army Ammunition Plant, Milan, TN, 766

Defense Contract Management Area Office

Sabana Seca, US Naval Security Group Activity, Puerto Rico, 1144

Defense Contract Management Area Operations, Brussels

80th Area Support Group, Belgium, 975

Defense Contract Management Command, Clearwater

Defense Contract Management Command, Clearwater, Saint Petersburg, FL, 229

Defense Contract Management Command, Cleveland

Defense Contract Management Command, Cleveland, Bratenahl, OH, 644

Defense Contract Management Command (DCMC)

Defense Supply Center, Columbus, Columbus, OH, 654

Defense Contract Management Command, GE Aircraft Engines Cincinnati

Defense Contract Management Command, GE Aircraft Engines Cincinnati, Cincinnati, OH, 646

Defense Contract Management Command, Hughes Los Angeles

Defense Contract Management Command, Hughes Los Angeles, Los Angeles, CA, 75

Defense Contract Management Command, Indianapolis

Defense Contract Management Command, Indianapolis, Indianapolis, IN, 333

Defense Contract Management Command, Indianapolis, Hughes Defense Communications

Defense Contract Management Command, Indianapolis, HDC, Fort Wayne, IN, 327

Defense Contract Management Command, Indianapolis-South Bend

Defense Contract Management Command, Indianapolis-South Bend, South Bend, IN, 337

Defense Contract Management Command International

Defense Contract Management Command, International, Dayton, OH, 657

Defense Contract Management Command, Lockheed Martin, Marietta

Defense Contract Management Command, Lockheed Martin, Marietta, Marietta, GA, 255

Defense Contract Management Command, PLAS (Performance Labor Accounting System)

Defense Contract Management Command, PLAS, Chicago, IL, 301

Defense Contract Management Command, San Diego

Defense Contract Management Command, San Diego, San Diego, CA, 110

Defense Contract Management Command, Saudi Arabia

Eskan Village, Saudi Arabia, 1145

Defense Contract Management Command, Seattle

Defense Contract Management Command, Seattle, Bellevue, WA, 912

Defense Contract Management Command, Sikorsky

Defense Contract Management Command, Stratford, Stratford, CT, 165

Defense Contract Management Command, Stratford

Defense Contract Management Command, Stratford, Stratford, CT, 165

Defense Contract Management Command, Syracuse

Defense Contract Management Command, Syracuse, Syracuse, NY, 609

Defense Contract Management Command, Wichita

Defense Contract Management Command, Wichita, Wichita, KS, 363

Defense Contract Management District Mid-Atlantic

Philadelphia Defense Personnel Support Center, Philadelphia, PA, 715

Defense Contract Management District North Central

O'Hare International Airport Air Reserve Station, O'Hare IAP ARS, IL, 311

Defense Contract Management District Northeast

Defense Contract Management District Northeast, Boston, MA, 433

Defense Contract Management District South

Defense Contract Management District South, Marietta, GA, 256

Defense Contract Management District West

Defense Contract Management District West, El Segundo, CA, 66

Defense Contract Management Office

Defense Supply Center, Richmond, Richmond, VA, 898

Defense Contract Management Office, Raytheon

Defense Contract Management Office Raytheon, Bristol, TN, 757

Defense Contract Management Agency

1st Marine Corps District Headquarters, Garden City, NY, 588

Defense Courier Service

Administrative Support Unit, South West Asia, Bahrain, 973

Charleston Air Force Base, Charleston AFB, SC, 737

Kelly Air Force Base, Kelly AFB, TX, 807

Rhein-Main Air Base, Germany, 1025

Defense Courier Service, HQ

Fort George G Meade, Fort Meade, MD, 422

Defense Courier Service Station, Guam

Andersen Air Force Base, Guam, 1043

Defense Criminal Investigative Service (DCIS)

Defense Supply Center, Columbus, Columbus, OH, 654

Defense Supply Center, Richmond, Richmond, VA, 898

Defense Depot Distribution Station, San Antonio

Kelly Air Force Base, Kelly AFB, TX, 807

Defense Depot, Mechanicsburg

Mechanicsburg Navy Inventory Control Point, Mechanicsburg, PA, 706

Defense Dissemination Program

Los Angeles Air Force Base, Los Angeles, CA, 76

Defense Distribution Depot, Anniston

Anniston Army Depot, Anniston, AL, 1

Defense Distribution Depot, Barstow

Barstow, Marine Corps Logistics Base, Barstow, CA, 57

Defense Distribution Depot, Oklahoma City

Tinker Air Force Base, Tinker AFB, OK, 678

Defense Distribution Depot, Red River

Red River Army Depot, Texarkana, TX, 818

Defense Distribution Depot, Richmond

Defense Supply Center, Richmond, Richmond, VA, 898

Defense Distribution Depot, San Joaquin

Defense Distribution Region West, Stockton, CA, 134

Defense Distribution Depot, Susquehanna

Defense Distribution Region East, New Cumberland, PA, 709

Defense Distribution Depot, Tobyhanna
Tobyhanna Army Depot, Tobyhanna, PA, 721

Defense Distribution Region East (DDRE)
Defense Distribution Region East, New Cumberland, PA, 709

Defense Education Supplies Procurement Office
Defense Supply Center, Richmond, Richmond, VA, 898

Defense Equal Opportunity Management Institute
Patrick Air Force Base, Patrick AFB, FL, 221

Defense Finance and Accounting Service Center, Kansas City
Defense Finance and Accounting Service Center, Kansas City, Kansas City, MO, 504

Defense Finance and Accounting Service, Cleveland
Defense Finance and Accounting Service, Cleveland Center, Cleveland, OH, 650

Defense Finance and Accounting Service, Columbus
Defense Finance and Accounting Service, Columbus, OH, 653

Defense Finance and Accounting Service, Columbus (DFAS-CO)
Defense Supply Center, Columbus, Columbus, OH, 654

Defense Finance and Accounting Service, Denver Center
Defense Finance and Accounting Service, Denver Center, Denver, CO, 149

Defense Finance and Accounting Service Financial Systems Activity (DFAS-FFAPE)
Naval Education and Training Professional Development and Technology Center, Pensacola, FL, 223

Defense Finance and Accounting Service, HQ
Defense Finance and Accounting Service, Headquarters, Arlington, VA, 844

Defense Finance and Accounting Service, Indianapolis
Defense Finance and Accounting Service, Indianapolis Center, Indianapolis, IN, 334

Defense Finance & Accounting Service, Omaha
Offutt Air Force Base, Offutt AFB, NE, 530

Defense Finance and Accounting Service, Redstone Arsenal
Redstone Arsenal, Redstone Arsenal, AL, 16

Defense Finance and Accounting Service, Rome
Northeast Air Defense Sector, Rome, NY, 604

Defense Fuel Middle East
Administrative Support Unit, South West Asia, Bahrain, 973

Defense Fuel Office
Fort Dix, Fort Dix, NJ, 555

Defense Fuel Office, UK
West Ruislip RAF Base, United Kingdom, 1170

Defense Fuel Support Point, Melville, Allied Management
Naval Education and Training Center, Newport, Newport, RI, 726

Defense Industrial Security Clearance Office (DISCO)
Defense Supply Center, Columbus, Columbus, OH, 654

Defense Information School
Fort George G Meade, Fort Meade, MD, 422

Defense Information Service Organization-Defense Megacenter
Rock Island Arsenal, Rock Island, IL, 314

Defense Information Systems Agency
Defense Information Systems Agency, Arlington, VA, 845
Wheeler Army Airfield, Wheeler Army Airfield, HI, 293

Defense Information Systems Agency, Defense Megacenter San Antonio
Kelly Air Force Base, Kelly AFB, TX, 807

Defense Information Systems Agency, Western Hemisphere
Fort Ritchie, Fort Ritchie, MD, 424

Defense Information Technology Contracting Office
Scott Air Force Base, Scott AFB, IL, 318

Defense Intelligence Agency
Bolling Air Force Base, Washington, DC, 173

Defense Investigative Agency
Seymour Johnson Air Force Base, Goldsboro, NC, 625

Defense Investigative Service
Camp Zama, Japan, 1071
Corry Station Naval Technical Training Center, Pensacola, FL, 222
Grand Forks Air Force Base, Grand Forks AFB, ND, 641
Kelly Air Force Base, Kelly AFB, TX, 807
Laughlin Air Force Base, Laughlin AFB, TX, 810
Minot Air Force Base, Minot AFB, ND, 642
Shaw Air Force Base, Shaw AFB, SC, 749

Defense Investigative Service, DOD Central Region, Midwest Sector
Army Armor Center & Fort Knox, Fort Knox, KY, 366

Defense Investigative Service, Ft Rucker
Fort Rucker, Fort Rucker, AL, 5

Defense Investigative Service, Investigative RA (D11NP)
Naval Education and Training Center, Newport, Newport, RI, 726

Defense Investigative Service, Savannah Field Office
Hunter Army Air Field, Savannah, GA, 260

Defense Language Institute
Presidio of Monterey, Monterey, CA, 85

Defense Language Institute English Language Center
Lackland Air Force Base, Lackland AFB, TX, 809

Defense Logistics Agency
Cherry Point Marine Corps Air Station, Cherry Point, NC, 621

Defense Logistics Agency, HQ
Defense Logistics Agency, HQ, Fort Belvoir, VA, 865
Fort Belvoir, Fort Belvoir, VA, 866

Defense Logistics Agency Operations Research Office (DORO)
Defense Supply Center, Richmond, Richmond, VA, 898

Defense Logistics Agency Operations Support Office (DOSO)
Defense Supply Center, Richmond, Richmond, VA, 898

Defense Logistics Agency Performance Standards Support Office (DPSSO)
Defense Supply Center, Richmond, Richmond, VA, 898

Defense Logistics Services Center
Defense Logistics Agency, HQ, Fort Belvoir, VA, 865
Defense Logistics Services Center, Battle Creek, MI, 451

Defense Manpower Data Center
Naval Postgraduate School, Monterey, CA, 83

Defense Mapping Agency
Sigonella Naval Air Station, Italy, 1059

Defense Mapping Agency Representative
Administrative Support Unit, South West Asia, Bahrain, 973

Defense Mapping College, Ft Belvoir, VA
National Imagery & Mapping Agency, Fairfax, VA, 860

Defense Mapping School
Fort Belvoir, Fort Belvoir, VA, 866

Defense Megacenter, Chambersburg
Letterkenny Army Depot, Chambersburg, PA, 699

Defense Megacenter, Columbus (DSIO)
Defense Supply Center, Columbus, Columbus, OH, 654

Defense Megacenter, Huntsville
Redstone Arsenal, Redstone Arsenal, AL, 16

Defense Megacenter, Ogden
Hill Air Force Base, Hill AFB, UT, 824

Defense Meteorological Satellite Program
Falcon Air Force Base, Falcon AFB, CO, 151

Defense Military Pay Office
Army Transportation Center & Fort Eustis, Fort Eustis, VA, 868
Fort Buchanan Army Garrison, Puerto Rico, 1141

Defense Military Pay Office and 1st Finance Bn
Fort Riley, Fort Riley, KS, 353

Defense National Stockpile
Defense Logistics Agency, HQ, Fort Belvoir, VA, 865

Defense Nuclear Agency's Field Command
Kirtland Air Force Base, Kirtland AFB, NM, 572

Defense Personnel Support Center, Philadelphia
Philadelphia Defense Personnel Support Center, Philadelphia, PA, 715

Defense Plant Representative
Defense Plant Representative Office, Air Force Plant No 4, Fort Worth, TX, 795

Defense Printing Reprographic Facility (DPS-RF)
Defense Supply Center, Richmond, Richmond, VA, 898

Defense Printing Service
Anniston Army Depot, Anniston, AL, 1
Great Lakes Naval Training Center, Great Lakes, IL, 308

Defense Printing Service Branch Office
Lakehurst Naval Air Engineering Station, Lakehurst, NJ, 560

Defense Printing Service Det Office
Army Transportation Center & Fort Eustis, Fort Eustis, VA, 868

Defense Printing Service Det Office, Knox
Army Armor Center & Fort Knox, Fort Knox, KY, 366

Defense Printing Service
Defense Supply Center, Columbus, Columbus, OH, 654

Defense Publications and Printing Service Det Office
Mechanicsburg Navy Inventory Control Point, Mechanicsburg, PA, 706

Defense Resources Management Institute
Naval Postgraduate School, Monterey, CA, 83

Defense Reutilization & Marketing Office
Anniston Army Depot, Anniston, AL, 1

Army Armor Center & Fort Knox, Fort Knox, KY, 366
Blue Grass Army Depot, Richmond, KY, 373
Defense Supply Center, Richmond, Richmond, VA, 898
Dover Air Force Base, Dover AFB, DE, 167
Grand Forks Air Force Base, Grand Forks AFB, ND, 641
Great Lakes Naval Training Center, Great Lakes, IL, 308
Lakehurst Naval Air Engineering Station, Lakehurst, NJ, 560
Laughlin Air Force Base, Laughlin AFB, TX, 810
Letterkenny Army Depot, Chambersburg, PA, 699
McAlester Army Ammunition Plant, McAlester, OK, 673
Minot Air Force Base, Minot AFB, ND, 642
Molesworth RAF Base, United Kingdom, 1168
Robins Air Force Base, Robins AFB, GA, 259
Seymour Johnson Air Force Base, Goldsboro, NC, 625
Tobyhanna Army Depot, Tobyhanna, PA, 721

Defense Reutilization & Marketing Office, Columbus (DRMO)
Defense Supply Center, Columbus, Columbus, OH, 654

Defense Reutilization & Marketing Office, Romulus Branch
Seneca Army Depot Activity, Romulus, NY, 605

Defense Reutilization & Marketing Service Operation East (DRMS)
Defense Supply Center, Columbus, Columbus, OH, 654

Defense Reutilization and Marketing Service
Defense Logistics Agency, HQ, Fort Belvoir, VA, 865
Defense Reutilization and Marketing Service, Battle Creek, MI, 452
Ellsworth Air Force Base, Ellsworth AFB, SD, 750

Defense Reutilization Management Office
Duluth IAP Air National Guard Base, Duluth, MN, 468
Rota Naval Station, Spain, 1149

Defense Satellite Communications System
Falcon Air Force Base, Falcon AFB, CO, 151

Defense Security Institute (DSI)
Defense Supply Center, Richmond, Richmond, VA, 898

Defense Special Representative Japan (DSRJ)
Yokota Air Base, Japan, 1085

Defense Special Weapons Agency's Field Command
Kirtland Air Force Base, Kirtland AFB, NM, 572

Defense Supply Center, Columbus
Defense Supply Center, Columbus, Columbus, OH, 654

Defense Support Program
Falcon Air Force Base, Falcon AFB, CO, 151

Defense Systems Management College
Fort Belvoir, Fort Belvoir, VA, 866

Defense Systems Management College, Western Regional Center
Los Angeles Air Force Base, Los Angeles, CA, 76

Delaware National Guard
Adjutant General of Delaware, Wilmington, DE, 168

Demil Technology Office
Savanna Army Depot Activity, Savanna, IL, 317

Dental Activity Japan
Camp Zama, Japan, 1071

Dental Command, Europe
Landstuhl Regional Medical Center, Germany, 1020

DOD Commissary, Fort Knox
Army Armor Center & Fort Knox, Fort Knox, KY, 366

DODDS
Yokota Air Base, Japan, 1085

DODDS, Superintendent's Office
80th Area Support Group, Belgium, 975

DOD Manned Space Flight Support Office
Patrick Air Force Base, Patrick AFB, FL, 221

DOD Medical Exam Review Board
US Air Force Academy, Colorado Springs, CO, 146

DOD Polygraph Institute
Fort McClellan, Anniston, AL, 2

DOD Print Service
Tooele Army Depot, Tooele, UT, 830

Department of Energy Det
Kirtland Air Force Base, Kirtland AFB, NM, 572

Dept of Transportation, James River Reserve Fleet
Army Transportation Center & Fort Eustis, Fort Eustis, VA, 868

Deployment Process Modernization Office
Army Transportation Center & Fort Eustis, Fort Eustis, VA, 868

Depth and Simultaneous Attack Battle Lab
Fort Sill, Fort Sill, OK, 671

Deputy Commander for Logistics Operations
Albany Marine Corps Logistics Base, Albany, GA, 239

DESRON 31 (NR)
Tyler Naval Reserve Center, Tyler, TX, 819

Destroyer Squadron 12
Mayport Naval Air Station, Mayport, FL, 210

Destroyer Squadron 14
Mayport Naval Air Station, Mayport, FL, 210

Destroyer Squadron 24
Mayport Naval Air Station, Mayport, FL, 210

Destroyer Squadron 24 (NR)
Sioux Falls Naval Reserve Center, Sioux Falls, SD, 754

Destroyer Tender (AD-41) Det 8 (NR)
Tuscaloosa Armed Forces Reserve Center, Tuscaloosa, AL, 17

Destroyer Tender, Det 3 (NR)
White River Junction Naval Reserve Center, White River Junction, VT, 834

Deuringen Training Area
Augsburg Military Community, Germany, 999

Dexheim Family Housing
Anderson Barracks, Germany, 998

Harry Diamond Laboratory
Adelphi Laboratory Center, Army Research Laboratory, Adelphi, MD, 405

Director of Auxiliary, Alameda
Alameda Coast Guard Integrated Support Command, Alameda, CA, 54

Director of Auxiliary, Curtis Bay
Curtis Bay Coast Guard Yard, Curtis Bay, MD, 420

Director of Auxiliary, Juneau
17th Coast Guard District, Juneau, AK, 29

Director of Auxiliary, New Orleans
8th Coast Guard District, New Orleans, LA, 380

Director of Auxiliary, San Pedro
San Pedro Coast Guard Support Center, San Pedro, CA, 131

Director of Logistics, Camp Shelby
Camp Shelby Training Site, Camp Shelby, MS, 478

Director of Logistics, Munitions Branch (US Army Support Command, Hawaii, DOL)
Lualualei Naval Magazine, Waianae, HI, 289

Directorate for Industrial Security Clearance Review (DSICR)
Defense Supply Center, Columbus, Columbus, OH, 654

Directorate of Clothing and Textiles
Philadelphia Defense Personnel Support Center, Philadelphia, PA, 715

Directorate of Information Management
Fort Dix, Fort Dix, NJ, 555

Directorate of Manufacturing
Philadelphia Defense Personnel Support Center, Philadelphia, PA, 715

Directorate of Medical Materiel
Philadelphia Defense Personnel Support Center, Philadelphia, PA, 715

Directorate of Tactics
Nellis Air Force Base, Nellis AFB, NV, 541

Dismounted Battleship Battle Lab
Fort Benning, Fort Benning, GA, 248

Distributed Interactive Simulation Center (AMCOM)
Redstone Arsenal, Redstone Arsenal, AL, 16

District Armory, Boston
Boston Coast Guard Reserve Center, Boston, MA, 432

District Corps of Engineers, Resident Engineer Office, Savannah
Hunter Army Air Field, Savannah, GA, 260

District of Columbia National Guard
Commanding General, DC National Guard, Washington, DC, 175

District of Columbia National Guard Aviation Det
Davison Army Airfield, Fort Belvoir, VA, 864

Division Artillery
Fort Stewart, Hinesville, GA, 252

Division Support Command
Fort Stewart, Hinesville, GA, 252

DPCA, HQ
Yakima Training Center, Yakima, WA, 941

Dragon Brigade
Fort Bragg, Fort Bragg, NC, 624

Drill Instructor School
Parris Island Marine Corps Recruit Depot/ Eastern Recruiting Region, Parris Island, SC, 747
San Diego Marine Corps Recruit Depot, San Diego, CA, 119

Drill Sergeant School
84th Division (IT) HQ, Milwaukee, WI, 960
Fort Benning, Fort Benning, GA, 248
Fort Jackson, Columbia, SC, 740

Drug Demand Reduction
Stead Training Center, Reno, NV, 545

Dunham Army Dental Clinic
Carlisle Barracks, Carlisle Barracks, PA, 698

Dunham Army Health Clinic
Carlisle Barracks, Carlisle Barracks, PA, 698

Ira C Eaker College for Professional Development
Maxwell Air Force Base, Maxwell AFB, AL, 8

East Camp Grafenwöhr
100th Area Support Group, Germany, 991

Eastern ARNG Aviation Training Site
Fort Indiantown Gap, Annville, PA, 696

Eastern Range
Patrick Air Force Base, Patrick AFB, FL, 221

Echterdingen Airfield
6th Area Support Group, Stuttgart, Germany, 988

Edigheim Beacon Site
293rd Base Support Battalion, Germany, 996

Edingen Radio Receiver Facility
Heidelberg Military Community, Germany, 1011

Egelsbach Transmitter Facility
223rd Base Support Battalion, Germany, 993

Ehrling Bergquist Hospital
Offutt Air Force Base, Offutt AFB, NE, 530

Einsiedlerhof Air Station
Ramstein Air Base, Germany, 1023

Dwight David Eisenhower Army Medical Center
Army Signal Center & Fort Gordon, Fort Gordon, GA, 249

Electric Shop, San Francisco
San Francisco Coast Guard Group, San Francisco, CA, 126

Electrical Maintenance Co, 4th Maintenance Bn
Wichita Naval & Marine Corps Reserve Center, Wichita, KS, 364

Electronic Combat Weapon School
Whidbey Island Naval Air Station, Oak Harbor, WA, 924

Electronic Combat Wing, Pacific Fleet
Whidbey Island Naval Air Station, Oak Harbor, WA, 924

Det 2, Electronic Maintenance Co, 4th Maintenance Bn
Indianapolis Naval & Marine Corps Reserve Readiness Center, Indianapolis, IN, 335

Electronic Shop, Cape May
Cape May Coast Guard Training Center, Cape May, NJ, 553

Electronic Shop, Ketchikan
Ketchikan Coast Guard Station, Ketchikan, AK, 30

Electronic Software Distribution Center
Gunter Annex, Gunter, AL, 6

Electronic Support Det, Alameda
Alameda Coast Guard Integrated Support Command, Alameda, CA, 54

Electronic Support Det, Buffalo
Buffalo Coast Guard Group, Buffalo, NY, 582

Electronic Support Det, Charleston
Charleston Coast Guard Group, Charleston, SC, 732

Electronic Support Det, Elizabeth City
Elizabeth City Coast Guard Support Center, Elizabeth City, NC, 623

Electronic Support Det, Galveston
Galveston Coast Guard Base, Galveston, TX, 798

Electronic Support Det, Ketchikan
Ketchikan Coast Guard Station, Ketchikan, AK, 30

Electronic Support Det, Miami
Miami Beach Coast Guard Group/Station, Miami Beach, FL, 212

Electronic Support Det, Milwaukee
Milwaukee Coast Guard Base/Group, Milwaukee, WI, 961

Electronic Support Det, Mobile
Mobile Coast Guard Group/Station, Mobile, AL, 10

Electronic Support Det, St Petersburg
St Petersburg Coast Guard Group/Station, Saint Petersburg, FL, 231

Electronic Support Det, San Pedro
San Pedro Coast Guard Support Center, San Pedro, CA, 131

Electronic Support Unit Det, Port Angeles
Port Angeles Coast Guard Air Station/Group, Port Angeles, WA, 926

Electronic Support Unit, Honolulu
Honolulu Coast Guard Base/Station, Honolulu, HI, 275

Electronic Support Unit, Kodiak
Kodiak Coast Guard Integrated Support Command, Kodiak, AK, 32

Electronic Systems Center, Headquarters
Hanscom Air Force Base, Bedford, MA, 430

Electronic Systems Support Unit, Seattle
Seattle Coast Guard Integrated Support Command, Seattle, WA, 929

Electronic Warfare Operational Programming Facility
Northwest Naval Security Group Activity, Chesapeake, VA, 858

Electronic Warfare Squadron 135
Whidbey Island Naval Air Station, Oak Harbor, WA, 924

Electronic Warfare Squadron 137
Whidbey Island Naval Air Station, Oak Harbor, WA, 924

Electronic Warfare Squadron 139
Whidbey Island Naval Air Station, Oak Harbor, WA, 924

Electronic Warfare Squadron 141
Whidbey Island Naval Air Station, Oak Harbor, WA, 924

Electronics Systems Support Unit, Cleveland
9th Coast Guard District Headquarters, Cleveland, OH, 648

Embrey-Riddle Aeronautical University, Giebelstadt
Giebelstadt Army Airfield, Germany, 1010

Energetic Manufacturing Technology Center
Indian Head Division, Naval Surface Warfare Center, Indian Head, MD, 426

Engineer Brigade
Fort Stewart, Hinesville, GA, 252

Engineer Brigade HQ, Camp Howze
Camp Howze, Korea, Republic of, 1101

Engineer District Japan
Camp Zama, Japan, 1071

Engineer Maintenance Co, 4th Maintenance Bn
Omaha Naval & Marine Corps Reserve Center, Omaha, NE, 531
Wichita Naval & Marine Corps Reserve Center, Wichita, KS, 364

Engineering Data Management Office, Army JEDMICS Component Office
Redstone Arsenal, Redstone Arsenal, AL, 16

Engineering Duty Officers School
Port Hueneme, Naval Construction Battalion Center, Port Hueneme, CA, 104

Engineering Field Activity, Midwest
Recruit Training Command Great Lakes, Great Lakes, IL, 309

Engineering Logistics Center, Curtis Bay
Curtis Bay Coast Guard Yard, Curtis Bay, MD, 420

Enhanced Fiber Optic Guided Missile
Redstone Arsenal, Redstone Arsenal, AL, 16

Enlisted Heritage Research Institute
Maxwell Air Force Base, Maxwell AFB, AL, 8

Enlisted Personnel Management Directorate
Army Reserve Personnel Center, Saint Louis, MO, 510

Enlisted Sailor Program
Recruit Training Command Great Lakes, Great Lakes, IL, 309

Environics Directorate
Tyndall Air Force Base, Panama City, FL, 220

Environmental Sciences Division
Navy Clothing and Textile Research Facility, Natick, MA, 442

EOT Det 2
Seal Beach Naval Weapons Station, Seal Beach, CA, 133

EOT Det 3
Seal Beach Naval Weapons Station, Seal Beach, CA, 133

EOT Det 4
Seal Beach Naval Weapons Station, Seal Beach, CA, 133

EOT Det 5
Seal Beach Naval Weapons Station, Seal Beach, CA, 133

EOT HQ Det 1
Seal Beach Naval Weapons Station, Seal Beach, CA, 133

Equipment Concentration Site 24
Fort Indiantown Gap, Annville, PA, 696

Equipment Concentration Site 67
Fort McCoy, Fort McCoy, WI, 954

Equipment Concentration Site 93
Army Transportation Center & Fort Eustis, Fort Eustis, VA, 868

Equipment Concentration Site (AMSA 27)
Fort Dix, Fort Dix, NJ, 555

Equipment Maintenance Center— Continental US
Camp Dodge Iowa, Johnston, IA, 346

Oklahoma Maintenance Shop (OMS) #3
Camp Gruber, Army National Guard Training Site, Braggs, OK, 669

Ernst Ludwig Kaserne
223rd Base Support Battalion, Germany, 993

Eselsfürth Quartermaster Facility
Kaiserslautern Military Community, Germany, 1013

European Confinement Facility
Coleman Barracks, Germany, 1006

Euro-NATO Joint Jet Pilot Training
Sheppard Air Force Base, Sheppard AFB, TX, 817

European Office of Aerospace Research & Development
European Office of Aerospace Research & Development, London, United Kingdom, 1163

European Stars & Stripes
Stars and Stripes Kaserne, Germany, 1031

European Tanker Task Force
Mildenhall RAF Base, United Kingdom, 1167

Everberg Armed Forces Network (AFN) Facility
80th Area Support Group, Belgium, 975

Executive Directorate
Naval Research Laboratory, Washington, DC, 182

Exercise Support Command
Fort Clayton, Panama, 1133

Expeditionary Warfare Training Group Atlantic
Little Creek, Naval Amphibious Base, Norfolk, VA, 880

Expeditionary Warfare Training Group, Pacific
Coronado Naval Amphibious Base, San Diego, CA, 109

Explosive Ordnance Department Mobilization Unit
Tallahassee Naval & Marine Corps Reserve Center, Tallahassee, FL, 234

Explosive Ordnance Disposal (EOD)
Earle Naval Weapons Station, Colts Neck, NJ, 554

Explosive Ordnance Disposal, Det Bahrain
Administrative Support Unit, South West Asia, Bahrain, 973

Explosive Ordnance Disposal (EOD)
Roosevelt Roads Naval Station, Puerto Rico, 1143

Explosive Ordnance Disposal, Group 2, Det ROTA
Rota Naval Station, Spain, 1149

Explosive Ordnance Disposal, Group 3, Det Fallon
Fallon Naval Air Station, Fallon, NV, 535

Explosive Ordnance Disposal Mobile Unit 2
Crane Division, Naval Surface Warfare Center, Crane, IN, 324
Yorktown Naval Weapons Station, Yorktown, VA, 910

Explosive Ordnance Disposal Mobile Unit 2 Det Newport
Naval Education and Training Center, Newport, Newport, RI, 726

Explosive Ordnance Disposal Mobile Unit 3
Pearl Harbor Naval Complex, Pearl Harbor, HI, 283

Explosive Ordnance Disposal Mobile Unit 5, Det Guam
Naval Station, Guam, Guam, 1047

Explosive Ordnance Disposal Mobile Unit 8 (EODMU EIGHT)
Sigonella Naval Air Station, Italy, 1059

Explosive Ordnance Disposal Mobile Unit 11
Whidbey Island Naval Air Station, Oak Harbor, WA, 924

Explosive Ordnance Disposal Mobile Unit 17
Whidbey Island Naval Air Station, Oak Harbor, WA, 924

Eygelshoven Reserve Storage Area
254th Base Support Battalion, Netherlands, 1127

Facilities and Services Division
Barstow, Marine Corps Logistics Base, Barstow, CA, 57

Facilities Technology Laboratory
US Army Corps of Engineers, Construction Engineering Research Laboratories, Champaign, IL, 300

Family Housing Welcome Center, Naval Station Washington
Anacostia Naval Station, Washington, DC, 171

Faulenberg Kaserne
98th Area Support Group, Germany, 990

Federal Aviation Administration
Edwards Air Force Base, Edwards AFB, CA, 63
Operating Location Alpha Bravo South East Air Defense Sector, Old Town, FL, 214

FAA, Oakdale
Charles E Kelly Support Facility, Oakdale, PA, 711

Federal Bureau of Investigation
Army Armor Center & Fort Knox, Fort Knox, KY, 366

Federal Bureau of Investigation Academy
Quantico Marine Corps Combat Development Command, Quantico, VA, 895

Federal Bureau of Prisons
Fort Dix, Fort Dix, NJ, 555

Federal Emergency Management Agency
Blue Grass Army Depot, Richmond, KY, 373
Cheyenne Mountain Air Force Station, Colorado Springs, CO, 145
US Army Corps of Engineers, New England District, Waltham, MA, 445

FEN
Yokota Air Base, Japan, 1085

FF-1084 McCandless Det 8406 (NR)
Cumberland Naval Reserve Center, Cumberland, MD, 419

FFG22 2207 (NR)
Augusta Naval & Marine Corps Reserve Center, Augusta, GA, 244

FH 500 CBTZ 23 Det C (NR)
Lincoln Naval Reserve Center, Lincoln, NE, 529

FH 500 CBTZ 23 Det K (NR)
Wichita Naval & Marine Corps Reserve Center, Wichita, KS, 364

FH 500 CBTZ23, Det F (NR) NMCB 25 Det 1425 (NR)
Dubuque Naval Reserve Center, Dubuque, IA, 344

FH 500 CBTZ23 O
Cheyenne Naval Reserve Center, Cheyenne, WY, 966

Field Command, Johnston Atoll
Army Chemical Activity Pacific, Johnston Atoll, 1086

Field Office, Caruthersville, MO
US Army Corps of Engineers, Memphis District, Memphis, TN, 765

Field Office, Wynne, AR
US Army Corps of Engineers, Memphis District, Memphis, TN, 765

Field Training Det 317
Charleston Air Force Base, Charleston AFB, SC, 737

Field Training Det 327
Hurlburt Field, Hurlburt Field, FL, 200

Field Training Site (GA ANG)
Savannah IAP Air National Guard Base, Garden City, GA, 251

Fighter Squadron 2
Oceana Naval Air Station, Virginia Beach, VA, 903

Fighter Squadron 11
Oceana Naval Air Station, Virginia Beach, VA, 903

Fighter Squadron 14
Oceana Naval Air Station, Virginia Beach, VA, 903

Fighter Squadron 31
Oceana Naval Air Station, Virginia Beach, VA, 903

Fighter Squadron 32
Oceana Naval Air Station, Virginia Beach, VA, 903

Fighter Squadron 41
Oceana Naval Air Station, Virginia Beach, VA, 903

Fighter Squadron 101
Key West Naval Air Facility, Boca Chica Key, FL, 191
Oceana Naval Air Station, Virginia Beach, VA, 903

Fighter Squadron 102
Oceana Naval Air Station, Virginia Beach, VA, 903

Fighter Squadron 103
Oceana Naval Air Station, Virginia Beach, VA, 903

Fighter Squadron 211
Oceana Naval Air Station, Virginia Beach, VA, 903

Fighter Squadron 201 (VF 201)
Fort Worth, Naval Air Station, Joint Reserve Base, Fort Worth, TX, 796

Fighter Squadron 143
Oceana Naval Air Station, Virginia Beach, VA, 903

Fighter Squadron 213
Oceana Naval Air Station, Virginia Beach, VA, 903

Fighter Squadron Composite 13 (VFC-13)
Fallon Naval Air Station, Fallon, NV, 535

Commander, Fighter Wing, US Atlantic Fleet
Oceana Naval Air Station, Virginia Beach, VA, 903

Finance Co, Det B
Barton Barracks, Ansbach, Germany, 1002

Financial Management and Comptroller Systems
Gunter Annex, Gunter, AL, 6

Finthen Airfield
221st Base Support Battalion, Germany, 992

Finthen Family Housing
221st Base Support Battalion, Germany, 992

Fintherlandstrasse Family Housing
221st Base Support Battalion, Germany, 992

Fire & Safety Test Det, Mobile
Mobile Coast Guard Group/Station, Mobile, AL, 10

Fire Support Armaments Center (FSAC)
Armament Research, Development, and Engineering Center, US Army TACOM, Picatinny Arsenal, NJ, 562

First Sergeant Academy
Keesler Air Force Base, Keesler AFB, MS, 487

FISC Yokosuka Det 116 (NR)
Sioux Falls Naval Reserve Center, Sioux Falls, SD, 754

FISC Yokosuka, Det 313 (NR)
Dubuque Naval Reserve Center, Dubuque, IA, 344

Fish & Wildlife Service
Rocky Mountain Arsenal, Commerce City, CO, 147

Fitzsimons Army Medical Center
Fitzsimons Army Medical Center, Aurora, CO, 144

Commander, Fleet Activities Okinawa (COMFLEACT)
Kadena Naval Air Facility, Japan, 1075

Fleet Activities Yokosuka
Yokosuka, Fleet Activities, Japan, 1083

Fleet Air Reconnaissance Squadron One
Whidbey Island Naval Air Station, Oak Harbor, WA, 924

Fleet Air Wing 31
Iwakuni Marine Corps Air Station, Japan, 1073

Fleet Analysis Center
Naval Warfare Assessment Division, Norco, CA, 86

Fleet & Industrial Supply Center
Fleet Industrial Supply Center, Norfolk, VA, 878
Jacksonville Naval Air Station, Jacksonville, FL, 205

Fleet & Industrial Supply Center, Cheatham Annex
Fleet & Industrial Supply Center, Cheatham Annex, Williamsburg, VA, 907

Fleet & Industrial Supply Center, San Diego
San Diego Fleet and Industrial Supply Center, San Diego, CA, 118

Fleet Antisubmarine Warfare Training Center
Fleet Antisubmarine Warfare Training Center, Pacific, San Diego, CA, 111

Fleet Area Control and Surveillance Facility (FACSFAC)
North Island Naval Air Station, San Diego, CA, 115

Fleet Area Control & Surveillance Facility, Virginia Capes
Oceana Naval Air Station, Virginia Beach, VA, 903

Fleet Aviation Specialized Operational Training Group, Atlantic (FASO)
Cherry Point Marine Corps Air Station, Cherry Point, NC, 621

Fleet Aviation Specialized Operational Training Group, Atlantic Fleet
Oceana Naval Air Station, Virginia Beach, VA, 903

Fleet Aviation Specialized Operational Training Group, Pacific
Lemoore Naval Air Station, Lemoore, CA, 74
North Island Naval Air Station, San Diego, CA, 115
Whidbey Island Naval Air Station, Oak Harbor, WA, 924

Fleet Combat Direction Systems Support Activity
Dam Neck, Fleet Combat Training Center, Atlantic, Virginia Beach, VA, 902

Fleet Combat Training Center
Fleet Combat Training Center, Pacific, San Diego, CA, 112

Fleet Combat Training Center, Atlantic
Dam Neck, Fleet Combat Training Center, Atlantic, Virginia Beach, VA, 902

Fleet Composite Squadron Eight (VC-8)
Roosevelt Roads Naval Station, Puerto Rico, 1143

Fleet Composite Squadron 12
Oceana Naval Air Station, Virginia Beach, VA, 903

Fleet Composite Squadron, Det 6
Dam Neck, Fleet Combat Training Center, Atlantic, Virginia Beach, VA, 902

Fleet Electronic Warfare Support Group
North Island Naval Air Station, San Diego, CA, 115

Fleet Hospital 500 CBTZ 23 Det Q
Sioux Falls Naval Reserve Center, Sioux Falls, SD, 754

Fleet Hospital 500 CBTZ Det O
Ebensburg Naval & Marine Corps Reserve Center, Ebensburg, PA, 702

Fleet Hospital Det F
Pocatello Naval Reserve Facility, Pocatello, ID, 299

Fleet Hospital Program Office
Naval Supply Systems Command, Mechanicsburg, PA, 707

Fleet Imaging Center, Atlantic
Oceana Naval Air Station, Virginia Beach, VA, 903
Rota Naval Station, Spain, 1149

Fleet Imaging Command, Whidbey Island
Whidbey Island Naval Air Station, Oak Harbor, WA, 924

Fleet Imaging Facilities Det Atlantic
Roosevelt Roads Naval Station, Puerto Rico, 1143

Fleet Imaging Facility, Pacific
Lemoore Naval Air Station, Lemoore, CA, 74

Fleet Industrial Supply Center Det
Sasebo, US Fleet Activities, Japan, 1080

Fleet Industrial Supply Center Norfolk, Newport Det
Naval Education and Training Center, Newport, Newport, RI, 726

Fleet & Industrial Supply Center, Puget Sound
Puget Sound Naval Shipyard, Bremerton, WA, 914

Fleet Intelligence Training Center
Fleet Antisubmarine Warfare Training Center, Pacific, San Diego, CA, 111

Fleet Logistic Support Squadron 22 (VR-22)
Rota Naval Station, Spain, 1149

Fleet Logistic Support Squadron 40 (VRC-40)
Sigonella Naval Air Station, Italy, 1059

Fleet Logistic Support Squadron 54 (VR-54)
New Orleans Naval Air Station Joint Reserve Base, Naval Air Station, New Orleans, LA, 384

Fleet Logistics Squadron 1 (VR-1)
Washington, DC, Naval Air Facility, Andrews AFB, MD, 408

Fleet Logistics Squadron 48 (VR-48)
Washington, DC, Naval Air Facility, Andrews AFB, MD, 408

Fleet Logistics Support Squadron 46 (VR-46)
Atlanta Naval Air Station, Marietta, GA, 254

Fleet Logistics Support Squadron 50 (VRC-50)
Administrative Support Unit, South West Asia, Bahrain, 973

Fleet Logistics Support Squadron 52 (VR-52)
Willow Grove Naval Air Station (JRB), Willow Grove, PA, 723

Fleet Logistics Support Squadron 59 (VR 59)
Fort Worth, Naval Air Station, Joint Reserve Base, Fort Worth, TX, 796

Fleet Mail Center, Yokohama
Yokosuka, Fleet Activities, Japan, 1083

Fleet Marine Force, Atlantic (FMFLANT), HQ
Camp Elmore, Norfolk, VA, 877

Fleet Marine Force, Pacific
Camp H M Smith, Camp Smith, HI, 266

Fleet Material Support Office
Naval Supply Systems Command, Mechanicsburg, PA, 707

Fleet Numerical Oceanography Center
Naval Postgraduate School, Monterey, CA, 83

Fleet Ocean Surveillance Information Facility
Rota Naval Station, Spain, 1149

Fleet Reconnaissance Squadron 2 (VQ-2)
Rota Naval Station, Spain, 1149

Fleet Satellite Communications System
Falcon Air Force Base, Falcon AFB, CO, 151

Fleet Support Division
Barstow, Marine Corps Logistics Base, Barstow, CA, 57

Fleet Support Services
Naval Supply Systems Command, Mechanicsburg, PA, 707

Fleet Surveillance Support Command
Northwest Naval Security Group Activity, Chesapeake, VA, 858

Fleet Training Center
Mayport Naval Air Station, Mayport, FL, 210
San Diego Naval Station, San Diego, CA, 122

Fleet Training Center, Norfolk
Fleet Training Center, Norfolk, Norfolk, VA, 879

Fleet Training Command
Fleet Training Center, Norfolk, Norfolk, VA, 879

Fliegerhorst Airfield Kaserne
414th Base Support Battalion, Germany, 997

Flight Services Division
Gunter Annex, Gunter, AL, 6

Florida Marine Patrol
Naval Coastal Systems Station, Panama City, FL, 219

Florida National Guard
Adjutant General of Florida, Saint Augustine, FL, 228

Florida Regional Training Institute (OCS)
Camp Blanding Training Site, Starke, FL, 232

FLT HOSPITAL 23 Det N (NR)
Omaha Naval & Marine Corps Reserve Center, Omaha, NE, 531

FLTSUPTRA 1007 (NR)
Greensboro Naval & Marine Corps Reserve Readiness Center, Greensboro, NC, 626

FLTSUPTRA Det 1409 (NR)
Louisville Naval Reserve Center, Louisville, KY, 371

Flynn Family Housing Area
Bamberg Military Community, Germany, 1001

Flynn Training Area
Bamberg Military Community, Germany, 1001

Food Service FUNC TM 2 (NR)
Cape Girardeau Naval Reserve Center, Cape Girardeau, MO, 500

Force Protection Battlelab
Lackland Air Force Base, Lackland AFB, TX, 809

Foreign Language Center
Presidio of Monterey, Monterey, CA, 85

Forest Service
Camp Navajo, Bellemont, AZ, 34

Fort AP Hill
Military District of Washington, Washington, DC, 179

Fort Belvoir
Military District of Washington, Washington, DC, 179

Fort Crowder
Fort Crowder, Neosho, MO, 507

Army Garrison
Fort Detrick, Fort Detrick, MD, 421

Ft Dix Resident Engineer Office
Fort Dix, Fort Dix, NJ, 555

Fort Fisher Air Force Recreation Area
Fort Fisher Air Force Recreation Area, Kure Beach, NC, 628

Fort Hamilton, NY
Military District of Washington, Washington, DC, 179

Fort McClellan Military Police Co
Fort McClellan, Anniston, AL, 2

Fort McNair
Military District of Washington, Washington, DC, 179

Army Garrison, Fort McNair
Fort Lesley J McNair, Washington, DC, 177

Fort Meade
Military District of Washington, Washington, DC, 179

Fort Myer
Military District of Washington, Washington, DC, 179

Fort Ritchie
Military District of Washington, Washington, DC, 179

Fort Story Community Clinic
Fort Story, Fort Story, VA, 871

Frankenthal
293rd Base Support Battalion, Germany, 996

Frankfurt AFN Station
223rd Base Support Battalion, Germany, 993

Frankfurt Mortuary
223rd Base Support Battalion, Germany, 993

Benjamin Franklin Village Family Housing
293rd Base Support Battalion, Germany, 996

Frasdorf Operations Area
Augsburg Military Community, Germany, 999

Frechetsfeld Radio Site
282nd Base Support Battalion, Germany, 995

Freihölser Training Area
282nd Base Support Battalion, Germany, 995

Fridley Naval Industrial Reserve Ordnance Plant
Fridley Naval Industrial Reserve Ordnance Plant, Minneapolis, MN, 471

Friedberg Training and Storage Area
Friedberg Area Support Team, Germany, 1007

Friedrichfeld Storage Area
293rd Base Support Battalion, Germany, 996

Friedrichsfeld Quartermaster Service Center
293rd Base Support Battalion, Germany, 996

Friendly Forces Coordination Cell
Eskan Village, Saudi Arabia, 1145

Friolzheim Communication Facility
6th Area Support Group, Stuttgart, Germany, 988

Fryar Circle Family Housing
Augsburg Military Community, Germany, 999

Funari Barracks
293rd Base Support Battalion, Germany, 996

G1/46th Adjutant General Bn (Reception)
Army Armor Center & Fort Knox, Fort Knox, KY, 366

Gablingen Kaserne
Augsburg Military Community, Germany, 999

Garmish Family Housing
6th Area Support Group, Garmish, Germany, 987

Geilenkirchen Airbase
254th Base Support Battalion, Netherlands, 1127

General Dynamics Land Systems (operating contractor)
Lima Army Tank Plant, Lima, OH, 658

General Science and Technology Directorate
Naval Research Laboratory, Washington, DC, 182

General Services Administration
Stockton Naval Communications Station, Stockton, CA, 135

GSA, Fleet Management Center
Charles E Kelly Support Facility, Oakdale, PA, 711

General Support-Motor Transport Co, 6 Motor Transport Bn
Naval Education and Training Center, Newport, Newport, RI, 726

Geophysics Directorate
Hanscom Air Force Base, Bedford, MA, 430

Georgia Army National Guard
Hunter Army Air Field, Savannah, GA, 260

Georgia National Guard
Adjutant General of Georgia, Atlanta, GA, 241

Georgia National Guard Armory
Fort Gillem, Forest Park, GA, 247

German Air Force Training Command
Fort Bliss, El Paso, TX, 790

Germersheim Army Depot
Germersheim Sub-Community, Germany, 1009
Heidelberg Military Community, Germany, 1011

Germersheim Rail Transportation Office Facility
Germersheim Sub-Community, Germany, 1009
Heidelberg Military Community, Germany, 1011

Gerow Army Reserve Center
Fort Lee, Fort Lee, VA, 869

Gerszewski Barracks
Germersheim Sub-Community, Germany, 1009
Heidelberg Military Community, Germany, 1011

GETN Training Site
Pine Bluff Arsenal, Pine Bluff, AR, 53

Global Combat Support System
Gunter Annex, Gunter, AL, 6

Global Operations Center
Beale Air Force Base, Beale AFB, CA, 58

Goex
Longhorn/Louisiana Army Ammunition Plant, Minden, LA, 379

Goodfellow NCO Academy
Goodfellow Air Force Base, Goodfellow AFB, TX, 801

Grafenwöhr Army Airfield
100th Area Support Group, Germany, 991

Grafenwöhr Army Training Area
100th Area Support Group, Germany, 991

Grand Bay Weapons Range
Moody Air Force Base, Moody AFB, GA, 258

Grefrath Kaserne
254th Base Support Battalion, Netherlands, 1127

Griesheim Airfield
223rd Base Support Battalion, Germany, 993

Grobbendonk Site
80th Area Support Group, Belgium, 975

Ground Combat & Support Systems
Army Tank-Automotive & Armaments Command, Warren, MI, 466

Grounds Intelligence Support Activity (CONUS)
Fort Bragg, Fort Bragg, NC, 624

Grunstadt AAFES Facility
293rd Base Support Battalion, Germany, 996

Grunstadt Communication Station
293rd Base Support Battalion, Germany, 996

Guam Air National Guard
Andersen Air Force Base, Guam, 1043

Guam National Guard
Adjutant General of Guam, Guam, 1042

Guard Co Pearl Harbor
Marine Barracks, Hawaii, Pearl Harbor, HI, 282

Gulf Strike Team, Mobile
Mobile Coast Guard Group/Station, Mobile, AL, 10

Gunpowder Target Range (ARNG)
Gunpowder Military Reservation, Glen Arm, MD, 425

Hainerberg Housing
221st Base Support Battalion, Germany, 992

Nathan Hale Quartermaster Area
223rd Base Support Battalion, Germany, 993

Hammond Barracks
Heidelberg Military Community, Germany, 1011

Hanau Army Airfield
414th Base Support Battalion, Germany, 997

Hardwood Air-to-Ground Weapons Range (Detached)
Volk Field Air National Guard Base, Camp Douglas, WI, 953

Harvey Barracks
Kitzingen Military Community, Germany, 1017

Hawaii Air National Guard
Barbers Point Naval Air Station, Barbers Point, HI, 265
Fort Kamehameha, Honolulu, HI, 274
Pacific Missile Range Facility, Kekaha, HI, 279

Hawaii Air National Guard, HQ
State of Hawaii, Department of Defense HQ, Honolulu, HI, 277

Hawaii Army National Guard, HQ
State of Hawaii, Department of Defense HQ, Honolulu, HI, 277

Hawaii ANG Military Academy
Bellows Air Force Station, Waimanalo, HI, 291

Hawaii National Guard
Schofield Barracks, Schofield Barracks, HI, 286

Hazardous Material Afloat Program
Naval Supply Systems Command, Mechanicsburg, PA, 707

HQ First United States Army forward (West)
Army Armor Center & Fort Knox, Fort Knox, KY, 366

HQ USAF Area Defense Counsel
Minot Air Force Base, Minot AFB, ND, 642

HQ Air Force Space Command
Peterson Air Force Base, Peterson AFB, CO, 156

HQ & HQ Det (ND ARNG)
Camp Gilbert C Grafton, Devils Lake, ND, 638

HQ & HQ Det Training Site
Camp Santiago, Puerto Rico, 1140

HQ & Maintenance Squadron 13
Yuma Marine Corps Air Station, Yuma, AZ, 45

HQ & Service Bn
Camp Elmore, Norfolk, VA, 877
Camp Foster, Japan, 1066
San Diego Marine Corps Recruit Depot, San Diego, CA, 119

Headquarters and Service Co
Marine Barracks, Hawaii, Pearl Harbor, HI, 282

Det 2, Communications Co, HQ & Service Co
Lehigh Valley Naval & Marine Corps Reserve Center, Allentown, PA, 694

Headquarters Bn
Barstow, Marine Corps Logistics Base, Barstow, CA, 57
Fort McClellan, Anniston, AL, 2

HQ Bn, Twentynine Palms
Twentynine Palms Marine Corps Air Ground Combat Center, Twentynine Palms, CA, 139

HQ, DC Air National Guard
District of Columbia National Guard, HQ, Washington, DC, 176

HQ, District Area Command, DC Army National Guard
District of Columbia National Guard, HQ, Washington, DC, 176

HQ State Area Readiness Command (CGTS) Det 3
Camp Gruber, Army National Guard Training Site, Braggs, OK, 669

HQ State Area Readiness Command, Det 1
New Mexico National Guard State Headquarters, Santa Fe, NM, 573

HQ State Area Readiness Command, Det 4 (Medical)
New Mexico National Guard State Headquarters, Santa Fe, NM, 573

HQ State Area Readiness Command (STARC), NM ARNG
New Mexico National Guard State Headquarters, Santa Fe, NM, 573

HQUSMEPCOM
Great Lakes Naval Training Center, Great Lakes, IL, 308

HQ WV State Area Readiness Command, Det 3
Camp Dawson, Kingwood, WV, 947

Health & Dental Clinic, Det 3 (DC ARNG)
District of Columbia National Guard, HQ, Washington, DC, 176

Health Care Region 12
Tripler Army Medical Center, Tripler AMC, HI, 287

Health Services Command
Fort Sam Houston, Fort Sam Houston, TX, 794

Heidelberg AFN Relay Facility
Heidelberg Military Community, Germany, 1011

Heidelberg Army Airfield
Heidelberg Military Community, Germany, 1011

Heidelberg Community Support Center
Heidelberg Military Community, Germany, 1011

Heidelberg Education Center
Patton Barracks, Germany, 1022

Heidelberg Hospital
Heidelberg Military Community, Germany, 1011

Heideneim Radio Relay Site
Barton Barracks, Ansbach, Germany, 1002

Helicopter Antisubmarine Light Wing
Mayport Naval Air Station, Mayport, FL, 210

Helicopter Antisubmarine Squadron 3
Jacksonville Naval Air Station, Jacksonville, FL, 205

Helicopter Antisubmarine Squadron 5
Jacksonville Naval Air Station, Jacksonville, FL, 205

Helicopter Antisubmarine Squadron 11
Jacksonville Naval Air Station, Jacksonville, FL, 205

Helicopter Antisubmarine Squadron 15
Jacksonville Naval Air Station, Jacksonville, FL, 205

Helicopter Antisubmarine Squadron Light 37 (HSL-37)
Barbers Point Naval Air Station, Barbers Point, HI, 265

Helicopter Antisubmarine Squadron Light 40
Mayport Naval Air Station, Mayport, FL, 210

Helicopter Antisubmarine Squadron Light 42
Mayport Naval Air Station, Mayport, FL, 210

Helicopter Antisubmarine Squadron Light 44
Mayport Naval Air Station, Mayport, FL, 210

Helicopter Antisubmarine Squadron Light 46
Mayport Naval Air Station, Mayport, FL, 210

Helicopter Antisubmarine Squadron Light 48
Mayport Naval Air Station, Mayport, FL, 210

Helicopter Antisubmarine Squadron Light 94 (HSL-94)
Willow Grove Naval Air Station (JRB), Willow Grove, PA, 723

Helicopter Antisubmarine Wing, US Atlantic
Jacksonville Naval Air Station, Jacksonville, FL, 205

Helicopter Combat Support Squadron 4 (HC-4)
Sigonella Naval Air Station, Italy, 1059

Helicopter Sea Control Wing, Atlantic
Norfolk Naval Air Station, Norfolk, VA, 882

Helicopter Support Squadron 2, Det 2 (HC-2)
Administrative Support Unit, South West Asia, Bahrain, 973

Helicopter Support Squadron 4, Det 1 (HC-4)
Administrative Support Unit, South West Asia, Bahrain, 973

Helicopter Support Squadron 5
Naval Station, Guam, Guam, 1047

Helicopter Training Squadron 8
Whiting Field Naval Air Station, Milton, FL, 213

Helicopter Training Squadron 18
Whiting Field Naval Air Station, Milton, FL, 213

Herongen Storage Area
254th Base Support Battalion, Netherlands, 1127

HHD Stare Area Readiness Command
Camp Keyes, Augusta, ME, 392

High Tech Regional Training Center
Tobyhanna Army Depot, Tobyhanna, PA, 721

Hill 365 Radio Relay Facility
Kaiserslautern Military Community, Germany, 1013

Hohenfels Combat Maneuver Training Center
282nd Base Support Battalion, Germany, 995

Hohenstadt Radio Relay Station
Augsburg Military Community, Germany, 999

Hollis Plaines (ARNG)
Hollis Plaines, Buxton, ME, 397

Holston Defense Corp
Holston Army Ammunition Plant, Kingsport, TN, 760

HQ & Service Bn
Quantico Marine Corps Combat Development Command, Quantico, VA, 895

HS-14
Atsugi Naval Air Facility, Japan, 1063

HSC, 16th Medical Bn, Area Support
Camp Hialeah, Korea, Republic of, 1099

HSL-51
Atsugi Naval Air Facility, Japan, 1063

Human Resource Management School
Maxwell Air Force Base, Maxwell AFB, AL, 8

Human Resources Office
Barstow, Marine Corps Logistics Base, Barstow, CA, 57

Human Systems Center
Brooks Air Force Base, San Antonio, TX, 815

Humphreys Engineer Center Support Activity
Humphreys Engineer Center, Fort Belvoir, VA, 867

Huntsville Virtual Reality Alabama
Redstone Arsenal, Redstone Arsenal, AL, 16

Hydromechanics Directorate
Carderock Division, Naval Surface Warfare Center, West Bethesda, MD, 429

Hythe Depot Activity
Hythe Depot Activity, United Kingdom, 1160

I & I Staff HQ Bn
Indianapolis Naval & Marine Corps Reserve Readiness Center, Indianapolis, IN, 335

I & I Staff (USMC)
Greensboro Naval & Marine Corps Reserve Readiness Center, Greensboro, NC, 626
San Diego Naval & Marine Corps Reserve Center, San Diego, CA, 120

I & I Unit (USMC)
Tacoma Naval & Marine Corps Reserve Center, Tacoma, WA, 937

I Corps
Fort Lewis, Fort Lewis, WA, 921

I G Brown Professional Military Education Center (ANG)
McGee Tyson Airport, Air National Guard Base, Knoxville, TN, 762

IBU-11
Seattle Naval Reserve Readiness Center, Seattle, WA, 930

IBU-12
Seattle Naval Reserve Readiness Center, Seattle, WA, 930

Idaho Army National Guard, HQ
Boise Air Terminal, Air National Guard Base, Boise, ID, 295

Idaho National Guard
Adjutant Genral of Idaho, Boise, ID, 294

Idar Oberstein Family Housing
Baumholder Military Community, H.D. Smith Barracks, Germany, 1003

Illinois Air National Guard, Headquarters
O'Hare International Airport Air Reserve Station, O'Hare IAP ARS, IL, 311

Illinois National Guard
Adjutant General of Illinois, Springfield, IL, 319

Immigration & Naturalization Service
Boston Coast Guard Reserve Center, Boston, MA, 432

Indiana National Guard
Adjutant General of Indiana, Indianapolis, IN, 332

Industrial Operations Command
US Army Corps of Engineers, Rock Island District, Rock Island, IL, 316

Industrial Operations Command, HQ
Rock Island Arsenal, Rock Island, IL, 314

Industrial Plant Equipment Machines
Defense Industrial Plant Equipment Facility, Atchison, KS, 351

Infantry Training Brigade
Fort Benning, Fort Benning, GA, 248

Information Management Directorate
Army Reserve Personnel Center, Saint Louis, MO, 510

Information & Management Support Team
Industrial Analysis Support Office, Philadelphia, PA, 713

Information Resources Management Directorate
Albany Marine Corps Logistics Base, Albany, GA, 239

Information Sciences and Technology Directorate
Adelphi Laboratory Center, Army Research Laboratory, Adelphi, MD, 405

Information Warfare Division
Point Mugu, Naval Air Weapons Station, Point Mugu, CA, 98

INSCOM Support Element
Zoeckler Station, Korea, Republic of, 1122

INSCOM Training and Doctrine Support Det
Fort Huachuca, Fort Huachuca, AZ, 35

Inshore Boat Unit 13
Portland Naval & Marine Corps Reserve Readiness Center, Portland, OR, 688

Inspector-Instructor 2nd Bn 25th Marines
1st Marine Corps District Headquarters, Garden City, NY, 588

Inspector-Instructor Staff
Fort Wayne Marine Corps Reserve Center, Fort Wayne, IN, 329

Inspector-Instructor (USMC)
Phoenix Naval & Marine Corps Reserve Readiness Center, Phoenix, AZ, 40

Installation Support Unit, Camp Shelby
Camp Shelby Training Site, Camp Shelby, MS, 478

Institute of Heraldry
Fort Belvoir, Fort Belvoir, VA, 866

Instrumentation Development Directorate
White Sands Missile Range, White Sands Missile Range, NM, 574

Integrated Combat System Test Facility, San Diego
Port Hueneme Division, Naval Surface Warfare Center, Port Hueneme, CA, 103

Integrated Logistics Support Directorate
Albany Marine Corps Logistics Base, Albany, GA, 239

Integrated Ship Defense Systems Engineering Center (ISDSEC)
AEGIS Combat Systems Center, Wallops Island, VA, 905

Integrated Support Command, Alameda
Alameda Coast Guard Integrated Support Command, Alameda, CA, 54

Integrated Support Command, Cleveland
9th Coast Guard District Headquarters, Cleveland, OH, 648

Integrated Support Command, Honolulu
Honolulu Coast Guard Base/Station, Honolulu, HI, 275

Integrated Support Command, Ketchikan
Ketchikan Coast Guard Station, Ketchikan, AK, 30

Integrated Support Command, Miami
Miami Beach Coast Guard Group/Station, Miami Beach, FL, 212

Integrated Support Command, San Pedro
San Pedro Coast Guard Support Center, San Pedro, CA, 131

Integrated Support Command, Seattle
Seattle Coast Guard Integrated Support Command, Seattle, WA, 929

Intel Programs Office (NR)
Honolulu Naval & Marine Corps Reserve Readiness Center, Honolulu, HI, 276

Intelligence Analysis System
Point Mugu, Naval Air Weapons Station, Point Mugu, CA, 98

Intelligence Systems Flight
Ramstein Air Base, Germany, 1023

Inter-American Defense College
Fort Lesley J McNair, Washington, DC, 177

Inter-American Naval Telecommunications Network
Panama Canal Naval Station, Panama, 1137

Inter-American Air Forces Academy
Kelly Air Force Base, Kelly AFB, TX, 807
Lackland Air Force Base, Lackland AFB, TX, 809

International Ice Patrol, Avery Point, Groton
Coast Guard Academy, New London, CT, 161

Investigative Services, Boston
1st Coast Guard District, Boston, MA, 431

Investigative Services, Chesapeake Region
Atlantic Area & Fifth Coast Guard District HQ, Portsmouth, VA, 890

Investigative Services, Gulf Region
8th Coast Guard District, New Orleans, LA, 380

Investigative Services, Pacific Region
Alameda Coast Guard Integrated Support Command, Alameda, CA, 54

Investigative Services, Seattle
13th Coast Guard District Office, Seattle, WA, 928

Ionizing Radiation Dosimetry Center
Blue Grass Army Depot, Richmond, KY, 373

Iowa Air National Guard
Camp Dodge Iowa, Johnston, IA, 346

Iowa Army Ammunition Plant
Iowa Army Ammunition Plant, Middletown, IA, 347

Iowa Army National Guard, Headquarters
Camp Dodge Iowa, Johnston, IA, 346

Iowa National Guard
Adjutant General of Iowa, Johnston, IA, 345

Ireland Army Community Hospital
Army Armor Center & Fort Knox, Fort Knox, KY, 366

Izmir AS
Izmir Air Station, Turkey, 1153

ISR Institute of Surgical Research
Fort Sam Houston, Fort Sam Houston, TX, 794

Thomas Jefferson Village Family Housing
293rd Base Support Battalion, Germany, 996

Jefferson Village Family Housing
223rd Base Support Battalion, Germany, 993

Jim Creek Regional Outdoor Recreation Area
Jim Creek Naval Radio Station (T), Arlington, WA, 911

Johnson Barracks
282nd Base Support Battalion, Germany, 995

Johnston Atoll Chemical Agent Disposal System
Army Chemical Activity Pacific, Johnston Atoll, 1086

Joint Analysis Center (USEUCOM JAC)
Molesworth RAF Base, United Kingdom, 1168

Joint Communications Support Element
MacDill Air Force Base, MacDill AFB, FL, 209

Joint Computer-aided Acquisition & Logistics Systems (JCALS)
Fort Monmouth, Fort Monmouth, NJ, 557

Joint Fleet Telecommunications Operations Center (JFTOC)
Naval Computer & Telecommunications Area Master Station MED, Naples, Italy, 1056

Joint Forces Brig, Okinawa
Camp Hansen, Japan, 1067

Joint Interagency Task Force East (JIATF East)
Key West Naval Air Facility, Boca Chica Key, FL, 191

Joint Interagency Task Force West
Alameda Coast Guard Integrated Support Command, Alameda, CA, 54

Joint Interoperability & Engineering Organization (JIEO)
Fort Monmouth, Fort Monmouth, NJ, 557

Joint Interoperability Test Center (JITC)
Cheltenham Naval Communication Detachment, Cheltenham, MD, 418

Joint Interservice Regional Support Group (North 14)
Fort Dix, Fort Dix, NJ, 555

Joint Language Training Center (JLTC)
Camp W G Williams, Riverton, UT, 827

Joint Logistics Systems Center
Wright-Patterson Air Force Base, Wright-Patterson AFB, OH, 667

Joint National Test Facility
Falcon Air Force Base, Falcon AFB, CO, 151

Joint Personal Property Shipping Office, Washington Area (JPPSOWA)
Military District of Washington, Washington, DC, 179

Joint Readiness Training Center
Fort Polk, Fort Polk, LA, 377

Joint Rear Area Coordinator (JRAC)
Eskan Village, Saudi Arabia, 1145

Joint Security Force
Joint Task Force—Bravo, Honduras, 1048

Joint Services Recreation Center
Kilauea Military Camp, Joint Services Recreation Center, Hawaii National Park, HI, 270

Joint Signal Group
Vecihi Akin Garrison, Turkey, 1154

Joint Special Operations Command
Fort Bragg, Fort Bragg, NC, 624
Pope Air Force Base, Pope AFB, NC, 629

Joint Targeting School
Dam Neck, Fleet Combat Training Center, Atlantic, Virginia Beach, VA, 902

Joint Task Force, Full Accounting
Camp H M Smith, Camp Smith, HI, 266

Joint Task Force, Southwest Asia
Eskan Village, Saudi Arabia, 1145

Joint Visual Information Activity
Tobyhanna Army Depot, Tobyhanna, PA, 721

Joint Warfare Center
Hurlburt Field, Hurlburt Field, FL, 200

Joliet Army Ammunition Plant
Joliet Army Ammunition Plant, Wilmington, IL, 322

JTUAV Protect Office
Redstone Arsenal, Redstone Arsenal, AL, 16

Jungle Operations Training Bn
Fort Clayton, Panama, 1133
Fort Sherman, Panama, 1135

Kaiserslautern Army Depot
Kaiserslautern Military Community, Germany, 1013

Kaiserslautern East Community Facility
Kaiserslautern Military Community, Germany, 1013

Kaiserslautern Equipment Support Center
Kaiserslautern Military Community, Germany, 1013

Kaiserslautern Law Center
Kleber Kaserne (Kaiserslautern Law Center), Germany, 1019

Kalb Family Housing
282nd Base Support Battalion, Germany, 995

Kansas National Guard
Adjutant General of Kansas, Topeka, KS, 359

Kapaun Air Station
Kaiserslautern Military Community, Germany, 1013
Kapaun Air Station, Germany, 1014
Ramstein Air Base, Germany, 1023

Kastel Housing Area
221st Base Support Battalion, Germany, 992

Kastel Storage Facility
221st Base Support Battalion, Germany, 992

Kastner Army Airfield
Camp Zama, Japan, 1071

Katusa Training Academy
Camp Humphreys, Korea, Republic of, 1102

Kefurt Family Housing
6th Area Support Group, Stuttgart, Germany, 988

Keller Army Community Hospital
West Point, Army Garrison, West Point, NY, 614

Kelley Barracks
6th Area Support Group, Stuttgart, Germany, 988
223rd Base Support Battalion, Germany, 993

Kentucky Army National Guard, Military Academy
Army Armor Center & Fort Knox, Fort Knox, KY, 366

Kentucky National Guard
Adjutant General of Kentucky, Frankfort, KY, 367

Kerzenheim Communication Facility
293rd Base Support Battalion, Germany, 996

Keesler Area Audit Office
Keesler Air Force Base, Keesler AFB, MS, 487

Kilbourne Kaserne
Heidelberg Military Community, Germany, 1011

Kimborough Ambulatory Care Center
Fort George G Meade, Fort Meade, MD, 422

Dr Martin Luther King Village
221st Base Support Battalion, Germany, 992

Kitzingen Family Housing
Kitzingen Military Community, Germany, 1017

Kitzingen Training Areas
Kitzingen Military Community, Germany, 1017

Kleber Kaserne
Kaiserslautern Military Community, Germany, 1013

Knowledge Engineering Group (KEG)
Carlisle Barracks, Carlisle Barracks, PA, 698

Königstuhl Radio Relay Station
Heidelberg Military Community, Germany, 1011

Kwajalein Missile Range
Kwajalein Missile Range, Marshall Islands, 1124

LA National Guard
Longhorn/Louisiana Army Ammunition Plant, Minden, LA, 379

Lakehurst Naval Air Engineering Station
Lakehurst Naval Air Engineering Station, Lakehurst, NJ, 560

Lampertheim Training Area
293rd Base Support Battalion, Germany, 996

Land Forces Southeastern Europe (LANDSOUTHEAST)
Vecihi Akin Garrison, Turkey, 1154

Land Management Laboratory
US Army Corps of Engineers, Construction Engineering Research Laboratories, Champaign, IL, 300

Land, Sea, Air, Simulators & Combat Support Operations Team
Industrial Analysis Support Office, Philadelphia, PA, 713

Landstuhl Hospital
Kaiserslautern Military Community, Germany, 1013

Langen Terrace Family Housing
223rd Base Support Battalion, Germany, 993

Large Cavitation Channel, Memphis Det
Memphis Detachment, Large Cavitation Channel, Memphis, TN, 763

Larson Barracks
Kitzingen Military Community, Germany, 1017

Laser and Surveillance Systems Group
Point Mugu, Naval Air Weapons Station, Point Mugu, CA, 98

Laughlin Civil Service Aircraft Maintenance (LCSAM)
Laughlin Air Force Base, Laughlin AFB, TX, 810

Law Enforcement Command
Fort Riley, Fort Riley, KS, 353

Lawson Army Airfield
Fort Benning, Fort Benning, GA, 248

Leadership Academy, 80th Training Support Brigade, 80th Division
Fort A P Hill, Bowling Green, VA, 855

Lechfeld Training Area
Augsburg Military Community, Germany, 999

Ledward Barracks
280th Base Support Battalion, Germany, 994

Lee Barracks
221st Base Support Battalion, Germany, 992

Legal Service Office Det, Cecil Field (NLSO)
Cecil Field Naval Air Station, Jacksonville, FL, 202

Leighton Barracks
98th Area Support Group, Germany, 990

Leistadt Communication Facility Hill 460
293rd Base Support Battalion, Germany, 996

Libby Noncommissioned Officer Academy
Fort Leonard Wood, Fort Leonard Wood, MO, 501

Light Armored Vehicle Test Directorate
Yuma Proving Ground, Yuma, AZ, 46

Light Station, Egmont Key
Egmont Key Coast Guard Light Station, Saint Petersburg, FL, 230

Lincoln Village Family Housing
223rd Base Support Battalion, Germany, 993

Lockheed Martin Skunk Works
Production Flight Test Installation, Air Force Plant 42, Palmdale, CA, 94

Logistics Group Western Pacific
Logistics Group Western Pacific, Singapore, 1147

Logistics Support Activity (LOGSA)
Redstone Arsenal, Redstone Arsenal, AL, 16

Logistics Transportation
Gunter Annex, Gunter, AL, 6

Lohnsfeld Communication Station
293rd Base Support Battalion, Germany, 996

Lone Peak Facility (UT Dept. of Corrections)
Camp W G Williams, Riverton, UT, 827

Long Range Surveillance Det
Camp Hovey, Korea, Republic of, 1100

Longare Communication Site
Caserma Ederle/Vicenza Military Community, Vincenza, Italy, 1060

Loran Monitor Station, Kodiak
Kodiak Coast Guard Integrated Support Command, Kodiak, AK, 32

Loran Station Narrow Cape
Kodiak Coast Guard Integrated Support Command, Kodiak, AK, 32

Louisiana Air National Guard, HQ
Jackson Barracks, New Orleans, LA, 382

Louisiana Military Academy (NCOA & OCS)
Camp Beauregard, Pineville, LA, 388

Louisiana National Guard
Adjutant General of Louisiana, New Orleans, LA, 381

LST-1184 Support Unit Det B (NR)
Lincoln Naval Reserve Center, Lincoln, NE, 529

Lualualei Naval Magazine
Lualualei Naval Magazine, Waianae, HI, 289

M1 Abrams Tank Materiel Fielding Team
Hunter Army Air Field, Savannah, GA, 260

MACG-48
Atlanta Naval Air Station, Marietta, GA, 254

Machinery In-Service Engineering Directorate
Carderock Division, Naval Surface Warfare Center, West Bethesda, MD, 429

Machinery Research and Development Directorate
Carderock Division, Naval Surface Warfare Center, West Bethesda, MD, 429
Naval Surface Warfare Center, Carderock Division, Annapolis Detachment, Annapolis, MD, 410

Madigan Army Medical Center
Fort Lewis, Fort Lewis, WA, 921

Mail Service Branch Postal Inspection & Audit Division
Army Postal Group Europe, Rheinau, Germany, 1026

Maine Military Academy
Camp Keyes, Augusta, ME, 392

Maine National Guard
Adjutant General of Maine, Augusta, ME, 391

Maintenance Activity #10 (WANG)
Vancouver Barracks, Vancouver, WA, 938

Maintenance Branch
Balikesir Air Field, Turkey, 1151

Maintenance Center
Barstow, Marine Corps Logistics Base, Barstow, CA, 57

Maintenance & Logistics Command, Pacific
Alameda Coast Guard Integrated Support Command, Alameda, CA, 54

Maintenance Readiness Branch
Camp Shelby Training Site, Camp Shelby, MS, 478

Mainz Area Support Team
221st Base Support Battalion, Germany, 992

Mainz Repair and Upkeep Area
221st Base Support Battalion, Germany, 992

Major Port Command
Charleston, Naval Weapons Station, Charleston, SC, 734

Major Shared Resource Center
Wright-Patterson Air Force Base, Wright-Patterson AFB, OH, 667

Malcolm Grow Medical Center
Andrews Air Force Base, Andrews AFB, MD, 407

Mannheim Class III Point
293rd Base Support Battalion, Germany, 996

Mannheim Law Center
Taylor Barracks, Germany, 1034

Mannheim Military Community
Funari Barracks, Germany, 1008

Det 5, MARFORPAC
Saint Louis Naval & Marine Corps Reserve Center, Bridgeton, MO, 499

Marine Aerial Navigation School
Randolph Air Force Base, Randolph AFB, TX, 814

Marine Aerial Refueler Transport Squadron 152
Futenma, Marine Corps Air Station, Japan, 1072

Marine Aerial Refueller Transport Squadron (VMGR 234)
Fort Worth, Naval Air Station, Joint Reserve Base, Fort Worth, TX, 796

Marine Air Control Group 18
Futenma, Marine Corps Air Station, Japan, 1072

Marine Air Control Group 28
Cherry Point Marine Corps Air Station, Cherry Point, NC, 621

Marine Air Control Squadron 2
Beaufort Marine Corps Air Station, Beaufort, SC, 730

Marine Air Control Squadron 4
Futenma, Marine Corps Air Station, Japan, 1072

Marine Air Control Squadron 7
Yuma Marine Corps Air Station, Yuma, AZ, 45

Marine Air Control Squadron 23 (MACS-23), MACG-48
Cheyenne Naval Reserve Center, Cheyenne, WY, 966

Marine Air Control Squadron 24
Dam Neck, Fleet Combat Training Center, Atlantic, Virginia Beach, VA, 902

Marine Air-Ground Task Force Warfighting Center
Quantico Marine Corps Combat Development Command, Quantico, VA, 895

Marine Air Group 12
Iwakuni Marine Corps Air Station, Japan, 1073

Marine Air Group 42 (MAG-42)
Atlanta Naval Air Station, Marietta, GA, 254

Marine Air Group 46 (Marine Reserve)
New Orleans Naval Air Station Joint Reserve Base, Naval Air Station, New Orleans, LA, 384

Marine Air Logistics Squadron 49 (MALS-49) MAG-49
Stewart Air National Guard Base, Newburgh, NY, 599

Marine Air Support Squadron 2
Futenma, Marine Corps Air Station, Japan, 1072

Marine Air Transport Refueler Group (VMGR-452)
Stewart Air National Guard Base, Newburgh, NY, 599

Marine Aircraft Group 11
Miramar Marine Corps Air Station, San Diego, CA, 113

Marine Aircraft Group 13 (MAG-13)
Yuma Marine Corps Air Station, Yuma, AZ, 45

Marine Aircraft Group 14 (MAG-14)
Cherry Point Marine Corps Air Station, Cherry Point, NC, 621

Marine Aircraft Group 16 (MAG-16)
Tustin Marine Corps Air Station, Tustin, CA, 138

Marine Aircraft Group 26 (MAG-26)
New River Marine Corps Air Station, Jacksonville, NC, 627

Marine Aircraft Group 29 (MAG-29)
New River Marine Corps Air Station, Jacksonville, NC, 627

Marine Aircraft Group 31
Beaufort Marine Corps Air Station, Beaufort, SC, 730

Marine Aircraft Group 36
Futenma, Marine Corps Air Station, Japan, 1072

Marine Aircraft Group 39 (MAG-39)
Camp Pendleton Marine Corps Base, Oceanside, CA, 91

Marine Aircraft Group 41 (MAG 41)
Fort Worth, Naval Air Station, Joint Reserve Base, Fort Worth, TX, 796
Washington, DC, Naval Air Facility, Andrews AFB, MD, 408

Marine Aircraft Group 42, Det a
Cecil Field Naval Air Station, Jacksonville, FL, 202

Marine Aircraft Group 46
Miramar Marine Corps Air Station, San Diego, CA, 113

Marine Aircraft Group 46, Det B
El Toro Marine Corps Air Station, Santa Ana, CA, 132

Marine Aircraft Group 49 (MAG-49)
Andrews Air Force Base, Andrews AFB, MD, 407
Willow Grove Naval Air Station (JRB), Willow Grove, PA, 723

Marine Aircraft Group 49, Det B (MAG-49)
Stewart Air National Guard Base, Newburgh, NY, 599

Marine Aircraft Support Det HQ (MASD)
Washington, DC, Naval Air Facility, Andrews AFB, MD, 408

Marine Attack Helicopter Squadron HMLA-773
Atlanta Naval Air Station, Marietta, GA, 254

Marine Attack Squadron 211
Wake Island Missile Launch Facility, Wake Island, 1172
Yuma Marine Corps Air Station, Yuma, AZ, 45

Marine Attack Squadron 214
Yuma Marine Corps Air Station, Yuma, AZ, 45

Marine Attack Squadron 311
Yuma Marine Corps Air Station, Yuma, AZ, 45

Marine Attack Squadron 513
Yuma Marine Corps Air Station, Yuma, AZ, 45

Marine Aviation Det
Patuxent River, Naval Air Station, Patuxent River, MD, 427

Marine Aviation Logistics Squadron 11
Miramar Marine Corps Air Station, San Diego, CA, 113

Marine Aviation Logistics Squadron 12
Iwakuni Marine Corps Air Station, Japan, 1073

Marine Aviation Logistics Squadron 36
Futenma, Marine Corps Air Station, Japan, 1072

Marine Aviation Logistics Squadron (MALS 41)
Fort Worth, Naval Air Station, Joint Reserve Base, Fort Worth, TX, 796

Marine Aviation Logistics Support Element, Kaneohe
Kaneohe Bay Marine Corps Base, Kaneohe Bay, HI, 278

Marine Aviation Training Support Command (MATSG)
Corpus Christi Naval Air Station, Corpus Christi, TX, 780

Marine Aviation Training Support Group
Cecil Field Naval Air Station, Jacksonville, FL, 202
Lemoore Naval Air Station, Lemoore, CA, 74
Meridian Naval Air Station, Meridian, MS, 489
Pensacola Naval Air Station, Pensacola, FL, 225
Whidbey Island Naval Air Station, Oak Harbor, WA, 924

Marine Band
Marine Barracks Washington DC, Washington, DC, 178

Marine Barracks, Guantanamo Bay
Guantanamo Bay, Naval Base, Cuba, 981

Marine Barracks, HI
Marine Barracks, Hawaii, Pearl Harbor, HI, 282

Marine Barracks, Japan, Sasebo Det
Sasebo, US Fleet Activities, Japan, 1080

Marine Corps Absentee Collection Unit
Great Lakes Naval Training Center, Great Lakes, IL, 308

HQ, Marine Corps Air Bases, Western Area
El Toro Marine Corps Air Station, Santa Ana, CA, 132

Marine Corps Air Facility Quantico
Quantico Marine Corps Combat Development Command, Quantico, VA, 895

Marine Corps Air Ground Combat Center
Twentynine Palms Marine Corps Air Ground Combat Center, Twentynine Palms, CA, 139

Marine Corps Air Station, Beaufort
Beaufort Marine Corps Air Station, Beaufort, SC, 730

Marine Corps Air Station, New River
New River Marine Corps Air Station, Jacksonville, NC, 627

Marine Corps Association
Quantico Marine Corps Combat Development Command, Quantico, VA, 895

Marine Corps Band, Marine Corps Logistics Base
Albany Marine Corps Logistics Base, Albany, GA, 239

Marine Corps Base
Camp Foster, Japan, 1066

Marine Corps Base, Camp Smedley D Butler
Camp Smedley D Butler, MCB, Japan, 1064

Marine Corps Base, Camp Lejeune
Camp Lejeune Marine Corps Base, Camp Lejeune, NC, 618

Marine Corps Base, Camp Pendleton
Camp Pendleton Marine Corps Base, Oceanside, CA, 91

HQ Bn, Marine Corps Base, HI
Kaneohe Bay Marine Corps Base, Kaneohe Bay, HI, 278

Marine Corps Base, Quantico
Quantico Marine Corps Combat Development Command, Quantico, VA, 895

Marine Corps Color Guard
Marine Barracks Washington DC, Washington, DC, 178

Marine Corps Combat Development Command
Quantico Marine Corps Combat Development Command, Quantico, VA, 895

Marine Corps Communication-Electronics School
Twentynine Palms Marine Corps Air Ground Combat Center, Twentynine Palms, CA, 139

Marine Corps Det
Goodfellow Air Force Base, Goodfellow AFB, TX, 801

Torii Station, Japan, 1082

Marine Corps Det, Newport
Naval Education and Training Center, Newport, Newport, RI, 726

Marine Corps Eastern Recruiting Region
Parris Island Marine Corps Recruit Depot/Eastern Recruiting Region, Parris Island, SC, 747

Marine Corps Expeditionary Warfare Training Group, Atlantic, Amphibious Reconnaissance School
Fort Story, Fort Story, VA, 871

Marine Corps Field Artillery
Fort Sill, Fort Sill, OK, 671

HQ Bn, HQ US Marine Corps
Henderson Hall, HQ USMC, Arlington, VA, 848

Marine Corps Institute
Marine Barracks Washington DC, Washington, DC, 178

Marine Corps Intelligence Activity
Quantico Marine Corps Combat Development Command, Quantico, VA, 895

Marine Corps Liaison Office
Army Transportation Center & Fort Eustis, Fort Eustis, VA, 868

Marine Corps Mountain Warfare Training Center
Camp Pendleton Marine Corps Base, Oceanside, CA, 91

US Marine Corps Naval Academy Co
Annapolis Naval Station, Annapolis, MD, 409

Marine Corps Operational Test and Evaluation Activity
Quantico Marine Corps Combat Development Command, Quantico, VA, 895

Marine Corps Program Office
Hawthorne Army Depot, Hawthorne, NV, 537

Marine Corps Readiness Center, Norfolk
Norfolk Naval & Marine Corps Reserve Readiness Center, Norfolk, VA, 883

Marine Corps Recruit Depot
Parris Island Marine Corps Recruit Depot/Eastern Recruiting Region, Parris Island, SC, 747

US Marine Corps Recruiting Office
Worcester Naval & Marine Corps Reserve Center, Worcester, MA, 448

Marine Corps Recruiting Station
Defense Distribution Region East, New Cumberland, PA, 709

Marine Corps Reserve Center
Camp Joseph T Robinson, North Little Rock, AR, 52

Roosevelt Roads Naval Station, Puerto Rico, 1143

Marine Corps Reserve Center, Brooklyn
Brooklyn Coast Guard Air Station, Brooklyn, NY, 579

Marine Corps Reserve Center, Washington
Anacostia Naval Station, Washington, DC, 171

Marine Corps Reserve Center, Youngstown
Youngstown-Warren Regional Airport, Air Reserve Station, Vienna, OH, 666

Marine Corps Reserve Readiness Center, Alameda
Alameda Naval & Marine Corps Reserve Readiness Center, Alameda, CA, 55

Marine Corps Reserve Readiness Center, Charleston
Charleston, Naval & Marine Corps Reserve Readiness Center, Charleston, SC, 733

Marine Corps Reserve Training
Corpus Christi Army Depot, Corpus Christi, TX, 779

Marine Corps Reserve Training Center
Fort Lewis, Fort Lewis, WA, 921

Milwaukee Coast Guard Base/Group, Milwaukee, WI, 961

Marine Corps Security Co, Puerto Rico
Sabana Seca, US Naval Security Group Activity, Puerto Rico, 1144

Marine Corps Security Force Co
North Island Naval Air Station, San Diego, CA, 115

Panama Canal Naval Station, Panama, 1137

Rota Naval Station, Spain, 1149

Sigonella Naval Air Station, Italy, 1059

Yorktown Naval Weapons Station, Yorktown, VA, 910

Marine Corps Security Force Co, Bangor
Bangor Naval Submarine Base, Silverdale, WA, 932

Marine Corps Security Force Co, Diego Garcia
Diego Garcia, Naval Support Facility, Diego Garcia, 982

Marine Corps Security Force Co, Kings Bay
Kings Bay Naval Submarine Base, Kings Bay, GA, 253

Marine Corps Security Force Co, London
West Ruislip RAF Base, United Kingdom, 1170

Marine Corps Security Force Co, Naples
Naples (Capodichino) Naval Support Activity, Italy, 1055

Marine Corps Security Force Training Center
Northwest Naval Security Group Activity, Chesapeake, VA, 858

Marine Corps Silent Drill Platoon
Marine Barracks Washington DC, Washington, DC, 178

Marine Corps Systems Command
Quantico Marine Corps Combat Development Command, Quantico, VA, 895

Marine Corps University
Quantico Marine Corps Combat Development Command, Quantico, VA, 895

Marine Drum and Bugle Corps
Marine Barracks Washington DC, Washington, DC, 178

Marine Fighter Attack Squadron 212
Iwakuni Marine Corps Air Station, Japan, 1073

Marine Fighter Attack Squadron 112 (VMFA 112)
Fort Worth, Naval Air Station, Joint Reserve Base, Fort Worth, TX, 796

Marine Fighter Attack Squadron 115
Beaufort Marine Corps Air Station, Beaufort, SC, 730

Marine Fighter Attack Squadron 122
Beaufort Marine Corps Air Station, Beaufort, SC, 730

Marine Fighter Attack Squadron 224
Beaufort Marine Corps Air Station, Beaufort, SC, 730

Marine Fighter Attack Squadron 232
Miramar Marine Corps Air Station, San Diego, CA, 113

Marine Fighter Attack Squadron 251
Beaufort Marine Corps Air Station, Beaufort, SC, 730

Marine Fighter Attack Squadron 312
Beaufort Marine Corps Air Station, Beaufort, SC, 730

Marine Fighter Attack Squadron 332
Beaufort Marine Corps Air Station, Beaufort, SC, 730

Marine Fighter Attack Squadron 451
Beaufort Marine Corps Air Station, Beaufort, SC, 730

Marine Fighter Attack Squadron 533
Beaufort Marine Corps Air Station, Beaufort, SC, 730

Marine Fighter Training Squadron 401
Yuma Marine Corps Air Station, Yuma, AZ, 45

Marine Forces, Pacific Band
Kaneohe Bay Marine Corps Base, Kaneohe Bay, HI, 278

Marine Forces Pacific (MARFORPAC)
Camp H M Smith, Camp Smith, HI, 266

Marine Heavy Helicopter Squadron 362
Kaneohe Bay Marine Corps Base, Kaneohe Bay, HI, 278

Marine Heavy Helicopter Squadron 363
Kaneohe Bay Marine Corps Base, Kaneohe Bay, HI, 278

Marine Heavy Helicopter Squadron 366
Kaneohe Bay Marine Corps Base, Kaneohe Bay, HI, 278

Marine Heavy Helicopter Squadron 463
Kaneohe Bay Marine Corps Base, Kaneohe Bay, HI, 278

Marine Heavy Helicopter Squadron 769
El Toro Marine Corps Air Station, Santa Ana, CA, 132

Marine Helicopter Squadron 1 (HMX-1)
Anacostia Naval Station, Washington, DC, 171
Quantico Marine Corps Combat Development Command, Quantico, VA, 895

Marine Helicopter Training Squadron 301
Kaneohe Bay Marine Corps Base, Kaneohe Bay, HI, 278

Marine Medium Helicopter Squadron 265
Futenma, Marine Corps Air Station, Japan, 1072

Marine Medium Helicopter Squadron 764
El Toro Marine Corps Air Station, Santa Ana, CA, 132

Marine Meteorology Division, Monterey
Naval Research Laboratory, Marine Meteorology Division, Monterey, CA, 84

Marine Observation Squadron VMO-4
Atlanta Naval Air Station, Marietta, GA, 254

Marine Reserve Units
Buckley Air National Guard Base, Aurora, CO, 142

Marine Safety Det, Kodiak
Kodiak Coast Guard Integrated Support Command, Kodiak, AK, 32

Marine Safety Office, Boston
Boston Coast Guard Reserve Center, Boston, MA, 432

Marine Safety Office, Buffalo
Buffalo Coast Guard Group, Buffalo, NY, 582

Marine Safety Office, Charleston
Charleston Coast Guard Group, Charleston, SC, 732

Marine Safety Office, Detroit (Captain of the Port)
Detroit Coast Guard Group/Base, Detroit, MI, 455

Marine Safety Office, Honolulu
Honolulu Coast Guard Base/Station, Honolulu, HI, 275

Marine Safety Office, Milwaukee
Milwaukee Coast Guard Base/Group, Milwaukee, WI, 961

Marine Safety Office, Mobile
Mobile Coast Guard Group/Station, Mobile, AL, 10

Marine Safety Office, Philadelphia
Philadelphia Coast Guard Marine Safety Office & Group, Philadelphia, PA, 714

Marine Safety Office, Puget Sound
Seattle Coast Guard Integrated Support Command, Seattle, WA, 929

Marine Safety Office, San Diego
San Diego Coast Guard Activities, San Diego, CA, 117

Marine Safety Office, San Francisco Bay
Alameda Coast Guard Integrated Support Command, Alameda, CA, 54

Marine Safety Office, Sault
Sault Ste Marie Coast Guard Group, Sault Ste Marie, MI, 462

Marine Safety Office, Seattle
Seattle Coast Guard Integrated Support Command, Seattle, WA, 929

Marine Safety Office, Tampa
Tampa Coast Guard Marine Safety Office, Tampa, FL, 235

Marine Security Guard Bn
Quantico Marine Corps Combat Development Command, Quantico, VA, 895

Marine Support Bn
Rota Naval Station, Spain, 1149

Marine Support Bn, Co K
Corry Station Naval Technical Training Center, Pensacola, FL, 222

Marine Tactical Control Squadron 18
Futenma, Marine Corps Air Station, Japan, 1072

Marine Unmanned Aerial Vehicle Squadron 1
Twentynine Palms Marine Corps Air Ground Combat Center, Twentynine Palms, CA, 139

Marine Wing Headquarters Squadron 1
Camp Foster, Japan, 1066

Marine Wing Support Group 27
Cherry Point Marine Corps Air Station, Cherry Point, NC, 621

Marine Wing Support Group 47
Selfridge Air National Guard Base, Selfridge ANG Base, MI, 464

Marine Wing Support Group 273
Beaufort Marine Corps Air Station, Beaufort, SC, 730

Marine Wing Support Squadron 171
Iwakuni Marine Corps Air Station, Japan, 1073

Marine Wing Support Squadron 172
Futenma, Marine Corps Air Station, Japan, 1072

Marine Wing Support Squadron 272
New River Marine Corps Air Station, Jacksonville, NC, 627

Marine Wing Support Squadron 371
Yuma Marine Corps Air Station, Yuma, AZ, 45

Det A, Marine Wing Support Squadron 471 (MWSS-471)
Minneapolis Naval Air Reserve Center, Minneapolis, MN, 472

Det B, Marine Wing Support Squadron 471 (MWSS-471)
Green Bay Naval & Marine Corps Reserve Center, Green Bay, WI, 955

Marine Wing Support Squadron 473
El Toro Marine Corps Air Station, Santa Ana, CA, 132

Maritime Defense Command 11, Coast Guard Pacific Region
Alameda Coast Guard Integrated Support Command, Alameda, CA, 54

Maritime Defense Command 13
13th Coast Guard District Office, Seattle, WA, 928

Maritime Defense Zone Sector Southern California Operations Center
Fleet Combat Training Center, Pacific, San Diego, CA, 112

Maritime Liaison Officer, Bahrain
Administrative Support Unit, South West Asia, Bahrain, 973

Maritime Prepositioning Force Program
Charleston, Naval Weapons Station, Charleston, SC, 734

Mark Twain Village Family Housing
Heidelberg Military Community, Germany, 1011
San Diego Fleet and Industrial Supply Center, San Diego, CA, 118

George C Marshall European Center for Security Studies
6th Area Support Group, Garmish, Germany, 987

George C Marshall Kaserne
Rose Barracks, Germany, 1027

George C Marshall Space Flight Center
Redstone Arsenal, Redstone Arsenal, AL, 16

Maryland National Guard
Adjutant General of Maryland, Baltimore, MD, 412

MASC MAG OPS Det 1
Seal Beach Naval Weapons Station, Seal Beach, CA, 133

MASC PIER OPS 3 (NR)
Greensboro Naval & Marine Corps Reserve Readiness Center, Greensboro, NC, 626

MASC PIER OPS Det 1
Seal Beach Naval Weapons Station, Seal Beach, CA, 133

Massachusetts National Guard
Adjutant General of Massachusetts, Reading, MA, 443

Massbach Quick Reaction Site
280th Base Support Battalion, Germany, 994

Material Operations Division, Army National Ground Intelligence Center
Aberdeen Proving Ground, Aberdeen Proving Ground, MD, 404

Materials Research Division
Navy Clothing and Textile Research Facility, Natick, MA, 442

Materials Science and Component Technology Directorate
Naval Research Laboratory, Washington, DC, 182

Materials, Structures & Survivability Directorate
Carderock Division, Naval Surface Warfare Center, West Bethesda, MD, 429

Materiel Readiness Support Activity (MRSA)
Blue Grass Army Depot, Richmond, KY, 373

Materiel Test Directorate
White Sands Missile Range, White Sands Missile Range, NM, 574

MATES
Camp Shelby Training Site, Camp Shelby, MS, 478

McAlester Army Ammunition Plant
McAlester Army Ammunition Plant, McAlester, OK, 673

McArthur Place Family Housing
Friedberg Area Support Team, Germany, 1007

McCully Barracks
221st Base Support Battalion, Germany, 992

McMullen Target Site (near Freer, TX)
Kingsville Naval Air Station, Kingsville, TX, 808

MEDEL (Medical Element)
Joint Task Force—Bravo, Honduras, 1048

Medical Department Activity Japan
Camp Zama, Japan, 1071

Medical Department Activity (MEDDAC)
Fort Benning, Fort Benning, GA, 248

Medical Equipment Maintenance Division
Defense Distribution Region West, Stockton, CA, 134

Medical Maintenance Operations Division-Pennsylvania
Tobyhanna Army Depot, Tobyhanna, PA, 721

Melibokus Radio Relay Station
223rd Base Support Battalion, Germany, 993

Mess Specialist School
Fleet Antisubmarine Warfare Training Center, Pacific, San Diego, CA, 111

Messel Small Arms Range
223rd Base Support Battalion, Germany, 993

METOC
Naval Station, Guam, Guam, 1047

Michigan National Guard
Adjutant General of Michigan, Lansing, MI, 459

Mid-Atlantic Electronic Warfare Range (MAEWR)
Cherry Point Marine Corps Air Station, Cherry Point, NC, 621

Miesau Ammunition Depot
Kaiserslautern Military Community, Germany, 1013

Military Academy, West Point
West Point, Army Garrison, West Point, NY, 614

Military Affiliate Radio System (MARS)
Honolulu Naval & Marine Corps Reserve Readiness Center, Honolulu, HI, 276

Military Air Traffic Coordination Unit
Charleston Air Force Base, Charleston AFB, SC, 737

MDW Engineer Co
Military District of Washington, Washington, DC, 179

Military District of Washington, HQ
Fort Lesley J McNair, Washington, DC, 177

MDW Military Police Co
Fort Myer, Arlington, VA, 847

Military Entrance Processing Station
Defense Distribution Region East, New Cumberland, PA, 709
Fort Buchanan Army Garrison, Puerto Rico, 1141
New York Area Command & Fort Hamilton, Brooklyn, NY, 581

HQ, Support Troop, Military Freefall School
Yuma Proving Ground, Yuma, AZ, 46

Military History Institute
Carlisle Barracks, Carlisle Barracks, PA, 698

Military Intelligence Bn
Joint Task Force—Bravo, Honduras, 1048

Military Operations Team
Industrial Analysis Support Office, Philadelphia, PA, 713

Military Personnel & Adjutant General Services
Fort Dix, Fort Dix, NJ, 555

Military Personnel Division Tripler Army Medical Center
Tripler Army Medical Center, Tripler AMC, HI, 287

Military Police Co B
Pittsburgh Naval & Marine Corps Reserve Readiness Center, North Versailles, PA, 710

Military Retiree Activities Program (RAO)
Defense Supply Center, Columbus, Columbus, OH, 654

Military Sealift Command
Naval District Washington, Washington Navy Yard, Washington, DC, 180
Panama Canal Naval Station, Panama, 1137

Military Sealift Command, Atlantic
Bayonne Military Ocean Terminal, Bayonne, NJ, 552

Military Sealift Command, Far East
Yokosuka, Fleet Activities, Japan, 1083

Military Sealift Command Office
Military Ocean Terminal, Sunny Point, Southport, NC, 633

Military Sealift Command Office, Southwest Asia
Administrative Support Unit, South West Asia, Bahrain, 973

Military Sealift Command Unit, Diego Garcia
Diego Garcia, Naval Support Facility, Diego Garcia, 982

Military Sealift Command, Western Pacific
Naval Station, Guam, Guam, 1047

Military Strategic and Tactical Relay (Milstar)
Falcon Air Force Base, Falcon AFB, CO, 151

Military Traffic Management Command
Fort Buchanan Army Garrison, Puerto Rico, 1141
Rota Naval Station, Spain, 1149

Military Traffic Management Command, Eastern Area
Bayonne Military Ocean Terminal, Bayonne, NJ, 552

Military Traffic Management Command, Europe
Military Traffic Management Command, Europe, Netherlands, 1129

Military Traffic Management Command, Gulf Outport
New Orleans Naval Support Activity, New Orleans, LA, 386

Military Traffic Management Command, HQ
Military Traffic Management Command, HQ, Falls Church, VA, 861

Military Traffic Management Command, Pacific
Wheeler Army Airfield, Wheeler Army Airfield, HI, 293

Military Traffic Management Command Transportation Engineering Agency
Army Transportation Center & Fort Eustis, Fort Eustis, VA, 868

Military Traffic Management Command, Western Area
Military Traffic Management Command, Western Area, Oakland, CA, 89

Military Traffic Management Command, Western Area, HQ
Oakland Army Base, Oakland, CA, 90

Mills Dental Clinic
Fort Dix, Fort Dix, NJ, 555

Mine Countermeasures Squadron 1
Ingleside Naval Station, Ingleside, TX, 806

Mine Countermeasures Squadron 2
Ingleside Naval Station, Ingleside, TX, 806

Mine Warfare Command
Corpus Christi Army Depot, Corpus Christi, TX, 779
Corpus Christi Naval Air Station, Corpus Christi, TX, 780

Mine Warfare Training Center
Ingleside Naval Station, Ingleside, TX, 806

Minimal Essential Airfield (MEA)
Northeast Air Defense Sector, Rome, NY, 604

Minnesota National Guard
Adjutant General of Minnesota, Saint Paul, MN, 475

Missile and Munitions Center and School
Redstone Arsenal, Redstone Arsenal, AL, 16

Missile Launch Facility, Wake Island
Wake Island Missile Launch Facility, Wake Island, 1172

Missile Warning Center
Cheyenne Mountain Air Force Station, Colorado Springs, CO, 145

Missiles School
Dam Neck, Fleet Combat Training Center, Atlantic, Virginia Beach, VA, 902

Mission Support Activity Korea, Configuration Management Office & Installation Team Pacific
Zoeckler Station, Korea, Republic of, 1122

Mississippi Air National Guard Field Training Site, HQ
Gulfport-Biloxi Regional Airport, Air National Guard Base, Gulfport, MS, 481

Mississippi National Guard
Adjutant General of Mississippi, Jackson, MS, 484

Missouri National Guard
Adjutant General of Missouri, Jefferson City, MO, 503

MIUW 106
San Diego Naval & Marine Corps Reserve Center, San Diego, CA, 120

MIUW 107
San Diego Naval & Marine Corps Reserve Center, San Diego, CA, 120

MIUW 213
Milwaukee Naval & Marine Corps Reserve Center, Milwaukee, WI, 962

MIUW Det 201
Toledo Naval & Marine Corps Reserve Center, Perrysburg, OH, 662

MIUWU 210
Baltimore Naval Reserve Readiness Center, Baltimore, MD, 413

MK 48/ADCAP Torpedo Division
Lualualei Naval Magazine, Waianae, HI, 289

MK 48 Shop Admin
Lualualei Naval Magazine, Waianae, HI, 289

Mobile Construction Bn 133
Lemoore Naval Air Station, Lemoore, CA, 74

Mobile Diving Salvage Unit TWO Det
Roosevelt Roads Naval Station, Puerto Rico, 1143

Mobile Equipment Ordnance Center
Albany Marine Corps Logistics Base, Albany, GA, 239

Mobile Mine Assembly Group, Det 5
Sigonella Naval Air Station, Italy, 1059

Mobile Mine Assembly Group, Det 10
Kadena Naval Air Facility, Japan, 1075

Mobile Mine Assembly Group OIC (MOMAG)
Lualualei Naval Magazine, Waianae, HI, 289

Mobile Mine Unit
Earle Naval Weapons Station, Colts Neck, NJ, 554

Mobile Undersea Warfare Unit
Fort Dix, Fort Dix, NJ, 555

Mobilization and Training Equipment Site (MATES)
Camp Blanding Training Site, Starke, FL, 232
Camp Grayling Maneuver Training Center, Grayling, MI, 458
Fort McCoy, Fort McCoy, WI, 954
Western Mobilization & Training Complex, Paso Robles, CA, 95
Yakima Training Center, Yakima, WA, 941

Mobilization and Training Equipment Site (MATES) (WA ANG)
Washington Army National Guard Mobilization and Training Equipment Site, Yakima, WA, 940

Mobilization, Operations and Training Directorate
Army Reserve Personnel Center, Saint Louis, MO, 510

Möhringen Family Housing
6th Area Support Group, Stuttgart, Germany, 988

Moncrief Army Community Hospital
Fort Jackson, Columbia, SC, 740

Monroe County Memorial, Army Reserve Center
Tobyhanna Army Depot, Tobyhanna, PA, 721

Montana National Guard
Adjutant General of Montana, Helena, MT, 522

Morale, Welfare and Recreation Support Activity
Quantico Marine Corps Combat Development Command, Quantico, VA, 895

Morale, Welfare, and Recreation Division
Barstow, Marine Corps Logistics Base, Barstow, CA, 57

Morale, Welfare, and Recreation Division (BUPERS)
Bureau of Naval Personnel Detachment, Memphis, Millington, TN, 767

Mörsfeld Storage Point
Rose Barracks, Germany, 1027

Motor Transport Maintenance Co
Lehigh Valley Naval & Marine Corps Reserve Center, Allentown, PA, 694

Mountain Warfare Training Center (USMC)
Marine Corps Mountain Warfare Training Center, Bridgeport, CA, 59

Mounted Maneuver Battlespace Lab
Army Armor Center & Fort Knox, Fort Knox, KY, 366

Multi-User Engineering Change Proposal Automated Review System
Redstone Arsenal, Redstone Arsenal, AL, 16

Munich AFN Facility
Augsburg Military Community, Germany, 999

Münster Ammunition Depot
Babenhausen Area Support Team, Germany, 1000

MWSS-472
Atlanta Naval Air Station, Marietta, GA, 254

Nahbollenbach Storage Area
Baumholder Military Community, H.D. Smith Barracks, Germany, 1003

NAMTRAGRUDET Mayport
Mayport Naval Air Station, Mayport, FL, 210

NAMTRAGRUDET Widbey Island
Whidbey Island Naval Air Station, Oak Harbor, WA, 924

NAS Cecil Field
Cecil Field Naval Air Station, Detachment Astor, Astor, FL, 190

NASA Ames Research Center/ Dryden Flight Research Facility
Edwards Air Force Base, Edwards AFB, CA, 63

NASA
Houston Coast Guard Air Station, Houston, TX, 804

NASA Flight Operations
Ellington Field, Air National Guard Base, Houston, TX, 803

NASA Transoceanic Abort Landing Site
Moron Air Base, Spain, 1148

NASA White Sands Test Facility
White Sands Missile Range, White Sands Missile Range, NM, 574

National Air Intelligence Center (NAIC)
Wright-Patterson Air Force Base, Wright-Patterson AFB, OH, 667

National Airborne Operations Center
Offutt Air Force Base, Offutt AFB, NE, 530

National Bureau of Standards
Pacific Missile Range Facility, Kekaha, HI, 279

National Defense University
Fort Lesley J McNair, Washington, DC, 177

National Guard Bureau, Installation Restoration Program Branch
Aberdeen Proving Ground, Aberdeen Proving Ground, MD, 404

National Guard Marksmanship Training Unit
Camp Joseph T Robinson, North Little Rock, AR, 52

NIMA, Dissemination Division
National Imagery & Mapping Agency, Dissemination Division, Bethesda, MD, 416

National Imagery and Mapping Agency (NIMA)
Fort Bragg, Fort Bragg, NC, 624
Molesworth RAF Base, United Kingdom, 1168

National Imagery and Mapping Agency, St Louis
National Imagery and Mapping Agency, Saint Louis, Saint Louis, MO, 511

National Naval Dental Center
National Naval Medical Center, Bethesda, MD, 417

NOAA Air Operations Center
MacDill Air Force Base, MacDill AFB, FL, 209

NOAA Weather Station
Fort Dix, Fort Dix, NJ, 555

National Range Operations Directorate
White Sands Missile Range, White Sands Missile Range, NM, 574

National Security Agency
Fort George G Meade, Fort Meade, MD, 422

National Strike Force Coordination Center
Elizabeth City Coast Guard Support Center, Elizabeth City, NC, 623

National Training Center
Fort Irwin, National Training Center, Fort Irwin, CA, 70

National Weather Service
Camp Navajo, Bellemont, AZ, 34

NAVAIRTERM Norfolk 307 (NR)
Greensboro Naval & Marine Corps Reserve Readiness Center, Greensboro, NC, 626

NAVAIRTERM NORVA Det 609 (NR)
Louisville Naval Reserve Center, Louisville, KY, 371

Naval Academy Preparatory School
Naval Education and Training Center, Newport, Newport, RI, 726

Naval Air Facility
Andrews Air Force Base, Andrews AFB, MD, 407
Mildenhall RAF Base, United Kingdom, 1167

Naval Air Facility, Detroit
Selfridge Air National Guard Base, Selfridge ANG Base, MI, 464

Naval Air Facility, Lajes
Lajes Field, Portugal, 1138

Naval Air Facility, Misawa
Misawa, Naval Air Facility, Japan, 1077

Naval Air Force, Atlantic Fleet
Norfolk Naval Air Station, Norfolk, VA, 882

Commander, Naval Air Force Pacific Fleet, HQ
Coronado Naval Amphibious Base, San Diego, CA, 109

Naval Air Maintenance Training Group
Pensacola Naval Air Station, Pensacola, FL, 225

Naval Air Maintenance Training Group Det
Cecil Field Naval Air Station, Jacksonville, FL, 202

Naval Air Maintenance Training Group, Det, Lemoore
Lemoore Naval Air Station, Lemoore, CA, 74

Naval Air Maintenance Training Group, Det ROTA
Rota Naval Station, Spain, 1149

Naval Air Maintenance Training Group Dets
Oceana Naval Air Station, Virginia Beach, VA, 903

Naval Air Maintenance Training Group Dets, North Island
North Island Naval Air Station, San Diego, CA, 115

Naval Air Mobile Mine Assembly Unit 15 (MOMAU-15)
Kingsville Naval Air Station, Kingsville, TX, 808

Naval Air Reserve
Rickenbacker IAP, Air National Guard Base, Columbus, OH, 655

Naval Air Reserve Center, Lemoore
Lemoore Naval Air Station, Lemoore, CA, 74

Naval Air Reserve Center, Minneapolis
Minneapolis Naval Air Reserve Center, Minneapolis, MN, 472

Naval Air Reserve, Jacksonville
Jacksonville Naval Air Station, Jacksonville, FL, 205

Naval Air Reserve, Point Mugu
Point Mugu, Naval Air Weapons Station, Point Mugu, CA, 98

Naval Air Reserve, Santa Clara
Santa Clara, Naval Air Reserve, Moffett Federal Airfield, CA, 82

Naval Air Reserve Unit
Jacksonville Naval Air Station, Jacksonville, FL, 205

Naval Air Reserve, Whidbey Island
Whidbey Island Naval Air Station, Oak Harbor, WA, 924

Naval Air Station
Patuxent River, Naval Air Station, Patuxent River, MD, 427
Pensacola Naval Air Station, Pensacola, FL, 225

Naval Air Station, Corpus Christi
Corpus Christi Naval Air Station, Corpus Christi, TX, 780

Naval Air Station, Dallas
Dallas Naval Air Station, Dallas, TX, 783

Naval Air Station, Fallon
Fallon Naval Air Station, Fallon, NV, 535

Naval Air Station, Jacksonville
Jacksonville Naval Air Station, Jacksonville, FL, 205

Naval Air Station, Keflavik, Iceland
Kaflavik Naval Air Station, Keflavik, Iceland, 1049

Naval Air Station, Lemoore
Lemoore Naval Air Station, Lemoore, CA, 74

Naval Air Station, New Orleans
New Orleans Naval Air Station Joint Reserve Base, Naval Air Station, New Orleans, LA, 384

Naval Air Station, Norfolk
Norfolk Naval Air Station, Norfolk, VA, 882
Norfolk Naval Base Complex, Norfolk, VA, 885

Naval Air Station, North Island
North Island Naval Air Station, San Diego, CA, 115

Naval Air Station, Whidbey Island
Whidbey Island Naval Air Station, Oak Harbor, WA, 924

Naval Air Station, Willow Grove
Willow Grove Naval Air Station (JRB), Willow Grove, PA, 723

Naval Air Systems Command (NAVAIR)
Patuxent River, Naval Air Station, Patuxent River, MD, 427

Naval Air Technical Training Center
Pensacola Naval Air Station, Pensacola, FL, 225

Naval Air Technical Training Center, Det
Lakehurst Naval Air Engineering Station, Lakehurst, NJ, 560

Naval Air Warfare Center Aircraft Division (NAWCAD)
Patuxent River, Naval Air Station, Patuxent River, MD, 427

Naval Air Warfare Center Aircraft Division, Trenton
Lakehurst Naval Air Engineering Station, Lakehurst, NJ, 560

Naval Air Warfare Center Det
Key West Naval Air Facility, Boca Chica Key, FL, 191

Naval Air Warfare Center Det (DAMO)
Charles Melvin Price Army Support Center, Granite City, IL, 307

Naval Air Warfare Center Weapons Division, China Lake
China Lake Naval Air Weapons Station, China Lake, CA, 60

Naval Air Warfare Center, Weapons Division Det
Yorktown Naval Weapons Station, Yorktown, VA, 910

Naval Air Warfare Center, Weapons Division (NAWCWPNS)
Point Mugu, Naval Air Weapons Station, Point Mugu, CA, 98

Naval Air Warfare Center, Weapons Division, White Sands
White Sands Missile Range, White Sands Missile Range, NM, 574

Naval Air Weapons Station
Point Mugu, Naval Air Weapons Station, Point Mugu, CA, 98

Naval Air Weapons Station, China Lake
China Lake Naval Air Weapons Station, China Lake, CA, 60

Naval Air Weapons Test Squadron
China Lake Naval Air Weapons Station, China Lake, CA, 60

Naval Amphibious Base, Coronado
Coronado Naval Amphibious Base, San Diego, CA, 109

Naval Amphibious Base, Little Creek
Little Creek, Naval Amphibious Base, Norfolk, VA, 880

Naval & Marine Corps Reserve Readiness Center
Naval Education and Training Center, Newport, Newport, RI, 726

Naval Atlantic Meteorology & Oceanography Det
Cecil Field Naval Air Station, Jacksonville, FL, 202
Patuxent River, Naval Air Station, Patuxent River, MD, 427
Roosevelt Roads Naval Station, Puerto Rico, 1143

Naval Audit Site
Naval Education and Training Center, Newport, Newport, RI, 726

Naval Auxiliary Landing Field, Fentres
Fentres Naval Auxiliary Landing Field, Chesapeake, VA, 857
Oceana Naval Air Station, Virginia Beach, VA, 903

Naval Auxiliary Landing Field, Orange Grove
Kingsville Naval Air Station, Kingsville, TX, 808
Orange Grove, Naval Auxiliary Landing Field, Alice, TX, 774

Naval Auxiliary Landing Field, San Clemente Island
North Island Naval Air Station, San Diego, CA, 115

Naval Aviation Depot
Cherry Point Marine Corps Air Station, Cherry Point, NC, 621
Coronado Naval Amphibious Base, San Diego, CA, 109
Jacksonville Naval Air Station, Jacksonville, FL, 205
Norfolk Naval Base Complex, Norfolk, VA, 885
North Island Naval Air Station, San Diego, CA, 115

Naval Aviation Depot, Norfolk
Norfolk Naval Aviation Depot, Norfolk, VA, 884

Naval Aviation Depot Operations Center
Patuxent River, Naval Air Station, Patuxent River, MD, 427

Naval Aviation Engineering Service Unit
Cecil Field Naval Air Station, Jacksonville, FL, 202
Lemoore Naval Air Station, Lemoore, CA, 74
North Island Naval Air Station, San Diego, CA, 115
Rota Naval Station, Spain, 1149
Sigonella Naval Air Station, Italy, 1059

Naval Aviation Maintenance Office
Patuxent River, Naval Air Station, Patuxent River, MD, 427

Naval Aviation Schools Command
Pensacola Naval Air Station, Pensacola, FL, 225

Naval Base Jacksonville, Commander
Jacksonville Naval Air Station, Jacksonville, FL, 205

NAVBASE Norfolk 0702 (NR)
Greensboro Naval & Marine Corps Reserve Readiness Center, Greensboro, NC, 626

Naval Beach Group 2
Little Creek, Naval Amphibious Base, Norfolk, VA, 880

Naval Branch Dental Clinic, Newport
Naval Education and Training Center, Newport, Newport, RI, 726

Naval Branch Dental Clinic, Wahiawa
Naval Computer & Telecommunications Area Master Station, Eastern Pacific, Wahiawa, HI, 288

Naval Branch Medical Clinic
Concord Naval Weapons Station, Concord, CA, 61

Naval Branch Medical Clinic, Wahiawa
Naval Computer & Telecommunications Area Master Station, Eastern Pacific, Wahiawa, HI, 288

Naval Center for Space Technology
Naval Research Laboratory, Washington, DC, 182

Naval Civil Engineer Corps Officers School
Port Hueneme, Naval Construction Battalion Center, Port Hueneme, CA, 104

Naval Civilian Personnel Data Systems Center
Randolph Air Force Base, Randolph AFB, TX, 814

Naval Combat Helicopter Support Unit 5
Andersen Air Force Base, Guam, 1043

Naval Command, Control and Ocean Surveillance Center, Headquarters
Fleet Combat Training Center, Pacific, San Diego, CA, 112

Naval Command, Control, and Ocean Surveillance Center, In-Service Engineering
Naval Education and Training Center, Newport, Newport, RI, 726

Naval Communications Station
Stockton Naval Communications Station, Stockton, CA, 135

Naval Computer and Telecommunications Area Master Station
Norfolk Naval Base Complex, Norfolk, VA, 885

Naval Computer and Telecommunications Area Master Station, Atlantic Det
Key West Naval Air Facility, Boca Chica Key, FL, 191
Naval Education and Training Center, Newport, Newport, RI, 726

Naval Computer and Telecommunications Area Master Station, Eastern Pacific
Naval Computer & Telecommunications Area Master Station, Eastern Pacific, Wahiawa, HI, 288

Naval Computer and Telecommunications Area Master Station MED, Naples
Naval Computer & Telecommunications Area Master Station MED, Naples, Italy, 1056

Naval Computer and Telecommunications Area Master Station (NCTAMS-Guam)
Naval Station, Guam, Guam, 1047

Naval Computer and Telecommunications Area Master Station WESTPAC
Naval Computer & Telecommunications Area Master Station, WESTPAC, Guam, 1046

MARS
San Diego Fleet and Industrial Supply Center, San Diego, CA, 118

Naval Computer and Telecommunications Command
Naval Security Station, Washington, DC, 183

Naval Computer and Telecommunications Station
Roosevelt Roads Naval Station, Puerto Rico, 1143
Rota Naval Station, Spain, 1149
Sigonella Naval Air Station, Italy, 1059

Naval Computer and Telecommunications Station, Cutler
Cutler Naval Computer & Telecommunications Station, Cutler, ME, 399

Naval Computer and Telecommunications Station, Diego Garcia
Diego Garcia, Naval Support Facility, Diego Garcia, 982

Naval Computer and Telecommunications Station, Puget Sound
Naval Computer and Telecommunications Station, Puget Sound, Silverdale, WA, 933

Naval Computer and Telecommunications Station, Washington, DC
Washington, Naval Station, Washington, DC, 189

Naval Consolidated Brig
Charleston, Naval Weapons Station, Charleston, SC, 734

Naval Construction Bn Center
Port Hueneme, Naval Construction Battalion Center, Port Hueneme, CA, 104

Naval Construction Bn Unit 403
Annapolis Naval Station, Annapolis, MD, 409

Naval Construction Bn Unit 415
Oceana Naval Air Station, Virginia Beach, VA, 903

Naval Construction Bn (USNR)
Rickenbacker IAP, Air National Guard Base, Columbus, OH, 655

Naval Construction Force Support Unit TWO
Port Hueneme, Naval Construction Battalion Center, Port Hueneme, CA, 104

Naval Construction Training Center
Gulfport Naval Construction Battalion Center, Gulfport, MS, 482
Port Hueneme, Naval Construction Battalion Center, Port Hueneme, CA, 104

Naval Criminal Investigation Service Office
Worcester Naval & Marine Corps Reserve Center, Worcester, MA, 448

Naval Criminal Investigative Service
Concord Naval Weapons Station, Concord, CA, 61
Corry Station Naval Technical Training Center, Pensacola, FL, 222
Great Lakes Naval Training Center, Great Lakes, IL, 308
Naval District Washington, Washington Navy Yard, Washington, DC, 180
Naval Education and Training Center, Newport, Newport, RI, 726
Roosevelt Roads Naval Station, Puerto Rico, 1143

Naval Criminal Investigative Service, Bahrain
Administrative Support Unit, South West Asia, Bahrain, 973

Naval Criminal Investigative Service, Lemoore
Lemoore Naval Air Station, Lemoore, CA, 74

Naval Criminal Investigative Service Resident Agency
Panama Canal Naval Station, Panama, 1137

Naval Criminal Investigative Service Resident Unit
Diego Garcia, Naval Support Facility, Diego Garcia, 982

Naval Dental Branch Clinic, Sasebo
Sasebo, US Fleet Activities, Japan, 1080

Naval Dental Center
Great Lakes Naval Training Center, Great Lakes, IL, 308
Roosevelt Roads Naval Station, Puerto Rico, 1143

Naval Dental Center, Camp Lejeune
Camp Lejeune Marine Corps Base, Camp Lejeune, NC, 618

Naval Dental Center, Newport
Naval Education and Training Center, Newport, Newport, RI, 726

Naval Dental Clinic
Concord Naval Weapons Station, Concord, CA, 61
Lakehurst Naval Air Engineering Station, Lakehurst, NJ, 560

Naval Dental Research Institute
Great Lakes Naval Training Center, Great Lakes, IL, 308

Naval District Washington
Naval District Washington, Washington Navy Yard, Washington, DC, 180

Naval Drug Screening Laboratory
San Diego Naval Medical Center, San Diego, CA, 121

Naval Education and Training Center
Naval Education and Training Center, Newport, Newport, RI, 726

Naval Education and Training Professional Development and Technology Center
Naval Education and Training Professional Development and Technology Center, Pensacola, FL, 223

Naval Education Support Center
Fleet Antisubmarine Warfare Training Center, Pacific, San Diego, CA, 111

Naval Electronic Systems Engineering Center
Norfolk Naval Shipyard, Portsmouth, Portsmouth, VA, 891

Naval Engineering Support Unit
Boston Coast Guard Reserve Center, Boston, MA, 432
Honolulu Coast Guard Base/Station, Honolulu, HI, 275

Naval Engineering Support Unit, Cleveland
9th Coast Guard District Headquarters, Cleveland, OH, 648

Naval Engineering Support Unit, Miami
Miami Beach Coast Guard Group/Station, Miami Beach, FL, 212

Naval Engineering Support Unit, Seattle
Seattle Coast Guard Integrated Support Command, Seattle, WA, 929

Naval EOC/DOD School
Eglin Air Force Base, Fort Walton Beach, FL, 197

Naval European Meteorology and Oceanography Det
Sigonella Naval Air Station, Italy, 1059

Naval European Meteorology and Oceanography Det, Souda Bay
Souda Bay, Naval Support Activity, Greece, 1040

Naval Explosive Ordnance Disposal Technology Division
Indian Head Division, Naval Surface Warfare Center, Indian Head, MD, 426

Naval Facilities Command Northern Division Philadelphia
Lakehurst Naval Air Engineering Station, Lakehurst, NJ, 560

Naval Facilities Engineering Command, Atlantic Division
Naval Facilities Engineering Command, Atlantic Division, Norfolk, VA, 881
Norfolk Naval Station, Norfolk, VA, 886

Naval Facilities Engineering Command, HQ
Naval Facilities Engineering Command Headquarters, Alexandria, VA, 838

Commander, Naval Facilities Engineering Command, Pacific Division
Pearl Harbor Naval Complex, Pearl Harbor, HI, 283

Naval Facilities Engineering Command, Southern Division
Naval Facilities Engineering Command, Southern Division, Charleston, SC, 735

Naval Facilities Engineering Service Center
Naval Facilities Engineering Service Center, Port Hueneme, CA, 102
Port Hueneme, Naval Construction Battalion Center, Port Hueneme, CA, 104

Naval Forces Central Command (COMUSNAVCENT)
Administrative Support Unit, South West Asia, Bahrain, 973

Commander Naval Forces Japan Det
Kadena Naval Air Facility, Japan, 1075

Commander, Naval Forces Korea (COMNAVFORKOREA)
Chinhae Fleet Activities, Korea, Republic of, 1114

Naval Health Research Center
Naval Health Research Center, San Diego, CA, 114

Naval Health Sciences Education and Training Command
National Naval Medical Center, Bethesda, MD, 417

US Naval Home
US Naval Home, Gulfport, MS, 483

Naval Hospital
Cherry Point Marine Corps Air Station, Cherry Point, NC, 621
Roosevelt Roads Naval Station, Puerto Rico, 1143
Rota Naval Station, Spain, 1149

Naval Hospital Beaufort
Beaufort Naval Hospital, Beaufort, SC, 731

Naval Hospital, Bremerton
Bremerton Naval Hospital, Bremerton, WA, 913

Naval Hospital, Camp Lejeune
Camp Lejeune Marine Corps Base, Camp Lejeune, NC, 618

Naval Hospital, Charleston
Charleston Naval Hospital, North Charleston, SC, 746

NAVHOSP CHASN 807 (NR)
Greensboro Naval & Marine Corps Reserve Readiness Center, Greensboro, NC, 626

NAVHOSP CHASN P0725 (NR)
Greensboro Naval & Marine Corps Reserve Readiness Center, Greensboro, NC, 626

Naval Hospital Corps School
Great Lakes Naval Training Center, Great Lakes, IL, 308
Recruit Training Command Great Lakes, Great Lakes, IL, 309

Naval Hospital Corpus Christi
Corpus Christi Naval Hospital, Corpus Christi, TX, 781

Naval Hospital Great Lakes
Recruit Training Command Great Lakes, Great Lakes, IL, 309

Naval Hospital Guam
Guam US Naval Hospital, Guam, 1045
Naval Station, Guam, Guam, 1047

Naval Hospital Guantanamo Bay
Guantanamo Bay, Naval Base, Cuba, 981

Naval Hospital Jacksonville
Jacksonville Naval Air Station, Jacksonville, FL, 205
Tallahassee Naval & Marine Corps Reserve Center, Tallahassee, FL, 234

Naval Hospital Lemoore
Lemoore Naval Air Station, Lemoore, CA, 74

Naval Hospital NTC
Great Lakes Naval Training Center, Great Lakes, IL, 308

Naval Hospital Newport
Naval Education and Training Center, Newport, Newport, RI, 726

Naval Hospital Oak Harbor
Whidbey Island Naval Air Station, Oak Harbor, WA, 924

Naval Hospital Okinawa
Camp Lester, Japan, 1069

Naval Hospital Pensacola
Pensacola Naval Hospital, Pensacola, FL, 226

Naval Hospital Pensacola 2110 (NR)
Tuscaloosa Armed Forces Reserve Center, Tuscaloosa, AL, 17

Naval Hospital Portsmouth Det (NR)
Watertown Naval Reserve Center, Watertown, NY, 611

Naval Hospital Sigonella
Sigonella Naval Air Station, Italy, 1059

Naval Hospital Yokosuka
Yokosuka, US Naval Hospital, Japan, 1084

Naval Hospital Yokosuka, Branch Clinic
Iwakuni Marine Corps Air Station, Japan, 1073

Naval Imaging Command
Anacostia Naval Station, Washington, DC, 171

Naval Inshore Undersea Warfare Group 2
Fleet & Industrial Supply Center, Cheatham Annex, Williamsburg, VA, 907

Naval Intermediate Maintenance Facility (NAVIMFAC)
Pearl Harbor Naval Submarine Base, Pearl Harbor, HI, 284

Naval Inventory Control Point
Kelly Air Force Base, Kelly AFB, TX, 807
Naval Supply Systems Command, Mechanicsburg, PA, 707

Naval Inventory Control Point Philadelphia
Philadelphia, Naval Inventory Control Point, Philadelphia, PA, 716

Naval Investigative Service
Lakehurst Naval Air Engineering Station, Lakehurst, NJ, 560
New London Naval Submarine Base, Groton, CT, 158
Quantico Marine Corps Combat Development Command, Quantico, VA, 895
Rota Naval Station, Spain, 1149

Naval Investigative Service Command
Cheltenham Naval Communication Detachment, Cheltenham, MD, 418

Naval Justice School
Naval Education and Training Center, Newport, Newport, RI, 726

Naval Legal Service Office Det
Great Lakes Naval Training Center, Great Lakes, IL, 308
Naval Education and Training Center, Newport, Newport, RI, 726

Naval Legal Service Office, Groton
New London Naval Submarine Base, Groton, CT, 158

Naval Legal Services Office (NLSO)
Roosevelt Roads Naval Station, Puerto Rico, 1143

Naval Magazine, Guam
Guam Naval Magazine, Guam, 1044

Naval Manpower and Analysis Center
Bureau of Naval Personnel Detachment, Memphis, Millington, TN, 767

Naval Media Center
Roosevelt Roads Naval Station, Puerto Rico, 1143

Naval Media Center Det, Diego Garcia
Diego Garcia, Naval Support Facility, Diego Garcia, 982

Naval Medical Center, San Diego
San Diego Naval Medical Center, San Diego, CA, 121

Naval Medical Clinic
Lakehurst Naval Air Engineering Station, Lakehurst, NJ, 560

Naval Medical Command, Mid-Atlantic Region
Portsmouth Naval Hospital, Portsmouth, VA, 892

Naval Medical Research and Development Command
National Naval Medical Center, Bethesda, MD, 417

Naval Meteorology and Oceanography Command
Naval Meteorology and Oceanography Command, Stennis Space Center, MS, 493

Naval Meteorology and Oceanography Command, Commander
Naval Research Laboratory, Stennis Space Center, Stennis Space Center, MS, 494

Naval Military Personnel Command
Anacostia Naval Station, Washington, DC, 171

Naval Mobile Construction Bn 27, Det 0927 (NMCB)
White River Junction Naval Reserve Center, White River Junction, VT, 834

Naval Mobile Construction Bn
Roosevelt Roads Naval Station, Puerto Rico, 1143
Rota Naval Station, Spain, 1149

Naval Mobile Construction Bn 3
Port Hueneme, Naval Construction Battalion Center, Port Hueneme, CA, 104

Naval Mobile Construction Bn 4
Port Hueneme, Naval Construction Battalion Center, Port Hueneme, CA, 104

Naval Mobile Construction Bn 5
Port Hueneme, Naval Construction Battalion Center, Port Hueneme, CA, 104

Naval Mobile Construction Bn 21
Lakehurst Naval Air Engineering Station, Lakehurst, NJ, 560

Naval Mobile Construction Bn (NMCB 22)
Dallas Naval Air Station, Dallas, TX, 783

Naval Mobile Construction Bn 25 (NMCB-25)
Fort McCoy, Fort McCoy, WI, 954

Naval Mobile Construction Bn 40
Port Hueneme, Naval Construction Battalion Center, Port Hueneme, CA, 104

Naval Mobile Construction Bn 24, Det 1224
Chattanooga Naval & Marine Corps Reserve Center, Chattanooga, TN, 758

Naval Mobile Construction Bn, Camp Olson Sigonella
Sigonella Naval Air Station, Italy, 1059

Naval Mobile Construction Bn Det
Sasebo, US Fleet Activities, Japan, 1080
Sigonella Naval Air Station, Italy, 1059

Naval Mobile Construction Bn Seabee Det
Diego Garcia, Naval Support Facility, Diego Garcia, 982

Naval Nuclear Power Training Command
Orlando, Naval Training Center, Orlando, FL, 218

Naval Nuclear Power Training Unit
Ballston Spa, Naval Nuclear Power Training Unit, Ballston Spa, NY, 577

Naval Ocean Processing Facility
Dam Neck, Fleet Combat Training Center, Atlantic, Virginia Beach, VA, 902

Naval Oceanographic Command
Whiting Field Naval Air Station, Milton, FL, 213

Naval Oceanography Command Facility
Jacksonville Naval Air Station, Jacksonville, FL, 205

Naval Oceanographic Office, Stennis Space Center
Naval Research Laboratory, Stennis Space Center, Stennis Space Center, MS, 494

Naval Oceanographic Processing Facility
Whidbey Island Naval Air Station, Oak Harbor, WA, 924

Naval Oceanography Command Center
Rota Naval Station, Spain, 1149

Naval Oceanography Command Det
Key West Naval Air Facility, Boca Chica Key, FL, 191
Oceana Naval Air Station, Virginia Beach, VA, 903

Naval Oceanography Command Det, Okinawa
Kadena Naval Air Facility, Japan, 1075

Naval Oceanography Command Facility
Jacksonville Naval Air Station, Jacksonville, FL, 205
North Island Naval Air Station, San Diego, CA, 115

Naval Office of Medical/Dental Affairs
Great Lakes Naval Training Center, Great Lakes, IL, 308

Naval Operational Medical Institute
Pensacola Naval Air Station, Pensacola, FL, 225

Naval Ophthalmic Support and Training Activity
Yorktown Naval Weapons Station, Yorktown, VA, 910

Naval Ordnance Center
Indian Head Division, Naval Surface Warfare Center, Indian Head, MD, 426

Naval Ordnance Center, Pacific Division
Concord Naval Weapons Station, Concord, CA, 61
Fallbrook Naval Ordnance Center, Pacific Division, Fallbrook, CA, 68

Naval Ordnance Center, Pacific Division Det, Port Hadlock
Port Hadlock, Naval Ordnance Center, Pacific Division Detachment, Port Hadlock, WA, 927

Naval Ordnance Station, Crane Division, Naval Surface Warfare Center
Louisville Naval Ordnance Station, Louisville, KY, 370

Naval Pacific Meteorology and Oceanography Det, Diego Garcia
Diego Garcia, Naval Support Facility, Diego Garcia, 982

Naval Pacific Meteorology and Oceanography Det, Lemoore
Lemoore Naval Air Station, Lemoore, CA, 74

Naval Pacific Meteorology Oceanography Command Det
Fallon Naval Air Station, Fallon, NV, 535

Naval Personnel Support Activity Det
Key West Naval Air Facility, Boca Chica Key, FL, 191

Naval Postgraduate School
Naval Postgraduate School, Monterey, CA, 83

Naval Radio Station, Jim Creek
Jim Creek Naval Radio Station (T), Arlington, WA, 911

Naval Reactors Facility
Idaho Falls Naval Nuclear Power Training Unit, Idaho Falls, ID, 297

Naval Readiness Command Region Four
Fort Dix, Fort Dix, NJ, 555

Naval Reconnaissance Support Activity
Rota Naval Station, Spain, 1149

Naval Recruiting (Reserve)
Honolulu Naval & Marine Corps Reserve Readiness Center, Honolulu, HI, 276

Naval Regional Contracting Center
Naval Regional Contracting Center, Italy, 1057

Naval Regional Contracting Center, Bahrain
Administrative Support Unit, South West Asia, Bahrain, 973

Naval Regional Contracting Center, Western Pacific
Logistics Group Western Pacific, Singapore, 1147

Naval Research and Development (NRAD)
Fleet Combat Training Center, Pacific, San Diego, CA, 112

Naval Research Laboratory
Naval Postgraduate School, Monterey, CA, 83

Naval Research Laboratory Flight Support Det
Patuxent River, Naval Air Station, Patuxent River, MD, 427

Naval Research Laboratory, Stennis Space Center
Naval Research Laboratory, Stennis Space Center, Stennis Space Center, MS, 494

Naval Reserve Center
Camp Joseph T Robinson, North Little Rock, AR, 52
Gulfport Naval Construction Battalion Center, Gulfport, MS, 482
Roosevelt Roads Naval Station, Puerto Rico, 1143

Naval Reserve Center, Brooklyn
Brooklyn Coast Guard Air Station, Brooklyn, NY, 579

Naval Reserve Center, Corpus Christi
Corpus Christi Naval Air Station, Corpus Christi, TX, 780
Naval Reserve Center, Corpus Christi, Corpus Christi, TX, 782

Naval Reserve Center, Denver
Denver Naval Reserve Readiness Center, Aurora, CO, 143

Naval Reserve Center, Pensacola
Pensacola Naval Reserve Center, Pensacola, FL, 227

Naval Reserve Center, Port Hueneme
Port Hueneme, Naval Construction Battalion Center, Port Hueneme, CA, 104

Naval Reserve Center, Roosevelt Roads
Roosevelt Roads Naval Reserve Center, Puerto Rico, 1142

Naval Reserve Center, Saufley Field
Naval Education and Training Professional Development and Technology Center, Pensacola, FL, 223

Naval Reserve Center, Seattle
Seattle Naval Reserve Readiness Center, Seattle, WA, 930

Naval Reserve Center, Washington
Anacostia Naval Station, Washington, DC, 171

Naval Reserve Center, Westover ARB
Westover Air Reserve Base, Chicopee, MA, 438

Naval Reserve, Charleston
Charleston, Naval Weapons Station, Charleston, SC, 734

Naval Reserve CHEMRADTECHLANT 108
Chattanooga Naval & Marine Corps Reserve Center, Chattanooga, TN, 758

Naval Reserve CINCUSNVAEUR (Commander in Chief U.S. Naval Forces Europe) Det 108
Tallahassee Naval & Marine Corps Reserve Center, Tallahassee, FL, 234

Naval Reserve FFG Support 208
Tallahassee Naval & Marine Corps Reserve Center, Tallahassee, FL, 234

Naval Reserve Force, Cheatham Annex
Fleet & Industrial Supply Center, Cheatham Annex, Williamsburg, VA, 907

Naval Reserve Guarded Missile Frigate Support Unit (FFG SUPPU 0)108
Chattanooga Naval & Marine Corps Reserve Center, Chattanooga, TN, 758

Naval Reserve MAC-G
Chattanooga Naval & Marine Corps Reserve Center, Chattanooga, TN, 758

Naval Reserve Naval Hospital, Jacksonville, Det 208
Chattanooga Naval & Marine Corps Reserve Center, Chattanooga, TN, 758

Naval Reserve, Naval Shipyard NORVA 308
Chattanooga Naval & Marine Corps Reserve Center, Chattanooga, TN, 758

Naval Reserve NSC (Navy Supply Corps) Pensacola 108
Tallahassee Naval & Marine Corps Reserve Center, Tallahassee, FL, 234

Naval Reserve Personnel Center
New Orleans Naval Support Activity, New Orleans, LA, 386

Naval Reserve Readiness Center
Buckley Air National Guard Base, Aurora, CO, 142

Naval Reserve Readiness Center, Alameda
Alameda Naval & Marine Corps Reserve Readiness Center, Alameda, CA, 55

Naval Reserve Readiness Center, Charleston
Charleston, Naval & Marine Corps Reserve Readiness Center, Charleston, SC, 733

Naval Reserve Readiness Center, Norfolk
Norfolk Naval & Marine Corps Reserve Readiness Center, Norfolk, VA, 883

Naval Reserve Readiness Command, Region One
Naval Education and Training Center, Newport, Newport, RI, 726
Region One, Naval Reserve Readiness Command, Newport, RI, 727

Naval Reserve Readiness Command, Region 4
Region Four, Naval Reserve Readiness Command, Fort Dix, NJ, 556

Naval Reserve Readiness Command, Region 5
Youngstown-Warren Regional Airport, Air Reserve Station, Vienna, OH, 666

Naval Reserve Readiness Command, Region 6
Region Six, Naval Reserve Readiness Command, Washington, DC, 184

Washington, Naval Station, Washington, DC, 189

Naval Reserve Readiness Command, Region 8
Jacksonville Naval Air Station, Jacksonville, FL, 205
Region Eight, Naval Reserve Readiness Command, Jacksonville, FL, 207

Naval Reserve Readiness Command, Region 10
New Orleans Naval Support Activity, New Orleans, LA, 386

Naval Reserve Readiness Command, Region 11
Region Eleven, Naval Reserve Readiness Command, Dallas, TX, 787

Naval Reserve Readiness Command, Region 13
Great Lakes Naval Training Center, Great Lakes, IL, 308
Region Thirteen, Naval Reserve Readiness Command, Great Lakes, IL, 310

Naval Reserve Readiness Command, Region 16
Minneapolis-Saint Paul IAP, Air National Guard Base/ARS, Minneapolis-Saint Paul IAP, MN, 474
Region Sixteen, Naval Reserve Readiness Command, Minneapolis, MN, 473

Naval Reserve Readiness Command, Region 19
Region Nineteen, Naval Reserve Readiness Command, San Diego, CA, 116

Naval Reserve Readiness Command, Region 22
Region Twenty-Two, Naval Reserve Readiness Command, Everett, WA, 918

Navy Reserve Recruiters
West Palm Beach Naval & Marine Corps Reserve Center, West Palm Beach, FL, 237

Naval Reserve Recruiting Command, Det Five (NRC Baltimore)
Baltimore Naval Reserve Readiness Center, Baltimore, MD, 413

US Naval Reserve Recruiting
Phoenix Naval & Marine Corps Reserve Readiness Center, Phoenix, AZ, 40

Naval Reserve SCONTGRP 0814
Tallahassee Naval & Marine Corps Reserve Center, Tallahassee, FL, 234

Naval Reserve Shore Intermediate Maintenance Activity, Det 908
Tallahassee Naval & Marine Corps Reserve Center, Tallahassee, FL, 234

Naval Reserve Training Center
Fort Lewis, Fort Lewis, WA, 921

Naval Reserve Unit
Boston Coast Guard Reserve Center, Boston, MA, 432

Naval Reserve, USS *Yosemite* (AD-19)
Chattanooga Naval & Marine Corps Reserve Center, Chattanooga, TN, 758

Naval Reserve Voluntary Training Unit (VOLTRAUNIT) 0802
Chattanooga Naval & Marine Corps Reserve Center, Chattanooga, TN, 758

Naval Reserve, Weapon Station Charleston 908
Chattanooga Naval & Marine Corps Reserve Center, Chattanooga, TN, 758

Naval Safety Center
Norfolk Naval Air Station, Norfolk, VA, 882

Naval School, Explosive Ordnance Disposal
Indian Head Division, Naval Surface Warfare Center, Indian Head, MD, 426

Naval School of Health Sciences
National Naval Medical Center, Bethesda, MD, 417
San Diego Naval Medical Center, San Diego, CA, 121

Naval Sea Combat Systems Engineering Station
Fort Story, Fort Story, VA, 871

Naval Sea Logistics Center, Det Pacific
Concord Naval Weapons Station, Concord, CA, 61

Naval Sea Logistics Support Engineering Center
Mechanicsburg Navy Inventory Control Point, Mechanicsburg, PA, 706

Naval Sea Systems Command, Field Office
Bath Supervisor of Shipbuilding, Conversion and Repair, Bath, ME, 395

Naval Sea Systems Command, HQ
Naval Sea Systems Command, HQ, Arlington, VA, 849

Naval Security Group Activity
Corry Station Naval Technical Training Center, Pensacola, FL, 222
Rota Naval Station, Spain, 1149
Sabana Seca, US Naval Security Group Activity, Puerto Rico, 1144
Sugar Grove Naval Security Group Activity, Sugar Grove, WV, 950
Winter Harbor Naval Security Group Activity, Winter Harbor, ME, 403

Naval Security Group Activity, Det Winter Harbor
Brunswick Naval Air Station, Brunswick, ME, 396

Naval Security Group Activity, Ft Meade
Fort George G Meade, Fort Meade, MD, 422

Naval Security Group Activity, Groton
New London Naval Submarine Base, Groton, CT, 158

Naval Security Group Activity, Guantanamo Bay
Guantanamo Bay, Naval Base, Cuba, 981

Naval Security Group Activity, Hanza
Kadena Naval Air Facility, Japan, 1075

Naval Security Group Activity, Lajes
Lajes Field, Portugal, 1138

Naval Security Group Activity, Northwest
Northwest Naval Security Group Activity, Chesapeake, VA, 858

Naval Security Group Activity, Whidbey Island
Whidbey Island Naval Air Station, Oak Harbor, WA, 924

Naval Security Group Department
Naval Computer & Telecommunications Area Master Station, Eastern Pacific, Wahiawa, HI, 288

Naval Security Group Det
Crane Division, Naval Surface Warfare Center, Crane, IN, 324

Naval Security Station
Naval Security Station, Washington, DC, 183

Naval Shipyard Portsmouth, NH 302 (NR)
White River Junction Naval Reserve Center, White River Junction, VT, 834

Naval Shipyard, Puget Sound
Puget Sound Naval Shipyard, Bremerton, WA, 914

Naval Small Craft Instruction & Technical Training School
Panama Canal Naval Station, Panama, 1137

Naval Space Command
Dahlgren Division, Naval Surface Warfare Center, Dahlgren, VA, 859

Naval Space Surveillance Center
Dahlgren Division, Naval Surface Warfare Center, Dahlgren, VA, 859

Naval Special Warfare Command (SEALs)
Coronado Naval Amphibious Base, San Diego, CA, 109

Navy Special Warfare Development Group
Dam Neck, Fleet Combat Training Center, Atlantic, Virginia Beach, VA, 902

Naval Special Warfare Unit 4 (NSWU-4)
Roosevelt Roads Naval Station, Puerto Rico, 1143

Naval Special Warfare Unit 8
Panama Canal Naval Station, Panama, 1137

Naval Station, Annapolis
Annapolis Naval Station, Annapolis, MD, 409

Naval Station Everett
Everett Naval Station, Everett, WA, 917

Naval Station, Guantanamo Bay
Guantanamo Bay, Naval Base, Cuba, 981

Naval Station, Ingleside
Ingleside Naval Station, Ingleside, TX, 806

Naval Station, Norfolk
Norfolk Naval Base Complex, Norfolk, VA, 885
Norfolk Naval Station, Norfolk, VA, 886

Naval Station, Panama Canal
Panama Canal Naval Station, Panama, 1137

Naval Station, Pascagoula
Pascagoula Naval Station, Pascagoula, MS, 490

Naval Station, Pearl Harbor
Pearl Harbor Naval Complex, Pearl Harbor, HI, 283

Naval Station, Roosevelt Roads
Roosevelt Roads Naval Station, Puerto Rico, 1143

Naval Station, San Diego
San Diego Naval Station, San Diego, CA, 122

Naval Station, Washington
Washington, Naval Station, Washington, DC, 189

Naval Strike & Air Warfare Center
Fallon Naval Air Station, Fallon, NV, 535

Naval Striking and Support Forces Southern Europe (STRIKFORSOUTH), Representative
Vecihi Akin Garrison, Turkey, 1154

Naval Submarine Base, Kings Bay
Kings Bay Naval Submarine Base, Kings Bay, GA, 253

Naval Submarine Medical Research Laboratory
New London Naval Submarine Base, Groton, CT, 158

Naval Submarine School
New London Naval Submarine Base, Groton, CT, 158

Naval Submarine Support Facility, New London/Groton
New London Naval Submarine Base, Groton, CT, 158

Naval Submarine Training Center, Pacific (NSTC)
Pearl Harbor Naval Submarine Base, Pearl Harbor, HI, 284

Naval Supply Center
Jacksonville Naval Air Station, Jacksonville, FL, 205

Naval Supply Center Det, Pensacola
Pascagoula Naval Station, Pascagoula, MS, 490

Naval Supply Systems Command
Naval Supply Systems Command, Mechanicsburg, PA, 707

Naval Support Activity Monterey Bay
Naval Postgraduate School, Monterey, CA, 83

Naval Support Facility, Diego Garcia
Diego Garcia, Naval Support Facility, Diego Garcia, 982

Naval Support Force Antarctica
Port Hueneme, Naval Construction Battalion Center, Port Hueneme, CA, 104

Naval Surface Force
Coronado Naval Amphibious Base, San Diego, CA, 109

Commander, Naval Surface Group Middle Pacific
Pearl Harbor Naval Complex, Pearl Harbor, HI, 283

Naval Surface Warfare Center
Crane Division, Naval Surface Warfare Center, Crane, IN, 324
Port Hueneme Division, Naval Surface Warfare Center, Port Hueneme, CA, 103

Naval Surface Warfare Center, Carderock Division
Annapolis Naval Station, Annapolis, MD, 409

Naval Surface Warfare Center, Dahlgren Division
Dahlgren Division, Naval Surface Warfare Center, Dahlgren, VA, 859

Naval Surface Warfare Center, Dahlgren Division Det
Fort Monroe, Fort Monroe, VA, 870

Naval Surface Warfare Center Det, Dahlgren Division
Naval Security Station, Washington, DC, 183

Naval Surface Warfare Center, Indian Head Det
Yorktown Naval Weapons Station, Yorktown, VA, 910

Naval Surface Warfare Center, Indian Head Division Det, McAlester
McAlester Army Ammunition Plant, McAlester, OK, 673

Naval Surface Warfare Center, Port Hueneme Division
Port Hueneme, Naval Construction Battalion Center, Port Hueneme, CA, 104

Naval Surface Warfare Center, Port Hueneme, East Coast Division
Dam Neck, Fleet Combat Training Center, Atlantic, Virginia Beach, VA, 902

Naval Technical Training Center
Corry Station Naval Technical Training Center, Pensacola, FL, 222
Meridian Naval Air Station, Meridian, MS, 489

Naval Technical Training Center Det
Goodfellow Air Force Base, Goodfellow AFB, TX, 801

Naval Telecommunications Center
Naval Postgraduate School, Monterey, CA, 83
North Island Naval Air Station, San Diego, CA, 115

Naval Telecommunications Center, Cheltenham
Cheltenham Naval Communication Detachment, Cheltenham, MD, 418

Naval Telecommunications Station, Washington
Cheltenham Naval Communication Detachment, Cheltenham, MD, 418

Naval Training Air Wing 5
Whiting Field Naval Air Station, Milton, FL, 213

Naval Training Center
Great Lakes Naval Training Center, Great Lakes, IL, 308

Naval Training Center, Orlando
Orlando, Naval Training Center, Orlando, FL, 218

Naval Training Meteorology & Oceanography Det, Newport
Naval Education and Training Center, Newport, Newport, RI, 726

Naval Training Meteorology Oceanography Command Det Kingsville (NTMOD)
Kingsville Naval Air Station, Kingsville, TX, 808

Naval Training Station
Norfolk Naval Station, Norfolk, VA, 886

Naval Training Systems Division
Naval Air Warfare Center, Training Systems Division, Orlando, FL, 216

Naval Trial Service Office Det
Great Lakes Naval Training Center, Great Lakes, IL, 308

Naval Undersea Medical Institute
New London Naval Submarine Base, Groton, CT, 158

Naval Undersea Warfare Center
Concord Naval Weapons Station, Concord, CA, 61
Fort Story, Fort Story, VA, 871
Hawthorne Army Depot, Hawthorne, NV, 537

Naval Undersea Warfare Center, Det
Naval Undersea Warfare Center, Detachment, Atlantic Undersea Test & Evaluation Center, Bahamas, 972
Pacific Missile Range Facility, Kekaha, HI, 279
Seneca Lake Sonar Test Facility, Lake Seneca, NY, 591

Naval Undersea Warfare Center Division
Naval Education and Training Center, Newport, Newport, RI, 726

Naval Undersea Warfare Center HQ
Naval Education and Training Center, Newport, Newport, RI, 726

Naval Undersea Warfare Center, Keyport Division
Keyport Division, Naval Undersea Warfare Center, Keyport, WA, 922

Naval Undersea Warfare Command (NUWC)
Lualualei Naval Magazine, Waianae, HI, 289

Naval Underwater Systems Center, New London Laboratory
New London Naval Submarine Base, Groton, CT, 158

Naval War College
Naval Education and Training Center, Newport, Newport, RI, 726

Naval Warfare Assessment Center
Roosevelt Roads Naval Station, Puerto Rico, 1143

Naval Warfare Assessment Division
Naval Warfare Assessment Division, Norco, CA, 86

Naval Weapons Station, Charleston
Charleston, Naval Weapons Station, Charleston, SC, 734
Charleston Naval Weapons Station, Goose Creek, SC, 742

Naval Weapons Station, Concord
Concord Naval Weapons Station, Concord, CA, 61

Naval Weapons Station Det 8 (NR)
Watertown Naval Reserve Center, Watertown, NY, 611

Naval Weapons Station, Seal Beach
Seal Beach Naval Weapons Station, Seal Beach, CA, 133

Naval Weapons Station, Yorktown
Yorktown Naval Weapons Station, Yorktown, VA, 910

NAVHOSP CLEJEUNE 0209 (NR)
Lexington Naval Reserve Center, Lexington, KY, 368

NAVHOSP CLEJEUNE 0309 (NR)
Cape Girardeau Naval Reserve Center, Cape Girardeau, MO, 500

NAVHOSP CLEJEUNE P0109 NR
Louisville Naval Reserve Center, Louisville, KY, 371

NAVHOSP CLEJEUNE P0921
Louisville Naval Reserve Center, Louisville, KY, 371

NAVHOSP GLAKES 513 (NR)
Evansville Naval & Marine Corps Reserve Center, Evansville, IN, 326

NAVHOSP GLAKES 1613 (NR)
Toledo Naval & Marine Corps Reserve Center, Perrysburg, OH, 662

NAVHOSP GLAKES Det 113
Decatur Naval Reserve Center, Decatur, IL, 305

NAVSEA RASO Det
Yorktown Naval Weapons Station, Yorktown, VA, 910

NAVSTA Panama Det 409 (NR)
Lexington Naval Reserve Center, Lexington, KY, 368

NAVSTAR Global Positioning System
Falcon Air Force Base, Falcon AFB, CO, 151

Navy Advancement Center
Naval Education and Training Professional Development and Technology Center, Pensacola, FL, 223

Navy & Marine Corps Intelligence Training Center
Dam Neck, Fleet Combat Training Center, Atlantic, Virginia Beach, VA, 902

Navy Band
Naval District Washington, Washington Navy Yard, Washington, DC, 180

Navy Band, Great Lakes
Recruit Training Command Great Lakes, Great Lakes, IL, 309

Navy Band, Jacksonville
Jacksonville Naval Air Station, Jacksonville, FL, 205

Naval Band, Newport
Naval Education and Training Center, Newport, Newport, RI, 726

Navy Broadcasting Service, Det Bahrain
Administrative Support Unit, South West Asia, Bahrain, 973

Navy Broadcasting Service Det, ROTA
Rota Naval Station, Spain, 1149

Navy Calibration Laboratory
Rota Naval Station, Spain, 1149

Navy Campus
Fleet Antisubmarine Warfare Training Center, Pacific, San Diego, CA, 111

Navy Cargo Handling and Port Group
Fleet & Industrial Supply Center, Cheatham Annex, Williamsburg, VA, 907

Navy Clothing and Textile Research Facility
Army Soldier Systems Command, Natick, MA, 441

Navy Communications Area Master Station Satellite Communications Atlantic Facility
Northwest Naval Security Group Activity, Chesapeake, VA, 858

Navy Computer & Telecommunications Det
Great Lakes Naval Training Center, Great Lakes, IL, 308

Navy Contracting Office (USNCD)
Ship Support Office, American Consulate General, Hong Kong, China, 980

Navy COOPMINE Unit
Boston Coast Guard Reserve Center, Boston, MA, 432

Navy Det, Ft Sam Houston
Fort Sam Houston, Fort Sam Houston, TX, 794

Navy Diving & Salvage Training Center (NDSTC)
Naval Coastal Systems Station, Panama City, FL, 219

Navy Drug Screening Laboratory
Great Lakes Naval Training Center, Great Lakes, IL, 308

Navy Education & Training Management Support Activity
Dam Neck, Fleet Combat Training Center, Atlantic, Virginia Beach, VA, 902

Navy Exchange
Yorktown Naval Weapons Station, Yorktown, VA, 910

Navy Exchange Newport
Naval Education and Training Center, Newport, Newport, RI, 726

Navy Exchange Service Command
Naval Supply Systems Command, Mechanicsburg, PA, 707

Navy Experimental Diving Unit (NEDU)
Naval Coastal Systems Station, Panama City, FL, 219

Navy Explosive Ordnance Disposal Training & Evaluation Unit Two
Fort Story, Fort Story, VA, 871

Navy Field Contracting System
Naval Supply Systems Command, Mechanicsburg, PA, 707

Navy Fleet Materiel Support Office
Mechanicsburg Navy Inventory Control Point, Mechanicsburg, PA, 706

Navy Flight Demonstration Squadron (Blue Angels)
Pensacola Naval Air Station, Pensacola, FL, 225

Navy Fuel Depot, Manchester
Puget Sound Naval Shipyard, Bremerton, WA, 914

Navy Head of Contracting Activity
Naval Supply Systems Command, Mechanicsburg, PA, 707

Navy—Marine Corps Military Affiliate Radio Station
Cheltenham Naval Communication Detachment, Cheltenham, MD, 418

Navy Maritime Prepositioning Ships Squadron 2
Diego Garcia, Naval Support Facility, Diego Garcia, 982

Navy Mobile Construction Bn 20
Army Armor Center & Fort Knox, Fort Knox, KY, 366

Navy Mobile Construction Bn 28 SEABEES (NR)
Barksdale Air Force Base, Barksdale AFB, LA, 374

Navy Mobile Dive and Salvage Unit TWO, Det 506
Fort Story, Fort Story, VA, 871

Navy Office of Information, East
Navy Office of Information, East, New York, NY, 596

Navy Office of Information, Midwest
Navy Office of Information, Midwest, Chicago, IL, 302

Navy Office of Information, New England
Navy Office of Information, New England, Boston, MA, 434

Navy Office of Information, Southeast
Navy Office of Information, Southeast, Atlanta, GA, 242

Navy Office of Information, Southwest
Navy Office of Information, Southwest, Dallas, TX, 786

Navy Office of Information, West
Navy Office of Information, West, Los Angeles, CA, 78

Navy Personnel Support Activity, Det Okinawa
Kadena Naval Air Facility, Japan, 1075

Navy Personnel Support Det Activity, Diego Garcia
Diego Garcia, Naval Support Facility, Diego Garcia, 982

Navy Petroleum Office
Naval Supply Systems Command, Mechanicsburg, PA, 707

Navy Public Works
Fort Story, Fort Story, VA, 871

Navy Public Works Center
Norfolk Navy Public Works Center, Norfolk, VA, 887
San Diego Naval Station, San Diego, CA, 122

Navy Public Works Center, Norfolk
Norfolk Naval Station, Norfolk, VA, 886

Navy Public Works Center, Oakland Det
Department of Defense Housing Facility, Novato, CA, 88

Navy Public Works Center, Pearl Harbor
Pearl Harbor Naval Complex, Pearl Harbor, HI, 283

Navy Publications and Printing Service Center
Yorktown Naval Weapons Station, Yorktown, VA, 910

Navy Radar Bomb Scoring Unit-Spokane (RBSU)
Spokane Naval & Marine Corps Reserve Readiness Center, Spokane, WA, 934

Navy Recreation Center
Solomons, Navy Recreation Center, Solomons, MD, 428

US Navy Recreation Park
Norfolk Naval Base Complex, Norfolk, VA, 885

Navy Recruiting
Defense Distribution Region East, New Cumberland, PA, 709
Reading Naval & Marine Corps Reserve Center, Reading, PA, 719

Navy Recruiting Area 1
Scotia Naval Administrative Unit, Scotia, NY, 608

Navy Recruiting Area 5
Great Lakes Naval Training Center, Great Lakes, IL, 308
Recruit Training Command Great Lakes, Great Lakes, IL, 309

Navy Recruiting Command
Navy Recruiting Command, Arlington, VA, 850

Navy Recruiting District, New England
Navy Recruiting District New England, Boston, MA, 435

US Navy Recruiting Office
Worcester Naval & Marine Corps Reserve Center, Worcester, MA, 448

Navy Recruiting Orientation Unit
Pensacola Naval Air Station, Pensacola, FL, 225

Navy Regional Branch Dental Clinic
Yorktown Naval Weapons Station, Yorktown, VA, 910

Navy Regional Branch Medical Clinic
Yorktown Naval Weapons Station, Yorktown, VA, 910

Navy Regional Data Automation Center, San Diego
North Island Naval Air Station, San Diego, CA, 115

Navy Resale
Whiting Field Naval Air Station, Milton, FL, 213

Navy Reserve, Guam
Naval Station, Guam, Guam, 1047

Navy Reserve Naval Air Station, Barbers Point Det 187
Barbers Point Naval Air Station, Barbers Point, HI, 265

Navy Reserve Training Center
Milwaukee Coast Guard Base/Group, Milwaukee, WI, 961

Navy Resident Officer-in-Charge of Construction (ROICC)
Barksdale Air Force Base, Barksdale AFB, LA, 374

Navy Security Assistance Office
Naval Supply Systems Command, Mechanicsburg, PA, 707

Navy Space Surveillance Station
Hunter Army Air Field, Savannah, GA, 260

Navy Special Warfare Group 2
Little Creek, Naval Amphibious Base, Norfolk, VA, 880

Navy Strategic Communications Wing 1
Tinker Air Force Base, Tinker AFB, OK, 678

Navy Submarine Torpedo Facility
Yorktown Naval Weapons Station, Yorktown, VA, 910

Navy Supply Center
Norfolk Naval Station, Norfolk, VA, 886

Navy Supply Corps School
Navy Supply Corps School, Athens, GA, 240

Navy Support Office, La Maddalena
La Maddalena Navy Support Office, Italy, 1054

Navy Technical Training Unit
Keesler Air Force Base, Keesler AFB, MS, 487

Navy Transportation Office
Naval Supply Systems Command, Mechanicsburg, PA, 707

NCFSU 3 Det E
Augusta Naval & Marine Corps Reserve Center, Augusta, GA, 244

NCR-20th Naval Construction Regiment, Det E
Tuscaloosa Armed Forces Reserve Center, Tuscaloosa, AL, 17

NCTAMS
Rota Naval Station, Spain, 1149

NDCL NORFOLK Det 809 (NR)
Louisville Naval Reserve Center, Louisville, KY, 371

NEAT (NR)
Omaha Naval & Marine Corps Reserve Center, Omaha, NE, 531

Nebraska National Guard
Adjutant General of Nebraska, Lincoln, NE, 527

NEMOC (Weather)
Rota Naval Station, Spain, 1149

Netherlands Law Center
Netherlands Law Center, Netherlands, 1130

Network Control Center (BUPERS)
Bureau of Naval Personnel Detachment, Memphis, Millington, TN, 767

Neubrücke Hospital
Baumholder Military Community, H.D. Smith Barracks, Germany, 1003

Neureut Kaserne
Heidelberg Military Community, Germany, 1011

Nevada Air National Guard, HQ
Nevada National Guard Headquarters, Carson City, NV, 534

Nevada Army National Guard, HQ
Nevada National Guard Headquarters, Carson City, NV, 534

New Argonner Family Housing
414th Base Support Battalion, Germany, 997

New Hampshire National Guard
Adjutant General of New Hampshire, Concord, NH, 547

New Jersey National Guard
Adjutant General of New Jersey, Trenton, NJ, 565

NM Air National Guard
Kirtland Air Force Base, Kirtland AFB, NM, 572

New Sanno Hotel, Japan
New Sanno Hotel, US Naval Joint Services Activity, Japan, 1078

NY ARNG-Class IX
Combined Support Maintenance Shop C/ US Property & Fiscal Office—NY, Rochester, NY, 602

New York City Recruiting Bn
New York Area Command & Fort Hamilton, Brooklyn, NY, 581

New York National Guard
Adjutant General/Commander of New York, Latham, NY, 592

NY Police Dept Aviation
Brooklyn Coast Guard Air Station, Brooklyn, NY, 579

Newport Defense Commissary Agency, Northeast Region
Naval Education and Training Center, Newport, Newport, RI, 726

NF FH-500 CBTZ 21 Det L
Tyler Naval Reserve Center, Tyler, TX, 819

NH Bethesda 1206 (NR)
White River Junction Naval Reserve Center, White River Junction, VT, 834

NH Bethesda 1306 (NR)
Williamsport Naval & Marine Corps Reserve Center, Williamsport, PA, 722

NH Bethesda Det 2606 (NR)
Cumberland Naval Reserve Center, Cumberland, MD, 419

NH Jacksonville 1408 (NR)
Augusta Naval & Marine Corps Reserve Center, Augusta, GA, 244

NH Jacksonville PO80 (NR)
Augusta Naval & Marine Corps Reserve Center, Augusta, GA, 244

Nickell Barracks Training Center (ARNG)
Nickell Barracks Training Center, Salina, KS, 357

Night Vision & Electronic Sensors Directorate
Fort Belvoir, Fort Belvoir, VA, 866

NIS Resident Agency
Yorktown Naval Weapons Station, Yorktown, VA, 910

NISE East Calibration Laboratory
Charleston, Naval Weapons Station, Charleston, SC, 734

NMCB 14, Det 1114
Tallahassee Naval & Marine Corps Reserve Center, Tallahassee, FL, 234

NMCB 15
Omaha Naval & Marine Corps Reserve Center, Omaha, NE, 531

NMCB 15 Det 1215
Wichita Naval & Marine Corps Reserve Center, Wichita, KS, 364

NMCB 17 Det 0317
Cheyenne Naval Reserve Center, Cheyenne, WY, 966

NMCB 21 Det 0921
Williamsport Naval & Marine Corps Reserve Center, Williamsport, PA, 722

NMCB 23 Det 0523
Ebensburg Naval & Marine Corps Reserve Center, Ebensburg, PA, 702

NMCB 24 Det 0924
Lexington Naval Reserve Center, Lexington, KY, 368

VTU 1606G (NR)
Dubuque Naval Reserve Center, Dubuque, IA, 344

NMCB 26 Det 1226
Toledo Naval & Marine Corps Reserve Center, Perrysburg, OH, 662

NMCB 26 Det 1326
Decatur Naval Reserve Center, Decatur, IL, 305

NMCB 26 Det 1826
Evansville Naval & Marine Corps Reserve Center, Evansville, IN, 326

NMCB 27 Det (NR)
Watertown Naval Reserve Center, Watertown, NY, 611

NMCB 28 Det 0428
Cape Girardeau Naval Reserve Center, Cape Girardeau, MO, 500

NMCB 28, Det 1628
Tyler Naval Reserve Center, Tyler, TX, 819

NOACT (NR)
Omaha Naval & Marine Corps Reserve Center, Omaha, NE, 531

Noble Army Health Clinic
Fort McClellan, Anniston, AL, 2

NCO Academy
Army Armor Center & Fort Knox, Fort Knox, KY, 366
Army Transportation Center & Fort Eustis, Fort Eustis, VA, 868
Fort Huachuca, Fort Huachuca, AZ, 35
McGuire Air Force Base, McGuire AFB, NJ, 561

Noncommissioned Officer Academy, Ft Benning
Fort Benning, Fort Benning, GA, 248

Noncommissioned Officer Academy, Ft Lewis
Fort Lewis, Fort Lewis, WA, 921

NCO Academy, Kisling
Kisling NCO Academy, Germany, 1016

Noncommissioned Officer Academy, Okinawa
Camp Hansen, Japan, 1067

NCO Academy, Ramstein
Ramstein Air Base, Germany, 1023

NORAD Systems Support Facility
Tyndall Air Force Base, Panama City, FL, 220

Norfolk Fleet Training Center
Norfolk Naval Station, Norfolk, VA, 886

Norfolk Naval Shipyard
Norfolk Naval Shipyard, Portsmouth, Portsmouth, VA, 891

North American Aerospace Defense Command
Peterson Air Force Base, Peterson AFB, CO, 156

North American Aerospace Defense Command (NORAD)
Cheyenne Mountain Air Force Station, Colorado Springs, CO, 145

North Atlantic Regional Dental Command
Walter Reed Army Medical Center, Washington, DC, 188

North Atlantic Regional Medical Command
Walter Reed Army Medical Center, Washington, DC, 188

NATO Communications and Information Systems Agency
80th Area Support Group, Belgium, 975

NATO HQ
80th Area Support Group, Belgium, 975

NATO HQ North
426th Air Base Squadron, Norway, 1132

NATO III
Falcon Air Force Base, Falcon AFB, CO, 151

North Atlantic Treaty Organization Satellite Communications Facility
Northwest Naval Security Group Activity, Chesapeake, VA, 858

North Atlantic Veterinary Command
Walter Reed Army Medical Center, Washington, DC, 188

North Carolina Air National Guard, HQ
145th Airlift Wing, Charlotte, NC, 619

North Carolina National Guard
Adjutant General of North Carolina, Ralcigh, NC, 630

North Dakota National Guard
Adjutant General of North Dakota, Bismarck, ND, 636

Northeast Air Defense Sector (NEADS)
Northeast Air Defense Sector, Rome, NY, 604

Northeast Army Regional Intelligence Support Center (NEARISC)
Fort Dix, Fort Dix, NJ, 555

Northeast Region Civilian Personnel Operations Center
Aberdeen Proving Ground, Aberdeen Proving Ground, MD, 404

NE Regional Fisheries Training Center
Cape Cod Coast Guard Air Station, Cape Cod, MA, 436

Northern Europe Veterinary Det
221st Base Support Battalion, Germany, 992

Northern Law Center
Northern Law Center, Belgium, 978

Northern Warfare Training Center
Fort Greely, Fort Greely, AK, 25

Northrop Grumman
Production Flight Test Installation, Air Force Plant 42, Palmdale, CA, 94

Northwest Regional Naval Intelligence Center
Whidbey Island Naval Air Station, Oak Harbor, WA, 924

NPMOD (Weather Det)
Fallon Naval Air Station, Fallon, NV, 535

NRC Baltimore (17 units)
Baltimore Naval Reserve Readiness Center, Baltimore, MD, 413

NSLC Det, Portsmouth, NH
Portsmouth Naval Shipyard, Portsmouth, NH, 551

Nuclear Effects Directorate
White Sands Missile Range, White Sands Missile Range, NM, 574

Nuclear Power Training Unit
Charleston, Naval Weapons Station, Charleston, SC, 734
Idaho Falls Naval Nuclear Power Training Unit, Idaho Falls, ID, 297

Nuclear Weapons Training Group, Pacific (NUWPNTRAGRUPAC)
North Island Naval Air Station, San Diego, CA, 115

NWS CHAS EOT Det 5 (NR)
Augusta Naval & Marine Corps Reserve Center, Augusta, GA, 244

NWS CON EOT Det 10
Cheyenne Naval Reserve Center, Cheyenne, WY, 966

NWS York Det 709 (NR)
Louisville Naval Reserve Center, Louisville, KY, 371

Oberdachstetten Training Area
Storck Barracks, Illesheim, Germany, 1032

Ocean and Atmospheric Science and Technology Directorate
Naval Research Laboratory, Washington, DC, 182

Ocean County Vocational Technical School
Lakehurst Naval Air Engineering Station, Lakehurst, NJ, 560

Oceanographer of the Navy
US Naval Observatory, Washington, DC, 186

Office of Commander Subsistence Field Activities and Director, Subsistence
Philadelphia Defense Personnel Support Center, Philadelphia, PA, 715

Office of Naval Intelligence Det
Naval Education and Training Center, Newport, Newport, RI, 726

Office of Naval Research
Office of Naval Research, Arlington, VA, 851

Office of Naval Research Asian Office
Asian Office of Aerospace Research & Development, Tokyo, Japan, 1081

Office of Naval Research Europe
Office of Naval Research Europe, London, United Kingdom, 1164

Office of Scientific Research
Bolling Air Force Base, Washington, DC, 173

Office of Special Investigations, Det 310
Charleston Air Force Base, Charleston AFB, SC, 737

Office of Special Investigations, Det 719
Charleston Air Force Base, Charleston AFB, SC, 737

Office of Special Investigations (USAF)
Defense Contract Management Command, Lockheed Martin, Marietta, Marietta, GA, 255

Office of Staff Judge Advocate, Mannheim
Taylor Barracks, Germany, 1034

Office of Telecommunications and Informations Systems
Philadelphia Defense Personnel Support Center, Philadelphia, PA, 715

Office of the Chief, Army Reserve
The Pentagon, Arlington, VA, 852

Office of the Surgeon General, USN
Naval Medical Command, Bureau of Medicine & Surgery, Washington, DC, 181

Office of Total Army Quality
Army Armor Center & Fort Knox, Fort Knox, KY, 366

Office of USAREUR Provost Marshal
Taylor Barracks, Germany, 1034

Officer Personnel Management Directorate
Army Reserve Personnel Center, Saint Louis, MO, 510

Officers Candidates School
Quantico Marine Corps Combat Development Command, Quantico, VA, 895

Offices of the Program Manager for Security Assistance with the Saudi Arabian National Guard
Eskan Village, Saudi Arabia, 1145

Oftersheim Small Arms Range
Heidelberg Military Community, Germany, 1011

Ogden AFB Material Command (Rivet Mile)
Grand Forks Air Force Base, Grand Forks AFB, ND, 641

Ogden Air Logistics Center
Hill Air Force Base, Hill AFB, UT, 824

Ohio National Guard
Adjutant General of Ohio, Columbus, OH, 651

Oklahoma City Air Logistics Center
Tinker Air Force Base, Tinker AFB, OK, 678

Oklahoma National Guard
Adjutant General of Oklahoma, Oklahoma City, OK, 674
Camp Gruber, Army National Guard Training Site, Braggs, OK, 669

OL A 366th Communications Squadron
Portland Air National Guard Base, Portland IAP, OR, 691

OL-AE, MSG (Software Development Agency)
Kelly Air Force Base, Kelly AFB, TX, 807

Olen Storage Facility
80th Area Support Group, Belgium, 975

On-Site Inspection Agency Europe
Rhein-Main Air Base, Germany, 1025

On-Site Inspection Agency (OSIA)
Yokota Air Base, Japan, 1085

Operating Location C, 18th Weather Squadron (USAF)
Army Armor Center & Fort Knox, Fort Knox, KY, 366

Operating Location Alpha, RAF Barford St John
Croughton RAF Base, United Kingdom, 1157

Operating Location France (OL-FR)
Istres Air Base, France, 986

Operation Joint Endeavor
San Vito dei Normanni Air Station, San Vito dei Normanni, Italy, 1058

Operation Northern Watch
Incirlick Air Base, Turkey, 1152

Operational Support Airlift Command, Det 44
New Mexico National Guard State Headquarters, Santa Fe, NM, 573

Operational Support Airlift Command (OSAC), Fort Knox Regional Flight Center
Army Armor Center & Fort Knox, Fort Knox, KY, 366

Operational Support Airlift Command (OSAC)
Military District of Washington, Washington, DC, 179

Operational Test and Evaluation Command
Fort Rucker, Fort Rucker, AL, 5

Operational Test and Evaluation Force, Pacific (OPTEVFOR)
North Island Naval Air Station, San Diego, CA, 115

Operations Airlift Command
Davison Army Airfield, Fort Belvoir, VA, 864

Operations Group, Ft Irwin
Fort Irwin, National Training Center, Fort Irwin, CA, 70

Operations Team
Industrial Analysis Support Office, Philadelphia, PA, 713

Ordnance Det Mobile Unit One
Lualualei Naval Magazine, Waianae, HI, 289

Ordnance Det Training and Evaluation Office
Lualualei Naval Magazine, Waianae, HI, 289

Ordnance Environmental Support Office
Indian Head Division, Naval Surface Warfare Center, Indian Head, MD, 426

Oregon Air National Guard, Headquarters
Portland Air National Guard Base, Portland IAP, OR, 691

Oregon Wing (CAP)
Portland Air National Guard Base, Portland IAP, OR, 691

Organizational Maintenance Shop 4
Camp Dawson, Kingwood, WV, 947

Organizational Maintenance Shop 5
Mitchell National Guard Complex, Mitchell, SD, 752

Organizational Maintenance Shop 8
Camp W G Williams, Riverton, UT, 827

Organizational Maintenance Shop 10
Camp Perry Training Site, Port Clinton, OH, 663

Organizational Maintenance Shop 16
Camp Smith, Peekskill, NY, 601

Organizational Maintenance Shop 20
Camp Smith, Peekskill, NY, 601

Osprey Class Coastal Mine Hunters (9)
Ingleside Naval Station, Ingleside, TX, 806

Osterfelderstrasse Housing
6th Area Support Group, Garmish, Germany, 987

OTH-B (Over-the-Horizon Backscatter) Program
Bangor IAP Air National Guard Base, Bangor, ME, 393

Pacific Air Forces, HQ
Hickam Air Force Base, Hickam AFB, HI, 271

Pacific Beach Resort
Pacific Beach Resort & Conference Center, Pacific Beach, WA, 925

Pacific Fleet Imaging Command (FLTIMAGCOMPAC)
North Island Naval Air Station, San Diego, CA, 115

Pacific Stars & Stripes
Pacific Stars and Stripes, Japan, 1079
Torii Station, Japan, 1082

Panzer Kaserne
6th Area Support Group, Stuttgart, Germany, 988
Kaiserslautern Military Community, Germany, 1013

Papago Military Reservation
Adjutant General of Arizona, Phoenix, AZ, 39

Patch Barracks
6th Area Support Group, Stuttgart, Germany, 988

Patent Counsel, Naval Undersea Warfare Center
Naval Education and Training Center, Newport, Newport, RI, 726

Patrick Henry Village Family Housing
Heidelberg Military Community, Germany, 1011

Patrol Squadron One
Whidbey Island Naval Air Station, Oak Harbor, WA, 924

Patrol Squadron 4 (VP-4)
Barbers Point Naval Air Station, Barbers Point, HI, 265

Patrol Squadron 5 (VP-5)
Jacksonville Naval Air Station, Jacksonville, FL, 205

Patrol Squadron 8 (VP-8)
Brunswick Naval Air Station, Brunswick, ME, 396

Patrol Squadron 9 (VP-9)
Barbers Point Naval Air Station, Barbers Point, HI, 265

Patrol Squadron 10 (VP-10)
Brunswick Naval Air Station, Brunswick, ME, 396

Patrol Squadron 11 (VP-11)
Brunswick Naval Air Station, Brunswick, ME, 396

Patrol Squadron 16 (VP-16)
Jacksonville Naval Air Station, Jacksonville, FL, 205

Patrol Squadron 23 (VP-23)
Brunswick Naval Air Station, Brunswick, ME, 396

Patrol Squadron 24 (VP-24)
Jacksonville Naval Air Station, Jacksonville, FL, 205

Patrol Squadron 26 (VP-26)
Brunswick Naval Air Station, Brunswick, ME, 396

Patrol Squadron 30 (VP-30)
Jacksonville Naval Air Station, Jacksonville, FL, 205

Patrol Squadron 44 (VP-44)
Brunswick Naval Air Station, Brunswick, ME, 396

Patrol Squadron 45 (VP-45)
Jacksonville Naval Air Station, Jacksonville, FL, 205

Patrol Squadron 47 (VP-47)
Barbers Point Naval Air Station, Barbers Point, HI, 265

Patrol Squadron 49 (VP-49)
Jacksonville Naval Air Station, Jacksonville, FL, 205

Patrol Squadron 56 (VP-56)
Jacksonville Naval Air Station, Jacksonville, FL, 205

Patrol Squadron 64 (VP-64)
Willow Grove Naval Air Station (JRB), Willow Grove, PA, 723

Patrol Squadron 66 (VP-66)
Willow Grove Naval Air Station (JRB), Willow Grove, PA, 723

Patrol Squadron 94 (VP-94)(NR)
New Orleans Naval Air Station Joint Reserve Base, Naval Air Station, New Orleans, LA, 384

Patrol Squadron, Diego Garcia
Diego Garcia, Naval Support Facility, Diego Garcia, 982

Patrol Squadron (PATRON SIG)
Sigonella Naval Air Station, Italy, 1059

Patrol Squadron Special Projects Unit 2 (VPU-2)
Barbers Point Naval Air Station, Barbers Point, HI, 265

Patrol Wing One, Det
Diego Garcia, Naval Support Facility, Diego Garcia, 982
Kadena Naval Air Facility, Japan, 1075

Patrol Wing 10
Whidbey Island Naval Air Station, Oak Harbor, WA, 924

Patrol Wing 11, Commander
Jacksonville Naval Air Station, Jacksonville, FL, 205

Patrol Wings Atlantic (Topsham Annex)
Brunswick Naval Air Station, Brunswick, ME, 396

Patrol Wings Pacific Fleet
Barbers Point Naval Air Station, Barbers Point, HI, 265

Patterson Army Health Clinic
Fort Monmouth, Fort Monmouth, NJ, 557

Patton Barracks
Heidelberg Military Community, Germany, 1011

Peace-Time War-Time Support Team (PWST) Fort Wayne
Fort Wayne Marine Corps Reserve Center, Fort Wayne, IN, 329

Peekskill Warehouse
Camp Smith, Peekskill, NY, 601

Pennsylvania Department of Military & Veterans Affairs
Fort Indiantown Gap, Annville, PA, 696

Pennsylvania National Guard
Adjutant General of Pennsylvania, Annville, PA, 695

Personal Support Activity Det (PSD)
Roosevelt Roads Naval Station, Puerto Rico, 1143

Personnel Actions & Services Directorate
Army Reserve Personnel Center, Saint Louis, MO, 510

Personnel Center (AFRES)
Air Force Reserve Command Personnel Center, Denver, CO, 148

Personnel Support Activity
Great Lakes Naval Training Center, Great Lakes, IL, 308

Personnel Support Activity Det
New London Naval Submarine Base, Groton, CT, 158
North Island Naval Air Station, San Diego, CA, 115
San Diego Naval Station, San Diego, CA, 122
Sasebo, US Fleet Activities, Japan, 1080
Yorktown Naval Weapons Station, Yorktown, VA, 910

Personnel Support Activity Det, Lemoore
Lemoore Naval Air Station, Lemoore, CA, 74

Personnel Support Activity Det, Mechanicsburg
Mechanicsburg Navy Inventory Control Point, Mechanicsburg, PA, 706

Personnel Support Activity Det, Newport
Naval Education and Training Center, Newport, Newport, RI, 726

Personnel Support Activity Det, Panama
Panama Canal Naval Station, Panama, 1137

Personnel Support Activity Det, Wahiawa
Naval Computer & Telecommunications Area Master Station, Eastern Pacific, Wahiawa, HI, 288

Reserve Readiness Command Region 19
San Diego Fleet and Industrial Supply Center, San Diego, CA, 118

Personnel Support Det
Dam Neck, Fleet Combat Training Center, Atlantic, Virginia Beach, VA, 902
Ingleside Naval Station, Ingleside, TX, 806
Lakehurst Naval Air Engineering Station, Lakehurst, NJ, 560
Navy Supply Corps School, Athens, GA, 240
Sabana Seca, US Naval Security Group Activity, Puerto Rico, 1144
Scotia Naval Administrative Unit, Scotia, NY, 608

Personnel Support Det, Naval Training Center
Great Lakes Naval Training Center, Great Lakes, IL, 308

Personnel Support Det Newport
Naval Education and Training Center, Newport, Newport, RI, 726

Personnel Support Det, Pearl Harbor
Pearl Harbor Naval Complex, Pearl Harbor, HI, 283

Personnel Support Det, Recruit Training Command
Great Lakes Naval Training Center, Great Lakes, IL, 308

PHIB CB 1 Det 309 (NR)
Louisville Naval Reserve Center, Louisville, KY, 371

PHIB CB 2 Det 205 (NR)
Toledo Naval & Marine Corps Reserve Center, Perrysburg, OH, 662

PHIB CB 2 Det 405 (NR)
Ebensburg Naval & Marine Corps Reserve Center, Ebensburg, PA, 702

PHIB CB 1 Det 313 (NR)
Evansville Naval & Marine Corps Reserve Center, Evansville, IN, 326

Phillips Laboratory
Edwards Air Force Base, Edwards AFB, CA, 63
Kirtland Air Force Base, Kirtland AFB, NM, 572

Phillips Laboratory, Maui
Maui Space Surveillance Complex, Kihei, HI, 280

Physical Fitness School
Fort Benning, Fort Benning, GA, 248

Pillar Point Air Force Station
Pillar Point Air Force Station, El Granada, CA, 65

Pine Bluff Arsenal
Pine Bluff Arsenal, Pine Bluff, AR, 53

Pinon Canyon Maneuver Site
Fort Carson and 4th Infantry Division (Mechanized), Fort Carson, CO, 152

Pioneer Kaserne
282nd Base Support Battalion, Germany, 995
414th Base Support Battalion, Germany, 997

Pioneer Village Family Housing
414th Base Support Battalion, Germany, 997

Planning & Management Laboratory
US Army Corps of Engineers, Construction Engineering Research Laboratories, Champaign, IL, 300

Pond Barracks
282nd Base Support Battalion, Germany, 995

Port Security Unit 309 (USCGR)
Camp Perry Training Site, Port Clinton, OH, 663

Port Security Unit Training Det (USCG)
Camp Perry Training Site, Port Clinton, OH, 663

Port Services, Kin Red Pier
Kadena Naval Air Facility, Japan, 1075

Portsmouth Naval Shipyard
Portsmouth Naval Shipyard, Portsmouth, NH, 551

Post Exchange
Tobyhanna Army Depot, Tobyhanna, PA, 721

Post HQ, Ft Story
Fort Story, Fort Story, VA, 871

Prepositioning Programs Support Directorate
Albany Marine Corps Logistics Base, Albany, GA, 239

Prior Service Recruiting (USMC)
Phoenix Naval & Marine Corps Reserve Readiness Center, Phoenix, AZ, 40

Production Center, Bethesda, MD
National Imagery & Mapping Agency, Fairfax, VA, 860

Production Center, Reston Center, Reston, VA
National Imagery & Mapping Agency, Fairfax, VA, 860

Production Center, St Louis, MO
National Imagery & Mapping Agency, Fairfax, VA, 860

Production Center, Washington, DC
National Imagery & Mapping Agency, Fairfax, VA, 860

Professional Education Center
Camp Joseph T Robinson, North Little Rock, AR, 52

Program Executive Office for Command, Control & Communications Systems (PEO C3S)
Fort Monmouth, Fort Monmouth, NJ, 557

Program Executive Office for Intelligence & Electronic Warfare (PEO IEW)
Fort Monmouth, Fort Monmouth, NJ, 557

Program Executive Officer, Armored Systems Modernization (PEOASM)
Armament Research, Development, and Engineering Center, US Army TACOM, Picatinny Arsenal, NJ, 562

Program Executive Officer, Field Artillery Systems (PEOFAS)
Armament Research, Development, and Engineering Center, US Army TACOM, Picatinny Arsenal, NJ, 562

Program Executive Officer, Ground Combat and Support Systems (PEOGCSS)
Armament Research, Development, and Engineering Center, US Army TACOM, Picatinny Arsenal, NJ, 562

Program Management Office Strategic Systems Programs Det
Program Management Office, Strategic Systems Programs Detachment, Magna, UT, 826

Program Manager Chemical Demilitarization
Aberdeen Proving Ground, Aberdeen Proving Ground, MD, 404
Army Chemical Activity Pacific, Johnston Atoll, 1086

Project Manager Abrams Tank Systems
Aberdeen Proving Ground, Aberdeen Proving Ground, MD, 404

Propulsion Training Facility
Charleston, Naval Weapons Station, Charleston, SC, 734

Provost Marshal, West Point
West Point, Army Garrison, West Point, NY, 614

PSD Miramar Reserve Dept
San Diego Naval & Marine Corps Reserve Center, San Diego, CA, 120

PSD SOEUR Support Unit (NR)
Greensboro Naval & Marine Corps Reserve Readiness Center, Greensboro, NC, 626

Public Works Center
Washington, Naval Station, Washington, DC, 189

Public Works Center/Engineering Field Activity
Great Lakes Naval Training Center, Great Lakes, IL, 308

Public Works Center, Great Lakes
Recruit Training Command Great Lakes, Great Lakes, IL, 309

Public Works Center, Guam
Naval Station, Guam, Guam, 1047

Public Works Center, Pearl Harbor
Pearl Harbor Navy Public Works Center, Pearl Harbor, HI, 285

Public Works Center, San Diego
Concord Naval Weapons Station, Concord, CA, 61

Public Works Center, Virginia Beach Site
Dam Neck, Fleet Combat Training Center, Atlantic, Virginia Beach, VA, 902

Puerto Rico National Guard
Adjutant General of Puerto Rico, Puerto Rico, 1139

Pulaski Barracks
Kaiserslautern Military Community, Germany, 1013

Pusan Storage Facility
Pusan Storage Facility, Korea, Republic of, 1119

Quality Assurance Division
Navy Clothing and Textile Research Facility, Natick, MA, 442

Quantico Marine Corps Band
Quantico Marine Corps Combat Development Command, Quantico, VA, 895

Quartermaster Center and School
Fort Lee, Fort Lee, VA, 869

Quartermaster Kaserne
Augsburg Military Community, Germany, 999

Quirnheim Missile Station
293rd Base Support Battalion, Germany, 996

Andrew Rader Medical Clinic
Fort Myer, Arlington, VA, 847

Radio Transmitter Facility, Lualualei
Lualualei Naval Magazine, Waianae, HI, 289

Ramstein Air Base
Kaiserslautern Military Community, Germany, 1013

Range Control
Quantico Marine Corps Combat Development Command, Quantico, VA, 895

Ranger Training Brigade
Fort Benning, Fort Benning, GA, 248

Ray Barracks
Friedberg Area Support Team, Germany, 1007

Readiness Group, Atlanta
Fort Gillem, Forest Park, GA, 247

Readiness Group, Bragg
Fort Bragg, Fort Bragg, NC, 624

Readiness Group, Dix
Fort Dix, Fort Dix, NJ, 555

Readiness Group, Knox
Army Armor Center & Fort Knox, Fort Knox, KY, 366

Readiness Group, Lee
Fort Lee, Fort Lee, VA, 869

Readiness Group, Meade
Fort George G Meade, Fort Meade, MD, 422

Readiness Unit (NR)
Lincoln Naval Reserve Center, Lincoln, NE, 529

Recruit Training Command
Great Lakes Naval Training Center, Great Lakes, IL, 308
Recruit Training Command Great Lakes, Great Lakes, IL, 309

Recruit Training Regiment
San Diego Marine Corps Recruit Depot, San Diego, CA, 119

Recruiters School
San Diego Marine Corps Recruit Depot, San Diego, CA, 119

Recruiting (DC ARNG)
District of Columbia National Guard, HQ, Washington, DC, 176

Red River Army Depot
Red River Army Depot, Texarkana, TX, 818

REDCOM ONE Activity
Albany Naval & Marine Corps Reserve Readiness Center, Albany, NY, 575
Bangor Naval Reserve Center, Bangor, ME, 394
Buffalo Naval & Marine Corps Reserve Center, Buffalo, NY, 583
Erie Naval & Marine Corps Reserve Center, Erie, PA, 703
Frankfort Naval Reserve Center, Frankfort, NY, 587
Glens Falls Naval Reserve Center, Glens Falls, NY, 589
Horseheads Naval Reserve Center, Horseheads, NY, 590
Manchester Naval & Marine Corps Reserve Center, Bedford, NH, 546
New Haven Naval & Marine Corps Reserve Center, New Haven, CT, 160
Plainville Naval & Marine Corps Reserve Center, Plainville, CT, 164

Portland Naval Reserve Readiness Center, Portland, ME, 400
Providence Naval & Marine Corps Reserve Center, Providence, RI, 729
Rochester Naval & Marine Corps Reserve Center, Rochester, NY, 603
Syracuse Naval & Marine Corps Reserve Center, Mattydale, NY, 593
Watertown Naval Reserve Center, Watertown, NY, 611
Worcester Naval & Marine Corps Reserve Center, Worcester, MA, 448

REDCOM FOUR Activity
Amityville Naval & Marine Corps Reserve Center, Amityville, NY, 576
Avoca Naval Reserve Center, Avoca, PA, 697
Bronx Naval & Marine Corps Reserve Center, Bronx, NY, 578
Ebensburg Naval & Marine Corps Reserve Center, Ebensburg, PA, 702
Harrisburg Naval & Marine Corps Reserve Center, Harrisburg, PA, 704
Kearny Naval Reserve Readiness Center, Kearny, NJ, 559
Lehigh Valley Naval & Marine Corps Reserve Center, Allentown, PA, 694
Moundsville Naval & Marine Corps Reserve Center, Moundsville, WV, 949
Pittsburgh Naval & Marine Corps Reserve Readiness Center, North Versailles, PA, 710
Reading Naval & Marine Corps Reserve Center, Reading, PA, 719
Williamsport Naval & Marine Corps Reserve Center, Williamsport, PA, 722
Wilmington (DE) Naval & Marine Corps Reserve Center, Wilmington, DE, 170

REDCOM SIX Activity
Adelphi Naval Reserve Center, Adelphi, MD, 406
Asheville Naval Reserve Center, Asheville, NC, 616
Baltimore Naval Reserve Readiness Center, Baltimore, MD, 413
Charleston Naval & Marine Corps Reserve Center, Charleston, WV, 943
Charlotte Naval & Marine Corps Reserve Center, Charlotte, NC, 620
Cumberland Naval Reserve Center, Cumberland, MD, 419
Greensboro Naval & Marine Corps Reserve Readiness Center, Greensboro, NC, 626
Huntington Naval Reserve Center, Huntington, WV, 945
Raleigh Naval & Marine Corps Reserve Center, Raleigh, NC, 631
Richmond Naval & Marine Corps Reserve Center, Richmond, VA, 899
Roanoke Naval & Marine Corps Reserve Center, Roanoke, VA, 900
Wilmington (NC) Naval & Marine Corps Reserve Center, Wilmington, NC, 635

REDCOM EIGHT Activity
Atlanta Naval & Marine Corps Reserve Readiness Center, Dobbins AFB, GA, 246
Augusta Naval & Marine Corps Reserve Center, Augusta, GA, 244
Columbia Naval & Marine Corps Reserve Center, Columbia, SC, 739
Columbus Naval Reserve Center, Columbus, GA, 245

Greenville Naval & Marine Corps Reserve Center, Greenville, SC, 744

Miami Naval & Marine Corps Reserve Readiness Center, Hialeah, FL, 198

Orlando Naval & Marine Corps Reserve Readiness Center, Orlando, FL, 217

St Petersburg Naval Reserve Center, Clearwater, FL, 193

Tallahassee Naval & Marine Corps Reserve Center, Tallahassee, FL, 234

Tampa Naval Reserve Center, Tampa, FL, 236

West Palm Beach Naval & Marine Corps Reserve Center, West Palm Beach, FL, 237

REDCOM NINE Activity

Baton Rouge Naval & Marine Corps Reserve Center, Baton Rouge, LA, 375

Bessemer Naval & Marine Corps Reserve Readiness Center, Bessemer, AL, 3

Cape Girardeau Naval Reserve Center, Cape Girardeau, MO, 500

Chattanooga Naval & Marine Corps Reserve Center, Chattanooga, TN, 758

Jackson Naval Reserve Center, Jackson, MS, 485

Knoxville Naval & Marine Corps Reserve Center, Knoxville, TN, 761

Lexington Naval Reserve Center, Lexington, KY, 368

Louisville Naval Reserve Center, Louisville, KY, 371

Memphis Naval Reserve Readiness Center, Millington, TN, 768

Mobile Naval & Marine Corps Reserve Center, Mobile, AL, 11

Nashville Naval Reserve Center, Nashville, TN, 771

New Orleans Naval & Marine Corps Reserve Readiness Center, New Orleans, LA, 385

Saint Louis Naval & Marine Corps Reserve Center, Bridgeton, MO, 499

Shreveport Naval & Marine Corps Reserve Center, Bossier City, LA, 376

Springfield Naval & Marine Corps Reserve Center, Springfield, MO, 515

Tuscaloosa Armed Forces Reserve Center, Tuscaloosa, AL, 17

REDCOM ELEVEN Activity

Albuquerque Naval & Marine Corps Reserve Center, Albuquerque, NM, 568

Amarillo Naval & Marine Corps Reserve Center, Amarillo, TX, 775

Austin Naval & Marine Corps Reserve Center, Austin, TX, 776

El Paso Naval & Marine Corps Reserve Readiness Center, El Paso, TX, 789

Harlingen Naval Reserve Center, Harlingen, TX, 802

Houston Naval & Marine Corps Reserve Readiness Center, Houston, TX, 805

Lubbock Naval & Marine Corps Reserve Center, Lubbock, TX, 811

Oklahoma City Naval & Marine Corps Reserve Readiness Center, Oklahoma City, OK, 676

Orange Naval Reserve Center, Orange, TX, 813

San Antonio Naval & Marine Corps Reserve Center, San Antonio, TX, 816

Tulsa Naval & Marine Corps Reserve Center, Broken Arrow, OK, 670

Tyler Naval Reserve Center, Tyler, TX, 819

Waco Naval & Marine Corps Reserve Center, Waco, TX, 820

REDCOM THIRTEEN Activity

Akron Naval & Marine Corps Reserve Center, Akron, OH, 643

Battle Creek Naval & Marine Corps Reserve Center, Battle Creek, MI, 450

Cincinnati Naval & Marine Corps Reserve Center, Cincinnati, OH, 645

Cleveland Naval Reserve Center, Cleveland, OH, 649

Columbus Naval & Marine Corps Readiness Center, Columbus, OH, 652

Dayton Naval & Marine Corps Reserve Readiness Center, Dayton, OH, 656

Decatur Naval Reserve Center, Decatur, IL, 305

Detroit Naval Reserve Readiness Center, Selfridge ANG Base, MI, 463

Evansville Naval & Marine Corps Reserve Center, Evansville, IN, 326

Forest Park Naval Reserve Center, Forest Park, IL, 306

Gary Naval & Marine Corps Reserve Center, Gary, IN, 330

Grand Rapids Naval & Marine Corps Reserve Center, Grand Rapids, MI, 457

Indianapolis Naval & Marine Corps Reserve Readiness Center, Indianapolis, IN, 335

Lansing Naval & Marine Corps Reserve Center, Lansing, MI, 460

Peoria Naval & Marine Corps Reserve Center, Peoria, IL, 313

Rock Island Naval & Marine Corps Reserve Center, Rock Island, IL, 315

Saginaw Naval & Marine Corps Reserve Center, Saginaw, MI, 461

South Bend Naval & Marine Corps Reserve Center, South Bend, IN, 338

Toledo Naval & Marine Corps Reserve Center, Perrysburg, OH, 662

REDCOM SIXTEEN Activity

Calumet Naval Reserve Facility, Calumet, MI, 454

Cedar Rapids Naval Reserve Center, Cedar Rapids, IA, 341

Des Moines Naval & Marine Corps Reserve Center, Des Moines, IA, 343

Dubuque Naval Reserve Center, Dubuque, IA, 344

Duluth Naval Reserve Center, Duluth, MN, 469

Fargo Naval Reserve Center, Fargo, ND, 639

Green Bay Naval & Marine Corps Reserve Center, Green Bay, WI, 955

Kansas City Naval Reserve Readiness Center, Kansas City, MO, 505

La Crosse Naval Reserve Center, La Crosse, WI, 956

Lincoln Naval Reserve Center, Lincoln, NE, 529

Madison Naval & Marine Corps Reserve Center, Madison, WI, 957

Milwaukee Naval & Marine Corps Reserve Center, Milwaukee, WI, 962

Omaha Naval & Marine Corps Reserve Center, Omaha, NE, 531

St Paul Naval & Marine Corps Reserve Center, Saint Paul, MN, 476

Sioux City Naval Reserve Center, Sioux City, IA, 349

Sioux Falls Naval Reserve Center, Sioux Falls, SD, 754

Topeka Naval & Marine Corps Reserve Center, Topeka, KS, 362

Wichita Naval & Marine Corps Reserve Center, Wichita, KS, 364

REDCOM NINETEEN Activity

Bakersfield Naval & Marine Corps Reserve Center, Bakersfield, CA, 56

Encino Naval & Marine Corps Reserve Center, Encino, CA, 67

Fresno Naval Reserve Center, Fresno, CA, 71

Honolulu Naval & Marine Corps Reserve Readiness Center, Honolulu, HI, 276

Las Vegas Naval & Marine Corps Reserve Center, Las Vegas, NV, 539

Phoenix Naval & Marine Corps Reserve Readiness Center, Phoenix, AZ, 40

San Diego Naval & Marine Corps Reserve Center, San Diego, CA, 120

Tucson Naval & Marine Corps Reserve Center, Tucson, AZ, 44

REDCOM TWENTY-TWO Activity

Anchorage Naval Reserve Center, Anchorage, AK, 18

Billings Naval & Marine Corps Reserve Center, Billings, MT, 517

Boise Naval & Marine Corps Reserve Center, Boise, ID, 296

Central Point Naval Reserve Center, Central Point, OR, 683

Eugene Naval & Marine Corps Reserve Center, Eugene, OR, 685

Everett Naval Reserve Center, Everett, WA, 916

Great Falls Naval Reserve Center, Great Falls, MT, 519

Missoula Naval Reserve Center, Missoula, MT, 524

Pocatello Naval Reserve Facility, Pocatello, ID, 299

Portland Naval & Marine Corps Reserve Readiness Center, Portland, OR, 688

Reno Naval & Marine Corps Reserve Center, Reno, NV, 542

Sacramento Naval & Marine Corps Reserve Readiness Center, Sacramento, CA, 106

Salem Naval & Marine Corps Reserve Center, Salem, OR, 693

Salt Lake City Naval & Marine Corps Reserve Center, Salt Lake City, UT, 829

San Bruno Naval & Marine Corps Reserve Center, San Bruno, CA, 108

San Jose Naval & Marine Corps Reserve Center, San Jose, CA, 129

Seattle Naval Reserve Readiness Center, Seattle, WA, 930

Spokane Naval & Marine Corps Reserve Readiness Center, Spokane, WA, 934

Tacoma Naval & Marine Corps Reserve Center, Tacoma, WA, 937

Redstone Scientific Information Center (RSIC)

Redstone Arsenal, Redstone Arsenal, AL, 16

Redstone Technical Test Center (RTTC)

Redstone Arsenal, Redstone Arsenal, AL, 16

Walter Reed Army Institute of Research

Walter Reed Army Medical Center, Washington, DC, 188

Walter Reed Army Medical Center
Walter Reed Army Medical Center, Washington, DC, 188

Regensburg Family Housing
282nd Base Support Battalion, Germany, 995

Regimental Noncommissioned Officer Academy
Army Signal Center & Fort Gordon, Fort Gordon, GA, 249

Regimental Officer Academy
Army Signal Center & Fort Gordon, Fort Gordon, GA, 249

Regional Civilian Personnel Center (CPOC), Redstone Arsenal
Redstone Arsenal, Redstone Arsenal, AL, 16

Regional Civilian Personnel Center, Redstone Arsenal
Redstone Arsenal, Redstone Arsenal, AL, 16

Regional Counterdrug Training Academy
Meridian Naval Air Station, Meridian, MS, 489

Regional Medical Command, Europe
Landstuhl Regional Medical Center, Germany, 1020

Regional Signal Intelligence Operations Center
Army Signal Center & Fort Gordon, Fort Gordon, GA, 249

Regional Support Group
Mayport Naval Air Station, Mayport, FL, 210

Regional Support Group, Ingleside
Ingleside Naval Station, Ingleside, TX, 806

Regional Training Brigade (AC)
Camp Shelby Training Site, Camp Shelby, MS, 478

Regional Training Institute
Camp Shelby Training Site, Camp Shelby, MS, 478
New Mexico National Guard State Headquarters, Santa Fe, NM, 573
Stead Training Center, Reno, NV, 545

Regional Training Site, Maintenance
Fort McCoy, Fort McCoy, WI, 954

Regional Training Site, Maintenance (Camp Dodge)
Camp Dodge Iowa, Johnston, IA, 346

Regional Training Site, Medical
Fort McCoy, Fort McCoy, WI, 954

Regional Training Site, Medical (RTS-Med)
Parks Reserve Forces Training Area, Dublin, CA, 62

Reinwarzhofen Radio Relay Facility
282nd Base Support Battalion, Germany, 995

Repair Division
Barstow, Marine Corps Logistics Base, Barstow, CA, 57

Commander, Republic of Korea/US Forces Korea Combined Forces
Chinhae Fleet Activities, Korea, Republic of, 1114

Reserve Antisubmarine Warfare Training Center (RESASWTRACEN)
Willow Grove Naval Air Station (JRB), Willow Grove, PA, 723

Research & Development Activity (night-vision & electronic sensing)
Davison Army Airfield, Fort Belvoir, VA, 864

Research & Development Center, Avery Point
Coast Guard Academy, New London, CT, 161

Research & Development Liaison Office London (USAF)
Research & Development Liaison Office London (USAF), London, United Kingdom, 1165

Reserve Component Enclave (13 US Army Reserve Units)
Army Transportation Center & Fort Eustis, Fort Eustis, VA, 868

Reserve Forces Center, Old Fort Benjamin Harrison
Old Fort Benjamin Harrison, Indianapolis, IN, 336

Reserve I & I (USMC)
Cincinnati Naval & Marine Corps Reserve Center, Cincinnati, OH, 645

Reserve Intelligence Programs Office Six (RIPO Six)
Dallas Naval Air Station, Dallas, TX, 783

ROTC Cadet Command HQ
Fort Monroe, Fort Monroe, VA, 870

Reserve Readiness Center
Great Lakes Naval Training Center, Great Lakes, IL, 308

Naval Computer & Telecommunications Center
San Diego Fleet and Industrial Supply Center, San Diego, CA, 118

Reserve Training Site, Medical
Reserve Base, Fort Chaffee, Fort Smith, AR, 48

Residence of Vice President
US Naval Observatory, Washington, DC, 186

Resident Integrated Logistics Support Activity
Defense Plant Representative Office, Air Force Plant No 4, Fort Worth, TX, 795

Resident Officer-in-Charge of Construction
Concord Naval Weapons Station, Concord, CA, 61

Resident Officer in Charge of Construction (ROICC)
Roosevelt Roads Naval Station, Puerto Rico, 1143

Resource Management Directorate
Army Reserve Personnel Center, Saint Louis, MO, 510

Resource Management Division
Barstow, Marine Corps Logistics Base, Barstow, CA, 57

RETRO FVR
Camp Shelby Training Site, Camp Shelby, MS, 478

Rhein Main Air Base
223rd Base Support Battalion, Germany, 993

Rheinau Coal Point D-1
293rd Base Support Battalion, Germany, 996

Rheinblick Recreation Annex
221st Base Support Battalion, Germany, 992

Rheingrafenstein Training & Storage Area
Rose Barracks, Germany, 1027

Rhine Ordnance Barracks
Kaiserslautern Military Community, Germany, 1013

Rhode Island National Guard
Adjutant General of Rhode Island, Cranston, RI, 725

RNCFSU 3 Det C (NR)
Greensboro Naval & Marine Corps Reserve Readiness Center, Greensboro, NC, 626

RNCMB 15, Det 0715
Sioux Falls Naval Reserve Center, Sioux Falls, SD, 754

RNMCB 15 Det 0415 (NR)
Lincoln Naval Reserve Center, Lincoln, NE, 529

RNMCB 24 Det 0824 (NR)
Greensboro Naval & Marine Corps Reserve Readiness Center, Greensboro, NC, 626

RNMCB 23 Det 0623
Cumberland Naval Reserve Center, Cumberland, MD, 419

Robinson Barracks
6th Area Support Group, Stuttgart, Germany, 988

Robinson-Grendadier Family Housing
6th Area Support Group, Stuttgart, Germany, 988

Rock Island National Cemetery
Rock Island Arsenal, Rock Island, IL, 314

Rocky Mountain Arsenal
Rocky Mountain Arsenal, Commerce City, CO, 147

Rodelheim Ordnance Facility
223rd Base Support Battalion, Germany, 993

Rome Laboratories
Northeast Air Defense Sector, Rome, NY, 604

RIPO/RIAC-14
Atlanta Naval Air Station, Marietta, GA, 254

Rose Barracks
Rose Barracks, Germany, 1027

Rotterdam Administration Facility
254th Base Support Battalion, Netherlands, 1127

Rottershausen Ammunition Storage Area
280th Base Support Battalion, Germany, 994

Sabre Drill Team
Gunter Annex, Gunter, AL, 6

Sacramento Air Logistics Center
McClellan Air Force Base, McClellan AFB, CA, 81

Sagami General Depot
Camp Zama, Japan, 1071

Sambach AFN Facility
Kaiserslautern Military Community, Germany, 1013

San Antonio Air Logistics Center
Kelly Air Force Base, Kelly AFB, TX, 807

San Gottardo Signal Site
Caserma Ederle/Vicenza Military Community, Vincenza, Italy, 1060

San Nicholas Island, Outlying Landing Field
Point Mugu, Naval Air Weapons Station, Point Mugu, CA, 98

Sandia National Laboratories
Kirtland Air Force Base, Kirtland AFB, NM, 572

Sandia National Laboratories, Kauai Test Facility
Pacific Missile Range Facility, Kekaha, HI, 279

Sanem Site
80th Area Support Group, Belgium, 975

Satellite Communication Station (SATCOM)
Western Mobilization & Training Complex, Paso Robles, CA, 95

Schinnen Army Base
254th Base Support Battalion, Netherlands, 1127

School of Engineering and Logistics (AMC)
Red River Army Depot, Texarkana, TX, 818

School of Military Packaging Technology
Aberdeen Proving Ground, Aberdeen Proving Ground, MD, 404

School of the Americas
Fort Benning, Fort Benning, GA, 248

Schwanberg Defense Communication Site
Kitzingen Military Community, Germany, 1017

Schweinfurt Training Areas
280th Base Support Battalion, Germany, 994

Schwetzingen Training Area
Heidelberg Military Community, Germany, 1011

Science & Technology Center
221st Base Support Battalion, Germany, 992

Sea-Air Land Team Two (SEAL, Amphibious Force, Navy Atlantic Fleet)
Fort A P Hill, Bowling Green, VA, 855

Commander, Sea Control Wing, US Atlantic Fleet
Cecil Field Naval Air Station, Jacksonville, FL, 202

Sea Girt National Guard Training Center
Sea Girt National Guard Training Center, Sea Girt, NJ, 564

Seabee Division
Kingsville Naval Air Station, Kingsville, TX, 808

Seabees
Anacostia Naval Station, Washington, DC, 171

SECGRU Greensboro (NR)
Greensboro Naval & Marine Corps Reserve Readiness Center, Greensboro, NC, 626

Secretary of Defense
The Pentagon, Arlington, VA, 852

Secretary of the Air Force
The Pentagon, Arlington, VA, 852

Secretary of the Army
The Pentagon, Arlington, VA, 852

Secretary of the Navy
The Pentagon, Arlington, VA, 852

Secure Communications Branch
Balikesir Air Field, Turkey, 1151

Security Bn
Quantico Marine Corps Combat Development Command, Quantico, VA, 895

Security Police Branch
Balikesir Air Field, Turkey, 1151

Selective Service System, Region III
Great Lakes Naval Training Center, Great Lakes, IL, 308

Self Defense Test Ship
Port Hueneme Division, Naval Surface Warfare Center, Port Hueneme, CA, 103

Sembach Annex
Ramstein Air Base, Germany, 1023

Seneca Army Depot Activity
Seneca Army Depot Activity, Romulus, NY, 605

Senior Army Advisor PR ANG
Fort Buchanan Army Garrison, Puerto Rico, 1141

SNCO Battle Skills Course
Camp Hansen, Japan, 1067

Sensors and Electron Devices Directorate
Adelphi Laboratory Center, Army Research Laboratory, Adelphi, MD, 405

Sergeants School, Okinawa
Camp Hansen, Japan, 1067

Service School Command
Great Lakes Naval Training Center, Great Lakes, IL, 308
Recruit Training Command Great Lakes, Great Lakes, IL, 309

Sheridan Barracks
6th Area Support Group, Garmish, Germany, 987

Sheridan Kaserne
Augsburg Military Community, Germany, 999

Ship Repair Facility Det
Sasebo, US Fleet Activities, Japan, 1080

Ship Repair Unit Det Bahrain
Administrative Support Unit, South West Asia, Bahrain, 973

Shipboard Electronic Systems Evaluation Facility
Fort Story, Fort Story, VA, 871

Shipton Kaserne
Barton Barracks, Ansbach, Germany, 1002

Shipyard, Ensley Engineer Yard
US Army Corps of Engineers, Memphis District, Memphis, TN, 765

Shore Intermediate Maintenance Activity
Mayport Naval Air Station, Mayport, FL, 210
Pascagoula Naval Station, Pascagoula, MS, 490
San Diego Naval Station, San Diego, CA, 122

Shore Intermediate Maintenance Activity, NY Det
Earle Naval Weapons Station, Colts Neck, NJ, 554

Shore Intermediate Maintenance Activity, Portsmouth
Shore Intermediate Maintenance Activity, Portsmouth, VA, 894

Shore Intermediate Maintenance Facility
Ingleside Naval Station, Ingleside, TX, 806

Sierra Army Depot
Sierra Army Depot, Herlong, CA, 73

Signatures Directorate
Carderock Division, Naval Surface Warfare Center, West Bethesda, MD, 429

SIMA San Diego 2318 (NR)
Cape Girardeau Naval Reserve Center, Cape Girardeau, MO, 500

Simulation & Analysis Facility
Wright-Patterson Air Force Base, Wright-Patterson AFB, OH, 667

Site Activation Task Force, Det 17
Charleston Air Force Base, Charleston AFB, SC, 737

Small Boat Station, Cape May
Cape May Coast Guard Training Center, Cape May, NJ, 553

Small Computer Division
Gunter Annex, Gunter, AL, 6

Smith Barracks
Baumholder Military Community, H.D. Smith Barracks, Germany, 1003

Soldier Show (Army Community & Family Support Center)
Fort Belvoir, Fort Belvoir, VA, 866

Soldier Systems Command
Fort Benning, Fort Benning, GA, 248

Soldier's & Airmen's Home
US Soldiers' and Airmen's Home, Washington, DC, 187

Soldiers **Magazine**
Fort Belvoir, Fort Belvoir, VA, 866

Sonar Test Facility Seneca Lake
Seneca Lake Sonar Test Facility, Lake Seneca, NY, 591

South Carolina National Guard
Adjutant General of South Carolina, Columbia, SC, 738

South Dakota Air National Guard, HQ
South Dakota Air National Guard Base, Sioux Falls, SD, 755

South Dakota ARNG
Fort Meade Military Reservation, Fort Meade, SD, 751

South Dakota NG
Camp Rapid, Rapid City, SD, 753

Southeast Air Defense Sector
Tyndall Air Force Base, Panama City, FL, 220

Southeast Air Defense Sector, Det 3
Cudjoe Key Air Force Station, Summerland Key, FL, 233

Southeast Air Defense Sector, OL-AB
Operating Location Alpha Bravo South East Air Defense Sector, Old Town, FL, 214

Southeast Civilian Personnel Center (CPOC)
Fort Benning, Fort Benning, GA, 248

Southeast Regional Veterinary Command
Army Signal Center & Fort Gordon, Fort Gordon, GA, 249

Southern Command Network
Fort Clayton, Panama, 1133

Southern Europe Veterinary Det
Caserma Ederle/Vicenza Military Community, Vincenza, Italy, 1060

Southern European Task Force
22nd Area Support Group, Italy, 1050

Southern European Task Force, HQ
Camp Darby, Livorno Military Community, Italy, 1052

Southern European Task Force Infantry Brigade
Camp Darby, Livorno Military Community, Italy, 1052

Space and Missile Systems Center
Los Angeles Air Force Base, Los Angeles, CA, 76

Space & Naval Warfare Systems Center, San Diego
Space & Naval Warfare Systems Command, San Diego, CA, 124

Space Defense Operations Center
Cheyenne Mountain Air Force Station, Colorado Springs, CO, 145

Space, Missile, Electronics, Computers, & Ammunition Team
Industrial Analysis Support Office, Philadelphia, PA, 713

Space Surveillance Center
Cheyenne Mountain Air Force Station, Colorado Springs, CO, 145

Space Warfare Center
Falcon Air Force Base, Falcon AFB, CO, 151

Special Boat Unit 22
New Orleans Naval Support Activity, New Orleans, LA, 386

Special Boat Unit 26
Panama Canal Naval Station, Panama, 1137

Special Forces Recruiting
Fort Benning, Fort Benning, GA, 248

Special Missions Operations Test & Evaluation Center
Hurlburt Field, Hurlburt Field, FL, 200

Special Operations Command, Pacific
Camp H M Smith, Camp Smith, HI, 266

Special Operations Forces Equipment Pool
Camp Dawson, Kingwood, WV, 947

Special Trials Unit
Patuxent River, Naval Air Station, Patuxent River, MD, 427

Spinelli Barracks
293rd Base Support Battalion, Germany, 996

St Barbara Village Family Housing
223rd Base Support Battalion, Germany, 993

Staff Judge Advocate
Army Armor Center & Fort Knox, Fort Knox, KY, 366

Staff Judge Advocate, Ramstein
Ramstein Air Base, Germany, 1023

Staff Noncommissioned Officers Academy
Quantico Marine Corps Combat Development Command, Quantico, VA, 895

Standard Systems Group, Headquarters
Gunter Annex, Gunter, AL, 6

Standardization & Evaluation Division (OGV)
Howard Air Force Base, Panama, 1136

State Area Command, AR ARNG
Camp Joseph T Robinson, North Little Rock, AR, 52

State Area Command, HQ
Boise Air Terminal, Air National Guard Base, Boise, ID, 295
Camp Rapid, Rapid City, SD, 753

State Area Command, HQ, ME ARNG
Camp Keyes, Augusta, ME, 392

State Area Command (STARC), HQ
Jackson Barracks, New Orleans, LA, 382

State Area Readiness Command, Det 2
Camp Perry Training Site, Port Clinton, OH, 663
R L Esmay Training Center, Guernsey, WY, 968

State Area Readiness Command, Det 3
Camp Lincoln, Springfield, IL, 320

State Area Readiness Command, Det 4
Camp Lincoln, Springfield, IL, 320

State Area Readiness Command, HQ
Fort William Henry Harrison, Helena, MT, 523
Nevada National Guard Headquarters, Carson City, NV, 534

State Area Readiness Command HQ, Det 3 (ARNG)
Camp Rilea, Oregon National Guard Training Site, Salem, OR, 692

State Area Readiness Command-NY, Det 2, HQ
Camp Smith, Peekskill, NY, 601

State Area Readiness Command (STARC)
Camp Lincoln, Springfield, IL, 320

State Area Readiness Command-VT, Det 2, HQ
Ethan Allen Firing Range, Jericho, VT, 833

State Environmental Section
Camp Grayling Maneuver Training Center, Grayling, MI, 458

State Headquarters, VA ANG
Richmond IAP Air National Guard Base, Sandston, VA, 901

State Maintenance Office (SMO)
Camp Blanding Training Site, Starke, FL, 232

Steinbachtal Ammunition Area
98th Area Support Group, Germany, 990

Stem Kaserne
Heidelberg Military Community, Germany, 1011

Steuben Family Housing
6th Area Support Group, Stuttgart, Germany, 988

Stocksberg Communication Station
Heidelberg Military Community, Germany, 1011

Storage and Distribution Directorate
Albany Marine Corps Logistics Base, Albany, GA, 239

Storck Barracks
Storck Barracks, Illesheim, Germany, 1032

Strassburg Kaserne
Baumholder Military Community, H.D. Smith Barracks, Germany, 1003

Strategic Maintenance Complex
Charleston, Naval Weapons Station, Charleston, SC, 734

Strategic Mobility Logistics Base (ARMY SMLB)
Charleston, Naval Weapons Station, Charleston, SC, 734

Strategic Studies Institute
Carlisle Barracks, Carlisle Barracks, PA, 698

Strategic Weapons Facility, Atlantic
Kings Bay Naval Submarine Base, Kings Bay, GA, 253

Strategic Weapons Facility, Pacific
Bangor Naval Submarine Base, Silverdale, WA, 932

Strike Fighter Maintenance Unit
El Centro Naval Air Facility, El Centro, CA, 64

Strike Fighter Squadron 22
Lemoore Naval Air Station, Lemoore, CA, 74

Strike Fighter Squadron 25
Lemoore Naval Air Station, Lemoore, CA, 74

Strike Fighter Squadron 27
Lemoore Naval Air Station, Lemoore, CA, 74

Strike Fighter Squadron 94
Lemoore Naval Air Station, Lemoore, CA, 74

Strike Fighter Squadron 97
Lemoore Naval Air Station, Lemoore, CA, 74

Strike Fighter Squadron 113
Lemoore Naval Air Station, Lemoore, CA, 74

Strike Fighter Squadron 115
Lemoore Naval Air Station, Lemoore, CA, 74

Strike Fighter Squadron 125
Lemoore Naval Air Station, Lemoore, CA, 74

Strike Fighter Squadron 137
Lemoore Naval Air Station, Lemoore, CA, 74

Strike Fighter Squadron 146
Lemoore Naval Air Station, Lemoore, CA, 74

Strike Fighter Squadron 147
Lemoore Naval Air Station, Lemoore, CA, 74

Strike Fighter Squadron 151
Lemoore Naval Air Station, Lemoore, CA, 74

Strike Fighter Squadron 192
Lemoore Naval Air Station, Lemoore, CA, 74

Strike Fighter Squadron 195
Lemoore Naval Air Station, Lemoore, CA, 74

Strike Fighter Squadron 204 (VFA-204)(NR)
New Orleans Naval Air Station Joint Reserve Base, Naval Air Station, New Orleans, LA, 384

Strike Fighter Super Hornet Team
Lemoore Naval Air Station, Lemoore, CA, 74

Strike Fighter Weapons School
Lemoore Naval Air Station, Lemoore, CA, 74

Strike Fighter Weapons School, Atlantic
Cecil Field Naval Air Station, Jacksonville, FL, 202

Strike Fighter Wing, Det Fallon
Fallon Naval Air Station, Fallon, NV, 535

Strike Fighter Wing, Pacific
Lemoore Naval Air Station, Lemoore, CA, 74

Commander, Strike Fighter Wing, US Atlantic Fleet
Cecil Field Naval Air Station, Jacksonville, FL, 202

Stuttgart Administration Facility
6th Area Support Group, Stuttgart, Germany, 988

Submarine Base, Pearl Harbor
Pearl Harbor Naval Complex, Pearl Harbor, HI, 283

Submarine Development Squadron 5
San Diego Naval Submarine Base, San Diego, CA, 123

Submarine Development Squadron 12
New London Naval Submarine Base, Groton, CT, 158

Submarine Force, US Pacific Fleet
Pearl Harbor Naval Complex, Pearl Harbor, HI, 283

Submarine Group 2
New London Naval Submarine Base, Groton, CT, 158

Submarine Group 10
Kings Bay Naval Submarine Base, Kings Bay, GA, 253

Submarine Maintenance Engineering Planning & Procurement (SUBMEEP)
Portsmouth Naval Shipyard, Portsmouth, NH, 551

Submarine Rescue Unit
North Island Naval Air Station, San Diego, CA, 115

Submarine Squadron 2
New London Naval Submarine Base, Groton, CT, 158

Submarine Squadron 11
San Diego Naval Submarine Base, San Diego, CA, 123

Submarine Squadron 16
Kings Bay Naval Submarine Base, Kings Bay, GA, 253

Submarine Squadron 17
Bangor Naval Submarine Base, Silverdale, WA, 932

Submarine Squadron 20
Kings Bay Naval Submarine Base, Kings Bay, GA, 253

Submarine Training Facility
San Diego Naval Submarine Base, San Diego, CA, 123

Sullivan Barracks
293rd Base Support Battalion, Germany, 996

Sullivan Heights Family Housing
Augsburg Military Community, Germany, 999

Sulzheim Training Area
280th Base Support Battalion, Germany, 994

Supervisor of Shipbuilding, Conversion and Repair
New London Naval Submarine Base, Groton, CT, 158
New Orleans Naval Support Activity, New Orleans, LA, 386

Supervisor of Shipbuilding, Conversion, and Repair, Pascagoula
Pascagoula, Supervisor of Shipbuilding, Conversion and Repair, Pascagoula, MS, 491

Supervisor of Shipbuilding, Conversion, and Repair, Portsmouth
Norfolk Naval Shipyard, Portsmouth, Portsmouth, VA, 891
Portsmouth Supervisor of Shipbuilding, Conversion and Repair, Portsmouth, VA, 893

Supervisor of Shipbuilding, Newport News
Newport News Supervisor of Shipbuilding, Conversion and Repair, Newport News, VA, 873

Supply Department NTC
Great Lakes Naval Training Center, Great Lakes, IL, 308

Support Bn
Parris Island Marine Corps Recruit Depot/Eastern Recruiting Region, Parris Island, SC, 747

Support Branch
Balikesir Air Field, Turkey, 1151

Support Center Pacific, Det 15
Kadena Air Base, Japan, 1074

Support Det, Cape May
Cape May Coast Guard Training Center, Cape May, NJ, 553

Support Det, Curtis Bay
Curtis Bay Coast Guard Yard, Curtis Bay, MD, 420

Support Det, Juneau
17th Coast Guard District, Juneau, AK, 29

Support Det, Woods Hole
Woods Hole Coast Guard Group, Woods Hole, MA, 447

Support Troops Bn
White Sands Missile Range, White Sands Missile Range, NM, 574

Support Troops, HQ
Dugway Proving Ground, Dugway, UT, 822

Supreme Headquarters Allied Powers Europe (SHAPE) HQ
80th Area Support Group, Belgium, 975

SUPSHIP 1122
Pocatello Naval Reserve Facility, Pocatello, ID, 299

Surface Force, Atlantic
Norfolk Naval Station, Norfolk, VA, 886

Surface Warfare Engineering Facility
Port Hueneme Division, Naval Surface Warfare Center, Port Hueneme, CA, 103

Surface Warfare Officers School Command
Naval Education and Training Center, Newport, Newport, RI, 726

Survivability, Structures and Materials Directorate
Naval Surface Warfare Center, Carderock Division, Annapolis Detachment, Annapolis, MD, 410

Systems Design Center
Defense Logistics Agency, HQ, Fort Belvoir, VA, 865

Systems Design Center (DSDC)
Defense Supply Center, Columbus, Columbus, OH, 654

Tactical Air Command Logistics Liaison Office
Defense Plant Representative Office, Air Force Plant No 4, Fort Worth, TX, 795

Tactical Air Control Group
Coronado Naval Amphibious Base, San Diego, CA, 109

Tactical Aircrew Combat Training System (TACTS)
Cherry Point Marine Corps Air Station, Cherry Point, NC, 621

Tactical Automated Mission Planning System
Point Mugu, Naval Air Weapons Station, Point Mugu, CA, 98

Tactical Electronic Reconnaissance Processing and Evaluation System
Point Mugu, Naval Air Weapons Station, Point Mugu, CA, 98

Tactical Electronic Warfare Squadron 131
Whidbey Island Naval Air Station, Oak Harbor, WA, 924

Tactical Electronic Warfare Squadron 209 (VAQ-209)
Washington, DC, Naval Air Facility, Andrews AFB, MD, 408

Tactical Exploitation Group
Point Mugu, Naval Air Weapons Station, Point Mugu, CA, 98

Tactical Support Center
Sigonella Naval Air Station, Italy, 1059

Tactical Training Group, Atlantic
Dam Neck, Fleet Combat Training Center, Atlantic, Virginia Beach, VA, 902

Tactical Training Group, Pacific (TTGP)
Fleet Combat Training Center, Pacific, San Diego, CA, 112

Tallahassee Training Unit
Tallahassee Naval & Marine Corps Reserve Center, Tallahassee, FL, 234

Tank Automotive Command (TACOM)
Lima Army Tank Plant, Lima, OH, 658

Team Alpha, Task Force 1-7 ADA (Patriot)
Prince Sultan Air Base, Saudi Arabia, 1146

Commander, Task Force 12
Pearl Harbor Naval Complex, Pearl Harbor, HI, 283

Task Force 72.2
Kadena Naval Air Facility, Japan, 1075

Tatalina Long Range Radar Site (LRRS)
Tatalina Air Force Station, McGrath, AK, 33

Taukkunen Barracks
293rd Base Support Battalion, Germany, 996

Taylor Barracks
293rd Base Support Battalion, Germany, 996

Team C4IEWS
Fort Monmouth, Fort Monmouth, NJ, 557

Technical Center for Explosive Safety
Indian Head Division, Naval Surface Warfare Center, Indian Head, MD, 426

Technical Center for Explosives Safety
Savanna Army Depot Activity, Savanna, IL, 317

Technical Information Innovation Center for JCALS/JEDMICS
Port Hueneme Division, Naval Surface Warfare Center, Port Hueneme, CA, 103

Technical Support Division
Navy Clothing and Textile Research Facility, Natick, MA, 442

Telecommunications Center, Zoeckler Station
Zoeckler Station, Korea, Republic of, 1122

Tennessee Army National Guard
Catoosa Area Training Center, Tunnel Hill, GA, 263

Tennessee National Guard
Adjutant General of Tennessee, Nashville, TN, 769

Test & Evaluation Command
White Sands Missile Range, White Sands Missile Range, NM, 574

Test & Evaluation Group, Det 2
Ellsworth Air Force Base, Ellsworth AFB, SD, 750

Test and Experimentation Command Experimentation Center
Fort Hunter Liggett, Fort Hunter Liggett, CA, 69

Test and Experimentation Command (TEXCOM)
Fort Hood, Fort Hood, TX, 792

TMDE Support Center
221st Base Support Battalion, Germany, 992
Fort Benning, Fort Benning, GA, 248
Fort Lewis, Fort Lewis, WA, 921
Pine Bluff Arsenal, Pine Bluff, AR, 53

TMDE Support Group
Fort Dix, Fort Dix, NJ, 555

TMDE Support System
Letterkenny Army Depot, Chambersburg, PA, 699

Test, Measurement, Diagnostics, and Evaluation Center
Fort Rucker, Fort Rucker, AL, 5

TMDE Support Center (MICOM)
Fort Bragg, Fort Bragg, NC, 624

Texas Air National Guard
Houston Coast Guard Air Station, Houston, TX, 804

Texas Air National Guard, HQ
Camp Mabry, Austin, TX, 777

Texas Army National Guard, HQ
Camp Mabry, Austin, TX, 777

Texas National Guard Academy
Camp Mabry, Austin, TX, 777

Texas State Guard
Camp Mabry, Austin, TX, 777

Tiergarten Training Area
414th Base Support Battalion, Germany, 997

TMC Team, Det 6, HQ STARC (AMMED)
Camp Grayling Maneuver Training Center, Grayling, MI, 458

Tompkins Barracks
Heidelberg Military Community, Germany, 1011

Total Army Warrant Officer Career Center
Fort Rucker, Fort Rucker, AL, 5

Total Quality Leadership Team, Pacific
Fleet Antisubmarine Warfare Training Center, Pacific, San Diego, CA, 111

Total Ship Systems Directorate
Carderock Division, Naval Surface Warfare Center, West Bethesda, MD, 429

TRADOC Analysis Command, Headquarters
Fort Leavenworth, Fort Leavenworth, KS, 352

TRADOC Contracting Activity
Army Transportation Center & Fort Eustis, Fort Eustis, VA, 868

TRADOC HQ
Fort Monroe, Fort Monroe, VA, 870

TRADOC Region G
Fort Lewis, Fort Lewis, WA, 921

TRADOC Regional Coordinating Element (DELTA)
Army Armor Center & Fort Knox, Fort Knox, KY, 366

TRADOC System Manager, Antitank Missiles
Fort Benning, Fort Benning, GA, 248

TRADOC System Manager, Bradley Fighting Vehicle System
Fort Benning, Fort Benning, GA, 248

TRADOC System Manager for Tactical Wheeled Vehicle Modernization
Army Transportation Center & Fort Eustis, Fort Eustis, VA, 868

TRADOC System Manager (TSM) for Abraams
Army Armor Center & Fort Knox, Fort Knox, KY, 366

TRADOC System Manager (TSM) for Force XXI
Army Armor Center & Fort Knox, Fort Knox, KY, 366

TRADOC Tactical Wheeled Requirements Management Office
Army Transportation Center & Fort Eustis, Fort Eustis, VA, 868

Training Air Wing 1
Meridian Naval Air Station, Meridian, MS, 489

Commander, Training Air Wing 2 (CTWII)
Kingsville Naval Air Station, Kingsville, TX, 808

Training Air Wing Four
Corpus Christi Naval Air Station, Corpus Christi, TX, 780

Training & Technical Assistance Center
Yorktown Coast Guard Reserve Training Center, Yorktown, VA, 909

Training & Training Technology Battle Lab (T3BL)
Fort Dix, Fort Dix, NJ, 555

Training Command, Atlantic Fleet
Norfolk Naval Station, Norfolk, VA, 886

Training Command, US Atlantic Fleet
Training Command, US Atlantic Fleet, Norfolk, VA, 888

Training Squadron 2 (VT-2)
Whiting Field Naval Air Station, Milton, FL, 213

Training Squadron 3 (VT-3)
Whiting Field Naval Air Station, Milton, FL, 213

Training Squadron 6 (VT-6)
Whiting Field Naval Air Station, Milton, FL, 213

Training Squadron 7 (VT-7)
Meridian Naval Air Station, Meridian, MS, 489

Training Squadron 19 (VT-19)
Meridian Naval Air Station, Meridian, MS, 489

Training Squadron 21 (VT-21)
Kingsville Naval Air Station, Kingsville, TX, 808

Training Squadron 22 (VT-22)
Kingsville Naval Air Station, Kingsville, TX, 808

Training Squadron 23 (VT-23)
Meridian Naval Air Station, Meridian, MS, 489

Training Squadron 27 (VT-27)
Corpus Christi Naval Air Station, Corpus Christi, TX, 780

Training Squadron 28 (VT-28)
Corpus Christi Naval Air Station, Corpus Christi, TX, 780

Training Support Bn, Pittsburgh
Charles E Kelly Support Facility, Oakdale, PA, 711

Training Support Brigade-Travis
Military Traffic Management Command, Western Area, Oakland, CA, 89

Training Support Squadron, Det 1 (ACC)
Luke Air Force Base, Luke AFB, AZ, 37

Transient Personnel Unit
Great Lakes Naval Training Center, Great Lakes, IL, 308
Norfolk Naval Station, Norfolk, VA, 886
San Diego Naval Station, San Diego, CA, 122

Transportation Engineering Agency, MTMC
Transportation Engineering Agency, MTMC, Newport News, VA, 874

Tri-Care Northeast Region
Walter Reed Army Medical Center, Washington, DC, 188

Trident Refit Facility
Bangor Naval Submarine Base, Silverdale, WA, 932

Trident Training Facility
Bangor Naval Submarine Base, Silverdale, WA, 932

Kings Bay Naval Submarine Base, Kings Bay, GA, 253

Troop Command, Tripler Army Medical Center
Tripler Army Medical Center, Tripler AMC, HI, 287

Turley Barracks
293rd Base Support Battalion, Germany, 996

Twin Cities Army Ammunition Plant
Twin Cities Army Ammunition Plant, Arden Hills, MN, 467

Uhlerborn Housing Area
221st Base Support Battalion, Germany, 992

Commander Undersea Surveillance
Dam Neck, Fleet Combat Training Center, Atlantic, Virginia Beach, VA, 902

Underwater Construction Team Two
Port Hueneme, Naval Construction Battalion Center, Port Hueneme, CA, 104

Underway Replenishment Test Site
Port Hueneme Division, Naval Surface Warfare Center, Port Hueneme, CA, 103

Uniform Distribution Center, Cape May
Cape May Coast Guard Training Center, Cape May, NJ, 553

Uniformed Services University of the Health Sciences
National Naval Medical Center, Bethesda, MD, 417

Unit Training Equipment Shop 2
Camp Perry Training Site, Port Clinton, OH, 663

Unit Training Equipment Site 3
Camp Swift Training Site, Bastrop, TX, 778

Unit Training Equipment Site (UTES)
Camp W G Williams, Riverton, UT, 827
Fort Dix, Fort Dix, NJ, 555

Unit Training Equipment Site (UTES) #1
Camp Gruber, Army National Guard Training Site, Braggs, OK, 669

United Defense
Western Mobilization & Training Complex, Paso Robles, CA, 95

United Nations Command
Yongsan Army Garrison, Korea, Republic of, 1121

Commander, United Nations Command Naval Component
Chinhae Fleet Activities, Korea, Republic of, 1114

United Nations Command (Rear), HQ
Camp Zama, Japan, 1071

USO of South Texas
Ingleside Naval Station, Ingleside, TX, 806

US Seventh Fleet
Yokosuka, Fleet Activities, Japan, 1083

USAFE Air Postal Squadron, Det 1
USAFE Air Postal Squadron, Det 1, Germany, 1036

USAFE Command Surgeon
Ramstein Air Base, Germany, 1023

USAFE Contracting Squadron
Ramstein Air Base, Germany, 1023

HQ USAFE/CSS
Ramstein Air Base, Germany, 1023

HQ USAFE/DP
Ramstein Air Base, Germany, 1023

USAF Europe, HQ
Ramstein Air Base, Germany, 1023

HQ USAFE/LG
Ramstein Air Base, Germany, 1023

US Air Forces in Europe (USAFE)
Alconbury RAF Base, United Kingdom, 1156
Lakenheath RAF Base, United Kingdom, 1161

US Army Europe (USAREUR), HQ
Campbell Barracks, Germany, 1005
Heidelberg Military Community, Germany, 1011

USAREUR Office of the Chaplain
Campbell Barracks, Germany, 1005

USAREUR Vehicle Registry
Taylor Barracks, Germany, 1034

USA Materiel Support Center-Korea
Camp Carroll, Korea, Republic of, 1088

US Atlantic Command
United States Atlantic Command, Norfolk, VA, 889

US Bullion Depository
Army Armor Center & Fort Knox, Fort Knox, KY, 366

US Central Command
MacDill Air Force Base, MacDill AFB, FL, 209

USCGC *Assateague*
Honolulu Coast Guard Base/Station, Honolulu, HI, 275

USCGC *Axe*
Mobile Coast Guard Group/Station, Mobile, AL, 10

USCGC *Barnof*
Miami Beach Coast Guard Group/Station, Miami Beach, FL, 212

USCGC *Bayberry*
Seattle Coast Guard Integrated Support Command, Seattle, WA, 929

USCGC *Bittersweet*
Woods Hole Coast Guard Group, Woods Hole, MA, 447

USCGC *Boutwell*
Alameda Coast Guard Integrated Support Command, Alameda, CA, 54

USCGC *Bridle*
Southwest Harbor Coast Guard Group, Southwest Harbor, ME, 402

USCGC *Bristol Bay* **(WTGB-102)**
Detroit Coast Guard Group/Base, Detroit, MI, 455

USCGC *Buckthorn*
Sault Ste Marie Coast Guard Group, Sault Ste Marie, MI, 462

USCGC *Buttonwood*
San Francisco Coast Guard Air Station, San Francisco, CA, 125
San Francisco Coast Guard Group, San Francisco, CA, 126

USCGC *Capstan*
Philadelphia Coast Guard Marine Safety Office & Group, Philadelphia, PA, 714

USCGC *Chandeleur*
Miami Beach Coast Guard Group/Station, Miami Beach, FL, 212

USCGC *Cheyenne*
Saint Louis Coast Guard Base, Saint Louis, MO, 513

USCGC *Chincoteague*
Mobile Coast Guard Group/Station, Mobile, AL, 10

USCGC *Clamp*
Galveston Coast Guard Base, Galveston, TX, 798

USCGC *Cleat*
Philadelphia Coast Guard Marine Safety Office & Group, Philadelphia, PA, 714

USCGC *Cuttyhunk*
Port Angeles Coast Guard Air Station/ Group, Port Angeles, WA, 926

USCGC *Dauntless*
Galveston Coast Guard Base, Galveston, TX, 798

USCGC *Durable*
St Petersburg Coast Guard Group/Station, Saint Petersburg, FL, 231

USCGC *Eagle*
Coast Guard Academy, New London, CT, 161

USCGC *Escanaba* **(WMEC-907)**
Boston Coast Guard Reserve Center, Boston, MA, 432

USCGC *Farallon*
Miami Beach Coast Guard Group/Station, Miami Beach, FL, 212

USCGC *Firebush* **(WLB-393)**
Kodiak Coast Guard Integrated Support Command, Kodiak, AK, 32

USCGC *Hatchet*
Galveston Coast Guard Base, Galveston, TX, 798

USCGC *Hornbeam*
Cape May Coast Guard Training Center, Cape May, NJ, 553

USCGC *Lewis* **(WLM-551)**
Naval Education and Training Center, Newport, Newport, RI, 726

USCGC *Ironwood* **(WLB-297)**
Kodiak Coast Guard Integrated Support Command, Kodiak, AK, 32

USCGC *Jarvis*
Honolulu Coast Guard Base/Station, Honolulu, HI, 275

USCGC *Juniper* **(WLB-201)**
Naval Education and Training Center, Newport, Newport, RI, 726

USCGC *Katmai Bay*
Sault Ste Marie Coast Guard Group, Sault Ste Marie, MI, 462

USCGC *Madrona*
Charleston Coast Guard Group, Charleston, SC, 732

USCGC *Mallow*
Honolulu Coast Guard Base/Station, Honolulu, HI, 275

USCGC *Manitou*
Miami Beach Coast Guard Group/Station, Miami Beach, FL, 212

USCGC *Mariposa*
Seattle Coast Guard Integrated Support Command, Seattle, WA, 929

USCGC *Matagorda*
Miami Beach Coast Guard Group/Station, Miami Beach, FL, 212

USCGC *Matinicus*
Cape May Coast Guard Training Center, Cape May, NJ, 553

USCGC *Maui*
Miami Beach Coast Guard Group/Station, Miami Beach, FL, 212

USCGC *Mellon*
Seattle Coast Guard Integrated Support Command, Seattle, WA, 929

USCGC *Metompkin*
Charleston Coast Guard Group, Charleston, SC, 732

USCGC *Midgett*
Seattle Coast Guard Integrated Support Command, Seattle, WA, 929

USCGC *Monomoy*
Woods Hole Coast Guard Group, Woods Hole, MA, 447

USCGC *Morgenthau*
Alameda Coast Guard Integrated Support Command, Alameda, CA, 54

USCGC *Morro Bay*
Yorktown Coast Guard Reserve Training Center, Yorktown, VA, 909

USCGC *Munro*
Alameda Coast Guard Integrated Support Command, Alameda, CA, 54

USCGC *Naushon*
Ketchikan Coast Guard Station, Ketchikan, AK, 30

USCGC *Obion*
Saint Louis Coast Guard Base, Saint Louis, MO, 513

USCGC *Papaw*
Galveston Coast Guard Base, Galveston, TX, 798

USCGC *Planetree*
Ketchikan Coast Guard Station, Ketchikan, AK, 30

USCGC *Point Batan*
Cape May Coast Guard Training Center, Cape May, NJ, 553

USCGC *Point Brower*
San Francisco Coast Guard Air Station, San Francisco, CA, 125
San Francisco Coast Guard Group, San Francisco, CA, 126

USCGC *Point Francis*
Coast Guard Academy, New London, CT, 161

USCGC *Point Franklin*
Cape May Coast Guard Training Center, Cape May, NJ, 553

USCGC *Point Hobart*
San Diego Coast Guard Activities, San Diego, CA, 117

USCGC *Point Ledge*
Mobile Coast Guard Group/Station, Mobile, AL, 10

USCGC *Point Lobos*
Pensacola Coast Guard Station, Pensacola, FL, 224

USCGC *Point Spencer*
Galveston Coast Guard Base, Galveston, TX, 798

USCGC *Point Steele*
Fort Myers Beach Coast Guard Station, Fort Myers Beach, FL, 196

USCGC *Polar Sea*
Seattle Coast Guard Integrated Support Command, Seattle, WA, 929

USCGC *Polar Star*
Seattle Coast Guard Integrated Support Command, Seattle, WA, 929

USCGC *Rambler*
Charleston Coast Guard Group, Charleston, SC, 732

USCGC *Red Wood*
Philadelphia Coast Guard Marine Safety Office & Group, Philadelphia, PA, 714

USCGC *Resolute*
St Petersburg Coast Guard Group/Station, Saint Petersburg, FL, 231

USCGC *Rush*
Honolulu Coast Guard Base/Station, Honolulu, HI, 275

USCGC *Saginaw*
Mobile Coast Guard Group/Station, Mobile, AL, 10

USCGC *Sanibel*
Woods Hole Coast Guard Group, Woods Hole, MA, 447

USCGC *Sassafras*
Honolulu Coast Guard Base/Station, Honolulu, HI, 275

USCGC *Seneca* **(WMEC-906)**
Boston Coast Guard Reserve Center, Boston, MA, 432

USCGC *Sherman*
Alameda Coast Guard Integrated Support Command, Alameda, CA, 54

USCGC *Spencer* **(WMEC-905)**
Boston Coast Guard Reserve Center, Boston, MA, 432

USCGC *Storis* **(WMEC-38)**
Kodiak Coast Guard Integrated Support Command, Kodiak, AK, 32

USCGC *Sumac*
Saint Louis Coast Guard Base, Saint Louis, MO, 513

USCGC *Sweetgum*
Mobile Coast Guard Group/Station, Mobile, AL, 10

USCGC *Tybee*
San Diego Coast Guard Activities, San Diego, CA, 117

USCGC *Valiant*
Miami Beach Coast Guard Group/Station, Miami Beach, FL, 212

USCGC *Venturous*
St Petersburg Coast Guard Group/Station, Saint Petersburg, FL, 231

USCGC *Vigorous*
Cape May Coast Guard Training Center, Cape May, NJ, 553

USCGC *Vise*
St Petersburg Coast Guard Group/Station, Saint Petersburg, FL, 231

USCGC *Washington*
Honolulu Coast Guard Base/Station, Honolulu, HI, 275

USCGC *White Pine*
Mobile Coast Guard Group/Station, Mobile, AL, 10

USCGC *White Sumac*
St Petersburg Coast Guard Group/Station, Saint Petersburg, FL, 231

USCGC *Willow* **(WLB-202)**
Naval Education and Training Center, Newport, Newport, RI, 726

USCGC *Yocona* **(WMEC-168)**
Kodiak Coast Guard Integrated Support Command, Kodiak, AK, 32

US Customs
March Air Reserve Base, March ARB, CA, 80

US Customs Miami Air Branch
Homestead Air Reserve Base, Homestead ARB, FL, 199

US Customs Service
Corpus Christi Army Depot, Corpus Christi, TX, 779

US European Command
Alconbury RAF Base, United Kingdom, 1156

US Forces Azores Joint Staff
Lajes Field, Portugal, 1138

US Forces Japan
Yokota Air Base, Japan, 1085

US Forces Korea
Yongsan Army Garrison, Korea, Republic of, 1121

US-ROK Combined Forces Command
Yongsan Army Garrison, Korea, Republic of, 1121

US Medical Activity, HQ Co
Heidelberg Military Community, Germany, 1011

United States Military Training Mission
Eskan Village, Saudi Arabia, 1145

Commander-in-Chief, US Naval Forces Europe
West Ruislip RAF Base, United Kingdom, 1170

US Naval Forces, Japan
Yokosuka, Fleet Activities, Japan, 1083

Commander in Chief, US Pacific Command
Pearl Harbor Naval Complex, Pearl Harbor, HI, 283

Commander in Chief, US Pacific Fleet
Pearl Harbor Naval Complex, Pearl Harbor, HI, 283

US Property and Fiscal Office
Camp Blanding Training Site, Starke, FL, 232
Nevada National Guard Headquarters, Carson City, NV, 534

US Property and Fiscal Office for California
Camp San Luis Obispo, San Luis Obispo, CA, 130

US Property and Fiscal Office for Texas
Camp Mabry, Austin, TX, 777

US Property and Fiscal Office—NY
Combined Support Maintenance Shop C/ US Property & Fiscal Office—NY, Rochester, NY, 602

US Property and Fiscal Office Warehouse Facility for LA
Camp Beauregard, Pineville, LA, 388

US Southern Command
US Southern Command, Miami, FL, 211

US Space Command
Cheyenne Mountain Air Force Station, Colorado Springs, CO, 145
Peterson Air Force Base, Peterson AFB, CO, 156

US Space Flight
Hammond Air National Guard Station, Hammond, LA, 378

US Special Operations Command
MacDill Air Force Base, MacDill AFB, FL, 209

US Strategic Command
Offutt Air Force Base, Offutt AFB, NE, 530

US Transportation Command, HQ
Scott Air Force Base, Scott AFB, IL, 318

US Southern Command
Homestead Air Reserve Base, Homestead ARB, FL, 199

USAMC Management Engineer Activity
Letterkenny Army Depot, Chambersburg, PA, 699

USASETAF Lion Brigade
Caserma Ederle/Vicenza Military Community, Vincenza, Italy, 1060

USNS *Mercy*
San Diego Naval Submarine Base, San Diego, CA, 123

USS *Abraham Lincoln* **(CVN 72)**
Everett Naval Station, Everett, WA, 917

USS *Arkansas*
Puget Sound Naval Shipyard, Bremerton, WA, 914

USS *Belleau Wood* **(LHA 3)**
Sasebo, US Fleet Activities, Japan, 1080

USS *California*
Puget Sound Naval Shipyard, Bremerton, WA, 914

USS *Callaghan* **(DDG 994)**
Everett Naval Station, Everett, WA, 917

USS *Camden*
Puget Sound Naval Shipyard, Bremerton, WA, 914

USS *Chandler* **(DDG 996)**
Everett Naval Station, Everett, WA, 917

USS *Constellation*
Coronado Naval Amphibious Base, San Diego, CA, 109

USS *Constellation* **(CV-64)**
North Island Naval Air Station, San Diego, CA, 115

USS *David R Ray* **(DD 971)**
Everett Naval Station, Everett, WA, 917

USS *Detroit* **(AOE-4)**
Earle Naval Weapons Station, Colts Neck, NJ, 554

USS *Dubuque* **(LPD 8)**
Sasebo, US Fleet Activities, Japan, 1080

USS *Ford* **(FFG 54)**
Everett Naval Station, Everett, WA, 917

USS *Fort McHenry* **(LSD 43)**
Sasebo, US Fleet Activities, Japan, 1080

USS *Frank Cable*
Naval Station, Guam, Guam, 1047

USS *Frank Cable* **(AS-40) Det E**
Decatur Naval Reserve Center, Decatur, IL, 305

USS *Thomas S Gates*
Pascagoula Naval Station, Pascagoula, MS, 490

USS *Germantown* **(LSD 42)**
Sasebo, US Fleet Activities, Japan, 1080

USS *Stephen W Groves*
Pascagoula Naval Station, Pascagoula, MS, 490

USS *Guardian* **(MCM 5)**
Sasebo, US Fleet Activities, Japan, 1080

USS *John L Hale*
Pascagoula Naval Station, Pascagoula, MS, 490

USS *Hayler* **(DD-997)(9709NR)**
Tuscaloosa Armed Forces Reserve Center, Tuscaloosa, AL, 17

USS Inchon **(MCS-12)**
Ingleside Naval Station, Ingleside, TX, 806

USS *Ingraham* **(FFG 61)**
Everett Naval Station, Everett, WA, 917

USS *John F Kennedy*
Mayport Naval Air Station, Mayport, FL, 210

USS *Kentucky* **(SSBN 737)**
Kings Bay Naval Submarine Base, Kings Bay, GA, 253

USS *Kitty Hawk*
Coronado Naval Amphibious Base, San Diego, CA, 109

USS *Louisiana* **(SSBN 743)**
Kings Bay Naval Submarine Base, Kings Bay, GA, 253

USS *Maine* **(SSBN 741)**
Kings Bay Naval Submarine Base, Kings Bay, GA, 253

USS *Maryland* **(SSBN 738)**
Kings Bay Naval Submarine Base, Kings Bay, GA, 253

USS *McKee*
San Diego Naval Submarine Base, San Diego, CA, 123

USS *Nebraska* **(SSBN 739)**
Kings Bay Naval Submarine Base, Kings Bay, GA, 253

USS *Patriot* **(MCM 7)**
Sasebo, US Fleet Activities, Japan, 1080

USS *Paul F Foster* **(DD 964)**
Everett Naval Station, Everett, WA, 917

USS *Pennsylvania* **(SSBN 735)**
Kings Bay Naval Submarine Base, Kings Bay, GA, 253

USS *Ranier*
Puget Sound Naval Shipyard, Bremerton, WA, 914

USS *Rhode Island* **(SSBN 740)**
Kings Bay Naval Submarine Base, Kings Bay, GA, 253

USS *Sacramento*
Puget Sound Naval Shipyard, Bremerton, WA, 914

USS *Seattle* **(AOE-3)**
Earle Naval Weapons Station, Colts Neck, NJ, 554

USS *Simon Lake* **(AS-33)**
La Maddalena Navy Support Office, Italy, 1054

USS *Supply* **(AOE-6)**
Earle Naval Weapons Station, Colts Neck, NJ, 554

USS *Tennessee* **(SSBN 734)**
Kings Bay Naval Submarine Base, Kings Bay, GA, 253

USS *Ticonderoga*
Pascagoula Naval Station, Pascagoula, MS, 490

USS *West Virginia* **(SSBN 736)**
Kings Bay Naval Submarine Base, Kings Bay, GA, 253

USS *Wyoming* **(SSBN 742)**
Kings Bay Naval Submarine Base, Kings Bay, GA, 253

USS *Yorktown*
Pascagoula Naval Station, Pascagoula, MS, 490

USSTRATCOM (NR)
Omaha Naval & Marine Corps Reserve Center, Omaha, NE, 531

Utah National Guard
Adjutant General of Utah, Draper, UT, 821
Tooele Army Depot, Tooele, UT, 830

Det 2, UT STARC (Army Garrison)
Camp W G Williams, Riverton, UT, 827

Utah Test and Training Range
Edwards Air Force Base, Edwards AFB, CA, 63
Hill Air Force Base, Hill AFB, UT, 824

Utilities & Industrial Operations Laboratory
US Army Corps of Engineers, Construction Engineering Research Laboratories, Champaign, IL, 300

Vancouver Barracks
Fort Lewis, Fort Lewis, WA, 921

VAQ-136
Atsugi Naval Air Facility, Japan, 1063

VAW-77
Atlanta Naval Air Station, Marietta, GA, 254

VAW-115
Atsugi Naval Air Facility, Japan, 1063

VC-6 UAC Det
Patuxent River, Naval Air Station, Patuxent River, MD, 427

Vermont National Guard
Adjutant General of Vermont, Colchester, VT, 832

Vessel Traffic Service, Puget Sound
Seattle Coast Guard Integrated Support Command, Seattle, WA, 929

Vessel Traffic Service, San Francisco
San Francisco Coast Guard Group, San Francisco, CA, 126

Vessel Traffic Service, Sault
Sault Ste Marie Coast Guard Group, Sault Ste Marie, MI, 462

VF-154
Atsugi Naval Air Facility, Japan, 1063

VFA-15
Cecil Field Naval Air Station, Jacksonville, FL, 202

VFA-27
Atsugi Naval Air Facility, Japan, 1063

VFA-34
Cecil Field Naval Air Station, Jacksonville, FL, 202

VFA-37
Cecil Field Naval Air Station, Jacksonville, FL, 202

VFA-81
Cecil Field Naval Air Station, Jacksonville, FL, 202

VFA-82
Cecil Field Naval Air Station, Jacksonville, FL, 202

VFA-83
Cecil Field Naval Air Station, Jacksonville, FL, 202

VFA-86
Cecil Field Naval Air Station, Jacksonville, FL, 202

VFA-87
Cecil Field Naval Air Station, Jacksonville, FL, 202

VFA-105
Cecil Field Naval Air Station, Jacksonville, FL, 202

VFA-106
Cecil Field Naval Air Station, Jacksonville, FL, 202

VFA-131
Cecil Field Naval Air Station, Jacksonville, FL, 202

VFA-136
Cecil Field Naval Air Station, Jacksonville, FL, 202

VFA-192
Atsugi Naval Air Facility, Japan, 1063

VFA-195
Atsugi Naval Air Facility, Japan, 1063

VFA-203
Atlanta Naval Air Station, Marietta, GA, 254

Vicenza Basic Load Storage Area
Caserma Ederle/Vicenza Military Community, Vincenza, Italy, 1060

Vicenza Family Housing
Caserma Ederle/Vicenza Military Community, Vincenza, Italy, 1060

Virgin Islands National Guard
Adjutant General of the Virgin Islands, VI, Virgin Islands, 1171

Virginia National Guard
Adjutant General of Virginia, Richmond, VA, 897
State Military Reservation, Camp Pendleton, Virginia Beach, VA, 904

Visioneering Laboratory
Point Mugu, Naval Air Weapons Station, Point Mugu, CA, 98

VMFA-134
Miramar Marine Corps Air Station, San Diego, CA, 113

VMFA-142
Atlanta Naval Air Station, Marietta, GA, 254

VMFA-314
Miramar Marine Corps Air Station, San Diego, CA, 113

VMFA-323
Miramar Marine Corps Air Station, San Diego, CA, 113

VMFA (AW)-225
Miramar Marine Corps Air Station, San Diego, CA, 113

VMFA(AW)-242
Miramar Marine Corps Air Station, San Diego, CA, 113

Vogelweh Cantonment
Kaiserslautern Military Community, Germany, 1013

Vogelweh Military Complex
Ramstein Air Base, Germany, 1023

Voluntary Training Unit
Pocatello Naval Reserve Facility, Pocatello, ID, 299
Tallahassee Naval & Marine Corps Reserve Center, Tallahassee, FL, 234

Volunteer Training Unit 0267 (NR)
White River Junction Naval Reserve Center, White River Junction, VT, 834

VTU 0416G
Williamsport Naval & Marine Corps Reserve Center, Williamsport, PA, 722

VOLTRAUNIT 0517 (NR)
Toledo Naval & Marine Corps Reserve Center, Perrysburg, OH, 662

VOLTRAUNIT 0706 (NR)
Greensboro Naval & Marine Corps Reserve Readiness Center, Greensboro, NC, 626

VOLTRAUNIT 0909 (NR)
Louisville Naval Reserve Center, Louisville, KY, 371

VOLTRAUNIT 0908 (NR)
Lexington Naval Reserve Center, Lexington, KY, 368

Volunteer Training Unit 0916 (NR)
Tuscaloosa Armed Forces Reserve Center, Tuscaloosa, AL, 17

Volunteer Training Unit 1307G (NR)
Evansville Naval & Marine Corps Reserve Center, Evansville, IN, 326

Volunteer Training Unit 1604G
Decatur Naval Reserve Center, Decatur, IL, 305
Dubuque Naval Reserve Center, Dubuque, IA, 344

Volunteer Training Unit 1801 (NR)
Cape Girardeau Naval Reserve Center, Cape Girardeau, MO, 500

VTU 1809G (NR)
Lincoln Naval Reserve Center, Lincoln, NE, 529

Volunteer Training Unit 3005
Yokosuka, Fleet Activities, Japan, 1083

Volunteer Training Unit Det 0605 (NR)
Cumberland Naval Reserve Center, Cumberland, MD, 419

VTU (NR)
Wichita Naval & Marine Corps Reserve Center, Wichita, KS, 364

VQ-5
Atsugi Naval Air Facility, Japan, 1063

VQ-6
Cecil Field Naval Air Station, Jacksonville, FL, 202

VRC-30
Atsugi Naval Air Facility, Japan, 1063

VS-21
Atsugi Naval Air Facility, Japan, 1063

VS-22
Cecil Field Naval Air Station, Jacksonville, FL, 202

VS-24
Cecil Field Naval Air Station, Jacksonville, FL, 202

VS-30
Cecil Field Naval Air Station, Jacksonville, FL, 202

VS-31
Cecil Field Naval Air Station, Jacksonville, FL, 202

VS-32
Cecil Field Naval Air Station, Jacksonville, FL, 202

Wackernheim-Schwabenwäldchen Training Area
221st Base Support Battalion, Germany, 992

Waldstadt AFN Facility
Heidelberg Military Community, Germany, 1011

Walson Air Force Medical Facility
Fort Dix, Fort Dix, NJ, 555

Warfare Assessment Laboratory
Naval Warfare Assessment Division, Norco, CA, 86

Warfare Systems and Sensors Research Directorate
Naval Research Laboratory, Washington, DC, 182

Warner Barracks
Bamberg Military Community, Germany, 1001

Warner Barracks Family Housing
Bamberg Military Community, Germany, 1001

Warner Robins Air Logistics Center
Robins Air Force Base, Robins AFB, GA, 259

Warrior Brigade
Fort Polk, Fort Polk, LA, 377

Warrior Replacement Co
Camp Mobile, Korea, Republic of, 1106

Washington National Guard
Adjutant General of Washington, Tacoma, WA, 935

Washington Naval Yard
Naval District Washington, Washington Navy Yard, Washington, DC, 180

Washington Navy Yard
Washington, Naval Station, Washington, DC, 189

Washington OSA Flight Det
Fort Lewis, Fort Lewis, WA, 921

Watervliet Arsenal
Watervliet Arsenal, Watervliet, NY, 612

Weapons and Field Training Bn
Parris Island Marine Corps Recruit Depot/Eastern Recruiting Region, Parris Island, SC, 747

Weapons and Materials Research Directorate
Adelphi Laboratory Center, Army Research Laboratory, Adelphi, MD, 405

Weapons Co, 1st Bn, 24th Marine Regiment
Toledo Naval & Marine Corps Reserve Center, Perrysburg, OH, 662

Weapons Department, Tengan Pier
Kadena Naval Air Facility, Japan, 1075

Weapons Test Squadron
Point Mugu, Naval Air Weapons Station, Point Mugu, CA, 98

Weapons Training Bn
Quantico Marine Corps Combat Development Command, Quantico, VA, 895

Weicht Village Family Housing
6th Area Support Group, Stuttgart, Germany, 988

Weierhof
293rd Base Support Battalion, Germany, 996

Weilimdorf Warehouse
6th Area Support Group, Stuttgart, Germany, 988

Weisskirchen AFN Transmittal Facility
223rd Base Support Battalion, Germany, 993

WEPSTA Concord
Pocatello Naval Reserve Facility, Pocatello, ID, 299

West Point School
West Point, Army Garrison, West Point, NY, 614

West Virginia ANG, HQ
Yeager Airport, Air National Guard Base, Charleston, WV, 944

WV Mountaineer Challenge Academy
Camp Dawson, Kingwood, WV, 947

West Virginia National Guard
Adjutant General of West Virginia, Charleston, WV, 942

Western Air Defense Sector
McChord Air Force Base, McChord AFB, WA, 923

Western Hemisphere Group
Mayport Naval Air Station, Mayport, FL, 210

Western Hemisphere Group (WESTHEMGRU)
Roosevelt Roads Naval Station, Puerto Rico, 1143

Western Mobilization & Training Complex
Western Mobilization & Training Complex, Paso Robles, CA, 95

Western Pacific Marine Corps HQ
Camp Courtney, Japan, 1065

Western Recruiting Region
San Diego Marine Corps Recruit Depot, San Diego, CA, 119

Western Regional Medical Command
Madigan Army Medical Center, Tacoma, WA, 936

Wetzel Family Housing
Baumholder Military Community, H.D. Smith Barracks, Germany, 1003

Wetzel Kaserne
Baumholder Military Community, H.D. Smith Barracks, Germany, 1003

White Beach Port Facility
Kadena Naval Air Facility, Japan, 1075

White House Transportation Agency
Military District of Washington, Washington, DC, 179

Wiesbaden Air Base
221st Base Support Battalion, Germany, 992

Wiesbaden Service Annex
221st Base Support Battalion, Germany, 992

Wiesbaden Small Arms Range
221st Base Support Battalion, Germany, 992

Windberg Barracks
254th Base Support Battalion, Netherlands, 1127

Wisconsin Air National Guard, HQ
Wisconsin National Guard, Office of the Adjutant General, Madison, WI, 959

Wisconsin Army National Guard, HQ
Wisconsin National Guard, Office of the Adjutant General, Madison, WI, 959

Wisconsin Military Academy
Fort McCoy, Fort McCoy, WI, 954

Wolfgang Kaserne
414th Base Support Battalion, Germany, 997

Womack Army Medical Center
Fort Bragg, Fort Bragg, NC, 624

Worms Quartermaster Area
293rd Base Support Battalion, Germany, 996

Worms Repair and Upkeep Area
293rd Base Support Battalion, Germany, 996

Wright Laboratories
Tyndall Air Force Base, Panama City, FL, 220

Wright Laboratory
Eglin Air Force Base, Fort Walton Beach, FL, 197
Wright-Patterson Air Force Base, Wright-Patterson AFB, OH, 667

Wright-Patterson Medical Center
Wright-Patterson Air Force Base, Wright-Patterson AFB, OH, 667

Würzburg Hospital
98th Area Support Group, Germany, 990

Würzburg Supply Point
98th Area Support Group, Germany, 990

Würzburg Training Areas
98th Area Support Group, Germany, 990

Wyoming Army National Guard Training Site
R L Esmay Training Center, Guernsey, WY, 968

Wyoming National Guard
Adjutant General of Wyoming, Cheyenne, WY, 964

Wyoming Regional Training Institute
R L Esmay Training Center, Guernsey, WY, 968

Yakima Training Center
Fort Lewis, Fort Lewis, WA, 921

Yokosuka Naval Base
Yokosuka, Fleet Activities, Japan, 1083

Yorkhof Kaserne
414th Base Support Battalion, Germany, 997

Yuma Proving Ground
Yuma Proving Ground, Yuma, AZ, 46

Zutendaal Site
80th Area Support Group, Belgium, 975